COMMERCIAL REPORTS

AREA STUDIES SERIES

EDITORIAL DIRECTOR   Professor J J O'Meara
RESEARCH UNIT DIRECTOR   T F Turley
ASSISTANT DIRECTOR   S Cashman

CHIEF EDITORIAL ADVISERS

P Ford
Professor Emeritus, Southampton University
Mrs G Ford

SPECIAL EDITORIAL CONSULTANT FOR
THE UNITED STATES PAPERS

H C Allen
Commonwealth Fund Professor of American History, University College, London
Director of the London University Institute of United States Studies

RESEARCH EDITORS
Johann A Norstedt
Marilyn Evers Norstedt

This Series is published with the active co-operation of
SOUTHAMPTON UNIVERSITY

IRISH UNIVERSITY PRESS AREA STUDIES SERIES

BRITISH PARLIAMENTARY PAPERS

UNITED STATES OF AMERICA

35

Embassy and consular
commercial reports
1890–91

IRISH UNIVERSITY PRESS
Shannon   Ireland

PUBLISHER'S NOTE

The documents in this series are selected from the nineteenth-century British House of Commons *sessional and command papers*. All of the original papers relating to the United States of America are included with the exception of two kinds of very brief and unimportant papers. Omitted are (1) random statistical trade returns which are included in the larger and complete yearly trade figures and (2) returns relating to postal services, which are irregularly presented, of tangential USA relevance, and easily available in other sources.

The original documents have been reproduced by photo-lithography and are unabridged even to the extent of retaining the first printers' imprints. Imperfections in the original printing are sometimes unavoidably reproduced.

Many papers in this reprint are enlargements from the original octavo format.

© 1971 Irish University Press Shannon Ireland
Microfilm, microfiche and other forms of micro-publishing
© *Irish University Microforms Shannon Ireland*

ISBN 0 7165 1535 0

Printed and published by
Irish University Press Shannon Ireland
DUBLIN CORK BELFAST LONDON NEW YORK
T M MacGlinchey *Publisher*   Robert Hogg *Printer*

Contents

For ease of reference IUP editors have assigned a continuous pagination which appears on the top outer margin of each page.

IUP Page Number

Commercial Reports

Commercial report no. 25 on aliens and foreign companies in the United States
1890–91 [C.6512] LXXXIII 9

F.O. annual series no. 823: report on Galveston, 1890
1890–91 [C.6205–54] LXXXVIII 17

F.O. annual series no. 827: report on agriculture of the New Orleans district, 1890
1890–91 [C.6205–58] LXXXVIII 31

F.O. annual series no. 833: report on New Orleans, 1890
1890–91 [C.6205–64] LXXXVIII 91

F.O. annual series no. 835: report on Baltimore, 1890
1890–91 [C.6205–66] LXXXVIII 117

F.O. annual series no. 843: report on Boston, 1890
1890–91 [C.6205–74] LXXXVIII 139

F.O. annual series no. 845: report on Charleston, 1890
1890–91 [C.6205–76] LXXXVIII 149

F.O. annual series no. 868: report on Savannah, 1890
1890–91 [C.6205–99] LXXXVIII 167

F.O. annual series no. 892: report on Chicago, 1890
1890–91 [C.6205–123] LXXXVIII 175

F.O. annual series no. 906: report on San Francisco, 1890
1890–91 [C.6205–137] LXXXVIII 217

F.O. annual series no. 910: report on the agriculture of the San Francisco district, 1890
1890–91 [C.6205–141] LXXXVIII 275

F.O. annual series no. 911: report on New York, 1890
1890–91 [C.6205–142] LXXXVIII 291

F.O. annual series no. 933: report on agriculture of the New York district
1890–91 [C.6205–164] LXXXVIII 315

Commercial report no. 7 on the protocols of the International Marine Conference at Washington, 1889
1890–91 [C.6255] XCVII 325

As most commercial reports are extracted from larger papers, the reader should note that a particular report may lack a proper title page.

COMMERCIAL. No. 25 (1891).
(UNITED STATES.)

FURTHER REPORT

ON THE

STATUS OF ALIENS AND FOREIGN COMPANIES

IN THE

UNITED STATES.

[In continuation of "Commercial No. 13 (1890):" C. 5969.]

Presented to both Houses of Parliament by Command of Her Majesty.
August 1891.

LONDON:
PRINTED FOR HER MAJESTY'S STATIONERY OFFICE
BY HARRISON AND SONS, ST. MARTIN'S LANE,
PRINTERS IN ORDINARY TO HER MAJESTY.

And to be purchased, either directly or through any Bookseller, from
EYRE AND SPOTTISWOODE, EAST HARDING STREET, FLEET STREET, E.C., AND
32, ABINGDON STREET, WESTMINSTER, S.W.; OR
JOHN MENZIES & Co., 12, HANOVER STREET, EDINBURGH; AND
88 and 90, WEST NILE STREET, GLASGOW; OR
HODGES, FIGGIS, & CO., 104, GRAFTON STREET, DUBLIN.

[C.—6512.] *Price* 1*d.*

Further Report on the Status of Aliens and Foreign Companies in the United States.

[In continuation of "Commercial No. 13 (1890):" C. 5969.]

No. 1.

Consul Boyle to the Marquis of Salisbury.—(Received July 29.)

My Lord, Galveston, Texas, *July* 16, 1891.

I HAVE the honour to inclose herewith copy of "Alien Land Laws," State of Texas, which I have been requested to forward your Lordship by Sir Julian Pauncefote.

I am, &c.
(Signed) JAMES BOYLE.

Inclosure in No. 1.

"ALIENS."

General Laws.—*State of Texas*

Passed 22nd Legislature, convened at Austin, January 13, 1891.

ARTICLE 9. An alien shall have and enjoy in the State of Texas such rights pertaining to personal property as are or shall be accorded to citizens of the United States by the laws of the nation to which such alien shall belong, or by the Treaties of such nation with the United States.

Art. 10. No alien or a person who is not a citizen of the United States of America shall acquire title to or own any interest in the lands within the State of Texas, and any deed or other conveyance purporting to convey such title or interest to any alien or unnaturalized foreigner, or to any firm, Company, or Corporation composed of such in whole or in part, shall be void.

Art. 10 A. This Chapter shall not apply to any alien who shall, at the time of acquiring title to lands in Texas, have declared his intention of becoming a citizen of the United States of America, and who shall, in obedience to such laws, become a citizen within six years from the time such intention was declared.

Art. 10 B. All aliens who shall hereafter take lands by devise or descent may hold the same for the space of six years and no longer, provided that any alien, minor, or person of unsound mind inheriting lands in Texas may have six years after such minor reaches twenty-one years of age, or person of unsound mind shall have had a legal guardian.

Art. 10 C. Any alien may, for a valuable consideration, take, hold, assign, foreclose, sell, or buy, under any mortgage or deed of trust, any lands within the State of Texas in which he has an interest by virtue of having heretofore made a loan of money, subject to the provisions of this Chapter in reference to alienating said lands within six years as herein required.

Art. 10 D. If any alien shall undertake to hold lands for a longer time, or in any way contrary to the provisions of this Chapter, such lands shall escheat to and vest in the State of Texas in like manner as is provided for the escheat of estates of persons dying without any devise thereof and having no heirs.

Art. 10 E. It shall be the duty of the Attorney-General and District or County Attorney, when they shall be informed or have reason to believe that any lands in this State are being held contrary to the provisions of this Chapter, to institute suit in behalf of the State of Texas in the District Court of the county where such lands are situated, praying for a writ of possession for the same in behalf of the State.

Art. 10 F. The escheat proceeding provided for in the next preceding Article shall, in the matter *scire facias*, appearance and default, judgment, execution, and sale, be governed by the provisions of Title 36 of the Revised Statutes of Texas, in so far as the same is applicable, except that the only question on the trial shall be whether or not the provisions of this Act have been violated.

Art. 10 G. All laws and parts of laws in conflict with this Title are hereby repealed.

Approved.
April 13, 1891.

No. 2.

Acting Consul Sadler to the Marquis of Salisbury.—(*Received August* 6.)

My Lord,   *Chicago, July* 27, 1891.

I HAVE the honour to report that an Act, copy of which is transmitted herewith, was this year passed by the Legislative Assembly of the State of Kansas, and is now in force, affecting the future status of non-resident aliens in that State with regard to the acquirement of land.

"Non-resident aliens, firm of aliens, or corporation incorporated under the laws of any foreign country, shall not be capable of acquiring title to or taking or holding any lands or real estate in this State by descent, devise, purchase, or otherwise, except that the heirs of aliens who have heretofore acquired lands in this State under the laws thereof, and the heirs of aliens who may acquire lands under the provisions of this Act, may take such lands by devise or descent, and hold the same for the space of three years, and no longer, if such alien at the time of so acquiring such lands is of the age of 21 years; and if not 21 years of age, then for the term of five years from the time of acquiring such lands; and if, at the end of the time herein limited, such lands so acquired by such alien heirs have not been sold to *bonâ fide* purchasers for value, or such alien heirs have not become actual residents of this State, the same shall revert and escheat to the State of Kansas the same as the lands of other aliens under the provisions of this Act: Provided, that minor aliens actually residing in the United States may acquire title to lands in this State by purchase, and hold the same for the term of six years after they might, under the Naturalization Laws of the United States, have declared their intentions to become citizens of the United States; and if at the expiration of said term of six years said aliens have not become citizens of the United States, the lands so acquired by them by purchase shall revert and escheat to the State, under the provisions of this Act; and it shall be the duty of the County Attorney of the county in which said lands are situated to enforce forfeitures of all lands mentioned in this section in the same manner as pointed out in this Act for other forfeitures."

I also transmit herewith an extract from a local paper of Topeka, Kansas, containing the results of an interview with Chief Justice Horton, of the State of Kansas, from which it would appear that various enterprises about to be inaugurated under alien capital and management will have to be abandoned.

I have, &c.
(Signed)   R. H. HAYES SADLER.

3

Inclosure 1 in No. 2.

In Relation to Aliens.

An Act in regard to Aliens, and to restrict their Rights to acquire and hold Real Estate, and to provide for the disposition of the Lands now owned by non-resident Aliens.

BE it enacted by the Legislature of the State of Kansas:—

Section 1. That a non-resident alien, firm of aliens, or corporation incorporated under the laws of any foreign country, shall not be capable of acquiring title to or taking or holding any lands or real estate in this State by descent, devise, purchase, or otherwise, except that the heirs of aliens who have heretofore acquired lands in this State under the laws thereof, and the heirs of aliens who may acquire lands under the provisions of this Act, may take such lands by devise or descent, and hold the same for the space of three years, and no longer, if such alien at the time of so acquiring such lands is of the age of 21 years; and if not 21 years of age, then for the term of five years from the time of so acquiring such lands; and if, at the end of the time herein limited, such lands so acquired by such alien heirs have not been sold to *bonâ fide* purchasers for value, or such alien heirs have not become actual residents of this State, the same shall revert and escheat to the State of Kansas the same as the lands of other aliens under the provisions of this Act; Provided, that minor aliens actually residing in the United States may acquire title to lands in this State by purchase, and hold the same for the term of six years after they might, under the Naturalization Laws of the United States, have declared their intentions to become citizens of the United States; and if at the expiration of said term of six years said aliens have not become citizens of the United States, the lands so acquired by them by purchase shall revert and escheat to the State, under the provisions of this Act; and it shall be the duty of the County Attorney of the county in which said lands are situated to enforce forfeitures of all lands mentioned in this section in the same manner as pointed out in this Act for other forfeitures. *[Not acquire title. Revert to the State. Minor aliens.]*

Sec. 2. That no corporation or association, more than 20 per centum of the stock of which is or may be owned by any person or persons, corporation, or association, not citizens of the United States, or of some District or Territory thereof, shall hereafter acquire, hold, or own any real estate in the State of Kansas. *[No corporation or association.]*

Sec. 3. Any alien resident of the United States who shall declare his intention of becoming a citizen of the United States in accordance with the Naturalization Laws thereof, and every alien female who shall in good faith become an actual resident of the United States, shall thereupon be authorized and enabled to take and hold lands and real estate of any kind whatsoever, to him or her and his or her heirs and assigns for ever, and may, during six years thereafter, sell, assign, mortgage, devise, and dispose of the same in any manner as he or she might or could do if he or she were a natural-born citizen of the United States: Provided that, in the case of an alien male, he shall, at the time of acquiring such lands, cause to be recorded in the office of the Register of Deeds of the county in which such lands are situated a certified copy of his said declaration to become such citizen; and in case of an alien female, her affidavit of the fact that she is in good faith an actual resident of the United States, shall be so filed; but no such alien, unless he or she be an actual resident of this State, shall have power to lease or devise any real estate which he or she may take or hold by virtue of this provision. *[Alien declaring his intention.]*

Sec. 4. If any alien who has declared his intention of becoming a citizen shall not become a naturalized citizen of the United States within six years after the declaration of his intention, and be living, shall not have sold said real estate to purchasers thereof for value and in good faith, such real estate acquired by him under authority of this Act shall revert to, escheat, and become the property of the State of Kansas. *[Shall not become a naturalized citizen.]*

Sec. 5. Any real estate held or owned in violation of this Act shall be foreited to the State of Kansas; and it shall be the duty of the County Attorney of any county in which such real estate is situated to enforce such forfeiture in a civil action brought in the name of the State as plaintiff, the same to be *[Forfeiture of real estate.]*

commenced, proceeded with, and disposed of in the same manner as other civil actions affecting real estate. The Court, upon the application of the Attorney and the presentation of a verified petition in proper form, shall appoint a receiver in any such action, who, upon being qualified as provided by law, shall have the usual powers of receivers in actions affecting real estate.

Final hearing.

Sec. 6. If upon the final hearing of such action the Court shall find that any portion of the real estate described in the petition is held or owned in violation of this Act, the Court shall adjudge such real estate forfeited to the State; and shall order the same appraised, sold, and conveyed by the Sheriff in parcels not exceeding 160 acres each, in the same manner provided by law for the sale of real estate upon execution.

Confirmation of sale.

Sec. 7. Upon the confirmation of such sale, the proceeds thereof, together with any moneys realized therefrom by the receiver, shall be applied to the payment of the costs of such action, including such allowance to the receiver for his services as the Court shall find to be just, and an allowance of 10 per cent. of the proceeds of such sale to the County Attorney for his services; and the residue of the money so realized shall be paid to the order of such defendant or defendants as the Court shall find to have been the owner of said real estate at the time of such forfeiture: Provided, that if the residue of said money shall not be paid to the persons entitled thereto within thirty days from the date of any such Judgment, the same shall be paid into the Treasury of the State of Kansas, where it shall remain subject to the order of the person or persons adjudged to be entitled thereto.

Rights of aliens or non-residents.

Sec. 8. Any alien, non-resident of the United States, who owns land in this State at the time this Act takes effect, shall have the right and power to dispose of the same during his lifetime to *bonâ fide* purchasers for value, and to take security for the purchase-money, with the same right to such securities as a citizen of the United States, except that if he or his non-resident heirs again obtain title to the said lands or any sale thereof made by virtue of any Judgment or Decree of any Court of Law or Equity, rendered in order to enforce the payment of any part of such purchase-money, he or his non-resident heirs shall only hold the title to said lands for three years after obtaining the same; and if said lands so acquired are not sold in good faith to *bonâ fide* purchasers for value within said time, then the said lands shall be forfeited and escheat to the State of Kansas, in the same manner as provided in this Act.

Valid title.

Sec. 9. Nothing herein contained shall prevent the holder of any lien upon or interest in real estate heretofore acquired from holding or taking a valid title to the real estate in which he has such interest or upon which he has such lien, or prevent any alien from enforcing any lien or Judgment for any debt or liability which may hereafter be created, or which he may hereafter acquire, or which may hereafter be adjudged in his favour, or from becoming a purchaser at any sale by virtue of such lien or Judgment: Provided, that all lands so acquired shall be sold within three years after title shall be perfected in him under such sales, or, in default thereof, that the same shall escheat as provided in this Act:

Shall not apply.

Provided further, that the provisions of this Act shall not apply to any lands which are now or may hereafter be used for the purpose of mining coal, lead, or zinc ore.

Sec. 10. That this Act shall take effect and be in force from and after its publication in the Statute Book.

Approved 6th March, 1891.

Inclosure 2 in No. 2.

Extract from a local Paper of Topeka, Kansas.

THE ALIEN LAND LAW.

Judge Horton's Opinion as to its Scope and Provisions.

[Special.]

Topeka, Kansas, July 23.

THE question having been raised that the Alien Land Law passed last winter would shut out all foreign capital, the "Journal" representative interviewed Chief Justice Horton respecting its provisions and its scope. Judge

Horton did not give his opinion as a member of the Court, nor did he enter fully into the Law, but he consented to give what he believed to be the effects of the Law upon the right of corporations to acquire or hold lands in this State. He said:—

"There is no question as to the disqualifications of foreign corporations, or corporations in which 20 per cent. of the stock is held by non-resident aliens, for holding or acquiring real property in this State. The limitations are clearly defined."

"Can such a corporation lease such lands as may be required?"

"My opinion is that they cannot. The Law says they cannot acquire, hold, or own. In regard to railroad property, this has always been held as an inhibition of long-time leases or holdings, and the Courts have so held. I do not see that a lease can help the matter any. It is unfortunate for the enterprises about to be inaugurated in Kansas City, but they cannot hold the land either as owners or as lessees."

"Could not the residents own the land and the corporation own the buildings as personal property?" was asked.

"There is no question as to the legality of such an arrangement. The owners of the land could hold and pay taxes on the land, while the corporation could pay the taxes on the personal property. The contract between the parties would have to be very carefully drawn, as it involves vast interests, extending over more than limited time. In this case the owners of the land would have the right to make such contracts as to its use as they deemed to their interests, while the owners of the personal property would be fully protected in all their rights of ownership. This is the only way a corporation of foreign persons or capital can enter the State. I have no doubt this arrangement could be made, as it would be legal, and the laws would protect all the parties. The Law is unfortunate in that it has not provided some exceptions, as it was drawn to prevent large holdings only."

While it is the rule for the members of the Supreme Court to decline to give their opinions, as the same question might possibly come before that body, in this case Judge Horton recognized the importance to Kansas City of this matter, and was willing to express himself briefly.

Speaking of the effects of the Alien Land Law, Judge Horton thought it directly opposed to the principles embodied in the McKinley Bill. "The latter," he said, "is directly in the interest of the manufacturing industries of this nation, while the Alien Bill has a tendency to drive them out, keeping as it does foreign capital from investing, unless hedged about by difficulties that capital will not usually stand."

The views taken by Judge Horton are fully indorsed by the Attorney-General, who gave much study to this subject when the measure was before the Legislature. There were two Bills under consideration at the same time, one in each House. The House Bill was practically the same as the Senate Bill, except that it provided that foreign corporations should not own more than 160 acres of land. After the passage by the House of the Senate Bill it was recalled, at the request of Mr. Douglass, but the recall message was too late to effect its purpose, as the Bill had been enrolled. Mr. Douglass intended to so amend it as to cover the very point that now drives from Kansas soil the vast interests contemplated at the mouth of the Kaw.

Able lawyers declare, however, that foreign capital can, through the means suggested and approved by Judge Horton, operate upon land owned by citizens of the United States, properly guarded by contract. The owner of the real property can grant any and all rights to the owner of the personal. This is the only way out of the difficulty.

COMMERCIAL. No. 25 (1891).
(UNITED STATES.)

Further Report on the Status of Aliens and Foreign Companies in the United States.

[In continuation of "Commercial No. 13 (1890):" C. 5969.]

Presented to both Houses of Parliament by Command of Her Majesty. August 1891.

LONDON:
PRINTED BY HARRISON AND SONS,

FOREIGN OFFICE.
1891.
ANNUAL SERIES.

N⁰ 823.

DIPLOMATIC AND CONSULAR REPORTS ON TRADE AND FINANCE.

UNITED STATES.

REPORT FOR THE YEAR 1890
ON THE
TRADE OF GALVESTON.

REFERENCE TO PREVIOUS REPORT, Annual Series No. 661.

Presented to both Houses of Parliament by Command of Her Majesty,
MARCH, 1891.

LONDON:
PRINTED FOR HER MAJESTY'S STATIONERY OFFICE,
BY HARRISON AND SONS, ST. MARTIN'S LANE,
PRINTERS IN ORDINARY TO HER MAJESTY.

And to be purchased, either directly or through any Bookseller, from
EYRE & SPOTTISWOODE, EAST HARDING STREET, FLEET STREET, E.C., and
32, ABINGDON STREET, WESTMINSTER, S.W.; or
JOHN MENZIES & Co., 12, HANOVER STREET, EDINBURGH, and
21, DRURY STREET, GLASGOW; or
HODGES, FIGGIS, & Co., 104, GRAFTON STREET, DUBLIN.

1891.

[C. 6205–54.] *Price One Penny.*

New Series of Reports.

Reports of the Annual Series have been issued from Her Majesty's Diplomatic and Consular Officers at the following places, and may be obtained from the sources indicated on the title-page:—

No.		Price.
697.	Calais	2d.
698.	Marseilles	1d.
699.	Brest	1d.
700.	Lisbon	2½d.
701.	Leghorn	2d.
702.	Rio Grande do Sul	1d.
703.	Tainan	1d.
704.	Kewkiang	4d.
705.	Fiume	1d.
706.	Odessa	2d.
707.	Suakin	½d.
708.	Hankow	½d.
709.	Amoy	1d.
710.	Buda-Pesth	1½d.
711.	Corunna	2d.
712.	Mogador	2d.
713.	Cadiz	½d.
714.	Cadiz	1d.
715.	Rio de Janeiro	2½d.
716.	Newchwang	½d.
717.	Chinkiang	½d.
718.	San Francisco	6d.
719.	Busserah	½d.
720.	Beyrout	1d.
721.	Adrianople	½d.
722.	Nantes	½d.
723.	Caracas	1d.
724.	Mogador	½d.
725.	Tientsin	1d.
726.	Foochow	1d.
727.	Port au Prince	½d.
728.	Callao	1d.
729.	Puerto Plata	½d.
730.	San Francisco	1d.
731.	Philadelphia	2½d.
732.	Pakhoi	1d.
733.	Bilbao	1d.
734.	Dunkirk	1d.
735.	Vienna	1d.
736.	Nantes	1½d.
737.	Paramaribo	1d.
738.	Honolulu	½d.
739.	Chicago	2d.
740.	Söul	1d.
741.	Brindisi	1½d.
742.	Mozambique	1d.
743.	Caldera and Lota	1½d.
744.	Nice	1½d.
745.	Aleppo	1d.
746.	Hakodate	1d.
747.	New York	2d.
748.	Cagliari	1d.
749.	San Salvador	1d.
750.	Gothenburg	2d.
751.	Nagasaki	1d.
752.	Sofia	3½d.
753.	Meshed	1d.
754.	Yokohama	2½d.
755.	Shanghai	2d.
756.	Lisbon	1½d.
757.	Teneriffe	½d.
758.	Noumea	½d.
759.	Tahiti	½d.

No.		Price.
760.	Bushire	1½d.
761.	Frankfort	2d.
762.	Palermo	2½d.
763.	Guatemala	1d.
764.	Smyrna	4d.
765.	Munich	2d.
766.	Hiogo	1½d.
767.	Alexandria	1½d.
768.	Maracaibo	½d.
769.	Macao	1d.
770.	Canton	1d.
771.	Bangkok	2½d.
772.	Stockholm	1½d.
773.	Jaffa	½d.
774.	Copenhagen	½d.
775.	Ningpo	½d.
776.	Stettin	2d.
777.	St. Petersburg	3d.
778.	St. Petersburg	½d.
779.	St. Jago de Cuba	1½d.
780.	Chefoo	1d.
781.	Christiania	3½d.
782.	Marseilles	½d.
783.	Baghdad	1d.
784.	Naples	1½d.
785.	Tunis	4d.
786.	Vera Cruz	1d.
787.	Tangier	1½d.
788.	Rome	2d.
789.	Stuttgart	1½d.
790.	Panama	1½d.
791.	Berne	1½d.
792.	Asuncion	½d.
793.	Bahia	7½d.
794.	Monte Video	1½d.
795.	Munich	2d.
796.	Bucharest	1d.
797.	Tokio	1d.
798.	Tabreez	1d.
799.	Antwerp	1d.
800.	Malaga	1d.
801.	Odessa	1d.
802.	Malaga	2d.
803.	Amsterdam	1d.
804.	Bogotá	1½d.
805.	Guayaquil	½d.
806.	Lima	1d.
807.	Rio de Janeiro	3d.
808.	Dantzig	1½d.
809.	Florence	1½d.
810.	Lisbon	1d.
811.	Quito	½d.
812.	Para	½d.
813.	Palermo	2½d.
814.	Copenhagen	1d.
815.	Serajevo	½d.
816.	Porto Rico	1d.
817.	Madrid	½d.
818.	Brussels	½d.
819.	Patras	½d.
820.	Stuttgart	1d.
821.	Taganrog	1d.
822.	Salonica	2d.

No. 823.

Reference to previous Report, Annual Series No. 661.

UNITED STATES.

GALVESTON.

Acting-Consul Heyworth to the Marquis of Salisbury.

My Lord,   Galveston, Texas, February 12th, 1891.

I HAVE the honour to enclose Consular Report (Commercial) for the past year 1890.

           I have, &c.
       (Signed)   O. HEYWORTH.

Report on the Trade and Commerce of Texas for the Year 1890.

The chief event of importance in Texas during the past year has been the passage of a Bill through Congress appropriating 6,200,000 dol. for the improvement of Galveston Harbour, from the results of which when completed the whole territory comprised within Arizona, New Mexico, Utah, Kansas, Colorado, Iowa, Nebraska, Oklahoma, and even as far north as the Dakotas, expects to reap great advantages in the way of cheaper transportation for their grain crops, as 71,000 miles of railway west of the Mississippi River—nearly one-half of the total mileage of the United States—now connects with the Texas system, whose natural port is Galveston. *[Grant for harbour.]*

As a seaport outlet through the Gulf of Mexico, instead of through the Atlantic, Galveston is nearer than New York to the points named as follows:—San Francisco, 900 miles; Denver, 700 miles; Lincoln (Nebraska), 400 miles; Topeka, 600 miles; Omaha, 400 miles; St. Louis, 250 miles; Little Rock, 700 miles; Kansas City, 483 miles.

This territory raised in 1889 a surplus in excess of feed, bread and seed, used in local consumption, corn, 150,000,000 bushels; wheat, 112,000,000 bushels; also of meat products, 126,000,000 dol., or about 750,000 tons. It is estimated the result of deep water at Galveston would be a saving to the producers of grain of 40,000,000 dol. per annum in rail haul, and 5,000,000 dol. in freight on meat products.

Railways.

The railroads of the United States being mostly controlled by Eastern capitalists have been worked for the last 15 years on what is known as the "long haul" system, *i.e.*, on the supposition that they could afford to carry produce from the south and west to the eastern ports of New York, Boston, Philadelphia, and Baltimore, say an average distance of 1,800 miles, at the same rate they would charge to carry it, say 600 miles, to a Texas port; but experience has shown that this theory is wrong, and stockholders are beginning to complain of the results.

Steamship communication.

A steamship line has been established during the past year between Galveston and Central America, and tropical fruit is now landed here in one to two days shorter time than in New Orleans, and shipped hence to the various cities of the west, as Los Angelos (California), St. Louis, Kansas City, Chicago, &c. The President, in his annual message to Congress of December, 1890, thus refers to the trade of this section of country:—

"The South Atlantic and Gulf ports occupy a very favoured position towards the new and important commerce which the reciprocity clause of the Tariff Act and the Postal Shipping Bill are designed to promote. Steamship lines from these ports to some northern port of South America will almost certainly effect a connection between the railroad systems of the continents long before any continuous line of railroads can be in operation.

"The very large appropriation made at the last session for the harbour of Galveston was justified, as it seemed to me, by these considerations. The great north-west will feel the advantage of trunk lines to the south as well as to the east, and of the new markets opened for surplus food products, and for many of the manufactured products."

Real estate.

The attention of the outside public having thus been called to Texas has resulted in a marked advance in the value of real estate in the principal cities, and a general desire to experiment as to what can be grown on lands along the coast previously considered almost worthless, but which now promise to become valuable for rice culture, just as lands a little further inland, which were of scarcely any value 10 years ago, are now found to yield an average revenue of 600 dol. per acre in various fruits, more particularly strawberries and pears, the former of which can sometimes be shipped north in mid-winter.

Manufactories.

There is a marked tendency to increase manufactories in Texas, which for some years have been in abeyance, probably owing to the difficulty of securing skilled labour; thus, in Galveston, there is a large cotton mill just completed, besides bagging and rope factories, and a wool-scouring mill. Cotton mills are also being built in several other cities in Texas, and there is no reason why this State should not in time manufacture all the cotton goods used by its inhabitants, as also their agricultural implements, as there are vast deposits of mineral wealth in various sections.

Cotton.

The cotton crop has undoubtedly been the largest ever grown in Texas, and is estimated to have yielded to the farmers about 60,000,000 dol. (12,000,000*l.* net cash). It is somewhat singular that this immense crop should benefit the ports of the State so little, as the bulk of it is now bought for European or Eastern spinners' account from the farmer himself, thus avoiding all charges to middlemen, while new machinery now enables the farmer to have his cotton compressed for stowing on board ship at the same time it is ginned, thus further depriving the port of even its compressing business.

This is only in accordance with a principle that has obtained in all the ports of the United States, with the exception of New York, during the past 20 years, the absence of imports having prevented them from being the trade marts that they are in other countries; thus, in Texas, lands worth 25 c. per acre 20 years ago are now worth 4 dol. to 5 dol. per acre, and city property in proportion; whereas in Galveston there has been no advance until lately.

Hence the inadvisability of Englishmen coming over to Texas, who have only been educated in office work, and expect to find situations in the cities, but are unable to work at any trade, or understand nothing about farming. There is simply nothing for them to do, whereas a labouring man usually gets along, and often becomes affluent, while a mechanic or skilled labourer invariably succeeds. *Hints to emigrants.*

The great bane of the interior of Texas, as of most of the States of the Union, is malaria, which invariably attacks strangers on arrival, who have not been accustomed to outdoor life and hard work. Of course it is in itself no worse than many diseases prevalent in colder climates, but it seems to have a singularly depressing effect on new comers, who have often been induced to emigrate by reading circulars whose great promises they would have known could never be realised in this world had they stopped to reflect. *Malaria.*

The question of the equitable adjustment of railroad freights on cotton and other produce has occupied the serious attention of the people of Texas, who do not understand why it should cost as much to haul a bale of cotton 170 miles as 400 miles, or any greater distance, within the State; the same maximum rate applying at present to all places over 170 miles from the coast. *Railway freights.*

This subject has engaged the attention of the Legislature at various times during the past 14 years; but owing to the fact that the Legislature only meets once in every two years, and then but for an average session of 60 days, no adequate laws have been passed, as in other States, to regulate this and other discriminations, and rebates made indirectly to large shippers.

At the biennial election of State officers, held last November, this question was submitted to the popular vote in the shape of an amendment to the constitution, which requires the Legislature to pass laws empowering a commission to regulate railroad freights and passenger fares, thus giving security to the railroads, freedom to commerce, and protection to the public, as is already done by similar means in 23 States of the Union.

(1045)

Railroads would thus, it is hoped, be removed from exerting political influence, and instead of eastern and foreign traffic managers levying the highest rates that local commerce can possibly bear, not for corporate purposes, but to support speculative schemes, there would be fair rates developing the interests of the public and railroads.

Financial status of railways.

The great drawback to the value of American railroad securities as an investment has been that the original proprietors have been allowed to issue bonds and stock for double or treble the amount that it cost them to construct the railroad, which naturally cannot be expected to pay a dividend on such increased sums; hence the reason why nearly all the Texas railroads are in the hands of receivers, though otherwise they would have been paying investments. In the annual message of the new Governor to the Legislature he thus alludes to this subject:—

"Restrictions should be imposed on the execution of railway bonds and mortgages.

"They are neither more nor less than public obligations that must be paid by the traffic of the country.

"For many years past they have been recklessly issued without regard to corporate demands or public interest at all, until now there are 263,000,000 dol. of interest bearing bonds secured by mortgages upon the 8,000 miles of railroad within this State.

"No such bond or mortgage should hereafter be permitted to be issued except in strict conformity with constitutional demand, which is, that it must be for property, labour, or money received for corporate use, and then it should be denied circulation or negotiation until after it had been tested by the Attorney-General and duly registered with the Secretary of State or Comptroller.

"In a nutshell, all public securities should have the stamp of honesty placed on them by the hand of the State Government, so that all investments in them shall be secure, and the honour of a just public shielded from opprobrium."

The present estimated cost of railroad construction in Texas is 20,000 dol. per mile; of course, it was much greater some years ago, but this will show the magnitude of the evil referred to, as the Governor only alludes to the bonded indebtedness of the railroads.

The Governor also alludes to the fact that the executive and most members of the Legislature are committed to the enactment of a law to prohibit corporate monopolies and perpetuities as to land and titles thereto, which have never been forbidden hitherto by the laws of Texas, nor perpetuities defined.

Land tenure.

These land corporations, the Governor points out, are hardly in any case originated in Texas, but many of them operate under charters granted by England, which contain an express provision that they shall not have the right to own land within the dominion of Great Britain, but that they may go to Texas for that purpose.

Thus the counterpart of primogeniture—viz., estates in perpetuity—is extending in Texas.

The Governor suggests that those corporations holding lands here do so in fee simple for the purpose of alienation, but have only a determinable fee for the purpose of enjoyment, on the will of the Government.

The Governor goes pretty lengthily into the laws relating to murders and other crimes, and strongly recommends such changes as shall cause a murderer to be as summarily dealt with as a horse thief, who is universally known to be shown no quarter in Texas. *Crime.*

The improvement of the public roads is a matter that is exciting the serious attention of the people, and it is proposed to issue bonds secured by the revenues accruing from a tax on the people of each county for such improvement, somewhat in a similar way to that in which the various gaols and court-houses have been built, the bonds of which have in many cases been paid, and which are considered as good security as United States bonds. *Roads.*

The question of irrigation is one that bids fair to be agitated as the population of Texas increases, but at present the unsettled portion of the State is so vast, and so much fertile land needs cultivation, that immigrants do not care to cast their lot in any but the best parts. *Irrigation.*

At the same time the fact is beginning to be perceived that the older lands do not yield anything like the quantity of cotton to the acre that they once did. There are no returns on this subject for Texas, but for the total cotton-growing region of the United States the increase of acreage has been about 20 per cent. since 1883, while the increase of cotton has only averaged about 2 per cent. until the present crop. *Agriculture.*

The fact that the Atlantic States and Tennessee use fertilisers more or less extensively, may probably bring them up pretty nearly to the average of Texas and the rest of the cotton-growing States.

Last year a considerable amount of cotton was grown in the south-western counties along and immediately north of the Rio Grande, which were previously thought to contain land only fit for stock raising.

The same thing may occur in time in that vast stretch of country between Abilene and El Paso, a large portion of which is now inhabited by prairie dogs, and if these lands do not prove suitable for cotton they may produce grapes or other fruits with proper irrigation like that around El Paso, whose grapes are famous all over the Union.

The extent of this western half of Texas is but feebly understood even by the inhabitants of the State, who commonly suppose that the centre point is somewhere around the town of Waco, because that is the centre of the eastern portion of cotton producing half of the State, which is alone taken account of in the Government weather reports, &c., whereas the true centre is some 20 miles west of Abilene on the Texas and Pacific Railway, the reason of this being that no crops are as yet grown in this western section.

UNITED STATES.

Of course, the appropriation made by Congress for Galveston Harbour (in accordance with the request of the deep-water convention, embracing delegates from all the States and territories interested in having a good harbour on the Texas coast, which unanimously selected Galveston as the most desirable port) has, for the time being, diverted public attention from the other harbours of Texas as Aransas Pags, Sabine Pags, &c., though considerable improvements have been made at the former place during the past year.

New Mexico.

The extent of the coalfields of New Mexico is not generally known, and consist of the Raton fields, an extension of the Colorado fields, and embrace about 600,000 acres of the best bituminous coal, of good coking quality. The mines have now a capacity of 500 tons per day. There are also other coalfields, besides deposits of gold, silver, and copper ore. The hills are full of undeveloped mines of iron, with coal enough to work them.

The sheep interest has been decreasing since 1887, when the number was estimated at 4,000,000 head, whereas it is now probably only half that number, owing to heavy losses by scarcity of grass.

Still the sheep business is usually very profitable, being estimated to yield an average profit of 20 per cent. on the capital invested; there need not be any expense for range as there are large tracts of public lands which, by their nature, must remain unoccupied for some years to come, because away from the streams, and where water for sheep can be easily stored by means of dams, commencing at the head of the ravines, and building a succession of small reservoirs.

As a proof of the correctness of this estimate of profit, it may be mentioned that the old custom among the Mexicans was to place their sheep on shares in the care of industrious men, who willingly paid a yearly rental of 20 per cent. to 25 per cent. to the owner.

Of course, the dryness of the climate prevents any such disease as "rot," which sometimes gives great trouble to the sheepmen of Texas.

It has been the custom in former years to ship steers from a New Mexican range to Missouri or Illinois, where they have been fed, and in due time slaughtered and shipped back in refrigerator cars for the consumption of, perhaps, the original owner.

This system is now being revolutionised by the "alfalfa" plant, which is a species of clover, a perennial of enormously prolific growth, containing a very high percentage of digestible, nutritive matter, and of such a hardy character that when once firmly rooted it requires little attention otherwise than an occasional irrigation, and harvesting of the heavy crops of hay which it produces.

GALVESTON.

On any good land in the Rio Grande Valley five tons of alfalfa per acre per annum may safely be counted upon, of which, experience shows, two tons fed during 90 days will fatten a range steer, or say two and a-half tons to make him in prime condition so as to bring the best market price. Thus two steers can be fattened on the produce of one acre.

An acre of land will cost 20 dol. to 25 dol. Add to this 10 dol. to seed it down to alfalfa and care for it during the first year of its growth, the profits on the hay harvested the first two years are estimated at 8 dol., after which it should yield as above.

Yucca palm. Tons of yucca palm, one of the best paper materials known, are shipped from New Mexico and Arizona to Europe, and thousands of tons lie rotting on arid, because unirrigated, plains.

Skins. Hides are shipped by train loads to the shoe and harness manufactories of the east, while thousands of acres of canaigres, the choicest tanning material known, grow up, die, and decay undisturbed.

Wool. Both Texas and New Mexico ship their wool to a large extent in the dirt, paying high freights on sand and soil to the woollen manufactories of the east, and after the fleeces have been washed, sorted, spun, and woven, pay more freight in blankets, &c., when there are pure streams close at hand in which to wash the wool, and coal also for its manufacture close at hand.

Irrigation. In a report to the Department of Agriculture on the irrigation of the United States, Mr. Richard J. Hinton estimates that it lies within the power of civil and hydraulic engineering, at a comparatively small cost, estimated by results, to make of the region called the great plains—whose eastern line will be the 100th meridian, while its western limit will be at 105 degrees; its north and south boundaries the border of Manitoba to Fort Ringgold, near Brownsville, Texas, say, 700 miles north and south and 250 miles east and west—a region which will give farms of 100 acres each to at least 25,000,000 people.

Fruit. New Mexico claims to raise better grapes, peaches, apricots, pears, quinces and apples, than even California, and as proof of this it may be mentioned that Los Angelos merchants tried to purchase New Mexican fruits to supply their own local demand.

Hot springs. The hot springs of New Mexico are beginning to attract the attention of invalids, notably those of Las Vegas, which are said to resemble the celebrated, though stronger, waters of Karlsbad in their medicinal qualities, and where every comfort has been supplied for the accommodation of visitors.

Health. As a health resort for consumptives the climate of New Mexico claims to rank first in the United States. Thus, according to census reports, the death rate from this disease is 25 per cent. in New England, in Minnesota 14 per cent., Southern States 5½ per cent., but less than 3 per cent. in New Mexico. In Yaos county land grants held by English investors cover some 200,000 acres, from which 25 per cent. is the usual return for wheat seeded.

UNITED STATES.

Pecos Valley. The Pecos Valley embraces 500,000 acres of arable land, and an ample supply of water for its irrigation. The great inducement that this section affords to the immigrant lies in the fact that all these lands were, until recent years, invested in the United States Government, and therefore titles are never questioned. From this valley, in the neighbourhood of Roswell, burst forth mammoth springs, which, flowing unceasingly, form good-sized rivers, from which the farmers have taken ditches, and through these arteries have made the arid land to grow with vegetation.

Fruit. In the older settled portion of the valley about Roswell apple trees six years old yield three to four barrels each year, pears as many bushels, plums four to six bushels, peaches 400 lbs. to 500 lbs., and it is not uncommon to see 25 dol. to 30 dol. worth of peaches or plums taken from a single tree.

Alfalfa. Alfalfa yields four to five crops per annum, or 8 to 12 tons per acre.

Articles.		Per Acre.	
Corn	Bushels	60 to	80
Wheat	,,	40	60
Oats	,,	50	70
Barley	,,	40	60
Rye	,,	30	40
Peas	,,	35	40
Sweet potatoes	,,	100	250
Beets	,,	175	400
Carrots	,,	175	300
Onions	Lbs.	23,000	25,000
Turnips	,,	20,000	22,000

Railways. Several railroads are being rapidly pushed forward to this fertile portion of the territory, so that there soon bids fair to be ample facilities to carry these products to market.

Education. The public schools of Texas are rapidly attaining a degree of perfection that will make them compare favourably with those of New England.

The following facts are from reports of the secretary of the Texas State Bureau of Immigration.

The permanent free school fund, invested in State and county bonds, is 5,873,174 dol.; 40,000,000 acres of land controlled by the State, and four leagues, or 17,712 acres, to each county organised and unorganised, controlled by the counties, making a total of 47,288,676 acres, which at 3 dol. per acre would give 141,866,028 dol., and added to the above makes a grand total of 147,739,202 dol.

The interest on the bonds and land notes for which school lands have been sold, rentals from the lands leased, one-third of the State tax, and 1 dol. on each poll, forms the available fund which is used each year for the maintenance of public free schools. This fund is rapidly increasing each year; in 1881 the amount appropriated was 103,933 dol. 44 c.; in 1885, 2,050,000 dol.; in 1887, 2,285,415 dol.; and in 1890, 2,645,524 dol, to educate a scholastic population of 565,672 children, say, at 4 dol. 50 c. per capita.

It is estimated that of this number of children only 402,000 availed themselves of the public schools during the past year.

The State University at Austin is one of the best endowed educational institutions in the United States, and is free to students of both sexes.

The University Permanent Fund is 523,411 dol., invested in bonds, with an available fund of 21,680 dol., and cash on hand of 10,825 dol., making a total university fund of 555,916 dol., besides which it has 2,221,400 acres of land, most of which was located in early times, and is very valuable, say worth 6 dol. per acre at least, or 13,328,400 dol., making a grand total of 13,884,316 dol. for university purposes.

The State Agricultural and Mechanical College, near Bryan, Brazos County, is endowed with 209,000 dol., invested in bonds, and has also a large endowment from the United States Government.

Here 94 students—half of whom take a mechanical, and half an agricultural course—receive free board and tuition.

The cost of board and tuition for other students is 130 dol. for the scholastic year.

UNITED STATES.

Exports.

	Cotton.		Lumber, &c.	Cotton Seed, Oilcake, and Meal.		Wheat Flour.		Corn.		Bottled Beer.	Sundries.	Total.
	Quantity.	Value.	Value.	Quantity.	Value.	Quantity.	Value.	Quantity.	Value.	Value.	Value.	
	Bales.	Dollars.	Dollars.	Lbs.	Dollars.	Barrels.	Dollars.	Bushels.	Dollars.	Dollars.	Dollars.	Dollars.
Great Britain	385,111	20,330,163	11,631	58,701,617	572,963	19,300	79,698	33,699	11,000	..	..	21,006,455
Germany	64,756	3,333,662	12,553	55,543,354	530,428	3	12	..	..	..	3,650	3,880,305
France	24,923	1,282,123	..	..	..	..	..	..	..	..	..	1,282,123
Russia	20,037	1,133,689	..	..	..	..	..	..	..	..	..	1,133,689
Mexico	4,362	223,763	176,416	..	..	130	518	1,547	989	14,378	32,471	448,535
Denmark	..	..	..	4,099,079	87,652	..	..	..	..	..	..	87,652
Sweden and Norway	..	..	..	1,460,095	11,736	..	..	..	..	..	..	11,736
Nicaragua	..	..	..	..	..	48	283	..	..	245	3,418	3,994
Total	499,189	26,303,400	200,600	Tons. 53,484	1,202,779	19,481	80,511	35,246	11,989	14,623	39,539	27,853,489

GALVESTON.

Vessels engaged in the Foreign Trade.

Entered.

Country.	Ballast. Number of Vessels.	Ballast. Tons.	Cargo. Number of Vessels.	Cargo. Tons.	Total. Number of Vessels.	Total. Tons.
America	38	7,179	29	9,159	67	16,338
Great Britain	76	86,267	36	46,475	112	132,742
Norway	24	11,664	4	1,494	28	13,158
Germany	5	3,522	2	532	7	4,054
Spain	4	3,422	...	...	4	3,422
Mexico	2	460	...	135	3	595
Total	149	112,514	71	57,795	221	170,309

Cleared.

Country.	Ballast. Number of Vessels.	Ballast. Tons.	Cargo. Number of Vessels.	Cargo. Tons.	Total. Number of Vessels.	Total. Tons.
America	3	333	65	17,291	68	17,624
Great Britain	...	...	120	149,943	120	149,943
Norway	...	...	22	8,922	22	8,922
Germany	...	...	7	4,344	7	4,344
Spain	...	...	3	2,398	3	2,398
Mexico	...	...	2	460	2	460
Total	3	333	219	183,358	222	183,691

Of course all the American tonnage is coastwise, and conveys cotton and wool to New York for eastern manufacturers, as well as large quantities of cotton on through bill of lading to Europe in connection with transatlantic steamers from New York.

Value of Imports in transit to Mexico.

		Dollars.
From Great Britain	..	368,618
Germany	..	165,890
Belgium	..	145,327
France	..	84,363
Mexico	..	2,455
Total	..	766,653

Other Imports.

Total value, 475,982 dol., of which Great Britain, 340,435 dol., principally cement and cotton ties; Mexico, 50,735 dol., principally coffee; Germany, 35,160 dol.

LONDON:
Printed for Her Majesty's Stationery Office,
By HARRISON AND SONS,
Printers in Ordinary to Her Majesty.
(1250 3 | 91—H & S 1045)

FOREIGN OFFICE.

1891.

ANNUAL SERIES.

No. 827.

DIPLOMATIC AND CONSULAR REPORTS ON TRADE AND FINANCE.

UNITED STATES.

REPORT FOR THE YEAR 1890
ON THE
AGRICULTURE OF THE CONSULAR DISTRICT OF NEW ORLEANS.

REFERENCE TO PREVIOUS REPORT, Annual Series No. 650.

Presented to both Houses of Parliament by Command of Her Majesty,
MARCH, 1891.

LONDON:
PRINTED FOR HER MAJESTY'S STATIONERY OFFICE,
BY HARRISON AND SONS, ST. MARTIN'S LANE,
PRINTERS IN ORDINARY TO HER MAJESTY.

And to be purchased, either directly or through any Bookseller, from
EYRE & SPOTTISWOODE, EAST HARDING STREET, FLEET STREET, E.C., and
32, ABINGDON STREET, WESTMINSTER, S.W.; or
JOHN MENZIES & Co., 12, HANOVER STREET, EDINBURGH, and
21, DRURY STREET, GLASGOW; or
HODGES, FIGGIS, & Co., 104, GRAFTON STREET, DUBLIN.

1891

[C. 6205—58.] *Price Threepence.*

New Series of Reports.

Reports of the Annual Series have been issued from Her Majesty's Diplomatic and Consular Officers at the following places, and may be obtained from the sources indicated on the title-page:—

No.		Price.	No.		Price.
705.	Fiume	1d.	766.	Hiogo	1½d.
706.	Odessa	2d.	767.	Alexandria	1½d.
707.	Suakin	½d.	768.	Maracaibo	½d.
708.	Hankow	½d.	769.	Macao	1d.
709.	Amoy	1d.	770.	Canton	1d.
710.	Buda-Pesth	1½d.	771.	Bangkok	2½d.
711.	Corunna	2d.	772.	Stockholm	1½d.
712.	Mogador	2d.	773.	Jaffa	½d.
713.	Cadiz	½d.	774.	Copenhagen	½d.
714.	Cadiz	1d.	775.	Ningpo	½d.
715.	Rio de Janeiro	2½d.	776.	Stettin	2d.
716.	Newchwang	½d.	777.	St. Petersburg	3d.
717.	Chinkiang	½d.	778.	St. Petersburg	½d.
718.	San Francisco	6d.	779.	St Jago de Cuba	1½d.
719.	Bussorah	½d.	780.	Chefoo	1d.
720.	Beyrout	1d.	781.	Christiania	3½d.
721.	Adrianople	½d.	782.	Marseilles	½d.
722.	Nantes	½d.	783.	Baghdad	1d.
723.	Caracas	1d.	784.	Naples	1½d.
724.	Mogador	½d.	785.	Tunis	4d.
725.	Tientsin	1d.	786.	Vera Cruz	1d.
726.	Foochow	1d.	787.	Tangier	1½d.
727.	Port au Prince	½d.	788.	Rome	2d.
728.	Callao	1d.	789.	Stuttgart	1½d.
729.	Puerto Plata	½d.	790.	Panama	1½d.
730.	San Francisco	1d.	791.	Berne	1½d.
731.	Philadelphia	2½d.	792.	Asuncion	½d.
732.	Pakhoi	1d.	793.	Bahia	7½d.
733.	Bilbao	1d.	794.	Monte Video	1½d.
734.	Dunkirk	1d.	795.	Munich	2d.
735.	Vienna	1d.	796.	Bucharest	1d.
736.	Nantes	1½d.	797.	Tokio	1d.
737.	Paramaribo	1d.	798.	Tabreez	1d.
738.	Honolulu	½d.	799.	Antwerp	1d.
739.	Chicago	2d.	800.	Malaga	1d.
740.	Söul	1d.	801.	Odessa	1d.
741.	Brindisi	1½d.	802.	Malaga	2d.
742.	Mozambique	1d.	803.	Amsterdam	1d.
743.	Caldera and Lota	1½d.	804.	Bogotá	1½d.
744.	Nice	1½d.	805.	Guayaquil	½d.
745.	Aleppo	1d.	806.	Lima	1d.
746.	Hakodate	1d.	807.	Rio de Janeiro	3d.
747.	New York	2d.	808.	Dantzig	1½d.
748.	Cagliari	1d.	809.	Florence	1½d.
749.	San Salvador	1d.	810.	Lisbon	1d.
750.	Gothenburg	2d.	811.	Quito	½d.
751.	Nagasaki	1d.	812.	Para	½d.
752.	Sofia	3½d.	813.	Palermo	2½d.
753.	Meshed	1d.	814.	Copenhagen	1d.
754.	Yokohama	2½d.	815.	Serajevo	½d.
755.	Shanghai	2d.	816.	Porto Rico	1d.
756.	Lisbon	1½d.	817.	Madrid	½d.
757.	Teneriffe	½d.	818.	Brussels	½d.
758.	Noumea	½d.	819.	Patras	½d.
759.	Tahiti	½d.	820.	Stuttgart	1d.
760.	Bushire	1½d.	821.	Taganrog	1d.
761.	Frankfort	2d.	822.	Salonica	2d.
762.	Palermo	2½d.	823.	Galveston	1d.
763.	Guatemala	1d.	824.	Rome	1½d.
764.	Smyrna	4d.	825.	Paris	1½d.
765.	Munich	2d.	826.	Bushire	½d.

No. 827.

Reference to previous Report, Annual Series No. 650.

UNITED STATES.

NEW ORLEANS.

Consul de Fonblanque to the Marquis of Salisbury.

My Lord,   *New Orleans, February 3rd,* 1891.

I HAVE the honour to enclose, herewith, Reports on Agricultural matters from this Consulate and from the Vice-Consulate of Pensacola.

Vice-Consul Barnewall, of Mobile, states that he is waiting for the publication of a Report from the Agricultural Department of Alabama, which he will utilise in his next Report.

I have, &c.
(Signed) A. DE G. DE FONBLANQUE.

Report on Agriculture, 1890.

The great floods to which the States in my district are liable, which form the subject of observations in my Trade Report, leave some slight compensation for the destruction they cause by leaving deposits which give an extra amount of fertility to the soil when they have subsided. Thus we find that the cotton crop of 1890 is from 5 per cent. to 7 per cent. larger than that of last year, though from 1 per cent. to 1½ per cent. inferior in point of quality. *[The flood. Compensation. Cotton.]*

Rice has followed the same course, and the result on sugar is phenomenal, as much as 7,000 lbs. of cane having been produced per acre; previous averages, 5,000 lbs. *[Rice and sugar.]*

I annex the last published Bulletin of Professor Stubbs on Field Experiments with Sugar Cane; also one on the Texas Screw Worm.

The United States Chemical Division of the Department of Agriculture has published the following instructions regarding the planting of sugar beets soil. The soil must be well drained, and with a good exposure to the light. It should be of loose texture, easily pulverised and of average fertility. *[Beets.]*

Fertilising.—Barnyard manure should not be applied immediately before planting, but if the soil has received a dressing of *[Fertilisers.]*

(1037)

well rotted manure the previous autumn, which has been well ploughed in and left over winter, it may be of advantage.

If fertilisers are employed, super-phosphates of lime, containing from 10 to 15 per cent. of available phosphoric acid, may be used at the rate of 250 lbs. to 300 lbs. per acre; if nitrogen is employed, it should be only in moderate quantities, and best in the form of nitrate of soda, at the rate of 100 lbs. to 150 lbs. per acre. Potash may be supplied in the form of kainite at the rate of 200 lbs. to 400 lbs. per acre, or a high grade sulphate at the rate of 50 lbs. to 100 lbs. per acre. It is probable that in most soils where experiments are made this year no fertilisers of any kind will be used, and very good beets can be grown on most of our western soils without the use of fertilisers at present. When fertilisers are employed they may be sown broadcast or drilled in the rows, and best at the time of planting.

Soil.

Preparation of Soil.—If the soil is deep and rich, it may be ploughed at once to the depth of 12 inches or 15 inches. In less fertile soils it is best to plough to the depth of 8 inches or 9 inches, and sub-soil to the depth of 4 inches or 5 inches. The land should be thoroughly harrowed, and reduced to a fine condition of tilth before planting.

Planting.

Planting.—For small patches the seed can be put in by hand. For larger fields drills can be provided. In general, the rows should be 18 inches apart, and the seed planted so as to give 1 inch for about every 3 inches. When the beets begin to show four leaves they should be thinned, so that they will stand at a distance of from 6 inches to 9 inches apart in the rows, according to the fertility of the soil. This regular thinning of the beets is absolutely necessary to secure a high sugar content, and it should be completed before they show six leaves. In very fertile soils the beets should be left closer together, while in less fertile ones they should be further apart. The object, in all cases, should be to grow a beet which will average about 1 lb. in weight after it is cleaned and topped.

Cultivation.—It is best to have the beets cultivated flat, and not planted in ridges. Any method of cultivation which will keep out the weeds, and keep the ground thoroughly stirred, will be sufficient. It is important that the hoe should be used, especially at the time of thinning, and to secure good results this method of cultivation should not be neglected. The cultivation of beets should be continued about the same time as for ordinary crops, and they should be laid by when the leaves begin to thoroughly cover the ground.

Exposure.

If beets are planted in small patches they should be in such a position as not to be shaded by other growing crops, especially corn, as the free exposure to sunlight is absolutely necessary to produce a beet containing a maximum percentage of sugar.

Ramie.

The production and preparation of ramie has passed out of the practical agriculture of this district. It had but a half-hearted support with the sole exception of General Sewell, whose faith remains unshaken. He is now engaged in large experiments in

Mexico, under the auspices and at the expense of its Government.

The following remarks on fruit as food may have some interest:—"So convinced am I of the extreme value of fruit in the animal economy," says an eminent physician, "that I hope to live to see the time when an orchard shall be an important part of every farm, and small fruit and berries shall be cultivated whenever there can be found space for them. I am more than convinced that a far too large proportion of meat is eaten in this country.

"The man who should bring about a change in this respect would be one of the greatest reformers of the day. There would be less poverty, less sickness, less sorrow and sin. Now, I will tell you what I claim for fruits as food, that is as complement for one's daily diet. First, that it is exceedingly palatable; secondly, that it causes, owing to this very palatableness, an increased flow of saliva; thirdly, that it thus assists us in digesting other food, both bread and meat; fourthly, that fruit is itself easily assimilated by the system; fifthly, that it keeps the system free and in good working condition; sixthly, that by its acids, salts, and essential oils the blood is purified and disease germs destroyed; and seventhly, that by its saccharine matter the body is nourished and the animal heat kept up. It would seem like a paradox to say that fruit both warms and cools the body, but such is the case.

"In summer its acids temper and equalise the heat, in winter its sugars warm. Sugar and acid, in fact, are so equally balanced in this food, formed in the greater laboratory of nature, that neither preponderates unduly or to the detriment of the other. 'To what extent,' it may be asked, 'would I propose cutting meat from the dietary?' 'To the extent,' I reply, 'of just one half.' If nothing else could be claimed for fruit, except its power of aiding the digestion of other food, it would be still worthy of our best consideration. It is indigestible or undigested food lying in the alimentary canal that causes people so much uneasiness, to say nothing of actual suffering. Fermentation takes place, and if the system is unable to disburden itself of the load, there is hardly a portion of the animal economy that does not come to grief. The liver is sorely distressed, the stomach chimes in with its sad complainings, the heart flutters or palpitates like an over-driven beast of burden, the blood is overheated, and the brain and nerves are affected. It is well if this last but for a night, and restlessness with bad dreams be the only results; but how seldom is this the case, when, after a night, the same effects follow the same indiscretions! No wonder the liver at last gives up the unequal struggle, or that the soured blood stores up its salt in joint or muscle, developing all the misery of rheumatism or gout."

One subject upon which the American agriculturist can (as it seems to me) instruct the British farmer is the growing and management of fruit trees. "The American Cultivator" says,

4. UNITED STATES.

Fruit trees. "for peaches, plums, and cherries sand soil is especially adapted. The only caution needed in growing these fruits is to make the land rich, and to supply large amounts of mineral fertilisers.

Fertilisers for stone fruit. These stone fruits are especially greedy for potash, and if wood ashes cannot be readily obtained the potash salts furnish a good substitute. In forming the seeds of any fruit, as in ripening the fruit itself, potash is indispensable. Lack of this or other mineral elements retard the fruit in ripening, and often after standing still for one or two weeks for lack of material to develop the fruit drops to the ground. Lack of mineral plant food is

Grape mildew. probably the original source of grape mildew and rot, though once established the disease flourishes under almost any conditions. Most cases of grape mildew originated in vines whose vitality was weakened by overbearing. But except when boughs break through being too heavily loaded there is no such thing as over-bearing, it means rather an insufficient supply of plant food for nature to perfect the fruit it has set and undertaken to ripen."

The "scale." For "scale" on fruit trees a correspondent of the "Florida Agriculturist" writes:—"I used potash and whale oil soap for scale, and the more I used the more I had to. I had occasion to tie up trees, and used, as a cushion, between the stake, string, and tree, grass, pine straw, or anything that would serve as a protection from chafing. I noticed that where pine straw was used there was no scale, while there was around where other articles

Wash for "scale." were used. That gave me the hint that a scale did not like turpentine. I prepared a wash as follows, and have used it five years:—Water, 2 gallons; sal. soda, ½ lb.; when dissolved add 1 gill of spirits of turpentine. Keep it well stirred while using. I never had to make a second application. In Government reports for 1888 they had best results from a preparation of rosin, but did not follow it up or they would have found the turpentine mixture."

Oranges. In colonies where oranges can be cultivated the following hints by a practical Florida planter may be of value:—"Not unfrequently do I see something about 'ploughing-in cow peas in their green state as excellent manure,' &c. However good advice this may be for North Florida and Georgia, it is very detrimental on all lands that I have observed in this portion of Florida. I do not stand alone in this matter. I and some of my neighbours have had land ruined for some time by turning under one heavy green crop during the hot rainy weather, and on high land at that. Fermentation takes place, and the land becomes sour and dead; while if the growth had been broken down and allowed to decay on the surface, and then turned over in October or November, the land would have been materially enriched.

Turning in green crops. "I have seen healthy orange trees greatly injured by turning-in green crops at this season of the year. The trees turn 'frenchy,' and remain so for some time despite the most careful attention afterward. For groves here it is far better to keep the ground worked till the June growth is well started, and then let the ground alone till the cooler weather in October and November, and even till December. It takes but a little time in hot weather by turning under such succulent growths as cow peas, to bring land to such a state that it will not grow even healthy crab-grass.

"I have found no time so desirable for fertilising a grove as the last part of October, and so on till the middle of December. This application should contain such elements as the tree requires to make perfect blooms, and not only to make the blooms, but leave vitality enough in the trees to hold the young fruit. More stress comes to the tree with such an amount of blooms as most trees carried last February and March than at the fruit-growing season. The stress comes all at once. It is not gradual. If a little more fertilisers were expended so as to be available at such times, there would be fewer complaints of trees dropping their fruit. *Time for fertilising.*

"My experience is that nothing takes the place of sulphate of potash, phosphoric acid, and magnesia, with ammonia. I never mix my fertiliser. I cannot do it thoroughly by hand, and that which brings me back commensurate results is cheapest in the end without regard to first cost. *Sulphate of potash.*

"Again, I fertilise the last part of May, 500 lbs., when I put 700 lbs. in November, and at any time from June, or when I see a tree that is off in colour, or in any way shows want of food, it gets it. If it is complete food for the wants of that tree it will do no damage, even though the amount be more than the tree requires. Any plant food which produces succulent growth on a bearing tree is at no time desirable.

"My belief and practice is to use in the nursery every such plant food as makes good strong wood that will stand heat or cold —the two extremes come near each other—that has all the elements which are required to put the tree in the condition for which I planted it, namely, to bring me results, good marketable fruit, and not only good, but the best. If I had only a few trees which I wanted to pet I would use, when they were well filled with fruit, fertiliser in August also, such as would not increase the size, but fill it full and round it out, and add to its juiciness and flavour. The tree never rests after bloom; its circulation is going on through every minute cell till the fruit is picked." *Plant food.*

Annex A.—REPORT of the Sugar Experiment Station, of the Louisiana State University and A. & M. College, at Audubon Park, New Orleans, La.

Experiment Station, Audubon Park, New Orleans, La.
Major T. J. Bird, *Commissioner of Agriculture, Baton, Rouge, La.*

Dear Sir,
I HAND you herewith Field Experiments with Sugar Cane, and ask that it be published as Bulletin No. 28.
Respectfully submitted,
WM. STUBBS, Director.

FIELD EXPERIMENTS.

With the end of the present season closes a series of experiments begun four years ago. It was contemplated in the beginning to extend them through five years, but the removal of this station from its old location near Kenner, to its new domicile at this place, has shortened the time.

These four years have been patiently spent in repeating the same experiments upon the same soil, and the aggregate results are far more suggestive and conclusive than those reached in one year. The bulletin will contain, therefore, a summary of the results of the four years, together with the detailed results of 1889. In comparing the yearly results the different seasons must be known and considered. The station has kept an accurate weather record and diary ever since March 1, 1886. The following is a condensed record of each year's rainfall and temperature.

NEW ORLEANS.

Condensed Weather Record of Sugar Experiment Station from March 1, 1886, to January 1, 1890.

Month.	Average Temperature	Maximum Temperature	Minimum Temperature	Rainfall.
1886.	Degrees.	Degrees.	Degrees.	Inches.
March	63	80	37	9·13
April	69	87	41	7·32
May	76	93	57	3·59
June	83	97	69	11·5
July	83	95	68	3·25
August	84	96	66	4·18
September	80	91	59	5·24
October	73	87	39	1
November	66	75	33	5·55
December	65	79	26	2·75
1887.				
January	57	82	22	3·31
February	65·4	80	30	5·23
March	58·2	81	40	3·27
April	71·7	89	57	2·21
May	78	94	59	6·56
June	84	94	62	10·35
July	84	97	68	7·86
August	82·5	95	69	6·7
September	79	92	56	3·3
October	69·5	86	40	6·39
November	60	80	30	·11
December	54·6	77	30	7·14
1888.				
January	56·6	77	30	3·77
February	59·8	76	37	9·8
March	59	78	36	5·79
April	73·4	85	54	·91
May	76·7	92	54	11·77
June	79·8	92	65	8·69
July	82	98	71	5·49
August	81·2	95	70	15·8
September	77·3	89	57	3·29
October	70·6	85	53	3·4
November	62·4	84	34	2·5
December	63·6	71	27	4·12
1889.				
January	54	71	34	8·3
February	55	75	31	3·21
March	63·6	79	40	2·38
April	72	86	47	3·28
May	78·1	91	48	·76
June	82·3	96	57	9·43
July	85·6	92	68	7·15
August	81	90	66	5·74
September	79·1	91	51	5·3
October	68·1	86	51	..
November	58·9	82	30	..
December	63	80	45	·43

In the following table is presented the four years in a comparative form, and it may be useful in determining some of the factors which go toward solving the problem of good crop years.

The winter of 1886 was very severe, destroying much of the seed and stubble; the spring was late and cold, and good stands of cane were not obtained till May. The subsequent seasons were fair, and where good stands prevailed the crop was medium.

The winter of 1887 was mild and conducive to excellent seed cane; the spring was moderately dry and warm; followed by a warm and wet summer grading into a cool dry autumn; conditions favourable to heavy tonnage.

The winter of 1888 was fairly propitious, but the spring was excessively wet, preventing the proper cultivation of the cane. The wet weather extended to July, causing a serious postponement or abandonment of the regular "lay-by" of cane. These rains were succeeded by a dry, cool fall, giving us light tonnage, but heavy sugar yield, due more to the low glocuse content than excess of sugar in cane.

The year 1889 will always be remembered as the year of drought. The rainfall for the year was only 46 inches, and this fell mostly in the winter and summer, giving us a spring and fall of unexampled dryness—a dryness which has been prolonged into the winter of 1890, and up to this time has scarcely been broken.

Taking the table and the seasons, we find that a dry, warm winter, followed by a moderately dry spring, and this, in turn, succeeded by a hot wet summer, shading gradually into a cool dry autumn are conditions favourable to a maximum growth of cane.

After the cane is laid by frequent showers of considerable intensity seem highly beneficial.

The following is the comparative weather statement for the four years:—

	Average Temperature	Maximum Temperature	Minimum Temperature	Rainfall.
	Degrees.	Degrees.	Degrees.	Inches.
1887	70·3	97	22	62·43
1888	69·3	98	27	75·33
1889	70·1	96	30	45·98
Spring months, 1886	69·3	93	37	20·04
,, ,, 1887	69·3	94	40	12·04
,, ,, 1888	69·7	92	36	18·47
,, ,, 1889	71·2	91	40	6·42
Summer months, 1886	83·3	97	66	18·93
,, ,, 1887	83·5	97	62	24·91
,, ,, 1888	81	98	65	29·98
,, ,, 1889	82·9	96	57	22·32
Fall months, 1886	73	87	33	11·79
,, ,, 1887	69·5	92	30	9·08
,, ,, 1888	70·1	89	35	9·19
,, ,, 1889	68·7	91	34	5·03
Winter months, 1887	59	82	22	15·68
,, ,, 1888	56·6	77	27	17·69
,, ,, 1889	57·3	82	31	11·94

The field experiments, extending over the four years, have been of the following:—
1. Germination questions.
2. Physiological questions.
3. Varieties best adapted to Louisiana.
4. Manurial requirements.

Germinating questions. The sugar cane has been so long cultivated from cuttings that it has, like the banana, lost its power of producing ordinary true seed, even though it passes through all the phases of fructification. Often in nature, when any organ is rendered useless, it ceases to exist. The fish in underground caverns are eyeless. The banana and some other plants, long propagated from shoots or suckers, produce seedless fruits. In the last year or two, however, the cane has been made to produce true seed. The idea by which this result was achieved was, in itself, a simple one, yet the thought may produce a revolution in cane culture. Profs. Harrison and Bovell, of Dodd's Reformatory, Barbadoes, conceived the idea that by placing in close proximity unlike varieties of cane from different parts of the world, by cross fertilisation, perfect fructification might result.

Experiments have verified this conception, and to-day a large number of true seedlings are growing (some on this station from seed kindly furnished by Prof. Bovell), and already several new varieties of great promise have been named and propagated. This discovery is of great value, since the cane plant, hitherto so refractory and susceptible to change only through bud variation, now becomes a pliant tool in the hands of the scientist, and soon we may expect varieties of great excellence as the result of the labours of the latter. Pending these researches and experiments, the Louisiana planters must continue to utilise a goodly part of each crop as seed, and economy often suggests the propriety of planting the upper part of the stalk, so poor in sugar, instead of the entire stalk, so valuable at the mill. This practice is, however, severely criticised by some, upon reasons drawn from known principles of vegetable physiology. The cane, say they, has only sterile flowers, and consequently gives no seed or grains. Therefore the eyes of the cane are intended to replace the true seed or grain. In all seed-bearing plants those seeds germinate and fructify best which are permitted to reach perfect maturity. Therefore, in immitation of this natural law, we must seek that part of the stalk which contains the largest and best developed eyes in order to secure seed which will produce the most vigorous plants. It is further claimed that where tops are universally used as seed a degeneracy of the cane will follow, since the latter is always reproduced with those parts of the cane where the juices are poorest in nourishment (sugar) and the eyes the most imperfectly developed. Hence, it is a practice with some of our planters never to plant fall cane until the polariscope shows at least 10 per cent. sugar in the cane. *Per contra* there are others who claim that the planting of the tops is justifiable from purely scientific reasons, besides the economy involved.

They regard the cane planted as "cuttings" rather than true seed, and the eyes as buds to be developed under proper conditions. They say that the florist when he wants to root new plants never uses the old or mature wood, but rather the young and succulent portion. Therefore, in planting cane, the youngest and most succulent portions will secure the best results. Which is right has not yet been decided by science. Experiments in the field have demonstrated that eyes from both the mature and immature parts of the stalk will germinate. But which are the best, i.e., which will insure the best and surest results under the varying conditions of our seasons, soils, and rainfall?

To determine this question the following experiments were instituted, with a view of continuing them through a series of years in order to eliminate, as far as possible, all the modifying factors incident to one year's experiment. Great pains were taken to select healthy stalks of uniform length. These were cut up into short pieces, beginning with the green immature top. Two eyes were left upon each cutting, and each stalk was selected so as to give eleven cuttings. Seventy-five of these cuttings, containing 150 eyes, were devoted to each experiment.

The land was in excellent order, having had a large crop of pea vines turned in early in the fall with a four-horse plough. The cuttings were carefully deposited in each row and covered by a hoe. The following are the experiments:—

Plat O.—Germination Questions.

1. Seventy-five white immature joints of two eyes each.
2. Seventy-five joints next to No. 1, partially white, two eyes each.
3. Seventy-five joints next to No. 2, full red, two eyes each.
4. ,, ,, ,, ,, 3, ,, ,, ,,
5. ,, ,, ,, ,, 4, ,, ,, ,,
6. ,, ,, ,, ,, 5, ,, ,, ,,
7. ,, ,, ,, ,, 6, ,, ,, ,,
8. ,, ,, ,, ,, 7, ,, ,, ,,
9. ,, ,, ,, ,, 8, ,, ,, ,,
10. ,, ,, ,, ,, 9, ,, ,, ,,
11. Seventy-five joints, butts, two eyes each.

In 1886 the severe weather, with a late unfavourable spring, so prevented germination as to vitiate results. All germinated badly, but No. 3 gave the largest number of sprouts, followed closely by No. 2.

In 1887 a fresh planting was made, which was closely followed through three years.

In 1887 and 1888 this plat was worked up during November; in 1889, in October. This year was one remarkable for immature cane, particularly in the early part of the season. The following tables will show the yield and sugar contents for each year:—

NEW ORLEANS.

Table 1.—PLAT O.—Germination Questions. Planting different parts of the Stalks of the Cane, February 9, 1887. First Year Plant Cane, Harvested November 3.

Part of the Stalk Planted.	Feb. 27.	March 10.	March 13.	March 17.	March 19.	March 25.	At Harvest, Nov. 3.	Weight of Stalks.	Average Weight of each.	Ton per Acre.	Number of Stalks per Acre.
								Lbs.	Lbs.		
1. Upper white joints	5	24	24	24	26	34	97	247	2·54	18·14	14,287
2. Next to white joints	12	39	41	41	45	45	140	407	2·91	32·06	21,050
3. ,, No. 2	10	45	48	54	63	69	165	485	2·94	38·18	25,987
4. ,, ,, 3	4	27	34	39	45	51	152	428	2·82	33·75	23,940
5. ,, ,, 4	1	27	36	45	51	53	154	442	2·87	34·08	24,255
6. ,, ,, 5	1	25	35	43	52	58	149	426	2·86	33·56	23,467
7. ,, ,, 6	0	19	20	25	33	40	147	400	2·72	31·48	23,152
8. ,, ,, 7	0	13	18	23	27	32	133	320	2·41	25·24	20,947
9. ,, ,, 8	1	19	23	28	34	39	130	340	2·61	26·82	20,552
10. ,, ,, 9	0	12	14	20	26	36	97	214	2·21	16·88	15,276
11. Butts*	0	11	15	20	41	41	73	160	2·19	12·62	11,520

* This row was seriously injured in the summer by proximity to a fig tree, and is not counted in stubble.

Table 2.—PLAT O.—First Year Stubble, Harvested November 14, 1888.

Part of Stalks Planted.	Number of Stalks Harvested.	Weight of Stalks.	Average Weight of each.	Tons per Acre.	Number of Stalks per Acre.
		Lbs.	Lbs.		
1. Upper white joints	76	136	1·79	10·71	11,970
2. Next to white joint	119	206	1·73	16·22	17,742
3. ,, No. 2	133	257	1·87	19·72	20,947
4. ,, ,, 3	127	226	1·07	17·79	20,002
5. ,, ,, 4	130	244	1·88	19·21	20,475
6. ,, ,, 5	142	238	1·68	18·74	22,305
7. ,, ,, 6	124	220	1·77	17·32	19,536
8. ,, ,, 7	132	256	1·94	20·16	20,790
9. ,, ,, 8	104	192	1·84	15·12	16,380
10. ,, ,, 9	89	146	1·64	11·49	14,017

Table 3.—PLAT O.—Second Year Stubble, Harvested October 15, 1889.

Part of the Stalk Planted.	Number of Stalks Harvested.	Weight of Stalks.	Average Weight of each.	Tons per Acre.	Number of Stalks per Acre.
		Lbs.	Lbs.		
1. Upper white joints	60	78	1·03	6·16	9,480
2. Next to white joint	90	167	1·72	13·19	14,536
3. ,, No. 2	110	182	1·66	14·37	17,380
4. ,, ,, 3	125	257	2·06	20·03	19,750
5. ,, ,, 4	92	125	1·36	9·08	14,536
6. ,, ,, 5	112	246	2·02	19·41	18,960
7. ,, ,, 6	124	235	1·09	18·56	19,592
8. ,, ,, 7	123	214	1·74	16·09	19,434
9. ,, ,, 8	90	165	1·84	13·03	14,220
10. ,, ,, 9	64	114	1·78	9·00	10,112

12 UNITED STATES.

Table 4.—PLAT O.—Field and Sugar House Results, November 3, 1887. First Year Plant.

Number and Kind of Experiments.	Yield per Acre in Tons.	Degree Baumé.	Total Solids.	Sucrose.	Glucose.	Purity Coefficient.	Glucose Ratio.	Per Ton.	Per Acre.
1. Upper white joints ...	18·14	7·4	13·31	10·3	1·24	77·38	12·04	118	2,141
2. Next to white joints	32·06	7·8	14·01	11·2	1·35	79·94	12·05	128	4,104
3. ,, ,, No. 2 ...	38·18	7·6	13·71	10·3	1·28	75·12	12·42	117	4,467
4. ,, ,, ,, 3 ...	33·75	7·3	13·21	10·0	1·06	75·07	16·00	99	3,341
5. ,, ,, ,, 4 ...	34·80	7·5	13·61	10·0	1·06	73·47	16·00	99	3,445
6. ,, ,, ,, 5 ...	33·56	7·8	14·01	10·9	1·35	77·80	12·38	124	4,161
7. ,, ,, , 6 ...	31·48	7·3	13·11	10·5	1·28	80·09	12·19	120	3,777
8. ,, ,, ,, 7 ...	25·24	7·8	14·01	10·6	1·35	81·36	12·73	120	3,029
9. ,, ,, ,, 8 ...	26·82	8·0	14·41	10·5	1·35	72·86	12·95	119	3,192
10. ,, ,, ,, 9 ...	16·88	7·9	14·31	11·5	1·35	80·36	11·73	133	2,245

Table 5.—PLAT O.—Field and Sugar House Results, November 14, 1888. First Year Stubble.

Number and Kind of Experiment.	Yield per Acre in Tons.	Degree Baumé.	Total Solids.	Sucrose.	Glucose.	Purity Coefficient.	Glucose Ratio.	Per Ton.	Per Acre.
1. Upper white joints ...	10·71	8·4	15·2	13·5	89	88·81	6·59	170·01	1,821·77
2. Next to white joints	16·22	8·2	14·8	13·3	75	89·86	5·63	169·75	2,753·34
3. ,, ,, No. 2 ...	19·72	8·4	15·1	13·5	77	89·04	5·07	172·27	3,397·16
4. ,, ,, ,, 3 ...	17·79	8·4	15·2	13·7	80	90·13	5·84	175·00	3,113·25
5. ,, ,, ,, 4 ...	19·21	8·3	14·9	13·5	82	90·06	6·07	171·78	3,299·89
6. ,, ,, ,, 5 ...	18·74	8·6	15·5	14·0	69	90·32	4·92	181·51	3,401·49
7. ,, ,, ,, 6 ...	17·32	8·3	15·0	13·0	82	86·66	6·03	164·78	2,853·98
8. ,, ,, ,, 7 ...	20·16	8·1	14·6	12·7	87	86·98	6·85	159·53	3,216·12
9. ,, ,, ,, 8 ...	15·12	7·5	13·6	11·4	89	83·82	7·08	140·91	2,130·56
10. ,, ,, ,, 9 ...	11·49	7·8	14·1	12·3	91	87·23	7·39	153·09	1,759·00

Table 6.—PLAT O.—Field and Sugar House Results, October 15, 1889. Second Year Stubble.

Number and Kind of Experiment.	Yield per Acre in Tons.	Degree Baumé.	Total Solids.	Sucrose.	Glucose.	Purity Coefficient.	Glucose Ratio.	Per Ton.	Per Acre.
1. Upper white joints ...	6·16	6·6	11·9	8·2	2·61	69	31·82	59·99	369·54
2. Next to white joints	13·19	6·7	12·2	8·2	2·67	67	32·56	58·66	773·72
3. ,, ,, No. 2 ...	14·37	7·6	13·7	8·4	2·46	61	29·04	65·99	947·56
4. ,, ,, ,, 3 ...	20·03	7·6	13·8	10·8	2·41	78	22·31	100·66	2,043·04
5. ,, ,, ,, 4 ...	9·88	7·0	12·7	9·6	2·37	75	24·68	84·07	836·84
6. ,, ,, ,, 5 ...	19·41	7·0	12·6	9·7	2·38	77	24·53	85·82	1,665·76
7. ,, ,, ,, 6 ...	18·56	7·7	14·0	10·7	2·63	76	24·57	94·64	1,756·52
8. ,, ,, ,, 7 ...	16·09	7·0	12·6	8·6	2·91	68	34·18	58·66	990·35
9. ,, ,, ,, 8 ...	13·03	6·5	11·7	7·0	3·23	59	46·14	30·24	394·03
10. ,, ,, ,, 9 ...	9·00	5·5	10·0	5·1	3·33	51	65·29	1·54	13·86

The following table will give the aggregate yield, and the available sugar on 70 per cent. extraction per acre for the three years:—

Yield Available Sugar.	Tons.	Lbs.
1. Upper white joint..	35·01	4,832
2. Next to ,, ,, ..	61·47	7,631
3. ,, ,, No. 2 ..	72·27	8,812
4. ,, ,, ,, 3 ..	71·84	8,497
5. ,, ,, ,, 4 ..	63·89	7,582
6. ,, ,, ,, 5 ..	71·71	9,228
7. ,, ,, ,, 6 ..	67·36	8,387
8. ,, ,, ,, 7 ..	62·03	7,235
9. ,, ,, ,, 8 ..	55·67	5,717
10. ,, ,, ,, 9 ..	37·37	4,018

Here No. 3 has given the largest tonnage, and next to No. 6 the largest available sugar. The upper white joints germinate much more quickly than the others, but these sprouts are incapable of withstanding prolonged droughts in early life. Many of these sprouts died in 886, and the stubble crops were therefore "gappy." Again the stubble of No. 5 was somewhat injured in 1888 by driving carts over it to obtain cane from the experiments beyond, and, hence, its yield was very low in 1889.

Conclusions.

These experiments clearly show that the upper portion of the the cane, barring the green, immature joints, is the equal if not the superior of the whole cane, or any other portion for seed, and suggests the propriety of search for some practical way of utilising the upper thirds of the entire crop for seed, and grinding the other two-thirds.

This question, propounded to the plant cane in 1887, has been followed through the first and second rattoons.

How many stalks of cane to plant?

Simultaneous with this question has been incidentally propounded another:—Which is best for seed—plant or stubble cane?

In the same plat were also tried a few experiments confirmatory of those already described, viz., what part of the cane is best for seed?

The following are the experiments in full:—
1. One cane with a lap, cut in the row.
2. Two canes ,, ,,
3. Three ,, ,, ,,
4. Four ,, ,, ,,
5. One cane, no lap, uncut.
6. Upper halves of canes, two and a lap.
7. Lower ,, ,, ,, ,,
8. Upper thirds ,, ,, ,,
9. Middle ,, ,, ,, ,,
10. Lower ,, ,, ,, ,,

Table 7. — Plat O. — Germination Questions. Planted February 10; and Gathered November 4, 1887. Plant Cane.

Number and Kind of Experiments.	March 13. No. of Sprouts. Plant.	March 13. No. of Sprouts. Stubble.	May 25. No. of Sprouts. Plant.	May 25. No. of Sprouts. Stubble.	November 4. Plant. No. of Stalks.	November 4. Plant. Weight of Stalks, Lbs.	November 4. Plant. Ton per acre.	November 4. Stubble. No. of Stalks.	November 4. Stubble. Weight of Stalks, Lbs.	November 4. Stubble. Tons per acre.
1. One cane (cut)	36	50	89	77	371	1114	33·42	420	1109	33·27
2. Two ,, ,,	87	83	172	154	409	1232	36·96	413	1338	40·14
3. Three ,, ,,	136	144	220	214	430	1144	34·32	440	1336	40·08
4. Four ,, ,,	120	158	250	279	409	1296	38·88	479	1410	42·03
5. One ,, (uncut)	30	48	53	77	357	1146	34·33	413	1132	33·96*
6. Upper halves	108	106	148	154	421	1360	40·08	436	1292	38·76
7. Lower ,,	53	57	123	109	388	1334	40·02	402	980	29·04*
8. Upper thirds	139	101	168	147	420	1278	38·34	344	918	27·54*
9. Middle ,,	100	109	165	180	385	1276	38·28	310	860	25·08*
10. Lower ,,	117	46	177	104	407	1134	34·02	296	740	22·02*

* Injured more or less by shade of a live oak tree.

Table 8.—Plat O.—First Year Stubble, November 14, 1888.

Number and Kind of Experiments.	Plant. Number of Stalks.	Plant. Weight of Stalks. Lbs.	Plant. Tons per Acre.	Stubble. Number of Stalks.	Stubble. Weight of Stalks. Lbs.	Stubble. Tons per Acre.
1. One cane (cut)	315	516	15·48	355	668	20·04
2. Two canes (cut)	355	578	17·34	419	770	23·01
3. Three ,,	377	544	16·32	433	719	21·57
4. Four ,,	433	691	20·73	461	866	25·98
5. One cane (uncut)	358	742	22·26	338	622	18·66
6. Upper halves	398	870	26·01	374	784	23·52
7. Lower ,,	400	804	24·12	209	521	15·63*
8. Upper thirds	405	826	24·78	310	492	14·76*
9. Middle ,,	414	750	22·05	298	454	13·62*
10. Lower ,,	373	604	18·12	277	432	12·96*

* Injured by shade.

Table 9.—PLAT O. Second Year Stubble, October 15, 1889.

Number and Kind of Experiments.	Plant. Number of Stalks.	Plant. Weight of Stalks.	Plant. Tons per Acre.	Stubble. Number of Stalks.	Stubble. Weight of Stalks.	Stubble. Tons per Acre.
		Lbs.			Lbs.	
1. One cane (cut)	275	572	17.16	307	767	23.01
2. Two canes (cut)	278	533	15.19	217	451	13.54
3. Three canes (cut)	262	490	14.70	257	596	17.88
4. Four canes (cut)	334	855	25.65	368	868	26.05
5. One cane (uncut)	297	867	26.01	156	522	15.66
6. Upper halves ..	321	674	20.22	241	520	15.61
7. Lower „ ..	334	835	25.05	217	503	15.69
8. Upper thirds ..	346	733	21.09	180	309	9.27
9. Middle „ ..	291	680	20.40	112	116	3.8
10. Lower „ ..	289	693	20.79	80	76	2.28

Table 10.—PLANT CANE. Harvested November 4, 1887.
PLAT O. Germination Questions.

Number and Kind of Experiments.	Yield per Acre in Tons.	Degree Baume.	Total Solids	Sucrose.	Glucose.	Coefficient Purity.	Glucose Ratio.	Lbs. of Available Sugar upon 70 per cent. Extraction. Per Ton.	Lbs. of Available Sugar upon 70 per cent. Extraction. Per Acre.
1 one cane-cut, plant ...	33.42	7.05	12.71	9.9	1.77	77.89	17.86	101.05	3,392
1 one cane-cut, stubble	33.27	7.03	13.24	11.3	1.57	85.35	13.88	125.30	4,169
2 two cane-cut, plant ...	36.96	7.04	13.39	10.2	1.84	76.17	18.03	104.16	3,850
2 two cane-cut, stubble	40.14	7.04	13.49	10.2	2.24	76.61	21.96	95.76	3,844
3 three cane-cut, plant	34.32	7.03	13.19	10.1	1.92	76.57	19.00	101.08	3,469
3 three cane-cut, stubble	40.08	7.05	13.69	10.3	1.09	75.23	18.44	104.82	4,180
4 four cane-cut, plant ...	38.88	7.05	13.59	9.9	2.04	73.58	20.06	95.76	3,723
4 four cane-cut, stubble	42.03	7.05	13.59	10.9	1.09	80.02	17.43	112.07	4,767
5 one cane uncut, plant	34.33	7.03	13.24	10.8	1.09	81.57	17.59	111.03	3,821
5 one cane uncut, stubble	33.96	7.04	13.49	10.4	2.00	77.83	19.23	103.06	3,418
6 upper halves, plant ...	40.08	7.03	13.24	10.8	1.09	81.57	17.59	111.03	4,541
6 upper halves, stubble	38.76	7.05	13.69	10.2	2.00	74.05	19.06	100.08	3,907
7 lower halves, plant ...	40.02	7.03	13.19	10.8	2.14	81.88	19.51	106.26	4,253
7 lower halves, stubble	29.04*	7.04	13.49	10.3	2.00	76.64	19.41	102.02	2,094
8 upper thirds, plant ...	38.34	7.03	13.14	10.4	1.09	79.09	18.26	105.07	4,053
8 upper thirds, stubble	27.54*	7.06	13.89	10.6	2.00	77.03	18.86	106.84	2,930
9 middle thirds, plant ...	38.28	7.04	13.44	10.5	1.09	78.12	18.09	109.01	4,100
9 middle thirds, stubble	25.08*	7.06	13.89	10.5	2.00	75.59	19.04	105.60	2,709
10 lower thirds, plant ...	34.02	7.06	12.74	10.0	1.86	78.49	18.06	101.00	3,436
10 lower thirds, stubble	22.02*	7.09	14.29	11.2	1.82	78.37	16.25	118.58	2,521

* Injured by proximity of live oak.

Through an accident in the laboratory the samples of juice were mixed, which vitiated the accuracy of results, and hence no correct table can be given for 1888. That for 1889 is, however, presented.

(1037)

16 UNITED STATES.

Table No. 11.—SECOND Year Stubble, Harvested Oct. 15, 1889.
Plat O—Germination Questions.

Number and Kind of Experiments.	Yield per Acres in Tons.	Degree Baume.	Total Solids.	Sucrose.	Glucose.	Coefficient of Purity.	Glucose Ratio.	Per Ton.	Per Acre.
1. One cane cut, plant ...	17·16	7·4	13·3	10·0	2·27	75	22·7	92·33	1,584·38
1. ,, ,, stubble	23·02	8·1	14·6	10·7	2·27	73	21·19	102·13	2,351·03
2. Two ,, plant ...	16·01	6·6	11·9	9·5	2·21	80	23·26	86·59	1,386·31
2. ,, ,, stubble	13·54	6·9	12·4	7·8	2·89	63	37·05	48·51	656·83
3. Three ,, plant ...	14·93	7·2	12·9	9·6	2·59	74	26·97	80·01	1,195·89
3. ,, ,, stubble	17·88	7·9	14·3	19·9	2·35	76	21·46	103·25	1,846·11
4. Four ,, plant ...	25·65	7·3	13·2	9·9	2·64	75	26·66	83·16	2,133·05
4. ,, ,, stubble	26·05	7·4	13·4	9·8	2·52	73	25·71	84·28	2,195·49
5. One cane uncut, plant	26·01	7·7	13·9	10·8	2·38	77	22·03	101·32	2,635·33
5. ,, ,, stubble	15·66	7·6	13·8	10·4	2·64	75	25·38	90·16	1,411·90
6. Upper halves, plant ...	20·22	7·8	14·0	11·5	2·38	82	20·69	111·02	2,244·82
6. ,, ,, stubble	15·61	8·0	14·4	10·7	2·72	74	25·42	92·68	1,446·73
7. Lower ,, plant ...	25·65	7·5	13·5	10·7	2·57	79	24·01	95·83	2,458·04
7. ,, ,, stubble	*15·11	7·9	14·2	11·0	2·64	79	24·00	98·56	1,488·24
8. Upper thirds, plant ...	22·00	7·3	13·1	10·2	2·56	78	25·09	89·74	1,974·28
8. ,, ,, stubble	* 9·28	7·5	13·6	10·3	2·48	75	24·07	92·12	854·87
9. Middle ,, plant ...	20·42	7·0	12·7	9·4	2·48	74	26·38	79·52	1,623·8
9. ,, ,, stubble	* 3·49	7·4	13·4	10·2	2·56	76	25·09	89·04	1,310·75
10. Lower ,, plant ...	20·8	7·1	12·8	9·6	2·70	75	28·12	77·7	616·16
10. ,, ,, stubble	* 2·3	7·3	13·1	8·7	2·95	66	33·93	61·95	142·48

Analyses. | Lbs. of Available Sugar upon 70 per cent. Extraction.

* Injured by shade.

In the above experiments several of those where stubble cane was used as seed were injured by shade. Eliminating these, we find that in an average year, with good seed, two stalks and a lap will be abundant seed; that stubble cane is as good, if not better seed, than plant, and that the upper halves or thirds of the cane are as good as the entire stalk for seed. It is also shown that there is no physiological benefit accruing from cutting the cane. Whatever benefit may arise from this practice, now almost universal, must be ascribed to care and efficiency of work in planting and covering, and to the decreased risk of unearthing the cane during early cultivation, especially when the latter is very crooked. When cane has to remain in the ground all winter, before germinating, it is best not to cut the cane at all if its physical condition will permit such a procedure, since every cut produces a wound which more or less induces fermentation and decay. It is the belief of those who practice cutting that when an eye on an entire stalk starts vigorously into growth, it can and may injure the vitality of the other eyes, and hence they recommend cutting the cane to prevent this destruction. That such is not the case has been shown by a number of experiments conducted by the station. In planting entire stalks it is difficult to cover each eye at the same depth. Those near the surface germinate first, while those at the greatest depth may never germinate at all, though perfectly sound and healthy, because ere the conditions necessary to germination at that depth are secured the earlier sprouts are being cultivated and more dirt thrown on them. It frequently happens in digging stubble that eyes on the mother cane are found sound and, in many instances, germinate after a burial of over twelve months. With a view of throwing more light on this subject, the following experiments were instituted and carried to successful completion:—

1. Two whole canes planted, tops three inches, butts six inches deep.
2. Two whole canes planted, tops three inches, butts ten inches deep.
3. Two whole canes planted, tops three inches, butts fourteen inches deep.
4. Two whole canes planted, tops three inches, butts sixteen inches deep.
5. Two whole canes planted, tops three inches, butts seventeen inches deep.
6. Two whole canes planted, tops three inches, butts eighteen inches deep.
7. Two whole canes planted, tops three inches, butts twenty inches deep.
8. Two whole canes planted, tops three inches, butts twenty-one inches deep.
9. Two whole canes planted, tops three inches, butts twenty-two inches deep.
10. Two whole canes planted, tops 3 inches, butts 24 inches deep.
11. Two whole canes planted, tops 18 inches, butts 3 inches deep.
12. Two whole canes planted, tops 22 inches, butts 3 inches deep.
13. Two whole canes planted, tops 24 inches, butts 3 inches deep.
14. One whole cane planted perpendicularly, top up, butt down.

Canes of about 4 feet in length were placed carefully in trenches properly prepared of above depth, on March 13, 1889.

On November 14 and 15 they were carefully dug up, the growing canes removed and counted, the mother stalk carefully washed and examined, and each eye carefully treated as regards germination and soundness. The following are the notes made:—

Experiment No. 1. Both mother canes rotten, 17 developed stalks, one stool coming from the eye deepest buried (6 inches).

Experiment No. 2. One mother cane rotten. The other perfectly sound with two well-preserved sound eyes on it: there were 24 well-developed stalks, one stool from eyes at depth of 6 inches, 8 inches, and 10 inches (lowest eye).

Experiment No. 3. Both mother canes sound, 28 growing stalks; one stalk had a stool at 14 inches depth, another at 10 inches, and another at 6 inches, with one sound eye. The other stalk had its lowest four eyes started, but not yet to surface, with stools at 10 inches, 6 inches. Every eye but one had germinated; this was dead and was at a depth of near 8 inches.

Experiment No. 4. Both mother canes rotten; only 12 stalks of cane. The lowest eye which germinated was at 6 inches.

(1037)

Experiment No. 5. Both mother canes rotten, 21 stalks of cane, one stool from an eye 12 inches deep, one at 8 inches, and another at 6 inches.

Experiment No. 6. Both mother canes rotten; 13 stalks of cane, one stool of two stalks from an eye 4 inches deep and another from eye 12 inches, and at the lower end (18 inches) was found a living sucker not yet out of the ground, coming from a dead sprout, which had doubtless been smothered in the spring.

Experiment No. 7. Both mother canes rotten; 11 stalks cane, one stool from eye 15 inches deep, and another from eye 14 inches deep.

Experiment No. 8. Both mother canes rotten, and no eyes germinated.

Experiment No. 9. One mother cane rotten, the other sound. No eyes germinated on rotten cane. Three stools from sound cane from upper eyes. 13 canes; three eyes still good.

Experiment No. 10. One mother cane rotten, and one excellently well preserved. 23 canes. Only one stool of three stalks from rotten stalk, from second eye from top of cane (about 5 inches). Four stools had developed on sound cane, from 12 inches up to 3 inches deep. Five eyes had developed on lower part of cane into short sprouts, which had been smothered. Two eyes still good.

Experiment No. 11. Both mother canes sound; 20 canes; one stool from an eye 24 inches deep, was very curious in its underground connection with the mother stalk. It ran out at an angle of about 45 degrees to mother stalk to a length of 17 inches, and then came perpendicularly to the surface. This forcibly illustrated the power of vitality. Three eyes on the two canes were still sound.

Experiment No. 12. Both mother canes rotten; 13 canes from only two eyes, at 8 and 6 inches deep.

Experiment No. 13. Both canes rotting; 12 canes from two eyes, 10 to 8 inches deep.

Experiment No. 14. This cane was still sound. Every eye from 18 inches deep to the top germinated, giving 21 fully-developed canes. After being dug up the stalk with its adherent growth was a great curiosity. It had the form of an umbrella inverted by the wind, only the ribs were placed at intervals along the stalk. At the depth of 25 inches there was found a sound eye. Below this the stalk was rotten, above sound and strong.

The sound eyes in every case were planted, and germination actually produced. It is to be regretted that the canes used in these experiments were defective. Our best seed had been planted before this work was projected, and in preparing for this work we had to select stalks from refused seed cane. However, enough is shown to controvert the opinion that an eye starting early into growth does destroy the other eyes on the same cane unfavourably situated. It also suggests the immense power resident in a good sound eye of cane. Last season was, however, a very dry one, and perhaps favourable to these experiments, while the seed used was defective and unfavourable. A wet season, with excellent seed cane, might give different results, especially upon stiff, undrained soil. Whenever a large number of stalks appeared above ground, the mother cane was nearly always sound.

Along with the above, another series of experiments was made. Canes were cut up into one and two joints and planted vertically at distances apart varying from 6 to 18 inches. The land was nicely bedded, and the joints were simply inserted by hand. A drought of unprecedented fury prevailed immediately after planting, with disastrous results to the experiments.

Row No. 1, where one joint was planted 12 inches apart, failed to germinate.

Row No. 2, where one joint was planted 18 inches apart, gave one stool of 15 stalks.

Row No. 3, where one joint was planted 6 inches apart, gave eight stools, aggregating 79 stalks.

Row No. 4, where two joints were planted 12 inches apart, gave six stools, aggregating 76 stalks.

Row No. 5, where two joints were planted 18 inches apart, gave five stools, aggregating 68 stalks.

Row No. 6, where two joints were planted 6 inches apart, gave seven stools, aggregating 83 stalks.

This cane came up very scatteringly and suckered enormously, giving very few well-developed stalks.

Physiological Experiments.

This question was experimentally begun with plant cane in 1888. This year it has been followed into stubble.

What distance apart shall we give our cane rows?

The following, taken from bulletin No. 20, gives an account of the original planting. This year the stubble has been treated in the same manner as regards fertilisers, the latter applied on May 2. Some difficulty was experienced in working properly the narrow rows, and they suffered in consequence:—

" 1. Three rows, three feet wide.
" 2.   „   four   „
" 3.   „   five   „
" 4.   „   six   „
" 5.   „   seven   „
" 6.   „   eight   „

"These rows were two acres long, and were divided into equal parts. Upon the upper part, plant was used for seed; and on the lower stubble. Each of these parts was again equally divided, and upon the southern half of each part manure was used, the same amount to each experiment. This gave each row the same amount of manure, but very varying quantities per acre. Bradley's fertiliser was used on the part planted with stubble, and Bowdker's fertiliser on that with plant. These goods were especially prepared in Boston for Mr. Frank Ames, for his sugar plantation, and by him presented to the station.

"Two attempts were made, after the cane had reached several

feet in height, to cultivate the narrow rows with a two-horse plough, by driving the mules "tandem," but a failure was made each time. The soil was too stiff. The other experiments were cultivated like the rest of the cane on the station in the usual way.

"The difficulty of cultivation must always remain as a serious objection to narrow rows for cane in stiff soils. In light soils a one-horse plough may do all the work effectually. However, in these experiments our narrow rows do not show any loss from lack of cultivation, nor from the absence of high ridges and deep middles, though the subsequent seasons were extremely unfavourable."

Results of both 1888 and 1889 are hereby given :—

RESULTS of Plat 13—Different Widths of Rows in Plant Cane for 1888.

Width of Rows.	Fertiliser Used.	Amount Fertilised per Acre.	Yield per Acre.	Degree Baume.	Total Solids.	Sucrose.	Glucose.	Purity Coefficient.	Glucose Ratio.	Per Ton.	Per Acre.
Feet.		Lbs.	Tons.								
3	Bradley	1,336	39·38	9·0	16·2	14·1	·78	87·03	5·33	181·02	7,128·57
4	,,	1,002	38·55	8·4	15·1	12·5	1·15	82·78	9·12	150·09	6,748 25
5	,,	800	34·04	8·8	15·8	13·4	·97	84·81	7·23	167·03	5,694·89
6	,,	668	30·87	8·5	15·3	12·8	1·15	83·66	8·97	155·12	4,788·55
7	,,	573	29·69	8·4	15·2	12·7	1·08	83 55	8·50	155·12	4,605·51
8	,,	504	21·59	8·2	14·8	12·4	·97	83·78	7·82	153·03	3,177·91
3	No manure	...	31·41	7·3	13·2	11·2	·75	84·09	6·75	141·12	4,432·58
4	,,	...	25·93	7·3	13·2	11·2	·75	84·09	6·75	141·12	3,659·24
5	,,	...	24·91	7·3	13·2	11·2	·75	84·09	6·75	141·12	3,515·03
6	,,	...	21·69	7·3	13·2	11·2	·75	84·09	9·75	141·12	3,060·91
7	,,	...	24·69	7·3	13·2	11·2	·75	84·09	6·75	141·12	3,516·48
8	,,	...	20·65	7·3	13·2	11·2	·75	84·09	6·75	141·12	2,914·13
3	Bowdker's	1,336	35·91	7·5	13·5	11·2	·86	82·96	7·67	138·79	4,982·15
4	,,	1,002	31·44	7·8	14·0	12·2	1·07	87·14	8·77	148·04	4,665·07
5	,,	800	27·72	7·4	13·4	11·2	·08	83·58	7·67	138·74	3,845·87
6	,,	667	21·29	7·9	14·2	11·9	1·06	83·08	8·90	144·34	3,023·00
7	,,	573	21·91	6·7	12·0	9·5	·87	79·16	9·15	114·08	2,515·27
8	,,	504	18·04	7·8	14·0	12·5	·96	89·28	7·68	154·84	2,849·06
3	No manure	...	31·37	8·0	14·4	13·0	1·01	90·27	7·76	160·86	5,040·18
4	,,	...	23·53	7·5	13·6	11·9	·96	87·05	8·C6	146·44	3,545·73
5	,,	...	20·82	7·9	14·2	12·0	·83	84·05	6·91	150·64	3,130·32
6	,,	...	16·22	8·2	14·8	12·7	·92	85·81	7·32	158·48	2,570·54
7	,,	...	17·01	8·0	14·4	12·3	·86	85·41	6·99	154·14	2,635·79
8	,,	...	19·75	8·4	15·1	12·9	·09	85·43	6·97	161·07	3,190·57

RESULTS of Plat 13—Different Widths of Rows in Stubble Cane, 1889.

Width of Rows.	Fertiliser Used.	Amount Fertiliser per Acre.	Yield per Acre.	Degree Baume.	Total Solids.	Sucrose.	Glucose.	Coefficient of Purity.	Glucose Ratio.	Lbs. of Available Sugar upon 70 per cent. Extraction. Per Ton.	Per Acre.
Feet.		Lbs.	Tons.								
3	Bradley	1,336	23·22	7·8	14·1	11·9	1·31	84	11·00	139·09	3,231
4	,,	1,002	19·74	7·8	14·1	12·1	1·11	85	9·17	146·16	2,885
5	,,	800	21·76	7·8	14·1	12·0	1·17	85	9·75	143·05	3,123
6	,,	668	20·31	7·8	14·0	11·9	1·13	85	9·49	142·94	2,903
7	,,	573	20·17	8·0	14·5	12·5	1·04	86	8·31	153·16	3,089
8	,,	504	15·88	7·9	14·2	12·4	1·14	87	9·19	149·66	2,377
3	No manure	...	15·63	8·0	14·5	12·3	1·06	84	8·61	149·94	2,343
4	,,	...	10·82	8·0	14·5	12·5	1·14	86	9·12	151·06	1,634
5	,,	...	12·64	7·8	14·0	12·0	1·15	85	9·58	143·92	1,819
6	,,	...	12·69	8·1	14·6	12·2	1·16	83	9·05	146·44	1,858
7	,,	...	14·04	8·0	14·5	12·1	1·22	83	10·08	143·78	2,018
8	,,	...	15·12	8·0	14·5	12·5	1·18	86	9·44	150·22	2,271
3	Bowdker's	1,336	24·45	7·9	14·2	12·0	1·03	84	8·58	146·44	3,580
4	,,	1,002	20·09	7·9	14·3	12·1	1·06	84	8·76	147·14	2,956
5	,,	800	17·02	7·9	14·2	12·0	1·07	84	8·91	145·06	2,504
6	,,	668	15·36	7·9	14·2	11·5	1·11	81	9·65	137·69	2,114
7	,,	573	14·61	7·9	14·2	11·8	1·19	83	10·08	140·21	2,048
8	,,	504	15·05	7·5	13·5	11·3	1·21	83	10·07	132·79	2,058
3	No manure	...	12·56	7·9	14·2	11·5	1·08	81	9·39	138·32	1,737
4	,,	...	13·68	8·3	15·0	13·0	1·01	87	7·76	160·79	2,199
5	,,	...	15·52	8·4	15·1	13·0	1·02	86	7·84	160·58	2,492
6	,,	...	15·02	8·0	14·5	12·5	1·11	86	8·88	151·69	2,306
7	,,	...	14·84	8·3	15·0	12·6	1·19	84	9·44	151·41	2,247
8	,,	...	13·76	8·3	15·0	12·7	1·13	85	8·89	154·07	2,120

COMPARISON of Aggregate Results of Plat 13 for Two Years.

	3 ft. Rows. Tons.	Available Sugar.	4 ft. Rows. Tons.	Available Sugar.	5 ft. Rows. Tons.	Available Sugar.	6 ft. Rows. Tons.	Available Sugar.	7 ft. Rows. Tons.	Available Sugar.	8 ft. Rows. Tons.	Available Sugar.
		Lbs.		Lbs.		Lbs.		Lbs.		Lbs.		Lbs.
Bradley	62·61	10,360	58·29	9,633	55·8	8,828	51·18	7,692	49·86	7,695	37·47	5,555
No manure	47·04	6,776	36·75	5,293	37·55	5,334	34·38	4,919	38·73	5,534	35·77	5,185
Bowdker	60·36	8,562	51·53	7,622	44·92	6,350	36·65	5,137	36·52	4,563	33·9	4,951
No manure	43·93	6,777	37·21	5,745	36·34	5,622	31·42	4,877	31·94	4,883	33·51	5,311
Average	53·48	8,118	45·94	7,073	43·65	6,534	38·33	5,656	39·26	5,668	35·16	5,250
Excess of 3 feet rows over	...	...	7·54	1,045	9·83	1,584	15·15	2,462	14·23	2,450	18·32	2,868
Excess of 4 feet rows over	...	...	...	...	2·29	539	7·61	1,417	6·68	1,405	10·78	1,823
Excess of 5 feet rows over	...	...	...	...	...	...	5·32	878	4·39	876	8·49	1,281
Excess of 6 feet rows over	...	...	...	...	...	...	...	...	...	...	3·17	406
Excess of 7 feet rows over	...	...	...	...	...	...	...	...	...	...	4·1	418

The sucrose content seems to depend upon factors other than width of rows, though the narrow rows have slightly the advantage. Attention was called in bulletin No. 20 to the defective drainage of the six foot plat, due to an old water furrow which once drained an oat patch. The decrease in yield due to this cause was also apparent this year.

To plant an acre in cane, with rows seven feet apart, using "two stalks and a lap" for seed, will require about four tons of cane; at the same rate there will be required for seed:—

In three foot rows, $9\frac{1}{3}$ tons per acre.
In four foot rows, 7 tons per acre.
In five foot rows, 5·6 tons per acre.
In six foot rows, $4\frac{2}{3}$ tons per acre.
In seven foot rows, 4 tons per acre.
In eight foot rows, $3\frac{1}{2}$ tons per acre.

Subtracting these qualities from average yield above will give net cane per acre over the amount used in planting, as follows:—

Three foot rows, 44·15 tons.
Four foot rows, 38·94 tons.
Five foot rows, 38·05 tons.
Six foot rows, 33·67 tons.
Seven foot rows, 35·26 tons.
Eight foot rows, 31·66 tons.

These results are so striking that we cannot avoid the conclusion reached last year.

It is unwise, as well as unscientific, to draw conclusions from a few years' experience, yet the above results strongly suggest thought and reflection. Have we not in our efforts at easy and thorough cultivation passed the boundary of maximum yield sugar content in the width of our rows? Do not wide rows and late cultivation also tend to large immature canes at harvest? The frequent remarks of planters that "cane never grows well until laid by," and "cane never grows fast until it shades the ground," cause the inquiring mind to ask the reasons for these popular axioms. May not the frequent rupture of the roots in cultivation, which wide rows permit to be extended (perhaps) beyond the requirements of the plane, and the growth of grass and weeds, which flourish longer, because unshaded, in wide rows (the killing of which often requires the late cultivation), have much to do with originating these popular beliefs?

It is certainly desirable in this climate to have early maturing cane. To do this obstacles or checks upon its growth must be presented in some form in order that it may do the only thing left it, i.e., mature. These obstacles may be found in want of drainage, or lack of fertility. The last obstacle may be presented by withholding fertilisers, absence of deep ploughing, want of rain, and crowding the land with cane, &c. May not a width of rows just sufficient for good cultivation, varying according to soil, be better than the conventional seven foot row now almost everywhere found. The station continues to test this question.

Varieties of cane. The station has now growing on it over 60 varieties of cane, collected from all parts of the world. It has received since our last report 35 varieties from the botanical gardens of Jamaica, kindly donated by the director.

It has also received from Professor Bovell, of Dodd's Reformatory, Barbadoes, a bottle of true cane seeds. These have been carefully planted. Many have germinated, but have been rapidly destroyed by ants. Preventive measures have been now introduced, and it is hoped that canes may ultimately be obtained here from seed, as has been so successfully accomplished at Barbadoes. To both of the above-mentioned gentlemen the station returns thanks.

Last year over 30 varieties of cane were grown to maturity, carefully analysed, and in several instances worked up in the sugar house. Our results so far are somewhat contradictory. Several canes which did well in 1888, a wet season, almost failed in 1889, a very dry one, and vice versâ. Again, several canes which were very promising the first year, have not fulfilled expectations in subsequent seasons, while others, entirely unpromising the first season, are gradually becoming acclimated and are growing in favour. No foreign cane has as yet attained that complete acclimation which will enable us to speak positively of its merits. It is, therefore, deemed best to withhold all remarks in regard to the different varieties until their merits and demerits have been more fully investigated.

One fact is here worthy of record: Every sample received is carefully examined, and an accurate description as to its botanical and physical properties noted in a book kept for that purpose. On harvesting the cane the next season, another thorough examination is made and entered in its appropriate place. From a record of such examinations, we find that many of these canes have either been changed greatly by planting here, or in their immature condition (only eight months old here) are quite different from the mature cane received. It is well known that many favourite varieties of cane are susceptible of variation in the same climate on different soils. Perhaps in a different climate and on a different soil variation may markedly occur. These thoughts have been suggested by receiving canes of marked similarity, and yet totally unlike, from different countries under different names. Have not the numerous so-called varieties originated by variations incident to climatic and soil influences, and cannot a patient investigation eliminate a large number of the present varieties and reduce the number to a few primordial types, with numerous slight variations unworthy of being styled varieties? The station is now trying to collect and bring together under a common influence all the noted varieties of cane, and to test the question of reduction of the number of true varieties. At an early day a bulletin covering the study already made of the numerous varieties now on the station will be issued.

Last April 30 varieties of cane were planted in adjacent rows in the hot room of the agricultural hall. These came from all parts of the world, and were planted in close proximity, in order that by cross fertilisation the fructifying power might be given to the seed. It is well known that all canes at a certain age go through the process of "arrowing" or "tasselling," but usually produce no true seed. Professors Harrison and Bovell have, by placing varieties of opposite character and habits in close juxtaposition, produced true seeds, which have germinated and given new varieties of cane. In humble imitation of their example, the station is now anxiously awaiting the tasselling of this cane, in hopes of obtaining true seed. As yet no sign of the arrow is visible, though the canes are immense and their sugar content has passed over 18 per cent. in several instances.

Manurial Requirements.

For four years the station has made strenuous exertions to determine a fertiliser suitable for cane on the sugar lands of Louisiana. A fertiliser is desired which will give simultaneously large tonnage with large sugar content. Unfortunately, these combinations are rarely obtained in this latitude, where the cane is harvested long before maturity. So far that class of manures which will ensure a large tonnage are known to give succulent watery canes, poor in sugar, while unmanured stunted canes are apt to be comparatively rich in saccharine. It is therefore, for the present at least, prudent to seek a fertiliser which will give a fair tonnage with chances in favour of high sucrose. The ingredients of value in every commercial fertiliser are nitrogen, phosphoric acid, and potash. These in different forms are combined in varying proportions to form the fertilisers offered on our market.

Do our soils need all three of these ingredients to make a remunerative harvest of cane? If so, in what forms shall they be presented, and in what proportions shall these combinations be made and what quantities of the mixtures shall be used per acre? To answer truly all these questions would be the solution of the chief agricultural problem to-day presented to our sugar planters. In experimenting to determine these questions, a seemingly insuperable difficulty confronts us. We are seeking sugar—a compound containing only carbon and hydrogen—without a trace of any of the above ingredients, and yet it is universally known that well-developed cane cannot be obtained when the soil is deficient in any one of them. What, then, are their relations to the elaboration of sugar in the cane? Their action is not nutritious. It may be physiological, but exactly in what way is yet an undetermined problem. Do excesses of all or any one of these ingredients tend to develop sugar in the juice? Nitrogenous manures alone certainly do not, for when offered in excess produce exceedingly poor canes in large quantities. Phosphatic manures may accomplish this end, yet there are seasons when they, too, utterly fail to augment the sugar content. Potassic manures in all forms have failed with us to affect the sugar content or tonnage in any way, though reported favourably as to the former in some foreign experiments. Experiments covering all of the above questions have been carefully and patiently made for four years, under the hopes that some light would be thrown upon this important problem. While the problem has been by no means solved, yet much valuable information has been gained, and we are enabled to report successful progress.

NITROGEN MANURES.

In 1886 a series of experiments were begun with the different forms of nitrogen, using nitrate of soda, sulphate of ammonia, cotton seed meal, fish scrap, and dried blood. All of these were used in such quantities as to give 24 lbs., 48 lbs., and 72 lbs. of nitrogen per acre, styled one-third, two-thirds, and one full ration. The results of 1886 and 1887 clearly demonstrated that the full ration of 72 lbs. per acre was excessive and wasteful, and hence, in subsequent years, only the one-third and two-thirds rations were used. The above forms were used with excesses of acid phosphate and potash.

At same time experiments with a mixture of these last two substances, called mixed minerals, were made to test their efficacy when used alone. In 1886 the stand was severely injured, and hence tonnage not secured; only analyses of canes obtained. Each subsequent year gave both. The following table gives the results for 1889:—

Result of Part XIV.—NITROGENOUS MANURES. First Year Stubble 1889, Harvested November 15.

Names and Quantities of Fertilisers Used.	Yield per Acre in Tons.	Total Solids.	Sucrose.	Glucose.	Purity Coefficient.	Glucose Ratio.	Per Ton.	Per Acre.
1. 350 lbs. cotton meal, 500 lbs. acid phosphate, 70 lbs. muriate potash (mixed minerals)	22·75	13·1	11·1	1·32	84	11·89	127·7	2,905
2. 700 lbs. cotton meal and mixed minerals	24·85	13·2	11·1	1·28	84	11·53	128·5	3,914
3. 350 lbs. fish scrap and mixed minerals	19·69	14·3	11·8	1·08	83	9·15	142·5	2,720
4. Mixed minerals	14·03	14·5	12·2	1·04	84	8·52	146·2	2,050
5. 700 lbs. fish scrap and mixed minerals	19·65	14·2	12·3	1·13	86	9·18	148·5	2,917
6. 180 lbs. dried blood and mixed minerals	18·66	13·1	11·3	1·07	86	9·46	135·7	2,533
7. 360 lbs. dried blood and mixed minerals	22·69	13·8	11·3	1·42	82	12·56	128·4	2,926
8. 120 lbs. sul. ammonia (mixed minerals)	19·68	12·9	11·2	1·07	87	9·55	134·3	2,640
9. 240 lbs. sul. ammonia (mixed minerals)	22·70	13·9	11·1	1·38	79	12·43	126·4	2,870
10. No manure	12·81	12·8	10·7	1·23	83	11·49	123·9	1,588
11. 150 lbs. nitrate soda and mixed minerals	17·05	13·9	12·0	1·00	86	8·33	147·0	2,505
12. 300 lbs. nitrate soda and mixed minerals	12·51	13·6	11·4	1·11	84	9·73	136·3	2,941

UNITED STATES.

COMPARISON OF RESULTS.

Average Yield per Acre.	No Manure. Tons.	No Manure. Average Sugar.	Mixed Minerals. Tons.	Mixed Minerals. Average Sugar.
		Lbs.		Lbs.
⅓ cotton seed meal over	7·62	1,288	7·75	1,115
⅔ cotton seed meal over	9·20	1,345	9·33	1,172
⅓ fish scrap over	5·48	..	5·61	..
⅔ fish scrap over	6·40	1,231	6·56	1,056
⅓ dried blood over	7·86	..	7·99	..
⅔ dried blood over	8·82	1,175	8·95	1,002
⅓ sulphate ammonia over	6·29	1,203	6·42	1,024
⅔ sulphate ammonia over	9·78	1,225	9·91	1,052
⅓ nitrate soda over	7·53	967	7·16	694
⅔ nitrate soda over	7·41	647	7·54	174
Average of all ⅓ rations over	6·85	1,150	6·98	944
Average of all ⅔ rations over	8·33	1,124	8·46	951

CONCLUSIONS.

It is evident, from the experiments of four years, that these soils require nitrogen to grow maximum crops. This is clearly shown by the constant increase of the nitrogen mixtures over both "no manure" and "mixed minerals." Either of the above forms are readily assimilable by the cane plant; hence the planter can, with impunity, purchase that form which will give him the cheapest nitrogen.

The third question propounded by these experiments is not yet satisfactorily solved, viz.: the quantity of nitrogen to be used per acre. The whole ration (72 lbs. per acre) is certainly excessive and wasteful. Whether the two-thirds ration (48 lbs. per acre) carries with it a profit over the one-third ration (24 lbs. per acre) is still doubtful. Though the tonnage is slightly enhanced, the sugar per acre is about the same, and future experiments must fully decide this question.

Phosphoric acid and potash. Experiments with the various forms and in different quantities of phosphoric acid and potash have been made, extending over three years, and the results have been published yearly. By comparing these results, it will be seen that phosphoric acid *is needed* on these soils to grow maximum crops, though not in as great demand as nitrogen. It has also been shown that the soluble forms are the most profitable for cane.

No form of potash used in moderate quantities has been productive of apparent good. The carbonate of potash and the ashes of cotton seed hulls have both produced results inferior to the other forms.

The following table gives the comparative results for four years:—

RESULTS of Four Years Compared.—Nitrogenous Manures.

		1886. Plant.	1887. Stubble.	1888. Plant.	1889. Stubble.	Average.
1. Mixed minerals, ⅓ ration of cotton meal	Yield per acre	...	19·18	26·83	22·75	22·92
	Sucrose	15·7	12·2	13·2	11·1	12·05
	Glucose	...	1·45	·83	1·32	1·2
	Lbs. available sugar	...	2,695	4,492	2,905	3,364
2. Mixed minerals, ⅔ ration of cotton meal	Yield per acre	...	22·4	26·25	24·85	24·5
	Sucrose	14·5	11·6	13	11·1	12·55
	Glucose	...	1·82	·89	1·28	1·33
	Lbs. available sugar	...	2,780	4,289	3,194	3,421
3. Mixed minerals, ⅔ ration of fish scrap	Yield per acre	...	17·7	25·55	19·09	20·78
	Sucrose	11·7	13·1	...	11·8	...
	Glucose	...	1·11	...	1·08	...
	Lbs. available sugar	...	2,816	...	2,720	...
4. Mixed minerals	Yield per acre	...	1·24	19·07	14·03	15·17
	Sucrose	1·29	12·2	12·2	12·2	12·37
	Glucose	...	1·56	·7	1·04	1·1
	Lbs. available sugar	...	1,719	2,979	2,050	2,249
5. Mixed minerals, ⅔ ration of fish scrap	Yield per acre	...	20·33	25·2	19·65	21·73
	Sucrose	13·5	12·7	12·9	12·3	12·85
	Glucose	...	1·56	·75	1·13	1·15
	Lbs. available sugar	...	2,948	4,156	2,917	3,307
6. Mixed minerals, ⅓ ration of dried blood	Yield per acre	...	26	21·81	18·66	22·16
	Sucrose	14	11·5	...	11·3	...
	Glucose	...	1·8	...	1·07	...
	Lbs. available sugar	...	3,203	...	2,532	...
7. Mixed minerals, ⅔ ration of dried blood	Yield per acre	...	26·84	22·75	22·79	24·12
	Sucrose	12·8	10·4	13·2	11·3	11·93
	Glucose	...	1·6	·81	1·42	1·28
	Lbs. available sugar	...	3,006	3,822	2,926	3,251
8. Mixed minerals, ⅓ ration of sul. ammonia	Yield per acre	...	21·31	23·8	19·68	21·59
	Sucrose	13·1	11·5	13·1	11·2	12·23
	Glucose	...	1·8	·79	1·07	1·22
	Lbs. available sugar	...	3,203	3,975	2,640	3,273
9. Mixed minerals, ⅔ ration of sul. ammonia	Yield per acre	...	29	23·56	22·7	25·8
	Sucrose	12·9	10·4	13·4	11·1	11·95
	Glucose	...	2	·8	1·38	1·39
	Lbs. available sugar	...	3,004	4·029	2,870	3,301
10. No manure	Yield per acre	...	15·22	17·87	12·81	15·3
	Sucrose	13·1	10·8	12·6	10·7	11·8
	Glucose	...	1·8	·65	1·23	1·22
	Lbs. available sugar	...	1,726	2,913	1,588	2,076
11. Mixed minerals, ⅓ ration of nitrate soda	Yield per acre	...	27·4	20·55	17·05	22·33
	Sucrose	13	10·6	12·9	12	12·13
	Glucose	...	2	·62	1	1·21
	Lbs. available sugar	...	2,913	3,411	2,505	2,943
12. Mixed minerals, ⅔ ration of nitrate soda	Yield per acre	...	21·77	24·35	21·51	22·71
	Sucrose	11·4	8·8	11·6	11·4	10·8
	Glucose	...	2·42	·72	1·11	1·41
	Lbs. available sugar	...	1,576	3,653	2,941	2·723

Another part of Plate 14 was devoted to the trial of various **Formulas for** formulas hitherto given to the public as adapted to cane. No. 13, **cane.** consisting of 130 lbs. nitrate of potash, 650 lbs. acid phosphate, 510 lbs. gypsum, is prescribed by Professor George Ville, of the Government school at Vincennes, France, as specially adapted to plant cane. It is an expensive compound, and experience here has shown excessive in phosphoric acid and deficient in nitrogen.

No. 14 is a formula prescribed by the Experiment Station upon St. Denis, on the Island of Reunion (formerly Bourbon), and is highly endorsed by the planters of this island and Mauritius. It too is expensive, and the quantity per acre much in excess of the ordinary requirements of our crops. It is as follows:—

No. 14, 140 lbs. sulphate of ammonia, 100 lbs. nitrate of soda, 120 lbs. dried blood, 560 lbs. acid phosphate, 80 lbs. muriate potash.

UNITED STATES.

Here the nitrogen is presented in three forms, which is believed to best meet the requirements of the plants.

Nos. 15, 16, and 17, which were fertilised last year respectively with Ohlendorff's "A" special cane manure, "B" early cane manure, and "C" dissolved Peruvian guano, were this year as stubble, in default of these goods, treated with the following mixtures:—

No. 14, 720 lbs. cotton seed meal, 500 lbs. acid phosphate, 320 lbs. kainite.

No. 16, 720 lbs. cotton seed meal, 500 lbs. acid phosphate, 80 lbs. muriate of potash.

No. 17, 720 lbs. cotton seed meal, 500 lbs. acid phosphate, 80 lbs. sulphate potash.

YIELDS of 1888–89.—Plat 14.

		Plant. 1888.	Stubble. 1889.
13. Ville's formula	Yield per acre	26·01	15·65
	Sucrose	13·2	11
	Glucose	·84	1·31
	Lbs. available sugar	4,357	1,979
14. St. Denis formula	Yield per acre	30·05	21·56
	Sucrose	13·1	10·9
	Glucose	·9	1·32
	Lbs. available sugar	4,943	2,692
15. Ohlendorff's special cane manure in 1888	Yield per acre	29·16	20·82
	Sucrose	11·7	11·2
Meal phosphate with kainite in 1889	Glucose	·9	1·22
	Lbs. available sugar	4,225	2,731
16. Ohlendorff's early cane manure in 1888	Yield per acre	24·73	19·13
	Sucrose	12·4	11·4
Meal phosphate with muriate potash in 1889	Glucose	·91	1·47
	Lbs. available sugar	3,825	2,462
17. Ohlendorff's dissolved Peruvian guano in 1888	Yield per acre	22	20·88
	Sucrose	15·7	10·9
Meal phosphate with sulphate of potash in 1889	Glucose	·85	1·22
	Lbs. available sugar	3,527	2,651

The St. Denis formula has furnished the largest tonnage each year, while No. 15 has given this year the largest sugar yield. The fertilisers used in Nos. 15, 16, and 17 are far cheaper than those prepared by the foreign formulas, and give equally as good results. Ville's formula is deficient in nitrogen and excessive in phosphoric acid, while St. Denis is excessive in both; both nitrogen and phosphoric acid in Nos. 15, 16, and 17 were greatly in excess of requirements last season, this being an unusually dry one.

A part of Plat 14 was used for these experiments.

What proportions shall nitrogen and phosphoric acid be combined for cane.

The object of these experiments was to determine, if possible, the proportions in which cotton seed meal and acid phosphate should be mixed to give the best results on cane.

Cotton seed meal has been used alone on experiment 18. In the other experiments it has been combined in such proportions with acid phosphate as to give the following ratios of nitrogen to phosphoric acid, viz.: 1—3, 1—2, 1—1, 2—1, and 3—1. In this combination no account has been taken of small amount of phosphoric acid in cotton seed meal, or of the still smaller amount in the insoluble form in the phosphate. The nitrogen is reckoned at 7 per cent. in the meal, and the soluble phosphoric acid at 14 per cent. in the phosphate. The combination was used at the rate of 750 lbs. per acre. The following are the quantities used:—

Experiments.	Nitrogen.	Phosphoric Acid.
No. 18—		
650 lbs. cotton seed meal	..	..
No. 19—		
300 lbs. cotton seed meal	1	3
450 „ acid phosphate		
No. 20—		
375 lbs. cotton seed meal	1	2
375 „ acid phosphate		
No. 21—Nothing.		
No. 22—		
500 lbs. cotton seed meal	1	1
250 „ acid phosphate		
No. 23—		
600 lbs. cotton seed meal	2	1
150 „ acid phosphate		
No. 24—		
650 lbs. cotton seed meal	3	1
100 „ acid phosphate		

The results of both years are herewith given:—

PLAT 14.

	1888 Plant.	1889 Stubble.
18. Cotton meal (alone). Nitrogen 7 to phosphoric acid 3—		
Yield per acre..	18·69	20 23
Sucrose	11·9	11·1
Glucose..	·71	1·19
Lbs. available sugar ..	2,839	2,638
19. Nitrogen 1 to phosphoric acid 3—		
Yield per acre..	19·48	19·79
Sucrose	14·2	12 6
Glucose..	·39	1·04
Lbs. available sugar ..	3,623	3,059
20. Nitrogen 1 to phosphoric acid 2—		
Yield per acre..	20·07	19·85
Sucrose	14·8	11·5
Glucose..	·56	·9
Lbs. available sugar ..	3,914	2,834
21. No manure—		
Yield per acre..	16·97	14·65
Sucrose	11·4	12·8
Glucose..	·76	·91
Lbs. available sugar ..	2,435	2,345
22. Nitrogen 1 to phosphoric acid 1—		
Yield per acre..	22·75	18·53
Sucrose	12·2	10·5
Glucose..	·75	·1
Lbs. available sugar ..	3,536	2,334
23. Nitrogen 2 to phosphoric acid 1—		
Yield per acre..	24·5	19·25
Sucrose	13·4	11·5
Glucose..	·71	1·21
Lbs. available sugar ..	4,241	2,610
24. Nitrogen 3 to phosphoric acid 1—		
Yield per acre..	33·8	26·55
Sucrose	13·4	11·3
Glucose..	·78	1·29
Lbs. available sugar ..	4,082	2,694

In 1883, No. 23, nitrogen two parts to phosphoric acid one part, gave the largest tonnage, and No. 20, nitrogen one part to phosphoric acid two parts, the largest sugar content. In 1889 No. 24 gives the largest tonnage, and No. 19 the highest sucrose period.

Tiled versus untiled land. In the fall of 1885 a plat of the blackest and stiffest land on the station, and perhaps as black and stiff as any piece in the State, was selected for testing the efficacy of tiles in ameliorating the physical and chemical properties of such soils. This plat was four acres deep and nearly one acre wide. It was divided into two equal parts—one was tiled and the other left undisturbed. After completing the work there was no sign or indication of the line of demarcation between the two pieces. These tiles were laid four feet deep and 20 feet apart. The work was performed by Mr. Oakes, of Ohio, and was well done.

Early in the winter of 1885–86 the plat was flushed and divided in two equal parts. The untiled part was named Plat

No. IV., and the tiled, No. V. They were carefully bedded and planted in cane in the early spring of 1886. These plats were in stubble cane when we obtained the place, and we were told that it had been in succession cane for years.

The seed cane used was defective and the stand was poor, except on the first group. Hence, only this group was harvested this year. On account of the poor stand of 1886 the stubble was ploughed up and land replanted in cane March 5, 1887. An excellent stand was obtained, which has subsequently been cultivated as first and second year stubble (1888 and 1889). The following are the manures used per acre on each plat:—

No. 1, 500 lbs. cotton seed meal, 500 lbs. acid phosphate, 500 lbs. kainite.

No. 2, 500 lbs. cotton seed meal, 500 lbs. acid phosphate.

No. 3, nothing.

No. 4, 500 lbs. cotton seed meal, 500 lbs. natural phosphate, 500 lbs. kainite.

No. 5, 500 lbs. cotton seed meal, 500 lbs. natural phosphate.

No. 6, nothing.

No. 7, 500 lbs. cotton seed meal, 500 lbs. bone dust, 500 lbs. kainite.

No. 8, 500 lbs. cotton seed meal, 500 lbs. bone dust.

No. 9, nothing.

No. 10, 500 lbs. cotton seed meal, 500 lbs. floats, 500 lbs. kainite.

No. 11, 500 lbs. cotton seed meal, 500 lbs. floats.

No. 12, nothing.

No. 13, 500 lbs. cotton seed meal, 500 lbs. ashes cotton hulls, 500 lbs. kainite.

No. 14. 500 lbs. cotton seed meal, 500 lbs. ashes cotton hulls.

No. 15, nothing.

No. 16, 500 lbs. cotton seed meal.

No. 17, 500 lbs. acids phosphate.

No. 18, 500 lbs. kainite.

No. 19, nothing.

Both plats have received the identical treatment through the four years.

The accompanying table gives the results of the four years:—

UNITED STATES.

RESULTS Plat 4 and 5, Untiled and Tiled Lands.

	1886.		1887.				1888.				1889.			
	Tons per Acre.	Sucrose.	Yield per Acre.	Sucrose.	Glucose.	Sugar per Acre.	Yield per Acre.	Sucrose.	Glucose.	Sugar per Acre.	Yield per Acre.	Sucrose.	Glucose.	Sugar per acre.
			Tons.			Lbs.	Tons.			Lbs.	Tons.			Lbs.
1. Untiled	6·72	12·1	18·92	12·2	1·06	2,811	14·49	14·7	·65	2,797	9·76	11·8	1·25	1,356
Tiled ...	12·08	12·4	27·1	12·5	1·05	4,144	22·49	13·6	1·1	3,756	17·1	11·3	1·24	2,259
2. Untiled	9·62	10·9	·5	12·5	1·05	3,823	20·44	13·7	1·07	3,454	18·6	11·5	1·37	2,459
Tiled ...	14·8	11·6	26·64	11·4	1·3	3,524	25·99	...	...	...	18·3	12	1·26	2,590
3. Nothing	7·64	10·6	14·95	13	1·05	2,600	9·75	13·4	·91	2,988	6·3	12·3	1·18	928
4. Untiled	...	...	23·26	12·4	1	3,549	17·68	13·6	·67	3,959	11·7	11·4	1·02	1,617
Tiled ...	...	...	26·14	12	1·05	3,815	22·37	14·6	·81	3,158	18·88	10·9	·98	3,492
5. Untiled	...	...	23·7	12·4	1·04	3,596	16·89	13·7	·77	4,163	12	12	1·26	1,698
Tiled ...	...	...	24·8	12·5	1·05	3,793	23·52	13·9	·79	1,888	15·9	10·6	1·28	1,907
6. Nothing	...	...	14·26	12·5	1·09	2,160	10·43	13·9	·66	2,961	4·7	12	1·28	663
7. Untiled	...	...	20·16	13·6	·8	3,330	16·45	13·9	·77	3,925	11·86	11·3	1·02	1,614
Tiled ...	...	...	24·64	...	...	...	21·93	14	·78	3,378	18·02	12·3	1·08	2,604
8. Untiled	...	...	23·68	12	1·4	3,198	18·87	...	...	...	13·6	12·3	1·21	1,996
Tiled ...	...	...	24·6	12·7	1·05	3,831	20·04	12·6	·62	1,700	14·36	11·8	1·14	2,028
9. Nothing	...	...	17·18	12·7	1·05	2,675	10·43	13·3	·69	2,318	3·2	12	1·13	462
10. Untiled	...	...	15·94	12·3	1	2,410	13·48	13·6	·63	2,949	7·7	12·6	·83	1,224
Tiled ...	...	...	26·36	13	1·35	4,234	16·66	13·7	·98	2,260	16·32	12·5	·92	2,540
11. Untiled	...	...	19·96	12	1·05	2,787	12·36	13·3	·53	3,706	8·5	12·8	1·19	1,310
Tiled ...	...	...	22·91	12·5	·92	3,504	21·18	13·1	·59	1,557	12	11·5	1·31	1,601
12. Nothing	...	...	14·86	18·9	1·3	2,604	9·1	14·6	·53	1,824	3·5	11·8	1·3	482
13. Untiled	...	...	15·1	13·4	·6	2,420	9·45	14·8	·58	3,208	5·8	12·5	1	892
Tiled ...	...	...	23·54	14·7	·9	4,549	16·45	14·4	·47	2,372	13·7	12	1·09	1,988
14. Untiled	...	...	17·84	15	·96	3,409	12·36	15·3	·55	3,575	7·3	10·6	1·08	844
Tiled ...	...	...	20·06	12·8	1·04	3,190	17·61	...	...	...	12·6	12·1	1·1	1,843
15. Nothing	...	...	13·78	12·9	·65	2,176	8·45	12·3	·6	1,568	2·7	10·4	1·11	330
16. Untiled	...	...	16·1	14·1	·78	2,978	9·8	13·2	·61	2,012	3·76	11·8	1·3	518
Tiled ...	...	...	20·1	13·6	1·04	3,328	11·7	12·8	·54	1,546	8·8	...	...	...
17. Untiled	...	...	12	11·1	1·04	1,602	9·2	14·3	·52	2,455	4·9	11·7	1·13	686
Tiled ...	...	...	15·92	13	·86	2,609	12·99	14·4	·57	1,250	7·16	11·3	1·27	941
18. Untiled	...	...	13·98	13·35	·77	2,386	6·58	11·6	·53	1,293	...	...	...	...
Tiled ...	...	...	19·17	12·6	·93	844	7·79	14·4	·54	1,402	...	...	...	...
19. Nothing	...	...	14·82	13·7	1	2,531	7·88							

There are in the above two sets of experiments. The second set runs within a few feet of the tiles, and hence the benefits of the latter are plainly apparent in the results. The first set more nearly represents the true difference between tiled and untiled lands. Taking the difference of yield for each year we have:— *Review of results of tile drained lands.*

FIRST SET.

	Cane.	Available Sugar.
	Tons.	Lbs.
Increase per acre of tiled over untiled for 1886 ..	5·36	..
" " " " 1887 ..	6·23	909
" " " " 1888 ..	6·06	758
" " " " 1889 ..	7·05	1,236
Average increase for the four years	6·17	968

SECOND SET.

	Cane.	Available Sugar.
	Tons.	Lbs.
Increase per acre of tiled over untiled for 1886 ..	5·18	..
" " " " 1887 ..	2·58	357
" " " " 1888 ..	2·68	551
" " " " 1889 ..	2·64	336
Average increase for the four years	3·27	415
" " of both sets for four years ..	4·72	691

	Tons.
The aggregate yield of first set tiled per acre for four years ..	61
" " " untiled per acre for four years ..	41
" " second set tiled per acre for four years ..	58½
" " " untiled per acre for four years	47
" " both sets tiled per acre for four years ..	59¾
" " " untiled per acre for four years	44

	Per cent.
The increase per cent. of first set tiled over untiled	48
" " second set tiled over untiled	24
" " both sets tiled over untiled	36

It may, therefore, be truly said that the increase in cane upon lands well tiled will be from 25 to 50 per cent. upon similar lands not tiled. These tiles are 20 feet apart, the distance recommended by many experienced engineers.

The actual benefits just enumerated are sufficient recommendations for the drains; but to them must be added that lands tile-drained are made warm, sweet, and mellow; roots penetrate easier and deeper, and thus provide themselves with better apparatus for procuring water in times of drought. In wet weather the excess is drained off instead of being evaporated. Evaporation is a cooling process, requiring much of the heat of the soil. Again, it takes a much larger quantity of heat to warm up a soil filled with water than a dry one. Water is also a poor conductor of heat, and, therefore, wet soils are warmed downward very slowly. As water drains from a soil air enters it and aids in warming. Snow melts at least a week earlier, on an average, upon drained than on undrained land similarly situated. Vegetation advances far more rapidly on drained land. Stiff soils are made open and porous, easier worked, and earlier handled after rains. The time and labour saved in a few years will pay for the tiles. The open ditches are objectionable for many reasons, some of which are constant cost of cleaning and waste of land. Ploughing can only be done one way; the loss of the cream of the soil by being constantly washed in small particles through the quarter drains into the ditches, and thence into the canal and swamps.

Drainage is of the first importance to the sugar planter, since cane revels in well-drained land. The successful sugar planter recognises the necessity of drainage, and a heap of it. The year before last there fell on this station 75 inches of rain. Each inch represents 27,154 gallons of water per acre, or, in round numbers, 2,036,550 gallons, or 8,485 tons by weight per acre for the year. This would give an average of 25 tons of water to be evaporated daily from each acre of land did none run off the surface. If it run off, what a powerful eroding and carrying power on our soils! If, as our engineers say, 1 lb. of coal will evaporate 8 lbs. of water, it would require over 3 tons of coal per day for each acre of land throughout the year to evaporate the water which falls on it. This enormous rainfall forces the necessity of drainage. But which is best—surface drains, with loss of soil, or under drains, which not only relieve the soil of excess of moisture, but make it warm and mellow? Tile drainage, like diffusion, is surely but slowly coming.

Plat 15.—Pea vines removed v. pea vines turned under. In the spring of 1886, plat 15 was sown broadcast in cow peas. A luxuriant growth of vines was obtained. The plat was divided into two equal parts. The vines were removed on the west half, and fed to stock. The entire plat was then fallowed with a four-horse plough, and cane planted in October, 1886. This gave a basis for similar experiments with and without pea vines. In order to determine the chemical value of the latter, together with its roots, the following experiment was made:—A square 10 feet × 10 feet near the centre of the plat, and fairly representing the average of the crop, was selected, and the vines carefully removed by a scythe. These were at once weighed, and thoroughly dried and analysed. Around this plat a ditch 18 inches deep was dug, and, with a strong spray pump, the roots were patiently washed up. It required three days with three labourers to successfully perform the operation. The vines were nearing maturity, and had passed the period most desirable for hay making.

The following are the results, with analyses:—

	Lbs.
Amount of green vines removed per acre	21,345
„ roots washed up per acre	3,464
Total green matter removed per acre	24,809
When thoroughly dried, the vines weighed	3,330
„ „ „ the roots „	1,040
Total dry matter per acre	4,370

It is proper to add here that, despite our careful efforts, a considerable quantity of the small rootlets escaped us. The following are the analyses:—

	Organic Matter.	Ash.	Nitrogen.	Potash.	Phos. Acid.	Lime.
Dried vines	90·26	9·74	1·7	2·77	0·48	1·01
„ roots	92·58	7·42	0·8	1·74	0·43	0·97

Applying the above, one acre of cow peas turned under gives to the soil 3970·38 lbs. organic matter, containing 64·95 lbs. nitrogen, 20·39 lbs. phosphoric acid, 110·56 lbs. potash, and 42·6 lbs. lime. Removing the vines for stock feed leaves in the roots at least 965 lbs. organic matter, containing 8·34 lbs. nitrogen, 4·43 lbs. phosphoric acid, 18·1 lbs. potash, and 10·16 lbs. lime. Good cotton seed meal contains 7 per cent. nitrogen, 3 per cent. phosphoric acid, 2 per cent. potash and kainite, and 12 per cent. of potash. Therefore the vines and roots combined contain more nitrogen than is contained in 900 lbs. of cotton seed meal, and more potash than is in the same amount of meal, additioned by 700 lbs. kainite. This amount of meal would contain a few pounds more of phosphoric acid than is found in the peas.

Removing the vines for feed would, therefore, decrease the supply of plant food to the acre by the following amounts:— Nitrogen, 56·61 lbs.; phosphoric acid, 15·96 lbs.; potash, 92·46 lbs.—amounts about equal to that contained in 800 lbs. cotton seed meal, and 640 lbs. kainite.

Therefore, in removing the vines, there is certainly a removal of a large supply of valuable plant food. Will the cane plant testify to the same fact? To decide this question, duplicate experiments were made upon each half of the plat. All the factors of planting, fertiliser, and cultivation were identical; the only variation was the "vines removed on one," and "turned under on the other."

There were other incidental questions also asked of this plat, but this was the leading object. These experiments, begun with plant cane in 1887, have been continued in 1888 and 1889 as first and second year stubble.

The table following gives the results for 1889, second year stubble:—

This plat was harvested October 3, and was too green to be successfully manipulated in the sugar house. The syrup could not be grained in the pan.

RESULTS Plat 15.—Second Year Stubble, Harvested October 3.

Manures Used per Acre.	Disposition of Pea Vines.	Yield per Acre in Tons.	Total Solids.	Sucrose.	Glucose.	Purity coefficient.	Glucose Ratio.	Lbs. Available Sugar on 70 per cent. Extraction. Per Ton.	Per Acre.
1. 500 lbs. cotton seed meal / 250 ,, acid phosphate / 100 ,, kainite	Turned in ...	16·03	11·09	8·02	3·03	69	36·95	47·04	760
1. Ditto ...	Removed ...	16·02	10·09	6·04	3·48	59	54·37	16·05	264
2. 500 lbs. cotton seed meal / 500 ,, acid phosphate / 100 ,, kainite	Turned in ...	17·17	10·07	6·06	3·44	62	52 33	20·02	346
2. Ditto ...	Removed ...	16·45	10·04	7·06	3·36	73	44·21	35·08	590
3. 500 lbs. cotton seed meal / 250 ,, acid phosphate	Turned in ...	15·99	10·09	7·00	3·06	64	43·71	33·07	540
3. Ditto ...	Removed ...	14·88	11·00	6·06	3·37	68	51·06	31·06	322
4. 500 lbs. cotton seed meal / 500 ,, acid phosphate	Turned in ...	17·05	11·07	6·04	3·41	55	53·28	18·00	307
4. Ditto ...	Removed ...	14·37	11·06	7·01	3·59	61	50·56	24·01	346
5. No manure ...	Turned in ...	11·41	11·08	7·03	3·42	62	46·84	30·04	347
5. ,, ,,	Removed ...	10·54	11·00	6·06	3·33	60	50·45	22·05	237
6. ,, ,,	Turned in ...	11·52	11·08	7·03	3·48	62	47·67	29·01	335
6. ,, ,,	Removed ...	13·07	10·06	5·07	3·55	54	62·38	5·03	56
7. 100 lbs. nitrate soda / 70 ,, sulph. am. / 150 ,, cotton seed meal / 300 ,, acid phosphate / 100 ,, kainite	Turned in ...	17·95	9·05	4·08	3·51	50	73·12	...	...
7. Ditto ...	Removed ...	17·57	10·07	5·05	3·33	51	60·54	7·01	124
8. 300 lbs. nitrate of soda / 300 ,, acid phosphate / 100 ,, kainite	Turned in ...	17·26	10·07	5·05	3·33	51	60·54	7·01	122
8. Ditto ...	Removed ...	15·54	10·07	5·06	3·57	52	63·74	3·05	53
9. 100 lbs. sulph. am. / 200 ,, dried blood / 300 ,, acid phosphate / 100 ,, kainite	Turned in ...	17·25	10·07	6·00	3·57	56	59·05	9·00	156
9. Ditto ...	Removed ...	18·06	10·05	5·08	3·07	55	63·79	3·05	63
10. 200 lbs. sulph. am. / 300 ,, acid phosphate / 100 ,, kainite	Turned in ...	17·68	10·05	5·08	3·07	55	63·79	3·05	62
10. ditto ...	Removed ...	15·83	10·06	5·03	3·85	50	72·64	...	...

Results for three years.

Taking the experiments with no manure, and where no known errors have influenced results, we have obtained the following per acre due to pea vines turned under.

In 1887, 2·91 tons; in 1888, 3·69 tons; and in 1889, ·82 tons: total, 7·42 tons.

Taking the entire plat, with several known modifying errors, we have, in 1887, 2·23 tons; in 1888, 1·08 tons; and in 1889, ·94 tons: total, 4·25 tons.

The former increase is perhaps nearer the actual gains than the latter. The vines removed would have given about two tons per acre of cured hay, worth, after the expenses of harvesting is deducted, 5 dol. per ton, or 10 dol. per acre. They were worth as a fertiliser the equivalent of 800 lbs. cotton seed meal, and 640 lbs. kainite. The former is now worth 20 dol. per ton, and the latter

15 dol., and these would give a fertilising value to pea vines of 12 dol. 80 c.

From this investment there has been an increase of 7·42 tons cane, worth, say, 4 dol. per ton, or 29 dol. 68 c. per acre.
It is believed that the average results from pea vines turned under are even higher than those obtained here.

However, the results obtained show conclusively that removing the pea vines for hay is to the detriment of subsequent crops, even to the third year.

The incidental questions involved in the above experiments are corroborative of others answered elsewhere. 1. Potash in small quantities is without effect on these soils. 2. That excessive quantities of phosphoric acid are without beneficial results. 3. That while sulphate of ammonia has given slightly better results, the increase is so slight and the price of this article, proportionately, so dear, that any form of nitrogen usually offered on our market can be used with safety by our planters. 4. That stubble cane makes just as good seed as plant.

In 1886 this plat was planted and fertilised with the following popular manures: cotton seed meal, acid phosphate, kainite, Charleston floats, gypsum, cotton hull ashes, tankage, and cotton seed. These experiments have been continued to third year stubble, and one remarkable fact has been shown conclusively by them, viz.: that when the proper manure in appropriate quantities has been used yearly, a profitable crop of third year stubble has been gathered. When an improper fertiliser has been used, or the soil has received no fertiliser, no crop has been gathered. An inspection of the following table will show this:— *Plat 2. Popular manures.*

RESULTS of Plat 2.—Third Stubble, 1889.

Manures Used per Acre.	Yield per Acre in Tons.	Total Solids.	Sucrose.	Glucose.	Coefficient of Purity.	Glucose Ratio.	Per Ton.	Per Acre.	When Harvested.
1. 200 lbs. cotton seed meal, 100 lbs. acid phosphate	5·5	13·5	9·3	2·78	69	29·3	71·8	396	October, 15
2. 333 lbs. cotton meal, 167 lbs. acid phosphate	8·64	12·8	9·1	2·82	71	31	68·2	589	,, ,,
3. 140 lbs. sulphate am., 120 lbs. dried blood, 200 lbs. cotton seed meal, 460 lbs. acid phospbate, 80 lbs. muriate potash	19·06	12·3	8·5	2·97	69	34·9	56·6	979	,, ,,
4. 466 lbs. cotton meal, 234 lbs. acid phosphate	17·2	12	7·7	3·06	64	39·7	43·5	997	,, ,,
5. 600 lbs. cotton meal, 300 lbs. acid phosphate	21·16	12·8	9·4	2·79	73	29·7	73	1,545	,, ,,
6. 600 lbs. cotton meal, 300 lbs. acid phosphate, 300 lbs. kainite	8·74	11·8	8	2·12	68	26·5	67·5	589	,, ,,
7. 600 lbs. cotton meal	5·78	13·3	9·6	2·51	72	26·1	81·7	472	,, ,,
8. 260 lbs. sulphate am., 460 lbs. acid phosphate, 80 lbs. muriate potash	7·05	12·5	8·5	2·36	68	27·8	69·4	489	,, ,,
9. 300 lbs. acid phosphate, 300 lbs. kainite	2·2	...	...	...	...	...	...	...	,, ,,
10. 300 lbs. kainite	1·8	...	...	...	...	...	...	...	,, ,,
11. 200 lbs. cotton seed meal, 100 lbs. floats	·6	...	...	...	...	...	...	...	,, ,,
12. 333 lbs. cotton seed meal, 167 lbs. floats	1·8	...	...	...	...	...	...	...	,, ,,
13. No manure	·9	...	...	...	...	...	...	...	,, ,,
14. 466 lbs. cotton seed meal, 234 lbs. floats	·3	...	...	...	...	...	...	...	,, ,,
15. 600 lbs. cotton seed meal, 300 lbs. floats	16·49	12·5	9	2·76	72	30·7	65·2	1,076	,, ,,
16. 600 lbs. cotton seed meal, 300 lbs. floats, 300 lbs. kainite	16·23	11·5	8·4	2·08	73	24·8	73·9	1,200	,, ,,
17. 600 lbs. cotton meal, 300 lbs. floats, 300 lbs. kainite, 200 lbs. gypsum	15·16	10·1	6·7	2·38	66	35·5	43·8	664	,, ,,
18. No manure	·8	...	...	...	...	...	...	...	,, ,,
19. 600 lbs. cotton meal, 300 lbs. floats, 300 lbs. cotton hull ashes	6·36	12·7	8·2	3·24	64	39·5	46·8	321	,, ,,
20. 300 lbs. tankage	2·2	12·9	9·1	2·35	70	25·8	78	772	November 25
21. 450 lbs. tankage	2·28	13·4	10·6	2·36	79	20·3	98·8	226	,, ,,
22. 700 lbs. tankage	3·53	13·2	10·4	2·14	77	25·8	100·6	355	,, ,,
23. No manure	...	...	...	...	...	...	...	...	Few stalks
24. 900 lbs. tankage	10·62	12·4	9·2	2·45	74	26·6	77·4	821	November 25
25. 900 lbs. tankage, 300 lbs. kainite	13·44	12·7	9·3	2·03	73	21·8	87·6	1,177	,, ,,
26. 900 lbs. tankage, 300 lbs. kainite, 200 lbs. gypsum	11·34	14	11·3	1·72	80	15·2	12·3	1,445	,, ,,
27. 900 lbs. tankage, 300 lbs. cotton hull ashes	1·1	...	...	...	...	...	..	...	,, ,,
28. No manure	1·1	...	...	...	...	...	...	...	,, ,,
29. 1,700 lbs. cotton seed (raw)	2·78	...	...	...	...	...	...	...	,, ,,
30. 1,700 lbs. cotton seed (raw), 300 lbs. acid phosphate	7·3	...	...	...	...	...	...	...	,, ,,
31. 1,700 lbs. cotton seed (raw), 300 lbs. acid phosphate, 300 lbs. kainite	5·6	...	...	...	...	...	...	...	,, ,,
32. 1,700 lbs. cotton seed (raw), 300 lbs. cotton hull ashes	5·5	...	...	...	...	...	...	...	,, ,,
33. No manure	·9	...	...	...	...	...	...	...	,, ,,
34. 1,700 lbs. cotton seed (raw), 300 lbs. floats	1·34	...	...	...	...	...	...	...	,, ,,
35. 1,700 lbs. cotton seed (raw), 300 lbs. floats, 200 lbs. gypsum	1·3	...	...	...	...	...	...	...	,, ,,

The four years just ended have been patiently and industriously spent in the investigations of the many problems underlying the successful growth of sugar cane and its manufacture into sugar. While everything hoped for has not been attained, the little accomplished, supplemented by the consciousness of the rectitude of our intentions and that generous support yielded by an indulgent patronage, gives consolation and lends encouragement for renewed efforts in the future. Nature yields her secrets with great slowness, and only to those who apply aright does she reveal them at all. Mindful that there are many, many facts yet to be learned before perfection in cane production can be attained, and relying upon that cordial support of the public so generously bestowed in the past, and a strong determination to accomplish its mission, the Sugar Experiment Station, in its new and handsome quarters, re-enters the experimental arena, confident of ultimate success.

Summary of results for four years.

The following are some of the conclusions taught by the results of the last four years:—

1. That the upper portion of the cane is the equal, if not the superior, to the lower part for seed, while the latter is vastly superior as a sugar producer.

2. That with good seed, two stalks and a slight lap will give an abundant harvest, and no more is needed.

3. That seed cane may be selected from either plant or stubble.

4. That suckering (tillering) is a natural function of all cereals, and should be encouraged to produce the best results.

5. That ratoons come equally as well from suckers as from the original stalk.

6. That cutting cane in planting is not necessary to ensure successful germination, the latter being dependent upon other conditions.

7. That the vital power of good sound eyes is enormous, enabling the latter, under favourable conditions of heat, moisture, and access of air to germinate at great depths, or even remain dormantly sound for over a year when properly protected.

8. That the present width of rows may be lessened (when the soil will permit of easy cultivation) with promise of increased production.

9. That several varieties of foreign canes promise adaptability to our wants.

10. That both nitrogen and phosphoric acid are needed by our soils to grow maximum crops of cane. That excessive quantities of each should be avoided, the former as being positively injurious and the latter as being redundant and wasteful.

11. That while sulphate of ammonia gives slightly the best results and fish scrap slightly the worst, it may be asserted that any form of nitrogen experimented with will give remunerative returns when properly compounded, and used in such quantities as to furnish from 25 to 50 lbs. nitrogen per acre.

12. That phosphoric acid, when applied at or after planting,

should be in a soluble state, in quantities of 32 to 64 lbs. per acre. Even the latter might, with propriety, be applied before the crop is planned. That insoluble phosphates should always be applied sometimes in advance of the planting.

13. That no form of potash is preferred by the cane plant, and that small quantities neither increase the tonnage nor the sugar content.

14. That mineral manures (phosphates and potash), when applied alone, are without much effect; to be available they must be combined with nitrogen.

15. That nitrogen is most cheaply supplied to the planters of Louisiana in the form of cotton seed meal, and experiments have demonstrated that its profitable limits are between 300 to 600 lbs. per acre under cane.

16. That tile drainage is a very valuable amendment to the soils of South Louisiana, and when properly done will pay a handsome dividend upon investment. Experiments indicate that best results are obtained when tiles are placed from 20 to 30 feet apart.

17. That pea vines turned under give an increased yield to the subsequent crops, extending even to the second year's stubble.

18. That the stubble from canes, properly manured, will give profitable crops for several years, while that unmanured, or unproperly fertilised, will fail in a year or two.

19. That manures can be prepared which will give tonnage, but no special manure has yet been found which will ensure a large sugar content. The latter seems to be largely dependent upon soil, sunshine, temperature, moisture, and climate.

These are the deductions from the work of the past four years, and may be modified by future investigations.

The question of the proper manuring of cane is not yet settled. Seasons, particularly rainfall, modify the benefits of fertilisers. If one could accurately foretell the season, then manuring could be done with some degree of intelligence. It seems quite well established that manures should be applied in such quantities and proportions to meet the requirements of a vigorous growth from the time of germination until September. At that time all available plant food should be exhausted, and growth should be suspended and the plant permitted to mature.

The proportions are independent of seasons, but the quantities assimilated by the plant are regulated almost entirely by the amount and distribution of rainfall. Therefore, what would be an excessive manuring in a very dry season might prove inadequate to the requirements of a plant in a very favourable one. Our experiments indicate that from 24 to 48 lbs. of nitrogen and 40 to 75 lbs. phosphoric acid to the acre are the quantities which can be successively assimilated during an average season. These are furnished by using from 350 to 700 lbs. cotton seed meal, combined with 300 to 600 lbs. acid phosphate, and this mixture is recommended both on account of its cheapness and its efficacy.

Upon new lands abounding in nitrogen, or pea vine fallow (see Plat XV.), less nitrogen is required than upon stubble or succession cane. Equal mixtures will do for the first, while two or even three parts of cotton-seed meal to one of acid phosphate may be required upon the latter. Each planter should study his soils, and, when found deficient in vegetable matter, should always increase his nitrogen.

There are very few seasons that will permit of the assimilation by the plant of over 900 lbs. of this mixture to the acre, and hence quantities above this should never be used. On the other hand, there are still fewer seasons when 500 lbs. cannot be easily assimilated; therefore a less quantity per acre will rarely ever be found profitable.

In the application of manure greater care is needed. It would by some means be thoroughly incorporated with the soil. The time of application is also important. Many planters apply nitrogenous manures at the time of planting, and mineral manures when the cane is well advanced. There is no objection to an application, at least in part, of the nitrogenous manures at the time of planting, but there is a decided loss in postponing the application of mineral manures. They should, by all means, be applied at planting, or, even better, before planting. These do not leach from the soil, and the sooner applied the more diffusible they become in the soil. This is particularly the case with potash. Nitrogenous manures may be applied at planting, and at any time during early growth.

Annex B.—TEXAS Screw-worm (*Compsomyia (Lucilia) macellaria*), by Professor H. A. Morgan, Entomologist.

State Experiment Station, Baton Rouge, La.

Hon. T. S. Adams, Commissioner of Agriculture, Baton Rouge, La.

Dear Sir,

I HAND you herewith a bulletin upon the Texas screw-worm fly (Compsomyia (Lucilia) macellaria), prepared by Professor H. A. Morgan, entomologist of the station. This bulletin is the result of a most patient and intelligent investigation of an insect which has occasioned great injury to the stock of this State: an insect long known in Texas, and believed to be imported into this State with Texas cattle in the last year. I most respectfully ask that you print this Bulletin No. 2, second series, and earnestly invite the careful perusal by every farmer of its contents. Respectfully,

WM. C. STUBBS, Director.

UNITED STATES.

Louisiana State University and A. and M. College,
State Experiment Station, Baton Rouge, La.

To Professor W. C. Stubbs, Ph.D., Director.

Dear Sir,

In accordance with your request, investigation has been made of the screw-worm fly (Compsomyia (Lucilia) macellaria) which has been so destructive to stock throughout the State during this season.

I herewith hand you a bulletin containing a report of the investigation made, and trust that benefit may be derived from the work done.

In the preparation of this bulletin I am indebted to Dr. Dalrymple for his assistance and information in the treatment of stock attacked and in the actions of the different agents used.

Yours obediently,
H. A. MORGAN.

SCREW-WORM FLY (COMPSOMYIA (LUCILIA) MACELLARIA).

Introduction.

During the present summer much alarm has been raised in connection with maggots, which at first were supposed to be those of the common blow-fly (Calliphora vomitoria), but afterwards determined to be those of the screw-worm fly (Compsomyia (Lucilia) macellaria).

Not only does this insect attack all the lower animals (fowl, dog, sheep, deer, pigs, cattle, and horses), but it attacks members of the human family, and from the statements of those who have suffered we learn that the pain is excruciating, and almost unbearable; thus we can easily account for the ready emaciation and rather sudden death of animals that have been attacked by screw-worms, and that have not received treatment and proper attention.

In order to become familiar with the habits and life-history of this insect, animals were purchased for the purpose of investigation, and although many things were discovered which will, I trust, be of value, yet the winter requires to pass over us before information can be given as to its complete eradication.

History of the screw-worm fly.

This fly has long been known in South America, where it is much dreaded on account of its attack upon the human race; and while it has been known to exist all the way from Patagonia to Canada, yet its effects were never seriously felt in North America, outside of Texas, until this season. In Texas its first appearance dates as far back as 1834, and from its long sojourn in that State it is commonly known in the South as the "Texas screw-worm fly." Since 1834 it has proven very troublesome during the summer season, but seems to cease its depredations at the coming of the frosts.

Life History.

Herewith is an engraving of the different stages of the screw-worm fly, as made from photos, magnified two diameters (except pupa, which is $2\frac{1}{2}$):—

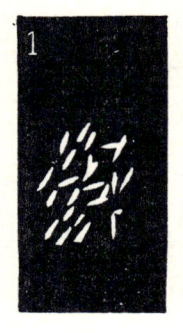

1. Eggs.   2. Maggot or larva.   3. Pupa or chrysalis.   4. Fly or adult.

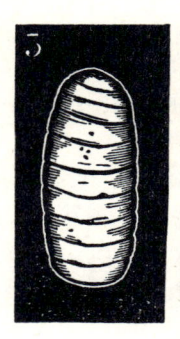

Eggs. Eggs, about one-sixteenth of an inch in length, and of a light yellow colour, are deposited in immense numbers (flies of the same family have been known to contain 20,000 eggs within the oviduct at once) usually in the evening, so that they may escape the sun's rays while hatching. Where a wound is present they are invariably deposited near it, but on dead animals they are placed on the under or shaded side, as eggs exposed to the hot sun soon lose their vitality. In order to prove that the eggs deposited were those of the screw-worm fly several flies were dissected, and the eggs found within the bodies were identical with those deposited. Since then, however, the screw-worm fly has been developed from eggs which I witnessed being deposited.

Larva or maggot. When full grown is three-fourths of an inch in length, and about one-eighth of an inch in diameter. The body, of a dull white colour,* is made up of segments, while between each segment is a ring of bristles, which causes the maggot to bear resemblance to a screw, and from which the name is derived. The head is pointed, and contains two strong, sharp-pointed, black hooks, bending ventrad. These hooks, together with the bristles, cause great irritation and flow of blood, as well as assist the maggot in its movements and in securing its food. The caudal end of the body is very much truncated. The larvae we had under our control remained in this condition from August 19 until August 24 and 25, when they entered into the pupa, or chrysalis condition.

Pupa, or chrysalis. When the larva is full grown it falls from the wound, and just below the surface of the ground assumes the pupa condition, in which it remains for seven or eight days (one lot remained from August 7 until August 14, while another from August 13 until August 20). The pupa is dark red in colour, about one-third of an inch in length, while the segment is plainly shown.

---

* The colour and size of larva is influenced to some extent by the character of the food. Those fed upon decaying animal and vegetable matter are darker, and not so large as those which prey upon living flesh.

Imago or fly.

When the fly emerges it is grey, but soon assumes its permanent colour, which is a bright metallic green; just behind the head (thorax) there are three distinct black stripes running from the head to the abdomen. The eyes are of a dull red colour and quite prominent. The wings are long, and in many instances lap one over the other on the body, presenting a narrowed appearance. The whole fly is a little larger than the ordinary house-fly (Musca domestica), and begins depositing her eggs the second day after emerging from the pupa.

Characters of the fly.

It is readily attracted by the odour of decaying animal and vegetable matter, and feeds very voraciously upon these until satisfied, when it will lodge upon plants in the immediate vicinity of its food. I have seen plants in the neighbourhood of a dead animal completely covered with these flies.

Will the screw-worm fly deposit her eggs upon decaying animal and vegetable matter, and will the maggots mature in those decaying substances.

There has been a very great deal of controversy on this point, and particular investigation was made in order to arrive at something conclusive regarding this. If it is so that they mature in decayed animal and vegetable matter, the knowledge of this will be of the first importance in aiding us to keep this terrible pest in check.

The first experiment to determine these points was as follows:—A large number of flies were captured on June 28, killed with gasoline, and put into a tin box, with cover. On June 29 the eggs, which were within the bodies of the female flies, hatched; no food whatever was given except the dead bodies of flies. On July 3 the young maggots, being nearly full-grown, were removed, with the hopes of carrying them through the different stages, but unfortunately they were placed in the hot sun, by mistake. Although the specimens could not be carried through the complete circle, they were sufficiently matured to prove that they would live upon decaying animal matter.

The maggots found upon decaying animal and vegetable matter were carefully examined under the microscope both by Dr. Dalrymple and myself, and while different species were found, blow-fly maggots (Musca (calliphora) Voritoria), flesh-fly maggots (Sarcophaga Carnaria), yet specimens (which were matured, by-the-way, to the perfect screw-worm fly) were generally found which seemed identical with the maggots taken from the living animals.

On August 18 a sheep died, and on the evening of the same day large masses of eggs was deposited on the underside of this animal. A cage was constructed so as not to allow the entrance of other flies, and provided with earth in the bottom that the maggots when full-grown might retire to this earth and pupate. On the same evening a portion of the dead animal was placed within the cage, as well as masses of eggs; in the course of 15 hours the egg hatched, when the young larvæ at once began feeding upon the decaying flesh, and continued feeding until August 23 and 24, when they pupated, coming out as perfect screw-worm flies on August 29 and 30; hence we may safely say that decaying animal and vegetable matter encourages the reproduction of the screw-worm fly.

Apart from the death caused by this insect in stock, there have been some deaths recorded in the human family, some in this State as well as some in other States; however, it is sufficient to know that the human family may be attacked—the openings of the head usually being the seats of attack, while the armpits or any exposed portion of the body are equally liable. Flies have been known to deposit their eggs during the dressing of a wound. The cases in this vicinity have in some instances caused death, while all caused the most excruciating pain. I have observed, on liberating a fly at night in a lighted room, that it is not as stupid as other flies are, but comparatively active; hence the necessity of mosquito bars in localities where the screw-worm fly is prevalent. *Its attack upon the human family.*

Questions have been asked if there is any danger in taking this insect into the system by means of food. There is a disease (Myiosis intestinalis) caused by the maggot of a fly of the family Anthromyidæ which enters the body with decaying vegetables, the decay being wholly unnoticed by the presence of some seasoning article, as vinegar, &c., but no cases have ever been recorded where the larvæ of flies of this family have ever caused any internal diseases.

All the natural openings of animals are liable to be attacked, particularly the sheaths of horses and mules, and the navals of newly-born stock, while in all animals where an abrasion of the skin is made an attack may be expected. *Are there some parts of animals more subject to attack than others?*

Among the worst cases that have come under my observation were when the horns of animals had been broken; the maggots penetrated the head, and when the animals were not at once attended to they soon died. The majority of cases throughout the country resulted from the deposition of eggs upon the animals in the vicinity of where ticks (Ixodes bovis) had been killed, the flies being attracted by the blood. I have observed that when sheep become sick and emaciated that the odour characteristic of sick sheep attracted the flies, and masses of eggs were deposited in the folds of the wool, and the young larvæ penetrated the skin where no wound had been made.

It is to the complete eradication (if possible) of this insect that we look to with the greatest interest, and it is not with the whole-souled and vigorous work of a few that the work is to be accomplished, but that of the untiring energies and assistance of every person throughout the State. *Remedies and preventives.*

Experience has proven that the tendency of the mass of mankind is not to resort to extreme measures until they are compelled, and few appreciate that time-honoured adage "that a stitch in time saves nine."

From the following facts conclusions may be drawn:—

1. The screw-worm fly has never given any trouble in Louisiana before this year, except during the war, when animals were removed from States where these flies were prevalent, to Loui-

siana and other States with impunity, and when communication throughout the Southern States was brisk.

2. There was importation of cattle into this State last season from places where screw-worm flies were prevalent, and from where the maggots were also imported.

3. Last winter was an exceptionally warm one, and one very propitious to the carrying through of insects that could not have endured our usual winters.

4. This fly did not remain in this State to do damage when introduced during the war.

Conclusions drawn. These must be taken for what they are worth, and not as positive.

1. The coming winter, if severe, may exterminate this insect.

2. If these insects are eradicated care should be exercised to forbid the importation of stock from districts where the screw-worm fly is always present. This may seem selfish, but every intelligent person cannot help but admit that insects of this order (many of them feeding and reproducing in decaying animal and vegetable matter), with unlimited range, will reproduce more readily than those kept within a limited range, and that where they are present in great numbers some are more liable to escape the winter than where these numbers are small. It is, therefore, wise that steps be taken to keep these pests within the borders where they are not influenced by the winters of those districts.

3. From the fact that this insect has been close to Louisiana for many years, and even here at one time, it would seem that there has been something which has had a checking tendency.

4. This tendency seems to have been the winter.

It is a very common practice throughout the South to allow dead animals to lie upon the surface of the earth to decompose, and to be devoured by buzzards. Now since the screw-worm fly lives on and reproduces its species in decaying animal and vegetable matter, it becomes of first importance, if not an absolute necessity, to have all decaying animal and vegetable matter buried. In connection with this a small experiment was made in order to ascertain to what depth an animal might be buried that the maggot might not mature. It was found that at the depth of from 2 to $2\frac{1}{2}$ feet (of course deeper) the eggs would hatch, but the larvæ would not mature, proving that the exclusion of air from the maggot will kill it. I cannot conceive of anything of more importance in the extermination of so vile a pest as having laws compelling stockowners to have all animals buried immediately after death. In many towns and cities it is quite a common practice to have a common "dumping place," where refuse of all kinds (animal and vegetable) is conveyed, let lie, decompose, thus causing stench and attracting flies, where they will feed and reproduce with great rapidity. From the great destruction of life, both of man and beast, caused by the prevalence of the screw-worm fly, it behoves every village, town, and city to adopt such means as to have all refuse either buried or so disinfected as to forbid the generation of these flies. Refuse from kitchens, which is left standing in barrels for a day or two, will become completely alive with maggots.

To reckon the number of descendants from a pair of these flies in a single season would be almost as endless a task as counting the sands upon the sea-shore. It cannot be made more practical and conclusive than by asking a question. Reaumur has observed 20,000 eggs, as stated previously, within the oviduct of a fly of the same family ("muscidæ") as the screw-worm fly. Now, supposing a pair of these screw-worm flies to be introduced into a locality early in April, what would be the number of descendants by the end of October, allowing 15 days to complete the circle from the egg to the fly, and 20,000 the number of young from each brood?

And now to discuss the particular remedies, and those within the grasp of every person, permit me to state that careful watch and prompt attention are the principal features in restoring your animals. If animals are worth having they are certainly worth taking care of. Should the fly remain within our State and continue to pest our people, as it has done this season, stock will have to be handled on a very different plan from the present one in order to make the raising of them profitable. The introduction of docile breeds of stock, and the herding of them in fields free from everything that would be liable to cause injury or abrasion of the skin, will have to be considered. Barbed-wire fence and the screw-worm fly go hand in hand.

In the use of agents for the destruction of screw-worm two things have to be taken into consideration, viz., the death of the worm, and the effect upon the wound that these agents necessary to destroy the maggot would have. Then, again, care has to be exercised in the too free use of mercurials, on account of animals licking the parts, or on account of absorption, thereby causing mercurialism and death. These maggots have wonderful vitality, as has been proven by taking them from a wound and subjecting them to the action of very powerful caustics, such as trichloride of antimony (butter of antimony), through which, for a short time, they seemed to move with impunity: such an agent as the above applied to a wound would, of course, destroy the vitality of the tissues and cause sloughing. So we see the necessity of bearing this fact in mind. *Treatment of stock attacked.*

The remedies which have been tried and in use are numberless, and nearly every experimenter believes his own the most efficacious. This seems to prove that the virtue does not altogether lie in the particular agent used, but in the careful application of it, and the untiring perseverance in attending to the stock which are the victims of this pest, as also those that have escaped, but which at any moment may be attacked.

Strong remedies, such as chloroform, crude carbolic acid, corrosive sublimate, &c., should be used with care, on account of their irritant properties when undiluted. Where the screw-worms are present in an animal, and have, by their boring, caused cavities or holes, the main object in view is to get rid of them, allow the

(1037)

wound made to heal up, and to prevent further attacks of screw-worm flies.

Chloroform. — One of the quickest agents to stupefy the maggots is chloroform (I say stupefy, because it has been proven that the maggots will recover in some instances after the applicacation of this drug); but, after filling the cavity with chloroform for the purpose of deadening the maggots, it should be washed out to prevent the irritating effect of the drug on the tissues, as well as getting out the dead or half-dead larvæ or maggots, and cleansing the wound.

Bichloride of Mercury (corrosive sublimate) is another powerful agent, caustic, corrosive, and irritant in its action, and is much too strong in its undiluted state, but when used as a diluted solution (60 grains to the pint of water) it may be left in the cavity without affecting the tissues for some time, and has the effect of not only making the maggots lose their hold, but, as it is the best antiseptic in use (in diluted state), it leaves the wound in a healthy state for healing.

Crude Carbolic Acid, when used alone, belongs to the irritant class. From experiment it appears to act almost as quickly as chloroform, and should be used in a similar manner; that is, use just sufficient to destroy the vitality of the maggots, and then wash out the wound and its contents.

Mercury Subchloride (calomel) is an agent much used, and with success. It has the desired effect upon the maggots, but in too large quantities, and often repeated, it over-stimulates the wound, becomes an irritant, and, if within the reach of the animal's tongue, may be licked and cause mercurialism.

Ether gives similar results to chloroform, although less powerful.

Spirits of Turpentine causes maggots to let go, but as its action is also irritant to the raw surface of a wound, it should be washed out afterwards. If carefully used it has antiseptic properties, and will assist the wound in healing.

Coal Oil.—Its actions and effects are similar to turpentine.

Cresylic Ointment.—This is a patent preparation. The name would imply its containing cresylic acid, which is much like carbolic acid, both being products of coal-tar. It is very much lauded in Texas as a destroyer of the screw-worm. Its action resembles that of crude carbolic acid, and from experiment we do not find that it supersedes that agent.

Air-slaked Lime.—This has been tried with varying results. Owing to its irritant action we do not recommend it.

Gasoline or Puroline Oil is a light volatile liquid-product obtained from the distillation of petroleum. It has a very deadly action on insect life, but, being extremely volatile, it becomes rather unreliable unless tightly corked. It may be used similarly to spirits of turpentine and coal-oil.

McDougall's Sheep Dip.—This is a patent medicine, and has been highly recommended for the destruction of the maggots of the screw-worm fly, but being unable to procure any of this preparation we cannot recommend it from experience. However, this may be said in its favour, that, being (when made into a wash) an invaluable remedy for the attack of vermin upon stock, it may be recommended as a remedy for the cattle-tick (Ixodes bovis), which seems to form the ground-work for the attack of the screw-worm fly.

Upon the recommendation of a number of parties decoctions of the following were tried:—

Leaves of china tree (Melia azederach).
Leaves of coffee plant (Cassia obtusifolia).
Sneeze-weed or bitter-weed (whole plant) (Helenium autumnaly).
Jamestown-weed (leaves) (Datura stramonium).
"Pyrethrum Insect Powder."
Leaves of the elder (Sambucus canadensis).
Leaves of smart-weed (Polygonum acre).

None of the above prove in any way destructive to the maggots, and thus cannot be recommended.

All these agents have been experimented with, but I think we are inclined to give the preference to crude carbolic acid. It is a cheap article, and does the work well when carefully used, as stated under the head of crude carbolic acid. *To sum up.*

When the maggots have been eliminated from the wound, the latter should be washed thoroughly with warm water, and dressed with carbolised oil (1 of carbolic acid to 16 of oil). If there is a cavity, lint cotton saturated with the oil should be inserted.

To prevent the attacks of the fly there is nothing simpler or more convenient than a mixture of tar and grease, or fish oil, smeared about the parts; so long as the smell lasts the flies do not seem to deposit their eggs.

For the treatment of stock attacked by this fly there is no specific virtue in any one agent (as previously stated) over another that will prevent future attacks, after one application, but by daily and careful attention to stock the mortality will be lessened to a very great extent.

PENSACOLA (FLORIDA).

Mr. Vice-Consul Hawe reports as follows:—

In my Report on Agriculture for the year 1888, I referred to the growth of the sugar cane, and to the manufacture of sugar therefrom in Florida. *Sugar-cane. Sugar.*

By a recent interesting paper in the "Florida Times Union Trade Edition," on the Florida sugar industry, it is claimed that sugar-cane can be grown in all of the forty-five counties of Florida, and that the sugar industry of this State is destined to become an important internal economy in the near future. The report gives particulars of a sugar-making establishment lately started—the Florida Sugar Manufacturing Company. *Sugar-cane can be grown throughout Florida. Sugar Manufacturing Company.*

It will be understood that in giving as follows, as briefly as I can, a description of the plantation, and mill, and yield of the

Florida Sugar Manufacturing Company, which is at St. Cloud, Florida, it is my aim and hope that the particulars given may not only prove interesting, but also be worthy of study, and thereby profit to sugar manufacturers and those that may be induced to open the untilled soil in British possessions over the world of like climate to that of Florida.

Sugar manufacturers.
British possessions.
Cultivation of the sugar-cane.
Best results.

In the article that I have referred to and am following, it is said that the cultivation of the sugar-cane heretofore in Florida had been pursued without any scientific knowledge of the conditions which lead to the best results, and that the profit formerly derived from it was attributable "to the evenness of the climate and good luck."

Fine grades of sugar.

The manufacture of the fine grades of commercial sugar, it is said, had never been thought of until a party of financiers, mostly from the Northern States of this country, under the name of the Florida Sugar Manufacturing Company, planted several hundred acres of cane in 1888, and erected a mill for the manufacture of sugar from the crop. The St. Cloud plantation, as it is called, is described as lying on the shore of East Tohopekaliga Lake, Florida, and on the line of the St. Cloud Sugar Belt Railway. The mill was first put in operation in the winter of 1888–89, "after an unprecedentedly wet season, and before the waters had really subsided." The plantation is described as being on a tract of "muck" land, which had been drained, but which, prior to the drainage, had constantly or frequently overflowed to the depth of several feet. The soil there is said to be composed almost wholly of decomposed vegetable matter, and yields a quality and an amount of sugar-cane which cannot be equalled anywhere in the world. Two drainage pumps have been established on the plantation, which can remove the surplus water at any time, and as quickly as desired.

Florida Company.
Mill erected.
St. Cloud plantation.
Sugar Belt Railway.

"Muck" land.
The soil.

Yields well
Drainage pumps.

The cane on this plantation is said to grow to an "enormous height," and its yield in sugar has been found to far exceed the expectations of the company. The first grinding season began in December, 1889, and continued until March following. The St. Cloud mill is referred to as an "immense business, with a capacity of 250 barrels of sugar per day." The cane field begins close to the mill, and its furthest confines are nearly two miles distant. The problem of transportation had, therefore, to be solved, and, as a result, the immense tract is penetrated by tramways, over which mules are constantly drawing car loads of the cane. The harvesters use the cane-knives common in Louisiana, which are manufactured in Philadelphia. On arriving at the mill the cars are unloaded on to a carrier worked by an endless chain, which conveys the cane into the mill for grinding. The mill consists of two sets of rollers, the first of which expresses the juice under a pressure of 265,000 lbs.; "the second set is the largest one in the country." As the residue of the cane passes between the two huge rollers, a pressure is exerted upon it of 621,000 lbs., which leaves only a dry substance called "bagasse." This is carried forward by the endless chain arrangement, and fed

Cane grows high.
Good yield.
Grinding season.
Immense business.

Transportation.
Tramways.
Cane-knives for harvesters.

Mill rollers.
Pressure.

"Bagasse."

into the furnace, where its combustion is complete. No other fuel is necessary, except to start the fires in the morning. *Combustion.*

The cane-juice passes through a chamber or receptacle, where it is bleached by being subjected to contact with the fumes of burning sulphur—sulphurous gas. Next comes the concentration of the juice into a syrup in vacuo; here it remains in an immense vat for 16 or 20 hours, in order that it may properly settle. After this it is conveyed through presses, or channels, into the strike pans, arranged in immense cylindrical vats of iron, not unlike cisterns. Here, under a temperature of from 160 degrees to 165 degrees, the syrup is grained; that is, it begins to take on a granular form like that of sugar, these grains being still a part of the syrup. Experts carefully trained to the work watch the boiling syrup, and keep testing it constantly during this process, for a little too much or not quite enough graining will spoil the whole mass. *Cane-juice bleached. Sulphurous gas. Syrup. Strike-pans. Vats of iron. Temperature. Experts.*

"From the strike-pans the syrup passes into centrifugal machines beneath, where the grains of sugar are separated from the syrup by centrifugal force. This process is repeated several times, the result being as follows:— *Keep testing. Centrifugal machines.*

"First grade of sugar.—Pure white, granulated, and yellow clarified. *Grades.*

"Second grade.—Brown sugar.

"Third grade.—Brown sugar.

"Molasses.—What remains after the above sugars have been separated from the syrup."

The report further states that there is a finely fitted-up laboratory in connection with the mill, and that a chemist is constantly engaged during sugar making in scientific investigation, in order to secure the best results in manufacture. The chemist "keeps a minute record of every development of interest as the process goes on, and at the end of each week makes an exhaustive report thereon." It thus appears that at the end of the eighth week after grinding operations commenced on the plantation, a report was made of the weekly yield of sugar each week, increasing in outturn. The record given is as follows:— *Laboratory. Chemist. Scientific investigation. Reports. Weekly yield.*

First week, 2,247 lbs. sugar to the acre.
Second week, 3,620 lbs. sugar to the acre.
Third week, 3,240 lbs. sugar to the acre.
Fourth week, 3,645 lbs. sugar to the acre.
Fifth week, 3,644 lbs. sugar to the acre.
Sixth week, 4,000 lbs. sugar to the acre.
Seventh week, 4,982 lbs. sugar to the acre.
Eighth week, 6,041 lbs. sugar to the acre.

Here is another table of the "partial results" at the St. Cloud plantation "for the week ending January 19, 1890." *Another table.*

UNITED STATES.

CANE.

Cane.	
Cane ground, number of acres	25·05
Number of tons	835·96

JUICE.

Number of pounds	1,260,462·5
Total gallons	141,625
Percentage, juice extracted	76·05
Degrees Beaume	9·05
Percentage, sucrose	15·01
„ glucose	1·20
„ total solids	16·94
„ impurities	0·73
„ ratio G. to S.	7·99
„ water	88·06
„ purity coefficient	88·60
„ available sugar	13·81

SYRUP.

Number of pounds	404,445
Total gallons	39,189
Degrees Beaume	28·03
Percentage, sucrose	43·47
„ glucose	3·76
„ total solids	51·34
„ impurities	4·11
„ ratio G. to S.	8·65
„ water	48·66
„ purity coefficient	85·06

DRY SUGAR.

Pounds of dry sugar estimated	161,452
„ sugar per ton of cane	194
„ „ acre	6,041

MOLASSES.

Gallons molasses, estimated	3,856
Pounds molasses, estimated weight	37,789

Louisiana planter. St. Cloud mill.

It is stated that a Louisiana planter of long experience, and a practical sugar manufacturer, is in charge of the St. Cloud mill, and this gentleman gives it as his opinion that Florida possesses a great advantage in the production of sugar beyond the other regular sugar-producing portion of the Southern States, from the

Cane not injured. From frosts or cold no danger.

fact that the cane is not injured by standing, as it may remain uncut until the secretion of "sucrose" is complete. There is no danger, it is said, from frosts or cold, and the stalks may, therefore, reach full maturity.

Twenty acres easily cultivated.

It is further stated that one man and a mule can cultivate 20 acres of cane on a plantation like the St. Cloud place, and that an acre properly cultivated ought to yield 30 tons of cane. "The cane, as it is harvested, is worth from 4 to 5 dol. per ton. Twenty acres, with the labour of one man and a mule will, therefore, bring the owner in 2,400 dol. in cash."

Value to owner.

Markets.

The St. Cloud Company finds a market in New Orleans, Savannah, and New York for its sugar. The "Times Union" hopes in its next trade issue to chronicle the establishment of several other mills of like magnitude. I see that one variety of the "agave" ("American aloe"), generally known in Florida as

"Sisal hemp," is attracting some attention, and has been referred to in a report of the Commissioner of Agriculture for Florida as the "jenequen," and which derives its name from the "Toltens," or "Mayas" (descendants of the Toltens, who are to be found in Yucatan and other Central American States), and has for many years been known as a valuable fibre plant. *Florida sisal hemp. Valuable fibre plants.*

Some years ago, on one of the keys between Bahia Honda and Key West, about 50 acres were successfully planted in "jenequen," or sisal hemp. That was the beginning of the culture or growth of sisal hemp in Florida. The plant "jenequen," as it is called, has, it appears, been especially investigated in Honduras, "the merits and habits of the plant," and it has been ascertained that it grows fully as well in Florida as in Central America. Among the plants there considered of most value is the agave Mexicana, from which the Mexican drink, called "pulque," is made, and which is "the celebrated drink of the country." The agava sisalana is supposed to be the best, for the fineness of its fibre. *Culture. Honduras. Merits of the plants. Makes Mexican drink. Fine fibre.*

It is said that these plants had been used for their fibre since before the discovery of America by Columbus; and that at one period it was thought that the plant might, to some extent, take the place of cotton, as it withstands drought as well as it does wet seasons. Experience proved, however, that it was susceptible to frosts; it therefore requires a warmer climate than does the cotton plant. It is believed that, as regards the intrinsic value of the two fibres, this is far superior to cotton for many purposes; but the cost heretofore of extracting the fibre has given cotton the supremacy. The several plants of the family of this fibre "will grow on high scrub lands." The fibre is, it is said, well adapted for the manufacture of twine, cordage, seines, and binding twine for grain, and it may be used for sail cloth; also, that the finer varieties will compare favourably with linen and other goods for domestic purposes. It has, it is said, "a fine gloss similar to that seen on linen." *Withstands drought. Susceptible to frosts. Superior to cotton for some purposes. Grows on high scrub lands. Makes twine, cloth, &c. Finer varieties. Compare with linen.*

The article from which I gather the above remarks about the sisal hemp in Florida goes on to say that the former drawback to the use of the plant for commercial purposes was owing to there being no machine to successfully work out, in good condition, the fibre from the plant, and, in the article, a full description is given of a recently manufactured "tropical fibre machine." It is advanced that this is the first really successful and practical fibre machine ever produced in this or any other country, so far as known; and "that it is both successful and practical," as stated, "is proven by the fact that the 10 machines recently made by the manufacturer, Mr. Van Buren, were the result of the satisfactory trial of three sent to the same party ordering the 10 in Bahamas in 1888. Also, that he has recently sent three to St. Domingo to a party who had seen them in operation in the Bahamas. The other machines in use there, and in Yucatan, are of English make, and do not give satisfactory results, as they *cut the fibre*. The tropical fibre machine does not cut the fibre, but takes out of the leaf all there is in it. This has been proved by rotting the leaf in *Machines to work fibre. Recently manufactured. Manufactured in America. Used in Bahamas. Machines of English make. Reported as cutting the fibre.*

the old way, and then cleaning by hand, and the tropical fibre machine shows the same results."

The article from which I gather the foregoing information about the fibre plant is published in "The Florida Times Union Trade Report" for 1890, and my object is twofold in embodying these particulars in this report. In the first place, I hope the subject may prove of interest to some of our agricultural people in latitudes and sails like of Florida; and, next, that the machines referred to of "English make," and which, it is said, "do not give satisfactory results, as they cut the fibre," will be looked into by the English manufacturers and improved upon, if it be *really the fact*, as regards the detrimental remarks to the English manufacture, when praising or "booming" the American machine.

The report on the fibre machine further states that "one advantage of the Van Buren machine is that, when the fibre leaves it, it is ready for market, except drying;" and that "in all other machines the fibre has to be washed after leaving them," and that "this injures the colour, and therefore the sale."

It is further given that the profit to the planter of this fibre, "at four or five years after planting, is 18 tons per acre, producing not less than 2,500 lbs. of fibre per ton, worth, at 10 c. a lb., 250 dol.," and that the cost of producing and manufacturing is about—"cultivating not over 10 dol.; manufacturing 18 days, one boy at 50 c. per day, 9 dol.; interest on machinery and other expenses about 5 dol.: total, 24 dol., making net profit per acre 226 dol."

Since writing the above, I see by the British Quarterly Review for November last that the "Times" has recently referred to this textile industry, as it is now being treated at a factory in Lambeth. The article from the "Times" is given, and is quite interesting on the subject, giving many details of manufacture, &c., of fibrous plants.

Cotton is almost an indigenous product of inter-tropical regions. The plant supplies the raw material for many important industries, particularly in some of the great manufacturing cities of Great Britain. It may be said that cotton is entitled to rank as one of Nature's most important products.

I have read that the origin of this plant has perplexed botanists, and that its "genealogy" is not quite clear. "The celebrated botanist, Lemas, gives five distinct species; other writers have added two more. The two great divisions are—the cotton of the new and of the old world, the oriental and the occidental (the Indian and the American). The botanical differences are slight, but sufficient to distinguish them. The seed of the eastern plant is never black or naked."

My present desire is to give some interesting information that I have gathered about the cotton principally produced in this portion of one of the great cotton-producing countries in the world.

It is said that Sea Island cotton is one of Florida's most important industries, and, for the benefit of those in the British tropical professions, I will confine my remarks to this one of the, if not the, most valuable species of the cotton plant. *British tropical possessions.*

Sea Island cotton, we are informed by writers, seems to be "A native of Honduras, whence it is supposed to have spread to the West Indies, and was then carried to the United States, about 100 years ago. This cotton requires a climate soft, mild, and maritime. *Valuable. A native of Honduras. Requires mild climate.*

"Before the present century the principal supply of this cotton was obtained from the West Indies. The finest ever brought to the English market, or probably ever grown, was raised on the Island of Tobago. The West Indian cotton was of superior grade. *West Indies. Tobago grew superior grade.*

"The abandonment of the culture of the Sea Island cotton in the West Indies left the Sea Island cotton region of America without a rival, unless we except a superior grade of cotton produced in Egpyt. *Growth abandoned in West Indies. Left America without a trial.*

"For years it was thought that this cotton could not be successfully cultivated on the mainland. But, shortly after Florida was ceded to the United States, it was found that the Sea Island cotton could be grown in Florida. *Successful cultivation.*

"The methods of cultivating cotton have too often been careless and shiftless, without due forethought and care. With proper culture and attention, as much cotton can be grown on an acre as is now grown on five, and at two-thirds of the cost. *Methods of cultivation. Requires attention.*

"In the cultivation of cotton, the thing of the first and vital importance is the selection of the seed. While Florida has and will produce the very finest grades of Sea Island, or long staple cotton, produced in the world, yet it is a fact that the quality rapidly deteriorates if the seed produced here is used continuously. *Selection of seed.*

"After the selection of good seed comes the question of cultivation. The more carefully and better any crop is cultivated, the better it is. Careful culture improves the quality and the quantity, the length, strength, and fineness." *Quality, &c., dependent on cultivation.*

Going beyond Pensacola and its surroundings on this subject —Tobacco—I see by the "Times Union Trade Edition" for 1890 (I have found this interesting and well-compiled publication of great service to me in this entire report) that "tobacco can be successfully and profitably grown in 'at least half the counties of the State of Florida.'" *Tobacco.*

The eagerness with which the people of Florida are engaging in the cultivation of tobacco, as it is said, has led to the purchase of thousands of acres of land in Florida for this purpose. Gadsden county, Florida, is the centre of these operations. The land there is unusually rich and fertile, it is said, and is especially adapted to the culture of tobacco. A company has been organised, and the planting of tobacco on a large scale has commenced. The capital stock of the company was placed at 300,000 dol. Over 14,000 acres of land has been bought; and, in addition to this company's land, other purchases of land for *Thousands of acres planted. Company formed.*

(1037)

UNITED STATES.

Florida dotted with tobacco fields.

tobacco planting have taken place. It is said that "Gadsden county, Florida, is now dotted with large tobacco fields."

The same report goes on to say that "the last revival in agriculture in the south is the cultivation of tobacco. It has been stimulated by Northern cigar manufacturers and others. They are investing in choice lands, and thousands of acres are in cultivation. Gadsden county, Florida, is the centre of these operations. The land is universally rich and fertile. It is especially adapted to the culture of tobacco."

Cigar manufacturers. Investing in choice lands.

Tobacco plantation, Santa Clara. Barns for storing. Seed. Different species. Luxuriant growth.

One of these large tobacco plantations, Santa Clara, embraces 4,000 acres. Immense barns for the curing and storing of the tobacco have been erected there.

The tobacco seeds used at Santa Clara are "Cuba, Pennsylvania, and Sumatra tobacco of the second year." So thick and luxuriant are the plants, it is said, that it is difficult to move through the fields soon after planting. There are from 16 to 20 leaves on each plant when the field is ready for cutting. All the leaves are valuable. Those directly in front are grown from Pennsylvania plants. "The superintendent claims that this part of the plantation, with first and second crops, will cut from 800 to 1,000 lbs." of tobacco to the acre. When the plant is first cut, what is known as a "sucker" puts out at the root of the stalk. It develops into a second great bunch of leaves, which are afterward added to the harvest. This is called the second cutting.

Large yield.

Sumatra seed.

Grows well.

Great results.

"Inquiry concerning the outcome of Sumatra seed was stimulated by a knowledge of its value; 70 acres were covered with the plants. They were growing luxuriantly. It was asserted that there were 6,500 to the acre. This made an aggregate of 455,000 to the 70 acres. They promise great results. The leaf is not so long as the leaf of the Pennsylvania plant. It is neither so long nor so wide, but it is of a deeper green in hue, and is more free from worms. The Cuban plants are still smaller. The leaf is thicker. It is preferable for cigar fillers."

Cuban plants smaller.

Profitable.

Agriculturists in British tropical places.

The above on tobacco may be found interesting, if not made profitable (by following some of the hints as to culture), by some of the agriculturists who dwell in British tropical places. It is true that this whole great business of large moneyed interests in tobacco planting, culture, &c., is of no apparent or actual necessity to mankind, and mostly ends in smoke; nevertheless, the human family will not do without tobacco, and there is no good any one moralising on the subject. The tobacco plant will ever be in the future, as it has been in the past, a source of large revenue to cultivators of the plant, manufacturers, and dealers generally in it. Some of the immense waste lands of the tropical places of the British colonies should, I think, be utilised for the purpose of taking a part of this great trade of the world. There are many of those places quite as well fitted in soil and climate to follow in the lines laid down in the impetus lately manifested in this tobacco industry in Florida. Why cannot

A source of revenue.

Waste lands in colonies should be utilised.

some of our people there form companies, the same as in Florida, and go largely to work in this great industry? *Should form companies same as in Florida.*

The work of the department of agriculture in Florida is provided for by law. There are various "bureaus" operated under its supervision. This lately organised agricultural department was agitated upon some years before it became law. Some sections of the State, it is said, demanded a Bureau of Agriculture, while in other sections it was strenuously and actively opposed. The spirit of progress and improvement finally succeeded, however, and the class of people who first opposed the movement, "wedded to the old ways" and "jealous of innovation," are now, no doubt, reaping the benefit of the advance in agriculture in Florida made through the agricultural department. *Department of agriculture. Bureaus. Beneficial in agriculture.*

The Commissioner of Agriculture in Florida is an administrative officer of the State Government, and performs his duties as provided by law. Among his duties he has supervision of all matters pertaining to the public lands; he also supervises immigration. *Supervising commissioner.*

A bureau in connection with the department of agriculture is for the inspection of fertilisers. It controls the quality and sale of fertilisers in the State. It provides a State chemist, and appoints inspectors of fertilisers. This bureau is under the immediate supervision and control of the Commissioner of Agriculture. The law requires that samples of all fertilisers analysed by the State chemist shall be kept; the law also requires that all manufacturers before offering their fertilisers for sale in the State shall first file a copy of the analysis of each brand sold by them, properly sworn to: thus purchasers of this important factor in agriculture are protected against spurious and worthless fertilisers, or any other than those approved after chemical test. *Inspection of fertiliser. Controls quality and sale. Samples of fertilisers. Analysis filed. Approved test.*

Referring to some remarks in the "Times" on this subject, the law of Florida in this respect appears to be very admirable.

The "Times," in one of its recent agricultural items, refers to "Manure adulteration," and points out that "The Royal Agricultural Society of England" have for some years past shown that the manure trade has much in it that is fraudulent. *Manure adulteration. Royal Agricultural Society of England.*

It appears that the law of Florida would, to a great extent, protect the agriculturist in the use of manure, giving him a good article, and value for his money.

It is said that the agricultural department will be of great benefit to the agriculturists here. Through this means the agricultural, mineral, and all industrial resources of the State are advertised to the world. "Being a friend of the farmer, it stands his most faithful and trusted guide and watchman." *Agricultural department great benefit.*

LONDON:
Printed for Her Majesty's Stationery Office,
By HARRISON AND SONS,
Printers in Ordinary to Her Majesty.
(1250   3 | 91—H & S   1037)

FOREIGN OFFICE.
1891.
ANNUAL SERIES.

No. 833.
DIPLOMATIC AND CONSULAR REPORTS ON TRADE AND FINANCE.

UNITED STATES.

REPORT FOR THE YEAR 1890
ON THE
TRADE OF THE CONSULAR DISTRICT OF NEW ORLEANS.

REFERENCE TO PREVIOUS REPORT, Annual Series No. 649.

Presented to both Houses of Parliament by Command of Her Majesty,
MARCH, 1891.

LONDON:
PRINTED FOR HER MAJESTY'S STATIONERY OFFICE,
BY HARRISON AND SONS, ST. MARTIN'S LANE,
PRINTERS IN ORDINARY TO HER MAJESTY.

And to be purchased, either directly or through any Bookseller, from
EYRE & SPOTTISWOODE, EAST HARDING STREET, FLEET STREET, E.C., and
32, ABINGDON STREET, WESTMINSTER, S.W.; or,
JOHN MENZIES & Co., 12, HANOVER STREET, EDINBURGH, and
21, DRURY STREET, GLASGOW; or
HODGES, FIGGIS, & Co., 104, GRAFTON STREET, DUBLIN.

1891.

[C. 6205—64.] *Price Twopence.*

New Series of Reports.

Reports of the Annual Series have been issued from Her Majesty's Diplomatic and Consular Officers at the following places, and may be obtained from the sources indicated on the title-page:—

No.		Price.	No.		Price.
709.	Amoy	1d.	771.	Bangkok	2½d.
710.	Buda-Pesth	1½d.	772.	Stockholm	1½d.
711.	Corunna	2d.	773.	Jaffa	½d.
712.	Mogador	2d.	774.	Copenhagen	½d.
713.	Cadiz	½d.	775.	Ningpo	½d.
714.	Cadiz	1d.	776.	Stettin	2d.
715.	Rio de Janeiro	2½d.	777.	St. Petersburg	3d.
716.	Newchwang	½d.	778.	St. Petersburg	½d.
717.	Chinkiang	½d.	779.	St. Jago de Cuba	1½d.
718.	San Francisco	6d.	780.	Chefoo	1d.
719.	Bussorah	½d.	781.	Christiania	3½d.
720.	Beyrout	1d.	782.	Marseilles	½d.
721.	Adrianople	½d.	783.	Baghdad	1d.
722.	Nantes	½d.	784.	Naples	1½d.
723.	Caracas	1d.	785.	Tunis	4d.
724.	Mogador	½d.	786.	Vera Cruz	1d.
725.	Tientsin	1d.	787.	Tangier	1½d.
726.	Foochow	1d.	788.	Rome	2d.
727.	Port au Prince	½d.	789.	Stuttgart	1½d.
728.	Callao	1d.	790.	Panama	1½d.
729.	Puerto Plata	½d.	791.	Berne	1½d.
730.	San Francisco	1d.	792.	Ascunsion	½d.
731.	Philadelphia	2½d.	793.	Bahia	7½d.
732.	Pakhoi	1d.	794.	Monte Video	1½d.
733.	Bilbao	1d.	795.	Munich	2d.
734.	Dunkirk	1d.	796.	Bucharest	1d.
735.	Vienna	1d.	797.	Tokio	1d.
736.	Nantes	1½d.	798.	Tabreez	1d.
737.	Paramaribo	1d.	799.	Antwerp	1d.
738.	Honolulu	½d.	800.	Malaga	1d
739.	Chicago	2d.	801.	Odessa	1d.
740.	Söul	1d.	802.	Malaga	2d.
741.	Brindisi	1½d.	803.	Amsterdam	1d.
742.	Mozambique	1d.	804.	Bogotá	1½d.
743.	Caldera and Lota	1½d.	805.	Guayaquil	½d.
744.	Nice	1½d.	806.	Lima	1d
745.	Aleppo	1d.	807.	Rio de Janeiro	3d
746.	Hakodate	1d.	808.	Dantzig	1½d
747.	New York	2d.	809.	Florence	1½d
748.	Cagliari	1d.	810.	Lisbon	1d.
749.	San Salvador	1d.	811.	Quito	½d.
750.	Gothenburg	2d.	812.	Para	½d.
751.	Nagasaki	1d.	813.	Palermo	2½d.
752.	Sofia	3½d.	814.	Copenhagen	1d.
753.	Meshed	1d.	815.	Serajevo	½d.
754.	Yokohama	2½d.	816.	Porto Rico	1d.
755.	Shanghai	2d.	817.	Madrid	½d.
756.	Lisbon	1½d.	818.	Brussels	½d.
757.	Teneriffe	½d.	819.	Patras	½d.
758.	Noumea	½d.	820.	Stuttgart	1d.
759.	Tahiti	½d.	821.	Taganrog	1d.
760.	Bushire	1½d.	822.	Salonica	2d.
761.	Frankfort	2d.	823.	Galveston	1d.
762.	Palermo	2½d.	824.	Rome	1½d.
763.	Guatemala	1d.	825.	Paris	1½d.
764.	Smyrna	4d.	826.	Bushire	½d.
765.	Munich	2d.	827.	New Orleans	3d.
766.	Hiogo	1½d.	828.	Buda-Pesth	½d.
767.	Alexandria	1½d.	829.	Hamburg	3d.
768.	Maracaibo	½d.	830.	Port Said	1d.
769.	Macao	1d.	831.	Samoa	½d.
770.	Canton	1d.	832.	Guayaquil	½d.

No. 833.

Reference to previous Report, Annual Series No. 649.

UNITED STATES.

NEW ORLEANS.

Consul de Fonblanque to the Marquis of Salisbury.

My Lord,   *New Orleans, February* 3, 1891.

I HAVE the honour to enclose herewith Annual Reports on Trade and Commerce of New Orleans, Pensacola, and Mobile for the year 1890.

        I have, &c.
    (Signed)   A. DE G. DE FONBLANQUE.

Trade Report, 1890.

The past year has been one of disaster and anxiety to the riverain States forming this consular district, but they have come out of their troubles much better than could have been expected during the first six months; and, upon the whole, have prospered. Unusually high water in the River Mississippi caused breaks in the levees of Arkansas, Louisiana, and Mississippi, not so wide as on former occasions, but occurring as they did at points upon which immense volumes of water impinged were sufficient to cause widespread suffering and loss. One of the most formidable of these breaks (Nita crevasse) is attributed to the reckless manner in which some rice planters perforated the levee with flumes for irrigating their crops. Other instances have been given in which levees were cut or lowered for the passage of waggons when the river was low, and not repaired in time to control the floods. Against this must be placed the manful spirit in which the raging waters were fought and brought into subjection when at their worst, the liberality with which help and subsistence was afforded to the sufferers, and the plucky, self-reliant manner in which they followed up the receding floods, foot by foot, and planked their devastated fields. At one time New Orleans itself was in peril, as the water lapped over her levees and ran in streams through some of the principal streets.

Most of this has occurred before, and will be repeated until the conservancy of our great river is placed under one responsible

The floods.

Injury to levees.

UNITED STATES.

No general system of levees.

system of control. Planters, parish juries, and State's boards acting piecemeal, and often actuated by selfish considerations, have been tried and found wanting; and hitherto the national government has expended fitful appropriations on the bed of the stream only, fearful lest the building of levees might benefit political opponents and give rise to election cries. The Mississippi river carries the commerce of 16 States. The floods of its lower portion are caused by the rainfall and drainage from 27 States and territories above. Every acre in the north-west opened to settlement and cultivation pours down more water for these southern States to contend against. No matter how much money any separate geographical or political division may spend upon levees it cannot prevent overflow, for the waters may pour down upon it through gaps in States above. Louisiana, for instance, is more or less flooded every high water by crevasses in Arkansas, over which it has no control, and which it cannot prevent; and the extraordinary proceeding was witnessed some years ago of the former constructing levees in the latter to protect its own lands. The maintenance of its levee system is beyond the control of the State, and to prevent floods it must enter into some levee treaty with Arkansas, and Arkansas similarly with Missouri. As it is now a different system prevails in every State, in every levee district, and in nearly every county and parish. A consistency of plan in location, construction, and administration can be secured only by placing the matter in the hands of the Federal Government. As long as the present system continues, the people of any district or State are at the mercy of those living above them.

Political considerations.

Causes of floods.

Federal control required.

If the levees were placed under Federal control the present defects, due to local influences and prejudices, would be avoided. There would be no break at Nita, because the Federal Government would not yield to the influence of the rice planters of St. James's, or other parishes, and permit rice flumes. It has been alleged that the Pecan Grove break was due to the improper location of the levee in consequence of local influence. This would be impossible with the levees under Federal control.

Loss by floods in general is not local.

In discussing levees in Congress there is always a disposition to make it appear that the matter is one of purely local concern, in which a small portion of the Union only is interested. It is true that the alluvial lands protected by levees (if that protection were perfect) would be able to raise 1,000,000 hogsheads of sugar and 10,000,000 bales of cotton, and add greatly to the wealth of the country; but aside from this, not the alluvial districts alone, but the whole Union suffers from these overflows. The Bonnet Carre crevasse alone carried its destruction along the Gulf Coast, and destroyed fisheries which had supported thousands of persons, and which they have revived since this break was closed. The flood of 1882, which interrupted traffic on all the railroads running east and west between Cairo and the Gulf, caused such injury to railroad property as to be distinctly felt on the New York Stock Exchange. And in 1884, the flood which affected our Pacific roads made itself felt as far distant as San Francisco.

The estimated damage by one crevasse (the Nita), as calculated by the police jury of the parish, was:— *Damage by one crevasse.*

Articles.	Acres Ruined.	Value.
		Dollars.
Sugar cane	5,620	599,400
Tobacco..	150	22,375
Corn	3,391½	33,915
Rice	6,170½	212,155
Potatoes, onions, and other crops ruined	..	81,325
Total losses on crops	..	1,113,040
Damage to drainage in filling ditches, &c.	..	82,325

Two plantations entirely destroyed and rendered useless, buildings levelled and washed away, 100,000 dol.; grand total of losses to crops and lands, 1,213,040 dol. (25,006*l.* 5*s.* 7*d.*); amount of land that could be reclaimed with good levees, 24,208 acres. This estimate did not cover the losses sustained by the Mississippi Valley and Illinois Central Railroads.

A proposal to appropriate 10,000,000 dol. for the improvement of the Mississippi River, without limitation, is now before Congress. *Expected appropriation.*

The President of the New Orleans Stock Exchange reports:— *Stock Exchange report.* "Although the year just passed has been, in its business relations, a disappointing one in many respects, and the volume of trade has not been what we hoped for, still the aggregate of sales at the Exchange have been, all things considered, fair.

"The sales of bonds for the past two years have not been large, but for 1890 they were 40 per cent. more than for 1889. In listed stocks the sales have decreased 15 per cent., while mining and other unlisted securities have been but little dealt in. The causes for the comparatively small amount of business done are not difficult to discover. State fours, which, after the discovery of frauds in over-issues and re-issues last year, dropped so rapidly, recovered and advanced, till in January last they sold at 99¼. The failure of the legislature to re-habilitate these bonds, and to provide in any manner for paying or funding the floating debt of the State, had necessarily a depressing effect, and when to this is added the stringency of the money market, which for the whole year has ruled higher than in 1889, and for four months past has been 8 per cent., with but occasional loans at 7 per cent., it is surprising that so many transactions have been made. *State stock.*

"City bonds, with the exception of premiums, which have advanced from 145¼ to 154⅜ at the close of the year, and since then to 156¾ bid, and gold sevens, which do not mature till 1922, having declined owing to the proposed constitutional amendment authorising a 50-year 4 per cent. bond to be issued. This will *City stock.*

UNITED STATES.

absorb over 9,000,000 dol. bonds maturing in 1892 to 1895, and which, having so short a time to run, have decreased in value. Notwithstanding the high rates of money, banks and other dividend paying stocks have advanced in price. You will see by the report of the secretary how largely the banks have added to their surplus and undivided profits ; and also that their value in the market has materially appreciated in the year. They have safely weathered the financial storm that has raged over the entire civilised world, and have come out of it stronger than ever.

Bank stock.
Rate of exchange, 4 dol. 84 c. to the 1l.

"The banks, 17 in number, with a capital of 5,855,200 dol., were valued at the end of December at 10,611,800 dol.; 932,980 dol. of this increase having been gained in the past year. Their surplus and undivided profits are 3,083,235 dol., of which 321,850 dol. were added in 1890. The bank clearings for the year were 528,833,431 dol., an increase over 1889 of 24,408,588 dol. Balances for 1890 were 63,177,656 dol., a gain over the year previous of 1,492,042 dol.

Insurance stock.

"Insurance stocks have, in the case of all but three of the companies, gained in market value. Although these three have depreciated, and the capital of another has been reduced from 500,000 dol. to 265,000 dol., the gain as compared with December, 1889, is 172,000 dol.

City railroad stock.

"City railroads, with a capital of 4,475,000 dol., are valued at 5,416,400 dol.; 360,900 dol. of the increase over par were added in 1890."

The values of stocks as given above are from prices bid in December, 1889 and 1890. Many securities have already advanced in the current year.

Insurance agents (foreign) liable to taxation.

The Supreme Court of Louisiana has decided that agents of foreign Insurance Companies doing business in the State are liable to taxation.

Manufactures.
Sugar.
Duty on sugar.
Bounty on sugar.

"Unless some alterations are made by Congress in the legislation respecting sugar, it is provided — "That on and after July 1, 1891, and until July 1, 1905, there shall be paid from any money in the Treasury not otherwise appropriated, under the provisions of section 3689 of the revised statutes, to the producers of sugars, testing not less than 90 degrees by the polariscope, from beets, sorghum, or sugar-cane grown within the United States, or from maple sap produced within the United States, a bounty of 2 c. per lb., and upon such sugar testing less than 90 degrees by the polariscope, and not less than 80 degrees, a bounty of $1\frac{3}{4}$ c. per lb., under such rules and regulations as the Commissioner of Internal Revenue, with the approval of the Secretary of the Treasury, shall prescribe.

Free sugar.

"All degrees of sugar under 16 Dutch standard in colour may be imported free, all above pay a duty of $\frac{5}{10}$th of 1 c. per lb., in addition to the rate herein provided for, when exported from or the product of any country, when and so long as such country pays, or shall hereafter pay, directly or indirectly, a bounty on the exportation of any such sugar, which may be included in this grade, which is greater than is paid on raw sugars of a lower saccharine strength, and the Secretary of the Treasury shall prescribe rules and regulations to carry this provision into effect.

"And provided further, that all machinery purchased abroad and erected in a beet-sugar factory, and used in the production of raw sugar in the United States from beets produced therein, shall be admitted duty free until July 1, 1892; provided that any duty collected on any of the above described machinery purchased abroad, and imported from the United States for the uses above indicated since January 1, 1890, shall be refunded. *Sugar-making machinery free.*

"On glucose the house rate of ¾ c. per lb. is retained. Whereas the Senate provided that the sugar schedule and bounty provision was to take effect March 1 next; the conference fixed upon April 1, as the date of operation, with a proviso that No. 13 sugar may be meantime refined in bond without duty." *Glucose.*

Some of our most enterprising planters seem to be sanguine in the belief that they can make sugar at a profit under these conditions, and I look for an active movement for the establishment of central factories, so often recommended in these reports. Since the abolition of slavery there never has been any good reason why a planter of sugar-cane must be a manufacturer of sugar, any more than that a planter of wheat should make bread, or a sheep farmer weave cloth. The quantity and quality of the last sugar crop will appear in my report on agriculture. *Central sugar factories.*

New Orleans has become an important centre for the manufacture of tobacco. The cigars made of Havana wrappers and domestic filling are excellent and second to none produced in this country. A fair quality may be had (retail) at 4 dol. per hundred, and are better than many that I have bought in London at 8d. each. *Tobacco.*

The expansion of this trade in the last three years will appear from the following table completed in the Internal Revenue Department:—

Tobacco Manufactured in the District of Louisiana, 1889-90.

		Quantity.	Value.
			Dollars.
Cigars	Number	49,299,446	1,484,980
Cigarettes	,,	84,796,660	169,952
Manufactured	Lbs.	1,393,879	348,467
Perique	,,	35,552	213,372
Snuff	,,	31,744	15,230
Total			2,232,001

UNITED STATES.

1888-89.

		Quantity.	Value.
			Dollars.
Cigars	Number	39,644,881	1,189,320
Cigarettes	"	60,699,160	157,747
Manufactured	Lbs.	1,434,435	430,320
Perique	"	111,300	66,780
Snuff	"	27,060	8,471
Total		..	1,846,638

1887-88.

		Quantity.	Value.
			Dollars.
Cigars	Number	32,120,669	993,620
Cigarettes	"	33,888,245	118,009
Manufactured	Lbs.	1,683,638	673,467
Perique	"	141,916	78,054
Snuff	"	37,842	18,912
Total		..	1,882,062

In this district there are now 115 manufactories of cigars and cigarettes (one of them the largest in the United States), seven of tobacco (for smoking and chewing), 31 of perique (a growth peculiar to St. James's parish, made into cakes something like Cavendish but stronger), and five of snuff.

Bricks, harness, and furniture. Manufactories of bricks, harness, and furniture have lately been established, and are doing well.

New Orleans improving. So far as private enterprise goes New Orleans is certainly on the rise. Under a strong and honest municipal government it would have a great future before it.

United States Navy yard. As I write, a new commission (appointed in the last session of Congress) is here selecting a site for a Navy yard for the Gulf States. A former one chose New Orleans. The banks thrown up by the sea on each side of the jetties are being surveyed with a view of erecting fortifications for the defence of the mouths of the river.

Shipping. *Shipping.*—Annex A. contains a return of British and foreign shipping at this port during 1890. The entrances of British ships are 465 against 471 in 1889, and the tonnage 584,488, against 589,895 tons during the same period. This, however, does not show any falling-off of legitimate British trade, because three steamships, the "Stroma" (518 tons), the "Marco Aurelio" (411 tons), and the "Joseph Oteri, Junior" (291 tons), which were only nominally British, were transfered to the American flag in September and October of last year. They are engaged in the fruit business, and make round trips of 14 days with about four days intermission; so taking their average in other years they will have counted—the "Stroma" and the "Joseph Oteri, Junior," five times, and the "Marco Aurelio" twice—for the country in

Transfer of fruiterers.

which they have been actually owned, and which alone has profited by them. If the statistics given to me by the custom house last year be correct, there has been a considerable falling-off of American shipping entered and cleared from foreign ports. *Decrease of American shipping.*

I notice that Mr. William Cliff, of Liverpool (whose long experience as a manager of steamships gives great weight to his opinions), in a pamphlet entitled, "The Incompetency of British Compared to Foreign Seamen," attributes the loss of life in our ships, compared with that in the average of foreign shipping, to the incompetency of our seamen. But why do we ship incompetent British seamen? The evil as far as my judgment goes lies:— *British seamen.*

(a) In the indiscriminate use of V.G. on certificates of discharge.
(b) In the carelessness of masters in selecting crews.
(c) In their subserviency (particularly abroad) to the crimps.

Why incapable seamen are shipped.

In my report for 1889 I remarked upon the shipment of sick, ruptured, and otherwise physically incapable men. The foreign seamen (as a rule) takes care of his money, and is consequently not in the hands of the crimp, whose interest is to ship the man who owes him most. Thus the dissolute and improvident get a preference over the sober and the thrifty. These are hustled on board without examination of any kind, and the master only knows when his ship is at sea that half his crew are "loafers." And this is not wholly his fault. His owner puts him under high pressure. As soon as a ship has her cargo on board, not a tide, not an hour is to be lost. She must go to sea instanter with so many head of crew (competency and condition unknown) to work her, or the master will be blamed for the delay. *Who is to blame?*

Direct imports from Europe to this port show an increase in 1890, probably in anticipation of the McKinley Tariff Bill. The exact effects of this measure upon the commerce of this district cannot at present be estimated; but upon general principles I look for an acceleration of the decline noticed in my last report in the quality of American manufactures. I have already considered the deterioration in all textile fabrics and in hardware. I can now add to this category—window-glass, paints, varnishes, cordage, and canvas, boots and leather goods, watches and agricultural instruments. None of these are as good as they were even a few years ago, though some of them are got up for sale in a very attractive appearance. If this be the effect of Protection, it may increase under the new and enhanced duties, and the question is, Will the people of America who desire first class goods, and are rich enough to pay for them, submit to the system in force, or revolt against it? On the other hand, manufacturers may be wise enough to expend a portion of their increased profits upon improving the quality of their productions. Time will show. *Imports. McKinley Act. Deterioration of American goods.*

UNITED STATES.

Exports.

The principal exports carried in British ships in 1890 are:—

Articles.		Quantity.
Cotton	Bales	1,221,615
„ seed	Sacks	4,159
„ „ oil	Barrels	48,445
„ „ „ cakes	Sacks	306,392
„ „ meal	„	470,345
„ „ soap stock	Barrels	16,944
Corn	Bushels	10,818,484
„	Sacks	72,443
Wheat	Bushels	812,700
„	Sacks	6,640
Flour	„	17,842
Staves	Pieces	1,460,341
Timber	Logs	1,271
„	Pieces	18,894
„	Feet	23,684
Lumber	Logs	Nil.
„	Pieces	16,065
„	Feet	204,500
Boards		23,306
Deals		21,466
Persimmon wood	Bundles	1,612
Satin wood	Pieces	28
Poplar	„	1,951
Boat oars		10,762
Pitch pine ties	Pieces	9,150
Tobacco	Hhds.	3,753
„	Cases	70
„ cuttings	Lbs.	15,739
Lead	Pigs and bars	111,614
Copper and copper ore	Sacks	1,841
Silver ore	Lbs.	22,500
Live cattle	Heads	913
Istle	Bales	434
Tallow	Pieces	1,588
Rice, Polish	Sacks	6,263
Horns	„	1,300
Pork	Barrels	100
Bran	Sacks	3,296
Moss	Bales	226

Frozen meat.

The Metropolitan Trading Company of London established a line of steamers to carry frozen meat from this port, and went to considerable expense in fitting out their ships with refrigerating appliances. The venture has failed for the present, but not, I think, upon its merits.

Police patrol waggons.

Having occasionally read in London papers that the police find difficulty in securing cabs for the conveyance of prisoners arrested in numbers to the lock-up, I beg to call attention to a system which is in force here and in several other American cities. This is the Police Patrol Waggon Service.

Signal boxes

Five open waggonettes, drawn by a pair of horses, with seating capacity for 12 persons, but capable of conveying 20, are engaged. Scattered over the city, at convenient intervals, are boxes (about the size of sentry boxes, but closed) with telephone communication to the patrol station corresponding to the district of each one.

NEW ORLEANS.

The constable of the beat has a key, and sometimes in the suburbs keys are intrusted to residents to be used in case of necessity. When an arrest is made, a "call" is turned in (just as in cases of fire from the fire boxes), and the patrol waggon, with one or more officers, according to the necessity of the case, comes to the scene and takes the arrested to the station.

Working of the system.

The advantages of this system are—the constable is not taken from his beat, unseemly struggles in the street with drunken or violent persons are avoided, and the risk of riot and rescue are reduced to a minimum.

Its advantages.

During the past year there were 6,312 "calls," and 9,415 prisoners were conveyed to the different stations. The waggons cost 275 dol. each; the horses averaged 350 dol. a pair; and the drivers are paid 40 dol. a month.

Cost of the system.

Wherever the American dollar is mentioned in this report it may be taken at the exchange of 4 dol. 84 c. to the 1l. sterling.

Annex A.—RETURN of all Shipping at the Port of New Orleans in the Year 1890.

ENTERED.

Nationality.	Sailing. Number of Vessels.	Sailing. Tons.	Steam. Number of Vessels.	Steam. Tons.	Total. Number of Vessels.	Total. Tons.
British	...	9,404	444	574,784	455	584,488
American*	6	11,049	145	89,739	151	100,788
Italian	37	18,423	24	15,688	61	34,111
Spanish	20	13,391	60	86,241	80	99,632
Norwegian and Swedish	6	4,500	52	54,018	58	58,518
German	...	...	...	...	26	38,565
French	1	655	18	47,068	19	47,723
Mexican	8	1,740	5	3,040	13	4,780
Austrian	4	2,419	...	...	4	2,419
Total	...	...	...	...	907	971,024
,, for the year preceding	...	...	...	...	1,149	1,329,150

CLEARED.

Nationality.	Sailing. Number of Vessels.	Sailing. Tons.	Steam. Number of Vessels.	Steam. Tons.	Total. Number of Vessels.	Total. Tons.
British	24	11,004	439	575,988	463	586,992
American*	33	12,716	126	13,623	159	26,339
Spanish	22	14,573	59	102,967	81	117,540
Norwegian and Swedish	6	4,500	82	54,018	88	58,518
French	1	655	18	47,068	19	47,723
German	...	...	...	...	23	34,446
Italian	34	16,429	24	15,908	58	32,337
Mexican	10	2,125	5	3,040	15	5,165
Austrian	7	4,422	...	...	7	4,422
Total	...	...	...	...	913	913,482
,, for the year preceding	...	...	...	...	1,069	1,289,346

* This is exclusive of coasting ships.

PENSACOLA.

Mr. Vice-Consul Howe reports as follows:—

It gives me pleasure to be able to state that the business proper of Pensacola—the trade in pitch-pine wood—continues at about its average prosperity. Some of the tables in this report will show the volume of the export trade for the past year; the bulk of which, as usual, went to the United Kingdom. Some cotton was shipped through Pensacola last year to Liverpool.

Several cargoes of salt were received here during the year from England; and some super-phosphate was imported from Cork, in Ireland. Some of this salt, and all of the phosphate, went on by rail from this receiving point to Alabama, Florida, and elsewhere. Several cargoes of fruit were received here from some of the British islands during the year.

The chief articles of import to Pensacola are received from the large markets of the United States, west and north.

In my last annual report I referred to the formation of an English company, "the Southern States Land and Timber Company, Limited," by which extensive saw-mills are operated. The company appears to continue in a prosperous condition, and I have heard of quite a respectable dividend being recently declared at the head office in London, on the occasion of the expiration of the company's first financial term.

In my last yearly report I referred to an act of the legislature of Florida, whereby British underwriters, and others concerned, were much relieved, in comparison with the position in which they formerly stood in respect to timber risks in the harbour of Pensacola. I pointed out that underwriters of these cargoes had to pay for much timber reported as lost that was actually picked up by unauthorised persons, and sold by them, and purchased for re-shipment. I am now in a position to make good my expectation then of the benefit that would be derived by the enactment, by showing the results of the fair test of one year's timber loading at Pensacola. I have secured from the legally appointed salvor of timber at Pensacola the following particulars:—

The quantity of timber reported to the public custodian of timber as having drifted away from vessels loading in the harbour of Pensacola, during the year 1890, amounted to 4,678 pieces. The quantity of timber recovered of drifted timber, and returned by the public custodian of timber to the vessels, amounted to 4,145 pieces. The value of the pieces of drifted timber amounted to about 32,746 dol. The amount of salvage paid was about 2,072 dol. Apparently the drifted timber unrecovered, or not returned to vessels, amounted to about 543 pieces, of which deficiency about 200 pieces were not recoverable, as this timber drifted to sea from cargo jettisoned from a vessel that grounded on the Pensacola bar. I say, again, that the law in this respect is working admirably in the protection of all concerned.

The quarantine system at this port goes on about the same as usual. Yearly proclamations are still issued, and vessels arriving are dealt with, as regards fumigation, detention at quarantine, &c., about as before.

Much dissatisfaction continues amongst British shipowners, and others concerned in British vessels, relative to the quarantine system of Pensacola; but I do not see that anything can be done to avoid what owners, masters, and charterers (and indemnity associations sometimes) deem as harsh and uncalled-for action of the Board of Health—that body claiming supreme control of these affairs. *Dissatisfaction. Board of Health.*

It will be observed by some of the tables in this report that British tonnage at Pensacola during the past year was about the same as the year preceding; and about up to its average. In keeping with the tonnage of other foreign flags British tonnage in 1890 at this port formed about 30 per cent.—somewhat beyond its proportion of the year preceding. *British shipping. Up to average.*

British sailing-vessels appear to diminish yearly. Many of the old British sailing-vessels, which some years ago were foremost in the Pensacola carrying trade, however, continue to come here under other flags, notably the Swedish and Norwegian flags. *British sailing vessels falling-off. Old British sailing vessels under other flags.*

British steam-tonnage is coming into the Pensacola trade steadily, if not rapidly, from year to year; and, as previously remarked in my former reports, the time is not far distant, I think, when the carrying-trade of Pensacola will be done largely by British steamers. *British steamers increasing at Pensacola.*

While writing on shipping at Pensacola, I regret exceedingly to state that I cannot add a word to show that the sailor is in any way better off than he ever has been, as regards his pursuers, the crimps. It appears that he never will be able to resist their wiles and temptations. Pleadings with the seaman on his own behalf are listened to, and he admits his follies and easy gullibility, nevertheless the allurements of the crimps are not resented. *Crimping at Pensacola. Sailors still pursued by crimps. Easily taken in by crimps.*

Another thing to be looked at in connection with this subject is the immense amount of money that yearly passes from the hands of the masters to the crimps in making good the desertions, or so-called desertions, from their ships. *Large amounts the crimps handle yearly.*

About the commencement of the present year the uniform amount of wages that had been prevailing at Pensacola for years previously, and which was an average of about 4*l.* per month to the United Kingdom and Continent of Europe, was increased to 6*l.* for such voyages. This advance was brought about by a "combination" of the crimps. The advance in wages was not meant for the benefit of the sailor, nor did it benefit him; but the object was to increase the advance wages fingered by the crimps, which always rule above the amount stipulated as monthly wages. Thus, the advance wages were at once put to the minimum of 7*l.*, engagements of officers at higher wages—being the highest rate of advance in proportion to that for the forecastle man. The rate of wages for other voyages was raised in proportion to the above, and the advance wages in like proportion. For South *Seamen's wages. Increased by crimps. Large advances of seamen's wages. Not beneficial to seamen. High rate of advance wages.*

UNITED STATES.

Blood money." Crimps' combination.

American voyages the rate was put to 20 dol., against 15 to 18 dol. before; and the rate of advances went up to about double that of monthly wages. Independently of the advance wages the crimps demand from 3 to 5 dol., which they call a shipping fee —vulgarly termed "blood money." The increased rate of wages and corresponding advances still remain in force, the "combination," as I am informed, still keeping intact their scheme for the robbery of the seamen.

Seamen poorly off.

It will be observed that at the end of a voyage to the United Kingdom or Continent, according to the above-given scale of advance wages, the seaman has little or nothing to receive. He then passes through about the same ordeal again, with, perhaps, lesser disadvantages. Nowhere, I believe, is he so badly fleeced by crimps as at Pensacola.

Sailor traffic. Not grappled with. Masters will not assist Consul.

I need not comment any further on this subject. It is outrageous the way that the sailor traffic goes on here from year to year, and still it is not grappled with and stopped. I believe it can be stopped, but I cannot do it alone. If British masters would stand by their Consul against the crimps, something —everything—might be done to check the evil even at this port, bad as it is, as regards crimping.

Indorsements. Reported desertions cannot be vouched for by Consul.

It is laid down to the effect that the Consular Officer shall indorse upon the articles of agreement the desertions reported to him by masters, and that in the event of his not positively knowing or believing that the desertion was actual, and not contributed to, he shall not vouch for it, but simply relate that it was reported. In very few cases do I see my way clear to actually vouch or give my belief of the positive desertion when making those indorsements.

Census. Increase of population. Enumeration does not please. Population said to be larger.

The census recently taken shows a large increase, over 100 per cent. in the population of Pensacola within the last decade. The return was made up, giving over 10,000 inhabitants; but the people here are not satisfied with the return, believing that errors have been made in the enumeration. It is claimed that in taking surrounding data the population of Pensacola should be at least 15,000.

Pensacola healthy. Port advancing in prospects. British capital coming in.

Pensacola has been particularly healthy during the past year —no epidemics of any kind. And, all in all, the well wishers of the place in the United Kingdom—those in direct business with Pensacola, as well as others—may be assured that all things look prosperous ahead. New schemes for the advancement of the port are now in discussion, such as increased capital being brought in (here British resources, I am informed, will be made largely available soon).

Coal. Steamers coal here. Shipments of coal.

The shipment of Alabama coal through Pensacola during the year 1890 assumed quite a large business. The steamers that ply to this port take large supplies of this coal for their bunkers. It will be observed by the following table, giving a comparative statement of shipments of coal during the year past, that there was quite a volume of trade this way. There was a strike at the mines that continued some weeks at the end of the year, which to some extent checked operations, but the differences have been settled. The value given per ton is for cargo lots, free on board. The retail price of this coal (very good bituminous it is) for domestic use here is at present from 6½ dol. to 7 dol. per ton, delivered at residences.

Value in lots.
Retail price.

TABLE giving the Shipments of Coal from Pensacola during the Years 1889-90.

Countries.	1890.	1889.
	Tons.	Tons.
Spain, Cuba	13,372	..
United States	7,673	..
Mexico	1,501	..
Central America	5,192	..
To various countries	..	4,205
Total	27,738	4,205

RETURN of Principal Articles of Export from Pensacola during the Years 1889-90.

Articles.	1890. Quantity.	1890. Value.	1889. Quantity.	1889. Value.
	Tons.	£ s. d.	Tons.	£ s. d.
Pitch-pine lumber	129,329,000	323,322 10 0	126,131,000	315,347 10 0
Sawn pitch-pine timber	12,528,440	313,211 0 0	14,609.244	380,449 1 3
Hewn ,, ,,	1,387,878	31,865 10 9	1,347,717	30,855 3 8
Cotton	21,713	229,506 11 3	...	...
Coal	31,738	18,780 18 9	4,205	2,628 2 6
Cedar	5,000	364 11 8	4,655	239 8 6
Other articles	...	1,854 19 2	...	312 10 0
Total	...	918,846 1 7	...	729,941 15 11

The following as regards the above table of exports is descriptive of the quantities, values, weights, and measures; the conversion of money into sterling being at the rate of 4 dol. 80 c. per 1*l*. Lumber at average of 12 dol. (2*l*. 10*s*.) per 1,000 superficial feet; sawn timber at an average of 12 c. (6*d*.) per cubic foot—basis 40 feet average; hewn timber at average of 11 c. (5½*d*.) per cubic foot—basis 100 feet average; cotton at average of 10 c. (5*d*.) per lb., in bales of 507 lbs., average weight each bale; 3 dol. 25 c. (13*s*. 6½*d*.) for the coal in 1890, 3 dol. (12*s*. 6*d*.) for the coal in 1889; cedar at 35 c. (1*s*. 5½*d*.) per cubic foot.

RETURN of Principal Articles of Import to Pensacola during the Years 1889-90.

Articles.	1890.	1889.
	£ s. d.	£ s. d.
Chief articles	..	..
Other ,,	11,521 5 0	..

NOTE.—The chief articles received at Pensacola are breadstuffs, grocery goods, hardware, and things generally required as necessaries of life, which goods are received from the large northern, southern, and western markets of the United States (see remarks elsewhere in this report in connection with this subject referring to British goods). In addition may be added as also received here from ports in the United States, railroad iron, fertilisers, &c. It is calculated that the entire receipts of chief articles are not less than 2,000,000 dol.—perhaps nearer 3,000,000 dol. per year. The exact articles, quantities, and values cannot be arrived at. As regards other articles of import, of which the value is given above, they comprise super-phosphate, salt, and fruit. The salt and some of the phosphate come direct from the United Kingdom. Some phosphate comes direct from Germany; and fruit from the British West India islands in small British vessels principally.

Three-fourths of Florida covered with timber.
Pitch-pine predominates.
Size for milling plants.

It is said that after deducting from the total area of Florida the aggregate area of her lakes, rivers, marshes, prairies, and hardwood forests, it will be found approximately correct to say that three-fourths of the State is covered with forests of pine, and mostly of the kind known as yellow or pitch-pine. South of Peace River, and along the Florida coast, pitch-pine predominates; but it is not till after crossing the Withlacochee and Ocklawaha Rivers that it attains the size and quality requisite for the establishment of large milling plants.

Counties where finest timber is found.
Estimates of quantity of pitch-pine timber largely conjecture.

It is said that the finest bodies of yellow or pitch-pine now in Florida are to be found in the counties of Suwanee, Columbia, Bradford, Alachua, and Levy. Late estimates of the quantity of pitch-pine timber in the State vary from 6,500,000,000 feet to 120,000,000,000 feet [I think this is an error in figures, most likely meant for 12,000,000,000 feet]; but all such estimates are so largely conjecture that they deserve little attention.

Destruction.
Supply.
Probable diminution of time timber will last.
Turpentine industry.
Forest fires.
Increasing demand.
Serious scarcity.

Again, it is said that although there are extensive bodies of virgin forest still untouched in Florida, it is very evident to lumbermen that at the present rate of consumption, or destruction, the supply cannot last more than 15 or 20 years longer. The saw mills have consumed all good timber within hauling distance of the railroads, and of streams on which logs can be rafted. Branch roads and tramways have been carried long distances in order to supply the larger mills with logs. It is said that the turpentine industry causes much destruction of pine timber, especially in connection with the forest fires, which also are a great obstacle to the natural renewal of the forests. Increasing demand at home and abroad is hastening the work of decrease it is also said; and that the approach of a time of serious scarcity is looked for.

Pensacola the exporting port.
Timber secured from Alabama.

Pensacola is the great timber and lumber exporting port of Florida; and, as I remarked in my trade report for the year 1887, a large quantity of the exports hence is secured from Alabama, an immediately adjacent State, and so convenient to railroads and watercourse for the transportation of timber to Pensacola mills, wharves, and harbour.

It may be safely said, I think, that the demand will go beyond the supply.

A short time ago quite an important discovery was made in Florida, which is not only contributing to the wealth of certain portions of the State, but is opening up a large export demand. I refer to the discovery of phosphate lands in Florida. The "Times Union Trade Report" for 1890 says:—"To tell one half of the wonderful phosphate story of Florida would require several pages of the trade edition. As it goes to press the whole State of Florida is stirred from centre to circumference over the wealth which this discovery promises. The business is not only in its infancy, it may be said to have hardly been born as yet. To present anything like an exhaustive review of it at present would be impossible."

To give some particulars about this interesting discovery, it may be related that about the middle of the year 1888 a gentleman, while digging a well in his yard at Ocala, Florida, found marly earth, which was examined and found to be a chalky lime substance not unusual in that portion of the State. It was, however, determined to have the "stuff" properly analysed, and a parcel of it was sent to eminent chemists of a large western city for analysation. The reports were that the stuff was rich in phosphorus acid, and advised that if there was much of it to look after it, as it was valuable. Other similar scientific establishments in large cities confirmed these reports, whereupon the land from which the sample was taken was searched, and the marly substance was found there in quantities, and also at several other places on adjoining properties. About 8,000 acres of these phosphate lands were immediately purchased in the "phosphate belt," followed by other purchases. A company was soon organised, which secured early in the year about 15,000 acres of choice phosphate lands. Other companies have since been formed which have also secured extensive quantities. I have heard of several vessels loading at some of the ports in Florida nearer to the phosphate beds, and among them some British steamers.

A house is, I am informed, about to be established at Pensacola by parties from the northern States of this country (and who are operators in fertilisers in Ireland for shipment abroad) for the purpose of putting up a regular factory there for the preparation of the crude phosphate into super-phosphate—or whatever the refined article may be termed—for general fertilising purposes. This phosphate business will, I am informed, add immensely to the circulation of money in Florida, and, of course, thereby be of general good to large portions of the State. The working population, it is supposed, will also materially benefit in the work of excavation, &c., that must go on in connection with the business. The original proprietors, or pioneers, in this new industry will also get rich, no doubt, in addition to the actual possessors of the phosphate lands.

It may be interesting, as well as stimulative, to those in British possessions of like climate and opportunities to that of

(1036)

UNITED STATES.

Statement. Florida for me to give a statement of some of the commercial products of Florida, and their values during the year 1889. The statement was published in the "Times Union," trade edition, for 1890, and is given as from an official source.

Annex A.—RETURN of all Shipping at the Port of Pensacola in the Year 1890.

ENTERED.

Nationality.	Sailing. Number of Vessels.	Sailing. Tons.	Steam. Number of Vessels.	Steam. Tons.	Total. Number of Vessels.	Total. Tons.
British	68	43,271	52	66,110	120	109,381
American	104	52,296	...	...	104	52,296
Swedish and Norwegian	190	157,134	3	2,465	193	159,599
Italian	103	66,371	...	...	103	66,371
German	16	14,291	...	...	16	14,291
Russian	18	11,647	...	...	18	11,647
Austrian	13	9,509	...	...	13	9,509
Netherlands	8	5,429	...	...	8	5,429
French	4	3,650	1	2,663	5	6,313
Spanish	4	1,609	2	3,018	6	4,627
Other countries (4)	6	1,747	...	...	6	1,747
Total	534	366,954	58	74,256	592	441,210
,, for the year preceding	606	392,178	50	60,400	656	452,578

CLEARED.

Nationality.	Sailing. Number of Vessels.	Sailing. Tons.	Steam. Number of Vessels.	Steam. Tons.	Total. Number of Vessels.	Total. Tons.
British	66	45,553	52	66,110	118	111,663
American	102	52,977	...	...	102	52,977
Swedish and Norwegian	177	147,099	3	2,465	180	149,564
Italian	104	67,133	...	...	104	67,133
Austrian	17	12,991	...	...	17	12,991
German	16	14,657	...	...	16	14,657
Russian	18	11,186	...	...	18	11,186
French	7	5,265	1	2,663	8	7,928
Netherlands	8	6,538	...	...	8	6,538
Spanish	5	2,490	2	3,018	7	5,508
Other countries (5)	8	3,709	...	...	8	3,709
Total	528	369,598	58	74,256	586	443,854
,, for the year preceding	587	378,510	49	59,248	636	437,818

Annex B.—TABLE showing the Total Value of all Articles Exported from Pensacola and Imported to Pensacola from and to Foreign Countries during the Years 1889-90.

Country.	Exports 1890. £ s. d.	Exports 1889. £ s. d.	Imports 1890. £ s. d.	Imports 1889. £ s. d.
United Kingdom	514,387 13 7	331,456 16 9	60,045 5 0	...
Italy	68,623 9 3	60,741 14 0	...	...
Netherlands	58,795 11 8	48,483 5 6	...	...
France	44,761 6 5	38,629 4 7	...	...
Spain and colonies	43,808 7 2	20,570 6 9	...	...
Argentine Republic	39,200 15 0	93,151 7 7	...	...
Brazil	26,967 10 0	9,020 0 0	...	...
Uruguay	19,582 10 0	29,395 0 0	...	...
Germany	17,919 14 6	23,014 9 0	5,517 0 0	...
Belgium	17,015 15 0	19,678 9 7	...	...
Portugal	7,874 0 0	3,873 17 3	...	...
Nicaragua	3,515 8 4	...	...	...
Mexico	2,774 6 5	...	...	...
Austria	1,981 0 3	3,899 17 2	...	...
Norway	1,247 9 10	2,417 7 9	...	...
United States of Columbia	...	902 10 0	...	...
Other countries	1,740 15 0	...	...	...
Total foreign countries	870,195 12 5	685,234 5 11	11,521 5 0	...
„ ports in the United States	48,650 9 2	44,707 10 0	...*	...
Total	918,846 1 7	729,941 15 11	11,521 5 0	...

* As stated elsewhere in this report, the exact value of imports from the cities of the United States to Pensacola cannot be obtained; but the receipts from those markets are calculated at over 2,000,000 dol. per annum, perhaps nearer 3,000,000 dol., comprising chief articles of import.

UNITED STATES.

Annex C.—STATEMENT of some of the Articles and Value of Products and Manufactures of the State of Florida during the Year 1889.

	Dollars.
Waggons, buggies, &c.	62,500
Ice	75,000
Artificial stone, &c.	25,000
Fish, oysters, and turtle	375,000
Firewood	475,000
Engines and boilers	45,000
Cedar	500,000
Manufactured iron	32,000
Books, pamphlets, &c.	55,000
Orange boxes and vegetable crates	235,000
Shoes, &c.	40,000
Piling timber	32,000
Tinware and sheet iron	45,000
Harness, saddles, &c.	25,000
Birds, feathers, &c.	20,000
Alligator hides and teeth	37,250
Lime	75,000
Brick, tile, and chimneys	275,000
Sponges	750,000
Ships, boats, &c.	140,000
Railroad cars, and repairing	300,000
Naval stores	825,000
Railroad sleepers	450,000
Furniture and mattresses	85,000
Manufactured clothing	275,000
Laths and shingles	595,000
Fence rails	390,000
Manufactured copper	5,000
Stone for building and cribbing	30,000
Sawed lumber and timber	13,750,000
Stone-made fertilisers	275,000
Florida curiosities	45,000
Total value	20,343,750

Total population at close of the year 1889 was estimated at 457,525. Income per capita (including value of agricultural products, 23,094,070 dol., given in my agricultural report for 1890), 95 dol.; assessed valuation, 1889, 92,000,000 dol.; actual valuation for year 1889, 276,000,000 dol.; wealth per capita, 600 dol.

MOBILE, ALABAMA.

Mr. Vice-Consul Barnewall reports as follows:—

Commercial year commencing September 1, 1889, and ending August 31, 1890.

Cotton receipts, prices. Receipts: 261,957 bales, valued at 13,341,013 dol. 67 c., against 229,184 bales, valued at 10,329,322 dol. 88 c., of the year preceding. Average price per bale, 51 dol. 31 c.; average price per lb., 10 dol. 19 c.; against 8 dol. 82 c. per lb. the year preceding.

Exports, cotton. There has been a falling-off this year in the direct exports to Liverpool of 5,709 bales, and an increase to other points of 37,666 bales, showing a net increase in exports of 31,957 bales.

Timber shipments, value, &c. Shipments of timber are again in excess of the year previous, in fact larger than any year. The total value of the foreign exports is about 90,000 dol. larger than last year, this was not caused by any improvement in prices over last season, but by actual increase in exports, and if the amount towed to Horn and Ship Islands were added to the exports, the trade of the year would be the largest on record, about 2,142,000 cubic feet of hewn, and 2,550,000 cubic feet of sawn.

The amount towed to Horn and Ship Islands were as follows—hewn, 868,958 cubic feet; sawn, 708,003 cubic feet.

The exports compared with last year show an increase of 765,000 cubic feet; all the increase is in hewn, the sawn being about the same as last year. Exports.

The value of foreign shipments shows the average price of hewn to be 14 c. per cubic foot, against 14½ c. last year; sawn shows an average of 13½ c. per cubic foot, against $13\frac{7}{16}$ c. last year. Foreign ships, prices.

The lumber trade of the past year was good and generally satisfactory, and the largest on record, about 65,000,000 feet were shipped from Mobile by vessels and railroads, against 55,000,000 feet last year; but if we add to the lumber the hewn and sawn timber shipments we will have a direct trade of over 111,000,000 feet. Then if we add to the above the amount of timber towed to Horn and Ship Islands, local consumption, river trade, &c., the trade of Mobile for the past twelve months will be about 136,000,000 feet, which is 25,000,000 feet larger than last year, and valued at about 1,650,000 dol. Lumber shipments.

The total exports, foreign and coastwise, is about 53,000,000 feet, against 48,000,000 feet last year, and 29,000,000 feet in 1887–88, and represents a trade of about 650,000 dol. The foreign exports, which are the largest on record, are about 8,000,000 feet larger than last year; and the coastwise shipments are 3,600,000 feet less than last year, but are larger than any previous year. Exports.

Compared with last year the exports show an increase of 868,000 feet to the United Kingdom, 4,644,000 feet to the River Platte, 280,000 to Rio de Janeiro, 515,000 feet to Mexico, 6,768,000 feet to Cuba, and 846,000 feet to New Haven. The principal decrease was 3,856,000 feet to the Continent, 1,743,000 feet to New York, and 1,219,000 feet to Boston.

Mobile offers splendid sites for mills, furnaces, and manufacturing enterprises of all kinds. Real estate is cheap, about 700,000 dol. has been invested in the past year. Mobile.

There are a number of manufacturing establishments in the city too numerous to mention in detail; but all doing a successful business, and materially aiding the prosperity of general trade. Manufacturing establishments.

Wholesale business.

The wholesale business of the city is estimated as follows:—

	Dollars.
Cotton	7,500,000
Lumber and timber	1,650,000
Shingles	500,000
Staves	135,000
Vegetables	458,000
Fruit	300,000
Fish and oysters	195,000
Naval stores	55,000
Wool	153,000
Groceries	5,000,000
Grain	1,000,000
Boots and shoes	1,000,000
Hardware	1,500,000
Cigars and tobacco	1,000,000
Dry goods	5,000,000
Fertilisers	400,000
Clothing	1,000,000
Hats	500,000
Drugs	150,000
Carriages, saddlery, and harness	350,000
Crockery	300,000
Jewellery	150,000
Country produce	150,000
Furniture	1,000,000
Miscellaneous	2,553,000
Total value of Mobile commerce	32,500,000

Annex A.—RETURN of all Shipping at the Port of Mobile in the Year 1890.

ENTERED

Nationality.	Sailing. Number of Vessels.	Sailing. Tons.	Steam. Number of Vessels.	Steam. Tons.	Total. Number of Vessels.	Total. Tons.
British	73	38,057	10	13,514	83	51,571
American	66	23,973	1	323	67	24,296
Austrian	1	468	...	...	1	468
German	2	1,363	...	...	2	1,363
Spanish	1	385	2	2,565	3	2,950
French	2	941	...	...	2	941
Russian	6	5,428	...	...	6	5,428
Danish	1	387	...	...	1	387
Italian	4	2,316	...	...	4	2,316
Dutch	2	1,149	...	...	2	1,149
Swedish	12	8,208	...	...	12	8,208
Hondurian	4	352	...	...	4	352
Norwegian	42	39,938	2	760	44	40,698
Total	216	122,965	15	17,162	231	140,127
Coastwise	...	...	...	...	121	80,946
Total	...	...	...	...	352	221,073
,, for the year preceding	...	...	...	...	258	142,396

NEW ORLEANS.

Cleared.

Nationality.	Sailing. Number of Vessels.	Sailing. Tons.	Steam. Number of Vessels.	Steam. Tons.	Total. Number of Vessels.	Total. Tons.
British	69	35,871	10	13,577	79	49,448
American	72	22,095	2	1,195	74	23,290
French	2	941	...	...	2	941
German	2	1,363	...	...	2	1,363
Spanish	1	385	1	1,108	2	1,493
Mexican	1	492	...	...	1	492
Norwegian	44	35,680	2	760	46	36,440
Russian	7	6,014	...	...	7	6,014
Swedish	13	8,680	...	...	13	8,680
Dutch	3	1,903	...	...	3	1,903
Austrian	1	468	...	...	1	468
Danish	1	386	...	...	1	386
Honduria	4	352	...	...	4	352
Italian	4	2,316	...	...	4	2,316
Total	224	116,946	15	16,640	239	133,586
Coastwise	...	...	...	...	64	38,177
Total	...	...	...	...	302	171,763
,, for the year preceding	...	...	...	...	265	142,332

Annex B.—Return of Principal Articles of Import to Mobile during the Years 1889-90 and 1889-90.

Articles.		1889-90. Quantity.	1889-90. Value. £ s. d.	1888-89. Quantity.	1888-89. Value. £ s. d.
Bagging	Pieces	21,554	...	25,306	...
Iron ties	Bundles	19,707	...	56,355	...
Bacon	Hogsheads	15,835	...	12,736	...
Cotton	Bales	261,957	2,800,211 3 7	229,003	2,150,242 14 2
Coffee	Sacks	15,749	...	15,135	...
Corn	,,	441,347	...	472,253	...
Flour	Barrels	142,536	...	133,049	...
Fertilisers	Sacks	195,597	...	200,817	...
Hay	Bales	75,016	...	80,960	...
Lard	Tierces	5,222	...	5,332	...
Molasses	Barrels	2,748	...	2,858	...
Oats	Sacks	132,338	...	130,741	...
Potatoes	Barrels	17,691	...	16,024	...
Pork	,,	916	...	1,196	...
Rice	,,	6,092	...	5,535	...
Salt	Sacks	18,067	...	46,416	...
Soap	Boxes	22,603	...	22,090	...
Sugar	Barrels	17,010	...	14,289	...
Tobacco	Boxes	28,290	...	29,030	...
Whiskey	Barrels	7,366	...	5,862	...
Coal	Tons	40,647	...	45,074	...
Wool	Lbs.	639,300	...	857,500	45,554 13 9

Value 1*l.* = 4 dol. 80 c.

I cannot enumerate articles imported from foreign countries, nor give the value of above enumerated articles, with exception of cotton and wool.

RETURN of Principal Articles of Export from Mobile during the Years 1889-90 and 1888-89.

Articles.		1889-90.		1888-89.	
		Quantity.	Value.	Quantity.	Value.
			£ s. d.		£ s. d.
Cotton	Bales	261,141	2,800,211 3 7	229,184	2,151,942 5 4
Timber	Cubic feet	3,893,916	110,931 3 2	3,122,943	92,174 9 5
Lumber	Feet	52,879,310	132,212 15 8	48,284,162	124,451 12 5
Rosin	Barrels	...	...	4,830	1,304 11 8
Staves	Mill	475,245	11,169 4 2	350,963	8,119 3 4
Shingles	1,000	757,950	655 0 0	520,510	380 11 5
Merchandise	...	...	5,405 9 8	...	2,094 3 8
Vegetables	...	...	95,430 4 2	...	77,315 4 2
Coton-seed meal	Sacks	...	...	6,720	1,437 10 0
		...	3,156,015 0 5	...	2,459,216 11 5

Annex C.—TABLE showing the Total Value of all Articles Exported from Mobile and Imported to Mobile from and to Foreign Countries during the Years 1888-89 and 1889-90.

EXPORTS.

	£ s. d.
1888-89	638,884 14 0
1889-90	702,229 7 4

IMPORTS TO JUNE 30, 1890.

| 1888-89 | 32,056 0 10 |
| 1889-90 | 20,880 4 2 |

I have no means of dividing the above exports as to countries, except as regards cotton included in above.

GREAT BRITAIN.

	£ s. d.
1888-89	474,155 3 7
1889-90	478,775 14 11

NEW ORLEANS.

Condition of Dredged Channel of Mobile Harbour, June, 1890.

Location of Cross Sections.	Distance from Initial Point.	Top Width of Cut.	Maximum Depth in Cross Section.
	Miles.	Feet.	Feet.
Initial point mouth of Mobile or Chain—			
Cluster, No. 1	..	690	21·4
Chain cluster, No. 2	0·06	650	21·6
Upper gap-light stake	0·45	700	20·5
Cluster, No. 2	0·64	700	21·9
Chain cluster, No. 3	1·07	700	20·4
Lower gap-light stake	1·48	700	20·3
Cluster, No. 3	1·96	700	22·2
,, ,, 4	2·46	700	20·2
,, ,, 5	3·25	700	20·6
,, ,, 6	3·50	700	20·8
,, ,, 7	4·02	700	18·8
,, ,, 8	4·59	700	19·6
,, ,, 9	5·09	700	20·2
,, ,, 10	5·61	700	20·0
,, ,, 11	6·11	700	19·8
,, ,, 12	6·60	700	19·0
,, ,, 13	7·08	700	19·3
,, ,, 14	7·54	700	19·4
,, ,, 15	8·03	700	19·3
,, ,, 16	8·54	700	19·3
,, ,, 17	9·03	700	19·2
,, ,, 18	9·52	700	19·1
,, ,, 19	10·01	700	19·0
,, ,, 20	10·52	700	19·7
,, ,, 21	11·00	700	20·5
,, ,, 22	11·41	700	19·6
,, ,, 23	11·99	700	19·2
,, ,, 24	12·45	700	19·5
,, ,, 25	12·94	700	19·2
,, ,, 26	13·42	690	18·7
,, ,, 27	13·91	700	18·2
,, ,, 28	14·41	700	18·4
,, ,, 29	14·99	700	17·9
,, ,, 30	15·39	700	18·3
,, ,, 31	15·91	700	17·2
,, ,, 32	16·21	700	17·7
,, ,, 33	16·71	700	17·4
,, ,, 34	17·24	700	16·7
,, ,, 35	17·75	700	17·3
,, ,, 36	18·27	700	16·6
,, ,, 37	18·77	700	15·9
,, ,, 38	19·25	700	16·5
,, ,, 39	19·71	700	16·6
,, ,, 40	20·27	700	15·9
,, ,, 41	20·69	700	16·2
,, ,, 42	21·29	700	15·8
,, ,, 43	21·83	700	16·6
,, ,, 44	22·33	320	16·7
,, ,, 45	22·94	430	17·8
,, ,, 46	23·35	700	17·5
,, ,, 47	23·89	700	17·9
,, ,, 48	24·40	510	18·3
,, ,, 49	24·94	600	19·5
,, ,, 50	25·49	690	20·4
,, ,, 51	25·91	700	18·6

No dredging has been done since the middle of February, 1890. The appropriation of 350,000 dol. by the last Congress is now available, and the work of dredging will shortly be resumed.

(1036)

LONDON:
Printed for Her Majesty's Stationery Office,
By HARRISON AND SONS,
Printers in Ordinary to Her Majesty.
(1250 3 | 91—H & S 1048)

# FOREIGN OFFICE.

1891.

ANNUAL SERIES.

Nº· 835.

DIPLOMATIC AND CONSULAR REPORTS ON TRADE AND FINANCE.

UNITED STATES.

REPORT FOR THE YEAR 1890
ON THE
TRADE OF THE CONSULAR DISTRICT OF BALTIMORE.

REFERENCE TO PREVIOUS REPORT, Annual Series No. 648.

Presented to both Houses of Parliament by Command of Her Majesty,
MARCH, 1891.

LONDON:
PRINTED FOR HER MAJESTY'S STATIONERY OFFICE,
BY HARRISON AND SONS, ST. MARTIN'S LANE,
PRINTERS IN ORDINARY TO HER MAJESTY.

And to be purchased, either directly or through any Bookseller, from
EYRE & SPOTTISWOODE, East Harding Street, Fleet Street, E.C., and 32, Abingdon Street, Westminster, S.W.; or
JOHN MENZIES & Co., 12, Hanover Street, Edinburgh, and 88 and 90, West Nile Street, Glasgow; or
HODGES, FIGGIS, & Co., 104, Grafton Street, Dublin.

1891.

[C 6205—36.]   *Price Three Halfpence.*

New Series of Reports.

Reports of the Annual Series have been issued from Her Majesty's Diplomatic and Consular Officers at the following places, and may be obtained from the sources indicated on the title-page:—

No.		Price.	No.		Price.
711.	Corunna	2d.	773.	Jaffa	½d.
712.	Mogador	2d.	774.	Copenhagen	½d.
713.	Cadiz	½d.	775.	Ningpo	½d.
714.	Cadiz	1d.	776.	Stettin	2d.
715.	Rio de Janeiro	2½d.	777.	St. Petersburg	3d.
716.	Newchwang	½d.	778.	St. Petersburg	½d.
717.	Chinkiang	½d.	779.	St. Jago de Cuba	1½d.
718.	San Francisco	6d.	780.	Chefoo	1d.
719.	Bussorah	½d.	781.	Christiania	3½d.
720.	Beyrout	1d.	782.	Marseilles	½d.
721.	Adrianople	½d.	783.	Baghdad	1d.
722.	Nantes	½d.	784.	Naples	1½d.
723.	Caracas	1d.	785.	Tunis	4d.
724.	Mogador	½d.	786.	Vera Cruz	1d.
725.	Tientsin	1d.	787.	Tangier	1½d.
726.	Foochow	1d.	788.	Rome	2d.
727.	Port au Prince	½d.	789.	Stuttgart	1½d.
728.	Callao	1d.	790.	Panama	1½d.
729.	Puerto Plata	½d.	791.	Berne	1½d.
730.	San Francisco	1d.	792.	Ascunsion	½d.
731.	Philadelphia	2½d.	793.	Bahia	7½d.
732.	Pakhoi	1d.	794.	Monte Video	1½d.
733.	Bilbao	1d.	795.	Munich	2d.
734.	Dunkirk	1d.	796.	Bucharest	1d.
735.	Vienna	1d.	797.	Tokio	1d.
736.	Nantes	1½d.	798.	Tabreez	1d.
737.	Paramaribo	1d.	799.	Antwerp	1d.
738.	Honolulu	½d.	800.	Malaga	1d.
739.	Chicago	2d.	801.	Odessa	1d.
740.	Söul	1d.	802.	Malaga	2d.
741.	Brindisi	1½d.	803.	Amsterdam	1d.
742.	Mozambique	1d.	804.	Bogotá	1½d.
743.	Caldera and Lota	1½d.	805.	Guayaquil	½d.
744.	Nice	1½d.	806.	Lima	1d.
745.	Aleppo	1d.	807.	Rio de Janeiro	3d.
746.	Hakodate	1d.	808.	Dantzig	1½d.
747.	New York	2d.	809.	Florence	1½d.
748.	Cagliari	1d.	810.	Lisbon	1d.
749.	San Salvador	1d.	811.	Quito	½d.
750.	Gothenburg	2d.	812.	Para	½d.
751.	Nagasaki	1d.	813.	Palermo	2½d.
752.	Sofia	3½d.	814.	Copenhagen	1d.
753.	Meshed	1d.	815.	Serajevo	½d.
754.	Yokohama	2½d.	816.	Porto Rico	1d.
755.	Shanghai	2d.	817.	Madrid	½d.
756.	Lisbon	1½d.	818.	Brussels	1d.
757.	Teneriffe	1d.	819.	Patras	½d.
758.	Noumea	1d.	820.	Stuttgart	½d.
759.	Tahiti	1d.	821.	Taganrog	1d.
760.	Bushire	1½d.	822.	Salonica	2d.
761.	Frankfort	2d.	823.	Galveston	1d.
762.	Palermo	2½d.	824.	Rome	1½d.
763.	Guatemala	1d.	825.	Paris	1½d.
764.	Smyrna	4d.	826.	Bushire	½d.
765.	Munich	2d.	827.	New Orleans	3d.
766.	Hiogo	1½d.	828.	Buda-Pesth	½d.
767.	Alexandria	1½d.	829.	Hamburg	3d.
768.	Maracaibo	½d.	830.	Port Saïd	1d.
769.	Macao	1d.	831.	Samoa	1d.
770.	Canton	1d.	832.	Guayaquil	½d.
771.	Bangkok	2½d.	833.	New Orleans	2d.
772.	Stockholm	1½d.	834.	The Piræus	1d.

No. 835.

Reference to previous Report, Annual Series No. 648.

UNITED STATES.

BALTIMORE.

Consul Segrave to the Marquis of Salisbury.

My Lord, *Baltimore, February* 10, 1891.

I HAVE the honour herewith to transmit to your Lordship Reports on the Trade and Commerce of Baltimore and Richmond for the year 1890, and of Norfolk (Va.).

I have, &c.
(Signed) W. F. SEGRAVE.

Report on the Trade and Commerce of Baltimore for the Year 1890.

There appears to be a generally expressed opinion throughout the mercantile community of Baltimore that, during the past year, the trade of the city has been disappointing. [Disappointment in past year's trade.]

It is not, of course, possible to please everyone, but an outsider would be induced to imagine that an increase in the foreign trade of over 10,000,000 dol. was a fairly satisfactory result, and might content even the most exacting. [Increase in foreign trade.]

The disappointment in which the mercantile community is said to indulge is probably occasioned by the reduction in the grain export, which at the commencement of the past year promised to be of colossal dimensions, but the destruction by fire of one of the largest corn elevators in the place caused a diversion of a considerable proportion of the trade to the comparatively (in the grain trade) insignificant port of Philadelphia, which had, as a result, the handling of nearly as large an amount of corn (maize) as Baltimore. [Reduction in grain export. Diverted to Philadelphia.]

This is, however, merely a temporary incident, which has not recently occurred at Philadelphia, and is not likely to recur, at least, in the near future.

The Baltimore Chamber of Commerce have reported strongly against the Tonnage Bill, or, as it is now termed, "a Bill to place [Tonnage Bill]

(1048)

UNITED STATES.

Chamber of Commerce opposes it.

the American Merchant Marine engaged in Foreign Trade upon an equality with that of other nations." They sensibly remark that "under the proposed Bill a sailing vessel of 1,000 tons would receive, on a voyage to Europe and back, a bounty of 1,800 doll. whilst a steamship of 5,000 tons would receive for the same voyage a bounty of 9,000 dol.

Its reasons.

The assurance of such a bounty continuing for ten years would give an artificial stimulus to shipbuilding, and, as a result, every line of business that needed assistance or bolstering up would clamour for a subsidy, and all to result in an unhealthy competition which would inevitably prove disastrous in the long run.

They continue: "If England will do our carrying trade at rates which we can afford to pay, why tax the people for an empty sentiment which will never be respected?

"There is no sentiment in trade, and every merchant will employ the cheapest bottom, regardless of its flag."

Revolution in ocean traffic.

But if the anticipations of some sanguine speculators are realised, there is little doubt that a great revolution in ocean steam traffic is impending.

New form of steamship.

Quite recently there has been launched from a Baltimore shipyard a new form of steamship, for which the inventor claims advantages not possessed by any vessel afloat.

The "Howard-Cassard."

She is stated to be a seagoing steamship, solely for passenger traffic, having no freight capacity whatever. Her builders assert that she can neither burn nor sink, and that, even if upset, she has in a high degree the property of righting herself, as she has 4 lbs. weight below water-line for every 1 lb. above it.

Her keel, which weighs 35 tons, acts not only as ballast, but as a centre-board, inasmuch as nearly half of its depth protrudes through the hull into the water.

In consequence of its extra rigidity the keel makes far safer and better engine and shaft bearings than those used in the ordinary methods of shipbuilding.

The difference between the safety compartment of the "Howard-Cassard" and those of vessels constructed under the existing system lies in the fact that this vessel has air as well as watertight compartments, whilst under the actual system vessels are provided with watertight compartments alone.

These safety compartments number 170, of which 136 are on either side of the ship's centre, thus forming practically three ships in one.

The motive power consists in an improved compound engine calculated to develop 1,600 horse-power, which would drive the ship at an average speed of 25 miles an hour on a consumption of one ton of coals.

The valve gear is so perfected that the valves may be opened and closed in the one-twentieth of a second, thus giving double power over engines of similar size.

The "Howard-Cassard" is 222 feet over all, or 206 feet between perpendicular. She has 16 feet beam, and 18 feet depth of hold. She is built of rolled iron plates on the cellular system

It is asserted that if an ordinary steamship be taken from the water, and supported only at the stem and stern, she would break in half, whilst the "Howard-Cassard," like a tubular bridge with a hull upon it, would support several times its own weight.

This vessel is only an experiment, and is only two-fifths of the proposed dimensions of the regular steamship which is to be built. The sister ship which will follow the "Howard-Cassard," if she proves the success which is anticipated, will have every luxury and convenience. There will be no disagreeable smell either from kitchens or engines. The decks will be air and water-tight, and the vibration of the ship minimised on account of the interlacing system of structure, and the power being all beneath the decks and on the rigid keel.

It is proposed to run these ships between Baltimore and Havanna, carrying passengers, mails, and express matter (parcels) only. Later a regular ocean steamship line will be started.

The promoters and builders assert that their system will completely revolutionise ocean traffic, and that in the future, instead of having a mixed service, there will be passenger and freight steamships only, just as on land there are passenger and goods trains.

For more than 20 years the preservation of the oyster has been a subject of paramount interest to the States Government of Maryland and Virginia. *Oysters.*

The question has been exhaustively discussed, as it is one of the gravest importance to the interests of the two States. Under existing conditions the depletion of the beds threatens the absolute extinction of the oyster. There appears to be a consensus of public opinion that the time has arrived when all sentiments on the subject must be laid aside, and it is probable that the next legislature may be called upon to pass more coercive laws on the subject, entailing confiscation of vessel and imprisonment of the owners and crews of such as may be convicted of poaching. *Destruction of beds.*

In the past year Maryland and Virginia instead of supplying, as in 1880, over 17,000,000 bushels of oysters (Maryland, 10,600,000; Virginia, 6,837,000), will not yield 6,000,000 bushels, although the two States have upwards of 1,500,000 acres of oyster beds. This deplorable condition of affairs results solely from the incapacity of the two States to enforce their own laws. *Destruction of oysters.*

The young oysters are being destroyed and the beds gradually depleted by over-dredging, so that unless prompt and energetic measures are adopted this great industry will utterly collapse, and the Chesapeake Bay oyster will follow the Buffalo into extinction.

According to public statistics last season's corn crop is worth more to the farmer than the preceding one, that is, to those farmers who have succeeded in raising a crop, which all have not done. *Agriculture.*

The mean price in December was 50·1 c. per bushel against 28·8 c. for the crop of 1889, or an increase in value of 75 per cent.

The average farm value of the wheat crop is estimated at *Wheat, value of.*

(1048)

Wheat re-imported.

84 c. per bushel, as against 69·8 c. for 1889, or an increase of 20 per cent.

Differing from the maize crop, whose price is not as a rule governed by the amount of foreign produce, the value of wheat is perceptibly affected by the harvest in other countries.

In connection with the grain trade a singular reversal of the ordinary course of business took place during the past season.

Future import of food.

Two cargoes of wheat were imported into Baltimore, or rather, to state the facts more strictly, were re-imported into Baltimore. The original shipper finding it more profitable to send his grain back than to dispose of it in England at the prices then ruling.

Desponding traders shook their heads and asked each other whether this transaction could be a forecaste of what might take place in the not too distant future; but if the past may be taken as any guide to the future there is but small reason to doubt that sooner or later this country will have to import food, that is, assuming that the population goes on increasing at its present ratio, and that the American farmer can devise no means whereby to extract from his land more than the average 12 bushels of wheat per acre.

Cattle and swine disease.

From reports presented to Congress it would appear that there has been no spread of contagious pleuro-pneumonia beyond the districts already reported as infected, and that the condition of cattle throughout the country shows the most gratifying improvement.

With regard to swine disease and the various processes for the prevention of hay cholera, the report shows that swine plague is more prevalent than was supposed.

Inoculation remedy.

On the subject of inoculation and the discovery by Dr. Koch of the bacillus of tuberculosis, the report states that the possibility of applying bacterial products to the prevention and cure of disease was made evident long ago through the investigations of the bureau of animal industry, and that if Dr. Koch's remedy is of the nature that it is assumed to be, his method consists in the application of a principle discovered in this country.

Koch process initiated in this country.

Respecting the effects of the substance which has this preventive power, it is stated to be very irritating upon the system of swine.

With the object of discovering some process by which swine disease might be prevented, or at least minimised, the bureau made exhaustive researches, and has succeeded in producing a drug which is said to have the same effect as the bacterial product. The report avers that this substance is not only similar to the bacterial product of the hay cholera germ in composition, but that it has the same faculty of conferring immunity from the disease.

Finance.

That Baltimore should have escaped practically scatheless from the effects of the financial crisis during the closing months of the past year, speaks well for the financial soundness of the city.

The banks were always ready to assist their customers within reasonable limits, and so tided over the difficult period in safety.

The increased volume of business is shown in the bank clearances, which are 102,509,622 dol. in excess of those of the previous year, as is shown by the subjoined statement.

Bank clearances at Baltimore :—

	Dollars.
1890	753,093,193
1889	650,583,571

The past year's finance must have been especially welcome to persons of limited incomes who depend on increased earnings, and consequently dividends, for support. Dividends have been paid on 1,000,000 dol. worth of securities in excess of 1889, and which has been the largest distribution in the history of this city.

Silver. The increase in the production of silver in this country during the past year was 21 per cent. out of a total of 31 per cent. for the whole world.

The price remained practically stationary, so that demand and supply must have gone on pari passu.

Silver Bill. Whether therefore the increased demand under the proposed "Silver Bill" with advanced prices depends on two unknown quantities, the course of supply, and the course of demand, other than that caused by the Bill.

If the price should fall there would be a strong tendency towards the depreciation not only of notes issued against silver, but on Government securities as well, and with an enhanced value of gold.

Baltimore clearing house opposed to. At the annual meeting of the Baltimore clearing house a resolution was adopted protesting against the pending Silver Bill.

The resolution states that, "should the Act become law, it would prove injurious to the agricultural, mercantile, manufacturing, and general business interests of the country at large, and would produce serious financial disturbance," and they call upon all banking, labour, and trade associations to take steps to defeat the measure.

Railway accidents. It is asserted that, in the United States, 20 railway servants are killed or injured every day in the year, and that only one in every five has, under present conditions, a chance of dying a natural death.

No wonder then that attempts are being made by legislation to remedy this state of things by forcing railway companies to adopt automatic couplers and brakes under the control of the drivers of the trains.

Safety brakes and couplers. An automatic coupler has been invented and adopted by the Car Builders' Association, which would only cost from 12 dol. to 25 dol. per car.

A safety brake has also been invented, which would work

UNITED STATES.

equally on goods trains, and the cost of the application of which per car would be from 25 dol. to 45 dol.

It is alleged that both of these inventions would minimise the risk to railway servants.

Baltimore, population of. The census of 1880 gave to Baltimore a population of 332,313 inhabitants, whilst that of 1890 finds the population to be 448,000, and which number is locally believed to be below the actual population. There are no doubt good grounds for this belief, as the census was taken in the middle of the summer, when large numbers of the inhabitants leave the city to escape the heat.

Post-office. Within four years the receipts of the Baltimore post-office have increased by 20,000 dol. a year, chiefly owing to the establishment of factories and workshops.

Harbour. The Federal Government recently appropriated 340,000 dol. for the improvement of the harbour, not before it was required, and it is estimated that, within the next three years, some 30,000,000 dol. will be locally expended in works of public improvement and utility.

Railway facilities. Nine railroads run into the city, and 50 passenger trains run daily between Baltimore and Washington, so that this city is fast becoming the market and shipping place of the national capital.

Foreign trade. Finally, Baltimore has become the third exporting and the sixth importing port of the United States, with a foreign trade in the past year aggregating 17,500,000*l.*, and showing an increase of 2,000,000*l.* over the previous year.

Manufactures. The fact that Baltimore has become a great manufacturing centre does not seem to be fully appreciated even in this country, yet many new industries have been established of late, and many long-established ones have quadrupled their production.

Manufactures, increase of. As an instance it may be stated that the amount of manufactured tobacco has increased in late years from 3,000,000 lbs. to 15,000,000 lbs.

Iron, steel, brass, and machinery were produced in 1890 to the value of 16,000,000 dol.; and tin, copper, and sheet-iron ware from 3,500,000 dol. in 1880 reached 7,000,000 dol. in 1890.

Foreign trade, increase of. But it is in its foreign trade that Baltimore maintains its ascendency, showing a larger percentage of increase than any other port in the country. The export trade has increased from 34,000,000 dol. in 1885 to 71,000,000 dol. in 1890, whilst imports have increased from 11,000,000 dol. in the former to 14,000,000 dol. in the latter year, and with the revival of the sugar-refining business imports will much largely increase in the present year.

Grain trade, increase in. The grain trade between 1882 and 1889 shows an average gain, whilst that of New York has a corresponding loss, amounting to 50,000,000 bushels in the past over the previous year.

Baltimore, advantages as a seaport. The future of Baltimore as a seaport is of great promise. It is the shortest and most accessible, and therefore the natural outlet for the products of the west.

BALTIMORE.

With large and increasing facilities for the economical movement of goods, with a channel deep enough for vessels drawing 27½ feet of water, and with manufactures daily increasing, it must, in the very nature of things, assume its place as the most important and safest Atlantic port in the country.

General trade.

The receipts of wheat have been very disappointing, though the export shows a slight increase over that of the previous year.

Grain and breadstuffs.

The receipts of flour, whilst showing an increase for the past year, have not been of such a character as to satisfy the local dealers. The export shows a moderate percentage of increase.

The corn trade opened brilliantly, and during the early months of the year the outlook was hopeful, but the competition with Russian, Danubian, and Argentine corn soon caused the trade to languish, and during the last six months the market lost more than was gained in the first six.

The stock of grain in the elevators at the close of the year was:—

	Bushels.
Wheat	513,137
Corn	164,711
Oats	99,136
Rye	22,609

Canned goods

For some years the canning business has been declining, but it appears to have fallen during the past year to the very lowest limit. This may be attributed, in part, to the total failure of the peach crop. At one time about 1,000,000 cans of this fruit were put up in a season. During the past year the entire pack did not amount to 500 cases. There was also considerable decline in tomatoes and corn, in the latter case mainly owing to the low prices prevailing in 1889.

Coffee.

The importation of coffee shows considerable decline. During the whole of the past year prices fluctuated rapidly.

There has been, however, little speculation on the market, and business has been fairly steady.

Cotton.

The lightness of the European money market had a marked effect on the Baltimore cotton trade. There was considerable increase in the amount received, but from the above cause a short export. 65,000 bales were taken by local mills, and 38,000 bales shipped coastwise.

The value of the cotton crop on the plantations is nearly the same as in the previous year, viz, 8 c. per lb., as the average export price is a trifle over 10 c. the difference may be assumed to represent the cost of transport, compressing, &c.

Fruit.

There were large increases in the import of tropical fruit during the year, and without doubt the trade has a great future in store for it.

Baltimore is so fortunately situated as compared with Philadelphia and New York that she can successfully compete with these ports. She is 24 hours nearer to the source of supply than the former, and 48 hours nearer than the latter, and has equal railway facilities to the west. No doubt there is room for con-

Cattle. siderable extension in this business in which English steamers are employed throughout the whole year.

The export of live stock goes on increasing by leaps and bounds, the increase during the past year amounting to 49 per cent., and being nearly quadruple that of 1888. The severe weather at the close of the year must have been very trying to the cattle, and serious losses are reported.

Iron. The establishment of the huge iron works at Steelton at the mouth of the Patassco river, a short distance from Baltimore, has had a marked influence on the shipping trade of the port.

The import of iron ore, chiefly from Spain and Cuba, and exclusively in English bottoms, has nearly doubled during the past year, as a natural consequence there has been a reduction in the import of manufactured iron and steel, though not to the extent one might have been led to expect.

Tin-plate. There has been a great deal of talk about the establishment of shops for the manufacture of tin-plate, as well at Baltimore as at other places.

As has been remarked elsewhere there is no sentiment in trade, and it is more than doubtful whether American tin-plate can be placed on the market at a sufficiently low price to compete with the Welsh article, even when loaded with the heavy duty imposed under the M'Kinley Tariff.

Tobacco. The business in leaf tobacco was smaller than for many past years, chiefly owing to an exceptionally short crop, as well in Maryland as in Ohio. The small quantity grown in Maryland, though of a very inferior quality, found ready sale, and the higher and better qualities at largely enhanced prices. The stock remaining in the warehouses at the end of the past year is the smallest since 1880, and amounts to only 6,584 hogsheads.

The Ohio crop was of a better quality, and nearly the whole of it was purchased by the French and Italian Governments at a considerable advance price over that ruling in 1889.

Baltimore customs receipts. The total receipts of the Baltimore customs for the past year amounted to 3,174,039 dol., showing an increase over 1889 of 124,926 dol.

There were 147 maritime disasters reported at the custom-house involving loss of human life in 68 cases, and destruction of shipping property to the amount of 50,000*l*.

Immigration During the past year 72 vessels (20 English and 52 German) brought 30,440 immigrants to this port, of whom 16,094 were males, and 14,346 females.

The following nationalities were represented:—

BALTIMORE.

England	329
Scotland	2
Ireland	163
British Possessions	12
	506
Austria	1,784
Belgium	14
Bohemia	1,797
Denmark	439
France	12
Hungary	1,528
Italy	2
Netherlands	14
Norway	26
Poland	220
Roumania	21
Russia	3,893
Sweden	192
Switzerland	35
Turkey	6
Germany	18,787

The balance being made up by American subjects.

Subjoined are transmitted :—

Annex A.—Return of all shipping at the port of Baltimore in the year 1890.

Annex B.—Return of principal articles of export from Baltimore for 1890.

Annex C.—Principal articles of import into Baltimore in 1890.

Annex D.—Table showing the total value of all articles exported from or imported into Baltimore to and from foreign countries in 1890.

Annex A.—Return of all Shipping at the Port of Baltimore for the Year 1890.

Entered.

Nationality.	Sailing. Number of Vessels.	Sailing. Tons.	Steam. Number of Vessels.	Steam. Tons.	Total. Number of Vessels.	Total. Tons.
British	22	8,692	605	839,161	627	847,853
American, foreign trade only	145	51,645	...	...	145	51,645
German	1	720	87	171,152	88	171,872
Italian	10	3,674	...	...	10	3,674
Swedish, Norwegian	...	...	24	22,156	24	22,156
Spanish	...	...	12	29,472	12	29,472
Other nations	5	1,287	2	2,740	7	4,027
Total, 1890	183	66,018	730	1,064,681	913	1,130,699
,, 1889	180	81,365	573	858,667	753	940,032
Increase in 1890	...	...	157	206,014	160	190,667

British increase, vessels 124
,, tonnage 142,656

UNITED STATES.

CLEARED.

Nationality.	Sailing. Number of Vessels.	Sailing. Tons.	Steam. Number of Vessels.	Steam. Tons.	Total. Number of Vessels.	Total. Tons.
British	22	8,692	592	884,419	614	893,111
American, foreign trade only	140	39,620	...	...	140	39,620
German	1	720	85	169,214	86	169,934
Italian	8	2,976	...	...	8	2,976
Swedish, Norwegian	...	...	24	22,156	24	22,156
Spanish	...	...	12	29,472	12	29,472
Other nations	4	1,427	2	2,146	6	3,573
Total, 1890	175	53,435	715	1,107,407	890	1,160,842
,, 1889	175	62,064	574	856,191	749	918,255
Increase in 1890	...	...	141	251,216	141	212,587

British increase, vessels 109
,, tonnage 187,914

Annex B.—Return of Principal Articles of Export from Baltimore in the Years 1889-90.

Articles.		1890. Quantity.	1890. Value.	1889. Quantity.	1889. Value.
Grain and breadstuffs—					
Wheat	Quarters	641,469		563,396	
Flour	Tons	257,179		228,113	
Corn (maize)	Cwts.	592,569		519,298	
,, meal	Tons	725		617	
Oats	Bushels	617,653		132,000	
,, meal	Tons	1,573		1,864	
Barley and malt	Bushels	772,177		628,359	
Rye	,,	28,890		...	
Provisions—					
Cattle	Head	88,172		59,357	
Beef, canned, salt, and fresh	Tons	28,458		16,019	
Pork, bacon, and hams	,,	9,523		4,794	
Lard, tallow, and stearine	,,	55,530		404,277	
Butter	,,	46		70	
Cheese	...	975		217	
Oils—					
Petroleum	Barrels	387,824	Total value of exports for 1890, 71,780,959 dol.; at 4 dol. 85 c. per 1l. = 14,800,185l. 10s.	239,791	Total value of exports for 1889, 61,131,509 dol.; at 4 dol. 85 c. per 1l. = 12,604,434l. 17s. 6d.
Mineral, vegetable, and animal	,,	173,853		120,000	
Oil-cake	Tons	27,926		25,548	
Minerals—					
Copper (matte)	,,	25,925		27,790	
,, sulphate of	,,	686		...	
Silver (ingots)	,,	460		...	
,, (matte)	,,	1,156		...	
Zinc (ore)	,,	318		...	
Coals	,,	61,491		55,796	
Timber—					
Lumber	M. feet	29,126		25,427	
Logs	Number	41,856		26,004	
Staves	M.	2,423		3,354	
Seeds—					
Clover, grass, Timothy	Tons	6,409		3,852	
Various—					
Apples (dried and evaporated)	,,	2,086		3,342	
Bark	Bags	46,304		...	
,, extract	Barrels	10,837		...	
Bones	Tons	1,951		...	
Cotton	Bales	146,573		170,110	
,, cloths	Yards	231,181		147,933	
Hair and bristles	Bales	6,790		...	
Hops	,,	12,200		...	
Leather	Lbs.	139,746		363,491	
Rosin	Barrels	116,181		57,853	
Sugar (grape)	Tons	1,205		...	
Starch	,,	1,721		2,417	
Tobacco	Hhds.	53,924		63,346	
Wax	Tons	1,173		566	
Whiskey	Barrels	2,516		...	

Note.—Exports increase, 2,195,751l.

BALTIMORE.

Annex C.—RETURN of the Principal Articles of Import into Baltimore in the Years 1889-90.

Articles.		1890. Quantity.	1890. Value.	1889. Quantity.	1889. Value.
Metals and minerals—					
Iron ore	Tons	515,382		289,252	
,, manganese	,,	9,192		...	
,, purple	,,	37,161		...	
,, speigle	,,	7,432		...	
,, pig	,,	18,725		20,589	
,, various	,,	3,240		8,640	
Steel, bitlets	,,	2,267		...	
,, varicus	,,	2,859		...	
Tin, plate	Boxes	1,199,408		1,249,055	
,, various	Tons	880		...	
Fertilisers—					
Guano	,,	2,686		6,290	
Salt-manure	Bags	75,785		...	
,, cake	Tierces	3,982		...	
Soda, ash	Casks	24,028		29,486	
,, caustic	,,	1,464		...	
Sulphur	Tons	15,964	Total value of imports for 1890, 14,519,041 dol.; at 4 dol. 85 c. per l. = 2,993,616l. 15s.	17,711	Total value of imports for 1889, 15,435,375 dol.; at 4 dol. 85 c. per l. = 3,182,551l. 11s.
Fruit—					
Bananas	Bunches	614,161		386,615	
Cocoanuts	M.	1,942		1,979	
Pineapples	Dozens	335,153		286,271	
Oranges	Boxes	9,272		22,490	
Coffee	Bags	190,085		308,547	
Rice	,,	39,882		41,775	
Pepper and spices	Cases	4,843		...	
Pickles	Casks	3,742		...	
Beans	Bags	22,297		...	
Potatoes	,,	5,964		...	
Onions	,,	1,837		...	
Salt	Tons	13,687		17,637	
Ashphalt	,,	2,221		2,096	
Clay (ball)	,,	1,212		...	
Bleaching powder	Casks	3,183		...	
Cement	Barrels	83,839		51,627	
Kainite	Tons	5,355		...	
Kaiserit	,,	4,348		...	
Plaster	,,	3,430		...	
Earthenware and china	Crates	19,305		...	
Toys	Cases	15,912		...	
Herrings, cured and salted	Kegs	23,978		...	
Beer	Barrels	3,233		...	
Mineral water	Cases	10,640		...	
Whiskey	Barrels	14,081		13,908	
Wines	Cases	4,945		...	
Woollen goods	Lbs.	136,135		104,001	
Cotton dress goods	Sq. yrds.	911,519		525,080	
,, cloths	,,	124,216		62,392	
Hides	Bundles	16,703		...	
Oilcloths	Bales	4,671		...	
Paints	Casks	4,712		...	
Marble	Blocks and slabs	20,039		...	
Bricks, fire	M.	499		...	
,, bath	Tons	350		...	
,, ordinary	Casks	3,165		...	
Iron bedstead	Packages	1,546		...	

NOTE.—Imports decrease, 188,935l.

Annex D.—TABLE showing the Total Value of all Articles Exported from and Imported into Baltimore from Foreign Countries in the Years 1889-90.

Country.	Exports. 1890.	Exports. 1889.	Imports. 1890.	Imports. 1889.
	£	£	£	£
Great Britain	9,000,000	8,400,000	1,750,000	1,800,000
Germany	1,850,000	1,000,000	200,000	250,000
Brazil	650,000	500,000	350,000	600,000
Netherlands	1,170,000	600,000	125,000	..
France	750,000	1,000,000	..	..
Belgium	620,000	500,000	..	40,000
Cuba	..	20,000	160,000	100,000
Italy	..	50,000	30,000	100,000
Spain	..	..	125,000	115,000
Algiers	..	..	..	..
Denmark	85,000	40,000	..	..
Sweden	..	20,000	..	..
Argentine	150,000	75,000	..	..
Other countries	100,000	21,302	150,000	3,200
Total	14,375,000	12,226,302	2,890,000	3,008,200

RICHMOND.

Mr. Vice-Consul Marshall reports as follows:—

Trade. The trade and commerce of Richmond for the year 1890 have been prosperous and increasing in all its material interests, and has suffered less than could be expected during the financial troubles that prevailed during the latter part of the year.

Industries. Factory. There has been an increase of 59 manufactories of all kinds compared with the preceding year, the total number of all manufactories for 1890 being 783, employing 21,618 hands, with a capital of 16,596,500 dol. The most considerable industries in Richmond are as follows:—

Tobacco. Tobacco, employing 8,792 hands, with a capital of 4,286,300 dol.

Iron. Iron industries, including foundries, nail works, machine work, rolling mills, locomotive works, &c.

Flour. Flour and meal flour mills, employing 209 hands, with a capital of 85,000 dol. The capital abovenamed is only cash capital, and does not include the real estate owned by the proprietors.

The stock of grain in the elevator on December 31, 1890, was:—

Grain.

	Bushels.
Wheat	40,935
Maize	3,910
Oats	22,298
Rye	564

Building during the year was very active, and 936 houses have been erected in Richmond and the suburbs. *Building.*

The population of Richmond by the late census was 83,000, but, with the suburbs adjoining, it is estimated at about 100,000; of this number, perhaps, about 35,000 are coloured, but it is almost impossible to ascertain their real number. *Population.*

The report of the President of the Board of Health states the whole number of deaths at 2,236, of which number 1,049 were white and 1,187 coloured. The rate of mortality of the whole population was $\frac{22}{36}$ per 1,000 per annum; rate of mortality of white population, $\frac{18}{73}$ per 1,000 per annum. *Vital statistics.*

Jobbing sales for the year 1890 amount to 22,042,000 dol., an increase of 2,902,000 dol. over the year 1889. *Jobbing sales.*

The direct imports are very small, merchants supply themselves with goods from the northern cities, shipped from thence coastwise to Richmond. *Goods from northern cities.*

Speculation has been great in all kinds of enterprises, in mining companies, development companies, and lots and land, and much capital has been withdrawn from its more legitimate employment to invest in such companies.

There has been some diminution in the number of vessels during the year coming in ballast from the United States, having landed their cargoes there, and they are all entered and cleared as foreign. *Shipping.*

Table showing the movement of shipping at the port of Richmond, without including the coasting trade in American vessels, and the return as to these vessels represents the entries and clearances to and from foreign ports only.

RETURN of all Shipping at the Port of Richmond for the Year 1890.

ENTERED.

Nationality.	Sailing. Number of Vessels.	Sailing. Tons.	Steam. Number of Vessels.	Steam. Tons.	Total. Number of Vessels.	Total. Tons.
British	8	1,747	28	44,853	36	46,600
American	4	1,576	...	...	4	1,576
Swedish	2	469	...	...	2	469
Norwegian	2	488	...	...	2	488
German	3	658	1	1,052	4	1,710
Spanish	...	...	5	8,190	5	8,190
Total	19	4,938	34	54,095	53	59,033
„ for preceding year	25	8,168	41	64,560	67	72,728

UNITED STATES.

CLEARED.

Nationality.	Sailing. Number of Vessels.	Sailing. Tons.	Steam. Number of Vessels.	Steam. Tons.	Total. Number of Vessels.	Total. Tons.
British	8	1,747	28	44,853	36	46,600
American	4	1,576	...	...	4	1,576
Swedish	2	469	...	...	2	469
Norwegian	2	488	...	...	2	488
German	3	658	1	1,052	4	1,710
Spain	...	...	5	8,190	5	8,190
Total	19	4,938	34	54,095	53	59,033
„ for preceding year...	26	8,168	40	62,941	66	71,169

RETURN of the Principal Articles of Export from Richmond during the Years 1889-90.

Articles.		1890. Quantity.	1890. Value.	1890. Value.	1889. Quantity.	1889. Value.
			Dollars.	£		£
Cotton	Bales	173,908	8,441,825	...	204,975	...
Flour	Barrels	46,169	225,717	...	39,607	...
Cattle	Heads	1,855	84,670	...	992	...
Staves	Pieces	144,600	45,870	...	500	...
Tobacco	Tierces	45	8,100	...	2,806	...
Shuttle blocks	Pieces	10,684	2,900	...	...	...
Total	...	...	8,808,682	1,761·36	...	2,023,456

NOTE.—5 dol. = 1l.

RETURN of the Principal Articles Imported into Richmond during the Years 1889-90.

Articles.		1890. Quantity.	1890. Value.	1890. Value.	1889. Quantity.	1889. Value.
			Dollars.	£		£
Salt	Sacks	5,550	3,811	...	6,761	...
Guano	Tons	1,200	25,000	...	786	...
Plaster	„	2,575	2,550	...	21	...
Bananas, pineapples, and sundries	„	...	950	...	...	...
Total	...	...	32,311	6,478	...	7,396

NORFOLK, VIRGINIA.

Mr. Vice-Consul Barton Myers reports as follows:—

Railways. During the last two or three years there have been added two new railroads to the already good transportation facilities of the port, and the lines heretofore existing have been extending their connections in the west and south, until now Norfolk has seven broad gauge railroads, and two narrow gauge railroads, controlling an aggregate of over 17,000 miles, which put her in connection with all points reached by railroads in the north, west, and south; while she is connected by first class steamship lines with Boston, Providence, New York, Philadelphia, Baltimore, Washington, Richmond, and other points on the coast and sounds. She is within 20 hours of Boston by rail, and 40 hours by water;

12 hours of New York by rail, and 21 hours by water; 10 hours of Philadelphia by rail, and 18 by water; 8 hours of Baltimore by rail, and 12 by water; 7 hours of Washington by rail, and 12 hours by water; and 2½ hours of Richmond by rail. She is within 23 hours of Cincinnatti, Ohio, and 34 hours of Chicago and St. Louis.

Steamship communication. The connection with Liverpool is by means of steamers known as "tramps," chartered mostly for the carriage of freight, there being no regular transatlantic line plying between this port and European ports.

City of Norfolk. The city of Norfolk has a complete system of sewerage, and is well paved. The healthfulness of the climate as exhibited by the death rate is not surpassed by any city in this country, the percentage being, in 1890, 16·90.

Water supply. The water supply of the city is derived from large lakes of spring water, seven miles distant, which is not only good for household use, but it is admirably adapted for manufacturing purposes, being absolutely free from all those substances which corrode boilers.

Climate. The climate, tempered by the proximity of the Gulf Stream, is mild, and there is rarely ever ice or snow to interfere with outdoor work or exercise.

Lighting. The city is lighted by electric lights, and has as fine a fire and police department as any in the country.

All denominations are well represented in churches.

Hospitals. There are two good hospitals, one under the care of the sisters of charity, and the other under the Protestant organisations of the city. *Education.* The educational advantages of the city are most excellent, there being a thorough system of public schools, together with numerous seminaries and private schools for both sexes. In the matter of amusements the city is well provided, having two good theatres at which the best companies stop on their pilgrimages from the larger cities of the north to the south.

The increase of the city in the matter of commercial importance deserves especial attention, and is best illustrated by statistics.

Trade. In 1883 the aggregate trade was placed at 38,200,436 dol., while five years later, in 1888, it had risen to 65,011,656 dol.; in 1889 it increased to 75,000,000 dol., and in 1890 to 100,000,000 dol.

Shipping. The tonnage of Norfolk in 1870 was 13,502 tons, valued at 886,594 dol.; in 1880 it increased to 103,608 tons, valued at 11,116,595 dol.; in 1887, 257,884 tons, valued at 14,714,404 dol.; for the year 1890 the tonnage reached 582,846, valued at 15,197,095 dol.

It will be hard to find a parallel case in this country in two decades showing an increase of tonnage from 13,502 tons in 1870, to 582,846 tons in 1890, and valued at 816,594 dol. in 1870, less than 1,000,000 dol., to 15,197,095 dol. in 1890.

The following tables give the entrances and clearances from this port, and the exports and imports for the year 1890.

UNITED STATES.

Harbour.

The port of Norfolk is attracting great attention, and has assumed control of a large part of the commerce of the south Atlantic seaboard.

It has the most magnificent natural harbour on the Atlantic coast, having no bar to block its entrance, being within 30 miles of the Atlantic Ocean, yet sheltered from all the vicissitudes of weather, always free from ice, and capable of any depth of water.

The sheet of water known as Hampton Roads, which is at the confluence of the James and Elizabeth Rivers with Chesapeake Bay, affords a harbour unsurpassed by any in the world, easy of access, and navigable for vessels of any size or draft.

Centenary of discovery of America.

It is here that the Congress of the United States has designated for the rendezvous of the navies of the world in 1892-3, to celebrate the fourth centennial of the discovery of America. A 26 foot channel, well marked with buoys and lighthouses, leads from the Chesapeake Bay to the wharves of Norfolk, and above the city to the United States Navy Yard.

Norfolk now has a population within its limits of 35,454 inhabitants, being an increase since the census of 1880 of 61 per cent. This, with the population of Portsmouth, Berkley, and other suburbs, makes a total population around the harbour of Norfolk of 70,000 souls. The increase in population of Norfolk in the last few years has been rapid, and the growth of business and increase in the value of property of all kinds are turning the attention of capitalists and investors to this point.

TABLE showing the Movement of Shipping at this Port, without including the Coasting Trade in American Vessels, and the Return as to these Vessels represents the Entries and Clearances to and from Foreign Ports only.

ENTERED.

Nationality.	Sailing. Number of Vessels.	Tons.	Steam. Number of Vessels	Tons.	Total. Number of Vessels.	Tons.
British	6	5,335	378	489,968	384	496,303
American	6	2,220	3	4,000	9	6,220
Spanish	...	...	36	58,925	36	58,925
Italian	7	3,464	...	...	7	3,464
Norwegian	...	...	13	7,363	13	7,363
German	...	...	2	2,669	2	2,669
Total	19	11,019	432	562,925	451	573,944

BALTIMORE.

Cleared.

Nationality.	Sailing.		Steam.		Total	
	Number of Vessels.	Tons.	Number of Vessels.	Tons.	Number of Vessels.	Tons.
British	7	7,085	376	488,038	383	495,123
American	28	10,268	5	5,034	33	15,302
Spanish	...	...	36	58,925	36	58,925
Italian	7	3,464	...	...	7	3,464
Norwegian	...	...	13	7,363	13	7,363
German	...	...	2	2,669	2	2,669
Total	42	20,817	432	562,029	474	582,846

TABLE showing the Principal Articles of Export and Import at this Port during the past Year.

Exports.

Articles.		Quantity.	Value.
			£
Cotton	Bales	286,666	..
Resin	Barrels	3,257	..
Tallow	,,	37	..
Cattle	Head	1,031	..
Tobacco	Hhds. and t'cs.	310	..
Factory sweepings	Bales	430	..
Machinery	Boxes	2	..
Grain	Bushels	38,728	..
Benzine	Cases	15	..
Flour	Sacks	5,450	..
Beef and pork	Barrels	50	..
Flour	,,	50	..
Poplar logs	Cars	2	..
,,	Numbers	3,044	..
Poplar plank	Cars	7	..
,,	Pieces	2,204	..
Ash logs	Number	1,160	..
Hardwood	Pieces	99	..
Gum Logs	Number	13	..
Dogwood	Tons	240	..
Persimmon and dogwood	Pieces	13,232	..
Spokes	Cases	105	..
,,	Number	21,969	..
Shuttle blocks	Crates	1,687	..
Oak plank	Pieces	27,032	..
,,	Cars	282	..
Oak lumber	Tons	210	..
Yellow pine	Pieces	16,282	..
Walnut logs	Number	1,058	..
,, lumber	Pieces	4,383	..
Clothes pins	Cases	2,000	..
Shingles	Number	800,000	..
Hickory logs	,,	814	..
Holly ,,	,,	36	..
Fence	Bales	146	..
Staves	Cars	19	..
,,	Pieces	4,267,164	..
Cedar	,,	520	..
Treenails	,,	12,573	..
Coal	Tons	140,478	..
Total	..	..	3,039,419

UNITED STATES.

Imports.

Articles.		Quantity.	Value.
			£
Salt	Lbs.	554,320	..
Ale	Barrels	100	..
Cotton ties	Bundles	39,600	..
Wine	Casks	4	..
,,	Octaves	16	..
Sylvenit	Lbs.	440,920	..
Kainit	,,	2,625,679	..
Manure salt	,,	672,403	..
Phosphate earth	Tons	375	..
Nitrate of soda	Bags	8,163	..
Sperm oil	Barrels	260	..
,, ,,	Gallons	9,000	..
Total		..	18,114

The foregoing indicates the growth of Norfolk's trade. Her prosperity is largely due to her cotton trade, in which she ranks the fourth in this country.

Cotton. Her location as a cotton market makes this one of the most desirable points for the manufacture of cotton goods in the United States, superior to the inland towns throughout the cotton belt in the south, because in each of these there is only marketed the product of the immediate neighbourhood; this is usually handled in three or four months, and a factory located there necessarily has in that time to purchase a year's supply, and if, for any cause, the quality of the cotton in the immediate neighbourhood is unsuited for its purposes, it is placed in the difficult position of having to draw its supplies from other localities; but Norfolk, being a large cotton market, not only furnishes an assortment of grades and quality, but enables the manufacturer to purchase his stock all the year.

Its advantages over southern seaport towns, as a manufacturing point, lies in its accessibility to New York and Boston, and other markets for the purchase of such supplies as the manufacturer frequently needs on short notice in connection with his business, while its railroad lines to the interior—north, west, and south—enable the manufacturer to distribute his goods to every point reached by rail in the United States.

Labour. Norfolk has thus far been exempt from those labour troubles and strikes which have characterised those other and larger manufacturing cities of the North.

In addition to the manufacture of cotton goods there is at Norfolk opportunity for profitable manufacture of furniture and all other articles made of wood, the close proximity of all kinds of lumber, such as ash, oak, pine, poplar, cypress, cedar, juniper, gum, &c., offer to such industries an abundant supply of cheap raw material.

Manufactures of stoves, sash, doors, and blinds, hardware, &c., will also find here raw material, cheap fuel, cheap labour, and everything necessary to profitable operating.

The cost of labour ranges from 1 dol. to 1 dol. 50 c. per day Wages. for unskilled men, and 2 dol. to 5 dol. for skilled men; females, 50 c. to 75 c. a day unskilled, and 75 c. to 2 dol. a day for skilled; boys, 33 c. to 1 dol. per day; girls, 25 c. to 1 dol. 25 c. per day. These quotations are for white labour, the negro not being adapted to labour in manufactories.

To those seeking commercial opportunities, Norfolk offers a field for the establishment of jobbing houses in dry goods, boots and shoes, hats, caps, notions, crockery, drugs, tinwares, and all other kinds, excepting wholesale groceries, in which she is fully supplied.

The cities lying to the south and west of the port of Norfolk are the markets to which goods from here are distributed in exchange for cotton, corn, oats, and wheat, and other crops.

LONDON:
Printed for Her Majesty's Stationery Office,
By HARRISON AND SONS,
Printers in Ordinary to Her Majesty.
(1250   3 | 91—H & S   1036)

FOREIGN OFFICE.
1891.
ANNUAL SERIES.

Nº 843.

DIPLOMATIC AND CONSULAR REPORTS ON TRADE AND FINANCE.

UNITED STATES.

REPORT FOR THE YEAR 1890
ON THE
TRADE OF BOSTON (MASS.)

REFERENCE TO PREVIOUS REPORT, Annual Series No. 664.

Presented to both Houses of Parliament by Command of Her Majesty, April, 1891.

LONDON:
PRINTED FOR HER MAJESTY'S STATIONERY OFFICE,
BY HARRISON AND SONS, ST. MARTIN'S LANE,
PRINTERS IN ORDINARY TO HER MAJESTY.

And to be purchased, either directly or through any Bookseller, from
EYRE & SPOTTISWOODE, EAST HARDING STREET, FLEET STREET, E.C., and
32, ABINGDON STREET, WESTMINSTER, S.W.; or
JOHN MENZIES & Co., 12, HANOVER STREET, EDINBURGH, and
88 and 90, WEST NILE STREET, GLASGOW; or
HODGES, FIGGIS, & Co., 104, GRAFTON STREET, DUBLIN.

1891.
Price One Penny.

[C 6205—74.]

New Series of Reports.

Reports of the Annual Series have been issued from Her Majesty's Diplomatic and Consular Officers at the following places, and may be obtained from the sources indicated on the title-page:—

No.		Price.	No.		Price.
725.	Tientsin	1d.	784.	Naples	1½d.
726.	Foochow	1d.	785.	Tunis	4d.
727.	Port au Prince	½d.	786.	Vera Cruz	1d.
728.	Callao	1d.	787.	Tangier	1½d.
729.	Puerto Plata	½d.	788.	Rome	2d.
730.	San Francisco	1d.	789.	Stuttgart	1½d.
731.	Philadelphia	2½d.	790.	Panama	1½d.
732.	Pakhoi	1d.	791.	Berne	1½d.
733.	Bilbao	1d.	792.	Asuncion	½d.
734.	Dunkirk	1d.	793.	Bahia	7½d.
735.	Vienna	1d.	794.	Monte Video	1½d.
736.	Nantes	1½d.	795.	Munich	2d.
737.	Paramaribo	1d.	796.	Bucharest	1d.
738.	Honolulu	½d.	797.	Tokio	1d.
739.	Chicago	2d.	798.	Tabreez	1d.
740.	Söul	1d.	799.	Antwerp	1d.
741.	Brindisi	1½d.	800.	Malaga	1d.
742.	Mozambique	1d.	801.	Odessa	1d.
743.	Caldera and Lota	1½d.	802.	Malaga	2d.
744.	Nice	1½d.	803.	Amsterdam	1d.
745.	Aleppo	1d.	804.	Bogotá	1½d.
746.	Hakodate	1d.	805.	Guayaquil	½d.
747.	New York	2d.	806.	Lima	1d.
748.	Cagliari	1d.	807.	Rio de Janeiro	3d.
749.	San Salvador	1d.	808.	Dantzig	1½d.
750.	Gothenburg	2d.	809.	Florence	1½d.
751.	Nagasaki	1d.	810.	Lisbon	1d.
752.	Sofia	3½d.	811.	Quito	½d.
753.	Meshed	1d.	812.	Para	½d.
754.	Yokohama	2½d.	813.	Palermo	2½d.
755.	Shanghai	2d.	814.	Copenhagen	1d.
756.	Lisbon	1½d.	815.	Serajevo	½d.
757.	Teneriffe	½d.	816.	Porto Rico	1d.
758.	Noumea	½d.	817.	Madrid	½d.
759.	Tahiti	½d.	818.	Brussels	½d.
760.	Bushire	1½d.	819.	Patras	½d.
761.	Frankfort	2d.	820.	Stuttgart	1d.
762.	Palermo	2½d.	821.	Taganrog	1d.
763.	Guatemala	1d.	822.	Salonica	2d.
764.	Smyrna	4d.	823.	Galveston	1d.
765.	Munich	2d.	824.	Rome	1½d.
766.	Hiogo	1½d.	825.	Paris	1½d.
767.	Alexandria	1½d.	826.	Bushire	½d.
768.	Maracaibo	½d.	827.	New Orleans	3d.
769.	Macao	1d.	828.	Buda-Pesth	½d.
770.	Canton	1d.	829.	Hamburg	3d.
771.	Bangkok	2½d.	830.	Port Said	1d.
772.	Stockholm	1¼d.	831.	Samoa	½d.
773.	Jaffa	½d.	832.	Guayaquil	½d.
774.	Copenhagen	½d.	833.	New Orleans	2d.
775.	Ningpo	½d.	834.	The Piræus	1d.
776.	Stettin	2d.	835.	Baltimore	1½d.
777.	St. Petersburg	3d.	836.	Trieste	2d.
778.	St. Petersburg	½d.	837.	Galatz	1½d.
779.	St. Jago de Cuba	1½d.	838.	Wênchow	1d.
780.	Chefoo	1d.	839.	Havre	2½d.
781.	Christiania	3½d.	840.	Rome	1½d.
782.	Marseilles	½d.	841.	Taganrog	2d.
783.	Baghdad	1d.	842.	Calais	1d.

No. 843.

Reference to previous Report, Annual Series No. 664.

UNITED STATES.

BOSTON.

Consul Henderson to the Marquis of Salisbury.

My Lord,   Boston, *March* 5, 1891.

I HAVE the honour to enclose a Report on the Trade and Commerce of Boston and the Boston Consular District for the year 1890.

I have, &c.
(Signed)   C. A. HENDERSON.

Report on the Trade and Commerce of Boston and the Boston Consular District for the Year 1890.

Throughout this consular district trade was, generally speaking, fairly active during the greater part of the year, and, whilst unaffected by any important or prolonged strikes, was, for some time, stimulated by the effort to forestall the increased duties and anticipated higher prices not only of foreign, but of home products, under the new tariff, which came into force on October 6 last. Owing, however, to a large increase in the number of firms in business, to close competition, and to losses occasioned by some heavy failures, profits were, in many branches, very small, and were further reduced during the latter part of the year by a stringent money market, which, while it lasted, seriously curtailed business transactions generally. [General condition of trade.]

Cotton continued high during the first seven months of the year, advancing from 11 c. ($5\frac{1}{2}d.$) in January, to $12\frac{1}{4}$ c. ($6\frac{1}{8}d.$) in July, and then gradually declining to $9\frac{5}{16}$ c. ($4\frac{5}{8}d.$) in December (the lowest price for eight years), in consequence of the large and rather poor quality of the year's crop, and, latterly, of the depressed condition of the money market. [Cotton and cotton goods.]

In cotton goods a fair business was done for home consumption, whilst a temporary advance in the price of silver increased exports of brown cottons and drills. Prices, however, ruled low, especially for print cloths, with which the market was overstocked.

Wool and woollens.

The price for wool was generally lower than in the previous year, from which, owing to a mild winter, large stocks of woollen goods and clothing were left unsold, whilst, in anticipation of the new tariff imposing higher duties, heavy importations were made of foreign goods. These circumstances rendered the demand for wool, on the part of the manufacturers, less urgent; but they took advantage, nevertheless, of the low market to make large purchases for future use, in the hope of being ultimately able to benefit from increased protection. The success of the low tariff party, at the recent political elections throughout the country, has, however, somewhat discouraged them from extending their operations, and they are not only greatly disappointed with the year's business, but less hopeful in regard to their prospects for the future.

Hides and leather.

The hide market fluctuated considerably during the greater part of the year, due principally to sharp alterations in supply and demand of domestic and foreign hides, but became more steady towards the end of the year, with light stocks on hand, and importations sold in advance.

The year opened with a large supply of leather unsold, and tanners found it necessary not only to curtail production, but to dispose of their old stocks at any price. By this means, which induced large purchases to be made for exportation, prices went up for a time, but late in the year a heavy decline again took place, followed, however, by a moderate advance at its close.

Boots and shoes.

The boot and shoe trade was very active, sales mounting up to 3,575,000 cases, or 140,000 cases in excess of those of 1889, which had been the largest business year on record. The low price of leather early in the year enabled manufacturers to fulfil large orders at low prices; but sharp competition, and the necessity of fulfilling previously-accepted orders, at a time when leather had advanced, reduced profits in many cases to a minimum.

Indiarubber.

Prices were unsteady throughout the year. From 80 c. (3s. 4d.) in January, fine Pará fell to 60 c. (2s. 6d.), then advanced as high as 1 dol. (4s.), declined again to 64 c. (2s. 8d.), and finally went up to 85 c. (3s. 6½d.) at the end of the year. These variations were, in great measure, due to foreign speculation, though also, to a certain extent, to the large stock of rubber goods on hand at the beginning of the year, to an occasional heavy demand for these goods later on, and to an increasing consumption for electrical purposes.

Iron and other metals.

The consumption of pig-iron was very large, but altogether the supply of native iron exceeded that of 1889, and prices were generally lower, with a steady market, during the whole year.

Steel rails were in good demand, and prices were steady at 30 dol. to 34 dol. (6l. to 6l. 16s.) during 10 months, when they fell to 28 dol. (5l. 12s.), in consequence of the demoralised condition of the money market.

Lumber was in demand at fair prices, a large amount of building, especially in and around Boston, having been undertaken to supply the increasing demand for dwelling-houses, stores, and offices—a new feature as regards the latter being the erection of blocks, 10 stories to 12 stories high, the uppermost of which are now easily reached by the universal use of elevators or lifts. The furniture trade has also been active owing to the general introduction, at moderate prices, of new artistic styles, hitherto rare and exceedingly costly. *[Lumber, building, and furniture trades.]*

Receipts of coal at Boston were 1,740,564 tons anthracite, and 964,857 tons bituminous, domestic, and 14,072 tons bituminous from Canada, being 150,000 tons more than in the previous year, notwithstanding an advance in prices. *[Coal trade.]*

The grain crops were all more or less reduced by an exceptionally hot and dry summer, and prices ruled higher than in 1889, especially for oats, which, with an increased acreage, only reached 70 per cent. of the average yield. *[Flour and grain.]*

The demand for fresh and packed meats was brisk throughout the year, both for consumption and exportation, and prices were well maintained. The produce market was also very active, and prices, on the whole, were satisfactory to farmers. *[Provisions and produce.]*

The mackerel catch of the New England fleet, which in 1889 had fallen to 22,000 barrels from 478,000 barrels in 1884, only reached 19,000 barrels in 1890. One vessel was sent experimentally to the South African coast, where in nine months she caught 900 barrels of mackerel; and the venture will probably be repeated in 1891 on a larger scale. *[Fish.]*

Imports of mackerel from Canada, Norway, and Ireland, were 73,000 barrels, against 39,000 barrels in 1889. Prices ranged from 10 dol. to 30 dol. (2l. to 6l.) per barrel, according to quality and packing. Norwegian brought the highest prices, and Irish the lowest, being, in fact, in some cases, unsaleable, from improper and careless packing.

The New England catch of cod and other ground fish was 436,650 quintals—a large falling-off from the average of the previous four years—prices for codfish ranging from 3 dol. 75 c. to 6 dol. (15s. to 24s.) per quintal, or somewhat higher than those realised since the year 1882.

Foreign imports at Boston in the year 1890 amounted to 13,213,000l., of which 3,605,000l. represented free goods, and 9,608,000l. dutiable goods. Foreign exports, of which 14,428,300l. were domestic, and 69,500l. foreign goods re-exported, amounted to 14,497,800l. These amounts, as compared with the previous year, show an increase in imports of 163,500l., and in exports of 328,300l. *[Foreign commerce.]*

The arrivals at the port of Boston in 1890 of vessels direct from foreign ports, as shown by the custom-house returns, were 2,335 vessels, of 1,464,797 tons. Of these, 1,793 vessels, of 1,156,922 tons, were British, 162 vessels, of 109,533 tons, were of other foreign nationalities, and 380 vessels, of 198,342 tons, were under the United States flag. Compared with the previous year, British vessels showed an increase of 21 vessels, and 52,251 tons; *[Foreign maritime trade.]*

(1058)

other foreign vessels, an increase of 6 vessels, and 9,842 tons; and American vessels, a decrease of 56 vessels, and 21,542 tons; the decrease in vessels being altogether 29 vessels, and the increase in tonnage 40,551 tons.

The total arrivals of British vessels at Boston from foreign and United States ports, as recorded at the Consulate, were 1,827 vessels, of 1,169,732 tons, namely, 604 steamers, of 1,030,771 tons, and 1,223 sailing vessels, of 138,961 tons; steamers showing an increase of 93 vessels, and 108,720 tons, and sailing vessels a decrease of 78 vessels, and 54,439 tons, or an actual increase of 15 vessels, and 54,281 tons.

Ocean freights. Ocean freights inwards averaged 4s. on pig-iron, 6s. on bar-iron, 9s. and 10s. on paper stock, 10s. on bleach, 5s. on soda ash, 6s. and 7s. 6d. on earthenware, 1s. and 4s. on salt, 20s. on wool in compressed bales, and 7s. on machinery.

Outward freights on live cattle were 65s. and 70s. per head; dead meat, on established contract rates for space occupied by refrigerators; grain, 5d. in January, 1d. in July, 3d. in December; flour in sacks, 18s. 9d. in January, 4s. in August, 12s. 6d. in December; provisions, 27s. 6d. in January, 8s. in July, and 17s. 6d. in December; cotton, 2s. 1½d. in January, 10d. in April, per 100 lbs.—$\frac{3}{32}$d. in September, $\frac{5}{32}$d. in December, per lb.; leather, 45s. and 50s. in January, 30s. and 40s. in December.

Sterling exchange. The rate of exchange for bankers' sight bills opened in January at 4 dol. 83½ c. per 1l., rose rapidly to 4 dol. 87¾ c., then fluctuated between 4 dol. 83½ c., and 4 dol. 89½ c. to December, and closed with the year at 4 dol. 83½ c.

Mercantile failures. The number of mercantile firms in this consular district which had declined in 1889 by 719 to 78,121, increased in 1890 by 599 to 78,720, whilst the number of failures was 886, a decrease of 211, and the amount of their liabilities 4,458,072l., a decrease of 76,928l. as compared with 1889.

Population, immigration, and education. The population of the State of Massachusetts, according to the hitherto unpublished United States Census of 1890, is reported to be 2,238,943, an increase of 455,853, or 25·57 per cent., since the date of the United States Census of 1880.

The number of immigrants into Massachusetts in 1890 was 51,367, of whom 20,336 came from the United Kingdom, 19,781 from Canada, and 11,250 from all other countries.

From the report of the Massachusetts State Board of Education for 1890, it appears that the number of persons between five and 15 years of age was 370,116, and that of pupils in the public schools was 371,493, or an increase on the previous year of 8,326 pupils, and the average attendance 273,910.

The number of public schools was 7,147, showing an increase of 700 in five years. In addition to these, 52 cities and towns maintained 201 evening schools, with an average of 13,972 pupils. The number of teachers in public schools was 1,017 men and 9,307 women. The average of monthly salaries of teachers was 25l. 2s. 4d. for men, and 8l. 19s. 2d. for women. The aggregate expense of public schools for the year was 1,657,212l., or an average of 4*l*. 11*s*. 6½*d*. for each child between five and 15 years of age.

The number of private schools in the State was 419, and of academies 92, or a total of 511, against 485 in the previous year. The number of pupils in private schools was 41,044, and in academies 17,135; and the amount paid for tuition was estimated at 145,000*l*., and 80,800*l*. respectively.

Annex A.—RETURN of all Shipping in the Foreign Trade at Ports in the Boston Consular District in the Fiscal Year ended June 30, 1890.

ENTERED.

Nationality.	Sailing. Number of Vessels.	Tons.	Steam. Number of Vessels.	Tons.	Total. Number of Vessels.	Tons.
Foreign	3,253	363,702	942	1,151,192	4,195	1,514,894
American	645	164,509	235	244,142	880	408,651
Total	3,898	528,211	1,177	1,395,334	5,075	1,923,545
„ for the year preceding	4,302	606,941	1,085	1,312,743	5,387	1,919,684

CLEARED.

Nationality.	Sailing. Number of Vessels.	Tons.	Steam. Number of Vessels.	Tons.	Total. Number of Vessels.	Tons.
Foreign	3,204	387,546	803	928,784	4,007	1,316,330
American	1,192	301,031	232	236,948	1,424	537,979
Total	4,396	688,577	1,035	1,165,732	5,431	1,854,309
„ for the year preceding	5,071	815,089	950	1,066,023	6,021	1,881,112

NOTE.—Sterling amounts in this report are given at the rate of 4*s*. to the dol.

UNITED STATES.

Annex B.—RETURN of Principal Articles of Export from and Import to Ports in the Boston Consular District during the Year ended June 30, 1890-89.

EXPORTS.

Articles.	Value. 1890.	Value. 1889.
	£	£
Meat and dairy products	5,824,578	4,510,951
Horned cattle	1,800,474	1,290,697
Corn, flour, and other bread stuffs	2,274,418	2,370,145
Raw cotton	1,558,497	2,636,909
Cotton manufactures	228,542	245,387
Tobacco in leaf and manufactured	305,855	196,517
Iron and steel, manufactures of	331,569	239,045
Sugar and molasses	22,638	19,298
All other domestic merchandise	2,894,782	2,809,567
Foreign merchandise re-exported	235,397	288,935
Coin and bullion	..	..
Total	15,476,750	14,607,451

IMPORTS.

Articles.	Value. 1890.	Value. 1889.
	£	£
Sugar and molasses	1,944,511	2,448,805
Wool	1,499,487	1,659,882
Woollen goods	711,165	890,009
Hides, goat and fur skins and furs	772,561	1,282,848
Iron ore, iron, and steel, manufactures of	945,971	1,063,358
Chemicals, drugs, and dyes	917,625	1,013,005
Flax, hemp, and jute	1,499,992	1,298,466
Cotton manufactures	302,579	265,696
Fish	407,300	371,518
All other goods (including domestic exports re-imported, valued in 1890 at 66,841*l*.)	5,559,517	5,111,511
Coin and bullion	9,863	15,844
Total	14,570,571	15,420,942

BOSTON.

Annex C.—TABLE showing the Value of all Articles Exported from and Imported to Ports in the Boston Consular District during the Fiscal Year ended June 30, 1890–89.

Country.	Exports. 1890.	Exports. 1889.	Imports. 1890.	Imports. 1889.
	£	£	£	£
United Kingdom and colonies	14,375,393	13,530,402	9,034,082	9,444,644
Spain and colonies	57,159	72,141	1,986,802	2,019,295
Germany	34,261	7,186	733,066	689,747
France and colonies	152,773	166,054	582,432	731,120
Argentine Republic	149,547	274,010	545,033	535,807
Belgium	282,608	173,890	285,547	272,790
Italy	6,121	..	262,367	253,913
Sweden and Norway	2,200	29,323	162,079	165,186
Chile	94,100	145,895	64,494	63,498
Netherlands and colonies	38,605	39,556	266,750	162,850
Brazil	1,716	1,074	32,127	142,955
Turkey	3,982	..	137,655	123,827
Mexico	..	..	84,654	246,251
All other countries	278,285	167,920	393,483	569,059
Total	15,476,750	14,607,451	14,570,571	15,420,942

LONDON:
Printed for Her Majesty's Stationery Office,
By HARRISON AND SONS,
Printers in Ordinary to Her Majesty.
(1250 4 | 91—H & S 1058)

FOREIGN OFFICE.
1891.
ANNUAL SERIES.

N°· 845.

DIPLOMATIC AND CONSULAR REPORTS ON TRADE AND FINANCE.

UNITED STATES.

REPORT FOR THE YEAR 1890
ON THE
TRADE OF CHARLESTON (S. CAROLINA.)

REFERENCE TO PREVIOUS REPORT, Annual Series No. 668.

Presented to both Houses of Parliament by Command of Her Majesty,
APRIL, 1891.

LONDON:
PRINTED FOR HER MAJESTY'S STATIONERY OFFICE,
BY HARRISON AND SONS, ST. MARTIN'S LANE,
PRINTERS IN ORDINARY TO HER MAJESTY.

And to be purchased, either directly or through any Bookseller, from
EYRE & SPOTTISWOODE, EAST HARDING STREET, FLEET STREET, E.C., and
32, ABINGDON STREET, WESTMINSTER, S.W.; or
JOHN MENZIES & Co., 12, HANOVER STREET, EDINBURGH, and
88 and 90, WEST NILE STREET, GLASGOW; or
HODGES, FIGGIS, & Co., 104, GRAFTON STREET, DUBLIN

1891.

[C. 6205—76.] *Price Three Halfpence.*

New Series of Reports.

Reports of the Annual Series have been issued from Her Majesty's Diplomatic and Consular Officers at the following places, and may be obtained from the sources indicated on the title-page:—

No.		Price.	No.		Price.
719.	Bussorah	½d.	782.	Marseilles	½d.
720.	Beyrout	1d.	783.	Baghdad	1d.
721.	Adrianople	½d.	784.	Naples	1½d.
722.	Nantes	½d.	785.	Tunis	4d.
723.	Caracas	1d.	786.	Vera Cruz	1d.
724.	Mogador	½d.	787.	Tangier	1½d.
725.	Tientsin	1d.	788.	Rome	2d.
726.	Foochow	1d.	789.	Stuttgart	1½d.
727.	Port au Prince	½d.	790.	Panama	1½d.
728.	Callao	1d.	791.	Berne	1½d.
729.	Puerto Plata	½d.	792.	Asuncion	½d.
730.	San Francisco	1d.	793.	Bahia	7½d.
731.	Philadelphia	2½d.	794.	Monte Video	1½d.
732.	Pakhoi	1d.	795.	Munich	2d.
733.	Bilbao	1d.	796.	Bucharest	1d.
734.	Dunkirk	1d.	797.	Tokio	1d.
735.	Vienna	1d.	798.	Tabreez	1d.
736.	Nantes	1½d.	799.	Antwerp	1d.
737.	Paramaribo	1d.	800.	Malaga	1d.
738.	Honolulu	½d.	801.	Odessa	1d.
739.	Chicago	2d.	802.	Malaga	2d.
740.	Söul	1d.	803.	Amsterdam	1d.
741.	Brindisi	1½d.	804.	Bogotá	1½d.
742.	Mozambique	1d.	805.	Guayaquil	½d.
743.	Caldera and Lota	1½d.	806.	Lima	1d.
744.	Nice	1½d.	807.	Rio de Janeiro	3d.
745.	Aleppo	1d.	808.	Dantzig	1½d.
746.	Hakodate	1d.	809.	Florence	1½d.
747.	New York	2d.	810.	Lisbon	1d.
748.	Cagliari	1d.	811.	Quito	½d.
749.	San Salvador	1d.	812.	Para	½d.
750.	Gothenburg	2d.	813.	Palermo	2½d.
751.	Nagasaki	1d.	814.	Copenhagen	1d.
752.	Sofia	3½d.	815.	Serajevo	½d.
753.	Meshed	1d.	816.	Porto Rico	1d.
754.	Yokohama	2½d.	817.	Madrid	½d.
755.	Shanghai	2d.	818.	Brussels	½d.
756.	Lisbon	1½d.	819.	Patras	½d.
757.	Teneriffe	½d.	820.	Stuttgart	1d.
758.	Noumea	½d.	821.	Taganrog	1d.
759.	Tahiti	½d.	822.	Salonica	2d.
760.	Bushire	1½d.	823.	Galveston	1d.
761.	Frankfort	2d.	824.	Rome	1½d.
762.	Palermo	2½d.	825.	Paris	1½d.
763.	Guatemala	1d.	826.	Bushire	½d.
764.	Smyrna	4d.	827.	New Orleans	3d.
765.	Munich	2d.	828.	Buda-Pesth	½d.
766.	Hiogo	1½d.	829.	Hamburg	3d.
767.	Alexandria	1½d.	830.	Port Said	1d.
768.	Maracaibo	½d.	831.	Samoa	½d.
769.	Macao	1d.	832.	Guayaquil	½d.
770.	Canton	1d.	833.	New Orleans	2d.
771.	Bangkok	2½d.	834.	The Piræus	1d.
772.	Stockholm	1½d.	835.	Baltimore	1½d.
773.	Jaffa	½d.	836.	Trieste	2d.
774.	Copenhagen	½d.	837.	Galatz	1½d.
775.	Ningpo	½d.	838.	Wênchow	1d.
776.	Stettin	2d.	839.	Havre	2½d.
777.	St. Petersburg	3d.	840.	Rome	1½d.
778.	St. Petersburg	½d.	841.	Taganrog	2d.
779.	St. Jago de Cuba	1½d.	842.	Calais	1d.
780.	Chefoo	1d.	843.	Boston	1d.
781.	Christiania	3½d.	844.	Bordeaux	2½d.

No. 845.

Reference to previous Report, Annual Series No. 668.

UNITED STATES.

CHARLESTON.

Consul St. John to the Marquis of Salisbury.

My Lord,   *Charleston, S.C., March* 9, 1891.

I HAVE the honour to transmit, herewith, a Report on the Trade and Commerce of Charleston for the year 1890.

I have, &c.
(Signed)   C. ST. JOHN.

Report on the Trade and Commerce of Charleston, South Carolina, for the Year 1890.

It will be seen from the facts and figures set forth in the following statements and tables that the general trade and commerce of Charleston for the year 1890 has undergone a marked improvement, when compared with the business of the port for the previous season; and while this improvement is undoubtedly due in part, at least, to the exceptionally fine cotton and other crops which have prevailed in this section of the country during the year, a fair proportion of the increased trade is also justly attributable to the improved terminal facilities that have been inaugurated and pushed forward with considerable energy and spirit towards partial completion, during the latter half of the season, by capitalists who have seen the necessities of the port in this respect, and have been enterprising enough to undertake this much-needed work. *General remarks.*

The improvements referred to, designed to connect by rail the different docks and wharves along the eastern and western water fronts, and place them in direct communication with the railway system of the country, have up to the present time only been completed as far south as the custom-house; but it is hoped and believed that they will be continued and extended so as to include all of the docks before the opening of the next commercial year. *Railways.*

This has been the first season in the history of Charleston when it has been possible for shipping to receive cotton directly *Cotton.*

(1064)

into their holds from the trucks at the town docks, without the necessity of breaking bulk for drayage or lighterage from the railway stations to the ships.

It is estimated that the total business of the past year amounted, in round numbers, to about 80,000,000 dol. (16,000,000*l.*), an increase of 4,000,000 dol. (800,000*l.*) over the year 1889. This increase in the cotton trade forms perhaps the most conspicuous feature.

From the opening of the cotton season on September 1, 1890, until December 31, 1890, the total receipts of cotton at Charleston amounted to 353,166 bales, against 294,564 received during the same four months of the previous year, and it is believed that before the end of the winter the receipts will have reached a figure approximating a total of 400,000 bales for the present year.

Shipping.

British shipping has naturally been favourably affected by this increase in the cotton traffic—as a reference to the shipping return for 1890 will show, 87 British ships (nearly all steamers) having arrived during 1890, against 63 in 1889.

While, however, there is much reason for a feeling of satisfaction at the improved condition which the trade here presents at the close of the season, and the better prospects which now give reasonable ground for hoping that a steady and permanent improvement will characterise the future, it is still, as it has been for many years past, a matter of great regret that no considerable increase has as yet been secured in the depth of water on Charleston bar.

The work on the jetties of the North or Swash Channel, which has been in progress for a number of years, continues to go forward with perhaps as much energy as it can be prosecuted by the Government engineers, who have this matter in charge; but the work has been a good deal retarded by insufficient appropriations on the part of Congress. It is expected, however, that a channel 22 feet deep will eventually be secured when the jetty system is finally completed.

A good deal of delay has been experienced by numbers of British steamers in getting to sea during the past winter, after they have taken in their cotton cargoes, for if their draught of water is but a few inches over 17 feet, it is only possible for them to get over the bar on the semi-monthly spring tides, and even then the conditions of a favourable direction of the wind and a moderate sea must prevail; otherwise, they must remain over until the next spring tides, and take their chances of having to face the same difficulties over again.

Hence, it has not unfrequently been the case days and weeks have been lost by British and other ships owing to detention from these causes, with the resulting loss to owners, charterers, or others concerned, in some instances of a serious nature.

It is not likely that the jetties can be completed, and the new or north channel opened up, for at least several years to come; but once this means of entrance to the harbour is finished, it will afford not only a deeper water channel, but also a very much more convenient and direct means of entrance to and exit from the port than the south channel route now used.

In addition to this the jetties, when completed, will doubtless prove an excellent breakwater; acting as a protection to the harbour against the south-east storms, occasionally prevailing in the autumn, causing sometimes a good deal of injury to the shipping and docks on the eastern side of the city.

There has been no material change in the conditions of the different railway feeders of Charleston from those which existed one year ago.

Railways. The South Carolina Railway, which is by far the most important of the three main lines entering this town, so far as the local interests and prosperity of Charleston are concerned, is still in the hands of a receiver, who will continue to manage and run the road until the courts decide to put the property up and sell it to the highest bidder.

The eventual result of the sale will probably be that the road will become absorbed by one of the three great railway combinations in this section known as the Louisville and Nashville, the Richmond and Danville, and the Georgia central systems, either one of which could doubtless use this property with great advantage to themselves, but whether it will be with advantage to Charleston or not remains to be seen.

The probabilities, however, are that great efforts will be made by local interests to have the road finally connected with one of the western lines, like the Louisville and Nashville Railway, in which case it would become a most valuable feeder, drawing to this port the products and commerce of the west.

Trade. The subjoined tables will show the amount and the money value of the trade of Charleston during the past commercial year:—

Amount of Trade, 1889-90.

Articles.		Quantity.
Cotton, Uplands..	Bales ..	342,572
„ Sea Islands	Bags ..	7,256
Rice	Barrels ..	97,240
Turpentine	Casks ..	50,548
Rosin	Barrels ..	219,773
Phosphate rock (crude)..	Tons ..	349,762
„ „ (ground)	„ ..	1,250
Fertilisers	„ ..	261,650
Lumber and cross ties ..	..	73,397,400
Cotton goods (domestics)	Bales ..	63,467

UNITED STATES.

Total Values.

	Dollars.
Cotton, Uplands	15,415,740
„ Sea Islands	719,230
Rice	1,458,600
Turpentine	1,010,260
Rosin	384,602
Phosphate rock (crude)	4,000,000
„ „ (ground)	10,000
Fertilisers	5,494,650
Cotton goods (domestics, &c.)	3,490,685
Lumber and cross ties	807,371
Fruits and vegetables	1,480,090
Manufactures, exclusive of fertilisers	9,527,879
Wholesale and retail trade	36,820,000
Grand total	80,619,717
	(16,124,000*l.*)

Foreign trade.

The foreign trade of the port is shown in the following tables:—

The value of the imports for the last year was as follows:

Imports.

	Dollars.
September	14,397
October	103,081
November	90,519
December	63,371
January	74,159
February	72,269
March	47,532
April	28,477
May	42,344
June	22,809
July	62,422
August	61,852
Total	683,232
	(136,646*l.*)

Exports.

	Dollars.
September	1,170,621
October	2,459,230
November	4,043,776
December	2,837,067
January	687,530
February	1,015,825
March	883,299
April	174,738
May	149,345
June	140,973
July	140,595
August	104,674
Total	13,807,673
	(2,761,534*l.*)

Cotton

The cotton trade one year ago was in a very depressed condition, the receipts of the port for the cotton year of 1889–90 amounting to but 349,828 bales, against 416,490 bales received the previous year, showing a decrease of 66,662 bales for the season.

Several causes contributed to this falling-off in the receipts; but the main reason was owing to the railway connection enabling the competing ports of Savannah, Wilmington, and Norfolk to greatly curtail the movement of the staple to this port, whose future prosperity was indeed so seriously threatened by this rivalry that it became evident, if not promptly met by an united effort on the part of the merchants and business men here, that Charleston would be unable to maintain her present position in the scale of American cotton ports. The depressed condition of this trade appeared to have reached a crisis last spring, when the South Carolina Railway was placed in the hands of a receiver.

There seemed, however, to have been a change for the better in the tide of affairs since the middle of last summer. The building of the east and west shore technical railways in the autumn, and the larger and more modern cotton compresses now being erected, caused an improvement to take place, which bids fair to work a new and more prosperous era in the cotton trade of the port.

The total cotton crop of the United States for the year amounted to 7,263,076 bales of the staple, of which 5,831,276 bales were received at the different ports for foreign and coastwise exportation; while 908,800 bales represent the net overland movement to Canada, the Eastern and Western States, the remainder, 523,000 bales, was consumed by the southern cotton mills.

Of the total port receipts Charleston received, as already stated, 349,828 bales, and the exports from this place were as follows:—

Exports—Foreign.

	Bales.
To Liverpool	48,706
Havre	24,070
Continental ports	164,802
Total foreign	237,578

Exports to Domestic Ports.

	Bales.
To New York	89,344
Interior points by rail	2,531
Total domestic	91,875
Grand total of foreign and domestic exports	329,453

The crop of long staple or Sea Island cotton for the season just closed, September 1, 1889, to September 1, 1891, has been one of the largest yielded in 25 years, owing to the favourable weather that prevailed throughout the year.

Carolina Sea Islands, of medium fine quality, opened at 27 c. per lb. in September, were quoted at 26½ c. in November, 27¼ c. in December, 26½ c. in January, 27 c. being the price paid for the last sales made.

Sea Island cotton.

UNITED STATES.

Extra fine Carolinas were in good demand at 34 c. to 35 c., and almost the entire production was sold before January 1.

Floridas of fine quality opened in September at 25 c., but declined by November to 23 c., advancing again to 24 c. before the close of the month, and ranging from that figure down to $23\frac{1}{4}$ c., the price paid in March.

Receipts and exports of Sea Islands.

The receipts and exports of South Carolina, Georgia, and Florida Sea Island cotton during the year 1889–90 at Charleston were as follows:—

RECEIPTS.

	Bags.
Receipts of Islands	7,170
Georgias and Floridas	86
Old stock	3
Total for year	7,259

EXPORTS.

	Bags.
Exports of Islands	7,108
Georgias and Floridas	86
Stock of Islands	67
Total for year	7,261

Of the exports of Sea Islands from Charleston, 4,673 bags were sent to Liverpool, 411 bags to Havre, and 2,108 bags went coastwise to New York.

The foregoing figures for the cotton year proper, ending September 1, 1890, may be supplemented by the following statements, indicating the trade in Sea Islands at this port from September 1, 1890, to December 31, 1890, these months being the first four of what is commercially known as the cotton season of 1890–91.

The total receipts of Sea Islands at Charleston from September 1, 1890, to January 1, 1891, amounted to 8,917 bags, showing an increase for these four months of the new season of 1,658 bags, over the total receipts of 7,259 bags for the entire 12 months of the previous year.

The total exports from September 1, 1890, to January 1, 1891, were 4,061 bags, leaving a stock on hand and ship board, January 1, 1891, of 4,967 bags, against 1,009 bags on hand for the corresponding date of the previous year.

The prices, however, for the first day of the new year for long staple cottons are not so good as they were 12 months ago, and although the market is quoted as active with sales of 634 bags for the last week of the year, the prices for medium fine Sea Islands are but 20 c. per lb., while 1 c. less is offered for cotton one grade lower in colour.

Phosphate mining, phosphates, and fertilisers.

The phosphate mining and fertiliser industry, so important a factor in the trade of this town and State, continues to add to their material prosperity, and has proved itself more profitable to those engaged in it this year than for any other in the history of this department of Charleston's trade; notwithstanding the fact that a widespread fear took possession of many of the Carolina miners, early in the year, by the discovery and partial development of the Florida rock deposits.

There are very good reasons, however, why the Carolina rock, in competition with the Florida article, should be able to maintain its own ground. In the first place, it is nearly chemically perfect as a source of supply, or basis, for the manufacture of acid phosphate and similar compounds; the supply, too, is regular and uniform as to quality; it contains no appreciable quantity of deleterious substances, has a high percentage of phosphate of lime, is low in carbonate, iron, and alumina, is of good colour when calcined, becomes crisp and dries well after being treated with acid, without afterwards absorbing moisture and becoming lumpy, and, moreover, it is easy to grind.

These reasons, being better understood now than a year ago, have naturally given rise to confidence and assurance to Carolina miners that they will hold their own individuality in the prospective competition with Florida rock.

Governor Tillman, who has recently been inaugurated into office as the Governor of South Carolina, has taken great interest in the phosphate industry, and has been recently engaged, together with the State phosphate commissioners, in making a series of inspections and investigations into the practical workings of the various phosphate mines and mills, with a view of so familiarising himself with this business as will enable him to recommend to the State Legislature the enactment of laws relative to the imposition of royalties.

Full particulars of the Carolina phosphate industry for the year are set forth in detail under their proper heading in the tables which follow, from which those interested in this business will perhaps be able to form a fair idea of the condition of the trade for the past year. These tables show that the business throughout the State in this industry has been very active, with a large increase in the amount of rock mined and manufactured compared to a year ago.

Some of the phosphate mines have become exhausted, and there has been a great consumption of slag. German and French buyers have dealt to a considerable extent with this market, and Hamburg is becoming, and seems likely to continue to be, a good and constant customer for the future.

The Carolina Land Mining Companies have sufficient regular demands from the local mills and manufacturers to keep them busy; but, in addition to this, they have to supply the wants of the neighbouring towns of Savannah, Wilmington, Atlanta, Augusta, Columbia, &c., besides the shipments to northern consumers and the amounts exported to foreign markets.

The stock of river rock has all been disposed of at advanced prices, and the Land Rock Companies, who have a home demand for at least 33 per cent. of their supply, cannot now sell any quantity of dry rock.

The phosphate lands in this State were unfavourably affected by the Florida discoveries during the early part of the year; but only a few comparatively small parcels or tracts of these lands changed hands during that period, and to-day holders have a firmer faith than ever in their value, more especially since the London circular was issued, stating that cargoes of Florida rock shipped abroad were found to be loaded with iron and alumina.

Prices for rock are very firm, owing to the fact that many cargoes gone forward during the season, when analysed abroad, showed between 62 and 63 per cent. of fertilising elements; rock sold for foreign shipment thereby netting 8 dol. 44 c. (1*l*. 15*s*.) per ton.

The price of land rock per ton has been:—For crude, 6 dol. 25 c. (1*l*. 6*s*.) to 6 dol. 50 c. (1*l*. 7*s*.); for hot-air dried, 7 dol. 25 c. (1*l*. 10*s*. 2½*d*.) to 7 dol. 50 c. (1*l*. 11*s*. 3*d*.).

River rock has commanded 6 dol. 50 c. (1*l*. 7*s*.) for crude, and 7 dol. 25 c. (1*l*. 10*s*. 2½*d*.) for hot-air dried.

Production.

The following statement will show the amount of phosphates and fertilisers produced during the year:—

	Tons.
Charleston Mining and Manufacturing Company	100,000
William Gregg	30,000
C. C. Pinckney, junr.	30,000
Charles H. Drayton	15,000
Rose Mining Company	20,000
William M. L. Bradley	30,000
St. Andrew's Mines	25,000
Bolton Mines	25,000
Wando Phosphate Company	15,000
F. C. Fishburne	20,000
C. O. Campbell	15,000
F. J. Hanahan	25,000
E. B. Fishburne	20,000
Horseshoe Mines	20,000
Meadeville „	20,000
Mount Holly Company	40,000
Palmetto Mines	10,000
Shier Mines	5,000
Beaufort Phosphate Company	25,000
Coosaw Company	100,000
Carolina „	50,000
Farmers' „	30,000
Fripp Fertiliser Company	5,000
Oak Point Mines	40,000
Sea Island Chemical Company	50,000
Williman's Island Company	20,000
E. C. Williams	5,000

Shipments.

The following statement shows the coasting shipments of crude and ground rock from Charleston for the year:—

CHARLESTON.

To Baltimore..	55,000	tons crude.
Philadelphia	14,900	,, ,,
Elizabeth Port	5,400	,, ,,
Wilmington (Delaware)	7,900	,, ,,
Barren Island	6,529	,, ,,
New York	6,500	,, ,,
,, ,,	750	,, ground.
Mantua Creek	3,715	,, crude.
Weymouth	18,980	,, ,,
Richmond	5,945	,, ,,
Seaford	1,800	,, ,,
Newtown Creek	1,646	,, ,,
Wilmington (North Carolina)	3,438	,, ,,
Other ports	2,285	,, ,,
,, ,,	500	,, ground.
Total coastwise	134,038	,, crude.
,, ,,	1,250	,, ground.

The total shipments of crude and ground rock from Charleston over the different railways to interior points and the west amounted to 65,748 tons; while the exports to foreign countries were 48,716 tons, and the amount consumed by the mills here 100,000 tons.

The year has been a very good one for the fertiliser business; the sellers having nearly their own way up to the end of the season. The companies have doubled their capacity during the year, new companies being formed, and the fertiliser interests more thoroughly advertised than ever among dealers and consumers. *Fertilisers.*

Some of Charleston's leading bankers have shown their confidence in the prospects of the business, and faith in the future of this town, by organising two new companies—the "Chicora" and the "Imperial."

These will add at least 50,000 tons to the supply for sale next year, and would seem to warrant the establishment of two mining companies to furnish the additional crude rock that will be required.

A favourable feature in this industry is the fact that the Western States, the great granary of the country, are beginning to use the Carolina fertilisers for the production of wheat, corn, barley, and oats. And it is believed that Chicago, Cincinnati, Detroit, Kansas City, and Minneapolis will soon become great fertiliser centres.

The total shipment of manufactured fertilisers from Charleston for the year was 261,650 tons.

The demand for commercial manures, constantly increasing in different directions, necessarily requires the importation of considerable quantities of chemicals used in their manufacture.

The imports of these chemicals are as follows :—

UNITED STATES.

IMPORTS of Chemicals into Charleston during the Year ending September 1, 1890.

	Quantity.	Value.
	Tons.	Dollars.
Kainit	13,619	93,376
Brimstone	19,302	324,938
Nitrate of soda	3,284	104,273
Muriate of potash	2,730	90,058
Total	38,935	612,645

Rice.

The rice season for 1889-90 was very favourable, and the yield both in South Carolina and Georgia exceeded that of the year before, the crop harvested being in excellent condition.

From September 1, 1889, to August 31, 1890, the town mills here received 799,144 bushels of rough rice, against 612,832 bushels for the same period of the year before, showing an increase for the season just closed of 186,312 bushels.

The total receipts at all the mills in the State for the year were 1,070,278 bushels, and those of the year before 867,060 bushels, an increase of 203,218 bushels.

The first shipment of new rice at the opening of the season last year was received on August 30: it was milled at the West Point Mills, and placed on the market for sale on September 2.

This was immediately followed by other shipments.

The market opened at $4\frac{1}{2}$ c. per lb.; later on, in September and October, good grades advanced to 5 c. Prices fell off a little during the winter, but became firmer in March, and continued so as the spring advanced.

At this time the high prices of foreign rice and the apparent probability that the stock of American rice remaining on hand would be insufficient to supply the wants of the country caused a sharp advance to take place, and high prices were maintained for the rest of the business season, towards the close of which 6 c. was freely paid for the light stock left in the mills. Before the end of the year the entire crop was disposed of, and the mills were thoroughly overhauled and put in good condition for handling the new crop.

The harvesting of the rice-crop for the season of 1890-91 was fairly under way by September 1, 1890, the weather up to this time having been as good as could be desired, and the yield on most of the rivers promising to exceed that of the year before, although there had been less rice planted on the Cooper River plantations than usual, and some further diminution from the ordinary yield was experienced from drought that prevailed during the spring months.

The Ashepoo River rice lands also suffered severely for want of water at a time when it was much needed, but from the

CHARLESTON.

plantations on the other rivers no serious losses have been reported.

The first parcel of the new rice crop for the season of 1890–91, consisting of 481 bushels, reached Charleston on August 25. It was immediately milled and sold on the 26th of the same month for 6½ c. per lb.

The quality was unusually good for such early rice.

Until the season of 1883–84 rice was usually packed for market in tierces, each having an average weight of 600 lbs. net; but for the past six seasons it has been packed in barrels weighing about 300 lbs. net each. *Receipts and exports of rice.*

The total amount of the South Carolina rice crop milled in this State during the year was 101,443 barrels, of which 76,095 barrels were milled in Charleston, and 25,348 barrels at Georgetown.

The total shipments of rice for the year were as follows:—

	Barrels.
To New York	4,153
Foreign ports	150
Interior points by rail	38,547
Town consumption	17,000

The total amount of rice received at Charleston from September 1, 1890, to January 1, 1891, was 26,462 barrels, while the total exported for the same period was 33,260 barrels, all being sent to domestic ports, or interior towns of the United States.

The receipts of naval stores have increased in volume during the past year, and the good prices prevailing in this branch of trade had a stimulating effect, and caused receipts to keep well up with the record of previous years, notwithstanding the fact that the pine forests in this section are being gradually exhausted. *Naval stores.*

The prices for turpentine have averaged higher than last year, owing to the fact that an advance took place earlier in this season, and have been well sustained since, although the closing price for spirits was lower than for the corresponding period of the previous crop year.

Rosin has also been higher in price throughout the entire season, and the outlook for the next year, as far as can be forecast, is encouraging.

The following statements show the receipts and exports of naval stores at Charleston for the period stated:—

RECEIPTS, Exports, and Stock of Naval Stores for the Year ended September 1, 1891.

	Spirits of Turpentine.	Rosin.
	Casks.	Barrels.
Stock on hand at the beginning of year	2,394	17,866
Receipts during year	50,548	219,773
Total	52,942	237,639

UNITED STATES.

Exports to Foreign Ports.

	Spirits.	Rosin.
	Casks.	Barrels.
To Rotterdam	4,812	12,873
Hamburg	1,872	27,965
Bristol	4,553	4,200
Goole	..	2,639
Cardiff	..	2,726
Trieste	100	22,877
Glasgow	1,750	4,020
Genoa	846	10,809
London	9,299	8,498
Garston Dock	150	5,082
Liverpool	..	3,158
Naples	..	2,352
Hull	200	3,700
Granton	..	3,613
Marseilles	..	2,375
Harburg	..	9,478
Riga	..	2,759
Barcelona	..	300
Venice	..	2,770
Stettin	..	5,033
Nordkopping	..	600
Sor's Helfors	..	2,156
Newcastle	..	3,200
Gottenburg	..	1,000
Total foreign	23,582	144,183

The coastwise exports of naval stores for the year were as follows:—

Coastwise exports.

	Spirits.	Rosin.
	Casks.	Barrels.
To New York	22,475	67,229
Interior by rail	3,175	6,453
Total	25,650	73,682

Recapitulation, 1889-90.

	Spirits.	Rosin.
	Casks.	Barrels.
Stock on hand September 1 and receipts to August 31	52,942	237,639
Total exports of foreign and domestic	49,232	217,865
Stock on hand	3,710	19,774

CHARLESTON.

Lumber. The lumber and timber business for the past year has been good, and the prospects are encouraging.

The hewn or ranging timber trade seems to have been less; the reason for this appears to lie in the fact that large resawn, or what is termed square and round timber, has been substituted for most purposes, because it is less expensive to handle, and this accordingly adds to the volume of the lumber trade.

There appears, however, to have been a falling-off in the foreign (transatlantic) shipments during the year, while the coast shipments show a large increase and good prospects for the future.

There has also been a substantial advance in the prices for all better grades of lumber, and inquiry is being constantly made for such.

The demand for home consumption for the ordinary purposes of building, as well as the improvements and extensive works on the water front, and manufactures now being carried on, has been largely supplied by mills situated on the lines of railways and rivers leading to Charleston, but this lumber is of an inferior quality generally, and is sold at correspondingly lower prices.

There are good opportunities for the supply of the very best grades of yellow pine and other lumber, while the recently acquired facilities for quick and inexpensive shipment must give to Charleston better chances hereafter to compete for this trade with ports that have heretofore been considered more highly favoured.

The completion of the terminal railway now partly built, together with the better prospective railway station and yard accommodations, will, it is believed, make it necessary to have a more extensive water front for the lumber trade of this port.

Exports of lumber. The exports of lumber, timber, and cross ties from the port of Charleston for the past year will be found in the following table:—

DOMESTIC.

		Feet.
To New York	..	30,638,452
Philadelphia	..	23,611,652
Baltimore	..	1,118,000
Other American ports	..	8,319,609
Total coastwise	..	63,687,713

FOREIGN.

		Feet.
To West Indies	..	4,268,437
Nova Scotia	..	430,000
Other foreign ports	..	11,250
Total foreign	..	4,709,687
Grand total	..	68,397,400

Manufactories and improvements. The manufacturing industries of Charleston have flourished during the year 1889-90, and show an increase on the figures of the preceding one both in the amount of capital invested and the value of the annual product.

14   UNITED STATES.

The total number of manufacturing enterprises have increased from 341 to 360, the number of hands employed from 4,838 to 5,722, and the capital invested from 6,946,000 dol. (1,450,000*l*.) to 8,997,500 dol. (1,900,000*l*.).

The value of the annual product has increased from 11,954,500 dol. (2,500,000*l*.) to 13,742,879 dol. (2,800,000*l*.), a gain for the year of nearly 1,788,379 dol. (300,000*l*.).

A large percentage of this increase is due to the heavy business done in commercial fertilisers, and the addition of new enterprises.

Two new fertiliser works have been organised this year, to which reference has already been made—the Imperial and the Chicora—and both of them will probably have their establishments completed and in operation during the coming season.

The business of manufacturing barrels has considerably increased, owing to the enlarged facilities which the Palmer Manufacturing Company have added to their works, and many of the other industries that have been in operation for less than 12 months contemplate starting the new year with increased capital and additional facilities; for instance, the Charleston ice factory will increase its capacity soon from 17 tons to 75 tons per day, while the mattress and woodware factory, the Imperial envelope and box factory, the Berkeley canning factory, and the Cosmos Fibre Company, will all operate, it is expected, during the year on a larger scale.

Two very important departments have been added to the Charleston cotton mill during the year—a bag factory and a Canton flannel factory. Both these departments are now completed, and will soon be able to fill orders for bags and flannel goods.

The cotton presses. The presses of Charleston have done a large business during the past year in compressing and handling cotton. Most of them have improved their plants, and the capacity of all has been increased.

Port Royal Harbour. During the past year the United States Government have taken the preliminary steps, and made the necessary subsidies of money, for the establishment of a large naval dry dock, and also a coaling station, at Port Royal, South Carolina.

This magnificent harbour, which is not only the finest in this State, but by far the best on the South Atlantic coast of the United States, has attracted a good deal of attention during the past year on account of the determination of the Government to avail itself of the advantages which Port Royal possesses as a commodious and deep-water harbour, easily accessible, and capable of accommodating the largest class of cruisers and other vessels now built.

It has also been brought into further prominence by reason of measures that have been taken by one or more projected lines of railways, which, it is understood, have in view the erection of necessary terminal facilities at this place for making it the South Atlantic port of entry and export for a considerable system of railways leading to the coal mines of Alabama and Tennessee, and the grain fields of the West.

In consequence of the proposed development of Port Royal, there has been a good deal of activity in the prices of lands and real estate in the locality, and some considerable transactions have taken place at good prices for suitably situated property.

An association of capitalists have recently applied for a charter for the incorporation of a company, to be called the Port Royal Company, whose purpose will be to buy lands as an investment, and to devote itself generally to the development of that port.

This company has recently purchased the Appleton estate in Port Royal, at a price, it is stated, of 100,000 dol.

In the event of Port Royal being able to secure the necessary railway connections with the Georgia, Alabama, and Tennessee coal regions, it would afford a very convenient coaling station for British ships.

Financial. The banks here, 13 in number, have done a fairly prosperous business this year, all of them paying dividends ranging from 6 per cent. to 10 per cent.

No new banks have been started, but those already established have, on the whole, done a business satisfactory to themselves and their depositors.

The rate of exchange for documentary bills of 60 and 90 days has averaged from 4 dol. 80 c. to 4 dol. 83 c. per £.

Money has been moderately well supplied for the necessities of trade, and no very serious effects were felt here in financial circles during the threatened panic of the money market last autumn in New York and London, beyond the difficulty that was naturally experienced for a few days in selling exchange bills on Europe.

LONDON:
Printed for Her Majesty's Stationery Office,
By HARRISON AND SONS,
Printers in Ordinary to Her Majesty,
1250   4 | 91—H & S   1064)

FOREIGN OFFICE.
1891.
ANNUAL SERIES.

N°. 868.

DIPLOMATIC AND CONSULAR REPORTS ON TRADE AND FINANCE.

UNITED STATES.

REPORT FOR THE YEAR 1890
ON THE
TRADE OF SAVANNAH.

REFERENCE TO PREVIOUS REPORT, Annual Series No. 691.

Presented to both Houses of Parliament by Command of Her Majesty,
APRIL, 1891.

LONDON:
PRINTED FOR HER MAJESTY'S STATIONERY OFFICE,
BY HARRISON AND SONS, ST. MARTIN'S LANE,
PRINTERS IN ORDINARY TO HER MAJESTY.

And to be purchased, either directly or through any Bookseller, from
EYRE & SPOTTISWOODE, EAST HARDING STREET, FLEET STREET, E.C., and
32, ABINGDON STREET, WESTMINSTER, S.W.; or
JOHN MENZIES & Co., 12, HANOVER STREET, EDINBURGH, and
88 and 90, WEST NILE STREET, GLASGOW; or
HODGES, FIGGIS, & Co., 104, GRAFTON STREET, DUBLIN.

1891.

[C. 6205—99.]   *Price One Halfpenny.*

New Series of Reports.

Reports of the Annual Series have been issued from Her Majesty's Diplomatic and Consular Officers at the following places, and may be obtained from the sources indicated on the title-page:—

No.		Price.	No.		Price.
744.	Nice	1½d.	806.	Lima	1d.
745.	Aleppo	1d.	807.	Rio de Janeiro	3d.
746.	Hakodate	1d.	808.	Dantzig	1½d.
747.	New York	2d.	809.	Florence	1½d.
748.	Cagliari	1d.	810.	Lisbon	1d.
749.	San Salvador	1d.	811.	Quito	½d.
750.	Gothenburg	2d.	812.	Para	½d.
751.	Nagasaki	1d.	813.	Palermo	2½d.
752.	Sofia	3½d.	814.	Copenhagen	1d.
753.	Meshed	1d.	815.	Serajevo	½d.
754.	Yokohama	2½d.	816.	Porto Rico	1d.
755.	Shanghai	2d.	817.	Madrid	½d.
756.	Lisbon	1½d.	818.	Brussels	½d.
757.	Teneriffe	½d.	819.	Patras	½d.
758.	Noumea	½d.	820.	Stuttgart	1d.
759.	Tahiti	½d.	821.	Taganrog	1d.
760.	Bushire	1½d.	822.	Salonica	2d.
761.	Frankfort	2d.	823.	Galveston	1d.
762.	Palermo	2½d.	824.	Rome	1½d.
763.	Guatemala	1d.	825.	Paris	1½d.
764.	Smyrna	4d.	826.	Bushire	½d.
765.	Munich	2d.	827.	New Orleans	3d.
766.	Hiogo	1½d.	828.	Buda-Pesth	½d.
767.	Alexandria	1½d.	829.	Hamburg	3d.
768.	Maracaibo	½d.	830.	Port Said	1d.
769.	Macao	1d.	831.	Samoa	½d.
770.	Canton	1d.	832.	Guayaquil	½d.
771.	Bangkok	2½d.	833.	New Orleans	2d.
772.	Stockholm	1½d.	834.	The Piræus	1d.
773.	Jaffa	½d.	835.	Baltimore	1½d.
774.	Copenhagen	½d.	836.	Trieste	2d.
775.	Ningpo	½d	837.	Galatz	1½d.
776.	Stettin	2d.	838.	Wênchow	1d.
777.	St. Petersburg	3d.	839.	Havre	2½d.
778.	St. Petersburg	½d.	840.	Rome	1½d.
779.	St. Jago de Cuba	1½d.	841.	Taganrog	2d.
780.	Chefoo	1d.	842.	Calais	1d.
781.	Christiania	3½d.	843.	Boston	1d.
782.	Marseilles	½d.	844.	Bordeaux	2½d.
783.	Baghdad	1d.	845.	Charleston	1½d.
784.	Naples	1½d.	846.	Manila	5d.
785.	Tunis	4d.	847.	Madeira	½d.
786.	Vera Cruz	1d.	848.	Paris	2d.
787.	Tangier	1½d.	849.	Tripoli	½d.
788.	Rome	2d.	850.	Swatow	1d.
789.	Stuttgart	1½d.	851.	Saigon	½d.
790.	Panama	1½d.	852.	Vienna	1½d.
791.	Berne	1½d.	853.	Algiers	2d.
792.	Asunsion	½d.	854.	Algiers	1d.
793.	Bahia	7½d.	855.	Mozambique	8d
794.	Monte Video	1½d.	856.	Antwerp	1½d.
795.	Munich	2d.	857.	Mogador	2d.
796.	Bucharest	1d.	858.	Ichang	½d.
797.	Tokio	1d.	859.	Calais	8½d.
798.	Tabreez	1d.	860.	Riga	2d.
799.	Antwerp	1d.	861.	San José	1d.
800.	Malaga	1d.	862.	Genoa	1½d.
801.	Odessa	1d.	863.	Warsaw	1d.
802.	Malaga	2d.	864.	Wuhu	1d.
803.	Amsterdam	1d.	865.	Marseilles	1d.
804.	Bogotá	1½d.	866.	Syra	1d.
805.	Guayaquil	½d.	867.	Jeddah	½d.

No. 868.

Reference to previous Report, Annual Series No. 691.

UNITED STATES.

SAVANNAH.

Consul St. John to the Marquis of Salisbury.

My Lord,   *Charleston (S.C.), March* 25, 1891.
I HAVE the honour to transmit herewith a Report on the Trade and Commerce of Savannah for 1890 by Mr. Vice-Consul Robertson.

I have, &c.
(Signed)   C. L. ST. JOHN.

Report on the Trade and Commerce of Savannah for the Year 1890.

The trade and commerce of Savannah for the year 1890 was in every way satisfactory. Savannahians have reason to be proud of their city, for she is becoming larger, richer, and more attractive every year. She compares favourably with any other city in the country, in the matter of health, and is second to none in the south in her promises of commercial importance.

In the last decade Savannah increased in population 41 per cent. The increase was almost wholly within the last three or four years. In view of her present promises of prosperity it is safe to predict that the city will have a population of 100,000 when the next census is taken. [Population.]

A rough estimate of the business of the port for the year under review amounted to 134,000,000 dol. (26,800,000*l.*), fully 25,000,000 dol. (5,000,000*l.*) more than it did the previous year. [Volume of business.]

Notwithstanding the large dealings in real estate, which have taken place during the past few years, at prices which at the time seemed excessive, the demand still keeps up, with a steady increase in value. In all categories the volume of business was far in excess of any previous year, one of the most gratifying signs of the times being the very great confidence shown by the people in buying real estate as an investment. Sales are constantly being recorded of lands purchased for the purpose of being held, and the purchasers of such property—irrespective of the [Real estate.]

Finance.

location—must, without doubt, realise largely on such investments.

Savannah is becoming more and more a financial centre, and although its banking facilities have increased during the past year, yet it is apparent to every class of business men that a large addition is still needed to meet the wants of the legitimate business of the place, and as the railroads continue to develop new territory, and to extend into more distant States, this need will be more urgently felt.

Railroads.

Three railroads have been completed within the year that will add greatly to the business and prosperity of Savannah.

They are the Alabama Midland, the Savannah and Western, and the Savannah, Americus and Montgomery. Much of the territory tributary to them has not been heretofore tributary to Savannah. These roads will greatly increase the commerce of the port. The country they traverse is rich in many things, and is susceptible of great development. Each year, therefore, their contributions to Savannah's prosperity will be greater than those of the previous year. The railroads now being built are the South Bound, and the Macon and Atlantic; both these roads will have river frontage, and will greatly aid the quick despatch of vessels loading at this port.

Quarantine.

The improvements at the quarantine station have been successfully pushed during the year, and the many complaints formerly made by the ship masters have ceased. Five vessels can now discharge at one time.

Harbour improvements.

The improvements in the river and harbour have been steadily carried on throughout the year, with the result that a 22 feet channel is now available for navigation. This depth is, however, inadequate to the growth of the port, and Congress has granted a large appropriation for the purpose of deepening the channel to 28 feet.

Crops,

The increase in Savannah's receipts of cotton over 1889-90 amounted to 127,000 bales, which is about 67,000 more than she ever received before in any one year.

The season was a good one for the planters: being open it enabled the farmers to gather and gin cotton rapidly.

Naval stores.

The year's business in naval stores was very gratifying. There was a large increase in both spirits and resin, and the total receipts were much larger than in any previous year.

The year's increase was as follows:—

	Spirits in Casks.	Resin in Barrels.
1889-90	185,000	685,000
1888-89	158,208	584,428
Increase	26,792	100,572

SAVANNAH.

Compared with previous years the business in rice should be considered satisfactory, while the yield per acre was less than was generally expected, the quality of the grain was remarkably fine, and during the whole season fairly good prices were obtained. This in a great measure made up for the short production. *Rice.*

The acreage planted was also slightly less than the previous year, and the dry weather in the early part of the season caused in some sections the stands to be very poor.

During the harvest the weather was unexceptionally fine, hence the entire crop was remarkable on account of its being entirely free from damage.

Savannah offers to investors a safe and profitable output for their capital. The rapid growth of the city has been the result of pure legitimate business. No fictitious booms have been created to enhance the value of property. Every foot of land in and about the city is to-day well worthy the attention of parties with spare capital to invest: more especially is this the case with parents wishing to make provision for their children. Property bought now in their names and allowed to stand must long before they reach legal years become very valuable. *Investments.*

Savannah buys annually from the northern markets millions of dollars' worth of cotton goods alone; and this in the face of the raw material growing within gunshot of the city. Although it seems surprising that such should be the case, the cause is not hard to discover. The capitalists are mostly engaged in the cotton business, and cannot afford to put out too much money in manufacturing enterprises to the detriment of their country constituents, who regularly require vast sums of ready money to prepare their lands and market their crops.

The imports and exports for the year have been generally satisfactory. *Imports and exports generally.*

The annexed tables A and B show a large decrease in the imports compared with 1889. *Imports.*

There is a marked decrease in this article of importation; this decrease is accounted for by the fact that several cargoes were received at the end of the year 1889, and not brought into use until 1890. *Fertilisers.*

The decrease which is noticeable in the importation of cotton ties I attribute to the same cause. *Cotton ties.*

The principal article of importation under this heading is fruit, which shows a small increase over the previous year. *Other articles.*

As will be seen by reference to the annexed returns nearly all articles under this heading show a large increase over the year 1889. *Exports.*

The exportation of cotton from this port continues to increase year by year. The crop was enormous, and Savannah with ever-increasing railroads and connections must naturally receive her share. *Cotton.*

The exportation of cotton seed continues to increase. *Cotton seed.*

UNITED STATES.

Lumber and timber. The value of the lumber and timber shipped from this port during the year was more than double that of 1889.

Spirits of turpentine. The shipment of this article of commerce during the year was very large, nearly 6,000,000 gallons were exported.

Resin. A large increase is shown in the exportation of this article.

All other articles. There was a considerable decrease for the year under this heading.

Annex A.—RETURN of Principal Articles of Export from Savannah during the Years 1889-90.

Articles.		1890. Quantity.	1890. Value. £	1889. Quantity.	1889. Value. £
Cotton	Lbs.	260,767,535	5,464,428	232,687,650	4,923,312
„ seed	„	2,026,718	4,162	1,336,680	2,452
Lumber and timber	Feet	32,006,065	59,396	15,011,786	27,083
Spirits of turpentine	Gallons	5,907,924	439,154	5,013,830	398,185
Resin (blls. of 280 lbs.)	Lbs.	659,320	212,847	627,289	152,959
Other articles	...	...	9,460	...	16,952
Total		...	6,189,447	...	5,520,943

RETURN of Principal Articles of Import from Savannah during the Years 1889-90.

Articles.		1890. Quantity.	1890. Value. £	1889. Quantity.	1889. Value. £
Fertilisers	Tons	8,053	17,296	17,815	40,162
Cotton ties	Bundles	32,509	6,465	80,885	11,747
Salt	Lbs.	11,228,736	2,825	12,880,379	3,068
Molasses	Gallons	44,625	1,433	61,100	1,937
Brimstone	Tons	4,960	14,993	3,200	11,913
Fruit and nuts	...	...	10,008	...	7,895
Other articles	...	...	28,143	...	20,963
Total		...	81,163	...	97,685

SAVANNAH.

Annex B.—TABLE showing the Total Value of all Articles Exported from Savannah and Imported to Savannah from and to Foreign Countries during the Years 1889–90.

Country.	Exports. 1890.	Exports. 1889.	Imports. 1890.	Imports. 1889.
	£	£	£	£
Britain	1,677,076	1,696,406	23,844	48,205
Germany	1,732,823	1,423,415	23,207	15,093
Spain	722,217	649,281	34	29
Russia	614,625	598,041	..	..
Netherlands	231,547	135,040	50	60
Belgium	102,756	242,170	2,260	1,685
Brazil	4,248	4,580	243	..
Italy	478,695	358,023	15,001	11,913
France	297,195	267,487	173	460
Other countries	328,265	146,500	16,351	20,240
Total	6,189,447	5,520,943	81,163	97,685

Annex C.—RETURN of all Shipping at the Port of Savannah in the Year 1890.

ENTERED.

Nationality.	Sailing. Number of Vessels.	Sailing. Tons.	Steam. Number of Vessels.	Steam. Tons.	Total. Number of Vessels.	Total. Tons.
American	60	32,302	390	327,469	450	359,771
British	24	13,020	81	106,958	105	119,978
Norwegian	121	66,725	9	3,196	130	69,921
German	34	18,895	...	...	34	18,895
Other countries	76	42,914	2	3,292	78	46,206
Total	315	173,856	482	440,915	797	614,771

CLEARED.

Nationality.	Sailing. Number of Vessels.	Sailing. Tons.	Steam. Number of Vessels.	Steam. Tons.	Total. Number of Vessels.	Total. Tons.
American	51	29,940	383	319,147	434	349,087
British	23	12,250	83	108,808	106	121,058
Norwegian	95	52,879	9	3,196	104	56,075
German	32	18,169	5	3,994	37	22,163
Other countries	77	46,642	2	3,292	79	49,934
Total	278	159,880	482	438,437	760	598,317

LONDON:
Printed for Her Majesty's Stationery Office,
By HARRISON AND SONS,
Printers in Ordinary to Her Majesty.
(1250 4 | 91—H & S 1083)

FOREIGN OFFICE.
1891.
ANNUAL SERIES.

N°· 892.
DIPLOMATIC AND CONSULAR REPORTS ON TRADE AND FINANCE.

UNITED STATES.

REPORT FOR THE YEAR 1890
ON THE
TRADE OF THE CONSULAR DISTRICT OF CHICAGO.

REFERENCE TO PREVIOUS REPORT, Annual Series No. 739.

Presented to both Houses of Parliament by Command of Her Majesty,
MAY, 1891.

LONDON:
PRINTED FOR HER MAJESTY'S STATIONERY OFFICE,
BY HARRISON AND SONS, ST. MARTIN'S LANE,
PRINTERS IN ORDINARY TO HER MAJESTY.

And to be purchased, either directly or through any Bookseller, from
EYRE & SPOTTISWOODE, EAST HARDING STREET, FLEET STREET, E.C., and
32, ABINGDON STREET, WESTMINSTER, S.W.; or
JOHN MENZIES & Co., 12, HANOVER STREET, EDINBURGH, and
88 and 90, WEST NILE STREET, GLASGOW; or
HODGES, FIGGIS, & Co., 104, GRAFTON STREET, DUBLIN.

1891.

[C. 6205—123.]   *Price Twopence Halfpenny.*

New Series of Reports.

Reports of the Annual Series have been issued from Her Majesty's Diplomatic and Consular Officers at the following places, and may be obtained from the sources indicated on the title-page:—

No.		Price.	No.		Price.
770.	Canton	1d.	831.	Samoa	½d.
771.	Bangkok	2½d.	832.	Guayaquil	½d.
772.	Stockholm	1½d.	833.	New Orleans	2d.
773.	Jaffa	½d.	834.	The Piræus	1d.
774.	Copenhagen	½d.	835.	Baltimore	1½d.
775.	Ningpo	½d.	836.	Trieste	2d.
776.	Stettin	2d.	837.	Galatz	1½d.
777.	St. Petersburg	3d.	838.	Wênchow	1d.
778.	St. Petersburg	½d.	839.	Havre	2½d.
779.	St. Jago de Cuba	1½d.	840.	Rome	1½d.
780.	Chefoo	1d.	841.	Taganrog	2d.
781.	Christiania	3½d.	842.	Calais	1d.
782.	Marseilles	½d.	843.	Boston	1d.
783.	Baghdad	1d.	844.	Bordeaux	2½d.
784.	Naples	1½d.	845.	Charleston	1½d.
785.	Tunis	4d.	846.	Manila	5d.
786.	Vera Cruz	1d.	847.	Madeira	½d.
787.	Tangier	1½d.	848.	Paris	2d.
788.	Rome	2d.	849.	Tripoli	½d.
789.	Stuttgart	1½d.	850.	Swatow	1d.
790.	Panama	1½d.	851.	Saigon	½d.
791.	Berne	1½d.	852.	Vienna	1½d.
792.	Asuncion	½d.	853.	Algiers	2d.
793.	Bahia	7½d.	854.	Algiers	1d.
794.	Monte Video	1½d.	855.	Mozambique	8d.
795.	Munich	2d.	856.	Antwerp	1½d.
796.	Bucharest	1d.	857.	Mogador	2d.
797.	Tokio	1d.	858.	Ichang	½d.
798.	Tabreez	1d.	859.	Calais	8½d.
799.	Antwerp	1d.	860.	Riga	2d.
800.	Malaga	1d.	861.	San José	1d.
801.	Odessa	1d.	862.	Genoa	1½d.
802.	Malaga	2d.	863.	Warsaw	1d.
803.	Amsterdam	1d.	864.	Wuhu	1d.
804.	Bogotá	1½d.	865.	Marseilles	1d.
805.	Guayaquil	½d.	866.	Syra	1d.
806.	Lima	1d.	867.	Jeddah	½d.
807.	Rio de Janeiro	3d.	868.	Savannah	½d.
808.	Dantzig	1½d.	869.	Suakin	½d.
809.	Florence	1½d.	870.	Berlin	1d.
810.	Lisbon	1d.	871.	Batoum	1½d.
811.	Quito	½d.	872.	Rosario	1d.
812.	Para	½d.	873.	Buenos Ayres	½d.
813.	Palermo	2½d.	874.	Mogador	1d.
814.	Copenhagen	1d.	875.	Tainan	6½d.
815.	Serajevo	½d.	876.	Pakhoi	1d.
816.	Porto Rico	1d.	877.	Odessa	2½d.
817.	Madrid	½d.	878.	Trebizond	1½d.
818.	Brussels	½d.	879.	Mollendo	½d.
819.	Patras	½d.	880.	Kiukiang	1d.
820.	Stuttgart	1d.	881.	Antananarivo	1d.
821.	Taganrog	1d.	882.	Stettin	2½d.
822.	Salonica	2d.	883.	Fiume	1½d.
823.	Galveston	1d.	884.	Batavia	1d.
824.	Rome	1½d.	885.	Samoa	½d.
825.	Paris	1½d.	886.	Cherbourg	1d.
826.	Bushire	½d.	887.	Cagliari	1d.
827.	New Orleans	3d.	888.	Hankow	1½d.
828.	Buda-Pesth	½d.	889.	Vienna	1½d.
829.	Hamburg	3d.	890.	Amoy	1d.
830.	Port Said	1d.	891.	Adrianople	½d.

No. 892.

Reference to previous Report, Annual Series No. 739.

UNITED STATES.

CHICAGO.

Consul Hayes Sadler to the Marquis of Salisbury.

My Lord,   *Chicago, April* 17, 1891.

I HAVE the honour to transmit herewith my Annual Report on the Trade and Commerce of Chicago during the year 1890.

I also enclose the Annual Reports of the Vice-Consuls at St. Louis, St. Paul, Denver, and Kansas city.

I have, &c.
(Signed)   J. HAYES SADLER.

Report of Consul Hayes Sadler on the Trade and Commerce of Chicago during the Year 1890.

THE CITY OF CHICAGO.

Each year shows a steady increase in the trade and business transactions of Chicago, which not only maintains its standing as the centre of manufacture and distribution in the west, but promises in time to acquire that position with regard to the whole of the United States. The geographical situation of the city, the richness of its agricultural surroundings, its railroad facilities as the centre of the greatest railroad system in the world, its extended water communication with the north, and its proximity to supplies required by manufacturing establishments unite in affording peculiar advantages. Each year shows an addition to the list of its numerous industries, and the untiring energy and enterprise of the business men furnish good reasons to predict a future of greatly increased importance. English capital has continued to flow in, and exercises a certain influence in the grain and provision markets, while many other branches of trade, notably the brewing business, have attracted investors. A large proportion of the 400,000,000*l.* said to have been invested in the United States during the last five years has been drawn

[marginal note: General remarks.]

Population and death-rate.

to enterprises here; very high prices were given for some of the businesses purchased, far higher probably than could have been otherwise realised, but many are said to be profitable investments.

The population of the city, the limits of which have been somewhat extended, increased from 503,189 in 1880 to 1,099,123 in 1890, and to this number may now be further added at least 65,000 since the census was taken last year. The number of deaths during the year was 21,856, or 18·21 per 1,000 of the population. Tubercular diseases carried off 2,231 persons; pneumonia, 2,073; consumption, 1,972; bronchitis, 1,189; diphtheria, 881; and typhoid fever, 1,008. Pulmonary affections from the changeable nature of the climate form one of the principal sources of illness and death.

Trade in general.

The total trade of the city, calculated on the same basis as on previous years, that is, on the first selling value of all goods arrived, except the precious metals, with the additional value they may have acquired by local manufacture, shows an increase in value of about 17½ per cent. over that of 1889 and 45 per cent. over that of ten years ago; it is estimated on the best authority to have amounted to 284,500,000*l.* sterling, including the produce, wholesale, and manufacturing trades. As, however, this advance in value may be partly credited to the rise in selling price of many commodities, which were unusually depressed in the preceding year, the actual amount of business done is calculated to have exceeded that of 1889 by about 10 per cent. This estimate does not include speculative business or transactions in real estate, and forms only 36 per cent. of the actual bank clearings. No doubt a portion of the business activity, especially the impetus given to the value of real estate, may be attributed to speculative transactions in view of the advantages to be derived from the World's Fair, and the prices of some commodities advanced in anticipation of the effects of the McKinley tariff, but towards the end of the season the stimulus given by these circumstances was in a measure checked by tightness in money, caused by financial difficulties in England; this tightness, however, was felt less heavily perhaps in Chicago than elsewhere, and was marked more by temporary decline in the value of stocks than by depression of local industrial enterprise or the value of property.

The advance has been general, not confined to any special trade, and is shown nearly evenly in all departments of trade. The receipts and shipments were larger, and the great increase of business in cereals from the large crops of 1889 has not been wholly lost. The receipts of cattle and hogs far exceeded those of the preceding year, and the packing business was correspondingly active. The wholesale business has been greater in every branch, the continued development and general prosperity of the west causing an ever increasing demand which is still largely supplied by the markets of Chicago; slackness was only shown in the sale of warm clothing, resulting from the mildness of the season. Manufactories have been actively at work, and fresh ones started; the demand for steel rails has been weak owing to less railroad building, but iron and steel are now employed for many new constructive purposes, greatly taking the place of lumber and other materials in building of almost all descriptions, and the industry has greatly developed. Where no official statistics have been available for this report the figures are taken from the best published authority.

Produce.

The receipts and shipments of the principal articles of produce at Chicago in 1890 are given in Annex A, together with the receipts in 1889. *Receipts and shipments.*

Notwithstanding the poor crops, compared with those of 1889, the movement of cereals was large, and shows that this city has not lost its hold as the great centre of distribution, though northern ports are actively competing in the shipping business. The wheat crop was short owing to unpropitious weather, except perhaps in the Red River valley. The average price of No. 2 wheat was 3s. 8½d. per bushel, against 3s. 6½d. in 1889. The corn crop was poor compared with the large yield of the preceding year, when farmers were compelled to sell at unusually low prices and in greater quantities than the railroads could at times find means to carry; some farmers indeed bought back last year at three times the price they had sold for. Buyers had to pay a higher price than usual, in consequence of the large consumption at low prices in the preceding year, and the reduction of reserves resulting from pressed sales of large quantities to meet liabilities. The average price of No. 2 corn was 1s. 7½d. against 1s. 4½d. in 1889, having stood as high as 2s. 2d. in November. The yield of oats was also poor compared with that of the preceding year, and the average price fetched was 1s. 3½d. against 11d. in 1889. Barley and rye advanced in sympathy with other cereals, and stood at enhanced prices. *Cereals.*

The receipts of live stock were by far the largest known in this city, nearly 13,000,000 animals having been delivered, and the year was generally a prosperous one. Pasturage was good in most parts of the country; the large corn crop of 1889 gave an impetus to stock raising, and there was a good supply of cattle, hogs, and sheep throughout the year. Large numbers of corn-fed cattle in good condition were received in the earlier months, but when it became certain that the yield of corn would be limited, many animals in poor condition were shipped for sale, and prices were low. The cattle were healthy and free from disease, and no case of Texas fever was reported during the year, which fact is greatly attributed to the recent quarantine regulations regarding the movement of cattle from the south-west. *Live stock. Cattle.*

The number of live hogs received was 7,644,000, exceeding that of the preceding year by 40 per cent., and that of any previous year by 600,000; the largest number previously received *Hogs.*

4   UNITED STATES.

having been in 1880. The shortness of the corn crop forced a large number of light hogs on the market in the latter part of the season, and prices were consequently lower than at any time for many years; the average weight of receipts was 234 lbs. against 246 lbs. in 1889. The hogs were mostly used up in the packing trade of the city.

Sheep.
Horses.
The number of sheep received was also the largest on record, and the dressed mutton business was active. Horses arrived to the number of 102,566, of which 94,362 were shipped eastward, by far the largest business done in one year.

Dairy products.
A satisfactory business was done in dairy products. The price of best creamery butter was 10½d., but a large quantity of inferior quality having been received the average price was only 7d. In cheese there was an increase of 6,000,000 lbs. received, and the quality is said to have been fair, low grades not meeting with encouragement. Early in the year full cream cheddars fetched about 5½d., while in the summer they were as low as 3½d. to 4d., at which figure large shipments were made to Europe. The total value of the produce trade is estimated at 95,340,124*l*.

Wholesale Trade.

Notwithstanding increased competition in some of the western cities, which have started business independent of Chicago, and extended their trade till they have themselves become centres of distribution within a certain surrounding limit, the wholesale trade of Chicago has kept pace with the increase in population. Trade has been opened out in fresh directions, and what has been lost in the west has been gained in other quarters; the year 1890 was a prosperous one, and prices of all goods, except sugar, were higher than they had been for two years. Millinery goods, furs, leather, and some other articles rose considerably in value on the passing of the McKinley Bill. Merchants also raised their charges for tobacco, hats, and carpets, and the effect of the new duties was felt in other branches of trade. The value of sales in the dry goods business during the year is calculated at more than 19,000,000*l*. sterling. Next to the dry goods the wholesale grocery houses did the largest volume of business, estimated at 11,500,000*l*. sterling. The total wholesale business of Chicago is said to have amounted to 92,500,000*l*. sterling.

Manufacturing Trade.

It is as a manufacturing city that Chicago shows the greatest advance, and in no manufacture has a greater stride been made than in that of iron and steel, especially in the branches connected with the building trade. There are now 6 rolling mills, 28 foundries, 67 machinery works, 22 boiler works, 70 galvanic iron, tin and slate roofing works, besides car-wheel, stove, steam-fitting

Iron and steel.

and many other manufactories, which turned out a product valued altogether at more than 14,000,000*l.* sterling, against 12,500,000*l.* sterling in 1889. Some orders for machinery for Africa were executed and forwarded to the Cape. What promises to be an important new branch of industry, the rolling of cold steel into wire, is being established, and an extensive manufacturing plant is being erected by the owners of the patent. The price of pig-iron ruled at 3*l.* 16*s.* 3*d.* against 3*l.* 14*s.* 2*d.* in 1889, and there was an increase of 20 per cent. in the volume produced which amounted to 1,100,000 tons.

The manufactories of iron and wood combined, including those of waggons and carriages, of which there are 70, elevators, agricultural implements, cars, sewing machines, &c., turned out a product valued at 8,500,000*l.* sterling. A considerable number of new works in this branch of manufacture were started during the year, and new railway car works are in course of construction on a very large scale. The scarcity of hides, and the advanced duty on cloth and other materials used in the manufacture of carriages, caused an advance of nearly 20 per cent. in the cost of those articles. *Iron and wood.*

The manufacture of glass, especially stained glass, has greatly developed, nearly all materials being furnished by this country, and the demand is almost wholly supplied by American manufacture. *Glass.*

The whole value of the product of Chicago manufactories, of which there are 3,250 in operation, is estimated at about 111,000,000*l.* sterling, equal to 28 per cent. advance on the value of products in 1889. *Total value of product.*

This includes the business of meat packing, which, owing to the abundance of live stock, was unprecedently large, as shown in the receipts and shipments. Three quarters of the cattle and most of the hogs received were slaughtered for the packing trade, and so great was the business done in dressed beef and pork that storage-room proved insufficient. The total product in this business amounted in value to about 28,000,000*l.* sterling; but, on account of the volume produced, prices were low. About 24,500 men were employed in this trade. *Packing trade.*

FREIGHTS.

Railroad freights varied greatly, the eastern lines competing for the transportation of many products which were formerly almost entirely in the hands of lake carriers. The Inter-state Commerce Commissioners have greatly stopped the discrimination which existed in favour of western and Missouri products. The rates for dressed beef were as high as 1*s.* 10½*d.* early in the year, and at one time stood as low as 11½*d.*; the rates on corn and oats increased towards the close of the year from 10*d.* to 1*s.* 0½*d.* per 100 lbs. *Railroad freights.*

Lake freights also fluctuated greatly: the rate for corn to Buffalo opening at about 1¾*d.* per bushel, and sinking at one *Lake freights.*

time to little over ½d. The quantity of iron ore carried last year was enormous. A good deal of lumber was carried, but the use of iron and steel is extending so widely that the imports seem not likely to increase now that the duties from Canada are heavier. The ports on Lake Superior yearly absorb more of the produce of the north-west, which is largely shipped by lake route to Europe.

Shipping.

Port of Chicago.
A return of all shipping at the port of Chicago, during the year 1890, is given in Annex B. It includes the vessels frequenting the small adjacent ports of South Chicago and Michigan city in the coasting trade, which ports are in the Chicago district. Every year shows some diminution in the number of sailing vessels, and an increase in the number and size of steam vessels.

Shipbuilding.
The first steel steamship built here was launched in February this year, from the yards of the Chicago Shipbuilding Company. It has a displacement of 4,600 tons, is 308 feet over all, 40 feet beam, and 24 feet depth; it is built for the Minnesota iron trade. There are three others of similar character which will be ready, it is said, for next season's iron trade. The cost of the four vessels will be about 160,000*l*.

Lake ports.
Some idea of the vast amount of trade on these great lakes may be formed from the statement that the aggregate entries and clearances in 1890 numbered 88,280, of which 21,054, 10,288,868 tons, were at the port of Chicago, and 20,038 at the port of Milwaukee in Wisconsin. The same statement gives the aggregate entries and clearances at New York at 15,283, and at the whole of the United States' seaboard at 37,756.

Port of Duluth.
The port of Duluth on Lake Superior is rapidly growing in importance. The total arrivals and clearances amounted in 1890 to 2,534 vessels, with an aggregate tonnage of 2,740,354 tons, more than double the tonnage of five years ago. The receipts by lake, according to customs returns, consist chiefly of coal, cement, lime, salt, and railroad iron, and amounted to 1,600,923; and the shipments, chiefly wheat, flour, other cereals, and iron ore, aggregated 1,079,131 tons; but this in some respects does not represent half the real trade of the place, as the manifests of vessels landing part of their cargo at Duluth, and then proceeding to Superior, are surrendered at the latter port, which is thus credited with much that is landed at Duluth; the same custom is followed with outward vessels, which clearing light from Superior are not credited in the customs records of Duluth with the cargo taken from that port. Superior, or West Superior, still further west than Duluth, only came into existence quite lately, and is fast rising into an important shipping port.

Customs Receipts.

The duties levied on imports at the customs of Chicago

amounted in 1890 to 1,068,582*l.*, against 1,040,984*l.* in the preceding year. On account of changes in the system of administration, the duties levied here are likely to increase in volume, and the importance of inland ports will probably be greater; but at present they give an imperfect idea of the quantity of foreign merchandise imported, as many goods pay duty at the seaboard, and are thence forwarded into the interior. The falling-off in customs receipts during the last three months of the year was caused by large quantities of merchandise having been imported during the few preceding months in anticipation of the new duties. It is early to form any opinion here as to what the effect of the new duties may be on imports; as yet there has been little perceptible difference, except that, since they came into force, an increase is said to have taken place in quantity, with a comparative decrease in amount of duty levied, which would imply a larger proportion of free goods entered.

The following is a return of merchandise entered for export with benefit of drawback at the port of Chicago during the year 1890:— *Drawbacks.*

Packages and Contents.			Quantity.	Articles and Quantities Entitled to Drawback.			Amount of Drawback.
			Lbs.				£
Canned meat	Packages	121,723	44,401,308	Tinplate	Lbs.	7,343,637	13,628
Salted meat	,,	268,190	29,665,114	Salt	,,	6,284,566	10,531
Flour	Bags	4,995	699,300	Burlaps	Yards	6,960	11
Barbed wire and spelter	Packages	174	21,533	Wire and spelter	Lbs.	20,523	19

IMPORTS AND EXPORTS.

Annex C is a return of the principal articles of import at the customs of Chicago in 1890, compared with the preceding year; and Annex D is a return of the direct exports by lake from Chicago for the same period. The returns of export by rail are not yet available. The customs returns are not drawn up so as to show the value of goods imported from or exported to different foreign countries.

REAL ESTATE.

Perhaps the most marked feature of the year has been an enormous rise in the value of city property, in great measure owing to the selection of Chicago as the site of the World's Columbian Exposition, to be held in 1893. More transfers of real estate took place than in the two preceding years, and invariably at enhanced prices. In the principal business part of the city frontage is of great value, as much as 4,000*l.* having been given per foot front; there are some stores which are now realising 50 per cent., and even 100 per cent., on their value a few *Rise in value.*

UNITED STATES.

months ago, and preparations are made for rebuilding on a vastly extended scale. In the suburbs, at least in the neighbourhood of Jackson Park, 6 miles from the centre of the city, where the exposition is to be held, the rise has been 200 per cent. to 300 per cent., and in some cases building lots, which had at the commencement of the year a value of 10*l.* to 20*l.* a front foot, changed hands four or five times in as many months, till they are now held at 60*l.* or more. Acres of land elsewhere have been divided into lots at almost an equal advance, and in many instances land originally bought for farming purposes has been realised at a far greater profit.

Rents. With regard to rents there has been a very general rise of from 10 per cent. to 15 per cent., and no houses, flats, or offices are now leased for more than one year in view of a further rise.

Building. A greater number of immense business and office buildings were erected than at any previous period, and, counting private houses, the value of new constructions in 1890 is estimated at 9,500,000*l.* There is one block in course of construction of an unusual height, on an area of 170 feet by 114 feet, where formerly stood what were once considered handsome office buildings. The roof is to be 275 feet above the street grade, and the building will cost 400,000*l.* The structure will be of steel, and absolutely fire-proof as far as material and skill can make it; the exterior facing of the first two stories being of granite, and that of the remaining 18 stories of grey brick and terra cotta. A rotunda with an area of 3,700 square feet will occupy the centre, and be opened to the height of the roof, finished with plate glass and white polished marble. There will be 18 elevators or lifts, capable of carrying 40,000 persons to 45,000 persons daily. The building will contain 700 offices, and more than 100 handsomely decorated lodge rooms, some of them capable of seating 1,000 persons, while an immense restaurant will occupy the basement.

Mode of. The common brick is now very little used in buildings of any dimensions, being replaced by hollow tile, pressed brick, and terra cotta, while many of the larger constructions are entirely built of steel with a veneer of tile or brick. Comparatively few hands are required; the steam crane does nearly all the work, lifting and placing the steel girders and columns, the latter being alternately of different height to ensure greater strength; and as the framework of each floor is riveted, the crane runs itself up an inclined plane to a rail on that floor, and proceeds to erect the next, till the whole is complete, a continuous chain of hods or buckets, like those of a dredging machine, worked by steam, raising all other material to the floor required. Steel wire netting takes the place of the lath to hold the plaster for ceilings and walls, and the windows, doors, and flooring, the latter often of hollow tile, furnish the only employment for the carpenter till the builders' work is done. Many houses it is said will soon be furnished with natural gas from the neighbouring State of Ohio, which will be conducted in pipes under pressure, and will, it is estimated, cost about 2s. the 1,000 feet. Owing to the mildness of the season building has continued uninterrupted during the winter.

RAILROADS.

Illinois has the greatest railroad mileage of any State in the Union, having 10,163 miles of main line, 926 of second, third, and fourth tracks, and 2,928 miles of sidings, &c., in the State. The total capital stock, funded debts, and current liabilities of the railway companies in Illinois for all mileage operated in 1890 amounted to 403,236,785*l*., or 10,833*l*. per mile, and the net income on 41 roads was 6,591,582*l*., while 21 roads showed a net deficit of 285,391*l*. The total earnings from operation in Illinois in 1890 amounted in the passenger department to 3,600,805*l*., in the freight department to 9,924,453*l*., and from miscellaneous sources to 390,266*l*., making the total earnings 13,915,524*l*., and showing a slight increase in the passenger traffic, and about 10 per cent. increase in freight returns over the preceding year. The operating expenses in 1890 were 2,646,438*l*. chargeable to passenger traffic, and 5,612,917*l*. to the freight department, total 8,259,355*l*., an increase of under 2 per cent. on the year 1889. The percentage of operating expenses to earnings per mile of road in Illinois was 63·09, against 66·90, and the net earnings per mile of road operated amounted to 461*l*., against 394*l*. in 1889. There were nearly 25,000,000 passengers carried in Illinois earning revenue, average distance carried 25 miles, and 48,364,653 tons of freight, average distance haul per ton $102\frac{1}{2}$ miles. The estimated cost of carrying one passenger 1 mile was under 1*d*., and 1 ton of freight per mile a fraction over $\frac{1}{4}d$. Only 12 lines paid dividends. There are 29 different railway lines which run to Chicago, and the number of passenger trains arriving and leaving daily are about 1,000. The number of miles of trackage in the city is about 1,100. A vast amount of stock changed hands towards the close of the year in consequence of financial stringency caused by the failure of Barings and Co., of London, and many stocks stand at a low figure.

In Illinois.

The increase of railway mileage during the year 1890 was not large; 223 miles of new line were laid down in Illinois, 421 in the State of Montana, 213 in Nebraska, and 211 in Colorado; but in other parts of this district railroad building has been carried on to a comparatively small extent.

Increase of mileage in the district.

There is continued tendency towards the better equipment of railroads, improved beds and structures, leading to greater safety, speed and comfort, the stronger lines in this State being well managed and constructed. Some of the weaker lines, however, are far from being in the safest condition. There are still 1,181 miles of iron rails, though 74,555 tons of steel rails were relaid during the year.

Condition of lines in Illinois.

A good many bridges have been lately reconstructed, and a fine new station has been built in Chicago for the use of three of the principal lines.

UNITED STATES.

Accidents.

The number of railroad accidents continues to be large, 568 persons having been killed in Illinois in 1890, of whom 176 were employés of the lines and 27 were passengers, while 1,564 persons, chiefly railroad employés, were injured. Many of the accidents to employés (who number 57,435 in this State) are caused in coupling and uncoupling cars, and in falling from trains and engines while engaged in setting brakes; this danger would be much reduced if continuous train brakes and automatic couplers were universally introduced. Almost all passenger trains are fitted with such brakes and couplers, but freight trains are much deficient in these appliances. Many injuries and deaths among non-employed persons are caused at the various level-crossings, where proper signals are non-existent; out of the estimated 700 graded crossings in the State only 34 are equipped with interlocking and signalling devices, and 1,477 miles of line are unfenced.

Grain inspection.

The State grain inspection department at Chicago transacted the largest volume of business yet shown in a single year. The department stands as an arbitrator between buyer and seller, producer and consumer, and practically fixes the value of the grain which passes under its supervision, appearing to execute its onerous duties with great success.

Live stock rate.

A new schedule of maximum rates to be charged for the transportation of live stock came into force on January 1 this year, in accordance with the provisions of a State law, and is based upon weight, freights being computed at so much per 100 lbs. of live stock transported, instead of the former carlot rates.

COAL MINES.

A large number of coal mines are worked in Illinois, there being 854 openings, but they are mostly small and only worked for local use on the spot. In 1889 the total output of lump coal was 11,598,000 tons, of which 90 per cent. was contributed by 217 of the mines. The average value at the mines was 4s. 7$\frac{1}{3}$d., the price of hand mining averages 3s. per ton, the number of mining machines is 235 in 35 mines, and does not increase. The rate paid for work in the machine mines rules about 9s. 3d. per day, 10s. 3$\frac{1}{2}$d. for machine operators, and 7s. 2$\frac{1}{2}$d. for labour. The sliding scale system is not adopted, having met with little favour, and being looked upon with suspicion by operatives here. On account of the mildness of the season there has been scarcely any increase of output. There are 30,076 men employed, of whom 23,583 are miners. This last year there has been no recurrence of trouble, but in 1889 a strike closed many mines for several months; the struggle arose from a proposed reduction of 10 per cent. in the price of mining, so as to enable the employers to compete with those of the adjoining States by reducing the cost of production. The difficulty was eventually compromised by the aid of mediation, the owners gaining the greater part of their demand, and the men accepting a reduction of 3$\frac{3}{4}$d. per ton, the majority being unable to get away or procure other work.

CHICAGO.

There were 42 fatal casualties in the mines in 1889 and 201 men were injured; the number of fatal accidents was far less than formerly, inspection and legislation having done much towards the safety of the miner. Among the most important of recent laws there are those which compel the owner, operator, or superintendent to cause an accurate map or plan to be made each year of the mine, showing the direction of the air currents, besides all other particulars of the mine, and also the date of each survey. A copy of the map is to be given to the inspector, which becomes the property of the State, and is open to the examination of the public. In all mines where more than six men are employed, in addition to the hoisting shaft, or opening, a separate escapement shaft at a certain distance from the opening, or underground communication with a contiguous mine approved by the inspector, is to be made within the limited time of one or two years, and to be afterwards maintained; and in mines over 100 feet in depth a suitable cage is to be substituted for the stairway in such escapement shaft with such hoisting apparatus as may be approved and considered safe by the inspector. With regard to ventilation it is enacted that all doors on main entries shall be constructed so as to close of themselves, and sufficiently tight to obstruct air currents, and in large mines a boy or trapper is always to be stationed to see the door securely closed, and the air currents controlled. Additional precautions are now taken in regularly sprinkling galleries, roadways, or entries where dust accumulates from dryness, and the inspector is to see that every precaution is taken against the careless handling of such powder as may be required; no loose powder and no prohibited tools are to be used, and no prohibited or inexperienced persons are to be employed where duties involve contact with inflammable gases or the handling of explosives.

CAPITAL AND LABOUR.

Trusts and monopolies continue to thrive, and are still a marked characteristic of the times, but in some instances the legal courts have shown themselves unfavourable to such combinations, which have been forced to adopt new modes so as to avoid collision with the law and meet the objections raised.* There is now scarcely any article of production or consumption the entire market for, and the price of, which is not affected or controlled by combinations of producers, and fresh organisations of associated capital are constantly in progress. Though there are still some branches of business conducted on a legitimate basis of competition the tendency of the last few years has been to crowd out the independent producer, while the dealer on a small scale has a poor chance to compete with the wealth of the larger houses. Both dealer and consumer are more and more compelled to pay the arbitrary prices fixed by combination of capital.

The recent higher duties, however much they may result in raising the profits of production, do not appear to have had the

* A full report on this subject is contained in No. 174, Miscellaneous Series of Foreign Office Reports.—[ED.]

effect of increasing the rate of wages paid for labour, except, perhaps, where combinations of labour have been able to dictate their own terms, and secure a preference to the prejudice of those outside their influence. In some instances a fall in the rate of wages given has been announced. No strikes of any importance took place to mar the prosperity of last year, though trade unions continue to make themselves felt, and to regulate the hours of work and rate of pay. Activity in the building and other trades has kept hands generally employed, but owing to the rush of workmen seeking employment here there has been in many cases great difficulty in securing work, especially among aliens, who are debarred from employment in any work paid from funds raised by taxation, and a good deal of distress existed in the winter months. It is not uncommon for the new arrival from England to find how delusive his hopes have been, and what little benefit he can expect from a higher scale of wages, which vanish from the increased cost of everything he requires except some of the actual necessaries of food; he often finds the difficulty of procuring employment greater as he has not the protection of American labour union, life and work harder, the climate trying, and the cost of clothing, tools, and many necessaries and luxuries far higher. There are not data sufficient to correctly estimate the rate of wages throughout this large district, but it may be safely said that there is, in general, great loss arising from unemployed days, owing largely to the hard winter season, and that the high scale of wages scarcely compensates for the lack of regular employment in the same service.

Wages in Wisconsin. From the able report of the bureau of labour statistics of the State of Wisconsin, where wages are quite up to, and in many instances above, the average of other States, and the position by no means unfavourable, the general rate of wages per hour for all branches of the building trade in Milwaukee in 1890 was 1s. 2d.; the higher grade, the masons, receiving 1s. 6¾d., and common labour 7½d. (The general rate at Chicago in the same trade was 1s. 7d.) Taking the year 1889 26·25 per cent. of working men were idle, the percentage rising in January to 70·67 per cent.; according to the pay rolls of firms in the trade the average number of working days for the year being 229. According to comparative statements of workmen the number of days worked during the year was 202, and the actual earnings for that period were 89l. 4s. 8d.; the average monthly wages in Wisconsin for 26 days' work was 11l. 16s. 1½d., while the same in Europe for 26 days' work are stated to have been 5l. 6s. 8½d.

In the Wisconsin factories 27·65 per cent. of daily wages range from 6s. 2½d. to 8s. 3d.; 22·83 per cent. from 5s. 2d. to 6s. 2½d.; 11·83½ per cent. from 8s. 3d. to 10s. 4d.; and 10·38½ per cent. from 4s. 1½d. to 5s. 2d. Scarcely 11 per cent. ranging above 8s. 3d. per day.

As regards the purchasing power of a day's wages it is calculated that earnings at 10d. (20 c.) an hour for 10 hours, or 8s. 3d. per day, will buy in Wisconsin 48 lbs. of wheaten bread, or 14 lbs. of meat, or 16 lbs. of pork, or 10 lbs. of butter, while in London or Glasgow it is said the day's wages at 6·35 pence for 9 hours, or 5s. 3½d. for the day, will purchase 40 lbs. of wheaten bread, or 9 lbs. of meat, or 11 lbs. of pork, or 5½ lbs. of butter.

In the West.

The prosperity, progress, and activity, so marked at Chicago, in a measure applies to the whole of this district, which now comprises 12 States: the territory of Montana having been created a State, and the territory of Dakota divided into the two States of North and South Dakota in 1889, and the territory of Wyoming admitted as a State in 1890. The population of these 12 States increased in ten years from 10,805,167 in 1880 to 14,979,942 in 1890. The rate of increase has been greatest in the north-west, the States of North and South Dakota, Wyoming, and Montana showing an increase of about 300 per cent. in that period. Agriculture and stock raising make rapid strides, as well as mining in the mineral localities; new enterprises are constantly springing up, and the value of property increases as fast as the towns and country districts fill up. Almost everywhere there is a scarcity of timber, and the demand for lumber is greatly in excess of the supply, though manufactures of iron take the place of wood for many purposes. The condition of live stock throughout the district has been healthy.

The new regulations, formulated in Illinois by the Board of Live Stock Commissioners on a greater knowledge of the Texas fever resulting from investigation and experiments, have kept the State free from the ravages of that disease; the Board was only established two years ago, and it has greatly protected the herds from other contagious diseases to which they are naturally exposed from the fact that the State of Illinois is the gateway for the livestock traffic of the great grazing districts of the west. The Board has condemned and destroyed for human food 2,548 head of cattle in the last two years infected with actinomycosis, and good results are reported of the efficiency of its work. The assessed value of domestic animals in Illinois is about 10,000,000l. sterling, or about one-third of the assessed valuation of personal property.

Iowa was admitted as a State 45 years ago; 10 years later its population only amounted to 220,000, and even then a great portion of the State was considered unfit for profitable agriculture. The population is now nearly 2,000,000, and it is a great agricultural country traversed by 8,230 miles of railway. Twenty years ago Sioux city did not exist, and now has a population of 37,862. Stock raising is one of the great industries, and Iowa contains more hogs than any other State, the number in 1890 having been 6,750,000, and the losses limited to 5 per cent. The hogs are chiefly shipped to Chicago, but packing is carried on at many points, particularly at Cedar Rapids and Sioux city; the total number of hogs slaughtered in the packing business in the State in 1889 having been 750,000. There is some interest taken in silk culture, cocoons can be economically produced, but until an automatic reel is perfected to substitute machinery for manual labour, hand reeling cannot successfully compete with other countries. The English sparrow, which was imported into the United States not many years ago, and spread so rapidly westward, has now overrun this State, and is considered a greater evil than an invasion of locusts, or the pleuro-pneumonia of cattle, as it is always present winter and summer. No remedy has yet made an appreciable effect upon the marvellous spread and growth of the sparrows, or successfully checked the destruction they cause in the fields, orchards, and gardens.

Wisconsin.

The city of Milwaukee has increased in population in 10 years from 115,567 to 204,150. Many other cities in Wisconsin show a good advance; the port of Ashland has now 16,000 inhabitants against 1,000 in 1880, and Superior has risen from nothing to 13,000 in 10 years.

Silos.

The silo in this greatly agricultural State is much appreciated, and has been in practical operation for nearly 10 years. The system has been gradually simplified, the cost reduced, and the production improved. Nearly every farming community in the south part of Wisconsin has a silo in or near it, affording opportunity for those who wish to do so to familiarise themselves with the process.

Montana.

Mining, stock raising, and agriculture are showing great development in Montana, and a tendency is visible towards the division of the stock interests among the ranchmen in smaller lots. Great irrigating enterprises are on foot to make the soil produce the prolific crops claimed for its fertility. The number of horses, sheep, and cattle is now 2,368,482 against 1,881,268 in 1889. The revenue of the State has increased nearly 100 per cent. in the last year, and the assessed valuation nearly 50 per cent. The mineral output in 1889 was 4,950,928*l*., and in 1890 it rose to 9,865,568*l*.

Nebraska.

The great increase in the population of the chief cities in Nebraska can be seen in the following comparison:—

	1880.	1890.
Omaha..	30,518	139,526
Lincoln	13,003	55,491
Beatrice	2,447	13,921
Nebraska city..	4,183	11,472

Sugar factories.

A large beet sugar factory, lately established and fully equipped, is now running in this State. The supply is obtained by contract with 600 farmers, within a distance of 100 miles, and though the yield last year was disappointing, the beet is said to have a high standard of sugar content, and the prospects of successful sugar-making is looked upon as encouraging, the country being considered well-suited to the growth of beet. The result of sugar-making in the other States has not been generally satisfactory, except perhaps in Kansas, and there the crop of sorghum cane, as well as of beet, was short last year; the factories of Fort Scott, Topeka, Medicine Lodge, and other places have however been running with few interruptions, and it is said to be satisfactorily proved that this industry can be carried on with good prospects of success in a commercial point of view, with the assistance of the bounty of 1*d.* per lb. granted by Government.

In North and South Dakota it is also stated that the soil is well adapted to the culture of the sugar beet, and that the percentage of sugar produced nearly equals the results in California, exceeding the percentage at which a profit is derived in Europe. Dakota.

An investigation of the extent of coal fields in North Dakota leads to the conclusion that the deposits are sufficient for the supply of the State, and for that of neighbouring States for centuries. It is chiefly lignite in quality, and in some cases bituminous. Coal.

In South Dakota the deposits of clay and chalk stone have been thoroughly tested, and a plant established at Yankton for the manufacture of cement. The product is said to be superior to Portland cement, and a sample one year old shows a tensible strength of 1,126 lbs. per square inch. There are other manufactories of cement in course of erection on the Missouri River. Cement.

The Black Hill mining district in this State embraces 100,000 square miles, or 64,000,000 acres, and yields every mineral known and most of the precious metals, notably gold, silver, and tin; more than 30,000 mining claims have been located, and 500 already opened sufficiently prove them capable of profitable operation. Four different geological formations show gold in various combinations. The Whitewood district, of which Deadwood and Lead city are the centres, in Lawrence county, is the most developed, the ore yielding about 4*l.* per ton. There were 600 stamps continually at work two years ago in that district, and the Homestake Company alone crushes 1,600 tons per day, and has paid up to 1889 900,000*l.* in dividends. Black Hill mining district.

Many other gold and silver mining companies have paid large dividends, and a number of mills owned by private persons have been profitably worked; the quartz mines having yielded up to January, 1889, a total of 8,804,120*l.* There are also a good many mills at work in Pennington county, but neither there nor in Custer county are the mines so developed as in Lawrence county. The Black Hills were first visited and surveyed, and ore discovered, little more than 15 years ago.

Tin and Tin Mining.

The new duties to be levied in July on tin plates, under the McKinley tariff, and the increase of about 15 per cent. in the cost of imported plates, which rise appears to be attributable more to the manufacture of sheets than to an increased value in tin, have attracted much attention, and tin plate manufacturing will Tin plates.

(1111)

soon be fairly started in Chicago as one of its many industries. Though for some years sheets have been tinned, and re-tinning has been practised in this country, the sheets have been imported, and the labour, if not imported, has been of foreign origin. Messrs. Norton and Sons, one of the largest manufacturers of cans, and importers of tin plate, have now nearly completed a steel furnace and rolling mills at Marwood, Chicago, which will soon be in operation, when they expect to turn out sufficient for their own use; the steel sheets being manufactured at the works, and the pig tin imported from Australia, if the mines of the country cannot supply it. This firm has for some years imported all the pig tin they require direct from Australia or Malacca. The principal part of the tin plate industry, the manufacturing the steel sheets, will thus be carried on here, and in time it is not doubted that the country will be independent of importing the metal which completes the operation. It is also expected that the substitution of machinery for hand labour, with which tinning is now done, will materially reduce the cost, and within three or four years plates will be made greatly cheaper than those now imported from England, and entirely of American material, and with American labour. The St. Louis Stamping Company are already making tin plates on a small scale for the market, and are proceeding to extend their works, while other factories are starting or proposed elsewhere. The Illinois Steel Company, of Chicago, are also said to be projecting the erection of mills for the manufacture of tin plates to supply the large demand of the local packing business, and the house and car roofing manufactories. It is confidently believed that the appliance of new processes invented, everything being done by machinery, will lower the cost of production to a point which will in a few years remove any fear of competition, and entirely exclude imported plate.

Tin mines in the Black Hills.

The greatest interest is taken in the tin deposits in South Dakota, with regard to which many conflicting reports have been circulated, and a definite opinion as to the commercial value of the tin found can scarcely be formed from the work that has been done. Professor Carpenter has made a second survey of the district. Professor Vincent and many American and English experts have visited the mines and written most favourable accounts of the richness of the deposits which are said to be inexhaustible, and Mr. Samuel Scott, mining engineer, recently furnished an able report from personal observation.

The Glendale mill, owned by the Tin Mining Company, of Chicago, is the first which has placed American tin on the market: it is the only mill which has yet cast any tin ore pigs, and is said to be working steadily on a small scale, capable of working only 30 tons a day, but a larger plant is being erected, and the statements of Mr. Richards with regard to the richness of the ore are said to be confirmed. The expense of mining and treating one short ton of ore is as follows:—Mining, 4s. 2d.; concentrating 2s. 1d.; smelting, 1s. 7d.; and incidental, 1s. 1½d.; total, 8s. 11½d., which compares favourably with the cost in

Cornwall, while the mines are considered many times richer. The work is done at present in a simple manner, by crushing and re-crushing the ore, and passing it successively through sieves till the required fineness is attained, a fine vanner being used to separate the ore and concentration effected by gravity methods. The smelting is done in a reverberatory or cupola furnace, and the molten metal is then cast into pigs.

Though tin deposits were discovered in the Black Hills some eight years ago, the excitement at once created by the discovery in a measure abated till the McKinley Bill has renewed the interest taken in the subject. At first no one in these parts knew much about tin, and some of the first capitalists who bought up claims appear, possibly for their own interests, to have discouraged the idea that mining could be successfully carried on as it would be found impossible to dress the ore. Samples, however, of acknowledged richness were sent to New York, and mining on a small scale was commenced; but the first mills were soon shut down and reports circulated that they could not be worked so as to be of commercial value. The Etta mine at that time bought up a great many claims, and after about three years this enterprise was consolidated into the Harney Peak Tin Mining, Smelting and Manufacturing Company, of New York and London, a great part of the capital being invested by English capitalists. This is the largest enterprise in the district and owns over 400 claims, which are being carefully prospected. There are 300 men or 400 men now employed, and about 500,000 tons of ore are in sight with, it is stated, an assay of 14 per cent., while selected specimens, it is affirmed, have shown as much as 30 per cent. or even 40 per cent. A large concentrating plant and smelting furnaces are being erected by this company, which will probably be ready for working in the summer. There are also in the district nine other companies, variously distributed, engaged in similar operations.

The chief deposits of tin are found in Custer and Tennington counties, where there are about 7,000 locations. The veins vary in width from 1 foot to more than 300 feet, the length from a few yards to 5 miles, and the outcrop ranges from a few feet to more than 150 feet above the surface. It is said that at least 4 per cent. of tin can everywhere be depended on. Numerous other minerals are found with the tin, but at present attention is almost exclusively drawn to the tin ore. The necessary fuel for working the mines is found in abundance in the immediate vicinity; inexhaustible resources of bituminous coal exist on the outskirts of the Black Hills, and the vast petroleum fields of Wyoming are at no great distance.*

---

* Exchange is calculated throughout this report at 4 dol. 85 c. per £ sterling.

18 UNITED STATES.

Annex A.—RETURN of the Principal Articles of Produce received and shipped at Chicago during the Years 1898-90.

Articles.		1890. Received.	1890. Shipped.	1889. Received.
Flour	Barrels..	4,358,058	4,134,586	4,410,535
Wheat	Bushels..	14,243,770	11,975,276	18,762,646
Corn	,,	91,387,754	90,574,399	79,920,691
Oats	,,	75,150,249	70,768,222	49,901,942
Barley	,,	19,401,489	9,470,971	12,524,538
Grass seeds	Lbs.	72,102,031	59,213,035	84,599,331
Canned meats	,,	300,198,241	823,801,460	279,317,936
,, ,,	Cases	36,324	1,767,654	23,569
Dressed beef	Lbs.	109,704,834	964,134,807	88,894,033
Pork	Barrels..	77,985	392,786	54,608
Lard	Lbs.	147,475,267	471,910,128	99,952,687
Cheese	,,	67,338,590	53,829,885	61,039,396
Butter	,,	140,548,850	156,688,837	156,315,245
Live hogs	Number	7,663,828	1,985,700	5,998,526
Cattle	,,	2,484,280	1,260,309	3,023,281
Sheep	,,	2,182,667	929,854	1,832,469
Hides	Lbs.	100,574,921	199,083,622	101,115,466
Wool	,,	22,281,570	39,006,263	28,839,182

Annex B.—RETURN of all Shipping at the Port of Chicago in the Year 1890.

ENTERED.

Nationality.	Sailing. Number of Vessels.	Sailing. Tons.	Steam. Number of Vessels.	Steam. Tons.	Total. Number of Vessels.	Total. Tons.
British—						
Foreign trade	11	4,412	36	33,438	67	37,450
Coasting trade	...	...	...	...	...	...
American—						
Foreign trade	71	21,086	15	7,075	86	28,161
Coasting trade	4,489	1,123,134	5,865	3,949,508	10,354	5,072,642
Total	4,571	1,148,232	5,936	3,990,021	10,507	5,138,253
,, for the year preceding	4,574	2,225,410	5,228	3,296,476	9,802	4,521,886

CLEARED.

Nationality.	Sailing. Number of Vessels.	Sailing. Tons.	Steam. Number of Vessels.	Steam. Tons.	Total. Number of Vessels.	Total. Tons.
British—						
Foreign trade	11	4,012	56	33,438	67	37,450
Coasting trade	...	...	...	...	...	...
American—						
Foreign trade	201	65,354	44	24,415	245	89,769
Coasting trade	4,423	1,097,674	5,812	3,925,722	10,235	5,023,396
Total	4,635	1,167,040	5,912	3,983,575	10,547	5,150,615
,, for the year preceding	4,721	1,257,563	5,302	3,371,621	10,023	4,629,184

Annex C.—Return of Principal Articles of Import to Chicago during the Years 1889-90.

Articles.	Value. 1889.	Value. 1890.
	£	£
Free goods	496,257	702,121
China and glassware	106,836	115,710
Caustic soda	13,280	18,838
Cigars and tobacco	112,309	136,744
Dry goods	933,980	991,231
Iron, pig, manufactures of, and wire, &c.	22,656	37,961
Leather manufactures	61,285	52,115
Metal	32,422	45,422
Musical instruments	39,704	43,216
Steel bars, bloom, &c.	310	183
Tin plate	296,925	336,599
Wines and liquors	67,381	76,178
Other articles, general	601,673	618,249
Total	2,785,018	3,174,617

Annex D.—Return of Principal Articles of Direct Export by Lake from Chicago during the Years 1889-90.

Articles.		1889. Quantity.	1889. Value.	1890. Quantity.	1890. Value.
			£		£
Wheat	Bushels	586,596	104,108	635,296	128,766
Corn	,,	5,540,524	415,617	2,638,334	231,082
Oats	,,	131,949	5,940	163,984	11,324
Rye	,,	...	...	40,028	41,153
Flour	Barrels	15,962	16,032	3,607	2,472
Cornmeal	,,	1,925	835	2,057	1,363
Pork	Lbs.	3,748,520	28,514	282,600	3,880
Cured meats	,,	14,880	185	550	14
Lard	,,	12,560	191	...	...
Tallow	,,	...	...	218,975	2,004
Steel rails	Tons	...	...	501	3,555
Other articles	...	...	1,579	...	570
Total	...	...	573,001	...	389,183

St. Louis.

Mr. Vice-Consul Western Bascome reports as follows:—

I shall endeavour in the following statement to give the statistics of the volume of business transacted, the improvement of the city, the increase in population, the condition of its leading industries and finances, which all point to the continual growth and importance of St. Louis. There are several indications which mark the commercial condition of the city, among which are the tonnage of its transportation lines, the records of its banking clearings, and the business of its post office.

Tonnage.

The table of tonnage on another page shows that the total amount of freight handled by the various railroad and steamboat lines entering in St. Louis during 1890 was 16,505,733 tons, being an increase over 1889 of 1,596,290 tons, and demonstrates that St. Louis is the centre of an immense system of rail and water transportation, the volume of which is increasing yearly.

Post office.

The statistics of the St. Louis post office on another page shows an increase over 1889 of 12·37 per cent. in amount received for sale of stamps, &c.

The amount of mail matter originating in St. Louis and dispatched to other points was 12,844,170 lbs., an increase of 1,383,542 lbs. The number of pieces of mail matter delivered and collected by carriers was 97,073,566 against 80,044,725 in 1889, and the number of pieces of registered mail was 1,683,588, an increase of 28,085.

Bank clearings.

The reports of the St. Louis clearing-house show the total bank clearings of the year to have been 223,714,642*l*., against 197,504,525*l*. in 1889, an increase of 13·38 per cent. The clearings of each of the last five years have exceeded each of the preceding years, so that comparing 1886 with 1890 the increase during that period has been nearly 38 per cent.

Capital.

The banking capital has been further increased during the year, and with the surplus now amounts to 4,327,400*l*., and, including the several trust companies, the combined capital at this time amounts to 5,327,480*l*. The deposits for the year amount to 12,158,800*l*., and loans, discounts, and bonds amount to 12,045,000*l*., and places St. Louis fifth in financial strength among the cities of the United States, which rank respectively— New York, Boston, Chicago, Philadelphia, and St. Louis.

The increase of the capital of the banks and trust companies, about 1,200,000*l*., helped to tide over during the financial stringency of the last quarter of the year, and although rates for money reached 8 per cent., yet all classes of borrowers were readily accommodated, except speculators, and little money was obtainable even upon the best collaterals.

City area.

The area of the city of St. Louis embraces 40,000 acres, or 61·357 square miles. The length of river is 19·15 miles, and of western limits 21·27 miles, and from east to west (air line) 6·62 miles.

Population

The population, as reported by the census of the United States taken in June last, was 451,000, and is now estimated at 460,000, an increase over the census of 1880 of over 100,000 in 10 years.

Buildings.

The report of the Commissioner of Buildings shows that there were erected during the year 3,994 buildings, which together with 57,820*l*. expended in additions to old buildings cost 2,730,540*l*., the largest amount expended in any one year; in addition to which was expended 220,000*l*. on public buildings.

Parks.

The parks of St. Louis comprise 2,268·30 acres, of which Forest, 1,371·94 acres; Tower Grove, 266·76 acres; Carondelet, 187·17 acres; O'Fallon, 158·32 acres; and Fair Grounds, 143 acres form the principal ones.

CHICAGO.

These are connected by boulevards constructed and in process: Delmar, running east and west, 100 feet wide, with glass plot extending down the centre; Kings' Highway, north and south from the natural bridge highway on the north, to the city limits on the south, 8½ miles, also 100 feet wide with grass plot down the centre, and tramway on either side, and grand avenue under reconstruction. There are 371·75 miles of paved streets, of which 41·35 miles are granite, 18·32 miles telford, 5·26 miles wood, 3·95 miles asphaltum, and 271·76 miles macadam. These streets are sprinkled by the city three times a day, using 10,000,000 gallons of water. Contracts for improvements and reconstruction during 1891 aggregated 303,310*l*. *Boulevards.*

Stree[ts].

The water supply is taken from the Mississippi River, passed through settling basins, and distributed through the city. This water is considered as wholesome as any in the world. Ship captains sailing from New Orleans assert that the water taken from the lower river keeps sweet and pure longer than any other. The daily consumption ranged from 28,500,000 gallons in February to 44,000,000 gallons in July. *Water.*

The mortality rate is low, being reported by the Health Commission at about 16 to the 1,000. Total births reported 11,419, and deaths 7,698. *Mortality.*

There are 214·36 miles of single track tramways, of which over 81 miles are operated by cable, 90 miles by electricity, and the balance by horse-power. The roads carried last year 68,105,561 passengers. *Tramways.*

The fire department of the city consists of 33 steamers, 3 chemical engines, 33 hose carriages, 8 hook and ladder trucks, 1 water tower apparatus, 6 fuel waggons, and 5 tool and hauling waggons. *Fire department.*

The salvage corps operated at the expense of the insurance companies is a valuable auxiliary. It consists of two companies with 2 salvage corps waggons, 6 Babcock fire extinguishers, 18 men, and 7 horses.

The total assessed valuation for taxation in 1890 was 49,166,970*l*., the total tax levy was 716,574*l*. *Assessed value.*

The total receipts were 1,989,980*l*., and total disbursements 1,374,807*l*.

The bonded debt at close of 1889 was 4,374,620*l*., the reduction during 1890 was 10,600*l*. *Debt.*

The lighting of the city was changed May 4, 1890, from gas to electricity. The total cost for nine months under the new system was 37,117*l*., or an average of 4,144 per month, and has effected a saving over gas in the proportion of 21 to 28. *Lighting.*

It was expected that the Census Bureau would have published their report of the manufacturing industries of St Louis in time for reference in this report, but the figures are unattainable. Enough, however, is known to warrant the belief that the increase in this line has been fully up to that in other lines of commerce. *Manufactures.*

The amount of grain handled was the largest in the history of *Commerce. Grain.*

Wheat. the city, showing St. Louis holds the second among the primary receiving markets of the country. Including flour reduced to wheat the receipts were 17,265,662 bushels.

Corn. The receipts of corn were 45,003,681 bushels.

Oats. The receipts of oats were 12,229,955 bushels.

Rye. The receipts of rye were 501,054 bushels.

The receipts of barley were 2,794,800 bushels.

Grain shipped to New Orleans. Of grain removed, 8,719,849 bushels of corn, and 1,409,440 bushels of wheat were forwarded viâ New Orleans.

Flour. The receipts of flour were 4,313,567 barrels, of which 1,872,005 barrels were manufactured in city mills, 1,229,975 barrels were received for sale by dealers, and the balance handled at country points; a falling-off from last year of 200,000 barrels, which was caused by the burning of the Anchor mills.

Cotton. The cotton business for the year was larger than for many years. The receipts were 587,187 bales, and shipments 578,327 bales, of which about 147,252 bales went to Europe. Prices ruled higher than for the previous year from $9\frac{1}{2}$ c. in February to $11\frac{7}{8}$ c. in September and October.

Provisions. The trade in provisions as shown by the shipments of hog product was 379,346,147*l*., a large increase over the previous year both in receipts and shipments. Prices advanced from January to June, and declined July to close of year 1890.

Cattle. The cattle receipts were the largest on record, being 25 per cent. above those of the previous year.

Tobacco. St. Louis is already the largest tobacco manufacturing centre in the world, the output for 1890 reaching 52,000,000 lbs., nearly 20 per cent. increase over 1889.

Cotton bagging. St. Louis is one of the principal interior points for the distribution of bagging-receipts with quantity manufactured here, the sales and shipments aggregating 13,000,000 yards, having a stock on hand at the close of the year of about 1,000,000 yards.

Cotton ties. The feature of the iron ties trade is that importations the past season were reduced on account of the largely increased tariff, the present duty being 65 c. per bundle, practically excludes importations. The stock at the close of the season was about 5,000 bundles, with prices 1 dol. 30 c. to 1 dol. 35 c. for arrow and 1 dol. 45 c. for delta.

Groceries. The merchants' exchange estimate of the grocery business for 1890 is 14,700,000*l*. to 15,800,000*l*., with an increase of 13 per cent. over 1889.

Sugar. The tariff has been reduced on all sugars above No. 16, Dutch standard in colour, from about 3 c. per lb. to $\frac{1}{2}$ c. per lb., to take effect July 1, 1891, and a bounty of 2 c. per lb. has been placed on all sugar grown in the United States to take effect at the same time. No sugar has been refined in this city during the past year.

Brewing. The brewing business of St. Louis is only exceeded in magnitude and prominence by the cities of New York and Philadephia. The beer manufactured in 1890 was 1,856,883 barrels, equal to 58,491,814 gallons.

CHICAGO.

Dry goods. The records of last year's business in dry goods shows an uninterrupted gain over previous seasons. The total volume of business for 1890 is estimated at 7,000,000*l.*, an increase over last year of about 15 per cent., and the outlook of the spring trade is very promising.

Boots and shoes. St. Louis is becoming a leading point for the manufacture as well as the distribution of boots and shoes, and now stands only second to Boston in magnitude. The trade of the past year is reported to show an average gain of 20 per cent. over that of 1889. Three new manufactories have been established during the year, and capacity of old ones materially enlarged. The output in 1890 is estimated at 3,750,000 pairs of shoes, representing a value of 1,400,000*l.*, being the product of 25 factories. The estimated value of boots and shoes received from the east is 2,800,000*l.*, making a total value in jobbing and manufacturing of 4,200,000*l.* for the year.

Hats and caps. The business of the year 1890 in hats and caps amounted to 600,000*l.*, being an average gain of 18 per cent. over 1889. The trade was good during the first half of the year, but fell off during the last six months.

Saddlery and harness. There was no increase in the business of saddlery and harness; the last six months were marked by dulness which resulted in the loss of the gain made in the first six months of the year. The volume of the business reached nearly 600,000*l.*, being about on a par with 1889.

Hardware. St. Louis has long stood among the leading cities in all lines of hardware, one of the local houses being acknowledged as the largest in the United States. The increase in business is reported as 10 per cent., and the value of the trade 2,800,000*l.*

Wood and willow ware. The importance of the wood and willow ware trade to St. Louis is shown in the report, claiming that one half of the entire wooden ware business of the United States is supplied from this city through one establishment, and although the actual figures are not public, a heavy gain over last year is reported.

UNITED STATES.

Foreign Shipments of Flour* from St. Louis viâ Atlantic Seaports.

Foreign shipments.

Destination.	1890.	1889.
	Barrels.	Barrels.
England	77,775	94,576
Scotland	48,224	137,885
Ireland	40,295	59,798
Germany	428	..
France	2,040	..
Holland	59,306	11,858
Belgium	43,127	24,719
South America	1,224	318
Mexico	..	102
Denmark	142	..
Norway	147	..
Portugal	..	3,825
Newfoundland	26,438	..
Canada	15,872	49,602
Cuba	510	8,440
Seaboard for export	3,158	..
Total	318,686	388,123

* Nearly all shipped in sacks, and shows a decrease of 69,437 barrels

Average Rates of Freight on Grain in Cents per Bushel by Barges and Steamers to Liverpool, viâ New Orleans, in 1889–90.

Freight rates. Grain.

Month.	St. Louis to New Orleans. 1890.	St. Louis to New Orleans. 1889.	New Orleans to Liverpool. 1890.	New Orleans to Liverpool. 1889.	St. Louis to Liverpool. 1890.	St. Louis to Liverpool. 1889.
January	7½	7½	13	12½	20½	19¾
February	7½	7½	14	12½	21½	19¾
March	7	6½	12½	13¼	19½	19¾
April	5½	6	11½	13	17	19
May	5½	5½	7	10¼	12½	16
June	5½	5½	6	8½	11½	14
July	6	5½	6½	8	12½	13½
August	6½	6	5½	11¾	12	17⅜
September	7	6½	4½	12¼	11½	19¼
October	7	6½	4	12½	14	18¾
November	7	7	2½	12	9½	19
December	7	7½	6	13	13	20½

The business of the rivers in tons shows a slight decrease, owing to the extreme low water from August to the close of the year 1890:—

	1890.	1889.
	Tons.	Tons.
Received by steamboats and barges	530,790	543,990
„ „ rafts	132,940	127,695
Shipped by steamboats and barges	601,862	712,700
Total	1,265,592	1,384,385

River tonnage.

VESSELS enrolled at the Port of St. Louis in the Year 1890.

Description.	Number.	Tonnage.
Steamers, wood	99	41,009·05
„ steel	5	1,735·89
„ under 20 tons	10	147·91
„ temporarily enrolled	2	168·77
Barges, permanently enrolled	95	88,491·01
„ under 20 tons	4	33·15
Total	215	131,585·78

Vessels enrolled.

SHIPMENTS of Bulk Grain to New Orleans by Barges for Export.

	1890.	1889.
	Bushels.	Bushels.
Wheat	1,409,440	1,672,361
Corn	8,717,849	13,315,952
Oats	..	89,707
Total	10,127,289	15,078,620

Bulk grain to New Orleans for export.

UNITED STATES.

Bank Clearing - House Statement—Business of the Year 1890 compared with 1889.

	Months.	Clearances. 1890.	Clearances. 1889.	Balances. 1890.	Balances. 1889.
		£	£	£	£
Bank clearings.	January..	18,943,028	16,839,961	3,516,193	2,416,305
	February	16,634,768	14,500,197	3,445,117	2,569,116
	March	17,447,358	15,954,946	3,123,289	2,938,256
	April	18,691,107	14,378,435	3,203,859	2,097,522
	May	20,185,128	16,747,729	3,799,983	3,326,212
	June	18,450,127	16,666,674	3,050,653	3,497,012
	July	18,588,180	16,441,577	2,449,666	2,788,322
	August	17,648,401	16,373,931	1,961,726	2,989,843
	September	18,706,585	16,102,251	2,302,984	2,775,647
	October	19,942,928	19,126,536	2,091,926	3,213,944
	November	18,906,806	16,804,149	1,862,684	2,080,306
	December	19,556,223	17,568,167	1,940,932	1,999,763
	Aggregates	223,714,642	197,504,526	32,756,019	32,692,251

N.B.—Increase in clearings in 1890 13·38 per cent., 26,210,116*l*.

UNITED STATES' Internal Revenue Collections 1889–90.

	Designation.	1889. £ s. d.	1890. £ s. d.
Internal revenue collections.	List, chiefly banks	259 14 0	969 8 0
	Spirit stamps	277,089 14 0	320,022 8 0
	Tobacco	719,434 13 0	839,242 17 0
	Cigars	28,839 19 0	30,824 8 0
	Snuff	629 11 0	509 10 0
	Beer	297,520 18 0	343,193 17 0
	Special tax	29,670 12 0	30,890 19 0
	Oleomargarine stamps	..	43 2 0

NOTE.—No oleo factories here. The collections made were on illicit goods seized at this point and released under compromise.

THE following increase in Mail Matter handled at the Post Office in 1890 was observed.

		Lbs.
Mail matter.	First-class mail matter, increase in lbs.—	
	Letters originating in St. Louis	134,514
	Postal cards	2,636
	Second-class matter—Newspapers and periodicals	1,017,025
	Third-class „ —Circulars, books, &c.	164,869
	Fourth-class „ —Merchandise	64,493
	Total	1,383,542

CHICAGO.

Comparative Business in Leading Articles at St. Louis for 1889-90.

Articles.		1889.	1890.	
Flour, amount manufactured	Barrels	2,066,442	1,872 005	Comparative business, 1889-90.
„ „ handled	„	4,249,261	4,313,567	
Wheat, total receipts	Bushels	13,810,591	11,730,774	
Corn „ „	„	34,299,781	45,003,681	
Oats, „ „	„	11,347,340	12,229,955	
Rye, „ „	„	679,364	501,054	
Barley „ „	„	3,070,807	2,794,880	
All grain received (including flour reduced to wheat)	„	68,466,596	77,795,232	
Cotton receipts	Bales	544,189	517,187	
Bagging, manufactured	Yards	13,000,000	12,000,000	
Hay, receipts	Tons	116,346	114,022	
Tobacco, receipts	Hogsheads	38,082	37,558	
Lead, receipts, in pigs of 80 lbs.	Pigs	2,018,483	1,756,850	
Hog product, total shipment	Lbs.	314,810,593	379,346,147	
Cattle, receipts	Head	508,190	630,014	
Sheep, „	„	358,495	358,496	
Hogs, „	„	1,120,930	1,359,789	
Horses and mules, receipts	„	78,104	82,071	
Lumber and logs	Feet	670,862,165	681,810,588	
Shingles	Pieces	111,080,500	64,173,150	
Lath	„	21,386,350	16,336,650	
Wool, total receipts	Lbs.	21,018,920	20,540,503	
Hides	„	29,732,042	28,245,828	
Sugar received	Lbs.	150,262,050	140,281,225	
Molasses, shipped	Gallons	2,131,080	2,467,060	
Coffee, received	Bags	211,789	222,765	
Rice, receipts	Packages	63,653	115,970	
Coal „	Bushels	65,403,025	69,477,225	
Nails „	Kegs	467,943	471,352	
Potatoes, receipts	Bushels	992,919	1,476,913	
Salt „	Barrels	293,663	326,189	
„ „	Sacks	21,316	33,848	
„ „	Bushels in bulk	304,080	160,030	
Butter	Lbs.	12,822,101	13,661,924	
Tons of freight of all kinds received and shipped		14,909,443	16,505,733	

UNITED STATES.

CUSTOM-HOUSE Transactions for 1890.—Condensed Classification of Commodities Imported into St. Louis in 1890, showing Foreign Values and Duty Paid.

Importations.

Commodities.	Value.	Duty.
	£ s. d.	£ s. d.
Ale and beer	3,813 16 0	1,571 0 0
Anvils	3,564 0 0	1,039 13 6
Art works	2,121 8 0	432 13 6
Books and printed matter	3,583 18 0	601 12 0
Bricks and tiles	547 0 0	92 2 6
Barley (44,150 bushels)	4,726 0 0	1,206 12 0
Brushes	1,802 8 0	611 2 6
Carpets	1,468 16 0	777 14 0
Cement (30,200 barrels)	6,343 0 0	1,068 12 0
Chemicals and drugs	17,112 16 0	4,211 6 6
China and earthenware	37,655 16 0	21,383 19 6
Corks, and manufacture of	7,026 16 0	1,883 2 6
Cutlery	21,130 0 0	10,169 19 0
Diamonds and precious stones	4,485 4 0	448 10 0
Fancy goods	11,357 0 0	4,160 10 0
Fish	3,806 4 0	976 0 0
Free goods	48,078 12 0	..
Glassware	11,824 12 0	6,485 4 0
Looking glasses	1,166 16 0	311 18 0
Guns and firearms	37,051 16 0	13,763 10 0
Hops	61,170 12 0	15,546 11 0
Jewellers' merchandise	5,874 16 0	1,530 13 0
Jute butts	7,439 12 0	2,150 4 0
,, ,, withdrawn free under new law	35,679 8 0	..
Manufactures of cotton	39,610 8 0	17,633 17 0
,, linen	29,386 4 0	10,500 10 0
,, iron—sheet, bars	4,559 8 0	1,990 5 0
,, leather	3,341 4 0	1,024 18 0
,, metals	9,411 12 0	3,992 14 0
,, paper	1,877 16 0	397 5 0
,, silk	6,434 16 0	3,276 2 0
,, wood	1,782 16 0	844 2 0
,, wool	11,250 12 0	7,294 5 0
Musical instruments	2,438 0 0	631 9 0
Nuts and fruits	5,257 16 0	1,905 19 0
Paints and colours	2,290 4 0	559 7 0
Philosophical apparatus	318 12 0	126 3 0
Rice, granulated	60,091 0 0	11,198 14 0
Seeds	2,898 16 0	656 5 0
Soda, caustic	3,829 0 0	1,791 3 0
Steel bars	1,758 4 0	562 14 0
Steel wire	22,585 16 0	11,365 9 0
Tin plate	81,485 0 0	25,669 18 0
Tobacco, cigars, and cigarettes	27,094 12 0	31,409 8 0
Varnishes	579 16 0	231 18 0
Wines	20,087 12 0	10,448 0 0
Window glass	30,354 12 0	8,857 17 6
Woollen dress goods	22,435 16 0	15,170 19 0
Liquors, spirituous	8,708 0 0	7,712 10 0
Miscellaneous	15,248 0 0	6,128 18 0
Total for the year 1890	754,445 18 0	271,802 19 0
,, ,, ,, 1889	649,838 0 0	242,540 10 0
Increase over 1889	104,607 18 0	29,262 9 0

MERCHANDISE Brought into St. Louis in Bond from Following Ports of Entry in 1890, showing Foreign Value and Estimated Duty.

Ports.	Foreign Value.	Duty.	
	£ s. d.	£ s. d.	
Baltimore	78,162 0 0	41,224 15 0	Importations in bond.
Boston	3,997 16 0	1,326 13 0	
Detroit	55,247 0 0	27,475 16 0	
New Orleans	77,449 5 0	23,554 16 0	
New York	395,696 16 0	122,164 3 0	
Philadelphia	126,884 0 0	48,377 2 0	
Portland	15,643 8 0	7,329 14 0	
Huron	823 8 0	231 6 0	
San Francisco	542 5 0	138 14 0	
Total	754,445 18 0	271,802 19 0	
In warehouse December 31, 1890	11,862 0 0	8,422 0 0	

ST. PAUL.

Mr. Vice-Consul Morphy reports as follows:—

In recording the comparative progress of the twin cities of St. Paul and Minneapolis, during the past year, it will be well in order to avert unfavourable criticism to draw attention at once, for the purpose of explanation, to the significant decrease in the population of both cities.

Their close proximity, which is but 12 miles from centre to centre, the desire of each one to enlarge its boundaries in the direction of the other has practically incorporated them as a federal city, in all but name. Each one in the hope of preserving its identity has cultivated a spirit of rivalry toward the other, which has become so strongly defined that it now amounts to antagonism. In order to sustain themselves in their contention and in the hope of attracting capital and population they each adopted a system of inflation which was largely fictitious, so much so that the United States Government on consideration felt called upon, at the close of the last census year, to order a recount, which resulted in a humiliating exposure on the one hand, and in a reduction of population to within proper bounds on the other hand. *Population.*

But notwithstanding the discipline inflicted by the readjusted census, the shrinkage in real estate and other values arising therefrom, together with the stringency in the money market which naturally affected the struggling north-west, more than the great money centres of the east, yet there has continued a buoyancy and living force everywhere abounding, which fully compensates these two communities for geographical or other disadvantages. *Real estate.*

One of the most noticeable features in connection with St. Paul is its splendid street car service, which now consists of 100 miles of cable and electric lines. The system of rapid transit *Tram car service.*

and transfer at one fare of 5 c. to any part of city has revolutionised the social system, to the extent of offering suburban life to all whose employments do not forbid such a luxury.

St. Paul.

Items.		Quantity.
Population	Number	133,156
Jobbing trade	Dollars	122,223,048
Manufacturing	,,	61,721,595
Bank clearings	,,	225,564,896
Imported goods	,,	1,110,240
Post office business	,,	5,240,804
Assessed valuation—taxable property	,,	121,499,930
Real estate transferred	,,	26,502,820
United States' internal revenue	,,	2,680,237
Cost of public works	,,	1,049,622
Electric and cable street cars	,,	100
Total graded streets	Miles	351
,, paved ,,	,,	41
Area of city	Acres	35,483
Length of city east and west	Miles	10
Width of city north and south	,,	5
Daily passenger trains in and out	,,	300
Daily United States' mail created at St. Paul	Tons	10

By the above table it will be seen that, with the exception of decrease in population already accounted for, decrease in expenditure for public works and of assessed value of taxable property, there has been a satisfactory advance; even real estate, which is always sensitive, has not yielded to pressure; this may be accounted for by the increased street car facilities.

The health department makes returns of 3,185 births, and 1,696 deaths, showing a death rate of 12 per thousand.

Building. Building last year was active: 9,500,000 dol. was expended by private enterprise, the amount was about equally divided between business blocks and residences. The Manhattan block and the metropolitan opera house are worthy of special notice, as being amongst the erections of last year.

Public works. The waterworks of the city have been constructed at a cost of 2,460,000 dol., the total mains now in are 193 miles with 10,458 connections. The daily consumption of water is 8,000,000 gallons, or equal to eight acres of water three feet deep.

The average rainfall for 32 years past has been 28 inches, that for 1890 was 23 inches.

The fire brigade consists of one chief, two assistant chiefs, 157 men, exclusive of officers, divided over 15 stations. The losses by fire during the year are reported at 261,263 dol. 92 c. as against 285,340 dol. the previous year.

The bonded indebtedness of the city is 7,000,000 dol., total assets 9,000,000 dol.

The customs duties collected at St. Paul for 1890 were 245,205 dol. 89 c., an increase of 15,819 dol. 77 c. over the previous year. Value of dutiable goods imported 675,345 dol. 53 c. Value of free goods imported was 434,895 dol. 28 c.; value of domestic exports 1,563,897 dol. 53 c.

MINNEAPOLIS.

Items.		
Population	Number	164,000
Assessed valuation	Dollars	124,045,000
Bonded debt	,,	6,486,300
Banking capital	,,	7,905,000
Bank clearings	,,	250,705,000
Jobbing trade	,,	184,209,000
Manufacturing	,,	64,592,000
Real estate transfers	,,	32,145,000
Wheat receipts	Bushels	43,500,000
Lumber, cut	Feet	343,573,762
Shingles	M.	162,217,500
Lath	,,	80,275,350
Annual capacity of mills	,,	500,000,000
Square miles in city	Miles	53½
Miles of streets	,,	810
Miles of water mains	,,	161

Tram car service. The street car service of Minneapolis is still of a mixed character, and is divided between horse cars, steam motors, and electric cars, but active measures are being taken to consolidate the whole system and adapt it to the electric. At the close of the year (1890) there were 80 miles of electric lines in operation, the construction of which was not commenced till August 23. The rapidity with which that portion of the system was changed augurs well for an early abandonment of the other two methods of locomotion.

The number of passengers carried during the year was 17,000,000.

In connection with street railways it must not be forgotten to call attention to the fact that there is an inter-urban line of 40 cars running at intervals every 10 minutes between Minneapolis and St. Paul at a fare of 10 c., with privilege of transfer at either end. This is a great boon to both cities.

The fire department is complete in all its details, and is composed of a force, exclusive of officers, of 167 men.

The losses by fire during the past year were—buildings, 130,067 dol. 95 c.; contents, 497,145 dol. 6 c. These amounts were fairly well covered by insurance, the total loss being 627,213 dol. 1 c.

Cereals. The wheat crop, which is the staple product for both Minnesota and Dakota, has only reached the aggregate of 68,767,000 of very inferior quality as against 87,108,000 of high grade the year previous; the comparative productiveness of other wheat-grow-

(1111)

ing countries, notably Manitoba, whose average crop last year was 30 bushels per acre, whilst these two States only make a showing of 12·5 bushels, has awakened an anxious interest in the breasts of millers in Minneapolis, and is causing them to revolve fresh schemes by which to guard against possible failures in future.

Proposed State legislature.

The Legislature of this State, which is now in session, has several Bills in suspension, which, if finally passed, will materially affect the future of the country. One is to reduce the rate of interest to 8 per cent., to tax all mortgages, whether foreign or local, 2 per cent., and to abolish commissions to loan agents under a heavy penalty. Another is to compel insurance companies to give security to a large amount before doing business in the State. The better opinion seems to be, however, that neither Bill will pass both Houses.

In conclusion, the evidences of prosperity in the district of this vice-consulate are apparent. There have been very few failures in business, the faith of the people in the future is unshaken, every preparation is being made to follow up past successes with renewed vigour, and, there is no doubt, with peace assured and a fair crop to reward industry, I shall have the pleasure next year to report another step in advance.

DENVER.

Mr. Vice-Consul Pearce reports as follows:—

The report for the year 1890, which I now have the honour of submitting, indicates that the State of Colorado and its varied industries still show evidences of rapid growth and prosperity.

Population.

It is my duty to correct the statement made in my last report in reference to the population of Denver, wherein it was estimated at 15,000. The report of the 11th Federal census, which was taken last year, shows the population to be 126,000.

It may be of interest to point out that the population of the whole State, as shown by the census report, amounts to 410,975, and some idea of the rapid increase in population may be formed by comparing the census reports of 1880 and 1870, which gave 194,327 and 39,864 respectively.

Value of new buildings.

The estimated cost of new buildings, which have been erected during the year, is somewhat in excess of the preceding year, viz., 3,308,325*l*., of which sum 927,427*l*. was expended in the construction of large business blocks, the balance being distributed among churches, colleges, schools, and dwellings. The business blocks have been constructed according to the most modern ideas of strength and durability, combined with good architectural taste; in fact, they compare favourably with similar modern buildings erected in the larger eastern cities. The most important of these buildings—the Boston block, eight stories, Masonic temple, seven stories, People's National Bank building, nine stories, and the Equitable building, now under construction—represent a total cost estimated at 633,000*l*.; this, in itself, is an indication of the steady growth and enterprise of Denver.

The transactions in real estate for the year were 13,185,985*l*., an increase over the previous year of 1,000,000*l*. *Transactions in real estate.*

The clearing-house records show a total of 51,119,000*l*.; increase, 31·4 per cent. *Clearing-house records.*

The value of taxable property in the whole State is said to be 44,110,813*l*., an increase over the previous year of 5,457,987*l*., or 14·1 per cent. *Value of taxable property.*

The general feeling prevails among capitalists that Denver offers favourable facilities for manufacturing. The amount of capital invested in the business of smelting alone increases every year, and Denver may be said to be the recognised centre for the smelting of gold, silver lead, and copper ores of the western portion of the continent. The estimated value of the products of all the manufacturing interests of the city for the year 1890 is 8,815,160*l*.; this is an increase of 28 per cent. over 1889. There are altogether 606 establishments, employing in the aggregate some 10,000 men, and the total amount of wages paid for the year is 1,416,992*l*. *Manufacturing.*

It is contemplated by local capitalists to erect a large plant for the reduction of iron and the manufacture of steel. The matter has during the past year come before the Board of Trade for discussion, and it appears to have assumed definite shape.

The extension of cable and electric motor railways has gone on increasing with great rapidity, as the following particulars will show. The two cable companies have adopted the electric system for the extension of their lines, and during the past year 49 miles of this system have been constructed and put in operation, the cost of which was 167,000*l*. The city has now over 100 miles of street railways covering the two systems, cable and electric, forming an extensive network over the entire city and its important suburbs. The electric system adopted is the Thomson-Houston overhead system, and the success of this system is assured beyond any doubt. *Cable and electric railways.*

The expenditure for the water supply of Denver has kept pace with other enterprises. 400,000*l*. has been spent during the year for increased water supply by the two companies in existence. *Water companies.*

The only change in the railroad situation during the past year which I have to report is the completion of the broad gauge system of the Denver and Rio Grande railroad, which connects with the Denver and Rio Grande Western railroad, and forms a continuous broad gauge route from Denver through to the Pacific coast by way of Salt Lake City, Utah. *Railroads.*

The total value of the product of the Colarado mines in silver, gold, lead, and copper during the year is as follows:— *Mining.*

	£
Silver	4,051,981
Gold	902,427
Lead	949,850
Copper	75,482
Total	5,979,740

UNITED STATES.

Coal.

The State Inspector of Coal Mines has, with his usual kindness, furnished me with a complete report of the coal industry of the State for the year; comparing it with the previous year there is an increase in the value of the output to the extent of 142,250*l*. The average value of the coal on the cars at the mines is estimated at 8*s.* per ton, making a total value of 1,230,312*l*.

PRODUCTION of Coal by Counties in Colorado for the Year ending December 31, 1890. The Month of December is estimated.

Counties.	Tons of 2,000 Lbs.	Increase.	Decrease.
Arapahoe	681	..	219
Boulder	409,130	115,037	..
El Paso	26,847	..	27,219
Fremont	392,570	112,715	..
Gunnison	238,139	..	16,669
Garfield	198,086	53,459	..
Huerfano	425,606	116,583	..
Jefferson	12,334	2,544	..
Las Animas	1,134,845	234,320	..
La Plata	33,045	..	235
Mesa	4,200	4,200	..
Park	67,203	20,198	..
Pitkin	74,362	28,181	..
Weld	42,603	16,427	..
Small mines, estimated	16,130	..	..
Total	3,075,781	..	..

Output for 1889, 2,373,954 tons; output for 1890, 3,075,781 tons, being an increase over 1889 of 701,827 tons.

PRODUCTION of Coke for 1890.

Counties.	Tons of 2,000 Lbs.	Increase.
Las Animas	149,503	30,067
Gunnison	44,521	1,663
Pitkin	34,463	12,338
Total	228,487	..

The above increase in the coke production is in comparing 1889 with 1890.

The following is a summary of the coal statistics for a number of years:—

	Tons.
1873	69,977
1874	87,372
1875	98,838
1876	117,666
1877	160,000
1878	200,630
1879	322,732
1880	375,000
1881	706,744
1882	1,061,479
1883	1,220,593
1884	1,130,024
1885	1,398,796
1886	1,436,211
1887	1,791,735
1888	2,185,477
1889	2,373,954
1890	3,075,781

Imports

Through the kindness of the collector of customs of this city, I am able to report a list of the principal articles of imports from Great Britain for the year 1890, wherein it will be seen that there has been an increase in value of imports of nearly 100 per cent.; this large increase is, in all probability, due in a measure to the fact that it is becoming better known every year that Denver is a port of entry, and goods which formerly passed through the eastern custom-house find their way direct to Denver in bond.

The following is a record of imports from Great Britain for the past five years since the establishment of this Vice-Consulate:—

Year.	£	s.	d.
1886	3,201	0	0
1887	5,043	12	0
1888	8,109	12	0
1889	17,585	7	0
Total value	33,939	11	0

UNITED STATES.

RETURN of the Principal Articles of Import to Denver during the Year 1890.

Articles.	Value.
	£ s. d.
Art works	146 0 0
Dolls and toys	60 4 0
Earthenware, decorated	995 4 0
" plain	1,357 16 0
Hats	372 8 0
Household and personal effects	581 16 0
Lace curtains	257 4 0
Linoleum	207 16 0
Liquors	1,080 12 0
Manufactured carpets	208 8 0
" wool cloths	4,925 16 0
" " clothing	199 0 0
" cotton	222 0 0
" glass	154 16 0
" linens	269 12 0
" metal	177 4 0
" silk	24 12 0
Paints	98 0 0
Pickles and sauces	508 8 0
Precious stones	14,190 4 0
Seeds, garden and other	75 12 0
Shot-guns, breach-loading	171 8 0
Sponges	220 4 0
Tea	182 0 0
Tin plates	5,334 12 0
Varnish	323 16 0
Miscellaneous	167 12 0
Total	32,512 4 0

KANSAS CITY.

Agricultural interests.

Mr. Vice-Consul Chandler reports as follows:—

The year 1890 was not a prosperous one for Kansas. Owing to the long and severe droughts, accompanied with hot winds of more than ordinary severity and frequency, all crops in the western half of the State were almost total failures, and a good deal of suffering both to the inhabitants and their stock has been the result. While the drought was not so severe in the eastern half of the State, its effects were general, and in no sections were the crops more than 50 per cent. of the average yield. Because of the general scarcity the prices of all farm products advanced on an average about 200 per cent. over those realised for the crops of 1889, and the farmers who were so fortunate as to have produce to sell found a ready market at prices that returned them greater aggregate profits than were derived from their crops of 1889.

Trade in general.

Owing to the unfavourable conditions surrounding the agricultural interest the cities and towns of Kansas have experienced a year of comparatively hard times, and commercial business generally has not been as good as is usual.

CHICAGO.

The area of the State of Kansas is 82,144 square miles. **Area.**

The population of the entire State is 1,423,485. **Population.**

The principal cities of the State are Topeka, the capital, Kansas City, Leavenworth, and Wichita. **Principal cities.**

The value of all taxable property as returned by the State Board of Equalisation is as follows, viz.:—Land, 168,285,199 dol.; town lots, 72,814,873 dol.; personal, 43,750,913 dol.; railroads, 57,866,232 dol. The assessments are made upon a basis of one-third of the actual value. The increase of taxable values over the returns for 1889 aggregate 99,555,626 dol. **Value of taxable property.**

The following table shows the population, assessed valuation of property, and indebtedness of the principal cities of Kansas:—

City.	Population.	Assessed Valuation. Land.	Personal.	Railroads.	Indebtedness.
		Dollars.	Dollars.	Dollars.	Dollars.
Topeka	35,662	7,682,460	2,040,945	353,654	500,525
Kansas City	30,950	7,941,933	804,999	206,387	1,807,466
Leavenworth	20,578	4,481,933	747,096	133,597	943,153
Wichita	23,500	7,822,700	1,532,535	181,989	402,000

The following statistics are taken from the report of the secretary to the State Board of Agriculture for the year 1890:— Wheat, 28,801,214 bushels, valued at 23,410,548 dol.; corn (maize), 51,090,229 bushels, valued at 21,491,961 dol.; oats, 29,175,582 bushels, valued at 9,174,400 dol.; rye, 2,274,879 bushels, valued at 1,136,463 dol.; barley, 247,918 bushels, valued at 123,959 dol.; potatoes, 2,817,288 bushels, valued at 3,152,514 dol. Total value of the sorghum cane crop, 4,217,757 dol. Buckwheat, cotton, flax, hemp, tobacco, and millet are all successfully grown to meet the local demands. **Crop reports and values.**

TABLE showing the Numbers of the Various Kinds of Live Stock and their Aggregate Value for the Year 1890. **Live stock.**

	Number.
Horses	716,459
Mules	78,346
Milch cows	674,705
Other cattle	1,696,081
Sheep	281,654
Swine	2,192,231
Value	$113,533,342

The total value of animals slaughtered, wool clipped, butter and cheese, poultry, eggs and milk sold, amounted to 366,997,463 dols.

38 UNITED STATES.

SALT MINING.

Salt. Extensive beds of rock salt exist in Southern Central Kansas, and mining on a large scale is carried on, principally at Hutchinson, in Reno County. There are 12 important salt marshes in the middle region of the State, and evaporating plants of considerable magnitude are in operation. The quality of the product is equal to any produced in the United States.

KANSAS CITY, MISSOURI, AND KANSAS CITY, KANSAS.

Location. The two Kansas Cities are separated by an imaginary line passing through the centre of State Line Street, and as far as their business interests are concerned they are practically one city.

Trade growing. The commercial prosperity of the two Kansas Cities during the past year has gradually increased in all lines over the business of any previous year.

Live stock. Kansas City ranks as the second live stock market in the world. The stock yards building has in it 121 offices, exclusive of the bank and yard company's office. The property has a daily yarding capacity of 20,000 cattle, 35,000 hogs, and 20,000 sheep.

Food animals. The receipts of all food animals during the year amounted to 4,864,360 head, and of horses and mules 35,856 head, of a total value of upwards of 75,000,000 dol. During the year the prices were generally lower than they were in 1889; this fact was largely due to the forced selling-off of all the cattle on the Cherokee strip. Range cattle varied in price from 1 dol. 30 c. to 2 dol. 80 c. per 100 lbs.; native cows from 1 dol. 60 c. to 3 dol. 25 c. per 100 lbs.; native stockers and feeders from 2 dol. 10 c. to 3 dol. 40 c. per 100 lbs.; native butcher and shipping steers from 3 dol. 25 c. to 4 dol. 80 c. per 100 lbs.

Horses and mules. Prices. Cattle.

Hogs. The price for hogs ranges from 3 dol. 15 c., the minimum reached December 2, to 4 dol. 20 c., the maximum reached October 1, per 100 lbs.

Packing trade. The packing trade for 1890 shows a large increase over that of 1889. This industry gives employment to 9,500 men. 493,000 cattle, 2,269,000 hogs, and 152,000 sheep were slaughtered during the year.

Banking. Capital increased from 9,207,300 dol. in 1889 to 11,617,300 dol. in 1890, and the surplus funds from 969,500 dol. to 1,063,813 dol. The bank clearings for the year reached 491,906,766 dol., an increase of 42,427,292 dol. over the previous year. For the first time cotton paper was handled in our market, and closer trade relations with Texas has drawn much trade from that State. The volume of business was satisfactory, and its character profitable.

Building operations. During 1890, 5,000,000 dol. were spent in new buildings in Kansas City, Missouri, and 3,000,000 dol. in Kansas City, Kansas.

The following table shows a comparative statement of the receipts of grain for 1889 and 1890, denoting bushels :— *Grain trade.*

Date.	Wheat.	Corn.	Oats.	Rye.
	Bushels.	Bushels.	Bushels.	Bushels.
1889	4,555,001	9,557,067	4,204,531	429,100
1890	5,797,400	18,050,300	4,767,000	336,000

Kansas City, Missouri, has a population of 135,000, and Kansas City, Kansas, has a population of 37,950 by the recent Federal census. *Population.*

The annual death-rate in Kansas City, Missouri, is 16·5 per 1,000 of population, as per the reports of the Marine Hospital Bureau of the United States. *Death rate.*

The total value of all merchandise imported directly to Kansas City is as follows :— *Imports.*

	Dollars.
Total value from all foreign points	484,929
Total value from Great Britain	391,933

The imports consisted chiefly of tin, terne plates, earthenware, manufactures of cotton, flax, hemp and jute, and salt.

(1111)

LONDON:
Printed for Her Majesty's Stationery Office,
By HARRISON AND SONS,
Printers in Ordinary to Her Majesty.
(1250 5 | 91—H & S 1111)

FOREIGN OFFICE.
1891.
ANNUAL SERIES.

Nº· 906.

DIPLOMATIC AND CONSULAR REPORTS ON TRADE AND FINANCE.

UNITED STATES.

REPORT FOR THE YEAR 1890
ON THE
TRADE OF THE CONSULAR DISTRICT OF SAN FRANCISCO.

REFERENCE TO PREVIOUS REPORT, Annual Series No. 718.

Presented to both Houses of Parliament by Command of Her Majesty,
JUNE, 1891.

LONDON:
PRINTED FOR HER MAJESTY'S STATIONERY OFFICE,
BY HARRISON AND SONS, ST. MARTIN'S LANE,
PRINTERS IN ORDINARY TO HER MAJESTY.

And to be purchased, either directly or through any Bookseller, from
EYRE & SPOTTISWOODE, EAST HARDING STREET, FLEET STREET, E.C., and
32, ABINGDON STREET, WESTMINSTER, S.W.; or
JOHN MENZIES & Co., 12, HANOVER STREET, EDINBURGH, and
88 and 90, WEST NILE STREET, GLASGOW; or
HODGES, FIGGIS, & Co., 104, GRAFTON STREET, DUBLIN.

1891.

[C. 6205—137.] *Price Threepence.*

New Series of Reports.

Reports of the Annual Series have been issued from Her Majesty's Diplomatic and Consular Officers at the following places, and may be obtained from the sources indicated on the title-page:—

No.		Price.	No.		Price.
784.	Naples	1½d.	845.	Charleston	1½d.
785.	Tunis	4d.	846.	Manila	5d.
786.	Vera Cruz	1d.	847.	Madeira	½d.
787.	Tangier	1½d.	848.	Paris	2d.
788.	Rome	2d.	849.	Tripoli	½d.
789.	Stuttgart	1½d.	850.	Swatow	1d.
790.	Panama	1½d.	851.	Saigon	½d.
791.	Berne	1½d.	852.	Vienna	1½d.
792.	Asuncion	½d.	853.	Algiers	2d.
793.	Bahia	7½d.	854.	Algiers	1d.
794.	Monte Video	1½d.	855.	Mozambique	8d.
795.	Munich	2d.	856.	Antwerp	1½d.
796.	Bucharest	1d.	857.	Mogador	2d.
797.	Tokio	1d.	858.	Ichang	½d.
798.	Tabreez	1d.	859.	Calais	8½d.
799.	Antwerp	1d.	860.	Riga	2d.
800.	Malaga	1d.	861.	San José	1d.
801.	Odessa	1d.	862.	Genoa	1½d.
802.	Malaga	2d.	863.	Warsaw	1d.
803.	Amsterdam	1d.	864.	Wuhu	1d.
804.	Bogotá	1½d.	865.	Marseilles	1d.
805.	Guayaquil	½d.	866.	Syra	1d.
806.	Lima	1d.	867.	Jeddah	½d.
807.	Rio do Janeiro	3d.	868.	Savannah	½d.
808.	Dantzig	1½d.	869.	Suakin	½d.
809.	Florence	1½d.	870.	Berlin	1d.
810.	Lisbon	1d.	871.	Batoum	1½d.
811.	Quito	½d.	872.	Rosario	1d.
812.	Para	½d.	873.	Buenos Ayres	½d.
813.	Palermo	2½d.	874.	Mogador	1d.
814.	Copenhagen	1d.	875.	Tainan	6½d.
815.	Serajevo	½d.	876.	Pakhoi	1d.
816.	Porto Rico	1d.	877.	Odessa	2½d.
817.	Madrid	½d.	878.	Trebizond	1½d.
818.	Brussels	½d.	879.	Mollendo	½d.
819.	Patras	½d.	880.	Kiukiang	1d.
820.	Stuttgart	1d.	881.	Antananarivo	1d.
821.	Taganrog	1d.	882.	Stettin	2½d.
822.	Salonica	2d.	883.	Fiume	1½d.
823.	Galveston	1d.	884.	Batavia	1d.
824.	Rome	1½d.	885.	Samoa	½d.
825.	Paris	1½d.	886.	Cherbourg	1d.
826.	Bushire	½d.	887.	Cagliari	1d.
827.	New Orleans	3d.	888.	Hankow	1½d.
828.	Buda-Pesth	½d.	889.	Vienna	1½d.
829.	Hamburg	3d.	890.	Amoy	1d.
830.	Port Saïd	1d.	891.	Adrianople	½d.
831.	Samoa	½d.	892.	Chicago	2½d.
832.	Guayaquil	½d.	893.	Brest	1d.
833.	New Orleans	2d.	894.	Smyrna	1d.
834.	The Piræus	1d.	895.	Cadiz	1d.
835.	Baltimore	1½d.	896.	Aleppo	1d.
836.	Trieste	2d.	897.	Foochow	1d.
837.	Galatz	1½d.	898.	Kiungchow	1d.
838.	Wênchow	1d.	899.	The Hague	1½d.
839.	Havre	2½d.	900.	Nice	1½d.
840.	Rome	1½d.	901.	Nantes	1½d.
841.	Taganrog	2d.	902.	Port-au-Prince	1½d.
842.	Calais	1d.	903.	Bengazi	1d.
843.	Boston	1d.	904.	Tahiti	½d.
844.	Bordeaux	2½d.	905.	Chinkiang	1d.

No. 906.

Reference to previous Report, Annual Series No. 718.

UNITED STATES.

SAN FRANCISCO.

Consul Donohoe to the Marquis of Salisbury.

My Lord, San Francisco, April 22, 1891.

I HAVE the honour to enclose herewith Annual Reports on the Trade and Commerce of San Francisco, Portland, Astoria, Port Townsend, Los Angeles, and San Diego for the year 1890.

I have, &c.
(Signed) DENIS DONOHOE.

Report on the Trade and Commerce of San Francisco for the Year 1890.

The year just closed has not in all respects met the expectations of the commercial community of San Francisco. The rainfall for the three last months of 1889, and the three first months of 1890, amounted to 43·49 inches in San Francisco, and was much heavier in the country. In the northern and central sections of the State of California, destructive inundations occurred and prevented early sowing of the grain crops, and destroyed many thousands of acres that had been already put under seed. The result has been a short crop of both wheat and barley, and a consequent advance in price. These heavy rains have, however, to a certain extent benefited the land by the thorough soaking which it has received. *Heavy rains. Short grain crops.*

The crop of wheat for 1890 is estimated, by the produce exchange of San Francisco, at 872,707 tons, which falls far short of that of 1889; the crop generally in the southern portion of the State has been a good one, that section of the country not having suffered so much as the northern from the unprecedented rainfall in the early part of the year. There have been large shipments of wheat to France and Belgium, and some cargoes to Brazil. *Wheat.*

UNITED STATES.

Flour. The export of flour for the year shows an increase of about 50,000 barrels; the total export being 1,187,552 barrels. Great Britain received 407,841 barrels, and China and Japan 459,515 barrels; the balance went principally to South and Central America and the Hawaiian Islands.

Barley. There was a very short crop of barley throughout the State; the receipts here are given as 92,511 tons, as compared with 112,932 tons in 1889. The new crop, however, was of excellent quality, and commenced to be received in this market in June, and opened at a high price, and with some fluctuations has steadily advanced. In consequence of the high prices prevailing in San Francisco, a great deal of barley has been sent here from the States of Oregon and Washington. The export to Great Britain has only been 2,209 tons.

Salmon pack. The total amount of tinned salmon received here by sea is 751,717 cases, which is a falling-off of about 100,000 cases as compared with 1889.

It is estimated that about 100,000 cases were still in hand in San Francisco at the end of 1890.

The total pack of the Pacific Coast is given by a mercantile house largely in the business as follows :—

	Cases.
Alaska	688,332
Columbia River	433,500
British Columbia	399,912
Sacramento River	35,006
Other small fisheries	67,117
Total	1,623,867

Dried fruits. The fruit crop of California has been a very large one for the year 1890, and, though it is not easy to make an exact estimate of the crop, the figures given for dried fruits by a reliable house here, which is extensively engaged in that business, are as follows:—

	Lbs.
Raisins, 20 lb. boxes, 1,215,000, or	24,300,000
Raisins in bags	8,000,000
Grapes in bags	9,000,000
French prunes	14,000,000
German and Hungarian prunes	5,000,000
Bleached and evaporated apricots	8,000,000
Bleached unpeeled peaches	8,000,000
Bleached peeled peaches	150,000
Sun-dried peaches	1,000,000
Bleached evaporated nectarines	500,000
Pitted plums	500,000
Pears	600,000
Evaporated apples	600,000
Sun-dried apples	300,000
Figs, black and white	200,000
Walnuts	2,000,000
Almonds	200,000
Extracted honey	4,500,000
Honey in the comb	500,000
Bees'-wax	30,000

SAN FRANCISCO.

The crop of raisins has been a heavy one, and there is a **Raisins.** notable increase in the quantity shipped in sacks; and, as the demand in the Eastern States has been good and prices high, the producers have had no difficulty in disposing of their product at good paying prices. I understand that inquiries have been made from Europe as to shipments from here, but, with the large demand and good prices in the home market, it would scarcely pay to ship at present.

The following is an estimate of the canned fruit pack of the **Canned fruits.** season by a leading packer:—

Articles.	Quantity.	Total.
Apples	7,000	
Apricots	130,000	
Asparagus	11,000	
Blackberries	16,500	
Cherries, white	38,500	
Cherries, black	27,500	
Currants	5,500	
Gooseberries	11,000	
Grapes	38,500	
Nectarines	5,500	
Pears	165,000	
Peas	27,500	
Peaches	255,000	
Plums	45,000	
Quinces	3,300	
Raspberries	11,000	
Strawberries	16,500	
		814,300
Miscellaneous—		
Pie fruits	56,500	
Tomatoes	270,000	
Jams and jellies	25,000	
		351,500
Grand total		1,165,800

The lumber receipts for 1890 show a slight reduction as **Timber.** compared with 1889, and are shown by the following table:—

Lumber Receipts for 1890.

	Feet.
Pine	242,086,120
Redwood	170,163,170
Spruce	37,500
Ash	96,700
Maple	37,576
Cedar	30,000
White cedar	25,000
Total	412,476,066
„ 1889	476,506,931

UNITED STATES.

Wine. United States census returns.

The wine production of the United States, as given by the census bulletin just issued, was 24,306,905 gallons, of which 14,626,000 gallons came from California, and 9,680,905 gallons from all the rest of the States. All the vineyards in the State are returned as a little over 200,000 acres. The estimated vintage for 1890 has been put at 19,400,000 gallons; a considerable deduction will have, however, to be made from this estimate, as a proportion goes to the still, as the brandy product is steadily increasing every year.

The price of grapes at the vineyards increased in vintage time from 30 to 50 per cent. over those prevailing in 1889. The quality of the new wine shows some improvement, and better prices were received for it. For ordinary wines sales were made at the vineyards from 6½d. to 8d. per gallon: for sweet wines from 1s. 5d. to 1s. 8d., and for brandies in bond 2s. 2d. to 2s. 6d. per gallon.

Sugar.

The principal sugar imports at this port came from the Hawaiian Islands, 112,952 tons having been imported from there and 7,605 from Manila.

Coal.

The receipts of coal from foreign ports have been as follows:—

	Tons.
From British Columbia	441,759
„ Great Britain	37,272
„ Australia	194,725
„ Japan	13,170
Total	686,926

The receipts in 1889 were 732,963 tons. There has been a falling-off in the receipts from British Columbia of about 60,000 tons, owing to the strike at the Wellington mines.

Quicksilver.

The total production of quicksilver in California in 1890 amounted to 22,926 flasks, as against 25,650 flasks in 1889. The average price for the year is about 11l. per flask.

Metal product.

From the annual statement of Messrs. Wells, Fargo, and Co., the net product of metals in the States and territories west of the Missouri River, excluding British Columbia and Mexico, for the last two years is given as follows:—

Year.	Gold.	Silver.	Copper.	Lead.	Total.
1890	6,359,072	12,586,166	4,113,818	2,301,914	25,360,970
1889	6,505,532	12,961,727	2,958,752	2,918,664	25,344,675

Silver export.

The export of silver from San Francisco during the past year to Japan, China, the Straits, &c., has been 1,360,173l.

Freights.

The following table gives the rates for freights current during each month of the year:—

SAN FRANCISCO.

Year.	Cork for Orders.						Liverpool.					
	£	s.	d.	£	s.	d.	£	s.	d.	£	s.	d.
January	1	18	9 to	1	14	9	1	15	0 to	1	12	6
February	1	17	6	1	14	9	1	16	0	1	11	3
March	1	17	6	1	11	3	1	15	0	1	11	0
April	1	17	6	1	13	9	1	16	9	1	11	6
May	1	18	0	1	14	6	1	15	0	1	12	6
June	1	17	6	1	15	6	1	15	0		..	
July	2	0	0	1	16	3	1	15	0		..	
August	2	3	9	1	16	9	1	17	6		..	
September	2	2	6	1	16	0	1	17	6		..	
October	2	6	3	2	1	3	2	2	6		..	
November	2	2	6	1	17	6	2	0	0	1	12	6
December	2	2	6	2	0	0	1	17	6		..	

Buildings and real estate. About 1,600 new buildings have been put up in San Francisco during the year, at a cost of about 2,000,000*l*., and the real estate market has been extremely active throughout the city, and much property has changed hands in the outlying districts within the city limits.

Population. By the United States census the population of the city, taken June 30, is given as 300,000 Caucasian, 282,000 African, and 18,000 Chinese. There were 6,880 deaths last year, as against 5,584 during 1889—an increase of 1,296. Of the deaths 4,338 were males and 2,542 females, and 1,390 died in public institutions.

The causes of death were as follows:—Casualties 228, suicides 99, homicides 16, alcoholism 64, croup 112, diphtheria 176, typhoid fever 133, cancer 234, phthisis 1,070, apoplexy 154, kidney disease 175, bronchitis 273, convulsions 185, heart disease 487, paralysis 273, pneumonia 732, inanition 407, old age 129.

The Board of Health gives the ratio of mortality at 1,000 per annum; white and African 20·50, Mongolian 18·50—aggregate 19·50.

The Bond-street Mercantile Agency reports 992 failures in the Pacific Coast States and territories for the year 1890, with assets 774,795*l*., and liabilities 1,448,631*l*., as compared with 813 of the previous year, with assets 473,474*l*., and liabilities 931,194*l*. The failures for the past year are divided among the States and territories as follows:—

States.	Number.	Assets.	Liabilities.
		£	£
California	645	375,523	786,800
Oregon	126	93,430	140,130
Washington	202	293,642	493,990
Nevada	9	6,060	14,380
Arizona	10	7,140	13,730
Total	992	775,795	1,449,030

Note.—All values in this report are reduced to sterling at the rate of 5 dol. to the 1*l*.

UNITED STATES.

The following causes are assigned for the failures, viz.:—Incompetence 256, inexperience 101, inadequate capital for the insurers undertaken 257, injudicious crediting 57, complication of indebtedness 14, personal extravagance 36, neglect of business and bad habits 37, excessive competition 34, unfavourable circumstances, floods, fires, &c., 86, speculation 13, and fraud 101.

Annex A.—RETURN of all Shipping at the Port of San Francisco in the Year 1890.

ENTERED.

Nationality.	Sailing. Number of Vessels.	Sailing. Tons.	Steam. Number of Vessels.	Steam. Tons.	Total. Number of Vessels.	Total. Tons.
British	169	281,148	46	86,769	215	367,917
American, from foreign countries	247	184,635	201	292,479	448	477,114
American, from Atlantic ports of Union	44	79,370	...	...	44	79,370
Hawaiian	18	11,701	24	42,356	42	54,057
German	22	27,168	1	1,703	23	28,871
Nicaraguan	9	8,113	25	22,500	34	30,613
Italian	5	8,457	...	...	5	8,457
Miscellaneous	5	4,025	2	923	7	5,548
Total	519	605,217	299	446,730	818	1,051,947
,, for the year preceding	612	683,039	281	443,217	893	1,126,256

CLEARED.

Nationality.	Sailing. Number of Vessels.	Sailing. Tons.	Steam. Number of Vessels.	Steam. Tons.	Total. Number of Vessels.	Total. Tons.
British	209	305,322	46	87,313	255	392,635
American, to foreign countries	264	225,571	182	296,829	446	522,400
American, to Atlantic ports of Union	11	18,580	...	...	11	18,580
Hawaiian	16	7,676	22	40,248	38	47,924
German	23	25,851	1	1,703	24	27,554
Nicaraguan	10	6,817	28	26,322	38	33,139
Italian	5	6,758	...	...	5	6,758
Miscellaneous	8	5,006	3	357	11	5,363
Total	546	601,581	282	452,772	828	1,054,353
,, for the year preceding	567	630,761	276	439,730	843	1,070,491

NOTE.—The entries and clearances of American ships do not include the coasting trade, or whaling and fishing voyages.

Annex B.—RETURN of Principal Articles of Export from San Francisco during the Years 1889-90.

Articles.		1890. Quantity.	1890. Value. £	1889. Quantity.	1889. Value. £
Wheat and flour	Tons	726,257	4,559,809	692,544	4,305,545
Tinned salmon	Cases	526,894	476,516	484,680	512,869
Wine	Gallons	4,027,848	333,906	3,649,441	307,063
Tinned fruit and vegetables	Cases	146,984	118,908	225,793	187,019
Barley	Centals	296,665	79,740	811,904	177,901
Timber	Feet	18,830,535	92,176	17,671,425	81,796
Quicksilver	Flacks	6,252	62,577	5,386	47,115
Brandy	Gallons	210,776	43,042	185,568	39,917
Other articles	...	...	2,240,010	...	3,795,594
Total	...	...	8,006,684	...	9,454,819

RETURN of Principal Articles of Import to San Francisco during the Years 1889-90.

Articles.		1890. Quantity.	1890. Value. £	1889. Quantity.	1889. Value. £
Sugar	Tons	146,673	2,705,944	141,758	3,035,229
Raw silk	Lbs.	2,227,517	1,740,204	3,689,133	2,633,575
Coffee	,,	20,023,557	691,444	20,272,586	584,760
Coals	Tons	563,531	405,102	732,963	515,861
Tin plates	Boxes	274,750	180,281	435,118	435,118
Rice	Tons	21,433	254,610	20,802	217,207
Tea	Lbs.	6,338,870	188,174	7,489,216	187,144
Cement	Bbls.	435,759	102,917	251,406	50,030
Scrap iron	Tons	20,025	51,492	18,105	58,836
Pig iron	,,	12,768	40,093	12,478	54,314
Bullion and coin	...	...	1,969,431	...	1,511,640
Other articles	...	...	789,133	...	993,947
Total	...	...	9,118,825	...	10,257,661

UNITED STATES.

Annex C.—TABLE showing the Total Value of all Articles Exported from San Francisco and Imported to San Francisco from and to Foreign Countries during the Years 1889-90.

Country.	Exports. 1890.	Exports. 1889.	Imports. 1890.	Imports. 1889.
	£	£	£	£
Great Britain	3,329,246	3,845,683	937,064	926,916
Hawaiian Islands	836,817	690,551	2,472,690	2,814,830
China	622,951	535,534	1,113,923	1,070,473
Australia	217,725	450,762	239,009	324,386
Mexico	294,129	360,736	160,012	163,210
Dutch, East Indies	..	..	297,158	..
Central America	371,541	279,532	602,503	562,002
Canada	183,292	186,508	314,604	382,295
Japan	143,472	165,672	1,569,594	2,287,766
France	439,094	115,629	249,319	351,069
Pacific Islands	93,750	106,933	53,773	46,951
Belgium	214,716	41,234	145,175	118,531
Germany	39,459	13,799	231,201	235,953
Spanish Possessions	11,933	10,998	273,052	522,835
India	1,418	5,974	79,989	297,867
Domestic ports and other countries	1,207,141	2,645,274	379,759	152,577
Total	8,006,684	9,454,819	9,118,825	10,257,661

PORTLAND.

Mr. Vice-Consul Laidlaw reports as follows:—

Trade generally. There has been a very considerable increase in the general trade of this district during the year 1890 in the value of manufactured produce and jobbing trade. The foreign import and export trade, however, have fallen off, and Puget Sound secured a very much larger percentage of the wheat export.

Harvest. The wheat harvest over the entire State was above an average, as well in quantity as in quality, and prices of produce, except wheat, were generally higher than last year.

British tonnage. The proportion of British tonnage employed in the foreign trade was 80 per cent. of the whole, which is 5 per cent. less than in 1889.

Imports. As usual the largest proportion of the import trade was done by sail and rail from the Eastern States and San Francisco. The customs returns show a diminished import of coal, salt, bagging, and an almost total absence of bar iron and manufactures thereof. On the other hand there has been an increase in tinplates, rice, pig-iron, and particularly in cement, beer, soda and chemicals, fire-bricks, tea, and window glass.

Glass and cement from Belgium. The larger proportion of the window glass and 20 per cent. of the cement came from Belgium.

Of the coals 2,246 tons were received from the United Kingdom, 4,368 tons from British Columbia, and 5,642 tons from Australia. From coast mines about 27,800 tons were brought to this port. This is a heavy decrease, and coal was scarce and high for the last few months of the year.

The total value of exports to foreign countries coastwise to San Francisco and by rail to the Eastern States was less than last year. The estimated values of all produce shipped to domestic points (exclusive of shipments viâ Yaquina Bay to San Francisco, of which I am unable to procure statistics) during the last three years are: 1888, 1,860,280*l.*; 1889, 1,666,000*l.*; 1890, 1,586,044*l.* <small>*Exports diminished. Coastwise and rail.*</small>

The flour trade with China and Japan has largely increased. 66,884 sacks were shipped, against 49,684 sacks last year. This is no doubt to some extent due to the regular sailings of the Canadian Pacific Company's steamers. <small>*Flour trade with China, &c.*</small>

A large proportion of the surplus grain of Eastern Oregon is being carried to eastern points by rail, and though the proceeds of this trade go to swell the volume of trade in this district they cut no figure in the export tables. Owing to a scarcity of tonnage at this port, many cargoes of wheat were carried by steamer to San Francisco for shipment to Europe on vessels chartered there for the purpose. The total shipments of breadstuffs, both foreign and coastwise, were 500,451 quarters of wheat, of an estimated value of 626,000*l.*, and of flour 365,935 sacks, valued at 383,060*l.* The average values during the year were about 25*s.* 10*d.* f.o.b. per quarter for Oregon Valley wheat, and 24*s.* 6*d.* f.o.b. per quarter for Walla-Walla. The blue stem wheat grown in the Palouse country, however, now commands almost equal prices with Valley wheat. <small>*Wheat. Shipments.*</small>

The decrease in receipts of wool is very marked. This is partly due to the increasing quantity which is now baled up at interior points and shipped direct by rail to the east. Formerly all the wool figured in the returns from this port. In the first months of the year there was a great loss of sheep in Eastern Oregon from severe weather and heavy snowstorms. Quality of wool improves yearly as the flocks are graded up. Prices ranged from 8¾*d.* to 10½*d.* per lb. for Valley, and 6¼*d.* to 8¼*d.* per lb. for Eastern. <small>*Wool trade. Quality improving.*</small>

The following are the receipts and shipments during the past two years:—

Year.	Receipts.		Shipments.	
	Valley.	Eastern.	Viâ San Francisco.	By Rail.
	Lbs.	Lbs.	Lbs.	Lbs.
During 1890	829,130	6,843,695	4,000,789	2,404,340
„ 1889	702,790	15,305,095	8,313,849	6,061,473

Consumption of Oregon woollen mills does not vary much, and was about 1,800,000 lbs

UNITED STATES.

Hop trade. Quality and prices good. The total crop of Oregon hops has been estimated about 3,700,000 lbs. Receipts were rather less than last year, being 2,124,566 lbs. Quality generally was fine and prices remunerative. Range of prices from 15 c. to 42 c.; probably the average was about 30 c. (14½d.).

Barley and oats. In demand. Barley and oats were in demand at satisfactory prices, and a large trade was done in flax seed.

Hides. Poor business. The receipts of hides were 75 per cent. more than in 1889, but prices were low and the trade unsatisfactory.

Timber. The foreign lumber trade was smaller than in 1889, but the total exports increased 15 per cent., reaching 94,250,000 feet. A large lumber trade was done to eastern cities, and it would have been much greater had the railway companies been able to provide adequate transportation. The extent of this business in and around Portland, and its rapid increase, is shown in the following table:—

Articles.	1890. Quantity.	1890. Value.	1889. Quantity.	1889. Value.
		£		£
Lumber cut (feet)	157,220,000	2,561,900	126,800,000	1,862,000
Lath „ „	35,000,000	..	27,300,000	..
Number of hands employed	1,004	..	670	..

Fisheries. Salmon product increased. The product of the salmon packing establishments of the Columbia River was 430,000 cases, while last year it was about 330,000 cases. The shipments to England were only 27,701 cases, all the rest of the pack being shipped by rail east or to San Francisco. Overland shipments from this were 286,732 cases. The average market price was about 5s. 2d. for tall tins, and 6s. 1d. for flat tins, per dozen 1 lb. tins f.o.b. here. I do not think the business last season was very profitable.

Fishing Company. The Deep Sea Fishing Company's steam schooner did a good business, and large quantities of salmon, halibut, and sturgeon were sent east fresh in refrigerator cars.

Financial. Banking capital. There has been quite an increase in the banking capital of this port, as shown in the following comparison:—

Banks.	Capital, Surplus, and Undivided Profits. 1890.	Capital, Surplus, and Undivided Profits. 1889.
	£	£
Oregon banks	1,319,860	624,380
British „	1,359,000	1,079,550

Clearing house. The clearing-house figures for the year were as follows, viz.:—

		£
Exchanges	.. ..	18,687,845
Balances	.. ..	3,557,015

Money market. At the close of the year the money market was very stringent, but there has been no financial embarrassment of any consequence.

Exchange. Exchange has been low during the year. Bills on London at 60 days fluctuated from 4 dol. 77½ c. to 4 dol. 85½ c. per £ sterling for bank, and between 4 dol. 75 c. and 4 dol. 85 c. for mercantile.

Freights. Rates of freight averaged rather lower than last year for iron ships, but the average for wooden ships was higher, 2l. 7s. 6d. and 2l. 3s. 9d. being the highest, and 1l. 17s. 6d. and 1l. 15s. being the lowest rates for iron and wood respectively. Average rate during the year for iron ships was 2l. 2s. 5d. and 1l. 19s. 10d. for wooden ships to a port in the United Kingdom, most of the charters being drawn with the option of Havre and Antwerp at the same rate as to the United Kingdom. The following table gives the tonnage engagements during the last two years, exclusive of coasting voyages:—

Shipping.

Articles.	Quantity.	
	1890.	1889.
	Tons.	Tons.
Grain and flour cargoes..	73,763	76,014
Salmon and assorted cargoes	3,271	5,334
Timber cargoes	2,528	5,129
Miscellaneous cargoes	1,656	1,152
Total	81,218	87,629

Of the above 48 were British ships, registering 65,765 tons. Of the engagements in 1889 58 were British, registering 74,274 tons.

Steamers, British. The British steamers "Danube" and "Mongkut" made regular trips between Vancouver, B.C., and this port.

Failure of Act against crimps. Owing to the difficulty in enforcing its provisions at Astoria, the most beneficent Act of the Legislature of 1889 against crimps has latterly become practically a dead letter, and the same exactions of bonuses as formerly practised has again become the rule.

Seamen's wages have been higher than last year, able-bodied men generally getting 6l. per month.

The number and changes in crews of British ships entering this port during the past year have been as follows, viz.:—

Total Number of Crews.	Deserted.	Discharged.	Engaged.	Reported Dead.	Percentage of Desertions.	Hospital Permits.
1,454	157	31	144	4	10·8	23

River bars and channels.

I am indebted to Major Thos. H. Handbury, U.S. engineer in charge, for the following information:—With the exception of some dredging work at Post Office bar, St. Helen's bar, Walker's Island, and Martin's Island, there has been no work done on the Lower Willamette and Columbia rivers, as the appropriation of 100,000 dol. voted by Congress, September 19 last, was not available for this season. The original project only contemplated 20 feet of depth at low water, but it is now proposed to get 25 feet from Portland to Astoria. Some improvements were made in the Upper reaches of the Williamette river, and a survey was made of the Upper Columbia.

Mouth of Columbia.

The most important work now in progress is the jetty at the mouth of the Columbia, which is now completed for a distance of three miles. The jetty tramway extends three-fifths of a mile further, and the jetty for this distance is partially finished, leaving only half a mile more to complete the work. There is now 26 feet of water on the bar at low tide, and results have been very satisfactory to the engineers, who expect to secure 30 feet of water at low tide. There is now but one channel instead of three, and it is straight, whereas the former channels were crooked. Major Handbury estimates that in one year more this most important work, which was begun in 1885, will be completed. The jetty is constructed of piling, filled in with brush mattresses and stone, and has cost so far 168,210*l*. To complete it 105,000*l*. more will be necessary. During the fiscal year ended June 30, 120,353 tons of rock have been dumped. The original estimate for this work in 1884 was 742,000*l*.

Minor harbours.

Captain Symons, U.S. engineer in charge, informs me that neither at Yaquina, Coos Bay, or Coquille has any work of consequence been done during the year for lack of appropriations.

Agriculture. Cereals, &c.

The past year has been a profitable one for farmers generally, the wheat harvest being fine in all sections. Oats, barley, potatoes, and all other farm produce brought good prices, and hop growers realised handsome profits. The fruit crops were unusually large, and prices very high, on account of an active demand for the Eastern States, to which four times as much was shipped as last year.

Sheep and cattle.

The losses of stock were very great in 1890. Conservative estimates give the loss of sheep on the Eastern Oregon ranges at 40 per cent., and of range cattle at 75 per cent. In the Willamette valley the losses were trifling. The business, therefore, has been far from profitable, though fair prices ruled during the year both for wool, mutton, and beef.

The immigration into this State is continuous, and the Board of Immigration estimates that 68,500 people have settled in the State during the year.

The general census, which in many instances has been very carelessly taken, gives the population of the State as 313,967.

In Portland and suburbs a careless and incorrect count gave the population as about 58,000, but on a recount it was fixed at 69,893, viz.:—

City proper	47,294
East Portland	10,615
Albina	5,169
Other suburbs	6,815
Total	69,893

A Bill will be brought into the next Legislature to consolidate Portland, East Portland, and Albina.

The increase in manufacturing enterprises of the city during the year has been very considerable. It is believed that the figures given below are very nearly correct:—

Year.	Capital Employed.	Persons Employed.	Estimated Value of Product.
1890	£ 3,968,300	10,217	£ 5,477,000
1889	2,560,700	7,862	4,036,600

The Oregon Iron and Steel Company's furnaces are all the year producing 12,305 tons of charcoal pig-iron. The cast-iron pipe works were kept running to their full capacity of 500 tons per month.

The gold product of Oregon in 1889 was 58,050 ounces, value 240,000*l.*, and silver 30,000 ounces, value 7,757*l.* In the past year it must have been much larger, as many small mines are worked in Southern Oregon, and in the Blue Mountain district of Eastern Oregon, the aggregate product of which must be considerable. New mines in the Cœur D'Alene district of Northern Idaho have been opened during the year, and this promises to be the great silver and lead producing district of the United States, or perhaps in the world. Concentrates average about 60 per cent. of lead, and 30 dol. in silver per ton. The principal producing mines are—the Bunker Hill and Sullivan, Stemwinder, Tyler, Sierra Nevada, Emma, and Last Chance, near Wardner, all in an area of about two miles long by less than one mile wide. They produce about 45,000 tons of concentrates per annum, averaging about 32 ounces of silver, and 65 per cent. in lead, or about 60 dol. per ton. On Canyon and Nine Mile creeks are—the Granite, Tiger, Poorman, Gem, San Francisco, Black Bear, California, and also the Sunset Peak mines, and other mines near Wallace, producing about 60,000 tons per annum of similar ore. Near Mullen are—the Morning, Evening, Hunter, Yolande, and others, producing about 100 tons of ore per day.

Gold. — The principal gold mines of Northern Idaho are on Pritchard Creek. The Mother Lode produces gold ore worth 80 dol. per ton, the Idaho produces free gold ore worth 24 dol. per ton, and the Treasure Box Company took out in six weeks 60,000 dol. in gold, using an arrastra. There are many other promising locations on the same lode.

In Eastern Oregon there are many small mines, but the best opened out are the Cracker Creek and Connor Creek mines, which have been worked for some years. Some of these mines are worked by British capital.

Baser metals. Copper. Chrome. Nickel. Manganese. Coal. — Copper is found in Baker and Josephine counties, but the deposits are not worked. Chrome ore is found in Southern Oregon, and nickel in Douglas, Josehpine, and Jackson counties. Manganese has been found in quantity in Columbia county. There are coal fields in Coos, Columbia, Clatsop, and Washington counties, but none of the deposits have been worked, except those of Coos Bay, which have been worked for years and yield a very superior quality of coal.

Iron. — About five miles north of this port, at Oswego, large deposits of brown hematite are found, the thickness of the vein varying from 6 feet to 15 feet. These mines have been worked for some years by the Oregon Iron and Steel Company. The ore analyses are as under:—

	Per cent.
Metallic iron	44·71
Phosphorous	0·666
Phosphorous, in 100 parts iron	1·490

There are other deposits of similar ore in other portions of the State, but they are not worked.

Public works. Cascades locks. — The important work on the canal and locks at the cascades of the Columbia river, under light appropriations, goes on slowly, and year by year approaches completion. The United States engineers are now laying down concrete, and building the walls of the locks. Three years at least will be required to complete the work. The appropriations by Congress for this work since its inception in 1876 have been equivalent to 375,400*l*., and the estimated amount required to complete the work is 349,000*l*.

The general plan adopted by the engineers calls for a canal with a clear width of 90 feet. One lock, with a length of 462 feet, a width throughout of 90 feet, and a lift of 24 feet, is to be constructed for lockage to a stage of 20 feet above low water at the foot of the canal. A navigable depth of 8 feet at low water is to be provided. A guard gate is to be placed below the lower lock gate. A second guard gate is to be placed a lock's length above the upper lock gate, the intervening space being left for a prospective extension of lockage to a stage higher than 20 feet. The gates are to be of metal, the lock is to be filled through the lock walls, and the sides of the canal are to be protected by dry stone walls to a stage of 20 feet on the lower gauge. Above that stage the slopes are to be riprapped. The tops of the slopes are to be placed 2 feet above highest water in the contiguous parts of the channel.

References of low water at the foot and head of the canal are respectively 72 and 96. The extreme river stages to be provided for are respectively 55·5 feet and 45·5 feet. A 20-foot stage at the foot of the canal gives references of 92 and 110 respectively (the latter is more recently found to be 109·4). The references fixed for the essential parts of the canal are as follows:—

Floor of lock, of sills of lower gates and of lower entrance..	64·0
„ upper entrance and sills of upper gates	88·0
Top of side walls of canal in lower entrance..	92·0
„ in canals in upper entrance	110·0
Top of lock-gates and lock masonry ..	110·0
„ lower guard-gates and masonry	100·0
„ upper guard-gates	141.5
„ „ guard-gate masonry	142·0

I have quoted the preceding from reports of Major Hanbury and Lieutenant Burr, the latter officer being in direct charge of the work.

Bridge. Another fine drawbridge has been completed during the past year across the Willamette River at this port. There are now three bridges in use.

Railway. During the year past the Union Pacific in conjunction with the Great Northern has been grading a line from Portland to a point on Puget Sound. A small amount of work has been done on a line between Portland and Astoria, which it is probable may be begun in earnest in 1891.

Terminal works. A large amount of work has been done, but the magnificent railway station projected has not yet been actually begun. The structures so far are mostly goods sheds and temporary buildings of wood.

Street railways. There has been a large amount of extension done during the year, principally of electric lines. There is now in service:—

	Miles.
Cable railroad lines ..	5¼
Electric „ „	39
Steam motor „	9
Horse car lines	19

These are all in Portland and suburbs. Many new lines are projected, and it is probable that electricity will supersede the horse on the line in service at an early date.

City finances. Water bonds. The water commission has now the equivalent of 140,000*l.*, 5 per cent. bonds issued having sold 10,000*l.* during the year at 10½ per cent. premium. Receipts from waterworks were equal to 36,190*l.*, and the disbursements of the operating department were 22,764*l.*, inclusive of 6,750*l.* interest on bonds. The total *Waterworks.* expenditures on waterworks since acquired by the city to *Receipts, &c.* December 31 last have been 150,030*l.*, and the estimated value

(1126)

of the plant is 190,320*l.* The next Legislature will be applied to for powers to sell bonds to bring in water from Bull Run, a pure stream 33 miles away.

Revenue. Exclusive of revenue from the waterworks, but including balances carried over from 1889, the total revenue of the city was equivalent to 75,491*l.*, and the expenditures were 74,100*l.*, exclusive of the amount received for sale of City Hall bonds and spent on construction.

City Hall bonds. During the year City Hall bonds were issued to the amount of 35,000*l.*, bearing interest at 5 per cent. These sold at a premium of 2½ per cent. The expenditure upon the building was 23,515*l.*

The following is the bonded indebtedness of the city:—

£
- 16,000 at 5 per cent.
- 4,000 at 6 "
- 35,000 at 5 " City Hall bonds.
- 140,000 at 5 " water bonds.

The cost of improvements paid by contiguous property owners was:—

Street improvements, 30,320*l.*; street extensions, 15,455*l.*; and sewers, 23,692*l.*

Taxation. The State, county, city, and school taxes aggregated 3·06 per cent. For assessment purposes property is valued at about 40 per cent. of its market value.

Real estate transactions. The transfers and sales of real estate recorded in Multnomah county during 1890 were—12,991,809 dol., equal to 2,598,360*l.* Nearly half of this was property in the city.

Buildings. All over the city and suburbs there has been great activity in the building trade, and magnificent brick business buildings, some of them eight stories in height, have been completed, or are in course of construction. The new City Hall will cost 100,000*l.*, and the Chamber of Commerce building very nearly as much. Many of these buildings are of a high order of architecture. Dwellings are still scarce and rents are high.

The following statement of buildings erected is compiled from the records of the superintendent of streets:—

	Number.	Value.
		Dollars.
Residences and tenements	522	1,286,200
Stores and office buildings	43	858,990
Hotels	6	636,000
Alterations and repairs..	..	40,600
Terminal buildings and improvements	4	286,000
Schools	2	165,300
Churches..	5	79,600
Street-car stables	2	28,000
Factories..	4	68,000
Total	..	3,448,600
Equivalent in sterling	..	689,720*l.*

Skilled labour has been in demand all the year, but at the close, owing to the cessation of railroad construction between this and Puget Sound, a large number of labourers were thrown out of employment, and for a time there was some distress. Quite a number of clerks and men brought up to no particular business have come out from England and the east, seeking employment. I would warn such against coming here unless they are so situated that they can afford to wait for some time, otherwise they are very apt to fall into distress.

The city and country generally are prosperous, and the general health has been good throughout the year.

The values given in this report are reduced to sterling at the average rate of 5 dol. per 1*l*.

Annex A.—RETURN of all Shipping at the Port of Portland, Oregon, in the Year 1890.

ENTERED.

Nationality.	Sailing. Number of Vessels.	Sailing. Tons.	Steam. Number of Vessels.	Steam. Tons.	Total. Number of Vessels.	Total. Tons.
British	46	62,384	16	10,764	62	73,148
American, foreign	2	2,389	2	1,998	4	4,387
,, Atlantic	7	10,032	...	...	7	10,032
,, coasting	28	7,926	293	211,380*	321	219,306
German	2	3,038	...	...	2	3,038
Total	85	85,769	311	224,142	396	309,911
,, for the year preceding	...	...	...	...	355	403,638

CLEARED.

Nationality.	Sailing. Number of Vessels.	Sailing. Tons.	Steam. Number of Vessels.	Steam. Tons.	Total. Number of Vessels.	Total. Tons.
British	45	62,187	17	11,325	62	73,512
American, foreign	11	15,293	...	...	11	15,293
,, coasting	9	2,681	277	207,512*	286	210,193
German	2	3,038	...	...	2	3,038
Total	67	83,199	294	218,837	361	302,036
,, for the year preceding	...	...	...	...	344	397,480

* Statistics of coasting steamers given in previous years have shown the gross tonnage, but the above is net register tons. There is, therefore, an apparent but not actual falling-off in the total tonnage.

UNITED STATES.

Annex B.—RETURN of Principal Articles of Export from Portland, Oregon, during the Years 1890–89.

Articles.		1890. Quantity.	1890. Value.	1889. Quantity.	1889. Value.
			£		£
Wheat	Quarters	280,418	354,296	293,885	393,085
„ flour	Sacks	296,910	308,493	297,287	328,470
Timber	1,000 feet	855	2,647	1,713	3,828
Tinned salmon	Lbs.	...	...	48,000	1,300
Other articles		...	16,061	...	...
Total foreign exports		...	681,497	...	726,673

RETURN of Principal Articles of Import to Portland, Oregon, during the Years 1890–89.

Articles.		1890. Quantity.	1890. Value.	1889. Quantity.	1889. Value.
			£		£
Coals and coke	Tons	12,655	9,635	25,035	17,760
Tin and terne plates	Lbs.	3,724,639	23,299	3,524,290	21,570
Rice	,,	3,282,516	11,804	2,818,305	10,171
Earthenware and glass		...	17,657	...	16,633
Salt	Lbs.	2,224,871	1,701	5,361,632	3,745
Cement	Barrels	58,989	14,791	24,579	4,981
Cigars and tobacco	Lbs.	40,939	14,482	40,147	17,289
Wines and liquors		...	2,898	...	2,659
Beer, porter, and ale	Gallons	31,220	4,436	13,033	1,779
Soda and chemicals	Lbs.	1,964,104	2,977	639,334	1,116
Oils	Gallons	21,239	1,694	15,437	492
Pig and scrap iron	Tons	1,828	4,543	1,054	2,923
Bar iron and manufactures of iron and steel cutlery		1,754	1,754	...	27,653
Firebricks	Number	1,427,705	1,134	399,725	432
Fireclay	Tons	208	308	...	...
Tea	Lbs.	411,005	12,475	193,741	4,537
Hemp	Tons	392	16,397	506	21,161
Window-glass	Lbs.	3,028,193	13,098	1,253,138	4,491
Bags and bagging		...	12,602	...	30,194
Pickles and sauces		...	1,691	...	1,350
Manufactures of silk		...	4,815	...	5,230
Matting		...	1,730	...	...
Manufactures of cotton		...	1,123	...	...
Lemons	Boxes	1,641	967	...	...
All other articles		...	14,454	...	10,748
Total foreign imports		...	192,465	...	206,914

N.B.—The above returns do not include exports or imports coastwise or by rail with the exception of articles transported in bond.

Annex C.—TABLE showing the Total Value of all Articles Exported from Portland, Oregon, and Imported to Portland, Oregon, from and to Foreign Countries during the Years 1890-89.

Country.	Imports. 1890.	Imports. 1889.	Exports. 1890.	Exports. 1889.
	£	£	£	£
Great Britain	569,309	640,619	77,418	100,396
Belgium	11,300	..	12,233	5,061
British Columbia	26,521	21,636	7,984	1,276
China and Japan	74,367	55,170	42,614	31,521
Australia	..	..	4,411	9,368
Peru and Chile	..	8,820	..	..
France	..	..	210	739
Cuba	..	..	14,032	17,032
Philippine Islands	..	..	17,621	22,348
India	..	..	11,377	18,769
Germany	..	..	3,598	..
Italy	..	..	967	..
All other countries	..	428	..	404
Total	681,497	726,673	192,465	206,914

ASTORIA.

Mr. Vice-Consul Cherry reports as follows:—

A large increase is to be noted in both city and district. *General business.*

Show a falling-off in values altogether on account of the low price of tinplates. *Foreign imports.*

The retail price was, during most of the year, quoted at 4 dol. 80 c. (19s. 6d.) per box, B.V. grades, but showed a sharp rise at the close of the year, going to 6 dol. (1l. 4s. 6d.). *Tin plates.*

More was imported, but at lower prices than last year, from 3l. 10s. to 3l. 16s. *Salt.*

A larger quantity was imported, all from Newcastle, N.S.W., selling at 1l. 8s. *Coal.*

Show a falling-off chiefly in the preserved salmon trade, the very great bulk of the pack going by rail for the United States' domestic market, and the balance by coasting steamers to San Francisco to be exported from there. *Exports.*

As already stated, does not appear in the custom-house statistics, as it leaves here for San Francisco by rail. *Canned salmon.*

Shows a somewhat larger export with lower values. *Wheat.*

Considerably less with lower values. *Flour.*

No new industries of any extent are to be noted. *Manufacturing.*

Sawing lumber and canning salmon still remain the only large manufacturing industries.

This industry was severely tried during the past year. The Fishermen's Union endeavoured to hold up the prices given in 1889, viz., 5s. per fish, but the very poor prices given for the preserved salmon would not admit of the price being given. *Salmon fishing.*

Before matters were adjusted there was some loss of life in the vain attempt of the Union party endeavouring to compel outsiders from fishing till the price was fixed. The result of the attempt was the loss of six or eight lives of the attacking party who were beaten back, and the price per fish was fixed at 75 c. (3s.).

Gill net fishing still goes on, but in decreasing number; seines, traps, and fish wheels taking most of the salmon. Nothing was done owing to the difficulties brought on about prices till late in May, notwithstanding which a very much larger catch is to be noted.

Salmon canning. The prices received for salmon canned ranged from 1*l*. 1*s*. 6*d*. to 1*l*. 3*s*. per case of 48 1 lb. tins.

The pack of the Columbia River was much larger than for some years past, nearly all of which was of good quality.

Columbia River, 433,000 cases, as compared with 364,000 cases in 1889, and 373,000 cases in 1888.

No salmon was put up on the coast north of Astoria, and to the south about 30,000 cases in the various harbours and inlets on the coast.

Sturgeon fishing. The catch of this fish still improves, and is still consumed entirely in the United States, being sent by rail mostly to the vicinity of New York.

I notice in this connection that sturgeon hooks of British manufacture are more used than those of American make.

Lumbering. The country within this Vice-Consular district shows a great increase in lumbering during the past year. In taking out logs for the saw mills there is some talk of the use of great rafts to be towed to San Francisco for manufacturing there, but so far nothing has come of it.

Lumber manufacture. Is increasing in the district both north and south of us, especially in the town; the output of the two mills was upwards of 21,000 met. feet broad measure, only a small proportion went abroad (Australian colonies), California taking nearly the whole output.

Box making. Two box making establishments make nearly all the boxes required for the preserved salmon trade, and send large quantities of fruit and salmon boxes to Mexico, California, and Alaska.

Openings for employment of capital. A paper pulp mill in the vicinity is turning out a steadily increasing quantity of wood pulp, all of it going to San Francisco. An opening is presented here for the employment of capital, as the resources and conveniences are practically unlimited.

Tile and pottery works. A good opening for the investment of capital lies here, a superior quality of pottery clay is worked from the bank of a tributary and navigable stream in the vicinity, 6,000 tons of which were taken out last year for works 125 miles from the source of supply.

Gunpowder. Within reasonable distance from this town, excellent sites on navigable streams for powder mills can be had with an unlimited and easy supply of good wood adapted for charcoal.

Shipping. I regret still to have to report a decrease in the foreign bound shipping for the Columbia River. This decrease is altogether of ships under the British flag, and to my mind is clearly traceable to the causes given in my report of 1889. I notice that the average tonnage of ships has greatly increased.

A feature of the good name of this port is the changing of the gang of crimps from here to Portland. I kept an accurate list taken from the articles of agreement during the year 1890 of the desertions of the two ports, and give the following of 45 British vessels with 1,200 men, the following desertions took place:— Astoria, 89 men ($7\frac{2}{5}$ per cent.); Portland, 172 men ($14\frac{1}{3}$ per cent.). *Seamen's abuses.*

The jetty for the improvement of the entrance to the Columbia River has been carried on with a slight halt during the past year, the trestle and the matrass work has been carried out to the distance of over 4 miles. The results during the past two years, as shown in the United States' survey charts, are the permanent straightening of the channel to the sea, also the increasing the depth in the deepest part of the channel from a maximum of 19 feet at average lowest low water of less than a quarter of a mile in width, to a 26 feet channel at the same stage of tide with a width of half a mile, and extending the 20 feet depth to nearly 4 miles on ground which before showed from bare at low water to 17 feet. All these soundings are taken at average lowest low waters. This gives a mean depth of 33 feet, at high water rising to 36 feet. The United States' engineer in charge has reported that there is no doubt of the permanent depth being increased by at least 4 feet, with an increased width of channel at that draft. Early this year (1891) depatches report the assurance of a sufficient appropriation to complete this work, and when finished will put the port of Astoria in the front rank of seaports for depth and ease of entrance for all classes of shipping, as hitherto only a particular build of vessels found it profitable to come to the Columbia river. *Government improvements.*

About 19 miles of road were finished of the Astoria and South Coast Railroad during the past year, connecting the town with a seaside resort, and as far as I can gather did very well. Surveys have been extended to the interior with satisfactory results, regarding grades and resources of country to be passed through. The late financial difficulties in money centres have threatened to retard the work, but it cannot be for long, as the increased population and the estimated low cost of construction warrant the early completion of the work. *Railroads.*

Have been more numerous and of a more permanent character than during any one year before. A far better class of buildings, both for business and residences, have been put up. *Improvements in Astoria.*

Four banks are doing a good business, as shown by their balance sheets. Two of these, a national and a savings bank, have been started during the year.

With the exception of the Russian influenza last winter has remained uniformly good. *Health.*

Annex A.—RETURN of all Shipping at the Port of Astoria, Oregon, during the Year 1890.

ENTERED.

Nationality.	Sailing.		Steam.		Total.	
	Number of Vessels.	Tons.	Number of Vessels.	Tons.	Number of Vessels.	Tons.
British	47	64,653	16	10,466	63	75,119
American, coasting	50	33,622	402	397,211	452	430,833
,, foreign	2	2,349	13	7,202	15	9,551
German	2	2,924	...	...	2	2,924
Total	101	103,548	431	414,879	532	518,427
,, for the year preceding	...	...	...	...	75	87,357

CLEARED.

Nationality.	Sailing.		Steam.		Total.	
	Number of Vessels.	Tons.	Number of Vessels.	Tons.	Number of Vessels.	Tons.
British	45	62,633	19	12,402	64	75,035
American, coasting	34	21,902	454	411,774	488	433,676
,, foreign	15	16,669	8	3,360	33	20,029
German	2	2,924	...	...	2	2,924
Total	96	104,128	481	427,536	587	531,664
,, for the year preceding	...	...	...	...	74	99,768

Annex B.—RETURN of Principal Articles of Export from Astoria, Oregon, during the Years 1889–90.

Articles.		1890.		1889.	
		Quantity.	Value.	Quantity.	Value.
			£		£
Salmon	Cases	27,701	32,540	135,614	189,900
Wheat	Bushels	578,805	92,700	559,090	91,800
Flour	Bbls.	35,638	27,503	54,210	44,450
Lumber	M. feet	3,981	8,600	52,300	10,353
Sundries	...	...	215	...	520
Total	...	...	161,558	...	337,023

RETURN of Principal Articles of Import from Astoria, Oregon, during the Years 1889–90.

Articles.		1890.		1889.	
		Quantity.	Value.	Quantity.	Value.
			£		£
Tin plates	Lbs.	36,712	24,456	35,300	35,650
Salt	,,	172	354	103	120
Coal	Tons	4,033	3,365	3,348	2,344
Sundries	...	...	150	...	285
Total	...	...	28,325	...	38,399

Annex C.—TABLE showing the Total Value of all Articles Exported from Astoria, Oregon, and Imported to Astoria, Oregon, from and to Foreign Countries during the Years 1889-90.

Country.	Exports. 1890	Exports. 1889.	Imports. 1890.	Imports. 1889.
	£	£	£	£
Great Britain	139,513	300,000	24,855	23,000
British Colonies	4,352	7,400	3,170	2,360
Other countries	13,717	3,450	..	..
Total	157,582	310,850	27,025	25,360

PORT TOWNSEND.

Mr. Vice-Consul Alexander reports as follows:—

Through the courtesy of C. M. Bradshaw, Esq., Collector of Customs at this port, who has allowed me free access to the records in the custom-house, I have been again enabled to procure correct data for the statistical portion of this report and the several annexes. To Allan Weir, Esq., Secretary of the State, and other persons I am also indebted for valuable information and suggestions.

General statistics.

The State of Washington embraces an area of 44,796,160 acres of land, forming the north-west State in the Union. The Cascade mountain range divides it into two regions entirely different in climate, in topography, and the character of its products. The region west of the Cascade is chiefly densely timbered, with a wild, humid atmosphere, and ample rainfall; that on the east, although milder than the same latitudes in the eastern States, is subject to greater extremes of heat and cold, with a dryer atmosphere; this region is generally treeless, and covered with bunch grass, the chief products being cereals and stock, here are the great wheat fields of the State. In the northern portion of the State the Cascade mountain range widens, extending eastward over that portion of eastern Washington lying north of the Columbia River. This northern mountainous region is known as the Okanogan county, and is rich in nearly every mineral known to commerce. The entire Cascade range in Washington is rich in coal and iron, while on its western slope and foot the hills are covered with a dense growth of mercantile timber.

Among the many indications to show the development and progress of this State during the past year I may mention, the increase in all taxable values according to official figures from about 24,959,089*l.* in 1889, to about 44,289,627*l.* in 1890, giving a gain of 20,330,538*l.*; the operating of 372·14 miles of new railway within the year, and 951·41 miles under construction, and many more projected. The sale by the Government of almost 2,000,000 acres of land, a large part of which will be made productive. From official reports, from the national bureau of agriculture, this State heads the list in average of wheat production to the acre, with an average of 23·5 bushels; and the same authorities show that the average per acre of hop production is greater in this State than any other, especially in the Puget Sound district, where also pasturage and dairy products are hard to be surpassed. An increase in both the imports and exports at Puget Sound ports show that the commerce of the country is growing and expanding. Consequently Washington presents a very inviting and promising future, not only to the business man, but to the mechanic and labourer desirous of seeking a new home.

Public domain. The State of Washington contains 66,880 square miles, or 44,796,160 acres of land, less than one-half of which is surveyed and in the market, of this amount 1,973,693 acres passed from the hands of the Government to that of private individuals within the past 12 months, according to the reports of the United States' local land offices in the State, and the Northern Pacific Railway disposed of 560,000 acres, making a total of 2,533,693 acres. The price paid for the Government lands, together with fees and commissions, amounts to 365,357*l.*, which added to the 600,600*l.*, the price received for the railway grant lands, makes a total of 965,957*l.*, expended for new lands and embraced in 7,870 entries, exclusive of those sold by the Northern Pacific Railway Company. Estimating each of these entry men to have expended 30*l.* in preliminary improvements on their claim, we would have a total expenditure of 236,100*l.*, which added to the amount paid for the land brings in a grand total of 1,202,057*l.* Of this sum over 800,000*l.* was sent east to the Government to pay for these lands. Computing each entry man to have a family of two, besides himself, we thus have an increase of 23,610 in the purely agricultural population of the State as directly shown from the land office records. It is thought that the total average of lands entered under the several Acts of Congress, and purchased from the Government, would have been very much larger had the Government granted the State a larger appropriation to keep the Government surveys up to the demands of settlers; out of an appropriation of 640,000*l.*, made by the last session of Congress for the survey of public lands for the year, this State was apportioned 17,000*l.*, to be expended in the survey of public lands already settled upon and occupied by actual settlers, and the lands granted to the State by the enabling Act. In western Washington there cannot be more than 200,000 acres that are now subject to entry, while there are about 2,500,000 acres as yet unsurveyed, of which a very large portion is now held by settlers under "squatters' rights;" these unsurveyed lands comprise some of the best agricultural timber and mineral lands.

There are within this State 18 Indian reservations, with an aggregate area of 7,126,593 acres.

The lands held by the State are of great value, and will enrich each of the various funds to which their proceeds are to be applied. Besides the common grant of the 16th section and 36th section of each township, for the support of the common schools, and the tide-lands which it acquired with its admission as a State, 668,000 acres of public land were granted for various purposes by the nation. Following is the table of all lands granted to the State:—

For What Purpose.	Acres.
For the support of the common schools	2,261,780
„ scientific school	100,000
„ agricultural college	90,000
„ State normal school	100,000
„ public buildings and State capitol	132,000
„ charitable, educational, penal, and reformatory institutions	200,000
„ State university	46,000
Total	2,929,780

The State is also entitled to 5 per cent. of the net proceeds of the sales of public lands sold after November 11, 1889.

Property assessments. — Judging from official figures the year's increase in taxable values gives a fair idea of the development and progress of this State, which has been from about 24,959,089*l.* in 1889, to about 44,289,627*l.* in 1890, a gain of 20,330,538*l.*

Census. — The federal census, taken in the month of June, 1890, shows for Washington a population of 349,390, against 75,116 in 1880.

Railways. — Nothing, possibly, has tended to advance the development of the country so much as railways. No other agency has been so powerful in adding to the population, in opening up new country, and in developing a market for surplus product. Until there were railways the greater part of the north-west was a region of remote and scattered settlements, with poor means of communication, the simplest ways of living, and without many of the better influences of modern civilisation. In this country of great rivers steamboats were only used to move the products of river lands, and the population was naturally confined almost exclusively to lands on the navigable rivers and waters. The fertile soil a few miles back was, to all practical purposes, a barren waste. The marvellous growth of trees spread over the entire region west of the Cascade range was the only part of the great wealth of the country that was at all available, and, therefore, lumbering, as it is called, was the earliest manufacturing industry. It has been necessary in later years, however, to penetrate these vast forests with logging roads—roads made through the forests to bring out the trees or logs—either by horses, oxen, or steam power, in order to procure the best timber; and, therefore, railroads have performed no small part in the growth and maintenance of this now important industry. Railways have brought here nine-tenths of the new population; it is expected that railways will be the chief factor in securing and transporting the immigration of the future. There are now three transcontinental lines within the State—the Great Northern, the Union Pacific, and the Northern Pacific, the latter controlling the largest number of branches or feeders; over 372 miles were constructed during the year, in the aggregate costing about 1,400,000*l*.; 451 miles of road were graded and levelled, but no rails laid, costing about 850,000*l*.; in machine shops and new surveys there was expended about 165,000*l*., and over 951 miles of road are under construction. The total mileage of railways in this State is over 2,080. The construction of railways in Washington has involved a vast expenditure during the year, and has contributed in no small degree to the general prosperity of the State. Many thousand men have been given steady work at good wages, and the effect has been felt in every branch of business.

Commerce.

The annexes marked respectively A., B., and C. show the extent of the commerce generally of this State, from which it will be seen that there has been a large increase during the past year, and one or two new features in connection with this subject are worthy of notice. The experiment of carrying timber to the Australian colonies in steamships was tried, two cargoes being taken, but I understand that the venture was not very remunerative to shippers, and I am not aware that any new charters have been made. The trade with other countries is rapidly growing, that with Alaska is quite important; China, Japan, Australia, the Sandwich Islands, South America, and England each do an increasing business direct with the ports on Puget Sound.

Agriculture.

The largest wheat crop ever grown in this State was grown this year, estimated to be about 20,000,000 bushels. The amount for export will be about 400,000 tons, or 13,000,000 bushels; owing to the scarcity of the rolling stock on the railways running through the district, which existed from the harvest time up to the middle of December, 1890, only a very small part of the surplus grain could be carried to the seaboard. The wheat area in eastern Washington is principally in the Palouse district, containing nearly 5,000,000 acres; about one-fifth of this land is under cultivation, and one-tenth devoted to wheat, with an average yield of 28 bushels to the acre. The largest quantity ever grown was 101 bushels to the acre, by a farmer in Whitman county in this district. The average yield throughout the State is 23 bushels over to the acre. The price ranges from 1*s*. 8*d*. to 2*s*. per bushel, whilst the cost of production is from 1*s*. to 1*s*. 6*d*. The wheat of this State does not make so white a flour as Californian wheat, but it is of a more nutritious quality, the percentage of nitrogen being from 4 per cent. to 6 per cent. greater. This flour is now being shipped to the United Kingdom and Europe, where it is gradually becoming known; the bulk finds its way to China and Japan in increasing quantities each year. During the year Puget Sound has shipped about one-third of the export of the Columbia River basin. The building of the

Union Pacific Railway to Puget Sound will connect it with the grain fields of eastern Oregon, and the building of the Great Northern Railway will open up to wheat culture the Big Band country and bring it into connection with Puget Sound. There can hardly be a reasonable doubt that with each succeeding year the business of exporting wheat and flour on Puget Sound will increase. No industry promises better results. Last year 26 cargoes of wheat and flour were shipped from Puget Sound to foreign countries, four of which were flour, and two parts flour and one part wheat, the total value of which approximated to the sum of 373,720*l*.

Hop growing is chiefly carried on in the Puget Sound district, where the climate and soil seem peculiarly adapted to this plant; they are also successfully grown in the Yaquina Valley in eastern Washington. The product for the year 1890 for the State has been about 38,000 bales, or 6,820,000 lbs., being a decrease from the previous year, although the acreage had increased about 10 per cent. to 5,000 acres. This is due to the ravages of the hop louse, which for the first time made its appearance in the Puget Sound country, and caused the yield to fall far below the average, only about 1,500 lbs. to the acre. The prices ranged from 15 c. (7*d.*) up to 1*s.* 8*d.* per lb., with an average of 1*s.* 3*d.* per lb.; as the cost of production does not exceed 5*d.*, the farmers have realised a good profit. Over one-fourth of the crop was shipped overland to London direct, the shipment taking up 30 days. It is estimated that the season's hop crop brought the sum of 500,000*l.* into the State.

Oats are grown very extensively on the dyked farms, which are made out of the reclaimed tide-lands situated on the eastern shore of Puget Sound, where over 100 bushels to the acre has been thrashed out. The local and San Francisco markets take most of the crop, which has averaged this year all through not less than 6*l.* per ton.

Almost every kind of root is grown, yielding enormously and commanding exceedingly good prices. Fruits and vegetables do well all over the State, and sell at remunerative prices and meet with a ready market; in fact the supply does not equal the demand, as California, Nebraska, and Iowa supplied vegetables, fruit, and poultry to the amount of 400,000*l.* More attention is, however, being paid to fruit-growing, market gardening, and dairying each year, and there will soon be no need to import in such large quantities.

The timber industry was, until lately, confined to the coast line, where transportation was easy, but as railways are built the inland forests are being reached. It still forms the chief staple of trade. As far as can be obtained from information 1,222,830,042 feet of timber were cut during the past year, making an increase of over 156,147,000 feet for the year preceding; the Puget saw mills contributing by far the largest proportion, two new saw mills being built during the year, and another under construction. The large amount of building done all over

Timber manufacture.

the State during the year, and the new railways requiring a very large quantity in their construction, made the domestic demand about the same as last year. Large quantities still continue to be sent by railway to the middle and eastern States. The foreign demand and distribution was about the same as last year. The shipments to the United Kingdom and Continent of Europe are increasing slowly in the number of cargoes, new markets being found principally in Belgium, Spain, and Germany. A large and steady trade has now sprung up with the interior of the continent of Australia, where the timber is used in railroad construction.

The supply of tonnage was not equal to the demand, which made the foreign trade suffer; vessels, however, owned by several of the mill companies on Puget Sound, were sent abroad with cargoes principally to the Australian colonies, who are the largest foreign customers, and it is quite possible that they will be kept in the foreign trade. Puget Sound fir still maintains its reputation, that no timber in the world equals it for the construction of bridges, warehouses, and all structures which are required to sustain great weight and strain, and it is unsurpassed for making ships' decks and spars. Proof of the value of fir for structural purposes may be found in a series of tests made by the United States Government, under the direction of the Secretary of the Interior, and published in the reports of the superintendent of census on the 10th census of the United States, made September 1, 1884, but space will not admit of my presenting them. The ruling price throughout the year was 2*l.* per 1,000 feet for rough timber, dressed and clear timber ranged from 2*l.* 11*s.* to 3*l.* 10*s.*, making the year's product considerably over 3,000,000*l.*

In this country houses are roofed with what are known as shingles, very similar in size and shape to the slate used in England, but made out of cedar wood; the trees being very abundant almost all over the western part of this State, and easily accessible. No branch of manufacture has grown so fast lately as the production of cedar shingles; a good shaved, that is hand-made, shingle made of Washington cedar will last a very long time, practically, with proper attention, never wearing out; these are principally shipped to the Sandwich Islands; the other kind are sawn shingles, made in a mill, they find a ready sale both at home and abroad, the eastern States taking large quantities, where the architectural style of dwelling houses has brought them into prominence. Hand-made shingles fetch a little better price than the sawn ones, which are worth about 8*s.* a 1,000.

Minerals.
Coal.

The year just closed has marked the greatest activity ever known in the coal industry of the State, not only in the extending operations upon old established mines, but the prospecting and developing of new mining properties. The coal fields of the State lie principally between the Cascade and coast ranges of mountains, those on the western slope of the Cascade being the most developed, and it is from them that the chief supply comes. The character of the coals, so far discovered, embrace lignite, semi-bituminous, and bituminous varieties, adapted for coking, steam, gas, and domestic purposes; some specimens of a very fine grade of coal resembling anthracite are reported as having been taken from Cowlits Pass, in Yaquina county. The most important mines are in the vicinity of Puget Sound, in King, Pierce, and Thurston counties; the output of the mines in King county for the year was 488,306 tons, being an increase of 97,123 tons over the previous one, and the output for the Pierce county mines during the same period was 403,354 tons. The mines in the Bucoda district, lying chiefly in Thurston county, are very little developed owing to their remoteness from railways. The Roslyn mine, situated on the east slope of the Cascade, about 20 miles from the summit, on the line of the Northern Pacific Railway, sells all its output locally in the eastern part of the State and Oregon, and also to the railways; the demand was greater than the supply. Outcroppings have been found in other localities in eastern Washington, notably at Ellensburg, and in Lincoln and Spokane counties. The coal fields are considered practically inexhaustible, what is needed are more railways to the coal fields, more coal-washing machinery for the heavy coking varieties, cheaper ocean transportation, and more capital to develop the country. Labour is well paid, and has been steady during the year, no labour troubles having taken place. The total output for the State during 1889 was 911,527 tons, for 1890 1,349,773 tons, an increase of 438,246 tons. Prices were steady, the minimum being 8s. 3d. per ton for screenings to 18s. 6d. for steam coal in large quantities, and 1l. 4s. 9d. to the retail trade; an average estimate of the market value will be 13s. 9d. per ton. Coal is shipped principally under steam and sail to California and Oregon, but there is a large consumption by steamships and tugboats plying on Puget Sound, and also for domestic purposes.

Iron ore is found in very large quantities in almost every part of the State, the character of the ores being hematite, limonite, magnetic, and bog ore. There are in process of development about 20 iron properties, but there being not much demand for iron now, the cost of mining and transportation retards much progress being made.

Gold, silver, copper, and other precious metals are found in some parts of the State, the want of facilities to get the ores to the smelters is badly felt.

Sandstone, limestone, marble, and deposits of various kinds of clay are continually being discovered.

The climate of western Washington is mild and humid, being influenced entirely by the ocean; during 1890 the highest temperature was 86 degrees, the lowest 10 degrees, rainfall 28·31 inches, snowfall 4 inches. During the winter months the prevailing winds are from a southerly direction, varying from southwest to south-east: in the summer months, westerly and northwesterly winds prevail, bringing in the cool ocean air, which tempers the heat.

Climate.

The mean annual temperature of eastern Washington is about 50 degrees, and the mean annual precipitation 18·13 inches. The climate is colder in winter and warmer in summer than the western portion of the State.

UNITED STATES.

Health.

The general health of the people has been good, no cases of serious epidemic diseases occurring, and there have been no cases of infectious or contagious diseases among the cattle, as far as I have been able to ascertain.

Buildings and works.

Many government and municipal buildings are under course of erection and contemplation. The United States Coast and Geodetic Service are actively employed, with most beneficial results to navigation, also the Lighthouse Service in buoying the the waters of Puget Sound.

The constitution of this State requires a bureau of agriculture, immigration, and vital statistics to be established in the office of the Secretary of State, but no provision has been made as yet to be of any service in this report, consequently it is extremely difficult to procure trustworthy information on many matters of interest in an annual report. I have, however, endeavoured to show as far as possible the development and progress of Washington, being conscious that it is very deficient in many respects.

Annex A.—Return of all Shipping at the Port of Port Townsend in the Year 1890.

Entered.

Nationality.	Sailing. Number of Vessels.	Sailing. Tons.	Steam. Number of Vessels.	Steam. Tons.	Total. Number of Vessels.	Total. Tons.
British	47	58,340	29	8,483	76	66,823
United States of America	179	150,601	1,215	950,243	1,394	1,100,844
Chilian	18	16,515	...	...	18	16,515
Norwegian	7	6,561	...	...	7	6,561
Dutch	2	2,328	...	...	2	2,328
German	2	1,700	...	...	2	1,700
Swedish	1	1,838	...	...	1	1,838
Hawaiian Islands	1	779	...	...	1	779
Ecuadian	1	778	...	...	1	778
Total	258	239,440	1,244	958,726	1,502	1,198,166
,, for the year preceding	151	128,476	859	621,855	1,010	750,331

Cleared.

Nationality.	Sailing. Number of Vessels.	Sailing. Tons.	Steam. Number of Vessels.	Steam. Tons.	Total. Number of Vessels.	Total. Tons.
British	51	55,065	28	9,337	79	64,402
United States of America	175	150,868	1,201	925,794	1,376	1,076,662
Chilian	17	14,813	...	...	17	14,813
Norwegian	6	5,750	...	...	6	5,750
German	3	3,319	...	...	3	3,319
Swedish	3	2,775	...	...	3	2,775
Dutch	2	2,332	...	...	2	2,332
French	1	879	...	...	1	879
Hawaiian Islands	1	779	...	...	1	779
Ecuadian	1	778	...	...	1	778
Total	260	237,358	1,229	935,131	1,489	1,172,489
,, for the year preceding	222	191,028	837	557,127	1,059	748,155

Annex B.—RETURN of Principal Articles of Export from Port Townsend during the Years 1890--89.

Articles.		1890. Quantity.	1890. Value.	1889. Quantity.	1889. Value.
			£		£
Cattle	Head	355	3,060	589	4,266
Hogs	,,	872	1,372	2,406	3,160
Horses	,,	153	8,848	273	13,799
Sheep	,,	20,940	9,397	30,513	14,384
Other animals	...	...	815	...	391
Wheat	Bushels	2,025,926	320,118	1,134,803	196,364
Flour	Bbls.	125,089	94,617	13,884	11,240
Other breadstuffs	...	...	4,801	...	4,517
Provisions, meats, &c.	...	...	22,120	...	18,475
Dairy produce	...	...	3,899	...	4,662
Vegetables—fresh, tinned	...	...	820	...	327
Fruits—fresh, tinned	...	...	2,361	...	2,844
Fish	...	...	2,411	...	1,357
Furs, hides (dressed)	...	...	13,313	...	6,762
Liquors and spirits	...	...	2,165	...	1,560
Oils	...	...	9,105	...	8,003
Tobacco, cigars	...	...	1,546	...	1,822
Agricultural implements, &c.	...	...	421	...	302
Manufactures of iron	...	...	22,260	...	16,229
Books, stationery, paper, &c.	...	...	3,549	...	2,916
Hops	...	...	77	...	821
Timber	...	...	721	...	...
Wood, and manufactures of	M. feet	...	258,714	109,765	235,773
,, doors, mouldings, &c.	...	...	6,007	...	6,350
Wool, woollen manufactures	...	...	736	...	4,489
Other articles	...	...	48,513	...	86,452
Total	...	...	841,766	...	627,256

NOTE.—In the import table the total value of free and dutiable goods together amount to 73,835*l*. Those in bond were shipped to other places in the United States and Canada. The 1*l*. sterling has been reckoned at 48,665 dol., the custom-house standard at this port.

UNITED STATES.

RETURN of Principal Articles of Import from Port Townsend during the Years 1890--89.

Articles.		1890. Quantity.	1890. Value.	1889. Quantity.	1889. Value.
Free—			£		£
Tea	Lbs.	229,750	6,742	...	995
Furs, skins (raw)	...	...	8,059	...	30
Arrowroot, flour	Lbs.	63,824	314	...	...
Other articles	...	...	1,239	...	507
		...	16,354	...	1,532
Dutiable—					
Liquors, spirits	...	...	2,366	...	2,175
Rice	Lbs.	3,067,901	10,160	...	3,178
Salt	...	...	1,150	...	1,172
Cement	Lbs.	70,813	18,587	...	6,472
Steel rails	Tons	151	701	1,500	6,918
Pig iron	,,	500	1,490	2,468	5,267
Coal	,,	3,174	3,635	5,364	3,867
Bricks—fire, common	...	...	1,150	...	1,181
Granite, rough	Tons	721	816	1,071	684
Tin plates	Lbs.	405,560	2,733	...	681
Nut oil	Gallons	4,481	331	...	...
Tobacco	Lbs.	5,853	103	...	65
Coke	Tons	26	29	...	...
Fire clay	,,	50	24	...	...
Cattle	Head	48	361	...	224
Fish	...	...	361	...	117
Furs (dressed)	...	...	129	...	355
All other articles	...	...	13,355	...	16,291
		...	57,481	...	48,640
In bond—					
Tea	...	...	166,920	...	135,129
Liquors	...	...	234	...	381
Wool	...	...	548	...	...
All other articles	...	...	27	...	10,159
In bond	...	...	167,729	...	145,669
Free	...	...	16,354	...	1,532
Dutiable	...	...	57,481	...	48,640
Grand total	...	...	241,564	...	195,841

Annex C.—TABLE showing the Total Value of all Articles Exported from Port Townsend and Imported to Port Townsend from and to Foreign Countries during the Years 1889-90.

Country.	Exports. 1890.	Exports. 1889.	Imports. 1890.	Imports. 1889.
	£	£	£	£
Great Britain	381,646	228,203	28,894	21,589
British Columbia	169,398	149,316	28,493	27,267
British Possessions—				
Australia	110,623	104,316	1,391	675
Chile	52,403	57,520	823	..
Hawaiian Islands	49,405	29,587	10	52
Peru	26,113	18,432	..	..
France	15,865	..	51	..
China	13,324	2,941	7,091	..
Mexico	7,584	3,904	..	330
Belgium	2,633	..	..	..
Guatemala	2,511	..	..	..
French Possessions—				
Australia	2,131	2,128	..	..
Argentine Republic	1,898	23,085	..	..
Germany	1,662	..	26	..
Spain	1,626	..	..	..
Bolivia	1,569	..	..	..
Ecuador	1,374	1,104	..	..
Japan	..	1,220	7,170	279
Other countries	..	5,500	37	..
Total	841,766	627,256	73,835	50,172

LOS ANGELES AND WILMINGTON.

Mr. Vice-Consul Mortimer reports as follows :—

The depression in business on which I commented in my last two reports still continues, and it is not now probable that there will be any marked revival for at least eight or ten months.

Introductory remarks.

In September and October there was some improvement, and it was hoped that the turning-point had been reached. Owing, however, to the financial panic last autumn, and some local causes, these hopes have not been realised. Business in this city still remains inactive, and the process of liquidation, which heretofore has been largely confined to "boom" transactions, is now being carried on with respect to mortgages made as investments, and residence property in this city is practically unsaleable, except at exceedingly low prices. Notwithstanding this state of facts, I am satisfied that the permanent prosperity of this city and district is assured, partly because the soil is more productive than elsewhere, and raises a great variety of valuable crops, partly because the climate is for delicate persons the best in the civilised world, partly because it is becoming the railroad centre

(1126)

of the Pacific Coast, and partly because the number and variety of raw materials gives promise in the future of great manufacturing industry. Since the "boom" of 1887 there has been a healthy growth, due to good crops, and the high prices realised in the Eastern States for the products of the orchards, and it is owing to the prosperity of the farmers I attribute the fact that the reaction from the "boom" was gradual, and not accompanied by a violent financial panic.

The following comparative statements indicate the progress made in the process of liquidation, which, I think, is now nearly at an end:—

The value of real property sold and conveyed in the city and county of Los Angeles during the year 1890, as shown by recorded deeds, was a little less than 4,000,000*l*. This amount was 45 per cent. less than the total for 1889, and only one-fifth of the total for 1887. The value of new buildings constructed in this city in the past three years was as follows:—

	£
In 1888	2,000,000
1889	900,000
1890	330,000

The assessed value of all property in the city and county of Los Angeles was—

	£
In 1888	20,600,000
1889	19,000,000
1890	15,700,000

(The figures for 1890 include Orange county, which was formed in 1889 out of the southern portion of Los Angeles county.) It will be seen from these figures that, according to the assessor's valuation, property has depreciated in value 25 per cent. in the past two years. This depreciation has been chiefly in town lots; in fact, the best orange lands and property in the business portion of this city has increased considerably in value. The Los Angeles clearing-house reports clearings as follows:—

	£
In 1888	12,600,000
1889	7,400,000
1890	6,200,000

The clearings for the first half of 1890 were 3,320,000*l*., and for the second half 2,880,000*l*. The fact that a system of electric tramways, 21 miles in length, is now being constructed here at a cost of about 400,000*l*., best indicates the confidence of capitalists in the future of this city. This venture is the more hazardous by reason of the fact that this city is already well-supplied with tramways, upwards of 20 miles of cable roads and about 40 miles of horse-car lines being now in operation. In this report I comment on many matters of apparently local interest only, owing to the number of inquiries I receive from persons in England who contemplate settling here. In so far as British interests are concerned the most important matters herein will be found under the following headings:—Beet Sugar, Advice to British Capitalists, Fraudulent English Companies, Estates of Intestates, Advice to Emigrants, and Injurious Truths. British interests.

The imports are shown in Annex B. The chief exports are oranges and other fruits, wines and brandies, and grain. Trade and commerce. Exports.

The orange crop for 1890 amounted to 2,600 car-loads (26,000 tons). The crop now being marketed is estimated at 3,780 car-loads (37,800 tons): a car-load consists of 300 boxes of about 70 lbs. each, at an average price of 8s. per box, the value of this year's crop being a little over 450,000l.

An Englishman engaged in orange growing here writes me with reference to the price of the best variety of oranges as follows:—"The average price for Navel oranges in 1890 was from 10s. to 11s. per box on the trees. This year the crop was light, and the fruit was very large, consequently not being so marketable. I should say that 9s. per box is a pretty accurate quotation; you will observe that it was the size of the fruit that caused the shrinkage in prices." A box contains from 90 to 300 oranges; the most marketable size is 160 to the box. The price of California oranges in New York has increased a little recently, owing, it is stated, to the reported loss by storms of a large portion of the Italian orange crop. The San Francisco Chamber of Commerce recently passed resolutions in favour of a reciprocity treaty with Mexico. This would admit Mexican oranges free of duty, and would cripple the industry here. It is not probable that such a treaty will be arranged. Oranges.

The duty on oranges under the new tariff is 1s. to 2s. per box, according to the size, or 6s. per 1,000 in bulk. The annual citrus fair just held in this city was the finest display of oranges ever seen in this country; the exhibit, some 40 tons, is now being transferred to Chicago for exhibition there. Tariff on oranges.

In the past two years there has been an extraordinary increase in the acreage planted in raisin grapes, and in consequence one of the viticultural commissioners prophesies that, within four years, over-production will result in very low prices. He is of opinion that the London market cannot be captured by California. At present prices raisin growers are reputed to make as much as 100l. per acre net profit. The manager of an English raisin vineyard writes me that "a full bearing raisin vineyard pays better than anything else in the fruit line known to-day." He states that some boxes of California raisins were recently sold in London at 1l. per box (20 lbs.), and adds, "with such prices we can of course nearly double our present profits, based on prices of from 8s. to 9s. per box in New York." Raisins.

The sale of pure California wines in the Eastern States is badly handicapped by the large amount of cheap adulterated stuff on the market there. The bad condition of the wine market has Wine.

been ascribed to the heavy tax on the producer, and the nominal tax on parties engaged in the adulteration of wines; the former paying a tax of 3s. 7d. per gallon on brandy, and the latter an annual license fee of only 40l.

Brandy. Under the new tariff the tax on brandy used in the fortification of sweet wines has been removed, and in consequence it is stated that sweet wines can now be made at about 6d. less per gallon than heretofore, and that brandy will now be used in fortifying, where formerly cheap corn spirits were employed. In 1876 California wines were so unsaleable that vineyardists in this district were much discouraged, and some rooted up their vines and planted grain and trees.

Price of grapes. From 1880 to 1884 the outlook was more encouraging; grapes sold readily at from 5l. to 7l. per ton, and many new vineyards were planted: over-production was the result, and partly on that account, and partly on account of a combination of the wine makers, the price of grapes was forced down to about 1l. 6s. per ton; the lowest price, 1l. 4s., being reached in 1889. The chief viticultural officer for this State is authority for the statement **Vineyards destroyed.** that in 1888–89 from 8,000 acres to 10,000 acres of bearing vines were destroyed in this district by the new disease described in my former reports. Owing to the lessened production in consequence of this heavy loss, and owing partly to a better demand for the wines of this district, and especially for brandy, the price of grapes advanced last season to an average of 3l. per ton. The demand for brandy is so good that it is now probable that 4l. per ton will be obtained this year. In 1885 this county produced 5,500,000 gallons of wine, and in 1890 only 3,000,000 gallons.

Canned fruits. The manager of the Southern California Packing Company writes me that his company packed in 1890 2,000,000 cans of 2½ lbs. each, consisting chiefly of apricots, peaches, pears, and plums. He estimates the total pack of this district at 3,500,000 cans, and adds: "The outlook for 1891 is better than any past season, for the reason that most of our orchardists are taking more pains with their fruit, and cultivating and pruning their orchards, and in consequence better results will be obtained."

Grain. The surplus for export was not large. I cannot ascertain the amount.

Shipping and navigation. British ships have almost ceased coming to San Pedro, the port for Los Angeles. In the past five years the number and tonnage of British ships arriving at the port were as follows:—

Number of British ships.

Year.	Number.	Tonnage.
1886	42	61,685
1887	46	66,440
1888	53	74,976
1889	22	30,441
1890	1	1,698

About nine-tenths of these vessels brought coals from

Australia for the Southern Pacific Railway. For the last 18 months that company has been drawing its supply of coals from Washington and British Columbia. The general manager writes me under date March 5, 1891:—"Our supply of coal received viâ the port of San Pedro continues to be largely drawn from the mines in the State of Washington, and from the district of Columbia. I cannot now say what our requirements of Australian coal may be over and above quantity imported from North Pacific Coast ports."

An inspection of the coast line of this district, from Point Duma to San Juan Capistrano (see map accompanying my report for 1889), was made some months ago by three officers of the corps of engineers under instructions from the Government to select the most suitable place for a deep-water harbour. Colonel Benyaurd, the chairman of the Board, writes me under date March 1, 1891, with reference to the improvement of San Pedro, and as to the selection of a harbour, as follows: "The amount on hand on the 1st of this month for the improvement of San Pedro harbour was in round numbers 24,600*l*. This amount will be expended under existing contracts in dredging the inner channel, and in raising and extending the west jetty. It is expected that these improvements will be continued in the future until the harbour receives the maximum depth possible to be obtained under existing tidal conditions. The report of the Board on the location of the deep-water harbour, between Points Duma and Capistrano, has not yet been submitted to the department." The Board examined the following embryo harbours:—Santa Monica, Ballona, Redondo, San Pedro, and Long Beach. The position of these places is shown on the map accompanying my report for 1889. I feel satisfied that the Board will select either Redondo or San Pedro. At the latter port upwards of 130,000*l*. has been expended by the Government without result, as far as foreign-going shipping is concerned. Heretofore the improvements at Redondo have been made by private enterprise; it is protected from the dangerous south-east gales to which San Pedro is exposed, but is unprotected on the west, and the water is too deep to admit of the construction of a breakwater.

Harbours.

New deep-water harbour.

Redondo.

The magnitude of the fruit industry in this (Los Angeles) county is well illustrated by the last report of the State Board of Horticultural Commissioners. That body states that there are nearly 23,000,000 fruit trees in the orchards of Los Angeles county, and upwards of 7,500,000 in nurseries and seedbeds. In Orange county, which was formed about a year ago out of the southern portion of Los Angeles county, there are nearly 1,000,000 fruit trees in the orchards. Returns are not given as to the other counties in this district. A London daily paper recently gave a long account of fruit culture in Southern California, with reference specially to oranges and raisins. This article, though in the main truthful and fair, and no doubt intended to be absolutely so, is calculated to give an erroneous impression to anyone ignorant of this country. The article concludes as

Agriculture.

follows:—"So far as the prospects of the intending fruit grower are concerned, the main point to be borne in mind is that no amount of glowing description—and in a land like California many truthful descriptions must necessarily be of that nature—should lead him to expect an earthly paradise, without the earthly qualifications of industry, common sense, and experience. With these kept steadily in view and in practice, success may be reckoned as sure as any branch of human labour can achieve. Gold mines may fluctuate, and other enterprises may partake more or less of a speculative character; but fruit production is a matter of well-attested facts and figures, regularly and profitably increasing year by year."

Speculative character of fruit culture. Fruit culture here is essentially speculative. Two years ago it seemed probable that the cultivation of the orange tree would cease here owing to the ravages of the "white scale," and although, as stated in my last report, the "white scale" has been exterminated by the "vedolia cardinalis," the orange grower has other pests to contend with, some of which are causing the growers a good deal of trouble and expense. Last year the profits of the orange growers were very large; this year, owing partly to a combination among the brokers, and partly to other causes, the growers are receiving a good deal less. The dangers from the various pests which attack the orange tree, the danger of combinations among the buyers, and the danger from storms, frost, &c., render the business of orange culture, and fruit culture generally, somewhat hazardous. This is patent from the fact that bearing-orange orchards, realising an annual profit of 30*l.* to 100*l.* per acre, can be purchased for 200*l.* to 300*l.* per acre. It is fair to say, however, that many persons who do not expect to realise more than a third of the present profits are engaging in the business. Mr. McNeil, a Canadian capitalist, is planting an orange grove of 450 acres; this when completed will be one of the largest in the world. He tells me that at 4*s.* per box for his crops the business will pay well. The price of land suitable for orange culture varies from 20*l.* to 100*l.* per acre. An English gentleman, who has owned and cultivated an orange grove here for the past seven years, gives me the following figures, which can be implicitly relied on:—"The best orange land, near the Foot Hills, with a good water right, is worth 60*l.* per acre. At present prices an orchard, planted to the best variety of fruit and well cared for, should net, when in full bearing, 70*l.* per acre. I mean, when in full bearing, a tree, say 12 years old from the bud. I consider such an orchard cheap at 200*l.* per acre."

Large orange grove.

Red scale. The "red scale" is doing a great deal of damage in the orange groves here. The secretary of the State Board of Horticulture writes me, under date March 7, 1891, as follows:—"I have no information as to the amount of damage done by the 'red scale,' 'aspidiotus aurantii' (introduced from Australia), but in Orange county, and also around Los Angeles, it has been a very serious pest. No internal parasite has been yet discovered to prey upon this scale. A Bill is now before the Legislature asking for an appropriation of 2,000*l.* to send a qualified agent in quest of parasites and predacious insects. The most successful remedy is hydrocyanic acid gas. . . . . An internal parasite is destroying a nearly allied species of scale, 'aspidiotus citrinus,' in the San Gabriel valley."

The gas treatment is applied by constructing a tent over each tree and generating hydrocyanic acid gas in the tent; this treatment kills all insects on the tree. I described this process in my report for 1888, and stated that the objection to its use was the expense, which at that time was 15*l.* per acre; the use of improved appliances has reduced the cost to about 3*l.* 10*s.* per acre. Many of the citrus fruit growers have kept their orchards comparatively free of red scale and other pests by spraying the trees twice a year with a wash recommended by the Horticultural Commission, the principal ingredient in which is resin. The objection to this treatment is that the liquid does not destroy all the scale bugs, many of those under the leaves escaping. The State Board of Horticultural Commissioners, in their report for 1890, after describing the four varieties of scale bugs recently brought here from Florida on young orange trees, adds:—"This commission is of opinion that these four pests are a serious menace to the citrus industry of the State, and nothing has as yet been adduced to convince us that it is either safe or wise to ignore the danger with which we are threatened." The various scale bugs multiply very rapidly, and when destroyed in one orchard by the gas treatment, the trees cleaned rapidly become again infested, unless the adjoining orchards be treated in the same way. In order to stamp out all scale bugs and injurious pests, it is now proposed to obtain legislation authorising the Horticultural Commissioners to apply the gas treatment to all infested orchards, and collect the cost in the same way as taxes are collected. *New varieties of scale bugs.*

The vine disease described in my last three reports has destroyed between 8,000 and 10,000 acres of bearing vines in this district, chiefly in Los Angeles county. Professor Dowlen, an expert employed by the Viticultural Commissioners, writes me under date March 2, 1891, with reference to this disease, as follows:— *Vine disease disappearing.*

"I may say that so far as my information goes the disease is disappearing. I have lately been through the seven southern counties, and all through this district the testimony was the same, viz., that there was nothing like so much disease present now as there had been 12 months previously. I do not know of more than three or four cases where it can be said that the disease has not decreased. In the district around Orange and Anaheim I found that many people were looking forward to the early replanting of the vineyards. I cannot state positively that the disease is the same as the Italian 'Mal Nero,' though, as far as my information goes, the two diseases resemble each other in nearly every particular. I still incline to the opinion that the disease may ultimately be traced to the action of a fungus."

UNITED STATES.

Reports of State Boards of Horticulture and Viticulture.

Persons interested should procure the annual report of the State Boards of Horticulture and Viticulture. They contain the fullest information on all matters of interest to orchardists and viticulturists. The report of the State Board of Horticulture for 1890 is a book of 500 pages, containing plates showing all the injurious pests, and the parasites that attack them. An Englishman who owns large orange and lemon groves in the province of Salenno, Italy, to whom I sent the report for 1889, writes me that it is more useful to him than any work on the subjects treated procurable in Italy.

Beet sugar

The cultivation of beets for the manufacture of sugar has been commenced in this district in the past two months. The Chino Valley Beet Sugar Company is constructing a factory on the Chino Ranch in San Bernardino county, 35 miles east of Los Angeles, at a cost of 100,000*l*. This company owns two factories in the State of Nebraska, and is now about to operate in California, because it is thought that this climate will admit of operations being carried on for about seven months in the year, whereas in Nebraska the season lasts only three months. The factory will have a capacity of 500 tons of beet per day, and will, it is stated, be the largest in the United States. It is proposed to keep it running by planting crops once a month, from February 1 to July 1. Mr. Gird, the owner of the Chino Ranch, has agreed to plant 5,000 acres in beets, and offers for sale or rent 23,000 acres in small tracts to farmers who will cultivate in beets. This is the first attempt at sugar beet culture in Southern California, and from the extensive preparations being made, the parties interested must be very confident of success. The United States Government has issued a pamphlet of about 250 pages on the sugar beet industry, entitled "Bulletin No. 27 of Chemistry Division of Department of Agriculture." From this publication I make the following extract:—"The area of soil suitable for beet cultivation in the county of Los Angeles is 1,480 square miles, and in the county of San Bernardino 465 square miles . . . . From the data of yield of beets per acre, and sugar per ton of beets (elsewhere than in Southern California), the average may be put at 15 tons and 9 per cent. respectively, or 2,700 lbs. of sugar per acre." This is 3 tons and 3 per cent., respectively, below the average results obtained by Mr. James Duncan, in Suffolk. On the other hand, the experiments made in the Chino Ranch in the past two years indicate that the results obtained there are far above the average in the most favoured beet districts of Europe or America. Mr. Gird writes me as follows:—"The highest percentage of sugar obtained in the beets grown for experimental purposes was 24 per cent. of the weight of the beet." The factory will be supplied chiefly by tenant farmers on Mr. Gird's estate. In the contracts with these farmers the prices to be paid for the beets are specified as follows:—"14*s*. per ton for beets containing an average of at least 12 per cent. of sugar to the weight of the beet, with a purity coefficient of 80 per cent., and an additional 1*s*. per ton for each and every per cent. of sugar contained above 12 per cent., as determined by daily lists to be made in Mr. Gird's laboratory." On this scale of prices it is thought that farmers will receive from 16s. to 1l. per ton, and at a maximum of 15 tons per acre the gross yield would be 12l. to 15l. Mr. Gird writes me that an industrious farmer can cultivate about 20 acres in beets, and on the terms on which he is prepared to rent a minimum net profit of 6l. per acre can be realised. It is stated that beets can be raised between the rows of fruit trees in young orchards, and that in this way farmers can realise a profit while their fruit trees are maturing. I always advise English farmers coming here to settle to rent for a year or two before purchasing land, and I now draw special attention to the beet sugar industry, because I think it offers a fair chance to strangers settling here to make a profit as tenant farmers, with the minimum of risk. In the recent changes in the United States customs tariff, sugar under No. 16 Dutch Standard was conditionally placed on the free list, and a bounty of $\frac{3}{4}d.$ to 1d. per lb. offered for all sugar produced in the United States. It appears from the Government publication, to which I have referred, that in California only has permanent success been obtained in the cultivation of beets for the production of sugar.

It has been a matter of surprise to me that the business of cultivating flowers for the manufacture of perfumes has not been carried on here. The pure olive oil necessary in the manufacture of perfumes is produced here in large quantities, and this climate is better adapted for the culture of flowers than that of the south of France, where the industry is carried on so extensively. I am now informed that Mr. Palmer, a perfume manufacturer of New York, is about to commence this business in this vicinity.

Perfumery.
Farming.

In my report for 1889, written in March 1890, I estimated the population of this city at about 80,000. The census taken in June following showed a little over 50,000. The difference is partly accounted for by the fact that 10,000 to 12,000 transient visitors spend the winter here, and at the time the census was taken these visitors had left, and many of the permanent residents were at the seaside: making these allowances, the population must have decreased from 12,000 to 15,000 in the past two years. In 1880 this city, with 11,000 inhabitants, was 211th in population among the cities of the United States. The census of 1890 shows that it is now 57th, a very remarkable increase.

Population and industries.

Population.

The great register, compiled for the elections in October, 1890, showed that the British-born persons resident in the city and county of Los Angeles, who are now American citizens, number 2,233 as follows:—Ireland, 836; England and Wales, 632; Scotland, 140; Canada, 555; other British possessions, 70. To these may be added between 700 and 800 British subjects who have not been naturalised, making a total of about 3,000. In estimates of population, five persons are usually allowed to each voter: allowing only three we get a total British-born population of about 9,000. In addition to 2,233 voters of British birth, there are 2,803 from other countries, making a total foreign vote of 5,036. The American voters number 18,626, making the total number of voters in this city and county 23,662.

British-born persons resident here.

There are 20 miles of streets in this city paved with asphalte, laid on concrete foundation, and 60 miles of graded and gravelled streets: about one-fifth of this work was commenced and completed in 1890. The cost of paving and grading streets is borne by the property owners on the streets so improved.

Borax. Borax is found in practically unlimited quantities in this district. The treasurer of the San Bernardino Borax Mining Company writes me that in eight months of 1890 his company manufactured 775 tons (2,000 lbs. per ton), and that the average price at the factory was 28*l.* per ton. I am informed that the cost of manufacture does not exceed 7*l.* per ton, that the borax fields are in a few hands, and that the price is kept up by limiting the output.

Tin. The San Jacinto Tin Mining Company, Limited, an English concern, has purchased the Temascal tin mines, about 40 miles east of this city, together with about 40,000 acres of land, for, it is stated, 300,000*l.* These mines undoubtedly contain a very rich body of ore, and are probably the richest tin mines in the United States. Fuel, however, is expensive, wages are high, and the maintenance of the new tariff on tin plates is possibly a little uncertain. In view of these conditions it will be interesting to see if British capital can enable the tin plate industry of America to successfully compete with that of the mother country. Owing to litigation the mines have never been worked until the present company commenced operations a few months ago.

Iron. In my last report I referred to vast deposits of iron, coal, and other minerals on the line of a proposed railway from Utah to Los Angeles. Analyses of samples of iron from the deposits I referred to, made recently by Thomas Price and Sons, assayers, San Francisco, and published here, show that the samples analysed contain from 62·40 to 67·30 per cent. of iron. The assayers state that "the highest percentage that chemically pure merchantable iron of this class could produce would be 72·45 per cent."

Oil. I cannot procure accurate statistics of the output of oil in this district in 1890. The estimates vary from 4,000,000 to 15,000,000 gallons. The price continues to be 8*s.* per barrel of 40 gallons, and at this price I am informed that it is cheaper for manufacturing purposes than coal at 1*l.* per ton. From the best information I can obtain I am satisfied that the supply of oil is practically unlimited, that when the oil fields are better developed the price will be reduced to about 4*s.* per barrel, and that at that figure manufacturing industries will be possible here. The present high price is due to the demand being greatly in excess of the supply. The English company referred to in my last report and elsewhere in this did not purchase the Puente oil wells.

Public works. Stoppage of railroad construction. Railroad construction in this district ceased suddenly in December, 1890. It was stated in the press that the stoppage of work was the result of a combination of the western roads, and it is not improbable that such a trust has been formed, as a complete community of interests would render it quite unnecessary to construct additional lines. In my last report I referred to the probable completion of a railway from Salt Lake City to Los Angeles by the Union Pacific. The line is in operation from Salt Lake City to Milford, in Southern Utah, and the assistant-general manager of the Union Pacific wrote me under date March 3, 1890:—" We shall construct this year from Milford to Pioche Nevada." He now writes me under date March 5, 1891:—"The Union Pacific have graded the line from Milford to Pioche; but it has not as yet been ironed, and I am unable to inform you when it will be. I have no information that leads me to believe that any other line is contemplating the construction of a line from Utah to Los Angeles, or a connection with the Atlantic and Pacific Road." The general managers of the Denver and Rio Grande, and the Carson and Colorado railways, write me to the same effect. The vice-president of the Atchison, Topeka, and Santa Fé railroad writes me that his company is not at present contemplating any extension whatever of its lines. In December this company was surveying a road from Los Angeles to San Francisco. The general manager of the Southern Pacific Company writes me under date March 5, 1891, that the coast line from San Francisco to Los Angeles, viâ Santa Barbara, will be completed by his company, " if the people interested along the route succeed in securing necessary right of way and depôt grounds." These concessions have been promised to the company, and will, I understand, be arranged for. This company again suffered heavy loss this year from washouts in the Solidad Cañon, on the main line between Los Angeles and San Francisco, and travel was suspended for several days. The line is being reconstructed above high water mark. *Railway to Salt Lake City.*

The terminal railway, connecting Los Angeles and Pasadena, is being extended from Los Angeles to the port of San Pedro. It is stated that this line will ultimately connect with the Union Pacific from Salt Lake City, and the fact that it is being extended to San Pedro gives countenance to the supposition, as on no other hypotheses would such an extension pay. Work was stopped on this road in December, and was recently resumed. In my last report I have pointed out the importance of a road from Los Angeles to Salt Lake City, and in what way it would affect British interests here, and the export of coals from Australia and British Columbia. I am satisfied, as I then stated, that such a road will be built within three to five years. Extensive public works have been carried on in this city in the past year, principally the construction of a system of sewers. Contractors were required, to employ citizens of the United States only; to work their men not more than eight hours per day; and to pay not less than 8s. per day to the labourers in their employ. I may add that the superintendent of streets has condemned some of the sewers contracted under these conditions. *Extension of terminal railway.*

Sewer construction.

UNITED STATES.

General remarks.

Advice to British capitalists.

In my report for 1889 I gave some particulars of a number of companies operating here which were then being floated on the London market, and added, dozens of schemes in this district, similar to the foregoing examples, are now being offered to the British investor. Those of them that are carried out will no doubt be further burdened with heavy promotion money in London. Apart from the promoters' charges, however, it is certainly not wise to pay 100 per cent. more than was asked during the "boom" of 1887, especially when local capitalists can buy at 50 per cent. below boom prices. Such great dangers beset the British investor in Southern California, from promoters in London, from mismanagement by English managers unfamiliar with this country—whose sole qualifications are possibly a reputation for honesty, and relationship to one of the directors—and from impositions by vendors and their agents here, that I am reluctantly compelled to advise British capitalists not to invest in Southern California companies. I give this advice unwillingly, as there are many openings here for the profitable investment of capital.

I am again most unwillingly compelled to reiterate this advice—unwillingly, because I am satisfied that this district offers excellent opportunities for profitable investment either by companies or individuals. The development of Southern California is in its infancy, and it is beyond question that all this part of the State will be very thickly populated. Unless, however, English investors can form joint stock companies without the aid of promoters, and can arrange for their management by responsible persons familiar with Californian business methods, it is useless to expect profits. "The San Francisco News Letter," a paper which makes a specialty of accurate information on mining matters, stated in its issue of December 27, 1890, that "of all the Pacific Coast mining properties floated in London during the past five years, none have turned out well, and many have developed into out-and-out swindles." "The San Francisco Evening Post" of July 11, 1890, accounts for the increasing difficulty in inducing English capitalists to invest in California mines by the statement that the history of these transactions for some years has been "one continued chain of financial disaster and miserable failure, without a solitary success as a redeeming feature."

Fraudulent English companies.

As far as my experience extends, English companies in Southern California have been either fraudulent ab initio, or through mismanagement, or, in a few cases, misfortune, have been unremunerative. In my report for 1889, I mentioned the proposed purchase by an English company of some valuable oil wells near this city. The sale was not carried out, and the vendor here (an Englishman who has lived here for a number of years, and who is incapable of unfair dealing) writes me as follows:—"The reason our oil property was not sold was on account of exorbitant demands of promoters. This property is one of the best ever placed on the London market, and would pay good dividends on price to be paid us, but the enormous amount required to be added to the purchase price to satisfy the rapacity of London promoters rendered it necessary to capitalise at such a high figure that we (my partner and myself) determined to withdraw the property from the London market."

<small>Estates of intestates.</small>

The estates of persons dying intestate here are administered by the public administrator if the decedent leaves no relatives entitled to administer. This official publishes a return every six months, showing *inter alia* the value of the estates in his hands. The return made by the public administrator here a few months ago showed that estates to the value of about 50,000*l*. had recently come into his hands: of this amount about 30,000*l*. belongs to heirs in England and Canada. He is not required to make efforts to find heirs, and as a rule does not do so, and unless friends of decedents interest themselves to find heirs the matter is speedily forgotten, and the money finally escheats to the State.

<small>Education.</small>

There are 34 public schools in this city, containing 178 rooms, and attended by nearly 8,000 male and female children. 14 of these schools were constructed in the year 1890, at a cost of upwards of 26,000*l*., to meet this expenditure; bonds to the amount of 20,000*l*. were issued and sold by the city, and the balance was paid out of the school fund. Grave charges of immorality, resulting from the co-education of the sexes, have been made by opponents of the public school system. I see by a recent Government report on education that one of the school superintendents meets another objection as follows:—"The mingling of the sexes in the school-room checks the tendencies both to romantic fancies and overwrought and unreal imaginings, engendered by attendance in separate schools, and this it does by substituting for such illusions the everyday commonplace reality of mutual rivalry in a common labour." This is no doubt the case, but it is at least doubtful whether it is well to dispel illusions which are possibly better than commonplace realities.

<small>Public schools.</small>

<small>University of Southern California.</small>

There is also a university here, which is advertised as "offering educational opportunities of the very highest and broadest character." An interesting correspondence between a Unitarian divine and a trustee of this university was published some months ago, the question at issue being whether this institution is in truth and in fact a university, or only a second-rate school. The former stated that an English gentleman brought his family here, believing that his sons could be educated at this university, and that he was much disappointed. The State university at Berkeley is probably the only institution in this State that would bear comparison with the universities in the Eastern States. There is a good deal of "unconscious education" in the press here, which is apt to have a bad influence on young men; for example, it is constantly alleged that legislation is procured by bribing the members of the Senate and House of Assembly, and in some instances the amount per capita alleged to have been paid to each legislator is openly stated. These allegations, as a rule, are probably untrue; true or false the subject is often treated

Treatment of vagrants.

with a degree of levity which is not likely to impress young men with the moral turpitude of such conduct.

In my last report I drew attention to statements made in the press here to the effect that labourers seeking employment were sometimes arrested as vagrants by the constables solely to obtain the fees allowed for making the arrest, and committed to the chain-gang. A gross case of this description was made public in April last. Two Mexicans proceeding to a farm where they were promised employment were arrested, convicted of vagrancy, and sentenced to a period of service in the chain-gang (constable's fees 10*l*.). When released they appealed to the Mexican Consul, and at his instance the constable was arrested and fined 15*l*. Persons convicted of vagrancy, and similar minor offences, are sentenced to a period of service in the chain-gang: that is, to work on the public streets with a cannon ball attached to the offender's leg by a chain. This is quite a severe punishment on a hot summer's day.

Taxation of mortgages.

The constitution of this State provides for the taxation of the interest of the mortgagee in property mortgaged to him. For example, if A owns property worth 600*l*., and borrows 200*l*. from B on mortgage, and the property be assessed for 250*l*.—property is generally assessed at about one-third of its value—B will pay the taxes on 200*l*., and A on the balance 50*l*. The taxation of mortgages was intended to lessen the burden of the debtor at the expense of the lender; the effect, however, has been just the reverse, as capitalists at once raised the rate of interest more than sufficient to cover any possible tax, and it is generally believed that the high rates of interest obtained here are due to the taxation of mortgages. Capitalists at a distance are unwilling to send money here for investment owing to the trouble in connection with the tax, and fearing also a sudden increase in the rate of taxation. The current rates of interest here on mortgage run from 8 per cent. to 12 per cent. gross, according to amount of loan and nature of security.

Advice to emigrants.

The classes likely to succeed here are industrious farm labourers and practical farmers with some capital. The former, if steady, industrious, and willing to work hard, and not too old to adapt themselves to entirely new conditions of life, can save enough money to rent a farm, and in a few years' time can become independent. Farmers with a little capital should seek employment at first, and not invest their money until, after some practical experience of the country, they have acquired some knowledge of values, modes of agriculture, &c. The sons of professional men, retired officers, and all that large class of English gentlemen, who have received a fairly good education, and yet are not specially fitted for any profession or occupation are not likely to succeed, and should not be encouraged to come here. It is downright cruelty to educate a boy at a public school in England, and then send him to California with a few pounds in his pocket to shift for himself; the chances are that he will soon sink to the level of a waiter in a restaurant, a farm labourer, or some similar position. It is almost incredible the number of sons of professional men (chiefly clergymen) who apply to me for advice or assistance. Nearly every one of them tells me that his father could not afford to give him a start in life in England, and in consequence he had to emigrate. As a rule they do not succeed as well as comparatively uneducated Englishmen of the lower classes. It is much the same in Canada and, I understand, in Australia, and I have come to the conclusion that English professional men, blessed with a number of sons for whom they are unable to provide, should be advised to send them away at 12 or 14 years of age, instead of 18 or 20, to finish their education in the colony or country in which their parents have determined to start them; three or four years at school will teach them the habits of the natives, and they will then have a fair start in commencing for themselves. The census of the United States, taken in June, 1890, shows that throughout the country generally the population in the cities is increasing at the expense of the country districts. Here the reverse is the case. A family can live comfortably on the produce of five acres in orange trees, and in consequence the settled portions of the country, that is, where there is water for irrigation, are very thickly populated, and the occupants of these small farms have the benefits of companionship and public schools, where their children can be educated without expense, except a few shillings for books.

It is a common saying that Southern California is no place for a poor man. The "Los Angeles Times," believing that this saying is a libel on the country, published interviews it had with a large number of prosperous American farmers, who, it is alleged, came here penniless. The following is a specimen interview:— *Southern California for poor people.*

"T. D. Cheney started in 1876, near Downey, in debt for his 40 acres of land. By work and good management he accumulated by 1887 a property which he sold for 42,000 dol., reserving seven thoroughbred cows, valued at about 3,000 dol. In other words, Mr. Cheney in 11 years made 45,000 dol. He commenced without money and in debt, and accomplished this by work, not speculation. His money was made from alfaifa and stock."

The qualities that ensure success here will ensure ultimate success in England or elsewhere, the only difference being that better opportunities are offered here. Persons who have a little capital can invest here now to better advantage than at any time for some years past, as, owing to the depression in business, many opportunities to purchase both city and country property at very low prices are now offering.

The expense of admission to the learned professions is nominal. For admission to the legal profession there are no fees, and no probationary period of study. It is necessary only to pass a not very difficult oral examination in open court, and procure a certificate of good moral character, to obtain a license to practise as a barrister and solicitor. One result is that the learned professions are somewhat crowded, and versatile men, not *Admission to learned professions.*

(1126)

UNITED STATES.

Exhibitions.

finding success in one profession, will sometimes leave it for another. There are few restrictions, and an intelligent man can be anything he is fit for.

A permanent exhibit of the products of Southern California is maintained in Chicago. The Atchison, Topeka, and Santa Fé provides the building in which the exhibit is held, and free transportation for all articles to be exhibited, and the principal fruit growers and business men here subscribe about 300*l.* per month to pay other necessary expenses. The exhibit attracts much attention, and no doubt induces many persons to settle in this vicinity. It is now proposed to maintain a similar exhibit in London for a couple of years. I mention the matter, as it is unquestionably advisable for newcomers to settle in a district which contains energetic and public-spirited men.

Climate.

Since my first report on this district in 1883 I have annually drawn attention to the climate of Southern California, pointing out that, owing to its equableness and dryness, it is superior to that of the south of France and Italy; that for persons in the earlier stages of consumption it is probably the best climate in the civilised world; and that owing to the fact that the greater number of those suffering from consumption are dependent upon their own exertions for support, this district offers greater advantages than the health resorts in the south of Europe, in that there is a fair chance for an intelligent man to make a living here when renewed health admits of his engaging in some occupation. The prosperity of this district in the past has been largely due to the fact that numbers of wealthy invalids come here annually for the benefit of their health. Of late years material prosperity has been based on the more solid basis of the large profits in fruit farming. When money, labour, and fuel are a little cheaper this city will be a manufacturing centre; in the meantime one of its mainstays is the climate. The total number of deaths here in 1890 was 844, from the following causes:—consumption (contracted elsewhere), 246; zymotic diseases, 122; suicides, murders, and accidents, 42; other causes, 434; total 844. The large number of deaths from zymotic diseases is due partly to defective and insufficient sewerage, and chiefly to the use of water condemned by the health officer as unfit for human consumption. The former cause will shortly be removed, as a large sum of money is now being spent in the construction of a complete system of sewers. In a filter attached to my kitchen faucet, after the water had been running half-an-hour, I caught to-day upwards of 40 worms, fish, and "creeping things" from $\frac{1}{8}$th inch to $\frac{1}{2}$ inch long. The city council is now asked to forfeit the franchise of the company supplying this water. The charge for this water is from 8*s.* to 8*l.* per month, according to the size of the house and number of occupants. Persons who can afford to do so purchase water by the gallon for drinking purposes. Water supplied by other companies in other sections of the city is fairly good. The death rate is about 13 per 1,000; excluding the deaths from consumption and other diseases contracted elsewhere,

Number of deaths.

Bad water.

and the deaths from preventible causes, the rate would not probably be more than 6 or 7 per 1,000. The rainfall for the last 10 years has averaged 18 inches per annum; it is, however, very irregular, the fall in 1881 being only 5½ inches, and in 1884 upwards of 40 inches. In the December and January numbers of Harper's Magazine, Mr. Charles Dudley Warner published articles on Southern California, which contain a good deal of valuable information about this district. These articles were republished by the "Los Angeles Daily Times," and can be procured from the "Times" office for 3d. Persons in delicate health, who contemplate coming to Southern California, should certainly procure and read these articles. Mr. Warner's estimate of the climate is a very fair one; in his estimates of the capabilities of the country, however, he falls into the common error of describing exceptionally large crops as normal returns. For example, he says that a fair average return from vines five years old is 7 tons of grapes per acre per annum. This is an exceptional yield; the average yield is under 4 tons. Making due allowance for similar exaggerations, these articles give briefly the most interesting account I have seen of Southern California; they have had an enormous circulation, and it is on that account I refer to them.

Death rate.

Mr. Warner on Southern California.

My reference to the subject of divorce in my last report was not well received here. I mention the matter partly because it is a subject of general interest, and partly because several persons in England have written me to ascertain if a valid divorce can be obtained without coming to California. The following cutting is taken from the "Los Angeles Evening Express," of December 20, 1890:—

Divorce.

"'DIVORCE DAY' IN DEPARTMENT TWO.

"Yesterday was what might be known as 'Divorce Day' in Department Two of the Superior Court. This is unquestionably true when one considers the fact that Judge Clark granted four divorces, and this within two hours.

"Lena Walker asked for a divorce from C. H. Walker on the ground of desertion. She demonstrated that for a number of years she had not seen her better half. She therefore was given a judgment by default.

"Nettie Cummings was given a divorce from Wellington Cummings on the ground of desertion. The testimony went to show that for 18 months Mr. Cummings had not shown up at headquarters. Default was therefore entered.

"Jessie Bassett was granted a divorce from David F. Bassett on the ground that he had in San Francisco been convicted of felony and sentenced to two years in San Quentin. In proof of this fact a copy of the commitment papers were presented in evidence."

In the city and county of Los Angeles about 200 divorces

were granted in 1890. This is about one-fifth of one per cent. of the total population.

In my last report, in commenting on the sale of lands in Kern county to persons in London, I stated that it was extremely unwise to purchase land in California without seeing it. The Kern County Land Company, with a capital of 2,000,000*l.*, and 400,000 acres of land, writes me as follows :—" The Kern County Land Company is the owner of the properties on which the English settlers, to whom you refer, are located. The work of colonising these lands was begun in the fall of 1889, and since that time this company has located nearly 20 families from England, and more than twice as many settlers from our eastern States. The English settlers are very desirable people, chiefly from mercantile and professional life, of more or less means, and have expressed themselves as much pleased with this section of the country, and their purchases here. . . . I enclose herewith copies of statements made by several of the representative families. . . . The system of irrigating canals on the lands of this company is the most extensive in California, comprising some 300 miles of main canals, and many times that length in laterals. . . . Water is furnished to each 20 acre tract. Water rates average about 6*s.* per acre per year." The "interviews" enclosed with this letter were had with Mr. Burnett, formerly of Woking, Surrey, head gardener to Lord Hope, Mr. Musser, and Mr. Arthur A. Wells. Without reflecting on this company, which as far as I am aware is thoroughly responsible and reliable, I still think that prospective settlers would be much wiser to reside in California for some months before purchasing land.

<small>Kern County Land Company.</small>

My last report on this district met with some hostile criticism here. The Chamber of Commerce, the Board of Trade, and the City Council, united in a request to the Government of the United States for my removal, alleging among other things that I had told "injurious truths" about this district. I have reiterated most of the "injurious truths" complained of in this report. Persons who contemplate investing in Southern California companies will find it to their advantage to discover the rest of the "injurious truths" by reading my last report.

<small>Injurious truths.</small>

I am indebted to Major Downing, United States Collector of Customs at San Pedro, for the statistics in Annexes A., B., and C.

Annex A.—RETURN of all Shipping at the Port of Wilmington (San Pedro), California, in the Year 1890.

ENTERED.

Nationality.	Sailing. Number of Vessels.	Sailing. Tons.	Steam. Number of Vessels.	Steam. Tons.	Total. Number of Vessels.	Total. Tons.
British	1	1,698	...	...	1	1,698
American	29	41,534	...	...	29	41,534
Other countries	3	1,135	...	...	3	1,135
Total	33	44,367	...	...	33	44,367
,, for the year preceding	35	44,838	6	7,980	41	52,818

CLEARED.

Nationality.	Sailing. Number of Vessels.	Sailing. Tons.	Steam. Number of Vessels.	Steam. Tons.	Total. Number of Vessels.	Total. Tons.
British	2	2,602	...	...	2	2,602
American	25	39,470	...	...	25	39,470
Other countries	2	1,157	...	...	2	1,157
Total	29	43,229	...	...	29	43,229
,, for the year preceding	35	45,426	6	7,980	41	53,404

NOTE.—This return does not include 468 sailing and steam coasting vessels, aggregate tonnage 290,733. The coasters for 1889 numbered 568, tonnage 489,500.

The following coasting vessels arrived at the port of Redondo:—Steam, 196; sail, 18; total, 214. Tonnage not stated.

Annex B.—RETURN of the Principal Articles of Export from Wilmington, California, during the Years 1889-90.

Articles.	1889. Quantity.	1889. Value.	1890. Quantity.	1890. Value.
	Tons.	£	Tons.	£
Wheat	..	..	..	..
Other articles	7	120	12	44
Total	7	120	12	44

The following is a summary of imports in coasting vessels (domestic trade):—

Articles.		Quantity.
Lumber	Feet ..	44,332,750
Railway ties	Number ..	9,545
Other articles..	Tons ..	16,758

And at port of Redondo :—

Articles.		Quantity.
Lumber	Feet ..	9,408,962
Other articles..	Tons ..	26,834

RETURN of Principal Articles of Import to Wilmington, California, during the Years 1890–89.

Articles.		1889. Quantity.	1889. Value.	1890. Quantity.	1890. Value.
			£		£
Coal	Tons	67,620	54,400	65,548	52,800
Pig iron	,,	200	...	...	...
Cement	Barrels	...	...	...	...
Other articles	Tons	209	...	...	230
Total	...	68,029	54,400	65,548	53,030

Annex C.—TABLE showing the Total Value of all Articles Exported from Wilmington and Imported to Wilmington from and to Foreign Countries during the Years 1889–90.

Country.	Exports. 1889.	Exports. 1890.	Imports. 1889.	Imports. 1890.
	£	£	£	£
Great Britain and British Possessions	120	44	54,400	53,030
Other countries	..	..	..	249
Total	120	44	54,400	53,279

SAN DIEGO.

Mr. Vice-Consul Allen reports as follows :—

General business. The depression in business, which began three years ago, still continues; but in many respects I am able to report an improvement in the outlook.

In 1888 many people were driven to seek an income from land bought for speculation only, and others, who had bought land for the purpose, planted large orchards, so that the country around San Diego is rapidly being made productive, and I think that in a very few years there will be a considerable fruit export trade.

San Diego county differs from most other counties of southern California in being very hilly. This makes transportation difficult and tends to retard progress. Before this county can be thoroughly developed it will be necessary to build railways through the main valleys to enable farmers and fruit growers to market their produce.

On the other hand, the hilly nature of the country affords many admirable sites for reservoirs for irrigating purposes.

These undertakings require large capital, and are beyond individual effort; but the profits are so large and so certain that there is little difficulty in finding capitalists ready to invest money in land and water companies. The usual method of operations is to buy, or bond, as much land as possible in the immediate vicinity of the projected reservoir, pipe water to it and sell it, with "water-right," at from two to four times the cost price. A yearly water rate is then charged, varying from 4 dol. to 6 dol. an acre.

Since the collapse of the "boom" much has been done to improve the town of San Diego. About 150,000*l.* has been spent on street grading and paving. A cable road 5½ miles long has been constructed at a cost of 73,000*l.* Coal bunkers have been built capable of storing 15,000 tons of coals, and the facilities for unloading and loading vessels are unequalled on the coast. A steam collier recently discharged her cargo at the rate of over 1,000 tons a day. There has been much building, both of business premises and dwellings.

As a place of residence San Diego is already attracting many people from the eastern States by its beautiful situation and incomparable climate. There are two seasons here. The warm winters attract visitors from the east, and during the summer Californians come from the hot inland towns and valleys to enjoy the cool sea breezes of San Diego Bay. The hotels are numerous and good, notably one that covers seven acres, situated in the suburb of Coronado.

Various industries in this and adjacent counties will also contribute to the building up of this city, *e.g.*, the Temescal tin mines, now working by a English company (the San Jacinto Mining Company). These are said to be the most valuable tin mines known. Cement also is manufacturing, though not yet on the market, to be known as Jamul Portland Cement; but I am as yet unable to form any opinion as to whether its quality will enable it to compete with the imported cements.

During the past year the number of British ships entering the port was 13, as against 11 for the previous year. Total number of all nationalities 212, as against 187.

It is probable that San Diego will become a shipping point

for wheat and barley to the United Kingdom. Two cargoes were shipped during the past season, and during the coming one there will probably be a larger number.

I pointed out in my last report that the exports for 1889 were largely increased by the mining excitement in Lower California. The exports for 1890 are accordingly less than for 1889; but a reference to Annex C. will show that they exceed those for 1888.

In 1889 there was a large falling-off in the amount of imports owing to the collapse of the "boom." The value of the imports during 1890 is more than double the value of imports during 1889, though not equal to the exceptionally high value for 1888.

In Annex C. I give the values for 1888 as well as those for 1889 to facilitate comparison.

The area of soil under cultivation has again been enlarged this season, and the recent rains should ensure plentiful grain crops, and this will tend to increase the exports for the current year.

The prospect of soon having another transcontinental railway built into San Diego has not improved during the past year, indeed it seems unlikely that there will be any railway building for several years to come. Projects are under consideration to connect San Diego with Yuma on the Southern Pacific; but I greatly doubt their being carried out.

The figures given in my last report were accepted as correct at the time; but the census of last year shows them to have been greatly over-estimated.

The population of San Diego and suburbs is now about 16,000, that of the county about 35,000. The gain for the city of San Diego since last census is over 500 per cent., and is the largest gain of any city in the Union.

The following table shows the increase of population, and assessed value of taxed property since 1880, for the three principal counties of southern California:—

County.	Population, 1880.	Population, 1890.	Ratio of Increase.	Assessed Valuation, 1880.	Assessed Valuation, 1890.	Ratio of Increase.
				£	£	
Los Angeles	33,381	101,140	3·04	3,273,730	13,895,005	4·24
San Bernadino	7,766	25,486	3·28	515,395	4,498,088	8·73
San Diego	8,618	34,878	4·05	705,052	6,023,701	8·54

A Bill providing for the establishment of a "military post" of ten companies, about 1,000 men, has been approved by the President.

For the information given in the subjoined annexes I am indebted to Major Bailhache, Deputy Collector of Customs for San Diego.

Dollars have been reduced to sterling in the following tables at the rate of 4·8665 dol. to 1*l*.

SAN FRANCISCO.

Annex A.—RETURN of all Shipping at the Port of San Diego, California, in the Year 1890.

ENTERED.

Nationality.	Sailing.		Steam.		Total.	
	Number of Vessels.	Tons	Number of Vessels.	Tons.	Number of Vessels.	Tons.
British	12	15,002	1	1,799	13	16,801
American	53	23,389	138	33,802	191	57,193
Other countries	5	592	3	1,236	8	1,828
Total	70	38,983	142	36,837	212	75,822
,, for the year preceding	63	42,245	124	35,680	187	77,925

CLEARED.

Nationality.	Sailing.		Steam.		Total.	
	Number of Vessels.	Tons.	Number of Vessels.	Tons.	Number of Vessels.	Tons.
British	11	13,803	1	1,799	12	15,602
American	32	10,865	141	35,838	173	6,703
Other countries	1	1,120	2	1,174	3	2,394
Total	44	25,788	144	38,811	188	64,599
,, for the year preceding	37	25,836	123	35,933	160	61,769

Annex B.—RETURN of the Principal Articles of Export from San Diego, California, during the Years 1889–90.

Articles.	Value.	
	1889.	1890.
	£	£
Wheat	..	11,569
Agricultural instruments	..	1,182
Fruit and nuts	..	1,370
Manufactures of iron and steel	..	5,981
Powder and explosives	..	874
Lumber	..	3,184
Lime and cement	..	702
Coals	..	1,373
Other articles	..	36,686
Total	87,909	62,921

(1126)

UNITED STATES.

RETURN of the Principal Articles of Import to San Diego, California, during the Years 1889-90.

Articles.		1889.		1890.	
		Quantity.	Value.	Quantity.	Value.
			£		£
Coals	Tons	56,527	33,949	46,226	30,788
Pig-iron	,,	...	...	458	1,603
Cement	Barrels	17,953	3,451	60,557	15,595
Other articles	...	...	11,319	...	52,707
Total...	...	...	48,719	...	100,693

Annex C.—TABLE showing the Total Value of all Articles Exported from San Diego from and to Foreign Countries during the Years 1888-90.

Country.	Exports.			Imports.		
	1888.	1889.	1890.	1888.	1889.	1890.
	£	£	£	£	£	£
Great Britain	...	...	11,569	...	3,451	24,884
British Possessions	...	...	...	...	33,949	28,208
Mexico	...	...	47,948	...	...	45,010
Not classified	...	...	3,404	...	11,319	2,591
Total ...	58,340	87,909	62,921	127,400	48,719	100,693

LONDON:
Printed for Her Majesty's Stationery Office,
By HARRISON AND SONS,
Printers in Ordinary to Her Majesty.
(1250 6 91—H & S 1126)

FOREIGN OFFICE.
1891.
ANNUAL SERIES.

No. 910.

DIPLOMATIC AND CONSULAR REPORTS ON AND FINANCE.

UNITED STATES.

REPORT FOR THE YEAR 1890

ON THE

AGRICULTURE OF THE DISTRICT OF THE CONSULATE OF SAN FRANCISCO.

REFERENCE TO PREVIOUS REPORT, Annual Series No. 730.

Presented to both Houses of Parliament by Command of Her Majesty,
JUNE, 1891.

LONDON:
PRINTED FOR HER MAJESTY'S STATIONERY OFFICE,
BY HARRISON AND SONS, ST. MARTIN'S LANE,
PRINTERS IN ORDINARY TO HER MAJESTY.

And to be purchased, either directly or through any Bookseller, from
EYRE & SPOTTISWOODE, East Harding Street, Fleet Street, E.C., and
32, Abingdon Street, Westminster, S.W.; or
JOHN MENZIES & Co., 12, Hanover Street, Edinburgh, and
88 and 90, West Nile Street, Glasgow; or
HODGES, FIGGIS, & Co., 104, Grafton Street, Dublin.

1891.

[C. 6205—141.] *Price One Penny.*

New Series of Reports.

Reports of the Annual Series have been issued from Her Majesty's Diplomatic and Consular Officers at the following places, and may be obtained from the sources indicated on the title-page:—

No.		Price.	No.		Price.
792.	Asuncion	½d.	851.	Saigon	½d.
793.	Bahia	7½d.	852.	Vienna	1½d.
794.	Monte Video	1½d.	853.	Algiers	2d.
795.	Munich	2d.	854.	Algiers	1d.
796.	Bucharest	1d.	855.	Mozambique	8d.
797.	Tokio	1d.	856.	Antwerp	1½d.
798.	Tabreez	1d.	857.	Mogador	2d.
799.	Antwerp	1d.	858.	Ichang	½d.
800.	Malaga	1d.	859.	Calais	8½d.
801.	Odessa	1d.	860.	Riga	2d.
802.	Malaga	2d.	861.	San José	1d.
803.	Amsterdam	1d.	862.	Genoa	1½d.
804.	Bogotá	1½d.	863.	Warsaw	1d.
805.	Guayaquil	½d.	864.	Wuhu	1d.
806.	Lima	1d.	865.	Marseilles	1d.
807.	Rio de Janeiro	3d.	866.	Syra	1d.
808.	Dantzig	1½d.	867.	Jeddah	½d.
809.	Florence	1½d.	868.	Savannah	½d.
810.	Lisbon	1d.	869.	Suakin	½d.
811.	Quito	½d.	870.	Berlin	1d.
812.	Para	½d.	871.	Batoum	1½d.
813.	Palermo	2½d.	872.	Rosario	1d.
814.	Copenhagen	1d.	873.	Buenos Ayres	½d.
815.	Serajevo	½d.	874.	Mogador	1d.
816.	Porto Rico	1d.	875.	Tainan	6½d.
817.	Madrid	½d.	876.	Pakhoi	1d.
818.	Brussels	½d.	877.	Odessa	2½d.
819.	Patras	½d.	878.	Trebizond	1½d.
820.	Stuttgart	1d.	879.	Mollendo	½d.
821.	Taganrog	1d.	880.	Kiukiang	1d.
822.	Salonica	2d.	881.	Antananarivo	1d.
823.	Galveston	1d.	882.	Stettin	2½d.
824.	Rome	1½d.	883.	Fiume	1½d.
825.	Paris	1½d.	884.	Batavia	1d.
826.	Bushire	½d.	885.	Samoa	½d.
827.	New Orleans	3d.	886.	Cherbourg	1d.
828.	Buda-Pesth	½d.	887.	Cagliari	1d.
829.	Hamburg	3d.	888.	Hankow	1½d.
830.	Port Said	1d.	889.	Vienna	1½d.
831.	Samoa	½d.	890.	Amoy	1d.
832.	Guayaquil	½d.	891.	Adrianople	½d.
833.	New Orleans	2d.	892.	Chicago	2½d.
834.	The Piræus	1d.	893.	Brest	1d.
835.	Baltimore	1½d.	894.	Smyrna	1d.
836.	Trieste	2d.	895.	Cadiz	1d.
837.	Galatz	1½d.	896.	Aleppo	1d.
838.	Wênchow	1d.	897.	Foochow	1d.
839.	Havre	2½d.	898.	Kiungchow	1d.
840.	Rome	1½d.	899.	The Hague	1½d.
841.	Taganrog	2d.	900.	Nice	1½d.
842.	Calais	1d.	901.	Nantes	1½d.
843.	Boston	1d.	902.	Port-au-Prince	1½d.
844.	Bordeaux	2½d.	903.	Bengazi	1d.
845.	Charleston	1½d.	904.	Tahiti	½d.
846.	Manila	5d.	905.	Chinkiang	1d.
847.	Madeira	½d.	906.	San Francisco	3d.
848.	Paris	2d.	907.	Brindisi	2d.
849.	Tripoli	½d.	908.	Beyrout	1d.
850.	Swatow	1d.	909.	Noumea	½d.

No. 910.

Reference to previous Report, Annual Series No. 730.

UNITED STATES.

SAN FRANCISCO.

Consul Donohoe to the Marquis of Salisbury.

My Lord, San Francisco, *April* 27, 1891.

I HAVE the honour to enclose herewith Reports on Agricultural matters from this Consulate, and from the Vice-Consulates of Portland, Port Townsend and Los Angeles, for the year 1890.

No report will be furnished this year by the Vice-Consuls at Astoria and San Diego.

I have, &c.
(Signed)   DENIS DONOHOE.

Report on Agriculture in the State of California.

The heavy rains at the commencement of the year placed everything in the farming way in a most backward state; serious floods occurred and much damage was done to the crops in the northern and central portions of the State.

Wheat. The long continued wet season prevented later sowing, the result has been one of the smallest crops ever had in this State, which is estimated not to have exceeded 900,000 tons.

The lower part of the San Joachin valley did not suffer so much as other parts of the State by the heavy rainfall, and as this portion of the State contains the best wheat lands, the farmer was tolerably well contented with the output.

Barley. The barley crop was a short one over a considerable portion of the State, and prices ruled high in consequence, and quality excellent. The grade known as "chevalier barley" was in some localities from 1 lb. to 2 lb. heavier this year than last.

Fruit. There never was in California a better year for fruit than 1890. The southern Pacific Railway carried to points in the eastern States, principally to Chicago, New York, and Boston, as follows:—

(1128)

	Lbs.
Canned fruit	77,738,250
Dried „	43,328,570
Raisins	27,370,330
Green fruit	86,527,900
Total	234,965,050

This quantity is nearly double that of 1889. Prices commenced at a reasonable figure, but after the opening of the season advanced nearly 50 per cent.

Wines. — In the report of the President of the Board of State Viticultural Commissioners, that very efficient officer says:—"The wine industry is just recovering from a period of over three years of depression caused by the largely increased production consequent on the extensive planting in the years prior to 1886." As a rule Americans in the eastern States are not a wine-drinking people, those who do not drink whiskey, drink beer, to which they are more accustomed than to wines; however, on the Pacific Coast, though the consumption of whiskey is large, wine is steadily making its way. The planting of grapes for wine-making has not increased of late, though large areas have been planted with vines which produce grapes suited for table use. I note a great improvement in the quality of red wines placed on the market here within the last two years. Wines that used to be sold for consumption formerly are now sent to the still, and a useful spirit is now produced, for which a fair demand is gradually springing up, and which is used for fortifying the wines that require it.

Brandy. — The production of brandy has steadily increased, and besides the home supply a considerable quantity is now shipped to the eastern States, England, and Germany. The success of the State Viticultural Commission in obtaining a gold medal for brandies for exhibit at Paris, in 1889, seems to have been a stimulus to the careful distiller. The internal revenue department gives the production for the fiscal year ending June 30, 1890, as 1,072,957 proof gallons in California. The same authority gives the number of registered distilleries of fruit brandy as 149, scattered over 28 counties of the State of California.

Raisins. — The planting of the raisin grape is making great progress in the State, and many thousands of acres of new vines have been planted in Fresno, Kern, Tulare counties, which are not yet producing. As I mentioned in a former report the Californian raisin crop will eventually drive the foreign raisins from the United States' market. The estimated crop of 1890 is given as 1,400,000 20-lb. boxes, whilst the import of foreign raisins is stated as 1,845,716 20-lb. boxes. This gives a total consumption for the year of 3,245,716 20-lb. boxes. In the year 1884 there were only 175,000 20-lb. boxes produced in California, and with the wonderful increase since then, it is easy to see that the foreign raisin will soon be unknown in the United States.

Dried wine grapes. — According to the President of the State Viticultural Commissioners an order was received from a London commission merchant offering 10*l*. per ton for all the dried grapes to be obtained in this State, laid down in French and North German ports. This offer was not, however, accepted, as from the short fruit crop in the eastern States far better prices could be realised in the home market. The demand was so great that it seriously reduced the wine yield of the year. Grapes for wine making, according to the same authority, will probably command a sufficiently high price in 1891 to deter any extensive contracts being made for dried grapes such as were made in 1890.

In Napa, Senorna, and Solano counties the phylloxera has made considerable havoc in the vineyards. Thousands of acres have been affected by this disease, and much apathy has been displayed in checking it. All affected vines should be promptly pulled up and burned on the spot, and resistant stocks of approved varieties should be substituted after leaving the spot bare for two years. *Phylloxera.*

The "Sweet Wine Bill," which has now become law, has been a great boon to the producers of sweet wines, as they can now use brandy for fortification free of internal revenue tax. *Sweet Wine Bill.*

PORTLAND.

Mr. Vice-Consul Laidlaw reports as follows:—

The Cascade mountains, extending north and south, divide the State of Oregon into two grand divisions known as eastern and western Oregon. The first division includes the counties of Wasco, Crook, Lake, Klamath, Morrow, Gilliam, Grant, Umatilla, Union, Wallowa, Baker, and Malheur; and the second division embraces the counties of Clatsop, Columbia, Washington, Clackamas, Marion Linn, Yamhill, Polk, Tillamook, Benton, Lane, Douglas, Coos, Curry, Josephine and Jackson. *Description of Oregon. Natural divisions.*

Western Oregon has an average width of 120 miles, and comprises the most thickly populated and wealthy portion of the State. *Western Oregon.*

Eastern Oregon has an average width of 230 miles, comprising a vast territory, a large portion of which is at present sparsely settled, and whose inhabitants are principally engaged in rearing horses, sheep and cattle; but of recent years the product of portions of this region in wheat is immense, as will be seen by reference to tables below. Along the coast extends a range of mountains from 3 to 4,000 feet high covered with timber. Streams flows from this range into the sea, and along them there is a great deal of land fit for cultivation and for grazing purposes. *Eastern Oregon. Coast range mountains.*

Between the coast range and the Cascade Mountains lie the Willamette, Umpqua and Rogue River valleys. The first two are separated by a short and low range known as the Calapooia Mountains. *Valleys.*

The Umpqua valley is named from the river which drains it, which stream flows through the coast range and empties into the Pacific Ocean. Rogue River drains the valley of the same name.

(1128)

It also pierces the coast range. The surface of the country from the Calapooia Mountains to the northern boundary of California is diversified by low hills and valleys, the whole fertile and adapted to agriculture, fruit growing, and grazing purposes.

Willamette valley.
The Willamette valley constitutes the wealthiest portion of Oregon. It is drained by the river of the same name, navigable for light draft steamers for a distance of 125 miles, which flows northward and empties into the Columbia River at a point a few miles below Portland, about 100 miles from the ocean. It has an average width of 60 miles, not including the mountain slopes, and comprises a beautiful sweep of valley containing about 7,800 square miles, all of which is highly fertile.

Rivers and streams.
From their sources in the Cascades flow westward the Clackamas, Molalla, Pudding, Santiam and Mackenzie Rivers, and empty into the Willamette. The coast fork is an important branch of this river. The Tualitan, Chehalem, Yamhill, La Creole, Lockiamute, Mary's, Long Tom and Calapooia Rivers all flow eastward from the coast range into the Willamette. These are all streams of importance, several of them navigable, and each drains a considerable country in the foot hills valuable for agriculture, fruit, stock, and timber.

Willamette valley lands.
The lands open to settlement in the Willamette valley are either United States Government, State, railroad and wagon-road grants, or school and university lands, and some 2,000,000 acres along the edges of the valley must be available, after deducting tracts, which are worthless as being too rocky or too steep. This does not include timber lands of which the extent is very great. Government land is held at 1 dol. 25 c. per acre, or within the limits of railroad grants at double this price. Railroad lands vary from 1 dol. 25 c. to 7 dol. per acre according to location.

Cost of clearing.
Cost of clearing is usually about 10 dol. per acre for felling and burning the growth and 85 c. per cord for chopping the sticks into cord-wood. Wheat grown in the new fields is clean. Not uncommonly farmers slash and burn the brush at the proper season, then sow wheat which they brush into the ashes by dragging a clump of bushes over it without either ploughing or harrowing. The result is often a crop of over 20 bushels per acre.

Umpqua valley.
The Umpqua valley lies south of the Willamette, and has an area of about 4,900 square miles.

Rogue River valley.
The Rogue River valley further south is about 35 miles long by 20 miles wide.

Fruit culture.
In both the Umpqua and Rogue River valleys much attention has been given of late years to the growth of fruit for which the soil and climate seems pre-eminently suited. There is much good land in all these valleys available for settlement, though not near the towns, and much of it is remote.

Increase of wheat culture in eastern Oregon.
In eastern Oregon there is much less rain, and until recent years nearly the whole country was given up to stockmen; but the wheat production is now immense and increasing annually. There is plenty of good land available for settlement under the

United States laws; but as in western Oregon, as a rule, such land will not be found near cities, or close to railroads.

As a whole, the year 1890 was a very profitable one for farmers in both eastern and western Oregon. The wheat harvest was much larger than last year. Oats were rather a light crop, but of potatoes and onions there was a good yield. The fruit crops were large and fine, but probably the hop crop was the most profitable of all. *Crops generally good.*

The wheat harvest in the Willamette valley was above an average, and that of eastern Oregon was immense. The market was depressed till opening of the cereal year, when there was a speculative demand, which afterwards declined. I think on the whole the farmers did better, but the average prices were hardly up to last year. *Wheat.*

The receipts of wheat and flour were as under during the cereal years ending July 31 each year:— *Receipts at Portland.*

Cereal Year.	Willamette Valley.		Eastern Oregon.	
	Wheat.	Flour.	Wheat.	Flour.
	Quarters.	Sacks.	Quarters.	Sacks.
1889-90..	283,536	195,455	320,300	91,378
1888-89..	199,095	251,614	571,403	81,425
August-December, 1890	124,673	101,177	378,406	41,852
,, ,, 1889	158,551	96,330	256,469	41,870

The oat harvest was fine in quality, but rather lighter in yield in the valley than last year. This cereal is not much cultivated in eastern Oregon, but the harvest there was greater. Prices were very high, and there has been a heavy demand all the year. The following is a comparison of receipts in centals:— *Oats.*

Cereal Years.	Quantity.	Calendar Years.	Quantity.	Five Months ending December 31.	Quantity.
	Centals.		Centals.		Centals.
1889-90 ..	479,654	1890 ..	486,710	1890.. ..	223,032
1888-89 ..	530,596	1889 ..	502,363	1889.. ..	215,976

The receipts of barley during the year ended December 31 were 154,597 centals, mostly from eastern Oregon. Last year receipts were only 18,865 centals. Prices were high. *Barley.*

Flax seed was a larger crop in the valley than last year, but appears to have varied little in eastern Oregon. Receipts during the calendar year were 9,009,433 lbs. In 1889, 10,210,763 lbs. were received. *Flax seed.*

In the first part of the year farmers received very high prices *Potatoes, &c.*

Fruit.

for potatoes, as much as 2½ c. per lb. being paid. The crop was good, and naturally prices fell materially after the new crop came in. Onions paid the growers handsome profits, and there was a good demand for farm produce generally.

Receipts of green fruit were very large, and the year was an exceedingly good one for owners of orchards. Yield generally was good, and prices high under an active demand for the eastern States. Apples were badly affected with the cadlin moth, but sound fruit was in demand, and at the close of the year is very high.

Tinned fruits.

Of tinned fruits the pack was small, the three factories at Salem, Oregon city, and east Portland working on peas, cherries, blackberries, strawberries, and pears. Prices were high.

Hops very profitable.

An increased acreage was planted, but the yield of hops was not quite up to an average. Dry weather in some sections during July and August lowering the average, and the hop louse on low lands damaging badly some crops. Average yield about 1,100 lbs. per acre, many reaching 2,000 lbs., and one large grower near Salem harvesting 2,500 lbs. to 3,000 lbs. per acre. On the other hand, some yards did not yield over 700 lbs. to 800 lbs. per acre. Crop was about 20,000 bales of 185 lbs. each. Quality exceedingly fine, except in yards where the hop louse had a hold. Growers are taking more care in curing and baling. The lowest sales were in July, after which there was a rapid advance, and in November as high as 42 c. or 1s. 8d. per lb. was paid. As it costs only about 4d. per lb. to grow and pick them, the profit is a very handsome one. It is, however, a very uncertain crop, as in 1889 only those who had contracted ahead realised much more than cost of picking.

Sheep and cattle — heavy mortality on ranges.

On the ranges of eastern Oregon, owing to cold weather, snow storms, and scarcity of food, the losses of sheep and cattle were very great at the beginning of the year. A reliable party tells me that 75 per cent. of the range cattle died, but I am inclined to think this ratio is much too large. Perhaps 40 per cent. of the sheep were lost. This branch of agriculture was, therefore, unprofitable in that large section.

Wool.

Of wool, in Wasco, Sherman, Gilliam, Morrow, Grant, and Crook counties, the clip was about 6,316,000 lbs., from about 902,000 sheep, and the loss was very nearly 220,000 sheep, which would be about 20 per cent. The ranges were, however, overstocked, and the flocks are in a much more healthy condition. Prices of sheep have advanced, and two year old wethers sell at 2 dol. 75 c. to 3 dol. per head after clipping. Receipts of wool here were 7,672,828 lbs. Last year 16,007,884 lbs. were received. Prices were higher in 1890.

Returns of animals in Oregon.

The following estimates of numbers of animals on farms and ranches in Oregon at the end of the year are taken from the census and assessors' returns.

	Number.	Average Price.	Value.
		Dollars.	Dollars.
Horses	181,236	47·44	8,598,230
Mules	3,647	62·69	228,618
Sheep	2,431,759	2·12	5,154,114
Cattle	368,081	12·38	4,654,031
Swine	101,311	2·15	218,636

Market prices of beef, cattle, and animals for slaughtering purposes were generally higher than in 1889.

Port Townsend.

Mr. Vice-Consul Alexander reports as follows:—

Introduction. I have the honour to present my report on agriculture in the State of Washington. This being my first special report on this subject, it will not be inappropriate to preface my remarks with a brief outline of the character and formation of the country.

Washington is divided unequally into two sections by the Cascade range of mountains, running north and south, known as eastern and western Washington, wholly different in climate and character. The eastern section may again be divided into a northern and southern part.

Description of country. The northern part. Of the northern part of this eastern section, comprising the counties of Stevens and Okanogan, I shall only say that it is mountainous and rich in minerals, but possessing fertile valleys suitable for grazing purposes, where stockmen still guard their numerous herds of cattle, which supply the markets of the eastern and western States. No railways have as yet penetrated these regions, so little cultivation of the soil is attempted, more than to supply the houses of the farmers.

The southern part. The remaining or southern portion of this eastern section is rolling prairie land, interspersed with timber towards the mountain ranges, through which the great Columbia River flows; here are the great wheat fields of the State, possibly the most productive in the world; their total yield for the year is estimated at 20,000,000 bushels. A failure in the crop has never been known, and scientific men who have analysed and studied the soil say it is not likely to occur, since it is formed by disintegrated rock, which is constantly renewing it from the bottom as it is exhausted from the top. Portions of this section, however, need irrigation to produce the best results, particularly the counties of Yakima, Franklin, Klickitat, and Douglas; but with irrigation magnificent crops of wheat, oats, Indian corn, rye, barley, tobacco, all the vegetables including sweet potatoes, peanuts, melons, and fruit in almost every variety, except the citrus fruits, can be grown successfully on the arable lands. Where no irrigation is required, in addition to wheat, which is the staple, the principal productions are oats, barley, rye, flax, buckwheat, hay, vegetables of all kinds, and nearly every variety of fruit both large and small, are successfully grown, and yield abundantly according to situation and exposure. The straw of wheat, oats, barley, and rye is very hard, and the heads very heavy, it being impossible to bind a sheaf with the straw. This peculiarity of the straw seems to be caused by the climate. There is very little rain during the growing season, and farmers say that they have grown good crops without a shower from the time the wheat appeared above the ground in the spring, until it was harvested. Generally, however, there are occasional light showers during the summer, but never heavy enough to beat down the grain, the stiffness of the straw would prevent lodging, even if the rains were heavier, it also lengthens the time of harvest, as the grain usually takes no harm from standing in the fields for several weeks after it has ripened, and even after being cut it will lie for some time without any appreciable loss. Last season harvesting begun about the middle of July and continued through September, and in some places as late as October. Some of the latest pieces cut had ripened early, but had taken little, if any, harm from its long wait for the harvesting machines. More or less grain is always lost in harvesting in gathering the crop, and this, if the ground is left unploughed, will produce about half a crop the following year. These "volunteer crops," as they are called, are quite common, nearly every farmer having more or less of them every year. One wheat field in Whitman county has never been sown but once, and has produced a volunteer crop every year for the last 13 years; this year's yield was 30 bushels to the acre. Very little rye is now sown, as it "volunteers" so readily that it becomes a weed, and is hard to get rid of.

A few years ago the cattle ranges in the Walla-Walla county in this eastern section had to give way to the wheat lands, and these in turn are fast giving way to orchards and gardens. Wheat farms worth 20*l.* per acre are now worth 100*l.* per acre in 10 acre tracts for orchards and gardens. On the warm gravelly bottoms, with plenty of irrigation, several crops are raised each season, and all are marketed at a good profit. The business has assumed such proportions that organisation has been found necessary to sell the crops, and the Walla-Walla Fruit-growers' Association has recently been formed to further this end; one of the needs of this part is practical gardeners and orchardists to develop these industries.

The Moxee experimental farm is situated in this section of the country also; it belongs to a company who have carried the science of irrigation to a high degree. The main ditch is 18 feet on the bottom, and calculated to carry a depth of 3 feet of water; it winds round the foothills of the Moxee valley. Alfalfa, producing three crops a year, hops, tobacco, grapes, apples, peaches, pears and cereals of all kinds are grown in great quantities and of fine quality on this farm.

The western section of Washington is mostly heavily

timbered, and the land has to be cleared before it can be utilised for agricultural purposes. This necessarily makes the arable lands very limited in extent, and proportionately very valuable when got into a thorough state of cultivation. The waters of Puget Sound extending inland over 100 miles, navigable to their head, drain this section of the country; to the northward is the San Juan Archipelago, studded with numerous islands of various areas, containing some of the oldest farms in the country; the land is now being cleared for orchards, for which it appears to be peculiarly adapted. *The western part.*

The soil of the valleys and river bottoms is very rich and most productive; that of the uplands, although not quite so rich as that of the valleys, will produce enormous crops of grain, hay, fruit, roots, potatoes, and vegetables, in some instances growing a better quality. This applies more particularly to the root crops, which are inclined to be too watery when grown on the bottom lands, there evidently being too much moisture in the soil. The farms are usually small, and general or mixed farming is the rule. Wheat is not grown in this section to any great extent as a staple crop, it not being profitable, better returns being made from other crops. On the reclaimed tide-lands on the eastern shore of Puget Sound there are astonishing yields of oats. Very large crops of hay, roots, vegetables, and fruits are grown in this section. The climate, which is very equable, seems to be adapted to fruit-growing and market gardening. This is an excellent country for the small farmer and market gardener, and to those who understand it no business offers greater advantages and more certain profits in a small way. The crop never fails, and the market is close by; the only drawback is the want of the right person to cultivate the land. Small farms containing a few acres under thorough cultivation bring in better returns than large ones, if advantageously situated to markets. The farmer who can do without hired men, except during the busy times, possesses a great advantage over his neighbour who has to hire. Labour as a rule is very expensive, and frequently very unsatisfactory.

Generally in the farming districts responsible buyers come round early in the season, and offer to purchase the crops when harvested, or any other farm produce, so the farmers need not seek the market.

The average yield of the State, as made up by the agricultural department in Washington, taken from the report for 1890, in bushels per acre is as follows:—wheat, 23; oats, 33·5; barley, 25; Indian corn, 90; potatoes, 91; hops (lbs. to the acre), 1,480. *Average yield of crop through State.*

Prices have been excellent for the farmer all through the year, and there is every prospect that the crops will be large and prices sustained, the winter having been very mild.

In the eastern section the wheat crop has averaged from 40 bushels to 60 bushels per acre, weighing from 5 lbs. to 9 lbs. more than the standard bushel of 90 lbs. in Douglas county, *Wheat.*

where the Little Club wheat is the favourite, requiring only half a bushel to the acre for seed, the yield was 31 bushels. In the western section wheat will average from 40 bushels to 80 bushels to the acre, price fluctuating from 5*l.* to 6*l.* per ton.

Oats. — In the eastern section oats average from 40 bushels to 60 bushels, and exceed the weight of the standard bushel per acre. In the western section oats are grown in immense quantities on the reclaimed lands on the shores of Puget Sound, where long dykes have been constructed to keep out the tide-water, on these tide lands the yield is from 80 bushels to 120 bushels to the acre; on other land from 40 bushels to 80 bushels. Price ranging from 5*l.* to 6*l.* per ton, now 9*l.*, and very scarce.

Barley. — In eastern Washington barley is a very profitable crop, averaging from 40 bushels to 60 bushels to the acre, weighs heavy, and commands a high price in the eastern markets for brewing purposes.

Hops. — The yield of hops for 1890 amounted to over 38,000 bushels, or 6,820,000 lbs., the production for the year 1889 was about 7,980,000 lbs.; the year 1890 shows a decreased production, although the area was increased to 5,000 acres; this shortage was due to the hop louse, which made its appearance for the first time in this State during the summer when the harvest was well underway. Average yield this year will not exceed 1,500 lbs. to the acre. The selling price opened at 6½*d.* per lb. and reached 1*s.* 8*d.* per lb., averaging about 1*s.* 3*d.* per lb., all above 4½*d.* per lb. being profit. The total value of the crop was over 500,000*l.*

Hay. — In eastern Washington grasses of various kinds grow luxuriantly. Timothy being the staple for hay, many fields attaining a height of 6 feet, hay dealers bought up all the crop at good prices that was available; clover, blue grass, and alfalfa grow well. Puget Sound timothy will cut from 1½ tons to 3½ tons to the acre, price ranging from 3*l.* per ton to 5*l.* per ton, and has been up to 8*l.* per ton. This grass has to be reseeded every third year, as it runs out.

Vegetables. — Vegetables of almost every kind can be produced in the greatest profusion in almost every part of the State with very little attention; they are unexceptionable in size, quality, and flavour. Potatoes will yield from 300 bushels to 500 bushels per acre, price ranging from 2*l.* 10*s.* per ton to 5*l.* 10*s.* per ton. Mangolds from 10 tons to 50 tons per acre, price from 2*l.* 10*s.* per ton to 3*l.* per ton. Carrots, beets, turnips, from 10 tons to 25 tons and 30 tons per acre, price 3*l.* per ton to 4*l.* per ton. Other vegetables fetch remunerative prices, especially when brought into market early in the season.

Fruits. — In eastern Washington, as a fruit region Yakima county, Franklin, and Klickitat, with the Walla-Walla county and the Wenatchee valley equal California, except in citrus fruits, producing apples, peaches, pears, plums, prunes, melons, figs, apricots, and grapes. Apples have been exhibited weighing 29 ozs., and peaches measuring 12 inches in circumference, with bunches of grapes weighing from 4 lbs. to 7 lbs. each. Peaches are a very profitable crop. Many varieties of grapes do well, small quantities of wine and peach brandy are made, but simply for home consumption by the farmer. In western Washington fruit grows both in the valleys and uplands. Apples, pears, prunes, plums, and cherries are easily grown; peaches and apricots require care; strawberries, raspberries, currants will grow anywhere, almost all over the State, and yield abundantly. For early fruits and choice varieties good prices were obtained, which fall as the season advanced.

Cattle and stock generally have done well; great attention is now being paid to the general improvement of all animals, as quality is asserting itself in the market values. The demand is good and fair prices have been obtained. No cases of serious infectious or contagious diseases so far have appeared in the State. *Cattle.*

The following statements in regard to the productiveness of land in western Washington have been made:— *Practical results.*

In 1890 the following products were sold off a farm of 100 acres in cultivation: 200 tons of hay at 4*l*. per ton (800*l*.); 7 tons of hops at 160*l*. per ton (1,120*l*.); fruits and vegetables, 178*l*.; pasture rental, 60*l*.; milk (22 head cows), 300*l*.; sundries, 83*l*.; total amount sold, 2,701*l*. From a farm of 30 acres there were grown 11¾ tons of hops, worth 1,656*l*., and 2½ tons of hay, worth 84*l*.; total, 1,740*l*. From a farm of 70 acres there were grown 10 acres of onions (250 tons), worth 2,400*l*.; 5 acres of carrots, 500*l*.; 20 tons of hops, 1,680*l*.; 60 tons of hay, 240*l*.; 92*l*. of oats; and market garden, 320*l*.; total, 5,232*l*. A farmer sold 15*l*. worth of strawberries from one-eighth of an acre, 14 cherry trees yielded 300 lbs. each, worth 5*d*. per lb. In Jeland county one farmer had 1,100 bushels of wheat on 15 acres; another had 285 bushels of wheat on 4 acres; and another had 97 bushels of oats per acre.

In eastern Washington a farmer had 160 acres that yielded 4,000 bushels; 115 acres yielded 4,125 bushels; and 45 acres of barley that yielded 2,800 bushels. From a farm in Whitman county, where the farmer hired everything done, the land produced 47,270 bushels of wheat, averaging 33⅓ bushels an acre, and fetched 5,011*l*. The expense of ploughing, seeding, harvesting, leading, &c., amounted to 3,401*l*., leaving a net profit of 1,610*l*.*

WILMINGTON AND LOS ANGELES.

Mr. Vice-Consul Mortimer reports as follows:—

In my trade report on this district for 1890,† I have written at some length on agricultural matters. In this report, confining myself to matters likely to be useful or interesting to agriculturists in England, I must necessarily write briefly, owing to the fact the products (excepting grain) and modes of

---

* The values given in this report are reduced to sterling at the average rate of 5 dol. to the 1*l*. sterling; and the bushel of oats weighs 32 lbs.—all other, 60 lbs.

† See No. 906 Annual Series.—ED.

Oranges.
Vines.

cultivation are essentially different. I beg, therefore, to refer to that report for information about the citrus and viticultural industries.

Wheat.

The average in wheat has diminished in the past five years, owing to the fact that farmers find it more profitable to plant fruit trees or vines. The present season is a favourable one, and it is probable that good crops will be harvested. The yield will not probably exceed 2,000,000 bushels, a decrease of 100 per cent. on the crop of 1884. Land suitable for grain can be purchased at from 3*l*. per acre to 10*l*. per acre. Grain farming is not profitable here on land costing more than 6*l*. per acre, that is to say, the net profits will not pay interest on more than that amount. This is to some extent due to failures of the crop in dry years. As, however, dry years are becoming infrequent, owing to increased cultivation of the soil, the industry may in the future prove more profitable. Steam ploughs capable of turning 20 furrows, are employed on the large ranches. Each plough is handled by three men, requires about one ton of coal per day, and ploughs about 45 acres a day.

Beet sugar.

The sugar beet factory referred to in my last report is now being constructed on the Chino ranch, and 5,000 acres are being planted in sugar beet. A sugar beet expert from Germany makes the following report on the prospects of the industry here:—

"As a rule I find the land in this and adjoining counties first class in every particular, being bounteously supplied with the essential elements for the growth of a perfect sugar beet.

"Having heard of experiments being made at the Chino ranch I went out there last week, and from personal observation and private test I find that 22 per cent. is about an average for the product I found there. This I consider good, and is in fact a much better showing than can be made by some of the famous beet-producing countries of the world.

"I find that you have good land, and plenty to spare here, and I think it safe to say that 200,000 acres can be found in this vicinity perfectly adapted to the growth of the sugar-beet. This land, with thorough cultivation, can be made to yield, on a fair average, 25 tons per acre annually, for which the farmer will receive from the factory about 5 dol. per ton, making an average income per acre of 125 dol., which I think cannot be surpassed by any of the cereals of southern California.

"I consider the climate well adapted to the industry, the greatest advantage being the long seasons which you have here, by means of which the beets can remain in the soil much longer than in most countries, the farmer having very nearly 12 months in the year in which to ply his vocation.

"Another important desideratum to be considered in the sugar-beet industry is the fact that not only the sugar obtained is of value as an article of food, but the pulp is of material importance to the farmer for feeding purposes. About one-third of the pulp is returned to the farmer. Its value as food for stock is unquestioned, and is valued by the European farmer at 2 dol. per ton."

The owner of Chino ranch estimates the gross yield per acre at from 12*l*. to 15*l*. The estimate of 125 dol. (25*l*.) in the foregoing report is probably excessive.

Many years ago cattle and sheep were raised here in such large numbers that Los Angeles county was known throughout the State as "cow county;" now, owing to the increased value of the land, consequent on the large profits made in fruit, comparatively few cattle are raised here.

Cattle and sheep.

LONDON:
Printed for Her Majesty's Stationery Office,
By HARRISON AND SONS,
Printers in Ordinary to Her Majesty.
(1250 6 | 91—H & S 1128

FOREIGN OFFICE.
1891.
ANNUAL SERIES.

Nº. 911.

DIPLOMATIC AND CONSULAR REPORTS ON TRADE AND FINANCE.

UNITED STATES.

REPORT FOR THE YEAR 1890
ON THE
TRADE OF THE DISTRICT OF THE CONSULATE-GENERAL OF NEW YORK.

REFERENCE TO PREVIOUS REPORT, Annual Series No. 747.

Presented to both Houses of Parliament by Command of Her Majesty,
JUNE, 1891.

LONDON:
PRINTED FOR HER MAJESTY'S STATIONERY OFFICE,
BY HARRISON AND SONS, ST. MARTIN'S LANE,
PRINTERS IN ORDINARY TO HER MAJESTY.

And to be purchased, either directly or through any Bookseller, from
EYRE & SPOTTISWOODE, EAST HARDING STREET, FLEET STREET, E.C., and
32, ABINGDON STREET, WESTMINSTER, S.W.; or
JOHN MENZIES & Co., 12, HANOVER STREET, EDINBURGH, and
88 and 90, WEST NILE STREET, GLASGOW; or
HODGES, FIGGIS, & Co., 104, GRAFTON STREET, DUBLIN.

1891.

[C. 6205—142.]   *Price Three Halfpence.*

New Series of Reports.

Reports of the Annual Series have been issued from Her Majesty's Diplomatic and Consular Officers' at the following places, and may be obtained from the sources indicated on the title-page:—

No.		Price.	No.		Price.
787.	Tangier	1½d.	849.	Tripoli	½d.
788.	Rome	2d.	850.	Swatow	1d.
789.	Stuttgart	1½d.	851.	Saigon	½d.
790.	Panama	1½d.	852.	Vienna	1½d.
791.	Berne	1½d.	853.	Algiers	2d.
792.	Asuncion	½d.	854.	Algiers	1d.
793.	Bahia	7½d.	855.	Mozambique	8d.
794.	Monte Video	1½d.	856.	Antwerp	1½d.
795.	Munich	2d.	857.	Mogador	2d.
796.	Bucharest	1d.	858.	Ichang	½d.
797.	Tokio	1d.	859.	Calais	8½d.
798.	Tabreez	1d.	860.	Riga	2d.
799.	Antwerp	1d.	861.	San José	1d.
800.	Malaga	1d.	862.	Genoa	1½d.
801.	Odessa	1d.	863.	Warsaw	1d.
802.	Malaga	2d.	864.	Wuhu	1d.
803.	Amsterdam	1d.	865.	Marseilles	1d.
804.	Bogotá	1½d.	866.	Syra	1d.
805.	Guayaquil	½d.	867.	Jeddah	½d.
806.	Lima	1d.	868.	Savannah	½d.
807.	Rio de Janeiro	3d.	869.	Suakin	½d.
808.	Dantzig	1½d.	870.	Berlin	1d.
809.	Florence	1½d.	871.	Batoum	1½d.
810.	Lisbon	1d.	872.	Rosario	1d.
811.	Quito	½d.	873.	Buenos Ayres	½d.
812.	Para	½d.	874.	Mogador	1d.
813.	Palermo	2½d.	875.	Tainan	6½d.
814.	Copenhagen	1d.	876.	Pakhoi	1d.
815.	Serajevo	½d.	877.	Odessa	2½d.
816.	Porto Rico	1d.	878.	Trebizond	1½d.
817.	Madrid	½d.	879.	Mollendo	½d.
818.	Brussels	½d.	880.	Kiukiang	1d.
819.	Patras	½d.	881.	Antananarivo	1d.
820.	Stuttgart	1d.	882.	Stettin	2½d.
821.	Taganrog	1d.	883.	Fiume	1½d.
822.	Salonica	2d.	884.	Batavia	1d.
823.	Galveston	1d.	885.	Samoa	½d.
824.	Rome	1½d.	886.	Cherbourg	1d.
825.	Paris	1½d.	887.	Cagliari	1d.
826.	Bushire	½d.	888.	Hankow	1½d.
827.	New Orleans	3d.	889.	Vienna	1½d.
828.	Buda-Pesth	½d.	890.	Amoy	1d.
829.	Hamburg	3d.	891.	Adrianople	½d.
830.	Port Said	1d.	892.	Chicago	2½d.
831.	Samoa	½d.	893.	Brest	1d.
832.	Guayaquil	½d.	894.	Smyrna	1d.
833.	New Orleans	2d.	895.	Cadiz	1d.
834.	The Piræus	1d.	896.	Aleppo	1d.
835.	Baltimore	1½d.	897.	Foochow	1d.
836.	Trieste	2d.	898.	Kiungchow	1d.
837.	Galatz	1½d.	899.	The Hague	1½d.
838.	Wênchow	1d.	900.	Nice	1½d.
839.	Havre	2½d.	901.	Nantes	1½d.
840.	Rome	1½d.	902.	Port-au-Prince	1½d.
841.	Taganrog	2d.	903.	Bengazi	1d.
842.	Calais	1d.	904.	Tahiti	½d.
843.	Boston	1d.	905.	Chinkiang	1d.
844.	Bordeaux	2½d.	906.	San Francisco	3d.
845.	Charleston	1½d.	907.	Brindisi	2d.
846.	Manila	5d.	908.	Beyrout	1d.
847.	Madeira	½d.	909.	Noumea	½d.
848.	Paris	2d.	910.	San Francisco	1d.

No. 911.

Reference to previous Report, Annual Series No. 747.

UNITED STATES.

NEW YORK.

Consul-General Booker to the Marquis of Salisbury.

My Lord,   *New York, May* 8, 1891.

I HAVE the honour to transmit herewith my Annual Report upon the Trade of New York, with some information in regard to other parts of my Consular District.

I have, &c.
(Signed)   WM. LANE BOOKER.

Annual Trade Report for the Year 1890.

General review of trade.

The trade of this port in 1890 has been satisfactory, and the demand for goods, except perhaps in a few specialties, has not been beyond the requirements of the country, so without anything unforeseen occurring we may look for a continuance of prosperity.

The grain crops were much below the average, but the prices realised for the leading cereals were such as to fully offset the reduced quantity harvested, which prevented an otherwise much diminished money circulation in the western grain-growing States.

The prominent features of the year were the legislative discussions on silver, ending by the passage of the Act directing the Government to purchase 45,000 ounces monthly, under which the first purchase was made in August, and the passage of the new Tariff Bill; the former affected the market for securities materially, and the latter necessarily had an important bearing on trade transactions.

The clearing-house returns show an increased volume of trade: the total clearings in 1890 at the New York clearing-house were 7,716,473,168*l.*, and, eliminating from these figures 2,048,497,060*l.* as representing stock transactions, the clearings in strictly trade transactions amounted to 5,667,976,110*l*., 7 per cent. advance on those of 1889. The total clearings at all the clearing-houses of the country, outside of New York, were 4,667,812,460*l*.

The gross earnings of the railroads of the whole country were considerably in excess of those of 1889, estimated at over 8 per cent., due to a considerable portion of the very large crop of 1889 having been left over, and to the general activity in trade, but the net receipts were not of so encouraging a character under lower freights and increased operating expenses. There was more activity in railroad building, and in the year about 6,200 miles were constructed, chiefly confined to the southern and western portions of the country. In the latter part of the year there was some difficulty in finding a market for the bonds of the new roads, otherwise the mileage would have been greater.

The value of merchandise imports (excluding specie) was 9,379,678*l*., or about 9 per cent. more than in 1889, but this may in a great measure be accounted for by the increased receipts of many articles of merchandise in anticipation of the higher duties under the new (McKinley) tariff, which went into operation on October 6.

In exports there was a falling-off of 1,309,240*l*., or about 2 per cent.

The value of all dry goods marketed in 1890—that is, entered for consumption and withdrawn from bonded warehouse—was 29,633,456*l*.; 1,629,900*l*. more than in 1889. These figures are fairly accurate, as all dry goods are dutiable; but it is impossible by the same or any mode of calculation to even estimate, with any degree of accuracy, the value of all merchandise marketed, as so large a portion—35·62 per cent. in 1890 and 33·40 per cent. in 1889—enters on the free list. The value of all goods entered for consumption and on the free list, and withdrawn from bonded warehouses was 109,327,316*l*., against 100,009,510*l*. in 1889. The imports on the free list in 1890 were 35·60 per cent. of the whole, and in 1889 33·20 per cent., while the average of the past 10 years was 31·40 per cent.

The customs receipts at this port in 1890 were 33,627,085*l*., against 33,420,610*l*. in 1889.

The demand for money varied a good deal; in the early part of January call loans ranged as high as 25 per cent. to 40 per cent., but the demand slackened by the middle of the month, and 6 per cent. was about the average rate. Good commercial paper ranged from 5½ per cent. to 6½ per cent. In February and March call loans were made at from 2½ per cent. to 6½ per cent., and commercial paper 5 per cent. to 5½ per cent. In April, May, and June call loans ranged from 2½ per cent. to 12 per cent., the latter rate only for a day or two, and commercial paper 5½ per cent. to 6 per cent. In July call loans were made at 2 per cent. to 9 per cent., and commercial paper at 5½ per cent. to 6 per cent. In August the bank reserves had disappeared, and there was a great demand for call loans, which were made at all rates varying from 2 per cent. to 25 per cent., and commercial bills 6 per cent.

to 6½ per cent. Through September there was a demand for call loans at from 3 per cent. to 15 per cent., and commercial bills ranged from 6 per cent. to 7 per cent. In October call loans were made at from 3 per cent. to 8 per cent., and commercial paper at 6 per cent. to 6½ per cent. till towards the close, when the demand was great at much higher rates. In the early part of November there was a great stringency in the money market, in consequence of numerous failures and great distrust, which was relieved by the New York clearing-house authorising the issue of loan certificates under approved guarantees, which was taken advantage of by banks to the extent in the middle of December of 3,132,200*l.*; this was the largest amount issued, and by the end of the year it was reduced to 2,677,000*l.* During November and December call loans commanded from 3 per cent. to 40 per cent., and commercial paper 7 per cent. to 9 per cent.

The condition of the associated banks of the city at different periods of the year is shown in the following table:— *Bank returns.*

Associated Banks of New York City.

Average Amount of

1890.	Loans.	Specie.	Legal Tenders.	Deposits.	Circulation	Surplus over Reserve required against Deposits.
	£	£	£	£	£	£
January 4.	82,335,996	15,950,086	5,508,708	84,388,394	770,130	361,736
March 29.	83,342,966	17,098,824	5,013,195	84,878,798	754,434	892,320
June 28.	81,796,750	15,534,666	6,718,587	83,538,727	770,028	1,368,530
September 27.	81,169,995	19,239,843	4,611,887	83,808,793	696,672	2,899,532
December 27.	79,276,290	16,029,334	5,237,591	78,702,156	739,540	1,591,386

The annual report of the superintendent of the State Banking Department for the fiscal year ending September 30, 1890, has been presented to the Legislature, and from it I extract the following items of interest:—15 new State banks were authorised to do business during the year, with a capital of 223,510*l.*; five of these with a capital of 123,600*l.* are located in this city. One of the country banks was converted from the national system. In the last 10 years the State banks have increased from 68 to 166, and their capital from 20,569,250*l.* to 52,338,000*l.* Three new trust companies have been organised during the year with a capital of 391,400*l.*; two of these are located in this city. There are altogether under the supervision of the State Banking Department 32 trust companies, with a capital of 4,879,500*l.*; of these 22 are in New York, and six in Brooklyn; the four companies outside of the two cities of New York and Brooklyn have a capital of only 171,400*l.* The superintendent, in his report, suggests to the Legislature that the State banking law should be amended so as to compel State banks to keep a money reserve always on hand and available. The *Banking report.*

superintendent does not consider it necessary that the State banks should keep as large a money reserve as the national banks are required to do, and is of opinion that for banks doing business in cities of over 500,000 inhabitants 20 per cent. of the deposits would not be too large a reserve, and for small cities from 10 to 15 per cent. The superintendent also suggests that legislation is desirable to distinguish with greater particularity the difference between private bankers, who have voluntarily placed themselves under the supervision of the banking department, and are subject to its requirements, and those who have not, and are not under any supervision whatever. In this connection he urges that a more complete method for the organisation of individual or private bankers be provided, and the minimum amount of the capital to be employed by them fixed.

Sterling exchange.

The savings banks of this city generally paid 3½ per cent. interest, a very few ¼ to ½ per cent. more. The following gives the rates of bankers' sterling exchange during the year 1890:—

Month.		At Sixty Days.	At Sight.
January	Highest ..	4·84½	4·88
	Lowest ..	4·80½	4·84½
February..	Highest ..	4·84½	4·88
	Lowest ..	4·81½	4·85½
March	Highest ..	4·85	4·88
	Lowest ..	4·81½	4·85½
April	Highest ..	4·86½	4·88
	Lowest ..	4·85	4·87½
May	Highest ..	4·85½	4·87½
	Lowest ..	4·84	4·86
June	Highest ..	4·86	4·88½
	Lowest ..	4·84½	4·86½
July	Highest ..	4·85½	4·89½
	Lowest ..	4·84½	4·88
August	Highest ..	4·85½	4·90
	Lowest ..	4·82½	4·86
September	Highest ..	4·83	4·86½
	Lowest ..	4·81	4·85
October	Highest ..	4·83	4·86½
	Lowest ..	4·81	4·85
November	Highest ..	4·82½	4·88½
	Lowest ..	4·80	4·85½
December	Highest ..	4·82	4·88
	Lowest ..	4·79½	4·84

Failures.

In the following table, taken from Dun's Commercial Agency, will be found the number of failures in the past two years in New York and Brooklyn cities, and the States of my district. It will be seen that although the number of failures in this city and Brooklyn is somewhat less than in 1889, the liabilities are much heavier. This is due mainly to the failures of large concerns during the financial disturbance in the last quarter of the year. The liabilities of those who failed in the first nine months were below the average, and this in the face of much higher rates for money than in the previous year:—

	Number of Failures.		Amount of Liabilities.	
	1890.	1889.	1890.	1889.
			£	£
New York and Brooklyn cities	576	585	9,077,410	3,574,426
New York, outside of New York city and Brooklyn	748	589	1,745,942	1,955,977
Connecticut	176	137	298,210	334,680
New Jersey	154	128	572,653	302,788
Rhode Island	107	130	831,550	2,070,022
Delaware	18	15	44,047	32,177

The dry goods trade during the year 1890 was marked by great activity, both domestic and foreign. The latter was of especially large volume during the last six months of the year. The tariff agitation in Congress influenced importers to order very liberally in anticipation of their wants, and European manufacturers also shipped largely in order to get their goods into the ports of the United States before the higher duty rates would take effect. The result was very heavy importations at a period between seasons, and a very large accumulation of stocks in first and second hands. *Dry goods.*

In anticipation of higher prices trade speculators purchased freely previous to October 1, but soon after that date the demand fell off sensibly, the market everywhere becoming languid. Consumers refused to pay the prices demanded, and the trade during the last months of 1890 failed to respond to the bright hopes and high prices anticipated, although at the close there were signs of a more active market.

Influenced by the new and higher duties afforded for the benefit of American manufacturing interests, new life has been imparted to the cotton, worsted, woollen, and knit-underwear industry. Everywhere, especially in the Southern States, new textile mills have been going up with surprising activity, and all the old corporations have been operated on full time. There have been very few strikes among mill operatives during the year, with one or two exceptions, and those were not caused by reduced rates of wages, or hours of labour, but merely through discipline of the workers. As a rule, all the cotton mills have had a year of unusual activity. The production has been of larger volume than in any previous year, and the goods have found a ready sale generally, but at comparatively low prices, considering the high prices which prevailed during the first six months of the year for cotton. Market prices, except in a few cases, did not vary with the price of cotton. Opening generally at low rates, cotton goods have been steady, the home and export demand being sufficient to absorb the supply of all standard and staple makers of brown, bleached, and coloured goods, if we except printing cloths and calicoes. The request for both the latter has been somewhat *Cotton.*

limited, and the mills at Fall River engaged in the production of print cloths will find it difficult to declare any dividends this year unless they draw from their sinking funds. The price of printing cloths was never so low, viz., 2 dol. 94 c. (12s. 2d.) net for 64 picks square, 7 yards to the lb., and some makes of 56 by 60 picks have been closed out as low as 3½ c. net, the lowest price ever recorded. The depression in calicoes is in a measure owing to fashion changes, the trade having turned largely to ginghams in Scotch styles, for which the demand has been unprecedented, and at fairly profitable figures. As a whole, however, the outlook for the cotton industry is exceedingly favourable. There are no large supplies of any make of goods in stock, and prices generally are established on a paying basis.

Worsteds and woollens. The worsted goods industry has been marked by fresh life, since the new tariff has to a great extent cut off the importation of the lowest grades of such goods. All the old factories have started up, and are making goods on safe orders; and new mills are being erected by European and British capitalists with a view to manufacturing a finer class of dress goods, &c., than ever before has been produced in this country. The woollen goods industry, apart from ladies' cloths, does not show any perceptible signs of improvement, but keeps on a slow, steady gait, apart from carpetings and woollen underwear. Both of the latter industries have been unusually busy during the last six months at fairly profitable prices.

Silks. The silk industry has been more or less depressed. Some of the causes leading to this included the fact that fashion changed largely to woollen dress fabrics; another was the large importations made in anticipation of the tariff changes, and also the high price of the raw material. Many of the silk factories have turned from the manufacture of dress fabrics to other lines; and the silk industry has not shown any improvement during the year. But few new plants have been started, and the outlook for the coming year in this line is not cheerful.

The following table shows the total grain shipments from this port, and the nationality of the vessels engaged in the transport:—

NEW YORK.

Grain shipments.

Nationality.	Number of Bushels.
Great Britain	30,455,226
United States	302,201
Germany	4,210,167
France	1,231,743
Belgium	3,894,581
Netherlands	1,485,144
Italy	1,076,717
Denmark	788,388
Portugal	489,092
Spain	445,940
Austria	115,511
Norway	97,849
Total	44,592,559

All of the above, except 494,023 bushels, were carried in steamships.

Ocean freights. The freights from this Continent during the year 1890 proved generally disappointing to owners, owing to the partial failure of the winter wheat and maize crops by drought; the high prices consequently ruling in our markets having practically prohibited the shipment of cereals, except in shape of flour, during the autumn and winter months.

The transportation of grain being the basis of freights for the regular liners, these vessels have likewise suffered, since the amount of provisions, cotton, and general cargo obtainable is not sufficient for any length of time to fill the room offering, in default of grain, as a considerable part cargo.

Early in January, 1890, a fair demand set in for grain vessels, lasting well into March, under which freights to Cork for orders ruled at an average figure of 4s. 3d. to 4s. 6d. from New York, Baltimore, or Philadelphia, about 3d. to 6d. higher for outports, and from New Orleans about 6d. to 9d. beyond our figures to Cork for orders. In April rates had declined to 3s., and owing to the rapid advance in prices of our cereals, shipments of grain in entire cargoes practically stopped, being limited to sporadic shipments—at about one-half the freight paid during the early spring—to such outports as Lisbon, Santander, &c. During the winter months not a single full cargo of grain was engaged for, except to Portugal.

Cotton freights were satisfactory during the latter part of the season of 1889–90, and the enormous crop of 1890–91 bid fair to give occupation to a very large amount of steam tonnage at good figures. This anticipation proved fallacious, however. The enormous crop staring them in the face caused purchasers in Europe to buy from hand to mouth under the pressure of continually declining prices for the article, while indirect shipments by liners, viâ Baltimore, Philadelphia, New York, and Boston, were unusually heavy, owing to low figures accepted by the liners from these ports named.

UNITED STATES.

These facts militated against freights from the southern ports, and it appears doubtful whether the cotton crop has ever before been moved on a lower range of freights than those ruling for last year's crop. Freights opened at 40s. to 42s. 6d. from Atlantic, 45s. to 47s. 6d. from Gulf ports, losing rapidly from 7s. 6d. to 10s. per ton on steamers' net register, charterers paying stevedoring and compressing, leaving, at the close of the year, an unusually large stock of cotton in the leading southern ports.

Freights by steam for other commodities have fluctuated mainly under the influence of the demand, and the rates obtainable for the transportation of the staples (grain and cotton) were fairly satisfactory to owners during the first, and disappointing during the latter half of the year.

The competition of Batoum in the shipment of petroleum in cases for the east by way of the Suez Canal is becoming more pronounced, and its primary effect has been a gradual reduction of freights towards the level of those ruling from the Black Sea ports.

Sailing vessels are continuing to lose ground by the encroachment of steam upon long distance trades, hitherto supposed to be practically closed to the competition of the latter. The exportation of petroleum in barrels is rapidly drawing to an end, owing to steady increase of tank steamers carrying oil in bulk, and freights, from this cause, were, in the main, very unproductive to owners.

Canals. The New York canals opened in 1890 for navigation on April 28 and closed December 1. The report of the superintendent shows that 5,246,102 tons (2,000 lbs.) passed through in 1890, 124,267 tons less than in 1889, and 303,154 tons more than in 1888.

Of the tonnage transported in 1890 there was carried by the

	Tons of 2,000 lbs.
Erie Canal	3,303,929
Champlain Canal	1,520,757
Oswego Canal	225,936
Cayuga and Seneca Company	63,419
Black River	132,061

Of the above amount 3,836,004 tons were eastward bound freight, 1,410,098 tons were westward bound, and 3,110,490 tons of this freight were through freight, and 2,135,612 tons were classed as way freight.

The tonnage of the canals was composed of the following described classes of articles:—

	Tons.
Product of the forest	1,397,862
,, agriculture	1,201,916
,, manufacture	139,310
Merchandise	769,672
Articles not otherwise described	1,737,342

During the year 1,435,189 tons (2,000 lbs.) were sent west- *Railroads.* ward to Buffalo, Pittsburg, &c., by the railroads from New York, and 3,736,995 tons were received, originating at or west of Buffalo and Pittsburg. In 1889 the westward freight was 1,245,710 tons and eastward 3,498,339 tons.

The railroads engaged in the above service were the New York Central and Hudson River, the New York, Lake Erie, and Western, the Pennsylvania, the Baltimore and Ohio, the West Shore, the Delaware, Lackawanna, and Western, the Lehigh Valley, and the New York, Ontario, and Western.

The total amount of grain received in this city in 1890 was 77,702,156 bushels, of which 30,082,900 bushels came by canals. The freight from Buffalo for wheat, by canal, averaged 3·87 c. (2d.) per bushel, for maize 3·50 c.

The shipments of grain by canal from Buffalo to New York and way places in 1890 were:—

	Bushels.
Wheat..	10,984,367
Maize..	21,372,670
Oats..	2,825,093
Barley..	2,685,346
Rye..	603,744

There is very little to report in connection with labour. Wages in my district have remained without change. Strikes of *Labour.* importance have been infrequent, and generally in connection with unionism; when they have been for advance of wages they have been in almost every instance a failure. In 1890 the Legislature of this State passed an Act for the weekly payment of wages by corporations, making it imperative on every manufacturing, mining or quarrying, lumbering, mercantile, railroad, surface, street electric and elevated railway (except steam surface railroads), steamboat, telegraph, telephone, and municipal corporation, and every incorporated express company and water company, to pay weekly each and every employé engaged in its business, the wages earned by said employé to within six days of the date of such payment. A violation of the Act subjects the corporation to a penalty not exceeding 50 dol., and not less than 10 dol. for each violation. An Act of 1886 in regard to the employment of women and children in manufacturing establishments was amended to read as follows:—

"No person under 18 years of age, and no woman under 21 years of age, employed in any manufacturing establishment, shall work therein more than 60 hours in any one week, nor more than 10 hours in any one day, unless for the purpose of making a shorter work day on the last day of the week, nor more hours in any one week than will make an average of 10 hours per day for the whole number of days in which such person, or such woman, shall so work during such week; and in no case shall any person under 18 years of age, or any woman under 21 years of age, work in any such establishment after nine o'clock in the evening, or before six o'clock in the morning of any day.

10 UNITED STATES.

"Every person, firm, or corporation employing any person under 18 years of age, or any woman under 21 years of age, in any manufacturing establishment, shall post, and keep posted, in a conspicuous place in every room where such help is employed, a printed notice stating the number of hours per day for each day of the week required of such persons, and in every room where children under 16 years of age are employed, a list of their names with their ages respectively.

"The words 'manufacturing establishment,' wherever used in the Act, shall be construed to mean any place where goods or products are manufactured, repaired, cleaned, or sorted, in whole, or in part; but no other person or corporation employing less than five persons or children, excepting in any of the cities of the State, shall be deemed a manufacturing establishment, within the meaning of this Act."

Immigration. There were 358,510 emigrants landed at this port, in 1890, of the following countries:—

Country.	1890.	1889.
Great Britain	29,225	35,055
Ireland	33,604	38,640
Germany	68,058	67,950
France	4,208	4,747
Russia	49,119	27,852
Sweden	24,291	24,638
Norway	9,569	9,677
Switzerland	6,436	7,130
Belgium	2,118	2,238
Holland	3,209	5,394
Italy	58,243	27,710
Spain	144	98
Portugal	863	19
Denmark	8,220	7,273
Hungary	23,003	15,440
Austria	30,442	21,619
Turkey	540	254
Greece	273	108
All other countries	6,945	4,274
Total	358,510	300,111

There were returned in the year under the Act of Congress regulating emigration, as convicts, lunatics, idiots, or likely to become a public charge, 272 persons, and under the Contract Labour Act, 160 persons; of the latter 123 were Italians, the remainder being Germans, French, Belgians, Russians, and Austrians.

On April 18 the business connected with emigration passed from the hands of the Board of Commissioners of Emigration of the State of New York, established under the provisions of an Act of 1847, to the United States Treasury Department, and the emigrants are now landed at a Federal wharf near "Castle Garden," the old landing-place.

NEW YORK.

Prisons. The report of the superintendent of the State prisons shows a great improvement in the condition of the prisoners, who had for two years been restricted from employment in any productive industries, as all such were regarded and legislated upon as an injurious competition with free labour. The Bill referred to in my last report, making some provision for the employment of prisoners, has been acted upon with marked success, and their condition is very much improved, both morally and physically. The prisoners have been employed both on the piece-price system and on State account, and the year's earnings amounted to 56,613*l.* There is also a good feature, in the law referred to, that the convicts are credited with a portion of their earnings, which has necessarily an excellent moral effect. The cost of the State prisons, in which there were, in 1890, 3,508 prisoners, was reduced from 76,060*l.* to 32,747*l.*, which is regarded as a very good showing, after the great demoralisation caused by the enforced idleness of the prisoners. One prisoner has been executed under the law, substituting electricity for hanging, and the physician, in his report to the Government, states :—" Notwithstanding the wide publication of unofficial reports of the execution of Kemmler, and the efforts which have been made to proclaim it a failure, and to invest it with an air of repulsion, brutality, and horror, it is confidently believed that, when all the facts in the case are rightly understood, the first execution by electricity will be regarded as a successful experiment, and that in time due credit will be accorded to those whose duty required them to act as principals in carrying out the law, the establishment of which is destined, in the not distant future, to be regarded as a step in the direction of a higher civilisation."

State finances. The State gross indebtedness at the close of the fiscal year (September 30) was 997,372*l.*, against which there is a sinking fund of 651,726*l.*, leaving a net debt of 345,646*l.*—a reduction during the year of 129,843*l.* The tax rate for the current year is 2·34 mills, which, on the assessed valuation, will yield 1,775,660*l.*, to be devoted to—

	£
School purposes	789,190
Canals	445,300
General purposes	541,170

City finances. The total funded debt of the city of New York amounted to, at the close of 1890, 30,152,432*l.*, against which there was a sinking fund of 9,993,842*l.*, leaving a net funded debt of 20,158,590*l.*

Valuation and tax rates for the past five years are given in the following table :—

UNITED STATES.

Year.	Real Estate.	Personal.	City Tax.
	£	£	Per cent.
1890	288,047,740	61,529,806	1·97
1889	274,305,127	56,085,729	1·95
1888	268,380,689	51,628,451	2·22
1887	258,425,300	52,148,655	2·16
1886	248,011,860	44,707,606	2·29

Vital Statistics.—New York City.

City vital statistics.

	1890.	1889.
Births	39,250	37,527
Marriages	14,992	14,400
Deaths	40,103	39,679

Of the deaths reported, 15,367 were of foreign birth, and 16,305 were under five years of age. The causes of death were principally as follows :—

	Number.
Phthisis	5,492
Pneumonia	4,989
Diarrhœal diseases	3,346
Bright's disease	2,024
Diphtheria	1,262
Heart diseases	2,139
Bronchitis	1,989
Scarlatina	408
Gastritis and peritonitis	440
Measles	730
Whooping-cough	487
Malarial fevers	176
Cancer	954
Typhoid fever	350
Violence	1,733

Death-rate, 24·66 per 1,000.

Census. The United States census reports, still incomplete, give the following information in regard to the population of the States of my district :—

Country.	Population. 1890.	Population. 1889.
	Number.	Number.
New York	5,997,853	5,082,871
New Jersey	1,444,933	1,131,116
Rhode Island	345,506	276,531
Connecticut	746,258	622,700
Delaware	168,493	146,608

An important change in the distribution of the population is shown by the following:—

Country.	Urban Population, 1890.	Urban Population, 1889.
	Per cent.	Per cent.
New York	59·50	50·98
New Jersey	54·05	43·82
Rhode Island	78·89	63·46
Connecticut	50·58	42·73
Delaware	36·46	28·97

The census of 1890 shows an increase in the population of New York city of 25·46 per cent. in 1890 over that of 1880, augmenting it from 1,206,299 to 1,515,301, and the accession would have been much greater were there facilities of rapid transit to the northern part of Manhattan Island and the annexed district beyond the Haarlem River. The want of speedy communication with this vast tract of land, only very partially built on, is now attracting the attention of the city authorities, and various schemes have been devised to this end, either by an extension of the elevated railroad system, or by an underground railroad. This portion of the city is from 7 miles to 12 miles from the commercial part, and many engaged in business in New York have been driven to find homes in outlying towns. Thus Brooklyn has increased its population nearly 42 per cent.—from 566,663 in 1880 to 804,377 in 1890; Jersey city nearly 36 per cent.—from 120,722 in 1880 to 163,997 in 1890; and many smaller towns have increased in a like proportion.

This city is supplied with water by the Croton waterworks, belonging to the city, and the supply has been increased in the past year from 110,000,000 gallons per day to 155,000,000 gallons per day by the completion of the new Croton aqueduct.

The new aqueduct was commenced in 1883, and before its completion the supply of water had become insufficient, flowing in many houses not above the ground floor, and except in favoured localities not above the first floor of any.

Water supply.

14 UNITED STATES.

Annex A.—Return of all Shipping at the Port of New York in the Year 1890.

Entered.

Nationality.	Sailing. Number of Vessels.	Sailing. Tons.	Steam. Number of Vessels.	Steam. Tons.	Total. Number of Vessels.	Total. Tons.
Great Britain	1,236	541,581	1,615	2,866,650	2,851	3,408,231
United States	1,142	467,068	287	465,124	1,429	932,192
Germany	112	120,303	388	933,796	500	1,054,099
France	...	...	93	258,924	93	258,924
Sweden and Norway	141	107,628	226	104,210	367	211,838
Belgium	4	6,836	81	254,404	85	261,240
Italy	153	93,075	22	32,866	175	125,941
Mexico	...	...	...	...	...	...
Netherlands	7	6,592	76	163,037	83	169,629
Austria	28	20,748	...	...	28	20,748
Spain	17	5,532	55	87,088	72	92,620
Denmark	3	687	25	53,753	28	54,440
Other European countries	14	7,392	15	16,038	29	23,430
South America	6	2,817	...	...	6	2,817
Central America	...	...	...	...	...	...
Other countries	1	138	...	...	1	138
Total	2,864	1,390,397	2,883	5,245,890	5,747	6,636,287
,, for the year preceding	3,080	1,677,303	2,548	4,635,176	5,628	6,312,479

Cleared.

Nationality.	Sailing. Number of Vessels.	Sailing. Tons.	Steam. Number of Vessels.	Steam. Tons.	Total. Number of Vessels.	Total. Tons.
Great Britain	1,239	533,156	1,607	2,888,452	2,846	3,421,608
United States	779	363,924	273	434,517	1,052	798,441
Germany	105	111,526	349	858,106	454	969,632
France	50	137,617	...	...	50	137,617
Sweden and Norway	115	86,428	218	95,104	333	181,532
Belgium	5	7,334	94	281,016	99	288,350
Italy	136	83,979	22	32,866	158	116,845
Mexico	...	...	1	11	1	11
Netherlands	...	...	6	13,987	6	13,987
Austria	25	17,719	...	...	25	17,719
Spain	17	4,998	51	80,428	68	85,426
Denmark	6	2,751	29	58,034	35	60,785
Other European countries	...	...	3	3,304	3	3,304
South America	5	2,580	...	...	5	2,580
Central America	...	...	...	...	...	...
Other countries	2	276	...	...	2	276
Total	2,484	1,352,288	2,653	4,745,825	5,137	6,098,113
,, for the year preceding	2,504	1,370,846	2,533	4,610,056	5,037	5,980,902

NEW YORK.

Annex B.—RETURN of Principal Articles of Export from New York during the Years 1890-89.

		1890.		1889.	
Articles.		Quantity.	Value.	Quantity.	Value.
			£		£
Agricultural implements	...	...	589,870	...	770,790
Bacon and ham	Lbs.	293,011,373	4,815,890	269,864,080	4,689,833
Beef, fresh	,,	114,663,946	1,867,745	110,561,262	1,806,208
,, canned	,,	51,789,037	792,661	31,107,216	475,705
Butter	,,	20,623,534	557,495	20,158,042	622,175
Cattle, live	Number	166,084	2,748,255	125,094	2,095,085
Cotton, domestic	Packages	185,630	2,036,315	164,030	1,861,20
,, raw	Bales	738,963	7,810,735	1,050,124	10,530,867
Cheese	Lbs.	70,208,270	1,271,420	70,616,136	1,275,310
Flour	Barrels	3,694,112	3,523,100	3,710,565	3,535,229
Hops	Lbs.	6,152,440	352,438	7,476,438	308,248
Indian corn	Bus., 56 lbs.	23,855,541	2,159,820	29,130,494	2,715,735
Lard	Lbs.	335,324,851	4,670,606	265,232,655	4,109,576
Oil cake and meal	,,	241,610,409	605,380	272,498,997	719,674
Oleomargarine	,,	84,805,836	1,660,970	42,954,590	841,215
Petroleum, refined	Gallons	399,097,169	6,095,170	392,551,146	6,174,605
,, crude	,,	48,101,235	757,550	50,123,443	773,780
,, lubricating	,,	27,714,259	870,480	11,585,652	209,180
Sewing machines	...	...	526,650	...	475,016
Sugar	Lbs.	53,406,617	710,130	7,614,695	128,827
Specie and bullion	...	...	8,752,250	...	14,781,236
Tallow	Lbs.	54,329,996	548,850	61,149,080	606,340
Wheat	Bus., 60 lbs.	12,607,484	2,481,443	10,853,078	2,014,328
Other articles	...	...	31,242,537	...	24,413,567
Total		...	87,447,760	...	86,033,737

(1135)

UNITED STATES.

RETURN of Principal Articles of Import to New York during the Years 1890-89.

Articles.		1890. Quantity.	1890. Value.	1889. Quantity.	1889. Value.
			£		£
Cocoa	Bags	112,162	446,090	88,989	348,476
Coffee	,,	3,113,253	13,906,165	3,126,243	12,906,394
China, glass, and earthenware		...	1,966,032	...	1,916,856
Cotton	Bales	17,967	274,133	12,526	222,645
Dry goods—					
Manufactures of cotton	...	...	4,991,800	...	4,393,605
,, flax	...	...	3,852,485	...	3,945,785
,, silk	...	...	9,996,230	...	9,043,710
,, wool	...	...	8,620,205	...	8,263,770
Miscellaneous	...	...	2,634,746	...	2,509,800
Furs	Packages	23,339	1,371,675	22,888	1,292,157
Fruits	...	...	3,582,588	...	2,767,950
Hair	Packages	27,122	316,992	28,932	280,720
Hemp	Bales	372,398	1,511,926	494,432	2,587,855
Hides, dressed	...	...	696,267	...	646,810
,, undressed	...	...	4,026,860	...	3,460,270
Hops	Bales	10,420	183,982	10,100	161,390
India rubber	...	...	3,164,378	...	2,316,442
Jewellery, watches, and precious stones	...	...	2,951,468	...	2,709,100
Jute and jute butts	...	...	605,350	...	639,980
Linseed	...	...	488,130	...	653,715
Molasses	...	...	251,115	...	312,185
Paper stock	...	...	513,034	...	633,600
Metals—					
Cutlery	...	...	445,897	...	438,755
Iron, pig	Tons	11,965	53,546	23,778	70,875
,, spiegel	,,	84,074	479,018	75,322	325,662
,, other	...	...	196,432	...	303,556
Metal goods	...	...	520,945	...	358,695
Steel	...	...	493,490	...	499,920
Tin	Boxes	2,365,488	2,016,750	2,312,171	1,718,385
,, slabs	Tons	13,864	1,070,790	14,220	1,338,940
Soda, ash	...	...	351,285	...	217,783
,, caustic	...	...	196,233	...	141,320
Spices	...	...	584,056	...	514,392
Stationery and books	...	...	1,190,712	...	1,100,720
Sugar	Tons	704,507	8,612,609	664,087	10,143,860
Specie and bullion	...	...	4,196,220	...	1,637,322
Tea	Packages	1,248,858	2,060,855	1,295,690	2,001,048
Tobacco and cigars	...	...	3,494,498	...	2,669,844
Wines, spirits, &c.	...	...	2,246,006	...	1,987,240
Wood	...	...	1,024,783	...	1,173,407
Wool	Lbs.	43,205,565	1,085,474	52,795,113	1,339,490
Other articles	...	...	23,132,690	...	13,564,845
Total	...	...	119,703,940	...	103,569,144

Annex C.—TABLE showing the Total Value of all Articles Exported from and Imported to New York to and from Foreign Countries during the Years 1890-89.

Country.	Exports. 1890.	Exports. 1889.	Imports. 1890.	Imports. 1889.
	£	£	£	£
Great Britain and Ireland	42,879,435	40,090,215	26,406,675	22,268,820
British possessions	6,024,545	6,138,228	7,895,215	7,056,865
Germany	8,185,285	6,991,392	18,781,715	14,468,825
France and possessions	4,302,855	9,805,033	15,529,990	13,406,468
Belgium	3,386,545	2,928,363	1,470,050	1,204,945
Spain and possessions	4,695,915	4,042,470	9,038,170	9,864,530
Netherlands and possessions	3,831,735	2,988,487	4,064,380	3,710,397
United States and Colombia	574,000	516,540	1,948,160	1,119,321
Central American States	799,525	579,472	826,605	712,593
Italy	1,177,015	926,385	3,515,935	2,798,387
Brazil	1,604,970	1,333,458	12,012,715	10,227,777
China	930,510	642,100	2,352,400	2,038,877
Denmark and possessions	716,285	681,664	190,025	164,495
Venezuela	1,549,110	1,385,900	2,045,475	2,568,990
Portugal and possessions	766,940	434,036	255,140	247,965
Argentine Republic	636,645	1,453,835	559,255	525,656
Mexico	877,255	963,143	2,027,040	1,957,735
Hayti	1,651,405	1,191,158	478,620	701,185
Sweden and Norway	526,515	428,545	520,805	418,866
Japan	500,900	516,965	1,349,110	1,411,788
Chile	538,465	473,087	463,260	330,375
San Domingo	218,015	288,880	539,580	381,408
Uruguay	245,420	529,005	382,500	432,800
Austria	87,460	21,143	2,037,450	1,350,380
Russia	68,140	135,300	615,580	524,662
Peru	299,155	203,825	82,975	64,755
Switzerland	5,775	4,520	3,002,675	2,478,716
Other countries	367,940	335,588	1,312,440	1,131,563
Total	87,447,760	86,033,737	119,703,940	103,569,144

UNITED STATES.

The specie included in the tables was exported to and imported rom the following countries during the years 1890-89:—

Country.	Exports. 1890.	Exports. 1889.	Imports. 1890.	Imports. 1889.
	£	£	£	£
Great Britain	6,375,345	7,095,880	949,050	123,755
British possessions	19,425	1,717	108,720	51,650
Germany	571,905	11,445	1,045,030	356,8:5
France and possessions	236,320	5,755,530	469,455	341,012
Spain „ „	740,360	929,504	683,115	181,495
Netherlands and possessions	..	6,352	41,800	16,660
United States and Colombia	35,425	23,423	567,865	391,905
Central American States	29,145	39,494	26,460	20,874
Brazil	93,855	100,428	2,575	235
Denmark and possessions	..	6,138	21,395	5,232
Venezuela	357,735	546,442	2,580	17,310
Portugal and possessions	..	..	860	..
Mexico	2,080	7,786	190,915	95,353
Hayti	265,965	196,376	4,540	10,345
San Domingo	16,450	57,787	81,200	13,044
Peru	6,180	..	210	..
Other countries	2,060	2,934	450	11,637
Total	8,752,250	14,781,236	4,196,220	1,637,322

PROVIDENCE, R.I.

Mr. Vice-Consul Stockwell reports as follows:—

General report on trade. A review of trade and commerce during the year 1890 at the port and in the city of Providence discloses nothing of extraordinary interest. The course of business was uninterrupted by any important fluctuation, except in the latter part of the year.

The volume of business was larger than in the year preceding, as shown by the bank clearings, which amounted to 55,017,100*l.* In 1889 the clearings were 54,001,232*l.* At the opening of the year the rate at banks for time loans was 6 to 7 per cent., and at the close, as the result of the fall stringency, ranged from 7 to 8 per cent.

Port statistics. The total number of vessels arriving at the port of Providence during the year was 139, of which 109 were British, 1 Dominican, 1 Italian, and 28 American.

TONNAGE of the Port.

Vessels.	Number.	Tons.
Sailing	78	11,900
Steam	40	14,819

NEW YORK.

	£
Amount of duties collected	58,735
„ „ tonnage dues collected	96
„ „ storage fees „	110
„ „ official „ „	168
„ „ miscellaneous fees collected	140
„ „ fines „	5

Trades generally have had full employment during the year at remunerative wages. There has been no disturbance in the labour market on account of wages. Among operatives in mills there has been some dissatisfaction expressed in regard to the hours of labour and in regard to the employment of non-union men, and, as a result, several strikes have taken place, but the interruption of labour in most cases has been brief. Final adjustment perhaps was not always satisfactory to all concerned. *Labour and wages.*

There has been no change of wages in trades generally, according to the report of the Commissioner of Industrial Statistics.

Improvements in terminal facilities for railways and sewerage are going forward as rapidly as circumstances will allow. When these are completed a great impetus and a greater volume will be given to the business of the city and State. The contemplated railway from Providence to Springfield, Mass., will bring the city nearer to the west, and the products of the west nearer to tide-water. Western freights to Providence come by the way of Worcester, Mass., the distance between Providence and Springfield, viâ Worcester, being 100 miles more or less, while the distance from Providence, by the railway proposed between Providence and Springfield direct, is only 37 miles. This project is, of course, opposed by railways that now have the monopoly, for if their system be tapped at Springfield, all freight for Providence will deviate at that point. *Public improvements.*

The building improvements generally have been unusually large. The number of buildings erected during the year was 558, and the improvements 199, at a cost of 494,030*l.*

Annex A.

ENTERED.

Nationality.	Sailing.		Steam.		Total.	
	Number of Vessels.	Tons.	Number of Vessels.	Tons.	Number of Vessels.	Tons.
British	109	10,638	...	...	109	10,638
American	28	7,211	...	...	28	7,211
Dominican	1	147	...	...	1	147
Italian	1	535	...	...	1	535
Total	139	18,531	...	...	139	18,531
„ for the year preceding	83	13,180	...	...	83	13,180

UNITED STATES.

CLEARED.

Nationality.	Sailing.		Steam.		Total.	
	Number of Vessels.	Tons.	Number of Vessels.	Tons.	Number of Vessels.	Tons.
British	95	7,032	...	...	95	7,032
American	12	2,108	...	...	12	2,108
Total	107	9,140	...	...	107	9,140
,, for the year preceding	72	8,538	...	...	72	8,538

Annex B.—RETURN of Principal Articles of Export from Providence, R.I., for the Years 1890-89.

Articles.		1890.		1889.	
		Quantity.	Value.	Quantity.	Value.
			£		£
Oil	Barrels	...	...	4,380	3,643
Vessel	...	...	413	...	342
Coal	Tons	16	15	...	...
Total		...	428	...	3,985

RETURN of Principal Articles of Import from Providence for the Years 1889-90.

Articles.	Value.	
	1890.	1889.
	£	£
Dry goods	39,210	68,865
Metals, and manufactures of	27,195	19,805
Rubber	28,188	..
Chemicals	25,707	23,730
All other	70,572	32,080
Total	190,872	144,480

Annex C.—TABLE showing the Total Values of all Articles Exported from Providence and Imported into Providence from and to Foreign Countries during the Years 1890-89.

Country.	Exports. 1890.	Exports. 1889.	Imports. 1890.	Imports. 1889.
	£	£	£	£
Austria	..	..	4,128	2,097
Belgium	..	..	556	..
Brazil	..	..	28,258	..
British West Indies	..	..	14,198	13,675
Canada	428	..	13,239	9,014
Cuba	..	..	12,509	8,949
England	..	..	71,544	70,052
France	..	..	18,907	17,840
Germany	..	..	7,443	10,376
Greece	..	..	..	2,730
Hayti	..	..	310	..
Italy	..	..	2,385	3,176
Ireland	..	..	207	..
Netherlands	..	3,985	428	914
Portugal	..	..	247	..
Scotland	..	..	1,318	1,265
Spain	..	..	372	..
Switzerland	..	..	3,803	5,180
All others	..	..	20	212
Total	428	3,985	190,872	144,480

22. UNITED STATES.

Return of the Number of Seamen who have been Engaged, Discharged, Left behind, reported Dead, or Deserted, or who have been Relieved at the British Consulate-General, New York, and showing the Total Number of British and Foreign Sailors who were Engaged, Discharged, &c., from British Ships, with the amount of Wages paid at the Consulate to Seamen on Discharge from their Ships, and from Hospital or Gaol; and also showing the number of New Agreements entered into during the Year 1890.

Seamen.									Nationality.		Total Number of Seamen.	Wages.			Agreements.
Engaged.	Discharged.	Left Behind.			Dead.			Deserted.	Relieved.	British.	Foreign.		Paid on Discharge from Vessels.	Paid on Discharge from Hospital or Gaol.	Total Wages paid.	Number opened.
		In Hospital.	In Gaol.	Total.	At Sea.	On Shore.	Total.									
13,324	9,949	205	25	230	58	34	92	3,517	96	16,084	11,103	27,187	Dollars. 430,574·13	Dollars. 4,948·03	Dollars. 435,522·16	291

(1250 6 | 91 — H & S 1135)

FOREIGN OFFICE.

1891.

ANNUAL SERIES.

N[o.] 933.

DIPLOMATIC AND CONSULAR REPORTS ON TRADE AND FINANCE.

UNITED STATES.

REPORT FOR THE YEAR 1890

ON THE

AGRICULTURE OF THE DISTRICT OF THE CONSULATE-GENERAL OF NEW YORK.

REFERENCE TO PREVIOUS REPORT, Annual Series No. 643

Presented to both Houses of Parliament by Command of Her Majesty,
JULY, 1891.

LONDON:
PRINTED FOR HER MAJESTY'S STATIONERY OFFICE,
BY HARRISON AND SONS, ST. MARTIN'S LANE,
PRINTERS IN ORDINARY TO HER MAJESTY.

And to be purchased, either directly or through any Bookseller, from
EYRE & SPOTTISWOODE, EAST HARDING STREET, FLEET STREET, E.C., and
32, ABINGDON STREET, WESTMINSTER, S.W.; or
JOHN MENZIES & Co., 12, HANOVER STREET, EDINBURGH, and
88 and 90, WEST NILE STREET, GLASGOW; or
HODGES, FIGGIS, & Co., 104, GRAFTON STREET, DUBLIN.

1891.

[C. 6205–164.]   *Price One Penny.*

New Series of Reports.

Reports of the Annual Series have been issued from Her Majesty's Diplomatic and Consular Officers at the following places, and may be obtained from the sources indicated on the title-page:—

No.		Price	No.		Price
811.	Quito	½d.	872.	Rosario	1d.
812.	Para	½d.	873.	Buenos Ayres	½d.
813.	Palermo	2½d.	874.	Mogador	1d.
814.	Copenhagen	1d.	875.	Tainan	6½d.
815.	Serajevo	½d.	876.	Pakhoi	1d.
816.	Porto Rico	1d.	877.	Odessa	2½d.
817.	Madrid	½d.	878.	Trebizond	1½d.
818.	Brussels	½d.	879.	Mollendo	½d.
819.	Patras	½d.	880.	Kiukiang	1d.
820.	Stuttgart	1d.	881.	Antananarivo	1d.
821.	Taganrog	1d.	882.	Stettin	2½d.
822.	Salonica	2d.	883.	Fiume	1½d.
823.	Galveston	1d.	884.	Batavia	1d.
824.	Rome	1½d.	885.	Samoa	½d.
825.	Paris	1½d.	886.	Cherbourg	1d.
826.	Bushire	½d.	887.	Cagliari	1d.
827.	New Orleans	3d.	888.	Hankow	1½d.
828.	Buda-Pesth	½d.	889.	Vienna	1½d.
829.	Hamburg	3d.	890.	Amoy	1d.
830.	Port Said	1d.	891.	Adrianople	½d.
831.	Samoa	½d.	892.	Chicago	2½d.
832.	Guayaquil	½d.	893.	Brest	1d.
833.	New Orleans	2d.	894.	Smyrna	1d.
834.	The Piræus	1d.	895.	Cadiz	1d.
835.	Baltimore	1½d.	896.	Aleppo	1d.
836.	Trieste	2d.	897.	Foochow	1d.
837.	Galatz	1½d.	898.	Kiungchow	1d.
838.	Wênchow	1d.	899.	The Hague	1½d.
839.	Havre	2½d.	900.	Nice	1½d.
840.	Rome	1½d.	901.	Nantes	1½d.
841.	Taganrog	2d.	902.	Port-au-Prince	1½d.
842.	Calais	1d.	903.	Bengazi	1d.
843.	Boston	1d.	904.	Tahiti	½d.
844.	Bordeaux	2½d.	905.	Chinkiang	1d.
845.	Charleston	1½d.	906.	San Francisco	3d.
846.	Manila	5d.	907.	Brindisi	2d.
847.	Madeira	½d.	908.	Beyrout	1d.
848.	Paris	2d.	909.	Noumea	½d.
849.	Tripoli	½d.	910.	San Francisco	1d.
850.	Swatow	1d.	911.	New York	1½d.
851.	Saigon	½d.	912.	Caracas	1½d.
852.	Vienna	1½d.	913.	Greytown	½d.
853.	Algiers	2d.	914.	Corunna	2d.
854.	Algiers	1d.	915.	Christiania	5½d.
855.	Mozambique	8d.	916.	Callao	1d.
856.	Antwerp	1½d.	917.	Macao	1d.
857.	Mogador	2d.	918.	Sŏul	1d.
858.	Ichang	½d.	919.	Dunkirk	1d.
859.	Calais	8½d.	920.	Tamsui	1d.
860.	Riga	2d.	921.	Bussorah	½d.
861.	San José	1d.	922.	Yokohama	3½d.
862.	Genoa	1½d.	923.	Bilbao	1½d.
863.	Warsaw	1d.	924.	Barcelona	2½d.
864.	Wuhu	1d.	925.	Netherlands India	1d.
865.	Marseilles	1d.	926.	Chefoo	1d.
866.	Syra	1d.	927.	Buenos Ayres	½d.
867.	Jeddah	½d.	928.	Santo Domingo	½d.
868.	Savannah	½d.	929.	Constantinople	½d.
869.	Suakin	½d.	930.	Erzeroum	1½d.
870.	Berlin	1d.	931.	Gothenburg	2d.
871.	Batoum	1½d.	932.	Tunis	1d.

No. 933.

Reference to previous Report, Annual Series No. 643.

UNITED STATES.

NEW YORK.

Consul-General Booker to the Marquis of Salisbury.

My Lord,　　　　　　　　　　*New York, June* 18, 1891.

I HAVE the honour to transmit herewith a Report upon the Agriculture of the States of New York, New Jersey, Connecticut, Delaware, and Rhode Island.

I have, &c.
(Signed)　　W. LANE BOOKER.

Report upon the Agriculture of the States of New York, New Jersey, Connecticut, Delaware, and Rhode Island for the Year 1890.

Agriculture.

In my last report on agriculture I referred to the elevation of the United States Bureau of Agriculture to an executive department of the Government, and to the probable more valuable information in future to be obtained in consequence of the change. The information furnished in the report of the secretary does not give so much statistical information as has been furnished in former reports, but it may be assumed that what is given is of a more reliable character.

The secretary in his annual report to the President states in this connection: "The operations of the statistical division have been replete with activity in various directions. The necessity of statistics in the work of legislation is becoming more and more imperative, as attested by the demands upon this office during the extended session of the present congress. The discussion of industrial and economic questions in the halls of legislation, in polemic discussion, in literature and journalism, makes constant demand upon the resources of the statistical bureau for the facts of production and distribution, prices of products, wages of labour, development of resources, and status of agriculture.

Agricultural experiment stations.

The report of the director of the office of experiment stations shows that there has been great activity at all the stations, and

(1165)

that the information collected has been of a highly valuable character as evinced by the enormous increase of applications from farmers in all parts of the country for publications of the department or information which may be given by supplying the publications.

New York.

The product of the cereals, &c., of the State of New York in 1890, and the two preceding years, is given in the following tables:—

Cereals.		1888. Number of Acres in each Crop.	1888. Quantity Produced.	1888. Average Yield per Acre.	1889. Number of Acres in each Crop.	1889. Quantity Produced.	1889. Average Yield per Acre.
Wheat	Bushels	660,214	9,309,000	14·1	647,010	8,929,000	13·8
Indian corn	,,	705,859	22,870,000	32·4	698,800	20,475,000	29·3
Barley*	,,	343,428	7,418,000	21·6	...	...	...
Oats	,,	1,398,957	40,570,000	29·0	1,384,967	36,009,000	26·0
Rye*	,,	236,851	2,724,000	11·5	...	...	...
Buckwheat*	,,	311,310	4,514,000	14·5	...	...	...
Potatoes*	,,	371,105	29,688,000	80·0	...	...	...
Hay*	Tons	4,933,415	5,426,757	1·10	...	...	...

* Official statistics incomplete.

Cereals.	1890. Number of Acres in each Crop.	1890. Quantity Produced.	1890. Average Yield per Acre.
	Bushels.	Bushels.	
Wheat	640,540	9,288,000	14·5
Indian corn	642,896	17,101,000	26·7
Barley*	..	..	..
Oats	1,343,418	23,913,000	17·8

* Statistics not available.

No statistics are furnished in the last two official reports in regard to the acreage and yield of the other cereals than those given in the foregoing tables, but the yield of barley and rye is stated to have been somewhat smaller in 1890 than the average, while that of buckwheat was unusually large. The table for 1888 shows the acreage of these cereals which has varied but little for several years. Tables furnished give the average value per acre of the following crops in New York:—

NEW YORK.

		s.	d.
Wheat		63	10
Indian corn		75	6
Oats		45	11
Rye		35	1
Barley		70	0
Buckwheat		34	1
Potatoes		155	10
Hay		56	8

Viniculture. From the census reports I have gathered the following information in regard to the viniculture of this State. In 1890 there were 43,350 acres in bearing vines, the product of which was 75,859 tons (2,000 lbs.); 60,687 tons were sold for table use and 15,172 to wineries. The largest supplies are from the Hudson River district and from the counties of Steuben and Chautauqua in the south-western part of the State.

Truck farming. The census reports all furnish an interesting report on truck farming; this is distinct from market gardening, and is described in the report as consisting in the production of green vegetables for market in parts remote from market, the truck farmer being dependent upon transportation companies and commission men for the delivery and sale of his products, and usually devotes himself to such specialties as are best suited to the soil and climate. The report is divided into districts which preclude me from giving the product specially of the States within my Consular jurisdiction, but two districts comprise them—New England district takes in Connecticut and Rhode Island, and New York and Philadelphia includes New York and New Jersey.

The number of acres of leading varieties of vegetable is given in the following table:—

Districts.	Asparagus.	French Beans.	Celery.	Cabbage.	Cucumbers.	Kale.	Peas.	Spinach.	Tomatoes.	Sweet Potatoes.	Miscellaneous.	Aggregate.
New England	242	65	443	1,586	272	...	1,476	310	305	...	2,139	6,838
New York and Philadelphia	6,592	2,710	4,058	41,054	870	110	9,446	3,262	6,990	4,660	28,383	108,135

The New York and Philadelphia district has one-fifth of the whole land in the United States devoted to this description of farming.

In the districts given there are 76,682 men employed, and 1,563 children, and the wages average 4s. 9½d. per day.

New York is a large producer of hops. In 1890 the product amounted to a little over 90,000 bales, about two-fifths of the total product of the United States.

Oleomargarine. The Dairy Commissioner, in his report, gives little information of interest beyond what has been furnished in my previous reports. He states that he can safely say that no oleomargarine,

(1165)

Milk inspection.

or imitation butter, is now made within the State; he believes that very small quantities of imitation butter have been from time to time shipped from other States into the State—generally shipped directly to the consumer. In regard to the inspection of milk, the report states:—"The work of inspecting the milk delivered to cheese factories, and shipped and exposed for sale as an article of food throughout the State, has been carried on as asual in previous years. Our force having been increased, and agents assigned to portions of the State where none had been at work before, we have been able to make a more thorough and frequent inspection than in previous years, and I am satisfied that the milk produced this year has been of better quality, and the percentage of adulteration has become so small as to be a very insignificant factor in the business of producing and selling milk."

Cheese brand.

With reference to the "cheese brand" the report states: "After an experience of nearly five years in the use by the manufacturers of full-cream cheese of a 'uniform stencil brand,' as authorised to be issued by the New York State Dairy Commissioner, under the provisions of Chapter 193, Laws of 1885, it has become evident that this enactment of the legislature was a wise one. While the number issued since and inclusive of 1885 has varied considerably in each year, yet the average has been a good one, and the number issued in 1889 is larger than any previous year. It would seem as if it had become an almost absolute necessity that full-cream cheese should bear the New York State brand before it is put on the market, if the manufacturer desires a good reputation as a cheese-maker, and the highest price for his product. In fact many buyers of cheese require such branding before they will purchase."

Brands were issued in the past season to 484 factories.

Land in New York State.

In the State of New York there are 30,746,800 acres of land of which 17,720,000 acres are in improved farms with an average of 3,650,000 acres devoted to grain. The production of hay is larger than in any other State of the Union, averaging over 5,500,000 tons.

New Jersey.

The product of the cereals, &c., of the State of New Jersey in 1890, and the two preceding years, is given in the following tables:—

Cereals.		1888.			1889.		
		Number of Acres in each Crop.	Quantity Produced.	Average Yield per Acre.	Number of Acres in each Crop.	Quantity Produced.	Average Yield per Acre.
Wheat	Bushels	141,652	1,785,000	12·6	140,235	1,711,000	12·2
Indian corn	,,	350,335	11,351,000	32·4	357,342	10,792,000	30·0
Barley*	,,	...	...	...	...	...	...
Oats	,,	140,218	3,688,000	26·3	144,425	3,408,000	23·6
Rye*	,,	105,588	1,098,000	10·4	...	...	...
Buckwheat*	,,	35,723	464,000	13·0	...	...	...
Potatoes*	,,	43,366	3,599,000	83·0	...	...	...
Hay*	Tons	488,655	586,386	1·20	...	...	...

* Official statistic incomplete.

Cereals.	1890.		
	Number of Acres in each Crop.	Quantity Produced.	Average Yield per Acre.
	Bushels.	Bushels.	
Wheat	138,833	1,680,000	12·1
Indian corn	357,342	11,185,000	31·3
Oats	141,537	2,449,000	17·3

Note.—No statistics are furnished in regard to other cereals, &c.

Connecticut.

The product of the cereals, &c., for the State of Connecticut in 1890, and the two preceding years, is given in the following tables:—

Cereals.		1888.			1889.		
		Number of Acres in each Crop.	Quantity Produced.	Average Yield per Acre.	Number of Acres in each Crop.	Quantity Produced.	Average Yield per Acre.
Wheat	Bushels	2,149	32,000	14·9	1,934	30,000	15·5
Indian corn	,,	56,977	1,788,000	31·2	56,977	1,766,000	31·0
Barley*	,,	638	14,000	21·9	...	...	...
Oats	,,	39,811	1,055,000	26·5	39,413	1,009,000	25·6
Rye*	,,	28,500	348,000	12·2	...	...	...
Buckwheat*	,,	10,974	134,000	12·2	...	...	...
Potatoes*	,,	33,459	2,677,000	80·0	...	...	...
Hay*	Tons	563,156	574,419	1·2	...	...	...

* Official statistics incomplete.

UNITED STATES.

Cereals.	1890. Number of Acres in each Crop.	Quantity Produced.	Average Yield per Acre.
	Bushels.	Bushels.	
Wheat	1,876	30,000	16·0
Indian corn	56,407	2,014,000	35·7
Oats	39,019	780,000	19·9

NOTE.—No statistics are furnished in regard to other cereals, &c.

DELAWARE.

The product of the cereals. &c., of the State of Delaware in 1890, and the two preceding years, is given in the following tables :—

Cereals.		1888. Number of Acres in each Crop.	Quantity Produced.	Average Yield per Acre.	1889. Number of Acres in each Crop.	Quantity Produced.	Average Yield per Acre.
Wheat	Bushels	94,790	1,194,000	12·6	94,790	1,100,000	11·6
Indian corn	,,	220,927	3,844,000	17·4	223,136	3,905,000	17·5
Barley*	,,	...	...	...	...	...	...
Oats...	,,	21,839	450,000	20·6	22,931	420,000	18·3
Rye*	,,	857	8,000	9·3	...	...	...
Buckwheat*	,,	...	...	...	...	...	...
Potatoes*	,,	4,224	317,000	75·0	...	...	...
Hay*	Tons	56,240	66,363	1·18	...	...	...

* Official statistics incomplete.

Cereals.	1890. Number of Acres in each Crop.	Quantity Produced.	Average Yield per Acre.
	Bushels.	Bushels	
Wheat	94,790	919,000	9·8
Indian corn	223,136	4,128,000	18·0
Oats	22,931	298,000	13·0

NOTE.—No statistics are furnished in regard to other cereals, &c.

Rhode Island.

The product of the cereals, &c., for the State of Rhode Island in 1890, and the two preceding years, is given in the following tables:—

Cereals.		1888.			1889.		
		Number of Acres in each Crop.	Quantity Produced.	Average Yield per Acre.	Number of Acres in each Crop.	Quantity Produced.	Average Yield per Acre.
Wheat*	Bushels	...	...	...	...	...	...
Indian corn	,,	12,588	382,000	30·4	12,558	393,000	31·3
Barley*	,,	848	20,000	23·6	...	...	...
Oats	,,	6,353	174,000	27·4	6,417	170,000	26·4
Rye*	,,	1,278	15,000	11·7	...	...	...
Buckwheat†	,,	...	...	...	...	...	...
Potatoes*	,,	6,889	668,000	97·0	...	...	...
Hay*	Tons	104,829	104,829	1·0	...	...	...

* Official statistics incomplete.

Cereals.	1890.		
	Number of Acres in each Crop.	Quantity Produced.	Average Yield per Acre.
	Bushels.	Bushels.	
Indian corn	12,307	402,000	32·6
Oats	6,545	153,000	23·3

Note.—No statistics are furnished in regard to other cereals, &c.

Barley. Barley has been largely imported into the United States from Canada, the receipts in 1890 amounting to 9,939,745 bushels of the value of 944,000*l.*; but under the new McKinley Tariff the duty is raised from 10 c. (5⅛*d.*) per bushel to 30 c. (15⅜*d.*) per bushel, which will stimulate its growth in this State and elsewhere. The total production of barley in the United States was in 1888 (the last year there is a record of) 63,884,000 bushels.

LONDON:
Printed for Her Majesty's Stationery Office,
By HARRISON AND SONS,
Printers in Ordinary to Her Majesty.
(1250   7 | 91—H & S   1165)

COMMERCIAL. No. 7 (1891).

PROTOCOLS OF PROCEEDINGS

OF THE

INTERNATIONAL MARINE CONFERENCE

HELD IN

WASHINGTON,

OCTOBER 16 TO DECEMBER 31, 1889.

[In continuation of "Commercial No. 20 (1890)": C. 6133.]

Presented to both Houses of Parliament by Command of Her Majesty.
March 1891.

LONDON:
PRINTED FOR HER MAJESTY'S STATIONERY OFFICE
BY HARRISON AND SONS, ST. MARTIN'S LANE,
PRINTERS IN ORDINARY TO HER MAJESTY.

And to be purchased, either directly or through any Bookseller, from
EYRE AND SPOTTISWOODE, EAST HARDING STREET, FLEET STREET, E.C.; OR
JOHN MENZIES & Co., 12, HANOVER STREET, EDINBURGH, AND
21, DRURY STREET, GLASGOW; OR
HODGES, FIGGIS, & Co., 104, GRAFTON STREET, DUBLIN.

Protocols of Proceedings of the International Marine Conference held in Washington, October 16 to December 31, 1889.

[In continuation of "Commercial No. 20 (1890)": C. 6133.]

Sir J. Pauncefote to the Marquis of Salisbury.—(*Received June* 16.)

My Lord,   Washington, *June* 6, 1890.

WITH reference to my despatch dated the 23rd ultimo, I have the honour to transmit Volume II of the Protocols of Proceedings of the Marine Conference, which have been presented to the Senate by the President.

                I have, &c.
          (Signed)   JULIAN PAUNCEFOTE.

Inclosure.

Protocols of Proceedings of the International Marine Conference held in Washington, D. C., United States of America, October 16 *to December* 31, 1889.

[The Protocols which follow are dated from December 2 to 31, 1889.]

CONTENTS.

PROGRAMME OF SUBJECTS.

				Page
Protocol, December	2.	General Division	I	5
,,	,, 3.	,, ,,	I	28
,,	,, 4.	,, ,,	I	52
,,	,, 5.	,, ,,	I	78
,,	,, 9.			98
		Interlocutory Report of Collocation Committee		99
		General Division	III	100
		,, ,,	XIII	102
		,, ,,	I	117
,,	,, 12.			121
		General Division XIII		125
,,	,, 16.			139
		Additional Report of Light Committee		139
		General Division	I	139
		,, ,,	V	148
		,, ,,	II	162
		,, ,,	IV	163
		,, ,,	VI	166
		,, ,,	VII	173
		,, ,,	VIII	178
,,	,, 18.	,, ,,	I	181
,,	,, 19.	,, ,,	I	206
,,	,, 20.	,, ,,	I	234
,,	,, 30.			261
		General Division	IX	263
		,, ,,	XII	264
		,, ,,	I	273
,,	,, 31.			276
		General Division	X	276
		,, ,,	XI	280

[93]

2

Programme of Subjects to be considered by the International Marine Conference.

OCTOBER 1889.

Department of State, International Marine Conference,
Washington, April 3, 1889.

Sir,

I HAVE the honour to inform you that, in conformity with the instructions of the State Department of the 27th February, 1889, the Delegates on the part of the United States to the International Marine Conference met on Monday, 25th ultimo, organized, and proceeded to the consideration of a detailed Programme of the subjects to be considered by the International Conference, for transmission to the several Powers.

This Programme was completed on the 30th ultimo, and is herewith inclosed.

The correspondence between the State Department and the British Government on this subject was examined, and, in conformity with the intentions of our Government therein expressed, a consideration of the "International Code of Flag Signals" was excluded from the Programme, and a consideration of the "load line" was included. With this exception and this addition, the entire subject-matter of the Act of Congress of the 9th July, 1888, was arranged in General Divisions, following as nearly as possible the precise language of the Act. These General Divisions were then carefully considered, and each was arranged under subdivisions and subheads.

It is believed that this arrangement in detail is sufficiently broad to include all matters bearing directly upon the principal topics, and care has been taken at the same time to avoid extending the field of deliberations of the Conference beyond the limits indicated in the Act of Congress, and its interpretation by the State Department.

Very respectfully,
(Signed) S. R. FRANKLIN, *Rear-Admiral, United States' Navy,*
President of the Board of American Delegates.

Hon. James G. Blaine,
Secretary of State.

Detailed Programme of Subjects to be considered by the International Marine Conference.

[Framed by the American Delegates in accordance with instructions from the Department of State, March 1889.]

GENERAL DIVISION I.

Marine Signals or other means of plainly indicating the Direction in which Vessels are moving in Fog, Mist, Falling Snow, and Thick Weather, and at night.—Rules for the Prevention of Collisions, and Rules of the Road.

1. Visibility, number, and position of lights to be carried by vessels:—

(*a.*) Steamers under way.
(*b.*) Steamers towing.
(*c.*) Vessels under way, but not under command, including steamers laying cable.
(*d.*) Sailing-vessels under way.
(*e.*) Sailing-vessels towing.
(*f.*) Vessels at anchor.
(*g.*) Pilot-vessels.
(*h.*) Fishing-vessels.

2. Sound-signals; their character, number, range, and position of instruments:—

(*a.*) For use in fog, mist, falling snow, and thick weather, as position-signals.
    For steamers under way.
    For steamers towing.
    For sailing-vessels under way.
    For sailing-vessels towing.
    (These signals to show the approximate course steered if possible.)
    For vessels at anchor.
    For vessels under way, but not under command, including steamers laying cable.
(*b.*) For use in all weathers as helm-signals only.
    For steamers meeting or crossing.
    For steamers overtaking.
    For steamers backing.
(*c.*) Whether helm-signals shall be made compulsory or remain optional.

3. Steering and sailing rules:—

(*a.*) Sailing-vessels meeting, crossing, overtaking, or being overtaken by each other.
(*b.*) Steamers meeting, crossing, overtaking, or being overtaken by each other.

(c.) Sailing-vessels meeting, crossing, overtaking, or being overtaken by steamers.
(d.) Steamers meeting, crossing, overtaking, or being overtaken by sailing-vessels.
(e.) Special Rules for channels and tide-ways, where no local Rules exist.
(f.) Conflict of international and local Rules.
(g.) Uniform system of commands to the helm.
(h.) Speed of vessels in thick weather.

General Division II

Regulations to determine the Seaworthiness of Vessels.

(a.) Construction of vessels.
(b.) Equipment of vessels.
(c.) Discipline of crew.
(d.) Sufficiency of crew
(e.) Inspection of vessels.
(f.) Uniform certificates of inspection.

General Division III.

Draught to which Vessels should be restricted when loaded.

Uniform maximum load mark.

General Division IV.

Uniform Regulations regarding the Designating and Marking of Vessels.

(a.) Position of name on vessels.
(b.) Position of name of port of registry on vessels.
(c.) Size of lettering.
(d.) Uniform system of draught marks.

General Division V.

Saving Life and Property from Shipwreck.

1. Saving of life and property from shipwreck at sea:—

(a.) Duties of vessels after collision.
(b.) Apparatus for life-saving to be carried on board ship. (Life-boats, life-preservers, life-rafts, pumps, and fire-extinguishing apparatus.)
(c.) The use of oil and the necessary apparatus for its use.
(d.) Uniform inspections as to (b) and (c).

2. Saving of life and property from shipwreck by operations from shore:—

(a.) Organization of, and methods employed by, life-saving institutions.
(b.) The employment of drilled and disciplined crews at life-saving stations.
(c.) The maintenance of a patrol upon dangerous coasts by night, and during thick weather by day, for warning off vessels standing into danger, and for the early discovery of wrecks.
(d.) Uniform means of transmitting information between stranded vessels and the shore.
(e.) Life-boats, life-saving apparatus and appliances.

3. Official inquiries into causes and circumstances of shipwrecks and other casualties.

General Division VI.

Necessary Qualifications for Officers and Seamen, including Tests for Sight and Colour-Blindness.

(a.) A uniform system of examination for the different grades.
(b.) Uniform tests for visual power and colour-blindness.
(c.) General knowledge of methods employed at life-saving stations.
(d.) Uniform certificates of qualification.

General Division VII.

Lanes for Steamers on frequented Routes.

(a.) With regard to the avoidance of steamer collisions.
(b.) With regard to the safety of fishermen.

4

General Division VIII.

Night Signals for communicating Information at Sea.

(*a.*) A Code to be used in connection with the International Code Signal Book.
(*b.*) Or a supplementary Code of limited scope to convey information of special importance to passing vessels.
(*c.*) Distress signals.

General Division IX.

Warnings of approaching Storms.

(*a.*) The transmission of warnings.
(*b.*) The uniformity of signals employed.

General Division X.

Reporting, marking, and removing Dangerous Wrecks or Obstructions to Navigation.

(*a.*) A uniform method of reporting and marking dangerous wrecks and derelicts.
(*b.*) The division of the labour, cost, and responsibility among the several maritime nations, either by geographical apportionment or otherwise—
Of the removal of dangerous derelicts;
And of searching for doubtful dangers, with a view of removing them from the Charts.

General Division XI.

Notice of Dangers to Navigation.—Notice of Changes in Lights, Buoys, and other Day and Night Marks.

(*a.*) A uniform method of taking bearings, of designating them (whether true or magnetic), and of reporting them.
(*b.*) A uniform method of reporting, indicating, and exchanging information by the several maritime nations—to include the form of Notices to Mariners.
(*c.*) A uniform method of distributing this information.

General Division XII.

A uniform System of Buoys and Beacons.

(*a.*) Uniformity in colour of buoys.
(*b.*) Uniformity in numbering of buoys.

General Division XIII.

The Establishment of a Permanent International Maritime Commission.

(*a.*) The composition of the Commission.
(*b.*) Its powers and authority.

Proposed Grouping of Subjects for consideration by Committees of the International Marine Conference.

1. Rules of the Road and signals—General Divisions I and VIII.
2. Saving of life and property from shipwreck by operations from shore—General Division V subdivision No. 2.
3. Construction and equipment of vessels, and saving of life and property from shipwreck at sea—General Divisions II, III, and IV, and subdivision No. 1 of V.
4. Qualifications of officers and seamen—General Division VI.
5. Steam lanes—General Division VII.
6. Official inquiries into shipwrecks and other casualties—General Division V, subdivision No. 3.

7. Transmission of warnings and information, buoys, &c.—General Divisions XI, X, XI, and XII.
8. Permanent Maritime Commission—General Division XIII.

All of which is respectfully submitted.

(Signed)   S. R. FRANKLIN, *Rear-Admiral.*
W. P. SAMPSON, *Commander, United States' Navy.*
S. I. KIMBALL, *General Superintendent, Life-Saving Service.*
JAS. W. NORCROSS, *Master Mariner.*
JOHN W. SHACKFORD, *Master, Merchant Marine.*
WILLIAM W. GOODRICH, *Counsellor-at-Law.*

Washington, Monday, December 2, 1889, 11 o'clock A.M,

THE Conference was called to order at 11 o'clock A.M., Rear-Admiral Franklin in the Chair.

The President.—The first business in order this morning will be the Reports of Committees. If there are no Reports to be made, the next order of business will be extra amendment No. 59. The Secretary will please read extra amendment No. 59.

The amendment is as follows:—

"All steamers under way may carry an additional white light, similar to the present light mentioned in Article 3 (*a*). These lights must be so placed in line with the keel that one must be at least 20 feet higher than the other, and should be in such a position with reference to each other that the lower light should be forward of the upper one, and for a vertical distance of 20 feet between them, there should be a horizontal distance of 30 feet, or in the proportion of 2 to 3, as near as practicable."

Captain Shackford (United States).—Mr. President, I find that there is some opposition to this proposed amendment among the Delegates, and I would like to have permission to change the amendment, in the manner in which I have it drawn up here.

The President.—The Secretary will please read the amendment as changed.

The amendment as changed is as follows:—

"All steamers under way may carry an additional white light, similar to the light mentioned in Article 3 (*a*). These lights must be so placed in line with the keel that one must be at least 15 feet higher than the other, and should be in such a position with reference to each other that the lower light shall be forward of the upper one. The vertical distance between these lights must be less than the horizontal distance."

Mr. Hall (Great Britain).—Mr. President, we understand the reasons for altering this amendment, and on behalf of my colleagues and myself we give our hearty support to this proposition. There were difficulties in the way of dealing with the amendment as it had been carried originally by the Conference; but now these difficulties appear to be surmounted; and, having regard to the evidence which has been given to us of the great use of range-lights in American waters, we cordially support the proposal that range-lights should be tried not only in American waters, but in all waters. Upon these grounds, we beg to support the amendment which is now before the Conference.

Captain Shackford (United States).—Mr. President, the amendment as it is at present has also the cordial indorsement of the Delegate from Germany, Captain Mensing, who I see is not present this morning.

The President.—If there be no objection to substituting the last proposed amendment of the Delegate from the United States, it will be considered the amendment which is now before the Conference. There seems to be no objection to the substitution, and the question will be upon the substituted amendment.

The question was put to the Conference upon the adoption of the substitute for amendment No. 59, proposed by the Delegate from the United States, and the substituted amendment was carried.

The President.—Extra amendment No. 60 is next in order. The Secretary will please read it.

Extra amendment No. 60 is as follows:—

"All vessels under way shall keep out of the way of coupled steamers engaged in trawling."

Captain Varela de Torres (Spain).—Mr. President, as Lieutenant Vega de Seoane is not here, I want to support this amendment, and I think that it will be scarcely necessary for me to say more than a few words in regard to it. Every man who has been at sea knows perfectly well that it is impossible for two steamers which are coupled together and are trawling to keep out of the way of other vessels; and on that account we think that these steamers must be treated as ships which cannot get out of the way. For that reason I think that such steamers as are described in this amendment should have the same privilege as a sailing-ship.

Mr. Goodrich (United States).—Mr. President, I think we have fully disposed of the subject of giving these vessels the right of way, and I think the Conference has practically settled this question. Of course, it is well to have discussion upon it if it is deemed desirable to have the matter brought up again before the Conference, but, as I understand it, that subject has been practically disposed of under the amendment of Dr. Sieveking. My idea is that the simple fact that steamers are coupled together makes no difference. It is reversing the whole Rule of the Road to compel a sailing-vessel to keep out of the way of a steamer.

Mr. Hall (Great Britain).—Mr. President, I quite agree with the learned Delegate from the United States that if we were to adopt this amendment we should be reversing completely the Rule of the Road at Sea, that a steamer should keep out of the way of a sailing-vessel. If a steamer chooses to couple herself for the purpose of trawling, let her do it and take the responsibility and inconvenience of it; then, if it be necessary, she must let go of the trawl to keep out of the way. I do not think we can possibly say that a sailing-vessel should keep out of the way of steamers when they are coupled together. As I say, it would be a very strong reversal of the ordinary principles. I am certain that the honourable Delegate will see himself that if we should adopt this amendment it would open the doors to making very great alterations in what is the accepted principle of the Rules of the Road at Sea, that steamers must keep out of the way of sailing-vessels.

The President.—The question is upon the amendment of the Delegate from Spain.

Mr. Hall (Great Britain).—Mr. President, perhaps I may point out that we refused to give this concession to steamers towing, and there are far more cases of steamers towing than of steamers trawling. The Conference decided by an overwhelming decision that they would not give such a privilege to a vessel towing.

The President.—Is the Conference ready for the question? The amendment will be read again. The amendment is as follows:—

"All vessels under way shall keep out of the way of coupled steamers engaged in trawling."

The President.—Is the Conference ready for the question?

The question was put to the Conference upon the adoption of extra amendment No. 60, and it was lost.

The President.—The next business in order is the new section proposed by the Delegate from the United States. It will be read.

The proposed new section is as follows:—

"In every case of collision between two vessels it shall be the duty of the master or person in charge of each vessel, if and so far as he can do so without danger to his own vessel, crew, and passengers (if any), to stay by the other vessel until he has ascertained that she has no need of further assistance, and to render to the other vessel, her master, crew, and passengers (if any), such assistance as may be practicable and as may be necessary in order to save them from any danger caused by the collision, and also to give to the master or person in charge of the other vessel the name of his own vessel and her port of registry, or the port or place to which she belongs, and also the name of the ports and places from which or to which she is bound. If he fails to do so, and no reasonable cause for such failure is shown, the collision shall, in the absence of proof to the contrary, be deemed to have been caused by his wrongful act, neglect, or default."

Mr. Kimball (United States).—Mr. President, this matter has been dealt with by the Committee on Life-Saving Systems and Devices, and I would suggest that it might be well to await the Report of that Committee before taking action upon it.

Mr. Goodrich (United States).—Mr. President, I have no objection to that. I call the attention of the Delegates to the fact that in the fourth line from the bottom the word "or" should be "and," so that it would read, "and also the name of the ports and places from which and to which she is bound." May I ask the Chairman of the Committee on Life-Saving Systems and Devices when the Report will be ready?

Mr. Kimball (United States).—It is now nearly ready to hand to the printer.

Mr. Goodrich (United States).—Mr. President, if the Chairman of that Committee desires to have this matter laid over, of course it should be done at once.

Mr. Kimball (United States).—I think my colleagues on the Committee would like to have it laid over.

Mr. Goodrich (United States).—I have no objection to that.

The President.—Does the Delegate for the United States desire to have the consideration of this matter withheld until the Report of that Committee?

Mr. Goodrich (United States).—Mr. President, the only possible reason that would be adverse to such a concession is that the Collocation Committee wants to lay the result of their work before the Conference, and any unpassed or unconsidered Rule delays that work just so much. Of course, if the Committee ask it we will have it lie over.

Mr. Kimball (United States).—I will say that the Committee approves of it with the exception of the last sentence. The Committee does not approve of the principle contained in the last sentence, and it states its reasons.

The President.—If there is no objection, the consideration of this section will be laid over for future consideration.

Mr. Hall (Great Britain).—Mr. President, I think there is great objection; because, as has been pointed out by the learned Delegate of the United States, it prevents the Collocation Committee from going on and completing their Rules, and laying them before the Conference. I am very glad to hear from the honourable Delegate of the United States that the principle of this amendment is to be reported on favourably by the Committee of which he forms so distinguished a member; that is, the amendment with the exception of the last four lines. I take it that—and I only speak from what I hear—there may be objection to the last four lines of this amendment. Of course, my colleagues and I will support this amendment in its entirety, because it is what the law is in England at the present time, and we should be very glad to see it made an international law if possible; but, at the same time,

I think we might possibly accept the amendment with the exception of the last four lines, if the learned Delegate for the United States thinks that would be desirable. Of course, this is a matter entirely for him to consider. But if we could practically test the principle, then I think we ought to do so without much loss of time, so that we shall be in a position to print the Rules as amended.

Mr. Goodrich (United States).—Mr. President, I have taken this amendment from the Statute of the 36th & 37th Vict., and it is, or is intended to be, in the exact words of that Statute, leaving out the penal clause which subjects the master who disobeys these laws to a penalty or punishment for a misdemeanour, that, of course, being a matter which must be dealt with by the several Powers which adopt the Report of this Conference. But it seems to me that, in the absence of that provision, it would be folly to leave out the punishment which is implied, and which results from the last few lines of this amendment. Therein lies the power of compelling obedience to the first part of it. The first part of the amendment simply says that the master shall stop, and the second contains the only punishment which the Rules can inflict, namely, that if he fails to obey the Rule, and no reasonable cause for such failure is shown, the collision shall, in the absence of proof to the contrary, be deemed to have been caused by his own wrongful acts. I do not think it is desirable to discuss this until we hear from the Committee.

Captain Richard (France).—Mr. President, I have two objections to the proposition of the Honourable Mr. Goodrich. The first is, it is not wise to introduce such a provision into the Rules themselves, of which it should not form a part. The second, the merits of which I will discuss when the proper time arrives, will be to ask the Conference to leave out the last four lines of the amendment as being not a proper subject for an international agreement. I will briefly examine, from this double standpoint, the wisdom of sending this amendment back when the Report of the Committee on Division V shall come up for discussion, and I will state that the necessity of so sending it back is self-evident, for the following reason :—

In France the Rules of the Road are simply directions for the guidance of navigators, and outside of cases of collision, of running aground, or of damage, in order to reach the captains who have infringed or neglected to observe these Rules, our legislation is obliged to resort to Article 471 of our Penal Code, which punishes with a fine of from 1 to 5 fr. those who offend against the Rules legally promulgated by the proper authority. Is that desirable or sufficient? Instead of an administrative Regulation, a Law should be demanded to prevent a repetition of such an offence, and in order to obtain such a Law it is necessary that the amendment should not be introduced into the Rules of the Road, but set forth in a special Report. I therefore think that we should be very careful not to insert this proposition into directions which are no doubt very important, but the non-observance of which is followed by punishment only in exceptional cases.

I would also ask you to omit the last phrase of the proposition, which, in our mind, is irreconcilable with strict justice.

It is evident that two distinct wrongs are confounded—collision, and the crime of inhumanity which is committed by speeding away after the collision and abandoning the vessel which requires assistance; because a captain is guilty of inhumanity he should not therefore be rendered responsible for the collision.

You should, therefore, leave to the Committee, which has maturely considered this question, the care of presenting their proposition, which, having been formulated by the Committee unanimously, may very probably be accepted by everybody.

Captain Mensing (Germany).—Mr. President, we have in Germany, as in Great Britain, a Law by which those persons who leave a ship in distress without rendering proper assistance can be punished. In this Law the last sentence of this amendment is not contained, although the rest of the Law is virtually the same as that which is in force in Great Britain. That points to the fact that the German Government thinks that the provision contained in the last sentence of the amendment is not acceptable. I believe, on that ground, that the German Government would not be in a position to accept the amendment as it is proposed here. One difficulty has been mentioned by the gallant Delegate from France, that there is a penalty inflicted by this Law in the Rules of the Road at Sea. I believe that it would be the best for everybody concerned if, as the gallant Delegate from France has suggested, this Law were not to be incorporated in the Rules of the Road; but it might be adopted as a principle to be called to the attention of the different Powers by the Report which we are expecting from the Life-Saving Committee.

Mr. Goodrich (United States).—Mr. President, I formally move that this matter be laid over until the coming in of the Report of the Committee on Life-Saving Systems and Devices, in order that we may have all the material before us necessary to a proper understanding of the arguments in favour of and against the proposition. I have thus far presented no argument in favour of it, which, of course, I should like to do in due season. I think, however, it will not be best to take up the time of the Conference to-day, as the suggestion has been made that it should be postponed until we hear further from the Committee on Life-Saving Systems and Devices.

The President.—It is moved that this subject be laid over until the Report of the Committee on Life-Saving Systems and Devices is received.

The question was put to the Conference upon the postponement of the new section proposed by the Delegate from the United States, and the further consideration of the subject was postponed.

The President.—The next business in order will be the Additional Report of the Committee on Sound-Signals. The Secretary will please read the Report of this Committee by sections. The Secretary will now read the first section of the Report.

The first section of the Report of the Committee on Sound-Signals is as follows :—

" Sir, " *Washington, November* 21, 1889.

" Agreeably with the reference of the Conference on November 8, for the Committee on Sound-Signals to consider and report the specific cases in which new fog-signals should be adopted, and to report specific signals for such cases, we beg to submit that in the opinion of the Committee it is desirable to adopt the sound-signals mentioned in the following Report for compulsory or permissive use as advised.

"To Rear-Admiral S. R. Franklin, United States' Navy,
"President of the International Marine Conference, &c."

Mr. Hall (Great Britain).—Mr. President, I think we might dispense with the reading of the preliminary part of the Report, because I think that all of us have read this very carefully before, several times. I would suggest, if it be agreeable to the Conference, that it be taken up at the middle of p. 4, where it says, "In accordance with our recommendations as above, we suggest, for the consideration of the Conference, the following readings of the Articles in the Regulations." I would suggest to the Conference whether it would not be a saving of time to begin at that paragraph.

The President.—If there be no objection, the course suggested by the Delegate from Great Britain will be pursued. The Secretary will please read the first paragraph, which is the addition to Article 9.

Addition to Article 9 is as follows:—

"A pilot-vessel wishing to attract attention may sound on her fog-horn, whistle, or siren three blasts, viz., short, short, long, with intervals of about one second between them."

Mr. Hall (Great Britain).—Mr. President, as the Conference has now determined to relegate the question of pilot-signals to the International Code-Signal Committee, and not to embody them in the Rules for preventing Collisions at Sea, I move that this addition to Article 9 be not inserted in the Rules for preventing Collisions at Sea. This is not because we think for one moment that the Committee which has made this valuable Report has not chosen the best signal which could be adopted for the purpose, but it is solely because of the decision of the Conference that the question of signals for pilots is not a proper matter to be inserted in the Rules for preventing Collisions at Sea. That there should be such a signal as this, and that it will find its way into the International Code-Signal Book, I have no doubt whatever; but at the present time I would move, having regard to the previous decision of the Conference, that this Article be not added to the Rules for preventing Collisions at Sea, the Conference having determined not to include pilot-signals in the Rules.

Admiral Nares (Great Britain).—Mr. President, before that is fully discussed I should like to say, on the part of the Sound-Signal Committee, that we first came to the conclusion that it was very desirable that a pilot should have a signal, so that he could make himself known in a fog when another vessel was not in sight. We also thought that a vessel wanting a pilot should be able to sound a signal if a pilot-vessel was not in sight. The reason why we put a communication signal of this kind into our Report is because the reference was to include all signals, which we would advise the Conference to allow on these occasions. Of course, whether or not such a signal is to come under the Rules of the Road is for the Conference to determine. Before that is decided upon, I would allude to the character which we have chosen for this signal, that is quite apart from the question as to whether this signal should be included in the Rules of the Road for preventing Collisions at Sea. If the Conference decide that there should be a signal for pilot-boats and a signal for vessels wanting a pilot, then we have done our duty.

It has come to my knowledge that the Signal Committee is dealing not only with the light-signals, but with sound-signals; and that this Committee has also considered this question, so that, in fact, two Committees which you have appointed are rather mixing with each other. Before their Report is handed in I would suggest that the two Committees might be amalgamated for the one purpose of choosing the best character for the several signals which they are about to propose to the Conference. It so happens that the Sound-Signal Committee have chosen the most simple signals of the characters that were left to their choice, and the other Committee are also looking about for the most simple signal to indicate to another ship: "You are standing into danger." We have both chosen the same signal, and I am quite certain we will not delay the Conference half-an-hour could the two Committees get together. If you will allow that plan, I am sure the Sound-Signal Committee will be most happy to put themselves under the Chairman of the other Signal Committee and talk the matter over. I will, therefore, ask you to allow the Sound-Signal Committee to reconsider this character for the signals.

There is one more subject to which I desire to call attention. We were so hard up for simple sound-signals, which is a very important matter, that we came to the conclusion that not only the pilot-boats, but the ship wanting the pilot, should make the same signal. When we talk this matter over with our other friends we can hit upon some signal, perhaps, which is separate, because there is no doubt that if we can do so it is desirable. Therefore, I should like that the Sound-Signal Committee might be permitted to reconsider this subject with the other Committee.

Mr. Hall (Great Britain).—Mr. President, perhaps I might put myself in order by moving, formally, that all signals by and to pilot-vessels be relegated to Committee No. 2, and that they be requested to confer with the Sound-Signal Committee upon that matter. I have no doubt they will be glad of the assistance, and with the combined efforts of these two Committees we ought to get a harmonious scheme of signals which would be satisfactory.

Captain Mensing (Germany).—Mr. President, I cannot fully agree with the gentleman who spoke before me. I believe that this should be discussed in the Conference, because the proposals made in regard to pilot-vessels and vessels requiring a pilot are, according to my idea, wrong in principle. I believe it is wrong in principle to give the same signal to a pilot-vessel and to a vessel requiring a pilot. Take into consideration, for an instant, the condition of things which would be brought about by the adoption of this Rule at the mouths of a number of rivers on the coast of the Netherlands and on the coast of Germany, at the Rivers Jade, Weser, Elbe, and Eider. On the coast we have four rivers or estuaries, where there are a number of vessels, steamers, and sailing-vessels—for there is an enormous traffic—which would be daily requiring pilots. Then there would be the same sounds or the same sound-signals over this whole region. In the one case, when the pilot gives the signal, it will signify, I am here and trying to reach you; I will get to you as soon as I can, because I want to put my pilot on board. In the other case, it will not only ask the pilot to come near you, but it will be a warning to other ships to get as far away as possible from you, since you are a source of danger. Therefore, the signal would mean in the two cases exactly opposite things. There is another reason which makes it doubtful whether we can adopt this Rule. If you will be kind enough to look at p. 2 of this Report, in the fourth paragraph from the bottom it says:—

"One, two, or three sound-blasts on a fog-horn are already in use by sailing-vessels under way. It is not laid down what the length of these blasts should be, but by the construction of the fog-horns used in the past, they are necessarily blasts of equal duration. We submit that they should be so regulated, and termed 'short blasts.'"

As I understand this—and I beg to be corrected if I am wrong—the Committee on Sound-Signals state distinctly that these sound-signals are now in use on sailing-vessels; that they make blasts of equal duration, and that they are short blasts. Now, if you introduce a single long blast, all the instruments, or by far the greater part of the sound-signal instruments, in use at present must become obsolete, and must be replaced by modern ones, able to give a short and long blast, exactly as they like, because otherwise this recommendation could not be carried out.

Now, the question with me is whether, if this signal deals with one class of ships, say, for instance, pilot-vessels, it would be possible to introduce a signal which is already in use in the Thames for an entirely different purpose—that is, a signal of four short blasts. The Committee on Sound-Signals have so strongly recommended the use of signals consisting of only short or long blasts that I, with all the respect which is due to the Report presented by such an eminent Committee, find it rather difficult to reconcile the two positions taken in the Report. In one place it is recommended to make blasts of equal duration, and in another place a short and a long blast are introduced. I believe that there is no other satisfactory means of multiplying these fog-signals than by the adoption of signals composed of long and short notes; but I believe that, before we begin with them, we ought to adopt all the possible combinations which may be made by using blasts of equal duration.

Captain Malmberg (Sweden).—Mr. President, I only want to ask whether or not it is a happy thought to provide the same signal for a pilot-boat and a ship wanting a pilot. A ship may be in want of a pilot and hear the signal, and thinking that she will find a pilot-boat, she will suddenly find herself alongside of another vessel of which she ought to keep out of the way.

Admiral Nares (Great Britain).—Mr. President, I have pointed out the difficulties in which the Sound-Signal Committee were placed, which required us to give the same signals to two vessels, the pilot-vessel and the vessel wanting a pilot. I think that, when we meet together in the two Committees, we can get over the difficulty with regard to that which is pointed out by the gallant Delegate from Germany. If you will look at the top of p. 2, the first principle adopted by the Sound-Signal Committee informs you that efficient mechanical fog-horns, capable of producing sounds of varying duration, are increasing in numbers on both sailing and fishing vessels. As I told you just now, we were so very hard-up for characters—and you will see how hard-up we were presently, when we come to discuss the signals which we have chosen for towing-vessels—that we were compelled to provide this signal as given in the Report. The signal provided for towing-vessels is a complicated one, and we were at our wits' end so long as we could only deal with single sounds. We have endeavoured to point out very clearly to the Conference the trouble we were in, and still we had to give character to the signals. To complete the character, as I said before, we could only adopt one signal for a pilot-vessel and for a vessel in want of a pilot.

I may say that the gentlemen sent by the Canadian authorities to give us information, and the gentlemen who came to give evidence from the pilots, both agreed that mechanical fog-horns capable of producing sounds of varying duration are increasing in numbers on board both sailing and fishing vessels. On that statement you may be sure that in a very few years the old single fog-horns, which only gave a single blast, will be gone, and you will have capable and efficient fog-horns on board of the ships; and if you agree to our signal of different sounds, long and short, you may depend upon it that before your Rules are promulgated these fog-horns will be used entirely. Now, arguing upon that statement, we have ventured to propose this signal. There are two signals in which we have given you different blasts, and that is the pilot-signal and a steam-vessel which is stopped, which will come up presently under Article 12. If the Conference will agree that the pilots must have a signal to be made when they cannot see another vessel, and if the Conference will agree that a steamer, when she cannot see a pilot-vessel, must have a signal, I have no doubt that we shall be able to lay two good and unmistakable characters before the Conference.

Mr. Goodrich (United States).—Mr. President, I have no desire to shut off discussion on an important principle like this, but I venture to call the attention of the President and members of the Conference to the fact that we are not discussing the Resolution of the learned Delegate from Great Britain, which was simply a question of reference, but we are consuming time which is going to be quite valuable, in view of the wishes of the Delegates to finish the Conference, which time will have to be used again when we come to discuss the Reports of the Committees as they shall be presented. So I venture to suggest that we had better take a vote on the proposition to refer this to the Committee, and unless some Delegate desires to speak upon that, I suggest that it had better be referred.

Mr. Hall (Great Britain).—Mr. President, I do not at all regret the discussion which has taken place, because of its very valuable bearing upon the principles which have been dealt with in this Report. In accordance with what has been stated by the Delegate from the United States I would point out that the question before the Conference is a very simple one. We have agreed that signals for pilots are not to come under the Rules of the Road at Sea. If so, why should sound-signals for pilots come into the Rules? We shall simply stultify ourselves and be reversing the action which we have previously taken if we put into the Rules anything about sound-signals for pilots. My sole object is to refer the question of signals for pilots to the Committee on General Division No. VIII.

Captain Mensing (Germany).—Mr. President, I think that this discussion should not be passed over in the Conference, because there is one point, upon which I have already touched, which, it seems to me, would make it most desirable that we should come to some sort of an understanding before we introduce these fog-horns, making long blasts and short blasts. In the present Rules, as we have passed them, it is required that they should only make one sound, and it is called an efficient sound-signal. Now, if we introduce here a signal which requires the instrument to be able to make short blasts and long blasts, then the other Article must be altered, according to my opinion. I wish to state that on principle I have nothing to say against the adoption of such a Rule as has been proposed, if there be a distinct signal for the pilot and another one for the vessel wanting a pilot.

The President.—The question now is upon the reference to Committee No. 2 upon General Division No. VIII. The Delegate for Great Britain moves that the sound-signals for pilot vessels be relegated to Committee No. 2 upon General Division No. VIII, with a request to that Committee to confer with the Sound-Signal Committee in choosing such signals. Is the Conference ready for the question?

Mr. Hall (Great Britain).—Mr. President, may I point out, that it may be clearly understood, that my motion is not merely to refer it. The word I used was "relegated," because we have decided that pilot-signals should not form a part of the Rules of the Road at Sea, as it was a matter for Committee No. 2 to deal with. If we use the word "refer" it will appear as if we ask them to report to us, and we shall have to deal with that Report. I want it to appear that the opinion of the Conference is that this question as to sound-signals has nothing whatever to do with the Rules of the Road at Sea, but that it is a matter to be dealt with by Committee No. 2 upon General Division No. VIII of the Programme.

Captain Salvesen (Norway).—Mr. President, I would like to know when the Rule was passed that these pilot-signals should not come into the Rules of the Road. It was ruled by the Conference that these pilot-signals should make a part of the Rules. Some days afterwards the learned Delegate of Great Britain asked permission from the gallant Delegate of the Netherlands to refer it to an International Code Signal Committee, but I do not think that such permission to refer it to this Committee alters the fact that the Conference has decided that these pilot-signals shall make a part of the Rules of the Road at Sea.

Mr. Hall (Great Britain).—Mr. President, I am speaking merely from memory, but I think it was on the last day we met that I pointed out the extreme undesirability of including pilot-signals in the Rules of the Road at Sea, and it was agreed that the pilot-signals and the Rules which had been actually adopted should be withdrawn. I think it was the Delegate who introduced them originally who agreed that this should be done, and it was done without any objection. I pointed out at that time the extreme undesirability of having pilot-signals in the Rules of the Road at Sea. If we include them in the Rules of the Road we might just as well have the whole international code signals incorporated into them.

Mr. Goodrich (United States).—Mr. President, I have it marked on my memorandum here, which may be a guidance, "Referred to the International Code Committee on General Divisions Nos. VII and VIII," which is Committee No. 2. I think that was done upon the motion of the Delegate from Great Britain.

Captain Hubert (the Netherlands).— Mr. President, the sound-signal for pilots was not mentioned in the amendment.

Captain Malmberg (Sweden).—Mr. President, I should like to be informed if there were ever proposed to the Conference any fog-signals to be made between pilot-vessels and vessels wanting a pilot. So far as I can remember, there has never been laid before the Conference any such proposition except what we find in this Report from the Committee on Sound-Signals.

Mr. Hall (Great Britain).—Mr. President, I am sorry that the Protocol of the last day is not yet put into the hands of the Delegates. I have a vivid recollection of what occurred, and it is confirmed by the note of the learned Delegate of the United States. If there is any doubt upon the matter at all, I am perfectly willing to move a substantive Resolution that it is undesirable, in the opinion of this Conference, that any signal, sound or otherwise, for or to pilots, be included in the Rules of the Road at Sea. I think that will clear up all possible doubt. I do not think it is necessary for me to occupy the time of the Conference with regard to this proposal. I think that originally the amendment with regard to the pilot-signals only crept in because the Delegates who proposed them, seeing the distress signals in, thought there might be no objection to putting in pilot-signals. If we put in the pilot-signals where are we to stop? Why should we not put in the other signals? Why should we not put in the whole International Code of Signals? I cannot see what the pilot-signals have to do with the Rules of the Road at Sea any more than any other signals. Perhaps it will be desirable, in order to clear the way, that I should move a substantive Resolution: "That this Conference is of opinion that it is undesirable to include, in the Rules of the Road for preventing Collisions at Sea, signals, sound or otherwise, for or to pilot-vessels."

The President.—The Secretary will please read the Resolution of the Delegate from Great Britain.

The Resolution is as follows:—

"*Resolved,*—That in the opinion of this Conference it is undesirable to include, in the Rules for preventing Collisions at Sea, signals, sound or otherwise, for or to pilot-vessels."

The President.—Is the Conference ready for the question on the Resolution of the Delegate from Great Britain?

11

The question was put to the Conference upon the Resolution of the Delegate from Great Britain, and the Resolution was adopted.

The President.—The question now is upon the proposition of the Delegate from Great Britain to relegate the subject of sound-signals to be made by or to pilot-vessels to Committee No. 2 upon General Division No. VIII of the Programme, with a request to that Committee to confer with the Sound-Signal Committee with regard to such signals.

Mr. Carter (Hawaii).—Mr. President, I was under the impression that had passed the Conference.

The President.—That Resolution had not been passed when the other Resolution was offered by the Delegate from Great Britain. It is now before the Conference.

Mr. Goodrich (United States).—It was passed, Mr. President, with the word "reference" in it.

The President.—The Chair read the word "relegated."

The question was thereupon put to the Conference upon the adoption of the Resolution of the Delegate from Great Britain, and it was adopted.

The President.—The Secretary will please read Article 10.

Article 10, paragraph (*a*), is as follows:—

"(*a*.) In fog, mist, falling snow, or heavy rain-storms, a drift-net vessel attached to her nets, and a vessel when trawling, dredging, or fishing with any kind of drag-net, and a vessel employed in line-fishing with her lines out, shall, at intervals of not more than two minutes, make a blast with her fog-horn, followed by ringing her bell."

Admiral Nares (Great Britain).—Mr. President, may I say, with regard to that signal, that the old Rule in Great Britain, under Article 10, is that such a vessel makes a blast on her fog-horn and rings her bell alternately? There has been some doubt as to whether the two-minute signal is to be a fog-horn, and two minutes afterwards the bell, and two minutes after that the fog-horn, and two minutes after that the bell, or whether it is to be a one-minute interval between them. To get over that doubt, the wording has been altered so as to read: "At intervals of not more than two minutes, make a blast with her fog-horn, followed by ringing her bell." So that, practically, every two minutes there would be a signal on the fog-horn and the bell.

Captain Mensing (Germany).—Mr. President, on p. 4, paragraph 2, the Committee express as their opinion on Article 12—

"We are of opinion that Article 12, prescribing what sound-signal apparatus should be carried by vessels, should be limited to vessels above 20 tons gross tonnage, smaller sailing-vessels and boats being allowed to make any efficient sound-signal."

This is referred to under Article 12 on p. 5 again, and will have to be discussed there. But I would like to call to the attention of the Conference the fact that, if this signal should be adopted, it would not be applicable at all to any vessel which is below 20 tons gross tonnage. It says: "Shall at intervals of not more than two minutes make a blast on her fog-horn, followed by ringing her bell." Now, as I read it, I am clearly of the opinion that under Article 12 small vessels would be allowed to make any efficient sound-signal. They might take a tea-kettle and beat upon it with a belaying-pin or anything else and make a kind of a noise. In a fishing-boat, then, that would take the place of the fog-horn and of the bell. If that be the case under Article 10, there can be only one signal given by the smaller fishing-vessels, which, I presume, are more numerous than those above the size of 20 tons gross tonnage. I desire to call the attention of the Conference to this, and to ask whether they think it desirable that such should be the case. A sailing-vessel cannot, even if she is properly equipped, according to these Regulations, follow the Rules laid down in this Article, because she has not two sound-signal apparatuses, but only one.

Admiral Nares (Great Britain).—Mr. President, the point which my gallant friend has just touched upon came up before the Committee, and they have provided for it on p. 5, which will come up presently under Article 12. Of course if Article 10 is to be reworded to allude only to vessels above 20 tons, that must be done; but we do not see the reason for it. We have provided for sailing-vessels and boats, which, of course, will include fishing-boats of less than 20 tons. Steam-vessels of that class must always have a whistle, and there is no reason why they should not sound it. As for a sailing-vessel, which is not obliged to carry a whistle, let her carry the belaying-pin and frying-pan. When we come to deal with a vessel, no matter how small she is, which is anchored in a fairway, we provide that she must sound a bell, and must have a bell on board to sound; and if she has no bell, she has no business to anchor in a fairway.

The President.—The question before the Conference is upon Article 10, paragraph (*a*).

Captain Richard (France).—Mr. President, I desire to submit to the Conference an objection to Article 10, in which I see that the old wording has been retained which orders the blowing of a horn and the ringing of a bell at intervals of two minutes. I cannot explain this provision. It was decided that steam-vessels under way shall blow their whistles at much shorter intervals (one minute instead of two) when they were under way in a fog, mist, or falling snow. This you decided, although the steam-whistles or sirens, when compared with the fog-horn and the bell, are very powerful instruments of sound. For the vessels which we are now discussing, whose bells and fog-horns can often not be heard beyond a few yards, the interval formerly adopted is retained.

It is my opinion that inasmuch as the noise of their sound-signals is carried a much shorter distance, and the speed of vessels with which it is possible for them to collide daily becomes greater—it seems to me that the necessity of repeating the sound-signals at minute intervals is even greater than in that of a vessel under way.

Mr. Hall (Great Britain).—Mr. President, the gallant Delegate from France has pointed out what is evidently, I think, an oversight, and that is, that the Committee have not adopted a principle which the Conference passed, that sailing-vessels should give a blast on the fog-horn at intervals of one minute, and not two minutes. I have no doubt that the Committee will agree that it is desirable that we should adopt that principle here and make this provision for intervals of one minute instead of two minutes.

Admiral Nares (Great Britain).—Mr. President, I am sorry to say that that is an oversight. It was taken down from the old Rule of the Road, and we have neglected to alter the word "two" into the word "one," in agreement with the decision of the Conference.

The President.—The oversight of the Committee will be corrected, and it will now read: "At intervals of not more than one minute make a blast with her fog-horn, followed by ringing her bell."

The President.—Is the Conference ready for the question? The paragraph will be read again.

Article 10, paragraph (*a*), is as follows:—

"(*a*.) In fog, mist, falling snow, or heavy rain-storms, a drift-net vessel attached to her nets, and a vessel when trawling, dredging, or fishing with any kind of drag-net, and a vessel employed in line-fishing with her lines out, shall, at intervals of not more than one minute, make a blast with her fog-horn, followed by ringing her bell."

The question was put to the Conference upon the adoption of Article 10, paragraph (*a*), and it was adopted.

Captain Mensing (Germany).—Mr. President, there is no alteration in Article 12, except as to the note.

Mr. Goodrich (United States).—Mr. President, there is another alteration to which I desire to call the attention of the gentlemen, and that is that the Committee has left out, purposely, I believe, the word "bellows." If the Conference will look at the original Rule you will find on the third line that the old Rule has it "to be sounded by a bellows or other means," if my memory serves me right.

Admiral Nares (Great Britain).—Mr. President, after the Rule is read I will explain what the intention of the Committee was.

The President.—Article 12 will be read.

Article 12 is as follows:—

"Article 12. A steam-ship shall be provided with a whistle or siren, sounded by steam or other efficient substitute for steam, so placed that the sound may not be intercepted by any obstructions, and with an efficient fog-horn to be sounded by mechanical means, and also with an efficient bell. A sailing-vessel of 20 tons gross tonnage and upwards shall be provided with a similar fog-horn and bell.

"NOTE.—In all cases where the Regulations require a bell to be used a drum will be substituted on board Turkish vessels, and a gong in Chinese waters, where such articles are commonly used on board small sea-going vessels."

Admiral Nares (Great Britain).—Mr. President, it is to be observed that we have left out the words "a bellows or other." We came to the conclusion that a fog-horn sounded by mechanical means included "a bellows or other." Hoping that the fog-horn would increase in efficiency we thought it would be better to take out the words "a bellows or other," and they are practically included in the words "sounded by mechanical means." The note with regard to the gong is rather important, because here we are rather asking the Conference to reconsider a decision which they came to. It was voted in the Conference that the term "gong" might be used in connection with the bell, and that vessels could ring the bell or sound the gong. Now, this is a very important case, as we are asking, in fact, the Conference to reconsider their vote. We go fully into the reasons for this, which are, shortly, that in certain waters gongs are still used very largely on board of light-ships. The sooner they disappear the better; but at the same time there they are, and it would be very perplexing if a vessel at anchor should be allowed to make the same signal that a light-ship makes. Therefore we have worded it, "and a gong in Chinese waters where such articles are commonly used on board small sea-going vessels." We first had it to read "in Eastern waters," but we thought that was rather vague. Still, we could easily include any waters which any Delegate wishes to include in these terms; and in those waters where the gong will not interfere with the sound-signal on board of a light-ship it would be practically, perhaps, a better sound-signal for a vessel at anchor than using a bell.

I can tell the Conference that the Liverpool pilot-boats have now adopted, and for many years have used, the gong as their sound-signal in a fog, and that is the way they attract a vessel to them; but it happens that in these waters there is no light-ship sounding a gong, and they are not interfering with any other signal in the local waters. The chief thing which I wish to point out to the Conference is that you have already passed a vote to adopt the gong in lieu of the bell anywhere, and if you now agree to the foot-note of the Committee you will be reconsidering that Resolution.

Captain Bisbee (China).—Mr. President, with reference to the asterisk after the word "bell" in the fourth line of Article 12 on p. 4 of this Additional Report of the Committee on Sound-Signals, and to the note at the bottom of that page, I would suggest that the part of that note following the words "Turkish vessels" be stricken out, and that reference marks be inserted after the word "bell" at the end of the next sentence and at the end of Article 10, to direct attention to a second foot-note, which shall read as follows: "Chinese vessels of native type may use a gong instead of a bell." Thus arranged it will at once be evident that the note refers to the native sailing craft, which are the only ones to whom the privilege would be of any value, as vessels of foreign type flying the

13

Chinese flag will be provided with all the appliances for producing sound-signals that are found on board those of other nations.

Mr. Hall (Great Britain).—Mr. President, as my gallant colleague has pointed out, we are asking the Conference to reconsider their vote. That is literally, perfectly true; but we all know that this word "gong" was put in purely for use in Chinese waters, because we understood that they used gongs instead of bells. With regard to the proposal of the Delegate from China it will make it, I think, a little more cumbersome, but if he will let us see it in writing we can, perhaps, come to some conclusion about it. It is merely a matter for the Collocation Committee.

Captain Bisbee (China).—I am willing to have it submitted to the Collocation Committee.

Mr. Flood (Norway).—Mr. President, I will take the liberty to make a remark about these words "efficient bell." I said on the first reading, and I think I have the right to point out now, that these terms do not properly express the requirements necessary in the bell. We all know that there are a great many of these bells which are made of cast-iron and can hardly be heard at all. In my country we have strict Regulations about this, and the bells are inspected by the Government Inspectors. The bell, the fog-horn, the signal-light, and everything is inspected. But I understand that there are a great many countries where this is not done. I think it would be very proper for us not to insert it exactly in the Rule, but in a short foot-note, stating that what we mean by an efficient bell is a bell made of a composite metal and not of iron. I think that in the English Regulations 10 inches in diameter is required in the bell; but that does not cover the point. I would submit that the Collocation Committee be directed to frame a foot-note for the purpose of defining what an efficient bell is, that it is to be a bell made of composite metal, and to have a good sound.

Mr. Goodrich (United States).—I would suggest to the gallant Delegate from Norway that if we do that we shall have to describe what "efficient" means in every other place in the Rules.

Mr. Flood (Norway).—Mr. President, I speak here from practical experience, and I think that some of my colleagues present will agree with me when I say that we have had a great deal of trouble from this cause. I will not say that I have heard bells made of tin, but I will say that I have heard them when made of iron, and I do not think they could be heard a ship's length.

Mr. Goodrich (United States).—Mr. President, it seems to me that the subject has already been discussed and passed upon by the Conference. If we are going to adopt the system of rediscussing a subject which has been thoroughly considered, the result will be the extension of this Conference for several weeks.

Mr. Flood (Norway).—Mr. President, that is the very reason why I did not propose any alteration in the Rule, but I simply submitted whether it would not be well to have a foot-note to explain what was meant by "an efficient bell." It should provide that the bell should be made of proper material, and not of cast-iron. It has been pointed out that this has been discussed in the Conference. I do not think that any one has stated at what distance the bell should be heard. We have the term "efficient light," but, at the same time, we have provided a range for the light. But there has been no Rule laid down as to what distance the bell should be heard.

Mr. Goodrich (United States).—Mr. President, may I suggest to the Delegate that if he will refer that to the Collocation Committee I am sure the Committee will be glad to consider it, as well as any other suggestions from other members?

Mr. Flood (Norway).—Mr. President, I only ask that it be referred to the Collocation Committee.

Mr. Hall (Great Britain).—Mr. President, may I point out that the business before us to-day is not the revision of the Rules which have been passed by the Conference? It is only to take into consideration such alterations as are necessary in these Rules in consequence of the Additional Report of the Committee on Sound-Signals. Now, we have discussed this question as to bells at very great length. We all agree with the gallaant Delegate as to the desirability of vessels being provided with proper bells, but we agreed that it was not necessary to put anything into the Rules beyond saying that the bell must be an efficient one, and that we must see that the Rule is enforced in our respective countries. If the Collocation Committee would put in a note to that effect it would be going contrary to the decision of the Conference. The Conference decided distinctly that the words "efficient bell" were sufficient, and that it should be left to the respective countries to see that that provision is properly enforced. I only rise to point out the extreme difficulty we shall be in if, when we are discussing the Report of the Committee on Sound-Signals, the whole of the Rules are to be reconsidered, without any motion for a reconsideration. There is nothing in the Sound-Signal Report with regard to an "efficient bell," and if we waste half-an-hour in the discussion over that we may just as well discuss every other Rule.

Mr. Verney (Siam).—Mr. President, I only rise to express the hope that the natives with small vessels in Siam shall be given the same privileges that are being claimed by the native boats in China. I am informed that the use of the gong is very common on board of these small boats in Siamese waters.

Captain Mensing (Germany).—Mr. President, I am very sorry to see that the introduction of the gongs is to be restricted in the manner proposed by the Committee on Sound-Signals, because it would have been much better for us to have voted upon the other proposition which was laid down, requiring that a gong might be used on all vessels. The wording of the amendment leaves doubt about it. I believe that only the first paragraph of Article 12 is under consideration at present, so I shall defer what I have to say about small boats until later on, when the second paragraph of Article 12 comes under consideration. If we have the gong introduced everywhere, it will have one advantage. I have stated before that the provision with regard to Turkish vessels was only upon religious grounds, and it was left optional with them to use the gong. I think very likely that the Turkish vessels will substitute the gong for their very inefficient sound-signals, because I believe that a drum used in a fog, or in wet weather, can scarcely be heard.

There is an insertion made here: "A sailing-vessel of 20 tons gross tonnage and upwards shall be provided with a similar fog-horn and bell." Those words are not in italics, though they are a change from the old text. Now, a question has been brought up as to whether mistakes would not result by confusing these gongs with gongs on board of light-vessels. The gongs which are used on board of these light-vessels, as has been so ably pointed out by the gallant Delegate from Great Britain, are very clumsy affairs. I believe that it would be just as difficult to make a mistake between a gong on board of a light vessel and a small gong on board of a merchant-vessel, as there would be in mistaking the sound of two bells. I believe the gong should be only introduced in the smallest kind of vessels. I wish to say that there is just as little difficulty in distinguishing between the notes of these two gongs as there is in distinguishing between the sounds of two bells. Very often a distinguishing signal used on board of a light-vessel is by ringing the bell a certain number of times, and then giving one, two, or three strokes of the bell afterwards. The same thing can be introduced here. Taking everything into consideration, I should object to having the change made as provided in the foot-note adopted by the Committee, and should be glad to have the Conference keep the Resolution which has been already adopted.

Captain Nares (Great Britain).—Mr. President, the terms, "a sailing-vessel of 20 tons gross tonnage and upwards shall be provided with a similar fog-horn and bell," were included there in consequence of the Conference having passed that part of Article 10 where it says, in connection with the light, "Paragraph (*a*) of this Article applies only to vessels and boats propelled by sails and oars of less than 20 tons gross tonnage." The Committee on Sound-Signals also thought it better to name the precise tonnage, and to make the largest of these vessels 20 tons. That should have been put into italics to draw attention to it, and I very much regret that it was not done. I may say that the first wording of the note was, "a gong in Chinese or other waters where such articles are commonly used aboard small sea-going vessels;" we were obliged to put in the words "sea-going" to distinguish from light-ships. But if the Conference think it necessary to include other than the Chinese waters, I am sure the Committee on Sound-Signals will not object. We are quite willing to allow the gongs to come into use wherever it can possibly be done without danger to navigation.

Commander Chen Ngen Tao (China).—Mr. President, I think it is very wise to leave out the words "in Chinese waters," because a Chinese vessel may use a gong and go out beyond Chinese waters.

Admiral Nares (Great Britain).—Mr. President, I am sure the Committee will be very glad of that alteration and to take out the words "Chinese waters."

Captain Mensing (Germany).—Mr. President, will the Committee on Sound-Signals be willing to strike out the word "commonly"? It would make a difference to the German Delegation with regard to the paragraph. If that could be done I believe there will be very little difficulty about accepting it as it stands now. If the use of the gong is made optional, I believe that we could accept the paragraph just as it stands here; if this is not done, we will find difficulty in the next paragraph. Of course, those vessels which are going up and down our coast would never be in a position to be mistaken for light-vessels, which, so far as I know, are only found in the vicinity of the coast of England.

Captain Malmberg (Sweden).—Mr. President, I may state that there are several light-vessels on the Swedish coast which sound the gong, and that is the reason why I opposed the use of the word "gong" when we discussed this Article before. I would greatly prefer that this gong should come in as the foot-note proposed by the Committee on Sound-Signals.

Captain Mensing (Germany).—Mr. President, I would like to move that the word "Chinese" and the word "commonly," in the foot-note of this paragraph, be struck out.

Admiral Nares (Great Britain).—Mr. President, I of course cannot speak for my colleagues on the Committee, but if any of them object I wish they would say so. According to my recollection of the conversation that went on in the Committee I should say that we are quite willing to take out those two words.

Mr. Hall (Great Britain).—Mr. President, may I point out that it is not necessary to have the words "in Chinese waters"? It will then read, "and a gong where such articles are used on board small sea-going vessels."

The President.—Is the Conference ready for the question?

Captain Mensing (Germany).—Mr. President, I propose that the word "will" be changed to "may."

The President.—If there is no objection the word "may" will be introduced in place of "will." Before putting the question upon this, the motion of the Delegate from Norway, to refer the words "efficient bell" to the Collocation Committee to prepare a foot-note, will be in order.

Mr. Flood (Norway).—Mr. President, I do not like to press my request. I thought it my duty to put it before the Conference and to give them my ideas with regard to the matter. I have done so to the best of my ability, and now that the learned Delegates, especially the learned First Delegate from Great Britain, have spoken against it, I suppose it is not worth while for me to try any more.

The President.—Does the Delegate withdraw it?

Mr. Flood (Norway).—Yes, Sir; I withdraw it.

Mr. Hall (Great Britain).—Mr. President, the Delegate from Norway says I spoke against his proposition. I pointed out that we were not entitled to discuss it without the Delegate moved a Resolution which was carried by a three-fourths vote to reconsider the question, which had been previously thoroughly discussed by the Conference.

Mr. Verney (Siam).—Mr. President, there is just one other little alteration to this foot-note, to change the word "and" to "or."

Mr. Hall (Great Britain).—Mr. President, I think the Delegate from Siam may safely leave that to the Collocation Committee.

The President.—The note will be read with these numerous alterations.
The note is as follows:—

"In all cases where the Regulations require a bell to be used a drum may be substituted on Turkish vessels, and a gong where such articles are used on board small sea-going vessels."

The question was put to the Conference upon the adoption of the foot-note to Article 12, and it was adopted.

The President.—The question now is upon the adoption of Article 12. Article 12 will be read.

Article 12 is as follows:—

"A steam-ship shall be provided with a whistle or siren sounded by steam or other efficient substitute for steam, so placed that the sounds may not be intercepted by any obstructions, and with an efficient fog-horn to be sounded by mechanical means, and also with an efficient bell. A sailing-vessel of 20 tons gross tonnage and upwards shall be provided with a similar fog-horn and bell."

The President.—Is the Conference ready for the question?
The question was put to the Conference upon the adoption of the first paragraph of Article 12, and it was adopted.

The President.—The Secretary will please read the next paragraph to Article 12.
The second paragraph to Article 12 is as follows:—

"Sailing-vessels and boats of less than 20 tons gross tonnage shall not be obliged to be provided with a mechanical fog-horn, but, if not so provided, they shall make, with any other instrument, an efficient sound-signal at intervals of not more than two minutes."

Admiral Nares (Great Britain).—Mr. President, that will be altered to one minute, in agreement with the decision of the Conference.

Captain Hubert (the Netherlands).—Mr. President, as the Conference has adopted the principle that sound-signals shall also be used in heavy rain-storms, it would be a burden upon the small fishing-boats in our colonial waters to make this Regulation apply to them, where, as I have stated, there is not room enough in the boats. Therefore, I will have it submitted to the Collocation Committee, as was our amendment which we offered a couple of days ago, when we asked that this Article should not apply to regions where its enforcement would prove too difficult in consequence of local conditions.

Admiral Nares (Great Britain).—Mr. President, we talked over this very subject in the Committee, and those members who have been employed in the South Pacific Islands and such places are well aware that the boats, all of them, do carry a very efficient fog-horn in the shape of a shell scooped out in the shape of a horn. Any boat that is in a navigable track ought to have some signal. This provision is worded so that these boats with their conches, which make a very efficient noise, would be considered as having an efficient sound-signal.

Captain Hubert (the Netherlands).—Mr. President, I am fully aware that they are used near these islands, but so far as I have seen in our colonial waters we never have had such a signal or instrument to make a noise. These boats have nothing. They only have a torch and a box of matches to light it; that is the only signal they can give. The boat is too small. There are two men with their fish-nets and their food for one day, and there is hardly room for the fish which they catch.

Admiral Nares (Great Britain).—Mr. President, our attention was also called to that. But there is no examination of such boats, and if they go off without their lights and fog-horns they do so at their own risk, and on their own responsibility.

The President.—Will the Delegate from the Netherlands state his proposition exactly, so that it can come before the Conference?

Captain Hubert (the Netherlands).—I desire it to be the same as our amendment offered on the 25th November, extra amendment No. 58.

The President.—Do you desire to have it referred to the Collocation Committee?

Mr. Hall (Great Britain).—Mr. President, I must suggest that it should not be referred to the Collocation Committee. Our shoulders are hardly broad enough now for the work we have got to do; and if, when some Delegate finds that he cannot get what he wants, he is to say, "I will refer it to the Collocation Committee," I cannot see where we are to end. I cannot help thinking that, after we have heard that the Committee considered this matter very carefully, and tried to do their very best to meet the difficulty, they proposed this Rule as the best they could do under the circumstances. When the gallant Delegate learns this, I dare say he will not consider it necessary to press his amendment. As my gallant colleague has already mentioned, these small boats are never examined or supervised. The law would say, if they choose to out and get in collision, and they do not take the trouble to give other vessels warning that they are in the neighbourhood, they take the risk themselves; but if they are provided with the proper sound-instrument to give a proper signal, they have complied with the law.

The President.—The question is upon the proposition of the Delegate from the Netherlands to refer this amendment to the Collocation Committee.

Mr. Goodrich (United States).—Mr. President, I also protest against that reference.

The President.—If the Delegate makes a proposition the Chair will entertain it.

Mr. Goodrich (United States).—Mr. President, I hope the gallant Delegate will withdraw that motion.

Captain Hubert (the Netherlands).—Mr. President, I will withdraw it.

The President.—The question now is upon the first paragraph upon p. 5. The Secretary will please read it again.

The first paragraph is as follows:—

"Sailing-vessels and boats of less than 30 tons gross tonnage shall not be obliged to be provided with a mechanical fog-horn; but if not so provided, they shall make with any other instrument an efficient sound-signal at intervals of not more than one minute."

The President.—Is the Conference ready for the question?

The question was put to the Conference upon the adoption of the second paragraph of Article 12, and was adopted.

The President.—Article 12, paragraph (b), will now be read.

Article 12, paragraph (b), is as follows:—

"(b.) A steam-vessel not at anchor, but with engines stopped, shall sound, at intervals of not more than two minutes, two prolonged blasts with an interval of about one second between them."

Admiral Nares (Great Britain).—Mr. President, I think there will be a little rewording required here. Under Article 13, the Conference adopted the words, "a vessel has stopped her engines," and then, at my suggestion, Article 12 was reworded much in the same way. The expression in (b) as it stands now is "stopped and having no way upon her." I may say at once that the majority of the Committee wanted to insert these words at the time, but I thought that we were going against the opinion of the Conference. We shall be complying with the opinion of the Conference if we alter the words, "with engines stopped," and make it read, "stopped and having no way upon her."

The President.—If there be no objection, it will be so altered.

Mr. Hall (Great Britain).—Mr. President, I have one suggestion to make, which I trust the Committee will think is one that they can agree to, and that is to use, instead of the word "prolonged," the words "such long blasts." Having regard to the fact that a prolonged sounding of the whistle is a signal of distress, it is desirable that there be no doubt as to what the long blast should mean. If we should use the word "prolonged," as is suggested here, a man might be blowing his whistle for some very considerable time and it would be taken as a signal of distress. So I venture to suggest that the Rule should read, "A steam-vessel not at anchor, but stopped and having no way upon her, shall sound, at intervals of not more than two minutes, two such long blasts with an interval of about one second between them."

Admiral Nares (Great Britain).—Mr. President, I may say that the intention of the Committee in altering this from "two such long blasts" into "two prolonged blasts" was in its connection with the short blast of one second's duration, more than in its connection with the long blast of four seconds' duration. I think the Committee would be quite content to have it two long blasts, provided they are to be of four seconds' duration. The Committee have provided this, so that it could not be confounded with two short blasts; because there is no doubt of the fact that the custom is to make short blasts considerably longer than one second, and that custom prevails everywhere. Now, if we can bring the short blast down to one second, the duration we have already adopted, so as to be very unmistakable, then, personally, I see no objection to the change. But at present the short blasts are considerably longer than a second, and that is the reason why we wanted to define it very clearly as "two prolonged blasts." If it is customary to make these short blasts of two or three seconds' duration, it will be a long time before they are brought down to the one second. If they do not make the blast of one second duration, there will be a very confusing signal; because, if a ship is giving two short blasts, indicating "I am putting my helm to starboard," and that the ship is turning to port, it will be confounded with this signal of a vessel being stopped altogether.

The President.—Does the Chair understand that the Delegate from Great Britain, who has just taken his seat, accepts the proposition of the Delegate from Great Britain who preceded him?

Admiral Nares (Great Britain).—Mr. President, I can scarcely accept it as Chairman of the Sound-Signal Committee. If the other gentlemen accept it I am quite ready to do so. It is more, I think, a question for the Conference. We have given our reasons, and if the Conference think that the term "two such long blasts" will be distinct enough from the helm signal of two short blasts, very well.

Mr. Hall (Great Britain).—Mr. President, I think we shall be able to suggest a wording which will relieve the Committee on Sound-Signals from any difficulty and from the possibility of the signals being mistaken for the starboard-helm signals, and that is by putting into this Article what the Conference has already inserted at the end of Article 19: "The term short blast in this Article shall mean a blast of about one second's duration." I think that will get over any possible objection which has been presented.

Captain Shackford (United States).—Mr. President, I trust that this word "prolonged" will be allowed to remain here. The ordinary port-helm signal blast in this country is from two to three seconds. They usually take that much time in sounding that blast. On sounding two blasts, my head is going to port. Each blast occupies from two to three seconds, and sometimes even longer. If this term "prolonged" should be permitted to remain, the Conference, if it sees fit, might provide that a prolonged blast could be six or eight seconds, to distinguish it from the other four-seconds blast.

The Conference thereupon took a recess until 2 o'clock.

After Recess.

Mr. Hall (Great Britain).—Mr. President, since the adjournment we have had an opportunity of considering the point which was raised by the Delegate from the United States with regard to the great importance of avoiding any risk whatever of allowing this signal, which is now under discussion, to be confounded with the starboard-helm signal; and with a view to that I have a proposition which I think will meet all the difficulties, and it is this: To make the long blasts or the prolonged blasts from four to six seconds. What I propose is this: To alter sub-section (*a*) to make it read:—

"A steam-ship under way shall make with her steam-whistle or other steam sound-signal, at intervals of not more than two minutes, a prolonged blast of from four to six seconds' duration."

I want to follow the decision of the Conference as far as possible, and yet to meet the difficulty pointed out by the Delegate from France, so that if we increase the long blast or the prolonged blast to a blast of from four to six seconds' duration, then in sub-section (*b*) we can say: "Two such prolonged blasts, with an interval of about one second between them." Then I think we avoid the difficulty of the possibility of confounding this signal with the starboard-helm signal.

The proposed amendments are as follows: Section (*a*). A steam-vessel under way shall make on her whistle or other steam sound-signal, at intervals of not more than two minutes, a prolonged blast of from four to six seconds. Then subsection (*b*) will read: "A steam-vessel not at anchor, but stopped and having no way upon her, shall sound, at intervals of not more than two minutes, two such prolonged blasts, with an interval of about one second between them."

Mr. Goodrich (United States).—Mr. President, if the members of the Conference will refer to the 38th amendment under Article 12, as we originally adopted it, they will see how this Article is to be worded.

Mr. Hall (Great Britain).—Will you kindly read the words?

Mr. Goodrich (United States).—"A steam-ship under way shall make with her steam-whistle or other steam sound-signal, at intervals of not more than two minutes, a long blast of about four seconds' duration."

Mr. Hall (Great Britain).—Mr. President, that is the way it was originally worded, and now we propose to alter that. I will read it again: "A steam-vessel under way shall make with her whistle or siren, at intervals of not more than two minutes, a prolonged blast of from four to six seconds' duration." Then section (*b*) will read: "A steam-vessel not at anchor, &c., shall sound, at intervals of not more than two minutes, two such prolonged blasts, with an interval of about one second between them."

Captain Shackford (United States).—Mr. President, I should be very glad to accept that, if the change is made in section (*a*) of Article 12.

Mr. Goodrich (United States).—Mr. President, I would suggest to the learned Delegate from Great Britain that it would be wise, for the purpose of bringing up the question, to move to reconsider section (*a*), Article 12.

Mr. Hall (Great Britain).—Mr. President, I am very much obliged to the learned Delegate from the United States for pointing that out to me. I move that Article 12, section (*a*) be reconsidered by the Conference.

The President.—It is moved by the Delegate from Great Britain that section (*a*), Article 12, be reconsidered.

Captain Van Steyn (the Netherlands).—Mr. President, I wish to state that I heartily agree with that portion of the Article which provides for the duration of the signal, because that would meet with the amendment proposed by the Delegates from the Netherlands. We proposed that the duration of the blast should be eight seconds.

The President.—The question is upon the motion to reconsider section (*a*), Article 12.

The question was put to the Conference upon the question as to the reconsideration of section (*a*), Article 12, and the question was carried.

The President.—The amendment of the Delegate from Great Britain will be read.

The amendment is as follows:—

"Article 12, paragraph (*a*). A steam-ship under way shall make with her whistle or siren, at intervals of not more than two minutes, a prolonged blast of from four to six seconds' duration."

Mr. Hall (Great Britain).—Mr. President, I will point out that that should read "a steam-vessel" and not a steam-ship.

The President.—The question now is upon the amendment of the Delegate from Great Britain to Article 12, paragraph (*a*).

The question was put to the Conference upon the amendment to Article 12, paragraph (*a*), and it was adopted.

The President.—The Delegate from Great Britain now has an amendment to paragraph (*b*), Article 12. Section (*b*), as amended, will be read again for the information of the Conference.

Article 12, paragraph (*b*), is as follows:—

"(*b*.) A steam-vessel not at anchor, but stopped and having no way upon her, shall sound, at intervals of not more than two minutes, two such prolonged blasts, with an interval of about one second between them."

The President.—Is the Conference ready for the question?

The question was put to the Conference upon the adoption of paragraph (*b*), Article 12, and it was carried.

The President.—The next subject for consideration is section (*c*).

Admiral Nares (Great Britain).—There is no change in section (*c*).

The Secretary.—When the Report was submitted you stated that the word "short" should be inserted before the word "blast" and "blasts."

[93]

Mr. Hall (Great Britain).—Mr. President, we propose to deal with that at the end of the Article in a general definition, as we have done in Article 19, and to provide that the term " short blast " in this Article shall mean a blast of about one second's duration. It is only in order to make it appear that the blasts should be made as short as possible.

Admiral Nares (Great Britain).—Mr. President, the Committee, as I informed the Conference the other day, had left out that proposal. The Committee has already decided that the signal for the starboard and port tack ought to be made compulsory, and therefore we have proposed that, as these signals will now be incorporated under Article 12, they should be worded so as to include the short blast, and so that there will be no mistake about it. I think that if the Secretary will read what we have proposed the Conference will understand it.

The President.—The Secretary will please read section (c).

Section (c), Article 12, is as follows:—

" (c.) A sailing-ship under way shall make with her fog-horn, at intervals of not more than two minutes when on the starboard tack, one short blast, when on the port tack, two short blasts in succession, and when the wind is abaft the beam, three short blasts in succession."

Admiral Nares (Great Britain).—Mr. President, there is a chance of the fog-horn being mistaken for the whistle, and we have thought it better to define it as a short blast, to make it quite distinct. The fog-horn may be mistaken for the fog-siren or fog-whistle of a steamer, which is the reason we propose to put in " short."

The President.—Is the Conference ready for the question upon section (c), which has just been read?

Captain Mensing (Germany).—Mr. President, I believe that it is not necessary to insert the word " short." I have been told that there are some of these instruments, devised for use on board of sailing vessels, which are more in conformity with the siren than the fog-horn. I would like to know whether the word " fog-horn," as used here, would cover all these instruments.

Admiral Nares (Great Britain).—Mr. President, if it is necessary to put in the word " mechanical " we can do so. Still, the words " her fog-horn " would include a mechanical fog-horn. We report to you that the fog-horns which are coming rapidly into use will be capable of producing long sounds and short sounds. Up to the present time they have been making only short sounds, and therefore the well-known signals to be used for the starboard and port tack and for running free have been short blasts. We think now, when they will be able to give long sounds, that it will be just as well for us to prevent them from doing so, and to state definitely what the signal is to be. They will be able to make long ones, but it will be better on the whole to make them short to agree with the other signals.

The President.—The question is upon section (c). The Secretary will please read it again for the information of the Conference.

Section (c) is as follows:—

" (c.) A sailing-ship under way shall make with her fog-horn, at intervals of not more than two minutes when on the starboard tack, one short blast, when on the port tack, two short blasts in succession, and when the wind is abaft the beam, three short blasts in succession."

Captain Shackford (United States).—Mr. President, I do not think this question of a short blast on a fog-horn has come up here before the Conference or before the Committee on Fog-Signals, and I would like to know if they propose to fix the short blast at only one second. It seems to me that a blast of one second is quite insufficient with a fog-horn used by sailing-vessels.

Mr. Hall (Great Britain).—Mr. President, this is referred to in the Report of the Committee, on p. 2, where they say, " One, two, or three sound blasts on a fog-horn are already in use by sailing-vessels under way." It is not laid down what the length of these blasts should be, but by the construction of the fog-horn used in the past they are necessarily short blasts of equal duration; we submit that they should be so regulated and termed short blasts; so that the Committee has considered the matter very carefully and is only carrying out the suggestion of the Conference that these words are put in.

Captain Shackford (United States).—Mr. President, I think that there was no length proposed for this blast in the Committee, and no length has been decided upon by the Conference.

Mr. Hall (Great Britain).—Mr. President, as the Conference has adopted one second as the time of a short blast, under Article 19, we thought it was desirable to adopt the same length in this Article, if we could.

Captain Shackford (United States).—Mr. President, I submit that one second is quite insufficient for short blasts on a fog-horn. It may possibly be a sufficient blast on a steam-whistle, but it is not long enough for a blast on a fog-horn, whether a mechanical horn or a mouth-horn.

Mr. Hall (Great Britain).—Mr. President, then possibly the best way of getting over it is merely to insert the word " short," as the Report of the Committee suggests, and give no duration or no definition as to the meaning of the word " short " in the Article. The great thing is to prevent vessels with some of the new mechanical fog-horns, which can be kept sounding for a long time, from giving signals which might be mistaken for a steamer's whistle, or the siren of a steamer.

Captain Shackford (United States).—Mr. President, the term " short blast on a steam-whistle " has been defined as one second. I submit that this might be understood as also to mean the length of a blast on a fog-horn unless we limit it or extend it to some definite length. I think that a blast of two or three seconds, certainly not less than two seconds, should be required of the fog-horn.

Admiral Nares (Great Britain).—Mr. President, the fog-horns, up to the present time, as we explained, until within the last two or three years, when the Norwegian fog-horn came up, were incapable of making a long blast. They were incapable of blowing more than about a second. It was impossible for any man's lungs to continue blowing this trumpet for more than a second at a time. We were informed by the fisherman who came to see us that out of all his crew he could only get two or three men who could blow it at all; that it depended upon the man's lungs, and that it was quite out of the question to talk of blowing it continuously for half-an-hour; and that, in fact, they only blew it when the vessels were coming near them. The words "of about one second" will include more than one second. If you leave out the word "short," and leave it as it stands, it is not a very material matter; but fog-horns are now coming into use which are capable of making long blasts and short blasts, and we thought it would be best to prevent them from making a long or a prolonged blast. I think, however, the Conference will be able to decide this question. I have tried to put it as clearly as possible. We adopt one second as "short" on a steam-whistle. If that same limit will not do for a fog-horn, then we had better leave out the word "short" altogether.

Captain Norcross (United States).—Mr. President, I think it is better to define that as "not to exceed three seconds."

The President.—Do you mean that as an amendment to section (c)?

Captain Norcross (United States).—I propose that as an amendment to Mr. Hall's amendment.

The President.—The Delegate from the United States proposes to define the term "short blast" in the amendment of the Delegate from Great Britain as "not to exceed three seconds."

Admiral Nares (Great Britain).—Mr. President, I am quite certain that if you are going to give one limit for a steam-whistle, and another limit for a fog-horn, then you must provide that there must be a long or a prolonged blast on the whistle of from four to six seconds, and if the Signal Committee are going also to define that long blast on the fog-horn as being only three seconds, then we shall get into a very serious scrape. On behalf of the Sound-Signal Committee, I will say that we would sooner leave out the word "short" altogether, if you are going to define two different shorts.

Captain Mensing (Germany).—Mr. President, I think it would be desirable to strike out the word "short." If that is done, then there is really no difficulty, and there can be no mistake made. So far as I know there are only made on the fog-horn two or three blasts, and it matters little whether they are long or short. I think it would be advisable to strike out the word "short" altogether, and leave the Rule as it is at present.

The President.—Does the Delegate from the United States consent to that?

Captain Norcross (United States).—I accept that, Sir.

The President.—The question then is upon the proposition of the Delegate from Germany to strike out the word "short."

Mr. Goodrich (United States).—Mr. President, it is not in yet. There is no necessity for that motion which has been made by the gallant Delegate from Germany. We are voting upon the proposition of the Committee to insert the word "short," and if the Conference do not like the word, then they will vote the proposition of the Committee down.

Admiral Nares (Great Britain).—Mr. President, I think the Committee will withdraw the proposition altogether, and leave out the word "short" in section (c), and let that section stand as it is at present.

The President.—The question now before the Conference is upon the adoption of section (e), which will be read by the Secretary.

Section (e), Article 12, is as follows:—

"(e.) A steam-vessel, when her engines are going full speed astern, shall sound on her whistle three short blasts."

Admiral Nares (Great Britain).—Mr. President, I may say that the word "short" is more important here. We have introduced here three decided short blasts, so as to make the signal unmistakable.

Captain Richard (France.)—Mr. President, I am surprised to find this clause placed in Article 12, instead of being placed in Article 19 only, which is its proper place. You now not only render these sound-signals obligatory in ordinary weather, instead of optional, as they formerly were in Article 19, but you also make them compulsory in fog, mist, falling snow, &c. Formerly you admitted that, in order to make these signals, it was necessary that the two vessels should see each other; now they are to indicate their manœuvre without seeing each other. I do not think that this is right. Will it not add to the confusion when a signal is repeated and the direction of the sound is not known? I understood the old Rule which governed a vessel's conduct in the matter of sound-signals, but now you set aside this Rule. We have been told here that, in order to avoid confusion at sea in a fog, when vessels do not see each other, that only long blasts will be used; short blasts to be used only when vessels are in sight of each other, the sailing-vessels to be distinguishable from steam-vessels in a fog by the character of the blast. This Rule was rational and clear. Why has it not been followed?

In my opinion, the Committee has gone too far, in that it has mixed the long and the short blast. What is the use of departing from a wise Rule for a vessel going full speed astern at sea? In the first place, I do not think that this manœuvre is a common one, but it may happen. Then I would like to know what advantage can be derived from the signal that the vessel is going astern when it is impossible to find out where she is? If you enter upon that path you will have to give notice of many other interesting facts; but this you cannot do, for then your signals will lose their simple character, which makes them valuable. Consequently I ask the Conference to confine itself to what is prescribed by Article 19, viz., when a vessel goes full speed astern in sight of another vessel, and that the paragraph which we are discussing be stricken from Article 12.

Captain Mensing (Germany).—Mr. President, I would simply like to state that the German Delegation agree with the gentleman who has spoken before me.

Captain Malmberg (Sweden),—Mr. President, I also do not see the necessity for introducing that signal in a fog when you do not see a vessel. If you do see a vessel, Article 19 will cover the case.

Mr. Verbrugghe (Belgium).—Mr. President, I am of the same opinion.

The President.—Is the Conference ready for the question? Section (*e*) will be read.

Section (*e*) of Article 12 is as follows:—

"A steam-vessel, when her engines are going full speed astern, shall sound on her whistle three short blasts."

Admiral Bowden-Smith (Great Britain).—Mr. President, before this is put to a vote, might we be quite certain whether it is only to apply in a fog when vessels are in sight of each other?

Mr. Goodrich (United States).—Mr. President, if the gallant Admiral will read the second subdivision of Article 12 as we have passed it, he will see that this subdivision (*e*) is part of the paragraph which commences: "In fog, mist, falling snow, or during heavy rain-storms, whether by day or night, the signals described in this Article shall be used as follows." That is to say, it must be in a fog or in thick weather.

Admiral Nares (Great Britain).—Mr. President, the intention of the Committee is this: Under Article 19 the signal has been made compulsory, provided a vessel does a certain action, provided she starboards, or ports, or goes full speed astern; but while Article 19 has been made compulsory, it is not to be allowed except when the other vessel is in sight. The Committee want to go beyond that. They will not allow the starboard or the port signal to be made to a vessel which is not in sight, but they see no reason why the signal "I am going full speed astern" should not be made whether the other vessel is in sight or not. You have already, under Article 12, told the vessel to stop her engines. Whether that will include that she will stop altogether will depend upon the captain. Suppose the captain goes full speed astern instead of merely stopping his way: why should he not indicate that action to the other vessel which is not in sight? You have already given him another signal: "You may feel your way past me with caution and I will stop by." So that it is all dovetailed together.

Under Article 19 you have made it compulsory to give the signals for the port and the starboard tack. I think they can only be made when the vessel is in sight; but yet this third signal, I am going full speed astern, may be made. While I am speaking about this there is one alteration which has been made. I am not quite clear whether we had a discussion about it or not; but I think we did. I think that it came up in the Conference, that the term "I am" was not definite, and we have altered it to "my engines" are going full speed astern. We have kept the three short blasts which have been in use for ages.

Captain Malmberg (Sweden).—Mr. President, I am still of the opinion that section (*e*) ought not to come into the Regulations, because if a steamer, according to the first paragraph in this Article, stops her engines and then goes astern, section (*b*) covers her situation as being stopped—no, I am mistaken in that. However, I should not like to introduce into Rules like these a manœuvre to be made by a steamer not having the other vessel in sight, as the issue of such a manœuvre may, in a fog, bring about a collision. The safest way in a fog is to lay the ship dead still and ascertain the position of the vessels in your vicinity. I still think that this subdivision (*e*) ought not to come into the Article.

Captain Sampson (United States).—Mr. President, I entirely agree with the last gentleman who has spoken. I think that some signal as provided in Article 19, to indicate that a vessel is going full speed astern, is very needful when two ships meet in a fog and approach each other to a point where they become visible. I think that signal would be a good one; but that case would be covered by Article 19. If the vessels are not in sight of each other it seems to me that no useful information can be conveyed by indicating that the ship is going full speed astern. That may be the direction to avoid a collision or it may be the direction to produce a collision.

The President.—Is the Conference ready for the question? The Secretary will please read section (*e*) again for the information of the Conference.

Section (*e*) is as follows:—

"(*e*.) A steam-vessel, when her engines are going full speed astern, shall sound on her whistle three short blasts."

The question was put to the Conference upon section (*e*) of Article 12, and the Chair being unable to decide, the yeas and nays were called for.

The Yea and Nay vote is as follows:—

Austria-Hungary .. .. Yea.	Mexico .. .. .. Nay.
Belgium .. .. .. Nay.	Norway .. .. .. Nay.
China .. .. .. Nay.	Portugal .. .. .. Nay.
Chile .. .. .. Nay.	Nicaragua .. ..
Denmark .. .. .. Yea.	Russia.. .. .. Nay.
France .. .. .. Nay.	Spain .. .. .. Nay.
Germany .. .. .. Nay.	Sweden .. .. .. Nay.
Great Britain .. .. Nay.	Siam .. .. .. Nay.
Hawaii .. .. .. Nay.	The Netherlands .. .. Yea.
Italy .. .. .. Yea.	United States.. .. .. Yea.
Japan .. .. .. Nay.	

The President.—Five have voted in the affirmative and 15 in the negative, so the paragraph is lost.

The next subject for consideration will be paragraph (*f*). The Secretary will please read it.

Paragraph (*f*) is as follows:—

"(*f.*) A vessel, if a steam-vessel, at anchor in a fairway at sea shall, at intervals of not more than two minutes, sound two prolonged blasts with her whistle or siren, followed by ringing her bell; or, if a sailing-vessel, two blasts with her fog-horn, followed by ringing her bell."

Mr. Hall (Great Britain).—Mr. President, I move to strike out the words "at sea." I think it is very important that vessels in a fog should know that there is anything in a fairway, whether it is at sea or in narrow waters. I think that as our object is to make these Rules applicable to all waters we ought to leave out the words "at sea." I must confess that I think the reasons given for this signal on the part of the Committee are very valuable and forcible. They point out the principle upon which the signal is chosen, and I must confess that their reasons lead me to think that it is not likely to be easily mistaken.

Captain Mensing (Germany).—Mr. President, I cannot see my way exactly to adopt the last amendment proposed. We have already, under Article 14, a Rule which provides that a steam-ship and a sailing-ship when not under way shall at intervals of not more than two minutes ring a bell. Now, we have got another Rule saying that a vessel, if a steam-vessel, at anchor in a fairway at sea, shall at intervals of not more than two minutes sound two prolonged blasts with her whistle or siren, followed by ringing her bell. I don't know where the difference is. I do not understand the expression, "a fairway at sea," and I would like to have it changed to "open sea," so as to read, "at anchor in the open sea." I think that a distinction ought to be made, and that if a steam-ship is met anywhere where a person would not expect her to be at anchor, but where she is at anchor, that she should make a different signal from one that is anchored in a fairway. Of course, one generally has in his eyes those things which are happening in the home waters. For instance, there are at the mouths of German rivers flats extending far out into the sea, where there are from 10 to 12 fathoms of water, perhaps 20 fathoms. It may be that a man-of-war in trying to make one of these ports drops her anchor. I think it would be an excellent thing to provide a signal for her. I do not see why upon going into fairways a steam-ship lying at anchor should make a different signal from a sailing-vessel. I would like to propose that it should read, "at anchor in the open sea."

Mr. Hall (Great Britain).—Mr. President, I think we could probably get over that difficulty by taking both the proposals, "at anchor in a fairway" or "at sea." I think it is much more important for a vessel, when she chooses to come to anchor in a fairway in the mouth of a harbour, where she would be more dangerous, to give notice that she is there, than if she were at anchor in the open sea. But if it is necessary to give a signal at anchor in the open sea, we will get over that by putting in the words "or at sea."

Mr. Goodrich (United States).—Mr. President, I confess I do not understand the connection between section (*d*) of Article 12 as we adopted it the other day and subsection (*f*) of the Committee's Report, and I call the attention of the Conference to it. Subsection (*d*) provides that a steam-vessel or sailing-vessel when at anchor shall at intervals of not more than one minute ring the bell rapidly or sound the gong for about five seconds. That is what was passed the other day. Now this is a proposition that a steam-vessel at anchor shall give an entirely different signal. The first provision covers every case of a vessel at anchor. There is difficulty in passing this amendment unless you make some other signal. Of course, subsection (*d*) as originally passed is more comprehensive and embraces all cases. Is that intended? I ask for explanation, for it seems to me that we have fallen into somewhat of an error, which, doubtless, the Committee can explain.

Admiral Nares (Great Britain).—Mr. President, it is a very common thing for vessels, particularly in a fog, to let go their anchors, and then, as we have explained before, they are in a most dangerous position, not only for themselves, but for any passing vessel. We have given them a special signal. At present the law provides, practically, they can only ring the bell, although they are in a dangerous position and have got other means on board by which they can give a very much better signal. We propose to give them the most powerful signal that they have on board in addition to their bell. Now, we cannot allow this signal to be used in any other place except where a vessel at anchor is an exceptional danger. The bell is quite sufficient, and perhaps more than sufficient, in a regular roadstead at sea, where we are expecting to find vessels at anchor, or in a harbour. When we go into harbour the bells are all around us, and some of them are very loud. If those vessels were also allowed to blow this prolonged blast, danger would be created instead of danger prevented. Whether our expression, "in a fairway at sea," is a good one I do not know. If it can be improved, we shall be very happy to have it improved. But our intention is, in a navigable channel, where vessels do not usually anchor, and where vessels navigating that fairway would not expect to find a vessel at anchor, to give such vessel the very loudest signal you can possibly give her. We have introduced the words "fairway at sea" to prevent any vessel at anchor, in a river or in a fairway, where they are expected to anchor, from making these signals, which would be a nuisance and would be a cause of danger.

Mr. Goodrich (United States).—Mr. President, the difficulty, as I apprehend it, has not been made quite clear by the gallant Delegate from Great Britain. The present Regulation provides that a steam-ship or a sailing-ship not under way shall, at intervals of not more than two minutes, ring the bell. That has been adopted by the Conference. The Article reads: "A steam-vessel or a sailing-vessel at anchor shall, at intervals of not more than one minute, ring the bell rapidly or sound the gong for about five seconds." The amendment which I have just read covers every case of a vessel at anchor, because it says a steam-vessel or a sailing-vessel when at anchor. It covers every case. Now you want to limit it. You are trying to define another set of cases by the amendment proposed by the Committee, that when a steam-vessel is at anchor in a fairway at sea she shall sound an entirely different signal. If you want to adopt that principle you must change the Rule as you have at present adopted it. One is comprehensive and embraces all cases, while the second embraces a separate case of a vessel at anchor in g fairway at sea.

Mr. Hall (Great Britain).—Mr. President, the difficulty which has been pointed out by the learned Delegate from the United States is perfectly correct. This, however, is purely a question of draughting. We can pass a Rule for vessels at anchor, and we can also pass a Rule for vessels at anchor in a special place. That can be met by making a new clause in the former Article and make it read as follows:—

"A steam-vessel or sailing-vessel when at anchor shall, at intervals of not more than one minute, ring the bell rapidly or sound the gong for about five seconds; but if such ships are at anchor in a fairway a steam-vessel shall sound two prolonged blasts on her whistle before ringing her bell, and a sailing-vessel shall give two prolonged blasts on her fog-horn before ringing the bell."

I think that the Collocation Committee will undertake to arrange that. We are very much obliged to the learned Delegate from the United States for pointing this out.

Captain Bisbee (China).—Mr. President, I propose the words, "an exposed condition," because I have known of one of the most serious cases of collision where the vessel was out of a fairway, but on account of the insufficiency of her bell a collision occurred and one hundred lives were lost. The wor "fairway" does not cover such a condition as that.

Captain Sampson (United States).—Mr. President, while this additional signal may serve a good purpose, it seems to me that we are going against a principle which we adopted when we first commenced the consideration of the subject of fog-signals. We are multiplying the number of signals to be used in a fog. It seems to me that every vessel, the moment she gets to soundings, should follow the rule laid down by the Conference that she is to proceed at moderate speed; and consequently the danger to a vessel on soundings would be less than to a vessel stationary at sea, where it was not possible to come to anchor. Will the Conference look a little more closely at the signal which is provided here: "Two prolonged blasts with her whistle or siren, followed by ringing her bell." Now, it seems to me evident that the length of the warning given by this signal is limited by the range of the sound of her bell. Consequently the object which it is intended to secure by using the two prolonged blasts serves no purpose except to confound it with the case of a vessel which is described in subsection (*d*). It is only when the vessel approaches one at anchor, to within the range of her sounding bell, that she becomes aware of the fact that it is a vessel at anchor, and not a vessel which is lying still in the water. It seems to me that if we allow the Rule to stand as it now exists, and which is reaffirmed in subsection (*d*) to Article 12, we shall have covered the case completely, and will not have multiplied the signals. We will have given all the warning of the presence of a vessel at anchor it is possible to give, so long as one of the limits of that signal is the ringing of her bell.

Admiral Nares (Great Britain).—Mr. President, I had better explain how we came to choose this character or signal. The argument of the Committee was this: On hearing a sound-signal of another vessel in a fog you have already ordered that the vessel hearing it is to stop her engines and proceed with caution. Then there is a provision that two blasts shall be: "I am stopped and have no way upon me." Now, it does not matter to me when I am approaching a vessel whether I hear two blasts given, coupled with the ringing of the bell, or whether I only hear the two blasts. I am proceeding with caution, and I have to proceed with caution until I get near enough to hear the bell. If I am not proceeding with caution it is, of course, a totally different thing; but a man must be proceeding with caution before he gets near enough to hear the bell. One of these long steamers swinging with the tide-way, instead of presenting 40 or 50 feet to a vessel going the opposite way, is presenting 500 feet, and there is ten times the chance of a collision. In addition to that there are many fishing-boats which anchor in a fairway, and it was very much in their favour that this was adopted. At present the law only provides that they shall ring their bells. They have a fog-horn on board; why not let them give the fog-signal at present approved, to show that they are stationary or stopped; the additional signal of a bell is to show that they are not only stationary and stopped, but fast to the ground.

Captain Donner (Germany).—Mr. President, there seems to be one more reason for adopting this section, because if two ships are near together and a double signal is given to the ship which has stopped her engines, both of these ships think that they are perfectly safe and that one cannot approach the other. But that is not really the case, because if one ship is at anchor the other will be swept down on her by the tide, and a collision will be inevitable. Therefore, there is a great necessity for the ship not being at anchor to know that the other ship is held fast to the ground. Therefore, I propose that this amendment be adopted.

Mr. Hall (Great Britain).—Mr. President, may I also point out just one matter to the gallant Delegate from the United States which I think may possibly have escaped his notice, and that is this: Take a vessel coming up a fairway in a place where she knows that there is anchorage on either side of the fairway where vessels bring up, as is the case in many of our rivers; if she merely hears the ringing of a bell she will say to herself: "This vessel is in the anchorage ground. I will go by her." Vessels are sometimes obliged to drop their anchors actually in a fairway when a fog comes on quickly and they are unable to move. In that case the vessel should be allowed to give the warning: "You must not go up this fairway; there is a vessel giving you a signal that she is at anchor in that fairway, and if you proceed you will do so at your peril."

Captain Richard (France).—Mr. President, when the Committee drew up this paragraph it evidently had in mind the necessity of giving to a vessel anchored in a frequented fairway more than ordinarily efficient means to give notice of her presence. I willingly admit that the ordinary means are insufficient; and although I protest against this classifying of vessels at anchor, I would have no objection to the principle of the proposition, if this new provision were characterized by a proper sound-signal. This would require a perfectly distinct and entirely new signal. Certainly the Committee has shown great ingenuity in drawing all the possible advantage from the sound-signals at their disposition. I think that they have even gone too far in that respect. The bell formerly indicated that the vessel was at anchor. This was a characteristic of it, in the same manner that the whistle indicated the vessel under way. This sensible arrangement has been upset.

The gallant Delegate from the United States just now remarked that the signal of two long blasts, followed by a ringing of a bell, indicated the position of the vessel making those sounds only so far as the sound of the bell could be carried, and beyond that confounded it with that of the vessel not under way, stopped, but not anchored. Cannot something similar be prescribed for the sailing-vessel at anchor in a frequented fairway? She makes two blasts with her fog-horn and then rings the bell. These instruments are not generally very powerful, and the said signal is not calculated to be heard at a great distance. When it is heard vessels are generally close together, and by reason of the difficulty of discovering the spot from whence the sounds of two different apparatus proceed, is it not easy to suppose that your vessel is in the presence both of a sailing-vessel on a port tack and of a vessel at anchor? If you are at a short distance from the signalling vessel you are in danger of seeing a sailing-vessel looming up on the port tack, and also a vessel at anchor.

I again repeat that the Committee showed great ingenuity in devising so many signals by coupling sounds which for that purpose have been diverted from their original meaning. In my opinion it has resulted in sowing the seed of confusion, which should have been avoided.

I therefore propose to the Conference to make paragraph 7 undergo the same fate as paragraph 6, by suppressing it.

Captain Sampson (United States).—Mr. President, it seems to me that, as the gallant Delegate from France has stated, this Rule lacks precision, not only in the signal which is given, but it lacks precision with regard to the place where it applies. The learned Delegate from Great Britain has stated the case of the ship which is forced to anchor in a channel in a fairway, and he says that the ordinary signal of ringing the bell might be mistaken for a vessel anchored in the usual place, adjacent to the fairway. A vessel has no business to anchor in a fairway when the usual anchorage is near at hand. It seems to me that the spirit of this Regulation is not quite so well defined as the others which we have adopted. The vessel would, in many cases, be in doubt whether or not she was anchored in a place which required her to make use of this signal.

Admiral Nares (Great Britain).—Mr. President, it is a mistake to suppose that in a fog a vessel which is in a fairway, in a channel, or in a line of route, can, with safety, put her helm to starboard or port and cross the channel or the course of navigation, thus exhibiting her whole broadside. She must anchor where she is, and if the soundings tell her that there is shallow water in-shore she cannot go towards the shore. She must keep her course straight on, as she was going before, or she must let go her anchor. She cannot safely present her broadside to the general line of navigation or go towards the shore.

Captain Shackford (United States).—Mr. President, I would like to ask how, after a vessel has been two or three days in a fog, it is possible to tell whether she is in a fairway or not? She may be in a fairway and she may not.

Mr. Goodrich (United States).—Mr. President, after all it seems to me that the more we discuss this question the more apparent it becomes that we are making a mistake in providing these two signals. I speak only with a landsman's knowledge, and not with a sailor's knowledge, of the circumstances of the case. I am not entirely clear that the Rule as we have adopted it is fixed to cover all cases; but I am growing more strong in the belief that one signal, either the signal in the old Rule or the signal in the proposed Rule, should be adopted for a vessel at anchor under all circumstances, whether in a fairway or elsewhere. I am very strongly impressed with the remark of my colleague a moment since that a vessel is not able to tell always whether she is in a fairway or not. The very case cited by the learned Delegate from Great Britain is an indication that it is not always certain where the vessel is or what her duty is. It seems to me that there should be one signal for a vessel at anchor under all circumstances. We certainly avoid the multiplicity of the signals by that arrangement. We avoid the possibility of the sailor mistaking the signal which he ought to give. If the signal which we have already adopted, in the judgment of sailors, is not sufficient, then change it for the one in the Rule presented by the Committee; but it seems to me that you had better have one signal for vessels at anchor.

Mr. Carter (Hawaii).—Mr. President, may I point out to the learned Delegate from the United States that we have one signal for vessels at anchor under all conditions? Now it has been clearly shown that there are conditions which require a signal to show that a vessel is anchored under unusual conditions, anchored in a place where she is not expected to be anchored. I move to substitute for this subsection (*f*) an addition to subsection (*d*), as follows: " When a vessel is at anchor in a fairway or other exposed position."

Mr. Goodrich (United States).—Mr. President, let us see what will be the practical result. What does the approaching vessel want to know? Whether she is in a fairway at sea or on soundings, or in a fairway in a river or in a strait? She simply wants to know that a vessel is at anchor there. Now, tell her that. Tell her by one signal. Why do you want two signals? You multiply the danger of misunderstanding the signals by having a number of them. All that she wants to know, it seems to me, is that there is a vessel ahead of her at anchor. Whether she is at anchor in a fairway, the approaching ship can tell. The man who is on the approaching vessel knows whether he is in a fairway at sea or in a river, and it is not necessary that the anchored vessel should add to that stock of knowledge a fact which he already knows.

Mr. Carter (Hawaii).—Mr. President, may I point out to the learned Delegate from the United States that it seems to me there is some difference here. A vessel is anchored on usual anchorage ground, in a fog; the approaching vessel will come at a slow speed, and of course will get near enough to hear the bell before there is any danger of a collision. Now, if a vessel is at anchor off the mouth of a river or in a fairway, she should be allowed to give a signal which will notify the approaching vessel long before the bell can notify her. That will lead the other vessel, naturally, to approach more slowly until she comes near enough to hear the bell signal.

Mr. Goodrich (United States).—Mr. President, the difficulty with that is that my learned friend the Delegate from Hawaii supposes that the vessel which is at sea disobeys the Rule which we enact. Now, do not forget this: You are directing a vessel in the open sea in a fog to do precisely the same thing that you are directing a vessel on the coast or in a crowded way to do; that is, to go at a moderate speed, and to proceed with caution when she hears a signal. This is a duty which you impose upon her in a crowded fairway, and you do not impose any other duty in a crowded fairway than you impose when the vessel is upon the broad sea. Now, all that vessel wants to know, it seems me, is that there is an object ahead of her, and that it is stationary. Just as you put up the white light to indicate in a clear night that there is danger ahead, so you could have a signal to indicate to an approaching vessel that there is a stationary object ahead.

Captain Mensing (Germany).—Mr. President, when the gallant Delegate from China spoke before, he mentioned that he thought the amendment might be necessary because he knew of a case where a ship had been in a very exposed position, and could only ring her bell, which was not sufficient to prevent a collision, and the loss of 100 lives. I would like to call attention to the fact that we have already adopted the signal of a gun, by which we call the attention of an approaching vessel in all such cases. I do not think it will be necessary to have this signal, and, as has been pointed out by a great many Delegates, this Rule is not exactly necessary for any other vessel than such as are in an exposed position. Now, if a ship in an exposed position finds that another ship is near her, she has already the right to fire a gun, and so warn the other ship which is coming near. The difficulty in adopting the amendment proposed by the learned Delegate from Hawaii is that if we adopt his words any steam-vessel at anchor would have to ring her bell, and at the same time blow her whistle, which, I think, might lead to confusion. Although I have been in favour of this amendment before, I must declare that I see a great many difficulties which have been pointed out, and which have not been set right by the gentleman who proposed it.

Admiral Nares (Great Britain).—Mr. President, may I speak in answer to what has fallen from the learned Delegate from the United States? In a fog we are to conduct our vessels with caution, and he argues as if we are both in calm waters and have merely to look after the rate of speed. This signal is specially directed to the case where we are at anchor in a tide-way, of perhaps 4 or 7 knots an an hour. Whatever precautions people take, when they only hear the present signal, they do not know whether the vessel is at anchor or not. What they want to know is that the vessel is at anchor in a place where vessels do not generally anchor, and then we know the tide, and we are able to calculate. If the tide is running past this vessel at anchor at 5 knots an hour, I may, although my vessel is not moving through the water, drift into her at the rate of 5 knots an hour.

Mr. Hall (Great Britain).—Mr. President, I have listened with great interest to the observations which have fallen from the various members of the Conference, and I only desire to say one or two words. The Conference has adhered to the principle adopted in its original Resolution not to extend this system of signals in fog to the very great extent which was proposed by some gentleman. We now see how very difficult it is to find one or two fresh signals. It is not a question of having thirty-two signals or forty-eight signals, but we now find ourselves at our wits' ends, almost, to find two fresh signals for use in a fog. I have listened with great attention to what has fallen from the various speakers, and I must confess that I have not heard anything as yet which has induced me to change my opinion that this is a good signal to indicate that a vessel is at anchor in a place where it would not be expected that she would be at anchor. Such information would be a great assistance to people who are navigating in a fog.

I have been considering whether I could devise some form of words which would meet the objections which have been made. I have already pointed out the case of a vessel being at anchor in a fairway, and that a man in charge of a vessel coming up that fairway or channel hearing the ordinary bell might at once think that the vessel was at anchor on either side of the channel, whereas that vessel might be at anchor blocking up the passage. There might be other cases, as, for instance, a steamer without steam on, or a vessel not under command, bringing herself to anchor. I think it is desirable for us to point out as specifically as we can all the cases which we desire to meet, and not merely the case which would possibly be included in the words "in a fairway." I would suggest this: "If such a vessel is not in the ordinary anchorage ground, or is in such a position as to be in the way of vessels using the ordinary channel, then she shall give these signals." I think that would include, so far as I can see, the case of a vessel anchored in a place where it is not expected to find her. So far as I can see, I think it is very desirable that a vessel which is at anchor in such a place should give some warning of her being there beyond merely the ringing of her bell.

Mr. Goodrich (United States).—Mr. President, I have listened, as usual, with a great deal of respect and attention to the First Delegate from Great Britain upon these topics, but I fail to be convinced that I am in error in the position which I have taken upon this Rule. We have adopted the principle in making these Rules to have them perfectly plain to the man who is, in the first instance, required to decide what they mean. Now, let us see if we are going to put any difficulty in the way. Here is a master coming into a harbour, when a fog suddenly shuts down upon him. There having been no fog before, and perhaps no reason to anticipate a fog, he has not his soundings exactly. He has been sailing by the shore line. He has been sailing, if at night, by the shore-lights, and he is called upon to anchor by reason of a fog. What has he to do? He has first to decide where he is, whether he is in a fairway, or whether he is not in a fairway, and according as he decides that question, he is to give a proper signal. Suppose the fog has been threatening, and he wishes to sail on through a light fog. You are to make the anchored ship decide where she is, and to give notice to a vessel approaching as to where she is, when that vessel knows just as well as she does, and has the same chance to know. The difficulty is that you are making the sailor decide as to what his position is, and what signal he should give. If you do not give enough notice by the signal which we have already adopted, then change the signal to the one which is proposed in the Report of the Committee.

Captain Donner (Germany).—Mr. President, I must declare that I formerly was in favour of this new Rule, but upon hearing the arguments advanced, my opinion has altered, and I am now ready to say that the Conference will make a great mistake if they allow this new Rule to pass. The reason is this: We are legislating for exceptions. That is wrong in the beginning. Such a case is only an exceptional one. Of course, ships sometimes may anchor in the open sea, but generally they do not do it, and to make a special law in these Regulations for exceptions does not seem to be right. There is another point to which I wish to call attention. If you hear in the open sea two prolonged blasts and a bell, what is to tell you that you have one ship or two ships before you, if you do not see them? I would say that we are producing a new danger. A man might say, " Here is one ship making two blasts, and here is another ship close by at anchor." How is he to manœuvre, and what is he to do? I, therefore, really think that this Article should be left out altogether.

Captain Shackford (United States).—Mr. President, I merely want to say to my learned colleagues that the six sailors on this Committee had no difficulty at all in arranging this and seeing through it clearly. It was only after it got into the hands of the Conference here, and the lawyers got to twisting it around, that we failed to understand it.

Mr. Hall (Great Britain).—Mr. President, as yet I have not heard from any sailor who was on that Committee that the arguments have induced him to change his opinion. I do not understand that the gallant Delegate from the United States has changed his opinion in regard to the matter. I presume that the Committee treated this matter very carefully. If I vote for this proposition, I shall vote for it as being the Report of the Committee. I quite see that there are arguments against it, as there will be against everything, and those arguments have been advanced as powerfully as they can be. But this is a carefully considered Report of the Committee, which has thoroughly inquired into the subject, and at present I can see no reason for not adopting that Report.

Admiral Nares (Great Britain).—Mr. President, before the question is put, may I say, on the part of the Committee, that if this signal is not carried it will mean that vessels anchored in these general places are left only with their bells to give warning to one another?

Mr. Verney (Siam).—Mr. President, may I suggest to the gallant Delegate who has just sat down whether, perhaps, the opinions of everybody might be met if some single signal rather better than that which is now adopted could be discovered to cover all cases? I am merely following out the suggestion which was foreshadowed by the learned Delegate of the United States.

Admiral Nares (Great Britain).—Mr. President, I can easily give you any amount of signals, but the difficulty is to give people memories to take the signals in. That we cannot do. We have adopted this signal as a danger-signal. Whenever you hear a vessel sounding two prolonged blasts, it is a known danger on the ocean. We have adopted that. Now, we only go one step beyond that and couple with it the known signal of a vessel at anchor. Now, there is very little for the memory to take in in that proposition; it will be long before a new signal becomes generally known. The Committee must stand or fall, if you please, upon this signal which we have adopted.

Mr. Hall (Great Britain).—May I ask the Delegate from Siam whether he can suggest a signal?

Mr Verney (Siam).—I am not a member of the Collocation Committee.

Mr. Carter (Hawaii).—Mr. President, it does seem to me that the Committee has followed out the logical result of the action of the Conference, and the practice on the sea. A vessel anchored in this exposed condition does constitute a danger on the sea, and she is to sound her blasts. She is a danger at anchor, and she rings her bell to show that she is at anchor. It seems to me a very simple proposition, and I confess that I have not been swayed at all from that idea by the arguments which I have heard.

Captain Sampson (United States).—Mr. President, suppose that this Rule is adopted. Suppose that the person in command of the ship has anchored in a fog. Now, imagine a case where he thinks he should make the ordinary signal of a ship at anchor. Another vessel approaching him would be misled because he would argue—if that ship is in a fairway or if that ship is in any danger of being run into by my vessel, she would make the signal which is required by this subsection (f). But if she only makes the ordinary signal she is out of my way, and the consequence would be that the vessel would be run down, simply because we have got another Rule. If the Rule which we have already adopted covers both cases, the approaching vessel would know that there was a vessel at anchor somewhere in her way, and she would be careful and cautious to avoid her. Subsection (f), as mentioned by the different speakers, seems to touch either the sea, the harbour, or a fairway, so that it is very difficult to find out what its application is. That is one of the fundamental objections to it, that it is not sufficiently definite to enable the master of a ship to say that he should make one signal or the other. There may be many cases where he would be certain which signal to make, but there will be cases where he will be uncertain, and where he might make a mistake which would be fatal.

Mr. Carter (Hawaii).—Mr. President, may I point out that the amendment of the learned Delegate from Great Britain meets that objection?

Captain Sampson (United States).—The spirit of it is the same. There are two signals to indicate a ship at anchor, and I think that is objectionable.

Captain Richard (France).—Mr. President, so far as I can judge, the intention of the Committee in proposing paragraph (f) is to give to the vessels at anchor in fairways, where they are more exposed to collision, greater security than that enjoyed by vessels at anchor under ordinary circumstances. I venture to say that the bell is not a sufficiently powerful instrument to give sufficient security. But what will be the consequence of the proposed Rule, if it is adopted? In my opinion it will become imperative to give the same signal to all vessels at anchor wherever they may be. Then the old proverb will immediately be recalled, " Qui peut le plus peut le moins;" that is to say, inasmuch as you intend to give additional security to vessels in frequented fairways because the bell is not sufficient security, why not give the same security to all other vessels at anchor which have bells of the same character, and which are also exposed, although to a less degree, to similar positions. The problem is therefore this—to give to an anchored vessel a sufficient signal. Have we for that purpose a proper sound-signal? I do not think so, and I do not observe any with the means now at our disposal. For that reason I object to these distinctions between vessels at anchor in some places and vessels at anchor in others. This may lead to further particularizing, and for each new case it will be necessary to find a new signal.

The President.—The last proposition with regard to this Article was by the Delegate from Great Britain.

Captain Shackford (United States)—Mr. President, if this Article should read, " at anchor in the open sea," I would like to know if it would meet the objections of the gentlemen.

Mr. Hall (Great Britain).—Mr. President, the words which I propose would include the open sea.

Captain Shackford (United States).—Mr. President, the opinion seems to be that words " in a fairway" should be stricken out.

The President.—If the Delegate has a proposition to make, he will be kind enough to make it in writing, so that it can be placed before the Conference.

Captain Shackford (United States).—Mr. President, I move that the Article read:—

" A vessel, if a steam-vessel, at anchor in the open sea, shall at intervals of not more than two minutes sound two prolonged blasts with her whistle or siren, followed by ringing her bell," &c.

Mr. Goodrich (United States).—Mr. President, there is a great difficulty about that, I suggest. It puts upon the sailor the difficulty of deciding what the open sea is. There is some difficulty in deciding what is the open sea, and where the limit of territory commences and where it ends. It strikes me that some nations have had very grave questions upon that subject, on both sides of this hemisphere.

Mr. Hall (Great Britain).—Mr. President, for that reason I proposed the words which I have the honour to propose, and I confess I prefer them to the words of the Delegate from the United States. The words are: " If she is not in ordinary anchorage ground or is in such a position as to be in the way of vessels using the ordinary channel."

I want to make one remark with regard to what has fallen from the gallant Delegate from the United States. He said, " A man may be mistaken as to where he is." Granted. But no Court of Law that I know of in any civilized country will ever hold a man to blame for not doing a thing unless he knew or ought to know that it was his duty. Then he will be perfectly excusable if he gives the wrong signal, being under a misapprehension, when he has only done what he believed to be right. You cannot hold a man to blame for breaking a Rule if he does not know what he ought to do. He must act as a reasonable sailor, and nothing else.

Captain Sampson (United States).—He might lose his vessel.

Mr. Hall (Great Britain).—He might lose that anyhow.

The President.—The motion of Captain Shackford will now be read.

Captain Norcross (United States).—Mr. President, I prefer the words as they stand here, " in a fairway at sea."

Captain Shackford (United States).—Mr. President, I withdraw my amendment in favour of the amendment of the Delegate from Great Britain.

The President.—The question now is upon the amendment of the Delegate from Great Britain, which will be read.

The amendment is as follows:—

" A vessel, if a steam-vessel, if she is not in the ordinary anchorage ground, or in such a position as to be in the way of a vessel using the ordinary channel, shall at intervals of not more than two minutes sound two prolonged blasts with her whistle or siren, followed by ringing her bell; or, if a sailing-vessel, two blasts with her fog-horn, followed by ringing her bell."

Mr. Goodrich (United States).—Mr. President, I think, as my friend on my right says, that this is worse than it was before. What would you call a vessel traversing the track of the North Atlantic steam-ships, if there is such a track? Would you include that in the word " channel"? Hardly, under the general acceptation of the term; and yet I suppose that the Delegate from Great Britain intends it to be included in his amendment.

Mr. Hall (Great Britain).—Mr. President, the officer in command of a vessel can generally have a pretty good idea as to whether or not he is anchored in a place where he is liable to be in the way of vessels which ordinarily ply in that neighbourhood. A man must know whether he is at anchor in an ordinary anchorage ground or in a place where he is liable to cause danger, and it is proper that he should be allowed to give a warning signal so as to show vessels that the way is not clear, as they would otherwise expect it to be.

Captain Sampson (United States).—Mr. President, it seems to me that the wording of the amendment as it stands now is less objectionable than it would be as amended by the learned Delegate from Great Britain, because the words which he has introduced bring the limit of the area in which this signal must be made much nearer to the shore. It brings it within the ordinary channels of a river or harbour. The amendment as it stands now says, " a fairway at sea." The term " at sea " may be indefinite, but still to my mind there is much less objection to adopting this special signal under such circumstances than there would be if we brought its limit into channels and rivers, nearer the shore than is provided for in the amendment as it stands now.

The President.—The question is upon the amendment of the Delegate from Great Britain, which will be read for the information of the Conference.

The amendment is as follows:—

"A vessel, if a steam-vessel, if she is not in the ordinary anchorage ground, or is in such a position as to be in the way of a vessel using the ordinary channel, shall at intervals of not more than two minutes sound two prolonged blasts with her whistle or siren, followed by ringing her bell; or, if a sailing-vessel, two blasts with her fog-horn, followed by ringing her bell."

Mr. Goodrich (United States).—Mr. President, I would like to ask the learned Delegate from Great Britain what he means by the word "channel."

Mr. Hall (Great Britain).—Mr. President, I will answer the learned Delegate at once. I think I could possibly make an alteration to meet that possible difficulty by using the words, "a fairway at sea." and inserting the words, "if not in the ordinary anchorage ground." So as to make it read: "When she is not in the ordinary anchorage ground, or in such a position as to be an obstruction to vessels in a fairway at sea."

Mr. Goodrich (United States).—Mr. President, I think that will be a good deal more definite. Will you repeat that once more?

Mr. Hall (Great Britain).—Make it read: "if she is not in the ordinary anchorage ground, or is in such a position as to be an obstruction to vessels in a fairway at sea."

Captain Richard (France).—Mr. President, it seems to me that the Conference could avoid a waste of valuable time by paying no attention to the wording of the Article itself. It would perhaps be better to know first whether the Conference desires to adopt the principle of the Article. If it does, it could be subsequently discussed. If, as I trust, the Conference does not approve the principle of the Article, it is not necessary to discuss its wording. I therefore take the liberty to propose that the Conference be consulted as to its views upon the principle of the Article.

Mr. Goodrich (United States).—Mr. President, it seems to me that we are in danger of passing on words the full force of which we are not prepared to appreciate. The great question here is whether the idea of the Committee will be adopted or not. I think we had better take the question first upon the principle. The matter of wording can very properly be referred to the Collocation Committee. I presume my friend the First Delegate from Great Britain will assume that responsibility. Certainly some of the rest of us will be quite willing to unite with him in doing it. I suggest that we take the question upon the principle, and then word this very carefully. I will move that the principle involved in this subsection (f) be adopted, and that the wording be referred to the Collocation Committee.

Mr. Hall (Great Britain).—Mr. President, as a brother member of the Collocation Committee, or I should say, as a very humble member of that Committee of which the learned Delegate from the United States is the Chairman, I am perfectly willing to assume the limited portion of the responsibility which attaches to a member of a Committee, and I shall look to my Chairman to assist us in the matter. I am very glad to support the proposition which he makes.

The President.—The motion is to adopt the principle of subsection (f), and if it be carried in the affirmative, to refer it to the Collocation Committee. Is the Conference ready for the question?

The question was put to the Conference upon the adoption of the motion to refer this paragraph (f) to the Collocation Committee.

The President.—The Chair is unable to decide.

The Yeas and Nays were called for.

The Yeas and Nays were as follows:—

Austria-Hungary	.. ..	Yea.	Japan	Yea.
Belgium	.. .. ..	Nay.	Mexico	Yea.
China	.. .. ..	Nay.	Norway	Yea.
Chile	.. .. ..	Nay.	Portugal	Yea.
Denmark	.. .. ..	Yea.	Russia	Nay.
France	.. .. ..	Nay.	Spain	Nay.
Germany	.. .. ..	Nay.	Sweden	Nay.
Great Britain	.. ..	Yea.	Siam	Yea.
Hawaii	.. .. ..	Yea.	The Netherlands ..	Yea.
Italy	.. .. ..	Yea.	United States	Yea.

The President.—Twelve have voted in the affirmative, and eight in the negative; so the principle is adopted.

Lieutenant Seoane (Spain).—Mr. President, I had the honour of proposing an amendment to the Rules of the Road in regard to coupled trawling-vessels. It was voted upon during my absence, while the printed amendments were being distributed to the Delegates. In view of the custom or the rule requiring a certain time to elapse between the distribution of the printed amendment and its discussion, I would ask the Conference to take up my amendment for a second reading.

The President.—The Delegate from Spain desires a reconsideration of his amendment, on the ground that it has not been long enough before the Conference, and that he was not present when it was considered.

The question upon the reconsideration of the amendment of the Delegate from Spain was put to the Conference and carried.

Lieutenant Beaugency (Chile).—Mr. President, the Conference has adopted paragraph (f) in principle, and has referred it to the Collocation Committee. It would be desirable to have the Committee report upon this subsection before their final Report is received.

Mr. Goodrich (United States).—Mr. President, will the gallant Delegate from Chile allow me to suggest the plan which the Collocation Committee will adopt? The Committee have had printed, and are using for their own information, the Rules as they have been passed. Some amendments are being made by the Collocation Committee.

These will be indicated in our printed Report in just the same manner as the amendments made by the Conference. The ordinary sections will contain the Resolutions as passed by the Conference, and the amendments made by the Collocation Committee will be in italics, so that every member, in due season, will have notice of what has been done.

Lieutenant Beaugency (Chile).—Mr. President, we will not have time to consider them after the final Report of the Committee comes before us. It would be better to have them in before the Report of the Collocation Committee, and have another reading before that time.

Captain Malmberg (Sweden).—Mr. President, if I understand rightly, the gallant Delegate from Chile wants the Conference to decide upon the wording of that, "in a fairway at sea." I will support the motion that it be decided here in the Conference how it is to appear in that paragraph. I wish that this Article, which has now been discussed in principle, should be fully discussed in the Conference.

Mr. Goodrich (United States).—Mr. President, I suppose that if the Committee do not agree with the views of the Conference, in their expression in the Report, the amendments can be made to the Report of the Committee.

Captain Malmberg (Sweden).—Mr. President, will it not save time if the Conference will decide that question?

Mr. Goodrich (United States).—The Collocation Committee will be delighted to be relieved from it.

The President.—The Chair understands that the Delegate from Chile wishes the Report on this paragraph made and printed by the Collocation Committee, so that it can be submitted before the final vote on the Report of that Committee.

Lieutenant Beaugency (Chile).—That is my motion, Sir.

The President.—So that it will be before the Conference before it comes up for final discussion. That is what I understand the Delegate from Chile wishes.

Mr. Goodrich (United States).—That will be done, Sir.

The President.—So that it will be submitted from twenty-four to forty-eight hours before it is finally acted upon.

Mr. Goodrich (United States).—Mr. President, that will be true of the whole Report. I think there should be forty-eight hours at least given for the consideration of that Report when it comes up, because that is final. In the meanwhile, of course, the Conference can be discussing some of the other subjects which are coming before it on some of the general subdivisions of the Programme.

The Conference thereupon, at 4 P.M., adjourned until Tuesday morning, 3rd December, 1889, at 11 o'clock.

Washington, Tuesday, December 3, 1889.

THE Conference was called to order at 11 o'clock A.M., Rear-Admiral Franklin in the Chair.

Captain Salvesen (Norway).—Mr. President, it may perhaps be rather late in the session to ask to have an Article reconsidered, but the more I have thought about it and spoken with other Delegates, the more I find it desirable to have the Article about the lights for a towing vessel reconsidered. As it now stands, a vessel towing more than one vessel shall carry three lanterns, without any exception. The consequence is that the three lanterns will be compulsory, even if only two small barges or boats are taken in tow. Under the discussion, all the arguments in favour of this additional lantern were based upon the long tows which might be met with, particularly on this coast. I beg to move that the length of the tow also should be taken into consideration, so that the Rule should be:—

"And when towing more than one vessel shall carry an additional bright white light 6 feet above or below such lights, provided that the length of the tow exceeds 600 feet."

The President.—The Delegate from Norway moves to reconsider Article 4 for the purpose of making it read as it has just been presented to the Conference. It will now be read by the Secretary.

Mr. Hall (Great Britain).—Mr. President, I hope that the Delegates will accede to the proposition of the gallant Delegate from Norway, because the amendment which he wishes to propose is one that, so far as I can see, is absolutely necessary. The amendment which was accepted some time since by the Conference did not take into consideration the fact that in the wording, as it stands at present, a tug would be obliged to hoist three lights if she took even a second barge in tow, which of course would be an absurdity. So this proposed amendment is merely to put some limit upon the Rule and say that a tug towing more than one vessel is not to be obliged to hoist a third light unless it is necessary. I hope, therefore, that the Conference will accede to the motion, as it is really to correct an oversight. Perhaps, therefore, the Delegates may be of the opinion that it is not necessary to have this amendment printed and laid before them, but that it may be adopted at this session of the Conference.

Mr. Goodrich (United States).—Mr. President, this subject was first brought before the Conference by an amendment proposed by Captain Norcross, of the Delegation from the United States, which practically provided for the same thing, and which was approved by the Conference. The amendment which is made to Article 4, which has just been referred to, is somewhat limited in its scope, for it was designed to apply chiefly to the great coal barges which pass from the southern ports along our coast to Boston and New York and farther to the eastward. We can see that the objection made by Captain Salvesen is a proper one, and the United States' Delegates are in favour of the amendment proposed by him.

Captain Norcross (United States).—Mr. President, in offering the amendment to Article 4, I had express view to steamers towing barges at sea at the end of a long hawser. I shall be very glad to accept the amendment offered by the gallant Delegate from Norway.

Captain Bisbee (China).—Mr. President, I desire to ask whether it will be necessary to indicate what the length of a tow is. Where do you begin to measure; from the stern of the tow to the stern of the aftermost vessel being towed?

Captain Shackford (United States).—Mr. President, I should say it would be from the bow of the tow-boat, the whole length of the structure.

The President.—The question is upon the reconsideration of the amendment to Article 4.

The question upon the reconsideration was put to the Conference, and was carried.

The President.—The Article is now before the Conference. The question is upon the passage of Article 4 as amended. The amendment will be read.

The amendment is as follows:—

To add to extra amendment No. 52, Article 4, the following words:

" Provided that the length of the tow exceeds 600 feet."

Mr. Goodrich (United States).—Mr. President, I suggest to the gallant Delegate from Norway that these words should come into the amendment at the end of the first paragraph. As the Collocation Committee have the Article, the first part of it reads: "A steam-vessel when towing another vessel shall, in addition to its side-lights, carry two bright white lights, one over the other, not less than 6 feet apart, and when towing more than one vessel shall carry an additional bright white light 6 feet above or below such lights."

Captain Salvesen (Norway).—Then should come in: "provided that the length of the tow exceeds 600 feet."

Captain Richard (France).—Mr. President, the amendment which has been read has been considered by the Conference, and I have an objection to its language. It seems to me that the expression, "600 feet," which is something like 180 metres, French measurement, is far too great a length. When a vessel tows another, the length of the hawser varies according to the weather. When the weather is fine, and the sea smooth, you can have a comparatively short hawser, say 60 to 80 metres long; and when the weather is bad, with a heavy sea, or under certain special conditions, you are obliged to have between the towing vessel and the vessel in tow, as we all know, longer hawsers. I do not think that, generally, in cases of towing the average length of the hawser exceeds 100 metres. I have had occasion, in my career as a seaman, frequently to tow three-decked vessels, and I have never seen the necessity of employing hawsers over 120 metres long. A three-decker is, moreover, a vessel of no little tonnage. I think that we should reduce this distance to 80 or 100 metres instead of 600 feet.

Captain Salvesen (Norway).—Mr. President, I think the gallant Delegate from France has misunderstood the word "tow," taking it to be the length of the tow-line. It means here the combined length of the tow-line and the length of the vessel or vessels in tow.

Captain Bisbee (China).—Mr. President, I beg to propose an amendment to Captain Salvesen's amendment in these words: " Provided that the length of the tow, measuring from the bow of the towing-vessel to the stern of the aftermost vessel being towed, shall exceed 600 feet."

Mr. Goodrich (United States).—Mr. President, I have suggested to the gallant Delegate from Norway that he put in the word "whole" before the word "tow," which I think will cover the point, so that it will read: " provided that the whole length of the tow exceeds 600 feet."

Mr. Hall (Great Britain).—Then that would include the towing-vessel.

Mr. Goodrich (United States).—In our language, as decided by the Courts, it would include it.

Mr. Hall (Great Britain).—Mr. President, I think the words which have fallen from the gallant Delegate from France show how necessary it is to use words which can be translated into other languages without any doubt, and it is clear that there is some doubt with regard to the translation of the language used in this proposed amendment as presented by the gallant Delegate from Norway. The word "tow" to him would mean only the scope of the hawser by which the vessel is towed. In our language the word "tow" includes not only the scope of the hawser, but the vessel which is being towed.

The President.—The amendment of the Delegate from China will be read.

The amendment is as follows:—

"To add after the words 'such lights' the following: 'Provided that the length of the tow, measuring from the bow of the towing vessel to the stern of the aftermost vessel towed, shall exceed 600 feet.'"

Mr. Hall (Great Britain).—Mr. President, I suggest that perhaps it would be better to have it read, "from the stern of the towing vessel to the stern of the vessel being towed," because you cannot call the towing vessel a part of the tow.

Captain Bisbee (China).—But you might have a vessel 500 feet long towing a vessel 50 feet long, or towing two vessels which are together 200 feet long.

Mr. Hall (Great Britain).—Then there is more reason for excluding the towing vessel if she is 500 feet long, because that would only leave 100 feet for the two tows.

Captain Bisbee (China).—If you make the tow to mean from the stern of the vessel towing, and the vessel towing is 500 feet long, you have got a tow of 1,100 feet, or, at least, you have got an obstacle to navigation of 1,100 feet.

Mr. Hall (Great Britain).—Mr. President, what we want to do is to gauge the distance from aft of the towing vessel to the end of the tow. We cannot do that if we are to calculate in that distance the towing vessel, because she may be a vessel 500 feet long, or she may be a vessel only 50 feet long. We want to have an ascertained distance behind the towing vessel. We get that at once if we take the length of the tow to be the length from the stern of the towing vessel; but it would appear to me to be a confusion of terms to say that the length of the tow is to be the length of the towing vessel and the length of the tow. The length of the tow is the length from the stern of the towing vessel to the stern of the last vessel which is towed. If we accept what the gallant Delegate from Norway originally proposed, that distance would be 600 feet from the vessel which is towing to the stern of the last vessel towed. I think that is clear.

The President.—Does the Delegate from China wish a vote upon his amendment?

Captain Bisbee (China).—Mr. President, there seems to be a difference of opinion among nautical men here, and I think it would be better to have a vote as to whether the definition of the tow should include the length of the towing vessel or not, and then we can make the Rule accordingly.

Captain Salvesen (Norway).—Mr. President, I think this distance of 600 feet would be rather too short a distance. The distance may be altered afterwards if the word "tow" is to include the towing vessel.

The President.—Does the Delegate from Norway make any proposition?

Captain Salvesen (Norway).—Mr. President, I only want to state that when I made my proposal I understood that the tow would be the distance between the stern of the towing vessel and the stern of the last vessel in tow.

Mr. Hall (Great Britain).—Mr. President, perhaps, in order to put the matter before the Conference, I may move, as an amendment to the words suggested by the gallant Delegate from China, the following, so that it will read: "from the stern of the towing vessel to the stern of the last vessel towed;" to substitute the word "stern" for the word "bow" in the first part of the sentence. I will point out to the Delegate from China that, of course, if you include the length of the towing vessel you would leave nothing behind for the tow, if it is a long vessel.

Captain Bisbee (China).—Mr. President, I have no objection to that. I will accept the amendment.

The President.—The Delegate from China states that he accepts the proposition of the Delegate from Great Britain, which amounts to the same thing as the proposal of the Delegate from Norway.

Mr. Hall (Great Britain).—Mr. President, perhaps I may say that I think this meets the views of the gallant Delegate from Norway. It is merely accepting his proposition. I would therefore suggest to him these words:—

"Provided that the length of the tow, measuring from the stern of the towing vessel to the stern of the last vessel towed, exceeds 600 feet."

Captain Salvesen (Norway).—That is exactly what I intended it to be.

The President.—Does the Delegate from Norway accept the suggestion of the Delegate from Great Britain?

Captain Salvesen (Norway).—Yes, Sir.

The President.—The amendment will be read.

The amendment is as follows:—

"To add after the words 'such lights' the following: 'provided that the length of the tow, measuring from the stern of the towing vessel to the stern of the last vessel towed, exceeds 600 feet.'"

The President.—Is the Conference ready for the question upon this amendment?

The question was put to the Conference upon the amendment, and it was adopted.

The President.—The question now is upon Article 4 as amended.

The question was put to the Conference upon the adoption of Article 4 as amended, and it was adopted.

The President.—The next business in order is the amendment proposed by the Delegate from Spain, extra amendment No. 60, which comes up this morning for consideration, and will be read by the Secretary.

Extra amendment No. 60 is as follows:—

"All vessels under way shall keep out of the way of coupled steamers engaged in trawling."

Lieutenant Vega de Seoane (Spain).—Mr. President, by accepting the amendment presented the other day by the Honourable Dr. Sieveking, Delegate from Germany, the Conference fixed in principle the Rules of the Road for trawling-vessels. You have imposed upon ordinary steam trawling-vessels the same duties as upon steam merchant-vessels, which is, in my opinion, too hard, and you leave the right of way invariably to sailing trawlers. But there is a third class of trawling-vessels which fish almost exclusively upon the banks in the Bay of Biscay, and which, although propelled by steam, do so under special conditions, which, in my opinion, prevent their being placed in the same category with ordinary steam trawling-vessels.

I will endeavour briefly to explain to you, with your permission, their mode of operation, and then you can judge for yourselves. These trawling-vessels are coupled for the purpose of dragging between them a single net. Placed parallel and at a short distance from each other, they cruize along the banks at a moderate speed, each of them dragging an end of the same net. Under those circumstances any rapid change of course exposes them not only to the risk of colliding with each other, but also—and this is more serious, and certainly more common—to entangling the nets which they are dragging with the propeller of one of the trawling-vessels. Such an occurrence not only means the loss of the net, whose value is from 5,000 fr. to 6,000 fr., but also disables one of the trawling-vessels. And in waters as dangerous as that part of the Bay of Biscay this amounts to exposing a vessel to a very probable collision.

I hope that the Conference, and especially nautical Delegates, whom I earnestly request to give an opinion on the subject, will consider that there is an essential difference between such vessels and ordinary steam trawlers and even sailing trawlers, which are to a certain extent always under command, and which can manœuvre with more or less difficulty, but without risk of being damaged, and which can get out of the way of vessels which they meet. This is not the case with the coupled trawling-vessels; they have less control of their movements than sailing trawlers, and I would ask you to extend to them the exception which you have made for the latter by accepting my amendment. I do not think that it would be just, and I do not even think that it would be possible, to compel these trawling-vessels to go out of the way for other vessels. If you accept my amendment you will not introduce anything new into the customs of seamen. You will only establish a law, the principle of which has been established by the common sense of the captains who navigate fishing-grounds frequented by these trawling-vessels, and which custom has already been sanctioned. All the vessels sailing from British ports and other countries in the north of Europe to the south-eastern ports of France and the northern ports of Spain, to Bayonne, to Passages, to St. Sebastian, to Bilbao, must cross the fishing-grounds of these vessels. Although the law does not now compel them to do so, and no one imposes the obligation upon them so to do, these vessels always give the right of way to these trawling-vessels. No one has ever made any complaint about it. This circumstance certainly ought to be taken into consideration by this Conference, which makes laws for the acceptance of all nations.

Mr. Goodrich (United States).—Mr. President, I was in favour of reconsidering the vote by which this amendment of the gallant Delegate from Spain was rejected, because he was absent from the Conference at the time of the vote, and because I think that the Conference desires that every opportunity shall be given to every one to discuss the proposals which have made an impression upon his own mind. It seems to me that this matter was thoroughly discussed yesterday in the absence of the gallant Delegate from Spain, and that the reasons which presented themselves to the Conference at that time will not be shaken by anything which he has said. In the first place, these coupled trawlers give no indication to approaching vessels of the fact that they are trawling; and in addition to that, it is giving to these vessels, which are steamers, a right of way over sailing-vessels of any kind whatever, and under all circumstances. That seems to me to be a very vicious proposition. The Conference has several times refused to give the right of way to steamers over sailing-vessels under various circumstances; and I think it would be a very wrong principle to engraft upon these Rules, and to overturn the whole system for the sake of giving the right of way to steamers engaged in fishing.

Lieutenant Vega de Seoane (Spain).—Mr. President, allow me to make one remark to the objection of the learned Delegate of the United States. The danger that these trawling-vessels will not be recognized by the vessels which they meet at sea should not be an obstacle to accepting my amendment. Two steam-vessels of about the same shape and the same size, very near to each other and steaming in the same direction, are without any further indications sufficient to show at a distance that they are trawling-vessels.

In regard to the difficulties which the adoption of my amendment would create in regard to sailing-vessels, to which we should always grant facilities, I would remark first that at present they give the right of way to these trawling-vessels, and they have never complained about it; and, secondly, I think that sailing-vessels are better under command than these coupled trawling-vessels. In my opinion we should give greater facilities to these vessels which are labouring under greater difficulties to manœuvre.

Captain Mensing (Germany).—Mr. President, I think there is a certain foundation underlying the proposal of the gallant Delegate from Spain. But as the learned Delegate from the United States has pointed out, there is great danger in allowing the right of way over sailing-vessels to coupled steamers engaged in trawling. It is scarcely possible for vessels in this position to get out of the way as easily as other vessels, for they have to wheel instead of turn, and are more or less hampered by the nets which they have out astern. It is likely that these nets will foul their screws if they manœuvre, and in addition they have to look after the hawsers used by both vessels to keep them in position with regard to each other. However, they are not in a more dangerous or difficult position than vessels which are under tow; large vessels being towed by small vessels are in a more dangerous position. But the Conference has adopted the principle that it should be left to the generosity of vessels meeting tows to get out of the way. I think it might just as well be left to the generosity of mariners, on finding these trawling steamers on the high seas, where there is no difficulty whatever for them to go to the right or left, and get out of the way if they choose. At the same time I should be glad if the gallant Delegate from France, who I believe has some interest in this matter as there are some French vessels which are engaged in these fishing operations, would give us his opinion.

Captain Richard (France).—Mr. President, the gallant Delegate from Germany has asked my opinion on that subject. I do consider that France is sufficiently interested in the Bay of Biscay to see that the operations of steam trawling-vessels which are coupled for the purpose of jointly fishing and for the purpose of dragging a trawling-net more easily and advantageously, should not be hindered. It is also true that France has a certain number of fishing-vessels engaged in that kind of fishing in the Bay of Biscay. Although I will vote for the proposition of the gallant Delegate from Spain, I deem it proper to state to the Conference that I do not consider this measure absolutely necessary.

I think that in our Rules of the Road we should only insert what is strictly necessary. I am afraid that in some of the Resolutions which have been adopted we have to a certain extent overlooked this principle. But if the Conference has infringed this principle, I do not think that a reason to depart from the general rule which I have adopted for my guidance, viz., invariably to consider the question from its widest and most liberal stand-point. Moreover, I am encouraged to continue in that path because, as it was observed by my gallant friend the Delegate from Spain, no complaint has been made on the subject, and the existing state of affairs is satisfactory. When a vessel sees two trawling-vessels coupled, she generally will get out of their way. This is all the more easy for her to do, inasmuch as in the Bay of Biscay, where these trawling-vessels are engaged in fishing, it is easy to manœuvre in one way or another and to change one's course without any trouble. But it may also happen that a strange vessel passing through the Bay of Biscay for the first time might encounter a group of these trawling-vessels, and produce a certain amount of trouble in the fishing operations of these vessels. There is no doubt that the cause is a worthy one. A fishing-vessel should, as far as possible, not be disturbed in her work; but should a Rule be made solely for her? I do not think that there are more than a hundred trawling-vessels engaged in the Bay of Biscay. I would state that I will vote in favour of the proposition of our colleague from Spain, for he champions a worthy cause, but I am unable to make any converts.

Mr. Hall (Great Britain).—Mr. President, it appears to me that there are strong arguments against the adoption of this proposal which has been brought forward by the gallant Delegate from Spain; and one of these has been advanced by the gallant Delegate from France. But the strongest argument of all, so far as I can see, is the argument upon principle which has been advanced by the learned Delegate from the United States. He has pointed out that in adopting this we would be running counter to the general principle of the Rules of the Road at Sea, which is that steamers are to keep out of the way of sailing-vessels. I think there should be a very strong case made out for any departure from that principle.

That is the ordinary principle, and now we come to a particular case. Can it be suggested that the exceptional cases which we have heard of, and which are referred to by the gallant Delegate from France, as well as by the gallant Delegate from Spain, can it be said that these individual circumstances are of such frequent occurrence as to justify us in altering the Rules of the Road at Sea? We know what the practice is. The captains of vessels know what is the meaning of the lights of two steamers together in these particular parts of the sea. They know that it means steamers coupled together and trawling, and they do keep out of the way, out of generosity. But there may be a person navigating in these waters who is not accustomed to such a thing and would not know what was meant. He might suppose that it was two steamers travelling in company. For such very exceptional cases ought we to vote for altering the general Rules of the Road at Sea? I myself, having regard to the fact that vessels do keep out of the way of steam trawlers when they are coupled and trawling, as much as they can, and having regard to the fact that this is an exceptional thing, am unable to vote for the proposition of the gallant Delegate from Spain. I do not think we ought to alter our Rules, as would be necessary if this proposal is adopted.

Lieutenant Vega de Seoane (Spain).—Mr. President, I agree with the gallant Delegate from France. As a matter of principle it is not proper to introduce special cases and exceptions into general Rules. But please observe that exceptions have already been made for squadrons and for sail trawling-vessels. I only ask for an extension of the exception which you have made for them, in favour of coupled trawling-vessels, which are more entitled to it than any other vessels. Leave the Rules as they are at present, and I will ask nothing better. With them the vessels leave the right of way to trawling-vessels. With those which are proposed you compel trawling-vessels invariably to go out of the way of sailing-vessels, and even trawling-vessels, when the Rules compel them to do so, must go out of the way of other vessels.

I must say that I am surprised that opposition to this amendment should come from the Honourable Mr. Hall, the First Delegate of Great Britain, and from the gallant Admirals who sit beside him. It is hardly eight days ago that with his usual eloquence he asked us to compel sailing-vessels invariably to go out of the way of squadrons consisting of more than two vessels, not for the purpose of giving a privilege to squadrons, but in order to avoid dangers which there may be for sailing-vessels to pass through their lines. The gallant Admirals Sir George Nares and Bowden-Smith, supported this proposition, which was adopted by the Conference. The gallant Admiral Bowden-Smith told us of the difficulties which a small sailing-vessel had occasioned last summer to a British squadron which left Queenstown, and especially pointed out the right of the sailing-vessel to keep her course. All the vessels of the squadron were obliged to manœuvre; their line was destroyed and the vessels scattered. I will not give you a description myself. I prefer to give you that of the gallant Admiral, which is far better—as is everything which comes from his lips—than anything that I could explain. The following are the gallant Admiral's own words:—

"I might mention that, the other day, when we were cruizing in columns, we had six heavy battle-ships in one column and five in the other. We were steaming along slowly off Queenstown when a small sailing-schooner went right through the line, which she had a perfect right to do, of course. We were manœuvring, and when she got through the lines we had all been scattered about. She had no sooner gotten through the lines when, for some unaccountable reason, she tacked and went through the lines again. Of course, these large ships were scattered all about, and it was a most ridiculous matter. It was really laughable; but if this had happened in the night it would not have been a laughing matter."

Supposing that the vessels of this squadron, instead of being under command, had been placed at a certain distance from each other and had been coupled, as is the case with trawling-vessels, each vessel being connected with her neighbour, unable to manœuvre except in one direction, unable to scatter as the vessels of the British squadron, and each couple of vessels dragging a heavy weight astern, then it would not have been a laughing matter either by night or by day. That would have been the case if a sailing-vessel were beating about a flotilla of these trawling-vessels so coupled; and it should be avoided by compelling sailing-vessels, for their own safety, to get out of the way of these trawling-vessels.

Another remark of the Honourable Mr. Hall, which I shall answer, is this: He said that Spain may make a local law which will compel vessels to give the right of way to trawling-vessels. This is impossible; for these trawling-vessels do not fish in territorial waters, but on the high seas 100 miles away from our coast, and we have no right to legislate here for vessels which do not belong to us.

Admiral Bowden-Smith (Great Britain).—Mr. President, as the gallant Delegate has been kind enough to mention my name in regard to what I said the other day about a fleet, I wish to remind him that if a vessel sees a fleet, either by day or night, in clear weather, she cannot possibly mistake it if there are three or more ships together. It strikes me that this arrangement of two small steamers with a net between them might be mistaken. If I am going about the sea in the night-time I do not think I should know that these two small steamers were trawlers with a net between them. But I think a fleet in clear weather, if the vessels are in formation, cannot possibly be mistaken for anything else.

Lieutenant Vega de Seoane (Spain).—Mr. President, I would only beg to observe to the gallant Admiral Bowden-Smith that this flotilla of trawling-vessels is generally more numerous and more easy to distinguish at sea than most squadrons.

Mr. Goodrich (United States).—Mr. President, may I occupy another moment of the time of the Conference to call attention to one point? The passage of this amendment so far alters the Rule, and the principle of the Rules which we have thus far adopted, that the adoption of it by the Conference would necessitate the adoption of a new Code of night-signals, so that these trawlers and coupled steamers would be known from steamers not coupled; and also a new set of fog-signals, perhaps, to indicate their presence. It is a little difficult to see how far the passage of this amendment would reach, and it should be rejected, unless the Conference is prepared to undo a good deal of its work and to do it over again. I think that we shall travel into unknown seas if we adopt this amendment.

Lieutenant Vega de Seoane (Spain).—Mr. President, only a few words to remark to the learned Delegate of the United States that the adoption of this amendment would not imply, as he thinks, any alteration in the lights and create the necessity of finding new and distinctive lights. You have already obliged these vessels to carry two side-lights, to carry a masthead-light, and, besides, another one with three colours, which makes four lights, that is to say, eight lights for each couple of vessels. Certainly that is enough to distinguish them without trouble; there are even too many.

In regard to fog, fortunately that is a very occurrence on our coast, but, at any rate, they could have the same fog-signals as vessels which are not under command, and then the difficulty would disappear.

The President.—Is the Conference ready for the question upon this amendment? The amendment will be read.

The amendment is as follows:—

"All vessels under way shall keep out of the way of coupled steamers engaged in trawling."

The question was put to the Conference upon the adoption of this amendment.

The President.—The Chair is unable to decide. The Yeas and Nays are called for.

The Yea and Nay vote is as follows:—

Austria-Hungary	Nay.	Japan		Nay.
Belgium	Yea.	Mexico		Yea.
China	Nay.	Norway		Nay.
Chile	Yea.	Portugal		Yea.
Costa Rica	Nay.	Russia		Nay.
Denmark	Nay.	Spain		Yea.
France	Yea.	Sweden		Nay.
Germany	Nay.	Siam		Yea.
Great Britain	Nay.	The Netherlands		Nay.
Hawaii	Nay.	Venezuela		Yea.
Honduras	Nay.	United States		Nay.
Italy	Yea.			

The President.—Nine countries have voted in the affirmative, and fourteen in the negative, so the amendment is lost.

The next business in order is paragraph (*g*), Article 12, of the additional Report of the Committee on Sound-Signals, on p. 5. The Secretary will please read the paragraph.

The paragraph is as follows:—

"(*g*.) A steam-vessel and a sailing-vessel when towing shall, and the vessel towed may, if necessary, at intervals of not more than two minutes, sound on the whistle, siren, or fog-horn four blasts sounded in pairs, the first two being separated from the last two by an interval of slightly longer duration than the intervals between the first and second blasts and the third and fourth blasts."

Admiral Nares (Great Britain).—Mr. President, the Committee desires to have the word "and" changed into "or," so that it will read, "A steam-vessel or a sailing-vessel."

On behalf of the Sound-Signal Committee, I would like to have this considered in two parts.

First of all as to the vessels which are to have and make use of the signals; and secondly, as to the character of the signal. It will be observed that we have proposed that the signal of the towing vessel is to be compulsory. The signal of the vessel towed is to be permissive. We consider that in almost every case the signal given by the vessel towing covers the line of vessels which she is towing, and that it would not be necessary for the vessels being towed, as a rule, to give their signals. In fact, the fewer signals which we have around us the better, so long as they are distinctive. Therefore, the principle we have adopted is that in almost all cases the towing vessel's fog-horn or sound-signal will cover the vessels being towed, just as the two lights, when they are visible by night, cover the length of the tow in ordinary cases. But still, if there is any danger, there is left a permissive signal.

Now, so far as regards the signal itself. In choosing the signal our desire has been to select the one which would be the easiest remembered, and so we selected four blasts. But that has been adopted in a very important place, where the navigation, I suppose, is as large as in any other part of the world—that is, in the London river; and, with the increasing size of steamers, it is a very important signal, and we do not like to prevent other local authorities from adopting it. It would be a great advantage, there is no doubt. There are cases in narrow waters which do not exist at sea. One case is that the large steamers cannot get out of the way of a barge on some occasions. Then, in the Thames, they have been given a signal to say, "I cannot get out of the way; I demand that you do." On giving this signal a sailing-ship or a barge under her bow has to move. Of course that is on the distinct understanding that if a signal is given unnecessarily the barge or sailing-ship can bring the steamer into Court. However, this has been working very well indeed for the last two years, and, in fact, I believe there has been no cause of trouble at all with either the steamer or the sailer. However, we have nothing to do with this signal, except for me to explain why we did not adopt the four single blasts. As we could not adopt the four single blasts we hit upon this plan, to give two blasts, and then a slight pause, and then two more.

Now, it is pointed out to us that if one of these two blasts is heard it might be mistaken for the starboard-helm signal. There is also another reason. In the American waters the present towing signal is three blasts in inland waters. We said, that is an old signal, do not let us interfere with it if we can possibly help it; and we thought that by adding one blast to it, making it four blasts, it would prevent accident in the interregnum while the new signal is being learned, a very important thing in changing a signal. Now, it has been pointed out that these two blasts might also be mistaken, and so, with the concurrence of the rest of the members of the Committee, we have thought of another description altogether for the signal. Our gallant friend from Germany pointed out how important it was with fog-horns giving a single sound, and that was another reason why we chose single sounds. But we have ventured to go further; whether the Conference will agree with us remains to be seen. We have adopted a long and a short sound, taking as a foundation for our Rule that before these Regulations are practically adopted, if sailing-ships have not got fog-horns that will make a long blast, they ought to have them. It is a very rare thing for sailing-ships to be towing; but still there are cases. The general case is that it is a steamer which is towing, and she is a steamer under way. Let her make the same signal as all other steamers under way, so that the first signal is a long blast. Then, as she carries two lights at night, we have added two short blasts for the additional fog-horn signal.

Therefore, practically, the signal we propose is a long blast for the steamer under way, followed quickly by two short blasts. We think that will be the easiest signal to remember. It is quite a new signal, and therefore it will have to be learned; but I think that if we accompany it by the long blast which is at present made by steamers, and then put the two short ones in agreement with the two lights, that it would be the best signal we can suggest. I do not know whether the Conference will be willing to take a vote first upon the two lines about having the signal, and then upon the character of the signal. If it is voted upon all together we want it to read as follows: In the third line, after "or fog-horn," strike out from the word "or" to the end, and add, "three blasts in succession, namely, one prolonged blast, followed by two short blasts." Let me state one further reason for choosing these three blasts. It might be said: Why can't you be content with one short blast. But we made this signal in agreement with the present signal in use in the United States' waters; but we say we will keep the three blasts of the United States' signal and will make it a long and two short blasts.

Captain Malmberg (Sweden).—Mr. President, although I was the original proposer that a sailing-vessel towing another vessel should be given a signal, I doubt very much if in this paragraph (e) there should be any mention made about sailing-vessels towing, for the reason that it will be almost impossible to find a proper signal. It was considered to be almost impossible to find a light-signal for a sailing-vessel towing, besides which it was such an exceptional case to find a sailing-vessel so engaged. Therefore, my motion to give a sailing-vessel towing a distinctive light was withdrawn. Now, in my opinion, it will look very strange to find in this Article a proviso that a sailing-vessel towing in a fog is to have a distinctive sound-signal, when you do not prescribe any proviso for the light to be carried when the sailing-vessel is towing. It seems to me that you ought to take the sailing-vessel out of this paragraph altogether, or else give a sailing-vessel towing a light-signal.

Mr. Hall (Great Britain).—Mr. President, I think I am correct in saying that the question of principle has already been decided by the Conference. I think that it was on the motion of the gallant Delegate who has just spoken that there should be a sound-signal for a sailing-vessel towing, and that principle was adopted.

Captain Malmberg (Sweden).—Mr. President, I have nothing to say against it. I only say that in my opinion it will look rather strange to read in this Article about a fog sound-signal for sailing-vessels towing when you do not find any light to be carried by them. You find in one place a signal for a sailing-vessel to make in a fog when she is towing; but there is no corresponding signal as to the light to be carried by a sailing-vessel towing.

Mr. Hall (Great Britain).—Mr. President, I confess, with all due respect to the gallant Delegate from Sweden, that the argument does not impress me very strongly, because it is a much more dangerous situation in a fog than in clear weather, and therefore it may be necessary to have a sound-signal for foggy weather. It is not necessary in clear weather. That, I presume, is one of the reasons for this paragraph. We are not now dealing with the question of lights at all. We are only discussing whether or not there shall be a sound-signal for sailing-vessels towing. I confess that I thought the principle had been adopted by the Conference beyond all doubt that such a signal should be adopted, and for that purpose the Committee have set to work to try and find a signal. I apprehend that this is the first question to be put to the Conference if the principle that sailing-vessels towing are to have a distinctive sound-signal has already been decided, as I think it has. Of course I am subject to correction by other Delegates whose memories may be better than mine.

Captain Malmberg (Sweden).—Mr. President, I do not object to its standing at all. I only want to point out that it will look very strange to find a fog sound-signal for sailing-vessels towing, and not to find any mention about what lights such a vessel is to carry.

Mr. Flood (Norway).—Mr. President, I will take the liberty to make a remark about the first part of this proposed Rule. I wish to propose that the sound-signal for vessels towing shall be made compulsory, and not as it is now, permissive. It has been pointed out by the gallant Delegate Sir George Nares that a signal given from a vessel towing generally covers the whole tow; that might be so except in special circumstances. We have already adopted this morning a Rule which states that 600 feet is about the maximum length of a tow that should carry two lights, and if we add the length of the vessel towing we get it up to very little short of 1,000 feet. When we remember that the siren or fog-horn of a vessel towing is in the fore part of the ship, we will find that really the distance is sometimes from 1,200 to 1,400 feet from the siren to the stern of the aftermost vessel.

I do not see why we should not make it compulsory for a vessel being towed, as soon as possible after the vessel towing, to sound the same signal. When a tow like that gets into a fairway, or when you meet a tow like that in the open sea, you hear the whistle or siren from the towing vessel and you have to give way to her. It is a matter of very great necessity to know how much you have to give way. There might be circumstances where a sailing-vessel would think she had to tack, when it would not be very easy or handy for her to do so; the channel might be narrow, and she might be anxious to get back into the track; upon hearing the noise of the signal she would know when she was clear of the tow. So I think that this little alteration is necessary in the proposed paragraph. It would make but very little alteration in the wording, because, according to my proposal, the first part of this paragraph would read as follows: "A steam-vessel or sailing-vessel when towing, and the vessel towed, shall at intervals," &c. I only intend to include the vessels towed, and to make the signal compulsory instead of permissive.

Admiral Nares (Great Britain).—Mr. President, we have considered this subject very closely. The consequence would be that if I heard the vessel towing and the vessel towed making the same signal, two or three cables apart, how am I to know that the sternmost sound is not the sound of another tow? I cannot distinguish them apart. At present the towing signal which we have prescribed provides that an approaching vessel, practically, in a fog, has to stop and get out of her way. You had much better leave it as it is than to give me a lot of musical sounds all around that I could not possibly distinguish. How could I know how many lines of towing vessels there were ahead of me? This point was very clearly put to us by the pilot that we examined, and he said, "For God's sake don't have a lot of musical sounds all around me. Give me one, and you may depend upon it I will take care not to go near that tow."

Mr. Flood (Norway).—Mr. President, I will only say that I think the towed vessel will generally be distinguished by the signal of the towing vessel; but that the towed vessel will in all probability be a sailing-vessel which will use a fog-horn, while a steamer is to use a siren. It is not often that sailing-vessels are towing other sailing-vessels. Therefore, I do not think that the argument will have very much effect. I admit the force of the other remarks about the number of sound-signals being confusing. But my reason for proposing this is based upon practical experience in my vocation formerly, and now as an insurance agent. I had an actual case of this kind in the Delaware River. A vessel came under the stern of a tow-boat with a very long tow. She got in between the tow and the vessels towing, and a collision and great disaster happened. The trouble is that the length of the tow differs so much in the open sea. There is sometimes from 90 to 120 fathoms in the tow-line. I had a vessel towed from Key West to New York which had 135 fathoms of tow-line. I think it is very necessary to have these signals. Of course, the Rule provides that they can be used, if necessary; but that is not enough. I think that they should be made compulsory. If they were made compulsory they would always be complied with.

Captain Mensing (Germany).—Mr. President, I am sorry that I cannot fully agree with the Delegate from Norway. I believe that what he wants done by these ships may be done under the amendment as it stands now. However, I think there is a good deal to be said on the other side, and for that reason I wish to have the provision left as it stands. It seems to me that this signal can only have one meaning: that there is a ship behind and that the ship approaching should be warned of this fact. I have already pointed out, when the subject was before the Conference some time ago, that in a collision of which I know, the "Frederick Charles," one of our iron-clads, came into collision during a fog with a vessel in tow. When another ship approached she blew her whistle and the other ship went around under her stern, and there was a second collision. On that account I believe the second signal is necessary. I do not see any reason why it should be made obligatory for such a towed vessel to make the signal, for there is nothing behind her. Why should she make such a signal? There is no Rule of the Road compelling anybody to get out of her way. I do not see that there is any obligation to make it compulsory; and I believe it will be good to limit the signals that we adopt here so as not to bring about confusion. Let us wait and find out if such a thing shall be necessary. Let us give the people time to think before we introduce more signals and so make these Rules more complicated.

The one thing which makes me sorry that the first amendment has not been kept as it stood is that we have in our navy this same signal for calling other ships in a fog—a long, short, short. I would most strongly advocate that we retain this signal, if it be deemed advisable that it be given by both sailing-vessels and steamers; though no doubt there will be very few cases where sailing-vessels will tow other vessels. These cases, however, may happen, and if they do happen and they get into the Law Courts, I do not know but what these Courts will ask: "Did you have such a fog-horn as to be able to give the long blast? Did you make the proper signal as prescribed by this Rule?" If you did not you would be found to be in fault. I do not doubt that the Courts would decide it in that way. From which it follows that every master would say: You may possibly get into a position where you have to use the long blast on the fog-horn, and you must provide yourself with a horn to make it.

Now, of course, in all small vessels where such a thing as a mechanical device is not known, it is impossible to make the long blast within the meaning of this law. Such fog-horns are not found on 90 per cent. of all the ships sailing from Germany. The invention which has been referred to is generally used on the Banks of Newfoundland. It is a most excellent signal and a very good invention, so far as I know; but it is not introduced to any large extent in any of our fleets in Germany. We put a great part of the responsibility of fitting out these vessels on the shoulders of the Government. If a long blast is to be given on the fog-horn, the German Government would come to the conclusion that it would be necessary to make it obligatory to fit out vessels with such an instrument, and a good many hundred thousand marks would have to be paid out on this account. I really do not see that there is any great necessity for it. If we have not adopted any distinguishing signal for a sailing-vessel towing another, or if we should think it unnecessary because, as has been pointed out here, such cases will be extremely rare, I think we might leave out altogether that signal for sailing-vessels.

Captain Sampson (United States).—Mr. President, it appears to me that if a vessel towed is to make the same signal as the vessel towing, the signal should be made obligatory. The Chairman of the Committee has pointed out that if such were the case it might be inferred by the vessel approaching that she was meeting a second tow. I believe that all that is required will be accomplished by the towing vessel giving the signal. It seems to me that if it is optional with the vessel being towed to make the signal or not, the vessel approaching the tow would not be able to decide whether she was meeting one tow or two. If she heard the signal of a vessel towing and subsequently the signal of a vessel towed, if the vessel towed is not *required* to make the signal, it would be impossible to say whether there was one tow or two. Therefore, if it be necessary that the towed vessel should make a signal, it should be made obligatory.

Captain Norcross (United States).—Mr. President, I would like to suggest that when approaching a tow at nearly right angles and hearing the same signals from three or four places, there would be difficulty in knowing which way the tow was going. Perhaps the vessel towed might blow a long and short blast (if it can be found a sa special signal for such a condition), and a hearer would then know which way to steer to go astern of the last vessel.

Mr. Carter (Hawaii).—Mr. President, I think it fair to assume that there is a certain amount of common sense on board of vessels that are towing and being towed, and that when it is necessary they will sound a signal. They are the best judges of that necessity. We cannot here legislate for all cases. We leave it optional with the second vessel, when the circumstances are such as require it, to sound the signal; and she will sound it, especially if she is a vessel which has already been in a collision, and is a little careful and sensitive upon that point.

Mr. Flood (Norway).—Mr. President, I agree with the learned Delegate from Hawaii that there is generally common sense on board of all vessels. But still we have found it necessary to have compulsory Rules for both light-signals and sound-signals. So I do not think that it will always do to depend upon common sense and let sailors do exactly as they please. With reference to what was said by the gallant Delegate from the United States, Captain Sampson, I desire to state that his point was stronger than any of the arguments I brought forward. The principal thing is that the signal should be made compulsory, because it is a great thing to be certain about the signal. If it is only made permissive it might be, as Captain Sampson pointed out, mistaken altogether for another tow. I think there are good reasons for having these signals made compulsory, and I hope the Conference will take them into consideration.

Captain Shackford (United States).—Mr. President, I would like to ask the gallant Delegate from the United States, Captain Sampson, what would be the result in a case of this kind: When a steamer was coming up a fairway towing six vessels at a time, and all of these six vessels were tooting their horns at the same time? It would be a regular pandemonium.

Captain Sampson (United States).—I do not advocate it at all.

Captain Shackford (United States).—Mr. President, I understand that the Delegate from Norway advocates that every vessel in the tow should blow her horn.

Mr. Flood (Norway).—Mr. President, I do not go so far as that. I will answer Captain Shackford that the same thing was discussed with regard to the lights, and it was objected to on the ground that you would see all these lights, and it would lead to confusion. On the other hand it was said: The more lights the better: they would show that there was an obstruction to navigation, and that you had better keep out of the way. I use the same argument with regard to fog-horns. Let them blow away and make the other vessels keep out of the way. I think that in a fog it is well to have the vessels keep out of the way, and they may sound as many fog-horns as they can, because these tows are an obstruction to navigation which should be avoided.

Mr. Goodrich (United States).—Mr. President, it seems to me that the gallant Delegate from Norway has advocated very strongly the converse of what he desires. If a vessel is towing half-a-dozen vessels he says that he would not have them all sound their horns, but he proposes that the after vessel only should sound her horn. That can be done if the Rule is permissive. But if you make it compulsory all of these towed vessels must sound their horns. Take the case of a steamer he has spoken of as being towed up from Key West. Does any one suppose that that vessel on a long hawser of 135 fathoms, towed astern, would not sound her fog-horn if she were permitted to do so under this permissive Rule? But suppose a vessel is towing in a crowded harbour half-a-dozen vessels on a hawser or in tiers, and each one of these vessels is sounding her horn. It would create a confusion to which the trouble at the Tower of Babel would not be a circumstance. You never could get through the harbour of New York if you allow all of these towed vessels, or rather if you compel all of these towed vessels, in a fog, to sound their horns. I suppose the gallant Delegate from Norway knows that tows in harbours are sometimes made up of twenty vessels. Is each one to sound a fog-horn? It is monstrous.

Mr. Flood (Norway).—Mr. President, I will answer that I am bringing this forward as a universal Rule for the whole world, and not alone for New York Harbour, or for any specially crowded waters. I know very well that there are tows of twenty and thirty and forty vessels.

Captain Shackford (United States).—Or even sixty vessels.

Mr. Flood (Norway).—Sixty or eighty. I have seen them strung along sometimes for half-a-mile or so. Of course no man of sense would say that each one of them ought to sound her fog-horn. But we have local Rules for arranging these things. When tows come down the North River or the East River they are governed by local Rules. I have seen a large steamer lying there for twenty minutes, and these tows did not use their sound-signals. They are under special Regulations. What I advocate is a general Rule to hold good for the whole world, and especially for vessels towing in the open sea.

Admiral Nares (Great Britain).—Mr. President, the position of the Committee is this. There is a signal to be made every two minutes. Now, we do not want that signal to be made every two minutes by both the tow and the towed. The towing ship is to make it every two minutes. Then whenever necessary the towed vessel is to make it, or may make it.

Captain Sampson (United States).—The Rule says "if necessary." It does not say whenever it is necessary.

Admiral Nares (Great Britain).—Mr. President, surely we are not going to take the command out of the hands of the captains, and tell them what they are to do to take care of their ships. We are putting the Rules as plainly as we can, and leaving to them, as sensible men, to act upon them. I am very sorry that we have chosen a signal which is already in use in Germany as a call for a vessel; but still it is so very difficult to give a new sound-signal which can be readily learned that I really ask the Delegate from Germany to consider whether the other signal could not be altered in some way, and let us keep this simple signal, provided it is considered by the Conference as a suitable one, and if they think it should be adhered to. If they think it will be better to have the four short blasts, and that it cannot be mistaken, why the Committee will give way on the subject, I am sure. We are in the presence of a great many nautical men here, and we have done our best to put it before the Conference.

Now as to the question of the price of reliable fog-horns. We are all, I believe, in agreement that it is very desirable to improve the present horn. Now, if they are to be improved they will have to get new ones, and all the difference in expense, so far as the cost goes, will be the difference in the cost between the new horn and the old one. The new horn will make a long and a short blast, and the old horn will make only a short blast. A fog-horn which will make a prolonged blast and a short blast, and which is thoroughly serviceable, can be had for 3*l.* or 4*l.*, as the Committee understand, and they will be serviceable three or four years. The unserviceable one will, I dare say, cost between 2*l.* and 3*l.* It will not be a matter of great expense to get a really serviceable horn.

Captain Sampson (United States).—Mr. President, I think that if the Committee would modify the amendment as suggested by the Chairman a moment ago, and make it read so that the vessel towed shall make the signal "whenever necessary," that it would make it obligatory, and at the same time it would not be necessary to make it so frequently. I think that is a very important point, and that it would remove the objection of so many sound-signals. A vessel approaching such a tow would hear the vessel towing make the signal at regular intervals, and she is at once put on her guard with reference to the length of the tow. If then, at longer intervals, she hears the last vessel in the tow make the same signal, it gives all the information necessary, as I stated before, and I think it is absolutely necessary to make it obligatory upon the vessel towed to make the signal, or else drop it out altogether.

Admiral Bowden-Smith (Great Britain).—Mr. President, I wish to say a very few words in support of the proposal of my friend and colleague Sir George Nares, on behalf of this Committee in regard to the change of the signal from what it is here in print to what they propose, for the following reason: I think it most desirable that the first noise a ship encounters in a fog should be a long blast. You say in this proposal that it shall be a short one. When this matter was before the Conference that was discussed, and when we proposed the long blast to be of about four seconds' duration, several Delegates thought that the sound would not penetrate a fog. Therefore, we altered it from four to six seconds. I think, therefore, that it is very desirable for the ship towing to make exactly the same noise that an ordinary steamer does when she is going along; and then by adding two short sounds to it it makes it very clear that there is something behind her.

With regard to what has fallen from the gallant Delegate from Germany, I do not think that it will really interfere with the signal in use in Germany. I do not, of course, know what the German arrangement of the signal is. It is the general rule that a steamer towing makes a loud and a prolonged blast, a longer blast than a fleet usually makes when they sound a long blast. I hope, therefore, he will see his way to allow the Committee to have these sounds as they propose. I think that possibly the short blast, as provided in the Report, might be confused with the helm signal. A ship would sound short, short, meaning, "I am directing my course to port." She sounds it again:

"I am directing my course more to port." That signal might be mistaken for the helm signal. Therefore, I am very much in favour of this change as proposed by the Committee.

Mr. Hall (Great Britain).—Mr. President, may I suggest to the gallant Delegate from the United States a way out of the difficulty, which I think, perhaps, will meet his views, and yet actually carry out the principle of the Committee? I understand, as has been pointed out by him, that it is undesirable that the vessel towed should keep on making this signal every two minutes as she would have to do under this Rule if she thought it necessary; but we could give her the option of merely being able to give that signal when there is necessity for it, if she sees another vessel approaching her. We might transpose the words "if necessary." Then it would read as follows: "All vessels towing shall at intervals of not more than two minutes, and vessels towed may, when necessary, sound," &c., and then go on and deal with the signal. That would provide for the vessel towing giving the signal regularly every two minutes, and give the option to the vessel towed to make the signal when necessity arises; but it would not compel her to make it every two minutes.

Captain Sampson (United States).—Will you allow me to suggest that it be made to read, instead of "may whenever necessary," "shall whenever necessary?"

Captain Richard (France).—Mr. President, I desire to know what is meant by "whenever necessary." It seems to me that it is very difficult to understand, and that you are introducing into the Article something very vague and hard to explain. I would like to point out to you the consequences of the Article if you adopt it. I refer to the signal championed by Sir George Nares. You give a special fog-signal to the vessel which is being towed and to the towing vessel. This is evidently an excellent thing; and there is not a sailor who will not be delighted, provided the signal works properly. But if you adopt this signal for the towing vessel and for the vessel which is being towed, you practically enter upon a path which may carry you very far. Why should we not do something similar for vessels not under command and for vessels laying telegraph cables? As you have given them a special system of lights, why should you not also give them special sound-signals? We all know that a vessel which is paying out a telegraph cable, or which is engaged in drawing one up, cannot manœuvre at will. For such operations she is obliged—for example, if she is laying a cable—to continue her way even in fog or mist, at a certain rate of speed, not less than 6 or 7 knots. There is, therefore, an evident advantage in knowing her presence in regions where she is engaged. Something should also be done for the vessel which is not under command. The consequence of having given a special sound-signal to the group consisting of the vessel in tow and the towing vessel is that you can no longer refuse to give a special signal to the vessel engaged in raising a telegraph cable, and a special signal to the vessel which is not under command.

Mr. Hall (Great Britain).—Mr. President, with regard to the suggestion of the gallant Delegate from the United States, of course if the word "shall" were put in, followed by the words "when necessary," I think that most sailors would say that it was not necessary, and practically they would not do it. I think that it will meet the difficulty if there is added at the end of the Article this provision: Leave out the first sentence about vessels being towed, and then add, "Vessels towed may also sound this signal." Then leave it to the prudent captain to sound it if he thinks there is any danger of collision or any necessity for it. Of course, first of all, any one approaching a towing vessel and hearing the towing signal will know that that vessel has got something behind her. He will know that she has got a vessel in tow, and he will proceed to give her a wide berth. If she has got more than one vessel in tow, then a prudent man on the tow would give the signal, and he ought to give it as an ordinary precaution as a seaman. I think that we are all agreed in principle that it is necessary that a signal should be given by vessels towing. If we merely say the vessels towed may also sound the signal, it carries out the intention of the Committee, and sets at rest some of the difficulties which have been pointed out as to the phraseology with regard to some of the proposals.

Mr. Flood (Norway).—Mr. President, may I suggest that we might put in the same limitation that we did this morning with regard to the white light, and make it obligatory for all tows over 600 feet to make the signal, in the same way as we did this morning with regard to the towing lights?

Admiral Nares (Great Britain).—Mr. President, I would point out that when the lights are in sight on the last vessel on the string of the tow, you also see at the same time the lights on the vessel towing. Now, the sound-signals you do not hear. You do not hear the whole string; and, therefore, they may be mistaken for a new string, as I pointed out before. The sounds and the lights are totally different things, and an argument with regard to one will not apply to the other.

Mr. Flood (Norway).—Mr. President, I will say that, as a general rule, a person hearing the signal from a vessel towing would also hear the signal from the vessel towed. It has been stated here by several experts that a good sound-signal could be heard from 2 to 5 miles. Now, when you can hear the signal from a towing vessel, I think, as a general rule, you will also hear the other. They ought to be sounded at the same time, so as to give the vessel approaching the distance between the vessel towing and the vessel towed.

Mr. Hall (Great Britain).—Mr. President, I hope the Conference will not assume that a sound-signal can be heard from 2 to 5 miles in a fog. It is possible that such a whistle may have been heard in a fog at that distance, but we all know that the atmosphere varies in a fog so that at other times you might not be able to hear sound-signals in a fog over 200 yards. It is absolutely impossible to lay down any rule as to the distance at which you can hear sound-signals in foggy weather, and so in a tow of a considerable length you might hear the signal of the vessel towing, and not hear the signal from the vessels being towed. But these difficulties make it all the more important for us to be careful. Now, the Delegate from Norway proposes that if the tow is over 600 feet the signal is to be made compulsory. Then exactly the same difficulty will follow which has been pointed out, that there will be a chorus from every vessel in that tow, and you will have to deal with that chorus, which has been properly likened to the Tower of Babel.

Captain Mensing (Germany).—Mr. President, may I read the amendment as I would like to propose it?

"A steam-vessel when towing, and a sailing-vessel when towing, shall, and the vessel being towed may, at intervals of not more than two minutes,—instead of the signal mentioned in Article 12, paragraph (*b*)—sound on her whistle or fog-horn three blasts in succession, one prolonged blast, followed by two short ones."

There is one addition made in this amendment, and one omission. The addition is in the paragraph regarding Article 12 (*b*). It says there:—

"A sailing-ship under way shall make with her fog-horn, at intervals of not more than two minutes, when on the starboard tack one blast, when on the port tack two blasts in succession, with the wind abaft the beam three blasts in succession."

Now, that is compulsory. The signal which is proposed here in the amendment of the Sound-Signal Committee is optional. It seems to me that it is doubtful whether the vessel under tow is not held, under the Rule as in Article 12 (*b*), to make the signal as prescribed there, and in order to do away with any mistake with regard to that I have put it in here. I have left out the words, "if necessary," because, as the gallant Delegate from France so ably pointed out, that is a source of mistake.

It is not desirable to make these signals when they are not necessary, because a steam-vessel towing two other vessels across the ocean has to listen to the signal that she is making on her own siren or steam-whistle, and this signal may now take about fifteen seconds from the beginning of the signal to the end of the last blast. She has to repeat that signal at least every two minutes. Now imagine that there is astern another vessel or two vessels, and they are blowing their fog-horns, a long blast and two short blasts. While these fog-horns are going the tower cannot hear the signal of any approaching vessel. If there are a great many vessels behind her she cannot hear anything; if there be but two ships behind her, the first one would take up the signal and blow it for fifteen seconds, and then the other one for fifteen seconds; and there are three-quarters of a minute gone out of two minutes. These are the reasons why I propose this change.

Regarding what fell from the gallant Delegate from Great Britain, Sir George Nares, as to the price of the different fog-horns, I should like to say that the case which he quoted here is not applicable to the case which I had in mind. Our ships are fitted out with mechanical fog-horns; they do not have to buy them. But they would have to get new fog-horns. Of course, 3*l*. or 4*l*. would be very little difference in the price of the new fog-horn and the old one, but this difference multiplied by 4,000 or 5,000 is quite a nice little sum, I should say. I do not know whether my Government would not feel bound to introduce them if this Rule is made compulsory to all vessels. I beg those Delegates who come from Governments where the case may be similar to remember this when we come to a vote.

Mr. Flood (Norway).—Mr. President, may I be permitted to say a word or two about what Captain Mensing has mentioned about the fog-horns? The fog-horn repeatedly mentioned in this Conference is used a great deal in these waters, particularly on the Newfoundland coast, and in Nova Scotia, where I was informed the other day that in the course of six or seven years there had been 1,500 or 2,000 of them sold. That fog-horn apparatus is a patent from Norway, called Hansen's Fog Apparatus. It is exhibited to the Committee; they have tried it and know the qualities of it. As to the price, I will correct a mistake. The price of that instrument as delivered here in this country is from 11 to 15 dollars, on account of the duty of about 50 per cent. The same instrument could be bought in Norway for about 8 dollars, and in countries where there is not such a heavy tax as in the United States it could be bought for a much less price. I think that in England it could be bought for about 1*l*. 10*s*. That is the price of the instrument, the same as it stands in the Committee.

Admiral Nares (Great Britain).—Mr. President, I will only say a few words. As I understand Captain Mensing's proposed change, the whole principle that we have adopted will be capsized. We say that if a sailing-ship is towing another she is even in greater danger than a steam-ship towing, and she must and ought to give a compulsory signal. If she is allowed to give only an optional signal, the whole of our proposal is gone at once. We are distinctly in agreement that the vessel which is towing, whether a sailing-vessel or a steamer, must give this distinctive signal.

Captain Malmberg (Sweden).—Mr. President, I only rise for information. If a sailing-vessel towing another vessel is to give the same kind of signal as is to be given for steamers towing, how will that interfere with the signal a sailing-vessel is to make according to the rules laid down in Article 14, where it is said that a sailing-ship has to make one signal according to the tack she is on, or according to whether she is running before the wind? Now you propose to give a sailing-vessel towing the same signal as a steamer towing. How is Article 14 then to be understood? I think this is very dangerous, to give a sailing-vessel towing the same kind of signal you give to a steamer towing.

Captain Mensing (Germany).—Mr. President, I must say that I fully agree with what has fallen from the gallant Delegate from Sweden. I think it is a most important point. We have just heard from the gallant Delegate from Great Britain that a sailing-vessel towing another vessel is a very dangerous object. Now, we send this dangerous object afloat without giving her these distinctive signals. I want to call the attention of this Conference to the fact that there is no Rule whatever in favour of a sailing-vessel towing or a steam-vessel towing. I have certainly tried my best to induce the Conference to adopt such a Resolution, but it has been negatived, and they have declared that a sailing-vessel towing or a steam-vessel towing shall have in no way and under no circumstances a right of way over other ships. If that is so, why is it necessary to introduce this system and make it compulsory for them to give these signals? As I have stated, I think the point which has been brought forward by the gallant Delegate from Sweden is a most important one, and should be fairly considered.

Mr. Verney (Siam).—Mr. President, may I suggest a point which I do not think has been before presented? I would ask the gallant Delegate from Great Britain whether he has anything to suggest in the case of a steam-vessel that is towing and that is stopped not having any way upon her? I would ask what is the signal for a towing vessel to sound in such a case? Would it not be very misleading to sound the signal which is laid down in Article 12 (*c*), or is there any other signal which she ought to sound under the circumstances?

Admiral Nares (Great Britain).—Mr. President, I think that we are dealing with vessels towing and moving. Really, we did not consider any other signals. The reference to the Sound-Signal Committee was that they were to report upon the specific cases in which new fog-signals were to be adopted. We have reported on them, and have brought them before the Conference. We have reported specific signals for such cases, and we have chosen the best signals we can; but if we are to be interrogated and asked what ships are to do under the most extraordinary circumstances we cannot tell you.

Mr. Hall (Great Britain).—Mr. President, I will give formal notice before recess of an amendment, and that is, to strike out the words in this paragraph, "and a vessel towed, if necessary," and to add at the end of the paragraph the following: "The vessel towed may also sound this signal." I will not, of course, pursue the argument which has been made on this point, although I have heard with the greatest interest the observations which have fallen from the gallant Delegate from Germany, yet I take it that we are bound by the vote of the Conference to adopt a distinctive signal—if we can find a distinctive signal—for a steamer and a sailing-vessel towing. As far as I remember, it was adopted by the vote of the Conference, in principle, that a steamer and a sailing-vessel towing should give a distinctive signal, provided such a signal could be found by the Committee. I do not see how we can reopen the question as to whether a sailing-vessel towing can give a signal or not. If the principle has been adopted, the only question is what the signal is which is to be given by a sailing-vessel towing. My motion is to leave out the words, "and the vessel towed may, if necessary," and to add at the end of the Article the following: "A vessel being towed may also sound this signal."

Captain Shackford (United States).—Mr. President, while this discussion is going on I trust the members will not forget what is contained in Article 13. It reads:—

"A steam-vessel hearing apparently before her beam the fog-signal of a vessel, the position of which is not ascertained, shall, so far as the circumstances of the case admit, stop her engines, and proceed with caution until all danger of collision is over."

I think that is a very important rule to take into consideration in this discussion. It is only necessary to find out what you are meeting in a fog, and then any prudent sailor will stop and go slow until he finds out what kind of vessel he is approaching.

Mr. Flood (Norway).—Mr. President, I think that is a very strong argument for my proposal that towing vessels shall always sound the signals, because when a vessel is feeling her way along there is great necessity for her to know when she can again go ahead. For a ship to get tangled up in a tow is not very pleasant.

Captain Shackford (United States).—That is exactly why we say, put in there the words, "if necessary."

Captain Malmberg (Sweden).—Mr. President, I do not think the objection I raised against giving a sailing-vessel towing the same kind of signal as you give to a steam-vessel towing has been properly understood. The Conference has voted that a signal should be given to a sailing-vessel towing, if such a signal could be obtained. When I proposed a signal for a sailing-vessel towing I, for my part, did not give such a signal as is now proposed. The signal I gave was that a sailing-vessel towing should give the signal according to the rule under Article 14, and that the vessel towed should repeat this signal. In the way in which we have got the signal in this proposal of the Committee, it is quite contrary to the rule laid down by Article 14. For my part, I object to introducing such a signal.

Admiral Nares (Great Britain).—Mr. President, I did not answer my gallant friend because it was so near recess that I was not able to meet his argument. I am perfectly ready to do so. It was no disrespect to him whatever that he has not been answered.

Mr. Hall (Great Britain).—Mr. President, may I point out, before recess, that perhaps it will be desirable for us to take into consideration whether we should give a special signal for a sailing-vessel towing at all? I confess I thought at first that the feeling of the Conference was that there should be such a signal. I have felt myself all along a very strong opinion that it was unnecessary to give a special signal to sailing-vessels towing, because these are cases of much more rare occurrence than steamers towing. I think it will be very desirable for us to consider whether or not we should provide for more than a distinctive sound-signal for steamers towing.

Captain Sampson (United States).—Mr. President, if it is in order, I would like to present a new reading of this Article, to be thought over during recess, as the learned Delegate from Great Britain has suggested. It is to strike out in the first line the words, "and a sailing-vessel," and in the second line to strike out the words, "may have," and in the third line the words, "or fog-horn," and to make it read in this way: "A steam-vessel towing shall, at intervals of not more than two minutes, and the vessel towed shall, whenever necessary, sound on her whistle or siren," &c.

Mr. Goodrich (United States).—Mr. President, under the rule of business as at first established, there will be no session of the Conference to-morrow. I propose to move that the Conference shall meet to-morrow at 11 o'clock, unless there is objection made to it. It seems to me that we are right in the midst of the discussion of the Report of the Committee on Fog-Signals, and that we had better finish it before we take any interval for other work. Therefore, I move that when the Conferenc adjourn this afternoon it adjourn till to-morrow morning at 11 o'clock.

Captain Mensing (Germany).—Mr. President, I should be sorry to have that motion adopted, because, otherwise, Committee No. 3 will have time to work to-morrow, and we are now in a position where we hope to have something printed. If the Conference is to sit to-morrow, we shall be postponed for another day. The Committee does not understand that it is its duty to sit extra hours, and to take up the evening for morning work. We shall have to postpone the work, and it will be a longer time before we will be able to lay our Report before the Conference.

Mr. Goodrich (United States).—Mr. President, will the gallant Delegate allow me to point out to him that to adopt the course indicated by him will delay the whole Conference; and if we take the course proposed by me for the work of the Conference, it will delay only Committee No. 3? The idea I have of this is simply that we may finish our work on these Rules, so that the Collocation Committee can lay before the members of the Conference the work as it has been done. Let me suggest to the gallant Delegate from Germany that it is probable, in the work of the Conference, that the Report of Committee No. 3 will not be reached until the latter part of next week. We have got to discuss two or three important subjects first. The uniform load-line comes first before Committee No. 3; and the Committee on Life-saving Systems and Devices, of which Mr. Kimball is the Chairman, has a very important Report to present.

The President.—The Chair suggests that, if this discussion is to last any time, the Conference had better take its recess now.

The Conference thereupon took a recess until 2 o'clock.

After Recess.

The President.—The first business in order is the motion of the Delegate from the United States, to hold a session of the Conference to-morrow.

Mr. Goodrich (United States).—Mr. President, will the Chair kindly allow that to lie over for a few minutes? Before the adjournment of the Conference this afternoon we will decide what course to take, depending upon the result of the day's work.

Admiral Nares (Great Britain).—Mr. President, I will answer the gallant Delegate from Sweden with regard to the different signals to be made by a vessel towed and a vessel towing. We considered his extra amendment No. 36, asking for four blasts to be given by the vessel towed. We considered that some signal could be adopted by the vessel towing and the vessel towed, and we adopted practically his four blasts. But for the reasons which I stated this morning we have changed the signals, I think with the acquiescence of the Conference. We considered all of his amendments very closely at the time, and our Report was the result to which we came. If you will allow me to say two or three words with regard to the position in which we are placed. The Committee have reported in accordance with the belief that the question which was referred to them was that towing vessels, whether a steamer or a sailing-vessel, sound a certain signal. Now, there is a disagreement about that. Several members of the Conference think it would be quite sufficient, when the blasts on the fog-horn come into play, to have the steam-vessel alone giving this signal. That is the first.

The second is the question as to whether the signal should be given to a sailing-vessel towing or not. If we could decide that I think we should get a little further ahead. Another question has been presented here by Captain Sampson. He says that the vessel towed ought to have a compulsory signal. I would suggest whether it would not be desirable to have a vote first on the question as to whether a special signal should be given to a sailing-vessel towing as well as to a steam-vessel towing; and then I should like to have a vote upon the question as to whether the vessel towed should make a compulsory signal. That would settle the question.

Captain Malmberg (Sweden).—Mr. President, as it is on my instigation that this fog-signal for a sailing-vessel towing has been brought under consideration, I, for my part, find it very difficult to agree upon a proper signal for such a case, and I will, therefore, take the liberty of proposing that what this Article contains about sailing-vessels towing should be stricken out.

Captain Mensing (Germany).—Mr. President, I believe that this morning the distinguished First Delegate from Great Britain told us that this had already been adopted in principle. Now, if it has been adopted in principle, we should have to reconsider that vote. Therefore, I think it would be quite as well to take up the question in the manner proposed by the gallant Delegate from Great Britain, Sir George Nares. I would like to submit whether it would not be well to begin with the question, that in case a sailing-vessel should be given a signal, it should be optional. I would be for an optional signal, and I think I would be against a compulsory signal for such a purpose. It seems to me that the advantages to be derived from such a system have been lost sight of entirely. They are very great. It often happens that a sailing-vessel has another in tow, particularly in the case where there has been a collision. There may have been a collision, and one sailing-vessel takes the other in tow; perhaps the other is sinking, or has lost her masts, and is being taken to the nearest port. What is she going to do on the way; is she going to have a signal to sound one, two, or three blasts?

Now, while she is proceeding on her way and making her signal, as prescribed by Article 12 (*g*), she sees a vessel coming, and that vessel, though out of her way, wants to round her stern, and pass close aboard. She sees that. Now, if you adopt the amendment as I have proposed it, this would be exactly the moment when she would give that signal—long, short, short. And at such a time there would be nothing against the signal. Is there any difficulty in adopting that? It is only at that moment when she sees the risk of collision that she makes the signal, and the other ship is warned that another ship is following her; and if she wants to avoid the risk of collision, she must look out, and not try to go astern of that vessel. I think that the principle we have adopted makes it necessary

[93]

for us now to have such a signal, and I do not see any reason why we should not introduce it, as long as it is optional. I think the various reasons I have mentioned would be very much against the compulsion of such signals.

Mr. Hall (Great Britain).—Mr. President, the gallant Delegate from Germany has pointed out that it is necessary for us to take a formal vote on the matter to be reconsidered, as to whether or not a sailing-vessel towing is to give a distinct signal. Probably it would be well to take a vote upon that so as to put ourselves in order. Then I will move the Resolution of which I gave notice before luncheon. I move that the question be reconsidered as to whether or not a sailing-vessel towing shall give a distinctive sound-signal.

Mr. Goodrich (United States).—Mr. President, I suggest to the learned Delegate from Great Britain that no such motion is necessary. I understand that no part of this Article has been passed.

Mr. Hall (Great Britain).—It was adopted in principle.

Mr. Goodrich (United States).—I thought you were speaking of something on this paragraph.

Captain Sampson (United States).—Mr. President, I would like to ask if the Conference decided that the same signal should not be given by both steamers and sailing-vessels towing, whether it would exclude the adoption of some other signal for sailing-vessels towing? If we vote for a reconsideration on the adoption of the principle, and vote against it because of the objection which some of the members of the Conference have to this particular signal, we would be likely to vote to exclude sailing-vessels from having any signal at all.

Mr. Hall (Great Britain).—Mr. President, I think that on a motion to reconsider a decision with regard to sailing-vessels giving sound-signals, the question will then be open to discussion as to whether they shall give any sound-signals at all, and, if so, what. That would clearly be open on a motion to reconsider.

Captain Bisbee (China).—Mr. President, I would ask if it would not save the time of the Conference if the question was put before them as to whether they considered it necessary for a sailing-vessel to have any distinctive signal to show that she is towing. I believe that there are men here who have been a generation at sea who have never seen a sailing-vessel towing another vessel. If the occurrence is so very rare, what is the good of making a Rule to provide for it?

Mr. Hall (Great Britain).—Mr. President, we cannot discuss that until we have agreed to reconsider it. I quite agree with the gallant Delegate from China in what he has said.

The President.—The Delegate from Great Britain proposes to reconsider the principle by which a sound-signal was adopted for a sailing-vessel towing.

The question on the reconsideration of the principle as above was put to the Conference and was carried.

The President.—The question now before the Conference is whether the signal shall be given to a sailing-vessel towing or not.

Mr. Goodrich (United States).—Mr. President, adopting the suggestion of the learned Delegate from Great Britain, I move the following Resolution: "That, in the opinion of the Conference, no special signal should be given to sailing-vessels while towing another vessel." That will bring out the question clearly and distinctly. Does that agree with the ideas of the gentlemen at the other end of the table?

Admiral Nares (Great Britain).—That would agree with my proposal, only it is putting it in a contrary form.

The President.—The proposition of the Delegate from Great Britain will be read.

The proposition is as follows:—

"Shall a special signal be given to a sailing-vessel towing as well as to a steam-vessel towing?"

Mr. Hall (Great Britain).—Mr. President, I do not quite see how we could discuss this without we have an affirmative or a negative proposition introduced into it. I pointed out before adjournment that it was a matter which I thought desirable to discuss, but I think it ought to be discussed on an affirmative or a negative proposition.

Mr. Goodrich (United States).—Mr. President, I call the attention of the gentleman to the fact that I made a motion for that purpose, following out the suggestion which I received from the other end of the Conference table, viz.: "That, in the opinion of the Conference, no special signal should be given to a sailing-vessel towing another vessel."

The President.—Does the Delegate from Great Britain accept that in lieu of his own proposal?

Admiral Nares (Great Britain).—Mr. President, on the part of the Committee I may say that our position is that we want to know the sense of the Conference as to whether a special signal shall be given to a sailing-ship as well as to a steam-ship when towing, and if any gentleman will move it in any words which will bring that question to a vote we will be very glad.

Mr. Carter (Hawaii).—Mr. President, may I point out that the word "special" there involves another matter. My position is that I am in favour of having a steam-vessel and a sailing-vessel, when towing another vessel, give the same signal. Now, if you say that a sailing-vessel shall give a special signal, different from the signal of a steamer, I would say, No. Would it not be better to put it: Shall a sailing-vessel have any signal?

Mr. Goodrich (United States).—Mr. President, I accept that suggestion. Strike out the word "special."

Mr. Hall (Great Britain).—Mr. President, that is what the learned Delegate from the United States really proposes; and I would like to say a few words upon that point. I cannot add anything to the force of what has been stated by the gallant Delegate from China, that these cases are practically few in numbers. It is a question for the Conference to decide whether or not it is desirable to put into our Rules a special Rule giving a sound-signal for such exceptional cases when we have regard to the very great difficulty experienced in getting sound-signals at all. It is difficult enough to get special sound-signals for cases which are not exceptional. We have been occupied now for a day and a half in discussing two sound-signals only. Now, if for exceptional circumstances we are to frame a third sound-signal, then I think it will become more difficult than ever. I confess myself that at first I was inclined to follow the proposal, because I felt, as I have no doubt others felt, that the principle having been adopted by the Conference, it was necessary to discuss it, and that the Committee had no alternative but to propose such a signal after the principle had been adopted. But now we have got the power to reconsider it, which unties our hands. I have had an opportunity of consulting my colleagues, and I shall cast my vote in favour of the proposal that it is not desirable to give any sound-signals to a sailing-vessel towing another vessel.

I ought to say with regard to my gallant friend on the right that of course he has done his best on behalf of the Committee to whom this matter was referred. The Committee have done their best. They have proposed this Rule, and he adheres to his opinion that this is a signal which could be given. I think it is right that I should state this. But I have also had an opportunity of consulting with my other colleagues, and we shall cast our vote against any signal being given, having regard to the fact that the occasions are rare when such signals are wanted, and to the difficulty of finding such a signal at all.

Captain Malmberg (Sweden).—Mr. President, I will now come back to what I have stated in the beginning of the discussion on this Article. It is found to be very difficult to find a suitable sound-signal for a sailing-vessel towing, and it has been found quite impossible to find a proper light-signal for a sailing-vessel towing. Then the whole concern about sailing-vessels towing ought to be stricken out of the paragraph.

Captain Mensing (Germany).—Mr. President, I would like to be informed whether the opinion expressed by the distinguished Delegate from Great Britain is meant to oppose even the introduction of an optional distinctive signal. It is true that this is a case which does not very often happen. The Delegate from China has pointed that there are men who have been going to sea for a very long period without ever having seen such a vessel. I would like to say that these occasions are not so infrequent as he thinks they are, particularly in those waters where the sea is rougher and where there are more fogs, as, for instance, in the North Sea. These cases are not unheard of. I remember quite a number of them which I have seen in such waters.

Now, what has struck me is that there has really not been any point brought against my proposal, which is to leave it optional, and to take the signal which a steamer already has to give, so that there would be no more for the sailor to learn. He knows that this signal is optional, and that it is given on the fog-horn, and that it cannot be mistaken in any other respect. Why could not the signal be given in that form? I may say that I am at a loss to understand why this change of opinion has taken place. I have not heard a single reason why I should change my opinion expressed at the first reading of this Article. Then it was, as I believe, unanimously accepted that we should adopt this principle. Then I thought it best not to endeavour to introduce a compulsory signal, but to make it an optional one. I am still of that opinion, and I hope that the Conference will adopt my amendment.

Mr. Carter (Hawaii).—Mr. President, we have, of course, listened with great respect to the remarks made by the learned Delegate from Great Britain. He advanced two propositions: one was the great difficulty of finding a new signal, and the other was the rarity of occasions on which it would be necessary. Now, it seems to me that quite controverts his position in the matter. He is in favour, as I understand it, of a signal being given to a steamer towing another vessel. Now, what is the necessity for a new signal? A steamer towing another vessel is a vessel towing another vessel, and why should not any vessel, under the same circumstances, give the same signal? That the cases are so very rare only weakens his objection. If you prove that they never existed, the objection would prevail; if you prove that they exist but seldom, then there is very little objection. But it seems to me that, under the circumstances of a vessel towing another vessel in a fog, it is highly necessary there should be, whether a sailing-vessel or a steamer, some signal to enable her to give notice that she is towing. There is no necessity for a second signal.

Captain Malmberg (Sweden).—Mr. President, as there has been an allusion made to me, I take the liberty to point out why I wish that the special signal for sailing-vessels towing should not be brought into the Article. As far as I can see, it is quite impossible to give to a sailing-ship towing another ship a signal which would not interfere with Article 14, prescribing the signals which a sailing-vessel has to make. The only way, as I said once before, to get out of that difficulty is to have the vessel towed by the sailing-vessel repeat the signal given by the vessel towing. As for introducing a new signal to be made by the sailing-vessel towing, it cannot be done, because it will conflict with Article 14.

Admiral Nares (Great Britain).—Mr. President, the seamen throughout the world must in the future learn a number of signals. You give them a signal for a steam-ship towing. Now, the Committee have chosen the same signal for a sailing-ship. There is nothing further to learn. The question has often been asked, what is a sailing-ship towed or towing to do? Is she to make her signal for the starboard tack or the port tack? The signal which we have chosen for a sailing-ship, whether she is towed or whether she is towing, is the same, but one is to be compulsory, and the other a permissive signal, which will largely override her starboard and port tack signals or free wind signals. It is such a distinctive signal that it completely overrides the old signal. It will not be an additional signal to learn, because every mariner must learn the signal for a steamer towing.

Captain Mensing (Germany).—Mr. President, from what has fallen from the gentleman who sat down just now, I apprehend that his idea is that if a vessel is towing in a fog everybody would have to get out of the way of that vessel. But that principle has not been adopted. The Conference has adopted the principle that, no matter whether a ship is towing or not, she has to get out of the way if it is her duty to do so. There is no distinction made in that respect between a steamer towing and a sailing-vessel towing. A sailing-vessel has to get out of the way, or she has to hold her course under certain conditions. Now, I have tried to explain how my amendment would work if it were adopted. If that amendment is adopted, a sailing-vessel which was towing would, under ordinary circumstances, make one, two, or three short blasts on her fog-horn when she heard another vessel coming near her. Then she might alternate and make two short blasts after a silence of about two minutes. The signal —long, short, short; then, after a while, two shorts, and so on.

I do not see what difficulty there would be for any ship meeting this vessel finding out her character and finding out what the ship is doing. That ship has to get out of the way if necessary, and she has to keep her course if necessary. That is the Rule adopted by this Conference, and in order that she may do so she must be warned by the other sailing-ship what she has got to do. I do not see any reason whatever, and there has been no reason brought forward, so far as I can see, against the introduction of this optional signal. I should be glad to hear if there are any reasons to give against the optional introduction of some signal.

The President.—The question is upon the motion of the Delegate from the United States, that in the opinion of the Conference no signal shall be given to a sailing-vessel towing another vessel. Is the Conference ready for the question?

The question was put to the Conference upon the motion of the Delegate from the United States, and it was carried.

The President.—Does the Delegate from Germany wish to introduce his proposition for an optional signal?

Captain Mensing (Germany).—Mr. President, I have voted upon the side which I did not mean to vote for. I would like to have my motion put to a vote.

The President.—The question would then have to be reconsidered. If the Delegate from Germany would like a reconsideration of the motion, the question will be put.

Captain Mensing (Germany).—Yes, Sir; I would ask to have that done.

The President.—The question is upon the motion of the Delegate from Germany to reconsider the vote upon the motion of the Delegate from the United States.

The question upon the motion to reconsider was put to the Conference, and carried.

The President.—The question now is upon the motion of the Delegate from Germany that an optional signal may be introduced for a sailing-ship towing another ship.

Mr. Goodrich (United States).—Mr. President, I do not know whether the Conference fully understands that proposition.

The President.—The question which was just put has been reconsidered. Then the Delegate from Germany moved that we should have an optional signal for a sailing-ship towing another ship, and the question is to be taken upon that motion.

Mr. Goodrich (United States).—Mr. President, I want to show what result would be worked out under that.

The President.—The result will be that it will be carried or not carried, and then the question will revert to the main question.

Mr. Goodrich (United States).—Mr. President, let us see how this will work out. The Conference has already given as its opinion that no signal should be given to a sailing-vessel towing another vessel. Now the proposition is to permit an optional signal, as I understand the proposition of the gallant Delegate from Germany——

Mr. Carter (Hawaii).—Mr. President, I do not think the learned Delegate from the United States quite understands the gallant Delegate from Germany, who has moved a reconsideration. He voted Aye, not understanding the motion. I was, myself, about to raise a question that the way the motion was put would probably mislead some of the Delegates. It being a negative question they voted Aye, thinking they were voting for an affirmative proposition; but, because of the fact that they were voting for a negative proposition, they were misled. The gallant Delegate from Germany was misled in giving his vote, and he asked that it might be reconsidered. Then a new motion comes in, that an optional signal is needed.

The President.—The Delegate from Germany moved before the vote was taken upon the motion of the Delegate from the United States, that this optional signal be given, and that he wished to have that question opened. The Chair suggested a reconsideration of the vote, so as to give the Delegate from Germany an opportunity to have a vote upon his proposition.

Mr. Goodrich (United States).—Mr. President, I understand the situation precisely as the gentleman from Hawaii stated it, but the result of a vote in favour of the proposition of the gallant Delegate from Germany to make an optional signal will put us in the same position we were in before we made this last vote.

Mr. Hall (Great Britain).—Mr. President, may I rise to a point of order? I think that we shall be drifting into a position of difficulty if we reconsider a question because one of the Delegates voted by mistake. By all means let that Delegate have an opportunity to correct that mistake, and have his vote recorded on the other side; but I do not see why, when the Conference has examined the question, that question is to be reopened because by mistake a vote was called Aye instead of Nay. Certainly all of us want every Delegate to have his vote cast on the side on which he wants it to be. The result would be, if we followed the course which is proposed now, that whenever a division is called, and an amendment is carried, we could be invited to discuss some previous proposal because one of the Delegates voted wrong. That is really the position in which we are at the present moment. I am certain the gallant Delegate from Germany should have an opportunity to correct his vote. That vote should be corrected; but I apprehended that the decision of the Conference is a distinct matter.

The President.—The Chair does not so understand it. The Delegate from Germany moved a reconsideration of the vote in order that he might get a test vote upon his proposition for an optional signal. The Chair gave him an opportunity to do so. Now the question is, as the Chair understands it, upon his motion that you have an optional signal for a sailing-vessel towing.

Mr. Goodrich (United States).—Mr. President, that is precisely the way I understood it, and precisely the way in which the gentleman from Hawaii so clearly stated it. My suggestion is that if we want to give no special signal to a sailing-vessel towing another, then we should vote *No* on the proposition even to give an optional signal, and that disposes of the whole question.

The President.—The Chair wishes to bring it before the Conference in order to give the Delegate from Germany an opportunity for a test vote.

Captain Sampson (United States).—Mr. President, I call for the Yeas and Nays.

The President.—The Yeas and Nays will be called. Will the Delegate from Germany be kind enough to state what his proposition is?

Captain Mensing (Germany).—I have already handed in the proposition to the Secretary.

The President.—Do you make a special motion?

Captain Mensing (Germany).—Yes, Sir; I make a special motion that an optional signal be introduced for use on sailing-vessels towing other vessels; and I would like to add, if it is permissive, that this signal should be the same as that used by steamers.

Mr. Verney (Siam).—Mr. President, I am very glad that the gallant Delegate from Germany has just stated that, because it may make a great difference in the vote given. I, personally, should vote in favour of that proposition, but not of the other proposition.

Mr. Hall (Great Britain).—Mr. President, I am not prepared to vote in favour of that proposition, because I cannot forget the very strong arguments that were advanced this morning by the gallant Delegate from Germany about the difficulty of sailing-vessels giving a prolonged blast, and the great expense they would be put to if they had to get fog-horns enabling them to give a signal similar to that proposed. I shall oppose this Resolution because of the difficulty, first of all, of finding such a signal, and, secondly, because of the rarity of the occasions on which such a signal is required, and, thirdly, because it seems possible that sailing-vessels may not be able to give the signal even if they wish to do so.

Captain Sampson (United States).—Mr. President, I hope the Conference will not adopt any such proposition, because it seems to me it is just as objectionable as to make the signal obligatory. The fog sound-signal sounded by any vessel gives her no right of way. The object is to warn an approaching vessel that she is there. Now, if you give a sailing-vessel and a steamer the same signal, how is a vessel approaching to know whether that vessel has the right of way or not? If she is a sailing-ship, she has, according to the previous Rules, certain rights over steamers; but if you give her the same fog-signal as a steamer, you set aside the advantages which you have given her in the previous Rules.

Captain Mensing (Germany).—Mr. President, I am very sorry I was misunderstood when I said that it was the same signal. It is in one sense. It is a long blast and two short, but in another sense it is not the same at all. The signal which I propose is one which is not compulsory, and the other one is compulsory. I have already twice explained this matter, and I am very sorry if I have to take up the time of the Conference again, but I suppose I will have to do so, as there seems to be no definite conception as to what I desire. If this signal which I proposed—an optional signal—should be adopted, then a vessel going in the open sea, without hearing any other fog-signals, should sound one, two, or three blasts, which are prescribed for her here under Article 12, paragraph (*g*). Now, this certainly can have no other meaning than that if she sees another vessel coming, and sees that she wants to go under her stern, which she may expect her to do, that she should warn her that there is something attached to her which will surely bring the other vessel into collision.

I do not know whether I made myself clear; but it seems to me that there can be no doubt that a sailing-vessel should have one, two, or three blasts to indicate her course in relation to the wind, and that this signal could only be used by her whenever she saw fit to do so and thought it was necessary, and whenever she thought that by blowing it it would be possible to avoid a collision. That is my proposition. I hope I have succeeded in making myself clearly understood. I am sorry to have to take up the time of the Conference with this matter.

The President.—The Secretary will please read the proposition of the Delegate from Germany.

The proposition of the Delegate from Germany is as follows:—

" That an optional signal shall be introduced for a sailing-vessel towing other vessels, and that such signal be made permissive, and to adopt the same signal for sailing-vessels towing as for steamers towing."

The President.—Upon that proposition the Yeas and Nays will be called.

The Yea and Nay vote is as follows:—

Austria-Hungary .. .. Nay.	Japan .. .. .. Yea.
Belgium .. .. .. Yea.	Mexico .. .. .. Nay.
China .. .. .. Nay.	Norway .. .. .. Nay.
Chile .. .. .. Nay.	Portugal .. .. .. Nay.
Denmark .. .. .. Yea.	Russia .. .. .. Nay.
France .. .. .. Nay.	Spain .. .. .. Nay.
Germany .. .. .. Yea.	Sweden .. .. .. Nay.
Great Britain .. .. Nay.	Siam .. .. .. Nay.
Hawaii .. .. .. Yea.	The Netherlands .. .. Yea.
Italy .. .. .. Yea.	United States .. .. Nay.

The President.—Seven have voted in the affirmative, and twelve in the negative; so the proposition is not carried. The question now is upon the amendment of the Delegate of the United States, which will be read.

The proposition of the Delegate from the United States is as follows:—

"In the opinion of the Conference no signal shall be given to a sailing-vessel towing another vessel."

The question was put to the Conference upon the motion of the Delegate from the United States, and it was carried.

The President.—The Secretary will please read section (*g*) as it now stands.

Section (*g*) is as follows:—

"(*g*.) A steam-vessel when towing shall, and a vessel towed may, if necessary, at intervals of not more than two minutes, sound on a whistle, siren, or fog-horn three blasts in succession, namely, one prolonged blast, followed by two short blasts."

The President.—Is the Conference ready for the question?

Captain Mensing (Germany).—Mr. President, I think that if we should adopt this we would come to the extraordinary conclusion that a vessel being towed by a sailing-vessel would have the right to make her presence known to other vessels by giving a signal, and that the other vessel would not have that right.

The President.—The words "sailing-vessel" have been struck out.

Captain Mensing (Germany).—Mr. President, it reads, "and the vessels towed"—of course by a sailing-vessel, as I take it.

The President.—The words "sailing-vessel" have been struck out.

Captain Mensing (Germany).—Mr. President, I beg your pardon. As I read it, it is a steam-vessel towing, that is the first; and a vessel towed, that is the second. Now, I take it that the vessel towed is the vessel towed by a sailing-vessel.

The President.—The Chair does not so understand it. It means a vessel being towed by a steam-vessel. The words "sailing-vessel" have been erased.

Mr. Hall (Great Britain).—Mr. President, to make it quite clear, it reads: "A steam-vessel when towing shall, and her tow may"—the Collocation Committee will deal with that.

The President.—If there be no objection that insertion will be made.

Mr. Verbrugghe (Belgium).—Mr. President, may I point out that it was remarked this morning that the words "if necessary" inserted there will be of no avail? I should propose to strike out the words "if necessary," because if a collision should occur it will then be pointed out by the very fact of the collision that it was necessary, and it will be quite as well to leave it out entirely.

Mr. Carter (Hawaii).—Mr. President, I will point out that it would simplify the matter to say that a steam-vessel when towing a steam-vessel shall——

Mr. Goodrich (United States).—Mr. President, I understand that the learned Delegate from Great Britain has a suggestion which would meet the suggestion of the honourable Delegate from Belgium.

Mr. Hall (Great Britain).—Mr. President, I think it is exceedingly simple. It reads: "A steam-vessel when towing, and a vessel towed by her may." As the word "towed" comes before the words, "at intervals of not more than two minutes," it would look as if the vessel towed were to give the signal and to keep on doing it every two minutes. I do not suppose that it is the desire of the Committee, and therefore I think it would be better to place that at the end of the sentence in this way: "A vessel being towed by a steamer may also sound this signal." That would get over the difficulty.

Captain Malmberg (Sweden).—Mr. President, I think we have got into a difficulty here. We have provided that a steam-vessel when towing shall make with her whistle or siren such and such a signal. That is all right. Now, we have put in this signal to be made by the vessel under tow, and we have got into the fog-horn trouble, because it ought to state in these Rules that a steam-vessel towing shall make with her siren such and such a signal, which signal may be repeated by the vessel under tow on her fog-horn; because if we do not say on her fog-horn, then a steamer towing another steamer could give two steam-whistles for a signal, which will not bring to your notice that there is a tow at all. The steamer towing should make the signal, which should be repeated by the steamer being towed, not on her whistle, but on her fog-horn.

Captain Sampson (United States).—Mr. President, what has just been said by the last Delegate who has spoken confirms me in the suggestion which I made this morning, and that is that this signal must be repeated by the vessel in tow; and it seems to me that would remove all these difficulties. If it is left optional, the vessel approaching such a tow can never tell whether there is one or two tows in front of him. If it is made obligatory that the vessel being towed or the last vessel in the tow shall repeat the signal of the vessel towing, a vessel approaching knows at once that it is a tow, and knows the length of it. Of course that information would not be given if she did not feel certain that the last vessel in the tow had to repeat the signal. As has been pointed out by the learned Delegate from Sweden, she could not tell whether it was one tow or two. But if it is obligatory upon the last vessel in the tow to repeat the signal, there is no doubt in the mind of the vessel approaching that tow that there is either one or two.

Now, no difficulty will arise from the fact that the signals are repeated. We have retained the words, "whenever necessary." Under such circumstances a vessel towing would make the signal according to this Rule, and repeat the signal at least once in two minutes. The vessel being towed would not make the signal until after hearing the fog-sound signal of another vessel approaching. When the tow found itself in the presence of another vessel, then the circumstances would arise when it would become necessary for the vessel being towed to warn an approaching vessel as to the length of the tow. I can see the point made by the honourable Delegate from Belgium, that it would place upon the vessel being towed the obligation of proving, in case she did not repeat the signal at the right time, that no necessity existed for sounding it. It seems to me that if the signal is made obligatory that difficulty will be removed.

The President.—If you will make that amendment, it will be put to a vote.

Captain Sampson (United States).—Mr. President, I have already made that this morning.

Captain Malmberg (Sweden).—Mr. President, I think this paragraph (*g*) would be properly understood if it should read in this way: "A steam-vessel when towing shall sound her whistle or siren at intervals of not more than two minutes," and then the signal decided upon, "and the vessel in tow shall or may, as hereafter will be decided, on the fog-horn, repeat the signal made by the steamer towing."

Mr. Goodrich (United States).—Mr. President, we are drifting into a great deal of confusion. Let me propose a sentence which will decide this question. I call attention to the fact that this contains the permissive signal—that in the opinion of the Conference a permissive signal should be given to a vessel being towed in a fog.

Admiral Nares (Great Britain).—And not compulsory.

Mr. Goodrich (United States).—That means not compulsory. I am perfectly willing to make it read "permissive, and not compulsory."

Mr. Carter (Hawaii).—That should be a vessel being towed by a steam-vessel.

Mr. Goodrich (United States).—I have no objection to that. I will read it again for the information of the Conference:—

"That in the opinion of the Conference a permissive, and not a compulsory signal should be given to a vessel being towed by a steam-vessel in a fog."

Admiral Nares (Great Britain).—Mr. President, there is one word more I desire to say. We were very strong about this permissive signal in the Committee, and as we said this morning, we leave it to the captain to make the signal when it is necessary. When there is a long tow, if there is a steamer approaching, the last vessel, or the middle vessel in the tow, when in sight of that steamer, will give her signal that there is something astern of her. But this is all leading to close shaves. Of course you cannot give the right of way to vessels towing. But really, in a fog, we all know that everybody goes out of their way. We never go near them. If you are not careful in this signal, you are leading to close shaves, and giving them signals so that they will be able to go close under the stern of a vessel.

Captain Richard (France).—Mr. President, it seems to me that the Conference entirely agrees upon the first portion, namely, to give to the towing vessel a distinct signal, produced by a long blast and two short ones in succession. That is one of the most practicable sound-signals which I know, because the prolonged blast followed by two short ones can generally be very distinctly made.

But as to the second portion, the Conference is at variance, viz., as to the wisdom of giving to the vessel in tow a distinct signal, either permissive or compulsory. It seems to me impossible to arrive at an understanding upon the latter point. Why then persist in establishing it; and why not be satisfied with the first portion, in regard to which we are nearly all agreed, and which is complete in itself, and establishes a principle by itself. The principle is the following: To give to the towing vessel the means of making herself known in fog and mist, without heeding the vessel which is being towed, whose presence is implied by the signal made by the towing vessel.

That is more than the existing Rule. It is a step forward, although thereby every one is not fully satisfied. Let us, therefore, leave out the second portion, and state that every vessel, whether a steam or sailing vessel, towing another shall indicate her presence by giving at two minutes' intervals a prolonged blast, followed by two short ones, with her whistle, her siren, or her fog-horn. Evidently the vessel which hears the signal will hear nothing from the vessel which is being towed, but she will know perfectly well that she has before her or on one side of her a towing vessel with a tow. This will be generally sufficient, and the necessity of the vessel which is being towed using her fog-horn or her whistle seems to me very doubtful. The necessity of it was insisted upon when a vessel tows a large number of other vessels; but this case, which is very frequent in the United States in or near territorial waters, seldom happens at sea.

I would, therefore, propose to modify the Article in the following manner: "A sailing-vessel or a steam-vessel when towing another shall, at intervals of two minutes, give a prolonged blast and two short ones with her whistle, her siren, or her fog-horn." If the Committee takes this view, I think that the adoption of this amendment will be the solution of our difficulty.

Mr. Flood (Norway).—Mr. President, I shall not occupy the time of the Conference much longer, but I will only say that I will strongly support what the gallant Delegate from the United States, Captain Sampson, has said in favour of making this signal compulsory. I desire to ask the Conference this question: What is the meaning of these words, "if necessary"? Does it mean if necessary for the safety of the vessels towing, or for the safety of the vessel approaching the tow? I would like to know what is meant.

Mr. Goodrich (United States).—Necessary to prevent risk of collision.

Mr. Flood (Norway).—There is no risk of collision when you do not see anything. I suppose that the meaning of this Article is that when there is a very heavy fog, they are now and then to sound the signal. But, I ask again, is it for the safety of the vessel approaching?

Mr. Goodrich (United States).—It is for both.

Mr. Flood (Norway).—It is not for the safety of both. There are tows in tide-waters that will be towed pretty nearly abreast of each other, or very nearly so, and I may be on the inside ship. A ship might run into the outside vessel so that I would not be hurt at all. It would depend upon her situation. I should like to ask the question whether "if necessary" means for my own safety or for the safety of the vessel approaching me?

Mr. Goodrich (United States).—It is both.

Mr. Flood (Norway).—Mr. President, if that is the answer, I can say that this will have to be left to the individual captain, whether he be a careful captain or a reckless captain, to decide whether it is necessary or not to sound this signal. Why, then, have we such a fixed rule for the lights? These lights are to be put out from sunset to sunrise. Now, in the summer time, when the sun sets at 7 or 7·30 o'clock, you can see for an hour after the lights are put out, but they must be put there, the lights have to be in their position. They are necessary to give a warning as soon as possible. Why not have those sound-signals for vessels being towed as well as vessels towing? It is argued that this is bewildering. The lights are bewildering when they are on three or four vessels; but, as it was said, they convey the information that there is an obstruction to navigation. If two or three vessels are under tow and they alternately sound the fog-signal, it will be a warning to keep out of the way.

Captain Malmberg (Sweden).—Mr. President, partly because I think the Conference will find it almost impossible to agree upon these signals and how they are to be made by a vessel in tow, and partly because I think it is quite sufficient that the steamer towing makes a signal telling that she is a steamer towing, I would very much like the Conference to accept the amendment of the gallant Delegate from France, and not to mention anything about the signal to be made by vessels under tow, but to be satisfied to have the steamer towing make the proper signal.

Mr. Hall (Great Britain).—Mr. President, with regard to the difficulty in the words, "if necessary," which has been suggested by the Delegate from Norway, may I remind him of this fact, that these words which seem to give him so much trouble are part of the Rule which I suppose has been discussed more than any Rule of the Road at Sea, and that is Article 18, as to the duty of vessels when they are approaching one another, with risk of collision, to stop and reverse their engines, if necessary? A great many hundred cases have been tried upon that Rule, and in which these words have been used, and I have never known it to be suggested by any living man that they meant anything but what one would suppose them to mean—if necessary to prevent collision. I do not suppose that it was ever the intention of the Committee to pass a Rule which would protect only one ship and not protect the other. We want to protect both.

Mr. Goodrich (United States).—Mr. President, might I call further attention to the fact that the same words are used in the Article headed "Lights and Signals to attract Attention," where it says that every vessel may, if necessary, in addition to the lights which she shows, show a flare-up light, &c.?

Mr. Flood (Norway).—Mr. President, I will challenge every lawyer present to say whether or not the first point would be, and the first question to be asked on coming into Court after a collision would be, "Did you sound your signal or not?" Then, if I said "No, I did not think it was necessary," I would lose the case.

Captain Shackford (United States).—And you ought to lose it if you did not sound your fog-horn.

Mr. Goodrich (United States).—Mr. President, I call attention to the fact that this discussion is foreign to the proposition before the Conference. The present proposition is that, in the opinion of the Conference, a permissive, and not a compulsory, signal should be given to a vessel being towed by a steam-vessel in a fog. I suggest that we take a vote upon this proposition.

The President.—The Delegate from France has made a proposal which will be read first. The vote will be upon the proposition of the Delegate from France.

The proposition of the Delegate from France is as follows:—

Paragraph (*g*) to read:—

"A steam-vessel when towing shall, at intervals of not more than two minutes, sound upon her whistle, siren, or fog-horn three blasts in succession, viz., one prolonged blast and two short blasts."

Captain Mensing (Germany).—Mr. President, I think that the word "fog-horn" should be stricken out there.

Mr. Goodrich (United States).—Mr. President, if you will allow me to suggest, I do not think that is a privileged question which overrides my proposition. My proposition is upon a principle, and I think it takes precedence of the proposition of the Delegate from France.

The President.—The Chair understands that the last proposition is the one to be entertained. If so, the proposition of the Delegate from the United States is in order.

Mr. Hall (Great Britain).—Mr. President, may I point out that if the proposition of the gallant Delegate from France is voted upon by the Conference there is nothing to prevent the Conference from adding a permissive signal to that section? He has pointed out that we had come to a conclusion with regard to this matter, and that we ought not to go any further. I think we are all agreed that a steam-vessel should give a signal, and the mere carrying of that proposition will not prevent the discussion on the proposition of the learned Delegate from the United States.

The President.—The Chair understands the proposition of the Delegate from the United States to be as to whether a signal should be given to a vessel being towed by a steam-vessel in a fog. If the Delegate from France wishes his motion put first, it will be in order.

Captain Richard (France).—Mr. President, I should add that at first I included in my proposition—and I think that quite a number of my colleagues must have understood that such was the sense of my proposition—vessels towing, whether steam or sail. I was told that the Conference had already formally excluded giving a signal to sailing-vessels, whether towing or being towed. I, therefore, have taken out of my amendment whatever was not in harmony with the measure adopted. But the object of this amendment is, according to my view, a distinctive signal to the towing vessel, and I think that upon that point I am in harmony with the majority of the members. If it is necessary to indicate the presence of a towing vessel, why make any difference between a steam-vessel and a sailing-vessel? I greatly regret that the Conference should have decided against establishing this principle, when they seem to be disposed to accept the principle itself. This principle is a rational one, and, moreover, forces itself upon us. We should have no difficulty in agreeing upon the wisdom of allowing a towing vessel to signal her presence. There are many difficulties in defining the duty of the vessel in tow. Some of us desire that any sound-signal prescribed for the latter shall be obligatory; others desire to make it only permissive. Moreover, it has been found necessary, simply to facilitate the wording of the Article, to say "if necessary," an expression which leaves the practical difficulty unsolved.

In my proposition the towing vessel, whatever may be her character, is given the means to indicate her presence and to announce that she is towing a vessel, whatever may be the character and the tonnage of such vessel. This is valuable information. It is better than what we have, and it is a step forward. Something better would certainly be desirable, but with a view of the difficulties with which we are hedged in, we should be satisfied with the best that we can do. I wonder whether the Conference would not be more satisfied by reopening the decision, in order the better to harmonize the Rules which it is desirable to establish. In my humble opinion it would be very wise to adopt the principle of distinguishing a towing vessel, whether she be a sailing-vessel or a steam-vessel. By so doing the Conference would satisfy us all—both those who desire to include in this Rule sailing-vessels and those who wish to include steam-vessels.

If the Conference decides to review its decision, we might introduce into the Article the first portion of the Article recommended by the Sound-Signal Committee, leaving out the second portion in regard to which an understanding is difficult to arrive at, namely, all that concerns the vessel in tow. Who knows but that in a few years something will be found which will regulate the duty of the latter? At present it is almost impossible. Under these circumstances I would, therefore, suggest that the Conference accept that the steam towing vessels announce their presence in the manner indicated by the Committee. I intend, thereupon, to present an amendment to the effect whether it would not be well to apply to the sailing-vessel towing the same right granted to the steam towing vessel.

Mr. Goodrich (United States).—Mr. President, may I ask the gallant Delegate from France if it will not be a solution of the difficulty in which the Conference finds itself if the principle which is involved in my motion should take precedence of his motion which he has just presented, because we have already eliminated, practically, all opposition to the whole of his Resolution except that part which relates to a special signal to be given? We have said that a sailing-vessel shall not have a special signal given to it. Then his amendment follows necessarily, except as to the special signal to be given to a steamer. Now, we are taking it step by step, and our next step should be to determine the question whether a sailing-vessel being towed shall have any special signal, either permissive or compulsory. If that is opposed, naturally we come to the proposition of finally deciding upon the signal to be given. It seems to me that would be a very much shorter method of reaching a result.

Mr. Hall (Great Britain).—Mr. President, might I suggest, with a view of saving time, that we all agreed upon the proposal of the gallant Delegate from France, which is that a steam-vessel should make the signal which is proposed? Let us adopt that at once.

Mr. Goodrich (United States).—Adopt the signal and all.

Captain Sampson (United States).—Mr. President, I do not understand that we are agreed to the proposition made by the gallant Delegate from France. It seems to me that a portion of it relates to a sailing-vessel towing.

Mr. Hall (Great Britain).—Mr. President, there is nothing in it about a sailing-vessel towing. It is only with regard to steam-vessels towing, and providing that she shall sound the signal.

The President.—The Secretary will read the proposition for the information of the Conference.

The proposition is as follows:—

"A steam-vessel when towing shall, at intervals of not more than two minutes, sound on the whistle or siren three blasts in succession, viz., one prolonged blast and two short blasts."

Mr. Goodrich (United States).—Will the gallant Delegate accept the words, "followed by two short blasts"?

Captain Richard (France).—Yes, Sir.

The President.—Is the Conference ready for the question upon that amendment?

Captain Richard (France).—Yes, Mr. President, the signal proposed by the Committee, the only difference being that I have left out of it the vessel in tow.

The President.—The question is upon the substitute proposed by the Delegate from France for paragraph (*g*).

The question upon the substitute proposed by the Delegate from France was put to the Conference, and it was adopted.

The President.—The Resolution of the Delegate from the United States will now be in order.

Captain Richard (France).—Mr. President, now that we have adopted the principle that a steam-vessel towing another shall have a special signal indicating her presence, without paying attention to giving a special signal to the vessel which is being towed, why should not we extend this principle to sailing-vessels towing? You have decided that you desired a sound-signal which, as a general rule, should only apply to the towing vessel. Why not extend that principle to its fullest extent, inasmuch as we can do so? At sea, you may find a sailing-vessel which tows another. It is not a very frequent thing, but it may happen. It is good to inform vessels in the neighbourhood of that fact. It is a matter which can very properly be inserted in your Rule, which will cost you nothing. What will it cost you to give to the sailing-vessel the right, or rather to impose the obligation, to sound her fog-horn, viz., one long blast and two short ones? That will cost you nothing. Your principle remains unaffected. For, inasmuch as you adopt the principle for steam-vessels, why not apply that principle

[93]

to sailing-vessels; and why then allow yourselves to be withheld simply on the ground of Parliamentary etiquette from reopening the discussion of the proposition which has been adopted under certain difficulties, arising from the fact that, instead of viewing the entire subject from all sides, but one side of the question has been considered. The Conference, on the other hand, up to a certain degree, is in harmony with the Committee, by adopting a portion of this proposiition. I therefore propose that there be introduced into the first paragraph, " a steam-vessel or a sailing-vessel.'

Mr. Hall (Great Britain).—Mr. President, may I point out that we have discussed this already for several hours to-day, and the vote has been taken, practically, twice upon it, and we have had the votes counted? I do not think that we ought to reopen this discussion. May I point out that the reasons which actuated some of us were that it was practically very difficult to find such a signal for such a purpose; and, secondly, that the occasions when it was wanted were very few indeed; and, thirdly, the difficulty in giving a similar signal by sailing-vessels, and the difficulty in the construction of the fog-horns, &c.? I can only say that, if any point has been argued by the Conference thoroughly, it is this one which has been referred to by the gallant Delegate from France.

Captain Richard (France).—Mr. President, the discussion has been very much prolonged. We desire to find a signal, and I agree that the number of signals is very much restricted. But the same signal is adopted for the steam-vessel as for the sailing-vessel, only, instead of making it with the whistle you make it with the fog-horn. There is, therefore, no difference. There is nothing which in that respect can inspire you with the slightest fear. It is of easy application. Evidently the real objection is the difficulty of arriving at a reconsideration of the proposition. But the Conference can always resort to the Rule, that is to say, to appeal from the decision and to obtain a three-quarter vote in favour of reconsideration.

Mr. Hall (Great Britain).—Mr. President, the original proposition was that a steam-vessel and a sailing-vessel towing should each give the same signal. We voted against that, and decided that sailing-vessels towing should not give any signal at all. Now it is again proposed that a steam-vessel towing and a sailing-vessel towing are to give the same signal. Therefore the proposition of the gallant Delegate from France is exactly the proposition contained in this paragraph of the Report of the Committee from which the words, "a sailing-vessel," were struck out. By all means let us reconsider everything upon which there is any doubt; but I want to point out that his proposal is to reconsider the proposition which we have discussed at great length to-day. We decided to strike out the words, " sailing-vessels towing," and not to give them a signal. Now we are asked to say that they are to be given a signal which we decided against this morning.

Captain Richard (France).—Mr. President, I think, as I have said before, that the confusion arises from the fact that from that moment there was taken into consideration the necessity of giving a special signal to the vessel being towed. The moment that you get rid of the vessel being towed the circumstances will be different, and I think that we can accept the entire first portion of the Article. Although this will not be absolutely satisfactory to every one, it will give moderate satisfaction to us all, and your Rule will not be a bad one.

Captain Settembrini (Italy).—Mr. President, as one of the Committee on Sound-Signals, I beg to state that I second the motion of the gallant Delegate from France. I quite agree with what he said and what he proposes.

Mr. Verney (Siam).—Mr. President, may I suggest that, before that question can be put, as a matter of order we must have a vote passed on the reconsideration of that question?

The President.—The amendment of the Delegate from France will be read, if he insists upon it, although it has already been passed upon.

Captain Sampson (United States).—Mr. President, I should like to point out that the proposition of the gallant Delegate from France does not quite meet one objection made to the proposal this morning, and that is, that the signal gives no information as to the direction in which the towing-vessel is moving with respect to the wind. It seems to me that, in order to retain a proper relation to the preceding Rules, it is absolutely necessary, if we adopt this regulation, that a sailing-vessel should give her signal to indicate that she is sailing in a certain direction with reference to the wind. It is absolutely necessary to give this information if it is necessary to give any information by a sailing-vessel towing.

Captain Richard (France).—Mr. President, it is very certain that the objection presented by the gallant Captain Sampson is a very serious objection. I do not think that it is insurmountable. It is evident that it may compel a slight modification of a signal which heretofore existed, if it is absolutely necessary to indicate the tack which the towing vessel is making. It seems to me that it might be possible to indicate the tack upon which the towing vessel is going by making one or two short blasts follow the prolonged blast, according to whether the vessel is on the starboard or port tack. We would then have these signals—a prolonged and a short blast for the starboard tack for a sailing-vessel having another one in tow, and a prolonged blast and two short ones for a vessel towing another on the port tack. I certainly would prefer a prolonged and two short blasts for the towing vessel, whatever may be the tack she is making; but I would remark that you would thereby be informed of the presence of a sailing-vessel towing, whereas with the Rule before you you are informed of nothing at all.

The President.—The question is upon the amendment of the Delegate from France.

Captain Sampson (United States).—Mr. President, I understand that he has withdrawn his amendment.

The President.—Has the Delegate from France withdrawn his amendment?

Captain Richard (France).—No, Sir.

Mr. Hall (Great Britain).—Mr. President, I apprehend that, to put ourselves in order, we must carry a Resolution to consider this question. Of course, I shall vote in favour of a reconsideration.

The President.—The Chair understands that the principle of this has already been decided; it is not a question upon the original proposition. It is a question which has arisen after the passage of the amendment of the Delegate from France, although the principle has been decided before. It seems to the Chair that the quickest way will be to take a vote upon the question.

Mr. Hall (Great Britain).—Mr. President, I think that, if the gallant Delegate from France will move that the question of principle as to whether or not sailing-vessels towing are to carry a distinctive signal be considered, that it will put us in order. I am most anxious that nothing should be passed, so far as we are concerned, in this Conference without ample discussion. Our feeling is that every matter ought to be fully discussed. What makes me more anxious to support the gallant Delegate from France, although I am opposed to his views, is that I am informed that it is very possible that not only my gallant friend the Delegate from Germany voted in error upon the call of the vote, but that other Delegates also voted in error. Therefore it is desirable that the whole matter should be thoroughly discussed, so that all of us shall be fully satisfied. If he will move to reconsider the question of principle as to whether or not a sailing-vessel towing shall give a distinctive signal, I shall cast our vote in favour of that reconsideration.

Captain Richard (France).—Mr. President, I agree to that.

The President.—The Delegate from France moves to reconsider the question as to whether sailing-vessels shall give a distinctive signal when towing.

The question as to the reconsideration of this principle was put to the Conference, and carried.

The President.—The question now is upon the amendment of the Delegate from France. It will be read for the information of the Conference.

Mr. Goodrich (United States).—Mr. President, what is the proposition of the gallant Delegate from France? I do not know what his proposition is yet. It is not formulated so that the Secretary can present it.

The President.—The Secretary will read the proposition of the Delegate from France.

The proposition is as follows:—

" To restore the words ' and a sailing-vessel ' in paragraph (*g*)."

Captain Mensing (Germany).—Mr. President, I have already tried to find out this morning why it was thought impossible to introduce the signal which I proposed for this purpose. Under Article 16 (*a*), (*b*), and (*c*), the rule is laid down that a ship which is running free shall keep out of the way of a ship which is close-hauled; a ship which is close-hauled on the port tack shall keep out of the way of a ship which is close-hauled on the starboard tack; when both are running with the wind free, the ship which has the wind on the port side has to keep out of the way of the other; when both are running free with the wind on the same side, the ship which is to windward shall keep out of the way of the ship which is to leeward.

Now, I want to know whether I am on the same tack as another vessel or not. What would be the result if a collision occurred when that case is taken into Court? I think that these reasons have not been in any way explained, and, therefore, I think that my presumption stands that we ought to keep this distinctive signal. On the other hand, there are difficulties which have been pointed out by the gallant Delegate from the United States if we introduce three more signals for sailing-ships under tow. I presented my proposal this morning, which has been negatived by a vote of this Conference, in which I proposed that these signals should be optional. I was very sorry at the time that my gallant friend the Delegate from France voted against it. Now, I really do not see what reason there can be, and I wish he would explain it a little, as to why he should vote against the optional introduction of the signals, and why he now proposes to make them obligatory or compulsory.

Captain Malmberg (Sweden).—Mr. President, it seems to me that we are beginning to mix up to a great extent the Rules to be followed when vessels are in sight of each other, and the rules in a fog when vessels are not in sight of each other.

Captain Richard (France).—Mr. President, I think that our honourable colleague the gallant Delegate from Sweden has struck the right key by saying that the Rules of the Road do not exist for vessels under way in a fog, but have been made for vessels in sight of each other.

My gallant colleague from Germany reminded me that I had voted against the introduction of a permissive signal in paragraph (*g*) in favour of sailing-vessels. I would answer him by saying that at that moment the matter was a great deal more mixed up than it is now, for the following reason—if you will now adopt my proposition, the entire Article will be adopted, and then we can proceed with the discussion of Article (*h*). I must admit that at first I did not see very well how a steam-vessel or a sailing-vessel towing another and blowing her siren or fog-horn, and the vessel in tow likewise blowing her fog-horn or whistle, I repeat that I did not very well see whether you would be led by this Article, which is the result of the labours of the Committee. I saw many objections against what was proposed to us; and need I say that I was at first very much opposed to all the additions which the Committee has proposed to us? It seemed to me that all these additions should be considered with a great deal of care and suspicion, and that, in foggy weather, we should be limited to signals which are absolutely indispensable.

I would have preferred myself, and I even tried to do so, to disregard all the propositions of the Sound-Signal Committee; but I noticed, and I think that I was right, that the majority of the members of the Conference desired that there be introduced into our Rules some of these signals to answer certain requirements. Under those circumstances, such being the opinion of the Conference, and whatever may be my dislike to adopt that view, it is my duty to help in a measure to my utmost extent in order to make those signals the best that can be had.

Admiral Nares (Great Britain).—Mr. President, so far as the Rule of the Road goes, we have already given to a steam-vessel towing a distinctive signal; but that distinctive signal does not give her any right whatever to the right of way. Now, if you go further and give a sailing-ship under certain circumstances a distinctive signal, that has nothing whatever to do with any right under the Rules of the Road.

Admiral Bowden-Smith (Great Britain).—Mr. President, I wish to say one word to express my entire feeling with the gallant Delegate from the United States, Captain Sampson, with regard to the danger of giving a signal to sailing-vessels towing. I thought that the gallant Delegate from Germany, Captain Mensing, had hit the right nail on the head when he proposed that a sailing-vessel should alternately sound her ordinary signal and then sound the long and two short blasts. I thought at one time that was the way out of the difficulty; but now I find I cannot approve of that, and I really think that we shall get into a mess if we give a sailing-ship a towing signal at all; because, if the proposition of the gallant Delegate from Germany is carried, you will at once see how it will result. For instance, a ship makes a signal of two blasts: "I am on the port tack." The next minute she makes the towing signal. We do not know that it is the same ship making these signals. It is two ships. I cannot see that this signal will do, and I think it is unwise to give a signal to a sailing-vessel towing at all.

Mr. Goodrich (United States).—Mr. President, I have tried to work out what the amendment to this Rule would result in, taking the suggestion of the learned Delegate from France and the very wise suggestion of my gallant colleague Captain Sampson. This is what would have to be the Rule, and the question is whether the Conference is prepared to adopt this Rule, because we must come to some vote upon this question: "A sailing-vessel, when towing another vessel, shall or may, at intervals of not more than two minutes, sound on her fog-horn, when on the starboard tack, one prolonged blast, followed by one short blast; and when on the port tack, one prolonged blast, followed by two short blasts in succession; and when with the wind abaft the beam, one prolonged blast, followed by three short blasts in succession." Now, I am not advocating this. I am simply trying to work out what this Conference will necessarily adopt, if it adopts the principle of giving a sailing-vessel which is towing another vessel this signal.

Captain Mensing (Germany).—Mr. President, I simply rise to point out that according to my opinion the Rules contained in Article 14 apply to vessels in a fog as well as when they are in sight of each other.

The President.—Does the Conference desire a vote upon this question now, or does it desire to postpone the vote until some future time?

Mr. Hall (Great Britain).—Mr. President, I want to point out one dilemma which has not yet been answered by any advocate of giving a sailing-vessel the same signal as a steam-vessel towing. Take the case of a steamer under way in a fog. She hears the signal. How is she to know whether this is the signal of a steamer or the signal of a sailing-vessel towing? If it is a sailing-vessel she has got to keep out of the way. If it is a steamer she has to keep out of the way of her if she is on her starboard side. How is she to know whether or not she is to treat that vessel as a steamer or as a sailing-vessel, if they are to give the same signal, and when we are told that frequently there is a great similarity between some fog-horns and steam-whistles?

Mr. Flood (Norway).—Mr. President, I will answer that question practically in this way. I will say that it will not do to sit here and talk about a sailing-vessel sailing by the wind when in real practice there is no question of towing a vessel sharp on the wind. The object then is to reach the nearest port, and the rule is to sail with the wind abaft the beam; so that these questions of sound-signals and the proper attention to starboard tack and port tack and all that will not raise any practical difficulty at all. I would again strongly recommend that this Article should read as Captain Sampson proposed it this morning.

Mr. Goodrich (United States).—Mr. President, the time for the adjournment having so nearly arrived, I now renew my motion that when the Conference adjourns it adjourn to meet to-morrow morning at 11 o'clock, with the understanding, as I stated in conversation with the gallant Delegate from Germany, that as soon as we finish the discussion of the matters relating to the Rules of the Road before the Conference we shall then take an adjournment to such time as may be deemed proper to enable the Committees to get along with their work, or so that we will substitute another day for Wednesday for Committee work.

The President.—Does the Chair understand that the Delegate from Norway made a motion before he took his seat?

Mr. Flood (Norway).—Mr. President, I did not make any motion. I only took the liberty to answer a remark made about sailing by the wind. That hurt my feelings, as a practical man, a little, because I know it is never attempted.

The President.—Is the Conference ready for the question on the adjournment until to-morrow morning at 11 o'clock?

The Conference thereupon adjourned until Wednesday, 4th December, 1889, at 11 o'clock A.M.

Washington, Wednesday, December 4, 1889, 11 o'clock A.M.
THE Conference was called to order at 11 o'clock A.M., Rear-Admiral Franklin in the Chair.

The President.—The first business in order this morning is the amendment of the Delegate from France to paragraph (*g*). Paragraph (*g*) will be read, and then the amendment of the Delegate from France.

Paragraph (*g*) is as follows:—

"(*g*) A steam-vessel when towing shall, and the vessel towed may, if necessary, at intervals of not more than two minutes, sound on the whistle or siren three blasts in succession, viz., one prolonged blast followed by two short blasts."

The amendment proposed by the Delegate from France is:—
To restore the words in the first line: "a sailing-vessel."

53

Admiral Nares (Great Britain).—Mr. President, I am sorry that one or two of the Delegates who spoke yesterday and took a very decided position in regard to this matter are not yet present, because I have a few words to say on this matter, on the part of the Committee on Sound-Signals, which I very earnestly wish to place before them before the vote is taken. I hope the Conference, after our very long discussion of yesterday upon this question, will not think I am guilty of stubbornness in saying a few more words and in pointing out why the Committee should stand by their guns. We are confident that all the members of the Conference are quite prepared to listen and to study any Rule, and to consider any good argument on either one side or the other side of the question before us.

May I say, Sir, that I think that yesterday one of the motions was put which was practically in agreement with that now before us as proposed by the gallant Delegate from France, but it was put in such a way that I am afraid a number of the Delegates did not quite understand the position which they were taking? In fact one, if not more, of the Delegates told us at once that there had been a mistake. After that mistake was made, it was generally understood that the same vote would be repeated; but it was not repeated, and it has only now come before us. The nations were not called on that question. I believe that if the members had been called the proposition of the Committee would have been then and there carried. However, it is no use to cry over spilled milk, and this morning we start afresh. We have now an unmistakable proposition before us. The Conference has decided that a steam-vessel towing shall have a decided signal. They are asked now to say that a sailing-vessel towing shall have a decided signal.

Now, as a side-wind I would say a few words, although it is not on the precise vote which we are going to take, and that is that the sailors who have drawn up this proposal before us have rather left out something which will be necessary to be introduced on the part of the Court. I will only go as far now as the Conference has gone. The Conference has decided that a towing steamer is to make one long blast followed by two short blasts. Now, you have given that signal to a steamer, and it follows at once that the signal you have provided in section (*a*) of one long blast disappears. It does not matter to me when I meet a towing vessel whether that one blast is given or not. I shall hear one long blast and two short blasts, and that is sufficient. If we go further and vote now that a sailing-ship shall also have to make a signal, that signal, whatever it is, will have to be subject to the signal in section (*c*). But I, the approaching vessel, do not care whether that vessel is on the starboard tack or the port tack, or has a free wind. All I want to know is whether there is a hawser astern and something fast again astern of that hawser; in fact, that she is towing.

Now, I will speak on the actual vote that is coming before us: Is a sailing-ship to have a signal as well as a steam-ship? I wish the members to be very clear what was before the Committee when they put these words, "a sailing-vessel and a steam-vessel." Of course, by-and-by, when the Article is to be reworded, after this vote is passed, it will follow that it will be "a vessel towing." We put in the words, "a steam-vessel towing and a sailing-vessel towing," so that the Conference can be quite clear what was in our minds, and so that there would be no mistake what you are voting upon. It has come to a head upon this question. I will take an example which will show you what I have to say, and I will take the very worst example in the case which I put to you. First of all, under Article 24 it was argued yesterday that we are making new Sailing Rules. We are doing nothing of the kind. I will put it to any of the learned gentlemen, as well as to any of the seafaring members, whether under Article 24, which provides that all reasonable seamanship and care shall be exercised, whether, if I am approaching a long tow and can get out of the way of that tow, but instead of doing so deliberately run into it, although I have got the Rule of the Road in my favour, I would like to know from the learned gentlemen which side they would like to be on in arguing that case. You may depend upon it that I should be condemned, and that they would argue that I was doing wrong under Article 24. So we are not altering the Rules of the Road; and I say now, positively, that a vessel which has the right of way, if she runs into a tow, is going against the Rules of the Road. This, again, is apart from the actual point before us.

Now I will give you an example. The towing ship is on the starboard tack. Another ship is approaching her on the port tack. I will place myself, and I will ask each of the Delegates to place himself in command of the vessel on the port tack. He hears two fog-signals somewhere ahead, at least he hears them on the starboard bow and starboard beam. At last the fog looms up and he sees a vessel on his starboard beam, unmistakably, but still the fog is not clear enough for signals, and they must depend upon the sound-signals. He sees unmistakably a vessel on his starboard bow and a vessel on the starboard beam. He can get clear of the vessel on his starboard bow, or he thinks he can; but the Rule of the Road demands that he either goes about or keeps his way under the stern of the vessel on the starboard bow. Now, if I am just laying my course, I do not want to go about. I shall be perfectly safe and shall not hurt anybody by keeping away and going under the stern of the vessel that is on the starboard bow. I can readily clear the one that is on my starboard beam. Well, I port my helm. I am not close-shaving. I am taking the proper precautions. The law allows me to go between these two ships, and if there is no hawser there is no danger. Very well; I am approaching the quarter of the towing vessel. Suddenly the other fellow calls out. I ask, "What in the world is that fellow holloaing and screaming about?" and my attention and the attention of my look-out is taken to that towing vessel. The vessel on my starboard beam, which is fastened to him, I know nothing about. I am perfectly clear of him. While I am listening to this fellow holloaing and screaming, and if it is light enough, waving his arms, but he cannot tell me what he is doing; suddenly I am against the hawser. Now, that is the example which I give you on the part of the Committee, and ask if you will not allow a sailing-vessel towing to sound some signal.

Mr. Goodrich (United States).—Mr. President, I think it would assist the members in their voting upon this proposition if we could hear the experience of the nautical men about this board as to how frequent the instances are of sailing-vessels towing another vessel. I have had some conversation which has given me a good deal of light upon this subject from several of the gentlemen, and I should like to hear from them. There are nautical men here who can say what their experience is during past years. The suggestion is also brought out that it makes very little difference whether we give this permission or do not give it, simply because these instances are so rare. It is with that in my mind that I ask the nautical men of this board to tell us how often they have seen a sailing-vessel towing another vessel.

Mr. Flood (Norway).—Mr. President, in answer to the question raised by the learned Delegate from the United States, I said yesterday that I thought a sailing-vessel towing another was a very rare occurrence, and only happened when one of the two vessels was in distress. That is also the reason why I said that I did not think there would be much trouble with the signals, because the vessel towing would always have the wind abaft the beam. She would never, as suggested yesterday, attempt to tow another vessel laying by the wind herself. That is almost impossible. So far as the question goes as to how often that happens, I will say that in my experience I have had only one case under my control—and I have a great many vessels to look after—where such a thing happened. So it is a thing of very rare occurrence.

I will just make one remark on what Sir George Nares has said about the imaginary case which he brought before the Conference to-day. I mentioned yesterday an exactly similar case which happened to one of my vessels in the Delaware River only a couple of years ago. I stated then exactly, how a three-masted schooner ran into one of my ships being towed by another vessel. The towing ship at that time was a steam-ship, and it was proved in Court that the vessel which was towed did not sound the proper signals, depending upon the steamer ahead of her to sound them. In consequence I had to pay the damages and costs. So by that very example I prove that the vessel towing has to give a signal of some description. I must also mention, in connection with this, that the greatest danger for a vessel approaching a tow is not the vessel towing, which is generally a small craft, a tug-boat, but the danger of collision lies in the vessel towed. She will generally be the thing that will cause the collision and cause the trouble. The tug-boat is generally a smaller craft, but the vessel towed may often be a 2,000-ton ship, and she is the real danger.

Captain Malmberg (Sweden).—Mr. President, as a direct answer to the question put by the learned Delegate from the United States, I may say that although not being an eye-witness to the cases, I have learned by the reports in our papers that twice within a very few years ships in distress have been brought into port by sailing-vessels.

Captain Donner (Germany).—Mr. President, I am obliged to read through all the verdicts given by our Marine Court in Germany, which is compelled to look after every mishap to a German ship; and so I have had an opportunity of seeing that this towing by sailing-ships is happening very often; much oftener than anybody would suppose. But so far as I know it is only in the North Sea. The North Sea is literally swarming with British fishers, trawling men; and these fishermen make a good bargain if they can bring into port a derelict vessel; for it happens very often that a ship brings in a vessel which has lost a mast in these heavy storms. But this towing is only done for a certain distance; as soon as they come near the coasts of Great Britain or Germany, they find tug-steamers to tow the vessel into harbour. But they manage to tow such ships quite a long way over the sea. That happens very often; how often I am not able to say, though I might say it is an every day occurrence in the North Sea.

Admiral de Spaun (Austria-Hungary).—Mr. President, in answer to the question put by the learned Delegate from the United States, I may state that in forty years' service I have twice seen a sailing-vessel towing other vessels. The last time I saw it was more than thirty-five years ago, when steamers were not so numerous as they are now.

Mr. Flood (Norway).—Mr. President, may I be allowed to corroborate what I said a little while ago about its being very seldom the case that sailing-vessels are found towing another vessel? When I said that, I was alluding to my experience on this side of the Atlantic. I must say, with the learned Delegate from Germany, Captain Donner, that in the North Sea and the Baltic it is a common occurrence to tow in vessels of that description, because those waters are swarming with a great many ships.

Captain Settembrini (Italy).—Mr. President, I wish to answer the question of the learned Delegate from the United States. I have been thirty-two years at sea, and I have never seen a sailing-ship towing another ship; still it may happen. As the honourable Delegate from Germany has stated, in the North Sea sailing-ships do tow other sailing-ships. If that is the case, I think it necessary to provide a signal for sailing-ships towing other ships.

Mr. Goodrich (United States).—Mr. President, may I call attention to the fact now that, having heard from these nautical men the instances of sailing-vessels towing other vessels, it will be quite manifest to the Conference that these statements embrace every instance that has fallen within the observation of these gallant Delegates; but there is a still further reduction of the frequency of these cases, namely, when you come to take the question as to how often this has occurred in a fog. I would like to know, and perhaps I should have asked the question before, if there is any Delegate at the table who ever heard or who ever saw within his own experience a sailing-vessel towing another vessel in a fog?

Mr. Flood (Norway).—Mr. President, I would answer that question by saying that in a fog it is very hard to see and it is very difficult to hear.

Captain Mensing (Germany).—Mr. President, I pointed out the other day that I have seen, myself, several of these cases, and I can assure the Conference that they are not as infrequent as has been supposed. The gallant Delegates from Sweden and Norway, and my colleague from Germany, have pointed out that these cases do happen. It is very easy to explain why these things should happen so often in the Baltic and the North Sea, and not so often in other waters. For instance, if a ship sails from New York for China she will go out of the harbour of New York and up the Shanghae River. In all that time she will see very few ships except while coming out of New York Bay and going into the Shanghae River. Lying off these places are swarms of tugs, and whenever any ship is in distress, the tugs will take her in tow.

Now, take the North Sea or the Baltic Sea, where there are no tugs. Look at the Chart and see all of these inlets upon these coasts, where they have very bad weather, with sudden changes, such as are not to be found, I believe, in the glorious waters of the Mediterranean. I desire, therefore, to state to the Conference that in these waters this towing is a thing of rather frequent occurrence. How many tugs are there along the coast of Sweden outside of the harbours? There are a few steamers which make it their business to tow derelicts and to save life; so that a vessel has to rely for that kind of help upon sailing-vessels; along this coast most of the traffic goes near the shore, and that they will fall in very soon with a steamer is not the point at all, as has been pointed out most ably by the gallant Delegate from Italy. We know this thing happens, and we ought to provide for it. We have under discussion in another General Division the removal of derelicts. I would like to know how many derelicts have been seen by the members of this Conference. I would like to ask them whether they do not consider them quite serious impediments to navigation, and whether they are not of opinion that something should be done with regard to them? I think the towing cases certainly happen as often as the others.

Mr. Hall (Great Britain).—Mr. President, I do not think we should be wise if we branched off into the discussion of matters which have been assigned to Committees upon other Divisions of the Programme, because I apprehend the question is as to whether or not this state of affairs should be provided for in the Rules of the Road at Sea, and that is a very different question than the question as to whether it can properly be discussed and provided for by other Divisions in the Programme of the Conference. I think we are all agreed that it is desirable to confine the Articles of the Rules of the Road at Sea as much as we can within bounds, and not to put anything in them unnecessarily. Whereas, in the other Divisions, we can discuss every possible matter which arises pertinent to the subjects which are provided for in those Divisions. Now, I wish to say in a very few words—I think we are agreed that this matter has been thoroughly discussed—how we propose to vote.

There is one matter which I think cannot have helped striking the minds of many of us at this table. We are told now that there is a demand for this signal. It is suggested that there is a great demand for it in certain places. It is a remarkable fact that we have been sitting here ever since the 16th October, and with the exception of one proposal, that made by the gallant Delegate from Sweden, who has withdrawn it because he sees the difficulties with which it is fraught, not one single Delegate at this table has made a proposal until this came before us in the present case in the Report of the Committee on Sound-Signals. One would have thought that, if there was such a demand for a signal, we would have amendments showered down upon us by the Delegates who are aware of the importance of having such a sound-signal. But with the exception of the gallant Delegate from Sweden, who gave notice of an amendment, and who, as I say, has withdrawn his application because he sees the difficulties standing in the way, no single amendment was handed in asking for anything of the kind.

Now, I would just refer to what we have heard to-day, and I admit that they are statements which require the very greatest attention. We now know that in certain parts of the North Sea such cases as are provided for here are not of infrequent occurrence. But is not that rather a local matter? Are we to frame Rules for exceptional cases such as this? I confess that I thought our object was to have International Rules, which related, practically, to the open sea; but to leave individual cases, as far as we could, to take care of themselves. Now, Mr. President, I, on behalf of my colleagues, shall vote against this motion for exactly the same reasons that we did yesterday. I admire, if I may say so, the consistency of my gallant friend on my right, who, with the natural tenacity of a sailor, sticks to his colleagues and to his Report. And I may point out that we are not showing the slightest disrespect to them, because their Report is merely made upon the suggestion of the Conference that sailing-vessels which are towing should give a distinctive signal. This is not their suggestion. They merely provided a signal in response to the request of the Conference, so that we are not disregarding their Report at all in that respect, and we are not discussing whether that is a good signal, but whether such a signal should be given at all. Having regard to the reasons which I gave yesterday, notwithstanding what we have heard this morning that there are cases in the North Sea, that this is practically an exceptional case met with on the sea; and having regard to the difficulty in getting a convenient signal, and having regard to the very important point which has been mentioned by the gallant Delegate from Sweden, I shall, on the part of Great Britain, vote against this proposal.

Captain Salvesen (Norway).—Mr. President, the learned Delegate for Great Britain stated that there has not been any great demand for any fog-signal for sailing-vessels towing. I beg to remark that as such an amendment was delivered in the beginning of the session, I do not see that it would be proper for other Delegates to propose other amendments to the same effect. And as this amendment was carried, and the Conference decided that the sailing-vessel towing should have a distinctive fog-signal, provided the Committee on Sound-Signals could find a proper signal, I do not see that the statement of the learned Delegate of Great Britain is just to the point.

Mr. Carter (Hawaii).—Mr. President, when the learned Delegate of the United States asked the nautical men to rise and give their experience, I kept my seat, not knowing exactly how to classify myself. The circumstances of my birth, residence, and business have taken me very much to sea; and I have made about sixty ocean voyages. I have also had much to do with the law. I kept quiet, waiting for the nautical men to state their experience first. I have regretted several times in this Conference that among the very able Delegates of the United States there is not a person acquainted with the peculiar circumstances of the Pacific coast. I venture to say that this Rule would have more relevancy upon the Pacific coast than in any other part of the United States of America. This coast is peculiarly subject to fog. It is a coast where hundreds of sailing-vessels in the lumber and coal trade are plying constantly. The departures from San Francisco to Honolulu are, you may say, almost a sailing-vessel every other day, besides the steamers. The cases are not at all infrequent when sailing-vessels come into collision with one another in a fog; and the result always is that they ask the other vessel to lie by, or, if the vessel is injured, to take her in tow until she can find a steam-tug. Take the waters of Puget Sound; there are hundreds of small lumber vessels running through those waters, and they are constantly helping each other in this way.

[93]

I should be very much impressed with the remarks made by the learned Delegate of Great Britain if this Conference had been asked to find a new signal, and in that case I think the rarity of the occasions—although I do not agree with him from my own experience—would have given some pertinency to the objections; but as we are not making any new signal, but are merely giving a sailing-vessel the right to make the same signal as the steamer, there can be no difficulty arising from it. The objection, it seems to me, goes into thin air. The only objection is that it is useless. We point out that it will be very useful. We do not ask for any new legislation or for any new signal. We simply wish that, under these circumstances (which are not infrequent, as some of the gentlemen imagine whose attention is drawn wholly to New York and to those places where there are any quantity of tugs), a sailing-vessel may be permitted to give the signal.

Now, let me put a practical case. A vessel is coming up and hears the signal in a fog. Those signals are generally heard at first very indistinctly, and with listening ear; their whole being is intent upon locating the sound. The first thought, then, is to locate the sound, and then to find out what it is. They listen to see whether that vessel is on the starboard tack or on the port tack, or running with the wind free. Now, the first thing that a man ought to be made to know is that the vessel is towing another vessel, if there is such a danger in his path; and it is necessary for him to know this, notwithstanding that it may be a rare case. But I venture to say that it happens ten times in a year in and about the Bay of San Francisco and Puget Sound, where temporary assistance may be given by one sailing-vessel to another. We do not hear very much about these collisions. They do not involve generally more than 3,000 or 4,000 dollars, and the damage is not like that of collisions in the port of New York between steamers where lives are in danger. But I am confident that these cases are not as rare as some of the gentlemen seem to think, and in addition to that they can be easily provided for without making any new signals, and they ought to be provided for; therefore I shall vote in that way.

Mr. Verbrugghe (Belgium).—Mr. President, we have had a very long discussion upon this subject, and I believe we all know about how we are to vote. I wish to explain my vote. I shall vote for the signal, and for the proposition made by the Committee on Sound-Signals to put in the Article that the provision should be made for sailing-vessels. A great deal of discussion has arisen upon the question as to whether this was a case of frequent or infrequent occurrence. If it is not so frequent, it does not matter if you give the signal; but there should be one provided for such a case when it occurs. I listened with the greatest attention to the speech given by the gallant Admiral the Chairman of the Committee. He is not of the same opinion as the learned First Delegate from Great Britain, and, therefore, the Delegates will be at a loss to know, or at least they will be obliged to make their choice between the two opinions. One opinion is given by a seafaring man who occupies a very high rank in the naval power of Great Britain, and I do not believe that he defended the Rule only for the sake of duty, and because he was the Chairman of the Committee. If he had done so he would not have illustrated it as he did, when he referred to the case of two sailing-vessels meeting. Certainly those sailors who will be in such a condition as this in a fog will not be satisfied with the Delegates if they do not provide for such a case, because they will be more in danger then than they would if there were no signal given. Therefore, I shall vote for the sailing-vessels having the signal, and I wish the President to put the question to a vote.

Mr. Hall (Great Britain).—Mr. President, may I, merely for the sake of explanation, point out that in what I have said I have been carefully guarded so that it should not be supposed that I was expressing my private opinion on any occasion? I have always spoken in the name of the Delegates from Great Britain. I should not presume to give my private experience on any nautical matter, and I am always careful to say that I am expressing the decision of the Delegates from Great Britain.

Mr. Verbrugghe (Belgium).—Mr. President, I hope I have not said anything which was not correct or respectful. I only meant to say that I was very much puzzled by the discussion that has gone on. I will say again that I was very much impressed by the illustration given by the gallant Admiral, Sir George Nares.

Captain Mensing (Germany).—Mr. President, as the learned Delegate from Great Britain mentioned that no amendment proposing a signal for a sailing-vessel towing another vessel had been made, I would like to ask him to look at amendment No. 85, which was proposed by the gallant Delegate from Sweden, Captain Malmberg.

Mr. Hall (Great Britain).—I said excepting the one proposed by the gallant Delegate from Sweden.

Captain Mensing (Germany).—Mr. President, quite a considerable discussion has taken place upon this question. I inferred from his remarks that he thought it had been overlooked. It has been brought up before, and it has been discussed to quite a considerable extent. I wish to say that if I vote against this amendment it will not be because I do not consider it to be a most useful signal, but I shall vote against it because I believe that under the circumstances of the German shipping trade it will be a great hardship to introduce sound-signal instruments for producing a long note on the fog-horn.

The President.—The question is upon the amendment of the Delegate from France.

Mr. Goodrich (United States).—Mr. President, I call for the Yeas and Nays.

The President.—The Yeas and Nays are called for. The amendment will be read for the information of the Conference.

Captain Malmberg (Sweden).—Mr. President, may I be allowed to say a few words before the vote is taken? I, for my part, have suffered perhaps under a misapprehension about the signal suggested to be made by a sailing-vessel towing. I stated yesterday the reason why I withdrew my proposition for such a signal, because, as I read this section (*g*), I thought that a sailing-vessel towing would have to make the signal according to Article 14, with regard to the way in which the ship was heading according to the wind, and then, in addition, give the signal of a sailing-ship towing, the additional signal to tell that she was towing. But if this proposed signal, to be made by a sailing-vessel towing, is to be made instead of the signal contained in Article 14, then the question stands, in my opinion, in quite a different light. If, by giving a sailing-vessel towing this signal, you dispense with the signal to be made under Article 14, it is quite a different thing; and I wish to put before the Conference the question before the vote is taken in regard to this matter. If I am to understand that the signal to be made is to dispense with the signal under Article 14, then I will vote for the adoption of the signal; but if the signals are to be made according to Article 14, and with this additional signal also, I will vote No. I would like to have that point clear before I vote.

The President.—Does the Delegate from Sweden propose that as an amendment?

Captain Malmberg (Sweden).—Mr. President, I ask to have the point made clear by the Committee on Sound-Signals, whether it is to be understood that the proposed signal for a sailing-vessel towing is to overrule the signals to be made under Article 14 as to how the ship is heading, relative to the wind; because I find it, for my part, quite necessary to have this question clearly answered.

Admiral Nares (Great Britain).—Mr. President, when I spoke before in the early part of this morning I distinctly said that this would follow afterwards. But it is a question whether we could not take a vote now on the principle of a sailing-ship having a signal, and then the question whether that signal is to be coupled with the signal which she makes under subsection (*c*). I have worked out how the Article would stand; but I do not want to put it before the Conference now, because really the matter is getting so complicated that we are getting much into the same way as we were yesterday. There is a distinct provision before the Conference. Let us settle that. We can discuss the other question afterwards to bring things together.

Captain Malmberg (Sweden).—Mr. President, if the vote should be that no such signal shall be given, that subject cannot be brought up again, and, therefore, I think it is quite necessary to settle that question first. As the proposal now is I cannot vote, because I do not know how I am voting. If it be voted that a signal is to be given to a sailing-ship, it makes a great deal of difference to me whether the signal is to be made so as to override the signal provided for in Article 14.

Mr. Goodrich (United States).—Mr. President, I suppose it will follow as a matter of course that if this proposal of the gallant Delegate from France is voted on affirmatively, and the words "a sailing-vessel" put back into paragraph (*g*), it will follow that the signal required by this Article, if it should be finally adopted, would override the provisions of Article 14, because this is a specific case and defines the circumstances which have arisen under it beyond those which are embraced in Article 14, so that the signal given by this Article must be given in a fog to the exclusion of any signal under Article 14. That, I understand, is the question propounded by the gallant Delegate for Sweden.

Captain Malmberg (Sweden).—Mr. President, I want to have it clear to my mind, because if it says that a sailing-vessel towing is to make her signal relating to the wind, then I object to introducing an additional signal. But if it is to be understood that she is not to make that signal, and the Conference does not think there is any need of stating it in the Rules, and if it is supposed to be quite clear that this Rule is to override Article 14, then I will vote for the proposition.

Mr. Goodrich (United States).—Mr. President, let me say that it follows that if this Conference vote to put a sailing-vessel within the provisions of subdivision (*g*), they will give her a signal which will override the signal contained in Article 14.

Mr. Hall (Great Britain).—Mr. President, that is a matter which is very easily met with, as my gallant colleague has already said, that if this question be carried in the affirmative it will be for a signal instead of the ordinary signal provided by clauses (*a*) and (*b*).

Captain Malmberg (Sweden).—Mr. President, I understand the question and I am ready to vote.

The President.—The Yeas and Nays will be called on the amendment of the Delegate from France, which will be read.

The amendment of the Delegate from France is as follows:—

To restore the words, " and a sailing-vessel," in paragraph (*g*), Article 12.

The Yeas and Nays were as follows:—

Austria-Hungary .. .. Yea.	Italy .. .. .. Yea.
Belgium .. .. .. Nay.	Japan .. .. . Yea.
China .. .. .. Yea.	Mexico .. .. .. Nay.
Chile .. .. .. Yea.	Norway .. .. .. Yea.
Costa Rica .. .. .. Yea.	Russia .. .. .. Nay.
Denmark .. .. .. Yea.	Spain .. .. .. Yea.
France .. .. .. Yea.	Sweden .. .. .. Yea.
Germany .. .. .. Nay.	Siam .. .. .. Yea.
Great Britain .. .. Nay.	The Netherlands .. .. Yea.
Guatemala .. .. .. Yea.	Venezuela .. .. .. Yea.
Hawaii .. .. .. Yea.	United States .. .. Yea.
Honduras .. .. .. Yea.	

The President.—The vote stands 18 in the affirmative, and 5 in the negative; so the proposition is carried.

The question now will be upon paragraph (*g*) as amended.

Mr. Goodrich (United States).—Mr. President, may I ask whether the gallant Delegate from Great Britain, Sir George Nares, has not another proposal to make before this proposition is adopted as to the signal to be given, or as to whether it is to be permissive or not?

Mr. Hall (Great Britain).—Mr. President, now that the Conference has decided that this signal shall be given, it is necessary to consider whether or not a vessel or vessels towed shall give a signal also. We have considered very carefully what fell both from the Delegate from Norway and the gallant Delegate from the United States with regard to making such a signal compulsory, and the conclusion we have come to is this: Of course it would not be necessary for one vessel being towed to make the signal, because immediately when any vessel hears another vessel giving a towing-signal she knows that the vessel has got a tow behind her. But we think that where there is more than one vessel under tow, which we are told is frequently the case, it is desirable that the vessels composing that tow should give the signal. Therefore, in order to meet the views of the Delegate from Norway and the gallant Delegate of the United States, we have this amendment to propose, which would probably meet the views of both; put at the end of the clause the following: "When more than one vessel is being towed, each vessel towed shall sound this signal on hearing the sound-signal of an approaching vessel."

Mr. Goodrich (United States).—On her fog-horn.

Mr. Hall (Great Britain).—It may be a whistle or fog-horn.

Mr. Goodrich (United States).—Let me call your attention to the fact that in the first Article as it is at present adopted, the word "fog-horn" has been stricken out.

Mr. Hall (Great Britain).—It must come back again if the sailing-vessel is to be included. I am now only dealing with the signal to be given by the vessel towed. I quite agree that the word "fog-horn" will have to come into the Article. It comes in *ipso facto* by the amendment which has been carried; but I am dealing with a different principle now. I am dealing with the principle as to whether or not the vessel towed is to give the signal. By the Report of the Committee it was made optional. It was pointed out yesterday by the Delegate from the United States and the Delegate from Norway that it was desirable that it should be compulsory in certain cases, so that any one approaching a vessel towing should know where the end of the tow was. Therefore, we thought this would meet all of these requirements. If the Conference will allow me I will read it again:—

"When more than one vessel is being towed, each vessel towed shall sound this signal on hearing the sound-signal of an approaching ship."

Captain Richard (France).—Mr. President, in so far as I have been able to understand, the Conference, by adopting the amendment which I proposed, has declared itself in favour of the principle which I have heretofore advocated. This principle was to confer upon the towing vessel alone the right and the obligation to signal her presence, whereas the same right was denied the vessel or the vessels in tow, whatever might be their number or the length of their hawsers. This was the principle upon which my amendment was based. If we should now adopt the proposition of the learned Delegate from Great Britain, we would again take up the original drafting of the Committee on Sound-Signals, and the entire discussion may have to begin over again.

When a towing vessel signals her presence, she thereby indicates that she is towing one or more vessels. This signal has been given to the towing vessel, whether she be a steam or a sailing vessel, in order to no longer consider the signal to be given by the vessel in tow, and thereby doing away with the difficulty which it is very hard to overcome. Will the Conference now give to the vessel in tow the same sound-signal as to the towing vessel, or shall we give her a different sound-signal? Yesterday the complaint was made that the number of efficient sound-signals was too limited. If the vessel in tow is given the same signal as the towing vessel, is it not likely that, when several vessels are being towed by another, there will be very great confusion? If all these vessels make sound-signals, how will it be possible to distinguish the position of the towing vessel? I think that it would be wiser to reject this amendment.

Captain Norcross (United States).—Mr. President, it seems to me that there is an easy way out of the difficulty regarding this signal by towed vessels. I must reiterate my objection to giving the same fog-signal as the steamer as being dangerous, which must be plain to the nautical members, for the following reason: Let us suppose a steamer going out from west or coming in from east and hearing two, three, or four sound-signals ahead, and absolutely the same, she would be in doubt which way the tow was proceeding. I certainly think it necessary that the towed vessel should make some signal, and I would suggest that the steamer should give a long blast, and the vessel towed a long blast followed by one short blast. Here is a distinct signal which serves two purposes. The steamer-signal shows which end she is on, and consequently which way she is going; and the signal from the tow will tell unmistakably how many vessels there are being towed. I believe this special signal has not been adopted anywhere else, and I submit the above for consideration.

The President.—If you make any proposition, hand it in as an amendment, and it will be considered by the Conference.

Mr. Flood (Norway).—Mr. President, I am sorry to say that the amendment proposed by the learned Delegate from England does not suit me very well. He proposes to put in that every vessel towed, when there is more than one, shall repeat the signal given by the towing vessel. I think that the great danger lies just as much in towing one vessel as in towing several vessels. One vessel can be at the end of a long tow; as I pointed out yesterday, one vessel was at the end of about 1,500 feet. I think it is as necessary for one vessel to sound the signal as for several. It might happen that there would be three or four small vessels towed, and according to this Rule they would all of them be sounding fog-signals. As pointed out yesterday, I think that common sense might come in somewhere; and in case of three, or four, or five vessels being towed, I should think that common sense would direct that one or two of these only should sound the signal, and not the whole lot of them be sounding in the ears of each other. It would be compulsory if this Rule should be adopted as proposed by the learned Delegate from England.

I very much wish that my amendment as proposed yesterday could be accepted by the Conference, but if it meets with objection I am willing to strike it out, if I can only get rid of those words " if necessary." The paragraph then would read: " And a vessel towed may at intervals of not more than two minutes." I pointed out yesterday that the words " if necessary " were awfully objectionable to me, because it is impossible for a man in a fog to decide for himself whether the necessity exists or not. When I am blindfolded I have to feel my way, and if I want to go in a fog I must use sound-signals. But the Courts will in every instance take up those words " if necessary," and condemn the sailor if he does not make the signal. I do not like to have the poor sailor keel-hauled in the Courts n that way, as is often done.

The President.—May I ask what are the actual words which are suggested by the Delegate?

Mr. Flood (Norway).—Mr. President, I suggest that the whole paragraph be as it is at present, only that the words " if necessary " be stricken out.

Mr. Hall (Great Britain).—Mr. President, may I point out that I submitted this amendment, after great consideration, to try and meet the suggestion of the Delegate from Norway yesterday, that this signal must be compulsory? That is one of the principal reasons why I have prepared this amendment to-day.

Mr. Goodrich (United States).—Mr. President, may I suggest that we had better pass upon each proposition as it occurs, and have a vote taken upon the proposition of the learned Delegate from England before we attempt to make any other amendment? We are drifting back to the condition of things which existed yesterday.

The President.—The last amendment is in order.

Mr. Goodrich (United States).—Mr. President, I am only suggesting to the Delegates that it will be wise not to offer other amendments until we pass upon this question. Now, will the honourable Delegate from Norway withdraw the amendment subsequent to this proposition of the learned Delegate from England, and let us pass first upon this? If it is not satisfactory, vote it down and take something else. We shall never finish this discussion if we are continually adding amendments to amendments.

Captain Mensing (Germany).—Mr. President, the signals we are giving for the towing vessels shall, as I understand it, be given instead of the signals prescribed by Article 12. But of course the steam-vessel would have to use occasionally the sound-signals provided under Article 19. I believe on that account that it would be well enough to insert the words, " instead of the sound-signals mentioned in Article 12." Then there would be no doubt left as to the proper meaning of this amendment.

Mr. Flood (Norway).—Mr. President, may I remark that I have not altered my opinion at all from what I stated yesterday? My sincere belief is that the right way would be to word it as I suggested yesterday. But I have heard so many objections to the wording that I thought, by striking out the words " if necessary," and letting the word " may " stand there, that it would be better than to have it as it is. I have learned in my lifetime that if I cannot get the whole hand to be satisfied with the finger.

Mr. Goodrich (United States).—Mr. President, let me call the attention of the Delegate from Norway to what this proposition is. When more than one vessel is being towed, each vessel shall make this signal on hearing the sound-signal of an approaching vessel. My suggestion is that we take a vote upon this question and establish the principle; and then, if we want to add anything further to the Rule, let us do it. But you are adding amendments to amendments, and many of the amendments are not germane to the subject under discussion. You never will arrive at a conclusion. I think we all know our own minds, and although some of us have been on both sides of the question, yet I think that we are all this morning pretty well advised as to what we are going to do.

Mr. Flood (Norway).—Mr. President, I am now on slippery ground, because I am not well versed in Parliamentary ruling. But I will say this, that I would be in a very bad position if this is taken to a vote just now, because I should have to vote against it. But, at the same time, if the words " if necessary " are to be stricken out, I would change my vote. I will repeat that I should be very glad to have them make some sound. I was thinking that we could vote on the principle that a vessel or vessels towed could repeat the signal from the towing vessel. That would at once settle the question of principle, and then afterwards we could vote as to whether it would be one vessel or two vessels, or how many vessels that were required to make the signal. You will excuse me for making the remark, but it looks very difficult for me to know how I shall vote in this case.

Admiral Nares (Great Britain).—Mr. President, on behalf of the Committee, I think I can get my honourable friend out of the difficulty. I move on behalf of the Committee that the words, " and the vessel towed may," be introduced in the clause as it stands before the Conference. The effect of that would be, if that is voted in the affirmative, to give a permissive signal to the vessel towed, and if any member likes to get up and propose that that signal shall be compulsory on one vessel or on the last vessel, or any one or more of the vessels, let him put it before us. We have been five hours now working away with the proposal of the Committee before you. That shows that we have studied the question very closely, and have not put a proposal before you at random.

I think, therefore, that we may demand now, at least, that our work shall be voted upon. All that we ask you to do is to leave out the words " if necessary." The clause will stand then: " A steam-vessel and a sailing-vessel," which, of course, will be a " vessel," " when towing shall at intervals of not more than two minutes sound a "—a certain signal. We want to introduce the words as they were originally. But we want to say that a steam-vessel and a sailing-vessel when towing shall, and the vessel towed may, at intervals of not more than two minutes, sound such a signal. Our position is this: You have given a signal to a towing vessel; when there are more than two, the second vessel becomes the towing vessel; when there are six, the fifth vessel in the string becomes a towing vessel; but still you have not said so. What we want is to clear the matter up, and let the first tow make the signal which will cover the second. But it will not clear five or six. What we want is that any one of these vessels which really becomes a towing vessel be permitted to sound some signal to say: "There is another vessel behind me; I am towing."

Mr. Verney (Siam).—Mr. President, yesterday I went across to the gallant Delegate from the United States, who is not in his place this morning, and I put before him almost the identical words which the learned Delegate from Great Britain read a few moments ago. The words as I read them were these:—

"When more than one vessel is being towed, each vessel being towed shall sound this signal on hearing the signal of an approaching vessel."

I put this proposition to the gallant Delegate from the United States, and his answer was this: "Such a proposition as that is impracticable because of the length of time consumed in making these signals, which would be a matter of confusion: such a proposition I could not possibly vote for." Seeing that the gallant Delegate is not in his place this morning, I venture to ask the Conference whether that objection is not a very real one, and I would ask whether, before we vote upon these words of the learned Delegate from Great Britain, this should not be taken into account.

Mr. Hall (Great Britain).—Mr. President, may I ask the learned Delegate from Siam whether or not in his proposition he limited it only to the case when the signal of an approaching vessel was heard? That is put in to prevent the Babel of sounds which would occur if every vessel should keep repeating the signal. It is only when the signal of the approaching vessel is being heard that the vessel being towed is to repeat the signal. We do not propose that each vessel should repeat it when they are merely being towed. When they hear a vessel in the vicinity then let them give the warning that they are there.

Mr. Verney (Siam).—Mr. President, I quite understand the limitation which the learned Delegate from Great Britain has stated, but it seems to me when there are several vessels in a tow almost all of them would hear the signal of the approaching vessel almost simultaneously.

Admiral Nares (Great Britain).—Mr. President, our copies have got so confused that I have not quite clearly stated the wording. I have stated the principle. We have all agreed that we do not want them to be making the signal every two minutes. If we take our wording it will be: "A steam-vessel and a sailing-vessel when towing shall, at intervals of not more than two minutes, and the vessel towed may, sound on her whistle, siren, or fog-horn," &c. I move that on behalf of the Sound-Signal Committee, and I really think that we should take a vote upon it.

The President.—The amendment of the Delegate from Great Britain will be read.

The amendment is as follows:—

Paragraph (*g*) to be as follows: "A steam-vessel and a sailing-vessel when towing shall, at intervals of not more two minutes, and the vessel towed may, sound on her whistle, siren, or fog-horn three blasts in succession, viz., one prolonged blast, followed by two short blasts."

The President.—Does the Delegate from the United States wish to amend that? An amendment was proposed just now to change the nature of the signal altogether. If that amendment be insisted upon it must be taken into consideration.

Captain Norcross (United States).—Mr. President, I will postpone that amendment until after we get a vote on this.

The President.—The question, then, is upon the amendment of the Delegate from Great Britain.

Mr. Goodrich (United States).—Mr. President, I call for the Yeas and Nays.

The President.—Upon the amendment as just stated by the Delegate from Great Britain, the Yeas and Nays will be called.

The Yea and Nay vote is as follows:

Austria-Hungary	Yea.	Italy	Yea.
Belgium	Yea.	Japan	Yea.
China	Yea.	Mexico	Yea.
Chile	Yea.	Norway	Yea.
Costa Rica	Yea.	Russia	Yea.
Denmark	Yea.	Spain	Yea.
France	Nay.	Sweden	Yea.
Germany	Yea.	Siam	Yea.
Great Britain	Yea.	The Netherlands	Yea.
Guatemala	Yea.	Venezuela	Yea.
Hawaii	Yea.	United States	Yea.
Honduras	Yea.		

The President.—Twenty-two States have voted in the affirmative, and one in the negative; so the proposition is carried.

Mr. Hall (Great Britain).—Mr. President, may I point out a matter which is a mere question of wording? We have decided in the Conference that a steam-vessel being towed is under the same circumstances as a sailing-vessel under way, and that she is not to carry a steamer's light nor give a steamer's signals. We shall have to provide that a vessel towed shall give some signal on her fog-horn, but she must not use her whistle, or siren, because a steamer being towed is in the category of a sailing-vessel. I merely point it out now so that it will not be supposed to be a fresh principle. We will deal with it in the Collocation Committee. We will take care to provide that such use of the signals for any vessels towed must be made by the fog-horn only, and not by the siren or whistle.

61

The President.—The Delegate from the United States has proposed to make a change in the signal.

Mr. Goodrich (United States).—Mr. President, Captain Norcross postponed his amendment until the question was decided upon the other amendment. He now wants the vote on his proposition to make a change in the form of signal.

Mr. Carter (Hawaii).—Mr. President, may I point out that perhaps the Delegate from the United States will not think it necessary when he comes to consider that in a vast majority of cases the sound is to be made on the fog-horn, and is to all intents and purposes a different signal?

Captain Norcross (United States).—Mr. President, I know it will be a different signal, and that is what I want; otherwise no one would know whether this was a sailing-vessel or a steamer.

Captain Shackford (United States).—The difference between the whistle and the fog-horn will tell that.

Captain Norcross (United States).—Mr. President, I would like to have a vote upon this signal.

The President.—The proposition of the Delegate from the United States will be read.

The proposition is as follows:—

"If a steamer is towing more than one vessel, such vessel shall sound on her fog-horn, at intervals of not more than two minutes a long blast, followed by a short blast. This signal shall be obligatory when necesssary."

The President.—The question is before the Conference. Is the Conference ready for the question?

The question was put to the Conference upon the amendment proposed by the Delegate from the United States, and the amendment was lost.

Admiral Nares (Great Britain).—Mr. President, on behalf of the Sound-Signal Committee, I think there is one more point which should be cleared up. It was pointed out by the gallant Delegate from Sweden that there was something more necessary in this proposal. There is something necessary. I have not had an opportunity to confer with the members of the Sound-Signal Committee, but I am sure that they will all agree to the principle that these signals are to be made instead of the signals provided for in sections (a) and (b). Whether these words we have introduced are proper words is a question more for the lawyers to decide upon than the sailors. But the sailors ought to understand that these proposals for signals which we have chosen now are distinctly towing signals. In fact, it does not matter to the approaching vessel, so long as I am under tow and have half-a-dozen vessels behind me, whether I am on the starboard tack or the port tack. So long as they know I am towing, I do not think it is necessary to repeat the old signal. So our wording would be to introduce the words, "instead of the signals provided for in sections (a), (b), and (c)." That will provide that a steamer towing shall not be obliged to make her one blast, and the vessel towed will not be obliged to make her starboard and port tack signal. The vessel towed has no sails up. In the majority of cases she is neither on the starboard tack nor the port tack, nor is she running free; so practically there is no signal to be made. We are only interfering with the steamer's signal; but I think it had better be stated here, so as to clear the matter up.

Captain Malmberg (Sweden).—Mr. President, I will vote for the amendment proposed by the gallant Delegate from Great Britain, because I am quite certain that the wording will remove any doubt as to the meaning of the proposition.

The President.—Is the Conference ready for the question upon the proposition of the Delegate from Great Britain?

The question upon the proposition of the Delegate from Great Britain was put to the Conference, and carried.

The President.—The Chair understands that the question now is upon the whole of paragraph (g) as amended.

Mr. Hall (Great Britain).—Mr. President, before the question is put upon the whole of paragraph (g), may I move formally an amendment, to clear up a difficulty which I pointed out? If the words, "a vessel towed may sound her whistle, or siren, or fog-horn," were left, it would be incorrect, because the vessel towed, as I pointed out, is in the nature of a sailing-vessel, and must not give the signal on the whistle or siren. I think it will make it clear to put it in this way: "The vessel towed may also give this signal on the fog-horn, but not on the whistle or siren."

The President.—Is the Conference ready for the question upon the proposition of the Delegate from Great Britain? The Secretary will please read it.

Mr. Hall (Great Britain)—Mr. President, it would be to leave out the words, "and the vessel towed may," and add the other paragraph which I have read.

Captain Malmberg (Sweden).—Mr. President, I should think that it would be better to divide it into two paragraphs, one relating to steamers towing, and the other to sailing-vessels towing. I think that will be less confusing.

Mr. Hall (Great Britain).—Mr. President, we will do that in the Collocation Committee.

The President.—The proposition of the Delegate from Great Britain is as follows:—

To leave out the words, "and the vessel towed may," and to add at the end of the paragraph—

"The vessel towed may also give this signal on her fog-horn, but not on her whistle or siren."

Admiral Nares (Great Britain).—Mr. President, I think, on behalf of the Sound-Signal Committee, that we will be quite willing to adopt that. That is a mere matter of wording, but it is the same principle.

The question was put upon the adoption of the amendment of the Delegate from Great Britain, and it was carried.

The President.—The question now will be on the adoption of the whole paragraph as amended. The Secretary will please read paragraph (*g*) as amended.

Paragraph (*g*) as amended is as follows:—

"(*g*). A steam-vessel and a sailing-vessel when towing shall, at intervals of not more than two minutes, sound on the whistle, siren, or fog-horn three blasts in succession, viz., one prolonged blast, followed by two short blasts, instead of the signal provided for under sections (*a*), (*b*), Article 14."

The vessel towed——

Mr. Goodrich (United States).—Mr. President, is not that section (*c*) and not (*b*) of this Article? I will call that to the attention of the gallant Delegate from Great Britain.

The President.—Will the Delegate from Great Britain be kind enough to read Article (*g*) as he proposes it?

Mr. Hall (Great Britain).—Mr. President, if you will allow me I will read it so as to make it clear. "A vessel towing shall"——

The President.—Will the Delegate kindly read the whole Article?

Mr. Hall (Great Britain).—"A steam-vessel and a sailing-vessel when towing shall, instead of the signals provided under sections (*a*) and (*c*) of this Article, at intervals of not more than two minutes, sound on the whistle, siren, or fog-horn three blasts in succession, viz., one prolonged blast, followed by two short blasts.

"A vessel towed may also give this signal on her fog-horn, but not on her whistle or siren."

Captain Mensing (Germany).—Mr. President, I would like to point out that if this verbiage be adopted, the vessel towed would have to make the signals mentioned under Article 12 (*c*). Of course that is merely a matter of collocation, as has been pointed out.

The President.—The question now is upon paragraph (*g*), as amended.

The question was put to the Conference upon the adoption of paragraph (*g*) as amended, and it was adopted.

The President.—The Secretary will now please read paragraph (*h*).

Admiral Nares (Great Britain).—Mr. President, before that is read I would like to be allowed to make one remark. We have for some reason misstated the signal. Instead of the words, "my engines are stopped," under the decision of the Conference, it must go back to the words, "the way is off my ship."

It is as follows:—

"A steam-vessel wishing to indicate to another the 'way is off my ship, you may feel your way past me,' may sound on her whistle or siren three blasts, viz., short, long, short, with intervals of about one second between them."

Admiral Nares (Great Britain).—Mr. President, I think the Conference would like me to explain our reasons for putting in this signal. We are going now beyond the signal giving information as to an impediment in the way of another vessel, and we are coming into a communication signal. It will be a question for the Conference to decide whether such a signal should be given in this place, or whether it should go back to the two Committees, or to the one Committee considering communication signals under General Division No. VIII, or whether it should be left where it is. Of course I am not talking now of the particular signal to be given. That will come before the Conference. Nor am I speaking of the character of the signal. I only want to explain why we introduced it here. Communication signals are practically to be made when vessels are in sight of one another.

Now, the Conference has ordered ships in a fog hearing a signal anywhere before the beam to stop their engines, and then proceed with caution. There is no doubt a very cautious captain would want to say to the other man: "I am stopped, and I will remain stopped, but come along with caution." For that a signal will be required; being required, it will have to be made when the other vessel is not in sight. Under Article 12 you have all the signals that are to be made and that may be made when a vessel is not in sight. So the first question is whether such communication signal as this should come in here, or whether it should be put in the ordinary signals that are going to be proposed by the Signal Committee, and let it stand or fall there. We are not quite decided about that. The advantage of putting it here is that it will come into use far quicker than if it is put amongst the ordinary signals. We think now that when you have ordered two vessels practically to stop, that there should be something to enable them to communicate with each other, and give them an opportunity of wriggling past each other.

Captain Malmberg (Sweden).—Mr. President, being quite opposed to inserting in the "Regulations for preventing Collisions between Vessels" any such signal as suggested by the Committee on Sound-Signals under Article 12 (*h*), I venture to state my reasons for this opinion. By introducing the signal in question, this Article will contain a Rule in its character quite opposed to all other Rules concerning how vessels are to manœuvre in order to avoid risk of collision. The present Rules for this purpose prescribe that vessels are to keep out of the way, one of the other, but by introducing a signal and thereby a depending Rule by which you induce a steamer to feel her way past another one, the proximity of which can only be judged by her sound-signal, steamers will be enticed to draw too near each other, and so engender risk of collision.

As I think the signal proposed to be wrong in principle, and dangerous in its application, I will vote against its adoption, and hope that the majority of this Conference will support my idea.

Admiral Nares (Great Britain).—Mr. President, might I ask the gallant Delegate if, instead of voting distinctly against the signal, he would ask us to vote whether it would be sent to the double Committee? There will be sixteen gentlemen on the two Committees, and probably they can thrash out any question there as to the advisability of the signal at all very much better than we can in the Conference. Then they will advise the Conference whether the signal is a desirable one to introduce or not. Unless we do that we will be in this position: I must get up and argue the value of the signal, which I do not want to do at present; and I am sure that a great number of the Delegates will have to get up and argue for or against the signal. I do not think the Conference is quite ready for that.

Captain Malmberg (Sweden).—Mr. President, it is not the signal, it is the Rule, to which I am opposed, because I think it is a dangerous Rule to introduce. By such a Rule you will induce steamers to draw so near to each other that instead of avoiding the risk of a collision, collisions will be very easily brought about.

Captain Mensing (Germany).—Mr. President, I would like to state that I do not think it is advisable to adopt this signal. I do not think that this signal would ever be used, because I believe every captain at sea would always deem it to be the duty of the other vessel to stop and feel his way past.

Mr. Hall (Great Britain).—Mr. President, may I point out that it is thought desirable that we should not put any such signal as this in the Rules of the Road at Sea? Let the International Code Signal Committee discuss it, and if they choose, put it into the National Code Signal-Book; but I hope that they will consult with the Sound-Signal Committee, who have devoted so much time and consideration to this signal. But do not let us put it into the Rules of the Road at Sea. We now know what enormous difficulty there is in providing signals which are to be observed compulsorily under the Rules of the Road at Sea. If the International Code Signal Committee think it desirable to introduce such a signal, let them do it, and then the vessels may use it if they choose; but they will use it at their peril. I do not know whether it is necessary to make a formal motion; but if it is necessary to make such a motion, I will move that it is inexpedient to insert this Rule in the Rules for preventing Collisions at Sea, but that it be referred to Committee No. 2, dealing with General Division VIII.

Mr. Carter (Hawaii).—Mr. President, as a member of the Committee to which this is going to be referred, I would ask the learned Delegate from Great Britain if his motion would not be better if the last clause were left out, and simply have the motion that it is unwise to put it in the Rules of the Road of Vessels at Sea. If it can be referred to our Committee by the Conference, the reference might be thought to carry with it a mandate that we should prepare such a signal. If it were left entirely with us it would be a question for us to consider.

Mr. Hall (Great Britain).—Mr. President, I quite assent to that proposition. I see the force of the argument. I will move that it is inexpedient to insert these signals in the Rules for preventing Collisions at Sea. We know that the members of the International Code Signal Committee are many of them present, and I have no doubt that they will deal with it if they think it is desirable.

Captain Bisbee (China).—Mr. President, there is one other objection to this Rule, and that is, that if two steamers meet they will both make the signal and then they will come to a deadlock.

Mr. Hall (Great Britain).—Mr. President, before coming to the discussion may I move that it is inexpedient to insert any such Rule as this in the Rules for preventing Collisions at Sea?

Mr. Goodrich (United States).—Mr. President, I am a good deal in doubt whether that is wise or not. The United States' Delegation is in favour of this signal, although the question has not been brought up in the way indicated by the motion of the learned Delegate from Great Britain. Let us consider for a moment whether it is not expedient to have this inserted in the Rules of the Road.

In the first place, do not let us be influenced by the fact that if this motion is voted down we are going to have another discussion upon the subject. We shall have that discussion when the Report of the Committee referred to in the Resolution is presented, and we may as well have it now, if we desire to discuss the subject at all. This Conference has already said that it is wise to give vessels as much certainty in regard to the movements of other vessels as it is possible to give.

In the second place, we have already adopted certain sound-signals. In the third place, this signal is not likely to be confused with any other signal which has been reported by the Committee whose Report we are discussing. In the fourth place, the subject has been very carefully considered by the Sound-Signal Committee, and they have recommended the passage of this Article. I do not understand that there is anything in the remark of the gallant Delegate who is at the head of that Committee to the contrary of that proposition.

Now, what is the objection to this signal going into the Rules of the Road? As the gallant Delegate from Great Britain said, and said wisely, it will come into use much quicker if it is put into the Regulation Code than it will if it is only relegated to the International Code. I think this is a question about which we had better hesitate a good deal, and also as to whether we should strike out from the Report of this Committee this Article and relegate the subject to an entirely different Committee, and then put it in an entirely different part of the Report of the Conference. I am inclined to think that it is a good provision, and that it is a good provision to put into the Regulations for preventing Collisions at Sea.

Captain Malmberg (Sweden).—Mr. President, I hope the Conference will excuse me, but I must say that in my opinion it is quite the opposite of the Rule for preventing Collisions at Sea. As I said before, it will entice steamers to draw unnecessarily near to each other, and that is a Rule which ought not to be put into practice at all. I still hope that the Conference will not adopt that Rule.

Captain Shackford (United States).—Mr. President, we have adopted extra amendment No. 47, which says: "Every steam-ship when approaching another ship, if necessary in order to prevent risk of collision, shall slacken her speed, or stop and reverse." Now, if this Rule is not incorporated with the other, it seems to me that you will have two vessels stopped at the same time, at some distance from each other, without any means of communicating to each other how they are to pass. It seems to me that something of this kind is absolutely necessary. I tried once, when the Committee first met, to get over this difficulty by permitting the signals under Article 19 to be applied in a fog; but that was voted down. Now, it seems to me absolutely necessary, after a long experience on steamships, that something of this kind should be provided so that one vessel can let the other vessel know what she proposes to do.

Captain Malmberg (Sweden).—Mr. President, under Article 12 (*a*) it is stated that the steamer shall stop on hearing before her beam the sound-signal of another vessel, and shall then proceed cautiously. I should not think that both vessels would have to remain stopped. They are to proceed with caution. They are not to be lying there for two or three hours as stated. They are to proceed with caution, as they ought to do, and not to be lying still.

Captain Richard (France).—Mr. President, I entertain the opinion which has been expressed by several orators who have preceded me, namely, that we should put this signal into the International Signal Code, and not in the Rules of the Road. Certainly I agree with the Delegates of the United States that the signal would be a very good one, but I do not consider it indispensable, and we should only insert into the Rules of the Road at Sea strictly indispensable matters, and even then we would still have to leave out some of them.

I was just now astonished to hear the gallant Admiral, Sir George Nares, state that the Committee, after having considered the dangers and obstacles which a vessel might encounter at a specified moment, and after having provided sound-signals which would indicate their presence, had thereupon considered the communications which could be exchanged between vessels. Is it a positive fact, then, that the Committee has so fortunately succeeded in clearly indicating, by means of precise and well-defined signals, all the conditions wherein a vessel is unusually interested in making her character known? If I have any criticism to make I would ask whether a special signal has been given to vessels which are not under command, and to vessels which are laying or picking up telegraph cables, and which are not able to manœuvre with ease. I would also add that the Committee, in the Articles submitted to us, have not succeeded in establishing signals which are sufficiently defined and clear to indicate, without any danger of an error, what it is intended to indicate.

It would be a wise and prudent thing to limit ourselves to strictly necessary sound-signals—I would even say to strictly indispensable ones—and to oppose the consideration of anything tending to give in separate specified cases a special signal, when it is admitted that it is impossible to give a signal which is not liable to confusion. I think that until now no want has been felt for the majority of the signals which are offered to us, and it is only since the sessions of this Conference have commenced that it was discovered to be absolutely necessary to give a special signal during fog and mist to a vessel at anchor in a fairway, to a towing vessel, to a vessel whose engine is stopped, &c. It is all well enough to increase the number of signals of doubtful quality, but you will have still more increased the requirements which you will have to meet by allowing the introduction of demands for special cases, which are fully as important as those for which you have provided. By combining the prolonged and short blasts, it is easy to find a variety of sound-signals, but by so doing the principle will be abandoned which until now had been followed in the use of the long and the short blasts, and I think that the situation has become more confused. The great practical difficulty is to invent signals which will be easy to distinguish and interpret.

If you will read the statistics you will notice that three-fourths of the collisions have taken place by reason of the difficulty of finding out where the signals heard proceeded from. You know that the hearing of a signal and its interpretation are not all-sufficient, but that it is also necessary to locate the point whence it comes. Why, then, increase the number of inefficient sound-signals, and create still more inefficient ones? You have managed to give a short blast followed by a prolonged blast, and then again a short blast. No one here present can tell me that the signal will be efficient in practice; that it will be properly made and properly heard. Therefore, in order to attain an advantage which is doubtful, which is not necessary, with which you can dispense, and the utility of which is not absolutely indispensable, you plunge into signals of the practical efficiency of which you have no proof.

A suggestion is made to introduce them into the Rules of the Road at Sea. Would it not be better to put these signals into the International Code Signals?

Admiral Bowden-Smith (Great Britain).—Mr. President, I am not going to say a word about the signal which has been proposed by the Sound-Signal Committee. I would rather leave to the Conference the duty of deciding whether the signal is good or not. But I wish to make a few remarks about what has fallen from one, if not two, of the Delegates as to the action of two steamers when they meet in a fog. I understood the Delegate from the United States to say that two steamers meeting in a fog should stop, according to the Regulations that have been passed by the Conference, and that they should remain stopped. I do not read it in that way. The Conference distinctly passed this Rule, adding these words to the moderate speed clause: "A steamer, hearing apparently before her beam the sound-signal of another vessel, shall stop her engines and then proceed with caution." So she would not stop altogether. Now, she is to proceed with caution, and I read it that she is to proceed and take any action which she thinks most desirable. It does not mean to proceed ahead, as I read it. It means to proceed with caution, and to go ahead or to turn astern. She is to proceed to take some action with caution. I do not understand at all that two steamers in a fog, hearing each other, are to stop until they are relieved from doing so by the fog lifting.

Captain Shackford (United States).—Mr. President, certainly the gallant Delegate must acknowledge that there will be instances when two steamers will be obliged to stop very close to each other. I would like to know if it is not desirable to have some signal by which one vessel will say that she will remain stopped.

Admiral Bowden-Smith (Great Britain).—They will both see each other, and go astern as hard as they can.

Captain Shackford (United States).—They might be within 50 yards and not see each other.

The President.—The question is upon the motion of the Delegate from Great Britain.

Mr. Hall (Great Britain).—Mr. President, I do not for a moment desire to send this to any Committee if it is desirable that the matter should be discussed here. I confess that I thought it was better that this should be dealt with by the International Code Signal Committee and put into the International Code, and not made a compulsory signal under the Rules for preventing Collisions at sea. It is only an optional Rule, as has been pointed out. If it is thought desirable to put it into the Rules of the Road at Sea, by all means let us discuss it. I do not care to express my opinion one way or the other. Most of these signals are in the International Code, and I thought that was the proper place for them.

Captain Malmberg (Sweden).—Mr. President, being one of the members of the Committee to which this Rule may be referred, I, for my part, should very much prefer to take the vote of the Conference upon the question as to whether such a Rule is to be introduced at all, and not to put the Committee to the great difficulty of deciding the matter.

Mr. Carter (Hawaii).—Mr. President, may I point out that the Committee to which it is proposed to refer this Rule is really to take cognizance of night signals? General Division No. VIII is for night signals for communication at sea. It is quite questionable whether we might not think that this was not a proper subject for consideration before that Committee; and it would be hardly useful to make this signal to be used at night only and not in a fog, If we are going to get into a fog at all I should prefer that we do it in the Conference rather than in the Committee. Therefore, as we are here, and the weather so far is clear, I think we had better vote on the matter and settle it. I think it is a matter which will not require very great discussion. The value of the signal is doubtful, to say the least, and the Committees themselves seem to have thought so in making it merely a permissive signal. This signal is already contained in the urgent or important signals which are recommended by the British Board of Trade, and so there is at the present time a signal which may be used. What I meant to say about the urgency is with regard to whether it should be in the Rules for preventing Collisions at Sea. I do not believe that this is a very urgent signal. Therefore, I think that the motion of the learned Delegate from Great Britain which is before us now is a very apt one, that it is inexpedient that this signal should be contained among the Rules for preventing Collisions at Sea. On that proposition I think it would be very well for the Conference to take a vote.

Mr. Hall (Great Britain).—Mr. President, I certainly did not move that amendment for the purpose of asking the Conference to decide against this signal. Nothing was further from my mind, and for fear that it should be thought by my learned friend on my right that such was my intention I withdraw that amendment. On the contrary, I shall give my vote in favour of this signal. It is an optional signal, and it will meet the case pointed out by the learned Delegate from the United States where vessels want to communicate with each other. It is recommended by our Board of Trade for use in urgent cases, and has been for some time; and I cannot see the difficulty which would arise from the adoption of it.

Thereupon the Conference took a recess until 2 o'clock.

After Recess.

Captain Malmberg (Sweden).—Mr. President, shortly before the Conference adjourned it was stated as a good feature of this proposed Rule that it was to be optional. I remember very well when we were discussing Article 19 how it was said that one of the very worst features of the Rule was that it was optional, and that it was quite necessary to make it compulsory. It was also the decision of the Conference that it should be so, although some of us opposed it. Now, this Rule to be introduced is to be optional. I will not repeat what I said before about my objection to introducing this Rule. I only wish to say that if ever I be in command of a steamer I will take very good care not to make that signal.

Admiral Nares (Great Britain).—Mr. President, it now falls to me as the Chairman of the Sound-Signal Committee to give the reasons for wishing to introduce this signal. But after the experience we have had for the last few days I would request you, Sir, to consider whether it would not be better, first of all, to consider the point whether there shall be such a signal at all, and afterwards to consider its character. If we are to discuss the two points together we may get adrift on one of them. Therefore, I would ask whether we might not consider the principle as to whether such a signal should be adopted at all.

Now, the history of this signal is as follows: In Great Britain for the last two years we have been considering in Committees the revision of the International Code Signal-Book. When this Conference was first proposed we had got to the stage of revising the signal-book preparatory to sending that revision abroad for consideration by the other Powers. Therefore, any papers which have come before any member of this Conference have come before them, you may say, by accident in a round-about way. These papers are all being sent to foreign countries for their consideration. This is a very large question, and replies, of course, will come back to us in regard to the matter,

In the consideration of this signal, the Committee in London came to the conclusion, after consulting the whole of the trade, that they were not ripe for adopting a general system of night signals. At the same time the trade wished to adopt a few distinct special signals. The main point they had against the adoption of signals generally was that they cannot afford to have the attention of their officers distracted from their real work of navigating their ship and looking out for a ship and for vessels directly ahead of them, and turn them into signal officers. So, practically, what the proposition of Great Britain and of the trade of Great Britain have come to is that there are a few signals which are very important and which they would like to have adopted. The whole correspondence is before the Committee in the First Report of the Sound-Signal Committee, in Appendix (D). There is a Table given of the replies of the prominent shipping firms and of their officers about these signals. But for my case about this signal, "The way is off my ship, you may feel your way past me," it is not tabulated there what the opinion of the various captains and people interested were with regard to this signal.

Now, it happened to be my duty at the Board of Trade to go through a of the replies, and in my own private tabulation I had, instead of the six headings which we have in the Report here, I daresay a great many more. Under one of those I had tabulated the number of practical seamen who had especially asked for any one of these six signals. Unfortunately, in changing our papers from the Brevoort House down to this place I have lost that tabulation. It was on a large sheet of paper, so I cannot give now the number of practical seamen, but it was a curious state of things which was shown by that tabulation. Of the six signals that were put forward for adoption as special signals, the only one which large numbers of seamen in command of ships actually asked to have was this one : " The way is off my ship ; you may feel your way past me." It was an astonishing thing that none of them asked to say : " You are standing into danger." You see it comes around to a personal question. It is rather a selfish view they all take. They all want to have something which they feel to be important to themselves, but they ask for no signal that is important to their neighbour. Of course the Department in authority considers the question in a totally different view, so that they adopt all the signals which they think are necessary for both sides.

I am perfectly certain that a large number of the seamen navigating ships—I will not say a majority of them—would have voted in favour of this signal; and without its being put to a vote at all, a very large number of them asked for this signal: " The way is off my ship ; you may feel your way past me." So we thought that sufficient to put before the Conference the value of this signal.

The question whether it is to be used in a fog or not I will consider. On p. 5 of the old Report it says : " These signals may be made at night or during fog either by flashes of white light or by a combination of long and short sounds on the steam-whistle, fog-horn, siren, bugle," &c. So you see that the Committee have been considering this, and, after considering the replies which came with regard to this signal, came to the conclusion that it may be made in a fog. That is the reason why I put it before my companions on the Committee on Sound-Signals, because it is the only signal which has been asked for by the trade generally.

Captain Mensing (Germany).—Mr. President, if the gallant Delegate from Great Britain should put the question to me as to whether I should like to see such a signal embodied in the signal-book as he has proposed, I would say *Yes* ; but still, when it comes to the proposition that is before us, I shall answer *No*. The difficulty seems to me to be that all of the practical seamen who have sent in their answers have not thought of a fog at all. They have thought of the light. It strikes me that it would be a most appropriate signal to give when two ships are coming to a very narrow passage. One is there at the entrance, and for some reason or other she thinks she had better wait at one end, and she wants to signal the fact that she is waiting, that the way is off her, and she wants the other ship to feel her way past her ; then she gives that signal, and it is a very good signal. I do not see very much in the way of it, although of course the short blast at the beginning of it is rather objectionable to me.

But take the case of a fog. We have already adopted a signal of two long blasts to mean, " The way is off my ship," and it has been thoroughly set forth that the other ship is to wait until she has located the sound of the other vessel, and then to proceed with caution. Now, on one ship there may be four officers, and on the other only one : these four, after deliberate consultation, find out that the vessel giving the signal is located in that direction [indicating]. They say, " Very well, we will make the signal for her to proceed and we will remain stopped." Now, there is a great difficulty in the way and a great danger may be brought about : as has been pointed out by one of the Delegates here, a long vessel of over 500 feet, carrying a steam-whistle 100 feet from her bow, has got 400 feet from her steam-whistle to her stern, so she may be struck, and very likely will be sunk. I have no idea whether I can locate a sound ; so I do not know whether she is moving or what course she is steering. Thus a very great danger is brought in.

Then if we adopt it for use as a fog-signal only, we exclude it for any other use. I think it would be advisable to have another note in the Rules of the Road referring to this signal, and making it for use under ordinary circumstances. As has been ably pointed out by the gallant Delegate from France, I believe that it will be necessary to add one or even two fog-signals to those which have already appeared. On looking at this signal in this light, I must myself strongly object to putting any signals in the Rules of the Road that are not absolutely necessary. It has always been maintained that we should make these Rules as simple as possible. I do not see any reason whatever why we should bring this signal in here and adopt it as a Rule of the Road, which might, under certain circumstances, possibly be desirable, but certainly is not absolutely necessary.

Mr. Flood (Norway).—Mr. President, I may say that I fully agree with what has been said by the gallant Admiral from Great Britain. If we alter the expression, " My engines are stopped," to " The way is off my ship," I think that the paragraph is in its right place. The argument brought forward that optional signals are very objectionable is not to the point, in my opinion. We have other optional signals. In the paragraph above we have agreed that vessels towing may sound a signal. We have not said that they *shall* sound it, as I propose, but we have said that they *may*, and that leaves it to a certain extent optional. Under such circumstances I think that it is very well that there should be such a communication between two steamers. The fact that it is optional is the safe part of the paragraph, to my mind, because a vessel hearing another steamer's signal will know that the way is off her ; and if she does not think it necessary, she need not make that signal at all. If this had been a compulsory signal then I should say that it might be dangerous ; but it is not compulsory. It is left to the common sense of the master as to whether it is necessary to make the signal or not.

The argument brought forward by the gallant Delegate from Germany, when he stated that he objected to it because there were some other signals wanted, which I admit is the case, does not convince me. I am sorry to confess that I have been forming here an amendment, or rather a proposal for an additional paragraph, which requires another signal. But I do not think that ought to affect this at all. The signal proposed here is, as I think, a very simple and a very clear signal, and, being optional, is not to be used by all vessels, but only to be used by steamers. I think the paragraph as it stands, on the whole, ought to be accepted as it is contained in the proposition of the Committee.

Mr. Goodrich (United States).—Mr. President, a remark fell from the learned Delegate from Hawaii this morning which is well worthy of consideration and which possibly may influence the vote upon this question. He suggested that a Rule of this kind might properly go into the International Code Signal-Book. But the difficulty will then arise that it is not in the Rules of the Road, and the fact that there is such a signal in the International Code Signal-Book does not point the attention of the sailor to the necessity of using this signal under proper circumstances. The Rules of the Road are laid before the master of a vessel and he governs himself according to them. He is not bound to go to the International Code Signal-Book to find what signal he may sound. He goes to the Regulations to see what he may or may not sound; and the fact that the signal is in the International Code would have no effect upon the construction of these Rules if a collision comes to be investigated in the Courts, because there are hundreds of other signals the use of which is permitted by the International Code. But it does not affect at all the duty of the vessel in regard to giving the signal either in a fog or where there is danger of collision.

Of course the question as to the propriety of using the signal is chiefly within the knowledge of nautical men; but the question of putting it into the Rules here or of relegating it to the International Code-Book is a question, perhaps, upon which the Conference may receive some light from the legal gentlemen around the board. As at present advised, I do not see that there is any very great question upon this Article, or I should be prepared to discuss it at some greater length. Let me say, however, that the experience of the last few days demonstrates the propriety under all ordinary circumstances of standing by the Report of a Committee composed, as the Sound-Signal Committee is composed, of as able men as there are in the Conference, who have given a subject most careful consideration; and especially when, as stated by the gallant Delegate from Great Britain, it is also the result of long investigation which the Committees of the Board of Trade have given to it for many months past. I am sure that, if we get into a discussion such as we got into upon paragraph (*g*) of the Report of the Committee, we shall gradually drift back to the Report.

Captain Malmberg (Sweden).—Mr. President, if these Regulations were denominated or headed, as they generally are, the Rules of the Road, I would have no objection, perhaps, to introducing the Rule in question; but these Regulations are for preventing collisions at sea; that is the reason I object to the introduction of the Rule.

Captain Mensing (Germany).—Mr. President, I would be very much obliged to the learned Delegate from the United States if he would point out to me what effect on the Rules of the Road it would have if we adopt this Regulation. I think he said something to that effect, that it would work a great advantage, but I am sorry to say that I have not been able to see the effect it would have upon the Rules of the Road. If that should be the case, I should be very much more inclined to vote against it than I am now.

Mr. Goodrich (United States).—Mr. President, I do not quite catch the point of the question.

Captain Mensing (Germany).—Mr. President, I think Mr. Goodrich pointed out to us that if this Rule was relegated to the Signal-Book it would have no effect on the Rules of the Road. From that I inferred that it might be the opinion that it would have some effect on the Rules of the Road, and I should be very glad indeed if he would kindly point out to us what it is.

Mr. Goodrich (United States).—Mr. President, my statement was that if this provision or this signal were made a signal which was adopted in the International Code, it would have no more force than any other signal that is embraced in that Code. If, however, you put it into these Rules, and if a set of circumstances arises which renders the use of this Rule necessary, and which renders it proper that the master in command of the ship shall exercise the option which he has under these Rules, the Courts in judging of a collision at sea caused by a failure to obey the Rules will take under the very gravest consideration the question as to whether the master ought not to have obeyed this Rule and given the proper signals under it. I do not know whether I make myself clear to the gallant Delegate from Germany. You may as well say, if you put this signal in the International Code, that any signal which is in the International Code must be resorted to and obeyed and made a rule of sailing, when occasion rises for it, as in the case of this one. If, however, you put it into the Rules of the Road, and an occasion arises when a master of a ship should not obey this signal, he would be found in fault for not obeying it, provided the Court shall be of the opinion that he ought to have given it. That is the reason for putting it into these Regulations instead of relegating it to the International Signal Code.

Admiral Nares (Great Britain).—Mr. President, the view of the Committee was this: That having practically two stationary steamers in a fog, having previously told each other that they are stationary, like two men in the street not quite certain which way to pass, one at last says, "I will remain stopped, you may come on." That is practically what the signal is. If any captain will put himself in that unselfish position then he has no signal, and if there is an unselfish captain who wants to make this signal that he will remain stopped and let the other one pass, we have given him the signal to do it. We really think that by adopting this signal you are making men more cautious and more inclined to go slowly or stop, because then they will know that when they are stopped there is a signal for them to pass each other, if they will give it.

Now, as to whether the signal should be included in the Rules of the Road or in the Code, I would point out that it is not an extra signal to remember. Wherever you put a signal it will have to be learned and remembered by all the officers, if it comes into play. If it does not come into play, it will disappear. Whether the signal is really in the Signal-Book, or whether it is in the Rules of the Road, if it is of any use it will have to be remembered. The idea of the Committee was to try and get it into use as quickly as possible, because we think it a very valuable signal.

Captain Mensing (Germany).—Mr. President, from what fell from the gallant gentleman who just spoke, I infer that he believes that everything which is in the Signal-Book would have to be learned. Now, I do not believe that everything that is in the Signal-Book has to be learned by the men who pass the examination for masters or mates. But I believe that everything which is contained in these Regulations must be known, if possible, by heart, or at least so that it is perfectly clear what decision he is to make either when he goes up on examination or is on board of his vessel. It has been pointed out here what a dangerous thing it is to bring into the Rules a number of signals.

I wish to call the special attention of my friend the Delegate from Norway to the fact that, the moment the word "may" comes in, the Courts will say: "You may, and, therefore, you *must* under certain circumstances." I think we heard that from the learned Delegate of the United States; but perhaps he thinks that this Rule which has been brought up is just like a bait. The fish nibble a little at it, and if it tastes right good they put their little jaws into it and bite it. The sailor comes to this Rule and he is at once gobbled up. Now, if it is nothing but a permissive Rule, then what reason is there in the world why it is not sufficient if we introduce the whole matter by putting it in the Signal-Book? Then nobody has to learn it. Nobody is confused by it, and it meets all that we intend to accomplish. If a man has not got his Signal-Book somewhere about the bridge, all he has to do is to send down to the captain's room and get it. I believe there is no great difficulty in doing this.

The gallant Delegate from Great Britain also stated that he believed this Rule would make people more inclined to be careful in a fog. I cannot agree with him about that. We have provided in our Rules that a steamer shall stop when she hears another's signal, and that she shall not proceed until she has located the sound and found the position of the ship. As I have stated, a steamer 500 feet long, with her whistle 100 feet from the bow, and with that whistle in front of her smoke-stack, when she makes that signal and there is another ship coming up about four points astern of her, does not know where the vessel is. She thinks the distance is an entirely different one, and she signals to her. Now, what is the use of such a signal? If you want to make it permissive, it can be very easily done by introducing it into the Signal-Book. If you want to make it obligatory and bring out all the advantages of a compulsory Rule, or if you want to make the behaviour of people on board of ships dependent upon this Rule, then speak out and say so; but let no mistakes be possible afterwards.

Captain Malmberg (Sweden).—Mr. President, I thank the gallant Delegate from Great Britain, Sir George Nares, for the parallel which he made a short time ago about two men in the street, and that they should be able to indicate, one to the other, "I am standing still; you may pass me." I suppose that refers to daylight, when they are in sight of each other. But I am of the opinion that when two persons meet in a fog—take, for example, in London—one of them will not be very apt to give the signal, "I will stand still, and you may feel your way past me."

Mr. Goodrich (United States).—Mr. President, there is another element in regard to this Rule which has not been clearly set before the Conference in connection with it. We have repeatedly adopted the principle to which I referred awhile ago, and I will call the attention of the Conference to it in this connection. It has been very ably argued by both the sailors and the lawyers of this Conference that one of the important necessities, when risk of collision was involved, was that there should be as much certainty as possible as to the course and action of the approaching vessel. In a fog, if that knowledge can be communicated, it is of especial importance and of very great value. Here are two vessels in a fog. If each vessel could know that her signals were heard and would be obeyed by the other vessel, there would never be a collision, provided, of course, that the signal was given at an early time during the process of navigation. If one of these vessels, or either of the vessels, can say to the other, "I heard you; I know where you are; I am guiding my course according to your signal or according to the signal I now give," the result would be a protection to each vessel. That, as I understand it, is the object of this Rule. The gallant Delegate from Germany, as I understand him, proposes to bury this Rule by relegating it to the Signal-Book. That certainly would be the effect of such relegation. No man will obey it. No man's attention will be pointed to it. He will have to search through 1,500 signals to get this one, and before he can find it the time when the necessity for the use of it has arisen will have passed away.

Now, one word about the construction of these Rules. The Courts have already considered similar Rules. Take the 19th Rule. It has been settled by the Courts over and over again that this Rule is not a mandatory one, but that it is optional; that you are not bound to give this signal. But if you do give it, then you will be held responsible for the consequences of proper action on the signal. I have in my mind a very important case where the very question was discussed. I adverted to that case in a previous session of the Conference. It was a case where a steamer came into collision with a sailing-vessel in a fog, and where, if the signal had been given, no collision would have ensued, and yet the Court, in a strong case like that, said that the authority to give or not to give the signal is optional, and because that option was not exercised there can be no Judgment against the vessel because she did not exercise it. If she exercises the option, then a new responsibility comes upon her. That I understand to be good sound law, and, so far as I know, it has never been changed. The object which I have in arguing for the adoption of the Report of the Committee is this: if you relegate this Rule to the Signal-Book it will never be heard from. As I said before, it will be buried. Put this before the sailor. Put it in the Code which is in their hands day after day to be studied by them, and their attention will be called to the Rule; and although it be at first an optional or permissive signal in its character, it will grow just as the 19th Rule grew, from similar circumstance, from a permissive Rule to a mandatory Rule, to which this Conference has set its seal of approval by changing the word "may" to "shall" in that Rule.

Another thing is suggested to me by my colleague Captain Shackford, and I call the attention of the gallant Delegate from Germany to the fact. You cannot make this Rule compulsory. It would be an absurdity to do it. To say that a vessel in a fog was to sound this signal under all circumstances would be absurd. Shall both vessels sound it? Under the 13th Rule, you have at sea a vessel going at a moderate speed in a fog, and you have a provision that she shall proceed thereafter with caution until she finds the position of her adversary. This Rule is a mere complement of that Rule. Having ascertained the position of the other vessel, either one may give this optional signal and remain stationary, but the other vessel feels her way past her. But if you say, "shall give that signal," it applies as much to one vessel as the other, and both may remain in the fog until the fog clears up, or, as my friend on my right says, for ever.

Mr. Hall (Great Britain).—Mr. President, I would like to state very briefly the reasons for which I am prepared to cast the vote of Great Britain in favour of the proposal of the Committee. It is urged that possibly the fact of relegating this signal to the International Code Signal-Book would have the effect of burying it, and I think that is a powerful argument for introducing it into these Rules. I do not think that anybody proposes that this should be a compulsory Rule on all vessels. With regard to the law, I quite agree with the learned Delegate from the United States, that when a signal like this is permissive only, the Courts would not hold any vessel liable for not having used such a signal, and the case which he has cited under the 19th Article is strongly in point. Now, Mr. President, I do not mean to weary the Conference at any great length with observations in regard to this matter. We have all made up our minds how we shall vote. I will only say that we shall vote for this proposition, because of the strong representation which has been made by the Board of Trade with regard to it, and the desire expressed for it by the sailors; and because of, so far as I can see, the absence of any danger in adopting such a signal.

Captain Norcross (United States).—Mr. President, it seems to me that there are two sides to this question. The gallant Delegate from Sweden has pointed out that the signal is, "Here I stand; you may feel your way past me;" but suppose the other steamer should say the same thing, which is to be obliged to accept the invitation?

Lieutenant Beaugency (Chile).—Mr. President, let me say a few words with regard to the great difficulty pointed out by the learned Delegate from the United States about finding this signal in the Signal-Book, if we adopt it. In my country, our merchant-ships (national and foreign) are obliged to have the Book of Signals; and they have, on a small piece of paper, the signals which are usually required in special cases, and they can find it in one second. That may not be the case in other countries.

Captain Malmberg (Sweden).—Mr. President, if this Rule is of such immense good as is stated here, I do not see much danger of its being buried in the Signal-Book; if it is a good signal, it will soon be brought forward and put into practice.

Admiral Bowden-Smith (Great Britain).—Mr. President, I only want to say, in answer to the learned Delegate from the United States, that if this signal were put into the International Code Book he would not have to search through 1,500 signals, because the signals proposed by the Board of Trade, this being one of them, are all on one page, in a very simple position, as I am going to take the liberty of showing him.

Mr. Goodrich (United States).—Mr. President, it seems to me that from the fact that this signal is considered to be of enough importance to separate it from the great body of signals, and put it upon a page by itself, it is a justification for adopting it and putting it in the Rules of the Road.

Captain Malmberg (Sweden).—It is in good company, too.

Captain Mensing (Germany).—Mr. President, I believe that nobody has spoken against the desirability of making the signal for the Signal-Book; and I would like to call the attention of the Conference to the fact that when Sir George Nares had the kindness to read from his Report of those men who, he said, were in favour of the signal, that they only answered the question as to whether they were in favour of adopting this signal in the Signal-Book, and not as a fog-signal.

Captain Wyatt (Great Britain).—Mr. President, as a practical sailor who has to travel some 70,000 miles every year, I take a great interest in this signal. It seems to me that when two ships are stopped in a fog it is very much safer for one ship to move cautiously past the other than for both to look for each other at the same time.

The President.—The question is upon the proposition of the Delegate from Great Britain, which will now be read.

The proposition is as follows:—

"Shall a signal be given to a steam-vessel to indicate to another: The way is off my ship; you may feel your way past me?"

The President.—The vote will be taken on that proposition of the Delegate from Great Britain.

Mr. Goodrich (United States).—Mr. President, I call for the Yeas and Nays.

The President.—The Yeas and Nays are called for. The nations who are in favour of this proposition will answer Yea, and those opposed to it Nay.

The Yea and Nay vote is as follows:—

Austria-Hungary .. .. Yea.	Japan .. .. Yea.
Belgium .. .. .. Yea.	Mexico .. .. Yea.
China .. .. Yea.	Norway .. .. .. Yea.
Chile .. .. Yea.	Russia .. .. Yea.
Denmark .. .. .. Yea.	Spain .. .. Nay.
France .. .. Nay.	Sweden .. .. Nay.
Germany .. .. .. Nay.	Siam .. .. Yea.
Great Britain .. .. .. Yea.	The Netherlands .. .. Yea.
Hawaii .. .. .. Yea.	United States .. .. Yea.
Italy .. .. Yea.	

The President.—Fifteen countries have voted in the affirmative, and four in the negative; so the proposition is carried. The next question in order will be the second proposition on the same paragraph.

Admiral Nares (Great Britain).—Mr. President, it will now be necessary to consider the character of the signals, and the reasons why we have chosen this signal. First of all, we will say that we must have a combination signal of long and short. I think the Conference will all agree to that. Then the question is whether we shall begin with the long or the short. The principle we have got to now is that all vessels in motion are giving a long sound for their first sound, and, therefore, it is an advantage for vessels which are stopped to give a short sound. So, we propose here to commence with the short sound. Then we thought that the best combination of all, in the characters that were chosen by the Committee in London, and the most important is: You are running into danger, or that you want assistance; and that this was the third. The danger signal they have chosen is practically a combination short and long. They made the signal as short as they possibly could make it, and two combinations are taken for that. Then the most distinctive of three signals was a short, long, short. That was considered. Of course the Committee on Sound-Signals do not stick positively to this character; but they have considered it practically in that direction. If any gentleman can give us a better signal that will not really prevent more important signals from being adopted, we will not interfere with them, but we should be very happy to consider it. But at present we think that the best signal in connection with other valuable signals is this combination: short, long, short. I move that this signal be adopted.

The President.—The question is upon the adoption of the signal as suggested by the Delegate from Great Britain.

Admiral Nares (Great Britain).—Mr. President, there have been remarks made that commencing the signal with a short sound it might be indistinctly given because of the steam in the pipes condensing and giving the sputtering sound as we all know it does. But this signal cannot be made until the vessels have been making their long signals before; so, practically, the steam-pipe ought to be pretty well cleared out; and if it is not cleared out well the captain is in fault, I should say. But, at all events, if the first signal is given badly, the second time it is made it will be all right.

Mr. Goodrich (United States).—Mr. President, this may be a matter for the Collocation Committee, but I call the attention of my gallant friend from Great Britain to the question as to whether the same language should not be used here as is used in the other portion of the Article. The principle being adopted, I suppose the Collocation Committee can fairly deal with that. The verbiage is a little different from the other paragraphs.

The President.—The question is upon the second proposition of the Delegate from Great Britain.

The question upon this proposition was put to the Conference, and carried.

The President.—The question now is upon the whole of paragraph (*h*). The Secretary will please read it.

Paragraph (*h*) is as follows:—

"(*h*). A steam-vessel wishing to indicate to another, 'The way is off my ship; you may feel your way past me,' may sound on her whistle or siren three blasts, viz., short, long, short, with intervals of about one second between them."

The question upon the adoption of paragraph (*h*) was put to the Conference, and it was adopted.

Mr. Flood (Norway).—Mr. President, before leaving this Article on fog-signals, I must ask the liberty to detain the Conference for just one moment.

The President.—Does the Delegate ask to reconsider some portion of the Article?

Mr. Flood (Norway).—No, Sir; I want to bring to the attention of the Committee the fact that we still have some vessels in a fog looming up in the distance, and that is vessels which are under way but not under command. What are you to do with them? We have not any signal yet as to what they shall do when they are in a fog, and I take the liberty to propose that they are also to be provided with a signal. I put this before the Conference as a principle, and am prepared to offer the amendment.

Mr. Goodrich (United States).—Mr. President, may I call the attention of the learned Delegate to subdivision (*d*) of Article 12, and recall to his memory the discussion which ensued upon the use of the words "at anchor," and may I ask him whether it is not fully covered by that Article? If not, a single word in that Article might accomplish what he wishes.

Mr. Flood (Norway).—Mr. President, I do not feel inclined to do it in that way. Perhaps there should be a paragraph coming in after paragraph (*h*), to be called paragraph (*i*), and to state that disabled vessels—or use the same words as in Article 5—"vessels under way and not under command," shall use the signal in a fog. I shall not detain the Conference any more just now, but I should like to have the Committee on Sound-Signals give me their opinion about the matter.

Admiral Nares (Great Britain).—Mr. President, on the part of the Sound-Signal Committee, I would ask the Delegate from Norway to refer to the bottom of p. 5 of our Additional Report, in which we propose a sound-signal to attract attention. We considered that if we took any more signals for any special case that we should be giving too many signals for the officers to remember. If the wording at the bottom of the page does not meet this case, then I will argue the case a little further. It says:—

"Article —. Every ship may, if necessary, in order to attract attention, in addition to the lights which she is by these Regulations required to carry, show a flare-up light, or use any detonating signal that cannot be mistaken for a distress signal."

If, in addition to this, the gallant Delegate wishes any further signal for the special case, I will be prepared to argue the question.

Captain Mensing (Germany).—Mr. President, I beg leave to offer the following motion:—

"(*i*). A vessel which from any accident is not under command, and a vessel employed in laying or picking up a telegraph cable, shall, at intervals of not more than one minute, sound on the whistle, siren, or fog-horn three prolonged blasts in succession."

I think that we ought to provide for such a signal. I have been very much against increasing the number of signals. We have just now adopted a signal the necessity for which I do not believe has been demonstrated by any gentleman here. None of the gentlemen who have spoken have called this a necessary signal. Now, if you will lend me your attention for a few moments, I would like to read from Article 5, under paragraph (*g*), where it speaks of the lights on vessels not under command. It says:—

"The lights required to be shown by this Article are to be taken by other ships as signals that the ship showing them is not under command and cannot, therefore, get out of the way."

Here we have two classes of ships, I am sorry to say, without any signal given, but there is a duty put upon the other ships to get out of their way.

I do not think, if any person reads this Article carefully, that there can be any doubt left in his mind what the business of another ship is which is going to meet such a vessel. If that vessel cannot get out of *my* way I must get out of *her* way. There can be no doubt about that. Now, is this ship to be able to make her presence known in a fog? The gallant Chairman of the Committee on Sound-Signals refers to this Article at the bottom of p. 5. But that has nothing to do with fog-signals. Imagine that a telegraph sailing-ship, or a ship not under command, is coming along, or, for instance, one of these long passenger steamers with her screw broken, which is unable to get out of the way, and which is only too glad that she has a little way on her—what signal is she going to make? Has she not a very good right to expect other vessels to get out of her way? If that be so, and we want to make it compulsory for vessels to get out of the way of this vessel, I think that the least we can ask is that she shall have a signal, and that the signal shall be a distinctive one and one which will last a little longer than the other signal, because vessels are not required to get out of the way of other vessels, except of vessels at anchor. On that account I have changed the interval to one minute, so that the three blasts on the siren or fog-horn shall have to be repeated every minute. I have done that in order to give every facility to a ship meeting that vessel to get out of her way as soon as possible.

Captain Shackford (United States).—Mr. President, I would like to ask the gallant Delegate from Germany if the signal which has just been adopted by the Conference would not answer that purpose?

Admiral Nares (Great Britain).—Mr. President, if the Conference will kindly turn to p. 2 of our Report they will find that we say there: "The most unmistakable and easily remembered sound-signal, like those now authorized, consists of a single sound or a combination of sounds of equal length; and the Committee advise the adoption of such characters for any new signals made by one vessel wishing to warn another of her presence, whether she is under way, not under command, or at anchor in a fairway at sea." So you see that we have considered the case of vessels not under command.

Now, with regard to the three long blasts. If that is an appropriate signal to adopt at all, we ought to have adopted it previously, if we acted on principle, before we got into the combination of "short, long, short," or longs and shorts combined. But we thought that the three long blasts might be mistaken for three shorts. We have gone a very long step, we argue, in allowing the two long blasts, and to such an extent that we have altered the word "long" to "prolonged." The Conference have agreed with us in that, so that if you have anything at all you must make it three prolonged blasts.

But there is another point. I do not know whether the members of the Conference have considered the number of signals. The commander has already actually got four signals in his mind. The Conference has already given him three others. Are they prepared to give him the fourth and make it double the number they have at present? We are going very far and very fast. If we are going to give a vessel not under command a distinctive signal, there will be an eighth signal for him to remember. If it is so important that he should have a distinctive signal, I direct attention to what we have already provided in making a signal to attract attention. The Committee considered that he ought to make the same signal as a vessel at anchor in a fairway, and you will remember that we argued that the two prolonged blasts could be joined with the anchor signal. But a vessel not under command will not be at anchor, so on principle they ought not to give that signal. Still, in preference to adding any more sound-signals to be remembered by the officers, I think the Committee would really sooner have the vessel not under command make the same signal as a vessel that was an obstruction in a fairway at sea or at anchor.

Therefore, I think that if this is considered at all, let us consider first of all whether a vessel not under command should have a distinctive signal in a fog. Let us go that far and then consider what the signal shall be. Do not let us consider both points together, because they are two totally different things. All the Conference will see now the number of signals we have given. I should propose now on the part of the Committee that this should be considered—if the gallant Delegate from Germany will accept that—on the principle whether a signal for a vessel not under command, a distinctive signal, should be provided.

Mr. Flood (Norway).—Mr. President, I must say that I am very much of the same opinion as that expressed by Captain Mensing. I will ask permission to read my amendment, or rather my proposal,

[93]

with regard to this paragraph as I have tendered it, and which, perhaps, might meet the views of the Conference. My proposal is this:—

"A vessel under way but not under command, for instance those mentioned in Article 5, may sound on her whistle, siren, or fog-horn, four blasts sounded in quick succession."

That is my idea. I must say that the trouble with these signals does not seem to me to be so much in the way of adopting them, because vessels are not every day in trouble.

It is not a signal that will be in every-day use. It is only in case of distress and when vessels are hampered or in trouble that such precautions have to be taken. I do not think that under those circumstances it would be any trouble for the officers on board to have these signals made in the proper way. The reason I suggested the four short blasts was because it is not only steam-vessels that get into trouble; sailing-vessels also get into trouble. They may be dismasted or partly dismasted. We have cases where vessels break their rudders, or get disabled and have to be given over to the mercy of the sea. Now, since they have to use their fog-horns, and as they have not very good mechanical horns, I thought the short blasts were the best to be used; they are not so easily misunderstood. But I may mention that sea-going vessels, I suppose of every kind, will after awhile be provided with mechanical fog-horns. Then they will have a good chance to sound these four blasts on the fog-horn as well as the steamer on her siren.

I have also noticed what Sir George Nares remarked about the last Article and about the detonating signal to be given; but I think that does not comply exactly with a case of this kind. I am also aware that under Article 27 we have the celebrated minute-gun to be fired, and of course that could be used under certain circumstances; but as I said before, there are generally on merchant-ships and sailing-ships not more than one or two guns, and if you have one or two guns and fire them every minute for an hour or two I think you will find that they will get hot. So I think it would be well to have a special signal for this case. I will wait to see what the Conference will say.

Captain Malmberg (Sweden).—Mr. President, as the principle of the signal to be introduced——

The President.—The Chair would state that the Delegate from Great Britain has proposed the question as to whether there should be a signal or not; after this the discussion will be in order.

Captain Malmberg (Sweden).—Mr. President, it is to that question that I want to call the attention of the Conference. It was stated by the gallant Delegate Sir George Nares that we would have too many paragraphs in Article 12. That is very true. We have already too many proposed, but they are fortunately not all passed. We have not adopted one Rule, the signal in paragraph (e), so that if we accept the signal for ships not under command, we will find that the numbers of the paragraphs to Article 12 are exactly in the same position as those given to us by the Committee on Sound-Signals.

Admiral Nares (Great Britain).—I may say, on the part of the Committee, that we considered all of the proposals that were brought up before us that have been placed before the Conference, and the fact that we have not recommended signals for any special case is because we considered that it was not necessary to give them special signals. There are a great many amendments which we have not approved, but we have not stated here distinctly in our Report that we recommend that such and such signals should not be given. We have left it to be inferred that if we have not proposed a signal we have considered the case, and thought, in fact, that we could not afford to give them a special signal.

Mr. Flood (Norway).—Mr. President, may I be allowed to add one word to what I said when I handed in the amendment to the Chair? I put in the four short blasts because I know the result of the voting to-day. I expected that the proposal made by the Sound-Signal Committee about four blasts used in Article 8 would be passed. If we are going to discuss only the first part of it I am very well satisfied. But I will explain that I proposed the four short blsats because I expected this to pass which has been proposed by the Committee. I am willing to take that which has been proposed by the Committee on Sound-Signals in Article 8, although I think that four blasts in quick succession will be better understood.

Mr. Hall (Great Britain)—Mr. President, we really never shall get to the end of this discussion if the Delegates will not kindly follow the suggestions made that we should first of all determine the question of principle. The Delegate from Norway has addressed us at considerable length to prove the desirablility of four short blasts. Let us try to keep the discussion confined to the question before the Conference, which, I take it, is, first of all: Shall there be a signal at all? It has been argued that because we have given signals for vessels at anchor in a fairway, and have given a signal in other cases, that, therefore, logically, we ought to give signals to vessels not under command and vessels laying telegraph cables. It is very true according to logic; but we have got to deal practically with the case. There have been certain cases cited where it has been thought desirable by the Conference that we should give sound-signals if they could be found. We have done so. We have already added two sound-signals. Does it follow that because we have done that we are to increase the number of sound-signals because there are cases provided for in the Rules in respect to lights?

Now, first of all, is it a very common occurrence? The Delegate from Norway tells us that it is not. It has been said you have passed a Rule for a vessel to say, "I am stopped, you can feel your way past me," which is not half so important as this case. The answer to that is that such a signal was asked for by a great number of sailors. The gallant Delegate from Germany says *No.* He may not have been in the room when my gallent colleague stated the replies to the Board of Trade letters. He did not hear my colleague say that he thought it most desirable that there should be such a signal, and that he travelled a yearly distance of about 70,000 miles, and thought it necessary to have the option of giving such a signal. But what practical sailor is there present who will tell us that he has been hampered at all by the want of a signal for a vessel not under command? If any sailor will tell us his experience, that he has ever had any difficulty, I should be glad to hear it in this Conference. It may be that there have been isolated cases; but not as a matter of general occurrence, or of such frequent occurrence as to justify us to include such a signal in the sound-signals of the Rules of the Road—if that is not the case why should we include it in our Rules? It is an exceptional case. I agree that the best way to deal with it, if it is to be included, would be in the way which has been suggested by the Delegate from the United States, to include it in some other Rule.

But that is the question as to the kind of the signal to be given. First of all it is desirable to decide whether we should give any signal at all. Until we have some ground for thinking that it is desirable and requisite, and as sailors of experience tell us that in their practical experience they have never wanted it, I do not think we ought to give it. I do not think the mere fact of some Delegate having moved an amendment in its favour shows that sailors want it. It only shows that his intelligence has been so accurate and so on the alert that he has provided in his amendment for every possible case which might arise. It does not show that he thinks it desirable or in the interest of navigation, but he is merely pointing out the want which is not supplied by the Rules. But first of all, before we determine in favour of such a signal, let us be satisfied by information that such a signal is really wanted at sea.

Captain Malmberg (Sweden).—Mr. President, I have listened to the argument of the learned Delegate from Great Britain, and I feel inclined to move that the Conference strike out Article 5 altogether.

The President.—Does the Delegate desire to make any motion?

Captain Malmberg (Sweden).—Mr. President, I said, and I repeat it, that, on taking up the reasoning presented by the learned Delegate from Great Britain, as to not introducing fog-signals for vessels not under command, on the very same reasoning I would feel almost obliged to vote that Article 5 should be eliminated from the Regulations altogether.

Mr. Flood (Norway).—Mr. President, I will not go quite so far as my gallant friend from Sweden. I will not move that Article 5 be stricken out.

Admiral Nares (Great Britain).—Mr. President, I have proposed a distinct motion, and I will ask you to rule whether such a proposition as has just been placed before us can be considered on my motion. I want to know whether the proposal to strike out Article 5 can be argued or considered now on my previous motion.

The President.—The Chair decides that it cannot be. It will come up at a different period of the session if the Delegate wishes to make a motion at another time. The question before the Conference is the consideration of the principle as to whether the Conference wishes to adopt a signal for a vessel not under command.

Mr. Flood (Norway).—Mr. President, may I not be allowed to make one further remark with regard to what was said by the learned Delegate from Great Britain, which relates exactly to that matter? I thought I had the right to bring my opinion before the Conference. It differs a little from what has been stated by the Delegate from Great Britain. It is only a couple of words. May I say it?

The President.—Yes, Sir.

Mr. Flood (Norway).—Mr. President, it is pointed out that this is rather a rare occurrence, and for that reason it is not adopted. We have lately adopted signals for a still more rare occurrence. We have adopted a special signal for one sailing-vessel towing another. Now when we find it necessary to adopt a Rule for that, I do not see why we should not feel it to be necessary to adopt a Rule in this case, which is not of such rare occurrence, but which happens very often. I again ask my colleagues in this Conference to back me up or to contradict me when I say that it happens very often that vessels are disabled at sea and are not exactly under command. But when they are in the open sea they are just as liable to get into a fog as any other vessel. Is it not necessary in conformity with Article 5, which provides for them in clear weather, to also provide for them during a fog?

Captain Mensing (Germany).—Mr. President, I believe that there are at least twenty steamers a year which put into the port of New York with disabled machinery. If they put in there it is a necessity that they meet a fog on the outside. I was very glad to hear the learned Delegate from Great Britain say that my proposition was at least true to logic, and that the only fault he had to find with it was that it was not practical. It has already been pointed out that one signal has been proposed by the Committee which has not been adopted, so that by this we do not propose any other signal except the same number which the Sound-Signal Committee have proposed. I see that the distinguished Chairman shakes his head. But if I leave out (*e*) this will be (*i*). If I add one and then substract one to a number, I believe that the original number remains the same; indeed, I would like to have it explained if it is different.

Now, we do not propose, as the distinguished member from Great Britain supposed, to extend this number of signals indefinitely. We bring here one distinct proposition, and we point to the fact that under Article 5 (*d*) the Rule is laid down that other vessels have got to get out of the way of such vessels; I cannot construe that Rule in any other way. If that is the case, if we do not provide for this signal I think that we shall not be doing our whole duty. The distinguished Chairman of the Sound-Signal Committee has explained to us that there were reasons in the Sound-Signal Committee why they had not discussed this; I should be very glad to hear them. So far I have not heard a single one of them, nor have I seen a word alluding to them in the Report, except casually to a proposition which has been handed in by the gallant Delegate from the Netherlands. In the 41st amendment he says: "A steam-ship which from any accident is not under command, but making way through the water, shall sound at intervals of not more than one minute two prolonged blasts in succession, with an interval of about one second between them."

Now, here was an amendment proposed. I ask where is the answer that the Sound-Signal Committee ought to have given to this very plain question? I have not heard it so far. I should be very glad to be informed if there are any reasons. It has been stated several times that the answer was given by the Board of Trade Report. I do not think so. In the Board of Trade Report the question was put whether the signal was necessary. I think I have been fully aware of all that has

[93]

fallen from the distinguished gentlemen the members of the British Delegation, and I hope that I have not been remiss in any way or inattentive to what they have said.

Admiral Nares (Great Britain).—Mr. President, first of all, about the number of signals. There are already, as I said before, four signals well known to all seamen. One of these is in the Morse Code, three short blasts, "I am going full speed astern." But that signal, at present, can only be made when one vessel is in sight of the other. The Fog-Signal Committee considered that it might be advisable and that the signal would be very useful if made when one vessel could not see the other. All that we have done in paragraph (*e*) is to shift out an old well-known signal, keep its character and keep its wording, and only make it apply when the vessels could not see each other. The Conference has thought differently about that, and has stricken out paragraph (*e*). Consequently it does not alter the number of signals. The signal is still in existence and still made every day. So far as the number of signals goes they remain the same.

Now, as far as regards the steam-ship which from any accident is not under command but making way through the water, which is mentioned in the 41st amendment. Very well; there you are in motion. Now, if you are making way through the water, why should you not make your long blast? So we considered that instead of giving some special signal you had better keep the old signal if you are making your way through the water. If you are not making your way through the water then you come under Article 12 (*b*), a steam-vessel not at anchor, but stopped, and having no way upon her, and you should sound at intervals of not more than two minutes two such prolonged blasts. Surely a vessel which is not in motion can make one of these two signals. If she has way upon her let her make a long blast; if not, let her make two blasts. The Committee considered this 41st amendment, and that was the conclusion to which we came.

Captain Malmberg (Sweden).—Mr. President, I only want to ask for information what signal a sailing-vessel is to make. That paragraph says steamers; but it does not say anything at all about sailing-vessels not being under command.

Admiral Nares (Great Britain).—Mr. President, there has been no amendment to that effect placed before us. That is a blot, I own. I admit it. But if the Conference considers this to be a blot, let them vote upon the question of principle which is before them. If it is adopted, the signal must be chosen for all vessels not under command, sailing-ships as well as steam-ships. If the Conference adopts the principle, I will help them and give them the signal if we can. But at the same time, speaking as Chairman of the Committee, I will say that we have not thought it necessary to provide for that case.

Captain Shackford (United States).—Mr. President, I would like to ask when a sailing-vessel is not under command.

Captain Malmberg (Sweden).—When she is laying or picking up a telegraph cable.

Captain Shackford (United States).—You do not use sailing-vessels for picking up telegraph cables. I should think that a sailing-ship was not under command only when she was dismasted, and then she would be in distress.

Admiral Nares (Great Britain).—Mr. President, just one word more. As to the telegraph-laying ships, that was considered. But a ship laying a telegraph cable is going at a good speed. If she is going at a good speed, why should she not make a blast? She is practically under command.

The President.—Is the Conference ready for the question? The Secretary will please read the proposition of the Delegate from Great Britain.

The proposition is as follows:—

"Shall a vessel not under command, or a vessel laying or picking up a telegraph cable, be given a distinctive fog-signal?"

Admiral Nares (Great Britain).—Mr. President, may that be read again?
The proposition is as follows:—

"Shall a vessel not under command, or a vessel laying or picking up a telegreph cable, be given a distinctive fog-signal?"

Mr. Flood (Norway).—Mr. President, I have put before the Conference an amendment, which has been delivered to the Chair in writing. I would ask if that could not be just as well voted on in principle.

The President.—Your amendment proposes a signal, and the question is whether a signal shall be adopted or not.

Mr. Flood (Norway).—Mr. President, we can put the question on the first part of it.

The President.—The motion of the Delegate from Great Britain is upon the principle as to whether there shall be a signal.

Mr. Flood (Norway).—Mr. President, I only wish the vote to be taken on the principle. It makes no difference to me how the vote is taken.

The President.—The Secretary will read again the proposition of the Delegate from Great Britain, which, I think, is about the same as the proposition of the Delegate from Norway.

Admiral Nares (Great Britain).—Mr. President, the wording of this proposition was as a test vote. I have spoken very strongly against it, both as Chairman of the Committee and personally; but I thought it was well to put the question as a test vote and as an affirmative vote. I think the Conference got into trouble yesterday by putting a negative vote. I think it is worded very properly as an affirmative test vote.

Mr. Flood (Norway).—Mr. President, I have no objection to what is proposed by the gallant Delegate from Great Britain. But I desire to say that, practically, before I reject a dish I always like to taste it, and so why not read my amendment and see if it is objectionable before we go to a vote?

The President.—If there be no objection, it will be read for the information of the Conference; but the vote will be taken upon the proposition of the Delegate from Great Britain.

The proposition of the Delegate from Norway is as follows:—

"A vessel not under command—for instance, those mentioned in Article 5, paragraphs (*a*) and (*b*)—may sound on her whistle, siren, or fog-horn——"

Admiral Nares (Great Britain).—Mr. President, that is not my motion at all. I think that will do to get a vote on, but it is not my motion. I had nothing to do with that.

The President.—The Chair understands that. It is the proposition of the Delegate from Norway. The first part of it is to be read.

The Secretary.—That is the first part of it. The second part of it is: "four blasts, sounded in quick succession."

The President.—The question is upon the proposition of the Delegate from Great Britain.

Captain Mensing (Germany).—Mr. President, I wish that that could be read over again. I must say that I have not heard this before. I do not know whether it differs in intention from the amendment which I handed in. I know that I had it in writing here this morning when the learned Delegate from Norway spoke of the principle, and I handed it in to shorten matters. If there is any difference in principle I would like to hear it read.

The President.—The Chair understood that the Delegate from Germany had accepted the proposition of the Delegate from Great Britain, to vote upon the principle as to whether there should be a signal.

Captain Mensing (Germany).—Mr. President, I have adopted the proposition of Sir George Nares, but that is not the one which has just been read.

The President.—The proposition of the Delegate from Great Britain will be read again.

The proposition is as follows:—

"Shall a vessel not under command, or a vessel laying and picking up a telegraph cable, be given a distinctive fog-signal?

Mr. Carter (Hawaii).—Mr. President, I want to point out that because a vessel has a light-signal it is not necessary that she should have a fog-signal. You can multiply your light-signals by the colours, but you cannot multiply your fog-signals without running into danger. We have adopted additional signals to-day, and if we adopt to-morrow another, and another, and another, we will find ourselves resolved into a school for establishing an alphabet.

Captain Richard (France).—Mr. President, most assuredly the statement of the learned Delegate from Hawaii is absolutely true, but his remarks should have been made before the Conference took up the propositions of the Sound-Signals Committee. Those propositions have been almost wholly adopted. The Committee then knew very well that it had at its disposal but a very limited number of signals, and it has lavished them in cases of doubtful utility; and now, after having scattered about these signals with a liberal hand, is it right to say that there are no more left to meet pressing needs? If more urgent cases have been examined the reasoning would have held good, but can it be now said, "It is too late; we can do nothing more; we are powerless?"

Now, let me mention some other objections which require to be answered. It has been said that the sound-signals proposed by the Committee were demanded by a great number of sailors, whereas no sailor has asked anything for vessels which are not under command or for the vessel laying a telegraph cable—is that true? Why have you, in Article 5 of the Rules of the Road, given special lights to those vessels? The entire maritime world has therefore admitted the necessity of a distinction for those vessels. Believe me, that was done only because it was indispensable. But now we are told that no one has asked anything for those vessels in a fog. Is it necessary that we should be guided solely by the demands which are addressed to the Conference, and should we only take them into consideration? Is it, therefore, necessary for sailors to come and tell us what cases we are to provide for, and must we omit to consider all subjects in regard to which no demand has been addressed to us?

We are an assembly wherein seafaring men are largely represented by experts and men of technical knowledge, who must know themselves what is proper and right. Who better than ourselves can judge whether vessels which are not under command, or which are laying a telegraph cable, should or should not receive the special provisions already sanctioned by Article 5? A vessel laying a telegraph cable, between England and New York, for example, can neither reduce her speed nor stop. Should she cut the cable which she is laying the moment she enters a fog? I do not think she should. She will continue on her course at the speed which is necessary to her. She will go at least 6, 7, or 8 knots, to be enabled to properly pay out the cable on the ocean's bottom, without making any twists in the cable and without being obliged to pay out more cable than is necessary. When the cable vessel is on the course of another vessel she is an actual danger to the latter, which should be notified. When the sound-signal of the cable ship is heard from its furthest distance, the best thing to do is get out of her way until all perception of the sound is lost.

You have adopted the proposition to give signals to a vessel anchored in a fairway, to a vessel which is being towed, to a vessel which wishes to indicate that she will stop; and now you find that besides those cases there are a certain number of other cases which not only have a great deal of merit, but which are still more worthy of attention. Those vessels, as well as others, require a distinction, a special sound-signal. By straying from the originally simple provisions of Article 12, in order to obtain the signals of paragraphs (*d*), (*e*), and (*f*), you have been obliged to go beyond the simple signals formerly in use. You have made new ones, and now you are obliged to find more, and you come and tell us: "We have exhausted all there are; our pockets are empty; we have nothing more to give."

The gallant Admiral Sir George Nares evidently feels where the difficulty lies. I know as well as he does that it is very difficult to give suitable and proper special signals for the cases which I have mentioned. It seems to me that, so far as the principle is concerned, we must all agree in saying that if we increase the number of sound-signals introduced or inserted in the Rules of the Road at Sea, we should first endeavour to find a special signal for vessels which are not under command, or which are laying telegraph cables and cannot stop. What! We are going to give a special signal to the vessel which has stopped, and we do not give any to the vessel which does not know where she is going, whose rudder is broken, perhaps, and which in certain cases may drift about without control, the toy of the sea and the winds. To be logical we should above all indicate the presence of a vessel which is not under command.

I will add but one word in regard to vessels which are laying telegraph cables. International Treaties have been made providing for these vessels. By those Treaties, if I am not mistaken, it has been endeavoured to keep away at a considerable distance from a vessel which lays a cable all the vessels which are in the same region; which goes to show how solicitous Governments are to favour the operations of such vessels. Can it be supposed that the Contracting Powers will favourably look upon any measure which does not protect those vessels, as well as certain other classes of vessels?

Lieutenant Beaugency (Chile).—Mr. President, before the vote is taken I would like to say a few words, as a young officer. The learned Delegates from Great Britain and Hawaii have pointed out the very great difficulty of having so many signals. I think that if the Conference adopts this one that the officer on duty will be obliged to tell the captain that the ship is in a fog, and make the signal for that situation. If he does not remember it at the first moment, he can take the book and see what the signal is. It is not a difficult matter, because the officer or captain is not obliged to put the Rule into operation at the first moment, as with regard to the other Rules of the Road.

The President.—The Secretary will now read the proposition of the Delegate from Great Britain.

The proposition is as follows:—

"Shall a vessel not under command, or a vessel laying or picking up a telegraph cable, be given a distinctive fog-signal?"

The President.—Is the Conference ready for the question?
The question was put to the Conference upon the above proposition.
The President.—The Chair is unable to decide.
Mr. Goodrich (United States).—I call for the Yeas and Nays.
The Yea and Nay vote is as follows:—

Austria-Hungary .. .. Nay.	Great Britain .. .. Yea.
Belgium .. .. .. Yea.	Hawaii .. .. .. Nay.
China .. .. .. Nay.	Italy .. .. .. Yea.
Chile .. .. .. Yea.	Japan .. .. .. Yea.
Denmark .. .. .. Nay.	Mexico .. .. .. Yea.
France .. .. .. Yea.	Norway .. .. .. Yea.
Germany .. .. .. Yea.		

Admiral Nares (Great Britain).—Mr. President, I rise to a point of order. There is some mistake here. There are gentlemen saying Yea who do not wish any signal.
Captain Settembrini (Italy).—And I am one.
The President.—The proposition has been read several times.
Captain Settembrini (Italy).—I answer, No.
Admiral Nares (Great Britain).—Mr. President, I am sure there are others voting wrong.
The President.—If the Delegate desires, it will be read again and the vote taken over again.
Admiral Nares (Great Britain).—Mr. President, yes, Sir; I wish it clearly understood that those who vote *Yea* are voting for the signal, and those who vote *No* are voting for the present signals which the Sound-Signal Committee have proposed as sufficient.
The President.—The proposition will be read again.
The proposition is as follows:—

"Shall a vessel not under command, or a vessel laying or picking up a telegraph cable, be given a distinctive fog-signal?"

The Yea and Nay vote upon the above proposition is as follows:—

Austria-Hungary .. .. Nay.	Japan .. .. .. Yea.
Belgium .. .. .. Yea.	Mexico .. .. .. Yea.
China .. .. .. Nay.	Norway .. .. .. Yea.
Chile .. .. .. Yea.	Russia .. .. .. Yea.
Denmark .. .. .. Yea.	Spain .. .. .. Yea.
France .. .. .. Yea.	Sweden .. .. .. Yea.
Germany .. .. .. Yea.	Siam .. .. .. Yea.
Great Britain .. .. Yea.	The Netherlands .. .. Yea.
Hawaii .. .. .. Nay.	United States .. .. Yea.
Italy .. .. .. Nay.	

The President.—Fifteen have voted in the affirmative, and four in the negative; so the question is decided in the affirmative.

Mr. Hall (Great Britain).—Mr. President, perhaps I may say that we have voted with the Yeas in the hope that one of the existing signals will be found to include this class of vessels. We quite see the logic of providing, if possible, for vessels not under command, but we are very much opposed to extending the number of signals. It was only because we felt that if we voted *Nay* on that proposition and the Nays carried it, then it would be impossible to utilize one of the existing signals for such a case; we therefore voted *Yea*; but in so doing we are not in favour of extending the number of signals. We hope the case may be provided for by one of the existing signals.

Captain Mensing (Germany).—Mr. President, I should be very glad if that could be possible. We already have the opinion of Sir George Nares that he would very likely be able to find a signal for us. I should, therefore, like to propose that this matter be referred back to the Committee on Sound-Signals. I do this not merely to get another signal, but because I think that it is a very good idea to try, if possible, to bring it in under one of the other signals, as the learned Delegate from Great Britain proposes. It could not be done with the reading as we have it now.

Captain Malmberg (Sweden).—Mr. President, could we not get it in under that unfortunate paragraph (*f*).

Mr. Goodrich (United States).—Mr. President, I make the following proposition or amendment: To insert in paragraph (*d*) of Article 12, after the words "at anchor," in the second line, the words, "or when disabled or not under command, or laying or picking up a telegraph cable." That does not multiply the signals.

Admiral Nares (Great Britain).—Mr. President, may I rise, as a member who has given very close study to this thing, and ask the learned Delegate from the United States to withdraw his motion? Do not suddenly force upon us the consideration of any special signal. That has been very closely considered. You are laying down a greater labour not only on the Committee, but on the whole Conference. We must have time to consider this. We are asked for a signal for a vessel not under command and a vessel laying a telegraph cable. It strikes me at once that we will be in a difficulty as to what to do for the much more common occurrence of a vessel hove-to, and there are two or three other cases of much more frequent occurrence than this of vessels not under command. You have opened the doors, and it will require much consideration.

Mr. Goodrich (United States).—Mr. President, upon the able and pathetic appeal of my gallant friend, which touched my heart, I will withdraw my motion, and move that the subject of selecting a signal be referred to the Committee to report.

Admiral Nares (Great Britain).—Mr. President, the Committee have reported against it. The Committee have reported decidedly upon the matter not to have a signal for a vessel not under command. The position that we are in now is that we have had eight hours' working at the signals which we have put before you. Now you ask us for two more. We have only put three before you, and now you are asking us for two more.

Mr. Goodrich (United States).—Mr. President, we are like Oliver Twist, demanding more. I make my motion refer to the subject of selecting a signal for this particular case.

Captain Mensing (Germany).—Mr. President, I think that in my amendment there is but one signal provided for telegraph ships and for vessels not under command. I think that under Article 5 (*d*) these two classes of ships have been classed together, and that one signal will do for them both. It would be wrong to introduce two signals on this account.

Admiral Nares (Great Britain).—Mr. President, I will point out that a vessel not under command is very nearly stationary, and a vessel laying a telegraph cable is going at a very considerable speed.

The President.—It is very evident that this discussion will not end this evening, and as the time for adjournment has arrived, I desire to give the floor to the Delegate of the United States.

Mr. Goodrich (United States).—Mr. President, I would ask whether the Delegates are willing to sit a few minutes longer to decide the simple question of this reference, because if you put it in the hands of the Committee it will enable them possibly to report in the morning.

Admiral Nares (Great Britain).—Mr. President, I only hope that we are to be left clean-handed in any reference that is sent to us. Do not require us to give one signal to both classes of vessels until we have considered the matter ourselves.

Mr. Goodrich (United States).—Would the Chairman of that Committee prefer that the subject of reference should not proceed this afternoon?

Admiral Nares (Great Britain).—No, Sir; it seems to be the general opinion of the Conference that we should undertake this duty, and we will do our best, but in doing so what we request is that you shall not tie our hands. Give us the significations which you want, and leave it to us to find the signals, whether it be one or a half-a-dozen.

Mr. Goodrich (United States).—Mr. President, I move that the subject which has been under discussion, that of the signals for the two classes of vessels stated, be referred to the Sound-Signal Committee to select a signal or signals as they see fit.

The President.—It is moved that the matter of obtaining a signal or signals for vessels not under command and vessels laying telegraph cables be referred to the Committee on Sound-Signals for report.

The question upon the above motion was put to the Conference, and carried.

Mr. Goodrich (United States).—Mr. President, I propose that without any motion the Conference adjourn until to-morrow morning.

The Conference thereupon adjourned until Thursday, December 5, at 11 o'clock A.M.

78

Washington, Thursday, December 5, 1889, 11 o'clock A.M.

THE Conference was called to order at 11 o'clock A.M., Rear-Admiral Franklin in the chair.

Admiral Nares (Great Britain).—Mr. President, at the latter part of the session of yesterday the Conference decided to refer to the Sound-Signal Committee the question of considering the characters for two new fog-signals, one to meet the case of a vessel not under command, and the other to meet the case of a telegraph-vessel laying or picking up a cable. The Committee have met and considered these two subjects. They are quite prepared now to advise the Conference what they consider to be the best characters; but we put it to you whether the subject should be discussed at once, while it is fresh in the memory of each of the Delegates, or whether our signal should be printed and wait two or three days before they are discussed. We thought that as the Conference had, I may say, demanded the characters for the special signals, there would not be very much trouble in placing our reasons for adopting the course we have adopted before the Conference at once, and we will be quite prepared to meet any proposals which are placed before us by the other Delegates. So, if the Conference are agreed, we are quite prepared now to put before you the characters which we have been asked for.

The President.—If there be no objection the Conference will consider the subject now.

Admiral Nares (Great Britain).—Mr. President, the Committee have been asked for two signals, one for a vessel not under command, and the other for a vessel laying or picking up a telegraph cable. Now, one is practically unable to get out of the way of an approaching vessel, and the other may be going with some speed through the water. They are not at all in the same position. We, therefore, thought that a single character would not be appropriate for the two ships, and that it would be more advisable for the approaching ship to know decidedly whether the vessel was not under command and whether he must keep out of her way, or whether she was in the position of a telegraph-ship. So we have to consider two characters.

In our former Report we have said that it was immaterial when an approaching vessel finds in her course another vessel not under command, whether that vessel was stationary or whether that vessel was at anchor; and we are quite right about that on principle. But the reason why we have not adopted the same signal now is this: A vessel at anchor in a fairway may be at anchor, and she often is, in a very strong tideway, and, therefore, it would not be a good thing to give that vessel the same signal as to a vessel not attached to the ground and drifting through the water. So we considered that the signal in (*f*) is not appropriate for either of these two cases.

We also considered that in Article 12 (*b*) the two prolonged blasts for vessels stopped and having no way upon them would not be appropriate. That signal will practically be given in this way: there will be two steamers meeting, and we have told them that they should stop, because all of this is in a fog. The two vessels will be stopped, and will want to give their two blasts, that is, two prolonged blasts; and that will be as much as to say, "Yes, I am stopped; I am an impediment in your way; but, at the same time, I can take care of myself, and at the proper time I can come on; in fact, I am only stopped temporarily." So that will not do for a vessel not under command. So, practically, we have got to give two new signals. Now, what shall they be? First, consider the vessel not under command. We mention in our Report that in the London river a vessel which is not able to manœuvre is required by these Regulations to give four short blasts. A vessel not under command is in precisely the same position. She is not able to manœuvre according to the Regulations. These four short blasts are known to a great number of mariners already. They have been very successful, and they will be easily remembered.

We venture to put it to the Conference that in all cases when a vessel under way is unable to get out of the way of an approaching vessel, that she shall sound these four blasts. But we do not intend to have this music continually. We intend that a vessel not under command should make her ordinary signals, which are well known, and that when she hears the fog-signal of an approaching vessel then she must give her distinctive signal, and that distinctive signal will be four short blasts. Four prolonged blasts are deafening, and it takes a long time to make them. The four short blasts is a signal which has been introduced in the London river, and it is a successful signal, and it is already pretty well known. We do not think it is necessary to include it in the wording of this Article, but this would practically include also a vessel becalmed or stationary, because she is unable to get out of the way of an approaching vessel. Whether our actual wording, as seamen, would be adopted by the gentlemen here who are to help us from the Courts we do not know; but we will place the wording before you as it comes from us as seamen. The wording is:—

"A ship under way which is unable to get out of the way of an approaching vessel through not being under command, or unable to manœuvre as required by these Regulations, shall, on hearing the fog-signal of an approaching vessel, sound on her whistle, siren, or fog-horn four short blasts."

We shall have to argue both signals separately, and I think it will be preferable to let the Conference know at once the whole rhythm of signals which will be before them, because presently, when we argue them, they ought to know what the other signal is. Practically, the not-under-command signal is four short blasts, and in that we include every case of vessels unable to manœuvre as required by these Regulations. If we have not worded it well, that at least is our intention.

Now we come to the telegraph-cable ship, and we think that the signal proposed by the gallant Delegate from Germany is a very appropriate one. It is rather against the principle we have argued, but practically we are put in this position. Since we argued the principle we have distinctly adopted two long blasts, and called them "prolonged blasts," and we have said that they should be from four to six seconds' duration; in fact, to prevent two prolonged blasts from being mistaken for the helm-signal of two short blasts. The Conference have already decided that we can adopt two short and two long, and that the two long are to be decidedly two prolonged blasts.

Now, the Conference having decided that, we think they can go a step further, although we have got three short blasts to indicate a steamer going full speed astern; that, of course, is not to be made in a fog. That is when two vessels are in sight of each other. But still one ship may be in sight of her and another ship may be in the fog, and so the three short blasts might be mistaken. It will be for the Conference to decide that question. If we can arrange to choose this prolonged blast, I think the whole rhythm is very simple. So we propose that a telegraph-cable ship shall give three prolonged blasts. In the same way as the not-under-command signal, a telegraph-vessel laying her telegraph cable would be practically sounding her single blasts. When another vessel is approaching her and she wants to declare her character, she gives three prolonged blasts. In the Committee it was considered if the three long blasts can possibly be mistaken for three short—of course there is a danger comes in there—but if the Conference thinks it cannot, then we propose to have three prolonged blasts. First of all, let her give her one long blast, that is a steamer under way, and follow it in a little while by two. I must say that a majority of the Committee think that now that you have adopted two blasts you may go a step further and take three prolonged blasts.

Now, we will go through for a moment the whole rhythm of signals which we have proposed. We have the one prolonged blast for a steamer moving. The Conference has adopted two prolonged blasts for the steamer stopped; she is an impediment in the way. Now, we tell you there is another impediment in your way, and a little worse impediment, and that she shall give three prolonged blasts; and then there is another man who demands the right of way. Then he gives you four short blasts, and you must get out of his way under all circumstances, if he demands it. So that, in principle, all blasts over one give you practically a vessel which you have to be careful about.

We think these signals will be easier remembered if they are in a sequence of this kind, and we have tried to introduce them in that way. Another reason why this signal may be easier remembered is that by adopting the three prolonged blasts we are giving a telegraph-ship the same number of blasts as she has lights. She has her three lights, and now she will have her three blasts. These are the steps which we have considered in Committee, and these are the signals which we have brought before you.

Mr. Goodrich (United States).—Mr. President, may I call the attention of the gallant Delegate from Great Britain to the fact that they have not indicated how often the signals are to be sounded? Do they desire to do that?

Admiral Nares (Great Britain).—Mr. President, it is distinctly worded. The wording is that o hearing the fog-signal of an approaching vessel—the approaching vessel would be sounding her signal every two minutes—and every time that signal is heard by a telegraph-ship or a vessel not under command, she is to give her distinctive signals. We do not wish these signals to be given oftener than can be avoided. The three prolonged blasts on the telegraph-ship will be a very severe tax on the officers on the bridge, and the fewer times it is sounded, so long as it is sounded often enough to give the warning, the better.

Mr. Goodrich (United States).—Mr. President, then I would suggest, after the word "sound," to insert the words, "in answer to each signal."

Admiral Nares (Great Britain).—Mr. President, of course that is all a mere matter of wording. We have worded it as seamen. The wording is not before the Conference yet. If the Secretary will read it, then perhaps you will arrange about that business afterwards. We were asked for two signals, and we have given them. Now we are in the hands of the Conference.

The President.—It will first be read for the information of the Conference.
The proposition is as follows:—

"A ship under way which is unable to get out of the way of an approaching vessel, through being not under command, or unable to manœuvre as required by these Regulations, shall, on hearing the fog-signal of an approaching vessel, sound on her whistle, siren, or fog-horn four short blasts."

Captain Richard (France).—Mr. President, it is evident to my mind that the subject in regard to which I am about to ask the gallant Chairman of the Sound-Signal Committee has been a matter of careful consideration in the Committee. I am not, therefore, offering any criticism; I am only asking for information, so that the Conference may be enlightened on the subject to which my attention is directed.

It has been demanded that vessels charged with the telegraphic service and with paying out their cables, or vessels no longer under command, should not sound their special signal until they should hear the vessel approaching them. I must say that this rather astonishes me, and for that reason 1 ask for an explanation. You will please observe that if they sound the special signal which has been given to them only when they shall hear a vessel in their vicinity, there may be some difficulty, for instance, in the case of a sailing-vessel which at the present time carries a sounding apparatus which cannot be heard very far; you allow them to give the special signal only when the vessels are very near to each other, and when a sailing-vessel cannot manœuvre. I think that the notice is then given at the eleventh hour, and inasmuch as those vessels have the privilege of using special sound-signals, they should be given the burden as well as the advantage of it. It is evident that the Committee has carefully discussed this question in its sessions. The explanation which I now ask is a résumé of that discussion and of the powerful motives which induced them to arrive at their decision.

The President.—Is the Conference ready for the question upon the first proposition of the Delegate from Great Britain?

Admiral Nares (Great Britain).—Mr. President, I intended to explain about not continually sounding the signal. It is far too great a tax on the officers of the watch; and if the signals are sounded too often and too much the officers cannot listen to the signals of the approaching ship; but it is far more important for them to be sure that another vessel is in that vicinity, or it is quite as important as for them to be sounding their own signal. But if there is no other way out of it than to jump from their first signal to the other character signal, I would like to suggest that we cannot see our way out of the difficulty. It is very certain that either they must keep on sounding them every two minutes, or we cannot give them the character at all.

Mr. Flood (Norway).—Mr. President, as the one who yesterday took the liberty of proposing a new paragraph to be added to the Rule, I beg to state that I am fully satisfied with what has been so ably said and explained by the gallant Delegate from Great Britain. I fully understand the difficulty of having a sound-signal of four short blasts continually repeated on board of a vessel, and the great tax it will be on the officers who have to stand in the continual sounding of the siren. So I think that the provision made use of, that this signal is only to be used when they hear an approaching vessel, will be practically satisfactory. It is just as necessary for the officers on the bridge to be able to hear a signal, as for the other vessel approaching to hear their signal. The officers on the bridge and the man on the look-out would be so deafened by hearing their own signal that it would make it very difficult to hear the signal of an approaching vessel.

The President.—Is the Conference ready for the question? The Secretary will please read the first proposition of the Delegate from Great Britain.

The first proposition of the Delegate from Great Britain is as follows:—

" A ship under way which is unable to get out of the way of an approaching vessel, through being not under command, or unable to manœuvre as required by these Regulations, shall, on hearing the fog-signal of an approaching vessel, sound on her whistle, siren, or fog-horn four short blasts."

Mr. Goodrich (United States).—Mr. President, it seems to me that, in accordance with the suggestion which I made, we had better make an altetation in this Rule. The first alteration would be, as a matter of course, in the first line, to use the words " a vessel." I would say in the last part of the proposition: " shall, upon hearing the fog-horn of an approaching vessel, answer on her whistle," &c. That will indicate that it is only to be an answer to each signal received from the approaching vessel. Is that satisfactory to the gallant Delegate from Great Britain?

The President.—Does the Delegate from Great Britain accept that suggestion?

Mr. Hall (Great Britain).—Mr. President, if the Chair will give my gallant colleague a few moments to consult with the gentlemen who have considered this matter very thoroughly, he will be able to give us their opinions.

Mr. Goodrich (United States).—Mr. President, Captain Sampson suggests that it should be read " sound in answer."

Captain Mensing (Germany.)—Mr. President, may I remark that if there are different persons around there and he had to answer every person, it would, perhaps, lead too far?

Admiral Nares (Great Britain).—Mr. President, on behalf of the Committee, as I said before, we have found the character, and we will leave it to the other gentlemen at the board to find the wording.

Mr. Goodrich (United States).—Mr. President, let me suggest to the gallant Delegate that the Collocation Committee would like to make as few alterations as possible, and if the Conference can adopt the language of the Rule, we would like to have it done. We shall have enough alterations to make which will provoke discussion.

Admiral Nares (Great Britain).—I can answer for myself, and I am sure the Sound-Signal Committee may be taken to agree with me unless any of the gentlemen get up and say they do not.

Captain Shackford (United States).—Mr. President, I would accept the words although I do not see the necessity for them.

Captain Malmberg (Sweden).—Mr. President, I do not see the necessity for introducing them. I do not think it would make the Rule any better by introducing those words; on the contrary, I think the Rule is better as it is.

Admiral Nares (Great Britain).—Mr. President, I may say, as I said twice before, that the Sound-Signal Committee are not prepared to take the full responsibility of every word. I said that we were asked for the characters of the signals, and we are responsible for them in advising the Conference; but we are not responsible for the wording, and we should be very glad of the assistance of any gentleman who can help us.

Mr. Goodrich (United States).—Mr. President, I have heard ungodly laymen say that lawyers would split hairs in Court. If you leave it as it is now, the requisition of the Rule is that, upon the giving of a single whistle, or a single response to the first whistle that is sounded by an approaching vessel, you comply with the Rule. Now, make it perfectly clear that that is not what you mean. If you mean that every time the approaching vessel sounds her whistle the vessel not under command must answer with the whistle, then say so, and make it read, " in answer to the signal from an approaching vessel in a fog." Then you have carried out the meaning of the Rule.

Mr. Hall (Great Britain).—Mr. President, I confess that I think this suggestion is a desirable one, simply for the reason which the learned Delegate from the United States has given—that unless these words were put in, a vessel would be complying with the Rule if she merely sounds that signal once. At present there is nothing put into the Rules to show how often she is to sound it. I am sure the gallant Delegate from Sweden will see that this is so.

The President.—Does the Delegate from the United States desire to offer that as an amendment?

Mr. Goodrich (United States).—I offer it as an amendment.

The President.—Does the Delegate from Great Britain accept it? If there be no objection to it, by general consent, it will be considered as accepted. Therefore, the vote will be upon the proposition as amended.

Mr. Verney (Siam).—Mr. President, may I ask whether the learned Delegate from the United States means this—that however often within a couple of minutes he hears these signals he is to reply to them?

Mr. Goodrich.—(United States).—Yes, Sir.

Mr. Verney (Siam).—Suppose she hears them six times in two minutes? Suppose there are four or five vessels there manœuvring at a time?

Mr. Goodrich (United States).—We must sound an answer every time.

Captain Shackford (United States).—Mr. President, we have heard a great deal about the poor sailors. I think somebody had better get up and say something about the poor masters.

Mr. Goodrich (United States).—This puts the Courts on the same plane as the masters.

The President.—Is the Conference ready for the question? It will be read again for the information of the Conference, with the amendment as accepted.

The proposition as amended is as follows :—

"A ship under way which is unable to get out of the way of an approaching vessel, through being not under command, or unable to manœuvre as required by these Regulations, shall, on hearing the fog-signal of an approaching vessel, sound in answer, on her whistle, siren, or fog-horn, four short blasts."

The President.—Is the Conference ready for the question?

The question was put to the Conference upon the adoption of the proposition of the Delegate from Great Britain as amended, and it was carried.

The President.—The second proposition of the Delegate from Great Britain will now be read.

The proposition of the Delegate from Great Britain is as follows :—

"A ship employed in laying or picking up a telegraph cable shall, on approaching or on being approached by another vessel, sound on her whistle, siren, or fog-horn three prolonged blasts."

Admiral Nares (Great Britain).—Mr. President, it would follow that the same wording will have to be adopted in that section, "shall sound in answer."

The President.—The same wording will be adopted in the second proposition. The second proposition is before the Conference. It will be read before the vote is taken.

Admiral Nares (Great Britain).—Mr. President, it may be necessary, after what was said just now, to state whether these blasts should be in succession, or whether they should be separate. We would word it, "three prolonged blasts in succession." That follows the wording of the other sections previous to this.

Mr. Goodrich (United States).—Mr. President, that is just what I was looking for.

Admiral Nares (Great Britain).—If you will look at section (*c*), where the sailing-vessel comes in, it says : "two blasts in succession, three blasts in succession." It is to be quite certain that they are to follow each other at equal intervals.

The President.—If there be no objection, the words "in succession" will be inserted, and the paragraph will be read before the vote is taken.

The proposition is as follows :—

"A ship employed in laying or in picking up a telegraph cable shall, on the approach of or on being approached by another vessel, sound in answer, on her whistle, siren, or fog-horn, three prolonged blasts in succession."

Admiral Kaznakoff (Russia).—Mr. President, I understand that the ship which is not under command, or the telegraph ship, when she does hear the sound of an approaching vessel, must use her usual fog-signals. That should be plainly set forth in the Rule.

Admiral Nares (Great Britain).—Mr. President, we considered that very closely. You see that if we introduce it here, unless it is carefully guarded from this character, you get a confusion of blasts, so that nobody will know what is happening. Take an illustration. These ships are generally steamers. It is very seldom that you have a sailing-ship laying or picking up a telegraph cable. It is a steamer moving, but when she is picking up the cable she is practically stationary. Then, I suppose, any captain of ordinary caution, if she is stationary, will be blowing two blasts, and if she is moving he will be blowing one blast. We did not think it was our place to consider that. We have specially to find the signal for a telegraph-cable ship. To us, although we were seamen, it followed as a necessity that this would be a separate signal. The sounding of a special signal is required when he hears a vessel approaching her. On all other occasions the ordinary signal should be sounded.

Mr. Goodrich (United States).—Mr. President, may I call the attention of the gallant Delegate to a fact which is suggested by Captain Sampson, that the words "in answer" are improperly placed in the second division, that is, with regard to a vessel employed in laying a telegraph cable, because it is not provided in the previous part of that Article for a fog-signal from the other vessel?

Admiral Nares (Great Britain).—It should be in answer to the signal of an approaching vessel.

Mr. Goodrich (United States).—Then it would read, "on hearing the fog-signal of an approaching vessel."

The President.—Is the Conference ready for the question? The Secretary will read it again.

The second proposition of the Delegate from Great Britain is as follows :—

"A ship employed in laying or picking up a telegraph cable shall, on hearing the fog-signal of an approaching vessel, sound in answer, on her whistle, siren, or fog-horn, three prolonged blasts in succession."

The President.—Is the Conference ready for the question?

The question was put to the Conference upon the adoption of the second proposition of the Delegate from Great Britain, and it was adopted.

The President.—The next subject before the Conference will be section 3—pilot-signals— on p. 5 of the Additional Report of the Committee on Sound-Signals.

Mr. Hall (Great Britain).—Mr. President, the Conference will recollect the passage of a Resolution on the day before yesterday that it was inexpedient to insert anything in the Rules for preventing Collisions at Sea with regard to pilot-signals. Therefore, I apprehend that this is disposed of. Of course, when the Committee treated it, they little thought that there was going to be such a Resolution carried by the Conference. But as we have determined to strike all signals for pilot-vessels out of the Rules of the Road at Sea, I apprehend that this Article is disposed of.

Mr. Goodrich (United States).—Mr. President, the other one was referred to Committee No. 2, dealing with General Division No. VIII.

The President.—Does the Delegate from Great Britain propose any action with regard to section 3? · Could it be disposed of in the same way as the other Article was disposed of?

Admiral Nares (Great Britain).—Mr. President, the reference to us was on sound-signals to be used in a fog, and, therefore, we were obliged to put this in; but as the Conference have referred a far more important signal to be made by a pilot to Committee No. 2, it follows, of course, that this must be taken out. This is of very little importance as compared with the one which you have already taken out of the Rules.

The President.—The other one was a pilot-vessel wishing to attract attention, and this is a vessel wanting a pilot——

Mr. Goodrich (United States).—Mr. President, the other section was referred to Committee No. 2.

Mr. Hall (Great Britain).—Mr. President, it was not referred; it was relegated. We distinctly decided that we had nothing to do with the pilot-signals in the Rules of the Road at Sea, but we ventured to point out to the Committee appointed to consider General Division No. VIII that it would be a matter which they would do well to consider under that Division, and that if they did consider it they might have the valuable assistance of the Committee on Sound-Signals, who have assisted us so much in considering the matter. Therefore I submit that the proper course would be to relegate section 3 in the same way. Of course we cannot attempt to dictate to that Committee as to what they shall do. We merely suggest that it be relegated to them, and I have no doubt they will take the matter under consideration.

Mr. Carter (Hawaii).—Mr. President, as a member of that Committee No. 2, I would call the attention of the Conference to the fact that General Division No. VIII, which is the only one we have anything to do with, connected with signals, is for night signals for communicating information at sea. Now, this is a question of a pilot-signal. It is a very broad and a very important one. There are two propositions here. One is that the pilot-boat should be given a signal, and the other is that the vessel wanting a pilot is to be given a signal also. It does not come under General Division No. VIII. Of course if the Conference desires that our Committee should meet with the other Committee and consider this subject, we will do so very readily; but it will be very much more agreeable to us if a vote could be taken in Conference upon the principle: Shall a pilot-boat be given a signal, or shall a vessel wanting a pilot be given a signal, or shall both be given a signal? They are rather important questions. Whatever the Committee might do, you will see that the question would have to come back to the Conference on the question of principle, and would have to be settled here. Therefore, it seems to me that the only question before the Conference is whether they shall consider this principle now or consider it after the Report has been brought in.

Mr. Goodrich (United States).—Mr. President, will the learned gentleman allow me to suggest that under General Division No. VIII there is the subdivision of a supplemental Code of limited scope to convey information?

Mr. Carter (Hawaii).—That is at night.

Mr. Goodrich (United States).—It is germane to this subject at any rate.

Mr. Carter (Hawaii).—Mr. President, I beg the pardon of the learned Delegate of the United States. That subdivision says, a Code to be used in connection with the International Code Signal-Book; and I take it that means at sea and at night. Of course we will take it under consideration if it is the wish of the Conference, and with such a strong Committee, if the other Committee will meet with us, there will be sixteen members to consider the subject. But our experience in the Conference is that discussion in the Committee does not shorten much the discussions in the Conference. Therefore, it seems to me that it will be just as well for the Conference to pass a vote upon the principle involved.

Admiral Bowden-Smith (Great Britain).—Mr. President, as one of the Committee of which the learned Delegate from Hawaii is the Chairman, I venture to hope that the Conference will now express an opinion as to whether there is to be this signal mentioned, because, if they do not, I foresee that we shall spend the afternoon, or perhaps the whole day, in the Committee, in settling the question, and when we have settled the question it will come back to the Conference, when one or two days will again be spent in the discussion of it. I venture to think the Conference could express an opinion after a short time as to whether a pilot-boat is to have a signal or whether the ship is to have the signal, or whether there is to be a signal for both or neither.

Mr. Hall (Great Britain).—Mr. President, as I pointed out only a few moments ago, the Conference has already decided that we will not discuss the pilot-boat signals under the Rules of the Road at Sea. Now it is pointed out by my learned friend the Delegate from Hawaii that he has doubts whether it is within the scope of their reference. I think there is a very simple way out of this difficulty, and that is for us to agree to request Committee No. 2, dealing with General Division No. VIII, to take this matter under their consideration. That will get over the difficulty pointed out by my gallant colleague and by my learned friend on my right.

But I wish to point out that we are out of order in discussing pilot-signals here. We have passed a Resolution that we will not discuss them under the Rules of the Road at Sea. Therefore we cannot discuss them now, but we can give any of the Committees extended powers if we choose. Then why should we not pass a Resolution requesting Committee No. 2, which deals with General Division No. VIII, to also kindly take into consideration the signals to be given by and to pilots, and to do so in conference with the Sound-Signal Committee? We shall stultify ourselves, after our Resolution of only three days ago, that we would not discuss the question of pilot-signals under the Rules of the Road at Sea, if we proceed to discuss them now. Therefore, I beg to move that Committee No. 2, dealing with General Division No. VIII, be requested to consider and report on the subject of sound-signals given by or to pilot-vessels, and to confer with the Sound-Signal Committee thereon.

Mr. Carter (Hawaii).—Mr. President, I was not anxious that the consideration of this principle should take place at once. I quite agree with the learned Delegate from Great Britain that discussion would be out of order until we have finished this Report which we have before us, and I believe that we should defer the consideration of this Resolution until this Report is finished. Then it would be in order for the Conference to take up and decide the principle as to whether pilot-vessels should have a signal or not. At present I quite agree with him that it would not be in order. If this Resolution is proposed and carried, and that is the wish of the Conference, as I said before we will be willing to take it; but it seems to me that although more time might be occupied to-day, in the end the Conference gains by establishing the principle upon which the Committee shall act.

The President.—The question is upon the motion of the Delegate from Great Britain.

Mr. Hall (Great Britain).—Mr. President, if it will be more consonant with the views of the learned Delegate from Hawaii, I will move that Resolution after we have finished our business with regard to the Rules of the Road at Sea. At present we are considering the Rules of the Road at Sea, and let us finish them. It is not necessary to move a Resolution, but if it were I would move to strike out this proposition. It is not necessary, because we have already passed a Resolution deciding that we shall not discuss pilot-signals. Therefore the matter is disposed of by that Resolution.

The President.—The question is upon the motion of the Delegate from Great Britain to relegate the matter to Committee No. 2, which is considering General Division No. VIII.

Mr. Hall (Great Britain).—Mr. President, I will postpone that Resolution until we have finished the Rules of the Road at Sea; then I will move the Resolution.

The President.—Then it is the sense of the Conference that this shall be passed over for the present. Article 19 will be next in order. The Secretary will please read it.

Article 19 is as follows:—

" In taking any course authorized or required by these Regulations, a steam-vessel under way shall indicate that course to any other ship which she has in sight by the following signals on her whistle or other steam sound-signal, viz.: one short blast to mean, ' I am directing my course to starboard;' two short blasts to mean, ' I am directing my course to port;' three short blasts to mean, ' My engines are going full speed astern.'"

Admiral Nares (Great Britain).—Mr. President, the only alteration in this Article is the insertion of the words "My engines are" instead of "I am," which is the old and very well-known signal, "I am going full speed astern," which has been, perhaps wilfully, misunderstood. The wording of the Article is very plain: "One short blast, 'I am directing my course to starboard'"—that is, the ship is directing its course to starboard; "Two short blasts, 'I am directing my course to port'"—that is, the ship is directing her course to port; "Three short blasts" means that the ship is going full speed astern. Now the question is, is it the ship or the engines? The ship practically is not going full speed astern. It was always intended that the engines should be going full speed astern. We have another signal for a ship being stopped, but no ship can go full speed astern. It is really intended that it is the engines which are to go full speed astern, and therefore we propose to make it quite clear by altering the words "I am" to "My engines are," so that it will read, "My engines are going full speed astern."

The President.—Is the Conference ready for the question? Article 19 will be again read.

" Article 19. In taking any course authorized or required by these Regulations, a steam-vessel under way shall indicate that course to any other ship which she has in sight by the following signals on her whistle or other steam sound-signal, viz.: One short blast to mean, ' I am directing my course to starboard.' Two short blasts to mean, ' I am directing my course to port.' Three short blasts to mean, ' My engines are going full speed astern.'"

The question was put to the Conference upon the adoption of Article 19, as amended, and the Article was adopted.

The President.—Article — will now be read.

Article — is as follows:—

" Every ship may, if necessary, in order to attract attention, in addition to the lights which she is by these Regulations required to carry, show a flare-up light, or use any detonating signal that cannot be mistaken for a distress signal."

Admiral Nares (Great Britain).—Mr. President, this was a reference especially made to the Fog-Signal Committee. It is rewording of the Article which I believe the Conference practically adopted. We wanted to specify clearly what the detonating signal was. Of course different countries will have different signals, but so long as they can make a noise I do not suppose that it makes much difference what the noise is if it cannot be mistaken for a distress signal. So it has been reworded by the Committee with that view. I believe that it was a detonating signal before, and it was provided how often it should be fired. But the practical outcome is that if a vessel is coming down upon you, you only make the noise once, if that is sufficient to attract attention, and if one sound is not enough you make two, or three, or four. You cannot lay down the number of times the signal shall be made, so we have adopted the term, "any detonating signal." But to prevent it from being mistaken for a distress signal it must not be made once a minute and it must not be continuous. We have got out of the difficulty as well as we could to prevent it from being mistaken for a distress signal.

Mr. Goodrich (United States).—Mr. President, I confess that I am not entirely clear about the propriety of this Rule. I want to call the attention of the Conference to the condition of things which exists in the United States to-day under the legislation which Congress has adopted upon this subject. When Congress adopted the English Rules of 1863 there was no provision in the Rules of Great Britain or the Rules adopted by the United States which permitted the showing of a flare-up light to an approaching vessel. In 1871 Congress passed an Act compelling a sailing-ship upon the approach of a steam-vessel at night to show a lighted torch upon the point or quarter of the sailing-vessel to which the steam-vessel was approaching. I am not aware whether Great Britain ever adopted that Regulation at all. I think not. And I think that no other country adopted it.

In 1879 Great Britain put into the Rules a provision which we have adopted, that is, old Article 11—a ship which is being overtaken by another shall show from her stern to the last-mentioned ship a white light or a flare-up light. In my judgment that is a very proper Rule. But the other Rule, which requires a sailing-vessel to show a flare-up light to an approaching steam-vessel, no matter what point she was approaching, whether forward or aft of the beam, was a very dangerous provision, and for the clear reason that if the lights upon the sailing-vessel were properly set and burning brightly there was no occasion for this flare-up light—forward of the beam, of course, I mean. And if the flare-up light was shown the effect was to blind the eye of the look-out on the steamer and so extinguish for a time the appearance of the coloured side-lights.

Now we are going back from the Rule adopted in England in 1879, and afterwards by Congress in 1885, to the old Rule of Congress, which never had any foundation in the English Rules nor in the Rules of any other country, so far as I am aware. I suggest that it is a very dangerous provision. Of course, I understand that this light is merely a flare-up light that is only shown for an instant, and is only shown in order to attract attention, and is only shown if necessary in order to attract attention. It is a very flexible Rule; but I doubt its wisdom very much indeed. If there is a vigilant look-out kept upon the approaching vessel, and if the lights which the Conference have now provided for both forward of the beam and aft of the beam are burning brightly, especially the stern-light, if it is fixed as the law permits it to be, then there is no danger. The question is, whether you are going to add to these lights another light, or whether there is any necessity for adding that light. I must confess that I have very grave doubts, especially in view of the fact that no other countries ever adopted that Rule of 1871, and also having regard to the fact, to which sailors can testify better than I, that the showing of this flare-up light will extinguish the side-lights.

Now, there is another point which rather goes to the wording of the Rule than to its principle, and which shows the great difficulty which the Committee found in introducing apt words to define exactly what they did mean. It says: "Every ship may, if necessary in order to attract attention." In the first place, this is a very general rule that might serve for a pilot-boat. If it said that "it may be shown, if necessary, to avoid collision," that would be another thing. But you have said, "if necessary to attract attention," and it covers the case of a pilot-signal; it covers the case of calling a tug-boat, &c. But the great principle which I object to lies back of that, that you are making the master of any vessel, a steam- or a sailing-vessel, the judge whether or not in impending danger it is necessary for him to show this flare-up light, and so adding to the uncertainty of these Rules.

I must confess that I am not in favour of that Rule as it stands at present, and I doubt whether the principle is a good one. I spoke to my learned brother, the Delegate from Great Britain, this morning upon that subject, and we may get a little light from him. His remark this morning made a good deal of impression upon me. Our Courts under the Act of 1871 were frequently called upon to decide whether the Rule of 1871 should have been obeyed; that is, whether a sailing-vessel should have shown a flare-up light to a vessel approaching forward of the beam, where a sailing-vessel's coloured light or lights could be seen, and for a long time there was a very decided attempt and desire on the part of the Court, as manifested in their opinions, to hold the sailing-vessel free from responsibility for not having shown that light, upon the ground that it was unnecessary to show it, because the circumstances of the case developed the fact that the approaching steamer had seen her far enough away to avoid collision, and, therefore, the showing of the light would not have helped the steamer to avoid a collision. But, all the same, there was put upon the sailing-vessel the burden of excusing herself, under similar language to this, or even under stronger language than this. There was put upon the sailing-vessel the burden of showing that she was not in fault for not exhibiting the light. Now we are putting that same burden back upon the vessel.

My learned friend says that was all very well when there was no such provision in the Rule. But we did have this provision in the American Rule, and it was under this Rule that our decisions proceeded, when there was not only no prohibition against carrying these lights and showing this flare-up light, but when there was an actual requirement that the flare-up light should be shown to an approaching vessel. I suggest that we are making these Rules a little uncertain by putting in this clause. I had a case recently under the present Rule where a sailing-vessel coming up the channel found a steamer getting very close to her and did show this light not authorized by the Rules. An attempt was made to justify it upon the ground of the language in the 23rd Rule, that it was perfectly evident that the approaching vessel did not see the sailing-ship nor her lights, and was not aware of her presence, and, therefore, the flare-up lights would give notice to the steamer that a vessel was there. But back of all this lies the principle whether it is wise for a vessel—take a steamer, for instance—exhibiting her bright masthead-lights and two powerful side-lights to show to a little sailing-vessel a flare-up light. The Rule embraces that case. It provides that every ship may, if necessary to attract attention, show a flare-up light. Suppose a steamer sees a sailing-vessel approaching her——

Mr. Hall (Great Britain).—She will have to keep out of her way.

Mr. Goodrich (United States).—Mr. President, I understand that, but we know they do not always keep out of the way. A steam-vessel may show this light, under this Rule, to attract the attention of the sailing-vessel. How often does it happen that the excuse is made in New York Harbour that three whistles are sounded to the sailing-vessel! I do not say that it is a good law, or that it is good reasoning, or that it is justified by the Rule; but the practice is that they sound three whistles to compel a sailing-vessel to do something. Judge Benedict within a few days decided a case upon these points. Of course, he stamped out the theory that a steamer could compel a sailing-vessel to do anything except hold her course. But the excuse was made, and made under the Rules. I suggest that it is a very dangerous provision to go into the Rules.

Mr. Flood (Norway).—Mr. President, may I be allowed to make a few remarks in regard to this matter? When the expression, "if necessary," or, rather, when the 40th amendment, which was originally intended to read, "at any time," was presented to the Conference, I took the liberty to propose an alteration so that it would read, "in an emergency." But that did not exactly meet with the approval of the Conference; and it was proposed by the learned Delegate from Great Britain to alter it to "if necessary." I gladly accepted that because I thought it was better than at first, although it was not so good as to definitely point out the emergency. I understood by the discussion that everybody was agreed that this extra flare-up or detonating signal should only be used when it was actually necessary, and not in such cases as were pointed out by the learned Delegate from the United States. I cannot understand how any such signal as the one proposed should cause any mistake or make any trouble. On the contrary, I think it will help to get rid of collisions.

Mr. Hall (Great Britain).—Mr. President, I have no doubt the Conference will all recollect what happened, as has been pointed out by the Delegate from Norway. I remember accepting, at his suggestion, the words "if necessary." It was originally drawn up, "Every ship may at any time," and that Rule was adopted in principle. I perfectly agree that it is open to the learned Delegate from the United States to discuss the nature of the signal. May I point out to him that there is a very great difference between the old Rule as used in the United States and this Rule?

But before I deal with that may I point out this: we considered this matter most carefully in London before we came here; we discussed it most thoroughly so as to see whether such a signal might be given. It was given to meet a general felt want that a vessel might be in the position of a sailing-vessel which sees a steamer coming down upon her but taking no steps to get out of her way, evidently with a bad look-out. Yet under the present Rules that sailing-vessel is to fold her arms, keep her course, and do nothing. That was put before us and we decided—and I think it is common sense—that the vessel might give a signal when it was necessary, but that she was not always to be doing it; and what sailor in the world would be burning a flare-up light when it was not necessary? I do not think that, as a rule, they are inclined to give these signals more than is necessary. We came to the conclusion that it is desirable to give to any vessel the power to give such a signal; but, of course, it is much more for the sailing-vessel, because, if a steamer sees a sailing-vessel she has to get out of the way; while a sailing-vessel has got to do nothing but keep her course.

We then considered what the nature of the signal should be, and we thought it should be a signal which a sailing-vessel could give at once. They have always got a flare-up light ready. They could say to a steamer approaching them, which was keeping a bad look-out, "Here I am. Don't you see me? Keep out of my way." The flare-up light is the quickest thing they can get at. I will not deal with the sound-signal at all for the present. I only want to meet the objection of the learned Delegate from the United States.

May I now ask the attention of the learned Delegate from the United States on his point, because I think he will see that there is a very broad distinction between the case he suggested and the present case? By your old Rule here, every sailing-vessel, as I understand it, was compelled to show a flare-up light to a vessel approaching her. I do not wonder that Rule was revoked. Such a Rule was a most dangerous one. When a vessel is approaching a sailing-vessel keeping a good look-out, the flare-up does not give her any assistance at all, and it is a most onerous thing to put upon a sailing-vessel the burden of burning a flare-up light whenever she sees a vessel approaching. I do not wonder that this Rule was done away with.

But this is a signal which will be used very rarely, and the sailor will only use it when he sees a vessel approaching him which he believes does not see him, and he wants to burn it in self-defence. If so, the sole point for us to consider is, what is the best signal he should give? We are all agreed that he should be allowed to give some signal. Can any one suggest a better one than the flare-up? You cannot give a sailing-vessel a white light. What are you to do? Is not the flare-up the simplest signal for her? I have pointed out the great difficulty of a sailing-vessel being always compelled to show a flare-up, and it might, if it was kept up, dazzle the eyes of the man on the approaching vessel and prevent him from seeing the side-lights of the sailing-vessel. But here it is only to be used when there is occasion for it. I think that if the Conference think it desirable to limit the Rule that I would be perfectly willing to insert the words which the Delegate from the United States suggests, so that it would provide, "if necessary to avoid risk of collision;" but I confess myself I do not think it is necessary. As I have said, it is such an exceptional case that I do not see how it can lead to any danger.

Captain Norcross (United States).—Mr. President, I differ with my learned colleague to this extent, that if this Rule was so changed that a sailing-vessel may use a flare-up light when making the lights of an oncoming steamer, it would be of great value to the steamer, as the light not only attracts attention but at the same time illuminates the sail and shows to the steamer that she is approaching the sailing-vessel. On the other hand, I perfectly agree with him that such a light shown when in immediate proximity is not only bewildering but dangerous.

Mr. Goodrich (United States).—Mr. President, I suggest that there should be put into this Rule these words; after the words, "if necessary," to add the words, "to avoid risk of collision;" after the word "flare-up" in the third line I think the time of the light should be stated. That is a suggestion of my colleague Captain Shackford, and I see the benefit of it, so that it should not extinguish the side-lights any longer than was necessary.

Mr. Hall (Great Britain).—Mr. President, the flare-up light has been used under these Rules before, and no one has ever thought of limiting the time of its burning.

Captain Shackford (United States).—Mr. President, I beg the pardon of the learned Delegate from Great Britain. When this matter was brought up before, I proposed to limit the flash, and I understood him to say the matter would receive some attention when it was called up finally. He may have forgotten it, but I have a very distinct recollection of it.

Mr. Hall (Great Britain).—Mr. President, may I point out that it is perfectly true that the Delegate from the United States did mention it in the discussion which arose on this subject before. I think it was pointed out then that the flare-up lights had been used under these Rules ever since they were first introduced, and nobody has ever thought of limiting the duration of the light. For instance, in the Overtaking Article there is a flare-up light to be shown, and under the Pilot Rule there is a flare-up light. I am speaking from recollection.

Captain Shackford (United States).—Mr. President, I can assure the learned Delegate that a great many sailors in this country have thought about limiting the length of the flare-up. The flare-up lights here sometimes burn for sixty seconds, and when we are running along and make a vessel's side-lights she shows a flare-up light for sixty seconds and then she may change her course. We cannot tell whether she has changed her course or not. I think it is a very important thing to limit the duration of this flare-up light.

Admiral Bowden-Smith (Great Britain).—Mr. President, may I point out to the honourable Delegate and to the Conference that whenever this signal is made as now proposed it will be made under great excitement, when a ship is in danger of a collision, and it would be almost impossible for them, when they are under great excitement, to limit the time of the duration of the flare-up? I think it would be impossible to limit the time the light is to burn.

Mr. Flood (Norway).—Mr. President, may I also add one word in this matter, based upon practical experience? This light is not like any other signal-light which burns an indefinite time. It is, as we all know, a mop, generally protected by some wire, dipped into some oil, or turpentine, or spirits, and it will not burn very long. Captain Shackford stated it would burn some sixty seconds, but I do not think I ever saw one that would burn more than thirty seconds, and when they are going to show a signal a second is not a very long time to warn another vessel to keep out of the way. So I think that practically the flare-up light is advantageous in itself, provided that it will not be used to any great extent or to an extent that will make it bewildering. When this light burns out it has to be lighted again, and they have to go off somewhere and get the lighting material, and it will take some time before that can be done.

Captain Shackford (United States).—Mr. President, in reply to the gallant Delegate from Great Britain, I merely want to say that what I would like to provide for is the contingency which arises when there is risk of collision. These lights are shown in great excitement, as he stated, but really I do not see any difficulty in having a light which only burns five seconds or ten seconds and then could not be shown any longer. There is no danger in having one of these torch-lights arranged so that it cannot burn more than five or ten seconds, instead of thirty or sixty seconds. I consider that a flare-up light which burns from thirty to sixty seconds is a very dangerous thing. The master, while under very great excitement, is liable to change the course of his vessel at any time, and a vessel approaching would not be able to know it. I should not have signed this Report of the Committee unless I had understood that this was to have been carefully considered when it was brought up.

Mr. Hall (Great Britain).—Mr. President, may I point out that this Committee has nothing whatever to do with the flare-up light. It merely has to deal with sound-signals. The only point before the Committee was the sound-signal. This discussion has arisen upon the motion of the learned Delegate from the United States with regard to the Rule itself. As I say, it is quite open to him to make that motion. I am quite willing to admit that the gallant Delegate who has just addressed us did point out at the time of the previous discussion that the flare-up lights in his country did last longer. But we cannot seriously propose that a vessel should carry any particular kind of a torch-light made in this country. We cannot provide that vessels all over the world should carry this particular kind of a torch-light.

Captain Malmberg (Sweden).—Mr. President, I have also had some experience in using the flare-up light, both in using it myself and seeing it used, and I think it is the very best kind of a signal you can have to show under such circumstances, when there is a risk of collision or when you wish to attract attention. As has been stated before, it is impossible to fix a certain time for the burning of such a light, because it depends upon the sort of a mop, the quality of oil you use, and other things. I, for my part, will vote for this Article as it stands.

Mr. Goodrich (United States).—Mr. President, I understood that the words, "if necessary to avoid the risk of collision," were acceptable to the Committee.

Mr. Hall (Great Britain).—Mr. President, the Committee have nothing to do with this.

Mr. Goodrich (United States).—Mr. President, we are talking about the Report of the Committee.

Mr. Hall (Great Britain).—Mr. President, the Report of the Committee is only dealing with sound-signals. I shall not oppose the insertion of these words at present, but I do not approve of them, because I do not think them necessary. I will not oppose the insertion of the words if my learned friend the Delegate from the United States insists upon it.

Mr. Goodrich (United States).—Mr. President, I do not want to press it unless it is deemed to be a wise provision to insert in the Rules. But it seems to me that the necessity of using this flare-up light, if it is to be used at all, should be confined to special cases of imminent danger, and that this should be made very clear in the Rules, because I think it is a dangerous signal any way, although I know that this is a question for the nautical men to decide, and not for landsmen; but I think that if it is to be used it should only be used in cases of urgent necessity. I think we ought to define it by using these words, or something like them. Therefore, I move to add, after the words "if necessary," the words, " to avoid risk of collision and."

Mr. Hall (Great Britain).—Mr. President, before the learned Delegate presses that amendment, may I make a few remarks? First of all, I feel perfectly satisfied that no vessel will be likely to use this signal any more than she can possibly help. I quite agree that it should only be used in exceptional circumstances; but do we really suppose that any vessel will be giving this when she can possibly help it? She will only give it when there is a necessity for it. Now let me point out an objection to it in a legal point of view, which, I think, will commend itself to the consideration of the learned Delegate from the United States. If you say every vessel may, if necessary to prevent risk of collision—and a collision occurs and that light has not been shown—will it not be argued that it was necessary for you to do it, and that you are to blame for not having shown the light?

It is dangerous to insert words like this without considering what the outcome will be. I am certain he will see that this is a well-founded observation, if I may say so. I admit that it is an optional Rule, but directly you say that every ship may, if necessary, in order to avoid risk of collision, show the light, the Courts might say, " You ought to have done it to prevent risk of collision. You had the power to do it, you were authorized to do it, and therefore you ought to have done it. You are to blame for not exhibiting that signal." I say that is a point which possibly might be made. Now let me ask any of the gentlemen here present whether there is any object in putting the words in, and whether this light will be burned any oftener than is necessary? Is there any reason to apprehend that any single vessel will give this signal except under circumstances that will justify his doing so?

Mr. Goodrich (United States).—Mr. President, let me say that I do not quite understand the point of the learned Delegate from Great Britain. I see the difference between the language of the Rules where the words " and if necessary " are referred to, because, if I understand it as it is written, it means when it is necessary to prevent risk of collision. You certainly do not mean to put it in for a pilot-signal or for any other purpose than that it shall be given when there is a danger of two vessels colliding. There cannot be another time when it would be called into interpretation by the Courts, and therefore the Rule refers to collisions and to cases where collision is imminent, where there is a chance for two vessels to collide. Therefore, I really do not see why the objection of the learned Delegate from Great Britain applies. You are giving this Rule still further prominence, and I urge this upon the Conference because I think I can foresee danger which will arise from this Rule, although of course I am looking rather at the construction of it by the Courts. You have got a Rule which permits the showing of a flare-up light to an overtaking vessel. Now here you are giving to this provision the special prominence which is given to it by putting it into an additional Rule. It is not as if it were tacked on as an Annex to the other Rule ; but you are giving it special prominence. The sailor will say, here is the 17th Rule, for instance; it says, " I must show a flare-up light whenever I want to attract attention."

Now, let us look into the practical working of the Rule along our coast. I take it that the first thing which attracts the attention of any lawyer who is called upon to commence an action for a collision which has occurred to a coasting schooner at night is, " Did she have her lights set?" And the impression among many of the members of the Bar is that the coasting schooners do not carry lights at night on the broad Atlantic. That may be unfounded, but I speak from my own experience. I know that in many instances they are not carried ; and we all know that the sailorman always says that his lights were burning, and burning brightly, the glass was clear, and there was nothing to intercept the view. Now, your Rule will permit the showing of this flare-up light. A coasting schooner wants to save a few cents' worth of oil or a little trouble in paying attention to her coloured lights, or the vessel is short-handed, is a small coasting vessel which perhaps has only two men on each watch, or at least not more than three, and instead of paying any attention to his coloured side-lights the master takes the chances of being able to show a flare-up light when another vessel is approaching.

That is the difficulty which I apprehend. I may be all wrong about this. As I said before, it is a question for the sailors rather than for the lawyers. But it is a difficulty which occurs to me from the fact that we have seen the actual operation of the old Rule of 1871, and heard the discussions upon it, and the decisions in regard to it. We are now putting into these Rules a new principle, extending the old Article 11 to new cases, changing the entire reading of Article 11, because they only required the flare-up light to be shown on that quarter or point of the vessel where no light was visible to an approaching vessel. That was a very wise provision. That is the time when the flare-up light should be shown, if ever. But now you are going further, and you are going to permit a vessel to show a flare-up light, and thereby extinguish her side-light, and to show it as often as she chooses. I say extinguish, and I mean blinding the sight of the approaching look-out. I use the word "extinguish" in that sense. I think that is dangerous. Take the case of two vessels approaching each other so as to involve risk of collision. One is a steamer and the other a sailing-vessel. The sailing-vessel has both of her lights burning brightly and properly, and here is an approaching vessel 2 miles away. Suppose the sailing-vessel is going 5 miles an hour, and the steamer is going 15 miles an hour. They are closing the gap at the rate of a mile in three minutes, or one-third of a mile in a minute. The interval of time is very short. Now, as the vessels approach each other, the sailing-vessel, recognizing the fact that there is no apparent change in the course of the steamer, attempts to change her course, and at the same time shows this flare-up light——

Mr. Hall (Great Britain).—She has no right to change her course.

Mr. Goodrich (United States).—But it is imminent danger, and the Courts justify a change when in imminent danger. It strikes me that you are blinding the sight of the steamer to changes which would be evidenced by the coloured lights if they could be seen. That is one difference which I see in the permission to use this flare-up light, because it practically extinguishes the coloured side-lights.

Mr. Carter (Hawaii).—Mr. President, I should like to put to the Conference an objection that I think underlies all Rules of this nature. Wherever you legislate for exceptional cases you simply create the exceptional cases. It seems to me that when a master is in a position which has just been described he will naturally make noises and show lights, and all the legislation to the contrary would not prevent him from doing so if he were in imminent danger. In addition to that, would not an Article like this seem to justify him in not taking the precautions laid down in the Rules for preventing Collisions at Sea? Would he not be likely to depend upon this action at the last moment? I grant you that in frequented waters, where they are constantly on the look-out, a man might not do this——

Mr. Hall (Great Britain).—Mr. President, I beg the pardon of my learned friend, but such a principle as this has already been adopted by the Conference, and the whole question is as to the nature of the signal. We have already adopted the principle. I hope he will forgive me for calling his attention to the fact, as I do not think we had the pleasure of his presence at the board the other day when this principle was adopted.

Mr. Carter (Hawaii).—Mr. President, I am obliged to the learned Delegate for calling this to my attention.

Mr. Goodrich (United States).—Mr. President, will my friend allow me to call attention to the fact that the Committee have added new words which justify amendment and discussion?

Mr. Hall (Great Britain).—But not as to the principle.

Mr. Goodrich (United States).—The Committee have added new words.

Admiral Nares (Great Britain).—Mr. President, allow me to say that we were obliged to transpose the words, "to attract attention," from the last part of the Article to where they are now. It came to us with the words, "to attract attention," at the end of the Article, and we have transposed them because we had to put in there a provision that it should not be mistaken for a distress signal, and we could not leave the words, "to attract attention," at the end.

Mr. Hall (Great Britain).—Mr. President, I confess that I cannot understand why the mere transposition of words could be understood to in any way change the principle of the Rule. The principle has been carried. The only question now is whether the flare-up light is the best signal that can be given. Now, may I just say a few words in reply to the remarks of the learned Delegate from the United States? He says that this light ought not to be used except under exceptional circumstances, and why not put in the words he proposes? The words "if necessary" were inserted at the time the Rule was under discussion, because it was pointed out that this light might possibly be shown when there were no circumstances which made it possible or necessary to show it. Now I have waited to hear whether or not there is any reason to apprehend that this light will be shown too frequently. The learned Delegate from the United States says that the vessels on his coast would not carry the side-lights if they could show this light, but we are legislating for careful mariners, and not for men who break the Rules. We are legislating for the men who keep the Rules and who want to attract attention to themselves.

The learned Delegate from the United States takes as an illustration a steamer going 15 miles an hour and a sailing-vessel 5 miles an hour, and he says that the sailing-vessel when she sees a steamer coming down upon her changes her course. He says that the Courts have decided that she has a right to do it. All I can say is this, that if a steamer has such a grossly bad look-out or is so careless as to come so near to the sailing-vessel as to drive her into changing her course, at such a time, the Courts will excuse her, and the steamer will be guilty of the greatest negligence. But when a sailing-vessel sees a vessel coming down upon her which is apparently guilty of the grossest negligence, why should she not be able to say to her, "Here I am;" and to burn a flare-up light?

Mr. Flood (Norway).—Mr. President, I simply want to state that I should be very sorry if this Rule should be altered in the way it stands here. It has been stated by the learned Delegate from the United States that it should be used in case of an emergency, and that there were no other cases before for showing a flare-up light. I think that there are other occasions to show this flare-up light. We have adopted Rules in behalf of vessels laying telegraph cables. Might it not be necessary for them, to make an approaching vessel know what they are doing, to show a flare-up light, and to show how she must go to avoid getting into the cable? I will also remind you that besides the Admiralty Courts we have another Court, the court of humanity. Suppose there is a man overboard! I want to use the flare-up light then. There are other occasions when it may be necessary; for instance, in saving a disabled or wrecked vessel, or taking wrecked sailors from a vessel; and the flare-up light is continually used under such circumstances. So I think the flare-up light should be used when necessary in order to attract attention. I think that language will cover all emergencies into which a seafaring man can come; but if we insert these words, "to prevent collision," we will get *into the soup.*

The President.—The question is upon the amendment of the Delegate from the United States to Article —, which will be read.

The amendment is as follows:—

"Insert in the first line, after the word 'attention,' the following words: 'to prevent risk of collision.'"

The President.—Is the Conference ready for the question?

The question was put to the Conference upon the amendment, and it was lost.

The President.—The amendment is lost. The question now is upon Article —. The Secretary will please read it as it now stands.

Article — is as follows :—

"Article —. Every ship may, if necessary in order to attract attention, in addition to the lights which she is by these Regulations required to carry, show a flare-up light or use any detonating signal that cannot be mistaken for a distress signal."

The President.—Is the Conference ready for the question?

Lieutenant Beaugency (Chile).—Mr. President, I desire to offer an amendment so that it will read, "any efficient detonating signal."

Captain Malmberg (Sweden).—Mr. President, may I ask who is to decide upon the efficiency of such a signal?

The President.—Is the Conference ready for the question upon the amendment of the Delegate from Chile to introduce the word "efficient" after the word "any"?

The question was to put to the Conference upon the amendment of the Delegate from Chile, and the amendment was lost.

The President.—The question now is upon the amendment. The Secretary will please read the amendment as it stands.

Article — is as follows :—

"Article —. Every ship may, if necessary, in order to attract attention, in addition to the lights which she is by these Regulations required to carry, show a flare-up light or use any detonating signal that cannot be mistaken for a distress signal."

The President.—Is the Conference ready for the question?

The question was put to the Conference upon the adoption of Article —, and it was adopted.

The President.—The next subject for consideration is Article 27. The Secretary will please read Article 27.

"Article 27. When a ship is in distress and requires assistance from other ships or from the shore, the following shall be the signals to be used or displayed by her, either together or separately; that is to say :—

"In the day-time—

"1. A gun fired at intervals of about a minute.

"2. The International Code-Signal of Distress indicated by N. C.

"3. The distant signal, consisting of a square flag, having either above or below it a ball or anything resembling a ball.

"4. Rockets or shells bursting in the air with a loud report, and throwing stars of any colour or description, fired one at a time, at short intervals.

"5. A continuous sounding with any fog-signal apparatus."

Admiral Nares (Great Britain).—Mr. President, I do not know whether it will be convenient to take up the day signals first. I think it would clear the ground quicker, if there is no opposition, to take the day signals, as we could argue it better.

The President.—If there is no objection the day signals will be considered first.

Admiral Nares (Great Britain).—Mr. President, I may say that in the additions we have put in about shells bursting in the air with a loud report and a continuous sounding with any fog apparatus we were practically adopting the four proposals that were put before the Conference, which were referred to the Sound-Signal Committee, as additions to these distress signals. The shells bursting in the air with a loud report and throwing stars of any colour comes into the day signals. That means that a vessel need only have one kind of shell or rocket on board. We do not want to require her to have different kinds of rockets. Practically all the rockets make a noise in bursting, and practically in bursting they throw out flame. So we combined the signal and provided for shells bursting in the air with a loud report and throwing stars. Then in regard to the fifth signal, the continuous sounding on any fog-signal apparatus, that practically came up in this way—there was a wreck in the channel and the poor fellow could not make any particular noise to attract the life-boat from the shore. The main point is that these distress signals are only made in case of necessity, and if any one of them is made, the person making them becomes liable for salvage and assistance. That has been the rule. So in adopting these two signals it is distinctly understood that they are distress signals and that the person making them does not only mean, "I want ordinary assistance," but that he wants decided assistance, and any person going off in his life-boat or in his vessel gets a certain payment.

The President.—Article 27, the signals for the day-time, is now before the Conference.

Admiral Nares (Great Britain).—Mr. President, I have a question handed to me in writing.

Mr. Goodrich (United States).—Mr. President, may I occupy a moment of the time of the Conference while the Committee is considering that question? Will the members of the Conference, each one of them, send to the Secretary his home address so that the list of Delegates may be printed, with their home addresses? I do not mean the Washington address; I mean their home residence and address.

Admiral Nares (Great Britain).—Mr. President, the Delegate from Japan pointed out that he wants to put in the words, "lights or signs." I think it will be taken for granted that stars would include throwing out flames and lights, and so this rocket bursts and makes a noise and it makes a light at the same time. Therefore, in the day-time we would hear the noise and in the night-time see the flame. It is in one Article to combine the two purposes. I do not think the Sound-Signal Committee are quite prepared to alter the word "stars."

[93]

The President.—Is the Conference ready for the question upon the first, second, third, fourth, and fifth signals to be used in the day-time?

The question upon the adoption of the five signals in Article 27 for use in the day-time was put to the Conference and carried.

The President.—The Secretary will please read the signals under Article 27, to be used at night.

" At night—
" 1. A gun fired at intervals of about a minute.
" 2. Flames on the ship (as from a burning tar-barrel, oil-barrel, &c.).
" 3. Rockets or shells, as described under Day-Signal.
" 4. A continuous sounding with any fog-signal apparatus."

The President.—Is the Conference ready for the question?

The question was put to the Conference upon the adoption of the first, second, third, and fourth signals to be used at night under Article 27, and they were adopted.

Mr. Goodrich (United States).—Mr. President, although the hour for adjournment has almost arrived, if the Conference will permit us to go over these Rules for a moment, I think we can adjourn without reassembling this afternoon.

Admiral Nares (Great Britain).—Mr. President, I may say on the part of the Sound-Signal Committee that we are quite willing to refer the pilot-signals to the combined Committee to report upon them, if the Conference shall see fit to do so. It was our duty to point out that there was a fog-signal wanting for a vessel asking for a pilot, and we have done our duty in pointing it out.

The President.—What is the motion of the Delegate from Great Britain?

Mr. Hall (Great Britain).—Mr. President, the motion of which I gave notice is this. I will preface it by saying that this signal has nothing whatever to do with the Rules of the Road at Sea; but it is possible that we ought to clothe the Committee which is to deal with General Division No. VIII with authority to deal with sound-signals, as it is pointed out that there is a doubt whether that comes within the scope of their reference. I therefore move that Committee No. 2 be requested to consider with General Division No. VIII the question of pilot-signals, and to confer with the Sound-Signal Committee thereon.

Captain Sampson (United States).—I second the motion.

Mr. Carter (Hawaii).—Mr. President, I am sorry that this vote is going to be taken just at this moment, when the Conference is about to break up, and when they would undoubtedly like to put this work on the Committee, and go home feeling that they had discharged their duty. Of course, I abide by the decision of the Conference, but I would have been very glad if, before this was sent to the Committee, a test vote could have been taken in the Conference. Of course I see that it is impossible to do it now before we adjourn for lunch. When is it intended that the Conference shall meet again?

Mr. Goodrich (United States).—Mr. President, I suppose there is no reason why the Conference should not adjourn presently for several days, until Monday, perhaps.

Mr. Carter (Hawaii).—Mr. President, then I suppose it may be considered that this will be a test vote, and that those who are in favour of referring this matter to the Committee are opposed to any test vote being taken on principle; and those who vote against it are in favour of having a vote taken before it goes to the Committee.

Mr. Hall (Great Britain).—Mr. President, I do not at all wish that to be the construction. I wish to assist my learned friend in every possible way. I think it is desirable that we should come to some decision with regard to the general principle as to whether a sound-signal should be given by pilots or to pilots. I am afraid that we will have to take up the discussion of this matter when we next meet. The only thing is that the Committee, of course, cannot commence work upon it until we have decided the principle. It has been suggested to me whether we could not consider this to-morrow morning; but then the Committees will have no time for their work.

Mr. Goodrich (United States).—Mr. President, why can we not vote on the principle right here?

Mr. Hall (Great Britain).—Very well, Sir.

Captain Sampson (United States).—Mr. President, if that is to be done, I think that probably the Conference will arrive at a decision more promptly if we were to vote upon these two questions separately; that is: Shall there be a signal to be made by a pilot? And, secondly, Is there to be a signal for a ship to make wanting a pilot? I think that, as far as my experience goes, it is not necessary that a pilot-boat should be enabled to make a signal other than the one she now has when there is no fog. It might be convenient for a ship to call a pilot-boat in a fog. But, however, I do not think the converse of that is necessary. If it is the sense of the Conference that we should vote upon this question, I make this motion: "That it is the sense of the Conference that no signal should be given to a pilot-vessel in a fog."

The President.—Is the Conference ready to vote upon the principle as to whether the signal shall be allowed to a pilot-vessel in a fog?

Mr. Carter (Hawaii).—Mr. President, is it to be a negative or an affirmative proposition?

Admiral Nares (Great Britain).—Mr. President, the Sound-Signal Committee would be very strongly in favour of putting it as an affirmative vote. I think we may consider that we are entitled to some consideration. We have proposed that you shall have a pilot-signal. Now, if you consider the matter at all, we request you to consider it on an affirmative vote; and I will ask you to put the vote upon the question, " Shall a fog-signal be given to a pilot-vessel wanting to attract attention in a fog?"

The President.—The question is upon the motion of the Delegate from Great Britain.

The question of the motion of the Delegate from Great Britain was put to the Conference.

The President.—The Chair is unable to decide.

Mr. Carter (Hawaii).—Mr. President, I would suggest that this subject be deferred until the next meeting of the Conference. It seems to me it would be taking what you might call a snap judgment to decide upon this matter now.

Mr. Hall (Great Britain).—Mr. President, I think that it is not desirable to take the decision now, for there is a very strong division of opinion upon the matter. I think we had better discuss it when we next meet.

Admiral Nares (Great Britain).—Mr. President, I may say that we have not had an opportunity to argue our case at all. We have not said one word about it. We have got a very strong opinion upon it.

The President.—The question will be taken on the motion of the Delegate from Hawaii that the consideration of this subject be deferred until some future meeting.

The question upon the above motion was put to the Conference, and carried.

Mr. Goodrich (United States).—Mr. President, as we have now finished the consideration of all the amendments to the Regulations, except that one to which reference has just been made, I present this Resolution. I move that the Regulations already passed be adopted, subject only to verbal alteration and arrangement by the Collocation Committee.

The President.—This will give rise to so much discussion, I would suggest that we adjourn. You cannot possibly get a vote upon it at present.

Mr. Goodrich (United States).—Mr. President, I would like to ask whether there is any objection to it.

Captain Richard (France).—Mr. President, my objection is as follows: We cannot in advance tie our hands by adopting this proposition, however anxious we may be to terminate our labour. We have a law to examine, and we cannot pledge ourselves in advance to be satisfied with it in its entirety without knowing it thoroughly. I repeat that we cannot allow our hands to be tied without knowing what we have before us.

The President.—The question now is whether the Conference adjourn until Monday, or whether it is to meet to-morrow. The Chair will entertain any motion in regard to the matter.

Mr. Goodrich (United States).—Mr. President, unless some motion is made the Conference meets at 2 o'clock this afternoon.

The President.—The Conference, then, stands adjourned until 2 o'clock this afternoon, unless some Delegate has a proposition to make.

Captain Sampson (United States).—Mr. President, what are we to do this afternoon?

The President.—That is for the Conference to decide.

Mr. Carter (Hawaii).—Mr. President, I move that the Conference adjourn, to meet at half-past 2 this afternoon.

The President.—The question is upon the motion of the Delegate from Hawaii.

Mr. Goodrich (United States).—Mr. President, I move that we now adjourn, to meet on Monday morning. There is nothing else to discuss this afternoon.

Mr. Carter (Hawaii).—Mr. President, we can discuss the pilot-signals this afternoon.

Captain Malmberg (Sweden).—Mr. President, I move that the Conference adjourn until Monday morning. There is a reason for doing it, not on behalf of the Delegates, but on behalf of the Secretaries. It is quite impossible for them to keep up their work in the way we are going now. That is the reason why I make the motion.

Mr. Carter (Hawaii).—Mr. President, I move that we meet at half-past 2 this afternoon, and that the Conference consider only the question of pilot-signals when we meet in the afternoon session.

The President.—Is the Conference ready for the question?

The question was put to the Conference upon the motion to adjourn, and the Conference adjourned until half-past 2 o'clock in the afternoon.

The President.—I desire to announce that Captain Sampson, of the United States' Delegation, will take the Chair this afternoon.

The Conference thereupon adjourned until half-past 2 o'clock.

After Recess.

In pursuance of the designation by the President of the Conference, Captain Sampson, of the United States' Delegation, took the Chair.

The Chairman.—The unfinished business before the Conference is the consideration of the principle which is embodied in the addition to Article 9, on p. 4 of the Report of the Committee on Sound-Signals, and in section 3 on the following page.

Admiral Nares (Great Britain).—Mr. Chairman, after the vote of this morning I rise with some trepidation, because I find myself in a position now of having to argue the case of absent people; that is the case of the pilot, who has got no representative whatever amongst the Delegates who are surrounding this table. I look upon all the Delegates as representing the pilots generally, but I am afraid the naval men may be taking the view as to how it affects them more than as to how it affects the pilot. I want to explain myself very clearly upon this point. I want to separate the pilot-signal that we have proposed in section 3 to be made by the vessel wanting a pilot completely away from the principle as to whether a vessel shall say that she wants a pilot. So, if the Conference will allow it, please put it on one side, as if there never was a proposition at all that a ship wanting a pilot is to have a signal.

The question before us now is purely the question—Shall the pilot-vessel wishing to offer pilotage services be allowed to have a signal? I think that objection may be taken to such words as we have proposed here. The principle is under discussion now, but I would prefer to practically discuss it on the words, "Shall a pilot-vessel wishing to offer her services" have a signal? and strike out the words "wishing to attract attention." That is the point I want to bring clearly before you. Really, Sir, it is so new to me to advocate a cause that I am afraid that I am losing certain points in the argument, and I am really rather in fear and trembling that I have to perform this duty. Therefore, I will ask the indulgence of the rest of the Conference, and ask them to help me out in this matter, and if I miss any points on the part of these pilots, please let them argue it on every side of the question. Let us approach it on both sides.

First of all let me take the naval view. I have been cruizing a good deal and I have never wanted a pilot. Personally, I have never taken a pilot, but have piloted my own vessels with the splendid charts which are provided for us now all around the world. I have never had a pilot on my ship unless I was forced to do it. Therefore, I cannot approach it as a personal matter, as a Captain of a man-of-war. It also cannot be approached personally by many fine officers in the Mercantile Marine who can push on if they do not pick up a pilot, and who go on and run their business so splendidly now that practically they are beyond the necessity of a pilot as a general rule. But still we will allow that there are numbers of them who cannot do anything like that, and in bad weather we are one and all very glad to hear the pilot call when we want him. Now, shall the pilot-vessel in a fog be able to say, "I am a pilot-vessel"? Now, we know that they cruize in great numbers, and as soon as they see a coming ship there will be a Babel of sounds perhaps. But what sounds are they making now? If they are steamers, they give their blasts. If it is a sailing-ship, it must make a signal. Now, if we can turn that signal which they are obliged to make every two minutes into an expressive signal which will say, "Never mind my tack; never mind whether I am a steamer or not; I am a pilot-boat." We argue that would be a good thing.

Now, the whole principle is already adopted by the Conference under Article 9. You have provided for every other part of the twenty-four hours except for the time when there is a fog. The pilots have got a special light. Very well; then surely in that part of the twenty-four hours when a fog comes on they ought to have a special sound. The principle is adopted so far as that goes. I do not think I need press that question. The point we are to vote upon is the principle: shall a pilot-vessel have a special signal? We have already voted that the signal shall not be contained in the Rules of the Road. If you vote No on the question before us, they will not have any signal at all. That is what you are going to say. Supposing that we are able to give them a simple signal; you are going to say that we shall not do it.

Now, as an example, I would give you the Liverpool pilot. We all know the trade of Liverpool. They are cruizing in certain districts. The Liverpool pilots have adopted, of their own accord, a fog-signal. They give this fog-signal. It is known to every trader with Liverpool, and we have never heard of a trader saying that the principle was a bad one. But I will tell you that when it was found out that they were sounding this signal and attracting attention the Board of Trade found it out, and because it was a question as to whether it was a legal matter or not they tried to interfere with it. So strong were the pilots of the opinion that a signal was necessary to be used in a fog by pilots that at last they induced the Board of Trade to give in, and they are making this signal at the present day.

When the Sound-Signal Committee were considering this matter, we thought it right to hear what the New York pilots thought of it, and what the Canadian pilots thought of it, because we will all agree that there are numerous cases of fog on those shores. A representative pilot was chosen by the New York pilots and sent to appear before the Sound-Signal Committee at Washington. The Canadian Government sent us an officer who has been cruizing in the waters amongst the fishermen and pilots for several years. We have the opinions of each of these gentlemen before us. We questioned them closely, and they both agreed as to the usefulness and necessity of allowing pilots to make some signal. I am not now talking about what the character of the signal will be. We are talking now about the principle, shall they be allowed to have any signal? When we finished our examination of the New York pilot we said to him, "From what you have told us we may tell you that the Committee is of the opinion that a pilot-signal should be provided during a fog." His answer was a rejoicing one. He said: "May I go back and tell them so?" I guarded myself at once, and luckily, as it turns out. I said to him: "No; you may tell them the opinion of the Committee; but mind you, it is not the opinion of the Conference; that has to come."

And now, Sir, after what has befallen us this morning I am afraid that I have spoken too soon. I have been nine years in a Department of London, and have learned by experience to hold my tongue; but I neglected to hold my tongue on that occasion, and I am afraid I went too far to even let him know what the opinion of the Committee was. It really struck me at the time, but I could not recall the words. But within a day or two I saw that this same language was repeated in the newspapers, and so, practically, I did not do much harm, and I have not given up the confidence of the Conference. Now, I think, so far as the Committee goes, I may leave you with the expression of opinion that to vote "No" as it is worded at present will not only strike out any signal from the Rules of the Road, but it will strike out any special signal for pilot-boats.

Mr. Verbrugghe (Belgium).—Mr. Chairman, I thank the gallant Delegate from Great Britain, the Chairman of the Committee on Sound-Signals, for having advocated the necessity of giving a signal to a pilot-boat. I believe that I have nothing to add with regard to this matter; but I will be glad, if you will allow me, to make a remark pointing out again the same necessity for the vessels seeking a pilot-boat. I believe that it is a great necessity for vessels during a fog, wishing a pilot-boat, to be able to locate the pilot-boat. Let me take, for instance, a steam-vessel. That steam-vessel is steering a course right into the wind, and, as pilot-boats generally are sailing-vessels, however slow the speed of the steamer may be, the pilot-boat will not be able to reach the steamer, nor the steamer the pilot-boat. But if the pilot-boat is able to give the signal, and so show her presence, then certainly the vessel will locate the pilot-boat, and she will be able to go to the vessel wanting the pilot.

If I understand the case, the principle upon that question has already been decided. I am not sure, however, because I see that it is discussed again. But, if it has not been decided, I hope that the Delegates will join the gallant Chairman of the Committee on Sound-Signals, and accept the signal which was already adopted in principle. I quite agree with the gallant Chairman of this Committee that this signal should be given to a pilot-vessel. The signal itself may be a different one after it comes from this double Committee, but for my part I will vote in favour of the principle, and I hope all the Delegates will do the same.

Captain Richard (France).—Mr. Chairman, after having carefully considered the proposition, I declare it to be my opinion that it would be difficult to adopt the principle without knowing how that principle would be applied. I cannot deny that the principle of giving to pilot-boats the means of making themselves known to vessels which may need them is a matter of great interest. But, on the other hand, I am rather embarrassed about adopting the principle. If I adopt the principle, I would like to know how it will be applied. I have no objection to the signal in question for calling a pilot, but I may have a whole series of serious objections to the signal which may be selected.

Up to this time, by following the footsteps of the Sound-Signals Committee, we have allowed ourselves to be led into adopting a series of signals of great importance; but after having adopted them I question whether they are very efficient, and whether we have not gone too far. I would, therefore, ask whether, after having adopted the principle, we will not adopt a signal which is going to be a new cause of confusion? We have turned the sound-signals to every possible advantage which could be derived from them. Perhaps we have gone even further than that. I, therefore, wonder whether it is wise and proper to adopt a principle which will bring us another sound-signal! If the signal is a good one, I would be glad to adopt the principle at the same time; but if you adopt a bad signal, I doubt whether it would not have been better for me to have voted against the principle.

I am ready to adopt the principle if you can invent a signal which is made neither with the siren, the whistle, nor the fog-horn. Otherwise, if the Committee can give me nothing better, I will vote against the adoption of the principle.

Mr. Verbrugghe (Belgium).—Mr. Chairman, allow me to say a few words in reply to the gallant Delegate who preceded me. The gallant Delegate from France declares that he is willing to adopt the principle of a sound-signal for a pilot-boat, provided he first knows the character of that signal. Will the gallant Delegate allow me to remark that the very condition which he imposes upon his vote must necessarily lead to his abstaining from taking a part in the vote? In fact, the selection of the signal in question is left to the Committee, which can evidently not yet declare itself, the more so as we have all recognized the difficulty of determining upon the sound-signal. I hope that the gallant Delegate from France will vote in favour of the principle. On the other hand, I venture to believe that the Committee will find inspiration in the suggestions which the gallant Captain has kindly made in regard to the selection of a signal.

Mr. Flood (Norway).—Mr. Chairman, may I be allowed to make a couple of remarks in reply to what the gallant Delegate from Great Britain said about pilotage? He said that he never had used a pilot, and he also stated that the merchant captains were growing more and more to the point of piloting their own vessels. With regard to the first part of what he said, of course I believe it, as it was stated from his own experience. But I think the gallant Delegate from England is a little mistaken when he speaks about the merchant captain not using pilots. I will remind him on this point that in my country, and, I think, in almost every maritime country, there are insurance laws which say that vessels are compelled to take a pilot in pilot waters, where he can be obtained, and they have to make signals for pilots for that purpose; and if they get into difficulty in narrow waters in crossing bars or anything of that description, which are under Pilot Regulations, and an accident happens to that ship in doing so, the damage will not be paid by the underwriters, but will fall upon the owners. Under these Regulations, I think that merchant-ships in general are very glad to get hold of a pilot. I am not prepared to say now what I have to say about these Regulations.

Captain Malmberg (Sweden).—Mr. Chairman, for my part I am against such a signal on principle. By giving such a signal to a pilot-vessel to say, "I am here," you thereby induce vessels to make for that pilot-boat, and so possibly in a good many places, while searching for that pilot-boat, they run into great danger, not only into danger of a collision with another vessel, but into the danger of running the vessel ashore. I object also to giving the signal on the fog-horn or whistle, or the introduction of any signal of that kind.

Admiral Nares (Great Britain).—Mr. Chairman, there was one point in this which I overlooked, and that is that without a special signal you are really discouraging the pilot to cruize out at a distance. If you do not give him a signal you deprive him of the whole advantage in going far away from port. Without a signal the approaching vessel will pass the outer man and pick up some fellow who has not taken the same courageous action; but by giving them this signal they will be able to obtain the benefit of their courage. It is not an additional signal. It is only in lieu of the present signal that they are making in a fog. By giving it to them we encourage good pilotage.

Mr. Carter (Hawaii).—Mr. Chairman, one always dislikes to differ with the gallant Delegate from Great Britain who has just spoken. The honesty of his convictions and the convincing tone of his voice is likely to lead us to follow him at all times. But he asks us to consider only one side of this question. That is the way with all tempters. It is the first step that counts, and he asks us to go into this matter and commit ourselves in the first place to giving the pilot-boat a signal; then we will come to the next step and we must give a signal to the vessel that is in want of a pilot, until I begin to entertain the fear that we shall so overload the Code with these fog-signals that cautious navigators will advise their Governments to throw the whole of our work out. This is something which we must avoid. The gallant Delegate has told us that we have provided the pilot-boat with a light-signal, and that we have provided for him at all times of the day and night except during a fog. But as has been mentioned by the gallant Delegate from Sweden, often times that is the time when, if we were taken on board of a vessel, the temptation would be very strong to run into danger. A captain approaching a port is very cautious until he gets his pilot on board, and then he is apt to take more risk than he otherwise would——

Cries of " No, no."

Mr. Carter (Hawaii).—I stand corrected. We always listen to these corrections, and especially from these nautical gentlemen. I was only speaking from my own limited experience. My own idea about giving a pilot-boat a signal is that it is unnecessary, because it is for the interest of the pilot to find a vessel, and it is for the interest of the vessel to find the pilot, and they will accomplish their purpose. The vessel will be giving her ordinary fog-signal as she is coming up, and the pilot, if he is anywhere within hearing of that signal and is not obliged to remain at his station to keep his bearings, will certainly go in search of that vessel, and he will generally find her and make himself known. Now where two parties are determined to get together, and this principle of natural selection is working, it seems to me that it is not necessary to legislate in any way with regard to the matter. It has been pointed out that there are places where a great number of pilots are seeking vessels, and that they really become a nuisance and offer their services before they are wanted ; but those are localities that I am not so well acquainted with. It has been stated with great force that the pilot has asked for this, and that one was overjoyed to think that they would get a signal——

Admiral Nares (Great Britain).—He was a representative pilot.

Mr. Carter (Hawaii).—I can well understand that the pilot would be very glad to have this granted. They would be very glad to be coming around all the time to offer their services, as the tug-boats do, and we would very naturally like to oblige all classes who would like to have a signal, and give one to every man who comes and asks for it. But we are limited to a certain extent unless we come to the conclusion that we will throw open the whole thing and adopt the Morse alphabet, and have the merchantmen carry a signalman so that they can communicate any kind of information they desire at sea, as I understand is now practised in the navy. But it seems to me that there have not yet been reasons forcible enough to lead us to give these two signals, because that is what it practically will amount to. Let us take a steamer coming to port. She has got to make her ordinary fog-signal. She has got to give her ordinary signal. Let us imagine she has got a vessel in tow. She has her ordinary signal to give; then she has a signal that she has a vessel in tow; then she may be stopped ; and then on the top of all this here is a signal for a pilot. Therefore, you see you have got the vessel navigated by the steam-whistle and the siren. It therefore seems to me, although I do not pretend it to be my ultimate conviction, that these signals should not be granted. Of course, I may change my mind, especially if it be the sense of the Conference that it should be granted. Yet it seems to me that the objections to giving them are weighty enough to require it to be considered seriously whether we should give them or not.

Admiral Nares (Great Britain).—Mr. Chairman, I did not intend to go into the argument about the ship question. But you see that we cannot well keep out of it. We have considered the ship side of the question. At present the ship is giving a single blast. Directly that she does so all the pilot-boats in the neighbourhood rush around her. If you give her a pilot-signal she will tell these vessels that she is the only vessel that wants a pilot, and as soon as she gets the pilot on board she will go on her way sounding her single blast again and will not be molested all the rest of her voyage. Then, as to remembering the signal. This will be only in special waters. Now, you will say that this is as much as to say : You have got a good signal to give us. I have got a good signal to give you at the proper time, and when the time comes to give you that signal. But whatever it is, suppose it is a difficult one to remember, or suppose we can give you as simple a one as we gave you this morning. It will only be applicable to these special waters, and it need not be remembered on the whole voyage by the captains on the look-out, when they were thinking of these other signals which represent dangers in their paths. I think that we could give you a distinct signal which will say, instead of being a danger in your path, there is a comforter there.

The Chairman.—Is the Conference ready for the question ? The proposition is to give a pilot-vessel wishing to offer her pilotage services a special fog-signal for that purpose.

The question was put to the Conference upon the adoption of the proposition.

The Chairman.—The Yeas and Nays are called for.

The Yea and Nay vote is as follows :—

Austria-Hungary	.. ..	Yea.	Japan	Yea.
Belgium	.. .. ..	Yea.	Mexico	Nay.
China ..	.. .. ..	Yea.	Norway	Yea.
Chile ..	.. .. ..	Yea.	Portugal	Nay.
Denmark	.. .. ..	Yea.	Russia	Nay.
France..	.. .. ..	Nay.	Spain	Yea.
Germany	.. .. ..	Nay.	Sweden	Nay.
Great Britain ..	.. ..	Nay.	Siam	Yea.
Hawaii	.. .. ..	Nay.	The Netherlands.. ..	Nay.
Italy ..	.. .. ..	Yea.	United States	Yea.

The Chairman.—Eleven have voted in the affirmative, and 9 in the negative. The proposition is carried. The next business is the principle involved in section 3 on p. 5: " Shall a signal be given to a vessel desiring a pilot ?"

Admiral Nares (Great Britain).—Mr. Chairman, I have now to argue the case on the part of the vessel approaching. I do not know whether I shall be allowed to say that many voted on this point just now, not directly against the interests of the pilot. I believe that several are wishing the pilot to come into communication with the ship wanting a pilot, but in some other way than by giving the pilot a signal. Now that the pilot-boat is to have a signal there is no doubt that it weakens the argument considerably on the part of the approaching vessel, because now that one of them should declare what she is, it is not of so much importance that the other should be able to make the signal; but we will leave it to the Conference to decide upon that question.

I believe that there are several members in the Conference who are of the opinion that so long as a pilot-boat has a signal it is not of so great importance to give it to the approaching vessel. I have already stated this morning that the Committee will not pin their faith to the signal which they have given, and especially after the extra signal which we had to provide for use this morning.

We shall certainly want to reconsider what that signal is to be. The signal for a pilot will have to be considered by sixteen members of the Conference, who have been sitting in Committee upon it. Still there is a signal on my brain; but I did not know whether the Conference would like me to let out what my idea is, and I can only speak, of course, as an individual.

I have still one signal left for a steamer moving, if we continue our principle that she shall make a long blast and then a short one. We have given her the long blast followed by two shorts. What I am personally prepared to argue in the Committee is that if we do give the signal, I think there is advantage in having something before us. You see I am talking now as if we had withdrawn the signal which the Committee had proposed, and therefore I am putting something new before you. What I am prepared to propose is a long blast given by a steamer still moving followed by one short. She will be coming up the channel, giving a long and a short instead of a single long blast every two minutes. I would give precisely the opposite signal to a pilot-boat. I would give to a pilot-boat a short and a long. The proposition of the Board of Trade Committee is that as the communication signal may not be learned so readily as the danger signal, they shall begin with the short. I propose to give to the pilot a short and a long. By transposing these two signals I think they would be readily learned, and there would be very little confusion amongst the signals which you have already chosen. But that is altogether apart. I only put out the characteristics of the signal with a view to counteracting the impression which might be in the minds of some of the Delegates when they see that we have proposed a short, short, long, for both boats.

Now, I will tell why we did not propose these simpler characters in the Committee. This simpler signal of two sounds, a short and a long, has been chosen in London by the Committee of which I was one of the members, and we did not like to interfere with one of the very important characters. But still we must not view it as a selfish business. These signals have only been put forward, and the several characters are not yet adopted by the several countries. Each country still has to consider them. And if we here consider that our signal for a pilot is of sufficient importance to adopt this signal, then we have the right to adopt it. I have been rather long, but I thought it was necessary just to allude to the character and then to leave it to the Conference. These characters will have to be adopted if the Conference is prepared to adopt a signal for a ship wanting a pilot.

Mr. Carter (Hawaii).—Mr. Chairman, I only rise to say that we are just in the position I prophesied. We have given the pilot a signal, and now we must give the boat wanting a pilot a signal. It seems to me that of the two parties the one anxiously seeking a pilot was the one to be preferred, and although I think we are, on general principles, multiplying the signals to too great an extent, I really do not see how I can stand before the Conference, which in the plenitude of its wisdom has deliberately voted to give the pilot a signal, and refuse to give the signal to the man who is seeking a pilot. My convictions are against it; but under the circumstances I am compelled to stop the argument.

Mr. Hall (Great Britain).—Mr. Chairman, in stating how I wish to vote upon this, I wish, if I may do so, to imitate my learned friend on my right, and to give a similar reason. It appears to me that we are rather putting the cart before the horse. We have determined that a pilot-boat shall give a signal without first determining whether the vessel who wants the pilot is to give a signal. It seems to me that it is much more important that the vessel which wants the pilot should give the signal for the pilot. In the first place, if she is a steamer she can give a much more powerful signal, which can be heard a much greater distance. A pilot-boat signal will not properly be heard half the distance of that of an ordinary steamer. I see at once that we are in favour of a vessel wanting a pilot giving the signal. But now you have put us into this position. You have increased the number of signals by giving a pilot-boat a signal. We are in this dilemma:

The Conference has just adopted what we think is an objectionable principle, that is, increasing the number of these signals so much. On the other hand, we do not like to refuse to give a signal to the vessel which we think ought to have it, and that is to the vessel which requires a pilot. If the vessel which requires the pilot gives the signal you may be certain the pilot-boat will come to it without sounding any signal at all, and the vessel wanting a pilot is able to give a much more powerful signal. She will not wait to hear the signal of the pilot-boat, but she will keep on sounding her own signal as she goes up.

Captain Norcross (United States).—Mr. Chairman, it does not seem to me that the vessel requiring the pilot wants a signal. When she hears the pilot-signal she will make her way in that direction. It has been many times in my experience after a long passage from the Pacific or Eastern seas to be obliged to heave-to and lie many hours because I could not locate a pilot. Certainly if I could have done so I should put my ship's head in the direction of the sound, thankful that such a signal was contained in the General Rules of the Road. With the difficulty of finding special signals I think this can be safely waived in favour of some greater requirement.

The Chairman.—Is the Conference ready for the question? The proposition is that a special signal shall be given to the vessel requiring a pilot in a fog.

The question was to put to the Conference upon the adoption of the principle, and it was carried.

Mr. Hall (Great Britain).—Mr. Chairman, I now move, in consequence of this decision, a Resolution to which I referred before the Conference adjourned for recess to-day. It has already been pointed out, I think, sufficiently clearly and distinctly that this discussion has no connection whatever with the Rules of the Road. My Resolution is as follows: "That the Conferdnce being of the opinion that sound-signals should be adopted to be given by and for pilots in thick weather and for a fog, that Committee No. 2 be requested to consider and report as to the nature of such signals and to confer with the Sound-Signal Committee thereon."

The Chairman.—You have heard the proposition of the Delegate from Great Britain?

The question on the Resolution of the Delegate from Great Britain was put to the Conference, and carried.

Mr. Carter (Hawaii).—Mr. Chairman, the time has come for the adjournment, and as this is the only business to be transacted this afternoon I beg to ask the members of the Committee No. 2 to meet immediately upon the adjournment of the Conference.

Admiral Nares (Great Britain).—The Sound-Signal Committee is to join them.

Mr. Goodrich (United States).—Mr. Chairman, while I know that the only subject before the Conference was the special order which has just been discussed, I think it expedient to present the following Resolution, with the permission of the members, and I present it for the purpose of having the subject brought before the Conference. The Conference may either discuss it now or wait until the next meeting. It is this:—

"*Resolved,*—That, in the opinion of the Conference, it is inexpedient to adopt course-indicating sound-signals in foggy or thick weather, because among the other strong reasons presented by the Sound-Signal Committee, if such signals were used in crowded waters dangers would result from the uncertainty and confusion produced by the multiplicity of signals and from the false security which would be created in the minds of mariners.

Mr. Hall (Great Britain).—Mr. Chairman, I beg to support that Resolution most heartily. I was under the impression, and I think many of us are under the impression, that the Conference has already decided in an unmistakable way upon that very point, but so far as I am aware, and I have endeavoured to look through my notes which I have made during the meetings of the Conference, we have not actually passed a Resolution to that effect. I think it would be most desirable if we were to put this matter completely at rest. We have had a very able Report from the Sound-Signal Committee, which is before us, and so far as I am aware, since the presentation of that Report, and the very conclusive reasons which were advanced therein, no member of this Conference has argued in favour of course-indicating sound-signals. I think we are all of one mind upon the fact. I certainly should not ask the Conference to give its decision upon it unless I thought that we were absolutely unanimous upon the point; but if that be so, let us put it upon the record so that there shall be no doubt as to the opinion of the Conference upon this important subject.

Mr. Goodrich (United States).—Mr. Chairman, I desire to call out no great discussion on this, but I want to call the attention of the Conference to the very strong Report of the Committee on Sound-Signals, which was dated 31st October, where, on the second page, at the bottom of the page, the Committee states:—

"Until seamen are able to localize a sound with as great precision as they can the position of a light or object seen visually, the results to the mercantile marine from the adoption of a system of course-indicating fog-signals are in the opinion of the Committee a doubtful advantage. The chief use would appear to be to give facilities to approaching vessels, when not in sight of one another, and therefore when not certain of one another's position, to continue their respective courses without having first localized the direction and distance off of the neighbouring ship, and for the two vessels to try to pass close to each other without taking the precaution of first reducing or, if necessary, stopping their way through the water."

Later on, on p. 3, the Committee say:—

"The Committee are of opinion that, however simple an adopted system of course-indicating sound-signals may be, and however distinct in character the symbols chosen are from the signals now authorized and used, if vessels were navigated in dependence on them, when neither can see the other, there would be a danger of the officer in charge reading the signal incorrectly; or, if read correctly, of interpreting it wrongly.

"Further, if such signals were in use in crowded waters, we apprehend that danger would result from the uncertainty and confusion produced by the multiplicity of signals, and from a feeling of false security that would be created in the minds of many."

I have imported into the Resolution the final paragraph which I have just read. It was stated to me with a good deal of force the other day, by a gentleman who was very urgent to have these course-indicating signals adopted, that the primordial protoplasm of this Conference was the necessity of having course-indicating sound-signals in a fog adopted. Therefore, I have presented this Resolution that the public may know, if this Resolution is adopted, that, although the Conference have given the most careful study to the subject, not only around the board, but in the Committee-room, they are of the opinion, perhaps unanimous, that the time has not come for the adoption of any such course-indicating sound-signals.

The Chairman.—The Chair understands that before recess it was decided to close the Conference after the business which has already terminated.

Mr. Goodrich (United States).—Mr. Chairman, I would ask unanimous consent to present this Resolution.

Mr. Carter (Hawaii).—Mr. Chairman, I would simply point out that some of the Delegates may have remained away this afternoon who would perhaps like to be present before any action was taken upon this Resolution.

Mr. Goodrich (United States).—Mr. Chairman, then I will postpone it. I will let it lie over and be printed.

Admiral Bowden-Smith (Great Britain).—Mr. Chairman, may I give notice, on behalf of my colleague, Captain Mensing, that he would like to have his Committee meet at 10 o'clock to-morrow morning? He is not well enough now to come himself.

The Secretary.—I am directed by the President of the Conference to say that, owing to the illness of Lieutenant Baba, he has appointed his colleague, Mr. Tsukahara, on the Committee on Collocation.

Mr. Goodrich (United States).—Mr. Chairman, I move that the Conference adjourn until Monday morning at 11 o'clock. The Collocation Committee will meet to-morrow morning at 10 o'clock.

Mr. Hall (Great Britain).—Mr. Chairman, may I suggest that for Monday we might perhaps fix some order of business so that we may be prepared? There are several Reports of Committees in the hands of the members, and have been for nearly a week. I suppose that we might deal with them on Monday morning after dealing with the Resolution as to course-indicating sound-signals, which I suppose will come first. I would suggest that we take up then the Reports of the several Committees which have sent them in, and which we have had time to consider, so that the Delegates may know what business to be prepared to discuss when we meet.

The Chairman.—Will the Delegate from Great Britain indicate what part he would like to have taken up?

Mr. Hall (Great Britain).—Mr. Chairman, there are two already in our hands, the Load Line Committee and the International Maritime Commission Report.

Mr. Goodrich (United States).—Mr. Chairman, I would like to have that arranged in such a manner that the Report of the Collocation Committee shall have precedence whenever it is ready for presentation; because, while we have the Rules of the Road in our mind, it is probably wise for us to finish with the Report. I think the Collocation Committee will be able to present the printed Report to members on Monday morning; and unless some one objects, I shall ask that it be taken up Monday morning.

Dr. Sieveking (Germany).—Mr. Chairman, I would like to remark that I do not think it would be very advisable to deal with the Report of the Collocation Committee as soon as it has been handed in. If it is handed in on Monday morning, as it will be perhaps, it would be wiser to allow the members of the Conference four, five, or six days' time to consider it, as it really is very important to consider every item and every word in that Report.

The Chairman.—The Chair would state that there are two Committee Reports, one on the load-line and one on Division No. XIII, which have been completed and handed in.

Mr. Hall (Great Britain).—Mr. Chairman, of course I am very anxious that the Delegates should have ample time to consider the Report of the Collocation Committee; but I should think that forty-eight hours would be ample time to consider simply a question of verbiage. No question of principle is involved in the Report of the Collocation Committee. It is merely verbiage, the principle being determined by the Conference. I apprehend that it is a matter which the Delegates will not require very many days to consider. It is a pure matter of verbiage and nothing else.

Captain Richard (France).—Mr. Chairman, I cannot agree with the learned Delegate from Great Britain in considering the work proposed to us strictly as a matter of verbiage. There is a work before us in its entirety, which we are going to review thoroughly. Before submitting this this law to our various Governments, it will be necessary for us to see how its various component parts are adjusted among each other. It seems to me that it will be necessary to cast a glance over the entire edifice, and to see whether it is well built. Possibly we may find things to add, and possibly other things to strike out. I think that we should give a very careful scrutiny to its final wording, which will establish a great number of new Rules. Under these circumstances I will ask the Conference to support the proposition of the learned Dr. Sieveking, and to give us several days to enable us to read attentively and with all necessary care a work which will come out of the hands of the Collocation Committee as the conclusion and the crowning of our laborious discussion.

Mr. Verney (Siam).—Mr. Chairman, I desire to say one word in support of what has fallen from the gallant Delegate from France. It does seem to me that, when we get the Report of the Collocation Committee into our hands, we shall have before us a document which will come before us for the first time. I desire to remind this Conference that the proceedings of the Conference have been unlike that of many other Conferences in this respect, that we have never had—perhaps it would not be possible—the minutes of each day's proceedings read at the commencement of each session, which is provided for in Crocker's Manual, which has been adopted as the Rules for the proceedings of this Conference. I think that there are several besides myself who find it impossible to go through the Protocol carefully during each day. Several of us have only had one copy of the Protocol, and that we have handed back to the Secretary for the purpose of revision. Therefore, perhaps, I may be allowed to say one word in support of what has fallen from the gallant Delegate from France, that we do want considerable time to look over the Report of the Collocation Committee, in order to do full justice to their very valuable labours.

Mr. Carter (Hawaii).—Mr. Chairman, I would suggest that this discussion would be more pertinent when the Report is handed in, and we see what it is and what we want time to consider.

Mr. Goodrich (United States).—May I ask through you, Mr. Chairman, whether there is any other Committee which is likely to hand in its Report in the early part of the week?

Mr. Carter (Hawaii).—I think Committee No. 2 will hand in their Report. In fact, a part of it has been ready for some days; but this new work has kept us back a little.

Captain Richard (France).—Mr. Chairman, the Committee on Life-Saving Systems will soon be ready to produce its Report. The President of that Committee not being in the room, I have taken upon myself the duty to answer and to give the Conference the necessary information. We have but a slight difference to smooth over, or, I should rather say, a certain adjustment to make in one part of our Report. It is a very small matter, and I think that it will soon be ready.

[93]

Mr. Goodrich (United States).—Mr. Chairman, would Committee No. 2 be able to present their Report upon General Divisions VII and VIII, leaving the subjects referred to them to-day as a matter of a Supplementary Report?

Mr. Carter (Hawaii).—I think so. The subjects referred to us to-day, I apprehend, would take a very few minutes, after the conclusion at which the Conference has arrived. We only have to consider what the signal should be that is to be incorporated in our Report.

Mr. Goodrich (United States).—Mr. Chairman, perhaps it is unnecessary for any special order to be provided for, except that there will be three Reports on Monday, and we can take them in their order as they are presented.

I move that when we adjourn we adjourn until Monday morning at 11 o'clock.

The Conference thereupon adjourned until Monday, December 9, at 11 o'clock A.M.

Washington, Monday, December 9, 1889, 11 o'clock A.M.

THE Conference was called to order at 11 o'clock A.M., Rear-Admiral Franklin in the Chair.

The President.—The Secretary will please read an invitation for the information of the Conference.

The invitation is as follows:—

"*Department of State, Washington, December* 6, 1889.

"The Secretary of State presents his compliments, and, at the instance of the Joint Committee of the Senate and House of Representatives, has the honour to invite you to be present at the ceremonies to be held in the House of Representatives, Wednesday, the 11th instant, at 1 o'clock P.M., in commemoration of the centennial inauguration of the first President of the United States, George Washington."

The President.—Any Delegates desiring to attend will please let the Secretary know, and they will be given tickets of admission to the House of Representatives.

The Chair now desires to announce that Señor A. P. Cheney, Delegate from Nicaragua, has appeared in the Conference and taken his seat.

The first business in order this morning will be the Reports of Chairmen of Committees. Are there any Reports to be submitted?

Mr. Goodrich (United States).—Mr. President, in order to save time, though a little out of order, I present a Resolution as an addition to the Resolution presented on the 5th December in regard to course-indicating sound-signals, which I will ask the Secretary to read.

The President.—Does the Delegate desire this addition to be printed for further consideration?

Mr. Goodrich (United States).—Mr. President, it may be read first to see whether the Conference is ready to adopt it now, or whether it shall be printed.

The President.—The Secretary will please read the addition to the Resolution proposed by the Delegate from the United States.

The Resolution is as follows:—

"*Resolved*,—That in the opinion of the Conference it is inexpedient to adopt course-indicating sound-signals in foggy or thick weather, inasmuch as, among the other strong reasons presented by the Sound-Signal Committee, if such signals were used in crowded waters danger would result from the uncertainty and confusion produced by a multiplicity of signals and from the false security that would be created in the minds of mariners; and if vessels were navigated in dependence on such signals, when neither could see the other, there would be danger that the officer in charge might read the signal incorrectly, or, if he read it correctly, would interpret it wrongly."

The President.—Is the Conference ready to consider this question now, or does any Delegate desire that it should be printed and laid over for further consideration?

Mr. Goodrich (United States).—Mr. President, I might say in regard to this matter that I have simply added to the Resolution which I offered the other day a few words, taken, with some slight changes of grammar rendered necessary by the language of the Resolution, bodily from the Report of the Committee on Sound-Signals. I have now embodied in this Resolution both of the grounds upon which the Committee saw fit to report that it was inexpedient to adopt these course-indicating sound-signals in foggy weather. If there is any desire to have it printed, I have no objection to having it laid over. I will, however, move the passage of this Resolution. I gave my reasons for presenting it at the last meeting of the Conference.

Mr. Hall (Great Britain).—Mr. President, I hope this Resolution will be passed, because I apprehend that the feeling of the Conference is practically unanimous on the point, and if any of us had doubts before, those doubts, I think, have been set at rest after consideration of the very able Report of the Sound-Signal Committee. The experience of the Conference during Wednesday and Thursday of last week, when we discussed and determined a very limited number of sound-signals, for cases which were admittedly cases of danger, will, I think, strengthen this feeling. Under these circumstances I hope that the Conference will not have any difficulty in coming to a determination upon this Resolution.

The President.—The Resolution will be read again for the information of the Conference.

The Resolution is as follows:—

"*Resolved*,—That in the opinion of the Conference it is inexpedient to adopt course-indicating sound-signals in foggy or thick weather; inasmuch as, among the other strong reasons presented by the Sound-Signal Committee, if such signals were used in crowded waters danger would result from the uncertainty and confusion produced by a multiplicity of signals, and from the false security that would be created in the minds of mariners; and if vessels were navigated in dependence on such signals when neither could see the other, there would be danger that the officer in charge might read the signal incorrectly, or, if he read it correctly, would interpret it wrongly."

The President.—The question is upon this Resolution.

Mr. Goodrich (United States).—Mr. President, upon that I call for the Yeas and Nays.

Mr. Hall (Great Britain).—Mr. President, might I point out if there was no expression of opinion against the Resolution it would be unanimous?

Mr. Goodrich (United States).—Mr. President, my reason for calling for the Yeas and Nays is that the members of the United States' Delegation have been approached and pressed by various bodies and by many individuals to secure from the Conference, if possible, the adoption of these course-indicating sound-signals in a fog; and while I know that the Committee have made a very strong Report, I still want to have it appear that the Conference, not hastily, but by the expression of each Delegate, have expressed their idea upon this Resolution.

The Yea and Nay vote is as follows:

Austria-Hungary	Yea.	Italy	Yea.
Brazil	Yea.	Japan	Yea.
Belgium	Yea.	Mexico	Yea.
China	Yea.	Norway	Yea.
Chile	Yea.	Nicaragua	Yea.
Denmark	Yea.	Russia	Yea.
France	Yea.	Spain	Yea.
Germany	Yea.	Sweden	Yea.
Great Britain	Yea.	Siam	Yea.
Hawaii	Yea.	The Netherlands	Yea.
Honduras	Yea.	United States	Yea.

The President.—Twenty-two have voted in the affirmative, there are no negatives, and five absentees; so the Resolution is unanimously adopted.

Mr. Goodrich (United States).—Mr. President, I will now present a Report of the Collocation Committee of an interlocutory character, which I am compelled to present without the signature of the Delegate from France, as he was not at the session of the Committee at which this subject was considered, and is not in attendance on the Conference this morning. I will ask the Secretary to read the Report.

The interlocutory Report of the Collocation Committee is as follows:—

"To Rear-Admiral Samuel R. Franklin,

"President of the International Marine Conference:

"The Collocation Committee have deemed it wise to make an interlocutory Report, calling attention to extra amendment No. 41 for Article 3, proposed by Captain S. W. Flood, of Norway, and adopted by the Conference November 14.

"It reads as follows:

"'Art. 3 (*g*). Said green and red side-lights to be placed in steam-vessels not forward of the masthead-light, and in sailing-vessels as near abreast of the foremast as practicable.'

"The Collocation Committee is aware that the Conference did not confer upon it the right to suggest or make any change of the principle contained in any of the Rules, but the proposed change is so radical and far-reaching in its results, that in the opinion of the Committee the attention of the Conference should be again called to the serious difficulties in the way of its adoption, and the great expenses to steam-vessels, and especially to war-vessels, which will result from this provision.

"The Committee therefore recommend that this amendment be reconsidered, and that if the proposed change of the position of the side-lights is approved of, the suggestion be made in a note, instead of being embodied in the Regulations.

(Signed) "SPAUN, *Austria-Hungary.*
"SIEVEKING, *Germany.*
"CHARLES HALL, *Great Britain.*
"S. TSUKAHARA, *Japan.*
"A. R. MONASTERIO, *Mexico.*
"T. SALVESEN, *Norway.*
"N. KAZNAKOFF, *Russia.*
"WM. W. GOODRICH (*Chairman*), *United States.*"

Mr. Goodrich (United States).—Mr. President, I do not know that the Conference will care at this time to hear the reasons which induced the Collocation Committee to present this Report, or whether it would be the desire of the Conference that this Report should be printed and laid upon the table for future action. I am prepared to take either course, according to the wish of the Conference, especially, I may say, in deference to the desire of the learned Delegate from Norway, who presented the amendment in question.

The President.—The question is upon the motion to reconsider.

Mr. Flood (Norway).—Mr. President, as this amendment, which was carried and accepted by the Conference, was presented by me, I most sincerely beg permission to have it laid over for future consideration. It was put into my hands about five minutes ago, and before that time I had no idea that it would be brought before the Conference. I think it only fair to give some little chance to think the matter over.

Mr. Hall (Great Britain).—Mr. President, I am sure that we shall all agree that this matter should stand over for future consideration, so that we may all of us be prepared to discuss it thoroughly when it is next reached. Might I suggest this, that we request the Committee on Lights to be so kind as to consider this point? I think they could aid us, without trespassing on their time to any great length, because we are aware that this was introduced in consequence of something which was included in the Report of the Committee on Lights. For that purpose I would move that the Committee on Lights be requested to give the Conference its views on the matter referred to in the interlocutory Report of the Collocation Committee of this date. That is, of course, assuming, as I take for granted will be the case, that the Conference will agree to reconsider the matter, but we must take a formal vote to that effect. As soon as we do that I will then move to request the Committee on Lights to assist us in the matter.

The President.—The question is upon the motion to reconsider.

The question was put to the Conference upon the motion to reconsider, and it was carried.

Mr. Hall (Great Britain).—Mr. President, I now move *pro formâ* that the Committee on Lights be requested to give the Conference their views on the matter referred to in the interlocutory Report of the Collocation Committee of this date.

The President.—The Conference has heard the motion of the Delegate from Great Britain. Is the Conference ready for the question?

The question was put to the Conference upon the motion to refer the principle contained in the interlocutory Report of the Collocation Committee to the Committee on Lights, and the motion was carried.

The President.—The interlocutory Report of the Collocation Committee will be printed and referred to the Committee on Lights.

The next business in order is the consideration of the Report of the Committee on Uniform Load-Mark. There seems to be no other business before the Conference which takes precedence of this matter. It was the ruling of the Conference some days ago that these Reports should be considered in order after the Rules of the Road had been disposed of. The Rules are now practically disposed of so far as the Conference can deal with them. Therefore, in order to keep up the continuity of the work, the next order of business appears to be the consideration of the Reports. The Report of the Committee on Uniform Load-Mark will be read.

The Report is as follows:—

"*Report of the Committee upon the subject of a Uniform Load-Mark, General Division No. III of the Programme.*

"*Members of the Committee.*—Brazil, Captain J. Maurity; Chile, Lieutenant Beaugency; China, Lieutenant Chia Ni Hsi; France, Captain Richard; Germany, Dr. Sieveking; Great Britain, Mr. Gray; Italy, Captain Settembrini; the Netherlands, Captain Hubert; United States, Mr. Griscom.

"Sir, "*Washington, November* 26, 1889.

"Your Committee, having been appointed to report on the subject of a uniform load-mark, have first of all endeavoured to obtain as much information as could be collected on this very important question.

"The British law, as laid down in 'The Merchant Shipping Act, 1876' (39 & 40 Vict., c. 80), gives certain powers to the Board of Trade to detain British and foreign vessels which, by reason of overloading or improper loading, are unfit to proceed to sea without serious danger to human life. These powers may be put into force against foreign ships when they have taken on board all or any part of their cargo at a port in the United Kingdom, and are, whilst at that port, unsafe by reason of overloading or improper loading.

"With the intention of carrying out this law in a way consistent with the interests of the mercantile community on the one side, and with the regard due to protection of life and property on the other side, certain general Rules, after careful investigations instituted by a Load-Line Committee appointed by the President of the Board of Trade, as well as by the Board of Trade, have been framed with the purpose of ascertaining whether a ship be overloaded or not. These Rules assign to ships a freeboard which, according to the experience collected on the subject, is considered sufficient to prevent dangerous overloading without unduly interfering with trade, and they contain Tables assigning such freeboard as is suitable for vessels of the highest class in Lloyd's Register, or of strength equivalent thereto, and which is to be increased for ships of inferior strength.

"The above-mentioned Rules have proved to be a good standard upon which to determine the proper loading of British vessels which are classed in Lloyd's Register, or for other vessels the particulars of whose strength and fitness to carry any particular cargo can easily be ascertained by the Surveyors of the Board of Trade.

"As regards foreign ships, however, which are loading in the United Kingdom, and which are either not classed in Lloyd's Register or the particulars of which cannot be ascertained without a minute examination, the difficulty exists that the law which intends to guard against the dangers arising from overloading cannot be enforced without serious disadvantages to the owners of ships and cargoes consequent upon the difficulty of ascertaining whether the ships are fit to carry the cargo in question.

"For these reasons it appears to be obvious that it would be very desirable if means could be found to ascertain, in a simple and easy way and without loss of time, the fitness of any vessel loading in a port of the United Kingdom to load a particular cargo.

"These remarks naturally apply also to vessels loading elsewhere, because it is a very high and important interest, common to all nations, to take every possible measure for the protection of life and property against the dangers arising from overloading.

"For these reasons it appears to deserve very serious attention whether, by providing for a certain load-line to be marked on sea-going ships, a trustworthy and simple method could be arrived at for deciding whether a loading vessel should be detained for overloading or ought to be allowed to go to sea.

"The British Government has recently invited the attention of other Governments to this question. But inasmuch as up to the present no progress has been made in this matter, the question arises whether something could be done to expedite an understanding by any action on the part of the Conference now here assembled.

"Now, as far as your Committee have been able to ascertain, the laws of many maritime nations contain provisos for dealing with the question of overloading and enabling the local authorities to detain overladen ships. But nowhere, except in Great Britain, as far as is known, have statutory rules been introduced for the purpose of ascertaining whether a ship be fit to carry a certain cargo by a load-mark or load-line.

"In order to arrive at such laws and to enforce them it would appear to be necessary to induce the Governments of the maritime nations not only to institute investigations similar to those made in Great Britain above referred to, but also to establish a sufficient staff of competent officials to insure the universal compliance with the laws to be given, and to establish Courts of Appeal authorized to decide on complaints against unjust detention, and to award damages to the ship-owners and shippers of cargo in case of an unjustifiable detention.

"It appears to your Committee that this would be surrounded with very serious difficulties, as it depends upon the varying conditions of each country whether the Governments would think it advisable to take steps in this direction or not. It must be kept in mind that a great display of scientific labour, and, moreover, a heavy expenditure of money, would be necessary to introduce a system similar to that which is used in Great Britain. Besides, it could be questioned whether it be necessary to make a law on load-lines or load-marks in order to guard against the danger of overloading, because it might be said that sufficient safeguards are given by the responsibility of the ship-owners towards the shippers of the cargo, and to their insurers, and by the control exercised by the underwriters and the various institutions for classing ships. There may also be circumstances peculiar to certain countries, as, for example, the fact that the goods which they export, generally, are light goods only, which do not endanger the stability of a ship, which may operate in favour of non-interference on behalf of the respective Governments.

"Your Committee is led to believe that on these grounds, notwithstanding the advantages which would be connected with the introduction of a uniform system of load-marks, this matter is not ripe for consideration of this Conference, and that it ought to be left to the negotiations to be carried on between the Governments of the maritime nations.

"We beg to remark, in concluding, that this Report has been sanctioned by the undersigned members of your Committee unanimously; and that Mr. Thomas Gray, who has been prevented from reading and signing it by the necessity of his departure, has, nevertheless, expressed his concurrence with its general views.

(Signed) " SIEVEKING, *Chairman of Committee.*
" J. MAURITY.
" R. BEAUGENCY.
" CHIA NI HSI.
" E. RICHARD.
" R. SETTEMBRINI.
" D. HUBERT.
" CLEMENT A. GRISCOM.

"To Rear-Admiral S. R. Franklin,
"President of the International Marine Conference, &c."

The President.—The Report is before the Conference.

Dr. Sieveking (Germany).—Mr. President, I beg to move the adoption of this Report. I do not think it is necessary to discuss it at present, and I beg to move that the Report may be adopted.

Mr. Hall (Great Britain).—Mr. President, before this matter is put to a vote, perhaps it is desirable that I should say a very few words with regard to the attitude which Great Britain has taken in this matter. It may be within the knowledge of the members of the Conference that this matter of a uniform load-line was especially included in the subjects to be discussed by the Conference at the suggestion of Great Britain. I need not say that, having regard to what we believe to be the beneficent results of the system which was carried out in England, we thought it would be a matter of great advantage if it could be adopted by the whole of the Maritime Powers. We came here under that opinion, and we are still of the opinion that, if such a matter can be carried out, it is most desirable, in the interest of all seafaring humanity, that it should be reduced into an international Rule

But, Mr. President, I am aware that this matter has been most carefully considered by a Committee who have investigated it thoroughly; and having regard to the nature of their Report—although, as I say, we are most anxious that this matter should become a subject for international agreement—that this matter is not ripe for consideration by this Conference, we bow to the decision of that Committee, and consider that it would not be becoming on our part to waste the time of the Conference by arguing a matter which the Committee have reported not to be ripe for decision at the present time.

The President.—Is the Conference ready for the question on the motion of the Delegate from Germany, to adopt the Report of the Committee on a Uniform Load-Line? Does the Delegate from Great Britain desire the Ayes and the Noes called on this question?

Mr. Hall (Great Britain).—No, Mr. President.

The question was put to the Conference upon the adoption of the Committee's Report on a Uniform Load-Line, and it was unanimously adopted.

The President.—The next business in order is the Report of the Committee on General Division XIII. The Secretary will please read the Report.

The Report is as follows:—

"*Report of the Committee upon General Division XIII.*

"THE ESTABLISHMENT OF A PERMANENT INTERNATIONAL MARINE COMMISSION.

" Sir, "*Washington, November* 26, 1889.

" Your Committee have considered the above matter, and beg to report as follows:—

" At the commencement of our proceedings we invited our colleagues and the Secretaries to the Conference to furnish us with the proposals, if any, prepared by Governments of the several Powers taking part in the Conference, or of any private societies or persons, bearing upon the subject in question. We have not succeeded in ascertaining that there are any such proposals in existence save the documents set out in the Appendices hereto (A), (B), (C), (D), and (E).

" We have considered whether such a Commission could be instituted with a practical result, and in such a manner as to lead to its adoption by the Maritime Powers.

" However desirable such a result would be, a majority of your Committee does not believe it to be possible to carry it into effect, and is of opinion that it cannot be regarded as one of practical feasibility at the present time.

" We have also decided, by a majority of votes, that it is not possible to create an International Tribunal to try questions of collisions between subjects of different nationalities.

" In coming to this conclusion we have been guided, amongst others, by the following considerations:—

" An International Commission could not be invested with any legislative power. It would be a consulting body only, constituted with the view of preparing universal legislation on maritime matters of international importance. Apart altogether from the difficulties connected with the formation of such a body, the questions as to its domicile, as to who are to be its members, and how and by whom the members are to be compensated for their labours—difficulties which by themselves seem to be entirely insurmountable for the present—it seems to your Committee that such a consulting body of experts would not serve the purpose for which it is intended to be created, viz., that of facilitating the introduction of reforms in maritime legislation, because the advice given by such a Commission would not in any way enable the Governments of the maritime nations to dispense with the necessity of considering the subjects laid before them, and laying the proposals made to them, if adopted, before the legislative bodies of the different States.

" The consequence of instituting a body like that in question, on the contrary, would, it appears, be this: that merely another investigation of any scheme proposed with a view to reforming International Maritime Laws would have to be gone through before the opinions of the Governments could be taken, and thus the course of procedure as it is now—by correspondence between the different Governments—would be made more complicated instead of being simplified. For these reasons your Committee beg to propose to resolve:—

" That for the present the establishment of a permanent International Maritime Commission is not considered expedient.

" We have, &c.

(Signed) " TH. VERBRUGGHE, *Delegate of Belgium.*
" OSCAR VIEL, *Delegate of Chile.*
" E. RICHARD, *Delegate of France.*
" F. SIEVEKING, *Delegate of Germany.*
" CHARLES HALL (*Chairman*), *Delegate of Great Britain.*
" F. MALMBERG, *Delegate of Sweden.*
" CLEMENT A. GRISCOM, *Delegate of United States.*

" To Admiral S. R. Franklin,
" President of the International Marine Conference, &c."

" I regret that I am unable to sign this Report, as its general tenour varies too much from the views entertained by the Maritime Associations in my country on the important question mentioned in General Division XIII of the Programme.

" I have endeavoured to explain the views in this respect of the said Associations, as well as my own opinion, in a letter to the present Committee, which is laid before the Conference as Appendix (C) to the Committee's Report.

" AUG. SCHNEIDER, *Delegate of Denmark.*"

Mr. Hall (Great Britain).—Mr. President, as Chairman of this Committee, perhaps I may say a few words pointing out the reasons which have induced us to come to the conclusions embodied in our Report. In the first place, it was desirable that the Committee should ascertain if there were any authoritative proposals made by any Delegate to the Conference to see whether any of the Maritime Powers had desired any proposal to be laid before the Conference; and, if so, what the nature of those proposals was. So far as we have been able to ascertain, there are no proposals whatever brought forward by any foreign Government, and we think there could hardly be a stronger illustration of the necessity for not dealing with this matter at present, because it is clear that the foreign Governments have been invited to do so, as I will show the Conference in a very few moments, and they have apparently not thought the matter ripe for discussion, or that any proposal could be made at the present time.

Now, I will give you my reasons for stating that the foreign Governments have been requested to consider this matter and to instruct their Delegates to make proposals at this Conference, and that they have all declined to do so. The Conference of the Scandinavian Powers took place in the month of July last year, a year and a half ago. That was a representative body; but the Delegates, who were representative ship-owners and underwriters, and so forth, had no authority as Representatives of any Government at all. They came to a general conclusion, which is embodied on the first page of their Report, p. 5 of the Appendix, in which, in giving their reasons, they say:—

"That the development of the shipping trade which has taken place during the last years having given rise to a great number of questions of which the satisfactory solution is of the utmost importance to the trade, the Conference resolves: That this object best can be obtained by the establishment of a Permanent International Commission, and requests the Committee of the Conference to present a Memorandum to this effect to the Maritime Congress, which is to be held at Washington in the last days of April next year, and to apply to the Governments of the Northern States to submit the said Resolution, with their recommendation, to the Great European Powers and the United States of America."

That was carried, and I have no doubt whatever that the Committee did as they were requested and brought the matter before the Governments of the various Maritime Powers. They went further. The Committee appointed four gentlemen, undoubtedly of considerable position in the maritime world in Denmark, to prepare a Report. One of them was our honourable friend the Delegate who represents Denmark in this Conference. They drew up a Report, and their Report is set out in the Appendix. I think I ought to say at the outset that our object in preparing this Report has not been merely to deal with the question at the present time and to report that the matter is not ripe for consideration now, but considering the desirability of giving to all the Maritime Powers all the information on the subject, we have thought it right, even at the expenditure of a considerable amount of printing, to print the whole of the proposals which have been laid before us as a Committee.

We have laid before this Conference in this Report all of the proposals which we are aware of, which have been made with regard to the establishment of an International Maritime Commission, because we have thought it desirable that when this Report is sent in as a part of the proceedings of the Conference, the attention of those who are responsible for the maritime trade of the respective countries will inquire into the matter, and they will have the materials before them at once. In that way a great deal of time will be saved which otherwise would be expended. We want to bring the matter before the various Powers so that they can consider it thoroughly. Now, as I say, these gentlemen were appointed by the Committee to draw up a Report, and they did so. They drew up one which is a very interesting document indeed; but the sole recommendation in it with regard to an International Maritime Conference is to be found on p. 44. The Conference will see at once that it was impossible for us to formulate any International Commission upon such a mere sketch of a proposal as is there given. It is at p. 44:—

"A Permanent International Merchant Shipping Bureau should be established in London, with a staff consisting of a Chief Secretary, two Assistant Secretaries, and the necessary number of clerks, &c. This Bureau—which should be the intermediate link between the Governments as to the regular and general communications respecting the international sides of merchant shipping questions—would, under control of the Commission, have to collect and arrange all sorts of information in respect to international maritime Laws or Regulations, to prepare the proposals received from the Contracting Governments, maritime institutions, or private persons, to be laid before the Delegates of the Commission, and, on the whole, to perform the different inquiries or other special tasks intrusted to it by the Commission. It should take charge of all the necessary publications, the Reports of the Conferences held by the Commission, and the correspondence (in the English language) with the Commission or its Sub-Committees, as well as with the different maritime institutions and the public in general. The Chief Secretary should attend the conferences of the Commission, and take part in the discussion, but without right of voting. The Bureau to prepare a yearly Report (in the English language) of its works, and to forward it to the Administrations of the Contracting States.

"The common yearly expenses of this Bureau might probably be estimated at the same sum as proposed for the expenses of the Bureau of the International Customs Tariff Commission at Brussels. The sum to be participated by the Contracting States in proportion to the *gross registered tonnage* of their merchant steam fleets, but otherwise in the manner settled by the other International Conventions. The Permanent Merchant Shipping Commission to be composed of two or three Delegates from each of the Contracting States, of which one should be an expert in practical maritime questions, and the other an expert in maritime law. The Commission to hold conferences with intervals of at least two years, alternately, in the capitals of the six most important Maritime States. The expenses of these conferences to be borne in equal proportions by the Contracting States."

[93]

These were the proposals of that Committee. I may state that our Committee has received very great assistance from the learned Delegate from Denmark, especially in the Memorandum which he handed to us, Appendix (C) to the Report of our Committee. If we look at that, we find at once the key-note to the whole of this Report, in which the learned Delegate himself points out that the time has not come, and will not come for many years, when there should be such an International Maritime Commission. That will be found at p. 6. He says:—

"The views entertained on the composition and mode of action of a Permanent International Maritime Commission seem at present to vary too much. For instance, in a Report presented to the present Conference by several French marine societies, dated Havre, 5th August, 1889, it is recommended to establish a great international Tribunal, established in a neutral country, composed of international Judges, to decide absolutely, in fact and law, all matters which will be referred to them."

Now, as the learned Delegate from Denmark pointed out, the time has not come, and will not come for many years, when there should be such an International Maritime Tribunal, and he suggests merely the establishment of a Bureau to collect information. As he properly points out, this would be a good thing for the countries which have not got an establishment like the Board of Trade of England. We have such a body already; they have to collect these facts, and to deal with and digest all of these questions. Then we communicate with the foreign Governments, as soon as we arrive at what we believe to be the key to any difficulty presented or any invention brought before us. I think it would be very desirable that, for instance, the Scandinavian Powers should combine to have a Bureau amongst themselves, and that countries which have shipping alike and which have uniform objects in common should also do so. I think it is very desirable that they should have a Bureau; but that is a very different thing from establishing a Bureau to sit in London which should be represented by Delegates from all the Maritime Powers. The establishment of such a Bureau is not the matter which was referred to us, but it was the question of an International Maritime Commission.

Now, we have a very interesting Report from Captain Augé, which was communicated to us by the gallant Delegate from France who formed a member of our Committee. I have read that also with great care. His proposal, I take it, is a proposal that an International Maritime Tribunal should be established to try collision cases. He does not attempt to go into details or to formulate any distinct proposals, but presents what I may call, without any disrespect, a Utopian theory that we should have a Maritime Conference to determine everything connected with maritime matters throughout the world, which is impossible. Let us see whether such a thing as he suggested is practicable. First of all, there is one matter which I think every person connected with the administration of maritime law can have no doubt about, and that is the principle that it is most important that collision cases should be tried with the utmost expedition and celerity. When a vessel comes into port, the crew is there and the witnesses are there. It is most important that you should have the matter decided before they are dispersed, whilst you can easily get your evidence. It has always been laid down by our Admiralty Judges that in the administration of Admiralty law there should be the utmost dispatch, so as to get the evidence while the men have the facts fresh in their minds, and before they can be tutored upon the subject.

In Captain Augé's very interesting work he deals with various proposals; but they are proposals which we could not deal with here. For instance, he proposes to have an original Tribunal which is to be composed of three experts. One is to be chosen by the country in which the litigation takes place, and the other two, one by each side. What would be the use of such experts, one appointed by the plaintiff and one by the defendant? They would agree to differ before they went into Court at all; so that the matter would be left to the third expert, who would be appointed by the State in which the litigation took place. After that, he proposes that there should be an international Court of seven Judges, with experts and Secretaries, who are to decide cases upon written reports, and who are not to receive assistance from any one learned in the law at all. That is a proposal which I do not think the lawyers of this Conference would receive with open arms. I think, possibly, that sometimes lawyers may be of assistance to a Court which is discussing maritime matters. But his proposal is that the seven Judges, with experts and with Secretaries, and having the printed evidence before them, should then decide upon the matter at once, without having any argument addressed to them on either side.

There are other proposals. I have before me the proposal of M. Riondel, that there shall be a Permanent International Commission, composed of members of each of the Governments which have accepted the International Regulations of 1879. I think there were sixteen Powers which sent in their adhesion to those Rules. Therefore, a Court of sixteen Judges would have to be sitting permanently; that is to say, they would have to be at some place where they could sit practically at a moment's notice. That, of course, is a matter which could not be arrived at practically. It is only a matter of theory.

Now, I do not propose to discuss any of these suggestions at any further length. I only wish the Conference to see that we have had the matter before us and that we have done our best to see that all of these suggestions are laid before the respective Governments of the Maritime Powers who take part in the Conference. We think we have taken the best way of doing that by having all of these suggestions printed and annexed to the Report on General Division XIII on the Programme. I think it will be clear to the gentlemen who are here at the present time that in the absence of some definitive proposal, or in the absence of definite matter, it is impossible for us to take any action. And I go so far as this: I venture to say that in order to deal with a matter of such magnitude as this it would require a year's careful preparation by persons who were devoting their minds to the subject, and that the matter should be most thoroughly considered and reported upon before any Conference, however distinguished, could reach any satisfactory determination upon the subject.

At present, as I say, we are all of us of the opinion that this cannot be properly dealt with at the present time. No single Delegate has got authoritative recommendations from his Government to make any proposal with regard to this General Division of the Programme, and having regard to the fact that we have no definite or substantial proposal before us, and no proposal which has been worked out carefully by any authoritative body, we have been obliged to come to the recommendations which we have made in our Report, and that is, that at present the matter is not ripe for discussion. It is practically the same Report as that which was made upon the subject of a uniform load-line. With regard to the subject of the load-line, at any rate we have had the advantage of the Report and of the Laws which have been acted upon by Great Britain for some time, and the data which were drawn up by a Committee which took evidence in all of the various sea-ports in Great Britain, and which was primed with information on the subject. But even then the Conference was of the opinion that the matter was not ripe for discussion. We also say that this matter is not ripe for discussion, because we are really not in the possession of any data upon which we can act.

Mr. Goodrich (United States).—Mr. President, I notice that there is annexed to the Report of this Committee a minority Report made by the very distinguished Delegate from Denmark, and I request that that Report should be read for the information of the Conference. I may say this, that I have taken extreme interest in this subject of a Permanent International Commission, and if it were at all practicable, or if I could see any way in which this object aimed at could be accomplished, I should be heartily in its favour. In regard to the position of the United States' Delegates upon this subject, I may say that we were led to insert this subject in our programme by the answer which had been sent to our Government by the Scandinavian Conference; and, while the United States' Delegates are quite willing to discuss it, we are of the opinion that the Report of the Committee is of such a nature as to require its adoption by the Conference.

The President.—The minority Report on General Division XIII will be read by the Secretary.

The minority Report is as follows:—

"*Appendix (C) to Report of Committee upon General Division XIII.—Programme of Subjects.*

"*General Division XIII.*—'The establishment of a permanent Maritime Commission.' (*a.*) The composition of the Commission. (*b.*) Its power and authority.

"As a member of the Committee appointed to consider and report on the above-named Division, I beg to submit, for the consideration of this Committee, the following remarks:—

"Section (*b*). The problem to determine the power and authority of any International Commission has always been considered to be most difficult to solve, and this seems particularly to be the case when a Commission shall have to do with maritime matters.

"The Second Northern Marine Conference held at Copenhagen July last year, which consisted of about 200 Delegates from the greater part of all the existing maritime institutions in Norway, Sweden, Denmark, and Finland, and which represented a merchant fleet of a registered tonnage, between two and three million tons, ranging in order of all merchant fleets as the second or third— unanimously passed a Resolution by which the establishment of a 'Permanent International Marine Commission,' with a Bureau, was recommended, and also that a Memorandum to this effect should be presented to the present 'International Marine Conference' at Washington.

"This Memorandum, which also has been distributed to the distinguished members of this Committee, will clearly show that it was not the intention of the Northern Conference that the proposed 'International Marine Commission,' with permanent Bureau, should have any power or authority at all, and, therefore, in no way would interfere with the sovereignty of the different Contracting Powers. On the contrary, it should only form the connecting link between the different Maritime Governments and countries in all maritime matters of an international character. It should also be composed as much as possible in conformity with the Commissions or Conferences and their permanent Bureaux, established under the Conventions about an international 'metre' measure, about the international 'postage,' and the international 'telegraphy,' which have acted with so much benefit to international intercourse.

"As before said, the 'Northern Conference' of 1888 proposed both a Permanent International Marine Commission, *consisting of Delegates* from all maritime nations, and a permanent 'Marine Bureau.'

"Though, in accordance with the principle of these proposals, I think it expedient at present, by the experience gained during the sittings of the present Conference, only to offer some suggestions as to the establishment of a Permanent International Marine Department or Bureau. The views entertained on the composition and mode of action of a 'Permanent International Maritime Commission' seem at present to vary too much. For instance, in a Report presented to the present Conference by several French Marine Societies, dated Havre, 5th August, 1889, it is recommended (pp. 104–126) to establish a 'Tribunal Suprême International établi en pays neutre, et composé de Magistrats Internationaux pour juger *souverainement*, en fait et en droit, les Jugements nationaux en dernier ressort, qui lui seraient déférés.' . . . .

"As far as I know the general opinion is that the time for such an institution has not come, and will not come for many years.

"In the Report presented by the Branch Hydrographic Office, New York City, it is only said about the Permanent Commission mentioned in Division (*b*):—

"'The establishment of such a Commission is to be generally desired, and much good can be done by providing for an annual meeting for the purpose of regulating maritime affairs.

"'The composition of the Commission and its powers and authority should be settled by the Conference, and can become a part of the international agreement.'

"Maybe the present International Conference will not be acutually dissolved, but only adjourned,

[93]

in order to assist in the further steps necessary for carrying into effect its proposals and recommendations, and so far, some time at least, could perform the part of an International Maritime Commission.

"In consideration of these circumstances the following remarks only apply to the establishment of an International Maritime Department or Bureau, which, of course, would have no other power or authority than that which would result from the knowledge that all international maritime matters taken up by such an institution would be treated with impartiality, and by the best practical and scientific experts which can be procured in the whole world.

"Section (a). As to the formation of said institution, I particularly wish to draw the attention of the Committee to the Rules for the International Bureaux established according to the 'Règlements annexés à la Convention Postale Internationale, Paris. 1er Juin, 1878, Article 16 ; et à la Convention Télégraphique Internationale de Saint-Pétersbourg. Révision de Berlin le 17 Septembre, 1885 ; et à l'Union Internationale pour la publication des Tarifs Douaniers. Bruxelles, 1888.'

"In accordance with the principles laid down in these Regulations, the International Department in question should be established in a great maritime city, presumably in London ; and should, if no International Marine Commission is established, be under the supervision of the Foreign Office in the country where it is domiciled. This Department would then be the intermediate link between the Governments as to the regular and general communications respecting the international sides of merchant shipping questions. Its principal data should be to collect and arrange all sorts of information in respect to international maritime Laws or Regulations; to prepare the proposals received from the Contracting Governments, maritime institutions, or private persons for the consideration of future International Marine Conferences ; and, on the whole, to perform the different inquiries or other special tasks intrusted to it by the Contracting Powers. It should take charge of all the necessary publications, and the correspondence with the different Governments, as well as with the different maritime institutions and public in general.

"The Department should also prepare a yearly Report of its labours, and forward it to the Maritime Departments in the Contracting States.

"It should have a Staff, consisting of a Chief Secretary, three or four Assistant Secretaries, and the necessary number of clerks, &c.

"The Chief Secretary should attend the future Maritime Conferences and take part in the discussion, but without the right of voting.

"The common yearly expenses of this institution might probably be estimated about 300,000 fr. yearly, which is 200,000 fr. higher than the yearly expenses for the International Postage Bureau at Berne, and 175,000 fr. higher than the expenses for the Bureau of the intended 'International Customs Tariff Commission' at Brussels; but, having regard to the importance of the Maritime Department, its more costly residence, and the practical trials with light and fog apparatus, &c., which must be expected, it is not safe to estimate the yearly expenses at a lower sum. This sum might, perhaps, be defrayed by the Contracting Powers in proportion to the number of their merchant-ships above 100 tons gross tonnage, or in the manner settled by other International Conventions.

"If it is asked who should appoint the officers belonging to such an institution, I should think that the simplest way would be to advertise over the whole world that an International Marine Department is to be established, with Secretaries and clerks; and then, if no International Maritime Commission is in existence, leave it to Delegates from the Contracting Powers, nominated expressly for that purpose, to make the selection among the applicants. The voting might perhaps be given according to the above-named proportion, and the said Delegates would no doubt be careful to select the officers from different countries in order to secure the greatest possible knowledge of the different languages.

"As will be seen, there is nothing new or original in this plan, as it is only continuing in well-known and tried paths laid down by earlier International Cnoventions.

"That such an institution would be a great benefit for all the countries which do not own such an excellent Department as the 'British Board of Trade' is self-evident. Almost every maritime reform which is asked for in the different countries must be considered also from an international point of view, but at present it is often rather difficult to get the necessary information in this respect ; while if such a Department existed, in a short time, and in the most reliable manner, the necessary information would easily be obtained. This would, no doubt, assist the various Governments considerably in carrying through the proposed new maritime laws, as certainly the advices and recommendations from such an international institution would be listened to with respect, and, if otherwise acceptable, followed by the Legislative Assemblies. I should also think that if such a Department had existed before the present Conference took place, much labour and time would have been spared. Many important questions raised, which are now dropped in want of any institution to get them inquired into and tried, would also then get a proper treatment. For instance, in looking into the valuable Report of the 'Committee on Systems and Devices,' I find the following remarks on several proposals on night signalling, &c. :—

"'No. 5. This signal lantern appears a good lamp, and is well reported on by United States' naval officers.'

"'No. 27. Lighthouse fog-horn.' 'Not within the scope of the Conference as regards lighthouses, but is worth a trial on board ship.'

"'No. 37. Lamp without a wick.' 'Committee cannot pronounce an opinion without comparing this lamp with others at sea.'

"'*On Miscellaneous Subjects.*

"'No. 23. New system of lamps and electric buoy.' 'Committee cannot pronounce an opinion without seeing them at sea.'

"'No. 25. White flash stern-light with model.' 'Worth the consideration of Conference if occulting stern-lights are introduced.'

"Here the question must strike every one, 'Who is to take care of these recommendations, and who is to make the necessary trials?'

"As a member of the 'Committee on Sound-Signals,' I have also had the opportunity of looking into a great part of the seventy or eighty inventions or proposals as to fog-signals. Though some of these must be considered as valuable, and when times are ripe perhaps will be introduced in practice, I am afraid that no official notice will be taken of them, and that they therefore will be lost for the maritime world. On the contrary, if such an international institution existed, all such proposals and plans would be forwarded to it, registered there, compared with other proposals in the same direction, and, if possible, tried in practice. If the Department should be unable to do so with its own means, there would certainly be many maritime countries which willingly would, on an application to them from the Department, take the matter in hand, and get the wished-for trials executed.

"The Reports from the other Committees have not yet been laid before the Conference, and it is therefore not easy to know if the matters treated by them have been found to be of such a character that they ought to be arranged by International Agreements, or should be left only to be made by local rules. If the questions are to be arranged according to International Agreements, I do not see how it at present can be done, whereas, if the said International Department existed, the valuable recommendations could be instantly acted on and carried into effect in a comparatively short time.

"If it is asked what maritime matters other than those contained in the Programme would by and by come under the care of said Department, I should wish to draw the attention of the Committee to the fact that, in the opinion of the oft-mentioned Northern Conference, there are several other matters which are of such a character that they ought to be arranged according to International Agreements.

"Of such matters there are named, and shortly treated in the Memorandum presented to the present International Conference, the following:—

"1. International tonnage measurement.
"2. Agreements for preventing the transfer of unseaworthy vessels to the flags of other nations.
"3. Uniform quarantine regulations.
"4. International uniformity in the law of damages caused by collision at sea.
"5. Uniform salvage regulations.
"6. International uniformity in the law of general average.
"7. International uniformity in the law of affreightment and bills of lading.

"I only mention these questions in order to show that there is a number of international maritime questions which should be prepared by a Department of the said kind to be laid before future International Marine Conferences.

"The maritime institutions in the north of Europe take the greatest interest in this question, and the standing Committees of the Northern Maritime Conference have expressly wished that I should do my best to gain the good-will of the present International Conference for the plan herein mentioned. I therefore sincerely hope that this important Committee will see its way to meet the wishes of the Northern Conference by recommending the establishment of an international institution of the described kind.

"Finally, I may add that the Scandinavian ship-owners have so keenly felt the want of a head-quarters that they, in this year, have established a common Central Maritime Bureau at Copenhagen, wholly at their own expense.

(Signed) "AUG. SCHNEIDER,
"Delegate from Denmark.

"Washington, November 25, 1889.

"To the Committee appointed to consider and report on
General Division XIII."

Mr. Schneider (Denmark).—Mr. President, may I be allowed to add a short epilogue to the letter just read? As the Report was unknown to me when I presented that letter to the Committee, naturally I wish to explain why I, though I agree in most points of the Report, still am quite unable to agree with the Resolution proposed by the majority of the Committee.

When it was known in the maritime circles in my country that one of the subjects on the Programme, as framed by the Board of American Delegates, concerned the establishment of a Permanent International Marine Commission, this event was hailed by many expressions of sincere satisfaction and of gratitude to the Government of the United States. There was this very natural cause for such feelings, that for the last two or three years a similar question had been discussed with great interest among the Northern Maritime Associations, of which interest the Memorandum laid before the Conference as Appendix (A) will bear witness. As I am in accordance with the principles on this question as represented in that paper, the Resolution proposed by the present Report has been a very great disappointment to me, and, as I believe, also to several other Delegates to this International Conference. The Committee have not seen its way to recommend any step at all, on account of the many difficulties which may arise against the realization of such a plan. Of course I admit that there will be many difficulties to overcome in its pathway. But may I ask, has the Conference not been summoned here expressly to cope with the many difficulties which surround almost every question it has had to deal with, and, if possible, to conquer such difficulties? I certainly think that the Conference has already with great success overcome at least as large difficulties in several other important respects. Why not try to do the same thing in this case?

If it were not my firm conviction, gained by over thirty years' experience in dealing with maritime matters more or less of an international character, that a Bureau of Information for International

Marine Affairs soon will show itself to be an inevitable necessity, I should certainly never have wasted a word on this proposal.

This conviction has been still more confirmed by the experience gained during the sittings of the present Conference, and particularly of late by examining the Reports of the Committees which hitherto have appeared, and which, in my opinion, clearly show the necessity of such a permanent institution, that can take up the proposals and recommendations of the Committees and lead them in the directions pointed out by the Conference.

Some years ago the general opinion certainly was that an "International Marine Conference," like the present, would be almost an impossibility; but now, thanks to the Government of the United States, it is an undeniable fact that such a Conference has taken place, and in a manner which, no doubt, will lead to several important results as to safety for life and property at sea.

I fully agree with the Report when it says, "An International Commission could not be invested with any legislative power," but I regret I am unable to agree when it states that the difficulties seem to be entirely insurmountable as to the formation of such a body, the questions as to its domicile, as to who are to be its members, and how and by whom the members are to be compensated for their labours. Here the ideas entertained by the Local Northern Conference last year must have been very much misunderstood. The plan was that the Commission should be composed of Delegates nominated just in the same manner as the Delegates to the present International Conference; also that it should have no fixed domicile at all, but only meet when a Conference should take place according to the arrangements in this respect by the Contracting Governments, and in the city pointed out by the Government who had proposed the Conference; and as they would only meet at intervals of years, members would not be entitled to any other compensation for their labours than what Delegates are entitled to during the sittings of all other Conferences, in accordance with the Regulations existing in the various countries. Therefore, the Delegates should only be considered as honorary members until a Conference was summoned; but nevertheless, it would be expected that they should keep themselves *au fait* with the international maritime questions brought to their knowledge at any time through the permanent Bureau.

It has been said that the British Board of Trade has done perfectly well the work of both the suggested Commission and of the proposed Bureau. No one conversant with nautical matters will deny that the maritime would is very much indebted to this most excellent Board for its painstaking and efficient labour, of course especially for the benefit of the English merchant fleet, and as a matter of fact also more or less for all other merchant fleets; but unfortunately this Board is not an international institution, and it can scarcely be expected that it will take up and deal with all unfinished subjects on the Programme, or the future international proposals which will continue to pop up, especially when such proposals do not have any particular interest for the British seamen. Besides, the more the international maritime arrangements get complicated, as, for instance, "The Rules of the Road at Sea," the greater number of doubtful points will be which are in want of an international elucidation. The British Board of Trade will not and cannot give any decided opinion on such questions as several of the gentlemen present will probably know of by personal experience; then please tell me, who shall answer such questions in times to come?

I am most anxious not unnecessarily to take up the precious time of the Conference, but at the same time I certainly think that the subjects under Division XIII already are, and in the future still more will be, of the greatest importance. The maritime circles, at least in my country, would therefore feel very much disappointed if the Conference agreed to the proposed Resolution, "That for the present the establishment of a Permanent International Maritime Commission is not considered expedient," without in some way or other adding an expression whereby this important matter can be kept up so that any Government, when the time is ripe, can launch the plan again.

The President.—The Chair will entertain a motion for the adoption of this Report.

Mr. Flood (Norway).—Mr. President, may I be allowed to say on behalf of the country which I have the honour to represent, and in behalf of its vast shipping interests, that we, in Norway, are very much in favour of the Resolution made by the learned Delegate from Denmark. The meeting of the Conference in Copenhagen, which has been repeatedly mentioned here, was held last year, with considerably over two hundred Delegates, and was composed of the cream of our seafaring ability, not only of ship-owners but also of our best Admiralty lawyers and insurance directors and adjusters. I have at the same time with great interest, and still more respect, followed the able words which have just been uttered by the learned Delegate from Great Britain against the advisability of such an International Marine Commission. I fully understand the argument which he presents, that there are so many obstacles in the way of the establishment of such a Commission, and that the time is not right for any Resolution in favour of it. I am fully aware of all that he has stated, and I would not for a moment detain this Conference by arguing in favour of passing a Resolution against the one already brought forward by the majority of the Committee.

The only thing I want to ask is that this matter should not be entirely put under the table; that it should not be entirely, so to speak, put on the shelf, as in the case of the Report of the Committee which is now before us. The Report of the Committee on the subject of a uniform load-line has been presented to us and we have unanimously declared that it is not desirable at the present time to adopt any principles; but the Committee when it closed the Report made the remark: "Your Committee is led to believe that on these grounds, notwithstanding the advantages which would be connected with the introduction of a uniform system of load-marks, this matter is not ripe for consideration by this Conference, and that it ought to left to the negotiations to be carried on between the Governments of the maritime nations."

Now, Gentlemen, if you are not willing, as I am sure you are not, to vote against the very able Report which has been laid before us by that Committee, I would ask you to show some good feeling to the proposal, and to give expression to your opinion in somewhat the same way as you have already done with regard to the Report of the Committee on the Uniform Load-Mark. I will take the liberty to propose that the following Resolution should be passed by this Conference :—

"*Resolved*,—That although for the present the establishment of a Permanent International Marine Commission is not considered expedient, this matter appears to be of such international interest that it is advisable it should be further investigated by communications carried on between the Governments of maritime nations."

That is the same recommendation as the one presented by the Committee on the Load-Line. I will ask the Conference to kindly take this into consideration before they vote one way or the other.

The President.—The Resolution of the Delegate from Norway will be read for the information of the Conference.

The Resolution is as follows :—

"*Resolved*,—That although for the present the establishment of a permanent International Maritime Commission is not considered expedient, this matter appears to be of such international interest that it is advisable that it should be further investigated by communications carried on between the Governments of maritime nations."

Dr. Sieveking (Germany).—Mr. President, I have listened with very great attention to the remarks which have fallen from the distinguished Delegate from Denmark, and I have also perused with great interest the Memorandum which is annexed as an Appendix to the Report of the Committee. I am sure that I am not the only one in this Conference to see that the arguments contained in this Appendix deserve great sympathy. I might even go a little further. I might venture to say that I hope that the ends which the learned Delegate from Denmark hopes to attain will be at some future time approached a little more nearly than we can do at present.

There can be no doubt, I think, that we are all of us imbued with a feeling that what we have done here for the past two months is to be the beginning only of a work which is to extend further, and which must attain a higher end than the mere forming of a Code for preventing collisions at sea; and although for the present we have declared that the matter is not ripe for discussion, yet I nevertheless think that the day will come, and that it will not be so very far distant, when the Governments will make serious efforts not only to make Rules to prevent collisions at sea, but also to make Rules for the prevention of collisions of laws. Commerce is uniting the nations now to such a degree that in fact nearly the same necessity which has now compelled the twenty-six Governments to unite for the purpose of agreeing upon certain Rules to be observed upon the high seas will compel them to try to give uniform laws on the most important subjects of maritime commerce, the general average, the contract of affreightment, &c. And I do not shrink at all for a moment from the difficulties which would surround the undertaking of such a vast plan.

But as we are assembled here for practical purposes, I think that instead of expressing such hopes and such convictions, we ought to look accurately at the question whether something practical can be done now; and I believe that notwithstanding the sympathy which the scheme laid before us by the Delegates of Denmark deserves on all sides, yet it has been sufficiently explained by the learned Delegate from Great Britain that it would be impossible even to realize only this part of the scheme—that is, the establishment of an International Bureau for the examining of questions of international importance in maritime affairs. As soon as you try to realize such an idea by putting it into certain words, you see that the difficulties are insurmountable, and that no great advantage could be derived from such a scheme being carried out. Let us even suppose that the twenty-six nations were to send one or two experts each—then a Commission of from thirty to fifty members would have to consider and prepare these questions. Or, to make it a little more practicable, let us say that five or six of the principal maritime nations consent to form a body of experts of from ten to twelve learned men. lawyers, and men of nautical experience, conversant with maritime affairs, provided with the necessary number of clerks, &c., and provided with the means not only of meeting at certain times, but also with means sufficient for printing, corresponding, &c. Let all of these difficulties be overcome, and let us think that such a body of from ten to twelve experienced and skilful and able men assemble in some capital, say in London, with the necessary number of clerks, and provided with the necessary means—then what would be accomplished? They certainly could not be invested with any authority to bind their Government, or to bind the Government of the nations which had no Delegates there. That is quite out of the question. It would have to be a body of experts, of prominent men, I dare say, who would be able to prepare such questions as were laid before them, to sift the schemes and to consider the questions, and then to work out some law which they might think it advisable to be accepted by the other nations. Now let us see, after they have done so, what will be the consequence. This law which they have prepared has to be laid before the Governments of all the maritime nations, and there, of course, this law, or this draft of a law, would have to be treated quite in the same way, as all draft laws and all questions on maritime commerce must be treated.

But the Governments of all maritime nations are more or less provided with officers whose duty it is to investigate these matters, to prepare laws, to examine plans which are laid before the different Governments, and then to prepare the legislation which is to be done by the several countries. Now, all of this would have to be done again. Of course the Government would not at once say that what this body of experts had settled upon would be acceptable without having carefully examined it. It would not be accepted. There would be alterations made, and then these alterations would have to be communicated to the different Governments. So, instead of simplifying the mode of proceeding, I am afraid, in fact I am quite sure, that the institution of such a body would actually tend to make more difficult the bringing about of an understanding between the different Governments.

Now, there is another and last point which I desire to mention. I do not think it is possible that a number of, say, ten or twelve—because we could not extend to an indefinite number of members—that a body of ten or twelve members could be composed so as to be really able to investigate and examine all the questions which are mentioned in this Memorandum, and which are certainly mentioned, and which deserve to be mentioned, as subjects of international maritime action by the separate Governments. The Governments, you see, are provided with their several officers. They have their own experts. The Board of Trade is not the only body of this kind—although the Board of Trade in this respect represents more than one-half of the tonnage in the world—but every Government has, more or less, its own staff of officers and experts, whose duty it is to go into these questions. Now, I will lay the question before any member of this Conference who knows anything about these affairs, whether this is not a considerable staff of officers—so numerous, in fact, as to require sometimes half-a-dozen experienced men to fill the positions of heads of the Departments, who can master these questions. There is no one man in the world who is able to say, when such a question is laid before him, I am the man to state how that question is to be dealt with without consulting anybody. So, you cannot get a body of experts of a limited possible number who are able to carefully prepare, as it should be done, all the questions which are laid before them.

Now, the end which the learned Delegate from Denmark wants to attain, and which we want to attain with him at some future time, could be attained much better by preparing the way for the discussion of this matter, but this must not be the work of Governments. It must be the work of private individuals and of Associations, the private individuals should do this work. Governments are rather slow, I agree; but then they sift with care, and they do, without mentioning it, greater work than many of us suppose they do. Many questions which are not brought before the legislative body at all, many questions which are not discussed in public at all, are carefully examined by the Governments, and because we do not hear of them we must not think that they are not busy, and that they do not do their duty in examining these questions. But still, to make the Governments a little more attentive and accurate, something could be done, and that, I think, could be done very well by private enterprise.

We have an example before us. We have seen the private ship-owners and insurers, and also the representatives of Chambers of Commerce and the Associations of Underwriters, &c., assembling and meeting at Glasgow, at York, and at Antwerp, to consider the subjects of general average. They have drafted Rules, and those Rules have been to a very great extent adopted in practice; and some of the Governments have followed in this matter. We have had, during the last year, a Conference assembled at Brussels, where the work has been begun of drafting a uniform Code of Commerce, or at least some Rules on the most important part of commercial law. And the Belgian Government has undertaken a very heavy work, which, if continued, will certainly merit the praise of all civilized nations, by communicating the results of this Conference to the different Governments, and trying to get their consent to it. This is the consequence of a movement which is brought about by private men, who are instigated by their common interests and by the common tie of commerce which now unites all nations, and which must make us clearly perceive that it is a necessity, greater or less, to have a uniformity of laws and uniformity of administration in regard to certain questions of maritime law.

We have not, and it was not our intention in the Committee, discouraged the idea of anything which would lead to the proposal made by the learned Delegate from Denmark. We have only recommended and resolved that for the present the establishment of a Permanent International Marine Commission is not considered expedient. I think that ought to be sufficient, without adding the words now proposed by the Delegate from Norway, because if we say that it is not expedient for the present to establish a Maritime Commission, still it is a matter of such interest as to make it advisable to investigate the matter further. That is only another expression for saying that at the present we have nothing to say about it. The discussion of the whole subject, I think, will lead the attention of the Governments to the subject, so far as the subject deserves their attention, and more than that this Conference cannot do. The necessities of uniting the laws of the different nations in certain respects will, I am sure, as it has done before, more and more in the future, bring the Governments to consider this question, and to try to bring about a unity, and this necessity will have a greater influence than any expression which could be made at this time by this Conference.

Mr. Hall (Great Britain).—Mr. President, might I ask the Delegate from Norway whether, after what has fallen from my learned friend, he wishes to press these words? I think I should tell him that the Committee has carefully considered whether we should be justified in inserting words such as he has suggested, so as to say that the matter should not be allowed to drop; and we inserted the words, " for the present," to meet the views which he has advanced. Of course, if we go further and adopt his words, we should be practically deciding by our vote that we were of opinion that it was desirable to introduce a Permanent Maritime Commission; and the Committee are not prepared to go as far as that until they can see how it can be done. Therefore, I think that, if he is content with the matter as it stands at present, the words, " for the present," would accomplish the object which he desires.

Mr. Flood (Norway).—Mr. President, it is really difficult for me to give a definite answer to what has just been stated by the learned Delegate from Great Britain. I am not a diplomatic man; I am a sailor, and as a sailor I am a little cautious about coming on to this rather slippery ground, in regard to these Parliamentary matters. I will only say that I heard and fully appreciated what was said by the learned Delegate from Great Britain. I fully appreciated every word he said. I would not attempt to repeat anything he said, but I understood every word of it, and for the most part I agree with him. The only thing I could not understand was in the last part of his address, when he said that he hoped the time would come when such a Conference would be more in use and be more general than hitherto. But I could not understand it when he said the last time that it would be impossible to go on and form a Commission like this on account of the very great difficulty in the

111

way. Upon the institution of the Metre Commission and the Telegraph and Postal Commission, established a few years ago, a great many able and wise men shook their heads and never thought that anything good would come out of universal postage all over the world. I do not see why we should not come to the conclusion that there might be some good in such a proposition as this.

Now, I repeat what I said. I do not desire this Conference to reject the Report of the Committee, because I admit that I feel the force of the expression used that the time is not ripe to consider the matter. But the only thing I ask for is this: Do not put the subject entirely under the table or on the shelf. Do not throw it entirely away. Just give it a little consideration to show that you acknowledge that the thing has been considered and not found ripe for the present, but that you *do* recommend that it be taken into consideration in the future. I speak not only for my own country, but I think I speak for the shipping world in general. There is not much sympathy for the load-line, but still, out of courtesy to the Board of Trade, and for the great Power which England represents, we have in the Report of the Committee on Load-Line voted that, although the matter is not ripe now, it be left for future consideration, and that it be left to the negotiations to be carried on between the Governments of maritime nations.

Now, if this Conference have already passed a vote on the load-line question that it should be passed for the consideration, not of private individuals, but as a subject of communication between maritime nations, I do not exactly see why we should strike out the whole of this question of a Maritime Commission, and say that we think it must not be brought forward for further consideration. I only ask for the same favour from the Conference that has already been given to the Committee presenting the Report of the uniform load-line. That is all I ask for, and as my proposal has already been before the Conference and has been read by the Secretary, I would like to have a vote upon it.

Mr. Hall (Great Britain).—Mr. President, may I point out to the honourable Delegate from Norway the difference between these two matters? The question of the load-line has been in operation in England, and it has been thoroughly discussed. The principle of it has been approved of by the Committee. The Committee having approved the principle, and being certain that it is a good thing, go so far as to report that they will leave it to the negotiations to be carried on between the different Governments, because, as is pointed out in the Report, there already have been negotiations with regard to the matter, and as it has already been in negotiation between the different Governments, they preferred to leave it to those negotiations. They are all agreed upon the principle. But here we are not all agreed that there should be a Permanent International Marine Commission, and if we adopt the words of the honourable Delegate from Norway we would be inserting words in the Report which would make every foreign Government believe that the Committee who made that Report were of the opinion that a Permanent International Maritime Commission was, to our minds, a good thing, and therefore we wished it to be discussed. We certainly have not come to any such conclusion; and there are so many difficulties in the way that we do not know whether it would be a good thing or not, and we cannot determine that until the matter has been brought into some definite form and some definite proposal has been made.

I will only say, with regard to the disappointment which has fallen upon certain Delegates with regard to this matter, that surely Great Britain is disappointed about the load-line not being adopted. But we certainly shall not occupy the time of the Conference in lamenting over that. We bow without further discussion to the Report of the Committee, and we adopt the decision of the Conference. But until we are satisfied that we ought to have an International Marine Commission, how can we say that it ought to be left to the negotiations of the different Governments? That would be approving the principle, without intending to do so. We have put in the words, "for the present," and we have left the matter open for discussion. With regard to the load-line, the Committee all agreed that it was a good thing, and the only question was as to how it could be carried out. The matter was under negotiation, and they said, Leave it to negotiation. But we have not come to such a conclusion here; far from it. At present there are a great many who think that it is impossible for a Marine Commission to be established, and until some definite proposal is brought forward showing how such a matter is practicable and possible, we cannot report in favour of it. Therefore, I think that the words, "for the present," are quite sufficient.

Mr. Garde (Denmark).—Mr. President, personally, I am not connected with this proposal one way or the other. I have no personal interest in this question. On behalf of our Government I would state that the Delegates from Denmark have no instructions to support and no instructions to oppose it. Why not? Simply for the reasons which have been explained by the learned Delegate from Germany. He has expressed his doubts as to the possibility of at present coming to any conclusion which might be favourable to the establishment of a Commission such as has been proposed in this Memorandum from the Northern Conference; and he has at the same time pointed out that such matters should be left to the action of members employed through private Associations. We have in our country no Board of Trade, such as Great Britain has; but, at the same time, Scandinavian countries represent a considerable amount of shipping, and feel very strongly the necessity of progressing in all of these directions which have been pointed out by the learned Delegate from Germany. Therefore, in our country, it is through the action of Associations and of private men, that these matters are considered, and they are able and conservative men in their business, who take into their hands the examinations of all these questions connected with the shipping business and commerce; they form just such Delegations as have been recommended by the honourable and learned Delegate from Germany. That is the way in which this Memorandum is at present before this Conference.

May I now call attention to what the learned Delegate from Great Britain, and the Chairman of the Committee, said in the commencement of his remarks to-day, that before this Conference there was no proposal on this matter in such a form as to entitle it to definite consideration? There was no proposal from any Government. There was no proposal from any authority. Now, that is our difficulty. We have no authority of any kind which can be taken into consideration, and no proposal which any Government must consider. The Government of Denmark is in the same position as any other Government. They say that we may take up such and such matters or such and such proposals, but they do not of themselves lay any proposal before this Conference. Therefore, I would point out that what we want is a medium of some kind for these proposals coming from private people of different kinds. Some of the proposals are of such a character that they ought to be considered very seriously, and all of those interested in the shipping business would be thankful for the work. I believe that the work of any future Conference which might meet would be advanced by such an institution.

On the other hand, there are very many proposals which, perhaps, it is not so desirable to lay before a Conference. I agree with the Committee that a permanent Commission, as it has been proposed, is not possible at present, and it is not advisable to recommend or propose such an institution. I will go further. I do not believe that a Commission of that kind is a necessity. There are so many difficulties in the way of establishing this Commission, as has been pointed out by the learned Delegate from Great Britain, that I do not believe any such recommendation will be possible. But that does not exclude the possibility of getting a medium, of which a large number of those who have an interest in the shipping business feel the want, a medium which is to meet and to collect the information and data, and which is to be, as my associate Delegate from Denmark has stated to-day, a Bureau. I may say at once I do not think that such a Bureau should be such a one as would have the necessary knowledge to determine every proposal, or to come with proposals framed by themselves as to the laws which deal with the shipping business; but it is to be an international institution, where everybody in the world who has anything to propose might refer it for examination and consideration.

Such a Bureau need not have its own experts of every kind; but what is of the most consequence is that the Bureau shall be able to lay before every International Marine Conference which may come in the future particular proposals which have been sifted by them before the meeting of the Conference. In special cases they may take the advice of experts. But if the Bureau is used in common by all the Maritime Governments, then it will be able to bring matters in regard to shipping interests to the knowledge of the different Governments before a Conference assembles, and the nations of the different Governments would have the proposals before them. I would say that it would be a benefit for any future International Conference to have these proposals examined and sifted in this manner. Therefore, I should think that the authority of such a Bureau and its duty would be to accept proposals from wherever they come, correspond with the different Governments, and get information from any source possible with regard to the matter, and then decide whether it is fit to be presented to any International Marine Conferences. I would say that it would be a great benefit to future International Conferences if at the same time it was stipulated that no proposal of any kind should have the right to appear before the Conference without having come through this International Bureau.

The President.—The time for recess having arrived, the Delegate will continue his remarks after recess.

The Conference thereupon took a recess until 2 o'clock.

After Recess.

Upon the reassembling of the Conference this afternoon one of the Delegates from Brazil resumed his seat.

The President.—The question before the Conference is the Resolution of the Delegate from Norway, upon which the Delegate from Denmark has the floor.

Mr. Garde (Denmark).—Mr. President, at the time of the recess I was calling attention to the fact that it would be a benefit to future Conferences if a Bureau of this nature could be established, and it was provided that no proposal should come before the Conference until it had been first examined and determined upon by that Bureau. Now, I may go a little farther in my idea about the establishment of such a bureau. I am perfectly aware that opinions might differ in regard to the manner in which a Bureau of this kind should be established. Of course, the different Powers would not be equally interested, but it has been pointed out by my colleague that we have examples to go by, and I would suggest that the course which is adopted in respect to the International Bureau for telegraph service is perhaps the one which is most desirable. I will point out that under such a plan the Conference would have to meet whenever there is a necessity for discussing questions of an international character, and, before the closing of the Conference, decide when the next Conference shall be held, the Bureau to be placed immediately under the authority of the Conference itself. The Conference decides where the Bureau is to be domiciled.

As to the establishment of the Bureau and its expenses I believe the rule is that the participating Powers are divided into six classes; each class counting a certain number of unities—as far as I remember the first class counts twenty-five unities, the following classes a diminishing number of unities. According to the number of unities the expenses of the Bureau are divided between the different countries. As for the division of the countries into the different classes, it is for the Conference to pass upon; but the practice is that different countries only announce themselves to be incorporated in such and such a class, and so far as experience goes it has never given any difficulty whatever. If any country should class itself either in a class too high or a class too low, it does not matter much. I mention this because, in my opinion, if a Rule of this kind could be adopted it would be of great value to International Marine Conferences. I am quite sure that we will have, perhaps within a short time, a new International Marine Conference, and therefore I am desirous that the Conference should be prepared to take this question up practically.

Therefore I do not feel satisfied with the recommendation which is contained in the Report of the Committee, although, of course, I fully admit that as the proposal stands the Committee could not come to any other result. I myself am of the opinion that the term "Commission" is not necessary, and might be done away with. The desire of my country is only that we should establish an International Bureau. I think that there should be a strong indication in the Report of this Conference that this matter should not be allowed to go to sleep, but should be taken up, and, therefore, I would submit that this matter should be referred to. I think that the vote should be upon the question whether it is advisable for the Conference in some way or other to give this desire an expression in the Report of this Committee, so as to encourage the different Governments to remember the question for the future.

The President.—The question is upon the Resolution of the Delegate from Norway.

Mr. Carter (Hawaii).—Mr. President, when the Report of the Committee was laid before us a few days since I was in hopes the members of the Conference would consider the Report carefully and be prepared when it came up for discussion to formulate their views. I do not think it incumbent upon myself, representing a very small nation, to prepare a Resolution, or to prepare myself in any way to discuss this subject thoroughly. The conclusions to which I arrived in my own mind, however, are the same in substance as the Report of the Committee, that a Permanent Commission as proposed would be found impracticable; that it would be found that a Permanent International Commission sitting at all times, or supposed to be at all times ready to be called together or to come together at stated periods, would be found impracticable; although I feel very strongly the weight of the reasons which have been so ably laid before us by the learned Delegate from Denmark; and they are reasons which would lead to some step being taken before another Marine Conference is called together for the digestion and consideration of the matters before them. Yet I think that all the members of this Conference have felt that exceedingly important subjects have come before us in our different Committees which we have been obliged to report were not at the present time ripe for action, which might have been so prepared that the Conference should have taken action upon them; but that any reasonable time which the Conference could be expected to sit would not permit of the thorough investigation and careful consideration of a Rule or principle which was to be adopted as an international principle.

My own thought has been that if it were decided among the nations that periodical Conferences should be held, say once in seven years, or once in ten years, or once in fifteen years, for the consideration of the Rules of the Sea or the Rules governing commerce generally, that the maritime nations would prepare themselves for these meetings, and that each nation then would create new Departments, somewhat analogous to the British Board of Trade, and so, when the Conference met they would not only have, as we have had, the great advantage of the deliberations of that notable body, but they would have also the well-digested and well-considered views of Powers somewhat smaller, who had considered these matters. Therefore, it seems to me that if this Conference simply pointed out to the different nations that International Marine Conferences should be held at stated periods it would be an advantage, and it would bring about the results which are aimed at by this proposition for a Permanent International Commission. These results would come about naturally, because the nations would prepare themselves for service, and send the Delegates thoroughly equipped to the Marine Conferences to be held.

I am not in favour of the Resolution of the Delegate from Norway. I do not think it wise to move an amendment to the well-considered Report of the Committee which practically negatives the Report itself. It would be, it seems to me, either better to vote to reject the Report, which I should vote against, because it deals simply with this question of a permanent Commission, or to move to defer the consideration of the subject until those who have some other proposition to propose shall be better prepared to lay it before the Conference.

Mr. Verbrugghe (Belgium).—Mr. President, the Committee to which I had the honour to belong were only called upon to examine into the establishment of a Permament International Maritime Commission. This question was made the subject of very careful consideration. We have heard the admirable discourses of the learned Delegates of England and Germany, who have thoroughly developed the matter. I think that on that subject we are all sufficiently enlightened and agreed to recognize the impracticability of establishing an International Maritime Commission, for the present, at least; and this is the only question as to which the Conference is called upon to declare itself.

The honourable Delegates from Denmark have, however, taken an entirely different view of the matter than that indicated by the programme which was submitted to our Committee, and although I hear that in the body of this Conference their plan meets with a certain amount of sympathy, I would remark that this plan is not well defined, and that it cannot be reasonably admitted that two distinct questions should be mixed in this discussion.

The honourable Delegate from Norway proposes an amendment which I, for my part, cannot accept, inasmuch as it invalidates the conclusions of our Report, which conclusions I am convinced will be adopted by the Conference; and I observe that in everything that has been said no one has combated them. These conclusions have even met with the approval of the Delegates from Denmark, and I repeat that I feel persuaded that all the Delegates will approve them. If the honourable Delegates from Norway and Denmark desire to make a proposition to the Conference in regard to the need of instituting a Permanent International Bureau, that is another thing. Let them take the first step to make such a proposition. I am not absolutely opposed to it, and the Conference can examine whether it will be proper to take it into consideration; but I demand that the Conference shall first take a vote in regard to the Report. I have risen solely for the purpose of giving the reasons which will influence my vote in regard to the amendment proposed by the honourable Delegate from Norway. If new questions must arise, let the Conference examine them if it considers them appropriate, but let them be embodied in a special Resolution.

[93]

The President.—The question is upon the Resolution of the Delegate from Norway.

Mr. Flood (Norway).—Mr. President, I will only say that this matter about the International Bureau has been brought up before the Conference to-day, and it is a new subject. I would ask permission that my Resolution and this question together be laid over for a couple of days for consideration amongst the members, and that they may be brought up for further consideration.

Mr. Hall (Great Britain).—Mr. President, I hope that Resolution will not be pressed. What are we to adjourn the discussion for? The Delegate from Norway says he wants to have time to consider the proposition. Are we to wait for an indefinite time while the Delegate tries to prepare something or other to put before the Conference? We must deal with it as a practical matter. If there are practical proposals, let us consider them. But no practical proposal has been put before the Conference at all. The Committee have dealt with this General Division XIII, and have published a Report. It would absolutely stultify that Report if we were to adopt the amendment of the Delegate from Norway. Now he proposes to adjourn the discussion of this Report. What are we to gain by the adjournment? What does he propose to do after a few days? Can he give the Committee any definite proposal for the Conference to consider? I venture to submit that the Committee have dealt with this matter thoroughly, and have given you a Report to which we have not heard one single word of objection in principle, and I submit that the Conference should proceed to vote upon that Report. I may also point out that this Report has been in the hands of the members for nearly a week.

The President.—The question is upon the motion of the Delegate from Norway to postpone the consideration of this question for two or more days.

Mr. Garde (Denmark).—Mr. President, I will say, as I have said once before, that I agree with the Committee; that as the question is laid before them they could not come to any other conclusion, according to my opinion, and therefore the Conference ought to vote upon the Report. Of course, what I desire to have considered is an international medium in some other shape than the proposal which has been laid before the Committee at present, and in that I sympathize with the aim which is laid down in the Resolution presented by the Delegate from Norway and the Delegate from Belgium, if I have understood it properly, which is that the vote of the Conference be taken upon the Report, and that then the Yeas and Nays be called upon the question as to the desirability of keeping this question alive for the future.

Mr. Flood (Norway).—Mr. President, may I be allowed to detain the Conference for a moment? I wish simply to state that I think I have expressed in the Resolution before the Conference that I fully agree with the conclusions to which the Committee has come so far as regards the possibility of establishing such a Commission; and that now the only thing I wish is to keep the question alive, and to have the principle brought forward in the future. I do this because we have just adopted the Report of the Committee about the load-mark, in which the consideration of the question was left to future negotiations, and the learned Delegate from Great Britain stated that he understood that most of the countries were in accordance with the English Board of Trade in their views on this question of load-mark. I differ greatly with him in that respect, because I do not think there are many Representatives here who have any authority from their Governments to favour that load-mark at all. I think, on the contrary, that it is not in favour. But still the Conference has expressed the desirability of keeping the thing open, and having it discussed among the Governments in the future. That is all I ask with regard to this proposal of the Conference at Copenhagen. I only ask that you frame a Resolution so that there will be a chance for us to bring forward this matter, and the door will be open for its consideration.

I bow before the Great Powers, especially before the greatest Power in the world, Great Britain, but you must remember that this Resolution is backed by one-sixth of the merchant fleet of the world, so that it really does not come from any single brain. This Resolution has come from the best of our ability amongst the seafaring men in the northern countries. So I, again and again, before you vote, ask you to remember that if you vote for the Report as it stands now you vote upon the question entirely, and do not leave it open for future consideration. While, on the contrary, if you adopt my humble and respectful Resolution, you only give an opportunity to bring the matter forward again to be taken into consideration.

Mr. Verbrugghe (Belgium).—Mr. President, I must again come back to the question on the subject of which I spoke a little while ago. It seems to me absolutely impossible to vote simultaneously upon the two questions in the manner in which they have been mixed, inasmuch as it has been claimed that they are distinct. We all admit that the conclusions upon the Report are perfectly admissible. Therein lies the whole question. What we should do now is to vote upon the question of knowing whether the establishment of an International Maritime Commission is possible. We all recognize the fact that it is not at all possible. We all think that it is dangerous to mix in with the Report subjects which it does not include. If you desire to put those subjects into a separate proposition, that is another matter. But as a member of the Committee, I insist upon a vote being taken upon the adoption of the Report.

The question raised by the honourable Delegate from Norway does not refer to the establishment of a Commission—of a sort of a Tribunal requiring jurists—but to the creation of a Bureau. If it be true that some of the members among us are in sympathy with such a Bureau, they must still vote against the amendment, for the reason that the Report bears upon the Permanent Commission, the sole subject which it was our duty to examine in our Committee, and not upon the establishment of a Bureau. Moreover, the Report of the Committee has been read by us all, and until now, I again repeat, no one has raised his voice in opposition to the conclusions of our Report. If the members desire to bring up a new question, let them take the initiative.

Mr. Verney (Siam).—Mr. President, may I be allowed to add one or two words to explain my vote upon this question? The proposal before us is inserted in the Programme as the establishment of a Permanent International Maritime Commission, and under subsection (*a*) its powers and authority are referred to. Now, Sir, I should vote against the establishment of such a Permanent

International Maritime Conference for the following, among other reasons, that it only can have power and authority after those powers and that authority are given to it by the several Governments who send Representatives to act as Commissioners. I have not heard a single definite proposal from those who are in favour of either this Commission or of a Bureau, which the learned Delegate from Belgium has so well pointed out is an entirely different thing from a Commission. I have not heard a single proposal as to the duties to be performed by an International Bureau; and before the establishment of any International Commission I should think that all of us would wish to know what are the powers and what is the authority which it is proposed to invest such a Commission with.

I think that the speeches which have been delivered this morning, certainly the speech delivered by the learned Delegate from Germany, has entirely annihilated any proposal of that kind. It appears to me that any International Maritime Commission, which could really be so called and have the right to the name of an International Maritime Commission, could not be appointed to deal with any matters until they have been the subject of diplomatic correspondence and action, but should deal with them only after they have been the subject of diplomatic correspondence. But that is not the subject before us. Whatever is meant by this International Maritime Commission, it does not mean the establishment of such a Bureau as has been referred to. The duty of such a Bureau, I would venture to suggest, is purely ministerial, and it has no powers of a representative nature, and no such powers as are given by Governments to Commissions especially appointed to meet and to discuss different subjects. That kind of Bureau is something entirely different and distinct from anything which is proposed here. Therefore, Mr. President, taking this Programme in my hand, and referring to the original proposition, which is the proposal to be discussed, I cannot see any reason why this Conference should vote for the establishment of such a Commission.

The President.—The question is upon the motion of the Delegate from Norway to postpone the consideration of this question—for how long?

Mr. Flood (Norway).—Mr. President, I would propose that it be postponed for three or four days, according to the time the Conference may see fit, so as to give us time for consideration.

The President.—Is the Conference ready for the question?

Mr. Hall (Great Britain).—Mr. President, may I ask the grounds for this postponement? We have not heard any as yet.

The President.—The Delegate from Norway is called upon to give his reasons for asking for this postponement.

Mr. Flood (Norway).—Mr. President, my reason is because I would like to talk with several of the Delegates about this special Bureau question which has been brought before the Conference to-day, and which has been spoken of before. I would like to have that question specially considered. I would like to state that my proposal is simply to keep this question open in some way or other, and to find the connecting link between this Conference and the future meetings of a similar character.

Mr. Hall (Great Britain).—Mr. President, I do not quite see how adjourning this for two or three days will have any effect upon bringing this up for consideration. If the Delegate from Norway supposes that any vote which we will come to here can prevent the Government from considering this subject in the future, I cannot agree with him. Of course, this matter can be considered without any vote of the Conference at all, and the Governments will consider it whenever any practicable proposals are laid before them. Some day a practical proposal may come forward, and then it can be discussed; but at present there is no practicable proposal, as it appears to us, and that is our Report. I confess that I cannot see how delaying for three or four days can have any effect whatever on that proposal.

Mr. Goodrich (United States).—Mr. President, I suggest that if any considerable number of the members of the Conference want time to consider any of the propositions before the Conference it certainly would do no injury to give them a reasonable time. Now let me suggest what might be done. Here are three or four nations who want to consider this matter a little further. We might take either one of two courses: we may either refer the matter again to the Committee to hear these gentlemen, or postpone the matter, say until Friday. The reason I suggest the latter course is this: We think possibly they may be satisfied to prepare a Resolution which, while it recognizes and adopts the Report of the Committee, shall refer to this matter or leave it open so that this Conference recommend the next International Conference to consider the subject, in the same way that the Northern Maritime Conference referred it to this Conference. I do not see that injury would come from that, and I do not really see much practical benefit to be derived from it. But if there are gentlemen who have a project which they think is for the benefit of the maritime world, I think they ought to have ample opportunity to discuss it. It is true that this Report has been laid upon our table for over a week, but yet here are four or five nations, representing the commerce of the world, who ask at the hands of this Conference a little further time to consider the matter amongst themselves, and it seems to me that it is wise and proper and courteous to give it to them.

While, at the present time, I am thoroughly in favour of the Report of the Committee, I do not see that any injury can come to us if this course should be taken. I may say now in the Conference that the Report of the Collocation Committee on the Rules will possibly be laid on the table of the members on Thursday morning. This I say after advice from the Secretary of the Committee as to some of the difficulties which have arisen in the way of printing. If this matter could be laid over until Friday I do not believe that any serious injury would come to any of us, nor do I believe that any great time would be taken up on Friday, at which time we shall probably dispose of all the Reports of the Committees which will be presented.

Mr. Hall (Great Britain).—Mr. President, may I point out the ridiculous position in which we are now placed? The learned Delegate of the United States said that three or four or five nations required this to be postponed. I have not heard such a desire expressed by any single Delegate except the Delegate from Norway. I asked for his reasons. I quite agree that whenever there is any ground for reconsidering or postponing a subject the privilege should be granted. But I have asked for his reasons, and I confess that I have not heard any reason for postponing this subject. There is no suggestion that the Report is wrong, because the Delegate from Norway says that he agrees with the Report. No one in the Conference has got up to say that he objects to this Report. Then what are we to adjourn it for? Because he says it is necessary to tell the Governments that this matter is not to be closed altogether, but that it can be reconsidered in the future. Who doubts that? Is it necessary for us to pass an amendment or a Resolution to that effect? Is it necessary for us to tell the Governments that they may or may not consider any proposal which is brought before them? Of course they may do so.

There is one further suggestion, Mr. President. I shall ask for your ruling on the question as to whether or not the question of establishing a simple Bureau comes within the meaning of this Division of the Programme; and whether such a Bureau is within the purview of the meaning of an International Maritime Commission? That is the question which is referred to the Committee, and that is what the Committee have reported on.

Captain Malmberg (Sweden).—Mr. President, as a member of the Committee upon General Division No. XIII, I move that the vote be taken upon the Report of said Committee.

Mr. Carter (Hawaii).—Mr. President, I would ask the learned Delegate from the United States whether the adoption of this Report on the question of a Permanent International Maritime Commission would preclude the consideration of the Resolution put forward looking to the establishment of a Bureau for preparing work for another Conference?

Mr. Goodrich (United States).—Mr. President, let me answer, following the judgment of the learned First Delegate from Great Britain, that I should say that it would not preclude the presentation of a Resolution in this Conference looking towards the establishment of an International Bureau, because I think that the learned Delegate from Great Britain has very properly said that is not the subject which was referred to the Committee.

The President.—There are so many propositions before the Conference that the Chair is undecided which proposition is now in order. It would seem to the Chair to be proper to take the sense of the Conference as to whether this matter should be postponed for future consideration or not.

Mr. Verbrugghe (Belgium).—Mr. President, I arose a while ago to propose that the Report of the Committee should be voted upon.

The President.—The Delegate is quite right; but the proposal which came after his must first be considered before his can be considered. The last proposal of all was that of the Delegate from Sweden, who proposed that a vote should be taken upon the Report of the Committee. The sense of the Conference will be taken upon that proposition.

The question was put to the Conference as to whether a vote should be taken on the Report of the Committee, and the question was carried.

The President.—The question is now upon the adoption of the Report of the Committee.

The question was put to the Conference upon the adoption of the Report of the Committee on General Division XIII, and the Report was adopted.

Mr. Flood (Norway).—Mr. President, I take the liberty to ask for a vote on my Resolution.

The President.—The Resolution of the Delegate from Norway will now be read.

The Resolution is as follows:—

"*Resolved,*—That although for the present the establishment of a Permanent International Marine Commission is not considered expedient, this matter appears to be of such international interest that it is advisable it should be further investigated through communications carried on between the Governments of maritime nations."

Mr. Flood (Belgium).—Mr. President, I call for the Yeas and Naes.

The President.—The question is upon this Resolution. The Delegate from Norway calls for the Yeas and Nays.

Mr. Hall (Great Britain).—Mr. President, before a vote is taken upon that may I point out, as I pointed out before, that it will really nullify a part of the Report as adopted? We have reported that at present it is impracticable, and now we are invited to ask the foreign Governments to discuss a question which is at present impracticable. When any well-digested scheme is brought forward it will be time to ask them to consider it. But we are now asking them to consider a scheme which we have just reported is impracticable. It would really reduce the whole proceeding to an absurdity.

Mr. Carter (Hawaii).—Mr. President, it seems to me that the idea aimed at is that this principle is one which still might be discussed between the Governments with advantage to future Conferences. Therefore I would suggest to the Delegate from Norway that he withdraw this present Resolution, which seems to deal solely with the question of a Permanent Commission, and take time to draft a Resolution which should simply embody the idea that some arrangement of this kind might be made if the principle were discussed between the different Governments.

Mr. Flood (Norway).—Mr. President, I should be most willing to do as proposed by the learned Delegate from Hawaii, but I understood that this discussion would be closed, and I did not think I would be allowed to open it again. That is the reason why I asked two or three times for a consideration of my Resolution, because I must confess that what has been pointed out by the learned Delegate has altered my view with regard to the Commission. I will be very willing to withdraw my amendment, if it be understood that there will be a chance to bring forward a Resolution in favour of the establishment of a Bureau. With that understanding I will withdraw my amendment for the present.

The President.—Does the Chair understand the Delegate from Norway to withdraw his amendment unconditionally? The Chair cannot speak for the Conference as to whether any Resolution will be adopted.

Mr. Flood (Norway).—Mr. President, then I will trust to the Conference, and I withdraw it unconditionally.

The President.—The Delegate from Norway withdraws his amendment unconditionally.

Mr. Flood (Norway)—Mr. President, I give notice that on Friday morning I will move another Resolution to take the place of this.

The President.—The Delegate from Norway gives notice that on Friday he will offer a Resolution instead of the one which has been withdrawn.

Mr. Goodrich (United States).—Mr. President, I may say, in addition to what I said a moment ago, that the Collocation Committee have been giving very careful attention to the drafting of the Rules upon the principles laid down by the Conference, and that their Report will probably be the subject of discussion early next week. But it seems to me that there should be some order of business in regard to that Report, and several members of the Committee, not officially, but informally, have requested me to present the following Resolution:—

"*Resolved,*—That all amendments to the Rules of the Road, as drafted by the Collocation Committee, must be in writing and handed to the Secretary of the Collocation Committee before 7 o'clock at night on the second day after the day on which the Report has been laid before the Conference, this latter day exclusive.

"That the Collocation Committee be vested with power to divide the amendments thus handed to them into two classes: First, such as refer to the verbiage only, or to the subjects which have been referred to the Collocation Committee for consideration; and second, such as are to be considered to involve a material alteration of, or an addition to, the Rules as adopted by the Conference.

"That the amendments thus divided be laid before the Conference on the morning of the second day after the expiration of the time for the handing in of the amendments to the Collocation Committee.

"That the amendments of the first class, referring to the verbiage only or to the subjects which have been referred to the Collocation Committee for consideration, be printed and discussed, and a vote taken on them on the third day and following days after the print has been laid before the Conference.

"That a discussion and voting upon the amendments of the second class, involving a material alteration of or an addition to the Rules as adopted by the Conference, be admitted only after the Conference, by a vote of the majority, to be taken without a previous debate (except that five minutes be allowed to the member offering the amendment and five minutes to members of the Conference to discuss the question of reconsideration), has decided upon admitting such discussion and voting, and that the amendments of the second class thus admitted be printed, and voted upon, after discussion, on the third and following days after the print has been laid before the Conference."

In other words, if the subject is not clearly understood by the members, the Collocation Committee are to be invested with power to divide all the amendments suggested and handed in to them into two classes: the one relating to verbiage in the Report and to certain subjects which have been omitted in the Collocation Committee; and the other relating to any suggestions for an alteration in the principles which the Conference have already passed upon, or which some member may see fit to bring before the Conference. The suggestions, of any character, are to be handed in to the Collocation Committee through its Secretary. For instance, if the Collocation Committee's Report is on the desk of the members on Thursday morning, and we think it will be, then these amendments must be handed in by Saturday evening. They will then pass through the Collocation Committee for their judgment. Questions of principle, changing the principles of the Rules, shall be presented in writing, and shall also be printed and laid before the Conference. Then any member proposing such an alteration in the principle shall have five minutes to explain to the Conference why he desires to present this new principle. I may say here that the time has been thus limited because it is believed by the Collocation Committee that already ample opportunity has been given to members to present amendments to these Rules. Then five minutes can be given to the members who do not think it wise to take up a new principle suggested. Then a vote on the Resolution is taken, and if the Conference decides to admit it the subject will have to be set down for discussion on some day or proceeded with at the time of the vote upon the question of reconsideration with regard to the principle.

We think that time will be saved by this method. Of course we understand that the Collocation Committee cannot pledge itself to present this Report on Thursday morning, but we will try to present it Thursday morning, or at any rate some time during the day. Then the members will have all of that day, and all of Friday, and all of Saturday to present their amendments. That will give the most ample opportunity, and will bring the discussion of the Conference on these Rules to a close.

Mr. Hall (Great Britain).—Mr. President, may I ask the Chairman whether or not it is not possible that the Report of the Committee should be distributed on Wednesday morning?

Mr. Goodrich (United States).—It is possible.

Mr. Hall (Great Britain).—If so, then the members of the Conference would have until Friday evening to present their amendments. That is to prevent any misapprehension in the minds of the Delegates that they will have until Saturday, at all events; because, if the Reports are presented on Wednesday, then Friday would be the limit of time, and the Collocation Committee could resume their work on Saturday and get the Report before the Conference.

The President.—Does the Conference wish a vote upon this Resolution now, or shall it be laid over until it is printed? The Resolution will be read.

The Resolution is as follows:—

"*Resolved*,—That all amendments to the Rules of the Road, as drafted by the Collocation Committee, must be in writing and handed to the Secretary of the Collocation Committee before 7 o'clock at night on the second day after the day on which the Report has been laid before the Conference, this latter day exclusive.

"That the Collocation Committee be vested with power to divide the amendments thus handed to them into two classes: First, such as refer to the verbiage only, or to the subjects which have been referred to the Collocation Committee for consideration; and second, such as are to be considered to involve a material alteration of, or an addition to, the Rules as adopted by the Conference.

"That the amendments thus divided be laid before the Conference on the morning of the second day after the expiration of the time for the handing in of the amendments to the Collocation Committee.

"That the amendments of the first class, referring to the verbiage only or to the subjects which have been referred to the Collocation Committee for consideration, be printed and discussed, and a vote taken on them on the third day and following days after the print has been laid before the Conference.

"That a discussion and voting upon the amendments of the second class, involving a material alteration of, or an addition to, the Rules as adopted by the Conference, be admitted only after the Conference by a vote of the majority, to be taken without a previous debate (except that five minutes be allowed to the member offering the amendment, and five minutes to members of the Conference to discuss the question of reconsideration), has decided upon admitting such discussion and voting, and that the amendments of the second class thus admitted be printed and voted upon after discussion on the third and following days after the print has been laid before the Conference."

Captain Richard (France).—Mr. President, the Resolution upon which we are going to vote seems to be an important one, and I would ask before it is voted upon that is should be printed and distributed among us.

The President.—The Delegate from France desires to have this Resolution printed and laid upon the table before a vote is taken upon it. It will be printed and laid on the Table of the Delegates tomorrow morning.

Mr. Hall (Great Britain).—Mr. President, I understand that the matter is disposed of and that we shall have the Resolution in print to-morrow morning. I only wish to say one word on a point of order before we adjourn, with regard to the Resolution notice of which has been given by the Delegate from Norway. I think that it is only right to state that I shall call for your ruling on a matter of order as to whether any such Resolution as the one of which notice has been given by the Delegate from Norway can properly be presented to the Conference. The Delegates are appointed by their respective Governments to discuss certain propositions which have been detailed in a Programme. We are here to discuss these proposals. It clearly would be most inconvenient if any Delegate were to propose any Resolution upon any matter which he sees fit and ask for a decision of the Conference upon the matter. The question as to the establishment of a Bureau has never been suggested to our Governments, and it has never been proposed. I doubt very much whether it has ever been proposed to any of the other Governments.

Under these circumstances, I shall ask for your ruling, when the Resolution is laid on the table, as to whether or not the Conference can discuss this Resolution. If we once admit that the Conference can discuss any question which any Delegate brings before it, what is the use of a Programme, and what are to be the instructions to the Delegates? I know what our instructions are and what we are instructed to discuss. We are not to meet here to discuss every abstract proposition that may be brought forward by any Delegate.

Mr. Goodrich (United States).—Mr. President, although I am a member of the Collocation Committee, I present the following Resolution in order to dispatch the business and to prepare for it in due season:—

"*Resolved*,—That the name of the Committee on Collocation of Rules be changed to the Committee on Collocation of Rules and General Report of the Conference, and that it be instructed to prepare such General Report in due season."

That is to be laid over and printed for to-morrow morning.

Now, Mr. President, I have one further suggestion to make. We have had an invitation presented to us this morning to attend the ceremonies in commemoration of the centennial anniversary of the inauguration of the first President of the United States, which is to take place at 1 o'clock on Wednesday. I suppose that a great number of the members of the Conference will desire to attend these ceremonies, which will be very interesting, and especially interesting to those of us who represent the United States. I shall, therefore, move that there be no session of the Conference on Wednesday. In order that Committees may understand that during a part of that day at least they will have an opportunity for the discharge of their own duty or for Committee business, I now move that there be no session of the Conference on Wednesday.

The President.—The Delegate from the United States moves that there shall be no session of the Conference on Wednesday, to enable the Delegates to attend the ceremonies at the centennial anniversary of the inauguration of the first President of the United States. The Chair will say in this connection that it is expected that those Delegates who are entitled to wear a uniform will wear it on that occasion. The State Department has so expressed its wish.

Mr. Hall (Great Britain).—Mr. President, may I ask when we shall have the Report of the Committee on Ocean Lanes? I understood that the Report of the Committee was intended to be sent to the printer some time ago, but it is not ready for the Committee yet. Can any member of that

Committee, or the Chairman, give us any information on that subject? The Report of the Committee was in draft a week ago.

Mr. Carter (Hawaii).—Mr. President, the Report is printed and has been handed to the different members of the Committee to-day. That part of the Report was held back, thinking that we would be able to add the night-signal part to it; then the Conference referred to us another matter, which deferred the whole Report. It is now in print, and will be laid upon the tables in a day or two.

Admiral Kaznakoff (Russia).—Mr. President, I would like to ask what is the programme for to-morrow? We have nothing more for discussion, I think, and we will have nothing to do; so why not adjourn until Friday?

The President.—The Chair knows of no business.

Mr. Goodrich (United States).—Mr. President, we can discuss to-morrow the Resolution in regard to the order of business which I presented a few moments ago.

Mr. Hall (Great Britain).—Mr. President, this is a matter which must be decided, for until it is decided we can do nothing. I am very sorry for it.

The President.—The Chair will state that the Resolution of the Delegate from the United States will be printed and laid upon the table to-morrow, so that the subject will be open for consideration to-morrow.

Mr. Goodrich (United States).—Mr. President, if the members prefer to discuss that now, we need have no session of the Conference to-morrow. If that is their desire, I have no objection. Is the gallant Delegate from France willing that course be pursued?

Captain Richard (France).—If you will give me a translation, I may be willing.

Mr. President, now that I have been able to read the entire proposition of the honourable Mr. Goodrich, I have no objection to take up the discussion of it at once. Some of our colleagues who have not read it as I have are perhaps in the same position I was in before, and have not been sufficiently informed in regard to its object and contents. However that may be, in order to save the time of the Conference, I am ready to vote now upon the proposition, but before doing so I ask permission to call attention to a paragraph which seems to me worthy of the consideration of the Conference. If I am not mistaken, that paragraph specifies that a period of not over five minutes shall be given to any Delegate who proposes an amendment, and that an equal period may be given to those who oppose it. I would like to know why it was determined that a maximum of five minutes would be given to the mover of an amendment in order to explain and defend it, and that a similar maximum of five minutes would be given to oppose it. Why is it necessary thus to clip the wings of a discussion? I think I can see through it a measure of precaution against needless speeches, but I think that our colleagues are as sensible as they are learned, and that they do not talk for the mere pleasure of talking. If they speak longer than five minutes, they will do so for very good reasons only. I would add as my own opinion that my colleagues discourse with such courteous grace that I always enjoy hearing them, whatever may be the length of their speeches. I consequently demand that the time limit be stricken out. If this concession is made to me, I am ready to vote for the proposition of the honourable Delegate of the United States.

Mr. Goodrich (United States).—Mr. President, I have not had the pleasure of fully understanding all the gallant Delegate from France has said, but as I read the Protocol I am quite sure that he can say in five minutes enough to convince us one way or the other on any proposition that is presented. We have discussed nearly every Rule in the old Regulations, and I think it would put the members to a good deal of trouble to make any new proposition. I do not believe that there is any new proposition to be presented; and if there is one of great importance it will be seen by the Conference, and the reasons can be advanced in a five minutes' speech by any Delegate in this Conference. I am not particular about the limit of five minutes; but I think that is enough.

Mr. Hall (Great Britain).—Mr. President, I apprehend that my gallant friend the Delegate from France is under a misapprehension. The limit of time is not to the discussion of the principle. That can be discussed fully, of course. It is only a question as to whether or not we shall allow such an amendment to be discussed. At present the vote is to be put at once, and a three-fourths vote is to be given. The only matter as to which there is a limit of time is that if any member wishes to propose an amendment to a principle then he is to state his reasons. He can do that in five minutes. Then if the Conference votes that we shall discuss it, he can discuss his principle at any length.

Captain Richard (France).—Mr. President, I should begin by saying that the proposition which I made is not at all for my personal advantage. I am firmly convinced that I could explain all that would come to my mind to say in less than five minutes. But if one of our colleagues has a new proposition to make, and it requires six or seven minutes to defend his proposition, I do not see how we can be so heartless as to oppose it, and to stop him at perhaps the most interesting moment. It is a matter of courtesy to, and confidence in, the speakers which they will appreciate. For that reason I repeat that I am opposed to that part of the proposition of the Honourable Mr. Goodrich which measures the time to be given to each speaker. I do not think that the Conference should adopt this five-minute limit. Moreover, I do not think that that measure will be availed of to its fullest extent.

The President.—The Delegate from France moves that the five-minute law be stricken out.

Mr. Goodrich (United States).—Would not the gallant Delegate from France accept a limit of ten minutes?

Dr. Sieveking (Germany).—Mr. President, because I have taken part in framing this proposal which has been read here, I think you will allow me to make a few remarks. I thought that on one side it would be but fair to give an opportunity to every member of the Conference for bringing in some new question, some new proposition, even if it should differ from the result which we have already adopted in the Conference, before the Conference had finally determined the matter. But before it was admitted, after the long time which we have had on the second reading of the Rules, to

[93]

discuss the whole subject, I thought it would be necessary and proper for us to take a vote of the Conference upon the admissibility of such a new amendment.

Now, I thought then and I think now that such a vote could be taken without any previous discussion. If an amendment is laid before the Conference, I think that after the two months' discussion which we have had that we would every one of us know whether or not we thought it worth while, or necessary, or advisable to open a discussion for this amendment after hearing the argument *pro* and *con*. I think that we are now sufficiently conversant with the subject to deal with the question at once. But it has been said against this that we ought to go a little further so as to allow a member to introduce a new principle, even at this late stage of our proceedings, and support the advisability of reconsidering a question of principle by an argument of five minutes.

Now, I think there must be some time given for debate on this question of reconsideration, or else the result will be that the discussion on the question of reconsideration will lead to a discussion of the whole subject, and everybody will try to form his opinion as to whether it was worth while to reconsider a subject according to what he hears about the importance of the subject, and then the subject itself would be entered into. There would then be no limit at all upon the discussion, which might embrace all of the subjects we have now been discussing for the past two months. I think there should be some limit as to the time, and if any time is to be given I think five minutes on both sides quite sufficient.

Captain Van Steyn (The Netherlands).—Mr. President, when I rise it is only to ask some information from the learned Delegate from the United States. It has been said before that after we received the printed Report of the Committee on Collocation we should have ample time to consider it for ourselves. I should like to ask Mr. Goodrich how many hours that means? We are sitting the whole day Thursday and Friday in the Conference, and perhaps on Saturday. How many hours are left to us before we can decide whether there are any amendments?

Mr. Goodrich (United States).—Mr. President, according to the reading of this Resolution, if the Report was handed in, for instance, on Thursday morning, it would give the members all day Thursday, except when they are in Conference, and Friday and Saturday night until 7 o'clock. There are really three days for them to consider the Report. I do not know that there will be any business to call the Conference together on Friday or Saturday. I will call the attention of the gallant Delegate from the Netherlands to the fact that we possibly shall have no session of the Conference on Friday, and certainly not on Saturday, because I do not believe that there is anything to discuss. On Thursday we shall probably discuss all of the Reports of the Committees which will come in on that day, as we have to-day disposed of all the Reports which have thus far been presented. I do not want to stand in the position here of driving the Conference unnecessarily or of imposing upon members burdens greater than they ought to bear. I am sure there are a great many of the Delegates who are anxious to finish their labours of the Conference and to adjourn.

I call your attention to another fact. The Christmas holidays commence in about two weeks, and we have only this week and next week before these holidays commence. If we do not finish our work by that time we will probably find it wise and desirable to adjourn through the holidays, and the Conference is therefore thrown over until the next year. Of course I only offer these Resolutions, as the Delegates well know, for the purpose of guiding the thought of the Conference to such course as it sees fit to adopt. I do not want to stand here in the position of attempting to work improperly. I think that we ought to make haste slowly under all circumstances.

The President.—The question is upon the amendment of the Delegate from France, to strike out the five-minute clause.

Mr. Hall (Great Britain).—Mr. President, I think, as there seems to be an objection to the limit of five minutes, that it would be unwise to vote in favour of keeping that limit in. I think that this discussion will be of use as it has been suggested that some of us need not be unnecessarily long in our remarks in the further discussion to take place. We have all argued these questions, some of us at very great length. And perhaps now that the Conference is in the possession of our views we shall be able to make our remarks very short indeed upon any further matter. Having regard to that, I think that perhaps it is undesirable to continue the limit at five minutes, especially as I myself think that if we give the limit of five minutes the speakers will be inclined to speak for five minutes; but if we do not put in any limit the probability is that they will not speak for more than one minute.

Mr. Goodrich (United States).—Mr. President, if there is no objection I will accept the proposition of the gallant Delegate from France, and strike out the words limiting the time to five minutes. So that the proposition reads:—

"That a discussion and voting upon the amendment of the second class involving a material alteration of, or an addition to, the Rules as adopted by the Conference be admitted only after the Conference by a vote of the majority, to be taken without a previous debate, has decided upon admitting such discussion and voting."

The President.—Does the Conference desire to vote upon the Resolution at the present time?

Mr. Goodrich (United States).—Mr. President, I move that the vote upon this proposition be now taken.

The President.—If there be no objection the vote upon the proposition will be now taken. The Conference have heard the Resolution twice read.

The question was put to the Conference upon the adoption of the Resolution presented by the Delegate from the United States, and it was adopted.

Mr. Carter (Hawaii).—Mr. President, I hope that this vote will not prevent its being printed.

The President.—No, Sir, it will be printed and laid on the table to-morrow.

Mr. Goodrich (United States).—Mr. President, if no other gentleman has any other business to propose, my friend on the right suggests that Chairmen of Committees may want to announce the time for their meetings. We are about to adjourn until Thursday morning.

Captain Sampson (United States).—Mr. President, I would like to have the privilege of asking Committee No. 1 to meet immediately after the adjournment. I give notice to Committee No. 3 to meet to-morrow morning at 11 o'clock.

Admiral Kaznakoff (Russia).—Mr. President, the Committee on Lights will meet to-morrow morning at 11 o'clock.

Captain Sampson (United States).—The Committee No. 1 will meet immediately after the adjournment, and Committee No. 3 will meet to-morrow morning at 11 o'clock.

Mr. Carter (Hawaii).—Mr. President, Committee No. 2 will be kind enough to meet immediately after the adjournement.

The Conference thereupon adjourned until Thursday morning, December 12, 1889, at 11 o'clock A.M.

Washington, Thursday, December 12, 1889, 11 *o'clock* A.M.

THE Conference was called to order at 11 o'clock A.M., Rear-Admiral Franklin in the Chair.

The President.—The first business in order this morning is the Resolution offered by the Delegate from the United States on the 9th December, 1889.

Mr. Goodrich (United States).—Mr. President, for the present I ask permission to lay that on the table. I do not know that there will be any necessity for its passage.

The President.—The Secretary will please read the Resolution referred to for the information of the Conference.

The Resolution is as follows:—

"That the name of the Committee on Collocation of Rules be changed to 'Committee on Collocation of Rules and on the General Report of the Conference,' and that it be instructed to prepare such a General Report in due season."

The President.—The Delegate from the United States proposes to lay that Resolution on the table.

The question was put to the Conference upon the motion to lay the Resolution on the table, and it was carried.

The President.—The next business in order will be the reading of the titles of the Reports which have been handed in.

The Reports presented to the Conference are as follows:—

The Report of the Committee on Life-Saving Systems and Devices, the Report of Committee No. 2, the Report of the Committee on Collocation of Rules.

Mr. Kimball (United States).—Mr. President, I wish to call attention to one or two errors in the Report of the Committee on Life-Saving Systems and Devices. On p. 3, next to the last paragraph, it reads: "The Committee are of the opinion that all vessels should be supplied with the proper quantity of animal or vegetable oil." Insert the word "sea-going" before the word "vessel" in the first line. On p. 6, in the third Resolution, second line, insert the word "sea-going" before the word "vessels." On p. 39, the last paragraph should read in this way: "Several ships steaming 10 or 11 knots head to wind," &c. Then in the last line erase the word "ahead," and insert the words, "over the bows." I would say, Mr. President, that it is a translation in which these errors occur. It is not a good translation, and if it could be reprinted in the original French, perhaps it would be better. I do not know whether that would be allowed or not.

The President.—The Delegate from the United States moves that this particular subject be reprinted in the original French instead of the copy which we have before us, because the translation is not a good one. Is the Conference ready for the question?

The question was put to the Conference on the motion of the Delegate from the United States, and the motion was carried.

The President.—The subject will be reprinted in the original French. The next question for consideration is the Report on General Divisions II, IV, and VI, of which Captain Sampson is the Chairman. Has he any suggestions to make in regard to the Report?

Captain Sampson (United States).—No, Sir.

The President.—The next Report in order will be the Report of Committee No. 2 on General Divisions VII and VIII.

Mr. Carter (Hawaii).—Mr. President, I would like to call attention to one or two errors which will be corrected in the subsequent edition of the Report on General Division VIII. In the note signed by the five members of the Committee, explaining their signature to the Report, the word "special" should come in the last line as to the desirability of giving special signals to be used with fog-horns. On the last page, in the Signal Code "J K" should come first. The signals "N P" and "J K" should be transposed.

The President.—Will the Delegate from Hawaii please state his corrections again?

Mr. Carter (Hawaii).—Mr. President, on p. 25 the word "special" should be inserted before the word "signals" in the third line of the note which is signed by the five members of the Committee, so that it should read:—

"The Undersigned desire to report that in signing the above Report they do so without prejudice to the opinions they hold as to the desirability of giving special signals to use with fog-horns on board pilot-vessels."

[93]

It should be "with fog-horns" instead of "on fog-horns." On p. 30, the signal "J K" should come before the signal "N P." Those two sentences should be transposed, bringing the signal "N P" in the second place instead of the first. The signal "J K," two short blasts and a long blast, should come before the signal "N P," three short blasts and a long blast.

The President.—The next Report for consideration is that of the Committee on Collocation of Rules.

Mr. Goodrich (United States).—Mr. President, on the first page of the Report of the Committee, in the last two paragraphs, reference is made to the note to be appended to the Report, marked Appendix (B). That Appendix is not yet printed, but probably will be handed in to-day or to-morrow. On p. 7, subdivision (*f*), the last line but one, after the word "anchor," insert a comma. On p. 12, the first heading, "Sound-Signals for vessels in sight of one another," should come in after Article 28; in other words, at the head of Article 29. The Conference will understand that the note to be appended to the Report, marked Appendix (B), is to embrace the recommendations dealt with by the Committee on Lights, of which Admiral Kaznakoff is the Chairman, and one or two notes which form no part of the Regulations themselves, but are to be appended to the Report; so that they are not necessary to be used in the consideration of the Rules as presented by the Committee.

The President.—These Reports are now before the Conference, and the Chair will entertain any motion with regard to them.

Mr. Goodrich (United States).—Mr. President, of course I understand that we shall want some little time to consider these Reports. Some of them are very important, and unless there is some special Report which the members are willing to take up to-day, they had better be suspended for the present. As they are important enough to form a Division of the Programme, I suggest that they be laid over. There is a subject with which we can occupy a part of the time this morning, and that is the Report of the Collocation Committee upon the amendment proposed by the Delegate from Norway.

The President.—The Report of the Committee on Lights with regard to that matter has not yet been received, and will not be in until midday.

Mr Goodrich (United States).—Mr. President, let me call the attention of the Conference to this fact. In the Interlocutory Report of the Collocation Committee, reference is made to that amendment as Article 3 (*g*). That, of course, is correct according to the condition of the amendment as it was submitted to the Collocation Committee; but that paragraph will now form, if passed, sub-division (*f*) of Article 2, the Articles having been renumbered. The Committee have left it out from their Report because it is not yet adopted, the Article having been reconsidered.

The President.—Does the Conference desire to have any of the Report read?

Mr. Hall (Great Britain).—Mr. President, I was about to make a motion to that effect with regard to one of these Reports, because I apprehend that it is very possible that the Report of Committee No. 2, dealing with General Division VII, the one with regard to lanes for steamers on frequented routes, might be dealt with, if it should be read by the Secretary. It might be possible that we would be able to have all the discussion which is required upon that Report now. I do not suggest for a moment that it should be taken up without discussion, for I do not know whether the Delegates have read it. I have read it myself this morning, and it appears to me that the matter is conclusively dealt with in the Report. It is very short, and perhaps the Delegates will be able to say whether they wish to have time to read it over again before dealing with it. I only want to take the sense of the Conference upon that. The Report appears to me to be very clear and concise, and to deal with all the matters which have been referred to the Committee. I would only suggest that we might consider this, as we have nothing to occupy the time until the receipt of the Report of the Committee on Lights, which will not be received until nearly midday. We might, therefore, occupy our time in reading this Report and seeing whether or not we could deal with it now, or whether, after it has been read, it is necessary to postpone it.

The President.—Does the Delegate suggest that the Report and the Appendices be read?

Mr. Hall (Great Britain).—No, Sir; only the Report of Committee No. 2, and only that part of the Report dealing with General Division VII.

Mr. Goodrich (United States).—Mr. President, may I ask, in order to finish all the amendments at present before the Conference, the attention of the Conference to the fact that the new section, proposed by myself on the 26th November, in regard to the necessity of requiring vessels to stand by each other in case of a collision, was postponed until the coming in of the Report of the Committee on Life-Saving Systems and Devices? That Report is now in, and I should like to have the matter considered, so that the subject can go to the Collocation Committee, unless the learned Delegate from Great Britain desires the other course to be pursued.

Mr. Hall (Great Britain).—Mr. President, I certainly prefer that the amendment of my learned friend the Delegate from the United States should be taken up for consideration.

The President.—You cannot consider that until you have read this Report.

Mr. Goodrich (United States).—Mr. President, I have had a moment's conference with the Chairman of the Committee on Life-Saving Systems and Devices, and he calls to my attention, as I call to the attention of the Conference, the first page of that Report. I will read the first paragraph in order that we may understand the bearing of it upon the amendment which I have offered:—

"Saving of life and property from shipwreck at sea.

"'(*a*.) Duties of vessels after collision.'

"What these duties are is obvious enough. Common humanity requires that the colliding vessels should remain by each other and render all needed assistance so long as they can do so consistent with their own safety. Experience shows, however, that masters of vessels frequently take advantage of the circumstances attending such disasters to escape from the scene without identification, in order to avoid responsibility. Several of the maritime nations have therefore imposed upon them the legal obligation of performing these natural duties. The extent to which they are evaded, where such legal requirements do not exist, is probably not generally appreciated. The Committee have had before them statistics of one such country, which shows that in 8 per cent. of the collisions reported the master got away without being known. In these instances there was loss of life upon some of the vessels so abandoned; some of them went down, and all suffered damage.

"It would seem, then, that any effective measure which might prevent such a practice, or make it less frequent, would not only be in the interest of humanity, but also aid in securing justice in regard to the rights of property. The Committee, therefore, are of opinion that in case of collision between two vessels, the master, or person in charge of each vessel, should be required, so far as he can without danger to his own vessel, crew, or passengers, to stay by the other vessel until he has ascertained that she has no need of further assistance, and to render to the other vessel, her master, crew, and passengers, such assistance as may be practicable and necessary in order to save them from any danger caused by the collision; and also to give to the master, or person in charge of the other vessel, the name of his own vessel, and of her port of registry, or of the port or place to which she belongs, and the name of the ports or the places from which and to which she is bound.

"So far as the Committee can learn, the laws of those countries which have taken action upon the subject are to the above effect, substantially agreeing in defining the duties of masters, although the infraction of the law is differently dealt with in the different countries.

"In expressing the foregoing opinion the Committee are unanimous, but a minority think the Conference should indicate what, in their opinion, the penalty of failure to comply with the duties prescribed should be. The majority, however, do not deem this necessary, believing that the consequences of disobedience to their laws can and will be properly taken care of by the several Governments, without suggestion from the Conference.

"For the information of the Conference, the enactments of Great Britain upon the subject, which prescribe severer penalties for disregard of the duties imposed than those of any other nation, are appended to this Report. (See Appendix A.)"

Now, Mr. President, in regard to this section——

Captain Richard (France).—Mr. President, I rise to a point of order. It was established by one of our Rules that no Report and no amendment should be discussed unless forty-eight hours had elapsed between the presenting of the amendment and its discussion. Now quite a number of Reports have been distributed among us. In order to be able to discuss them it will be absolutely necessary that we have time to read them. I certainly would have no objection to discuss the amendment itself were not a question of principle involved which it is important to observe. We are at this moment on the point of discussing one of the Reports with which we were furnished this morning. Therefore, if we discuss this one we may be led to discuss all the other Reports. I have no special objection to discuss the amendment itself as it was presented some time ago, but the Conference having previously decided that this amendment should be taken up for discussion simultaneously with the Report on Life-Saving Systems and Devices, pursuant to the Rule with which our discussions are governed, we should not discuss it until at least forty-eight hours after the said Report has been presented.

The President.—The Delegate from France desires the matter to lie over.

Mr. Goodrich (United States).—Mr. President, I have no objection to its lying over if any Delegate desires it.

Mr. Hall (Great Britain).—Mr. President, I apprehend that there is some slight mistake here. I did not understand that the learned Delegate for the United States wants to discuss this Report at all, but he proposes to discuss his amendment. This amendment was postponed until this Report should be handed in, and unless there is something in the Report which would make it undesirable to discuss that amendment, or something against the principle of that amendment, I do not see why we cannot discuss it, as we have had it before us for a fortnight. I understand that there is practically no difference of opinion about it, except with regard to the last three or four lines, and I apprehend that that would hardly be pressed without there was a reasonable possibility that the Powers would agree to it. I am sure that everybody will agree in this: That it is very undesirable for any of us to attempt to carry any Resolution against the sense of a considerable portion of the Conference, because it would be a waste of time. As I say, the amendment of the learned Delegate for the United States has been before us some time, and now surely we can express our opinion upon it, especially as we have no reason to suppose that anything can occur to change our opinion with regard to the matter.

Mr. Goodrich (United States).—Mr. President, if the gallant Delegate from France desires to have the amendment laid over, of course I must assent to it; but I do not think the difference between the Committee or the gallant Delegate from France and myself is so essential as to make it necessary to postpone. But that, of course, I leave absolutely to the gallant Delegate from France so far as I am concerned, and if he desires the amendment laid over I shall at once assent.

Captain Richard (France).—Mr. President, I look upon this matter simply as a measure of precaution. We cannot refuse to discuss the amendment of the Honourable Mr. Goodrich, which was presented a fortnight ago; but, in order to discuss this amendment, Mr. Goodrich commences by reading the Report of the Committee on Life-Saving Systems and Devices. But this Report cannot be discussed until forty-eight hours have elapsed. If we discuss it now I think that we enter upon the wrong course, and that, after having violated our Rule once, we will hereafter be more easily led to violate it again.

Under those circumstances, I ask that the discussion upon the life-saving systems and devices and the amendment of Mr. Goodrich be both adjourned forty-eight hours, not because we have not the right, when necessity requires it, to discuss the amendment—inasmuch as it was presented a **fortnight ago—but because** the Conference has decided that it should be discussed simultaneously with the Report, and that, by reason of such decision, its fate is irrevocably cast with that of the Report.

I, therefore, think that we should await the discussion of the Report of the Committee on Life-Saving Systems and Devices.

Mr. Verney (Siam).—Mr. President, I desire to make one remark, not only as regards this amendment, but as regards all of the amendments which have been put over until the Reports have been put on the table. I would ask the Conference what that means? Surely the fact that it has been laid over and put on the table means that the members of the Conference should have an opportunity of reading the Report before they discuss the amendment, otherwise what is the use of referring any amendment until the Report of the Committee is laid on the table? I have not had the opportunity which the learned First Delegate from Great Britain has had of reading through any of these Reports, and I do, therefore, support the proposition of the gallant Delegate from France, not only as regards this amendment, but as regards any amendment which was deferred until the Report had been laid on the table, and I hope that the common sense of that proposal will commend itself to this Conference.

Mr. Goodrich (United States).—Mr. President, personally I have not the slightest objection to assenting to laying over the consideration of this amendment until some future day. I only wanted to occupy the time of the Conference, if we had no other business before us.

Mr. Verney (Siam).—Mr. President, I sincerely hope that this will not in any way waste our time, because I think we have before us an enormous mass of material with which our time can be occupied.

The President.—The Delegate from France moves to postpone the consideration of this amendment for forty-eight hours, and then to have it considered with the Report of the Committee on Life-Saving Systems and Devices.

Mr. Goodrich (United States).—Mr. President, I think that instead of being postponed for forty-eight hours, it had better be laid over until Monday, because a certain day had better be fixed for its consideration.

Captain Richard (France).—Mr. President, I have no objection to that. I simply demand that the forty-eight hour rule be observed.

Mr. Hall (Great Britain).—Mr. President, might I suggest that the forty-eight hours would elapse, and we need not sit to-morrow, but could sit on Saturday? So far as I can see we shall have nothing at all to do this week if we lay over this amendment until Monday. I do not see why we could not sit on Saturday, and do a day's work. We shall not have anything to do to-morrow.

Mr. Goodrich (United States).—Mr. President, I shall not be able to be in attendance on the Conference on Saturday, and I would like to be heard on this proposition before it is decided.

Captain Mensing (Germany).—Mr. President, I would like to point out that the time would not be entirely wasted. Committee No. 3 have before it a large amount of work, and have been given very little time indeed for its work. There has not been sufficient time for the Secretary and Chairman of the Committee to enable them to get on with their part of the work. If the Conference will adjourn we would find the time; and, I dare say, it would not be found to be lost time.

The President.—The Delegate for the United States proposes to put off this discussion of the amendment and the Report of the Committee connected with it until Monday. Is the Conference ready for the question upon that motion?

The question was put to the Conference upon the motion to postpone the consideration of the proposed new section until Monday, and the motion was carried.

Mr. Hall (Great Britain).—Mr. President, might I point out that although it is most desirable that wherever time is desired all possible time should be extended, yet of course we have the power to discuss any subject by unanimous consent at once? I quite understand that the gallant Delegate from France pointed this out, because he thinks that the principle ought not to be established; but I do not apprehend that any one at this table requires any more time to consider this question of the Standing-by Rule, which is the amendment of the learned Delegate from the United States. We have really nothing to go on with except this, unless some Delegate really wants time to consider the matter, we might, by unanimous consent, agree to discuss it now.

I think I am right in saying that my gallant friend the Delegate from France did not make this motion with regard to this particular Rule, but it was more in order to guard against matters being discussed without our having time to consider them. The Conference, therefore, by unanimous consent, could agree to discuss the amendment of the Delegate from the United States and proceed with the discussion of it at once, unless any Delegate wishes more time to consider it. I certainly will not propose it if there is any dissenting voice, but not hearing any, I would suggest that we can take this amendment at once and discuss it. This matter has been before us for a long time, and I apprehend that all of us have made up our minds on the point, one way or the other. I would move, therefore, Mr. President, that the discussion of the amendment of the learned Delegate from the United States be proceeded with now, notwithstanding any rule to the contrary which has been adopted by the Conference.

Mr. Goodrich (United States).—What does the Delegate from France say?

Captain Richard (France).—Mr. President, we have heard our learned colleague from Great Britain, with his persuasive eloquence, tell us that he desired to make no exception, but he, notwithstanding, immediately thereafter proposed to violate the rules which govern our discussions. The reasons which he gave us were so strong that I myself felt fully convinced as to the propriety of adopting the measure which he advocates. But if to-day we depart from the rule, there will be nothing to prevent us from departing from it subsequently, and that is why I demand that the rule be strictly followed.

Mr. Hall (Great Britain).—Mr. President, I will only point out that we have on several occasions, where matters have come up when it was not necessary to wait forty-eight hours, dealt with them at

125

once when it was the general sense of the Conference that we could discuss them immediately. I certainly should not propose it unless it would appear to everybody that we could discuss it without any harm to any one at all. We have done this frequently. We have discussed cases absolutely in principle without waiting for the delay of forty-eight hours.

The President.—The Delegate from Great Britain proposes to discuss the amendment of the Delegate from the United States at the present time, if there be no objection on the part of any member of the Conference. If the Chair hears any objection on the part of any member of the Conference the question will not be proceeded with.

Captain Richard (France).—Mr. President, I still have the same objection, namely, that the proposition is directly contrary to the rule. If we infringe the rule for any reason which we may present, though the same may be overwhelming, we will violate the rule every time. I think that we should abide, as I said before, by our rule, and not introduce alterations into it. The amendment which is suggested to us for discussion will not, I think, lead to a long discussion. In our Committee we were unanimous upon its subject, and I hope that this unanimity will be shared by the Conference.

Consequently my objection is absolutely an objection to violating the rule; if we violate it to-day we will again do so later.

Mr. Hall (Great Britain).—Mr. President, I withdraw my proposition, as it is opposed by the gallant Delegate from France.

The President.—The proposition is withdrawn, and the discussion of the amendment will be postponed.

Admiral Kaznakoff (Russia).—Mr. President, if it is decided to postpone it until Monday, can we not begin on Monday earlier and sit later, so that, instead of sitting four hours a-day, we may work for five or six hours a-day?

Mr. Goodrich (United States).—Mr. President, I do not know why the suggestion of the learned Delegate from Great Britain might not be adopted, and that the Conference proceed and read the Report of Committee No. 2.

The President.—The Delegate from France has just objected to the consideration of any Report until sufficient time has been given to the Delegates to consider and read it.

Mr. Flood (Norway).—Mr. President, during our last meeting I took the liberty to ask permission to lay before the Conference a Resolution intended to be a modest supplement to the Report given by the Committee on General Division XIII of the Programme. During the discussion on that subject I, however, found that I must have been very much misunderstood, or perhaps I should say that I had not been able to use proper or happy words to make myself understood. After a short discussion of this subject I, therefore, asked leave to withdraw my Resolution, and asked the Chair to permit me to bring in an amendment or another Resolution at the next meeting—I said on Friday. But now we have come together to-day, and as it does not seem that there are many urgent things on the table, and as we are all very anxious to make the work as quick and as easy as possible, so as to get through at a reasonable time, I would ask that my Resolution be considered. I have, with the assistance of my learned friends the Delegates from Denmark and others, tried to draw a Resolution which I beg to lay before the Conference to-day. I would say that if the Conference are willing to discuss the matter at once, we are most willing to do so. The matter was so ably laid before the Conference at the last session that I do not think there is any necessity for spending much time in the discussion. I therefore ask your permission, Mr. President, to lay this Resolution before the Conference, to be read by the Secretary.

The President.—The Resolution of the Delegate from Norway will be read by the Secretary.

The Resolution is as follows:—

"The Report of the Committee on General Division XIII, on the establishment of a Permanent International Marine Commission, having been adopted by the Conference, it is further resolved that the Conference recommend that the advisability of a Bureau of Maritime Information be considered by the Governments of maritime nations."

The President.—The Resolution is before the Conference.

Captain Mensing (Germany).—Mr. President, I would like to ask for information whether this Bureau is to be one in which information may be sought regarding the dangers of navigation? If so, then I would like to point out that it would be proper to discuss this proposition when the Report on General Division XI is laid before the Conference. It will come up and be discussed in Committee, I suppose, to-day, and as the honourable Delegate from Norway is a member of this Committee he will certainly have every facility given to him to explain his plan, and then we will act upon it.

The President.—Does the Delegate from Norway desire to await the Report of the Committee just mentioned by the Delegate from Germany before his Resolution is discussed and put upon its passage?

Mr. Flood (Norway).—Mr. President, of course I am very willing to have any time given to consider this matter, but I would simply say that our idea of the Bureau of Information was ably pointed out by Governor Garde, the Delegate from Denmark, at our last meeting. There was to be a General Bureau of Information which would be of interest to seafaring mankind in general. So, as we already have before us the Report on General Division XIII, I thought that the right moment had come to have this subject discussed and to have an expression for or against it from the Conference, together with this Report on General Division XIII. Of course, when I offered to have it discussed to-day it was simply to get an expression of opinion from the Conference in regard to the matter, and to show our willingness to do what we could to facilitate business, so that it should not be said that we ran this in at the last moment, and that we intended to detain the Conference with it. I understood that there was not much for discussion to-day, and I think we could fill out a few moments of our time in hearing my Resolution and in giving us a few moments to further explain what we mean by this Bureau.

Mr. Hall (Great Britain).—Mr. President, I see no reason why we should not discuss this. We have discussed it for half a day already, and I think that all of us have formed our own opinions on the subject. I do not think it is necessary to postpone it. We have nothing to go on with at present unless we take this up, because we shall not get the further Report of the Committee on Lights until nearly midday, although we have the proof in our hands.

The President.—The Chair understands that the Committee, when they do receive the Report, wish to consider it before they lay it before the Conference. Does the Delegate from Germany, Captain Mensing, make any motion with reference to this Resolution?

Captain Mensing (Germany).—No, Sir; I do not make any motion with regard to it.

The President.—The Chair will state that the Report of the Committee on Lights, with reference to the motion of the Delegate from Norway, will not be read to-day at all. The Secretary has just informed me that the Report will not be ready. The Chairman of the Committee says that the Committee will have to meet before they can lay the Report upon this amendment before the Conference.

Mr. Hall (Great Britain).—Mr. President, then I propose that it would be desirable to take that up to-morrow, and not to-day, if that be the case, and to take up the Resolution of the Delegate from Norway to-day. That will give us something to occupy our time.

The President.—The Resolution of the Delegate from Norway is now before the Conference.

Mr. Garde (Denmark).—Mr. President, may I be permitted to say a few words as to the proposal of the honourable Delegate from Norway? I will say that it is only necessary for me to make a very few remarks, as I have already explained the view I took of this matter at our last meeting. Of course I will not detain the Conference longer than is necessary, so I will not repeat what I have already said. I will only remind you that during the discussion of the Report on General Division XIII, which was proposed by the Committee, the establishment of this Bureau was opposed. I suppose that the reason for doing so was that it was understood that the Commission should be a permanent Commission; and, I therefore explained that what we wanted in our country was not a permanent Commission, but a link or medium between the different countries, where proposals can be sent from any country. In order to explain what is meant by this Bureau, I mentioned a Telegraphic Convention, and I will take the liberty to read here an Article of the Convention about the telegraph which was signed in Berlin on the 17th September, 1885, and which at present has done so much good for the telegraphic service; and I apprehend that something in the same direction might be done for these maritime questions which are of an international character. The XIVth Article of the Convention says:—

"A central institution, placed under the supervision of a superior administrative authority of one of the Contracting Governments, as designed to this effect by the Regulations, is charged with the collection, preparation, and publication of all sorts of information as to the international telegraph service, the formulation and treatment of proposals as to amendments in the tariffs and in the regulations of service, to publish the amendments carried, and, on the whole, to take care of the investigations and execution of the work entrusted to it in the interest of international telegraphy.

"The expenses caused by this institution are to be reimbursed by all the Telegraph Administrations in the contracting countries."

This Convention has been supplied with Regulations for the service of the Bureau, and this reads in French:—

"Les frais communs du Bureau International des Administrations Télégraphiques ne doivent pas dépasser, par année, la somme de 70,000 fr., non compris les frais spéciaux auxquels donne lieu la réunion d'une Conférence Internationale. Cette somme pourra être augmentée ultérieurement par consentement de toutes les Parties Contractantes.

"L'Administration désignée, en vertu de l'Article XIV de la Convention, pour la direction du Bureau International, en surveille les dépenses, fait les avances nécessaires et établit le compte annuel, qui est communiqué à toutes les autres Administrations intéressées."

The reason I have brought this forward is that a Bureau for maritime matters would have to agree upon the principle as to the division of expenses, and this Convention about the telegraphic service is the only one where the classification has taken place in such a manner that the different countries announced, themselves, what classes they wished to enter, and thereby is obtained in a very simple manner what in practice has been shown to have no difficulties, whatever the division of expenses. The next Article mentioned is the different classes into which the respective countries are to be entered, and then we come to the last one:—

"Les Offices des États Contractants se transmettent réciproquement tous les documents relatifs à leur administration intérieure et se communiquent tout perfectionnement qu'ils viendraient à y introduire.

"En règle générale, le Bureau International sert d'intermédiaire à ces notifications.

"Les dits Offices envoient par la poste, par lettre affranchie, au Bureau International, la notification de toutes les mesures relatives à la composition et aux changements de tarifs, tant intérieurs qu'internationaux; à l'ouverture de lignes nouvelles et à la suppression de lignes existantes, en tant que ces lignes intéressent le service international; enfin, aux ouvertures, suppressions et modifications de services des bureaux. Les documents imprimés ou authographiés à ce sujet par les Administrations sont expédiés au Bureau International, soit à la date de leur distribution, soit, au plus tard, le premier jour du mois que suit cette date.

"Les dites Administrations lui envoient, en outre, par télégraphe, avis de toutes les interruptions ou rétablissements des communications qui affectent la correspondance internationale.

"Elles lui font parvenir, au commencement de chaque année et aussi complètement qu'il leur est possible, des tableaux statistiques du mouvement des correspondances, de la situation des lignes, du nombre des bureaux et des appareils, &c. Ces tableaux sont dressés d'après les indications du Bureau International, qui distribue, à cet effet, les formules toutes préparées.

"Elles adressent également à ce Bureau deux exemplaires des publications diverses qu'elles font paraître.

"Le Bureau International reçoit, en outre, communication de tous les renseignements relatifs aux expériences auxquelles chaque Administration a pu procéder sur les différentes parties du service."

Of course I have no desire to propose here that a Bureau should be established exactly upon this basis; but I read this only to show how in practice a similar Bureau at present works. I then take the liberty to call attention to the fact that what we want is not a Commission with any decisive power or with any administrative power or authority on all questions which are concerned with international maritime interests. Those, of course, will remain where they are now, with the different Governments. But what we want in our country is a medium through which we can address these Governments in such a manner that the proposals can be brought there from single persons or from organizations, and have them called to the attention of the respective Governments.

These Associations, public and private, I am convinced will desire such a medium, and if they do not get it they will be forced to unite in a smaller degree. For instance, Denmark, Sweden, and Norway will have to combine for this purpose, and they will be forced not to take as much interest as they ought to do, and so much as the common interests of mankind require should be done, in International Conferences. I move that it be understood that we bring this matter before the Conference, not because we intend to espouse the present system, but because we want to be assisted in a fair way by this Conference, so that in the future other Conferences can work with interest for this question, which we think is for the common interest of all seafaring people, and to obtain that interest we must know that the work we do will be fairly considered and fairly treated in the future. We cannot apply to our Governments, for our Governments cannot lay before this Conference any proposal as to one course or the other.

Now, we are not the only country which is in this condition. There is no country which has a Board of Trade like Great Britain. Of course we cannot work so carefully or so thoroughly consider these questions as is done by a Board of Trade; and therefore it is the more necessary for us to work on a smaller scale, so that we can, in an official way, come into communication with all other countries and give our proposals and get the proposals from them, which will be communicated to all of the different Governments; and then all future International Conferences will know what they have to consider before the Conference meets. I therefore recommend this to the adoption of the Conference, and ask that it will take into consideration whether it would not be in the interest of all countries that such a Bureau should be established. We do not propose that the Conference shall take any action as to the establishment, practically, of such a Bureau at the present time. We only propose that the Conference will recommend the advisability of a Bureau of Maritime Information to be considered by the Governments of the maritime nations. Then it is left entirely to them to act if they desire, and to come into communication with each other with regard to the matter.

Mr. Hall (Great Britain).—Mr. President, I certainly cannot vote in favour of this Resolution, and I cannot help thinking that the Delegate from Norway, perhaps, has not read very carefully the Report of the Committee which has already been presented. Any one reading that Report carefully will see this. We treated, not only the question of an International Maritime Commission which should dispense international law, but we also considered the very interesting Memorandum which was handed in by one of the Delegates from Denmark, and which is an Appendix to that Report, dealing entirely with the question of a Bureau. In that Report he says: "I do not propose an International Commission to deal with international law. I know that that is practically impossible. I would suggest that there should be a Bureau." Now, it is perfectly true that there is a distinction there, as has just been pointed out by the learned Delegate who has addressed us, when he says that this is not to be a permanent Commission, but it is merely to be a Bureau. But we have discussed the question whether or not it was desirable to have a Bureau, and any one reading that Report will see that the reasons which are given against the establishment of a permanent Bureau are against the establishment of a Bureau at all.

I say that the Report deals with the question as to whether there should be a Bureau at the present time, and whether it would be a good thing or not. We point out that it would be simply wasting time, because after the Bureau had made recommendations they would be obliged to have communication with the Governments, and the recommendations would merely come before the Governments again They would be sent backwards and forwards from one Government to another, and there would be more circumlocution than there is at present. Now let us look at this and see what it is, practically. So far as I can see it comes to this: The proposers of the Bureau say, "We have not got a Bureau in Norway or Denmark. Why should you not have a Permanent International Bureau in London, as is proposed here? Great Britain and the other Powers shall pay according to their tonnage, and we will pay our respective shares." Well, we are very much obliged to them for the suggestion. But do they propose that we should do away with our Board of Trade?

[Cries of "No, no."]

Mr. Hall.—Then, if we are not to do away with our Board of Trade, why are we to pay about 65 per cent. of the expenses of this Bureau to sit in London? Can it reasonably be supposed that any Power with a proper Bureau or a proper Board of Trade will undertake to pay a large share of the expenses of any Bureau, to be analogous to the Board of Trade, because it so happens that there may be some Powers which have not got a Board of Trade or anything corresponding thereto? That is what it comes to. The suggestion is this: "We have not got a Board of Trade, so we want to have an international one, and we will pay our share towards it." We are very much obliged to them for the suggestion; but can they suppose that any Power will undertake to consent to anything of the kind, when it has all of the proper appliances for considering the matters for itself? Now, allow me to deal with one further question. I do not mean to discuss this at very great length. I think the Report speaks for itself. What is the use of our advising the foreign Governments? Surely they can consider the question of a Bureau without our giving them permission or even suggesting it to them.

It is not a part of our province to instruct foreign Governments how they should do their work; and I cannot help thinking that if we pass this Resolution it would meet with a reception at the hands of foreign Governments which perhaps was not intended by the mover of it. I think they might very properly say, "Thank you for nothing. We can do our work in our own way, and we do not want any nstruction from you how to do it." But, I say, why should we or any Powers which have got ordinary Boards of Trade or Bureaux join in the establishment of another Bureau against our wish? We are told that the Scandinavian Powers cannot make proposals to foreign Governments. If they cannot, let them put themselves in order at once to be in a position to be able to do so. Let them have a joint Bureau if they like. There is nothing to prevent them from doing it at all. Let them have a joint Board of Trade. We know from that interesting Memorandum which was handed in by the Delegate from Denmark that the Scandinavian ship-owners have formed a Bureau, but that is, of course, an unofficial one. What is there to prevent those Powers from combining together and having a Bureau like the Board of Trade. Then, if they have an official Bureau, they can make their recommendations to foreign Governments perfectly well, and clothed with proper authority.

But I want to know this: is there one single Delegate who has got instructions from his Government to propose anything like this to this Conference at the present time? So far as the Committee know, and we made inquiries, we do not find one single Government which has authorized anything of the kind; and yet in the face of that it is suggested here that we are to vote to recommend the advisability of a Bureau of Maritime Information to be considered by the Governments of the Maritime Powers. Where is the Maritime Bureau to be? What is it to do? How is it to be composed, and how is it to be paid for? The whole of that is left in the dark, and we are asked to make a recommendation to foreign Governments as to the advisability of such a Bureau! Certainly, having regard to the matters which I have stated, and having regard to the Report of the Committee on General Division XIII, I think we would be very foolish to support any such proposition as this.

Mr. Flood (Norway).—Mr. President, it would be sheer madness in me to stand up and try to answer the different questions asked by one of the first Admiralty lawyers of the age, and I will not attempt it in any way, because I am entirely at his mercy in eloquence and everything else. But I will point out that when the learned Delegate from Great Britain says that it is such a strange act to propose this, that there was handed in upon the same day a Report of the Committee upon the Load-Line, Division No. III of the Programme, and there they use words which are stronger even than I have dared to use in my Resolution, that this matter is not ripe for consideration by this Conference, and that it should be left to negotiations to be carried on between the Governments of the maritime nations.

Mr. Hall (Great Britain).—Mr. President, that is because the Committee state in the Report that negotiations are going on between the Governments, that proposals have been submitted between foreign Governments, and, therefore, it is better not to take it out of their hands, and we ask them to go on with it. That is the reason for that recommendation. There are no proposals with regard to a Maritime Bureau.

Mr. Flood (Norway).—Then, Mr. President, I would simply state that our thought in having such a Bureau established is simply following up the argument of the learned Delegate from Great Britain. He says, "We have got a Board of Trade, and we do not need any other. Let those nations that have not got such an institution join together and get up a similar Bureau." Well, in that lies the very strength of what I am pointing out in our Resolution. I do not for a moment expect that Great Britain, with her Board of Trade, should grasp this at once or in any way, perhaps, join us in this matter. But I do say that the other countries which are in want of such a splendid institution as the Board of Trade should join together in forming such an institution as that Board of Trade; not one or two or three countries, but the most of the European Powers should join together in that way, and so have this chain made of links and links until at last it will encircle the whole world. A central institution of this kind would be a source of communication between them, and would be a great blessing for mankind.

While I have the floor may I be permitted to say only a few words more? I am not trained in speaking before such an august assembly as this, and I therefore take the liberty of framing my idea in a few lines which I will read, if you will allow me. Speaking about this Bureau, it has already been ably stated by Governor Garde that the expenses of it could be provided for as the expenses of the Telegraphic Bureaux have been provided for, and it could be carried on like those Bureaux, which are now acting as such a blessing all over the world. I am not claiming to be original in this idea, but simply have tried to point out that various Bureaux of this kind are already working and doing much good in the world. In doing this I desire to say, Mr. President, that from my modest Resolution it will be clearly seen that we never thought of establishing a Board of Commissioners with any legislative or executive power whatever. We only thought of a Board for information, to examine and report upon all inventions or other matters of interest which might be laid before the same through the interested Governments, through the many Maritime Associations or institutions of a similar kind, or from private individuals, and after careful examination report on the same to the different Governments or parties interested.

We have, however, bowed before to the decision of the Committee of General Division XIII, and loyally given our vote to the Report to the effect that, for the present, the establishment of a Permanent International Maritime Commission is not considered expedient.

We did this, however, with the fond hope, so ably and earnestly expressed before this Conference by both the distinguished Delegates from Denmark during our late debate on this subject, that the Conference would not altogether turn its back upon us and our supporters by denying us a recompense in recommending to the different Governments the adoption of a Maritime Bureau, a simple medium between the maritime nations which would be neither costly nor difficult to compose.

This idea is not original or in any way an invention by us. We have already many such Bureaux, and who will deny that all and each of them, in one way or another, are a blessing to the whole civilized world? How could or would, for instance, our splendid postal or telegraph institutions be carried on in an international spirit if each of them had not its own Central Bureau, and what nation has ever complained of difficulties in organizing or arranging these Bureaux? Why, then, not also extend this idea to the maritime world? You all see and acknowledge it would be a useful thing, and that even this Conference would have had a far easier task, and its results perhaps have been more satisfactory, if such a Bureau had existed already, which not only would have formed a programme for us, but also laid before us Reports on many things, not only inventions, but also other matters of interest, which would have shortened our stay here considerably, and, before all and everything, helped a good many of us to a more thorough knowledge of the matters laid before us and decided upon in this Conference.

Now, if this Conference is supposed to be the last as it is the first in the history of mankind, then, of course, let us drop the matter at once; and if our visit to this Western Hemisphere is to have that result, then by all means vote down my Resolution immediately. If, on the contrary, you wish to continue this intercourse at certain intervals, if you wish to invite your Western brethren to visit the Old World in years to come for the same purpose as we are gathered here from all parts of the world, then I do not see how you can vote down our modest proposal to try to establish a kind of medium, simply a connecting link, between this and coming Maritime Conferences.

You may all be proud of what you have done here, for I have no doubt this Conference will accomplish much for the benefit of humanity and safety of trade and commerce in general. But the world will hardly turn any year in its ethereal orbit without bringing new ideas, and new inventions will spring up or come forward which we cannot even conceive of now, and which before long will make a new Maritime Conference a necessity. Why not, then, foresee this by proposing, or at least favouring, the idea of establishing a kind of Bureau to watch our maritime interests for all of us; a Bureau to follow the development of science and knowledge in the same spirit and in the same way in which we see other Bureaux work to be useful and to be a blessing for mankind in general?

By voting for our Resolution you only give your consent to the brotherly thought, let us not part never to meet; and to forget each other. Let us, on the contrary, continue to work together; let us jointly watch how our ideas, formed in recommendations to new Rules and Regulations, operate in practice: and let us, in parting from each other for the present, take our modest Resolution as an acceptance of brotherly love extending over all the civilized world, and as a heartfelt and sincere " We will meet again."

Dr. Sieveking (Germany).—Mr. President, speaking on behalf of the German Delegates, I desire to say that we certainly cannot agree to the Resolution which has been proposed by the Delegate from Norway. I may say with some certainty that I know what will be the answer of our Government in case such a Resolution were laid before them, or in case a recommendation were laid before them that the advisability of a Bureau of Maritime Information should be considered by the Governments of the maritime nations. The German Government at once would say that they did not consider it advisable or did not consider it expedient; or perhaps, to be a little more polite, they would answer that they did not desire to have it at the present time.

Now, that is the very answer which the Conference has given to this question by adopting the Report of the Committee, which has stated that, for the present, the establishment of a Permanent International Maritime Commission is not considered expedient, because in fact the change from a Commission to a Bureau is a mere change of words. It is a mere change of words, in my opinion, to say, " We do not want an International Maritime Permanent Commission, but we want a Maritime International Bureau, not a Permanent Bureau." A Permanent Bureau is one which would have a continuous sitting without interruption. A Bureau which was not permanent would work when it was called together. Now, what is said in support of this Bureau? It has been ably explained to us that this Bureau is intended only to meet when it is called together, and all of the arguments which are brought forward in support of this Resolution tend to show that the intention is to have a certain body of experts who are to prepare maritime questions for the consideration of future Conferences. They will not sit every day, but their task will be a continuous one. It has been stated that it is to be a sort of an International Board of Trade, and is to do the work of a Board of Trade. Therefore it is, in fact, a Permanent Bureau.

Now, what is the difference between a Bureau and a Commission? There is no difference whatever except in words. What is a Commission? A Commission is certainly not a body with power of legislation or authoritative power as to legislation; but it is a body which is vested with a certain work to do, a body of men and experts, lawyers, mariners, and so forth, intrusted with a certain work, and that work would be the preparing of subjects for future Conferences, and for bringing about a unity of law and a unity in the administration of laws in certain maritime affairs. This is the work of a Commission, and it is the very same work which it is declared now is to be done by what is called a Bureau. When any one mentions a Bureau we think of a kind of an office with inkstands, &c., and when we speak of a Commission we think of something higher. But in fact it is quite the same thing. There is a body of men to consider matters brought before them, to do the appropriate work, and to lay the work before the different Governments.

Now, I will not press this point any further. It leads to this: We have rejected a Permanent Commission, and this rejection implies the rejection of a Permanent Bureau or of a Bureau. I will not press that. If we have made a mistake, let us correct it. Let us reconsider the question. If any harm has been done by that, if we can go a step farther in the promotion of civilization and of commercial interest to all nations, let us do so. Let us, then, annul the Resolution we have taken. But we cannot do so before we have convinced ourselves that the arguments which led us to the adoption of that Report were not sound ones. I have not heard a word to-day to prove this. It has not been tried to prove it. On the contrary, the Resolution begins with the words, "That the Report of the Committee having been adopted," so it confirms the Report of the Committee.

It has been put forward and pressed somewhat by the Delegate from Denmark that there is a precedent for this proposed Bureau contained in the Telegraph Convention. But I may point out that there is a great and decided difference between these cases. The Telegraphic Convention is a Convention or Treaty between nations, an existing Treaty. In order to carry out the principle of that Treaty it is quite natural to appoint a Commission of the contracting nations empowered to collect information and report from time to time what experience shows it may be necessary to do for the common interest, and to report all measures which might, by experience, be shown to be advisable for the common welfare. That is a necessary work for which there is a given basis. But what are we to do here? We have no Conventions. We have no Treaties. We have only to prepare certain subjects for promoting civilization in the interest of mankind and for the advancement of the commercial and maritime interests of the world. That is general and without any limit. It is a body of men to try whether they can do something to promote unity of legislation.

Now, it has just been said that this is to prepare the work for future Conferences, and some very sanguine hopes have been expressed with regard to the calling and meeting of future Conferences. But there is quite a difference between this Conference and other future Conferences. Before this Conference there was one certain subject which, in fact, was already regulated by International Regulations, not founded upon Treaties, but Regulations which were common to the whole maritime world. Practically all of the nations had the same Regulations or Rules of the Road, and therefore it was quite natural that a Conference was called, after a lapse of time, to consider whether in the light of experience some alterations ought to be added, or some reforms could be arrived at with regard to these Rules.

There was a certain subject which was to be considered by the Delegates, and there was a reasonable cause for the Governments to send their Delegates here. But now we are asked to convene a body of men to prepare questions, without any limit being given to it except that it must be a question of importance to the commercial nations. But that is, in fact, only doing what all of the separate Governments are now doing for themselves. Let us see how this would work. I will not repeat what has been said as to who is to select the Delegates and who is to compensate them, and so forth. All of these are questions which make it quite inadmissible that such a thing could be realized at all. I will not repeat, but will see how this will work. It has been said the British Board of Trade is the very thing which we have in view. It is an excellent body, composed of experienced experts in great numbers. A country which has such a Board of Trade of course would not want an International Bureau, because they have one of their own.

But, say the Scandinavian Powers, we have not; and when it is mentioned to them that Great Britain would be very little inclined to pay 65 per cent. of the expenses of such a Bureau, which she does not want and does not need, it is said that the other European Powers may join in something like the Board of Trade. Now I beg to point out to the Delegates from Norway that the German Government has its institution just as well as Great Britain has its Board of Trade. The Departments in Berlin and other maritime places of Germany entirely fulfil, or they try to fulfil, all of the necessary requirements. Of course their experience is not so large as that of the Board of Trade, but they try to fulfil the very same duties which the Board of Trade fulfils in Great Britain, and I am sure that France will have the same, and Spain the same, and Portugal the same, and Austria the same. I am sure that every civilized Government will have the necessary Departments and necessary officials to investigate such matters as are laid before them by private men or Associations; and that they will investigate them and prepare legislation when it is their duty to do so. Then there is correspondence between different Governments.

In Germany, when some theme is discussed, the Government writes to the Board of Trade and asks for its opinion, so the Board of Trade writes to Berlin. I am sure there is an interchange of correspondence and of opinions not only between the British Government and the German Government, but also between the Governments of all maritime nations. Now, if this proposal is adopted, there would be another Board of Trade, a Scandinavian Board of Trade or an International Board of Trade. I do not know what nations will participate, but that will be another body for the Governments to correspond with. I do not think they would be very much inclined to correspond with such a body. They have enough to do to correspond with each other. This would not dispense with any of their work. They would not save a minute of time. They would lose an enormous amount of time, because if this body had to report to the Governments, they would have to discuss it in the same way as they do now and ask the opinion of other Governments in regard to it. In that way a vast deal of correspondence would be added to that which is now already carried on.

I therefore, myself, am very positively of the opinion that such a Bureau would not be the proper way in which to prepare for international legislation. This preparation which has been referred to must be done in another way. The Governments cannot be expected to call together such a body and to pay for it because there is not such a body in the Scandanavian country. Now, in conclusion, I only want to add a few remarks about the position which we as Delegates would be put in if such a Resolution were passed. Let us look at the words of the Resolution. The Report of the Committee having been adopted, that is to say, although for the present a Permanent International Maritime Commission is not considered expedient, it is further resolved that the Conference recognizes that the

131

advisability of a Bureau of Maritime Information should be considered by the Governments of the maritime nations. In other words, we say that we do not consider it expedient for the present to have such a body, but we recommend that the Governments consider the advisability of the establishment of such a body. Now, what would our Governments say when we go home and bring such a result? They would say this: We sent you to Washington to consider whether it was expedient or not—that formed a part of the programme—as to the establishment of a Permanent International Commission; but we did not send you to say, after consideration, that it is not expedient, but still it is advisable to consider it. If you think it is advisable to consider it, point out how you want us to carry it out.

We are not meeting here as a body of philanthropists. We are not meeting as a body of philosophers. We are not meeting here as a body of the friends of mankind; but we are the Delegates of Governments, for a certain mission. The Governments have sent us here to consider whether or not it is expedient, and we must give them a reason, and we must give them an answer to that mission. We have given an answer, and we have said that we do not think it is expedient to establish such a body. That is what we have said to them. Now I think it would not be too strongly expressed if it were said that it would be a ridiculous position for the Delegates to be placed in if they should now say that they, nevertheless, think it advisable that the maritime nations should consider it.

Mr. Garde (Denmark).—Mr. President, may I make a few remarks in reply to the assertions made by the learned Delegate from Germany? I stated at the last session that we should vote against the establishment of a Commission. Now, a Commission and a Bureau are quite different things. A Commission has been proposed, to consist of a body of experts to do their work, &c. The Conference has not agreed to that. That question has been dealt with and we shall say nothing more about it. But that does not prevent the Conference from proposing something entirely different, that is, the establishment of a Bureau of Information. Now, with regard to the necessity for such an institution, we know perfectly well that Great Britain and other countries do not need it. But they may need it some time, because we have had experience with Great Britain, and we know that she has very often taken advice as regards questions of an international character. She has always been ready, more than any other nation, to say, This is an international question, and we wish to work together. Therefore I am not at all sure that the British Government would not take the view of this matter that it is a matter of international importance, and therefore they will consider it.

The learned Delegate from Germany has taken strong grounds against this proposal, and it does not deserve the strong cutting which he has given it. I say that because the intention has not been such as has been stated. I would take the liberty to say to the learned Delegate from England that of course I understand it to be a hard case for Great Britain, when she does not need a Bureau of this kind, to contribute to the expense; but, on the other hand, as I stated a while ago, she can make use of international work such as would be done there. In addition to that, I will say it is only a trifling expense, and I do not believe the economical rule will have any weight whatever in Great Britain. It would serve to benefit the smaller nations, and would draw all nations closer together. They would come into such intimate connection that they would have advantage to themselves. On the other hand, I agree that this Conference ought not to frame an absolute definite proposition with regard to such a Bureau. There, I believe, the learned Delegate from Germany is right.

Therefore we have proposed only to call to the attention of the different Governments that these Powers which are represented here felt the want of something of this kind, and would ask the Governments to take it into consideration and to carefully examine the question; and if they come to the conclusion, from their experience in other directions, that such a Bureau would not be as useless as has been stated here, and if they come to the conclusion that it would be beneficial that they should enter into correspondence or enter into a Convention in regard to the matter, then that would be the time to decide how this Bureau should work and how it should be constituted. I am quite sure that in proposing this here we are proposing something which in our country and in many other countries would be accepted as something useful. Do not forget that those countries which do not wish to join in this movement need not join, and then they do not pay. But the other Powers, which are not so well situated as they are, would then have a chance to get a connecting link, with an official stamp on it, to enable them to communicate with the different Governments better than at present, and that is what we want. Therefore I recommend once more that the Conference shall, in voting on this Resolution, have a kind regard to those different Maritime Powers who at the present time feel the necessity of the establishment of such a Bureau.

Mr. Flood (Norway).—Mr. President, for the same reason that I stated a short while ago, when I answered the question asked by the most distinguished Delegate from Great Britain, I also must refrain from answering the question asked by the learned Delegate Dr. Sieveking, the First Delegate from Germany. I will only take the liberty to ask one question. He says that each Government already has such a Bureau of Navigation as is referred to in our Resolution. He tells us what we all knew beforehand, that Germany has an excellent institution of this kind, and in fact every one of the other countries has such a Bureau, and that they all work well in their own country. Now, if that idea is followed out I take the liberty of asking the learned Delegate if we did no tin the olden times have in each country its Post Office and its own Telegraph Office, and after that we had a General Post Office for each country and a General Telegraph Office for each country, and for a long time it worked comparatively well? We paid half a thaler or half a Norwegian dollar for a letter from this country, and it worked very well. But as time progressed it was found out that "*E pluribus unum*" was a good motto not only in this country but all over the world, and it was found that these different Bureaux, by joining together and talking over the matter and trying to arrange different interests, constituted a Central Bureau that did very well, and it has been a blessing so far as these things go. Now, I repeat again, why should not a Central Bureau work very well in maritime matters in the same way as has been pointed out with regard to other matters?

The learned member has said that as far as a Commission is concerned this has already been disposed of by a Resolution of the Committee, and it would seem ridiculous to enter into another vote with regard to a Bureau, which he says is the same thing. In that I also take the liberty to differ with him. But he says that this matter has been disposed of, and that this proposal for a Bureau is not under consideration at all. Now, I want to ask the learned Delegate whether or not this General Division XIII is, officially, exactly a part of the Programme? So far as I have been able to find out, it is not. It is pointed out to me that the Act of Congress which provided the money for starting this Conference, and also gave the power to the President to invite the other nations, did not take General Division XIII into this Programme. But the Delegates for the United States, in going through the subject, have considered it important to lay before the Conference this question of the formation of a kind of Bureau or Commission in order to connect the different seafaring nations more closely together. They gave it the name of a Commission; but we are told here to-day that a Bureau and a Commission are the very same thing.

Dr. Sieveking (Germany).—Mr. President, I will only rise because the question has been put to me. Mr. Flood, the Delegate from Norway, has drawn attention to the fact that formerly there were several postal offices, telegraph offices, &c.; and in Germany we have considered it expedient to have one, instead of many in different places. That is true, and it has been done because the Empire of Germany has been formed. Now, if you will form an Empire of the whole world, I think you will have an international rule at once.

Mr. Carter (Hawaii).—Mr. President, it seems to me that we have gotten into a discussion, not upon the principle, but upon the method in which certain objects should be attained. As I read the very able and interesting document laid before us by the Representatives of the Scandinavian nations, their desire was to produce or to try to bring about a uniformity of laws among the maritime nations with regard to certain subjects affecting maritime interests—the safety of life and property at sea, freightage, general average, &c. They propose a general Commission for that purpose. I think the Committee have very clearly shown us that a permanent Commission is impracticable, and we have adopted that Report. Then the suggestion follows that a Bureau be established. I think the Delegate from Germany has shown us that this is impracticable. Now, I may say that I sympathize with the spirit of the Resolution, and I sympathize very strongly with the desire of the gentlemen that this uniformity of laws should be established. I think I may speak with very great freedom upon this subject, because I represent only a small nation which will have very little to do with framing any Regulations in this respect. The smaller nations see, of course, the necessity that the great maritime nations should settle these principles; then, when it is necessary to make them universal, they invite us to join them in adopting these laws.

Now, I have no doubt the courteous Representatives of Great Britain and Germany will agree with the Scandinavian nations that this uniformity is desirable, so far as is practicable and possible. Allow me to say that I quite agree with the learned Delegate from Germany that we are placing ourselves in a peculiar position in recommending to the Governments that they should consider this matter. The Governments instruct us, and we obey their instructions. But it is within our province to express an opinion and say what is the sense of this Conference, although it is not within our province to say how it should be carried out. If the Governments saw fit to take into kindly consideration the proposal made by the Delegate from Norway, I have no doubt they would find a way to bring about this very desirable result. Therefore I have prepared a Resolution which I have no doubt my gallant friend the brilliant Delegate from France would say was simply a measure of conciliation. The idea in my own mind is that something of this sort would express the views of the Conference without putting the Conference in any questionable position:—

"That it is the sense of this Conference that, so far as it is possible, there should be a uniformity in the laws of maritime nations providing for the safety of lives and property at sea, for the inspection of vessels and apparatus, for the enforcement of laws, and for the administration of laws; and this Conference trusts that all efforts for such uniformity will receive careful consideration."

I have worded that hastily. It may be better done; but it seems to me that it expresses the underlying convictions and opinions of all the Delegates who have put before us their views upon this subject. I do not know that it will meet the views of the Scandinavian Delegates, although I hope that it will. I do not know that it is a matter of great importance. I bring it forward, as I said before, as a measure of compromise or conciliation.

Mr. Flood (Norway).—Mr. President, I would ask to have that read again.

The President.—The Secretary will please read the Resolution again for the information of the Conference.

The Resolution is as follows:—

"That it is the sense of this Conference that, so far as it is possible, there should be a uniformity in the laws of maritime nations providing for the safety of lives and property at sea, for the inspection of vessels and apparatus, for the enforcement of laws, and for the administration of laws; and the Conference trusts that all efforts towards such uniformity will receive careful consideration."

Mr. Hall (Great Britain).—Mr. President, I quite recognize the kind spirit which has actuated my learned friend to endeavour to pour oil upon troubled waters; but may I ask him and the Conference to consider for one moment what would be the result if we passed this Resolution, which, I may say with very great respect to my learned friend, is no more than a sort of philosophical preamble to an essay, and which is a matter upon which every civilized man is agreed? We, all of us, want uniformity of law, but we know that at the present time it is absolutely impossible to have uniformity of law providing for the enforcement and the administration of the laws. We all know that such a thing is absolutely impossible at present. It is a thing to be striven after by all means; but is it a part of our duty here at this Conference? We are to deal with practical questions. If we are to branch off into passing abstract Resolutions as to what is desirable in the interests of mankind we could string together some very fine Resolutions, and we could string together a great many sentences such as we heard only a few hours ago in another place; but ought we to pass them as Resolutions of this Conference? I am certain that my learned friend has proposed this merely to enable us to get out of this trouble; but I think we should be getting out of the frying-pan into the fire. For myself, I do not like, because one Resolution is brought forward for which I cannot vote, to vote for another Resolution which I do not think could be seriously entertained by this Conference.

The Conference thereupon took a recess until 2 o'clock.

After Recess.

Mr. Garde (Denmark).—Mr. President, I only desire to remark that I believe there is some misunderstanding on the part of the learned Delegate from Germany and myself as to what we mean by this proposal. I will only say a few words to explain what our view of the matter is, and that is that the Commission has been done away with entirely, and that the Bureau shall be substituted for it, if the Governments choose to do so, and that when future Conferences come together, it is, in our opinion, desirable that they should be furnished with proposals which have been made in the different Governments before the Conference meets, so that the Governments and the Delegates will know what view they are to take in such proposals as are to come before them.

Now, it may be said, will any Conferences take place in the future? That I cannot say anything about; but I believe that they will take place, because the interests are of such consequence that it will be necessary to come to a discussion of them by the different Powers. But even if the Conferences do not follow, I believe that in daily life it will be of use to the different Administrations in different countries who now have to correspond with the Government on every question regarding the shipping interests; whereas if you had a Bureau of that kind you need not address the Administration directly. It will be a place where proposals coming from single persons or Associations can be considered. It will be sent to the Government, and the Governments may send them and form an opinion upon them before they come to any conclusion in regard to the matter. If such a Bureau is properly managed, in my opinion it can do a great deal. I cannot see the harm in a recommendation of the kind such as we have proposed, and I cannot see that there is a great deal of difference between the proposal of the Committee and this proposal.

Mr. Verney (Siam).—Mr. President, having voted the other day against the formation of a Permanent International Maritime Commission, and now being about to vote in favour of the proposal which has been made by the learned Delegate from Denmark, I desire, as briefly as I can, to lay before the Conference what, in my opinion, is a distinction of very great importance, and a vital one, between the Commission on the one side and the Bureau on the other. I am the more led to do this because the learned Delegate from Germany has informed us that, in his opinion, the two are practically identical. I do not for one moment venture to intrude my opinion on such a point as that in opposition or rivalry to one of so much greater experience on the subject than I am, but at the same time I feel that it would be almost like cowardice to sit still and give a silent vote when I feel very strongly upon the matter.

So far as I am concerned, there seems to me to be a most vital distinction between an International Commission and a Bureau such as is now proposed by the gallant Delegate from Norway, and that distinction is this: that an International Commission would be representative, and a Bureau cannot be. There is no such a thing as power or authority in a Bureau, as I understand it. The Boards of Trade of the various countries have been cited to-day, but the Boards of Trade in no country have any international authority or power whatever. A Commission, as I understand it, would be clothed with authority and with powers, and that authority and those powers would only come to various Governments represented on such Commission. It is clear to me that the Commission which was originally intended by those who drew up this Programme was such a Commission as I have tried to describe, because we read of its powers and authority in the very Programme itself.

I stated the other day that it seemed to me that there could be only one source for these powers and that authority, and nothing which has fallen from any of the Delegates to-day has shaken my conviction in the least. What is it that is proposed to us? It seems to me that it is a very modest proposal, and that it is with regard to something that is very different from that which is shadowed forth in this Programme. It might have been ruled by you, Mr. President, that we were entirely out of order in discussing something outside the Programme, and if you had ruled that I should not have been very much surprised. But after the discussion which has taken place with regard to this matter I apprehend that it is beyond your province, at this moment, to rule that this question is out of order.

Now, what is it that we have proposed here? It is this, that there should be a Central Office for the receipt and distribution of information. Now, Sir, I am the subject of a Great Power, but I have the honour to represent a small Power. As a subject of a Great Power I can quite understand what the learned Delegate from Great Britain and the other Delegates representing the Great Powers have said this morning. They have Boards of Trade and great offices to conduct their business, and they want nothing in the world more for themselves. We all know with what wonderful activity and patience the business of the Boards of Trade is conducted. I have personally an opportunity of knowing something of the operations of the Board of Trade, because I had the honour to be employed by them on more than one occasion when I was a member of the Bar in London. Now, I do not understand that this is to be a permanent Bureau, but only that it should have a permanent existence.

A permanent existence is a very different thing from being in permanent session. I would suggest to this Conference that we might take a very apt simile from one of those revolving lights which go round slowly and flash out their full brilliancy into the surrounding darkness at intervals. I would suggest the existence of such a Bureau might be continuous, but that its flashes might succeed each other at intervals to be settled by correspondence between the different Governments.

I cannot say that it seems to me there is anything so absolutely ridiculous in this Conference adopting a proposal of that kind. If I remember correctly at the outset of this Conference it was told to us that all of our work was to be *ad referendum;* that the proposals made around this table were not to be adopted as conclusive, but that we were vested with authority to go up to a certain point and no further, and that all of the conclusions which we arrived at would be referred to the various Governments for acceptance or rejection. It seems to me that this proposal might also be referred along with the others to be treated of by the various Governments accordingly as they see fit. It does not seem to me that we are in the least trenching upon the independent action or power of any Government by making such a proposal as this. If this Conference should think fit to adopt some such proposal as this I cannot but think it would be a very great advantage to the smaller nations, and if one thing is characteristic of this Conference above any other, I will venture to suggest that it is its generosity and—I was going to say chivalry—which is shown toward the smaller nations and Powers. I think that we may go as far as we can to try to get uniformity of such a kind as is here proposed without going from the domain of the practical into the domain of the dreamy and the ideal.

It has been said that there have been existing cases and that there is such a thing as this International Telegraph Convention. I quite understand that there is a radical difference between a Convention which has already been the subject of a Treaty between various nations and a mere proposal such as this is. But how would an International Treaty come about? What is the best means of getting the nations to act together? I venture to suggest that the best means is to collect facts upon which they can act together, and a collection of facts such as would be gained through the establishment of a Bureau of this sort could, I think, be of very great use in dealing with that question hereafter internationally. As I understand this Resolution it is a mere suggestion that this should be taken up by the various Governments, and that they should enter into diplomatic correspondence with each other as to whether it is advisable or not to press the matter. Before sitting down I may say that, representing an Eastern Power here, information which will be collected and distributed throughout the world by such a Bureau would be of very great use to at all events one Eastern Power, which is always forward in the path of progress and knowledge, as far as it can go. Therefore, Mr. President, I do desire to record my vote in favour of this proposal, believing it to be an extremely modest one. I also venture to think that in doing so I am not inconsistent in having voted against the formation of an International Commission, which I thought was impracticable and perhaps inexpedient.

The President.—The question is upon the Resolution of the Delegate from Norway. The last proposition was a proposition of the Delegate from Hawaii.

Mr. Carter (Hawaii).—Mr. President, I offered that not intending that it should be pressed upon the attention of the Conference unless it was accepted by the Delegate introducing the first Resolution.

The President.—Does the Delegate from Norway accept that?

Mr. Flood (Norway).—Mr. President, after consulting with my fellow Delegate from the Scandinavian countries, I must say that I cannot accept that as a substitute for the proposal made by us this morning.

The President.—The Delegate from Norway declines to accept this as a substitute; therefore the question is upon the Resolution of the Delegate from Norway. Is the Conference ready for the question?

Captain Sampson (United States).—Mr. President, I would like to say one word. It seems to me that this whole matter is very much in the air. A good deal can be said on both sides. I cannot, however, agree with what has been said as to the entire similarity or the similar objects to be accomplished by what has been proposed to the Conference in the way of an International Commission and the proposal which has since been made by the Delegate from Norway. It seems to me, as has been stated by the learned Delegate from Siam, that there is a great difference, and I would like to call the attention of the Conference to the fact that an International Bureau of a similar nature now exists—the International Bureau of Weights and Measures. It has been in existence for a number of years, and it has been participated in by, I think, all the principal Powers of Europe, as well as by the United States.

It has been forcibly brought to my mind in the last few days that if such a Bureau as is proposed here had existed, one of the Committees, of which I have the honour to be a member, would have been saved a great deal of labour. If such a Bureau or such an office had existed to which the matter of buoyage, for example, could have been referred, it would have been a very great advantage. The Committee which is now considering that subject finds itself in the curious predicament of being unable to recommend a uniform system of buoyage, simply because each nation has heretofore been working out its own system. Now, the result has been that there is a great diversity, without any reason for it, because each system has acted very well. For example, whether red or black is to be used as the distinguishing colour of the buoys on the starboard hand is a matter of no importance whatever, and yet we find that different nations have adopted different systems in this respect, and the result is that it would cost a great deal of money to bring them into harmony. If, however, such a Bureau had existed at one time, to which this very simple matter could have been referred, we would probably have a uniform system of buoyage all over the world.

While I agree with the learned Delegates from Great Britain and Germany who have so ably explained to us the objections to an International Commission, yet the fact that an International Bureau already exists and has been practicable for a number of years shows very clearly, I think, that the object which is aimed at in this case is also practicable. I would not be willing to commit myself to any particular scheme at this moment; but it seems to me that there is a germ in it which ought to be given a chance.

The President.—Is the Conference ready for the question on the Resolution? The Secretary will please read the Resolution.

The Resolution is as follows:—

"*Resolved,*—That the Conference recommend that the advisability of a Bureau of Maritime Information should be considered by the Governments of the maritime nations."

The President.—Is the Conference ready for the question?
The question was put to the Conference upon the adoption of the Resolution.
The President.—The Chair is unable to decide.
Mr. Goodrich (United States).—Mr. President, I call for the Yeas and Nays.
The President.—The Secretary will please call the roll.
The Yea and Nay vote is as follows:—

Austria-Hungary	.. ..	Nay.	Honduras	Nay.
Brazil	.. .. ..	Nay.	Italy	Nay.
Belgium	.. .. ..	Nay.	Japan	Yea.
China	.. .. ..	Nay.	Norway	Yea.
Chile	.. .. ..	Nay.	Russia..	Nay.
Costa Rica	.. .. ..	Nay.	Spain	Did not vote.
Denmark	.. .. ..	Yea.	Sweden	Nay.
France	.. ..	Did not vote.	Siam	Yea.
Germany	.. .. ..	Nay.	The Netherlands	Yea.
Great Britain	.. ..	Nay.	United States..	Yea.
Hawaii	.. .. ..	Yea.		

The President.—Seven have voted in the affirmative, and 12 in the negative; so the Resolution is lost.

Mr. Goodrich (United States).—Mr. President, I desire to say, on behalf of the Collocation Committee, that Appendix (B) will be handed in to-morrow morning at 11 o'clock, whether the Conference is in session or not, and will be ready to be delivered to the members. It will be laid on the Secretary's desk. I propose now, there being no special business before the Conference, that it would be wise to make some arrangement to expedite business as far as may be in connection with the adoption of the Rules as they have been presented in the Report of the Collocation Committee. I think it would be quite desirable if these Rules should have precedence over all other questions, so far as that course can be taken without wasting the time of the Conference. There is an amendment of the Delegate from Norway which is still undecided. There is also a Resolution which I presented in regard to the standing-by of vessels after collision.

I wish that the gentlemen who desire to be heard, *pro* and *con*, on these Resolutions would make up their minds to give their attention to these subjects to-morrow morning, and then we shall be prepared on Monday morning to attend at once to the Rules presented in the Report of the Collocation Committee. I am sure I voice the wish of a great many members of the Conference who want to free their minds with regard to these Rules, and who want to finish with that part of the business of the Conference as speedy as possible. I think I can say, without any very great stretch of the imagination, that this Conference is going to be prolonged over the Christmas holidays. I think the gentlemen will have to make up their minds to give us the benefit and pleasure of their company at least during a part of January.

The Collocation Committee will meet on Saturday, at 7 o'clock in the evening, and will, as the order of business requires, divide these Rules into two classes, and they will be laid on the table for the Delegates on Monday morning. We can then proceed to discuss the amendments which deal with principles, if the Conference sees fit. After these principles are established, the verbiage of the Rules as they have been presented by the Committee can be discussed. I really think that we ought to be able to get through with these Rules during the whole of next week. I am very anxious that that course should be taken unless some one in the Conference has a different view; and to that end it seems to me desirable that we should proceed to-morrow with the discussion of the two subjects which I have already referred to, namely, the amendment proposed by the Delegate from Norway, and the amendment which I proposed in regard to vessels standing by each other. It would be a great deal of assistance to all of us to decide this afternoon as to what course is to be taken, whether we are to adjourn until to-morrow morning, or until Saturday, or until Monday, or until Tuesday.

Mr. Hall (Great Britain).—Mr. President, I think it would be desirable for us to deal with the reconsideration of the amendment of the Delegate from Norway to-morrow morning, because then the Collocation Committee can act upon the decision of the Conference, and to insert into the collocation of the Rules of the Road at Sea the results of such decision. I think, therefore, that we should well occupy our time in dealing with that. I am perfectly well aware that this course will not give to-morrow to the only remaining Committee which, I understand, has not completed its labours. But I think we are all agreed with the learned Delegate of the United States that it is desirable to follow what was almost the first Resolution passed by this Conference, and that is that the Rules of the Road at Sea should have precedence over all other work. I may mention that this is a matter of great importance and desirability for this reason.

It has been pointed out during the deliberations of the Conference that there are some subjects that have been referred to the Committee which are technical matters, upon which it has been pointed out by the gallant Delegate from France that experts would be required to discuss and decide them;

because I remember when he introduced a motion asking the Conference to decide which matters should be gone on with, it was with a view that some of the gentlemen who are assisting us here were idle, as we were not dealing with the specific subjects for which they had been sent here by their respective Governments to assist us. I think that we are all agreed that we should deal with the Rules of the Road at Sea, and deal with them to the very best of our power. If we finish them it is possible that it may not be necessary for all the Delegates to remain until the Reports of one or two of the Committees, perhaps, which have not been finished up to this time, should be handed in unless they are handed in before we adjourn, which, I presume, will be on Tuesday week. If these Committees are not then finished, the Conference will have to adjourn for some few days, and it may not be necessary for all of the Delegates to remain to consider such technical matters.

Mr. Flood (Norway).—Mr. President, may I be allowed to say a couple of words connected with the late vote on this Resolution which has just been lost? It may seem ridiculous that the Danish Delegates and myself have stood here a whole day talking about the Scandinavian interests; that has already been whispered over the table, and whispered so loud that I have heard it. It seems very strange that we have dared to stand up here and represent the Scandinavian interest when we have tried to forward this Resolution, which is now lost, and one vote from one of the Scandinavian Powers has fallen against us. I may say that I hold in my hand the Minutes of that meeting in Copenhagen when it was unanimously decided by 200 Delegates, of whom 61 were the ablest and best men in Sweden connected with seafaring interests, from insurance directors and adjusters to the able captains, commanders, and the best Admiralty lawyers; so that when Captain Malmberg gave his vote against our Resolution, he must have given it individually as a Representative of his Government, but not of the maritime opinion of his country.

Mr. Hall (Great Britain).—Mr. President, I rise to a point of order. I want to ask whether it is proper for one Delegate to discuss and to canvass the reasons of another Delegate for giving a vote. I venture to submit that it is highly improper.

The President.—There is no subject which the Delegate is discussing before the Conference at the present time, and it would seem to the Chair that he is out of order.

Mr. Goodrich (United States).—Mr. President, in justice to a suggestion made to me a moment ago by a Delegate, I am bound to call attention to what I said a few days ago. I did say on Monday what I understand one of the gallant Delegates desires me to continue to support. I did not know whether there would be any business to call the Conference together on Friday or Saturday. I apprehend at that time that a disposition would be made of the Resolution of the Delegate from Norway. I do not want to stand here, as I said before, in the position of driving the distinguished and gallant Delegates to this Conference into undue work. I simply want to utilize our time and expedite the work as far as the proprieties of the situation will permit; so please do not consider me as being unduly anxious to hasten your exit from this Conference.

The President.—There is no proposition before the Conference at the present time.

Mr. Goodrich (United States).—Mr. President, I have only made this sugggestion. That is entirely within the power of the Conference. If any gentleman has business which renders it impossible for him to attend, I have nothing to say about it. But I really think that, unless there are outside duties for the members of the Conference, we might utilize to-morrow in the discussion of these two propositions.

Captain Richard (France).—Mr. President, at this present moment I do not see before the Conference a great deal of work which can be discussed with advantage to-morrow. I ask that the Conference decide that we adjourn until next Monday. Between now and that time we will have to consider the Report of the Collocation Committee, and it seems to me that we will hardly, even on Monday, be in a condition to go on with our work.

In making this proposition I indorse the proposition made by Admiral Kaznakoff, of increasing the number of hours of session of this Conference. We could begin at 10 o'clock and discuss until 5. Moreover, it would seem desirable to me for the Conference to enter upon the order of the day the order in which we shall discuss the various Reports, so that we may arrive at the Conference well prepared for the subject which shall be taken up for discussion.

I therefore propose to adjourn our sessions until Monday next, and then to consult the Conference in regard to increasing the number of working hours of our daily sessions, in order to bring our labours to a speedy termination; and thereupon to determine upon the order of the day, so that we may know in advance the order in which the various portions of the Programme shall come up for discussion. This is a proposition which I have the honour to make to the Conference, and I think that it will harmonize the interests of all.

Mr. Hall (Great Britain).—Mr. President, I quite agree with the gallant Delegate from France that we should come to some conclusion as to the order in which the work should be taken up. That, I apprehend, was practically suggested and provided for by the remarks of the learned Delegate from the United States. Having regard to what he has said, I should not propose to take anything to-morrow which would not be reached in the ordinary course. There is an amendment from one of the Delegates from Norway with regard to the lights, and of course that must be decided before we can finally finish with the Report of the Committee on Collocation. If there were any reasonable ground for supposing that the discussion of that would occupy only a short time, I would say by all means let us adjourn until Monday. But let me remind the Conference of the length to which such discussions extend. On Tuesday morning, at half-past 11 or a quarter to 12, the Delegate from Norway proposed to insert in the Report of the Committee on General Division XIII some words to make it appear more strongly that it was only for the present that we did not think it necessary to discuss those matters. We discussed that up to half-past 3 o'clock on Tuesday afternoon. We then had the amendment which we have just voted on, which began at 11 o'clock this morning. It is now about twenty minutes of 3; the discussion took until about half-past 2. Having these examples before us, I confess that I cannot look forward to a very short discussion of the amendment of the Delegate from

Norway. Therefore, I think that we ought to sit to-morrow to discuss and dispose of it. When we have disposed of it we have got all the materials for collocation.

Now, I am very glad to support the proposal of the gallant Delegate from France, that next week we shall take up the Report of the Collocation Committee in the order provided for in the Resolution already passed. On Monday morning we will discuss, first of all, which, if any, of the amendments in principle be considered. That will require a majority vote, as the Rule provides. The Collocation Committee will have those amendments in print, although under the Rule it is not necessary to have them in print until leave has been given to discuss them; we can then determine whether or not such amendments are to be reconsidered. After that, if we have time unoccupied, we can proceed with the Reports in order, the first of which, I apprehend, would be the Report next in number numerically, that is Report of Committee No. 2. If, on the other hand, the discussion of amendments on principles should occupy until Wednesday, we should then proceed with the amendments which have been handed in to the Collocation Report with regard to the Rules, and discuss them, until we have concluded our labours on the Rules of the Road at Sea, leaving the Reports and matters not already dealt with up to that time to be dealt with after we have finished the Rules of the Road at Sea. This order of business appears to me to be consistent with the Rules which we have already passed.

Captain Mensing (Germany).—Mr. President, I should like to point out that, in order to take up the discussion of the amendment of the gallant Delegate from Norway, it will be necessary that the Report of the Committee on Lights should be printed and should be distributed. I think the question may be raised again whether the Report should not be for some time before the Conference. The Committee have not met, although the Report has been talked over. I do not doubt that our Chairman will call us together as soon as the conference is ended, but before that it is impossible to agree upon this Report. It is not printed and it is not before the Conference.

Mr. Hall (Great Britain).—Mr. President, of course it would be impossible to discuss it thoroughly until we have the Report of the Committee on Lights before us, but if they meet this afternoon I apprehend that there will be no difficulty in letting us have the Report by to-morrow morning.

Admiral Kaznakoff (Russia).—I hope to have it ready to-morrow morning.

The President.—Does the Delegate from Great Britain make a motion to take up the amendment of the Delegate from Norway to-morrow morning, in case the Report of the Committee on Lights can be laid on the table?

Mr. Goodrich (United States).—Mr. President, I wish we could make the decision on that final. If to-morrow morning, when the Report comes in, the Delegates are going to say that they want time to look over this Report and consider it before proceeding with the discussion of the amendment of the Delegate from Norway, we might as well adjourn over until Monday at once. It interferes somewhat with the business of the Delegates to the Conference to simply come here for the purpose of adjourning. We, of course, cannot apprehend what the nature of that Report is going to be, or whether it will be such a Report as will require the consideration of the members for a time to-morrow. But if, when we come here to-morrow to consider this amendment, some member is going to say that he wants time to consider the Report before the discussion of the amendment is proceeded with, we might just as well save our time and adjourn until Monday at once.

Mr. Hall (Great Britain).—Mr. President, of course such a course might be adopted by some member, but such a course has not been adopted yet. We have referred matters from time to time to the Committee on Sound-Signals, and in some instances we have discussed their Reports without their having been put into print. Of course a long Report, dealing with a variety of matters, requires time for us to consider it. But this is merely a Report on an amendment with regard to a suggestion which has already been made by the Committee on Lights. I quite agree that if any Delegate says that this is so involved a matter that he cannot understand it without a short time to consider it, that we ought to give way, but when we have merely asked the Committee to report and advise us on one point, and we have that before us in print, I should hardly think that any Delegate would suggest that he wants forty-eight hours to consider the matter. As I said before, if there was any reason to hope that this amendment could be dealt with in the ordinary time which the majority of amendments have taken which have been before the Conference, then I should say by all means let it go over until Monday. But we have bought our experience, and we know how long it is likely to take. Under these circumstances there is all day to-morrow not provided for. Why not try to utilize that time? It is not as though we had a lot of Committees at work. There is only one Committee which has not finished its labour. But are all of us to be idle except the gentlemen who constitute that Committee? If I thought that by adjourning until Monday we could get the Report of that Committee in, then I would say by all means let us do so.

Mr. Goodrich (United States).—Mr. President, the learned Delegate and myself are thoroughly in accord. I made the remark which I did for the purpose of forestalling any attempt to-morrow to adjourn the Conference for the consideration of the Report. If any gentleman thinks that the nature of that Report is likely to be such that the Conference should be adjourned to enable the members to consider it before voting upon the amendment of the Delegate from Norway, I think it is just to the Conference that that opinion should be stated now and not to-morrow morning, after we have adjourned the Conference until that time.

The President.—The question before the Conference is whether the amendment of the Delegate from Norway shall be considered to-morrow morning if the Report of the Committee on Lights is made to the Conference by that time.

Mr. Verney (Siam).—Mr. President, perhaps I may be allowed to remark to the Conference that we have in our hands the Report of the Collocation Committee, which is the most important Report, I should say, which comes before us. I do not think that any member of this Conference will be idle with that Report in his hands; at least, I do not expect to be idle with it in my hands. Other members of the Conference have told me that they most decidedly wished to have what we understood we were going to have, not only two days but two clear days. When the learned Delegate from the United States got up and proposed that we were to have two days I understood—perhaps I was wrong—that we were going to have two clear days, and not two days taken up by Committee work and Conference work. I thought we were going to have two clear days to consider this Report, and I think that would have been enough. Perhaps I am more stupid than anybody here—I do not deny that—but I cannot master this Report in less time than that. I confess I am unable to do it, and I get up and announce my incompetency to accomplish it.

Mr. Goodrich (United States).—Mr. President, my object is to get the ideas of the Delegates. I am perfectly willing to do anything which the Delegates want. If the Delegates think they want until Monday without a session of the Conference, I am agreed to it. If you want to work to-morrow I will work with you from 9 o'clock until 7 if you desire it.

Mr. Verney (Siam).—Mr. President, then I venture to propose that this Conference shall adjourn until Monday.

Dr. Sieveking (Germany).—Mr. President, I desire to support the proposition made by the Delegate from Siam. I think that would be the best way to save time. I am quite sure that it is very important to consider the Report of the Collocation Committee, and the time is very short until Saturday night at 7 o'clock. I think it is but fair to give the members of the Conference an opportunity to look very carefully over the Report of the Committee, so that nobody will be idle, and then the Committee which has not yet finished its work will have time to go on with the work and prepare the Committee Report. I am sure that if we now adjourn until to-morrow morning only, in order to consider the amendment of the Delegate from Norway, that the Report of the Committee on Lights will come before us for the first time and somebody will want time to consider it.

Mr. Hall (Great Britain).—Mr. President, like my learned friend the Delegate from the United States, I only want to propose what is for the convenience of the majority of the Delegates. Certainly all of us want to meet the views of the majority, and that is the only course which ought to be pursued in a Conference of this nature. I shall, therefore, not oppose the proposition, but I will move to add a rider to it according to the suggestion of the gallant Delegate from France and the gallant Delegate from Russia, and that is that we meet at 10 o'clock on Monday and sit until 5 o'clock, and that we do so on each day during the week.

Mr. Goodrich (United States).—Mr. President, before the question is taken on that motion, may I ask the gallant Chairman of the Committee on Lights whether that Report will be ready to-morrow morning?

Admiral Kaznakoff (Russia).—Mr. President, we hope to have it ready to-morrow morning. The Committee on Lights will sit after the Conference adjourns. The Report is all drawn up, and I think it will be adopted in a few minutes and be printed this evening.

Mr. Goodrich (United States).—Mr. President, I call the attention of the Delegates to the fact that this Report will be ready for them at 11 o'clock to-morrow morning at the Secretary's desk. As I have stated before, Appendix (B) of the Report of the Collocation Committee will be printed and the Delegates can get it here. It will not be sent out to them, but it can be obtained at the desk of the Secretary. May I ask the Delegates to send in as early as possible to the Secretary these amendments, which will be sent to the printer not at 7 o'clock on Saturday night, but just as rapidly as they can be sent, having due regard to sending a proper number at once? So that if the Delegates have any amendments to make they will send them in to the Secretary early. They are not thereby precluded from sending other amendments which they may see fit to make.

The President.—The question is upon the amendment of the Delegate from Great Britain on the motion of the Delegate from Siam that the Conference adjourn until Monday, to meet at 10 o'clock and sit until 5. Is the Conference ready for the question?

Mr. Hall (Great Britain).—Mr. President, and on each day thereafter. I move as a substantive Resolution that we adjourn until 10 o'clock Monday morning and sit until 5 o'clock on that and on each succeeding day.

Mr. Verney (Siam).—Mr. President, can we not omit "each succeeding day"? Can we not see how many of us are alive at the end of the first day before we provide for the whole week?

The President.—The Delegate from Great Britain moves that the Conference adjourn to meet on Monday at 10 o'clock and sit until 5 o'clock on that day and each succeeding day thereafter. Is the Conference ready for the question?

The question was put to the Conference upon the motion of the Delegate from Great Britain, and it was carried.

The President.—The Conference has not yet adjourned. There was a motion that when it did adjourn it adjourn until Monday.

Lieutenant Beaugency (Chile).—Mr. President, I wish to ask whether we are to sit from 10 till 5 during the whole time, or only to consider the Report of the Committee on Collocation?

The President.—That has already been voted upon, and it is determined that the Conference sit from 10 o'clock till 5 o'clock on Monday and each day thereafter.

Mr. Goodrich (United States).—Mr. President, I move we adjourn.

The Conference thereupon adjourned till Monday, December 16, 1889, at 10 o'clock A.M.

139

Washington, Monday, December 16, 1889, 11 *o'clock* A.M.

THE Conference was called to order at 11 o'clock A.M., Rear-Admiral Franklin in the Chair.

The President.—The first business in order this morning will be the Additional Report of the Committee on Lights with reference to the amendment of the Delegate from Norway in regard to the position of the side-lights and the masthead-light. The Secretary will please read the Report.

The Additional Report of the Committee on Lights is as follows :—

" Sir, *Washington, D. C., December* 12, 1889.

" In accordance with the Resolution passed by the Conference on the 9th instant, your Committee have again considered the question whether it would be advisable to assign a certain position to the side-lights, as has been done by extra amendment No. 41 to Article 3, which has led to the Rule adopted by the Conference, viz. :—

" ' The said green and red side-lights to be placed in steam-vessels not forward of the masthead-light, and in sailing-vessels as near abreast the foremast as practicable.'

" Doubts have been raised by the Collocation Committee on the advisability of this Rule, on the ground that it involves a radical change and leads to great expense by compelling a very material alteration of the present construction of many ships, consequences which are said to outweigh the slight advantage of the introduction of the Rule in question.

" Your Committee after having most carefully considered the subject are unanimous in reporting that in their opinion the Rule passed by the Conference ought to be maintained.

" In the Report dated November 4, 1889, the reasons have been given why in principle it would be advisable to have the side-lights of all steam-vessels so placed that a vertical plane through the line drawn from them to the masthead-light would form a certain known angle with the keel. It has at the same time been acknowledged to be practically impossible to give the side-lights a certain fixed position in regard to the foremast-light, but it has been thought practicable and, therefore, has been recommended to introduce a Rule by which steamers are compelled to carry the side-lights abaft the foremast-light, the connecting line forming an angle of six points with the keel, or as nearly so as possible.

" The considerations which have led to this recommendation appear to your Committee to be sound, and whilst confirming what has been said in the former Report, we beg to add the following remarks :—

" The Rule as adopted by the Conference does not, it is true, go quite so far in assigning to the side-lights a certain fixed position with regard to the masthead-light as the recommendation contained in our Report of the 4th November. Nevertheless, by preventing steam-vessels from carrying the side-lights forward of the masthead-light, it will serve to give more certainty to the respective position of the regulation lights, and thus in our opinion will mark a decided improvement of the means of ascertaining the course of an approaching steamer, which improvement will gradually be increased when experience shows the advantages of the system.

" On the other hand, the difficulties connected with the introduction of the Rule appear to be not at all insurmountable. Many ships are even now constructed so as not to require any changes in consequence of the adoption of this Rule. Others might easily comply with the Rule by changing the position of the masthead-light, by placing it more forward of the foremast. And even if the position of the side-lights should have to be altered, this could, in most cases, be done without incurring too heavy expense.

" We therefore recommend to let the Rule stand as it is ; provided, however, that the Rule be adopted universally. Having regard to the difficulties which some ship-owners may justly feel if they had to comply with the new Rule at once, your Committee think that sufficient time should be allowed for the effecting of the changes necessitated by the Rule, so as to enable ship-owners to carry out these changes under the most convenient conditions. Vessels now in course of construction will, of course, be able to adopt the new principle at once.

As regards sailing-vessels, the Committee do not consider it necessary to adopt the above-mentioned Rule.

" We have, &c.
(Signed) " Vice-Admiral N. KAZNAKOFF, *Chairman, Russia.*
" E. RICHARD, *France.*
" B. VEGA DE SEOANE, *Spain.*
" JAS. W. NORCROSS, *United States.*
" HENRY WYATT, *Great Britain.*
" F. MALMBERG, *Sweden.*
" A. MENSING, *Germany.*

" To Rear-Admiral S. R. Franklin, United States Navy,
" President of the International Marine Conference, &c."

Mr. Hall (Great Britain).—Mr. President, as the learned Delegate for the United States who is Chairman of the Collocation Committee is not able to be in his place this morning, perhaps I may state very briefly what our action has been in the matter, and what the views are that we have taken in regard to this amendment. It may be remembered that originally a proposition was brought forward to assign a fixed position to the side-lights abaft of the foremast. That was discussed at considerable length ; but it was withdrawn by the gallant Delegate for Germany, who said that at a future time he would bring forward a Resolution in the words of the recommendation of the Committee on Lights. So the matter stood when the amendment of the Delegate for Norway was brought forward. It was not stated to the Conference then that this amendment—or rather it was stated that this amendment was the recommendation of the Committee on Lights ; but there were matters which were not stated in connection with it, and one was that the effect of this amendment, if carried, would be that every existing vessel which has not got a light in the position mentioned in the amendment would have to be altered for that purpose; and it was also not mentioned that the Committee on Lights had not made any suggestion whatever with regard to sailing-vessels, and this amendment included sailing-vessels as well as steamers. It was at once seen that by this amendment, if it stood as it was framed by the mover of it, all steam-vessels would have to be altered which had their lights forward of the masthead-light, and all sailing-vessels would be obliged to put their lights abreast of the foremast.

I need not point out to this Conference that the words, "if practicable," mean, in a legal sense, "if possible," and no sailing-vessel could excuse herself for not putting her lights in that position, if it were possible to do so. So that every sailing-vessel on the sea now would have to put her lights abreast of the foremast and carry them there. That formed such a far-reaching proposition, as it appeared to us, especially as it had not been called to the attention of the Conference at all—not one single word had been said by the mover of the amendment pointing out this proposition with regard to sailing-vessels—and as the Report of the Committee on Lights was silent on the point and made no suggestion about sailing-vessels—it appeared to us that it was not thoroughly considered by the Conference. I will only deal now with the proposition as it stands. The matter was referred to the Committee on Lights, and they have made a further Report. They say: "Your Committee, after having most carefully considered the subject, are unanimous in reporting that in their opinion the Rule passed by the Conference ought to be maintained." But that is clearly an oversight, because they say on the next page that as regards sailing-vessels they do not consider it necessary to adopt the above-mentioned Rule. So that the Report of the Committee on Lights is against that part of the amendment which applies to sailing-vessels. I do not think we shall have any difficulty about that, because, as far as I am concerned, I am at a loss to see what advantage could be gained with regard to sailing-vessels which do not carry a masthead-light, and therefore would not give you the slightest information with regard to the position of the side-lights.

Now, with the regard to the position of the lights on steam-vessels. We have been most anxious, my colleagues and myself, and I think our actions have proved it, to defer, in every case where we can, to the Report of the Committees appointed by this Conference. We have recognized the fact that the Committees which have dealt with the matters referred to them by the Conference have dealt with them most carefully and thoroughly; and in all cases where their recommendations have been made, if I may say so, upon actual experience, we have bowed to the decisions of the Committees. But with regard to the question of having a position, whether fixed or not fixed, on board of a steam-vessel, of course the Conference will have noticed this: that in the Report of the Committee on Lights it does not say that they are satisfied that such a matter would be productive of great good. All they say is that they think at least some advantage might be gained by placing the side-lights abaft the mast, and the change probably could be made without great expense. Well, so far as we are concerned, we cannot vote in favour of a proposition of this kind, which would compel every steam-vessel to be altered which at present carries her lights forward of the foremast simply because the Committee say they think some advantage might be gained by it. We do not think it is a sufficiently strong recommendation to justify voting in favour of the amendment, which, as I say, would compel a very large number of vessels now afloat to be in some cases almost reconstructed so as to alter the way in which these lights were carried.

I only want to point out the reasons which are given, not only by us from Great Britain, but by Delegates from other Powers, against the adoption of any position, either forward or aft of the mast, being laid down in a Rule. We discussed this most exhaustively before, when the original proposition was before the Conference on the motion of my learned friend the Delegate from Germany. I regret that we should be obliged to dissent at all from any recommendation of a Committee of this Conference, as we are anxious to support the Committees in their views; and I think we have given the very best evidence of that in our acquiescence in the Report of the Committee on the Load-Line, without demurring at all to the decision. Therefore, having regard to the fact that the Committee themselves only point out that they think some advantage might possibly be gained if this proposal were adopted, and having regard to the fact that if the proposal is adopted, existing vessels will have to be altered, in some cases, as I am told, at a very great expense, amounting sometimes, it is said by those who know best, to 1,000*l.* a vessel, we cannot feel justified in voting for the adoption of this amendment in regard to steam-vessels. As I say, with regard to sailing-vessels I take it that after the further Report of the Committee on Lights it is unnecessary to argue the question on this point. I think that is a proposition which cannot be supported.

The President.—The Additional Report of the Committee on Lights is before the Conference for consideration.

Mr. Flood (Norway).—Mr. President, I ask to be excused for again taking the liberty of occupying the time of this Conference. I have once before discussed this matter, and I have very little to say with regard to it in addition; but I will ask permission of the Conference, in view of my opinion, to say a few words on the subject, and to be allowed to make a short retrospect as to the manner in which this question has been put before the Conference, and how it has come up to-day. I will remind you, Mr. President and Gentlemen of the Conference, that this amendment was, as has already been stated before, brought before you in an amendment proposed by the German Delegation. It was brought before this Conference on the 4th November and discussed. Captain Mensing, in a very able and strong speech, showed how this arrangement would be very advisable; and how, in fact, it would be a benefit to shipping in general to adopt this amendment as it was then brought before the Conference. On the same day the Report of the Committee on Lights was placed before us, and after discussion it was decided to have the matter laid over until a further Report of the Committee on Lights, as there seemed to be some kind of misinterpretation concerning one of its expressions.

On that occasion, Mr. Hall, the learned First Delegate from England, then admitted that *primâ facie* this was the best position in which the side-lights could be carried. That is in the Protocol of the 4th November. Then he goes on to try to weaken the Report of the Committee on Lights by saying: "Can we propose to pass an International Rule because the Committee think it probable that some good would result from it, without any experiments being made?" Why! the Light Committee have never said they think it only *probable* that good may result; the Committee never use the word "probable" in their recommendation; but, on the contrary, they unconditionally recommend that such lights should be placed abaft the masthead-light. The word "probable" which Mr. Hall uses there I cannot find; I can only find on p. 9 of the Report of the 4th November the opinion expressed that this change could be made "*probably*" without incurring great expense; that is all. Further on the learned counsellor continues: "Our Admirals studied this very point, and they found that it was not practicable, having regard to the build of modern men-of-war." Indeed! Even if this were the case, which I take the liberty to doubt, how many men-of-war of this modern type are there in the world? And what percentage would they make of the combined merchant fleets of the world?

But what does the English Admiral say on the same subject? In the Protocol of the 4th November Admiral Bowden-Smith states:—

"I am very sorry to have to oppose this amendment, because I believe that if the lights were changed that is the right position for them."

Then it was proposed to consider further the Report of the Committee on Lights; and on the 14th November I took the liberty to propose to bring before the Conference my extra amendment No. 41, which is practically identical with Captain Mensing's, or with the proposal of the German Delegation; and I tried then, in recommending the same, to give practically the same reasons for adopting this amendment. In that I was very ably and forcibly assisted by the gallant Delegate from Germany, Captain Mensing. I do not desire to trouble the Conference with repeating here what has been said, but I will take the liberty further on of making some remarks particularly concerning sailing-vessels which would strengthen my argument.

The learned First Delegate from England again comes forward against this amendment, and he commences with stating that this proposal has already in reality been disposed of by the Conference. Further on he again quotes the Report of the Committee on Lights, and says:—

"But this is only a recommendation made without any practical experiments having been made and without any knowledge on the subject; and as has been pointed out here over and over again, a great many vessels would have to be reconstructed in order to provide for complying with any hard and fast Rule."

Why, Gentlemen, think of it! Shall we require the reconstruction of a man-of-war or a 5,000-ton vessel in the merchant fleet in order to hang out over their sides a tiny little thing in the shape of a side-light lantern? I forgive him his expression on the subject, without daring to call it exactly want of knowledge, as he is not a practical sailor or a ship-constructor; but I appeal to any practical sailor in this room, yea, even in the whole world, and ask him, Is the reconstruction of a vessel necessary? Or are changes even costly for this purpose? I am sure I will score a decided "No;" and I have it already in the Second Report of the Committee on Lights, made the 12th December, 1889.

I am well aware that the learned counsellor, on Captain Mensing's referring to the Conference to decide if the Committee had acted with or without knowledge on the subject, retracted the use of the words "without knowledge;" but further on he again repeats that he would consider it madness to pass International Rules simply because it was suggested by the Committee that some Rule might be adopted without having any knowledge that it would be practically good, or what the result would be. I leave it to the Conference to decide if the Committee's expression on this subject is only a suggestion or a direct recommendation.

Notwithstanding these strong arguments against my amendment, it was voted on, on the 14th of last month, and thirteen Powers, including Germany, Russia, Spain, Portugal, the Netherlands, and the Northern countries, voted for the same, upon which the President decided, "The amendment is adopted."

But, not satisfied with having the matter twice before the Conference, and the second time legally adopted, which created great satisfaction all over the shipping world, as many reports in the newspapers bear witness, the same case is now for the third time before the Conference, and this time it is brought by the Collocation Committee, of which three members have before cast their votes for the adoption of the amendment. Now, the reasons for this reconsideration are pointed out to be that this new Rule is too radical and far-reaching in its results, and particularly that it will entail great expense to sea-vessels and especially to war-vessels. The Committee on Lights are therefore again asked to reconsider this matter, this time assisted by the distinguished expert in naval architecture and ship-building lately added to Great Britain's brilliant representation. This Report is now before us in the Committee's Report dated the 12th December, and I can only find what I expected, that this able Committee, consisting of Representatives from the greatest Maritime Powers on earth, England, France, Germany, Russia, United States, &c., still stronger agree to their former Report, and recommend the adherence to this adopted Rule concerning steam-vessels. And they so forcibly point out the advantages of doing so that it would only be a waste of time for me to say more on this subject. To my great disappointment, however, the Committee closes its Report by saying:—

"As regards sailing-vessels, the Committee do not consider it necessary to adopt the above-mentioned Rule."

I am very sorry for this, and I frankly confess that I cannot understand how the distinguished Committee have come to this conclusion; and especially that this seems to be unanimous, as there is no dissenting vote, since, as before stated, four of the Representatives have heretofore cast the vote of their respective countries in favour of the Rule for sailing-vessels as well as for steam-vessels. I have not heard a single argument to prove that they voted wrong at that time; and I would respectfully ask them why they have altered their opinion about this matter? I will ask the opinion of the Conference and of yourself, Mr. President, as to whether you will take these two matters into consideration at the same time. If so, I will ask permission to consume a few minutes more time with regard to sailing-vessels.

The President.—I see no objection to the Delegate's proceeding with the subject of sailing-vessels.

Mr. Flood (Norway).—Mr. President, I shall not detain you much longer, because, as I stated before, I have said about all I can say with regard to this matter. With regard to sailing-vessels the Committee did not consider it necessary to adopt the above-mentioned Rule; I confess that I am very sorry for this; and I confess that I cannot see how the distinguished Committee have come to this conclusion, which seems to be unanimous, since, as I before stated, four of the Representatives have already cast the vote of their respective countries in favour of the amendment as at present adopted, which applies to sailing-vessels as well as to steam-vessels. I can only say that I am very sorry that the overwhelming majority of the merchant sailing fleet afloat at present is so thinly or so weakly represented in this Conference. It may be that the merchant-steamers and also the Bar are very ably represented, but the sailing masters are very poorly represented among us; if there had been some more, perhaps there would have been better words than mine brought forward in this matter.

The Committee say in this Report that they do not wish to force this Rule on sailing-vessels; so far as my experience goes, there is more reason for applying it to sailing-vessels than to steamers. Sailing-vessels are, of course, in some ways hampered and bothered by their sails; so the practice is to place the side-lights so that they cannot be obscured by the sails, and at the same time so that they can shine right forward free from any obstacle. For that purpose the side-lights must be placed on the broadest beam, or, if not, they must be hung in davits, clear of the ship's side. We all know that the broadest part of a vessel will be somewhere abaft or abreast of the foremast. Every vessel of modern construction, so far as I know, is more or less narrow aft, and placing the lantern right abreast of the mizzen-rigging would not be the broadest part of the ship, and would be at once the nail in the coffin in case of a collision or of any trouble of that kind. The only remedy for this is to hang them in davits outside.

Now, may I make you aware that nothing hung outside of a ship's side is insurable in any Company that I know of? Life-boats, or anything else hung in davits, are not insurable as long as they are outside of the ship's side. Why? Because experience has shown often and often that, during heavy weather, even the life-boats and other boats hung in davits are liable to be washed away by the heavy sea. Now, a tiny lantern must be so fixed that a man can reach it with his hand. The davits are made of about 1-inch iron, and the whole thing is of such a construction as to render it liable to be carried away immediately. I have had several cases of that kind in my experience. I had a bad case of that sort, where a vessel lost her lantern and tried to cross the Newfoundland Banks without the port lantern. She had no spare lanterns on board, and she ran into a fishing-schooner on the Newfoundland Banks on a dark night. She ran her down at sea, and of her crew of twenty only seven were saved. My Company had to pay very heavy damages to the owners of the schooner, and the owners are still under heavy penalties for the lives lost, all because she had her lantern slung in davits, and the sea took it overboard.

In addition to that, the learned First Delegate from England says that he cannot see any benefit in having the lights fixed at a certain place on board sailing-ships. I again, Gentlemen, appeal to your common sense. When we have vessels of from 250 to 300 feet long, can you say that it makes no difference to know where those lights are on board of that vessel, when there may be a difference from the cathead to the taffrail of over 200 feet? Does it not make any difference, in your judgment, where the lights are on a vessel on a dark night, when it comes to an emergency? I think that every man of common sense and practical knowledge with regard to this matter will answer that it is very necessary to know this.

It was further stated by the learned First Delegate from England that the expense of changing the lights would be as high as 1,000*l.*, in making the alterations and putting the side-lights from forward to abaft of the head-light. I would take the liberty to ask if that really is so, and if there is any practical ship-builder present, or any ship-owner, who will stand up here and say that it will cost 1,000*l.*? I am told by a man who ought to know very well that 100*l.* to 150*l.* would be the utmost that it would cost to have an alteration like that made. In connection with this I will only make one further remark. I ask the steam-ship owners and the steam-ship captains here present if I am not telling the truth when I say that, in crossing the Atlantic in the winter-time, their turrets during snow-storms and in wintry weather become covered with ice, so that the whole turret looks like a big snow-man; and if they do not have to move the side-lights to near the bridge on account of the spray coming over the bow more than over any other part of the ship? I will ask the present steam-ship captains and the steam-ship owners if this is not the case? That is a strong point for having the side-lights placed in a less exposed position.

Admiral Bowden-Smith (Great Britain).—Mr. President, I should just like to repeat again what I believe I said before with regard to placing the side-lights in a uniform position with the masthead-light. If I did not say it before I desire to state it now. I took the trouble, before I left England, to communicate with the Admiralty semi-officially, thinking that this question might come up here, because the principle as stated in this amendment certainly does give certain information. After consulting all the dock-owners, I found that they did not see their way to making this change, especially on men-of-war. I quite agree with what the honourable Delegate from Norway says, that men-of-war are a very small percentage of the ships; but, on the other hand, we say that the men-of-war ought to comply with the Regulations as well as any other ship. Of course, the British Government would pay great attention to anything that is passed by this Conference; but I can only say that, as to men-of-war, I do not think we could very well do it. Some of them carry only one mast, and that mast is right amidships.

With regard to sailing-ships, I do not quite follow the honourable Delegate from Norway, because I understand him to say that when some of these small ships put their lights aft, the sails obscure them. In that case, of course, they do not carry out the Regulations, because the Regulations say that these side-lights are to show from right ahead to so many points abaft the beam. Therefore, if a little vessel feels that she cannot carry her side-lights where other ships do, she puts them in davits, as many of the small boats do, and as many of the Scandinavian small boats do; and if she does not, then, of course, she does not carry out the Regulations. But it appears to me that this is a matter for the Inspectors to determine. I think the Inspectors might settle that. Surely if a sailing-ship carries her side-lights in any place where they cannot be seen, or where they are obscured by the sails, it is a question for the Inspectors to determine and stop, if necessary. Although I do see some good in such lights being carried in a uniform position with the masthead-lights on the steamers, because it gives you a certain kind of information, I do not exactly see the point with regard to sailing-ships carrying their side-lights in a certain fixed position, without you know on which end of the ship they are. I presume that they really carry them where they can best be seen, and that seems to me to be a mere matter for the Inspectors rather than for the Rules of the Road.

Mr. Flood (Norway).—Mr. President, first of all I must beg to be allowed to correct myself, if I expressed myself so wrongly as to say that I was against having them hung in davits because they would be obscured by the sails. Of course I understand that, according to the Regulations, and also by the Board of Trade Regulations, the side-lights are to be placed on the vessel where she has the broadest beam. Now, some vessels do not find it convenient to have them on the broadest beam, especially as mentioned by the gallant Admiral, in small ships, and for that reason they have them in davits on the outside of the ship, and it is for the purpose of not obscuring the light by the foresail, especially when they sail with free sheets or before the wind. So I do not see that there is any force in what has been said with regard to that.

Captain Shackford (United States).—Mr. President, in regard to the side-lights on steamers, it does not seem to me to make any difference to them at all, as I read this amendment, because they can carry their side-lights anywhere from the knight-head to the taffrail. As to sailing-vessels I am very sorry to differ with the gallant Delegate from Norway. It seem to me that the position he has assigned to the side-lights is the very worst place on the whole vessel in which he could place them. Abreast of the foremast on a large vessel 250 feet long is all very well, because they might be carried there, and that is the widest part of the ship; but on small vessels they certainly could not be carried below the lower dead-eye, and in bad weather they must be raised up into the rigging, and, as they are raised up, they must be carried inside, and on square-rigged vessels they are then immediately obscured by the foresail. They cannot be carried below in small vessels except in very fine weather, and as they are raised up they are carried inside of the line of the ship, and they must be obscured by the square sails. Again, as the gallant Admiral from Great Britain has just stated, it seems to me that the majority of the Scandinavian vessels carry these lights aft in davits. I have seen several carry their lights in that way, and they would not carry them there unless that was the best place for them. I agree entirely with the gallant Delegate from Great Britain that all small sailing-vessels should carry their lights in the position where they can best be seen by other vessels and also by the officer in charge of the vessel showing the light. Therefore, as I said before, I think this is about the worst place possible to select to put these side-lights. If they are abreast of the foremast they must be in the rigging.

Dr. Sieveking (Germany).—Mr. President, after what has fallen from the learned First Delegate from Great Britain I think it is quite clear that we may consider it to be certain that Great Britain would not accept the Rule if it was brought into the Regulations as a Rule. Now, the Committee on Lights in their Additional Report say that they recommend to let the Rule stand as it is, provided, however, the Rule be adopted universally. I think, as far as I understand the matter, that it is quite obvious that there will not only be no advantage derived from the Rule, but that even great uncertainty will be established if there is not a universal and uniform action in this matter taken by all the maritime nations. Under these circumstances, although the German Delegation is of the opinion (and this opinion is confirmed by the Additional Report of the Committee on Lights) that it would be advisable and that it would even be possible to carry out the Rule as a Rule, still, under the circumstances, I beg to say on behalf of the German Delegation that we would not insist on this Rule being embodied in the Regulations, and we shall not vote for inserting it in the Rules.

I see that the Collocation Committee in their Report recommend that this amendment be reconsidered, and if the proposed change of the position of the side-lights is approved, that the suggestion be made in a note instead of its being embodied in the Regulations. I think there will be some advantage at least obtained for the future if we insert a provision in the note providing for such a position of the side-lights instead of putting it into the Rules and Regulations. This principle could be printed in the Resolutions which are embodied in Appendix (B) of the Report of the Committee on Collocation, and that would, perhaps, be of some advantage. Therefore I should propose a Resolution to this effect: "That it is approved by the Conference and recommended to the attention of the Powers represented thereat that the green and red side-lights should be placed in steam-vessels not forward of the masthead-lights." That would refer to steam-vessels only. After what has been said here about sailing-vessels we think that such a provision should not be made a part of this recommendation. So we shall vote against the amendment of the Delegate from Norway being a part of the Rules of the Road, and we would propose to have it recommended as I have just read it, and to have it embodied in Appendix (B) for the future.

Lieutenant Vega de Seoane (Spain).—Mr. President, the honourable Delegate from Norway has manifested some astonishment because some of the Delegates who voted in favour of his amendment when it was voted upon in the Conference opposed in the Committee on Lights the second portion of the said amendment, which bears upon the position of the running-lights on sailing-vessels. I am one of them, and I desire to explain this apparent contradiction, which is not a contradiction in fact.

The Spanish Delegation voted in favour of the amendment, and it is still disposed to sustain it with its vote, because in its opinion the advantages which it introduces into the present system of lights on steamers are so important and so easy to effect that they largely compensate for the disadvantage of making a recommendation—there being nothing mandatory in the second portion of the amendment—that all sailing-vessels should have their side-lights placed in a certain position; which change, in the opinion of the Spanish Delegation, presents an advantage of but secondary importance, and which is insufficient to be made a Rule. I, therefore, propose to the Committee to separate the amendment into two portions, the one referring to steam-vessels, and the other to sailing-vessels. When this separation was accepted, I advocated and voted for the first portion, which makes an addition in the present Rules which is of great advantage, and I was thereby enabled to vote against the second portion, which is merely a recommendation in which I see no advantage worthy of consideration.

Now that I am speaking, allow me to reply to a remark made by the learned Dr. Sieveking. He thinks that we should not support this amendment, because it seems to him that it has not been accepted by Great Britain, and that therefore its advantages disappear. But that is the way with all the Articles; if any Government does not adopt them, the advantages of unanimity do not exist. But this consideration should in no wise cause us to change our opinions. We recommend what we think is good, what we consider necessary to modify, what the majority in this Conference desire to have unanimously adopted. It concerns our respective Governments, and not ourselves, to keep an account of the objections which some Governments may have to what we agree upon.

Captain Salvesen (Norway).—Mr. President, there have been remarks made to-day in the Conference about members of the Collocation Committee voting for the amendment who still recommend it to be reconsidered. I am one of these members. I voted for the Rule, but would not in the Collocation Committee oppose its reconsideration, as I think it of much more importance that the Rules should be correct than that my vote should be correct. But as I still consider the Rule good, I will once more in the Conference have to vote for it, but I have no objection to the Rule as it stands being inserted in the Appendix which is to be sent to different Governments as a recommendation.

Captain Malmberg (Sweden).—Mr. President, I will not take up the time of the Conference. I will only state that I am of exactly the same opinion as the learned Delegate from Germany, Dr. Sieveking. I will vote against inserting the amendment into the Rules of the Road as long as it is not universally adopted, but I will vote for its insertion in Appendix (B).

Mr. Hall (Great Britain).—Mr. President, I do not wish to prolong this discussion. I will only point out that we have all along expressed our willingness to vote in favour of such a proposition as this with regard to steamers' side-lights being placed in a certain position, and that it should be placed in a recommendation at the end of the Rules. That suggestion was thrown out, I think it perfectly fair to say, to the Delegate from Norway, who moved this amendment a very long time ago, and we have always been ready to do that. We opposed the Rule because it makes it obligatory upon vessels at the present time to carry the lights in this position. I will point out in reply to the learned Delegate from Germany, who states that he does not want this Rule adopted because Great Britain refuses to comply with it, that it is not Great Britain alone, but there are a great many more Powers which have voted against this Rule, and we have not heard anything which would lead us to suppose that they had changed their views any more than we have.

Mr. Flood (Norway).—Mr. President, may I be allowed to make a remark in regard to what has fallen from Captain Shackford, the gallant Delegate from the United States? He said a while ago that he thought a majority of the Scandinavian ships carried their side-lights aft. As a representative of over 3,000 Norwegian vessels, and having been for fifteen years an insurance director and insurance general agent, I ought to know a little more about that than the gallant Delegate from the United States, and I repeat that a very small percentage of the Scandinavian vessels carry their side-lights aft. I ask the honourable Delegates here present from Scandinavian countries to back me up in this matter. I forgot when the gallant Admiral Bowden-Smith spoke about the side-light question, whether he said that it should be a matter of inspection as to placing them—then I would say if we are to leave one thing to Inspectors why should we discuss whether the lamp should be of a certain size, and the range of the lamp? Why could not that also be left to Inspectors? We have different Rules about that in every country. Our lights are measured; the size of the wick is measured, and the length of the screen is given in centimetres, not only in feet. All that is subject to inspection. I do not see why this matter should be left to the Inspectors of the different countries any more than the question of lights should be left to the Inspectors.

Mr. Verbrugghe (Belgium).—Mr. President, I voted the first time against the amendment. I will do so again on this occasion for the following reason : Most assuredly the position of the lights on board of a steamer is a very important question. It would be desirable to arrive at a solution. If the three lights of a steamer could be placed in the same vertical plane, or in such a manner that the side-light should form a given angle with the vertical line passing through the white light, then, in case of the steamer manœuvring, the change in her course would be easily ascertained ; but it was found that great difficulties would prevent the adoption of such radical measures. These difficulties already exist in regard to the modifications proposed by the amendment now under discussion. I think that the real solution would be found in the proposition of the Honourable Dr. Sieveking. For the present moment we must limit ourselves to recommendations, which will certainly be taken into consideration in new constructions. If such difficulties exist for steamers, still more so are they encountered in sailing-vessels, and it is absolutely impossible to apply the measure as a general rule, which is the object of the Conference. As there are various categories of sailing-vessels and different tonnages, it would be dangerous to prescribe a Rule when we know in advance that it could not be applied to all.

For these reasons, I repeat that I will by preference vote for the amendment of the honourable Delegate from Germany.

Mr. Verney (Siam).—Mr. President, may I be allowed to support the proposition made by the learned Delegate from Germany for the following reason? It seems to me that it is extremely important to distinguish what is the duty of a master of a vessel and what is the duty of an Inspector. I think myself that some things have crept into these Rules connected with the construction of lights which should not have properly been in the Rules at all. I think that the main object and the sole object of the Rules to prevent Collisions at Sea, such as you are to put into the hands of sailors, should be to tell the sailor how to act under certain circumstances. Can the sailor, under any circumstances, have anything whatever to do with the construction of the lights? I think not. As regards sailing-ships, I admit there is a responsibility which is never absent, and can never be absent, from the master as to where these lights should be placed, and it seems to be quite right to leave that responsibility with him, as has been so ably explained to us by the gallant Delegate from the United States, Captain Shackford.

With regard to the steam-ship, the place where a steam-ship should have to carry a light can easily be determined beforehand, and should be determined before she leaves port. That being so, is it not right and fair to have it so determined? It is a very fair proposal which has been made to us by the learned Delegate from Germany that this proposal should be put into Appendix (B) and not inserted in the Rules. The gallant Delegate from Norway has argued that in other Rules these questions are dealt with. We must admit that he is right. There is no doubt that there are questions of construction brought into the Rules of the Road as regards lamps, &c. But because there happens to be one blot in the Rules should we put in another? Because construction is spoken of in certain Rules, is it necessary to put in another Rule dealing with construction? Is it not more logical to allow the question of the position of the lamp on board of the steam-ship to be dealt with in the Appendix, where it will always be before the minds of the Government, and some day or other, when the custom becomes more general and more uniform, to adopt that custom and make it a part of the Rules of the Road at Sea? Therefore, while I should cordially vote for the proposal of the learned Delegate from Germany, I do not feel able to support the proposal as originally made by the gallant Delegate from Norway.

Mr. Flood (Norway).—Mr. President, may I be allowed to make a remark? The First Delegate from Great Britain said that a long time ago I had been advised that they would agree to have the proposition put into a note, and that they had approached me on that subject. That is so, Mr. President. About a fortnight ago the learned Delegate Dr. Sieveking did me the honour to speak to me about this matter outside in the lobby, as did also the learned Delegate from Great Britain some days afterwards in this room. I answered both of the gentlemen in the same way, and I said: "Gentlemen, I have nothing to do with this amendment any more. It belonged to me before I put it before the Conference; but after being adopted by the Conference it belongs to the Conference, and I have not a word to say in the matter. If you think it necessary to have it brought before the Conference I shall not say a single word against it until I have heard what the Conference have to say in the matter." I answered both of the gentlemen the same thing, and they are here and will corroborate my statement. So I do not understand the force of what the learned First Delegate from Great Britain said when he stated that long ago the Delegate from Norway had been advised in this matter. But that matter has been decided by you, Mr. President. You stated from your chair that the amendment had been adopted. Then it became no longer mine; it belonged to the Conference and not to me. All that I said was that I would not oppose it until I heard what the Conference had to say about the matter, and I have kept my word. I did not say a word before the First Delegate from England made his elaborate speech.

Captain Norcross (United States).—Mr. President, I placed my name on the Additional Report of the Light Committee because really it makes no change in present conditions. If it is the meaning and intent of the amendment to have one uniform position on all vessels in which to carry the lights, then in view of risk of collision I perfectly agree with the Delegate from Norway, that the calculation of the ship's length is often an important factor. The Delegate from the United States has pointed out the risk attending the carrying of lights abreast the foremast on sailing-vessels. On larger vessels, however, the cage is always in the fore channels forward of the rigging, but in bad weather the lights are invariably placed aft. If this amendment pointed out the desirability of carrying the lights in that position, and recommended a note calling attention to future construction, I would give it my decided support.

Mr. Flood (Norway).—Mr. President, only one word. I hope I can say that it will be my very last in this Conference. It is this: When this proposition from the two learned Delegates from Great Britain and Germany was presented to me by them, neither of them said that he would strike out the provision in regard to sailing-ships. They proposed to take my amendment adopted by the Conference as it stood; but not a word was spoken about sailing-vessels. To-day I read that this is to be stricken out.

The President.—The question before the Conference is the Resolution of the Delegate from Germany as to placing this Resolution in a note in Appendix (B). The effect of the passage of this Resolution would be that the amendment of the Delegate from Norway would be lost, and this would be placed in Appendix (B) as a suggestion; that is, the first part of it which refers to steamers. It would not be the amendment of the Delegate from Norway.

Dr. Sieveking (Germany).—Mr. President, of course we leave that to your decision, but I think it fair to take a vote upon the amendment offered by the Delegate from Norway.

The President.—The Chair would prefer that course, but the Resolution comes first in order.

Dr. Sieveking (Germany).—Mr. President, my object in bringing forward this Resolution was, in case the amendment of the gallant Delegate should be lost, that this might be carried. Of course there will be no use for it if the amendment of the Delegate from Norway is carried.

The President.—If the Delegate from Norway so proposes the Chair will first put the question upon that part of the amendment which refers to steamers, and afterwards upon that part of it which refers to sailing-vessels.

Mr. Flood (Norway).—Mr. President, I have nothing more to say in the matter; I leave it entirely to your decision.

Mr. Verbrugghe (Belgium).—Mr. President, may I remark that if the Conference proceed in that way we shall be obliged to bring it under the Rules of the Road, and I believe the majority are against voting for it under the Rules. I would propose that the amendment as it stands should be voted upon, and then, whether it is carried or not, the Conference will vote upon the Resolution of the learned Delegate from Germany.

The President.—The question which has been discussed this morning is the Additional Report of the Committee on Lights. The Chair desires to have a motion with regard to that Report which has just been dealt with.

Captain Malmberg (Sweden).—Mr. President, may I have the honour to propose that a vote shall be taken upon the Report of the Committee on Lights?

The President.—Will the Delegate from Sweden be kind enough to propose that it be taken separately upon the two propositions?

Captain Malmberg (Sweden).—Mr. President, my proposition is to vote upon that Report as a whole.

The President.—Does the Delegate from Sweden move the adoption of the Report of the Committee?

Captain Malmberg (Sweden).—Mr. President, I move that the vote be taken upon the adoption of the amendment.

The President.—The question before the Conference is upon the Additional Report of the Committee on Lights, which is to be adopted or rejected.

Mr. Hall (Great Britain).—Mr. President, I think we might perhaps get into a difficulty if we adopt such a course, because there are two distinct propositions in the Report. One is that the Committee adhere to its former action with regard to the lights of steamers, and the other proposition is that it is not desirable to pass this Rule unless it can be accepted universally. I understand that the Report of the Committee on Lights is that they do not recommend that this amendment be accepted, unless there is reason to suppose that the Rule will be adopted universally. That, I apprehend, is the purpose and intent of their Report. I cannot help thinking that the proper course for us to pursue is to vote Yea or Nay upon the amendment of the Delegate from Norway, which was brought before us on a motion for reconsideration. I therefore move that the question be upon the amendment of the Delegate from Norway which is up for reconsideration by us this morning.

Captain Mensing (Germany).—Mr. President, I would like to submit that if the vote were taken upon the Report of the Committee on Lights, the German Delegates would vote against it, simply because in the Report of the Committee on Lights there has not been pointed out in a practical way any proposition which is made or any time fixed for the introduction of the Rule. It is quite impossible to take the Report of the Committee on Lights as it stands, and insert it into the Rules at any place. I think the proposition made by my colleague, Dr. Sieveking, covers the whole point. It gives the Conference all that is important and attainable, and I think it would show the direction in which we would like to have this matter move. I do not doubt that in a few years we will be in a much better position to discuss this proposition than we are at present. We do not know when this Rule is to come into force. If it is put into Appendix (B), the different nations may at once issue Regulations to their Supervisors to see that, so far as possible, those Rules mentioned in Appendix (B) are carried out, and it will come into use much sooner than the Rules can be put into force all over the world. Therefore, the German Delegates will vote against the Report, because there is no proposition made in it, and because in this form we find it is impossible that it should be adopted in the Rules.

Mr. Verney (Siam).—Mr. President, may I ask whether we should depart from our universal rule? May I ask the learned Delegate from Germany whether he will not allow his Resolution to come first?

Dr. Sieveking (Germany).—Mr. President, I think it is a mere matter of courtesy. I think it is but fair to the Delegate from Norway to put his amendment to a vote. If the amendment is carried, the Resolution will fall to the ground.

The President.—Does the Delegate from Great Britain accept the Resolution of the Delegate from Germany, that the question should be put upon the amendment of the Delegate from Norway?

Mr. Hall (Great Britain).—Mr. President, I understand that my learned friend the Delegate from Germany, who moved the Resolution, wishes the division to be taken first on the amendment, and, therefore, that perhaps should be done.

The President.—The Chair wishes to do what the Conference desires. The question will then be upon the amendment of the Delegate from Norway. Is the Conference ready for the question?

Lieutenant Beaugency (Chile).—Mr. President, I would like to have the amendment of the honourable Delegate from Norway postponed until after considering the Resolution of the Delegate from Germany.

The President.—The Resolution can be considered after the vote upon the amendment. The question is upon the amendment of the Delegate from Norway.

The question was put to the Conference upon the amendment of the Delegate from Norway, and it was lost.

The President.—The question will now be upon the Resolution of the Delegate from Germany, which will be read by the Secretary.

147

The Resolution of the Delegate from Germany is as follows:—

Resolved,—That it is approved by the Conference, and recommended to the attention of the Powers epresented thereat, that green and red side-lights should be placed in steam-vessels not forward of the masthead-light, and that this Resolution be inserted in Appendix (B) of the Report of the Committee on the Collocation of Rules."

Mr. Hall (Great Britain).—Mr. President, I desire to state on behalf of Great Britain that we shall support that Resolution. We think it most desirable to favour any matter that shall be brought before this Conference which we believe will lead to good, and will lead the Powers to investigate the matter and make the Rules in accordance with the results of experiments and experience. The sole reason, if I may say so, why we have opposed the amendment which has been dealt with is that it is a Rule dealing with vessels at the present time, and not to merely pointing out advice for the future. We wish to advance the investigation of this very important matter, and we shall give our very cordial support to this Resolution, as we should have done at the outset if the matter had been brought forward in the manner in which it is now.

Captain Richard (France).—Mr. President, the Delegation which I represent have decided to vote for the amendment proposed by the learned Dr. Sieveking, because it is the only means, I think, of harmonizing the Report of the Committee and the amendment presented by Mr. Flood. From a practical standpoint we cannot go any further. We cannot adopt the amendment of Mr. Flood, because that would lead us to do a thing which is not practicable. If, therefore, we accept the amendment of Dr. Sieveking, we show that we adopt the principle proposed by Mr. Flood, which has been adopted both by the Conference and by the Committee, to the extent allowed us by practical requirements. In that manner I think we will sanction it in the only manner possible to us. For that reason, I repeat, we will vote for this amendment.

The President.—The question is upon the Resolution of the Delegate from Germany. It will be read again by the Secretary.

The Resolution of the Delegate from Germany is as follows:—

"*Resolved,*—That it is approved by the Conference, and recommended to the attention of the Powers represented thereat, that the green and red side-lights should be placed in steam-vessels not forward of the masthead-light, and that this Resolution be inserted in Appendix (B) to the Report of the Committee on Collocation of the Rules."

Mr. Flood (Norway).—Mr. President, may I ask, for information, whether when this is voted on there will be another vote as to what shall be done with sailing-vessels?

The President.—The Chair does not so understand it.

Mr. Flood (Norway).—Is it understood now, Sir, that by the vote sailing-vessels are thrown out of the question altogether?

The President.—Unless there is some additional proposition, that will be the case.

Mr. Flood (Norway).—Mr. President, may I ask the question whether there is any chance to put in a proposition with regard to that now, or is it too late?

The President.—The Chair decides that a proposition of that kind is in order at any time the Conference is in session. The question now is upon the Resolution which has just been read.

The question was put to the Conference upon the adoption of the Resolution of the Delegate from Germany, and it was adopted.

The President.—There has been no disposition made of the Additional Report of the Committee on Lights. It is still before the Conference, and there must be some disposition made of it on the records, as it has been considered by the Conference.

Mr. Hall (Great Britain).—Mr. President, I apprehend that there being no proposal made upon this, it will merely appear upon the Minutes of our proceedings as having been handed to you, as President; and of course it will take its place among the various documents, and can be studied by the Powers.

The President.—It has been called up and has been under consideration. Therefore I think it might be inserted in the Minutes as having been considered by the Conference.

Mr. Hall (Great Britain).—Mr. President, I would submit that that should be done.

The President.—It is moved that the Additional Report of the Committee on Lights be inserted in the Minutes as having been considered by the Conference.

The question was put to the Conference upon the motion as above, and the motion was carried.

The President.—The next business in order will be the Report of the Collocation Committee.

Mr. Hall (Great Britain).—Mr. President, I apprehend that the next matter before the Conference is that we should determine whether or not the amendments in the nature of amendments on principle should be discussed by the Conference. Might I perhaps ask the indulgence of the Conference if I say a very few words on this point? The Delegates will see that the Collocation Committee have separated the amendments, as they were requested to do, into two classes. We have separated those in principle from those which are mere questions of verbiage, and the Delegates now have before them, bound up together, these two classes. As I say, it was agreed that the question should be considered whether or not amendments on questions of principle should be considered and entertained by the Conference, and it was pointed out that any gentleman moving or asking for leave to have amendments on principle discussed should confine his observations to as short a space of time as possible.

Now, Mr. President, I apprehend that really we can shorten this very considerably if we make up our minds what course we wish to pursue. With regard to Great Britain I may say this: We are anxious that every matter which any Delegate thinks it right to bring up for discussion again should be thoroughly discussed. We do not wish that by a mere majority, which we could do under the present Rule, to throw out any question which a Delegate, taking upon himself the responsibility for taking up the time of the Conference, thinks it right to bring before us, and accordingly we do not intend to vote against one single one of these amendments on principle being entertained by the Conference. As I say, we shall leave it to the Delegates to consider whether or not they are justified in occupying the time of the Conference in such discussion. Therefore I venture to make this suggestion, that the mover of each amendment, instead of making an introductory speech upon the matter, which can lead to nothing, because we are not empowered by our rules to discuss the amendments of principle here to-day—we cannot discuss them until Wednesday—but if the mover of each amendment will move *pro formâ* the adoption of his amendment and then wait to see whether there is any objection to proceeding to the discussion of it when the proper time arrives, it will save a great deal of time. We shall thus avoid speeches being made a second time.

I think myself that we are all of us practically actuated by the desire to have these important matters thrashed out to the utmost and thoroughly considered. If so, I apprehend that there will not be much disposition to vote against the discussion of these amendments in principle, although a great many of us may feel, certainly with regard to some of them, that they have been adequately discussed and adequately disposed of. But having regard to our desire that the matter should be thoroughly dealt with, I would venture to suggest that the mover of each amendment should merely move *pro formâ* that the amendment, for instance, No. 1, should be considered by the Conference and then wait to see whether any one objects. If there be no objection it can be put to a vote at once, and we can get through with a vote on what is purely a formal matter of business, and then be able to go on with the other matters before us.

Dr. Sieveking (Germany).—Mr. President, may we not go a step further and resolve that all the amendments of principle which have been handed in are to be reconsidered? I think that would save a great deal of time. I would like to move that the Conference resolve to take into reconsideration all of the amendments brought in under Class 2. Then we would go on with the discussion of the amendments the day after to-morrow, after forty-eight hours have elapsed, and we could take some of the Committee Reports to-day to occupy our time.

Mr. Hall (Great Britain).—Mr. President, I will willingly second that proposal. I confess that I had not seen the way to cut the Gordian knot which my learned friend has pointed out. As I said before, I think we are all anxious that every Delegate should have his opinion thoroughly considered and discussed; and therefore I second the Resolution of my learned friend the Delegate from Germany that we may discuss the matters proposed in Class 2 when the time arrives for that discussion.

The President.—It is moved that the Conference agree to discuss all the amendments, from 1 to 32, inclusive, of Class 2.

The question was put to the Conference upon the motion of the Delegate from Germany, and it was carried.

The President.—The next business in order is the Report of the Committee on Life-Saving Systems and Devices.

The Secretary will please read the Report.

The Report of the Committee on Life-Saving Systems and Devices is as follows:—

"*Report of the Committee on Life-Saving Systems and Devices.*

" Sir, "*Washington, December 5,* 1889.

"The Committee on Life-Saving Systems and Devices, appointed under a Resolution of the Marine Conference, were at first in doubt whether the terms of the Resolution gave them authority to consider and report upon all the topics embraced in General Division V of the Programme, but the subsequent action of the Conference in appointing Committees to report upon all the subjects of the other Divisions, yet making no further provision for those of General Division V, seemed clearly to imply that it was intended that this Committee should deal with them. They have accordingly done so, and herewith submit their Report. The various subjects will be taken up in their order upon the Programme.

" 1. Saving of life and property from shipwreck at sea.

" '(*a.*) Duties of vessels after collision.'

"What these duties are is obvious enough. Common humanity requires that the colliding vessels should remain by each other and render all needed assistance so long as they can do so consistently with their own safety. Experience shows, however, that masters of vessels frequently take advantage of the circumstances attending such disasters to escape from the scene without identification, in order to avoid responsibility. Several of the maritime nations have, therefore, imposed upon them the legal obligation of performing these natural duties. The extent to which they are evaded where such legal requirement does not exist is probably not generally appreciated. The Committee have had before them statistics of one such country, which show that in 8 per cent. of the collisions reported the master of one of the vessels left the other to take care of herself and her people, and got away without being known. In these instances there was loss of life upon some of the vessels so abandoned, some went down, and all suffered damage. It would seem, then, that any effective measure which might prevent such a practice, or make it less frequent, would not only be in the interest of humanity, but also aid in securing justice in regard to the rights of property. The Committee, therefore, are of the opinion that in case of collision between two vessels the master or person in charge of each vessel should be required, so far as he can without danger to his own vessel, crew, or passengers, to stay by the other vessel until he has ascertained that she has no need of further assistance, and to render to the other vessel, her master, crew, and passengers, such assistance as may be practicable and necessary in order to save them from any danger caused by the collision; and also to give to the master or person in charge of the other vessel the name of his own vessel, and of her port of registry, or of the port or place to which she belongs, and the name of the ports and places from which and to which she is bound.

"So far as the Committee can learn, the laws of those countries which have taken action upon the subject are to the above effect, substantially agreeing in defining the duties of masters, although the infraction of the law is differently dealt with in the different countries.

"In expressing the foregoing opinion the Committee are unanimous, but a minority think the Conference should indicate what, in their opinion, the penalty of failure to comply with the duties prescribed should be. The majority, however, do not deem this necessary, believing that the consequences of disobedience to their laws can and will be properly taken care of by the several Governments, without suggestion from the Conference.

"For the information of the Conference, the enactments of Great Britain upon the subject, which prescribe severer penalties for disregard of the duties imposed than those of any other nation, are appended to this Report. (See Appendix A.)

"'(b.) Apparatus for life-saving to be carried on board ship. (Life-boats, life-preservers, life-rafts, pumps, and fire-extinguishing apparatus.)'

"The Government of Chile has made the most liberal provision that the Committee have knowledge of for the safety of life on shipboard, requiring her vessels to be furnished with boats sufficient in number and capacity to afford the greatest security possible to everybody on board in case of disaster. (See Appendix B.) The Committee, however, do not regard the universal application of this provision as practicable under existing conditions. They believe that the basis upon which an agreement between the several nations is most likely to be established is to be found in the 'Rules of of the Board of Trade' of Great Britain, under the Merchant Shipping (Life-Saving Appliances) Act of 1888, which are to go into effect on the 31st March, 1890. These Rules provide for almost all cases that may arise under the vicissitudes of navigation, while they are sufficiently elastic to admit of adjustment to the various conditions existing in the countries interested, without violating their spirit. (See Appendix C.)

"The Committee also recommend the extension of the principle of these Rules to all smaller craft as far as practicable, and that each vessel of this class should carry at least one life-buoy of approved pattern and material, and for every person on board an efficient life-belt or jacket.

"The means of extinguishing fire on vessels has become to a considerable extent a matter relating to their construction, and the observation of members of the Committee is that in most vessels recently built great care is taken to make due provision in this respect, it being for the interest of the owners to do so. Most of the maritime nations have also enacted laws which provide for a suitable equipment of pumps and other devices. Perhaps, therefore, there is now no great necessity for action upon the subject by the Conference. However this may be, it would be impracticable for the Committee to prescribe any definite system, as it would involve a careful classification of vessels and a thorough study of a variety of apparatus, the necessary information and data for which it would be impossible to procure, properly consider, and report upon in season to be of avail to the Conference.

"'(c.) The use of oil and the necessary apparatus for its use.'

"There has been placed before the Committee much matter relating to this subject, consisting chiefly of reports from vessels that have used oil for calming dangerous seas, accounts of trials and experiments made under various conditions, deductions drawn from such reports and experiments, and directions for the application of oil under various conditions and circumstances.

"An examination of this material, and the information the Committee already possessed, have led to the conclusion that there need be no longer any doubt that the proper application of oil is efficacious on the open sea, but that there are conditions under which the action of breaking waves is not thereby much, if at all, modified. Its effect on the surf over bars at the mouths of rivers and those lying off beaches is especially doubtful. A Circular letter relative to the 'use of oil at sea,' issued by the Board of Trade of Great Britain, says: 'In a surf, or waves breaking on a bar, where a mass of liquid is in actual motion in shallow water, the effect of the oil is uncertain, as nothing can prevent the larger waves from breaking under such circumstances; but even here it is of some service.' Other official documents declare that in an exhaustive series of experiments no effect whatever was produced upon the surf breaking over the outlying bars of beaches.

"The Committee are of the opinion that all sea-going vessels should be supplied with a proper quantity of animal or vegetable oil (which seems to be more effective than mineral), and with suitable appliances for its distribution. For ordinary voyages the quantity need not be large. The best means of distributing it that have been brought to the attention of the Committee appear to be those specified by Vice-Admiral Cloué, published in a Circular issued by the French Government. (See Appendix D.)

"'(d.) Uniform inspections as to (b) and (c).'

"If the maritime nations should agree upon uniform requirements in respect to life-saving apparatus to be carried on board ship, and to the use of oil and the necessary apparatus for its use, uniform inspections might perhaps be advantageous; but it would be impossible to formulate an adequate system for this purpose without knowing definitely what these requirements might be, and even then it would be doubtful, considering the great diversity of administrative methods and machinery in different countries, whether any practicable system could be devised that would be acceptable to all.

"2. Saving of life and property from shipwreck by operations from shore.

"The Committee have had before them a number of valuable papers describing the organization and methods of institutions for the saving of life from shipwreck, and indicating the extent and results of their work. These will be found in Appendices (E) and (F). An examination of them clearly shows that these institutions are all managed by men whose hearts are in their work, and who may be trusted to use every means known to them for perfecting the apparatus and methods employed for the rescue of unfortunates cast upon their shores. The organization of the service in each country must necessarily vary according to the condition and temper of the people and the character and habits of the coast population from which the men constituting the effective life-saving force must be drawn. It is, therefore, deemed impracticable to formulate any definite Rules which would be applicable to all alike. It appears desirable, however, that the officers of every organization should study the features of the others, in order that they may adopt such improvements as seem suitable for their own. Some of the establishments appear to have been brought to a high degree of excellence.

"It seems desirable that careful attention should be given to the frequent drilling and exercising of life-saving crews. It is also deemed important that a watch or patrol should, wherever practicable, be established upon dangerous coasts at night, and during thick weather by day, not only for the early discovery of wrecks, but in order to warn off vessels that may be incautiously standing into danger. Coastguards are established in various countries for the prevention of smuggling, and where this is the case they can be utilized to give timely notice and assistance to life-saving crews, or even to constitute such crews, as is already done in some countries.

"With regard to special varieties of life-boats and other appliances, the Committee believe that the matter can be safely trusted to the judgment and discretion of the officers in charge of the life-saving institutions of the several countries. The requirements vary so greatly upon different coasts that boats and appliances effective in one place are often ill-adapted or useless in another. Besides, the preferences of the men employed have to be considered; they usually having greater confidence in particular models because they are accustomed to them. Confidence in the appliances a crew is required to use is, in general, an admitted essential to success. No one can judge of these matters so well as the officers whose duty it is to study the local conditions, and who are thoroughly acquainted with the prejudices and habitudes of the men.

"It is desirable that officers of life-saving institutions should generally communicate freely with each other with reference to any improvements that may occur to them, either in apparatus, methods, or organization, with a view both to the diffusion of information concerning such matters, and to establishing an international comity with regard to a beneficent work.

"With reference to subsection (d), 'Uniform means of transmitting information between stranded vessels and the shore,' the Committee would say that co-operation between mariners upon a wrecked vessel and those who wish to assist them upon shore is of the highest importance. The most earnest attempts at aid may be rendered nugatory if the shipwrecked are not aware of what is required of them. In order to secure this co-operation various means have been devised in maritime countries, such as attaching tally-boards to the lines of the beach apparatus, the publication of instructions in the official log-books distributed to vessels, the issuing of pamphlets or cards of such instructions, or the very excellent method of posting, in the forecastle, or some convenient place in the vessel, a durable placard showing by illustrations the manner in which life-saving lines are to be secured on board, and giving necessary instructions relative thereto.

"All these measures are good, but the instructions have not been as generally distributed among vessels of all nationalities as they should be, and with a view to the universal diffusion of this information it is recommended that a uniform system of issuing and distributing such instructions be adopted by the several maritime nations.

"The Committee are also of the opinion that the instructions generally issued do not adequately provide for co-operation between the ship and the shore, and that they should be supplemented by a few simple signals for the purpose of direct communication. The International Code can often be used in the day-time, but a still simpler system should be provided for the few signals required. It is believed that the signals absolutely necessary can be reduced to very few, and that the adoption and publication of such a system would be of great benefit in the emergencies of shipwreck.

"If it be determined to establish an International Code of Night Signals, such as is referred to in General Division VIII of the Programme—('Night Signals for communicating Information at Sea')—the signals needed for communicating at night between wrecked vessels and the shore ought to be incorporated therein. If it should prove impracticable to adopt a system of night signals for the International Code, it may yet be worth considering whether the few signals needed for use at wrecks ought not to be adopted. Such a system is recommended by the Committee, and will be found described in detail in the fourth Resolution at the close of this Report. Every signal there mentioned has been found necessary in emergencies that have actually arisen in service.

"3. Official inquiries into causes and circumstances of shipwrecks and other casualties.

"For countries which have not already provided by legislative enactments for official inquiries into the causes and circumstances of shipwrecks or other accidents to vessels that are of serious importance, the adoption of such laws is recommended, as it is believed that they are the most effective means by which masters and officers of vessels can be impressed with a proper sense of the serious responsibility that rests upon them, and that they therefore constitute one of the most important safeguards for life and property afloat that it is possible to devise. They would also add to the efficiency of laws designed to prevent the sending out of unseaworthy and overloaded vessels where such laws exist, and where they do not, would, to a certain extent, operate in their stead. They would, moreover, give information which might be of great value in showing the general causes and distribution of wrecks, and indirectly indicate the methods by which casualties might be averted or lessened.

"The Committee have formulated the foregoing recommendations into the following propositions, which are submitted for the consideration of the Conference:—

"1. *In every case of collision between two vessels, it shall be the duty of the master or person in charge of each vessel, if and so far as he can do so without danger to his own vessel, crew, and passengers (if any), to stay by the other vessel until he has ascertained that she has no need of further

---

* *Note.*—This proposition is stated in the form and language of the "New Section," proposed November 26, 1889, to be added to the "Rules of the Road;" the consideration of which the Conference have voted to postpone, pending the presentation of this Report.

assistance, and to render to the other vessel, her master, crew, and passengers (if any), such assistance as may be practicable, and as may be necessary in order to save them from any danger caused by the collision; and also to give to the master or person in charge of the other vessel the name of his own vessel, and of her port of registry, or of the port or place to which she belongs, and also the names of the ports and places from which and to which she is bound.

"2. *Resolved*,—That the Conference approve of the principle of the 'Rules made by the Board of Trade of Great Britain under the Merchant Shipping (Life-Saving Appliances) Act, 1888,' relating to boats and appliances to be carried on board ship for saving life; and recommend that the several Governments adopt measures to secure compliance with this principle in regard to such boats and appliances for vessels of 150 tons and upwards gross tonnage.

"It is also recommended that the principle of these Rules be extended to all smaller craft, as far as practicable; and that each vessel of this class should carry at least one life-buoy, of approved pattern and material, and for every person on board an efficient life-belt or jacket.

"3. *Resolved*,—That the Conference recommend that the several Governments require all their seagoing vessels to carry a sufficient quantity of animal or vegetable oil, for the purpose of calming the sea in rough weather, together with suitable means for applying it.

"4. *Resolved*,—That the Conference recommend that all institutions for saving life from wrecked vessels prepare uniform instructions to mariners with reference to their co-operation with those attempting their rescue from the shore, and that said instructions include the following signals:—

"Upon the discovery of a wreck by night the life-saving force will burn a red pyrotechnic light or a red rocket, to signify, 'You are seen; assistance will be given as soon as possible.'

"A red flag waved on shore by day, or a red light, red rocket, or red Roman candle displayed by night, will signify, 'Haul away.'

"A white flag waved on shore by day, or a white light slowly swung back and forth, or a white rocket or white Roman candle fired by night, will signify, 'Slack away.'

"Two flags, a white and a red, waved at the same time on shore by day, or two lights, a white and a red, slowly swung at the same time, or a blue pyrotechnic light burned by night, will signify, 'Do not attempt to land in your own boats; it is impossible.'

"A man on shore beckoning by day, or two torches burning near together by night, will signify, 'This is the best place to land.'

"Any of these signals may be answered from the vessel as follows: In the day-time, by waving a flag, a handkerchief, a hat, or even the hand; at night, by firing a rocket, a blue light, or a gun, or by showing a light over the ship's gunwale for a short time and then concealing it.'

"And it is recommended that the several Governments take measures to keep all their seagoing vessels supplied with copies of such instructions.

"5. *Resolved*,—That the Conference recommend that the several nations provide by legislative enactments for official inquiry into the causes and circumstances of all shipwrecks and other serious casualties happening to their vessels.

"The Committee have examined a large number of devices and projects relating to the saving of life from shipwreck, a list of which will be found below. Many of them indicate considerable ingenuity, and their number and variety show the great amount of interest and attention that this subject is receiving. The Committee have consulted them freely in reaching conclusions relative to the topics placed before them, but have not deemed it advisable to make specific recommendations regarding any particular device or plan, believing that such action is not expected of them by the Conference. Furthermore, to reach conclusions with regard to many of them would involve experiments or trials beyond the power of the Committee. To recommend those whose merits were already known to the Committee, or which required no such tests, might be unfair to the others.

(Signed) "S. I. KIMBALL, *Chairman*,
"*Delegate for the United States.*
"THO. VERBRUGGHE,
"*Delegate for Belgium.*
"O. VIEL, *Delegate for Chile.*
"A. M. BISBEE, *Delegate for China.*
"E. RICHARD, *Delegate for France.*
"A. FEIGEL, *Delegate for Germany.*
"HENRY WYATT,
"*Delegate for Great Britain.*
"VAN STEYN,
"*Delegate for the Netherlands.*
"B. VEGA DE SEOANE,
"*Delegate for Spain.*

"To Rear-Admiral S. R. Franklin, United States' Navy,
"President of the International Marine Conference, &c."

Mr. Kimball (United States).—Mr. President, I suppose the proper course of action upon this Report would be to consider the several propositions which have been formulated by the Committee, commencing with the first proposal on p. 6. That proposition relates to the duties of vessels after collision. It is in substance the new section which was proposed by my colleague, Mr. Goodrich, on the 26th November, 1889. He is not present, and perhaps we ought not to go on with the discussion of the proposition in his absence. The Committee are in favour of his proposed new section, with the exception of the last four lines. These last four lines are in the nature of a penalty, to prescribe a penalty for disobedience to the provisions of the proposition. We have imposed no penalty for the violation of any of the Rules of the Road, and the Committee are not in favour of the Conference providing a penalty here. If the Conference think this matter should not be discussed without the presence of the Delegate from the United States, I will drop it. I would inquire whether any one of my colleagues of the United States' Delegation is empowered to speak for Mr. Goodrich in regard to this matter. I do not know how much importance he attaches to the last clause.

I find that my colleagues of the Delegation of the United States are willing to strike out the last four lines and go on with the discussion.

The President.—The Delegate can make a motion to strike out the last four lines, and let the Conference decide it.

Mr. Hall (Great Britain).—Mr. President, perhaps I may say that we are very anxious not to consider any amendment which is handed in by any Delegate in the absence of such Delegate. I apprehend that perhaps it would be better that the proposition of including this in the Rules should be discussed when the learned Delegate from the United States is able to come back and take his place at our table. But of course that will not prevent us from discussing the Resolutions in this Report, and I apprehend that in discussing them it will not be necessary for us to consider whether or not any of these Resolutions are to be drafted into the Rules. We will leave that for the learned Delegate from the United States to propose when he next appears at the Conference, if he sees fit to do so.

Mr. Kimball (United States).—Mr. President, then I suppose that we are to discuss the proposition of the Committee which does not contain the last four lines in the new section proposed by the Delegate from the United States.

The President.—The Chair understands that these four lines are not in this proposition. The Delegate from the United States will proceed with this discussion upon the proposition as it stands here.

Mr. Kimball (United States).—Mr. President, in reference to this proposition, I apprehend that it is not necessary for me to say much, if anything, in addition to what has been said in the Report. It appears to me that it having once been known that there is a necessity for such a Rule as is proposed here, there can scarcely be any objection to it. The Report states that the statistics of one country have shown that in 8 per cent. of the collisions which happened between vessels, one of the vessels got away without being identified, and left the other to take care of herself and her people. In the United States that amounts to about twenty a year, there being, as statistics show, about 250 collisions annually. I find by the Report of the statistics in regard to maritime disasters issued by the Board of Trade of Great Britain that last year there were 1,231 collisions on and near the coasts of the United Kingdom, or to British vessels at sea. Eight per cent. of this number, or nearly 100, escaped without identification. As nearly as I can ascertain there are somewhere between 200 and 300 vessels a-year in collision which get off without identification. It seems to me that there should be some way to prevent this, and I know of no more effective means than those which have been adopted by Great Britain. How the law works in that country I am unable to say.

Mr. Hall (Great Britain)—Mr. President, before proceeding to discuss these Resolutions, may I say, on behalf of my colleagues and myself, that we feel that we are very much indebted to the Committee, and to the Chairman of this Committee, for the most careful and interesting Report which they have laid before us? We were aware, before we studied these documents, of the great interest which the United States takes in the life-saving service, and that has been testified by this most interesting document, which is annexed as an Appendix to the Report, compiled by the Chairman of this Committee, giving an account of the life-saving service of the United States. I may prophesy this—although I believe we are told that we never should prophesy unless we know—I think I may prophesy that this Report will be studied most attentively and carefully by all the Governments of the Maritime Powers taking part in this Conference.

Now, with regard to this Resolution. I apprehend that it is one which will practically meet the views of all who take an interest in the saving of life at sea, and it is in accordance with the very natural feeling which every right and fair-thinking man must entertain as to the character of those in charge of vessels who go away and desert a vessel they have been in collision with, without stopping to inquire whether or not there is danger to human life. I apprehend that no one in this room can entertain a contrary opinion as to that; and the only question is as to how we can emphasize our opinion on that matter best.

As I said, the proposition of the learned Delegate of the United States is not before us at the present time; but I am aware that this Resolution is taken word for word from an English Statute on the subject. It is not for that reason alone that I support it. I support this Resolution because I think it is a proper Resolution, which ought to be carried, even if there were no existing Statute to this effect; and I believe that I shall be supported in that view by practically everybody here present. How that is to be enforced is a different question, which we have not got to discuss under this Resolution. Whether it is possible to make any International Rule for the enforcement of it I very much doubt, although I wish it were possible. But upon the proposition as it stands, I cannot apprehend that any one sitting at this table can have the slightest difficulty or can find the slightest fault with the proposition which is presented to us by this Committee. Therefore, we shall vote in favour of the Resolution just now submitted to us by the Delegate from the United States.

Dr. Sieveking (Germany).—Mr. President, may I ask, for information, whether it is intended to have this Resolution embodied into the Rules of the Road? There is some doubt about it. In the second and third paragraph there is the word "Resolved," and they are pointed out as being Resolutions only. If this was a Resolution only I would not have a word to say about it; but if it is to be put into the Rules of the Road at Sea I would like to make a few remarks in regard to it.

153

The President.—The Chair understands that the discussion with regard to its being placed in the Rules of the Road will come on at some future time.

Captain Salvesen (Norway),—Mr. President, in Norway we have a Law, dated the 3rd June, 1874, which is of exactly the same import as the British Statute, as far as the present Resolution goes; but as to the penalty in our country, it is to be a fine, prison, or hard labour in the fifth degree. It is with us a common law, and has not its place in the Rules of the Road.

The President.—The question is upon the adoption of the first proposition in the Report of the Committee, which the Secretary will please read.

The proposition is as follows:—

"In every case of collision between two vessels it shall be the duty of the master or person in charge of each vessel, if and so far as he can do so without danger to his own vessel, crew, and passengers (if any), to stay by the other vessel until he has ascertained that she has no need of further assistance; and to render to the other vessel, her master, crew, and passengers (if any), such assistance as may be practicable and as may be necessary in order to save them from any danger caused by the collision; and also to give to the master or person in charge of the other vessel the name of his own vessel, and of her port of registry, or of the port or place to which she belongs, and also the names of the ports and places from which and to which she is bound."

The President.—Is the Conference ready for the question?

The question was put to the Conference upon the adoption of the first proposition of the Committee on Life-Saving Systems and Devices, and the proposition was adopted.

The President.—The Secretary will please read the second proposition.

The second proposition is as follows:—

"2. *Resolved,*—That the Conference approve of the principle of the 'Rules made by the Board of Trade of Great Britain under the Merchant Shipping (Life-Saving Appliances) Act, 1888,' relating to boats and appliances to be carried on board ship for saving life; and recommend that the several Governments adopt measures to secure compliance with this principle in regard to such boats and appliances for vessels of 150 tons and upwards gross tonnage.

"It is also recommended, that the principle of these Rules be extended to all smaller craft, as far as practicable; and that each vessel of this class should carry at least one life-buoy of approved pattern and material, and for every person on board an efficient life-belt or jacket."

Mr. Kimball (United States).—Mr. President, by reference to Appendix (B), on p. 17, it will be seen what the provisions made by the Chilean Government are:—

"Crew of from 2 to 5 men, including the captain, 1 boat, with capacity for 10 men.
"Crew of from 6 to 10 men, including the captain, 2 boats, with capacity for 20 men.
"Crew of from 11 to 20 men, including the captain, 3 boats, with capacity for 40 men.
"Crew of 21 to 30 men, including the captain, 4 boats, with capacity for 50 men.
"Crew of 31 to 50 men, including the captain, 4 boats, with capacity for 70 men.
"Crew of 51 to 70 men, including the captain, 5 boats, with capacity for 100 men,
"Crew of 71 to 100 men, including the captain, 6 boats, with capacity for 150 men.
"For each gang of 30 men exceeding 100, a larger boat shall be required, with a capacity for 50 men."

These are certainly very ample provisions; and it seemed to the Committee that they were rather more ample than the variety in the construction of vessels throughout the world and the variety of service required of them would justify. The Committee, however, deemed it necessary and proper to make every provision that consistently could be made for the safety of passengers and other people on board vessels, and after considerable examination of the subject and consideration of the literature which could be found upon it, they concluded that the course adopted by the English Government was perhaps the one upon which the maritime nations would be the most likely to agree. The provisions of that Government are found in the Rules made by the Board of Trade of Great Britain under the Merchant Shipping (Life-Saving Appliances) Act of 1888, and will be found on p. 23 of Appendix (B), and it is proposed that this Conference should approve of the principle of those Rules. What that principle is can perhaps best be understood by reading the three propositions on p. 21, incorporated in the Report of a Committee which was appointed by the Board of Trade to consider this matter. They are as follows:—

"1. The arranging of British ships into classes, having regard to the services in which they are employed, to the nature and direction of the voyage, and to the number of persons carried.

"2. The number and description of the boats, life-boats, life-rafts, life-jackets, and life-buoys to be carried by British ships, according to the class in which they are arranged, and the mode of their construction; also the equipments to be carried by the boats and rafts, and the methods to be provided to get the boats and other life-saving appliances into the water; such methods may include oil for use in stormy weather.

"3. The quantity, quality, and description of buoyant apparatus to be carried on board ships carrying passengers, either in addition to or in substitution for boats, life-boats, life-rafts, life-jackets, and life-buoys."

In the next paragraph the Committee say:—

"These Rules, if adopted, will, we think, insure that ships of different classes shall be provided with such appliances for saving life at sea as (having regard to the nature of the services in which they are employed, and the avoidance of undue incumbrance of the ships' decks) are best adapted for securing the safety of their crews and passengers."

I presume that the members of the Conference have all examined the Rules referred to, and it is not necessary for me to explain them.

Mr. Hall (Great Britain).—Mr. President, I apprehend that the Conference will have no difficulty in agreeing to the Resolution which has been proposed by the honourable Chairman of this Committee. I do not desire to occupy the time of the Conference, as I am certain that we all of us have read with very great interest the various provisions which are recommended by this Committee. I would only say this with regard to the Rules which the Committee recommend, the Board of Trade Rules, that they are the result of investigations extending over about a year. Tha Committee were composed of men whose names are household words in the history of the mercantile shipping. If any one looks down the list he can find the names of the representatives of the largest ship-owners in the various parts of the United Kingdom. They investigated the matter very thoroughly, and took evidence upon the points. Their deliberations continued for about the space of one year. The principle which is now recommended is the final outcome of their deliberations. I can only say this, we shall always hail with pleasure any suggestion which can improve these Rules whenever it may be made, and we shall certainly be amongst the first to adopt any improvement which can be made in them.

Mr. Kimball (United States).—Mr. President, I perhaps should call to the attention of the Conference that the Committee have gone further and suggested that the principle of these Rules be extended to smaller craft as far as possible, and that each vessel of this class should carry at least one life-buoy of approved pattern and material, and for every person on board an efficient life-belt or jacket. I now move the adoption of this Resolution.

The President.—The Delegate from the United States moves the adoption of Resolution No. 2. Is the Conference ready for the question?

The question was put to the Conference upon the adoption of Resolution No. 2 in the Report of the Committee on Life-Saving Systems and Devices, and the Resolution was adopted.

The President.—The Secretary will please read the third Resolution.

"*Resolved,*—That the Conference recommend that the several Governments require all their seagoing vessels to carry a sufficient quantity of animal and vegetable oil, for the purpose of calming the sea in rough weather, together with suitable means for applying it."

Mr. Kimball (United States).—Mr. President, it strikes me that it is a great wonder that the practice of carrying oil for calming the waves in rough weather has not been long ago adopted by mariners. It has been known for a great many years that oil does have a certain effect in quieting rough waters. It was known as long ago as the days of Aristotle; Pliny speaks of it, and recommends its use by vessels, and Dr Franklin recommended its use very strongly. But for some reason or other it has never been used to any great extent until recently. Within a few years there have been many experiments made with oil, and, so far as the Committee could learn, with a great deal of success. I believe there are several reasons why it has not been generally used before. Perhaps it has been considered unseamanlike. Perhaps mariners have been incredulous as to the effects claimed for it, and in the absence of an explanation of the phenomenon, have not believed that so great results as are claimed could arise from so apparently trivial a cause. The true explanation is still, perhaps, a mystery, although Dr. Franklin suggests that the oil operates simply as a lubricator between the wind, as it is forced against the water, and the water itself, and instead of tearing it up, as it does on a quiet sea, it simply glides along over the surface. This appears to me to be a very rational explanation.

At any rate, the Committee found that out of 179 trials reported, 173 of them produced the desired effect. In the other six instances petroleum was used in three; in one colza oil, which is a very thin oil, and in the other two it is stated that probably the lack of favourable results was due to the thickening of the oil by the temperature. These data seem to me to afford sufficient warrant for the action of the Committee in recommending the general use of oil. I may say, furthermore, that three of the great maritime nations have already approved of its use, and one of them, Great Britain, makes its use compulsory, particularly on life-boats, as will be seen by reference to pp. 29 and 32 of the Report of the Committee. With so excellent a showing for its use as has been made by these experiments, and after its adoption by these nations, I am inclined to think that there should be no objection to its general use. I therefore move the adoption of the Resolution.

Captain Malmberg (Sweden).—Mr. President, although I am in no way disputing the advantages of using oil for the purpose of calming rough seas, I for my part, cannot vote for any recommendation to the various Powers to use it on seagoing vessels, or that all seagoing vessels should be supplied with a considerable quantity of suitable oil. I think that this may be very well left to the different Powers without any admonition from this Conference. Therefore I shall vote against the Resolution.

Captain Salvesen (Norway).—Mr. President, as the Resolution reads and as it is printed it recommends that all the Governments require all their vessels to carry it. I presume that the word "vessel" here has the same meaning as in the Rules of the Road, so the smallest craft or boat would be required to carry oil. The word "seagoing" ought to be inserted here, as well as on p. 3.

Mr. Hall (Great Britain).—Mr. President, I understand that it was pointed out by the honourable Chairman of that Committee that the word "seagoing" has been omitted in the print and that the word "seagoing" was intended to be inserted.

The President.—Is the Conference ready for the question?

The question was put to the Conference upon the adoption of the third Resolution of the Committee on Life-Saving Systems and Devices, and the Resolution was adopted.

155

The President.—The fourth Resolution will now be read.
The fourth Resolution is as follows:—

"4. *Resolved,*—That the Conference recommend that all institutions for saving life from wrecked vessels prepare a set of instructions to mariners with reference to their co-operation with those attempting their rescue from the shore, and that said instructions include the following signals:

"Upon the discovery of a wreck by night the life-saving force will burn a red pyrotechnic light or a red rocket to signify 'You are seen; assistance will be given as soon as possible.'"

The President.—These signals will be considered by paragraphs. The first paragraph, which has been read, will now be considered.

Mr. Kimball (United States).—Mr. President, the object of this fourth Resolution is to overcome, as far as possible, just such difficulties as life-saving institutions encounter in their operations in saving life from stranded vessels. A great deal of difficulty is experienced on account of the ignorance of the people on board of stranded vessels with regard to the methods employed by life-saving institutions. Many of them do not know what to do with a shot-line when sent to them. I have known instances where, instead of hauling in the line, as you would naturally suppose they would do, they have actually payed it out, having previously fastened a warp to it on board, thinking that the life-saving crew was to haul a line from the vessel to the shore. In such a case they would be entirely without the aid of the shore apparatus.

In other instances they have not understood what to do with what is called the whip-line or the second line sent, to which the tail block is attached, and particularly they have not known what to do with the hawser, a line which is subsequently sent. They have even made it fast to the mast below the block on the whip-line, a course which embarrasses operations very much and sometimes entirely stops them. To overcome this difficulty, which all institutions have experienced, the various Governments in which there are life-saving institutions established have, as stated in the Report, adopted various methods, such as posting up a placard on some part of the vessel—on the mast or in the forecastle—with illustrations showing what should be done. That is a very excellent plan; but the trouble is that the distribution of these instructions has not been sufficient. So this Resolution recommends that all institutions prepare proper instructions, and that the several Governments shall see to their distribution and take care to have them placed on board of every vessel in their service, and kept on board. This is a very important thing, and one of the most important provisions of this series of Resolutions.

In reference to this matter there is one other thing which is proposed. It is thought necessary to assure the wrecked crew on the ship that help is at hand just as soon as possible, in order to encourage them to remain by their vessel and wait for help from the shore. There is quite an inclination on the part of a panic-stricken crew on a stranded vessel to attempt to land in their own boats. Nothing could be more fatal, generally, because the sailors are ignorant of the conditions with which they have to deal. They are used to rowing boats in deep water and not to going through the surf. Furthermore, their boats are not surf-boats, and are not suited to pass through surf. If they undertake it, in most instances they are liable to lose their lives. So it is thought necessary to have the wrecked crew informed as soon as possible that assistance is coming, and of course, assistance does come as soon as possible. The red pyrotechnic light or the red rocket is provided for this case. In most life-saving institutions when the line-carrying rocket or the gun is about to be fired to send a line over a vessel, a signal is made, if at night, by firing a red rocket, which signifies, "Be on the look-out for a line." Some institutions do not take this precaution, if it may be called a precaution, thinking that the firing of the rocket itself which carries the line, or the discharge of the gun, if a shot is fired, is sufficient; and indeed it would, it appears, be sufficient. This provision is not at all in conflict, I believe, with any signal which is given in any country. There can, therefore, be no objection to this signal that I am aware of. I will move the adoption of this Resolution.

Mr. Hall (Great Britain).—Mr. President, I would only venture to suggest the insertion of a single word to carry out what was, perhaps, the intention of the Committee, that these instructions should be uniform. In order to be of assistance it is desirable that they should all have the same instructions, and then, of course, they can be printed in the official log or on the back of shipping papers, so that they will always be on board of vessels. It is, of course, important that vessels should know that all life-saving institutions have the same instructions. So I would venture to suggest that it should read the Governments should be requested to prepare "uniform instructions" to mariners.

Mr. Kimball (United States).—Mr. President, I would say that I have no objection whatever to that. All life-saving institutions, so far as I am aware, have already issued such instructions, and they are uniform. The fact is that the operations for saving life from stranded vessels by the breeches-buoy is the same throughout the world, and has been adopted from the Manby method instituted in Great Britain about a century ago, and also by the French Government about the same time. I have no objection to the word and will accept the suggestion.

Mr. Hall (Great Britain).—It is only to provide for a vessel off a foreign coast, where she might not be certain that the instructions were the same as in other places.

Mr. Kimball (United States).—I accept the amendment.

The President.—If there be no objection the amendment will be made.

Mr. Hall (Great Britain).—So that it will read: "prepare uniform instructions."

The President.—The question will be, first, upon Resolution No. 4, and afterwards upon the first paragraph. Resolution No. 4 will be read.

Mr. Hall (Great Britain).—Mr. President, I think the word "uniform" should be substituted for the words, "a set of," so as to make it read: "prepare uniform instructions."

The President.—With the consent of the Delegate from the United States, the Resolution will be read as amended.

The Resolution is as follows:—

"4. *Resolved*,—That the Conference recommend that all institutions for saving life from wrecked vessels prepare uniform instructions to mariners with reference to their co-operation with those attempting their rescue from the shore, and that said instructions include the following signals:—

"Upon the discovery of a wreck by night the life-saving force will burn a red pyrotechnic light or a red rocket to signify, 'You are seen; assistance will be given as soon as possible.'"

The President.—Is the Conference ready for the question upon the fourth Resolution and the first paragraph after it.

The question was put to the Conference upon the adoption of the fourth Resolution and the first paragraph, and it was adopted.

The President.—The next paragraph will be read.

The paragraph is as follows:—

"A red flag waved on shore by day, or a red light, red rocket, or red Roman candle displayed by night, will signify, 'Haul away.'"

Mr. Kimball (United States)—Mr. President, in the remarks made upon the preceding paragraph, I think I showed the necessity for having the means of instructing a stranded crew to haul away. For instance, if they undertake to pay out the shot-line, the displaying of a red flag by day or a red light by night would inform them that they must haul it on board. I think I need not make any further explanation, except to say that the use of this red flag and red light, &c., will interfere with no other signal that I know of. In relation to this matter of signals, I believe that the gallant Delegate from Great Britain, Admiral Bowden-Smith, is the best posted man here, and if any of these signals will conflict with any of the signals of which he has knowledge, I would be pleased to have him state it.

Admiral Bowden-Smith (Great Britain).—Mr. President, having been on the Committee for revising the International Code-Book, I may say that we sent for our Director of Life-Saving Apparatus and asked him if he could propose any signals to be inserted in the Code. I sincerely wish that we had had the assistance of the honourable Delegate from the United States, and also the benefit of his suggestions; but, of course, it is impossible for foreign countries, one by one, to make recommendations. I am sure that the additional signals which he proposes will be carefully considered by the Board of Trade. I must say that so far as they have gone as yet the Board of Trade Committee did not see their way to put these signals into the little Code which they have prepared for night-work, and I do not see how they could do it. But I am sure that any signals which are proposed by the honourable Delegate from the United States will receive the consideration of the Board of Trade.

Mr. Kimball (United States).—These signals will not interfere with any others?

Admiral Bowden-Smith (Great Britain).—Mr. President, these will take the place of those which are of no use, I should think.

Mr. Kimball (United States).—I move the adoption of this second paragraph to the fourth Resolution.

The President.—The second paragraph will be again read by the Secretary.

The second paragraph of the fourth Resolution is as follows:—

"A red flag waved on shore by day, or a red light, red rocket, or red Roman candle displayed by night, will signify, 'Haul away.'"

The President.—Is the Conference ready for the question upon this paragraph?

The question was put to the Conference upon the adoption of the second paragraph of the fourth Resolution, and it was adopted.

The President.—The Secretary will now read the next paragraph, which will be the third paragraph of the fourth Resolution.

The third paragraph of the fourth Resolution is as follows:—

"A white flag waved on shore by day, or a white light slowly swung back and forth, or a white rocket or white Roman candle fired by night, will signify, 'Slack away.'"

Mr. Kimball (United States).—Mr. President, I apprehend that it will be understood at once that the same necessity exists for having the power to make a signal to a wrecked crew to "slack away" as to "haul away." We have had actual cases where the operations have been interfered with, and even entirely prevented, because the wrecked crew could not be made to understand that they must "slack away," and we have had our lines parted in consequence. You will notice that we speak of a white and red light slowly swung back and forth. We adopted that in order to distinguish the signal from lights flitting about the shore. If there is no objection, I move the adoption of the paragraph.

The President.—The Secretary will read the paragraph again for the information of the Conference.

The third paragraph of the fourth Resolution is as follows:—

"A white flag waved on shore by day, or a white light slowly swung back and forth, or a white rocket or white Roman candle fired by night, will signify, 'Slack away.'"

The question was put to the Conference upon the adoption of the third paragraph of the fourth Resolution, and it was adopted.

The President.—The Secretary will now read the fourth paragraph.

The fourth paragraph of the fourth Resolution is as follows:—

"Two flags, a white and a red, waved at the same time on shore by day, or two lights, a white and a red, slowly swung at the same time, or a blue light burned by night, will signify, 'Do not attempt to land in your own boats; it is impossible.'"

Mr. Kimball (United States).—Mr. President, this is one of the most important signals in the series, if not the most important. I think I can safely say that more lives are lost within the scope of our life-saving stations through this cause than from any other; I had almost said than from all others. If you will examine Appendix (F), p. 86, and the following pages, and look at the statistics furnished by the Government of Denmark, you will find it is stated that a certain number lost their lives in attempting to land by their own efforts. I find upon examination of these statistics that out of 935 lives lost, 227 of them—or 24 per cent.—were lost by mariners attempting to land in their own boats. That is a very large percentage, and, to my mind, shows the necessity of some such means as we have recommended. I move the adoption of this paragraph.

Captain Mensing (Germany).—Mr. President, so far as I know the blue light is one that is used by pilot-boats; and the blue lights which we have in our country are very much like white lights. I think they might be very easily mistaken for the white Roman candle mentioned before. I believe that the meaning of this paragraph is that a blue pyrotechnic light should be burned, and it should be expressly so stated. If that is the wish of the Committee, I would move that the word "pyrotechnic" be inserted.

Mr. Kimball (United States).—Mr. President, I do not think there would be any danger of mistaking the blue light burned on the shore for a blue light used on a pilot-boat.

Captain Mensing (Germany).—Mr. President, I wish to state that it is not because it might be mistaken for a pilot-vessel, but it might be very easily mistaken for the white light, at least, that is the case with those we have in our service.

Mr Kimball (United States).—Mr. President, there might be danger of that perhaps at a great distance; but it must be remembered that a vessel stranded is very near the shore, and whenever such a light is to be used it would be within a few hundred yards, or half-a-mile probably, at the outside. I do not imagine there will be any difficulty on that account. The green light, however, might be substituted perhaps.

Captain Mensing (Germany).—Mr. President, I have no preference whatever. I only want to state that our blue light is really, even at half-a-mile, easily mistaken for a white Roman candle. Now, if it were stated here that it should be a blue pyrotechnic light, everybody would know that this is a light which is blue in its character, or green, or anything else. But if we adopted the blue light, and we were to translate that into German by "*blau*," then it would be very easily confused with the white light, and a white Roman candle might be taken for the blue light, or *vice versâ*. If there is no objection I will move to have this word "pyrotechnic" inserted there, and then a mistake could not occur.

Mr. Kimball (United States).—Mr. President, there is no objection that I know of to the word "pyrotechnic" being inserted there. I suppose a blue light is a pyrotechnic light.

Captain Mensing (Germany).—Mr. President, of course the blue light which I mean is a pyrotechnic light. But "blue light" is a generic term for these lights, and it is in fact something which looks very much like a white Roman candle. It is a thing encased in wood, which burns very slowly, and which gives out a white flame, a little bluish. These lights have received with us the name "blue lights." You have used the words, "red pyrotechnic light," above; why cannot we adopt it here and make mistakes impossible?

Mr. Kimball (United States).—I will accept the suggestion.

The President.—If there be no objection, the suggestion of the Delegate from Germany will be received.

Captain Richard (France).—Mr. President, I do not think that there can be any objection on this important point. The idea of the Committee in prescribing this Rule was solely and simply to devise a signal which can be understood by everybody. Consequently, all that we have to come to an understanding about is in regard to the kind of light which is to be adopted. I see no objection whatever to adopting another light, whether pyrotechnic or otherwise, provided it satisfies everybody and is beyond the reach of criticism.

Mr. Kimball (United States).—Mr. President, I suppose it is understood that when I say I will accept the suggestion, I mean with the approval of my colleagues on the Committee.

The President.—The question is upon the fourth paragraph of the fourth Resolution, with the amendment suggested by the Delegate from Germany. As the Chair hears no objection, that suggestion will be accepted. The question now is upon the paragraph as amended, which will be read by the Secretary.

The fourth paragraph of the fourth Resolution is as follows:—

"Two flags, a red and a white, waved at the same time on shore by day, or two lights, a white and a red, slowly swung at the same time, or a blue pyrotechnic light burned by night, will signify, 'Do not attempt to land in your own boats; it is impossible.'"

The President.—Is the Conference ready for the question?

The question was put to the Conference upon the adoption of the fourth paragraph of the fourth Resolution, and it was adopted.

The President.—The Secretary will please read the next paragraph.

The fifth paragraph of the fourth Resolution is as follows:—

"A man on shore beckoning by day, or two torches burning near together by night, will signify, 'This is the best place to land.'"

Mr. Kimball (United States).—Mr. President, it is probably unnecessary for me to say anything in regard to the necessity for this signal. It seems to be almost self-evident. If a landing has to be made, as sometimes happens in the contingencies of shipwreck, then it is very desirable that the people on board should know where the best place to land is, and that can be pointed out by the signals proposed here. I move the adoption of the paragraph.

The President.—Is the Conference ready for the question upon this paragraph? The Secretary will please read it again before the vote is taken.

The fifth paragraph of the fourth Resolution is as follows:—

"A man on shore beckoning, by day, or two torches burning near together, by night, will signify, 'This is the best place to land.'"

The President.—Is the Conference ready for the question?

The question was put to the Conference upon the adoption of the fifth paragraph of the fourth Resolution, and it was adopted.

The President.—The Secretary will please read the sixth paragraph of this Resolution.

The sixth paragraph of the fourth Resolution is as follows:—

"Any of these signals may be answered from the vessel as follows: In the day-time, by waving a flag, a handkerchief, a hat, or even the hand; at night, by firing a rocket, a blue light, or a gun, or by showing a light over the ship's gunwale for a short time and then concealing it."

Mr. Kimball (United States).—Mr. President, I would simply say that these are the answering signals now accepted by all life-saving crews in operating from the shore, under instructions which have already been published by all life-saving institutions, as I have stated. I move the adoption of this paragraph.

The President.—Is the Conference ready for the question? The Secretary will please read the sixth paragraph again, before a vote is taken.

The sixth paragraph of the fourth Resolution is as follows:—

"Any of these signals may be answered from the vessel as follows: In the day-time, by waving a flag, a handkerchief, a hat, or even the hand; at night, by firing a rocket, a blue light, or a gun, or by showing a light over the ship's gunwale for a short time and then concealing it."

The question was put to the Conference upon the adoption of the sixth paragraph of the fourth Resolution, and it was adopted.

The President.—The Secretary will please read the next paragraph of the Report.

The paragraph is as follows:—

"And it is recommended that the several Governments take measures to keep all their seagoing vessels supplied with copies of such instructions."

Mr. Kimball (United States).—Mr. President, I move the adoption of the recommendation.

The President.—Is the Conference ready for the question?

The question was put to the Conference upon the adoption of the above recommendation, and it was adopted.

The President.—The fifth Resolution will now be read.

The fifth Resolution is as follows:—

"5. *Resolved,*—That the Conference recommend that the several nations provide by legislative enactments for official inquiry into the causes and circumstances of all shipwrecks and other serious casualties happening to their vessels."

Mr. Kimball (United States).—Mr. President, such legislative enactment exists in some countre already, and, I understand, is found very effective in the prevention of wrong by the operation which it has in enforcing compliance with the Rules of the Road. Mr. Gray, the Delegate to this Convention from Great Britain, who has gone home, was before our Committee with reference to this, and he pronounced it one of the most satisfactory Statutes upon the English Statute-book. I move the adoption of this Resolution.

Mr. Hall (Great Britain).—Mr. President, I can bear my personal testimony to the fact that the legislative enactments with regard to the official inquiry into the causes and circumstances of stranded vessels has certainly been productive of a very good effect indeed, and I believe it exercises a wholesome influence over the masters and officers in the marine service, when they know that if they infringe the Rules which are laid down, either the Rules of the Road at Sea or the instructions which are laid before them by the Board of Trade, that they are liable to have their certificates either suspended or cancelled. These inquiries take place in Great Britain before a Judge, who is assisted by three experts, who advise him upon all nautical matters, and the whole conduct of the officer in charge of the vessel that is wrecked or stranded is inquired into very carefully. That Court does not hesitate, in a case where they find that the provisions which are laid down by the law or by the State Departments are violated, to inflict a very serious punishment, as I am sure you will all agree it is, which in many cases amounts to depriving a man of his certificate, or of degrading him from the position of master, and giving him a certificate of a second mate, or, in some cases, depriving him of his certificate for a long space of time. As I say, I believe this enactment has been one of very great use indeed, and we should be very glad to see similar enactments adopted by all the Maritime Powers.

Captain Shackford (United States).—Mr. President, I want to say that I am somewhat familiar with the operation of this Act of Great Britain, and I very strongly recommend its adoption by this Conference.

The President.—The Secretary will please read the fifth Resolution again, before taking a vote.

The fifth Resolution is as follows:—

"*Resolved,*—That the Conference recommend that the several nations provide by legislative enactment for official inquiry into the causes and circumstances of all shipwrecks and other serious casualties happening to their vessels."

The President.—Is the Conference ready for the question?

The question was put to the Conference upon the adoption of the fifth Resolution, and it was adopted.

The President.—The question would seem to be upon the adoption of the Report of the Committee.

Mr. Kimball (United States).—Mr. President, I move that the Report of the Committee on Life-Saving Systems and Devices be adopted.

The President.—The question is before the Conference as to the adoption of the Report of the Committee as an entirety.

The question was put to the Conference as to the adoption of the Report as an entirety, and it was adopted.

Lieutenant Beaugency (Chile).—Mr. President, I will ask permission now to present an amendment to the Report of the Committee on Collocation.

The President.—By general consent it can be done. The Chair understands that the Conference made a rule upon that subject, but if there be no objection the amendment will be admitted.

Lieutenant Beaugency (Chile).—Mr. President, I desire to present an amendment, because in the Conference it has now been decided by unanimous consent that a red rocket shall be used as a signal. I presented an amendment before this Conference that the red rocket should be used as a distress signal, and it was overruled because it was said that the red rocket was dangerous, and they now adopt it. Let me take one expression from the learned Delegate from Germany, Dr. Sieveking: "At this moment I fall in love with this amendment."

Mr. Hall (Great Britain).—Mr. President, I apprehend that we are somewhat out of order in discussing such an amendment. I will point out, however, that the red light is a very different thing on shore from the red light carried on board the vessel in very warm latitudes.

The President.—It is only by general consent of the Conference that any other amendment with regard to the Rules of the Road can be admitted. If there be no objection, it is admitted. Does the Chair understand that there is an objection to this amendment of the Delegate from Chile?

Dr. Sieveking (Germany).—Mr. President, I think that we ought not to allow any exceptions. There has been ample time for the amendment to be brought in up to 7 o'clock on Saturday night, and if we, by courtesy, allow any one Delegate to present an amendment after that time I do not see any reason why we shall not do this in other cases.

The President.—The Chair desires to state to the Delegate from Chile that time was given to hand in amendments until 7 o'clock on Saturday evening, and as this amendment was not handed in prior to that time it is out of order.

Lieutenant Beaugency (Chile).—Mr. President, I do not propose the amendment now, but I propose it only for consideration with the Report of the Committee on Collocation, because the Conference unanimously adopted previously the principle that the red rocket is dangerous, and now they have adopted it as a signal. I will state to the learned Delegate Mr. Hall that after my amendment was voted down I received information from pyrotechnic manufacturing houses, and they told me that these lights were not dangerous and they did not know of any case of their exploding; and many of the officers around our table have said the same thing.

Mr. Hall (Great Britain).—Mr. President, I will only say, in answer to the gallant Delegate, that of course the fact that any gentleman has written and said that he does not know of a case of this kind occurring does not necessarily outweigh the testimony of those who have known of such cases occurring, and I am told that in some cases the use of red rockets has been given up in warm latitudes because it has been found that they go off spontaneously. I do not care to lengthen this discussion, as I apprehend that it is not in order. I only desire to state that the practical fact has occurred, and that we are aware of it.

Lieutenant Beaugency (Chile).—Mr. President, I will withdraw the amendment.

The Conference thereupon took a recess until 2 o'clock.

After Recess.

The President.—The first subject for consideration this afternoon will be the Report of the Committee on General Divisions II, IV, and VI of the Programme. The Secretary will please read the Report.

The Report of the Committee on General Divisions II, IV, and VI is as follows:—

"Sir, "*Washington, D.C., December 5*, 1889.

"The Committee appointed to examine and report upon the subjects contained in General Divisions II, IV, and VI of the Programme proposed by the United States' Delegates beg to submit the following Report:—

"GENERAL DIVISION II.

"*Regulations to determine the Seaworthiness of Vessels.*

" (*a.*) Construction of vessels.
" (*b.*) Equipment of vessels.
" (*c.*) Discipline of crew.
" (*d.*) Sufficiency of crew.
" (*e.*) Inspection of vessels.
" (*f.*) Uniform certificates of inspection.

" It is the opinion of the Committee that, upon the subjects contained in the sections of this Division, no International Rule could be made which would secure beneficial results. It is thought that the Conference would be limited in each case to a recommendation fixing a minimum for the objects which it is desired to secure under each of these sections. If such a minimum were made the legal requirement, it would have an injurious effect upon the present standard of efficiency in many countries.

" 2. In other countries, where such efficiency does not exist, it is thought that it will be best secured by the same means which have secured it elsewhere, leaving each nation to modify such means in ways which will best adapt them to the particular methods of the respective Governments.

" 3. Again, it is found that the present Rules existing in different countries upon several of these questions are different in many respects, though probably equally efficient. It would therefore become necessary, in forming an international Rule in such cases, to recommend changes in the existing Rules of several countries, which to some of them might be impracticable. This is thought to be undesirable. However, the Committee earnestly recommend that—

" All vessels, whether propelled by steam or sail, should possess a margin of strength over and above that which is required to enable them to perform the work for which they were designed and built. A chain, a bridge, or any other structure, the failure of which would entail the loss of human life, invariably has a considerable reserve of strength provided; in other words, the admitted working load is always much less than the computed strength, or the strength ascertained by actual test; certainly it is no less important that the hull of a vessel should contain a similar reserve.

" 5. To attempt to formulate rules for the construction of vessels of all sizes and for all trades would far exceed the province of this Committee; and, besides, any arbitrary rules would probably much hamper the advance in design and the method of construction.

" 6. Therefore, to obtain as much as seems to be practicable in this direction, it is desirable to rely upon efficient and oft-repeated inspection, when, upon the least indication of distress or of rupture showing, very substantial additions should be made before the vessel is allowed to again proceed to sea.

" 7. Ocean-going steam-vessels which carry passengers should be additionally protected by having efficient bulkheads, so spaced that, when any two compartments be filled with water, the vessel will still remain in a seaworthy condition, and two at least of the amidships bulkheads should be tested by water pressure to the height of the deck next above the water-line.

"GENERAL DIVISION IV.

" *Uniform Regulations regarding the Designating and Marking of Vessels.*

" (*a.*) Position of name on vessels.
" (*b.*) Position of name of port of registry on vessels.
" (*c.*) Size of lettering.
" (*d.*) Uniform system of draught marks.

" 1. The name of every registered merchant-vessel shall be marked upon each bow and upon the stern, and the port of registry of every such vessel shall be marked upon the stern.

" These names shall be marked in Roman letters in a light colour on a dark ground, or in a dark colour on a light ground, and to be distinctly visible.

" The smallest letters used shall not be less than 4 inches high.

" 2. The draught of every registered vessel shall be marked upon the stem and stern-post in English feet or decimetres, in either Arabic or Roman numerals. The bottom of each numeral shall indicate the draught to that line.

"GENERAL DIVISION VI.

' *Necessary Qualifications for Officers and Seamen, including Tests for Sight and Colour-Blindness.*

" (*a.*) A uniform system of examination for the different grades.
" (*b.*) Uniform tests for visual power and colour-blindness.
" (*c.*) General knowledge of methods employed at life-saving stations.
" (*d.*) Uniform certificates of qualification.

" 1. Every man or boy going to sea as a seaman, or with the intention of becoming a seaman, should be examined for visual power and colour-blindness; and no man or boy should be permitted to serve on board any vessel in the capacity of seaman, or where he will have to stand look-out, whose visual power is below one-half normal, or who is red and green colour-blind.

" 2. Every man who shall qualify as an officer of a registered vessel after the adoption of these Rules, except engineer officers, shall be required to have a certificate that he has the necessary visual power, and that he is not red and green blind. He shall also have a certificate that he is familiar with the Regulations for preventing Collisions at Sea, and with the duties required of him in co-operating with a life-saving station in case his vessel is stranded.

"It is recommended that each country provide means which will enable any boy or man intending to go to sea to have his eyes examined for visual power and colour-blindness, and to obtain a certificate of the result; also to enable the master of any vessel to have the eyes of any of his crew tested for the same purpose.

"It is the opinion of the Committee that defective visual power and colour-blindness are sources of danger at sea. The first, both by day and night, because of the inability of the short-sighted to see objects at a sufficient distance. Colour-blindness is a source of danger, more especially at night, because of the inability of a colour-blind person to distinguish between the red and green side-lights. The inability on the part of an officer or look-out to distinguish the colour of buoys may be a cause of accident in broad daylight.

"It is the opinion of the Committee, however, that tests for these defects need not be enforced in the cases of masters and mates who already occupy such positions.

"The Committee purposely avoid making any recommendation as to the methods to be used in making such tests for visual power and colour-blindness, or in conducting the necessary examinations for officers. It is thought that the desired objects will be best secured by leaving each country to employ the methods which may seem most suitable.

(Signed) "CHEN NGEN TAO.
"MAN'L ARAGON.
"CHR. DONNER.
"JAMES WIMSHURST.
"H. SETTEMBRINI.
"W. T. SAMPSON, *Chairman*.
"Captain H. LANNÉLUC.
"Captain L. SALDANHA DA GAMA.
"T. SALVESEN."

"To Rear-Admiral Samuel R. Franklin, United States' Navy,
"President International Marine Conference, Washington, D.C."

Captain Mensing (Germany).—Mr. President, I would simply like to say for myself that I understood the other day that the Report of the Collocation Committee would take precedence of all other Committee Reports. I understood that this was so, and that we should not take up the discussion of any of these Reports before the Report of the Collocation Committee was finally disposed of, and on that account I have not been reading any of these Reports. I do not doubt that it is my own fault, and I am very sorry for it, but it is so, and I do not think I would be able to take any responsibility for this Report if it be adopted now. Therefore, I would state this fact here, because I think there may be several points to come up for discussion in the Conference, or the whole Report may be adopted without giving rise to any discussion whatever. I wish to ask, personally, that a little time be given to consider thirty-two distinct amendments which have been laid before us in the Report of the Collocation Committee, and which I have been unable to look at. If we have five hours' discussion to-day and five hours to-morrow, and if we attend the delightful entertainment at which I am to be present as a member of this Conference, I do not see how I would have any time in which to prepare myself, so that, when the Report of the Collocation Committee comes under discussion the day after to-morrow, I should have nothing to say on the subject, or should be in no way prepared as I would like to be under the circumstances.

Captain Sampson (United States).—Mr. President, I desire to state that perhaps the difficulties which have been mentioned by the gallant Delegate from Germany will be met by the consideration of the two Reports which are now before the Conference, and it may then be possible to give all of those who desire it all day to-morrow to consider the Report of the Committee on Collocation, and to prepare for its discussion.

The President.—Is the Delegate from Germany prepared to go on with the Report that has just been mentioned?

Captain Mensing (Germany).—Mr. President, I only wanted to point out that it would be on record that I have not taken any part in this discussion, and I have had no chance to study this Report, and have had no opportunity to inform myself about it. I would, therefore, be glad to have it appear on record that I have taken no part in this discussion, in case any point should be brought up by my Government, so that they should not hold me responsible in the matter.

The President.—The Chair does not understand the Delegate to make any motion with regard to it.

Captain Mensing (Germany).—Mr. President, I do not make any motion.

The President.—The Chair desires to know the sense of the Conference as to whether they should proceed with this Report under the circumstances or not.

Mr. Hall (Great Britain).—Mr. President, it was pointed most clearly that we should give precedence to the Report of the Collocation Committee, but that we should take up the Reports when we had time unoccupied by that work. I pointed out distinctly that the order of business to-day and to-morrow would be, when we had finished the discussion of the question as to whether the reconsideration of principle should be accepted by the Conference as worthy of discussion, and we should occupy the rest of our time in dealing with such Reports as have been handed in. Of course it would be a great loss to us not to have the assistance of the gallant Delegate from Germany; but I think that we are all of us agreed that we ought to take these Reports up to-day, after we have finished with the question as to the consideration of amendments upon principle. I pointed out that that would not

[93]

occupy all of our time to-day and to-morrow, and therefore we ought to go on with the Reports now before us.

The President.—The Delegate from the United States moves to take up the Report on General Divisions II, IV, and VI of the Programme.

The question on the motion of the Delegate from the United States was put to the Conference, and carried.

Captain Sampson (United States).—Mr. President, I would propose that the Report of the Committee on General Divisions II, IV, and VI be considered by Divisions. As no positive Rule has been recommended under General Division II, I would move that the Report of the Committee with regard to that Division be adopted.

The President.—The question is upon the adoption of the Report of the Committee with regard to General Division II.

Captain Van Steyn (the Netherlands).—Mr. President, as no Resolution has been put into this Division, I would like to ask whether it is not wise to say something about the boats to be carried on board of these vessels. We have dealt with that under the Report of the Committee on Life-Saving Systems and Devices on General Division V, but I think that we should refer to that subdivision in this Report, with regard to the boats to be carried on board of vessels.

Captain Sampson (United States).—Mr. President, this subject of the equipment of vessels with regard to her boats, life-rafts, &c., was the subject of careful consideration by the Committee, and we were unable to see our way to making Rules. In different vessels of the same size the requirements would be very different, depending upon whether they carried passengers or not. The only thing upon which the number of boats can be prescribed would be [the number of people on board. But here again we are met with a difficulty that in many of our large passenger vessels it is impossible to carry boats sufficient to float all of the persons on board in case the vessel should sink. The number of boats which it would be necessary for a ship to carry would depend very much upon the method of construction used in the vessel herself. If a ship is constructed with several watertight compartments, the necessity for boats is not so great as in a vessel where this method of construction does not exist. Consequently, in prescribing the number of boats to be carried, we would have to enter into the question of the construction of the vessels themselves, in order to decide how many boats in any particular case a vessel should carry; and as it seemed impossible to make a Rule which would meet such a variety of circumstances, the Committee are of the opinion that it would be best to leave it to the Inspectors of the Service in each Government.

Captain Van Steyn (the Netherlands).—Mr. President, may I only point out that in dealing with the Report of the Committee on Life-Saving Systems and Devices, the Committee adopted the second Resolution :—

"That the Conference approve of the Rules made by the Board of Trade of Great Britain under 'The Merchant Shipping (Life-Saving Appliances) Act, 1888,' relating to boats and appliances to be carried on board ships for saving life, and recommend that the several Governments adopt measures to secure compliance with this principle in regard to such boats and appliances for vessels of 150 tons and upwards gross tonnage.

"It is also recommended that the principle of these Rules be extended to all smaller craft as far as practicable, and that each vessel of this class should carry at least one life-buoy of approved pattern and material, and for every person on board an efficient life-belt or jacket."

We have made that recommendation in that Report, and it seems to me that it would be better to refer to it here.

Captain Sampson (United States).—Mr. President, I see no objection, as that Rule has already been adopted, and it decides the question, as far as the Conference is concerned, with reference to the equipment of vessels with boats, life-rafts, &c.; although I do not think it covers the ground.

Mr. Hall (Great Britain).—Mr. President, may I point out to the gallant Delegate from the Netherlands that the Report which we have before us this morning will form a part of the Protocol, from which it will appear that they have dealt with this matter, so that it will be merely a repetition for other matter to be inserted in this Report, when we already have it in the Report of the Committee on Life-Saving Systems and Devices? I think he will see that it will not be necessary to have it inserted in here as well, because both of these matters will form part of the proceedings of the Conference in the Protocol.

Captain Van Steyn (the Netherlands).—Mr. President, it was not my opinion that these words should be inserted, but I only desired to refer to it as appearing in the Report of the Committee on General Division V.

Mr. Hall (Great Britain).—Mr. President, that of course will be met by the reference made to it by the gallant Delegate from the Netherlands. What he has said this afternoon will appear in the Protocol and form a part of it, and that will attract the attention of foreign Governments who look at the Report of the Committee which we passed this morning, and read it in conjunction with this Report, so that he will attain his object by having brought the attention of the Conference to the matter just now.

The President.—The question then will be upon the adoption of the Report of the Committee on General Division II. Is the Conference ready for the question? The Chair takes it for granted that the Delegates are all familiar with it, and will put the question without having it read a second time, if there be no objection.

The question was put to the Conference upon the adoption of the Report of the Committee upon General Division II, and that Report was adopted.

163

The President.—The Report upon General Division IV will now be considered, and it will be considered by paragraphs. The first paragraph will be read:—

"GENERAL DIVISION IV.

"*Uniform Regulations regarding the Designating and Marking of Vessels.*

" (*a.*) Position of name on vessels.
" (*b.*) Position of name of port of registry on vessels.
" (*c.*) Size of lettering.
" (*d.*) Uniform system of draught marks.

" 1. The name of every registered merchant-vessel shall be marked upon each bow and upon the stern, and the port of registry of every such vessel shall be marked upon the stern.

" These names shall be marked in Roman letters in a light colour on a dark ground, or in a dark colour on a light ground, and to be distinctly visible.

" The smallest letters used shall not be less than 4 inches high."

Captain Sampson (United States).—Mr. President, it is only necessary for me to point out that in submitting this Rule the Committee have followed what seemed to be the general practice among those nations which have a Rule upon the subject. Of course the object aimed at in marking vessels in this way, or in any way, is to enable other vessels to recognize them and know their names and ports of registry in case of a collision, or where for any other purpose it is necessary to know the name and port of registry of a vessel. The size of the letters and the method of placing them, of course, have for their object to secure the greatest possible distinctness, and not to make a Rule too limited, but so as to allow a certain latitude for large vessels. Therefore, the lower limit in regard to the size of the letters is the only one which has been prescribed. In some countries it is the practice to fix the size of the letters of vessels of different classes, but the Committee thought that so long as the name would be distinctly visible, and as the inclination would be in marking vessels to proportion the size of the letters to the size of the vessel, the object desired would be secured if the Rule which the Committee recommend should be adopted.

Captain Richard (France).—Mr. President, in our country we consider that the length or the dimensions of the letters, in order to be perfectly visible, should attain 20 centim. That amounts to something like 8 inches, or about double that which is proposed by the Committee. In establishing this dimension the Committee probably were led by very good reasons; but it seems to me that the object which is sought, by prescribing that a vessel's name shall be marked either on the bow or on the stern, is especially to render that name visible at a certain distance. There are many circumstances when it may be necessary for such a name to be recognizable at a distance, and for that reason you have placed it on the bow as well as on the stern. Following that order of ideas, I maintain my opinion that it would be a great advantage to increase the dimensions of those letters, and to make them 20 centim.

There is another point to which I desire to call your attention. The general custom in the merchant navy—I am not speaking of the military navy—is to mark the name of the vessels on the boats and on the life-buoys, so that if the vessel is lost some wreckage may be found bearing the name of the vessel, which can indicate her sad fate. By so doing we will not prevent collisions, but we can render a service to humanity. In some countries, when, in consequence of a shipwreck or a disaster at sea, men disappear beneath the ocean, a certain period must elapse after the accident in order that, if their bodies are not found and identified, they shall be declared legally dead, so as to enable the consequences resulting therefrom to proceed, such, for instance, as the opening of their estates. It is true that the necessity of officially establishing such disappearances does not directly concern this Conference. But, nevertheless, it is a matter which we should provide for, and which, I think, would be well for us to settle.

I, therefore, propose that the Conference should admit that it would be proper to paint the name of the vessel likewise on her boats and on her life-buoys.

Captain Sampson (United States).—Mr. President, I think that the remarks of the gallant Delegate from France are very appropriate for vessels of a certain size. But the Committee had in view the smallest letters which would be employed, and of course they should be adapted to the smallest vessels requiring them. I imagine that in all cases where the size of the vessel would warrant it that the smallest letters used would be probably larger than 4 inches, which is only about 10 centim. high. But this only places the limit on the very smallest letters for small vessels. It is probable that some of the letters will be larger, even on small vessels, than is prescribed in this Rule.

Mr. Carter (Hawaii).—Mr. President, I would like to point out that the legibility of a vessel's name does not always depend upon the length of the letters. I have seen vessels at sea where we could not make out their names, because the letters were crowded so closely together. Although they may have been 4 to 6 inches high, yet they were crowded so closely together that we could not make them out. I speak of this merely that it may go upon the Protocol that attention was drawn to this fact, and it would have been well, I think, if the Committee, when they discussed the minimum length of the letters, had also fixed how near they should be to each other, so that each letter might stand out prominently by itself to enable another vessel to read it. Perhaps the words, " shall be distinctly visible," in the preceding line cover that point.

Captain Sampson (United States).—Mr. President, I would like to point out that that was what the Committee had in view. A proposition was made to fix the proportion between the length and the height of the letters, but in many cases, of course, the length of the name would naturally modify that, and the Committee were all of the opinion that this clause, " be distinctly visible," if it were inserted, would cover the ground, as suggested by the learned Delegate from Hawaii.

Mr. Hall (Great Britain).—Mr. President, I am sure we shall all agree with the gallant Delegate from France that it is desirable that the names should be painted in letters of a sufficient size, but as the gallant Delegate from the United States has pointed out, this is a minimum Rule for all vessels, and therefore the smallest vessels will be compelled to have letters of this size. Now, is this not a matter which we can leave to the authorities of each country, to see, first of all, that they are of a proper size, and, secondly, that they are properly printed and properly coloured, as the Rule provides? In England we have a minimum size of 4 inches for our letters, and our Surveyors will not give a certificate to a vessel to clear until they are satisfied that her name is printed properly and legibly. Until the Surveyor is satisfied of that, he does not give a certificate to enable a vessel to clear the Customs.

I think that if we pass this general Rule, and leave it to the authorities of the respective countries, that it will be the better course, and that we will leave it in safe hands, so that the safeguards suggested by the Delegate from France will be properly carried out. I think he will see that we could not resolve upon a larger figure than this, for the reason that in some very small vessels it would be a very great advantage to provide for this limit. Under this provision the smallest vessels can comply with the minimum size of the letters, and then the other vessels can increase the size in ratio. But we could not very well classify them and give a distinct number of inches to vessels of different tonnages. I think we ought to leave that to the Governments of each country or to the Supervisors, and adopt this general Rule, that they are to be marked distinctly with letters of a minimum size of 4 inches.

Captain Van Steyn (the Netherlands).—Mr. President, I rise merely to ask for information. As I understand it, all vessels under this Rule are to have their names printed somewhere. If I am not mistaken, there are some vessels at present which are not compelled to have them; for instance, fishing-vessels duly registered; inland vessels which are only marked on the stern; and yachts belonging to recognized clubs. They are not compelled to have these names.

The President.—The question will be upon the motion of the Delegate from France. The Secretary will please read the motion.

The motion of the Delegate from France is as follows:—

"That 8 inches be the height of the smallest letters."

Captain Richard (France).—Mr. President, I desire to say a word in regard to the subject which has been developed by the eminent Delegate from Great Britain, that it is not here a question of tonnage. In fact, I do not think that we should stop to consider this question of tonnage, for the only question here is visibility. Whatever may be the tonnage of a vessel, her name should be so marked upon her as to be plainly distinguishable. That is why I propose 20 centim., or 8 inches, instead of 4 inches. For fishing-vessels we need not have the same consideration, because they have besides certain characters (letters or numbers) marked on their sails which enable them to be distinguished. In fact, they generally have a number on their sail with a letter which indicates the port or the maritime district to which they belong. But the Rule now before us would apply to coasting vessels as well as to merchant-vessels in general. I think we can adopt the Rule which has been adopted in France, namely, to require lettering 20 centim. in height.

Captain Van Steyn (the Netherlands).—Mr. President, in our country we have made some experiments, and according to these the visual test adopted is that these letters are to be visible with the naked eye 60 metres. We do not object to the height of 4 inches if that will render them visible with the naked eye 60 metres.

Captain Richard (France).—Mr. President, will you allow me to make a remark? I do not say that the letters could not be made 20 centim, 25 centim., or 30 centim. if you wanted to, but I intend to say this, that with 4 inches, which is 10 centim., those letters are too small and are not sufficiently visible.

Mr. Carter (Hawaii).—Mr. President, I would like to point out to the gallant Delegate from France that 8 inches as a minimum would be a very long letter, and to make the proper proportions the letters would have to be almost 6 inches apart. Now, with a proper allowance for space between the letters it would take 7 inches, and for a name of ten letters it would require 70 inches, which would be, on ordinary vessels, more than they could spare on the stern. It should also be remembered that a great many names run over ten letters.

Captain Richard (France).—Mr. President, if the honourable Delegate from Hawaii will allow me, I would state that if that is the only practical difficulty which embarrasses him, I am quite ready to solve it for him. The 20 centim. which I propose are used in France. That is the rule which until now has been applied by us, and we have found no difficulty whatever in applying it. I, therefore, think that the difficulty pointed out by the honourable Delegate from Hawaii is solved by its being in actual practice. The consideration is solely limited to the question of visibility. If you think that with 4 inches visibility is perfect, then vote for 4 inches. If you think that 4-inch letters are not absolutely visible, make it 6 inches; make it 7 inches if you do not want 8 inches, but increase the size.

The President.—The question is upon the motion of the Delegate from France to increase the size of the letters proposed by the Committee to 8 inches in height. Is the Conference ready for the question?

The question was put to the Conference upon the motion of the Delegate from France.

The President.—The Chair is unable to decide.

Captain Sampson (United States).—I call for the Yeas and Nays.

The Yea and Nay vote is as follows:—

Austria-Hungary	Nay.	Japan		Nay.
Belgium	Yea.	Mexico		Nay.
China	Yea.	Norway		Nay
Chile	Yea.	Russia		Yea.
Denmark	Nay.	Spain		Yea.
France	Yea.	Sweden		Yea.
Germany	Nay.	Siam		Yea.
Great Britain	Nay.	The Netherlands		Yea.
Hawaii	Nay.	United States		Nay.
Italy	Nay.			

The President.—The vote is 9 in the affirmative, and 10 in the negative, so the motion is lost.

The question will now be on proposition No. 1, which the Secretary will read for the information of the Conference.

The proposition is as follows:—

"1. The name of every registered merchant-vessel shall be marked upon each bow and upon the stern, and the port of registry of every such vessel shall be marked upon the stern.

"These names shall be marked in Roman letters in a light colour on a dark ground, or in a dark colour on a light ground, and to be distinctly visible.

"The smallest letters used shall not be less than 4 inches high."

The President.—Is the Conference ready for the question?

The question was put to the Conference upon the adoption of the first proposition contained in the Report of the Committee on General Division IV, and it was adopted.

The President.—The Secretary will now please read the second proposition.

The second proposition is as follows:—

"2. The draft of every registered vessel shall be marked upon the stem and stern-post in English feet or decimetres, in either Arabic or Roman numerals. The bottom of each numeral shall indicate the draught to that line."

Captain Sampson (United States).—Mr. President, it is hardly necessary for me to say that the Committee in recommending this Rule have followed the usual practice in marking the draught of vessels. We have not prescribed that a vessel should be marked on both sides of the stem and stern-posts, as we thought that was unnecessary. Probably in most large vessels this would be the practice. I might also say that the size of the letters was not prescribed, as it is usual in marking in feet to make the figures 6 inches high, so that the top of the figure shall mark one-half a foot or 6 inches. But on small vessels this might not be considered best, and as the draught is simply for the information of those who are concerned in the draught of water of the ship, as a pilot when taking her into a harbour or in docking a ship, it was not deemed necessary to make the figures so large as in marking the name of the vessel.

The President.—The question is upon the adoption of the second proposition of the Report of the Committee on General Division IV.

Admiral Bowden-Smith (Great Britain).—Mr. President, may I ask for information why they are to be marked in Roman and Arabic characters? If they are to be marked in that way, why not in Chinese or Siamese?

Captain Sampson (United States).—Mr. President, I will answer the gallant Delegate from England that the Committee were of the opinion that they should be marked in either one or the other, and that either would be well understood. Of course, a ship marked in Chinese numerals would hardly be understood by pilots in other parts of the world.

The President.—The Secretary will please read the second proposition.

The second proposition of the Committee on General Division IV is as follows:—

"2. The draught of every registered vessel shall be marked upon the stem and stern-post in English feet or decimetres, in either Arabic or Roman numerals. The bottom of each numeral shall indicate the draught to that line."

Lieutenant Beaugency (Chile).—Mr. President, I think it would avoid confusion if the marking of these ships were made in feet or centimetres, and that those marked in English feet were marked in the Arabic numerals, and those in centimetres were marked in the Roman numerals.

Captain Sampson (United States).—Mr. President, I will say that this was a subject of discussion in the Committee and they thought it best not to place that restriction upon the method of marking vessels. It has its advantages, as pointed out by the gallant Delegate from Chile, and I am sure that the Committee will have no objection to adopting such a Rule if the Conference see fit to do so. Of course, this would probably necessitate the changing of the marking on vessels now afloat.

Lieutenant Beaugency (Chile).—Mr. President, it would change the marking on the ships now afloat, but that is a very easy matter. When they come into dock there can be a new marking put on them.

The President.—The Delegate from Chile proposes that vessels marked in feet shall be marked with Roman numerals, and those marked in centimetres shall be marked with Arabic characters.

Captain Sampson (United States).—Mr. President, it is just the other way, I think.

The President.—Will the Delegate from Chile be kind enough to put his motion in writing, so that we can understand it? The Delegate from Chile proposes to mark the vessels whose draught is given in English feet with Arabic characters, and those given in centimetres with Roman characters.

Captain Sampson (United States).—Mr. President, I would like to point out that that would necessitate very great changes.

Captain Shackford (United States).—Nearly all vessels in England are marked just exactly the contrary way now.

Mr. Hall (Great Britain).—Mr. President, I think the vast majority of vessels are marked in Roman numerals, and the result of this proposition would be that a great many vessels would have to be changed.

Captain Sampson (United States).—Mr. President, I do not think that it would be practicable to do that, because a ship which is drawing 60 or 70 centim. would require very large numbers, which would take up a foot or two, to mark the draught of a ship.

The President.—Is the Conference ready for the question?

Mr. Verbrugghe (Belgium).—Mr. President, will the gallant Delegate from Chile limit his amendment to a recommendation, as I consider it to be very good? But I am unable to vote for it, because there is no way that we can oblige all vessels to change their marks. Perhaps the gallant Delegate from Chile would be satisfied if we should say that such a thing was recommended. But if we have to vote upon the proposition as it stands, I shall be obliged to vote against it.

The President.—Does the Delegate from Chile accept the suggestion of the Delegate from Belgium, to let it be inserted in the Proctocol as a recommendation, or does he wish to have a vote taken upon it?

Lieutenant Beaugency (Chile).—Mr. President, I am very sorry I cannot accept the suggestion of the honourable Delegate from Belgium, because I think it important to know whether a ship is to be marked in feet or centimetres. I hope you will allow me to have a vote upon my amendment.

The President.—The question is upon the amendment of the Delegate from Chile, who proposes that ships whose draught is given in English feet shall be marked with Arabic characters, and those given in centimetres with Roman characters.

Captain Shackford (United States).—Mr. President, before a vote is taken upon that I would like to call attention to the fact that this is exactly the contrary to the way in which vessels are marked now.

Lieutenant Beaugency (Chile).—Let them change.

Mr. Hall (Great Britain).—Mr. President, may I point out that there is no proposal here to mark them in centimetres?

The President.—The Delegate from Chile proposes to have a ship's draught which is given in English feet marked in Roman characters, and those given in centimetres in Arabic characters. That is the proposition now before the Conference. The Chair has put the proposition the other way, and it was decided that it was not the correct way. Now I put it in this way, which the Delegate from Chile proposes.

Captain Richard (France).—Mr. President, I have no objection to vote for the decimetres in Arabic figures, because that is the method which we employ in France. Consequently our interests are entirely protected, and we would have to make no change, and therefore no expense in order to conform to the Rule laid down in the proposition of the honourable Delegate from Chile. But if you ask us to mark our decimetres in Roman numbers, then I will vote against the proposition, because we would be obliged to change our system of numbering. If, therefore, the decimetres should be marked in Arabic numbers I see no reason to make any objection in behalf of our Delegation. It will only be for our colleagues from Great Britain to show how they will accommodate themselves to Arabic numbers to express in feet how much water a vessel draws.

Mr. Verbrugghe (Belgium).—I will vote in the same manner.

Mr. Hall (Great Britain).—Mr. President, may I represent the other horn of the dilemma? My gallant friend the Delegate from France objects to the proposal to mark centimetres in Roman letters because he says the vessels are numbered in a different way now in his country. In England it is just the reverse. The Roman letters are used, and I shall object if the proposal is for the figures to be marked in Arabic letters. So I am sure that my gallant friend the Delegate from Chile is on the horns of this dilemma, and either France must vote against him or England must vote against him, and I think he must take his choice.

Captain Sampson (United States).—Mr. President, it seems to me that this discussion shows very clearly that the Rule which the Committee recommended is the only one which can be adopted.

The President.—The question is upon the motion of the Delegate from Chile that the English feet should be designated in Roman letters, and the centimetres in Arabic numerals.

Lieutenant Beaugency (Chile).—Mr. President, in this case, after the very important reasons which the Delegate from England has advanced, I withdraw my amendment.

The President.—The question is upon the second proposal of the Committee.

The question was put to the Conference upon the adoption of the second proposal of the Committee on General Division IV, and it was adopted.

The President.—The Secretary will please read the first paragraph of the Report upon General Division VI.

The first paragraph is as follows:—

"GENERAL DIVISION VI.

"*Necessary Qualifications for Officers and Seamen, including Tests for Sight and Colour-Blindness.*

"(*a.*) A uniform system of examination for the different grades.
"(*b.*) Uniform tests for visual power and colour-blindness.

"(c.) General knowledge of methods employed at life-saving stations.
"(d.) Uniform certificates of qualification.

"1. Every man or boy going to sea as a seaman, or with the intention of becoming a seaman, should be examined for visual power and colour-blindness; and no man or boy should be permitted to serve on board any vessel in the capacity of seaman, or where he will have to stand look-out, whose visual power is below one-half normal or who is red and green colour-blind."

Captain Richard (France).—Mr. President, I hope that my colleagues on the Committee will bear me no grudge if I allow myself a slight criticism on General Division VI. This Division contains, as you will see in the Programme, four subdivisions (*a*), (*b*), (*c*), and (*d*), which must be treated separately. In the first place there is a system of general examination for the various grades; then that which concerns visual power and colour-blindness; third, the general knowledge of the methods employed at life-saving stations, and lastly, fourth, what may be said in favour of uniform certificates for masters of merchant and coasting vessels, &c. I do not know whether the Committee was embarrassed in its work, but I clearly see that in this entire chapter there is no question of anything else than colour-blindness. It considers that there is no other impediment to sailors exercising their calling than colour-blindness, and it starts in by saying: "That every man or boy going to sea with the intention of becoming a sailor shall be examined for visual power and colour-blindness, and no man may serve on board of a vessel if he suffers from colour-blindness."

Very well. Is it always in every one's power to choose his profession, and can any one be a sailor who wishes to be? Most assuredly the majority of those who go to sea would prefer, probably, to be bankers, barristers, advocates, or presidents of some large corporation. But they are born of a family of sailors; they are well built, vigorous, they have a good constitution, and they go to sea because their family has a craft to receive them and to teach them the hard apprenticeship of their life's calling. Should there be any worry as to whether they are afflicted with colour-blindness? Never since the world's existence has it been possible to claim that a person afflicted with colour-blindness should not be a sailor. Does colour-blindness unfit him for a fisherman; does it prevent him from holding a line; does it prevent him from throwing out a net, from cutting open a cod, from harpooning a whale, or from any other occupation of the same kind? I would like to know what induced the Committee to make this Rule. I would like to know why you are going to prevent men from earning their bread and to say to them, " My son, inasmuch as you cannot distinguish a red light from a green light, you are forbidden to earn your bread in the only way that it is easy for you to do." I, for my part, cannot accept such a theory.

In France there is the "Inscription Maritime," and from Dunkirk to Nice we have sailors who are sailors because they are born of sailors' families, and who commenced their calling in their tender years. They cannot change their profession, as you seem to think, because they are afflicted with colour-blindness. Instead of being so severe on colour-blindness the Committee should have shown itself more indulgent, and it should have allowed its severity to rest upon the examination for various grades. It should have told us that there are in this world improvised merchant captains who have no certificate and who command vessels without any guaranty, thereby endangering the existence of their own crew and threatening the existence of the crews of other vessels. I think that the attention of the Committee should have been directed with greater severity towards paragraph (*a*), which treats of that subject, than to paragraph (*b*). They might then have better earned the gratitude of humanity.

Because a person is afflicted with colour-blindness he is not blind; his eye-sight is not bad. Such a person can see very clearly in the day-time, and also during the night. And if we make of colour-blindness a latent defect so as to prevent a man from pursuing his calling, we might, on the other hand, reproach ourselves and say that, inasmuch as there are people who are afflicted with colour-blindness, instead of prescribing red or green lights, the Conference should have invented a system of lights which will allow of no possible confusion even to persons afflicted with colour-blindness. But to say that a man may not follow the sea because he is afflicted with colour-blindness is enough to nullify the entire paragraph. I think that the Committee made a mistake by recommending such a measure. You cannot make sailors as you can tin soldiers. A man is a sailor because he has been trained that way. If you can assure those whom you reject a happier means of existence, one which is easier and less burdensome, certainly no one will hesitate to adopt your proposition. But until such a thing is practicable let it rest.

Mr. Verbrugghe (Belgium).—Mr. President, I think that the discussion has elucidated the question as to how we are to understand the paragraph in regard to which we are about to vote, but the argument presented by the gallant Delegate from France remains entirely intact. It only remains to be explained why the Committee limited itself to requiring only certain physical conditions from sailors. It does not say why it has not imposed conditions of capacity upon those who are intrusted with the management of a vessel. I confirm absolutely all that has been said on that subject by the gallant Delegate from France.

In regard to voting for the conclusions of the Report, I am not at all embarrassed. In my country an examination is required for colour-blindness and visual power, and no person is admitted into our service who has any defect of the eyesight. I, however, think that the demand made by the Representative of a Great Power will be heeded. It may be objectionable for some of us to vote for Resolutions in which the Committee have given no reasons for having made such limits.

Captain Sampson (United States).—Mr. President, when the Committee took up this General Division VI and discussed it thoroughly, as I think they did, they found it was not practicable to follow the order in which the headings are laid down in this General Division VI. I think the gallant Delegate from France will find that there are other recommendations followed in this General Division than this rule with regard to defective visual power. I wish to call his attention to the fact that this paragraph is a recommendation. It does not say that every seaman and boy, &c., shall be examined for colour-blindness; but it is a recommendation by the Committee to the Conference, as a recommendation to be made by the Conference, that every man who goes to sea who is liable to be stationed as a look-out shall be tested for his visual power, and with reference to his ability to distinguish between the red and the green light. Now, there are ample statistics to show that this is a visual defect, and, granting that colour-blindness must be a source of danger at sea when a man on the look-out is unable to see whether the light is green or red, it is certainly a difficulty which ought to be removed.

The object of the Committee in making this recommendation is that this idea should be promulgated, so as to induce every man and boy who proposes to adopt the sea as a profession to determine in the first place whether he is colour-blind or not. It certainly would be very unjust, as the gallant Delegate from France has pointed out, to shut out a man after he has been following the sea as his profession all his life simply because he was colour-blind. But the Committee have made no such recommendation. They do not propose that the men and officers who are now at sea should be interfered with in any way whatever; but it is recommended, as will be found in a subsequent Article, that each Government should provide a place where men and boys who propose to go to sea can have their eyesight tested. It then becomes a voluntary matter with them.

Captain Malmberg (Sweden).—Mr. President, there is a provision in this paragraph to which I, for my part, must object, and, therefore, I will vote "No" on the adoption of this paragraph. There is, up to the present time, no uniform test for colour-blindness. We have in Sweden such an examination for a certain class of individuals; but, according to our system, we do not know any such expression as a visual power below one-half normal, because, according to the test in our country, we have normal visual power, and we do not know anything about half normal power. That is the reason why I object to this paragraph and the reason why I shall vote "No" upon it.

Captain Sampson (United States).—Mr. President, perhaps I should have explained that this expression, "half normal power," refers to the distance at which objects can be seen, and has nothing whatever to do with colour-blindness. It has been decided that a man has normal vision under certain given circumstances, that he sees objects at a distance distinctly; and a man who has only half normal power can see the same objects only half the distance. The man who is so short-sighted that he can see only one-half the usual distance is not fit to take the position of a look-out. For instance, he would be unable to see which way a vessel was steering or to judge from the heights of her masts, or to tell whether her masts were in line or not, or to tell whether a buoy was a conical buoy or a can buoy. It is very unusual to find a man who is so near-sighted as this, but when he is found he certainly should not be put in a position where the safety of lives and property depends upon his visual power.

Captain Bisbee (China).—Mr. President, with regard to this proposition I would like to ask for information. What has been the result of examining seamen for colour-blindness in any country where such examinations have been instituted; that is, what percentage of the total number examined has it been found necessary to reject?

Captain Sampson (United States).—Mr. President, the only statistics we have with reference to the examination of seamen is the examination in Great Britain, where in the case of 21,000 examinations there were 89 who were colour-blind, and who could not distinguish the red light from the green light. I would state that the percentage of colour-blind people among males is usually taken as from 2 to 5 per cent.*

Mr. Hall (Great Britain).—Mr. President, I have not got our Tables here. I lent the Report to the learned Delegate from the United States and have not yet received it back. But, so far as I remember, the figures given by the gallant Delegate from the United States, are, as one would expect, accurate. Now, Mr. President, with regard to the first paragraph, which is the only paragraph before us, it is quite open to the objection pointed out by the gallant Delegate from France. There is no doubt that if that stood as an affirmative Resolution it would become a mandatory Rule, and there would be very grave difficulties in the way of its adoption. I quite agree with him that it might be practically impossible to carry it out in practice. But after all it seems to me that this sentence is merely an abstract proposition for the purpose of the guidance of Departments of the various countries, and the Rule proposed is really the one which comes in the next sentence, to provide means to enable men and boys intending to go to sea to be examined and get certificates with regard to their eyesight. That, I apprehend, is a practical question which we have to deal with in this Report. The first sentence, which is before us now, is really incomplete to deal with at the present time, because it is really an abstract proposition, and one which we should all like very much to see carried into execution if it were possible. But I agree with the learned Delegate from France that to make it a Rule would be practically impossible. But we shall support this because we know that it is merely stated as a suggestion to guide us and enable us to deal with the practical proposition to provide the means for men and boys who desire to go to sea to obtain certificates as to their eyesight.

Captain Malmberg (Sweden).—Mr. President, I only wish to thank the gallant Delegate from the United States for the information which I have received with regard to this matter, as I had misunderstood the expression.

Captain Sampson (United States).—Mr. President, the view which the Committee took of the question submitted to it was this: That in the Rules for preventing Collisions at Sea the action of this Conference and the action of all the countries which are represented by the Delegates here is controlled by a majority vote of the Conference. If the Conference vote to adopt the Rules of the Road, when those Rules are adopted by the countries they become obligatory upon all of us. Now it is a very different matter when we come to consider such questions as we have before us here. The Committee were of the opinion that it was useless to recommend an international Rule which we thought all the members or all the Delegates of the Conference would not subscribe to. Such Resolutions cannot be enforced, and the different nations which are represented here are not under

---

* Since 1880 *pilots of steam-vessels* have been examined for colour-blindness in the United States.

the same obligation to receive those recommendations as they are to follow the Rules of the Road which this Conference may adopt. Consequently, when any country has under this first head made such an examination for the different grades they are unwilling to modify the Rules which they are now pursuing, and it is certainly useless for this Conference to establish a uniform rule. That was the action of the Committee in regard to this matter.

Each country has Rules under this heading, and we could not say that the Rule followed by any country should be the uniform international Rule, because no member of the Committee was willing to give up the Rule which his country had already adopted, and which was thought to be very efficient. Consequently, the Committee, when they found this to be the case under these different headings simply remained silent, and where we have made no recommendations under these different headings it was because we could not agree. The different members of the Committee were not willing to recommend to their Government or to this Conference a system of examinations or forms of certificates of qualification which should be uniform, and, therefore, the Committee deemed it best to remain silent about them.

Captain Richard (France).—Mr. President, I am ready to vote in favour of the first two lines of the paragraph, but I ask that the last three be taken out. It is evidently a very good thing to know whether a man on board of a vessel is afflicted with colour-blindness, but I do not think that you can, simply because he is afflicted with colour-blindness, close the profession of seaman against him. In our country young children living on our coasts have frequently no choice of their profession. They become sailors because their father and their kinsmen are sailors, and because that is the only means of eking out an existence. My gallant colleague, Captain Sampson, perhaps thinks that we admit our ordinary seamen into the "Inscription Maritime," with the same care which we apply in admitting pupils to the Naval School. In that school they undergo a very strict examination, and they are not admitted until they have undergone very decided proofs in regard to their distinctness of vision.

For our merchant captains and our pilots proofs of distinctness of vision can be demanded, but it should not be said, "that no man or boy should be permitted to serve on board any vessel in the capacity of seaman, &c.," because he is afflicted with colour-blindness. When you endeavour to point out all the disasters which may happen because some one may mistake a red light for a green one, I think you are going too far when you rest the fate of a vessel upon the perfection of sight of a simple sailor, even though he may be on the look-out forward. The man on the look-out, as a rule, only sings out to the watch officer: "A light ahead," or "A light to port," or "A light to starboard." It is not a simple sailor who commands the vessel; such an idea never entered the head of the staunchest enemies of Daltonism; it is the watch officer or the captain. Demand guarantees for master mariners, for coasting masters, and watch officers, and we shall be ready to grant them to you.

Captain Sampson (United States).—Mr. President, if the gallant Delegate will read the remainder of this recommendation he will find that these are the only persons to whom it is proposed to apply a test. I would call his attention to the fact that if this Rule of the test for colour-blindness is applied only to mates and masters, what is to become of the man who starts in as a boy or common sailor and rises to the position of a master, only to find himself thrown out because the Rule has been applied to him at that late date in his profession? I think it is very much better that he should see when he enters it what will be expected of him when he becomes a master or a mate, if he had ambition to become one. It was with that very thing in view that the Committee made the recommendation that the test, if possible, should be made when the boy first starts in to go to sea. It is not even intended to apply this Rule to those who are now in the service.

As he has questioned the possibility of accidents arising from this, I would call his attention to at least two cases which I recall now in connection with the study of this subject. In 1885 a vessel going into the port of Fernandina was run ashore by a pilot, and he confessed that he made a mistake in the colour of the buoy. When he was examined it was found that, while he was not really colour-blind, and he could distinguish colours when near at hand, at a distance of 9 feet he could not tell one colour from another. In 1875, at 9 o'clock in the evening, a steam-ship came in collision with a tug-boat inside the Capes of Virginia; one vessel was sunk and ten lives lost. The officers of the steamer testified that the tug was in a position where she could see only their green light. The captain of the tug, on the contrary, declared that he saw the port light. The captain of the tug was subsequently found to be colour-blind, and could not tell red from green.

Mr. Verbrugghe (Belgium).—Mr. President, I thank the gallant Delegate from the United States for the explanations which he has kindly given us in regard to the motive which prevented the Committee from imposing certain conditions for obtaining an officer's certificate. We will all understand that the reasons given were of such a nature as to block the way of the Committee in arriving at a practical solution. I venture to believe that the Conference will ratify the reasons stated by the Chairman of the Committee. It was, however, indispensable that they should be submitted to the appreciation of the Conference, in order to guide us before voting in favour of the Resolution of the Report.

Mr. Hall (Great Britain).—Mr. President, I am now, owing to the courtesy of Mr. Cottman, able to answer the question put by the gallant Delegate from China, and to state, very shortly, what the results of those examinations have been; they have carried out in a most remarkable way the hope which has been expressed by the gallant Delegate from the United States, that, if such examinations as these are instituted, it will prevent many a man going to sea when he rises to the grade of an officer, being disappointed when he finds that he is not fit for his calling, and I think that is assistance which we ought to give to men when they start into a profession, whether it be that of the sea or any other.

The first examinations extend over a period of ten years, and are for officers and men. They show 5·3 per cent. Of course, that is a small percentage. The number of men who were rejected out of those who came up for examination to be tested as to colour the first year was 6·78 per cent., about 6¾ percentage, and they were rejected for what is called colour-blindness. But these examinations have had very good effects in lowering the number of persons in the service who came up for examination and were rejected on account of the visual defects, and, accordingly, we find among the officers in the following year, which was last year, that the number declined from ·53 to ·41, that is, a decline of about 10 per cent. in one year alone; and the number of men who came up to be examined voluntarily declined from nearly 7 per cent. to 3·94 per cent., about 4 per cent. There is a decline of about 40 per cent. of the number of men rejected in the space of one year after these examinations had been thoroughly instituted and carried out.

I cannot imagine a more striking illustration of the desirability, which has been pointed out by the gallant Delegate from the United States, for having some such a test as this provided for. May I add one word more? Some of our steam-ship lines will not allow a man to be put on the look-out until they are satisfied that he is not colour-blind; and some of our very large Steam-ship Companies now decline to take men who have not got a certificate with regard to their eyesight. There was an examination in the mercantile marine at Tilbury Docks, and it was found that, in only four months of last year, no fewer than 16 out of 320 men were found unable to distinguish between the red and green lights, that is, 5 per cent. in three months only, showing the very great importance of attention being paid to this matter.

Mr. Carter (Hawaii).—Mr. President, I would like to suggest to the gallant Delegate from the United States if there will be any objection to taking out " or," so that it should read: " should be permitted to serve on board any vessel in the capacity of seaman where he will have to stand look-out." As it stands now, with the comma and the word " or," it is subject to the criticism of the gallant Delegate from France, that it might refer to a man already in the service. Therefore, if it is possible, I would suggest that the comma and the word " or " be stricken out.

Captain Sampson (United States).—Mr. President, I will only say that I think if that " or " is stricken out, it would better express the view of the Committee than to leave it in.

Mr. Carter (Hawaii).—Then I move that the word " or " be stricken out.

Captain Donner (Germany).—Mr. President, I fear that some of the members of the Conference are under the impression that the Committee have proposed to make it obligatory to have an examination for all men, and, therefore, I would like to say that this was not the opinion of the Committee. The Committee have only proposed an obligatory examination in colour-blindness for officers, masters, and mates, and not that every man is to have his eyesight tested. There is a great difference. I have declared in the Committee that it would be impossible for me to vote for a compulsory examination of all men who have an intention of going to sea or being seamen; and the only thing to which I could agree was that the ship officers should have to pass a compulsory examination. I only say this because I thought the gentleman speaking before me said something which might lead the Conference to infer that a man now actually being a seaman could not follow out his profession if he was not in the possession of a certificate. I think that no certificate could be asked for from a common sailor. He might get a certificate, but he need not be compelled to take out one. If we make such a proposition as that, I should be obliged to vote against it, because we do not intend in Germany to make any examinations compulsory for common seamen. We only want to make it compulsory for the ships' officers.

Mr. Carter (Hawaii).—Mr. President, I quite understand the idea of the Committee, that this was not compulsory. It is, however, a recommendation, and in the recommendation they say that no man or boy shall be permitted to serve, &c. Therefore, I think that the recommendation would commend itself more to the different Powers if the word " or " was stricken out. I, therefore, move that as an amendment to this Report.

Captain Sampson (United States).—Mr. President, I second the motion.

The President.—The Delegate from Hawaii moves that the comma and the word " or," in paragraph 1, in the line next to the last, should be stricken out.

Captain Sampson (United States).—Mr. President, if it is in order, I think I can answer for the Committee in accepting that amendment without putting it to a vote.

Mr. Carter (Hawaii).—Mr. President, in that case probably there is no necessity for a vote being taken.

The President.—If there be no objection on the part of any of the members of the Committee, and the Chairman will vote for the Committee, it will stand as amended.

Mr. Verney (Siam).—Mr. President, if I understand the proposal of the gallant Delegate from France, it was to strike out the last three lines, and it is in these last three lines that the word " or " and the comma occur. Therefore, if the suggestion of the Delegate from France were adopted, that question would not be before the Conference. I understand the Delegate from France to propose definitely to this Conference that the last three lines be stricken out, and I have not heard any counter-proposition to that.

Mr. Carter (Hawaii).—Mr. President, I think the amendment which I have made renders it more acceptable. I think that the gallant Delegate from France and all the Delegates will agree that persons who are colour-blind should not be permitted to stand as a look-out, and this is a suggestion to that effect. As I understand the remarks of the gallant Delegate from France, they were that the last three lines should be stricken out because they would bring about such matters as I mentioned awhile ago, and it struck me that to take out the word " or " would remove the objection to the paragraph.

Captain Richard (France).—Mr. President, I propose to divide the paragraph into two portions, and to have both portions of the paragraph successively voted upon. For my part I am decided to vote for the first two lines. The last three lines I cannot accept. Our gallant colleague of the United States has mentioned the fact of two vessels having collided, but that has nothing to do with the men who were on the look-out, because it was the pilot who was suffering from colour-blindness. For the pilot you can introduce the directions contained in the paragraph which I am discussing. For pilots and officers it is absolutely essential that they should see clearly, but, I repeat, it is not so for the man on the look-out, for all he has to say is: "I see a light to starboard, to port, or right ahead." It is the watch officer who must distinguish the colour of the light which is in sight, and determine upon the course. Let the Conference, therefore, confine itself to adopting the first two lines of the paragraph.

Mr. Verney (Siam).—Mr. President, may I be allowed to say that it seems to me to be a very difficult thing to lay it down that a boy who goes to sea shall not serve as a look-out? I would venture to ask the sailors here present whether a boy, who is allowed to go to sea with the intention of not standing as a look-out, might not be very easily put on the look-out? Therefore, do we not run some danger, even if we do strike out the word "or"? It is a question whether that is really a valuable alteration in the amendment.

Captain Sampson (United States).—Mr. President, I would answer that question by saying that it was the opinion of the Committee that it was not necessary to submit people who were habitually below, like the servants and men belonging to the engineer force, to the operation of this Rule.

The President.—The question will be upon the amendment of the Delegate from Hawaii. The Chair understands that the last motion was by the Delegate from Hawaii.

Captain Sampson (United States).—Mr. President, I do not think he made any motion.

The President.—Then the question will be upon the motion of the Delegate from France. The Delegate from France proposes that the vote be first taken on the first two lines of the paragraph. Those who are in favour of taking the vote in this way will say "Aye."

The question was put to the Conference upon the motion of the Delegate from France, and the motion was carried.

The President.—The question now is upon the first two lines of the paragraph. The Secretary will please read the first two lines.

The first two lines of the paragraph are as follows:—

"Every man or boy going to sea as a seaman or with the intention of becoming a seaman should be examined for visual power and colour-blindness."

Captain Donner (Germany).—Mr. President, I must observe that this does not express the opinion of the Committee, as I understand it, and I shall not be able to vote for it. The intention of the Committee, in my opinion, was only to state in general terms that it was desirable that everybody who went on board a ship and was liable to act as a look-out should have good eyes and not to be colour-blind. I do not agree to the principle contained in these two lines, and I declared in the Committee, in very strong terms, that I could not allow my country to be in any way bound to make it obligatory for a common seaman to show that he was not colour-blind; and that would be done, if this vote is in substance as it now stands.

Mr. Carter (Hawaii).—Mr. President, I should vote for the two lines, with the expectation that the rest will be added by the Conference; because I think the Conference will be obliged to add the rest. I think the position of the Conference would then be to carry out its intentions, to add the rest of the paragraph, and I would suggest to the gallant Delegate from France that perhaps it would be the better way to take a vote on his proposition to strike out the last three lines, rather than to vote to accept the first two. If the last three lines are stricken out, then the Conference are at liberty to strike out the whole of this, which I think they will be obliged to do. But if the first two lines are accepted and the last three lines are not received, then we shall have to reconsider the two lines again.

Captain Richard (France).—Mr. President, my intention is misunderstood by my honourable colleague from Hawaii. I asked that the Article be divided, and that the two portions be voted upon, simply because I can accept only the first two lines, and that I have decided to vote against the last three. I have no objection to accept that every sailor should be examined for colour-blindness. It is an advantage to know who is afflicted with it, and that the sailor in that case should have upon his service book a note stating that fact. When his captain knows that he will turn it to such advantage as he shall judge proper, and if he places him on the look-out forward, he will know in advance that such a man cannot distinguish colours. We cannot give any advice as to the manner in which he should be employed. By making sailors undergo a test as to visual power you will thereby gain an additional element of information, and you will be the better able to find out what each man is capable of.

Mr. Carter (Hawaii).—Mr. President, I would simply ask what is the use of an examination for colour-blindness if they are to be permitted to serve when they are found to be colour-blind?

Mr. Verney (Siam).—Mr. President, if a man is examined for colour-blindness and is known to be colour-blind, would any captain then employ him as a look-out? He would know that this man was colour-blind, and would never permit him to be put on a look-out. Therefore it would largely put the responsibility on the captain, where I think it ought to be.

Captain Sampson (United States).—Mr. President, it would be very embarrassing to the master of the ship if he always had to be acquainted with the men who were colour-blind on board his ship, and had to be careful that they were not put on the look-out. This is simply a recommendation, and it is made as emphatic as a recommendation can be made. I think the circumstances of the case show the desirability of accomplishing this object, and are sufficient to warrant the Committee in making the recommendation as strongly as it has been made. Therefore, Mr. President, if it is perfectly proper to do so, I move to amend the motion of the gallant Delegate from France, and move the adoption of the whole paragraph.

The President.—The Conference has already decided to vote upon it separately.

Mr. Hall (Great Britain).—Mr. President, I think that at present, unless we take your ruling upon this matter, that some of us will be in a difficulty to know how to vote. May I point out how that difficulty arises? If we vote for the first two lines and they are carried, and then by chance the vote of the Conference should be to strike out the remaining three lines, we shall all of us be voting for what we do not want, because I think that these two lines by themselves certainly do not express the opinion of the Committee, or what the most of us wish to see passed. On the other hand, if we vote against the first two lines because we wish to have the whole paragraph, it might be argued it was not open to us to have the whole paragraph, because we have voted against the adoption of the first two lines. So that we are now put in rather a fix by the gallant Delegate from France. Might I suggest to him that it would be better if we should take the sense of the Conference upon this motion to strike out the last three lines? I have no doubt he will assist us under these circumstances.

Captain Richard (France).—Mr. President, after the considerations which have been developed by the eminent Delegate from Great Britain, I should state that the proposition which I have made was in conformity with my desire to adopt but a portion of the paragraph, divided as I have asked it. As the remarks which I have made are just, and as I, on the other hand, do not desire to take the Conference by surprise, I accept the proposition made by the learned Delegate from Great Britain.

The President.—The Delegate from France moves to strike out the last three lines of paragraph 1 of the Report of the Committee on General Division VI, which is under consideration. The Secretary will read the last three lines, so that there will be no misunderstanding.

The last three lines of paragraph 1 are as follows:—

"And no man or boy should be permitted to serve on board any vessel in the capacity of seaman, or where he will have to stand look-out, whose visual power is below one-half normal, or who is red and green colour-blind."

The President.—Is the Conference ready for the question?

The question was put to the Conference upon the motion to strike out the last three lines of paragraph 1.

The President.—The Chair is unable to decide.

Captain Shackford (United States).—Mr. President, I call for the Yeas and Nays.

The President.—The Yeas and Nays are called for. The Secretary will please call the roll.

The Yea and Nay vote is as follows:—

Austria-Hungary	Nay.	Italy	Nay.
Belgium	Nay.	Japan	Nay.
China	Nay.	Mexico	Nay.
Chile	Nay.	Norway	Nay.
Denmark	Nay.	Russia	Yea.
France	Yea.	Sweden	Nay.
Germany	Yea.	Siam	Yea.
Great Britain	Nay.	The Netherlands	Nay.
Hawaii	Nay.	United States	Nay.

The President.—The vote stands 4 in the affirmative, and 14 in the negative; so the motion is lost.

Commodore Monasterio (Mexico).—Mr. President, I would ask the Secretary to change my vote. I vote for the affirmative.

The President.—The Delegate from Mexico has changed his vote from Nay to Yea, so that the vote now stands 5 in the affirmative, and 13 in the negative. The motion is lost.

The question now is upon paragraph 1, as it originally stood. Is the Conference ready for the question?

The question was put to the Conference upon the adoption of paragraph 1 of the Report of the Committee on General Division VI, and it was adopted.

The President.—The Secretary will please read paragraph 2.

Paragraph 2 is as follows:—

"Every man who shall qualify as an officer of a registered vessel after the adoption of these Rules, except engineer officers, shall be required to have a certificate that he has the necessary visual power and that he is not red and green blind. He shall also have a certificate that he is familiar with the Regulations for preventing Collisions at Sea, and with the duties required of him in co-operating with a life-saving station in case his vessel is stranded."

Captain Richard (France).—Mr. President, I now hope to present an amendment which will be more fortunate than his predecessors. I would like to introduce after the words, "Every sailor who shall undergo an examination for officer"—I would like to add the word "pilot." I think that we will be all unanimous on this point that a pilot should not suffer from colour-blindness.

Captain Sampson (United States).—Mr. President, I am sure the Committee would be very glad to accept the amendment of the gallant Delegate from France to introduce the word "pilot," so that it will read: "Every man who shall qualify as an officer of a registered vessel, or as a pilot."

The President.—The Chairman of the Committee accepts the suggestion of the Delegate from France. The paragraph will be read as amended.

The paragraph as amended is as follows:—

"Every man who shall qualify as an officer of a registered vessel, or as a pilot, after the adoption of these Rules, except engineer officers, shall be required to have a certificate that he has the necessary visual power and that he is not red and green blind. He shall also have a certificate that he is familiar with the Regulations for preventing Collisions at Sea, and with the duties required of him in co-operating with a life-saving station in case his vessel is stranded."

The President.—Is the Conference ready for the question?

The question was put to the Conference on the adoption of paragraph 2 of the Report of the Committee on General Division VI, and it was adopted.

The President.—The Secretary will please read the next paragraph of the Report upon General Division VI.

Said paragraph is as follows:—

"It is recommended that each country provide means which will enable any boy or man intending to go to sea to have his eyes examined for visual power and colour-blindness, and to obtain a certificate of the result, also to enable the master of any vessel to have the eyes of any of his crew tested for the same purpose."

The President.—Is the Conference ready for the question on this paragraph?

The question was put to the Conference upon the adoption of the third paragraph of the Report of the Committee on General Division VI, and it was adopted.

The President.—The Secretary will please read the next paragraph.

Captain Sampson (United States).—Mr. President, I do not think it is necessary to have a vote upon the next paragraph. I now move the adoption of the Report.

The President.—It is moved that the Report as amended be now adopted as a whole.

The question was put to the Conference upon the adoption of the Report of the Committee as a whole, and the Report was adopted.

Lieutenant Beaugency (Chile).—Mr. President, at the last meeting of the Conference I called your attention to the time taken up in the Conference. It is my case, and I think the case of many of the other Delegates who do not thoroughly understand the English language, that we have not had time to consider the Report of the Collocation Committee, and I, therefore, think that we ought to adjourn at 4 o'clock and meet to-morrow at 11 o'clock and sit until 4.

Mr. Hall (Great Britain).—Mr. President, I am most anxious, in making any proposal, to meet the views of the majority of the Delegates. But I would point out that the next Report we have to deal with is not a Report in which there are any Resolutions at all. It is a very interesting Report; but it is a Report which I apprehend will be adopted by the Conference. It will not be necessary to take it up sentence by sentence, there being no Resolutions in it. Therefore, if we were to take that up now and finish it before 5 o'clock, we would not have to meet to-morrow at all. I would only suggest that we should do whatever is most consonant with the views of the Delegates. Of course, if they decide that we adjourn to-day at 4 o'clock and meet to-morrow at 11, be it so. I would only say this with regard to the hours, that several of the gentlemen have expressed to me the opinion that the hours from 10 to 5 will be too long, and have expressed the desire that we should revert to our original hours of from 11 to 4. Of course, if they think so, I shall vote for that proposal at once. As I say, on the part of Great Britain, we only want to meet the views of a majority of the Delegates. We are ready to work from 10 to 5 if the rest of the Delegates are willing; and if they wish to sit from 11 to 4, we shall support that proposal. But I would venture to suggest that, after to-day, we should sit our regular hours, from 11 to 4. Perhaps the Conference might now decide whether it is worth while to sit for an hour and finish this Report.

Lieutenant Beaugency (Chile).—Mr. President, I will accept that.

The President.—The Report of Committee No. 2, General Division VII, is now in order. The Secretary will please read the Report.

The Report of Committee No. 2, on Lanes for Steamers on frequented Routes, General Division VII, is as follows:—

"Sir, "Washington, December 6, 1889.

"Committee No. 2 beg leave to report on General Division VII, entitled 'Lanes for Steamers on frequented Routes,' that after consideration of various routes they concluded to report only upon the North Atlantic route between ports of North America and ports of Northern Europe as the route upon which there was apparently the greater demand for such lanes, if such could be advantageously laid down on any ocean or sea.

"It appears that the adherence of fast steam passenger-vessels to certain southerly routes would tend to the avoidance of fog and ice; and the Committee adopted a Resolution to the effect that it was desirable during the spring and summer months that such vessels should follow a southern route which would clear the Banks of Newfoundland, and be likely to be clear of fog and ice; but when it came to proposing any plan to make such ocean lanes compulsory the Committee found the subject one of such difficulty that they do not recommend a proposition of that nature.

"The difficulty of enforcing the present Rule providing for moderate speed in thick weather suggests what greater difficulties would be met with in enforcing lane routes if made compulsory, and it was not thought desirable to lay down routes by international agreement unless they were to be made compulsory for swift steamers.

"Routes that might be proposed would be in danger of invasion by ice during the spring and summer months, and at all times would be crossed by sailing-vessels and steamers going north and south. If laid down on parallels of latitude which seemed to favour one seaport at the expense of another, or the ports of one country at the expense of the ports of another country, they would arouse opposition that would probably prevent their adoption.

"It is possible that even in the near future vessels may be employed of such power and speed that all such considerations may have to give way to the paramount consideration of safety, but, so far as shown to the Committee, present conditions do not seem to justify an international agreement to that effect. It was not shown to the Committee that collisions in mid-ocean between fast ocean steamers had taken place, or that the danger was great enough to justify enforced adherence to certain lanes. Collisions between fast steam-ships so far have occurred nearer the coasts where all tracks must converge.

"The Committee believe, however, that the voluntary establishment of, and adherence to, particular routes by the different Steam-ship Companies for different seasons of the year is very desirable. In fact, the Committee are of opinion that such action by the Steam-ship Companies, with the experience to be gained thereby, would be quite essential before any concerted action by the Maritime Powers could be profitably taken.

"The Committee, therefore, strongly recommend that the Companies interested should, by mutual agreement, after consultation together, establish routes for the different lines, and make them public, in order that the Hydrographic Offices of the various Governments may publish them for the information of navigators.

"The Committee have considered the opinions of several persons in the printed matter that has been laid before them. With the exception of one or two definite propositions, the literature before the Conference does not show how such lane routes could be laid down. Even those containing such propositions arrive at the conclusion that such routes could not be made compulsory. In Appendix (A) will be found extracts or copies of the papers laid before them.

"Subsection (*b*). With regard to the safety of fishermen upon the North Atlantic Ocean, the Committee are of opinion that their safety would be best promoted by unceasing vigilance on the part of the fishermen, and by careful compliance by all with the present Rules for the prevention of collisions, especially as to the efficiency of lights and sound-signals. If lanes were established which carried the fast steamers clear of the Banks frequented by the fishermen it might promote such a sense of security on their part as would tend to carelessness with reference to the Rules as at present laid down, and lead to danger from the slower vessels which would still frequent the Banks.

"During the months when the fishing-vessels most frequent the Banks the fear of encountering fog and ice leads many of the steamers to go south of them.

"Quick passages are what the steam-vessels aim at in response to the public demand for swift passenger and mail service, and if they were compelled to obey existing Rules regarding moderate speed in fogs at all times and in all places, they would avoid the Banks still more, in order to go clear of fogs; and thus it seems that the solution of the problem before the Committee, namely, of how to induce steam-ships of great speed to take safer routes to avoid fogs, ice, and danger of collision with fishermen and other vessels, is in compelling obedience to the present Rules regarding moderate speed in thick weather. The enforcement of these Rules would make it for the interest of such vessels to take routes comparatively clear of fogs and ice, and thus attain the end which compulsory legislation might fail to do.

"In Appendix (B) will be found some correspondence regarding the dangers of fishermen upon the Banks, from which it will be observed that vigilance regarding lights and sound-signals have been found efficient safeguards in most instances.

(Signed)   "AUG. GARDE, *Delegate for Denmark.*
"HENRI LANNÉLUC, *Delegate for France.*
"CHRISTIAN DONNER,
    "*Delegate for Germany.*
"N. BOWDEN-SMITH,
    "*Delegate for Great Britain.*
"H. A. P. CARTER, *Chairman,*
    "*Delegate for Hawaii.*
"T. DE SOUZA ROZA,
    "*Delegate for Portugal.*
"FREDERICK MALMBERG,
    "*Delegate for Sweden.*
"D. HUBERT, *Delegate for the Netherlands.*
"JOHN W. SHACKFORD,
    "*Delegate for the United States.*

"To Rear-Admiral S. R. Franklin, United States' Navy,
"President of the International Marine Conference, &c."

The President.—Before any discussion takes place upon this subject the Chair desires to lay before the Conference a communication from a very distinguished member of Congress, Mr. Cabot Lodge, upon this subject. The Secretary will please read it.

The communication is as follows:—

"[Commonwealth of Massachusetts, in the year One thousand eight hundred and eighty-nine.]

"*Resolutions relative to an International Convention in relation to Ocean Steamers crossing the Grand Banks.*

"Whereas the fishermen of this Commonwealth are subject to serious danger and great loss of property and life from the fact that the path of the ocean steamers lies directly across the Grand Banks: Therefore

"*Resolved,*—That the Senate and House of Representatives of the Commonwealth of Massachusetts, in General Court assembled, do most respectfully and earnestly urge upon Congress the immediate necessity of holding an International Convention, which body shall legislate upon the subjects and agree upon Laws which shall be binding upon all ocean steamers of the nations which have Delegates in attendance at such Convention, and which shall make it compulsory to pursue certain courses on all their passages, in order to avoid the fishing banks frequented by fishermen.

"*Resolved*,—That a copy of these Resolutions be transmitted to the Senators and Representatives in Congress from this Commonwealth.

"*Senate, April* 5, 1889.

"Adopted: Sent down for concurrence.

(Signed) "Henry D. Coolidge, *Clerk.*

"*House of Representatives, April* 11, 1889.

"Adopted in concurrence.

(Signed) "Edward A. McLaughlin, *Clerk.*

"A true copy. Attest:

(Signed) "Henry D. Coolidge, *Clerk of Senate.*"

The President.—I promised Mr. Lodge that I would have this read for the information of the Conference. The Report of Committee No. 2 is now before the Conference.

Captain Shackford (United States).—Mr. President, it seems to me there is something omitted from this Report, and that is the letter from the Gloucester fishermen to the Secretary of State. This is the first time that I have noticed that it is not here. I notice the replies of the fishermen, but I do not see this letter. I simply desire to call the attention of the Conference to the fact that they could not give a single instance of a fisherman having been run down on the Banks.

Mr. Carter (Hawaii).—Mr. President, I have no desire to take up the time of the Conference in presenting this Report. The Report speaks for itself. I will simply say that we have very carefully examined all the subjects before us. We considered carefully and particularly the question of lanes along the Mediterranean and the Red Sea. But we thought at last that perhaps the North Atlantic offered the best opportunity for laying down lane routes. But when we came to consider the subject we found it was quite the contrary. The fishing banks on the north and the Gulf Stream on the south put difficulties in the way. It is very hard to compel vessels to run south and encounter the Gulf Stream. They object to that. The northern routes were encumbered by numbers of fishermen. It was quite out of the question for us to consider what has been called the neutralization of the fishing banks. These banks cover a very large surface of the sea—some thousands of square miles—and, as we have stated here, to lay down Rules that would favour any port at the expense of any other port, or the ports of one country at the expense of those of another, would delay rather than invite the adoption of such Resolutions by the different Powers. Therefore, we did not make that recommendation which I understand is asked for by the Senate and House of Representatives of the State of Massachusetts. The reasons which we give are before you in the Report, and I really do not know that there is any use of my repeating them here, unless the members of the Conference desire to ask some questions as to why we arrived at the conclusions we did.

Captain Richard (France).—Mr. President, it would evidently have been desirable if a means could have been found for establishing special routes for avoiding collisions. After a long discussion and careful examination the Committee have determined that it is an impossibility, and I respectfully submit to their decision. But, on the other hand, there is a passage in the Report of this Committee in regard to which I must insist upon calling your attention. It is the first phrase of subsection (*b*), relating to the security of fishermen: "With regard to the safety of fishermen in the North Atlantic Ocean, the Committee are of opinion that their safety would be best promoted by unceasing vigilance on the part of the fishermen and by careful compliance," &c. It seems to me that the Committee have, in this first phrase, evidently gone beyond the idea. Is it not grimly humorous to tell a being who, in case of a collision, is destined to play a passive and sacrificial part, to increase his vigilance? Let us take the fishermen on the Banks of Newfoundland—inasmuch as it is they in particular who are aimed at in that portion of the Report—and let us speak of them. Have not they, in fact, the right to complain? And the number of vessels which have been run down, and of families in mourning for them, for collisions with steamers traversing the Banks, is certainly in harmony with the recommendations as to vigilance which your Committee have been so prodigal with by way of consolation.

Allow me to make a few remarks concerning our fishermen. There are every year about 20,000 fishermen on the Banks, of whom but 10,000 are French; the other 10,000 are English and American. So far as the French are concerned: in 1884 the "Rocabey" disappeared, with eighty-eight men of her crew; on the 25th May, 1885, the "Georges et Jeanne," being at anchor on the fishing grounds, was run down at 5 o'clock at night by the steam-ship "City of Rome;" only two men out of twenty-four escaped from the disaster; on the 20th July, 1886, at 10 o'clock at night, the "Sibylle" was cut in two by the steam-ship "Nova Scotia," going at full speed; on the 8th June, 1886, the "Michel Ernest" was sunk under the same circumstances, losing seven men; the "Saint Pair" underwent the same fate on the 9th August, being at anchor; the "Marie" was run down by the steam-ship "Parisian" at about the same date; finally, the "Medellin" was run down by the steam-ship "Queen," with her entire crew.

There are certainly more examples which I could gather, next to which could probably be placed a certain number of vessels which have disappeared and whose fate has never been ascertained. But I do not insist upon that point. I only desire to show the dangers to which fishermen upon the Banks of Newfoundland may be exposed by the passage of steamers upon those Banks. After having done so I take the liberty to state that the Committee have gone too far in inserting that sentence which has nothing better to say than to advise fishermen that the best means to avoid danger is to increase their vigilance. I really ask, what can they do? Of what use can this vigilance so highly championed be to them? A vessel is at anchor, and, as in all that class of fishing-vessels, it is a sailing-vessel, whose only way of making her presence known is the fog-horn or the bell. Generally the fishermen have adopted a mechanical fog-horn. They do all they can to make themselves heard and to prevent their being run into. It would be another thing if you were to give them a proper fog-horn, or some other sounding instrument, but you merely give them the excellent advice to be still more vigilant.

Is it not true that the idea of the Committee has been extended beyond what was intended? It seems to me that in that case the parts should have been reversed, and that it should have been said, as we cannot, in spite of our most generous intentions, prevent steamers from crossing the Banks of Newfoundland, the captains of such steamers should be told, "When you are about to enter upon the Banks of Newfoundland, where you are likely to meet fishing-boats, you must go with the greatest caution." When the question of speed during a fog was discussed, an endeavour was made to limit the speed of such vessels during fog and mist; and if a limit had been accepted these very vessels would not have hesitated to go farther south in order to avoid the possibility of having to slacken their speed to so considerable an extent. But the Conference accepted no proposition of that kind, and, consequently, as you have authorized them to go ahead, without ever allowing their speed to go below a considerable rate, I consider that it is a very bold thing to say to the fishermen, "Now, pay attention—as you have everything to fear, and you will have everything to lose—therefore, redouble your attention." But the steamer should have been told, "We cannot prevent your going at full speed on the Banks of Newfoundland, but pay attention, for it is at your peril."

According to the laws of most nations, fishermen must be neither troubled nor molested in carrying out their occupation. When the question came up of lights on small craft and fishing-vessels, you did all in your power to enable fishermen to pursue their occupation in peace. Why should you be less favourably disposed to those on the Banks of Newfoundland? I, therefore, do not think that you have been consistent in inserting that phrase. It is the steamer which should be careful, and not the fishermen—that inoffensive being who can do nothing to prevent collision.

Admiral Bowden-Smith (Great Britain).—Mr. President, I would like to ask whether I understood the gallant Delegate from France to say that the latest disaster to fishing-boats was in 1886?

Captain Richard (France).—In 1887.

Admiral Bowden-Smith (Great Britain).—Mr. President, that is two years ago. I am very happy to hear that there have been no disasters in the last two years. That shows, I think, that they are not an everyday occurrence. The gallant Delegate from France objects to the first two lines in subsection (*b*) of our Report, because, he said, we have advised the fishermen to keep a sharp look-out as the best way to avoid a collision. But we have also advised the steamer to take every precaution possible, especially with regard to lights and sound-signals. Now, I think that if he cannot quote any case of collision with fishing-vessels in the last two years, it is rather a clear case that they do not occur so very, very often as might be supposed. But I do not think my learned friend in his remarks proposes any way of getting out of the difficulty. The Chairman of our Committee has said, when he presented this Report, that he would not say very much more than we have said in the Report, but that if anybody had anything to offer he would be very glad to answer him. Why do not the gentlemen present some proposition or plan? We could not think of any plan to avoid this danger.

I should like to draw the attention to the answers of certain fishermen in Appendix (B). Questions were put, as Captain Shackford has mentioned, and the answers were rather curious. They show that they do avoid collision by keeping a sharp look-out. The question asked was, "Have any vessels disappeared under circumstances which induced the opinion that they had been run down by any steamer or steam-ship and are a total loss? Do you know of any that have had narrow escapes? Give the names of such vessels, the dates and situations when last seen, and also state the circumstances so far as you have learned them." Here is a man who says, "On the north-east part of George's, had a very narrow escape from being run down by a steamer at night, it being thick fog at the time. She came within 75 feet and would have run over the vessel if it had not been for our torches and fog-horns." So you see the steamer avoided the collision by doing what we have suggested. There was a very curious thing came out in our Committee which we had not the right to put in the Report, because it was a newspaper report; but one of our Delegates brought a letter from fishermen who said that they welcomed steamers upon the Banks of Newfoundland.

Captain Shackford (United States).—Mr. President, I was going to ask permission to read that letter.

Admiral Bowden-Smith (Great Britain).—Mr. President, I will not take up the time of the Conference in further discussing this matter. If the gallant Delegate from France, or any other Delegate, can propose any plan for these steamer routes, I have no doubt the Chairman of the Committee will be able to answer them.

Captain Richard (France).—Mr. President, the gallant Admiral Bowden-Smith has not understood my idea. If I had a better solution to propose I would have proposed it to the Committee. I only object to the phrase in subsection (*b*), which, in my opinion, would have been better placed elsewhere. The only comfort which it gives to fishermen is to advise them to watch with great vigilance, when they can do nothing and when all their vigilance cannot turn aside from them a vessel which is about to run into them. I have named a number of vessels sunk on the Banks of Newfoundland, and among the testimonials which are in the Appendix I find one of Mr. Charles Peterson, that according to his knowledge no vessel has ever been sunk by a steamer. This is evidently the testimony of a simple-minded being who could not see farther than his own vessel, and Appendix (B) oes not seem to be able to throw any new light upon the question.

Mr. Carter (Hawaii).—Mr. President, with regard to the subject of the fishermen, I would not ц the Conference for one moment suppose that the Committee neglected the consideration of what was best for the safety of the fishermen. The Committee felt that there lay upon them a very heavy responsibility. They all acknowledged the importance of the case of the fishermen. They all acknowledged their importance as contributors to the world's supply of food. We regret that their vocation leads them in the midst of dangers and parts of the ocean where steamers are going, and where there is danger to them; and we desired to do all that we could and to suggest anything that we could for the safety of the fishermen. But the subject was surrounded by insurmountable obstacles the moment we came to lay down any practical Rule. As I said before, it could not for a moment be thought of that we should lay down a Rule which would practically shut out from the commerce of the world 33,000 square miles of ocean. On the Grand Banks alone there are 8,000 square miles. On the Banks of George's there are 5,000 square miles.

Then there came the consideration: What are the dangers? And we let the fishermen answer that for themselves, and that answer is contained in the replies to this Circular letter, which was sent out for the purpose of getting replies of the fishermen, and for the very purpose, probably, of influencing the legislation of Massachusetts. But we found in every case that the fishermen themselves said that their safety lay in the care with which they used their apparatus and fog-horns. In one case they say that a steamer came within 75 feet of them, and then they were saved from collision by the prompt action of the steamer. In another case I think that even a shorter distance is mentioned. In another case she came within 25 feet of the vessel, and the steamer changed her course. Another answer says: " I do not know of any vessel being run down by a steamer, but have had several narrow escapes." But as soon as they use their apparatus and sound their fog-horns, it appears that the vigilance of the steamer has been sufficient to prevent collision. Therefore we point out that in this lies their safety, in unsleeping vigilance with regard to the use of their fog-horns and other apparatus.

Now, with regard to the steamers. We have pointed out here distinctly that if Rules for preventing collisions at sea, at present laid down, were properly enforced, and these vessels were always compelled to go slow or to go at moderate speed in a fog or thick weather, they would keep out of the way of the fishermen, naturally, because they would want to avoid the fog, and where the fishermen frequent they meet these fogs. Therefore, we have borne just as hard upon the steamers as we have upon the fishermen. And we have pointed out, I think it will strike you at once, that if you attempt to make a lane route which will force steamers to go south, you will be building up the commerce of Philadelphia at the expense of New York and Boston; or you may injure the commerce of Philadelphia by forcing them to go to Norfolk and Baltimore. You will, by establishing other lane routes which have been proposed before us, completely destroy Halifax as a commercial port.

Therefore, we find that we cannot lay down this hard and fast rule upon the ocean, and we believe that this vast expanse of the world's surface must be left free to the commerce of the world, and must be left without such Regulations as would neutralize the benefits which now come to mankind from having it as a common highway. We could hardly expect nations which draw a part of their bread-stuffs and food from the United States to declare that the great ocean between the United States and those nations should be closed to the ships which carried these bread-stuffs across the ocean. No one will propose that the Banks should be kept entirely free from steamers.

It will be clearly seen that we have drawn a distinction between the slow and swift steamers, because if we had laid down ocean lanes the Rules would only refer to the swift steamers. But if we take them off the Banks the great danger is that the fishermen would say: There is no longer any danger; we can save our oil; we will not burn our torches; we will go to sleep; we will not sound our fog-horns; and the result would be they would be run over by the slow steamers or tramps which would still take that course. Every time we attempted to lay down some rule which should be applied we found ourselves confronted by insurmountable obstacles. I believe it can be shown that the collisions between the steamers themselves going east and west which have taken place in mid-ocean are very few. They have taken place near the shores, on both sides, and there they would be liable to take place under any rules laid down. If we adopted a Rule which caused them all to cross the meridian of 50° on certain parallels of latitude, it would bring together a large number of vessels every day and cause so many lanes or routes to converge at certain points that we fear we should simply be increasing the danger, which we have shown is not so very great now as is supposed.

The collisions between the fast steamers are infrequent, and we think that is due to the fact that the great steamers, the fast steamers, are so carefully managed, and that it is so much in the interest of the captain and owners to manage them carefully, that the number of collisions between them have been small. The collisions have been generally between the fast and slow steamers, or between the slow steamers themselves. Therefore we did not feel justified in bringing forward to this Conference any Resolution which would commit them, or commit the Powers represented here, to the establishment of these lanes, or to change the custom and practice now prevailing. We think that if you enforce the law that steamers shall go at a moderate speed in a fog, you are arriving, as near as you can arrive, at the best way of providing for the safety of the vessels themselves, and especially for the safety of the fishermen.

Captain Sampson (United States).—Mr. President, I move the adoption of the Report of the Committee.

Captain Shackford (United States).—Mr. President, before it is adopted, I would like to have a letter read. We have heard a great deal about the desirability of ruling the steamers off the Banks. I have something here showing the desirability of keeping them on; and with your permission I would like to have this letter read by the Secretary.

The President.—If there be no objection on the part of the Conference. The Chair has none.

The letter is as follows:—

"*Gloucester, March* 20, 1889.

"The Gloucester skippers are by no means unanimous in wishing the steam-ships barred off from the Grand Banks. Indeed, the men engaged in fresh halibut fishing are the ones who encounter the most danger from these leviathans of the sea, as they fish a great deal on the southern edge of the Grand Banks where steamers frequently pass, and they generally oppose the proposition to compel the steamers to take a more southern course. Many of them say that they are always glad to see the steamers pass them while fishing, for, take it in winter time, the prevailing wind is from the northward, and there are no vessels but halibut fishermen on the Banks, and if any members of the crew get astray while tending trawls the only chance for rescue is by drifting to the southward and being picked up by a passing steamer, which is of common occurrence.

"Captain James McKinnon and crew, of the schooner 'Lillian Baxter,' who were rescued while the vessel was in a sinking condition by the Cunard steamer 'Umbria,' and landed at Liverpool, England, says that he would not care if twice as many steamers crossed the Banks. Captain Edward Blackburn and crew were rescued from the sinking schooner 'Gettysburg,' and carried to Liverpool, and they do not hesitate to say that the steamer saved their lives. Captain Daniels and crew, of the schooner 'Carl W. Baxter,' makes the same statement, for when in a sinking condition they were rescued by a steamer and landed in New York. Captain George W. Pendleton, of the schooner 'Cleopatra,' was dismasted in a gale on the southern edge of George's, and four of the crew were lost; he was taken off by the steam-ship 'Lord Gough,' and landed at Philadelphia. Captain Gray and crew, of the schooner 'Ivanhoe,' were rescued from a sinking vessel by a steamer and landed at New York. Captain Marr, of schooner 'Phil Sheridan,' was rescued by a steamer and landed at Boston. Captain Daniel Gray was rescued from the schooner 'Abbie S. Heath' by a steamer and landed in Havre, France. Captain Nicholson and crew were rescued from the sinking schooner 'Daniel A. Burnham' by the Allan line steamer 'Scandinavian,' and landed at St. John's, Newfoundland.

"Other cases could be enumerated where steamers have rendered valuable assistance in rescuing shipwrecked and suffering fishermen, and those who have been fortunate in thus being rescued say it should be remembered that not one case can be given where the steamer is known to have run down a Gloucester fisherman on Grand Banks. 'It is a shame,' said Captain Daniel McDonald, 'to accuse the steamers of running down vessels when there is no proof of it, for there are a great many ways in which vessels are lost, the chief of which is keeping a poor look-out.'

"Captain James Forrestall, who has been going to Grand Banks for seventeen years, says that he is always glad to see the steamers, in winter-time especially.

"The cases of the schooners 'Edwin C. Dolliver,' which sprung a leak on Grand Banks in a gale in winter, and the 'Charles Haskell,' which ran down a fisherman on George's, drowning all the crew, were cited as proofs that steamers did not run down all the vessels reported lost, and it is the general opinion among the halibut fishermen that the route cannot be improved upon."

The President.—The question now is upon the adoption of the Report of the Committee on General Division VII.

The question was put to the Conference upon the adoption of the Report on General Division VII, and it was adopted.

The President.—The Secretary will now read the Report of Committee No. 2 upon General Division VIII.

The Report of the Committee upon General Division VIII on Night Signals for communicating Information at Sea is as follows:—

"Sir, "*Washington, December* 6, 1889.

"With regard to subsections (*a*) and (*b*) of General Division VIII, the Committee have considered systems of night-signals with ordinary coloured lights, but the objection exists that they cannot be seen so far as a white light. It is the opinion of the Committee that night-signalling at sea can better be carried on by a system of long and short flashes from a white light than by any system in which coloured lights are used.

"The Committee have concluded that the systems of signalling by pyrotechnic lights which have been brought to their notice are too expensive for general use.

"The Committee have had before them a 'Supplementary Code of limited scope to convey information of special importance to passing vessels,' which has been prepared by a Committee of the British Board of Trade, and has been presented by the British Government to the various Powers for their consideration.

"Your Committee, after careful consideration, suggest that the Conference recommend the adoption, for optional use, of that Supplementary Code, with the following change, which will become necessary if the Conference adopt the signal suggested by the Joint Committee on Pilot Signals, viz.: To strike out signal 'P G,' 'Beware of derelict dangerous to navigation,' and substitute in its place 'N P,' 'I want assistance; remain by me.' Appendix (A) contains this Supplementary Code as amended.

"To illustrate the importance attached to the subject of night-signals the Committee refer to the great number of proposals on that subject mentioned by the Report of the Committee on Systems and Devices.

"That part of the proposed amendment to Article 27, entitled extra amendment No. 6, which reads as follows:—

"'Vessels in want of a pilot have to display their national flag with a white border or make the signal indicated by 'P T' at the fore.

"'At night, together or separately.

"'The pyrotechnic light, commonly known as a blue light, every fifteen minutes, or a bright white light, flashed or shown at short or frequent intervals just above the bulwarks for about a minute at a time'—which was referred to this Committee, the Committee find is already included in the International Code Signal-Book under the head of pilot signals; the Committee, therefore, recommend no further action on the amendment.

"With reference to the 23rd amendment to Article 4, viz., 'A tug wishing to offer her service to a vessel shall exhibit to such vessel, in addition to the ordinary lights, a white and red flare-up alternately,' which was referred to this Committee, the Committee beg leave to report that they do not think it expedient to allot any special signal to vessels of this class.

"Subsection (e), referring to distress-signals, was not considered, as it has been disposed of by the Conference.

"In compliance with the Resolution of the Conference referring to this Committee, assisted by the Committee on Sound-Signals, the subject of fog-signals to be allotted to pilots and to vessels seeking pilots, the Joint Committee met and decided upon the following signals:—

"For vessels requiring pilots, a prolonged blast followed by a short blast;

"For pilots wishing to offer their services, short blast followed by a long blast.

"And the Committee recommend that they be inserted in the International Code Book under the pilot-signals.

"While considering the subject of signals to convey information of special importance to passing vessels, the decision of the Conference in adding to the signals now in use, consisting of short and long blasts, and the favour in which such signals seem to be held, and the convenience which an extended use of such signals would be to mariners, have led the Committee to consider the benefits which might accrue from the more general use of the Morse system now in use by the navies of various Powers.

"Up to the present time no better system seems to have been devised for signalling purposes; it is one which can be used under all circumstances; it is readily acquired by young persons of ordinary ability, and is already taught on some training-ships. If its use were encouraged, it might lead to the study of the Code by more young men qualifying as officers of the merchant marine, or as signal-men, and thus come into more general use.

"Such studies are beneficial in developing the intellectual activity of seamen, and every accomplishment of the kind acquired and made necessary by the requirements of the service helps to develop the *morale* of the sailor.

"To thus encourage the use of the system the Committee suggest to the Conference that the complete alphabet of the Morse Code be inserted in the revised edition of the International Code Book for optional use.

(Signed)
"AUG. GARDE, *Delegate for Denmark.*
"HENRI LANNÉLUC, *Delegate for France.*
"CHRISTIAN DONNER, *Delegate for Germany.*
"N. BOWDEN-SMITH, *Delegate for Great Britain.*
"H. A. P. CARTER (*Chairman*), *Delegate for Hawaii.*
"T. DE SOUZA ROZA, *Delegate for Portugal.*
"FREDERICK MALMBERG, *Delegate for Sweden.*
"D. HUBERT, *Delegate for the Netherlands.*
"JOHN W. SHACKFORD, *Delegate for the United States.*

"To Rear-Admiral S. R. Franklin, United States' Navy,
"President of the International Marine Conference, &c."

"The Undersigned desire to record that in signing the above Report they do so without prejudice to the opinions they hold as to the desirability of giving special signals to use with fog-horns on board pilot-vessels.

(Signed)
"CHRISTIAN DONNER, *Delegate for Germany.*
"N. BOWDEN-SMITH, *Delegate for Great Britain.*
"T. DE SOUZA ROZA, *Delegate for Portugal.*
"FREDERICK MALMBERG, *Delegate for Sweden.*
"D. HUBERT, *Delegate for the Netherlands.*"

The President.—As the time has nearly arrived for the adjournment, the Chair would suggest that some disposition be made by the Conference as to the session to-morrow.

Mr. Carter (Hawaii).—Mr. Chairman, I was in hopes that we could finish this Report to-night, so that we would not be obliged to meet to-morrow. I do not know whether any of the members wish to discuss any part of the Report, but if they do, of course it will have to lie over. If not, I think we might act upon it in a very few minutes. There are no Resolutions that are absolutely adopted here. We make a suggestion to the different Governments that they should adopt this Supplementary Code, with the amendments which have been rendered necessary by the action of the Conference; and we have printed a suggestion which we would make with regard to the Morse alphabet. But they are merely suggestions and have no legal force at all; therefore, I do not know whether there is anything in the Report which would give rise to any discussion of sufficient importance to require us to meet specially for that discussion to-morrow.

Captain Salvesen (Norway).—Mr. President, I have only a few remarks to make. I want to suggest that the words, "in the revised edition," should be taken out, and that all of the signal letters in the Report should be taken out. I have many reasons for this, but if the Committee will agree to this without discussion, I shall not inflict a long speech upon you.

Captain Van Steyn (the Netherlands).—Mr. President, I also wish to make a few remarks, but I would like to know whether it is the decision of the Conference to go on with the session now?

The President.—The Chair sees no objection to continuing after 5 o'clock if the Conference desire to discuss this matter. The Chair would suggest that it be finished to-night.

Mr. Hall (Great Britain).—Mr. President, may I point out to the learned Chairman of the Committee that it does not appear to us to be important to keep the lettering in? The signals are merely suggested, and the lettering, as is pointed out by the gallant Delegate from Norway, is not material, because they must be decided upon afterwards.

Mr. Carter (Hawaii).—Mr. President, we would accept the suggestion to strike out the words, " in the revised edition," and let it read so that they might be inserted in the International Code Book. We also accept the suggestion to strike out the letters from the signal, because when the Governments adopt them they will rearrange the lettering.

The President.—If there be no objection it will be so ordered. The Delegate from the Netherlands has the floor.

Captain Van Steyn (the Netherlands).—Mr. President, I have a few remarks to make, but I do not know whether the Conference has decided to go on or not.

The President.—The Conference has decided to continue.

Captain Van Steyn (the Netherlands).—Mr. President, on p. 24, in that part which relates to the amendment to Article 27, it reads:—

"Vessels in want of a pilot have to display their national flag with a white border or make the signal indicated by 'P T' at the fore."

I would like to ask if it would not be possible to put in the signal-book a signal which the pilot makes answer to a vessel which is in want of a pilot?

Mr. Carter (Hawaii).—Mr. President, I did not quite catch the remark of the gallant Delegate from the Netherlands, but I believe it was whether it would not be possible to put in an answering signal for pilots?

Captain Van Steyn (the Netherlands).—Yes, Sir.

Mr. Carter (Hawaii).—Mr. President, we considered that the Conference had settled this question to its own satisfaction. This matter came to us from the Conference. The Conference voted absolutely that a vessel requiring a pilot and a vessel which wishes to offer her services as a pilot should be provided with signals by us, in connection with the Sound-Signal Committee. The Sound-Signal Committee very kindly met with us and we agreed upon these two signals, and that was all that we had to do. I think that the question of a pilot-signal was thoroughly discussed before the Conference, and I doubt whether it would be of any value to the Conference to take it up and to discuss it again. At all events we had nothing to do with that matter. We were instructed to find these two signals, which we did.

Captain Van Steyn (the Netherlands).—Mr. President, I was not speaking about the two sound-signals for a vessel wanting a pilot and for the pilot-vessel, but about the signal with regard to displaying the national flag. I want to ask whether it is not necessary that an answering signal should be given. The other signal is only a sound-signal.

Admiral Bowden-Smith (Great Britain).—Mr. President, the pilot comes in answer to the signal. I do not quite know what the gallant Delegate means.

The President.—He wants a signal provided for a reply by a pilot-boat.

Captain Van Steyn (the Netherlands).—Mr. President, I do not want the sound-signal answered, but when the national flag is displayed as a signal for a pilot the pilot ought to have a signal to answer it.

Mr. Verney (Siam).—Mr. President, there is one very small matter which I desire to bring before the Conference with reference to this subject. If long lines and short ones are to be put into the Reports in any way to indicate the signals, I would suggest that that kind of a mark [indicating] is a much more definite one than the short and long mark used in the Report. That is a semicircle, and they are not likely to run into one another as these other lines are. These will never run together. It is the well-known mark of a school-boy for scanning his Latin verse.

Mr. Carter (Hawaii).—Mr. President, that part of the Report, as we understand it, is before the Governments now for their consideration; and all that we have done was to recommend certain changes in compliance with what the Conference have recommended; therefore, I think we had better leave it to them.

The President.—Is the Conference ready to entertain the proposition of the Delegate from the Netherlands as to the adoption of an answering signal by a pilot-boat?

Captain Van Steyn (the Netherlands).—Mr. President, I only lay before the Conference the question whether it is not proper that an answering signal should be given to a certain signal which everybody understands. Everybody understands that the letters "P T" indicate "I want a pilot;" therefore, why not give the pilot an answering signal that everybody can understand?

Mr. Hall (Great Britain).—Mr. President, does not the pilot give the most practical answer in the world by coming when he hears a signal? If he is willing to come he comes. He approaches the vessel giving a signal that she wants a pilot. If he does not mean to come he does not come. That is the most practical answer you can give. On hearing the signal he changes his course at once, and bears down upon the vessel which signals for him, if he means to come; if he does not he stands off.

Admiral Bowden-Smith (Great Britain).—Mr. President, I do not think that we have any power whatever to add a day signal in our night signals Report. We were only told to give certain sound-signals in two cases, where the Conference decided to have signals, and I do not think the Committee had any power at all to deal with signals for pilots or anybody else.

Captain Shackford (United States).—Mr. President, I think the pilot-boats in our country carry an answering flag, and probably the answer would be to hoist the answering pennant in answer to the signal "P T."

Mr. Hall (Great Britain).—Mr. President, I think the point is perfectly clear that this Committee have only authority to deal with night signals.

The President.—I do not think the Delegate from the Netherlands insists that they have. He merely asked for this proposition independently from the Report of the Committee.

Captain Van Steyn (the Netherlands).—Mr. President, I do not insist upon this, but I found here this signal "P T," a day signal, and I thought it just as well to give the pilot-boat an answering signal by day.

The President.—In a fog they cannot see each other, while in day-time they can.

Mr. Hall (Great Britain).—Mr. President, may I suggest that we dispose of the Report from the Committee, and then if the gallant Delegate from the Netherlands has any Resolution to propose with regard to a pilot-signal, let him make it?

The President.—Does the Delegate from Great Britain move to adopt the Report?

Mr. Hall (Great Britain).—Yes, Sir.

The President.—Is the Conference ready for the question?

The question was put to the Conference upon the adoption of the Report of the Committee on General Division VIII, and it was adopted.

Captain Sampson (United States).—Mr. President, if there is no further business I move that the Conference adjourn until 11 o'clock on Wednesday morning.

The Conference thereupon adjourned until Wednesday morning, 18th December, 1889, at 11 o'clock.

"*Washington, Wednesday, December* 18, 1889, 11 *o'clock* A.M.

THE Conference was called to order at 11 o'clock A.M., Rear-Admiral Franklin in the Chair.

The President.—The first order of business this morning should be the two Resolutions presented by the Delegate from the United States, Mr. Goodrich; but he is necessarily absent on duty in connection with the Conference at the Capitol, and, therefore, they will be deferred until his return. The next order of business will be the Report of the Committee on Collocation of the Rules.

The Secretary will please read the Report.

The Report of the Committee on Collocation of the Rules is as follows:—

" Sir,   "*Washington, December* 11, 1889.

"The Committee appointed to collocate the Rules of the Road, as adopted by the Conference, report as follows:—

"The Committee have done their work on the following principles:

" 1. To retain the text of the existing Rules as far as it was feasible.

" 2. To avoid unnecessary repetitions.

" 3. To use similar words or sentences in expressing similar ideas in each of the Rules.

" 4. To make the Articles as short as possible.

" 5. To group together all Rules upon cognate subjects.

"The Regulations and notes are hereto annexed in Appendices (A) and (B) respectively.

"Particular attention is called to the changes made in Articles 7, 8, and 9, which, though differing in arrangement, embrace the precise principles of the amendments adopted by the Conference.

"We have, &c.
(Signed)   " W. W. GOODRICH (*Chairman*), *United States.*
      " Rear-Admiral DE SPAUN, *Austria-Hungary.*
      "Dr. SIEVEKING, *Germany.*
      "CHAS. HALL, *Great Britain.*
      " S. TSUKAHARA, *Japan.*
      " Commodore MONASTERIO, *Mexico.*
      " Captain SALVESEN, *Norway.*
      " Vice-Admiral KAZNAKOFF, *Russia.*

" To Rear-Admiral Samuel R. Franklin, United States' Navy,
 " President of the International Marine Conference, &c."

The President.—The first amendment in order is amendment No. 1, under Class 2. The Secretary will please read the amendment.

The amendment is as follows:—

Amendment to Collocation Report, proposed by Captain Shackford (United States), on the 14th December, 1889:

"Article 2, (*b*) and (*c*). Strike out '2,' and substitute '3,' in last line."

Captain Shackford (United States).—Mr. President, I only want to say that this distance of 2 miles was put in in 1863, more than twenty-six years ago; and it seems to me that in twenty-six years, with the improvements that have been made in lights, illuminating oil, &c., that such lights should be seen a great deal farther than 2 miles, and that the minimum standard should be higher. I believe that this is the most important subject which has come, and can come, before the Conference. A light which can be seen only 2 miles in clear weather, in misty or hazy weather can be seen certainly only a very short distance; in weather when it is not thick enough to slow down, such lights can only be seen perhaps half-a-mile. All the letters which I have received from ship-masters and persons connected with vessels have laid more stress on this subject than on any of the other subjects which have been mentioned before in the Conference. It seems to me that the minimum standard should be raised from 2 miles to 3 miles. As I said once before in the Conference, I am sure that I have seen side-lights 4 and 5 miles distinctly and plainly.

Mr. Hall (Great Britain).—Mr. President, I am sure that we all sympathize with the wish of the Delegate of the United States that these lights should be visible at as long a range as possible. But, of course, we must deal with this as with all other matters, in a practical way, and the Report of the Committee on Lights is conclusive on this point. I may point out from the Protocol—and I think it is always desirable to refer to what took place in these matters—that we discussed this matter thoroughly before. If the Delegates will turn to the Protocol of the 4th November, they will see that it was pointed out to the Conference that it was impossible to lay down a Rule that every vessel was to be provided with such lights, visible at a minimum distance of 3 miles in clear weather, because, at present, we were not in possession of sufficient data to satisfy the Powers that such lights could be got at a proper and moderate expense. When this matter came before us before, the Report of the Committee on Lights was referred to, and, if I may do so without occupying the time of the Conference unduly, I will give a summary of their Report upon this very interesting point. It is this:—

"It appears very difficult, if at all possible, to increase the power of a ship's side-light from the present range of 2 miles to that of 3, as proposed, without at the same time increasing the size of the lantern in a manner which would make it too cumbersome and expensive for use on board ship where the conditions are such as to make the construction of lanterns particularly difficult. The range of a light increases only in the ratio of the square root of its power, and it would be necessary to increase the latter in the ratio of 4 to 9, or 1 to 2·25, in order to get the desired range mentioned above.

"The Committee had no exact data before them on which they could safely base a more detailed investigation of this important and difficult question, and they therefore took the liberty to suggest that a number of experiments be carried out by the Lighthouse Board of the United States in order to furnish the material necessary for further discussion.

"Probably the construction of a more powerful light would necessitate the use of a wick of much larger diameter than that used at present, if not of a second wick; and this addition would again make it much more difficult to screen the lights properly. An electric light, on account of its smaller diameter, could no doubt be more easily arranged in such a manner as to meet the difficulty, but, in the opinion of the Committee, such a light cannot be made compulsory at the present day.

"The Committee therefore come to the conclusion that, though they cannot but consider an increase in the power of the side-lights most desirable, they do not find themselves at the present moment in a position to recommend any means by the adoption of which the desired end could with certainty be obtained. This, however, may, as they hope, result from the experiments now undertaken by the Lighthouse Board of the United States."

Now, Mr. President, the Lighthouse Board, I understand, sent in a communication to this Conference which it has not been thought necessary by the Committee to print with the Report, but I may point out this. The Lighthouse Board might report that it is possible to make side-lights visible 3 miles; but we have to decide whether or not we shall pass a Rule compelling every vessel to carry side-lights visible 3 miles. That would be a most onerous burden to cast upon small vessels. It is the small vessels that we have got to think about here. There is no difficulty about the larger vessels. These vast Atlantic steamers have magnificent lights, and there is nothing to prevent their lights being made visible at a very great distance. But it is not these big vessels for which it is important that strong lights should be provided. It is the small vessels which the big vessels overtake. They want to have the strong lights. It is the vessel out of the way of which you have to get, on which it is important that there should be powerful lights; not the big vessels, which, as a rule, have to keep out of their way.

As I say, when we have got so many small vessels—even assuming that one Board, however eminent, has found that it is possible to make side-lights visible more than 2 miles—can we, without experiments in our respective countries, make a hard and fast rule that vessels shall carry side-lights visible at a distance of 3 miles? I would venture to think, as has been pointed out by the Committee on Lights, that, in order to obey such a Rule as this, these vessels would have to carry very much larger lights, and so cumbersome that, practically, it would be out of the question. I hope the gallant Delegate from the United States will not think for one moment that any expression of opinion is going to fall from me, or from any one in this Conference, against the desirability of the lights showing farther, if it can be done; but we are not in possession of the material to justify this being done at present. Therefore, as much as I wish to see the range of the side-lights increased, I am unable to support the amendment of the Delegate from the United States.

The President.—The Chair would state that the Report of the Lighthouse Board was handed to the Chairman of the Committee on Lights.

Admiral Kaznakoff (Russia).—Mr. President, yes, Sir; the Report of the Lighthouse Board was handed to me, and the Committee did not find it necessary to report on it, because there is nothing leading to a certain conclusion in the Report. The trials were very well made, and were very, very good; but the officers who made these trials themselves remarked about the immense difference between the results obtained by them in New York Harbour and the results obtained in Hamburg by Germany. So that the Report only shows that the question is so difficult that it is not possible to advise any action upon the trials made; but that further trials should be made very carefully, and extending over a long period. So, since these experiments are made, we are in the same position as we were before they were made.

Therefore, the Committee on Lights are of the opinion that we cannot recommend anything based upon those experiments. But foreseeing the difficulties, the Committee on Lights have already made a Resolution, which is now put into the notes, desiring to have a longer distance at which the side-lights can be seen; and the Committee have adopted a Resolution, which has been accepted by the Conference, that the minimum power only of each such light should be definitely fixed, leaving it to the judgment of the parties responsible for fitting out the ship with proper lanterns to employ lamps of this or of a higher power. Therefore, under the Rules now it is stated, "at *least* 2 miles," or "at *least* 1 mile." So I think we give a very large margin to inventors to make lights visible for 5 miles, if they can do it.

Captain Sampson (United States).—Mr. President, I would like to point out with regard to the Report of the Lighthouse Board that the questions which were submitted to the Board were not such as to bring out anything with regard to the possibility of increasing the range of the lights. The question, as I understand it from reading the Report, was: Can the power be obtained required to make the side-lights visible 2 miles, and the white masthead-light visible 5 miles? These questions were answered by proper experiments to determine the actual candle-power required to make a light plainly visible at these distances, and no experiments were made to determine whether these same lights could be rendered visible at a greater distance. I am sure that if such experiments had been made as the learned Delegate from Great Britain has pointed out, they would have probably succeeded.

Without asking the Conference to attach any great importance to experiments made, I would like to point out that since this question was before the Conference I have made some experiments, and by using a lamp of 32 candle-power in the ordinary side-lights with the Fresnel lamps, both the red and green lights have been rendered visible as far as they could be seen above the horizon, with the lights fixed at a distance of 50 feet apart, horizontally, and 25 feet above the water; and I saw the lights distinctly for the distance of $5\frac{1}{4}$ miles, and as near as I can estimate it, they might have been seen 7 miles if they had not dipped at such a distance. Now, the lamp which was used in this case was what we call in this country the Rochester burner, and perhaps would not be well adapted, as it is now constructed, for use on board ships. But I am firmly convinced that it is only necessary to employ a good lamp in order to make the side-lights visible a distance of 5 miles, without any trouble, in clear weather. The lantern in which this was placed was an ordinary lantern, and there was no trouble about the light whatever.

It seems to me that this question is a very broad one and a very important one. There might be some difficulty in compelling the small vessels to provide themselves with such powerful lights—although indeed I do not think it would require a very powerful light to be visible 3 miles—but the subject is of sufficient importance for us to make some positive Rule on the subject a little in advance of the old Rule. There is no point in all of these Rules of the Road which has such a bearing upon the prevention of collisions at sea as this question of the range of the lights which a ship carries. Evidently if two vessels are capable of seeing each other at a distance of 5 miles, the danger of a collision is largely diminished below what it would be if they could see each other only at a distance of 2 miles. I am not positive that we have not done all that we can do; but it seems to me that vessels of a certain tonnage might be required to carry very much more powerful lights than those which the Rule requires them to carry. I think it is perfectly possible, and I think the importance of the point which is recommended by this amendment is sufficient to warrant us in making two Rules, if necessary; that is, one for large vessels and one for small vessels.

Admiral Bowden-Smith (Great Britain).—Mr. President, I listened with great interest to what has fallen from the gallant Delegate from the United States, and, as our First Delegate said, I sympathize with the desire to increase the range of the side-lights. What has fallen from him is of peculiar interest to me, because some experiments took place in England a short time ago when the candle-power tried in the side-lights was so near the candle-power mentioned by the gallant Delegate from the United States that the experiments will be very interesting. I think he said that the candle-power which he tried was 32. The experiments which were made in England were made with two red and green lanterns—modern lamps; and the candle-power tried was 30. The lights were upright, and they were tried on the range where the distances are marked off in hundreds of yards. The lamps were placed 50 feet apart, and the observer, an experienced officer, was sent off to examine them with signalmen as is usually done. The red and green lamps showed their full distances, 2 miles, from every point. I wish to state that the lamps were put on turn-tables, so that every point could be examined—the point of the greatest intensity and the point of the least intensity. The red and the green light both showed their full distances, but at a distance of 5,600 yards the green light failed; that is, it could still be seen, but it appeared nearly white.

Therefore I have come to the conclusion that, as the candle-power was so very near the same power as that used by my friend Captain Sampson, possibly the red and green glasses that he used were quite thin ones and not ordinary ship's glasses. I have listened with great interest to what he says; but I cannot look upon any experiments as, if I may say so, efficient experiments unless they are tried with actual ship lamps, because for sea purposes the glasses must be very thick, so that they will withstand the shock of the waves and all that sort of thing. These lamps were of 30 candle-power. Now, you must remember that the lights in the lamps deteriorate a little after they have been burning, say, for the first four hours; the lights deteriorate slightly after four hours; and you must also remember that the lights were then upright. Generally our lamps are tried at 10 degrees heel, so that if these lamps had been heeled you would not have seen them more than 2 miles. But I think the question to be considered by this Conference is whether we can expect sailing-ships and small steamers to carry lights of more than this power; and it appears to me that in order to get the Regulations through now they would have to have their side-lights of a 30 candle-power. I think that what we ought to try to do is to get the present Regulations better carried out than they are now.

Captain Sampson (United States).—Mr. President, I would like to say that the lamps with which I experimented were ship's lanterns, and that they were made with white lenses, with green and red screens, the red and green screens being about one-tenth of an inch in thickness. The red light, when tried with a spectroscope, was a good red light, without any other colour except a slight tinge of orange. But the colouring of the green did, however, continue into the orange, and it showed in the orange part of the spectrum. They were what I should consider good colour for side-lights, much better than is ordinarily used in the merchant service. I have since tried those used in the ordinary merchant service, and I find that the colour of the lights is very much inferior.

Captain Mensing (Germany).—Mr. President, I want to say, first, that I am very thankful that this discussion has taken place, as there has been considerable light thrown on this question by the discussion this morning which we have not had before. I believe that the difference in the results which have been obtained here and in England may be in a great measure attributable to the state of the atmosphere. In the North Sea and in the Channel we have, unfortunately, not the same clear weather that you have in the United States, and a clear night here means something entirely different from what we consider to be a clear atmosphere in our waters. Therefore, if the difference in the power of the lights was only so small as it was here, I can understand perfectly well how it was that in England they could only see the range of the light about 2 miles, whereas under very similar circumstances here we could get a range of 5 miles.

Captain Sampson (United States).—Mr. President, I understood him to say 3 miles.

Captain Mensing (Germany).—Mr. President, I think it was 2 miles. He said it was only 5,600 yards, and that was only when the lantern was upright. The gallant Delegate from Great Britain stated that when the lamp was heeled over to 10 degrees the range of light could not have exceeded 2 miles. I would like to point out that, so far as I know, the side-lights which are used in the United States' navy are of a particularly excellent quality. Those lights, shown in the depôt on Staten Island, were formerly used not as side-lights, but as regular fixed lights of the sixth class; they were particularly large, and constructed of beautiful cut glass. Now, such lights are extremely expensive, and I do not believe that even the great Transatlantic Companies would think of getting lanterns of that excellence in their service.

However that may be, I believe that there are two other drawbacks to the adoption of such powerful lamps as the gallant Delegate from the United States has spoken of. The Rochester lamp is the one to which he refers. I have the pleasure of sitting near one at home every night, and I like it exceedingly. But this lamp has an interior draught, and the air is not only let in to the flame from the outside, but from the inside. Now, that gives a very perfect combustion; and it would be a most excellent form to introduce into our navy but for one thing, and that is, that it requires that the draught should be regulated in the most careful manner, and if it is not regulated in the most careful manner, the lamp begins to smoke, and of course the moment the glasses are smoked there is no reliance to be placed upon them whatever. It was to this particular point that our attention was drawn in the Committee on Lights by the gallant Delegate from France. He pointed out this fact, and said that if we wanted to have a draught coming from the inside of the wick, then we would have to make a very cumbersome lantern.

There is another point to which I would like to call the attention of the gallant Delegate from the United States, and that is this: that such a light with such perfect combustion consumes an awful amount of oil. Of course I will not go into detail, because, after all, the expense of such matters may be considered very trifling; but you must make a reservoir for such a large lamp. I would like to point out that the reservoir for a Rochester lamp of about 32 candle-power is about that high [indicating], and about that large around [indicating]; this reservoir is emptied about two-thirds when the lamp has burned four hours. Now, take a long winter night, when you have to keep the lamp lighted for at least fourteen hours; then you would have to have a reservoir of perhaps this depth [indicating], and you would require a wick to suck up the oil from this point way down to here [indicating]. On this account we all know that it has been necessary to introduce pumping machines or other devices for providing these lamps that we are using in our lighthouse apparatus with oil so as to bring it up to the level of the wick.

I do not believe that it is impossible to make a better lamp. I do not believe that it is impossible, even keeping the lenses as they are now and the reflectors as they are now, to make a lamp which will show in the ordinary side-lights of a vessel the distance of 3 miles; but, so far as I know, there has not been any such lamp constructed just for side-lights or for the running lights of a steamer, and I think it would be rather risky to adopt such a Rule as this before we have such a lamp. Let such a lamp be introduced or invented, and I think that every country would find it very easy, under the Rules as they now stand, to introduce such instructions to their Surveyors as to require that the light should be visible 3 miles on board of all vessels in their service; but let us wait until that lamp has been invented; let us wait until it is fairly tried; let us wait until we are sure that this aim, which we all desire, is attainable.

Captain Bisbee (China).—Mr. President, I would like to ask Captain Sampson if, in the experiments which he made, the lamps were placed on a turn-table so as to show the minimum power as well as the maximum power, so that they could be turned to the observers to see the minimum power of the lamp?

Captain Sampson (United States).—Mr. President, I will answer that question by saying that no reflectors were used in the lights, but there was a uniform light through the whole horizon. There was no reflector in the lantern.

Captain Shackford (United States).—Mr. President, I want to say from my own knowledge that there are vessels in this country which have side-lights that can be seen over 3 miles; but whether it is due to the character of the glass or the nature of the oil I do not know. But I am positive that there are scores of vessels which carry lights of that description which can be easily seen 3 miles; and the side-lights in this country, I know, cost very little more than they do in Great Britain. The additional cost is very slight. As to the side lights not being seen in the North Sea in fair weather as far as they are in this country, it seems to me that we have no more powerful lights in lighthouses here than they have there. I do not know of any part of the world in which I have been where lights can be seen any farther than they can on the coast of Great Britain. I have seen the red flash on Tuskar 15 miles, and they must have pretty clear atmosphere to see a light at that distance, and a coloured light at that.

The President.—The question is upon amendment No. 1, Class 2. Is the Conference ready for the question? The Secretary will please read the amendment.

Amendment No. 1, Class 2, is as follows:—

Amendment to Collocation Report proposed by Captain Shackford (United States), the 14th December, 1889:

"Article 2 (*b*) and (*c*). Strike out '2' and substitute '3' in last line."

The President.—Is the Conference ready for the question?

The question was put to the Conference upon the adoption of amendment No. 1, Class 2, and it was lost.

The President.—The next amendment is amendment No. 2, Class 2, which the Secretary will please read.

Amendment No. 2, Class 2, is as follows:—

Amendment to Collocation Report proposed by Dr. Sieveking on behalf of the German Delegation, the 14th December, 1889:

"In Article 2 (*d*), insert the words, 'more than half a point,' after the word 'seen.'"

Dr. Sieveking (Germany).—Mr. President, may I ask permission to say a very few words about this amendment in order to explain what we intended in laying this amendment before the Conference, and what our reasons are for thinking that this is a subject of sufficient importance to be carefully considered, even at this late stage of our proceedings? There are two different points of view which are to be taken into consideration in this amendment. If I may use the expression, there is the legal or legislative point of view, and there is the technical point of view. The first is the legislative proposition. I should like to point out that I think there can be no doubt that under the Rules, as they stand at present, there is a contradiction. We say, in Article 2, subdivision (*d*):—

"The said green and red side-lights shall be fitted with inboard screens projecting at least 3 feet forward from the light, so as to prevent these lights from being seen across the bow."

Now, the meaning of this Rule, I think, is pretty clear. The Rule certainly means that the lights are not to be seen from any point across the bow, and the screens are to prevent the rays from crossing the bow altogether, or in other words from crossing the prolonged keel line or the prolonged longitudinal axis of the vessel. That is the meaning which must be connected with the words as they stand. But, of course, it is quite clear, if that were done, that there would be a patch before the vessel which would be left in the dark, a patch limited by the line going parallel with the keel line, and beginning on both sides of the vessel, so that the part of the sea before the vessel to a breadth corresponding with the breadth of the vessel would be left in the dark. That certainly would be very impracticable; and there can be no difference of opinion about that, I think. The Rules themselves show clearly that it is not the intention.

In Article 18 it is said: "When two vessels under steam are meeting end-on or nearly end-on, so as to involve risk of collision," and then it is explained that this Article applies to cases where by night each vessel is in such a position as to see both of the side-lights of the other vessel. So the Rules are very clear to the effect that they suppose it to be the regular case that both the side-lights are to be seen when the vessels are nearly end-on; and that can be done only if the rays of the side-lights cross the bow. In the beginning, in Article 2, the Rule is given which prohibits them from being seen across the bow, and in Article 18 a Rule is given which rests on the basis that the lights must be seen across the bow. That is what I call the legislative point of view. If it could be avoided, I do not think it advisable that Rules should be confirmed which contain such a contradiction. The question then would be, whether subsection (*d*) would have to be changed in a way so as to leave it to the discretion of ship-builders and constructors of lights, and Surveyors to have the lights screened so as to show any distance across the bow that they liked. But this, of course, would not be desirable, because then the end which Article 2 tries to attain would be far from being attained, and there would be no certainty whatever. So there must be a certain limit.

Now, the question as to what way a certain limit could be given has been before the Conference already on the 4th November, and I beg to call your attention to the Proctocol of that date, when the amendment bronght in by the Delegate from the Netherlands was considered, and which provided, "that the said green and red side-lights should be fitted with inboard screens so as to prevent these lights from being seen across the bow within a certain distance in front of the bow, say 100 metres." That amendment was discussed and was lost. You see that our amendment does not repeat this language, but rests on a different principle. We tried to define the limit at which the rays of the side-lights are to be allowed to cross the bow, by defining a certain angle; or to put it quite clear, by indicating a certain boundary-line, the line which is formed by drawing this line at an angle to the keel-line, and which angle we propose shall be an angle of half a point. So by drawing this line at the angle of half a point to the keel-line we arrive at the boundary-line which, according to our amendment, should be the boundary-line beyond which the side-lights are not allowed to be seen.

This principle has been also mentioned already in the discussion to which I referred. The learned First Delegate from Great Britain has mentioned it, and said that in his opinion it would be better to take the angle of vessels from the keel, and that it would be more advisable than the other principle of defining the distance from the bow at which the rays should be allowed to cross. On the second reading of the Rules no amendment to this effect has been brought in. These are the reasons why we have thought we would be allowed to lay this amendment before the Conference without repeating what has been thoroughly discussed already on a former occasion.

In the course of the second reading of the Rules it has also been mentioned as a fact, without having been contradicted, that cases have occurred where the side-lights crossed at such a wide angle that they could be seen even at a point and three-quarters across the bow, and that happened with a man-of-war, which, of course, must have been fitted out with particular care and attention. So it might happen that, as the Rule stands now, even a greater distance might practically occur than one and three-quarters points, because it does not give any limit at all. I think this is quite obvious, and I believe that it will be more fully explained by my friend on my left, as a technical point.

But I think it is quite clear and obvious, even to laymen, that very great danger must be caused by this uncertainty. If you take a vessel "A," proceeding on her course where the screens are so constructed as to allow the rays to cross at a very sharp or narrow angle only, so that they cannot be seen beyond a half a point across the bow, and this vessel meets another vessel "B," a little on her starboard side, whose screens are not so constructed, but which allow the rays to cross at a wider angle, say, at a point and three-quarters, then "A" sees the two side-lights of the vessel "B," and the vessel "B" only sees the green light of the vessel "A," and keeps her course in order to pass "A" on her starboard side. The consequence will be that, following the Rule laid down in Article 18, the vessel "A" will turn to starboard, or port her helm, while the vessel "B" keeps her course, because vessel "B" only sees the green light on her starboard bow, and thinks that she is in perfect safety and may pursue her course. So vessel "A" just turns into the course of vessel "B," and thereby collision may ensue.

It has already been mentioned, on the second reading of the Rules, that several cases have occurred where it has been ascertained that this was in fact most probably the cause of the collision where a great number of lives were lost. Therefore, from this technical point of view, which I have only tried to explain in order to show the importance of the matter, and from the other point of view which I mentioned, that the Rules, if possible, should be framed in such a way as not to contain an uncertainty or contradiction, it is very important to have this question settled, and we have thought it desirable to lay this amendment before the Conference.

Mr. Hall (Great Britain).—Mr. President, I am sure there is no need of any apology from my learned friend the Delegate from Germany in bringing this very important matter to the attention of the Conference. It is a matter which has attracted the attention, I think I may say, of all the Maritime Powers, as being a matter of very great importance, and we recognize it as such. But as I pointed out when this matter was first discussed before the Conference, our Board of Trade Regulations contain directions to Surveyors, covering, I think, about four pages of small print, pointing out the way in which they must see that the lights are screened, so as to prevent the rays from crossing the bows at more than a certain angle, and there are tabulated forms in these Regulations dealing with vessels above 20 feet in beam and vessels above 40 feet in beam. I should like to follow the example, because it is an example which it is always well to follow, of the learned Delegate from Germany in dealing with this question.

First of all, I will refer to the Rule as it stands as present. Now, Mr. President, of course I am unable to say what was in the minds of the original framers of these Rules, but I venture to think, and I have considered it very carefully, that when this Rule was framed the question of the rays of light crossing the bow never came within their minds at all. This Rule was that the light should be so placed that a man standing ahead of that vessel should not see the starboard light on the port side or the port light on the starboard side. That was the object, I have no doubt. But by experience it was found that however you screened the lights, if you screened them so that they showed their full light ahead, the rays would cross; and when we found that out our Board of Trade set to work to minimize that evil as much as possible. I think that the real question which we have to consider here is not whether or not the Conference shall come to a conclusion on the point—I think we shall all agree that this is most desirable—but the real question to be considered is the way in which it shall be done.

It was pointed out by one of the Delegates who spoke at our last meeting that these Rules are Rules for preventing collisions at sea, which should be rightly understood by sailors. They are not Rules for Surveyors. It is impossible for us to put into our Rules all the details necessary to show how these Rules are to be carried out in practice. I venture to think that this matter is a matter which could not be really dealt with in the Rules themselves. I think it is a matter which will require to be worked out very carefully by the respective Departments in the various countries of the Maritime Powers, because, as I have pointed out, it will require the greatest care to lay down definitions for the guidance of Surveyors as to how these lights should be screened. I did, when I addressed the Conference before upon this subject, make a suggestion that perhaps the angle was the best way to determine it, and I find that the gallant Delegate from Germany also expressed the opinion that perhaps that would be the better method to adopt. But we do not at all wish to adhere to that view. We want to come to a conclusion which will meet with the views of all, or the great majority, of the Delegates.

I would point this out: the Committee on Lights have studied all these matters very carefully, as we know from the gallant Chairman, the Delegate from Russia, and they studied this point also, but they did not find that they could come to any conclusion upon it. It is, however, very possible that the matter of the distance in front of the bows of the vessel was the question which was discussed before them, rather than the angle or the number of degrees or points at which the rays of light should be allowed to cross the bow. But, however that may be, I think it is possible for us to come to a conclusion upon the point, and I would venture to suggest to the learned Delegate from Germany that a Resolution might be set out in Appendix (B) as a recommendation to the various Maritime Powers in regard to the way in which these lights should be screened. I think it will certainly assist those Powers which have no Regulations on the subject at present, and I think it will be desirable if we can in the recommendations adopt, as far as possible, the practice which has been adopted, so far as I am aware, in all of the countries which have considered this question. The angle which we have thought desirable is an angle of 5 degrees, which is practically the same amount as the gallant Delegate from Germany proposes in his amendment. These two are so near to one another that we will willingly adopt the suggestion of half a point.

But then, the question comes, how is that to be measured? And that is an all-important question. That matter, I see, did come before the Committee on Lights, because my gallant friend the Delegate from Russia has pointed out the very great importance which should be attached to the spot from which the distance should be calculated, and that it should be from the centre of the flame, because, unless you take it from the centre of the light, the distance may vary. The great object, I assume, would be to have practically a uniform distance, and so it should be measured in the same way. Therefore, Mr. President, I would venture to suggest that this is a matter to be dealt with in a note to Appendix (B). Of course I only suggest this for the purpose of discussion, and very possibly suggestions may be made which will very much improve upon the words which I venture to submit. But so far as we can see, my colleagues and I think that perhaps we are meeting with the views of those who have studied this question, and having read the very interesting speeches of the gallant Delegate from Germany, and other speeches made upon this point when the matter was first raised, we propose this Resolution:—

"Side-lights should be so screened as to prevent the centre of the flame of the lamp from being seen across the bow more than half a point."

That, I think, will meet the various views which have been suggested. But, as I say, we shall be very glad if any one can suggest an improvement upon it.

Mr. Verney (Siam).—Mr. President, I want to make one or two observations on this subject, as I had the honour to address the Conference upon it on a former day. The remark which I have to make is this: I think our whole difficulty arises from what the learned Delegate from Great Britain has just said, that no Regulation of this kind should be found in the Rules for preventing collisions at sea. It may seem a startling proposition to some of the members of the Conference to hear that so boldly proclaimed; but it does seem to me that this is a mere matter for Surveyors. The responsibility for the way in which the lights are screened does not rest with the sailors. No master on board ship has any power whatever to alter these screens to the slightest degree, and I think that to put into the hands of a sailor who is to navigate a ship a Rule which he cannot possibly have anything to do with, is to insert in the Rules for preventing Collisions at Sea something which certainly should be excluded from them.

I venture to think that this applies not only to this subject but to some other matters, where construction has crept into the Rules for preventing Collisions at Sea. The responsibility of a sailor is one thing, and the responsibility of a Surveyor is another; and if you are going to mix up in this Rule two responsibilities, you will come into confusion which was born years ago, when these Rules were first made. I sincerely hope that the suggestion thrown out by the learned Delegate from Great Britain will be adopted, and that we shall not have in the Rules for preventing Collisions at Sea something which is entirely foreign to them, as this Rule is.

Captain Sampson (United States).—Mr. President, I would like to point out to the learned Delegate from Siam that the guidance of these Rules, so far as the sailor on board ship is concerned, must, of course, depend upon how these lights are placed, and the discussion now, as I understand it, is as to whether these lights shall cross the bow or whether the nearest rays shall be parallel with each other. The rays of the light do meet across the bow. They may be parallel, as the Rules require them to be, or they may be divergent. Of course there can be no objection to the rays crossing each other beyond the point at which they are visible. There can be no objection to that, because the lights are not visible. If we suppose that the light crosses the bow or is seen across the bow at the angle of half a point, necessarily in front of that vessel there will be an arc of a whole point over which both lights will be visible, and consequently a vessel approaching another will be uncertain as to the direction of that vessel within that arc. If we suppose these lights to be visible at the distance of 2 miles, you will see that the length of the arc at that distance will be considerable; that is, it will be a large fraction of a mile.

Hence I think that the Rule as it now stands is altogether the safer one. When you see a vessel headed for you you must remember that the distance between the lights is comparatively small. The visual angle subtended by these two lights, as you recede from the ship, at the distance of 2 miles, is very small. On a ship of 50 feet beam, at a distance of 2 miles, the arc subtended by the two lights is extremely small. I think that there can be no danger from the fact that both lights will not be visible at the proper distance from the ship. The visual angle is so small at some distance from the ship that the distance between the two eyes of the person is sufficient to subtend the arc between the two lights themselves; and where you have two look-outs, or the man is not perfectly stationary, I do not think it is possible that a position can be taken where both of the lights will not be visible directly in line with the keel of the ship.

Of course, if we are to fix an angle at which the light shall be seen across the bow of the ship, it ought to depend upon the beam of the ship, because the nearer the lights are together the nearer to the position of the lights will those rays cross each other. Not only that, but if we are to fix such a limit, it ought to depend upon the length of such a ship, because, as has been pointed out by the gallant Delegate from the Netherlands, the point at which the rays cross each other in a long ship may be very near the bow of the ship, and that would be objectionable. It seems to me, therefore, that the safer rule for us to follow is the one which is laid down here in the Rules of the Road.

Captain Mensing (Germany).—Mr. President, the aim of the amendment before us is to do away with the uncertainty which we have found under the Rule as it now stands. We have found that the expression "across the bows" means either too much or too little. The difficulty which we have found is shown very conclusively by what we have just heard from the gallant Delegate from the United States. If I am not mistaken, he pointed out that it was not desirable to have these rays cross before the limit of visibility, that is to say, 2 miles, and he believes that in order to secure this object we ought to allow the Rule to stand as it is now. Now, let me read to the gallant Delegates from the United States the Report on the Trials of Running Lights and Sound-Signals proposed for trial by the American Delegation of the International Marine Conference, and submitted by Commander F. E. Chadwick, United States' Navy, because I would like to point out how very high authorities have interpreted this Rule. He says:—

"It will be observed that there are large discrepancies between the estimates of observers and the actual bearings in some of the double-light observations. This arose largely from the fact that lights show over greater angles than intended. I have had a trial made of the arc of illumination of the side-lights of this ship, and find that the light itself will show (actually) as far aft as three points on the quarter (the reflection of the lights on the side of the light-box—the lights are electric and very brilliant—showing considerably farther aft), and across the bow one and three-quarter points. I think very few, if any, of the lights used are accurate in regard to the illuminated arc. Every portion of the flame throws a ray, and tangents drawn from its circumference to the edges of the light-box mark properly the limits of illumination."

Now, the gallant Delegate from the United States says that the law is that they shall not cross at all except in a limit of 2 miles, and that would make the angles just one degree. But here we have got it proved by actual measurement that in one of the latest ships this angle has been increased to one and three-quarter points, so that in front of the ship these lights have three and a-half points on each side. In order to point out the very great danger which might arise from such a state of things, I have made a diagram to-day, to which I desire to call your attention. In this diagram you

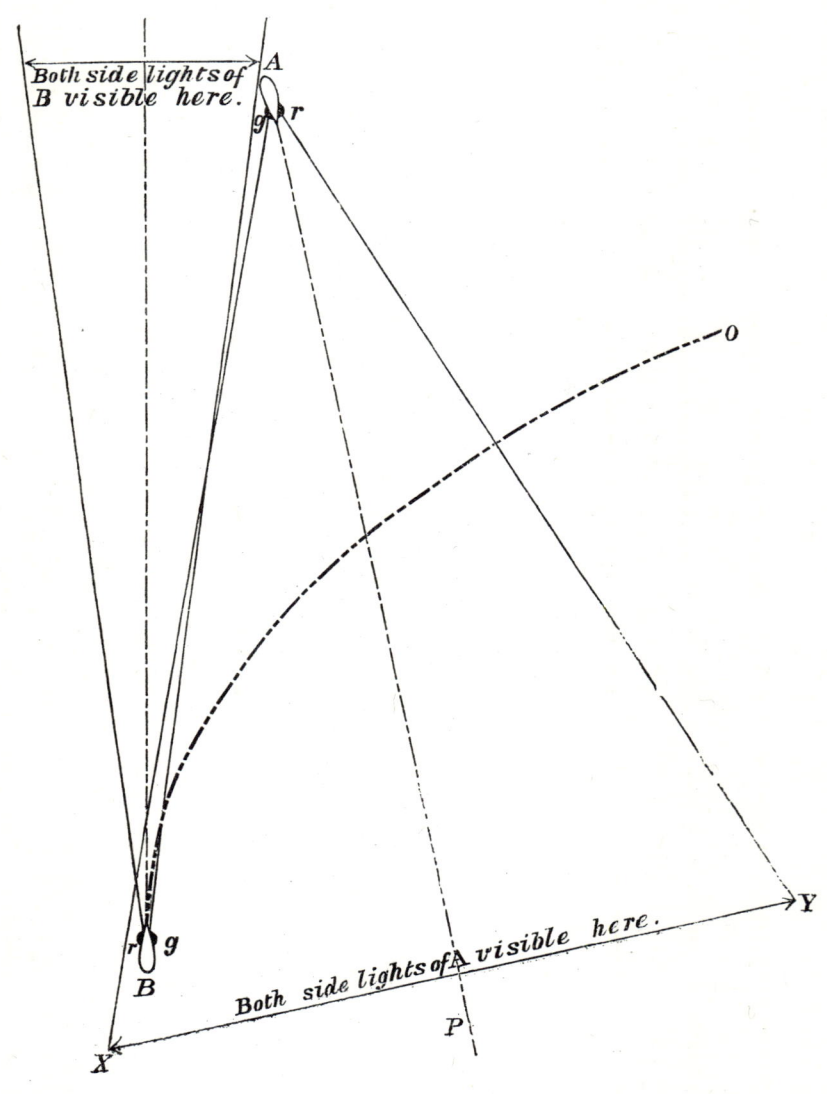

will find there are two ships, marked "A" and "B," which are both steamers. The side-lights of "A" are both visible over an arc of one and three-quarter points on each bow; the side-lights of "B" are screened so as to be both visible over an arc of half a point on each bow. Consequently, "A" sees only "B's" green side-light and holds her course; "B" sees both side-lights of "A" and steers to starboard. In this way imminent risk of collision is brought on.

I believe that, if you will study the diagram which I have submitted to you, you will see that the ships have to keep off, as I have pointed out here, under the instructions of Article 15, where it says that, "if two ships under steam are meeting end-on, or nearly end-on, so as to involve risk of collision, each shall alter her course to starboard so that each may pass to the port side of the other." That is the case with "B." "B" sees the red and green light of "A" nearly ahead, only a little, not more than half a point on her side, and, therefore, she has to turn to starboard. But "A" sees the green light of "B" on her starboard bow nearly a point and a half, and under the provisions of Article 15 she is to keep her course. I think you will remember that, in cases of collisions, the case is not infrequent where the ship says: "I proceeded, keeping my course, and saw the green light on my starboard bow; all at once I saw that the ship was turning across my bow and I saw both lights." That is the case which happens very often, and I believe that a part of the collisions which have been brought about may be explained in this way. Now, we wanted to deal with this subject to see whether this danger could not be removed, and we have brought this amendment before you.

There is very little more to be said except to explain how we came to adopt the angle of a half a point. As far as I know, there are only two countries in which the Rule where the lights should cross each other before the bow is accepted. One is Denmark, in which country the distance is settled to be about a cable's length, which would be 185 metres, so the angle would be much less than the one which we propose now; and the other country is Great Britain. There is a Table here from which I get the French translation, in which it says that, for the beam of a ship 20 feet broad, the shortest distance at which these rays should cross each other is about 200 feet; that is to say, the rule laid down by the Board of Trade comes practically to this—that, at the distance of ten beams, or ten times the breadth of the beam, there should be a distance before which these rays of the side-lights should not cross. That makes a half a point.

I should not at all oppose having this removed from the paragraph where we propose that it should be inserted, and inserted in Appendix (B), as I believe it makes but very little difference, and these gentlemen have said they would rather have it printed in Appendix (B). But I would like to ask you how it will be with those countries where there are no Surveyors who are surveying the vessels, and where the survey of vessels is entirely out of the question? I think there are a number of countries having very large fleets which do not have Surveyors, and I suppose they do not intend to have them, or that they cannot have them. If they cannot think of having every ship that goes to sea inspected by a Surveyor, how is the captain of a ship to know that, when he brings his ship into British waters, he will meet with a Rule under which he has not got his side-lights in the proper place, and that the rays cross at some other point than that prescribed by the Board of Trade? That his lights are entirely wrong, and that he will be blamed by the Court if he comes into collision? I think that Appendix (B) will have to be brought just as much before the sailor as the Rules, and then he will know what it is.

But there are a good many little details which we have already decided in the Rules. The captain does not fix these side-lights, therefore you might just as well say: Leave them altogether to the Surveyor; and so, all of these other statements about different points might be left out and the Rules be made so much the shorter; but, as I said before, I do not oppose having this put in Appendix (B), so far as I am personally concerned.

There is one thing in the proposition of the learned Delegate from Great Britain which makes me extremely doubtful whether that would be of any help to us. He proposes that the angle should be measured from the centre of the flame. Now, let us understand how this thing is. We have a flame, and he thinks that the line drawn from the centre of the flame to the edge of the screen should form an angle of not more than half a point. But that is merely a theoretical deduction, and is of no practical value whatever, for more than half the candle-power, or more than half the light, will be seen on the other side. We all know that half of a light is visible at not a very much less distance than the whole of it, and, therefore, it would come to about the same thing.

Now, remember that we have to make use of wicks of rather a large diameter; remember also that the lantern itself becomes in a feeble way an illuminator, owing to the light reflected on the inside from the glass, and I believe you will agree with me that this is rather a dangerous proceeding. I should have nothing to say against it if the learned Delegate from Great Britain will word this Regulation so that it shall be measured from the outside of the flame; or so that no part of the flame shall be visible for more than half a point. If half a point would not be acceptable to any of the Governments, I think it would be very easy to alter it accordingly, or so as to make it one point. I would state here that it really makes but very little difference whether the limit is given at half a point, or a point, or a point and a half, if only one can rely upon it that in every ship the limit is complied with. Whether it is to be half a point or a point, it seems to me may be safely left to the judgment of the Governments after they have made careful study of the matter, which I believe will be necessary. But I wish very much indeed that the learned Delegate from Great Britain would take out the reference to the centre of the flame, because that is nothing but a mathematical deduction, and does not practically affect it in any way whatever.

Captain Sampson (United States).—Mr. President, I would like to point out to the gallant Delegate from Germany that his very able argument seems to me to be all against the amendment which his Delegation has proposed. The Rule as it stands now says distinctly that the light shall not be seen across the bow. The gallant Delegate from Germany has taken an exaggerated case; one from actual practice, to be sure, but it is an exaggerated case of the amendment which the German Delegation has proposed. He has shown very clearly the evil effects of having the lights show across the bow. It seems to me that he has stated a case to prove that the amendment should not be adopted.

Captain Mensing (Germany).—Mr. President, there is a practical difficulty in adopting the proposition of the gallant Delegate from the United States, which I am sorry it may take me some time to explain, but I hope I will be able to do it without any drawings or diagrams. Imagine the wick of a lamp, and at some distance a screen which cuts off the flame, then you will understand how the line connecting the edge of that screen with the centre of the lamp will be gradually screened, and also, that there will be some light towards the last until it is cut off altogether. Now, if we adopt the Rule as Captain Sampson proposes it, the lights will have to be screened so that they cannot be very well seen at any such distance as 2 miles, and it is only as we turn farther to the starboard that the lights will become more distinctly visible. This, I believe, will always happen if we adopt a screen of the length which has been proposed here, say, from about 1 metre up to 2 metres. If I have a screen that is 100 feet long I can cut it off very well; but we have not these screens on our ships; the screens on board our ships are from 1 to 2 metres in length, and with such screens you cannot screen the light properly without weakening it in the sector which is nearest the screen.

Mr. Hall (Great Britain).—Mr. President, I have listened with great interest to the speech of the gallant Delegate from the United States, and also to the speech of the gallant Delegate from Germany, who has just sat down. I think we could meet the views of both. As I said before, with regard to the existing Rule, it has been pointed out by the gallant Delegate from the United States that this would practically be a contradiction in terms. But I still adhere to what I said at the outset. I believe that the Rule as it stands at present refers to a man standing at the bow, and not some distance in front of the bow. It is a mere direction that the light should not show across the bow. But it does not deal with the question of the rays of the light crossing the bow. I think that we can meet the views of both the gallant Delegate from Germany and the gallant Delegate from the United States by leaving out the words, "the centre of," so that it will read as follows: "Side-lights should be so screened as to prevent the rays of the light being seen across the bow more than half a point." That will be an instruction which will be given to Surveyors to be carried out, and I think that will obviate this difficulty as much as it possibly can be obviated.

The President.—The question is upon the proposition of the Delegate from Great Britain. The Secretary will please read it.

The proposition of the Delegate from Great Britain is as follows:—

To be inserted as a note to Appendix (B) the following:

"Side-lights should be so screened as to prevent the rays of light being seen across the bows."

Dr. Sieveking (Germany).—Mr. President, on behalf of the German Delegation I beg to say that we accept this proposal made by the learned Delegate from Great Britain.

Mr. Goodrich (United States).—Mr. President, I have not been able to attend during the progress of this whole discussion, but I do not see why the suggestion of the learned Delegate from Great Britain makes any serious change in that principle; and furthermore, I can see that it weakens the force of the present Rule, which is a direction to the sailor embodied in the Rule. The notes are recommendations to the Powers, and do not become Rules of the Sea. If I understand it, the desire of the learned Delegate from Great Britain is to take these words out from the Rule?

Mr. Hall (Great Britain).—No, Sir.

Mr. Goodrich (United States).—The idea is, then, to leave the Rule just as it is and to add an additional note?

Mr. Hall (Great Britain).—Mr. President, I do not think any of us want to alter the principle of the Rule. We merely want a latent difficulty explained, and it will be explained by this recommendation to the different Powers.

Mr. Goodrich (United States).—Mr. President I call the attention of the learned Delegate to the fact that the notes in Appendix (B) are not necessarily to be included in the Rules themselves, so they do not cover a latent difficulty or explain it to the sailor's mind. While the Board of Trade of England has its Inspectors and Surveyors, many nations have no such Board of Trade, and no such Inspectors, and no such Surveyors, and in all of these countries where there are no such officers such a note would be of no value. The Rule itself expresses the position of the lights, which are to be looked after by the owners or masters when the ship sails, and not by any officials. It seems to me also that you are explaining what does not require an explanation.

Mr. Hall (Great Britain).—Mr. President, I am only referring to what the learned Delegate from the United States himself suggested when this matter was discussed, when it was proposed to alter the Rule by putting in the amendment. He then said that he thought it would be far better for it to be made the subject of investigation by the proper authority in the respective countries, and not to put it in the Rules. We do not propose to alter the Rule at all. We do not propose to make any alterations in the instructions to sailors. This is merely a matter with regard to the instructions to Surveyors in surveying vessels and when vessels are being fitted out. We think it is a matter of importance that this should be brought to their attention. The only object is to try and get some uniform distance at which lights should cross the bow.

Captain Sampson (United States).—Mr. President, I think that perhaps the proposition of the learned Delegate from Great Britain will be entirely acceptable to all of us, as it does not affect the present Rule, whatever may be done to carry it into effect by the different Powers. I am sure that will be acceptable to all of us.

The President.—The proposition of the Delegate from Great Britain will be again read. The Chair understands that the Delegate from Germany accepts this in lieu of his amendment.

Dr. Sieveking (Germany).—Yes, Sir; we have accepted it.

The proposition of the Delegate from Great Britain is as follows:—

To be inserted in Appendix (B) as a Resolution:

"Side-lights should be so screened as to prevent the rays of light being seen across the bow."

Mr. Hall (Great Britain).—Mr. President, that should be "more than half a point across the bow."

Captain Sampson (United States).—Mr. President, I did not understand that the words, " more than half a point," were in there.

Mr. Hall (Great Britain).—Mr. President, I read it out twice distinctly. If there is any mistake about it by all means let us discuss it again.

Mr. Goodrich (United States).—Mr. President, I venture to call your attention to the fact that we have adopted one principle in the Rule, and now we are adopting another in a note to the Rule, which puts this Conference in rather a singular attitude.

Captain Mensing (Germany).—Mr. President, I do not understand the statement of the learned Delegate who has just sat down, because, as I have pointed out, the Dockyard authorities of the United States' Navy, which I believe are the highest authorities in the matter, have decided otherwise; and one of the latest ships of the United States' navy, the ship "Yorktown," had her lights so fitted that the rays crossed the bow at a point and three-quarters. If there is any member here who will be able to point out a single case where there is a ship that is screened in such a way that her lights can be seen at a distance of 2 miles when shining with full force ahead and still not cross between that distance and the bow of the boat I should be very glad if he would mention it, because I will be willing, if I have to travel 500 miles, to go and see this miracle of the world. I do not believe there is such a ship existing.

Mr. Goodrich (United States).—Mr. President, my gallant friend the Delegate from Germany does not seem to apprehend the suggestion which I have just made. The Conference have put into the Rule a provision that the lights shall be so screened as to prevent their being seen across the bow.

Mr. Hall (Great Britain).—Mr. President, no, it is the old Rule.

Mr. Goodrich (United States).—Mr. President, the Conference have adopted it. There is no change. It is an old-established Rule, which has worked well and which is fully understood, and the Conference have adopted the principle after a long discussion. They adopted the principle by refusing to change the Rule. That principle is that the lights shall be so screened that they shall not be seen across the bow. Now it is proposed to add a note to Appendix (B), which says that they shall be so screened as not to show more than half a point across the bow.

Mr. Hall (Great Britain).—Mr. President, that the *rays* shall not cross more than half a point before the bow, not the light.

Mr. Goodrich (United States).—Mr. President, I take it that the rays of the light and the light are the same thing. Some gentlemen shake their heads. If you can see the light you can see the rays of light. If you can see the rays of light you can see the light. That is my assertion, and it is true. It does not make any difference whether you see the light or the rays of light; to the sailor it is a light. Now, you are putting in the Rule one principle that the light shall not show across the bow at all, and you are putting into the recommendation to be inserted in this Appendix a principle that they shall not show more than half a point across the bow. The two things are utterly inconsistent, and I must very respectfully say that I should think, speaking only for myself, that if I voted on that subject in the affirmative I would be put in a very ridiculous position.

Mr. Hall (Great Britain).—Mr. President, the learned Delegate from the United States says that we are proposing something which is inconsistent. If that is the case we have been inconsistent ever since the Board of Trade published the Regulations upon this subject. Now, this is a practical question, and not a theoretical question. We know that you can put the lights so that you cannot see either of them across the bow, if you are standing at the head of the vessel. But if you put these lights so that they shall show a full light ahead, the rays of them must eventually converge, unless you have a vessel built which is a perfect parallelogram. As long as a vessel has bows and a stern you cannot possibly place this light so that the rays of light will not eventually converge at some distance or other. But you can place these lights so that if you stand at the head of the vessel you cannot see the port light on the starboard side or the starboard light on the port side. You must go a long distance off before these rays will converge.

Now, that is a practical difficulty which every thinking nation has seen. All that I can say is, that if we have been inconsistent, as the learned Delegate from the United States says, we have four pages of printed matter dealing with this difficulty and pointing out how it is to be avoided. The only object of this note in Appendix (B) is to call the attention of the Powers to this same difficulty which has been seen by all the Maritime Powers who have considered the question carefully. There is a latent difficulty which is to be guarded against. You can perfectly well put your lights at present so that they cannot be seen across the bows if you stand at the bow of the vessel. This is a question of dealing practically with a fact which has been ascertained by experience and which can only be dealt with in a practical way.

Captain Malmberg (Sweden).—Mr. President, as I read this Rule proposed by the German Delegation it appears to my mind that if we adopt it the lights, or the rays of the side-lights, would be allowed to be seen across the bow as long as they did not cross more than half a point. It does not at all provide that the rays should cross not more than half a point before the bow. As it is worded here the rays may be allowed to cross inside of the bow, as long as it is not more than half a point.

Admiral Nares (Great Britain).—Mr. President, a few words about the fact of the lights showing and the rays showing. The practice has come to be in all countries for the screen to be practically about 3 feet long from the centre of the light to where the angle will cut, on purpose to cut off the rays as much as possible. If you will adopt a longer screen of course you can get over the difficulty and the rays will not cross. If you can get a 20-foot screen they would not cross. But practically the limit of the screen is now, in all countries, about 3 feet. With regard to the light and the ray, I will bring forward the fact of the revolving light in the lighthouse. A first-class revolving light will show 20 miles, and as it revolved the whole light is taken away from the mariner. But it is actually blended inside the lantern and you can see that blending 5 or 6 miles; so much so, in fact, that correspondence has been going on with regard to the light on Cape Finisterre for about twenty years,

[93]

because mariners cutting around the corner within 5 or 6 miles of this light do not see the light revolving at all; they only see the rays of the light, and therefore they complain that it is a fixed light.

Captain Shackford (United States).—Mr. President, I hope that this will not be carried. We have no Surveyors in this country; every master and ship-builder fixes the lights to suit himself. We build the front part of the screen to the same distance from the screen that the centre of the light is from it. If we come to any such suggestion as this, that the light shall be screened so that it may be seen not more than half a point across the bow, the result will be that in a short time we shall be having lights seen across the bow two or three points, because the masters and ship-builders will begin to experiment on the position and angle of the light.

Mr. Hall (Great Britain).—Mr. President, may I point out that possibly the discussion of this and similar questions will have one very beneficial effect which I am sure will be hailed by all the Representatives who so ably represent the United States here, and that is that the United States, which is always ready to adopt anything that is of great benefit in its public service, will think it desirable to institute a Board of Trade in this country to look after these matters?

Mr. Goodrich (United States).—Mr. President, I might say in answer to that suggestion that we have shown our common sense in having adopted the Rules of the Road precisely as they were passed as proposed by the English Board of Trade. We have already a provision in the Statutes which authorizes the survey of vessels by the Collectors of Customs at the various ports. But, although this Statute has been on the Statute-book for nearly twenty years, there never has been an instance, so far as I know, where the Rule has been obeyed. In an interview which I had with the Collector of Customs at New York, within two or three weeks, I told him that I thought I could show him a power in the Statute which neither he nor any other Collector in the United States knew of. There was also a prominent Treasury official present, and I am bound to say that neither one of them knew of this provision. And no one ever heard in this country of any attempt being made to carry it out.

But the point which I make now is this: Why do you make a hard and fast rule, as you do make it now, that these lights shall be so screened as not to show across the bow, and then make a recommendatory Resolution that they shall not show more than half a point across the bow? Of course I understand that there must come a point forward of the lights where the lights are both shown. That must be so. But that does not make any difference in the suggestion that I make, that you must not make your recommendation inconsistent with the Rules, nor must you weaken the force of the Rules by permitting the lights to show, or by suggesting that the lights may show, or by recommending to the Powers to consider the question as to whether the lights should show more across the bows than the Rule provides for, because the Rule itself says that they shall not show across the bow at all. Now you are recommending that they shall not show more than half a point across the bow. This is weakening the effect of the Rule. Take a collision case where this subject comes up for consideration. The Rule says that the light shall not cross the bow, and to that point any careful lawyer would specifically address himself when he attempts to describe the position of the lights of the ship which he represented.

Now you come to the recommendation of the Conference that the light should not show more than a half a point across the bow. Supposing it is proved that these lights did show a half a point across the bow. Will the Court go to this recommendation and say, although the Rule says that the light shall not show across the bow, the recommendation of this distinguished Conference says that it shall not show more than half a point across the bow? Which is the correct Rule, the recommendation or the Rule itself? Either make the Rule a hard and fast one, and make the recommendation of the same kind, if you want to make any; or make the Rule that the light shall not show more than half a point across the bow, and make the recommendation to conform to that. In other words, amend the Rule as suggested by the learned Delegate from Germany, and leave out your recommendation, or have the two consistent. Now, a word with regard to what the gallant Admiral of Great Britain said about the Cape Finisterre light. I still insist that my suggestion is right, that the light and the rays of the light mean the same thing in these Rules. The instant the look-out sees the ray of light he begins to see the light itself, and by that ray of light he guides the direction of his vessel or his vessel guides its direction on his report, just the same as if he saw the light itself. It is a fainter light, that is all; but the ray of light must come directly from the light itself.

Captain Sampson (United States).—Mr. President, it seems to me we have wandered away from the amendment with which we started out. We have here, in the first place, a Rule which says that the light must not be seen across the bow. The learned Delegate from Germany has proposed an amendment by inserting the words, "more than half a point." It seems, after the discussion which has taken place, that the sense of the Conference, so far as I can make it out, is that the Rule is a proper one, and that the light, without any restriction, should not show across the bow. When it comes to considering the diameter of the flame, or the size of the light, it becomes evident that if you screen the light so that the rays from the centre of the flame shall not show across the bow, then the rays from the out-board half will cross the bow. The discussion comes to the question as to whether we shall make a recommendation with reference to the outside rays of the lantern or not. I believe it is the sense of this Conference that the Rule, as it stands, is a good one, and if we wish to make any recommendation with regard to this matter we must state distinctly that, owing to the size of the wick of the flame, it becomes necessary in building these lights to so place them that the centre rays from the flame shall not cross the bow. Under these circumstances we shall have a light showing across the bow or perhaps meeting near the bow of the ship.

I do not think it is necessary to modify this Rule or to put into a note any reference to the matter. Any one who has the intelligence to place the lights in a ship so that the rays shall not show across the bow will understand this matter. The light must be screened so as to comply with the Rule. I think it is unnecessary to adopt even the Resolution that the rays of the light, by which is meant the rays from the outer portion of the wick on each lantern, the outer rays on the starboard side and the outer rays on the port side, shall cross the bow at a distance of an angle of one half a point. So long as the flame has any magnitude there must be a certain amount of latitude for the divergence of the rays.

Captain Mensing (Germany).—Mr. President, I would like to ask the learned Delegate from the United States whether I understood him to say that the United States had adopted the Rules for Surveyors published by the English Board of Trade? I thought he said so.

Mr. Goodrich (United States).—No, Sir; I simply said this: In 1871 there was an Act passed by Congress which in two lines stated that the Collectors of Customs are directed to inspect the lights on board vessels, and it ended there. It is a very indefinite Act. Of course I give the words as near as I can, although I do not give them precisely. That was the beginning and the end of the subject. It was the beginning and end of the whole matter so far as any practical application of it was made to ships.

Captain Mensing (Germany).—Mr. President, I am obliged for the information given to me. It seems to me that the Delegates from the United States have not taken into consideration and have not answered the argument brought forward by the distinguished First Delegate of Great Britain. He pointed out that the words, "across the bow," had no meaning in a practical way. I would like to call to the attention of the learned Delegate of the United States that this does not seem to be the opinion of Great Britain alone, but that other countries have adopted the same principle. If you will look at the most interesting paper which has been submitted to the Conference lately by the Delegates from Chile, you will find there the expression used in their recommendation of "across the ship." There it is distinctly said that these lights must not be seen across the ship.

I would like to call the attention of the Conference to Article 15, in the end of which it speaks about two vessels meeting end-on or nearly end-on, and to the case in which by day each ship sees the masts of the other in line or nearly in line with her own, and at night to the cases in which each ship is in such a position as to see both of the side-lights of the other. Now, that Rule points very clearly to this one thing, that the side-lights of an approaching vessel should not only be seen in a line with her keel, but also when the observing vessel is nearly in a line with her keel; not only when her masts are in line, but when they are nearly in line; and, as has been pointed out awhile ago, the instructions to the Surveyors which have been adopted and published by the English Board of Trade have all approved of this matter. I do not see how we are bringing in anything new. We only express the opinion that this point should be settled; that there should be no double meaning left in the Rule. I think if you will look at the discussion which took place here before you will see that it is most desirable, and I may say almost absolutely necessary, that such a declaration shall be adopted by this Conference one way or the other.

The Conference thereupon took a recess until 2 o'clock.

After Recess.

The President.—The question is upon the Resolution of the Delegate of Great Britain.

Dr. Sieveking (Germany).—Mr. President, I desire to say a few words only to try to remove the difficulty under which the learned Delegate of the United States is labouring. He says that he does not object to the wording or intention of the Resolution which has been proposed by the Delegates of Great Britain and accepted by the German Delegates. He only points out that there would be a contradiction between the two: the Rule as it stands and the Resolution which is proposed. I think that could be very easily removed by voting first on the principle of the Resolution, and then considering afterwards whether it should be made a Rule or not.

If we first vote on the principle whether it would be desirable or whether it should be resolved that such lights should be so screened as to prevent the rays from being seen or the lights from being seen across the bow for more than one half a point—if we vote upon that principle it could be left an open question whether it is to be included in Appendix (B) or made a part of the Rules. There could be a vote taken upon that question afterwards, I think. Then if this proposition would, either as a part of Appendix (B) or as a Rule, be rejected, then, of course, the other question is dealt with. If it be adopted, then the question would arise whether it is to be made a part of the Rules or a part of Appendix (B). Then, perhaps, the question might be raised whether, after it was inserted in Appendix (B), the Rule ought to be altered or not. I think that would remove the difficulty of the Delegate from the United States, which I must agree exists, because there is a possibility of a different interpretation of the Rule as it stands. I should propose to have a vote upon this Resolution, leaving it an open question as to whether the Resolution should be put into Appendix (B) or be made a part of the Rules.

Captain Sampson (United States).—Mr. President, it seems to me that the proposition of the learned Delegate from Germany would not overcome the difficulty. The question which is involved in this discussion is as to the point at which the outside rays shall cross in front of the ship. This difficulty arises if we fix either an angle or a distance. If you have a wick of 1 inch in diameter and it is so screened that the outside rays from that wick shall cross the line of the keel of the ship at an angle of one half a point, it will result that the full effect of the beam of light will have a certain direction with reference to the line of the keel of the ship. For illustration, let us suppose that the wick is 1 inch in diameter and the light is so screened that the outer rays shall cross at an angle of a half a point with the keel of the ship, if we suppose that the centre rays are then parallel with the keel of the ship. Then let us suppose that the size of the wick is 2 inches in diameter and is so screened that the outer rays shall cross at the same point. Then the centre rays of that same lamp will diverge from the line of the keel of the ship.

This question is a complicated one. The Rules which have been adopted by the Board of Trade take into consideration all of these points: the size of the wick, the distance between the lights, and all of these questions upon which the proper solution of the problem depends, and unless we shall adopt some complete system of Rules for governing the placing of these lights, it seems to me that we had better let the matter rest without prescribing how the lights shall be placed, and leave the Rule as it stands, for the guidance of sailors, and let each nation adjust its lights so that the Rule shall be carried out as far as it is practicable to do so. If we attempt to fix a point at which the rays shall cross in front of the ship, it will result that the central rays from the different lamps will make a different angle with the keel of the ship; that is, the strongest beam of light may diverge from the direction of the keel of the ship, and that, I think, would be a very objectionable thing to bring about.

Mr. Goodrich (United States).—Mr. President, a suggestion made by the learned First Delegate from Great Britain is quite new to me, that is if I understood him that there has been judicial discussion upon the question of what point was intended as the point where the light is to be seen across the bow.

Mr. Hall (Great Britain).—Mr. President, no; I am not aware that this point has ever been raised. So far as I am aware no question has ever been raised as to the meaning of this Rule. It has been one of the Rules of the Road now for a great many years. There has been no question raised upon it so far as I am aware. But our Board of Trade found, in point of fact, that after a certain distance had been covered the rays of light converge and eventually cross. Accordingly they published an elaborate series of instructions to Surveyors, so as to minimize that to the smallest amount possible.

Mr. Goodrich (United States).—Mr. President, I have never heard of any judicial determination in our Courts of this Rule. For a great many years this Rule has been in existence, and it has worked without trouble. I am very much afraid that if we attempt to change it in the Rule itself or by inserting the words in a note, or if we attempt to construe it or to limit it, we are going to get into a difficulty which I cannot see my way clear to avoid, except by voting against the proposition. Even if we adopt the suggestion of the learned First Delegate from Germany, and adopt the principle of the Resolution first, and then decide on the question of putting it into the Rules or not, we shall still be met by the same objections that we labour under now, that we are making two inconsistent Rules. I think myself that the Conference had better decide whether they want to change the old Rule in the manner suggested by the amendment of the learned Delegate from Germany, or whether they will adhere to the old Rule as it stands.

I was not present during the discussion of this subject by the Collocation Committee; but I really do not see any benefit in changing this Rule, which has worked well and which is fully understood. Of course it is perfectly manifest that there must be a point somewhere where both lights will cross the bow, as seen by an approaching vessel. That must be so, and you cannot put the lights in any other position where only the breadth of the beam intervenes between the two lights; the two lights will cross at a quarter of a mile, or a half a mile, or 2 miles, or somewhere, no matter how you put them. Are we not doing well enough under the Rule as it now stands? Did we not fully discuss the principle when this subject came up on a former occasion? Are we going to do anything to the service of the public by making a change in this Rule? The Rule has worked well. Everybody understands it. Vessels are built in that way and lights are set in that way. I am sure that I am unable to see any benefit to arise from any change either in the Rule itself or by the Resolution in the way of a note to be added to Appendix (B).

Captain Mensing (Germany).—Mr. President, I am very sorry that the learned Delegate from the United States was not present when we began the discussion this morning, because I think that some of the points which he made just now would not be made if he had heard it. I am very glad to hear that it is admitted that it is impossible to put the two side-lights in a position so that the rays of light will not cross before the ship somewhere. Now, they make the point, as the gallant Delegate from the United States pointed out, that it is impossible to make such a construction, and that if we take a wick of 1 inch in diameter and another wick of 2 inches in diameter, the same instructions would not apply. Now these are extreme cases. A wick of 2 inches in diameter may be used in a Rochester lamp, but could scarcely ever be used in any other. A wick of 2 inches in diameter is a diameter which is not meant for illumination in the side-lights of a ship, but for the purpose of illumination of apparatus on shore. But what would be the difference if there should be such a lamp fitted up? Very fortunately I have this little book here, and I find that all the difference there would be is 1 degree and a little over.

I am sure that the gallant Delegate from the United States will allow me to say that such a small difference ought not to make any practical difference whatever. I do not believe that he will stand up here and say that he believes that this is a difference worth mentioning. It is simply 1 degree and a little over. It has been admitted now that the lights have to cross somewhere before the bow, and it is admitted that under the present Rule they may cross wherever they choose. I have been able to point out that in one case at least it has been brought to the attention of the Conference, by an officer well qualified to judge of such matters, that in some cases they cross at a point and three-quarters before the bow. Now, I would most earnestly point out that I believe this is the case with at least 10 or 15 per cent. of the vessels afloat, and if there are any gentlemen present who have any other opinion about this matter I would be very glad if they would kindly state what their opinion is. I for one am of opinion that a very large number of the vessels afloat, under the present Rules and Regulations, have their lights screened at such an angle that the rays cross at about one and three-quarter points, if not two points.

The dangers which are brought about by the present state of affairs I have tried to point out by the diagram which I have laid before you. If any member will say that this diagram is exaggerated, or that the case as I represent it is not correct, I wish to be corrected. Under the present state of things it has become possible that ships go to sea with this angle practically undetermined, and I think that it is time something was done. You will admit that the danger which I have tried to impress upon you is a real one. It has not only been pointed out by me, but by a greater authority in the matter, by the French book which is published by Captain Banaré.

I can honestly say that this point struck me three or four years ago, because I know of a collision which took place in the Baltic where one ship ran into another. It was a case which was brought officially to my knowledge. One ship was sunk and eighty lives lost. I had to look over this case most carefully, and I came to the conclusion that it could only be explained by assuming that the lights had been so fixed in one of the ships that they could be seen where the ship did not expect them to be seen. Now the amendment proposed by the learned Delegate from Great Britain has to me only one meaning, and that is, it calls attention to the fact that under the present Regulation a state of affairs has come about which is dangerous to navigation. If you say that this is not the case, all right. You can vote in the negative. But I believe that you must be careful in doing so. I believe that by voting in the affirmative on this Rule you declare that the Rule is a good one, and that no change is advisable under the circumstances.

I am at a loss to understand exactly what is meant by this present Rule. Article 15 is against it. Article 15 speaks about the rays of light crossing before the bow, by inference. The English Board of Trade has already fixed the angle; this angle has been adopted by the German Delegation, and has been put forward in this amendment which is now before you. If you declare that the present state of affairs is satisfactory, then I have nothing to say, except that there is a difference of opinion about it. If you say it is not satisfactory, then I think it will follow that you are either to adopt this, or to bring in some other amendment which may deal with the difficulty. I believe that the learned Delegate from Great Britain has declared here that he would accept anything which might differ in mere verbiage, to meet the difficulty.

Mr. Carter (Hawaii).—Mr. President, I would like to ask the gallant Delegate from Germany whether this unsatisfactory state of affairs which he alludes to does not arise from disobedience to the present Rule, and would not that disobedience continue even if this one half point were inserted? Would there be any less danger than there is at the present time? That is, would it practically obviate the difficulty?

Captain Mensing (Germany).—Mr. President, the Board of Trade of Great Britain, I believe, is considered a body of some authority, and if the case be as represented by Mr. Carter, it would imply that they have been in the wrong. They have stated in their printed books and in their instructions that there should be no greater angle than half a point. Now, these are gentlemen of the highest authority. The only other country which has taken up this position and has given a clear answer is Denmark. Denmark says they may cross the bow at about one cable's length. Now, what are you going to do? How are you to get around these two facts? You cannot get around them. The beneficial result of this Rule is shown by the application of it by the different Governments.

It is shown by paragraph 3 of Article 15 that the lights must cross at a certain distance. I think it would be a good thing to find the extreme limit within which they must not cross. What that limit is, is the difficulty. I will adopt anything if you will only put it so that the uncertainty which exists at present will be avoided. While that uncertainty exists, it cannot be put out of the way without declaring that the lights shall not cross at all, as it is in the present Rule. But they do cross. Does any gentleman here know of any vessel where the lights are so fixed that they do not cross before the bow? As I pointed out to you, there was one case where collision was caused by this difficulty, and let me assure you that there are many others, and, if so, this difficulty ought to be remedied. You will say, perhaps, how do I know? I have not made any experiments. But have you made any experiments? Can you tell me that I am wrong? If not, go to the instructions of the Board of Trade with regard to this. Go to the book of Mr. Banaré for information upon it. Then tell me whether you do not think it is advisable to have this thing settled in one way or the other. That is all I ask for. Settle it; do not leave undecided such a very important matter. Settle it one way or the other.

Mr. Goodrich (United States).—Mr. President, the remarks of the gallant Delegate from Germany apply now to another subject, it seems to me, than that which we are discussing. We are discussing the question whether you are going to make a hard and fast rule of parallel screen boards, so that the lights do not show across the bow, and then put into the Appendix a Resolution that they shall not show more than half a point across the bow. The difficulty which it seems to me arises from the instance which he has given in this Memorandum is this: if a collision occurs with lights which do not show across the bows, what advantage will result from having lights which are to be shown a half point across the bows? There always is a point whether you screen a light so as to be only seen by a person standing at a long distance off, or so as to be seen by a person standing at a short distance; there always is an instant when in turning the vessel the light begins to be seen. That is the danger point; and it makes no difference whether it is at the time when the vessel is a mile away or when the vessel is a half a mile away, there is the same difficulty and trouble about the screening. Of course I am not discussing the question whether there is more danger when the vessels are within half a mile of each other than there is when the vessels are within a mile of each other. All I mean is that the same difficulty will arise in each case, and that there is a time when there is some doubt over what arc the light begins to show.

I am not so sure that the gallant Delegate from Germany in his last argument has not opened a subject which it is well for the Conference to discuss. But it is not, it seems to me, a subject of present discussion. The thought which I adverted to in reference to the suggestion of the learned Delegate from Great Britain might be the solution of the whole difficulty, that is to define the point where the light shall be visible to a person, as the gallant Delegate from Germany said, about a cable's length away, or at a point at the knight-heads, or some point which will make it perfectly definite, so that the observer or inspector examining the lights of ships can see whether the lights, or the rays of light, meet across the bow. That might obviate the whole difficulty. But what makes an impression upon my mind is that these Rules have stood the test for a great many years. They never have been the subject of judicial discussion at all, which indicates that they have worked very well. Why should we attempt to alter it, or why should we attempt to make a difficulty where none exists? Everybody understands the Rule. Make your screen boards as nearly parallel with the keel as you can, and then let them trend out a little at the forward end, so as to prevent the light from crossing the bows. It seems to me the Rule is well understood and well obeyed; and that a change from two points to a point and a half, as the point where the rays of light cross the bow, is not going to get over the difficulty.

Mr. Hall (Great Britain).—Mr. President, I regret that the learned Delegate from the United States was prevented by public business from being here this morning. What we have been discussing now for some very considerable time is not a proposal to alter the Rules at all. There has been practically no such proposal. When I had the honour to move the amendment, I stated that we all agreed that it was not desirable to alter the Rules, and we finally adopted the opinion of the Committee on Lights on that very important point. But as we were aware of the fact that the rays of light must cross the bow at a certain distance from the vessel if these lights are screened so as to show their full light ahead, we thought it desirable to put in an amendment to this effect.

Now that is the sole point. We are trying to do that which the learned Delegate from the United States has just stated is a very desirable matter, and that is to minimize the amount which such lights shall show across the bow. That is the object of this Resolution. Now may I point out the very great importance of this? At present when a man sees two lights nearly ahead, slightly on his starboard bow, he does not know whether these lights cross at an angle of half a point or a point and three-quarters, or of a point and a half. Therefore he cannot be perfectly certain about that vessel. If we should agree to make it an angle of not more than a half a point, this man can know perfectly well when he sees this vessel coming that her lights do not cross more than a half a point ahead of the bow, and he can tell within a half a point exactly what the vessel is doing. We do not propose to alter the Rule at all. We only want to deal with the difficulty which has been found out. I do not think it would be becoming in me to make an amendment which has just been suggested to me, and I should prefer that it should be moved by the Representative of some other Delegation.

Of course I do not want for one moment to suggest that our Rules and Regulations are infallible; but we have found them to work most excellently, and our Surveyors have not had any difficulty in applying them. It might be possible that the Conference might think it desirable to recommend the adoption of the Board of Trade Rules with regard to this matter. That could be dealt with in a Resolution, directly. It would not interfere with the Rules. That possibly may be the solution of the difficulty. As I say, I do not think it would be becoming for a Delegate from Great Britain to make any such suggestion; but that has been suggested to me just now. Of course, if such a Resolution should be made, I need not say that we should support it heartily. I think it is a matter worthy of consideration, perhaps, but I will not say any more about it.

Captain Salvesen (Norway).—Mr. President, I have had some experience in screening lights. I have found it necessary to have definite Rules for it. We have no such official Rules in our country, but have had recourse to the British Rules, and have found them, in principle, very good. But as it stands in our country and in different countries we have no official Rules; I beg to move that the Conference recommend that the different Governments adopt the Board of Trade Rules about the screening of the side-lights.

Mr. Goodrich (United States).—Mr. President, is that Resolution to be moved and argued now? Because I am not familiar enough with the British Board of Trade Rules to say that, as a member of the United States' Delegation, I should be willing to adopt these Rules and recommend them to our Government. That is an entirely different subject from the principle contained in this Resolution. I think the learned Delegate from Hawaii has pointed out the difficulty of the situation, that these collisions which the gallant Delegate from Germany referred to resulted from a disobedience of the Rules in placing the lights. I do not see why there would not be just as much danger and just as much disobedience to the Rules suggested by the German Delegation as there is now. It will be obviated if you let the observer take his position at a given point ahead of the vessel as she is moored to the shore, and to take an actual observation of the lights, and see where they cross the bow. That is a very simple method of determining where these rays really do cross. It is the disobedience to this Rule which makes the trouble. If the lights are placed so that they do not cross the bow, according to the present Rule, there is no difficulty, and you will not benefit yourselves at all, it seems to me, if you provide that the light shall not show more than half a point across the bow. You will not then be in any better situation than you are now when you provide that the lights shall not cross the bow at all.

Captain Richard (France).—Mr. President, the discussion has been so extended, and all the arguments for and against the amendment which is proposed have been developed so fully, that I think it is unnecessary for me to enter into the details of this discussion. I will confine myself to saying that the two systems, whether the rays do or do not cross the bows, have their disadvantages as well as their advantages. In the former case you have a dark zone in which a collision may occur. In the latter case, when the rays cross, there is the light zone, which may also lead to a collision; by a strict observation of the Rules of the Road, each one of us will know the special cases to which I allude. Consequently, under those circumstances, it seems to me that uncertainty is made still more uncertain when we do not know with what system we are dealing; and it is an important point that, whatever be the system which is adopted, our vessels are placed in the same conditions. That is all we can ask.

Under those circumstances I am ready to support a solution which shall be adopted by all of us; for then we will have the same Rule and the same Laws, which will be a guaranty of security. I think that it is evident that we must not wantonly destroy the old Rules, for they are so well known that from that mere fact we have an element of security resulting from a common interpretation, and if you appear before a Court you will know in advance how the matter will be judged. Some nations —and not the smallest ones, if we consider their tonnage—have adopted a crossing of the lights. Great Britain is one of them. Inasmuch as it is an existing fact, and this measure, which is more or less justified and more or less contestable, has not been adopted by every country, I ask that we come to an understanding upon that question, which is not unimportant.

I have one thing to oppose to the number of degrees proposed by the gallant Delegate from Germany to obtain the crossing of the lights. I would say that we have not been given a very precise indication. The point where the red and green lights will cross will vary with the width of a vessel. For small vessels the dark zone, where the lights will not cross, is of little importance, because small vessels generally do not steer along a mathematically straight course. Their red and green lights are alternately seen when you are in the dark zone. Two systems are in the presence of each other—one in which the lights do not cross except at an infinite distance, the other where the lights cross at a defined distance. But what matters the system, provided the solution be uniform? Until now nothing has been proposed to arrive at such uniformity. I, therefore, think that we should, as much as possible, support a uniform measure for the whole world, and that is why I support the Article proposed by the learned Delegate from Germany.

Mr. Goodrich (United States).—Mr. President, if there is any further discussion upon this subject I would suggest that the best way to arrive at the sense of the Conference upon the several propositions stated will be to present the following Resolution :—

"*Resolved,*—That the Conference approve of Article 2 as reported by the Collocation Committee."

That is a little unparliamentary, yet it is an easy manner of arriving at the judgment of the Conference upon the proposition as to whether the Conference will adhere to the Rule as it now stands reported by the Committee, or whether it wants changing either by the amendment to the Rule itself or by a recommendation to be attached to Appendix (B).

Dr. Sieveking (Germany).—Mr. President, as far as my experience goes it is a general Parliamentary rule that whenever an amendment is brought forward it is to be put to vote, and the vote is not to be taken upon the question which is to be amended. So when the Report of the Collocation Committee is brought in, this amendment must be voted upon, and not the Report of the Committee. That is a general Parliamentary rule. Therefore, I think that the amendment which has been brought in by the German Delegates must be put to a vote. In the course of discussion a doubt has been raised whether this amendment should be put in the form of a Resolution only, or be inserted as a Rule. And therefore, it seems to me, as I said before, that the only correct proceeding would be to put the vote on the question as to whether the side-lights should be so screened as to prevent the rays of light from being seen more than half a point across the bow; and then afterwards to decide the question whether it is to be made a Rule, or to be recommended only in Appendix (B).

Mr. Goodrich (United States).—Mr. President, I was aware that my course of proceeding was not quite Parliamentary, but I thought it was the best way to arrive at the sense of the Conference. Of course, after the suggestion of the learned Delegate from Germany, I will withdraw the Resolution.

Mr. Hall (Great Britain).—Mr. President, I apprehend that, at present, the matter which is before the Conference, because I understand the gallant Delegate from Norway did not propose an amendment, but only to offer a suggestion in regard to the Board of Trade Rules, is the one which I had the honour to propose, and that is the Resolution instead of a Rule. I did that because I wanted this important matter to be discussed, and I thought it very desirable that if it was dealt with it should be dealt with in a Resolution and not in a Rule. I did not propose to alter the Rule at all; but proposed the Resolution, to call the attention of the Conference to this important fact. Therefore, I submit that the amendment which I have proposed, that is, that there should be a Resolution in Appendix (B), in the words which I have already read, is the matter before the Conference. I proposed it, because I thought it the best way of ventilating this question; to bring the matter before the Conference and to the attention of the foreign Powers.

Mr. Carter (Hawaii).—Mr. President, I would like to suggest to the German Delegation whether, after all, it makes any difference from what point you are looking at the light? The desire of the gallant Delegate of Germany is that there should be something definite and decided; some rule which is something definite to go by. If it says that the rays of these lights are not to cross at more than half a point before the bow, that depends entirely upon the point of view of the person judging it. The person near the light might find it exactly right, and a person a mile off would find it at a very different angle. I merely throw this out as a way out of the difficulty.

Captain Mensing (Germany).—Mr. President, I would like to point out that if this amendment proposed by the learned Delegate of Great Britain should be adopted, it would simply mean that an observer standing at about ten lengths of the beam forward of the ship in the line of the keel could see both of the lights, and that he could see no light if he stood on one side or the other. That is the proposition, as I understand it, which is before us, as an amendment.

The President.—The question is upon the amendment of the Delegate from Great Britain to the amendment of the Delegate from Germany. The Secretary will please read it.

The amendment of the Delegate of Great Britain to the amendment of the Delegate of Germany is as follows :—

"To be inserted as a Resolution in Appendix (B) the following :—
"Side-lights should be so screened as to prevent the rays of light being seen more than a half a point across the bow."

Captain Sampson (United States).—Mr. President, I would like to ask the learned Delegate from Great Britain whether he will substitute the word "light" for "rays"?

Mr. Hall (Great Britain).—Mr. President, I am afraid we could not do that. That would extend it so very much more if the light were to be allowed to cross. Of course the gallant Delegate can see that it would extend it to a very considerable distance. You could not tell when you saw both vessels' lights, practically, whether it was a point and a half, or a point and three-quarters, or two points, and then you would assume that the vessel was end-on, when she might be a vessel crossing.

Captain Sampson (United States).—Mr. President, that is the very point to which I wish to call attention—that when the rays of the light are seen it means that you see both lights. That is all there is to it. I think if we adopt this expression, "rays," in place of "lights," which we have used heretofore, we will be introducing a little uncertainty and ambiguity in the Rules. When a person is placed on the line of the keel of a vessel so that he sees the rays he sees both lights, neither more nor less. Then, when he goes further away, or goes to one side, he sees a greater number of rays from one light than from the other. But, as a matter of fact, whenever he is in a position to receive upon his eye the rays from either lamp he sees the light. I think it would be a mistake for us to adopt language different from that which is used throughout the Rules in every other case. If this Rule should be adopted, then say that the "light" shall not cross at a greater angle than half a point.

Mr. Hall (Great Britain.)—Mr. President, I see at once that there would be a great objection to putting this word "rays" in the Rule at all. And we would not propose to do it. This is merely an instruction which would be followed by the Surveyors, who would understand the meaning of the word. I do not propose for one moment to put the word "rays" into the Rule. I quite see the objection to doing so; but the Surveyors would understand that it meant a good deal more than the light, the ray of light crossing the bow and not the light itself, because the lights are expected to show their full light head, and as far ahead as possible; but you cannot prevent the rays crossing. The Surveyors understand that point and will so understand the meaning of this Resolution.

Captain Sampson (United States).—Mr. President, I think, although we have discussed this matter very thoroughly, there is still some misunderstanding about the difference between light when it first becomes visible and the full effects of the light. As I pointed out some time ago, if you are going to make such a Rule as that we ought to adopt, as has been suggested by the gallant Delegate of Norway, some complete system of Rules similar to those adopted by the English Board of Trade; and I, for one, speaking for myself alone, would be perfectly willing to adopt the Rules which Great Britain follows. In these Rules there are so many conditions to be taken into account that we cannot adopt the part without adopting the whole. As I pointed out before, the size of the wick, if it is a flat wick the width of it, or if it is a circular wick the diameter of it, will make a difference, if we refer to the point of the crossing of the outside rays, and greatly modify the direction in which the main beam of light shows, and I am sure we do not want to do anything of that sort. We have got to make a Rule so that the size of the illuminating surface shall enter into this problem, and if we do not, we shall make a change in the main beam of light which we do not want to make.

Mr. Hall (Great Britain).—Mr. President, I think I can make a suggestion to the gallant Delegate of the United States which will perhaps make it meet his views. I propose to insert the words which we have used in our Board of Trade Rules, and say the "most convergent rays of light."

Captain Sampson (United States).—Mr. President, I understand that the learned Delegate from Great Britain says that if the rays are more convergent from one lamp than they are from another, then the main beam whose direction depends upon the most convergent ray will differ in the two different lamps. That would not mean a beam parallel to the keel of the ship; but if the wicks are of different sizes then the most convergent rays will make a change in the direction of the main beam.

Admiral Bowden-Smith (Great Britain).—Mr. President, I should like to say one word in favour of the amendment proposed by the learned Delegate of Germany, and amended by the learned Delegate from Great Britain, and it is in reference to something which fell from the gallant Delegate of the United States just now. He said that every sailor knew exactly what this Rule meant. Then I must be one of the simple sailors who do not know what it means. I know that these lights are supposed to show right ahead; but, for the life of me, I do not know whether the entire light is supposed to be cut off at a half a point or a point and a half. I have not the slightest idea at this time. I *know* what the Board of Trade Regulations are, but whether the entire light is supposed to be cut off at half a point, or a point and a half, or two points, I do not know as a sailor, and I would very much like to have it told to me.

The President.—Is the Conference ready for the question on the amendment of the Delegate from Great Britain to the amendment of the Delegate from Germany?

Mr. Hall (Great Britain).—Mr. President, before that is put to a vote I was going to insert the words, "the most convergent rays of the light."

The President.—The Secretary will please read the Resolution.

The Resolution is as follows:—

"Side-lights should be so screened as to prevent the most convergent rays of the light being seen more than half a point across the bow."

The President.—Is the Conference ready for the question?

The question was put to the Conference upon the adoption of the Resolution proposed by the Delegate from Great Britain.

Mr. Goodrich (United States).—I call for the Yeas and Nays.

The Yea and Nay vote is as follows:—

Austria-Hungary	.. ..	Nay.
Brazil	.. .. ..	Yea.
Belgium	.. .. ..	Yea.
China	.. .. ..	Yea.
Chile	.. ..	Yea.
Denmark	.. . ..	Yea.
France	.. .. ..	Yea.
Germany	.. .. ..	Yea.
Great Britain	.. ..	Yea.
Hawaii	.. .. ..	Yea.
Italy	.. .. ..	Yea.
Mexico	.. .. ..	Yea.
Norway	.. .. ..	Yea.
Russia	.. .. ..	Nay.
Spain	.. .. ..	Yea.
Sweden	.. .. ..	Yea.
Siam	.. .. ..	Yea.
The Netherlands	.. ..	Yea.
The United States	.. ..	Nay.

The President.— Sixteen have voted in the affirmative, and 3 in the negative, so that the amendment to the amendment is adopted. Does the Chair understand this to be a substitute for the amendment offered by the Delegate from Germany?

Mr. Hall (Great Britain).—Mr. President, this is a Resolution offered instead of the amendment of the Delegate from Germany.

The President.—Then the next question is upon amendment No. 3.

Captain Shackford (United States).—Mr. President, I ask permission to withdraw that amendment.

The President.—The Delegate for the United States desires to withdraw amendment No. 3. If there be no objection it will be withdrawn. The next subject for consideration will be amendment No. 4, Class 2, which will be read by the Secretary.

Amendment No. 4, Class 2, is as follows:—

"Amendment to Collocation Report proposed by Captain Norcross (United States), December 14, 1889:

"Article 2 (*e*). To add a note to the effect that if the forward range-light be carried on the foremast, it be permissible to carry it lower than prescribed under (*a*)."

Captain Norcross (United States).—Mr. President, as my colleagues in the American Delegation have convinced me, against my will, that the range-lights can be carried on the foremast in all cases as high as is required by subsection (*a*) of Article 2, for the masthead-lights, with your permission I will withdraw this amendment.

The President.—If there be no objection, the Delegate from the United States desires to withdraw amendment No. 4, Class 2. The amendment is withdrawn. The next subject for consideration is amendment No. 5, Class 2, which will be read.

Amendment No. 5, Class 2, is as follows:—

"Amendment to Collocation Report proposed by the Delegates of Chile, 13th December, 1889:

"Art. 3. Strike out the words, 'and when towing more than one vessel, shall carry an additional bright white light 6 feet above or below such lights, if the length of the tow measuring from the stern of the towing vessel to the stern of the last vessel towed exceeds 600 feet. Each of these lights shall be of the same construction and character, and shall be carried in the same position as the white light mentioned in Article 2 (*a*), excepting the additional light, which may be carried at a height not less than 14 feet above the hull.'

"Art. 5. Strike out the words, 'and any vessel being towed.'

"New Article. Vessels being towed shall carry the ordinary side-lights, and the last vessel of the tow shall carry, in addition, two white lights 6 feet apart, in a vertical line abaft her aftermast."

Admiral Viel (Chile).—Mr. President, the proposition which I have made to strike out after the word "apart" in the Report of the Committee on Collocation, I consider a necessary one; for it is difficult at sea, and especially during the night, to appreciate a distance of 600 feet, unless it be marked in some distinctive manner. For that reason I have proposed this amendment, the more so as ordinary tow-boats cannot carry three lanterns by reason of their small masts; and if trouble should arise which would oblige them to tow, it would be very difficult for them to obtain three lanterns of regulation character. If the proposition which I have submitted should be adopted, it would be necessary to strike out from Article 5 the words, "and any ships towing," and to replace them with another phrase drawn up in accordance with my proposition.

Captain Norcross (United States).—Mr. President, I hope this radical change in the Rule as adopted by the Conference will not be made. With two lights at the two ends of the tow, how are you to tell which is the steamer and which the vessel towed? Such an arrangement would lead to the greatest confusion that possibly could be imagined. It seems to me that the Rule as it stands is the proper one, with the warning light on the steamer and the side-lights on the vessel towed, and the stern-light to be shown to an overtaking vessel. This constitutes a series of well-distinguished warnings, which will be able to guide a vessel past a tow, however long. I hope the Rule as passed will be retained, as reported by the Committee on Collocation.

Mr. Goodrich (United States).—Mr. President, of course I am not desirous of shutting off debate either upon any new principle or upon any old principle which has not been thoroughly understood by the Conference; but this subject, as I remember, was thoroughly discussed. Amendment after amendment was proposed, and it seems to me that the Conference have already expressed themselves very decidedly upon the change suggested by the gallant Delegate from Chile. For that reason I do not take up the time of the Conference in rehearsing strong arguments made *pro* and *con* on this subject.

Lieutenant Beaugency (Chile).—Mr. President, I will point out to the learned Delegate from the

United States that the Conference decided this amendment not in the same way in which it is now. The original amendment was to take out the side-lights of the ship being towed. That is what the Conference decided.

Mr. Hall (Great Britain).—Mr. President, I do not wish to occupy the time of the Conference, especially after what has fallen from the learned Delegate for the United States. But I think I should be expressing the feeling of all the Delegates when I express our thanks to the Delegates from Chile for their courtesy in presenting us each with a copy of their Rules, which I observe they have been so good as to have translated into English for our use.

The President.—The question is upon the amendment of the Delegate from Chile.

Captain Richard (France).—Mr. President, I have only a very short remark to make in regard to the amendment presented by our gallant colleagues from Chile. It is evident that the idea which inspired this amendment is an excellent one, in this sense: that at sea it is important to know, in a group formed by a towing-vessel and one or more vessels in tow, where the group commences and where it ends. Evidently the head of the group is at present indicated by special lights, but if it is necessary to know where the bow of the towing vessel is it is no less important to know where the stern is of the vessel which is in tow. I think that the amendment presented by our gallant colleagues is unassailable as to the principle. But in the proposition the towing vessel has absolutely the same lights as the vessel which terminates the group. It is exactly the same, viz., two white lights placed vertically at a distance of at least 6 feet——

Admiral Viel (Chile).—It is forward and not at the end.

Captain Richard (France).—Exactly, but a spectator who is a distance away will make no difference between the two white lights of the towing vessel and the two lights of the last vessel which is being towed. Perhaps to the eyesight a difference in the intensity of the two sets of lights will be noticed, because in the one case special lanterns are used and in the other ordinary lanterns are employed; but this difference is not sufficient, for the brilliancy of the lights varies with the oil, the length of time during which the lantern has been lighted, smoke, &c. The principle merits our earnest consideration, but its application should be rejected because there would be confusion between the lights of the towing vessel and the vessel being towed. That is the only objection I have to make

Lieutenant Beaugency (Chile).—Mr. President, I will point out to the gallant Delegate from France that the two white lights on the steamers are very near to the side-lights, and if the ship is being towed you can see the side-lights ahead of the two white lights on the after part, and you cannot make a mistake between the ship which is being towed and the ship which is towing.

Admiral Viel (Chile).—Mr. President, I have heard from the gallant Delegate from France that it is a good thing in principle, but that it is not so in practice. Since I have been in the naval service I have conducted convoys of vessels, and I have seen that the lights at the end greatly facilitated the looking after the convoys, and I think that this measure will be a very advantageous one to adopt; that is why I have proposed to strike out those words.

Captain Richard (France).—Mr. President, I fear that I have been misunderstood by the gallant Admiral. I do not dispute the principle, which I consider a very correct one; but I object to the lights themselves—to their character, which I find insufficient, because it leads to a confusion which may have serious consequences.

Admiral Viel (Chile).—Mr. President, I have been unable to find any other signal. The signal has been so variously applied, that I could find nothing but the two white lights. But as Captain Richard does not find it practicable, I do not insist upon them.

Mr. Verney (Siam).—Mr. President, may I ask whether the gallant Delegate from Chile would not accept as a signal the ordinary overtaking light. I understand that the gallant Delegate from Chile says that he would accept the signal-light of an overtaking vessel.

Mr. Hall (Great Britain).—Mr. President, has any one proposed such a thing? Would it be right to give a towed vessel the overtaking light signal? I doubt it very much, unless a vessel was approaching and overtaking her. We cannot put into this Rule a special light for the vessel being towed, without great consideration.

Captain Sampson (United States).—Mr. President, the question which the learned Delegate from Siam asked was whether the overtaking light which the vessels are required to carry would not be a sufficient indication of the end of the tow.

M. Verney (Siam).—Mr. President, that is what I intended to say. I hope the gallant Delegate from Chile will accept that.

The President.—Has the Delegate from Chile any proposition to make with reference to his amendment?

Admiral Viel (Chile).—Not anything further, Sir.

The President.—The question will first be upon the amendment. The Delegate from Chile, as the Chair understands it, accepts the usual stern-light as the signal which he proposes in his amendment.

Mr. Goodrich (United States).—Mr. President, will you please explain what is meant?

The President.—I cannot until it is put down in black and white. If he desires to change his amendment so as to admit that principle, he will have to write it out.

Admiral Viel (Chile).—I accept it, Sir.

Mr. Goodrich (United States).—Accept what?

Admiral Viel (Chile).—I accept one light.

Mr. Goodrich (United States).—Mr. President, my two distinguished friends are arranging these lights between themselves, and I do not quite undestand it. Formulate your proposition, if you please, Gentlemen, and let us see it. While we accept, of course, your good judgment in these matters, I think we would like to have a little voice in the discussion of it ourselves.

Admiral Viel (Chile).—Mr. President, it is to have one light in the place of two.

The President.—So that it will read one light instead of two.

Captain Sampson (United States).—Mr. President, I would like to point out that if the gallant Delegate from Chile is satisfied with the light which the vessel carries when there are several vessels being towed, and that the last vessel shall carry the ordinary overtaking light, and if that light sufficiently marks the end of the tow to satisfy him, the difficulty is solved by simply withdrawing his amendment.

Admiral Viel (Chile).—Mr. President, I withdraw my amendment.

The President.—The Delegate from Chile withdraws his amendment. If there be no objection it will be so considered. The next subject for consideration is amendment No. 6, Class 2. The Secretary will please read it.

Amendment No. 6, Class 2, is as follows:—

"Amendment to Collocation Report proposed by Dr. Sieveking on behalf of the German Delegation, 14th December, 1889:

" In Article 4 (*a*), instead of the words 'in the same position,' insert the words, 'at the same height,' and after the words, 'Article 2 (*a*),' insert the words, 'where they can best be seen.'"

Dr. Sieveking (Germany).—Mr. President, I desire to say a few words in regard to this amendment. This amendment refers to vessels out of command. Article 4 (*a*) as it now stands prescribes that the two red lights are to be carried in the same position as the light mentioned in Article 2 (*a*). That is to say, that the two red lights are to be carried on or in front of the foremast. Now, we did not think that would be wise for vessels out of command. There may be vessels which have lost their foremast, and which, therefore, are not able to place them in such a position. There may be other vessels which are in such a position, when they find themselves out of command, that the two red lights, in the position assigned to them under Article 2 (*a*), would be seen at a shorter distance than if they were placed in some other position; so that we thought it would be better to leave it to the judgment of the master, according to circumstances, and to prescribe only that these two lights are to be carried at the same height as the light mentioned in Article 2 (*a*); instead of assigning them a certain position on or in front of the foremast, to say that they shall be placed where they can best be seen.

Mr. Hall (Great Britain).—Mr. President, I think this is a very desirable alteration. It may be difficult for a vessel out of command to hoist the lights in a position in front of the foremast, or it may be desirable for her to hoist them aft. So far as I can see they could not be mistaken for any other signal; and, if so, I think this is a great improvement upon the old Rule.

Captain Richard (France).—Mr. President, I do not share the optimistic view expressed by the eminent Delegate from Great Britain. Allow me to express the opinion that the learned Delegate from Germany, by inserting the words, "at the same height," instead of "in the same position," has not improved the wording of the text of our Rules. Without demanding that this text shall be couched in academical terms, is it desirable to replace bad wording—which assigns to two lights, distant 6 feet from each other, the same position as to a single light placed in a well-defined position—with wording which is no more explicit and which has the disadvantage of being new? Every one of us knows how the expression, "the same position," can be criticized, but the expression, "the same height," is entitled to still less regard.

Now, on the other hand, I would respectfully submit to the Conference that we can derive no advantage from saying, "where they can best be seen," because what is the object in placing lights on the forward part of a vessel which is not under command? The intention evidently is to indicate the dangerous end of a vessel, namely, her bow.

Her bow is specially dangerous, because such a vessel wanders about aimlessly, without any definite plan which can clearly indicate her course. The lights are given her to warn you of such a vessel. I, therefore, think that it would be better to let the old Rule stand, namely, to retain the lights, indicating that a vessel is not under command, forward of the foremast. If the foremast has been carried away that will evidently be the case of *force majeure*, and you will be obliged to place them on the mainmast.

But I do not think that you should enter into an examination of these special cases. We will then have to examine the cases where one, two, or three masts have been carried away. As a matter of fact, in such a case there will always remain a spar to be erected at the spot where the mast was. In other words, it seems that generally it will be possible to rig up some arrangement which will enable you to place the lights in their proper position. But I think that those two lights should be placed forward of the foremast, on a line with the keel, to show the direction in which the vessel is going, and when her bow points to the neighbouring vessel then you will still better show the special lights of this vessel which is not under command, and you will offer sailors the best indications to avoid collisions. In such a case, above all, you should avoid the collision, and for that reason the two red lights should be placed forward of the foremast, in the position which was heretofore assigned to them by the Rule of 1884 and by the Collocation Committee.

Dr. Sieveking (Germany).—Mr. President, I should like to point out that it would be quite a correct expression to say that these two red lights are to be carried at the same height as the white light mentioned in Article 2 (*a*), because this Article 2 (*a*) only gives the minimum height. It says the height must not exceed so and so, or it must not be less than so and so. So the two lights can be put in such a position as to be at not less than a certain height. As to the other point raised by my gallant friend the Delegate from France, he says, so far as I understood him, that it would be better to leave it as it is with the two lights, which show the out-of-command situation, to be carried in the fore part of the vessel, because the fore part of the vessel is the most dangerous one. But it is not always the most dangerous one. A vessel may be out of command in a very dangerous situation. She might be shut up in the ice or be aground, or there may be other reasons to make the after part the most dangerous part of the vessel.

In such a case I should think it would be only common sense to say that the red lights should be shown in the after part, because that is the most dangerous part of the vessel. On the other hand, if the fore part of the vessel should be the most dangerous, then that would be the best place for the lights. The very object of the two red lights is that they should be distinguished and be seen as far as possible to make other vessels aware that there is an obstacle in their way. This leads to the conclusion, I should think, that these lights are to be placed in the position where they can best be seen. It must also be considered that these are lights which are shown all around the horizon, so that they are seen from all points.

Mr. Hall (Great Britain).—Mr. President, may I take the opportunity, before the gallant Delegate from France rises to his feet, to also add my contribution to the academical discussion which he has started? We are not all members of the Academy, I admit, and I apprehend that the original framers of these original Rules were not members of the Academy. But they were so foolish as to make the same great blunder which we are told we have made, because they said in the old Rule that both the lights were to be in the same position. The answer then was just the same that it is now, the height is a minimum height. I never heard of any sailor being puzzled by the old Rule when he was told to put the two lights in the same position. He knew perfectly well that he was to put them at a minimum height.

Admiral Bowden-Smith (Great Britain).—Mr. President, although it does not say so in the Rule, I apprehend that these two red lights are supposed to be visible all around the horizon, because it says that they are to be in globular lanterns. That is the reason, I suppose, that the learned Delegate from Germany has proposed to change the position of the lights, because if they are placed in the ordinary position they would not show all around the horizon.

Captain Richard (France).—Mr. President, it is a fact that custom has sanctioned this Article. The old Rule of 1863 did not in any manner provide for vessels not under command. It was only subsequently that the words, "in the same position," were adopted; and this expression has never been clearly defined. Must the lower light be placed at least 20 feet above the deck, or the upper light? I wish that some one here would give me a distinct explanation, supported by an explanative text. I am very much afraid that no will rise to do so. In practice, two lights are hoisted in such a manner that the upper light is in the place of the white light because the halyards and block are handy which are used in hoisting up the white light. I do not, therefore, see why we should change the words, which are misleading, for words which are no better. But I will not enter into an academical discussion, and this is not the place for it, as the learned Delegate from Great Britain wittily remarked.

I think the learned Dr. Sieveking has not quite understood the argument which I addressed to him. There was a question of a vessel which might be aground, and of the necessity of placing the two red lights where they could best be seen. But you have made Article 11, which provides for that eventuality. I heard the remark made that Article 11 only refers to vessels aground in a fairway. Even so! My objection nevertheless maintains its force, and I again take it up. A vessel not under command is dangerous, because she cannot be mastered, as, for instance, her rudder may be broken and her course may be tortuous. To indicate such course I think that it is of great advantage to have lights which are on the line with the keel and which indicate the course of the vessel. We should not alone endeavour to indicate the vessel's course, but also the condition of such a vessel when she is not under command. Moreover, what does "where the lights can best be seen" mean? Is it in general a position which will be visible from all the points of the horizon? When, for example, a vessel is under sail, how can she show those two red lights more effectively than according to the Rule of 1884?

Captain Mensing (Germany).—Mr. President, the reason why this amendment was brought forward is principally that if a ship is under sail, with all her sails set, it is very difficult to find a position in front of the foremast where the lantern could be hoisted, and it is only to give liberty to the master to place it in some other position.

Captain Malmberg (Sweden).—Mr. President, if the Conference should adopt this amendment proposed by the German Delegation I think it ought to state that these lights in sailing-vessels should at least be hoisted in the fore part and not anywhere where she might see fit to do so. She might see fit to hoist them in the after part, and that would convey no information to another vessel meeting that ship as to which way the sailing-vessel was heading. It ought at least to provide that the lights should be hoisted in the fore part of the ship.

Mr. Verney (Siam).—Mr. President, I do not wish to trouble this Conference about a mere matter of wording when we are going to discuss the verbiage of the Report of the Collocation Committee later, but I reserve to myself the privilege of discussing what is the most accurate description to be used here.

The President.—The Secretary will please read amendment No. 6, Class 2.

The amendment is as follows:—

"Amendment to Collocation Report, proposed by Dr. Sieveking on behalf of the German Delegation, 14th December, 1889:

"In Article 4 (*a*), instead of the words, 'in the same position,' insert the words, 'at the same height,' and after the words, 'Article 2 (*a*),' insert the words, 'where they can best be seen.'"

The President.—Is the Conference ready for the question?

The question was put to the Conference upon the adoption of amendment No. 6, Class 2.

The President.—The Chair is unable to decide. The Secretary will please call the roll.

The Yea and Nay vote is as follows:—

Austria-Hungary .. .. .. Yea.	Italy .. .. .. Yea.
Brazil .. .. .. Nay.	Mexico .. .. .. Nay.
Belgium .. .. .. Nay.	Norway .. .. .. Yea.
China .. .. .. Nay.	Russia .. .. .. Yea.
Chile .. .. .. Nay.	Spain .. .. .. Yea.
Denmark .. .. .. Yea.	Sweden .. .. .. Nay.
France .. .. .. Nay.	Siam .. .. .. Nay.
Germany .. .. .. Yea.	The Netherlands .. .. Nay.
Great Britain .. .. Yea.	United States .. .. Yea.
Hawaii .. .. .. Yea.	

The President.—Ten have voted in the affirmative, and 9 in the negative, so the amendment is adopted. The next subject for consideration is amendment No. 7, Class 2, which will be read by the Secretary.

Amendment No. 7, Class 2, is as follows:—

"Amendment to Collocation Report proposed by Dr. Sieveking on behalf of the German Delegation, 14th December, 1889:

"In Article 4 (a), strike out the words, 'in globular lanterns, each not less than 10 inches in diameter,' and insert, after 'visible' the words, 'all round the horizon.'"

Captain Mensing (Germany).—Mr. President, I tried to point out before that the words, "in globular lanterns," have no real meaning whatever, and I would only move that these words be stricken out. Our amendment is about the same as that proposed by the gallant Delegate from the Netherlands. I would like to point out also that by prescribing such a form of lantern it would make it impossible for any ship, or it would be against the Rules for any ship, not to use a globular lantern, but to use one of any other sort. A globular lantern, as I take it, is one in which the glass is of the same thickness all around the lantern at the same height. We do not use them in our navy at all. We have adopted the French system, and we have got a most excellent lantern, which shows a uniform light all around the horizon. By having a certain profile, we get a much better and stronger light. Now, with a telegraph ship laying a cable, it would be of great interest to show as powerful a light as possible, in order to give warning, as far as possible, that she is coming to get out of the way. The red lantern is of course of a diminished power, and, as a great authority has stated, the light is diminished to such an extent that all there is left of it is not very efficient. It is probably visible 2 miles; but as it has been adopted, we should allow the use of these lanterns. By striking out the words, "in globular lanterns, each not less than 10 inches in diameter," and inserting the words, "all around the horizon," I think we shall come to the desired result.

Captain Salvesen (Norway).—Mr. President, I would suggest that it should read, "two red lights in lanterns, &c., and so constructed as to show the light all round the horizon." A vessel may be so constructed as to enable the light to be seen all around the horizon.

Mr. Hall (Great Britain).—Mr. President, in England we have found that the best lanterns are not globular, but cylindrical: they are flat at the top and flat at the bottom, but they are circular. They certainly throw a better light than what is called the ordinary globular lantern. I am told that our Board of Trade holds that this is a lantern within the Rule. But of course it is an open question as to whether or not they are globular lanterns. As we find that these lights are very effective and better than any globular lantern, I do not see the object of maintaining this epithet. Therefore, we shall support the proposition which has been made by the Delegates for Germany and the Delegates for the Netherlands.

The President.—Is the Conference ready for the question? The Secretary will please read the amendment.

Amendment No 7, Class 2, is as follows:—

"Amendment to Collocation Report, proposed by Dr. Sieveking on behalf of the German Delegation, 14th December, 1889:

"In Article 4 (a), strike out the words, 'in globular lanterns, each not less than 10 inches in diameter,' and insert, after 'visible,' the words, 'all round the horizon.'"

The question was put to the Conference upon the adoption of amendment No. 7, Class 2, and it was adopted.

The President.—The next subject for consideration is amendment No. 8. No. 8 seems to be the same as amendment No. 7.

Mr. Goodrich (United States).—It is under Article 4 (b).

The President.—The question now will be upon amendment No. 8.

The question was put to the Conference upon amendment No. 8, and it was carried.

The President.—Amendment No. 9 is the next subject for consideration.

Captain Van Steyn (the Netherlands).—Mr. President, that has been disposed of.

The President.—Amendment No. 9 has been disposed of by the action of the Conference on a previous amendment.

The next subject for consideration is amendment No. 10. The Secretary will please read it.

Amendment No. 10, Class 2, is as follows:—

"Amendment to Collocation Report, proposed by Dr. Sieveking on behalf of the German Delegation, 14th December, 1889:

"In Article 7, 1 (a), strike out the words, 'or in front of.'"

Captain Mensing (Germany).—Mr. President, this proposition is not of very great importance, I take it. I think that, perhaps, small vessels have got no other place where they can place this lantern than the funnel. If they do not want to have a mast they will place it on the funnel, and very likely they will have a kind of hook rigged on which they may hang it. I would state that this is rather mere matter of expression. We do not want to change anything in the meaning of the Rules. The words, "in front of," might be stricken out and still the sense of the whole paragraph left.

Mr. Hall (Great Britain).—Mr. President, I think it is hardly necessary for the gallant Delegate from Germany to press this amendment. There may be cases where it is desirable to carry the lights not on the funnel, but in front of it. It might be in a small steamer using bad coal, and there would be smoke coming out of the funnel, and this might obscure the light. Therefore, if these words are left in, the light might be carried on or in front of the funnel. It is a very small matter, and I think we might as well leave in the words.

Captain Bisbee (China).—Mr. President, I will point out another difficulty. In using mineral oil, if the lantern were placed close to the funnel it would very often be so hot there that the oil would explode.

Dr. Sieveking (Germany).—Mr. President, we attach very little importance to this amendment, and I beg leave to withdraw it.

The President.—The Delegate from Germany withdraws amendment No. 10.

Captain Shackford (United States).—Mr. President, I would like to call attention to the language of this Rule. If these words, "or on," are left in there they can carry the light on the after part of the funnel, as far as I can see.

Captain Malmberg (Sweden).—Mr. President, in such case they would not comply with the Regulations under Article 2.

Captain Shackford (United States).—Mr. President, I still do not see why these words, "or on," should be left in there.

Mr. Hall (Great Britain).—Mr. President, it is to be carried as laid down in Article 2 (*a*), as the gallant Delegate from Sweden has pointed out.

Captain Shackford (United States).—Mr. President, it seems to me that this is a pretty broad Article. It applies to steam-vessels of less than 40 tons. I would like to inquire why the words, "or on," should be left in there; what is the use of them?

The President.—The Chair hears no motion.

Captain Sampson (United States).—Mr. President, then I will vote to strike out the words, "or on," after the words, "the forward part of the vessel."

Dr. Sieveking (Germany).—Mr. President, that would be a separate amendment, and, as the amendment has not been brought in in time, I think it would be inadmissible.

Mr. Hall (Great Britain).—Mr. President, I am afraid that we are out of order in discussing this matter. There is no amendment before us, but if the gallant Delegate from the United States will read through subsection (*a*) he will see that Article 2 prescribes where the masthead-light is to be. It is to show a light a certain number of points ahead over the horizon, which it would not be possible to do if it was fixed on the after part of a funnel.

Captain Sampson (United States).—Mr. President, I am probably very stupid, but I still fail to see why these words, "or on," are in there. A half a dozen of us discussed this matter very carefully yesterday, and did not see the necessity for these words.

The President.—This will be in the nature of an amendment, and the Chair is of the opinion that no amendment can be considered which is not adopted by a three-fourths vote.

Captain Bisbee (China).—Mr. President, these words originated in the Committee on Lights for Small Vessels. There are circumstances, no doubt, where it would be of advantage to carry this light on the funnel, and if there is an advantage they ought to be allowed to do so. As the learned Delegate from Great Britain has pointed out, no man can fulfil the Rule and place it abaft of the funnel.

The question was put to the Conference as to whether or not the motion of the Delegates of the United States should be entertained, and the motion was lost.

The President.—The next amendment will be No. 11.

Amendment No. 11, Class 2, is as follows:—

"Amendment to the Collocation Report, proposed by Dr. Sieveking on behalf of the German Delegation, 14th December, 1889:

"In Article 7, 1 (*b*), instead of the words, 'such lanterns shall be carried not less 3 feet below the white light,' insert the words, 'such lantern shall be carried vertically below the white light at a distance from the same of not less than 3 feet.'"

Dr. Sieveking (Germany).—Mr. President, this amendment is only to express a little more clearly what was intended by the words as they now stand. At any rate, at present the Rule does not say anything about the position in which these red and green lanterns are to be placed with reference to the white light. It says only such lantern shall be carried not less than 3 feet below the white light. That would allow the coloured lanterns to be carried upon one side or the other of the white light. And that would, of course, give quite a false idea as to the position of the vessel. The two coloured side-lights are replaced by one coloured lantern, with a green light on one side and a red light on the other, showing their respective coloured lights from right ahead to two points abaft the beam on their respective sides. That cannot be carried out in any other way than by placing the coloured lights vertically below the white light. Besides, if we allowed these different coloured lanterns to be carried in front of the white light or abaft of the white light, the distance between the lights, seeing them from some distance ahead, could be so lessened as to make their lights mix up with each other and prevent other vessels from distinguishing them. Therefore, this distance of

3 feet is only of importance and useful if the coloured light is carried vertically below the white light.

Mr. Hall (Great Britain).—Mr. President, there is a practical difficulty with regard to this which I dare say my friend has not foreseen, and that is, if the funnel has any rake at all you could not carry it vertically below. It would not be possible, if the light were fixed to the funnel. You take a funnel like that [indicating] with a masthead-light there [indicating]; you cannot put this light vertically below it, unless you put it inside of the funnel; and I do not suppose that is the proposition.

Dr. Sieveking (Germany).—Mr. President, I think it is very easily arranged by putting the white light a little in front of the funnel, and by having an arm of iron extend out in front of the funnel to which the white light could be attached at the end of the arm.

Mr. Hall (Great Britain).—Mr. President, I would suggest that it might be expressed in this way: "in the same fore-and-aft line." It would then read, "The light shall be carried in the same fore-and-aft line, and not less than 3 feet below the white light.

Mr. Goodrich (United States).—Mr. President, I may say that the United States' Delegation thought it would meet the desire of other parties if the word "vertically" was inserted after the word "carried;" so that it would read: "Such lantern shall be carried vertically not less than 3 feet below the white light." The suggestion made by the learned Delegate from Great Britain about its being in the same fore-and-aft line does not indicate how far forward of the other light it would be. One might be at the stern, and the other might be at the place indicated in the Article. They might be 100 feet apart.

Admiral Bowden-Smith (Great Britain).—The white light must be before the funnel.

Captain Shackford (United States).—It might be 20 feet forward of it.

Dr. Sieveking (Germany).—Mr. President, it is the very same meaning which we have expressed in other words. Of course we do not attach any importance to this wording; but we wish to have it vertically below the white light, and in distance not less than 3 feet. I do not think this is a question which is quite without importance. On these small steamers this is the light which replaces the sidelight. Steamers of this size need not carry the side-lights, but they certainly should indicate their heading to other vessels, so as to enable other vessels to distinguish them. Now, if the white light is carried in the after part of the vessel, and the other light, although placed at a vertical distance of 3 feet below it, is still placed in the fore part of the vessel, the more you widen the distance of the two lights, the more the lights will appear to you to be one light when seen from a distance. They will come nearer to each other, and it is a great obstacle in the way of distinguishing the lights. The only difficulty which is now pointed out is that if the white light is allowed to be carried on the funnel, and the funnel is not in a vertical position, then the coloured light might not be carried vertically below it. But that could be remedied by hanging the white light on a stanchion or arm, so as to enable the coloured light to be placed on the funnel, vertically, 3 feet below the white light.

Mr. Hall (Great Britain).—Mr. President, I think this is merely a question of words. The learned Delegate from the United States has suggested a form ; and I think I can suggest one which is even more simple, and that is to transpose the word "vertically" to the end of the sentence, so that it will read: "Such lantern shall be carried below the white light at a distance from the same not less than 3 feet vertically." You cannot get it vertically below, because that means 3 feet exactly below. I think that will carry out my learned friend's wishes.

Dr. Sieveking (Germany).—Mr. President, to say that the lantern shall be carried not less than 3 feet vertically below the white light would convey the meaning, so far as I see, that it must be carried vertically below the white light, and at a distance of not less than 3 feet. At any rate, that is what we propose, and what we think best.

Admiral Bowden-Smith (Great Britain).—Mr. President, I hope my friend will not press for a hard and fast Rule for these little boats. It might be the best plan to place this second light on the stem of the boat in some cases. You would have the little white light before the funnel, when it might be the best place to put the second little light on the stem. The second light is placed very low in any case, and if a man should stand up he would obscure the light. I really hope that he will not make the Rule too hard and fast for these little boats.

Captain Salvesen (Norway).—Mr. President, I think it looks rather queer that we, who have not been able to decide upon a place for the side-lights on board the big steamers, now shall be obliged to give an exact place for them upon this small craft.

Mr. Goodrich (United States).—Mr. President, does the Conference desire a vote upon this amendment before it adjourns?

The President.—Is the Conference ready for the question upon this amendment? The amendment will be read.

Dr. Sieveking (Germany).—Mr. President, after consultation with my colleagues, I beg to say, on behalf of the German Delegation, that we agree to have this altered in the way which has been proposed by the learned Delegate from Great Britain. I do not exactly remember the words.

Mr. Hall (Great Britain).—Mr. President, it is to put the word "vertically" at the end of the sentence.

Mr. Goodrich (United States).—Mr. President, on behalf of the Delegates for the United States I must say that we are very much impressed by the remark of the gallant Admiral from Great Britain, that we should not make a hard and fast Rule for these little boats. That was the intention of the Collocation Committee.

The President.—Does the Delegate from Germany modify his amendment?

Dr. Sieveking (Germany).—Mr. President, I think it quite clear if we put the word "vertically" at the end of the sentence.

The President.—The Secretary will please read the amendment as proposed by the Delegate from Germany.

206

The amendment is as follows:—

"Such lantern shall be carried not less than 3 feet below the white light, vertically."

The President.—Is the Conference ready for the question?

The question was put to the Conference upon this amendment, and it was lost.

The President.—The question now is upon the amendment. This was an amendment to the amendment. Is the Conference ready for the question?

The question was put upon this amendment, and the amendment was lost.

Mr. Goodrich (United States).—Mr. President, I rise to obtain, for the benefit of the Conference, the views of the majority of the members as to the length of time during which the Conference will sit during the holidays. The Delegates will remember that next Wednesday is Christmas, and, for the purpose of obtaining the views of the Conference, I wish to make a motion for adjournment from Friday of this week until the 6th January. Do not understand me as favouring that proposition. I do not favour it. I am making the motion, as I stated, deliberately for the purpose of obtaining the views of the Conference. It makes no difference to me what day is inserted. I only desire to meet the views of the Conference. For myself, I am willing to sit right up to the day before Christmas, and sit the day after Christmas, until we finish the work of this Conference. I distinctly state that this is not my wish, nor is it the wish of the Delegates from the United States.

Mr. Carter (Hawaii).—Mr. President, I move to amend that by moving that when the Conference adjourn on Friday it adjourn to meet on Monday at 11 o'clock.

Mr. Goodrich (United States).—Mr. President, I accept the amendment if that be the view of the Conference. What I want to get at is the time for the adjournment.

Mr. Carter (Hawaii).—Mr. President, I will withdraw my amendment.

Mr. Goodrich (United States).—Mr. President, I take it that no Delegate wants to sit on Christmas. If any member will make a motion—or I will make it myself, that we sit until Tuesday at 1 o'clock and then adjourn until the following Thursday. I am simply desirous of meeting the views of the foreign Delegates.

Dr. Sieveking (Germany).—Mr. President, I beg to move that we adjourn on Saturday at 1 o'clock. I do not say until what time. That depends upon how far we get along with the work on Saturday. Perhaps we can get through with the Rules of the Road and finish with them by Saturday. Then we can see what work we have before us. I should not like to have to attend a meeting on the day before Christmas, and I think we ought to be free on Monday. If it can be arranged to let us sit on Saturday, and take away our free Saturday which the rules allow, and give us a free Monday, that, I think, would be desirable.

Mr. Hall (Great Britain).—Mr. President, I quite agree with the learned Delegate from Germany that in deciding the length of the recess we ought to be governed by the work which is done. If we get on with our work, as there seems every possibility of our doing, we shall finish this matter by Saturday. We have got two more days before us, and we have got through already with one-third of the amendments which have been brought before us on principle. Among that one-third was the second amendment with regard to the crossing of the rays of light, which was a matter of very great importance, and occupied more than one-half of the day.

I do not think there are any other amendments likely to occupy so long. I think, giving a fair time for the discussion of amendments, that we can get through the amendments not only on principle, but the verbiage amendments, in a short time. The verbiage amendments are mere questions of words, and the Collocation Committee have considered these words very carefully indeed. I will only say for the Collocation Committee that they have done their work as best they can. I think the holiday should depend upon the condition of the work. If we get through the amendments to the Collocation Report on principle, and as to verbiage, there will then be nothing left with regard to the Rules of the Road, and it would merely remain for us to see that there are no errors in the final Report. After we have done that we have only the Report of one remaining Committee to deal with. That Report has not yet been finished. I think that we might then be able to adjourn, say, from Saturday until Friday of next week.

The Delegates should remember this: however much some of them might like to have a holiday, we are foreigners in a distant land, and we have not got our homes to go to to spend Christmas. Christmas and holidays are a mockery to us who want to go home to our friends and spend what time we can with them, whether it be at Christmas or whatever time it may be. Therefore, we want to go on and finish the work. I would venture to suggest that we adjourn on Saturday, and that the question of the duration of the holiday be left open until we know how we stand with regard to the work, because I certainly think that if we have not finished these amendments in relation to the Rules of the Road by Friday we ought to meet again as early as possible to go on with them and finish them.

Mr. Goodrich (United States).—Mr. President, I very heartily agree with the remarks which have fallen from the learned Delegate from Great Britain. It seems to me that I had better withdraw entirely the motion for adjournment, or for any arrangement of the sessions, and that we shall proceed along *die, diem*, until such a time as we shall finish with the Rules of the Road.

The Conference thereupon adjourned until Thursday, 19th December, 1889, at 11 o'clock A.M.

Washington, Thursday, December 19, 1889, 11 *o'clock* A.M.

THE Conference was called to order at 11 o'clock A.M., Rear-Admiral Franklin in the chair.

Mr. Goodrich (United States).—Mr. President, I think it is proper for me to present a new amendment. Of course, I am aware that it requires a three-fourths vote to permit the consideration of it by the Conference.

Dr. Sieveking (Germany).—Mr. President, it requires general consent.

Mr. Hall (Great Britain).—Mr. President, by the new rules I take it that no amendment can be now introduced without the unanimous consent of the Conference.

The President.—The Chair was under the impression that the old three-fourths rule still existed with reference to any matter which had been passed upon by the Conference.

Mr. Hall (Great Britain).—Mr. President, referring to the words of the Resolution passed on the motion of my learned friend the Delegate from Germany, I think it was provided that every amendment must be handed in before 7 o'clock on Saturday night. I am, of course, only speaking from memory.

Dr. Sieveking (Germany).—Mr. President, I am certainly under the impression that it was the intention of that Resolution to preclude every amendment which had not been brought in up to a given time on Saturday night.

Mr. Goodrich (United States).—Mr. President, I am inclined to think that in this case it will not make any difference, because it is such a palpable oversight that the Delegates will probably agree as to the necessity of discussing it. The amendment which I propose was one which was proposed by the English Delegates, and the Delegates will find it in the printed amendments to Article 22, the original amendment.

Mr. Hall (Great Britain).—Mr. President, it was amendment No. 61, I think.

Mr. Goodrich (United States).—Mr. President, it reads:—

"When, in consequence of thick weather or other causes, two ships find themselves so close to each other as to make it doubtful whether by the action of one ship alone collision can be avoided, the ship which, by the above Articles, is directed to keep her course and speed shall also take such action as will best aid to avoid collision."

Now, if the Delegates will remember, the propositions which were made by Great Britain, and which were printed and supplied to each of the members, embrace all the amendments which were suggested by Great Britain at that time, and they will find that this Article was one of such amendments. They also suggested an amendment to old Article 18 in such a way as to leave out the words, "when approaching another ship," relying upon the fact that such case would be provided for by the adoption of new Article 22. I submitted these Rules as reported by the Collocation Committee to one of the most able and painstaking Judges, Judge Brown, of the United States' District Court for the Southern District of New York, and he called my attention to what seems to me at this moment to be a very serious omission. I do not care whether I discuss the matter now or later; but I ask consent to the printing of this amendment, that it may be considered, perhaps to-morrow, for I do think there is a very serious omission here. The wisdom of the English Delegates was a great deal better than that which they displayed when they permitted myself amongst others to persuade them to withdraw this amendment, because it was at that time deemed unnecessary. I desire to have this amendment printed, and in due season will present my reasons to the Conference.

Dr. Sieveking (Germany).—Mr. President, I am sorry to say that I must object to the discussion of this amendment.

Mr. Goodrich (United States).—Do you object to the proposition?

Dr. Sieveking (Germany).—No; I object to discussing the amendment or to admitting the amendment. I think it is one of the most dangerous amendments. Of course, I shall be opposed to the principle; but I think it is an amendment of the kind which would make the Rules of the Road as at present framed, so far as my judgment goes, entirely unacceptable. It is undesirable at this stage to bring in any such important addition, which, after careful consideration, has been left out, and which I am very glad has been left out. I am sorry to say that I must object to this.

Mr. Goodrich (United States).—Mr. President, then I must ask a vote on the proposition, and to that end I must explain the proposition a little more carefully, as I think it requires a three-fourths vote to secure the consideration of this amendment. If the Delegates will turn to old Article 18 they will see that this is the provision:—

"Every steam-ship, when approaching another ship so as to involve risk of collision, shall slacken her speed, or stop and reverse, if necessary."

The English Delegation proposed to amend that by adding two Articles. Article 20 provides:—

"Every steam-ship that is directed by these Regulations to keep out of the way of another ship shall, on approaching her so as to involve risk of collision, slacken her speed if necessary, or stop if necessary, or reverse if necessary."

The Delegates will observe that that amendment only imposed upon the ship that was directed to keep out of the way the burden of doing that which was necessary to avoid collision, and by that no duty, under any circumstances, whether a collision was imminent or not, was imposed upon the privileged vessel. I suppose that the English Delegates, in connection with the exclusion of that whole Article 18, as amended by a new Article 20, believed that it was provided for by new Article 22, which reads:—

"When, in consequence of thick weather or other causes, two ships find themselves so close to each other as to make it doubtful whether by the action of one ship alone collision can be avoided, the ship which by the above Articles is directed to keep her course and speed shall also take such action as will best aid to avoid collision."

[93]

Couple these two Articles together and you have imposed upon the privileged ship, in case of imminent danger, where the giving-way ship has not obeyed the Rules, a still further duty to avoid collision, just as old Article 18 directed her to do. Of course, I am aware that we inserted in Article 28 of the Collocation Report the words, " and collision," so that it reads :—

" In obeying and construing these Rules, due regard shall be had to all dangers of navigation and collision, and to any special circumstances which may render a departure from the above Rules ecessary in order to avoid immediate danger."

Thus gentlemen will see that the pointed necessity of Article 18, as it originally stood, has been taken out of the Rules, and does not catch the eye of a mariner. You make it necessary for him to refer to three Rules in order to discover his duty, as it was provided by old Article 18. Now, will you permit me to read what Judge Brown, the Judge to whom I referred, says, in a communication which he has addressed to me? He says :—

" Article 23, in modifying the existing Rule, very much limits its application. By these proposed Rules I do not find any explicit requirement that a steamer that has the right of way shall stop and back when that would avoid a collision seen to be otherwise unavoidable; that is, when the vessel bound to keep out of the way has failed to take proper measures in time, and can no longer avoid collision if the other holds her course unchecked. Existing Rule 18 covers this obligation explicitly, by providing that 'every' steam-ship approaching, &c., shall slacken, stop, or reverse, if necessary. The exclusion of this express obligation in the substitute, with nothing to supply the place of this exclusion in any other part of the Rules, naturally raises the question whether the Conference intended to modify that obligation. I do not suppose for a moment that there was any such intention. The obligation itself is of the most fundamental character, constantly applied by the Courts; and in the very last number of the 'Times' Law Reports (4th December, 1889, p. 87), Lord Esher, in the case of the River Derwent, in the Court of Appeal, says that this obligation is 'paramount over all statutory Rules,' and, again, declared it ' superior to all written Rules.'

" In preparing a written Code for the guidance of mariners, ought a Rule so fundamental, of so frequent application, and ' superior to all others,' to be omitted from any distinct enunciation, or left to the vague generalities of Articles 28 and 30, affected in construction, as they might naturally be, by the suppression made through the modification of existing Article 18? Any doubt thrown on the duty of a vessel having the right of way to avoid a collision when she can do so, that would be otherwise unavoidable through the failure of the other vessel to do her duty, would be most unfortunate.

" The general duty, as I understand it to be universally enforced by the Courts, may be stated as follows : When a vessel bound to keep out of the way can no longer avoid collision unassisted, through disregard of her duty or any other cause, the other vessel shall do all in her power to avoid collision, notwithstanding any other provision in the Rules."

Now, the English Delegates, after their very careful consideration of these Rules and the amendment which they proposed, supplemented their amendment to old Article 18 and new Article 20, and rectified the omission by the provision of Article 22, as they proposed it. Now, the Delegates will see in a moment that the two Articles, as England proposed them, made a perfect Code, and made clear what was intended by old Article 18. But when you take the first of their amendments proposed, Article 20, and leave out the proposed new Article 22, you have emasculated the intention of the English Delegates and taken out all the vitality of this Rule and destroyed—although I am sure that is not the intention of this Conference—the Rule which has been laid down by the Courts, even in the absence of any written Rule, that where two vessels are in such a position as to involve risk of collision, although one is privileged to hold her course, she cannot hold it into the jaws of hell, when timely action on her part could have avoided collision.

As my friend the learned First Delegate from Great Britain said to me last night when we were discussing the subject—it is like the donkey case in the English Courts. If a donkey is hobbled on a highway, an approaching carriage has no right to run over it because it is improperly in the highway and hobbled; there is a duty upon the carriage which is approaching. The same Rule is laid down in cases of negligence against Railroad Companies in this country. A man may be walking on the track of a railroad where he has no right to walk. He is negligent in walking there. Under the common law, if a man is negligent, he cannot recover damages if he is injured, whether the other person has been guilty of negligence or not. But there is a higher rule than that which sometimes applies, where a Railroad Company, even where a stranger is negligent, can avoid collision and damage which it sees is imminent, and then the duty is imposed upon the Railroad Company to avoid that damage if they can do so. That is the rule which ought to apply here, and which for twenty-five years has been applied under these Rules.

Think what will be the effect of striking out this eminently clear and well-pointed provision of the old Rule! The sailor looks at these Rules and compares them with the old Rule. The old Rule, he says, directs me, in a case of imminent danger, although I am the privileged ship, to avoid a collision if I can by making some manœuvre. The Conference has stricken this provision out. What is my duty now? The Conference has said: " Hold on, and let the other vessel provide for herself; you are not responsible for damages." It is not enough to say that, by the construction of three or four Rules, the Courts thereafter will construe the liability of the negligent vessel. It seems to me that we either ought to strike out both the amendments of Great Britain and leave the old Rule, or we ought to adopt both the amendments suggested, and so point the necessity of obedience to this Rule to the mariner upon the deck of the ship. I think this amendment is exceedingly important, and if we do not at least consider it, as suggested by the learned Delegate from Germany, I think we shall fail in our duty.

Mr. Hall (Great Britain).—Mr. President, this is a striking illustration of the difficulty into which the Conference may sometimes be led by being told what is the opinion of a distinguished lawyer. I do not want to minimize at all the great importance of the opinions of gentlemen who hold distinguished places in their professions in this or any other country, but we must remember that they are not present at our deliberations. They do not know the reasons which have induced us either to propose or withdraw amendments. They have not studied the other Rules, or the principles substituted by us to take the place of the amendments which have been proposed. Therefore their opinions, of course, must be taken with a certain amout of reserve.

Now, what position are we in here? The learned Delegate for the United States is accurate, as he always is, when he says that he spoke to me last night about this matter; but I was not aware until a few moments ago that this motion was going to be made. I say at once we shall be very glad indeed if the Conference will insert this new Article. But how do we stand? Great Britain considered this and thought it a desirable Article to be put into the Rules. We acted upon the principle which we have acted upon throughout this Conference. We unreservedly presented at the outset every proposition we intended to make to the Conference. We thought it desirable to put the Conference into possession of all of our proposals at the very earliest possible moment, and we printed the whole of our amendments which we intended to make, side by side with the original Rules, and distributed them to the members of the Conference. Amongst them was this new Article.

Now, what is done? We are told that a most eminent Judge says that this Rule is perfectly unnecessary, and it is argued: Why do you put it in when it is provided for under general Article 23? We are told that it will meet with strenuous opposition, and we acted, as I think the Conference will bear me out in saying, as we have always acted; we thought it useless to attempt to force down an Article against the wishes of many of the Delegates; that it was no use getting a bare majority in order to carry a new Rule; and we felt that, if there was really strong opposition to the new Rule, we would not feel justified in pressing it on the Conference, although, as I say, we thought this Article a most desirable one, and although we prepared it with the greatest care before we came here. We found what we believed to be the consensus of opinion of the Conference, and we said: "We will withdraw the amendment; but we will ask permission to introduce words into the general Rule so as to make that Rule clearly apply to cases of collision as well as to other cases." We did that, as I say, not solely upon the opinion of an eminent Judge, because I do not think we should act upon such matters solely in deference to the opinion of one man, whoever he may be.

But, as we knew, my learned friend the gallant Delegate from Germany and other honourable Delegates had very strong opposition to this Rule, and, as I say, we withdrew it because we thought that we could attain our end as well, or perhaps nearly as well, by adding the words to the general Article. So we withdrew that amendment, and then inserted words, which the Conference adopted, in the general Article to meet the circumstances of the case which we had intended to provide for in the new Article. Those words were accepted by the Conference. They were accepted more than a month ago. They were accepted on the 19th November, just one month ago, and they were printed and have been ready for discussion during the whole of the time since then. Now, what happens? We are told that another eminent Judge thinks that it is most desirable that this Article should be put in, and his arguments are read to us in the form of a letter. As I say, I want to pay the greatest respect to the opinion of that learned Judge; but there is not one single word in that letter which has been read to us here to-day which practically has not been argued in this Conference. It was pointed out that we were taking a very serious step. When I introduced the Resolution with regard to vessels keeping their course and speed I said it was a most serious question, and that I hoped it would not be passed without the most careful consideration and discussion, and I do not think that any amendment before the Conference received more careful discussion.

My learned friend on my left addressed us a most interesting speech in regard to the importance of the change, and he pointed out the difficulties and dangers. It was pointed out over and over again that if we passed this Rule it might be necessary to say something which would point the minds of sailors to the fact that although there was this Rule they must not stick to it as a hard and fast Rule; but when they saw that there was danger of collision, which could not be avoided by the action of the keeping-out-of-the-way vessel alone, then the holding-on vessel must act also. That was pointed out, and there is no doubt that is the law. Under these circumstances, we introduced these words into Article 23. I will only say this: we should be very glad if the Resolution of the learned Delegate for the United States is carried, because we adhere to our former opinion. But I do not want it to be thought, and I think I am justified in saying that I decline to have it thought, that in this matter Great Britain is acting like a weather-cock. We withdrew our Article in deference to the expressions which we heard in regard to it; and therefore we do not think we are justified in attempting to get the vote of the Conference in its behalf, knowing that there was strong opposition to it. It is perfectly true now that some of the strongest opposition is withdrawn, and it is difficult for us to know how to act, for we do not know what the feeling of the Conference is.

As I say, we should gladly hail the insertion of this new Article if it could be inserted, and then it will not be necessary to add the words, "or collision," to old Article 23. I observe there is an amendment by the gallant Delegate from the United States to strike out those words. He will remember that those words were inserted partly for this particular and express purpose. If this new Article is carried it will not then be necessary to insert them in Article 23 (*b*), but if it is not, I think the Conference has expressed its mind pretty clearly that it is desirable to insert them, and they have been inserted accordingly. This is the way the matter stands at present. I say we hope you will insert this new Article; but whether or not the Conference will vote for it is, of course, a matter to be determined by its vote.

Dr. Sieveking (Germany).—Mr. President, allow me to make a few remarks upon a formal point. It has been resolved that all amendments to the Rules of the Road as drafted by the Collocation

Committee must be put in writing and handed to the Secretary of the Collocation Committee before 7 o'clock at night on the second day after the day on which the Report has been laid before the Conference. It certainly was the intention of this Resolution, and up to to-day it has not been doubted, that all amendments which had not been brought in by 7 o'clock at night on that day should not be admitted. The old rule of a three-fourths vote was passed at a time when nobody could have thought of the third reading of the Rules. It only intended to preclude those amendments with reference to Resolutions and subjects which had been dealt with by the Conference on the second reading. Therefore, I think I am quite right on that point, and unless there is unanimous consent of the Conference, such a subject should have been brought in by an amendment on the day appointed, before 7 o'clock at night; and if it was not presented in that time, the amendment is inadmissible.

You see, Mr. President, that it is very annoying for me to have to discuss this point, because I should not like to be the only one to oppose, from a formal point of view, any discussion on subjects which deserve the attention of the Conference, and for this reason I should like to say that if I am the only one who raises this formal point, I should like to be considered as if I consented to the admission of the amendment. But I cannot let this discussion end without drawing the attention of the Conference to the consequences into which we will be led. This amendment which is now proposed by the learned Delegate for the United States opens a subject which has been very carefully considered by the Conference, and it is of the utmost importance, because this Article 22 of the original draft made by the Delegation from Great Britain, which is now brought forward in the form of an amendment, is in very close connection, and cannot be dealt with separately from other Rules which have been considered by the Conference, and especially from the Rule according to which the holding-on vessel is to keep her speed.

When that Resolution was under discussion I pointed out that such a subject was of the very utmost importance, and that it would be a source of litigation; that there was a very heavy duty imposed upon the holding-on vessel by passing this Rule. These reasons and other reasons which have been given against the holding-her-speed Rule have been carefully considered by the Conference, and they have not been thought to be sufficient. Well, we bowed to that decision. We did not bring in any amendments except an amendment which we think supplies an oversight with regard to the duty which, by the wording of the Resolution, is imposed on an overtaken vessel to keep her speed, because we thought it was not the intention to make the Rule apply to overtaken vessels, but only to crossing vessels. But now, if this question is raised, I think I should be only right to claim the same privilege which is asked for in this new amendment to open the whole question again with regard to the keeping-her-speed Rule, because they cannot be separated. Where would that lead to? That would lead us not only to open the question of keeping her speed, but also other questions and other Regulations which are in close connection with it, and which were discussed a month ago very carefully, and are now before the Conference in the draft of the Report of the Collocation Committee.

The reasons, which have been dwelt upon at some length by the learned Delegate from the United States, which make it in his eyes desirable to have this amendment introduced, in my opinion are not at all sufficient to induce us to reconsider the matter. I must say a word about it. I would not have gone into the matter at all if it had not been that the learned Delegate from the United States had dwelt upon the merits of the case. It is one of the most important principles that the Steering and Sailing Rules should be so clear that there cannot be the slightest doubt upon the part of either vessel as to what is its duty. This is made quite clear now. One is to keep out of the way, and the other is to keep her course and speed. The learned Delegate from the United States says that this may lead to the consequence that the holding-on vessel must keep her speed even if she sees that nothing is done on the part of the other vessel to avoid a collision. Now, I beg to call the attention of the Conference to old Article 23, the meaning of which has not been altered by the new wording, which is to the effect:—

"In obeying and construing these Rules due regard shall be had to all dangers of navigation and collision, and to any special circumstances which may render a departure from the above Rules necessary in order to avoid immediate danger."

That Rule has always been interpreted in an innumerable number of cases by the Courts to mean that where the holding-on vessel sees that immediate danger would ensue unless she makes some manœuvre to avoid the collision, she not only has the right, but she has the duty, by old Article 23, to take such action in order to avoid immediate danger, and to depart from the Rules. That covers the case where, by the holding-her-course-and-speed Rules, risk of immediate danger is brought about. Therefore, considering besides the other Rules which have been added by the Delegates from Great Britain, and which were very good Rules, and which have been proposed and accepted after very careful consideration, of which I only beg to mention the one that vessels are now compelled to avoid crossing the bows of another vessel, and another that a vessel is allowed to give a warning signal, and a third Rule that the vessel which is to keep out of the way is to indicate her manœuvre—the holding-her-speed Rule will not lead to any serious or dangerous consequences. But the whole of these Rules form a system, and you cannot take out a part of it without discussing the whole system over again.

Now, what is proposed instead of this? It is this: When, in consequence of thick weather or other causes, two ships find themselves so close to each other as to make it doubtful whether by the action of one ship alone collision can be avoided, the ship which by the above Articles is directed to keep her course and speed shall also take such action as will best aid to avoid collision. So that a Rule which is clear and precise is deprived of its clear and precise character which it has now, and in doubtful cases the ship is allowed or is compelled to take action and to take notice of these doubtful cases. It has been a Rule which has been most strictly construed by the most eminent Judges of Great Britain. The Rule is that every vessel must know how to act, and that the holding-on vessel is bound to hold on and keep her course, and now also to keep her speed until she sees that immediate danger would ensue if she did not manœuvre. But now she is to be compelled to manœuvre, if it is doubtful, by any cause, whether a collision will be avoided by the manœuvre of the other ship. Think of the endless litigation which will ensue when such a Rule is introduced. We have no basis to rest upon, and instead of a clean-cut and uniform system which we have now we have a Rule the application of which is doubtful. There is now an uncertainty to be introduced in the Rules. In my opinion the whole system which has been adopted by the Conference will become unacceptable if we adopt this new principle.

These are my reasons in regard to this matter. The reasons may be wrong or they may be right, but there can be no doubt that if this amendment is admitted we ought to have the right to consider, if the amendment be carried, the whole of the new Regulations which have been brought into the Steering and Sailing Rules, and to decide whether or not they should be amended. I very much doubt if that would be an advisable proceeding. We are invited now to consider this amendment, which is one, in my opinion, of the most dangerous amendments that can be presented. We are asked to consider it to-morrow without having any time to consider it, and consequently without being able to bring in any amendment which may be the consequence, in our opinion, of the adoption of this amendment. These are the reasons why I think we ought to adhere to the Resolution which we have adopted, which I confess is a merely formal objection, but which is a formal objection not without very strong reasons to support it. I repeat, that if I am the only one here in the Conference who proposes this formal point I shall not press it. But if the amendment is admitted I think that at least we ought to be allowed a fortnight to consider it and to consider the consequences of it, and to bring in amendments to the whole system of Steering and Sailing Rules as they are now adopted.

Mr. Verbrugghe (Belgium).—Mr. President, I believe there is nothing to add to the very able speech delivered just now by the learned Delegate from Germany. I only rise to say that I quite agree in every respect with what he has said. I, for my part, was very glad that this sixty-first amendment was withdrawn, because it upset the Rule and the interpretation of the Rule as it formerly was. As was so ably said, every vessel knew what she had to do. She had to keep on her course until certain circumstances justified her in doing otherwise. Let me point out one thing. I will not discuss the question of principle; I will only state a question of fact. If this amendment is brought again under discussion and is accepted, then there is no longer any Rule at all, because there will always be some instances in which the sailor may think proper to depart from the Rule, and then what becomes of the Rule? We may say that we are really lost. For this reason I shall vote against taking into consideration the motion of the learned Delegate from the United States.

Mr. Hall (Great Britain).—Mr. President, I said at the outset of my remarks that we should be very glad to see this Article passed; but we cannot blind ourselves to the great force of the remarks which have fallen from the learned Delegate from Germany with regard to the right which any one would have who was opposed to this Article to propose to alter all of the Articles in connection therewith. We are strongly opposed to such a proceeding. We feel that we ought to bow to the decision of this Conference with regard to all of the Rules which we have discussed. Therefore, sooner than agree to any course which would imply that we think any of these Rules which have been passed by the Conference ought to be altered, we will cast our votes against the reconsideration of this question. We have acted as best we could upon the authority that was given to us and on what we were told. when we were told that there was strong opposition to this Article, we set to work to frame a Rule without the Article. We did not consider that Article necessary, and therefore we do not think now that we ought to vote in favour of this proposition, although, as I said, we should like to have seen the Article introduced as it was originally.

Mr. Goodrich (United States).—Mr. President, I hope the Conference will pardon me if I am somewhat strenuous in presenting my views upon this subject. In the first place, as I understand the reconsideration of this proposition, the Conference has adopted no rule, as far as I know, which affects this matter, with the possible exception of the old three-fourths rule, and the rule of action upon the Report of the Collocation Committee, to which the learned Delegate from Germany has referred, the Resolution offered on the 9th December. Of course it is a very simple matter to take either one of two courses, namely, to move to reconsider the Article or to reconsider this Resolution of 9th December. How this is done is an immaterial matter to me. I shall discharge my duty if I present to the Conference my views upon this subject. All the world is wiser than any man in it. But it seems to me that when a learned Judge, than whom there is no more able, experienced, and distinguished Judge in America, suggests the defects in the Rule as adopted by the Conference, it is well worth while for sailors and lawyers to pause and consider the suggestions of that Judge. We are agreed upon the principle. There is no difference, Gentlemen of the Conference, between the learned First Delegate of Great Britain and myself. There is not a particle of difference as to the propriety of a Rule which he thinks is already provided for by the Articles to which he refers, namely, new Articles 21, 23, and 28. I am free to say, with great deference to his superior judgment and experience, that I differ with him. In the first place the decisions of the Court already announced were pronounced upon the old Rule. They were founded upon the old Rule, they were enunciated with distinct reference to the fact that old Article 18 made a provision that every vessel under circumstances of imminent necessity was obliged to take the precautions which that situation required.

Now, what will the Conference do? Must they strike out that old provision under which the Courts have construed the duty upon the privileged vessel? They have absolutely stricken out that which, taken in connection with Article 23, imposed upon the privileged vessel a duty of avoiding collision in case of imminent danger, when she could. You have taken out the keystone of the arch of the old system, and what have you put in the place of it? Not a word except that in Article 28, as now proposed, you have the words, "and collision," which my gallant colleague on my right says do not belong there, and which he proposes to strike out in due season. I submit, Gentlemen, that when my learned friend the Delegate from Germany says that this will cause endless litigation, if you adopt the principle suggested by Judge Brown of New York—I prophesy that if you leave it out you will cause endless litigation in the construction of this new system. The old system was perfect in this regard. The system proposed by the Delegates from Great Britain with the two amendments was a perfect system. The system as now proposed, when you take one of the amendments and leave out the other, is totally inadequate to the situation.

I am as anxious to finish the work of this Conference as any gentleman here. I am just as anxious to have my good friends from the other side get home to their families. But it is worth our while to consider whether we had better keep this Conference in session a week or two weeks longer to consider this important proposition than it is to abjourn and go home, leaving our work in such a condition that some Legislature of some nation will refuse to adopt it on account of a defect in it. Of course we all agree to that. I must say frankly that this proposition of the learned Delegate from Germany does not startle me. If it is necessary to amend the other Rules, let us amend them, if we have made a defect which we ought to cover and cure. At any rate I do hope that the Conference will not close the door upon the consideration of this amendment. It is very easy to vote it down in due season, to-morrow or next week or any other time, if you do not like it; but it seems to me very unwise to refuse to even consider the question, especially when the learned Delegate from Great Britain says that they stand by their recommendation originally made to the Conference and that they deem it an important Rule, although now the learned First Delegate says that he is inclined to believe the system, as it is now, meets the necessities of the situation. I do hope the Conference will not refuse to consider this question and permit the printing of the amendment for further discussion.

Mr. Hall (Great Britain).—Mr. President, I am very unwilling to add anything more to this discussion. But what is the reason given now for the reconsideration of this matter? The sole reason that is given, I think, is that a learned Judge, whom we are told is the most eminent man in the State of New York, has expressed an opinion in a letter. He has not been present at our deliberations; he has not heard any of the arguments which weighed upon us in dealing with that Article. We are told that this is the opinion of the most learned man in New York; we were told a month before that the most learned Judge in the United States of America thought that this was a useless Rule, and said that he did not see why it was inserted. Now, if we are to act upon the opinion of this learned Judge or that learned Judge every time that we have a reprint of the Rules, what will be the result? Although we are very glad to have the assistance of these distinguished gentlemen, we really must act for ourselves. We must consider whether or not the matter has been thoroughly discussed, and whether we have carefully considered the matter. I venture to say that the learned Judge to whom the Delegate from the United States has referred has not heard what arguments have been presented. He has not had copies of the Protocols. He cannot tell why that Article was withdrawn, or why the alteration was made in other Articles in consequence of such withdrawal. I think that the mere opinion of a learned Judge, however learned he may be, is not a sufficient argument to induce us to reconsider a series of Rules which we have discussed with great care and at very great length, and which I believe the vast majority of the Delegates now think are good and workable Rules.

Mr. Goodrich (United States).—Mr. President, let me correct my learned friend. I either did not say, or if I did I did not intend to say, that the Judge to whom I referred was the most learned Judge in the State of New York. That would be an invidious comparison of which I certainly should not be guilty. But I spoke of him as one of the most able, experienced, and distinguished Judges in the State of New York.

The President.—What is the motion of the learned Delegate from the United States?

Mr. Goodrich (United States).—Mr. President, I do not know whether I had better pursue the Parliamentary rule here and ask a reconsideration of the proposition, or ask permission to introduce this amendment. Unless some member objects, I will ask permission to introduce this amendment.

Dr. Sieveking (Germany).—Mr. President, I have objected to the consideration of this amendment. I have said that if I was the only one who objected I would not object. I have not been the only one, and I shall have to object. The Conference must therefore decide, or the Chair will be good enough to decide, whether the unanimous consent of the Conference is necessary, as I think it is, or whether only a three-fourths majority is required. Of course I bow to the decision of the Chair.

The President.—The Chair was under the impression that a three-fourths majority was necessary in order to reconsider a matter which had already been decided upon, and the Chair would prefer to take that course in an important matter of this kind.

Mr. Goodrich (United States).—Then, Mr. President, I move that this amendment be printed for consideration, which will raise the question whether there are three-fourths of the members of the Conference who desire to have it presented. Unless a three-fourths vote is received, of course the subject is ended.

The President.—The Delegate from the United States moves that this amendment be printed for consideration.

Mr. Goodrich (United States).—Mr. President, let me say one word. Although I am aware it is very late in the discussion and in the work of the Conference, yet if this subject is refused consideration it is the first time in the history of the Conference that this course has been taken.

Mr. Hall (Great Britain).—Mr. President, upon that may I point out, and I have the Protocols before me, that this matter has been discussed previously at very great length? There is not one single item of novelty in the proposal which has been discussed to-day upon the question as to whether a vessel should keep her speed, and upon the question as to what she should do when she is keeping her course and speed and finds that a vessel is about to come into collision with her. We have never refused to reconsider any matter which had any element of novelty in it; but I think we ought to say that if an old subject is brought up, in which there is no element of novelty, we ought not to waste the time of the Conference in discussing it. This matter has been carefully thought out and argued. The rules have been carefully drawn up to meet the various requirements; and I confess myself that I cannot see that the letter of the learned Judge has imparted any novelty whatever to the subject.

Mr. Verbrugghe (Belgium).—Mr. President, I rose a moment ago to state the way in which I should vote, but the remark which has fallen from the learned Delegate from the United States obliges me to make a distinction. Out of courtesy I may admit that some new Rule or proposition might be recommended, even if I am opposed to it. But I am opposed to the consideration of this old amendment No. 61.

The President.—Is the Conference ready for the question? The Secretary will please call the roll.

The Yea and Nay vote is as follows:—

Austria-Hungary	.. ..	Nay.
Brazil	.. .. ..	Nay.
Belgium	.. .. ..	Nay.
China	.. .. ..	Nay.
Chile	.. .. ..	Nay.
Denmark	.. .. ..	Nay.
France	.. .. ..	Nay.
Germany	.. .. ..	Nay.
Great Britain	.. ..	Nay.
Hawaii	.. .. ..	Nay.
Italy	.. .. ..	Nay.
Norway	.. .. ..	Nay.
Russia	.. .. ..	Nay.
Spain	.. .. ..	Nay.
Sweden	.. .. ..	Nay.
Siam	.. .. ..	Nay.
The Netherlands	.. ..	Nay.
United States	.. ..	Yea.

The President.—The vote is 1 in the affirmative, and 17 in the negative, so the Conference have decided not to have the amendment printed. Amendment No. 12 will now be taken up for consideration. The Secretary will please read amendment No. 12, Class 2.

Amendment No. 12, Class 2, is as follows:—

"Amendment to Collocation Report proposed by Admiral Bowden-Smith (Great Britain), 14th December, 1889:

"Article 7, subsection (*c*).—Small steam-boats, such as are hoisted in on board vessels or hung to their davits, may carry the combined lantern mentioned in subsection (*b*) without the white light."

Admiral Bowden-Smith (Great Britain).—Mr. President, before speaking in regard to this amendment I would ask your kind permission to allow me to inform the Conference why the amendment stands in my name instead of in the name of the Delegates from Great Britain, in whose name I think all amendments ought to be presented. When we had our meeting last Friday evening to consider the Rules so ably drawn up by the Collocation Committee, I pointed out this to my colleagues, that I thought these little steam-boats ought not to be required to carry this light 9 feet above the gunwale. But, unfortunately, I had mislaid some of the papers containing the Regulations which are now carried out and have been carried out for the last two years with regard to this matter; so that I could not draw up the amendment then. The next morning I found my papers, but fearing that I could not have a meeting that day, before the time would expire at 7 o'clock in the evening, I put the amendment in my own name.

I may mention that the Regulations to which I referred go into this matter so very particularly that they state the candle-power, and that the light, when upright, should be seen at the distance of nearly a mile. It is usual to carry this light on the funnel. The funnel is usually made with a hinge, to lie down on the top of the boiler, to permit these boats to be hoisted inboard. Funnels are not built high enough to permit them to carry this light 9 feet above the gunwale. These boats are carried in large numbers now by men-of-war, yachts, and passenger-steamers. It is a very common thing, in rough weather, to get steam up at the davits and lower the boat down into the water with the men in it. If, then, the mast is stepped it will probably first of all go through the bottom of the next boat to it or be carried away against the ship's side. If the boat finally gets away from the ship with her light and mast attached the light will not be so well placed as it would be on the funnel, if the boat is knocked about considerably.

With regard to the second part of this, as to the nature of this light, I of course leave that to the Conference. I wish to point out that if the white light is carried 5 or 6 feet above the gunwale, if you put the second light 3 feet below the white light, it will be so low that it will not be seen. The men will probably hide it altogether, and it will not show. You could put the second light, as I pointed out yesterday, just inside of the stem in still water, but as these boats are used in the middle of the sea, of course it cannot be carried there on ordinary occasions. Therefore, if the second lights are carried so low that they cannot be seen, or if you put it immediately under the white light, naturally the white light would obscure it altogether. As regards the nature of this light, I would leave that entirely in the hands of the Conference. I do not in the least wish to claim for these boats any privilege as to the right of way. I think that whenever they do any damage they are responsible for it. I think my naval colleagues will bear me out in saying that these little boats cannot carry lights 9 feet above the gunwale.

Mr. Hall (Great Britain).—Mr. President, my gallant colleague submitted to my colleagues and myself the amendment which is handed in, and we think that perhaps it will meet his desire and be more consonant with the rule if we alter it somewhat. I think we are all agreed that you cannot make small steam-launches carry their light 9 feet above the gunwale. I do not think it necessary to mention any particular height for the white light, so long as it is carried higher than the combined light. Of course it need not be in the same vertical plane, because, as my colleague has pointed out, it might be necessary to put the combined light forward. I think that this will meet the views of my gallant colleague, and I hope it will commend itself to the good sense of the Conference:—

"Small steam-boats, such as are carried by seagoing vessels, may carry the white light at a less height than 9 feet above the gunwale, but it shall be carried above the combined lantern mentioned in subsection (b)."

We should be very glad if any sailor would give us his views on this point. It is a practical question for sailors to deal with.

Admiral Kaznakoff (Russia).—Mr. President, I am quite in accord with the gallant Admiral Bowden-Smith, and am ready to support the amendment. In my opinion it is impossible to carry the light 9 feet above the gunwale on small boats that are to be hoisted on board.

The President.—Does the Delegate from Great Britain accept the amendment?

Admiral Bowden-Smith (Great Britain).—Mr. President, I accept the amendment. The height was really what I wished to call attention to, and to point out that there is a certain difficulty about these lights blending if they are put close together.

The President.—The question is on the amendment of the Delegate from Great Britain as substituted for the amendment of the other Delegate from Great Britain.

Mr. Goodrich (United States).—Mr. President, in reading the amended suggestion of the learned Delegate from Great Britain I think he read it—

"Small steam-boats, such as are carried by seagoing vessels or on board."

Mr. Hall (Great Britain).—Mr. President, I think "carried by seagoing vessels" would be better, because the words, "on board," might not include a launch swinging at the davits. So we put in the word "by" to include those boats. It is only to save any unnecessary repetition.

The President.—The Secretary will please read the amendment as now proposed.

The amendment is as follows:—

"Small steam-boats, such as are carried by seagoing vessels, may carry the white light at a less height than 9 feet above the gunwale, but it shall be carried above the combined lantern mentioned in subsection (b)."

Captain Richard (France).—Mr. President, the matter pointed out by the gallant Admiral Bowden-Smith is so evident that we can all support the proposed amendment; but, besides the boats included in that amendment, there is quite an extensive class of small craft of a similar nature which labour under the same difficulty, but which are excluded from this favour. Consequently, I think that it should be extended not only to boats and launches which are hoisted on board of vessels, but to all kinds of boats of the same tonnage. The amendment should be applied to all boats and launches, whether they be hoisted on the vessel or not. The Conference, by endeavouring to make too general a Rule for all small crafts, have gone too far, and this omission we now propose partly to remedy. There may be small boats in the passenger service which carry three or four passengers. How are you going to compel them to carry their lights at a height of 9 feet?

Mr. Hall (Great Britain).—Mr. President, the reason why this limitation is made to launches such as are carried by seagoing vessels is that these vessels have a difficulty in carrying a mast, because they are alongside of a vessel and are raised and lowered. There is no difficulty for a steamer, however small, if she is not going to be raised and hoisted on board another vessel, in always having a small mast. I may point out that on the River Thames very small vessels carry the masthead-light and the side-lights. In these vessels that are hoisted and lowered the difficulty is that the spar or mast, whatever it is, would be likely to do great damage, especially when they are lying alongside in a heavy sea and are knocking about. But in launches that go about in the Mediterranean, as the gallant Delegate has pointed out, there is no difficulty in having a small spar or a small mast to carry the masthead-light 9 feet above the gunwale, because they are not hoisted or lowered into other vessels.

Captain Richard (France).—Mr. President, I ask permission to repeat what I have said. On board of war-vessels we use awning stanchions forward to hold the lantern containing the light. They are placed in a socket in the bows, and the light is fixed to the extremity of this awning stanchion, about 3 or 4 feet above the taffrail. It is a good thing to suppress the white light prescribed by subsection (b), Article 7. But if you suppress it why not allow small boats of the same tonnage, which neither have any masts, to benefit by it? What you do for one you might do for the other, for their situation is the same. If, therefore, I have any wish to express in the matter, I would ask that the amendment be extended to boats of all classes.

Captain Sampson (United States).—Mr. President, I would like to suggest to the gallant Delegate from France that probably the words of this amendment cover the case completely. It does not say the boats of a man-of-war or of any other vessel, but it says, "such boats as are to be hoisted on board a ship." That does not limit it necessarily to boats which are carried on board ship, but they are "such boats," presumably boats which are so small that they have not the necessary height to carry the white light 9 feet above the gunwale. It seems to me that the word "such" will cover the case.

The President.—Is the Conference ready for the question? The amendment will be read for the information of the Conference before the vote is taken.

The amendment is as follows:—

"Small steam-boats, such as are carried by seagoing vessels, may carry the white light at a less height than 9 feet above the gunwale, but it shall be carried above the combined lantern mentioned in subsection (b)."

The President.—Is the Conference ready for the question?

The question was put to the Conference upon the adoption of the amendment, and it was adopted.

Captain Hubert (the Netherlands).—Mr. President, I only desire to ask for information. Sub-section 2, Article 7, is adopted by the Conference. I wish to know if boats, which are to be carried by other vessels afloat, must have the lantern with the green and red glass?

The President.—It has been so decided by the Conference.

Mr. Hall (Great Britain).—Mr. President, the Collocation Committee—and I speak in the presence of the Chairman, and I think he will bear me out—very carefully considered what was passed by the Conference with regard to small boats. The Report of the Committee on Lights for Small Craft was adopted by the Conference, and we have not altered it at all.

The President.—The next subject for consideration will be amendment No. 13. The Secretary will please read it.

Amendment No. 13 is as follows:—

"Amendment to Collocation Report proposed by Dr. Sieveking on behalf of the German Delegation, 14th December, 1889:

"To Article 7 and Article 9 add the words: 'The vessel referred to in this Article shall also not be obliged to carry the lights prescribed by Article 4 (*a*), and Article 11, last paragraph.'"

Dr. Sieveking (Germany).—Mr. President, this amendment is brought in to correct what appeared to us to be an oversight. These small boats referred to in Article 7, and the fishing-vessels referred to in Article 11, certainly were not intended, at least in our opinion, by the Conference to be obliged to carry the out-of-command light, because a much greater facility has been given to them, having regard to the poverty of fishermen and to the fact that it was not necessary for these small vessels to carry side-lights. The facility has been given to them, therefore, that they need not carry side-lights, but instead of the side-lights they are allowed to carry a red and green lantern. Now, it has been omitted to say here that they are also not obliged to carry the out-of-command light; that is to say, the two red lights mentioned in Article 4 (*a*), and the lights mentioned in Article 11, last paragraph.

The Report of the Committee on Lights for Small Craft shows, I think, that it was not the intention to impose this duty of carrying the out-of-command lights on small vessels, because even for vessels of less than 40 tons gross tonnage it is said that they shall not be obliged to carry the lights prescribed for other vessels under steam. So that covers all lights; but the wording of the Rule as it stands does not cover all lights, and the consequence would be that these small boats, fishing-boats, would have to carry the out-of-command lights. Therefore, we have brought this amendment before the Conference. There is a misprint in the amendment. It reads "the vessel"—it should read, "the vessels." It is mentioned to me now that the word "also" might be omitted, as it is superfluous. I fully agree with that. I do not think there is any reason to keep it in. So I would like to strike out the word "also;" it does not alter the meaning of the amendment in any way.

The President.—The Secretary will please read the amendment before the vote is taken.

Amendment 13 is as follows:—

"Amendment to Collocation Report proposed by Dr. Sieveking on behalf of the German Delegation, 14th December, 1889:

"To Article 7 and Article 9 add the words: 'The vessels referred to in this Article shall not be obliged to carry the lights prescribed by Article 4 (*a*) and Article 11, last paragraph.'"

Mr. Verney (Siam).—Mr. President, may I ask whether it would not be rather more simple for sailors reading this Article just to define the lights of vessels out of command and vessels aground? Would it not make the amendment a little more perfect to refer to it by words, instead of by numbers? It is not so clear in its present form, to sailors, I think.

Dr. Sieveking (Germany).—Mr. President, I do not think that would be advisable, because it would introduce terms which are quite new in the Rules. "Out-of-command light" is an expression which does not occur in the Rules. I think a simple reference to the respective Articles is better.

Captain Sampson (United States).—Mr. President, I would like to ask the learned Delegate from Germany if it is necessary to make an exception in the case of Article 11? Of course this refers to very small vessels, and a vessel of less than 40 tons could not get aground in a fairway unless it was one of very little importance.

Dr. Sieveking (Germany).—Mr. President, I quite agree that they are not to be compelled to carry these out-of-command lights; but if we do not say so, the Rule, as it stands now, would be false. Article 9 compels "fishing-vessels and fishing-boats, when under way and when not required by this Article to carry or show the lights therein named, shall carry or show the lights prescribed for vessels of their tonnage under way." That is the Rule, which does not make any exception. It is, in fact, a mere matter of wording.

The President.—Is the Conference ready for the question upon this amendment?

The question was put to the Conference upon the adoption of the amendment, and it was adopted.

The President.—The next amendment is No. 14, which will be read by the Secretary.

Amendment No. 14, Class 2, is as follows:—

"Amendment to Collocation Report proposed by Captain Malmberg (Sweden), 14th December, 1889:

"Article 8. At the beginning of the second paragraph, instead of the words, 'On the approach of or to other vessels,' insert the words, 'When manœuvring to put a pilot on board a vessel.'"

Captain Malmberg (Sweden).—Mr. President, although it is, in my opinion, very desirable that pilot-boats should be allowed, when on their station on pilotage duty under such conditions, to show the side-lights temporarily to another vessel, it is, on the other hand, quite necessary that these conditions should be restricted and well defined, and I do not think that is the case as the wording of the second paragraph now stands. Every vessel is approaching another vessel in sight, whatever the distance between them may be, as soon as their respective courses tend to draw the vessels nearer to each other. A pilot-boat showing, therefore, under such undefined conditions, the side-lights temporarily may very easily be mistaken for a steamer under way. And a sailing-vessel, acting upon the rule that a steamer has to keep out of the way of a sailing-vessel, may easily enough be brought into collision with the pilot-boat.

It is perfectly true that the pilot-boat has to show at intervals not exceeding fifteen minutes a flare-up light; but the flare-up light is not a special signal-light to be used only by pilots. Every vessel has a right to use it in order to attract attention. There is, in my opinion, only one occasion when there is any need that a pilot-boat on her station on pilotage duty should be allowed to show the side-lights to another vessel, and that is when they are manœuvring or approaching a vessel to put a pilot on board, because the attention on board the pilot-boat and on board the vessel is very often taken up to such a degree that it has several times occurred, to my own knowledge, that a pilot-boat has been run down by the vessel, because the pilot-boat, according to the present Rules, is not allowed to show the side-lights, and thereby to indicate the way the pilot-boat is heading. There is, so far as I can see, a great deal of difference between allowing a pilot-boat to show the side-lights temporarily, whatever the distance is between the boat and the vessel in the vicinity—may be, say, a mile or two.

Now, that is the reason why I have proposed the amendment to substitute the words, "When a pilot-boat is manœuvring to put a pilot on board," for the words, "On approach of or to a vessel." But if there should be any real objection to the words proposed by me, I should wish to have at least the word, "near," inserted, so that it would read, "On the near approach of or to another vessel," because then the pilot-boat would be allowed to show the lights when they were manœuvring in the proximity of another vessel. If that will be acceptable to the Conference, I will move that instead of my own amendment.

Mr. Goodrich (United States).—Mr. President, after a hasty meeting of one or two members of the Collocation Committee, I may say on its behalf that there will be no objection to putting in the word "near" as suggested by the gallant Delegate from Sweden, if he will be satisfied with that in place of his amendment. Unless some member of the Collocation Committee objects, I will make that as a statement of the views of the Committee.

The President.—The Secretary will please read the amendment as a substitute for the other amendment.

The amendment is as follows:—

"On the near approach of or to other vessels."

Captain Malmberg (Sweden).—Mr. President, would it be acceptable to alter my amendment to read: "When manœuvring to put a pilot on board, or on the near approach of or to other vessels"?

Mr. Hall (Great Britain).—Mr. President, may I point out that the words, "On the near approach of or to other vessels," would include every case of "manœuvring to put a pilot on board."

Mr. Goodrich (United States).—Mr. President, may I call the attention of the gallant Delegate from Sweden to the fact that in various portions of the Report of the Collocation Committee the same terms are used, and we have thought it best to use the same terms wherever vessels are in the same situation. I think that if you emphasize this Rule by adding the word "near" you will meet precisely this need, because it differentiates it from the other Rules.

The President.—The Secretary will please read it as accepted by the Delegate from Sweden.

The amendment is as follows:—

The paragraph to read: "On the near approach of or to other vessels."

The President.—Is the Conference ready for the question?

The question was put to the Conference upon the adoption of the amendment, and it was adopted.

The President.—Amendment No. 15 is next in order. The Secretary will please read it.

Amendment No. 15 is as follows:—

"Amendment to Collocation Report proposed by Dr. Sieveking on behalf of the German Delegation, 14th December, 1889:

"In Article 8, paragraph 2, instead of the words, 'have at hand, ready for use, two lights, one green and one red, and shall show them temporarily,' insert the words, 'show their side-lights, but not longer than twenty seconds at a time,' and strike out paragraph 3."

Dr. Sieveking (Germany).—Mr. President, this amendment has been introduced by us in order to define a little more clearly the word "temporarily," by using the expression, "not longer than twenty seconds at a time." I see that there is an amendment, which is amendment No. 13, proposed by Captain Norcross. I think that amendment must be taken in connection with this one. There it is proposed to say in Article 8, paragraph 2, instead of using the words "temporarily," "shall flash them at short intervals," the Collocation Committee recommends, "show them at short intervals." I would only like to say that we did not propose to press the limit of twenty seconds at all. It might be objected that it could hardly be determined, unless a man had a watch in his hand all the time when he was showing a light. We only mention that it would perhaps be advisable to insert another expression instead of the word "temporarily," so that if the Conference prefer to have the words, "flash or show at short intervals," we shall not object to it.

Mr. Hall (Great Britain).—Mr. President, we agree in the principle of the amendment of the learned Delegate that it is desirable to point out that these are only to be shown at short intervals of time, and we think that the words suggested by the learned Delegate of the United States in his amendment, "flash them at short intervals," are very good words indeed. But we venture to propose to add another word and to make it, "flash or show them at short intervals." I will give the Conference a reason for that. These are the actual words used for the instruction of pilots at the present time in the Signal-Book. So that if we say, "shall flash or show them at short intervals," and in the third paragraph say, "shall flash or show at short intervals," it will meet the desire of the Delegates from the United States and the desire of the Delegates from Germany.

Captain Norcross (United States).—Mr. President, in making that amendment I objected to the word "temporarily" because it might be shown for an hour, and then they would call it temporarily. I therefore made use of the word found in the Report of the Committee on Small Lights. But I am very much obliged to the Collocation Committee, and I think that their word is much better. I accept it with great pleasure. I think that the words, "show or flash," would be sufficiently comprehensive.

Mr. Hall (Great Britain).—Mr. President, we want to have both "flash or show."

Captain Norcross (United States).—Mr. President, I have no objection.

Mr. Verbrugghe (Belgium).—Mr. President, I beg to support the suggestion of the learned Delegate from Great Britain. This question of the side-lights was the subject of discussion by the Committee of Lights for Small Craft, and we took good care in adopting it that no confusion should arise on account of these side-lights being shown with the white light of a pilot-boat, so as to be taken for a steamer. I believe that if this suggestion is carried out it will meet the desire and the idea which was expressed in the Report of the Committee on Lights for Small Craft.

Dr. Sieveking (Germany).—Mr. President, there is one point to which I would like to call attention which I had forgotten. If you will look at our amendment as altered it will read: "flash or show their side-lights at short intervals." You see that in the draft of the Collocation Committee pilot-boats are supposed to have two lights, one green and one red, besides the side-lights, and the Collocation Committee was right in using such an expression, because the Resolution as passed by the Conference was quite in accordance with the proposal of the Committee on Lights for Small Craft, as it is worded. It says: "When approaching a vessel to put a pilot on board, or when there is risk of collision with another vessel, such pilot-vessel shall have at hand two lights, one red and one green, so constructed that they can be flashed instantaneously, which shall be kept either in their places, screened, or on deck, on their respective sides of the vessel, always ready for use, and shall flash one of them (in order to show the direction in which she is heading) in sufficient time to prevent collisions, so that the red light should only be shown on the port side, and the green light only on the starboard side." Of course, that can be read so as to mean that the pilot-vessels might use their side-lights, and were supposed to have also two other lights of the character described here. But that was not, in fact, the meaning of the Committee, because it is said here: "Such pilot-vessels shall have at hand two lights, one red and one green, so constructed that they can be flashed instantaneously, which shall be kept either in their places, screened, or on deck, on their respective sides of the vessel, always ready for use." Of course, it is quite well understood that vessels never will have a store of unnecessary lanterns on board when they may make use of their side-lights, and, therefore, they will do this without going to the expense of having more lights.

There is another reason which commends this amendment, and I think it a very strong reason. If we say they are to flash or show the red and green light and the side-lights, but do not define the visibility of their lights, they may have two other lights which are visible at a very short distance only. But the intention is that pilot-vessels must have side-lights which are visible at the prescribed distance, because when they are not on pilotage duty they are to carry the side-lights, and they must be visible at the same distance that other side-lights are. Therefore, I think it would be wrong for us to say that they should have two lights, one green and one red, without saying that they are to be visible at a distance of 2 miles, and then we ought to say that the side-lights may be used for this purpose. For these reasons I would ask that the amendment should run as follows:—

"Article 8, paragraph 2, instead of the words, 'have at hand ready for use two lights, one green and one red, and shall show them temporarily,' insert the words, 'shall flash or show their side-lights at short intervals.'"

Then strike out paragraph 3.

Mr. Hall (Great Britain).—Mr. President, the gallant Delegate from Germany has called my attention to the Report, and I think it is clear, as was pointed out by the honourable Delegate from Belgium a little while ago, that it was the intention of the Committee that the side-lights should be used for this purpose, and I think, perhaps, that if the Conference are all agreed upon this point, it is unnecessary to refer to any other set of lights except the side-lights. I think that can be done, if I may venture to say so, very easily by making the paragraph read as follows:—

"On the approach of or to other vessels they shall have their side-lights lighted ready for use, and shall flash or show them at short intervals."

It has been pointed out that they must have their side-lights lighted, and then they can flash them when they want to.

Mr. Goodrich (United States).—Mr. President, I would be very glad to point out that the United States' Delegates approve that proposition, for it is precisely the principle which they argued at some length in the original consideration of this question. I think it is a very wise provision. The last mention of that Article, as approved by the Collocation Committee, shows that pilot-vessels must at all times carry their side-lights, and, therefore, we approve of the proposition to strike out the first paragraph.

Mr. Hall (Great Britain).—Mr. President, paragraph 3, of course, comes out. I do not know whether the Secretary has the wording. It is: "On the near approach of or to other vessels they shall have their side-lights lighted ready for use, and shall flash or show them at short intervals to indicate the direction in which they are heading."

Mr. Goodrich (United States).—What is the use of the words, "ready for use"?

Mr. Hall (Great Britain).—Because they might be lighted and put away underneath the hatch or somewhere. As we stated in the discussion about small vessels, they ought to be at hand ready for use, so that men can catch hold of them and hold them up. I have put in the word "lighted" in deference to the objection of the gallant Delegate for the United States, to the effect that a man might say, "I have got my lantern ready for use," and yet not have it lighted. Therefore, it is perhaps desirable to put in this word.

Captain Norcross (United States).—Mr. President, there is one thing to which I would like to call attention. I think we have provided for some classes of pilot-boats that they should not be compelled to carry side-lights at all. I would suggest whether it would not be well to say that they should have their coloured lights lighted and ready for use.

Dr. Sieveking (Germany).—Mr. President, that would be provided for in the fourth paragraph, where it is said: "A pilot-vessel of such a class as to be obliged to go alongside of a vessel to put a pilot on board may show the white light instead of carrying it at the masthead, and may, instead of the coloured lights above mentioned, have at hand ready for use a lantern with a red glass on one side and a green glass on the other, to be used as prescribed above."

The President.—The Secretary will please read the amendment again.

The amendment is as follows:—

"On the near approach of or to other vessels they shall have their side-lights lighted ready for use, and shall flash or show them at short intervals to indicate the direction in which they are heading, but the green light shall not be shown on the port side, nor the red light on the starboard side."

The third paragraph to be stricken out.

The President.—Is the Conference ready for the question?

The question was put to the Conference upon the adoption of the amendment, and it was adopted.

The President.—The next amendment is No. 16.

Captain Shackford (United States).—Mr. President, that amendment is disposed of by the last amendment.

The President.—Amendment No. 17 will be the next for consideration. The Secretary will please read it.

Amendment No. 17 is as follows:—

"Amendment to Collocation Report presented by Dr. Sieveking on behalf of the German Delegation, 14th December, 1889:

"In Article 9 (*b*) 1, instead of 'four' points abaft the beam, insert 'two' points abaft the beam."

Dr. Sieveking (Germany).—Mr. President, our reason for presenting this amendment is that we really do not see any reason why the green and red light should exceptionally show over an arc of the horizon from two points on either bow to four points abaft the beam, while the other side-lights are only to show two points abaft the beam. Perhaps this might not be considered important, but we must take into consideration that an overtaken vessel is now defined in Article 24, where it is said that "every vessel coming up with another vessel from any direction more than two points abaft her beam, that is, in such a position with regard to the vessel which she is overtaking that at night she would be unable to see either of that vessel's side-lights, shall be deemed to be an overtaken vessel; and no subsequent alteration of the bearings between the two vessels shall make the overtaking vessel a crossing vessel within the meaning of these Rules, or relieve her of the duty of keeping clear of the overtaken vessel until she is finally past and clear." That Rule would have to be changed, because it is said here, "every vessel coming up with another vessel in any direction more than two points abaft her beam." If we give side-lights now which show four points abaft the beam, then this overtaking Rule would not be correct. In our opinion there is no reason whatever why this light should show four points abaft the beam, and there is no advantage to be derived from this Rule, that trawling steam-vessels shall carry side-lights which should show further abaft than other side-lights show. For these reasons we have proposed this amendment.

The President.—Is the Conference ready for the question?

The Secretary will please read the amendment.

The amendment is as follows:—

"In Article 9 (*b*) 1, instead of 'four' points abaft the beam, insert 'two' points abaft the beam."

The President.—Is the Conference ready for the question?

The question was put to the Conference upon the adoption of th amendment, and it was adopted.

The President.—The next is amendment No. 18, which the Secretary will please read.

219

Amendment No. 18 is as follows:—

"Amendment to Collocation Report proposed by Captain Settembrini (Italy):

"In Article 9 (*b*) 2, insert at the end of the first paragraph: 'In the Mediterranean Sea, all vessels mentioned above shall carry only the white light in a globular lantern.'"

Captain Settembrini (Italy).—Mr. President, I hope that my honourable colleagues will not say that I am trespassing again upon their patience if I come now with an amendment. When we were discussing paragraph (*d*) to Article 10, I proposed to strike out the second part of the paragraph. The reasons in support of my proposal were such that it was adopted by a large majority, and although there never existed the confusion which was made by the learned Delegate from the United States, yet on the further reconsideration of that Article by the Conference extra amendment No. 57 was lost; but I did not lose hope that upon this question coming before you again you would not deny me your support. I shall not repeat what I said then. The North Sea fishing-boats are large and numerous, and a crowd of them work on the banks. For them it may be proper and useful to have a distinction —that is, a distinction by the red pyrotechnic light. But in the Mediterranean, all of my colleagues will bear witness we have not such large and numerous fishing-boats as they have in the North Sea. We have no banks where a crowd of them are at work, and we have not so many different ways of fishing as to impose upon some boats the necessity of giving way to others. We do not think it necessary to have any distinction whatever made. The white light in a globular lantern would be more than enough for them. I may point out, also, that every vessel seeing that white light would soon know that there is a fisherman. That light cannot be mistaken for that of a pilot-boat, because, with the exception of the Venice estuaries and the pilots in the ports of Marseilles, we have no other in the Mediterranean, and every sailor can go safely and boldly into any port.

But you will say we are here to make international laws for the whole world, and in consequence of that the fishing-boats must have the red pyrotechnic lights already in use in the Northern Sea. Let me point out for your consideration that we are here *ad referendum*. We can make as many laws as we please, but many that we propose will not be accepted by the several nations. Therefore, such laws will lose all their internationality. The reasons for the use of the red pyrotechnic lights in the North Sea are not strong enough to lead us to believe that they should be adopted by the fishing-boats in the Mediterranean Sea. Let the industrious fisherman in the North Sea be provided with the red pyrotechnic light; they may be required for the safety of the vessels they may meet. But let the Mediterranean fishermen carry only the white light. The amendment which I have submitted to your high judgment is very short and will not alter the Rules or make them any more complicated. I am sure that you will unanimously adopt it.

Mr. Hall (Great Britain).—Mr. President, I am certain that——

The President.—The hour for recess having arrived, the Delegate from Great Britain will postpone his remarks until after recess, when he will have the floor.

The Conference thereupon took a recess until 2 o'clock.

After Recess.

The President.—The question before the Conference is amendment No. 18. The Delegate from Great Britain has the floor.

Mr. Hall (Great Britain).—Mr. President, I am sorry to see that the gallant Delegate from Italy is not in his place.

The President.—We will wait a few moments if you will suspend your remarks.

Mr. Hall (Great Britain).—Mr. President, I was only waiting for the gallant Delegate to resume his seat to make a few observations on this point. It will be seen at once that this is a very different amendment to the one which the gallant Delegate from Italy moved before, because it applies only to the Mediterranean. This is a matter which affects only the Mediterranean Powers, and we should be most anxious to consult their opinion upon this matter. So far as we are concerned, we see no objection whatever to the proposal that the fishing-boats in the Mediterranean, where there are very much fewer pilot-boats than there are elsewhere, should be at liberty to carry the masthead-light and not be compelled to carry the pyrotechnic light. But if so, I would suggest that they should show the flare-up light, like small vessels under 7 tons. That I understand my friend the gallant Delegate from Italy will agree to; and I would submit this amendment should read as follows:—

"In the Mediterranean Sea all vessels mentioned above shall use the flare-up light instead of the pyrotechnic light."

Of course we shall await with interest the opinions of the Mediterranean Powers and what they have to say about it, but so far as we are concerned we are perfectly willing that they should be absolved from using the pyrotechnic light.

Captain Richard (France).—Mr. President, I am ready to vote for the amendment proposed by our gallant colleague from Italy in regard to fishing-boats in the Mediterranean. But, on the other hand, France has also fishing-boats on the Atlantic Ocean, which are in about the same condition. We have been unable to arrive at an understanding on the subject of the red pyrotechnic light, and I think that the discussion, if it were reopened, would not bring about a better result. Everything has been said on the subject, and a new discussion is unnecessary. I will therefore refrain from reopening it, but by so doing, in order not to prolong an endless debate, I think it necessary to make certain reservations. When our Government sent us to Washington we were given instructions of a most liberal nature, directing us to freely and frankly discuss all the Rules which should be proposed, to consider them only from the stand-point of their actual value, and to accept those which were valuable, by whomsoever proposed.

Under those circumstances I am quite satisfied to accept the amendment proposed by the gallant Delegate from Italy. I think that his amendment is a good one, and I will vote for it. I consider that the question has been solved in a satisfactory manner, in so far as the Mediterranean is concerned, but I will ask the Conference to note that I make all possible reservations concerning the Atlantic Ocean, and the Rules which this Conference have imposed upon fishermen, should the results which we are promised not be realized as they have been held out to us. Again, there is a certain amount of difficulty to legislate here for the Mediterranean and the Atlantic Ocean. Some of my honourable colleagues are in that respect in the same position that I am. In order, therefore, not to prolong an endless discussion, I think we should make all reservations which may seem necessary to us, in order not to tie the hands of our Governments, in that they may subsequently establish a better Rule for lights to be given to fishing-boats. In the North Sea and elsewhere we will thereby leave an open field for a more suitable solution of the difficulty.

Under those circumstances I will vote for the amendment, and I will not further discuss the question.

M. Varela de Torres (Spain).—Mr. President, the interests of Spain being identical with those of France in this matter, both nations having an equal interest in the Mediterranean and the Atlantic Ocean, I rise to support the views expressed by my distinguished friend the gallant Delegate from France with the reservations pointed out by him.

Captain Van Steyn (the Netherlands).—Mr. President, the Delegates from the Netherlands have offered an amendment to make an exception for their Colonies. So I heartily support what has been said by the gallant Delegate from France.

Captain Salvesen (Norway).—Mr. President, I have no objection to the amendment of the gallant Delegate from Italy, as I have no objection to any of the adopted Rules for fishing-vessels, having, according to the clear statements in the Conference of lawyers present, always understood that Norway could for its territorial waters make any Rule it liked for its fishing-vessels.

Commander Chen Ngen Tao (China).—Mr. President, may I be permitted to make a few remarks on Article 9, about the light required for fishing-vessels? When this Article came under discussion I intended to ask the Conference to have some alterations made, but at that time I heard that some members of the Conference said that if other Governments think the Rules of Article 9 will not suit them, they may establish their local Rules for their fishing-boats, &c. I therefore remained silent. But, Mr. President, I, on behalf of the Chinese Delegation, would like to mention before you and the Conference that we hope the work of this Conference will be adopted by all maritime nations. The Chinese Government is quite willing to adopt, if possible, any Rules we are now preparing, but I am aware that it is quite impossible for my Government to adopt Article 9; for two reasons: (1) Chinese fishing-boats are so numerous, and hosts of them are so small, that they are unable to carry lights in such a way as described in subsections (*a*) and (*c*) of this Article; (2) all Chinese fishermen are very poor, and they certainly cannot afford to keep up so many lights as described in subsection (*b*) 2 and 3 of this Article. I therefore beg, if the Conference will agree, to add this foot-note to this Article.

Mr. Verney (Siam).—Mr. President, I desire to say one or two words on this subject in the line pointed out by the gallant Delegate from China. I feel quite sure that the Siamese fishing-vessels and small boats will not be able——

Mr. Hall (Great Britain).—Mr. President, I do not want to be discourteous to the Delegate from Siam, but may I point out that there has been no notice of such an amendment as this? I apprehend that this is clearly not a consequential amendment, and we should have notice of any such a proposal as this. We have had a notice in regard to the Mediterranean, and we have had time to make inquiries and find out about it, and we did find out that there was an exceptional case in regard to it, which will allow the sailing-vessels to use the same signal-lights as pilot-boats, because there are very few pilots there. But we cannot go into the question of all fishing-boats. The gallant Delegate from China has pointed out that it is of course open to China to object to any particular Rule or to frame local Rules. That is certainly true. Of course the gallant Delegate from China has made his protest by the speech which he has just made, but I venture to point out that we cannot consider the question whether fishing-vessels in the Chinese waters and Siamese waters are to be exempted from the operation of the Rules. The sole point here is as to the Mediterranean waters, and of course anything fairly connected with that amendment would be matter for discussion.

The President.—The Chair will decide that this amendment can only be accepted by a three-fourths vote. Any amendment not germane to the present amendment can only be accepted by a three-fourths vote.

Mr. Verney (Siam).—Mr. President, do you consider that this is not germane?

The President.—I do not consider that the amendment is germane to the one with reference to the Mediterranean waters.

Mr. Goodrich (United States).—Mr. President, the Conference may remember that when this Report was under consideration on the 26th November, that exactly the same amendment now proposed by the gallant Delegates from Italy had been passed. I stated to the Conference that I foresaw very great difficulty in the way of the adoption of that Rule as suggested by him, and thereupon I moved a reconsideration of it. The vote was reconsidered and the subject was very carefully discussed. The Conference voted to reject the amendment of the gallant Delegate from Italy. He made a very humorous remark to me when he invited me to partake of the hospitalities of his house if ever I should go to Naples. He said to me that he was assured of one thing, if ever I came to Italy the fishermen would make the tail of a sardine cost me more than the Delegates pay for a dish of terrapin in Washington.

After a good deal of consideration on this subject I have come to the conclusion that, inasmuch as the Powers represented in this Conference which border on the inclosed Mediterranean Sea are satisfied with this amendment the United States will not interpose any objection to it; and moreover, I am informed that there are very few pilot-boats sailing in the Mediterranean Sea, and the lights would cause no misunderstanding with the lights which this amendment proposes shall be used by the fishing-boats. So the subject of the Rule, as it is confined to the Mediterranean alone, does not seem to me to be open to the objection which would arise against a general proposition of this kind. In looking over the Protocol of the 26th November, I find that to have been the real purpose of my objection; that is, that upon the open sea there will be a confusion between the lights suggested by this proposition and the lights of smaller vessels.

Captain Settembrini (Italy).—Mr. President, it has been suggested to me to change the wording of my amendment in the following manner:—

"In the Mediterranean Sea, the vessels referred to in this subsection (b) shall not be obliged to show the pyrotechnic light therein mentioned, but they may show the flare-up light."

The principle is just the same as the amendment which I have the honour to submit to the Conference; the wording only is different.

Mr. Hall (Great Britain).—Mr. President, may I point out that the wording is not quite consonant to the wording which I suggested, because that would leave it open to them not even to show the flare-up light? The wording which I suggested carried out what I think was agreed upon; and it is this:—

"In the Mediterranean Sea, the vessels above may show the flare-up light instead of the pyrotechnic light."

Under the wording suggested by the gallant Delegate from Italy they would not be compelled to show the pyrotechnic light and they would not be compelled to show the flare-up light; so they need not show any light. This was what was agreed upon, and I have no doubt the gallant Delegate from Italy will adopt the wording which I have suggested.

Captain Settembrini (Italy).—Mr. President, I accept the amendment proposed by the learned Delegate from Great Britain.

Mr. Hall (Great Britain).—Mr. President, I will read it to the Secretary:—

"In the Mediterranean Sea, all vessels referred to in subsection (b) 2 may show the flare-up light instead of the pyrotechnic light."

The President.—The question is upon the substitute amendment of the Delegate of Great Britain for the amendment of the Delegate of Italy, which will be read.

The amendment is as follows:—

"In the Mediterranean Sea, all vessels referred to in subsection (b) 2 may show the flare-up light instead of the pyrotechnic light."

The President.—Is the Conference ready for the question?

The question upon the adoption of the substitute amendment was put to the Conference, and it was adopted.

Commander Chen (China).—Mr. President, may I be permitted to say a few words more with regard to Chinese fishing-boats? They are exceedingly small, and in my opinion——

The President.—The Delegate is not in order. If he wishes to offer an amendment, upon a three-fourths vote he is at liberty to do so.

Commander Chen (China).—Mr. President, may I be permitted to hand in a foot-note, if it is agreed to by the Conference?

The President.—You may offer an amendment on a three-fourths vote, the Chair decides.

Mr. Goodrich (United States).—Mr. President, I understand that the gallant Delegate from China desires a little time given him to prepare his amendment.

Commander Chen (China).—Mr. President, I move it in regard to Article 9.

Mr. Goodrich (United States).—Mr. President, I understand that the Delegate wants time to prepare that amendment.

The President.—He does not say so. He has his amendment in his hand.

Commander Chen (China).—Mr. President, in the Chinese boats, wherever they are unable to carry the light as prescribed, I desire to have it stated in a foot-note that they need only carry the bright white light. It will not interfere with the general Rule in this Article. I only hope that it may be added as a foot-note to that Article.

The President.—The Delegate from China wishes to offer an amendment, which will be read, and upon a three-fourths vote it will be considered.

The Secretary will please read the amendment.

The amendment is as follows:—

"Chinese fishing-boats that are unable to carry the light as prescribed in this Article may only carry the bright white light."

The President.—The discussion is upon accepting for consideration the amendment of the Delegate from China; it can only be received on a three-fourths vote.

Mr. Hall (Great Britain).—Mr. President, may I suggest to the gallant Delegate from China that his protest will appear upon the Protocol, and of course China can except this Rule? She can accept all of the other Rules and except this one. She can do that perfectly well without carrying an amendment to that effect. I think we should get into difficulty by jumping to a conclusion upon this matter with regard to this amendment. The gallant Delegate from China has already made his point perfectly clear, and it will so appear upon the Protocol. China will at once say, We will accept all the Rules except the fishing Rule, which we object to.

Commander Chen (China).—Mr. President, I thought that it was just as well to bring this matter to the notice of the Powers that are represented in the Conference, and if the Conference agree, to put it in in a foot-note.

Mr. Goodrich (United States).—Mr. President, I hope this courtesy will be granted to the Delegate from China. It is the first time in the history of nations that China has appeared in a Conference, and, as she asks this, I hope the permission to have the amendment printed will be granted. I doubt whether there is a possibility of having any such amendment passed; but inasmuch as the Chinese Representatives are desirous of having that course taken, why should their request not be granted? It might be brought in and voted upon at once, so that the protest of China shall appear clearly in the Protocol. I beg to say, however, that I do not quite agree with the effect of the remarks of the learned Delegate from Great Britain in regard to the protest by China upon these Rules. Of course every word which he said is exactly correct, but perhaps he does not go quite far enough. The suggestion which I have to make is that China may not except from the operation of these Rules anything but her territorial waters. China, in her adoption of the whole Rules, may except this particular Rule which we have just passed, or the Article which we have just amended, and the effect of that would be that her own boats would be governed by the Rule so long as they were in territorial waters. If China simply dissents from the operation of the Rule it raises the old question as to what will be the effect of a collision occurring under the circumstances referred to in the Rules, and that would depend, I fancy, somewhat upon whether the collision was tried in Chinese Courts or in the Courts of some other country.

Mr. Hall (Great Britain).—Mr. President, may I point out what we are coming to if we follow the suggestion of the learned Delegate from the United States? I do not think he has quite foreseen what the logical result of this will be. It is that every member who was in the minority when we first voted on this Rule will get up and propose an amendment to except the particular waters of his particular State. That is what we shall come to. I think it is quite clear that any Power can accept these Rules and except certain Rules. She can accept a certain number of Rules, but she is not obliged to accept them all. If China objects to the fishing Rule she can accept the rest and reject that, and that would not be only with regard to her territorial waters, but it would be with regard to her vessels wherever they may be. She may say: "I decline to be bound to have my fishing-vessels carry any particular light wherever they may be." So China has the power to act as other Powers undoubtedly will act with regard to Rules to which they object; but if we now propose to vote upon this, what is there to prevent my learned friend the Delegate from Germany from getting up and objecting to its application to the Baltic? What is to prevent my learned friend on my right from objecting to its having any operation within the dominions of the Power he so ably represents, and so on *ad infinitum* with regard to any one of the Powers which require their waters to be excepted? The Conference adopted this Rule and have voted on it, and I think we ought to leave it to the Powers to object to it and to state their objection in the ordinary way, and not by a side-wind, by moving amendments which are absolutely a side-wind and nothing else. I am sure that the learned Delegate from the United States will see that this is the conclusion to which we might arrive if we take this course. There was a special reason given with regard to the Mediterranean Sea. We had plenty of time to consider that reason and it seemed to be a well-founded objection.

Commander Chen (China).—Mr. President, I think that this little foot-note would not interfere with the general Rule in Article 9, as now adopted; but after what has been pointed out by the learned Delegate from Great Britain, I will ask permission to withdraw my amendment.

The President.—Amendment No. 19 is next in order. It will be read by the Secretary.

Amendment No. 19 is as follows:—

"Amendment to Collocation Report proposed by Dr. Sieveking, on behalf of the German Delegation, 14th December, 1889:

"In Article 9 (*d*), strike out the words, 'all flare-up lights,' &c., to the end of the paragraph. Eventually strike out the words, 'or fishing with any kind of drag-net.'"

Captain Donner (Germany).—Mr. President, we have made this proposal because it has not been possible for us to see a reason why the flare-up lights should be shown in a certain defined place, as is done here, and at different places if the ship is under way, or if she is fast to a rock or any obstruction on the bottom of the sea. Every vessel, sailing or steaming, which is trawling, has the trawl on her stern and drags it along the bottom of the sea. Now, if such a trawl becomes fast to a wreck or a rock at the bottom of the sea, the ship will swing to the wind just in the same way that any ship will which is anchored by the stern, and she actually remains in the same position as a ship sailing before the wind with her trawl out. The only difference is that, when the ship is stationary, there is no way upon her; she is not going ahead. I cannot find out what reason there is to compel stationary vessels to show the flare-up light over the bow, and vessels under way to show it over the stern.

In my opinion, the first thing to be done is to show the light where it can best be seen, especially by a closing-up vessel; and that may be very often impossible, if I am obliged to show the flare-up light on the bow of the vessel because the ship has sails on, and the flare-up cannot be seen by the ship which is closing up with the wind aft. We therefore propose to strike out this clause altogether and leave it for a man to show the flare-up light where he chooses; that is, to show it in the place where the light can best be seen. The second part of the amendment is to strike out the words, " or fishing with with any kind of drag-net." We propose to strike out this because a drag-net is only a small trawl. In the North Sea they call a drag-net a small trawl; it is used to scrape oysters and such things. That is included in the word "trawl-net," because we have to find what is meant by the expression "trawl-net;" and then, every net which is drawn on the bottom of the sea by a vessel's motion comes under that definition, and there is no reason, therefore, to say, "trawl or drag-net."

Mr. Hall (Great Britain).—Mr. President, these words were inserted for the benefit of the fishermen, because it was said that a screw-steamer going near the stern of a trawl, if she had her nets out, was liable to get into these nets and destroy them. So it was originally proposed, in the interests of fishermen, and I am told by practical sailors who form part of our Delegation that invariably, when steamers are approaching fishing-vessels that are trawling, they try to pass the trawler in such a way that they will not go through the net; and if the trawler gives any indication by a flare-up light, they can see perfectly well which is the stern of the vessel, and they can therefore pass either ahead or astern so as to avoid getting into the net with their propellers. I think it would be a pity to strike out those words. I have no doubt the honourable Delegate from Germany who has proposed this was not aware that, in practice, they are found to be very useful, and that steamers were thus able to avoid getting into the nets. With regard to the latter part, his criticism is perfectly accurate; but it appears to us that this word "drag-net" is a mistake, although, of course, it was so printed in the old Rule. It appears to us that it was a mistake for "drift-net," because vessels have drift-nets out sometimes a mile long, and it is equally as important to avoid getting into the drift-net as to avoid getting into the drag-net. Therefore, what I would suggest is, not to strike out these words, but to alter the word "drag-net" into the word "drift-net."

Mr. Goodrich (United States).—Any net.

Mr. Hall (Great Britain).—Mr. President, simply strike out the word "drag." I think I may say that captains of steamers are very careful and considerate, and that they always try to avoid doing harm to fishing-vessels when they can, and it is an assistance to them to have the fishing-vessels show this light.

Captain Mensing (Germany).—Mr. President, I would like to point out that this is an entirely different proposition from the one which is presented in the Rule. It says here that all flare-up lights shall be shown in the after part of the vessel, except when the vessel is hanging by her fishing-gear, then the light shall be exhibited over the bow. Now, Captain Donner has pointed out very clearly that a trawler has always over her stern a trawl, so that the Rule as it stands here would practically come to this, that every trawler is to exhibit her flare-up light over her bow. If that is the meaning, it ought to be expressed in those words. But the point has been made that in such case a steam-trawler, having her foresail set, running before the wind and being overtaken by another vessel, would be obliged, under the Rule as it stands now, to exhibit the flare-up light in the bow, which, of course, would be the most unfortunate position she could possibly select. I understand but very little about drift-net fishing, but such an alteration as is proposed would alter the whole meaning of the paragraph as it stands here.

Mr. Hall (Great Britain).—Mr. President, I think we could provide for it, so as to prevent any doubt, by saying, "at the end of the boat farthest from the net." We are dealing here with a question of fact. There is one matter which, I am sure, all experienced sailors will appreciate, and that is, that it is not only for the interest of the fishing-vessels to avoid damaging the nets, but that this light enables steam-vessels to avoid damaging their own screws. I think that, if we make it read, "should be shown at the end of the boat farthest from the net," it will make the matter perfectly clear, if there should be any doubt about it as it stands at present.

Captain Donner (Germany).—Mr. President, I think that we cannot insert the word "drift-net" for "drag-net," because that has never been the meaning. A drift-net is a net sometimes 2 miles long that is fastened to the middle of the ship. The ship is lying broadside on at an angle of eighty points to the net, and drifts slowly to leeward. If you see the Dutch hookers, as we call them, you will see that they have an iron bar just in the middle of the ship, and that is the place to which they fasten their drift-net. The ship is actually lying-to. The hookers used, in the North Sea, to take down their foremast, and only hoist up a small sail to keep the ship just drifting with the wind abeam. Therefore, only to show the flare-up light to make it possible for the vessel to clear the net would actually be without any sense at all with regard to a drift-net vessel. Everybody, if he sees a drift-net vessel knows directly that she is to the leeward of her net, or that the nets are standing out to the windward. But as to trawls it is quite another thing. You can pass a trawler very close to her stern without damaging her net or getting the propeller screw into it, because the net is sunk on the ground, and the line extends down to the bottom of the sea in such a way that you can go close up to the stern of such vessels without coming in contact with the net.

The two cases are quite different. We cannot put "drift-net" in here in any way. This provision is taken out of the old English Regulations. The English Regulations make a distinction between a trawl-net and a drag-net; but that distinction has now been given up. We have made a new definition for a trawl-net, and have included a drag-net. There is, in my opinion, no necessity for keeping these two words, "drag-net," and we might strike them out altogether. I am not sure that the Rule requiring a trawling-vessel to show a flare-up light is not a good one; but I am of the opinion that the best thing we could do is to leave it to her to show the flare-up where it can best be seen, and every reasonable man will show it from the stern when he gets near the stern, and he will show it over the bow when he comes near the bow, or when he thinks that the ship's flare-up will not be seen if he shows it otherwise. I can only hope that the Conference will adopt my proposition. I dare say it is not a very material one; but still I think it is better that it should be adopted.

Mr. Hall (Great Britain).—Mr. President, I quite agree that this is not a matter of any great importance, but the Rule has been in existence for a good many years, and practical sailors tell us that it is of great use to them to enable them to avoid the nets of vessels fishing; so why should we strike it out?

Captain Malmberg (Sweden).—Mr. President, may I say a word to point out the reason why I should not like to have the amendment proposed by the German Delegation carried? I have had some experience as to the necessity of fishing-boats showing a flare-up light from the proper place on

[93]

board the vessel, because once I got into a drift-net on account of a fisherman not caring to use his flare-up light. If he had shown that flare-up I would not have got my propeller tangled up for three or four hours as I did. I hope this paragraph will be allowed to stand as it is, and not to strike out the flare-up light.

Captain Sampson (United States).—Mr. President, the amendment does not strike out the flare-up light.

Mr. Goodrich (United States).—Mr. President, the gallant Delegate from Sweden wants the Rule left as it is.

Captain Malmberg (Sweden).—Yes, Sir.

Captain Donner (Germany).—Mr. President, it is not our intention to strike out the use of the flare-up light altogether, as I understood the gallant Delegate from Sweden to state. The Article still permits fishing-boats to show the flare-up light.

The President.—Is the Conference ready for the question? It seems to the Chair that the first part of this amendment will have to be put to a vote. The word "eventually" is used; that is, in the event of the other not being passed. The question will be upon the first division of the amendment.

Captain Donner (Germany).—Mr. President, there are two different questions. You can strike out the first and leave the second, or *vice versâ*.

The President.—The Chair will put the questions separately. The first part of the amendment will be read.

"In Article 9 (d) strike out the words, 'all flare-up lights,' &c., to the end of the paragraph."

The question was put to the Conference upon the amendment, and it was lost.

The President.—The second division will be read.

The second division of the amendment is as follows:—

"Eventually strike out the words, 'or fishing with any kind of drag-net.'"

The President.—Is the Conference ready for the question?

Captain Shackford (United States).—I call for the Yeas and Nays.

The President.—The Yeas and Nays are called for on the second part of this amendment.

Mr. Hall (Great Britain).—Mr. President, may I point out, before a vote is taken, that if this is carried we could not put in the word "drift-net"? We should not be able to help the fishermen by taking care of their drift-nets.

Captain Mensing (Germany).—Mr. President, I would like to ask the learned Delegate from Great Britain whether he considers that a drag-net is the same thing as a drift-net?

Mr. Verbrugghe (Belgium).—Mr. President, I believe it is pointed out by the learned Delegate from Great Britain that this is a fault of the print, and that it means "drift-net." If it is "drag-net," it is of no use here, because there is a definition given for trawlers, which includes a drag-net, and I certainly agree that it ought to be taken out. But if it is "drift-net," then the provision made for showing this flare-up light is applied to drift-nets, and then I maintain the use of the word "drift-net." The question now is whether it is the fault of the print, or whether it meant drag-net. In the first instance, it must be maintained. In the second instance, it is of no use, because trawl means the same as drag-net.

Mr. Carter (Hawaii).—Mr. President, I would like to point out that if we pass this amendment we shall leave this Article reading, "That a flare-up light exhibited by a vessel when trawling" and there it will stop, having refused to adopt the first amendment.

Captain Salvesen (Norway).—If it is a misprint, and should be "drift-net," instead of "drag-net," it is not only a misprint in the Report of the Collocation Committee, but also a misprint in the Report on Lights for Small Vessels, and a misprint in the present Rules of the Road.

Mr. Hall (Great Britain).—Mr. President, I stated distinctly that it was not a misprint. I said that the word "drag-net" was in the old Rule. It is clear that it is more important for steamers to be able to keep out of the way of drift-nets than of trawl-nets, which are upon the ground. The drift-net is very near the surface of the water, and the whole object of this Rule is to prevent the nets of fishing-vessels being damaged, and therefore it applies more to the drift-net vessels than to trawlers. The Delegate from Belgium has pointed out most clearly that if it means trawls then the words are not wanted, and if it means drift-net then the words are wanted.

Captain Donner (Germany).—Mr. President, I dare say it is impossible to put in the word "drift-nets." A vessel fishing with a drift-net must never hang to her nets in the sense of this Rule. This Rule is only made for trawlers or for ships dragging an apparatus over the bottom of the sea, and that, for a net like a drift-net, is absolutely impossible. There is no sense whatever, in my opinion, in ordering fishing-boats with drift-nets to show a flare-up light over the bow when the drift-net is not fastened to the bow, but is fastened to the side of the vessel. Therefore, if you say anything you must say he must show it on the side of the vessel. It is no indication of her situation at all. If I show a flare-up light that will not be a mark for me that I am in the situation of a vessel fishing with drift-nets, because, as soon as I see the light and the distinctive light of a vessel fishing with a drift-net, I actually know where the nets are, and I must pass that vessel to the windward. That is the only thing I can do. Now, any fishing-vessel can show a flare-up light as much as she likes, but what reason is there to give her a certain place to show that light, and to give her a wrong place to show it? The old Article will not read correctly if you put in the word "drift-net," instead of "drag-net." Therefore, I beg the Conference will accept the proposition to leave out the word "drag-net" altogether

Admiral Nares (Great Britain).—Mr. President, I would like to say a few words as a seaman. The term "drag-net" is evidently applicable to a net dragging through the water. For the first time now you have defined that a vessel engaged in trawling is a vessel dragging an apparatus on the bottom of the sea. Now, there is a confusion. There is no doubt that the proper term for a floating net is a drift-net, and the actual practice is that the drift-net fishers are attached to their nets and drift with them, dragging them through the water. Supposing that they were not dragging them through the water, the net would not be in one line, but they keep way on, in some way or other, and keep a strain on their nets, dragging them along through the water. That is the practice. Now, we want to know in which direction the net is from the boat that is fast to it. What I would like to ask the mover of this proposal is which place would he choose for the flare-up light to be shown? It does not matter if it is the custom to show the flare-up light at the end nearest the net. Let it be so, if that is the custom; or if it is the custom to show it at the end farthest from the net, why not keep that custom? If we want to alter the custom let us alter it, but let us understand what we are doing. It is the custom all over the North Sea for the flare-up to be shown at the end farthest from the net. What is the consequence? A steamer coming along can then pass close to the end of the boat that shows the flare-up, and if it passes on the other side it winds the whole of that net around its screw, and he entangles himself and has destroyed the net. So there must be a flare-up light. Where shall it be shown? The practice is now to show it over the end of the boat farthest from the net, and unless you can get a better place you had better leave it alone.

Dr. Sieveking (Germany).—Mr. President, I think we ought to be very cautious in altering the words which have been used in the old Rules. I see in the old Rules the expression is used that the flare-up light is to be exhibited by a vessel when trawling, dredging, or fishing with any kind of drag-net. There the word "drag-net" is used. If it is a misprint only, we are to correct it. But we have not been told it is a misprint. On the contrary, the First Delegate from Great Britain has told us that he could not say it was a misprint. I do not think it is a misprint, because the words are repeated in the old Rule. Again, although I confess I do not understand anything about these technical questions, still I think it is quite clear that the word "drag-net" is purposely used, and that it was not the intention to say "drift-net." If we say "drift-net" instead of "drag-net" I am sure that would be a new amendment, and would come under the three-fourths majority rule. It has not been brought in as an amendment in time. It appears quite clear to me that if we say "trawling or fishing with any kind of a drag-net," the words, "any kind of a drag-net" are surplus, because the word "trawling" includes fishing with any kind of a drag-net. If I am wrong in that, or if there is any kind of a drag-net which is not included in the definition of the word "trawl," of course the words must be left as they stand now. If not, they are superfluous.

Therefore, I think that these are two different questions. First, are we to say "drift-nets," instead of "drag-nets"? If so, then the words of course cannot be eliminated, and the amendment now under discussion falls to the ground. But the question whether we shall use the word "drift-net" or not includes two questions, one of which is formal, requiring a three-fourths majority, and the other the question as to whether it is right or not.

Mr. Hall (Great Britain).—Mr. President, I do not want to set the example of moving any amendment whatever which the Conference has not had notice of. I moved this because it appeared to me to be a clerical error originally, and I believe so still, but I shall not make a motion to adopt this amendment. I object to striking these words out, because I believe that even in these words "drift-net" might be included. It says, "trawling or fishing with a drag-net." It may be that a drift-net is a drag-net within the meaning of these words. Therefore I shall oppose striking them out.

Mr. Goodrich (United States).—Mr. President, let me call the attention of the learned Delegate from Germany to the fact that every man is supposed to know the meaning of the amendment which he proposes, and that he will derive some information as to what drift-net means if he refers to extra amendment No. 54, proposed by the German Delegation, where he uses the word "drift-nets." I notice also that in old Article 10, subdivision (*b*), the word "drift-nets," are used. The same language is used in the proposition of the Committee on Lights for Small Craft on p. 3, where, in Article —, subdivision (*b*), they use the word "drift-nets," which seems to be identical with the provision as it stood in the existing Rule. From this it would seems to me that we might derive a knowledge sufficient to guide us in deciding what drift-nets are, and what drag-nets are. It seems to me that there ought to be some one at this table who knows the difference between a drift-net and a drag-net. At any rate, if the matter comes to that, you can express the same idea as was intended, in my judgment, to be expressed in this subdivision by giving apt words to define what you mean, and say, "vessels dragging the net after them," or something of that kind, which, I suppose, would include both drift-nets and drag-nets.

Captain Richard (France).—Mr. President, may I ask permission of the Conference to explain why I think there has been no mistake in the printing of the Rules, and that the word "drag-net" is the word which it was actually intended to put there. I think that it was intended to say "drag-nets," as the text shows us. In Article 1 of the old Rules—I mean in subsection (*b*)—reference is made to fishing-boats fishing with "drift-nets." In subsection (*e*) another class of fishermen was aimed at, namely, those who trawl or drag on the bottom of the sea drag-nets of every description, because this category of fishermen includes not only those who fish with trawls, and those engaged in dredging, but likewise those who fish with other nets which rest upon the bottom, or which are dragged along the bottom, such as seines and other apparatus of the same kind known as "drag-nets." Those drag-nets vary in kind according to whether these fishermen are engaged in the Mediterranean, on the coast of the Bay of Biscay, or in the Channel. I think, therefore, that in inserting the word "drag-nets" here, the intention of those who drew up these Rules had been complied with. Moreover, allow me to observe that if subsection (*b*) is addressed exclusively to drift-net vessels, subsection (*e*) specially aims at fishing-boats using the trawl, the dredge, or something similar, which can be classed in the same category, namely, that of nets dragging on the bottom of the sea. There is, therefore, a certain amount of logic in the sentence, which disappears if we introduce into it the word "drift-net" instead of "drag-net."

In my opinion an endeavour has been made to provide in the Article for the lights of the fishing-vessel in the various categories by dividing them into classes and by giving each suitable lights. This same order of ideas has led me to find an explanation of why the flare-up has been ordered to be shown on the stern. When a vessel trawls, dredges, or uses a drift-net she uses, in order to drag her fishing apparatus, a rope, which, being attached on the side or on the stern of the boat, extends behind her at a depth which varies with the distance at which this rope is fastened to the stern. A vessel passing astern of the fishing-boat at a short distance might entangle her screw in this fishing-rope and cut it, or drag off the fishing-vessel if it is not cut. In either event the fishing apparatus is lost. The author of the Rule intended to place the flare-up astern, in order to avoid, as much as possible, a vessel from crossing that rope. It is, moreover, not a bad plan to be able to distinguish the stern of a trawling-vessel or a dredging-vessel, for she does not act as an ordinary vessel does. When you see the direction of her longitudinal plan, it is easy to understand her course, but a trawling-vessel is entirely different. By reason of her trawling or dragging she does not go as other vessels do; she rather goes in a lateral direction. That is what I think has led to the making of this Rule, and I would be unwilling to change it.

Mr. Hall (Great Britain).—Mr. President, I have already said that I do not propose for a moment to press the word "drift-net," and the sole question before us is whether we shall strike out these words as proposed by the honourable Delegate from Germany. The speech of the honourable Delegate from France has shown a still stronger argument against striking these words out. I shall certainly vote against it. These words were inserted for a purpose, and I hope we shall have the benefit of that purpose.

Dr. Sieveking (Germany).—Mr. President, I am very much obliged for the information which has been given to me by the gallant Delegate from France. When it is once shown that there might be a difference between drag-nets and trawlers, of course these words ought to be left as they stand. If that is not the case they may be superfluous, but they would not do any harm, so that under both suppositions it would be better to leave them as they are, and I beg leave to withdraw the amendment.

The President.—The amendment is withdrawn. The next will be amendment No. 20.

Amendment No. 20, Class 2, is as follows:—

"Amendment to Collocation Report proposed by Dr. Sieveking, on behalf of the German Delegation, 14th December, 1889:

"In Article 9, strike out paragraph (*e*); and in Article 11, strike out the words printed in italics."

Dr. Sieveking (Germany).—Mr. President, this amendment has been rendered necessary for the reason that there was a difference between the anchor-lights as prescribed for all other vessels and the anchor-lights as prescribed for the fishermen. I have proposed to strike out paragraph (*e*) because we have brought in an amendment to the effect that the words describing a globular lantern of so many inches in diameter should be eliminated. That is in accordance with the amendment which we have brought. It has been suggested to us, however, that it would be advisable to have all the Rules for fishing-vessels included in this one Article, and we see that there are good reasons for having all of the Rules relating to fishermen together inserted in one Article. So I do not see any reason for pressing this amendment, and I beg leave to withdraw it.

The President.—The next amendment will be No. 21.

Amendment No. 21 is as follows:—

"Amendment to Collocation Report proposed by Captain Shackford (United States), 14th December, 1889:

"Article 10. First paragraph, after 'flare-up light,' insert 'or an occulting light.'

"Second paragraph, first line, after 'white light,' insert 'or occulting light,' and in the second line strike out 'fixed and.' In fourth line, after 'unbroken light,' insert 'or occulting light.'"

Dr. Sieveking (Germany).—Mr. President, my remarks in regard to the last amendment applied only to the first part of it. Of course in Article 11 we will strike out the words printed in italics, because if they were to remain they would be quite superfluous.

Mr. Hall (Great Britain).—Mr. President, we would strike out the words in Article 11. They are unnecessary because the lights for fishing-vessels and the lights for other vessels are the same. So long as there was a difference in the shape of the lantern it was necessary to put in these words in italics calling the attention to the fishing anchor-lights.

Dr. Sieveking (Germany).—I made a mistake. I move to have the second part of amendment No. 20 adopted.

The President.—The Secretary will please read what is proposed by the Delegate from Germany.

The amendment of the Delegate from Germany is as follows:—

"In Article 11 strike out the words printed in italics."

The President.—Is the Conference ready for the question?

The question was put to the Conference upon the second part of the twentieth amendment, and it was carried.

The President.—The next amendment is amendment No. 21.

227

Amendment No. 21 is as follows:—

"Amendment to Collocation Report proposed by Captain Shackford (United States), 14th December, 1889:

"Article 10. First paragraph, after 'flare-up light,' insert 'or an occulting light.'

"Second paragraph, first line, after 'white light,' insert 'or occulting light,' and in second line strike out 'fixed and.' In fourth line, after 'unbroken light,' insert 'or occulting light.'"

Captain Shackford (United States).—Mr. President, the only object of this amendment is to permit vessels to carry a fixed light which may be made a flare-up light whenever another vessel is coming up astern. The argument against the light before was that the occulting light was one which was operated by machinery and was likely to get out of order. My excuse for reopening this is that during the last two weeks we have had before the Signal Committee a light which can be used for a night signal and can be used for a fixed light to be carried astern, and can also be flashed or uncovered by hand. Every sailor knows the advantage of recognizing at once what a light is when it is first seen. This will be a purely distinctive light, to which I cannot see any objection at all. It can be carried as a fixed light; it can be uncovered or made occulting when necessary. I merely want the privilege of doing this. And this light will be of a definite character. It cannot be mistaken for any other light. It does not depend upon machinery, and, in my opinion, it ought to be allowed. I would like, with your permission, to read a list of Petitions which were handed in for the adoption of this distinctive stern light. They are as follows:—

1. The Vessel-Owners' and Captains' Associations, representing about 1,800 ship-owners and masters of the New England and Middle States, and between 5,000,000 and 6,000,000 dollars of vessel property.
2. The Petitions of owners representing 575 American vessels.
3. Another similar Petition representing 96 vessels.
4. Another similar Petition representing 53 vessels.
6. Petitions of ship-masters representing the following steam-ship lines: the White Star Line, Liverpool; the Pacific Mail Steam-ship Company, the West India and Pacific Steam-ship Company, the International Steam-ship Company, the Portland Steam-packet Company, the Maine Steam-ship Company, the Honduras and Central America Company, the Providence Line, the Newhaven and New York Line, the Merchants' and Miners' Company, the Neptune Line, the Weems Line, the Philadelphia and Reading Company, the agents or owners of the Wilson Line, the Baltimore Steam-packet Company.
7. Forty additional Petitions numerously signed by the masters of foreign and domestic ships in the ports of San Francisco, California; New Orleans, Louisiana; Galveston, Texas; Savannah, Georgia; Pensacola, Florida; Mobile, Alabama; Baltimore, Maryland; Philadelphia, Pennsylvania; New York; Boston, Massachusetts, and other ports; and by Delaware, Pennsylvania, and Sandy Hook pilots.

Mr. Hall (Great Britain).—Mr. President, so far as I am aware this is the only amendment which has been brought forward at this stage of the proceedings which has absolutely nothing new about it. We discussed this at great length when it was brought before us by the gallant Delegate from the United States. I find that not one single person voted in favour of this occulting light except the Delegate from the United States, and I find that when the vote was taken he did not venture to ask for the Ayes and Noes, for the simple reason that, so far as I am aware, there was not one other Delegate who answered "Aye" when it was put to a vote. But even in the face of that overwhelming decision of this Conference we are now asked to take this question up and discuss it again. And why are we asked to do so? Because some Petitions have been sent in. Why, any active clerk of a patenteee could get Petitions signed by the thousand in a month, and he would not be worth his salt if he could not. Is there any reason for us, when we have come to a positive determination upon this subject and we have discussed the matter at the very greatest length, when it has been pointed out by expert after expert that we have no positive data and no public experiments showing that there is an occulting light in existence which would work at sea so as to be relied upon—is there any reason for us to reconsider this matter?

We find that the gallant Delegate from Germany, who has studied this question of lights as much and perhaps more than any one in this room, has told us that at sea it is very difficult to keep an ordinary occulting light burning when there is a sea running. In face of all these facts we are told that the Committee on Systems and Devices have had a lamp before it. We remember when a patented light was brought into the other building six weeks ago, and when one of the Delegates turned it over-at an angle like that [indicating] it went out. That was one of the brilliant inventions which we were asked to adopt for use at sea. I venture to say that such a matter never has been advised by the Conference. It has been thoroughly discussed and carefully considered, and I do not think we ought to entertain it again, or that we ought to again consider a question which has been passed upon by a practically unanimous vote of the Conference.

Captain Shackford (United States).—Mr. President, I think that this is another proposition entirely; I think that the learned Delegate from Great Britain referred to a light occulted by machinery. I believe that almost every sailor in this Conference has been at least once knocked out by the silvery tongue of the learned Delegate from Great Britain. I acknowledge to having been bowled out several times; but, however, I come up every time more or less smiling. I certainly think that there are arguments in favour of this distinctive light which ought to be considered by the Conference. I ask only this, that a light purely distinctive in its character may be permitted to be shown, and that it may be made a fixed light or a flare-up light, whenever another vessel is coming up astern. I cannot see how any sailor can object to this word "occulting," when the terms "flashed and fixed" are kept in the Rule. If Great Britain does not care to use it, very well. But certainly there could be no objection to the vessels of small nations like Siam and the United States carrying this distinctive light.

The President.—Is the Conference ready for the question upon this amendment?

Mr. Goodrich (United States).—Mr. President, as Chairman of the Collocation Committee I propose, personally, to stand by the Report of the Collocation Committee. Not having the pluck which my colleague manifests, I did not care about making this fight on the occulting light twice. But the Delegates from the United States have voted "Aye" on this amendment, and, therefore, whatever be my own view, whether it has changed or not by what has happened in the Conference a few days since, I am bound to vote with my Delegation and to express their opinion by voting "Aye" upon this proposition.

Captain Shackford (United States).—Mr. President, before the vote is taken I hope it will be clearly understood that this light is merely a fixed light that can be flashed and can be occulted. It is a fixed light on the stern, in compliance with the present Rule; and when a vessel is approaching it can be flashed or occulted.

Mr. Hall (Great Britain).—Mr. President, surely the Delegate from the United States does not mean that we are to have a fixed light at the stern, and that if you put your hand in front of it you can then call it an occulting light.

Captain Sampson (United States).—Mr. President, I understand that a light is an occulting light when it is hidden, and it does not make any difference how it is done. Although I have not given this matter very much thought, it strikes me that the principle which is brought up is quite different from the one which was so very thoroughly discussed by the Conference when we went over this matter before. The principle involved in this question is this: We have now given vessels permission to carry a fixed light at the stern which is so screened as to show over an arc of twelve points. Now a difficulty might arise from this permission. Of course we assume that this permission having been once given will be availed of by the vessels because it removes them from all responsibility for keeping a look-out so far as it relates to an overtaking vessel. If that fixed light is shown astern, a vessel overtaking assumes all the responsibility of any collision or any damage which may result from overtaking the other vessel. It therefore follows, as I stated, that this light will be very generally used.

Now, then, we have fixed upon the stern of every vessel a white light. We use white lights in a good many places, and they have a particular significance, which is that a vessel carrying a white light is to be avoided. The difficulty is this: that the white light may be misunderstood. At a distance a vessel seeing it for some time will think it is the top light of a steamer whose side-lights are not yet visible. It may be an anchor-light. It may be several different things. But if we give the vessel carrying this light permission, when she thinks it necessary, or at any time when she sees a vessel coming up astern, to simply occult that light in any way, it then removes from the vessel overtaking her all possible doubt as to what that light is. It seems to me that that is a very small thing, and if it is found that it is not desirable to do it the Rule will not be followed. This light, as it stands now in the Rule as adopted, is a permissive light. There is a possibility that a vessel carrying a fixed light on her stern may mislead other vessels by taking it for the top light of a steamer whose side-lights are not visible, or for the white light of a picket-boat or a pilot-boat, and all of these difficulties will be removed if the light is permitted to be occulted.

Captain Malmberg (Sweden).—Mr. President, it is certainly stated that this occulting light, as is proposed, is to be moved by hand, but if we adopt the word "occult" as it stands here, there is nothing to hinder such a light being afterward constructed to be moved by machinery, and that is a thing which we do not want; at least, I do not want it for my part. So I think it would be better not to adopt the amendment at all.

Mr. Hall (Great Britain).—Mr. President, may I point out that the situation has not been changed by allowing the stern-light to be fixed, because that was decided upon before we took up the amendment of the Delegate from the United States as to whether an occulting light should be permitted? We first of all decided that the light might be carried fixed, and then we discussed the question of an occulting light. It is now suggested that an occulting light means a light which you may hide with your hand or your hat. But I take it that that certainly would not mean the occulting light which we have had submitted to us, and which we have had discussed here, whether the light be worked by hand or by machinery. It cannot be seriously said that it is necessary to have an occulting light because the steamer carrying the fixed light astern might be mistaken for a pilot-boat or a fishing-boat. If you want to hide the light for some time, there is nothing to prevent a man from putting his hand or his hat over it and hiding it. You propose that a vessel is to be allowed to show an occulting light; I take it, that is a light which is shown and then is dark, and then is shown again. I confess that to my mind that is the meaning of the word "occulting." It is not a light which is capable of being put out, because every light is capable of being put out.

The President.—The question is upon amendment No 21, which will be read by the Secretary. Amendment No. 21 is as follows:—

"Amendment to Collocation Report proposed by Captain Shackford (United States), 14th December, 1889:

"First paragraph, after 'flare-up light,' insert 'or an occulting light.'

"Second paragraph, first line, after 'white light,' insert 'or occulting light;' and in second line strike out 'fixed and.' In fourth line, after 'unbroken light,' insert 'or occulting light.'

The President.—Is the Conference ready for the question?

The question was put to the Conference upon the adoption of amendment No. 21, and it was lost.

The President.—The next amendment is No. 22.

Lieutenant Beaugency (Chile).—Mr. President, may I call the attention of the Committee on Collocation to the last paragraph of Article 4, which says: "These signals are not signals of vessels in distress and requiring assistance. Such signals are contained in Article 32"? Now, in amendment No. 20, proposed by the Delegate from Germany, the Conference has decided to strike out these words because they are superfluous. I think the same thing applies to this last paragraph of Article 4.

The President.—Does the Delegate from Chile offer an amendment?

Lieutenant Beaugency (Chile).—Mr. President, I would call the attention of the Chairman of the Committee on Collocation to the fact that amendment No. 20, proposed by the Delegate from Germany, has said that these words should be stricken out because they are superfluous, and I think that for the same reason these words which are in Article 4, in the last paragraph, should be stricken out.

Mr. Hall (Great Britain).—Mr. President, may I point out that the Conference decided that it was important to state in the not-under-command Rule that these were not signals of distress? That is why these words were inserted originally. It is still necessary to tell sailors that these are not signals of distress.

The President.—Amendment No. 22 is before the Conference. It will be read by the Secretary.

Amendment No. 22 is as follows:—

"Amendment to Collocation Report proposed by Dr. Sieveking on behalf of the German Delegation, 14th December, 1889:

"In Article 11, instead of the words, 'in a globular lantern of not less than 8 inches in diameter and so constructed,' insert the words, 'of such a character.'"

Mr. Verney (Siam).—Mr. President, may I propose that the third Rule of the Committeee on Collocation will be observed, which is to use similar words or sentences expressing similar ideas in each of the Rules, and under that Rule the same words which are used in subsection (a) should be used, that is, "so constructed"?

Dr. Sieveking (Germany).—Mr. President, a light cannot be "so constructed."

Captain Salvesen (Norway).—Mr. President, I would like to have it changed so it would read, "a white light in a lantern so constructed," because it is only a lantern which can be constructed.

Mr. Goodrich (United States).—Mr. President, may I call the attention of the gallant Delegate from Norway to the fact that the old Rule and the Rules as reported by the Collocation Committee in Article 2, subdivision (a), used the same language, "a bright white light so constructed"? That was simply a reprint of the old Rule, if I remember it.

Captain Salvesen (Norway).—Mr. President, but this light is to show all around the horizon. A light can never show all around on board a vessel, but the lantern can be so constructed that it can show all around. The anchor-lights on a vessel cannot be hung in a place where they can be seen all around, but a lantern can be constructed so that the light can show all around.

Mr. Verney (Siam).—Mr. President, I venture to press my original proposition, because I see in subsection (d) the words, "a green light so constructed as to show an unbroken light over an arc of the horizon."

The President.—Does the Delegate from Norway offer any amendment?

Captain Salvesen (Norway).—Mr. President, I only desired to ask whether it should not read that the lantern should be so constructed.

Dr. Sieveking (Germany).—Mr. President, is not that a mere matter of collocation?

Captain Salvesen (Norway).—Mr. President, if so, I have nothing to say at present.

Mr. Goodrich (United States).—Mr. President, I think we had better save the Collocation Committee the trouble of making a new Report by adopting whatever words we want to use now in the Conference. There is this difference, as the gentleman will see: In subdivision (a) of Article 2, and subdivision (b) of Article 2, and in subdivision (c) of Article 2, the words, "a light so constructed as to show," refers to a light which shows over an arc of the horizon. But when you come to a light which is to show all around the horizon, the words may properly be used, "of such a character." There are two descriptions: one relating to the lantern which shows over an arc, and the other to the light which shows all around the horizon.

Dr. Sieveking (Germany).—Mr. President, we are now between three alternatives, and I leave it to the choice of the Conference. I do not pretend to express any particular words or to give preference to any particular words. We have the expression, "a white light in a lantern so constructed as to show," &c. We have the wording, "a white light so constructed as to show," and we have the wording as proposed by the amendment, "a white light of such a character as to show;" there are precedents, I think, for all three. I do not see any reason for changing the amendment, and I think the simplest thing would be to take a vote upon the amendment.

The President.—The question is upon the amendment. The Secretary will please read it.

Amendment No. 22 is as follows:—

"In Article 11, instead of the words, 'in a globular lantern of not less than 8 inches in diameter, and so constructed,' insert the words, 'of such a character.'"

The President.—Is the Conference ready for the question?

The question was put to the Conference upon the adoption of amendment No. 22, Class 2, and it was adopted.

Captain Van Steyn (the Netherlands).—Mr. President, the next amendment has been practically disposed of, the first part of it yesterday and the second part of it to-day, so it is not necessary to bring it again before the Conference.

The President.—Amendment No. 23 having been practically disposed of, the Conference will proceed to consider amendment No. 24, which the Secretary will please read.

Amendment No. 24 is as follows:—

"Amendment to Collocation Report proposed by Captain Bisbee (China), 14th December 1889:

"Article 11. Instead of the last paragraph, insert the wording passed by the Conference (Protocol, p. 263), viz., 'a vessel aground in or near a fairway shall carry, where they can best be seen, two red lights in globular lanterns, one over the other, not less than 6 feet apart, in addition to the above-mentioned anchor-light or lights."

Captain Bisbee (China).—Mr. President, my object in proposing this amendment was to allow the officer in charge of any vessel aground to exhibit these red lights where they could best be seen. The amendment proposed by Dr. Sieveking, No. 6, to Article 4, having been adopted, alters the wording of Article 4, so that it really makes the provision which I desired to obtain by this amendment.

The President.—Do you therefore withdraw the amendment?

Captain Bisbee (China).—Mr. President, my object is accomplished in another way, and I withdraw the amendment.

The President.—Amendment No. 25 is next in order. The Secretary will please read it.

Amendment No. 25 is as follows:—

"Amendment to Collocation Report proposed by Captain Shackford (United States), 14th December, 1889:

"Article 15. Add as preliminary paragraph after 'fog-horn and bell'—

"All steam-whistles must be capable of producing a sound that can be heard in ordinary weather at least 2 miles, and all fog-horns at least 1 mile."

Captain Shackford (United States).—Mr. President, I propose to read from the Protocol of the 19th November:—

"*Mr. Goodrich* (United States).—Mr. President, I move that we proceed to the discussion of extra amendment No. 16.

"*Mr. Hall* (Great Britain).—Mr. President, might I point out to the Delegate from the United States that this matter will be better dealt with in a note to the various Powers, that it would be desirable that an attempt should be made to secure sound-signals to be used in a fog that would be heard at a certain distance? Of course some Powers already have their tests, and would not give certificates for fog-signals without being satisfied that they were thoroughly efficient. But I do not see how we can frame any International Rules upon the point. I think it would be better that we should adopt this principle in the same way that we have adopted the principle with regard to the standards of candle-power, and have it embodied in a note, suggesting that it is desirable that the whistles should be of such a power, if possible, as to be heard over low ground at a certain distance. Let it be in a note similar to the note with regard to the lights. I think the Delegates will see that it will be practically impossible, so far as the International Rules are concerned, to embody this in the Rules. We will certainly agree upon a note calling the attention of the various Powers to the utility and desirability of having such supervision."

Mr. Goodrich (United States).—Mr. President, I think that the desire of my gallant colleague from the United States is met by the ninth paragraph of Appendix (B) of the Collocation Committee's Report, which reads:—

"All steam-whistles, sirens, and fog-horns should be thoroughly tested as to their efficiency, and should be capable of being heard at a stated minimum distance, and should be so regulated that the tones of whistles and sirens should be as distinct as possible from the sound of fog-horns."

In the first Report of the Committee on Sound-Signals, in their first recommendation, they say:—

"We are of the opinion that many of the steam-whistles and fog-horns and bells now generally used cannot be heard at a sufficient distance, and we therefore recommend the use of instruments making a louder sound."

It seems to me that the note which the Collocation Committee have appended to their Report exactly meets the recommendation of the Delegate from the United States.

Captain Shackford (United States).—Mr. President, I thought that there had been a reference made to that in Appendix (B) of the Report of the Collocation Committee; but I understood from the remarks of the learned Delegate from Great Britain that some minimum distance would be mentioned. If he did not mean that, of course I entirely misunderstood him, and, therefore, I beg to withdraw the amendment.

Mr. Hall (Great Britain).—Mr. President, I quite understand how the mistake has arisen. I have explained to the Delegate from the United States that we wished to carry out loyally what we undertook with regard to this matter.

The President.—The amendment is withdrawn. The next matter will be amendment No. 26. The Secretary will please read it. Since the amendment has been printed it has been changed, and the Secretary will read it as changed.

Amendment No. 26 is as follows:—

"Amendment to Collocation Report proposed by Dr. Sieveking on behalf of the German Delegation, 14th December, 1889:

231

"In Article 18, strike out paragraph 2, and instead of the word 'It,' in the first line of paragraph 3, insert the words, 'This Article.'"

Dr. Sieveking (Germany).—Mr. President, I think it will be useful to make a few remarks in order to prevent any misunderstanding which might otherwise be brought about. The amendment, as it is printed, says, instead of the word "it," with the letter "I" as a capital letter. That would lead one to think that it is the word "It" which is contained in the fourth paragraph. But that is not our intention. Our intention is to have the second paragraph eliminated, commencing with the words, "This Article only applies to cases where vessels are meeting end-on," &c. Then, of course, instead of the word "it," in the first line, it must read, "This Article applies." So the aim of this amendment is to have the second paragraph eliminated. We have thought it right to bring in this amendment, because we thought it really was unnecessary to use so many words and to say the same thing twice or three times over. You see this is repeated in the third paragraph. Now, it is a well-known fact why this Article has been framed in such a redundant manner of expression. The old port Rule, as it continued for a long time, was a Rule which was very much revered by sailors, who always thought they had to obey the port Rule.

Now, when the port Rule was abolished, which was more than a quarter of a century ago, it was thought necessary to draw the attention of sailors to this Rule, and in this way the abundant use of words which we have before us was brought about, so as to attract attention to the fact that the port Rule had been abolished, and that instead of the port Rule this Rule (Article 18) gave the only case where vessels had to port their helm or to go to starboard. You will see that these words: "This Article only applies to cases where vessels are meeting end-on," are repeated in the third paragraph. The second part of paragraph 2 is also repeated. So it seems to us that this second paragraph is quite superfluous. As I have stated, it was the intention of this Rule to call the attention of sailors to the fact that the old port Rule had been abolished, but now we think it could be shortened a little. I think that no harm could be done by striking out this paragraph and giving it a wording which is a little more in accordance with the general rules of style and drafting and common sense.

Captain Malmberg (Sweden).—Mr. President, if this paragraph is to be stricken out, in accordance with the amendment of the Delegate from Germany, I hope that at least the last lines of the paragraph will be put into the first part of the Article, because I know that they are very necessary. Those words are: "does not apply to two vessels which must, if both be upon their respective course, pass clear of each other." I should very much object to having those words taken out of this Article.

Mr. Hall (Great Britain).—Mr. President, I hope the learned Delegate from Germany will not think it necessary to press this amendment. I think he is not aware of the circumstances under which these notes were framed. The port-helm Rule, it is quite true, was done away with by the Regulations of 1863; but sailors were still so wedded to the port-helm Rule that they would not regard this Rule. They did not treat it as sufficiently binding and they did not understand it, and the consequence was that, five years afterwards, a lengthy correspondence took place between France and Great Britain, the Powers which had drawn up these Rules originally, and after six months these two Powers devised the means of explaining this Rule so clearly that a sailor could not possibly say that he was mistaken about the meaning of it; and it was thought desirable to put it and to repeat it, and, at the risk of being accused of tautology and repetition, to say the same thing perhaps over and over again in such a way that no sailor, however ignorant, could say: "I do not understand that Rule." I apprehend it might be argued that the time has gone by for these explanations; but I certainly must hope that we shall not vote for doing away with these notes, which certainly do away with any responsibility of doubt as to the meaning of the Rule, simply because a few more words are used than are absolutely necessary.

I quite agree with the gallant Delegate from Sweden, that if a part of this Article were omitted we ought to keep the three lines of the first Article; and I think we ought not to mutilate the note and take two or three lines out of the first part, although they are lines which, I admit, are contained in other parts of these notes. But that would mutilate the note, and I think we can very well afford to leave these two or three lines, even at the risk of being accused of a little tautology, when we can retort, in answer to that accusation, that, at any rate, no sailor can make a mistake about what it means.

Mr. Goodrich (United States).—I may state that the Collocation Committee have already had the very question raised by the Delegate from Germany under very careful consideration, and, of course, in that consideration we had the benefit of the experience and suggestions of the learned Chief Judge of Germany. But still the Collocation Committee was of the opinion that the Rule had better be maintained in the condition in which it had stood for twenty-five years. There is another thing which I desire to suggest to the Conference, and that is, in all of the hundred amendments which have been proposed to the Regulations there was not a single one to this Article, except that the Delegate from Siam did propose to insert the words, "so as to prevent risk of collision," in the first part of this Article, which he afterwards withdrew. It is a pretty good rule not to attempt hastily to break an established Rule, nor to break a Rule where the Courts have given it a construction.

This Rule is designed not only for the construction of the Court—because the Courts have already given a construction to the words, "end-on or nearly end-on"—but to the sailor, inasmuch as the position is quite a frequent one to vessels crossing the Atlantic, and it was desirable that attention should be pointed and repointed to the necessity of obeying the Rule which provided for the case of vessels meeting end-on. The difficulty is that if you attempt to strike out one of these paragraphs and leave another, or to insert something new, you are going to destroy the symmetry of the Rule as it at present stands. It seems to me to provide against every case which a sailor can meet with at the time of his meeting a vessel end-on, or nearly end-on, and so prevent collision. I may further say that, so far as I know—and if I make a mistake I can be corrected by the learned First Delegate from Great Britain—in all the judicial constructions on this Rule there is only one case, and that a recent one, where the verbiage of this Rule has been criticized. I must say that my opinion has not been changed by what has been so ably said by the learned Delegate from Germany; and I think it is very wise to let this Rule stand as it has stood for twenty-five years.

Captain Mensing (Germany).—Mr. President, it is not my learned friend Dr. Sieveking who has proposed this amendment, but it is a sailor; and from a sailor's standpoint I would like to say something with regard to it. When I began to follow the sea I never could make anything out of this Rule, though I have read it over and over again. Whenever I came to these paragraphs Nos. 1, 2, and 3, I said: "Why are all these words stuck in here? There is a long row of words strung one after another, and they must have some meaning." After a while I said: "Very well; perhaps there is no meaning to them, as there is often a long string of words without any meaning; and so there is no meaning to them." I would ask any one of the gentlemen of this class (to which I have the honour to belong) of practical seamen whether they find that there is anything in this second paragraph which is not repeated in paragraphs 3 and 4? Now, I do not know anything about how this language originated, but it seems to me that it is the most natural way to suppose that the first Article was written, and then that it was found necessary to make a further declaration in the second Article, and, in order to make that declaration, paragraph 2 was inserted. But after a while the learned Judges found out that that was not sufficient, so they brought up paragraphs 3 and 4. Paragraphs 3 and 4 are nothing but a repetition; and it confuses the sailor to read the same thing over and over again.

The other Rules, as they stand now, seem to me to be very well defined, any sailor can make sense of them; but in this case I think it is doubtful, and I have taken the liberty to propose this amendment to my colleagues, and they have adopted it. I am sorry that this amendment has been included in the amendments on principle, for there is no principle about it. It is a simple matter of collocation. I think that it might be shorter, and then the Article would be more easily understood. That is the reason why I have proposed it.

Now, the gallant Delegate from Sweden has said that there was something in this paragraph which was not in the other Article. I beg to differ from his opinion, because in Article 4 he will see that it does not apply to the cases where, by day, a vessel sees another ahead crossing her own course; or by night to the cases where the red light of one vessel is opposed to the red light of the other; or where the green light of one vessel is opposed to the green light of the other; or where a red light without a green light, or a green light without a red light, is seen ahead; or where both green and red lights are seen anywhere but ahead. Now, I think that every sailor will understand that when he sees a green light on the starboard side he is clear and has to keep his course; and if he sees a red light on his port side he is clear and has to keep his course. If that meets the case, then you will see that the whole paragraph is nothing but a repetition and reiteration of what has been said in paragraphs 3 and 4. Now, it has been very ably explained in the Report of the Committee on Collocation that the Rules and Regulations should be as short as possible, and if that be true and there be really nothing in paragraph 2 but what is contained in paragraphs 3 and 4, I think the paragraphs might safely be omitted.

Mr. Verney (Siam).—Mr. President, perhaps I may be allowed to add one or two words to this matter. The Collocation Committee have put themselves into this dilemma. They say on the title-page of their Report that they are going to retain existing Rules as far as possible, and at the same time they are to make the Articles as short as possible. To do both is impossible. I shall not support the proposition of the Delegate from Germany, because in my opinion I think this Article might be made a great deal shorter and a great deal clearer, but it is not to be made so by merely taking out one paragraph. I think that if the Collocation Committee laid profane hands on this Rule and had ventured to deal with it, I venture to say that any one of them would make a much clearer and a much shorter Rule; at least I think they would. As they have not done that, and as it has been considered a Rule that nobody in this Conference has any business to touch, or at any rate that it is better to leave it alone, I prefer to leave it alone in its entirety rather than to cut out one part of it. There is an immense lot of tautology in it, and I think tautology does not tend to clearness. I think that same principle applies whether you are dealing with seamen or any other class of men.

I should very much prefer to have seen this Rule made more clear and explicit; and if the learned and gallant Delegates from Germany had brought us in a really carefully drawn up Rule, in a way which they are so abundantly able to do, I should have been willing to support it. I do not think that these last two lines in paragraph 2 are to be found in any other part of this Rule as it now stands; and I venture to think that they are a very valuable part of the Rule. Therefore, although I cordially agree with much that has fallen from the gallant Delegate from Germany, I still feel unable to support his proposition to cut out the second paragraph.

Mr. Goodrich (United States).—Mr. President, may I suggest in the first place that the gallant Delegate from France has an important Resolution to move; and in the next place, is it not worth while for the Delegates to consider whether they had not better continue our session a little later this afternoon? It is barely possible that we may discuss the remaining six or seven amendments before we separate to-night; and on behalf of the Collocation Committee, which will have to make some changes in the Rules as ordered by the Conference, I submit that it would perhaps be wise for us to go on until some member moves to adjourn. Therefore, I move that we prolong the session of the Conference until the motion to adjourn shall be carried.

Captain Richard (France).—Mr. President, I would, on the contrary, ask that the members of this Conference be allowed to go home. But in making this proposition, I would ask the Conference, in order that we may arrive at a prompt conclusion of the work which is imposed upon us, to adopt the proposition which I will now have the honour to submit to you. The discussion has progressed so far to-day in regard to the Rules of the Road, the opinions of all have been expressed so freely and a tlength, that we should now look to the means and the necessity of arriving at a conclusion. Under those circumstances I would ask the Conference that all amendments adopted by it be sent to the Collocation Committee, to enable it to give us a final Report. We have now discussed more than 200 amendments; we have for more than two months sat from 11 to 4 o'clock, and sometimes from 10 to 5, and I think that the time has come to make a final Report, and to cause to appear in such Report without further delay all the amendments which have been adopted by the Conference, so that the end may not be retarded. We will not learn very much more from further discussion, and we cannot allow amendments to be brought up for an indefinite period. The third reading has now taken place. The time has arrived for the final Rules to be presented.

I would, therefore, propose that all amendments adopted by the Conference be placed in the Rules by the Collocation Committee, and that they make a final Report. I will now ask the Honourable Mr. Goodrich not to propose prolonging our session beyond the regular hour, but to adjourn immediately, with the understanding that to-morrow we shall resume our regular session.

Captain Shackford (United States).—Mr. President, we have been sitting here four hours dealing with fifteen of these amendments. That is about four an hour, and we still have six, and the one which is now before us is not finished; so at the lowest calculation it will take an hour and a half or two hours to finish these amendments. Therefore I move to adjourn.

Mr. Goodrich (United States).—Mr. President, will my friend not give way, that we may take a vote upon this proposition of the Delegate from France?

Captain Shackford (United States).—Mr. President, if my motion is in order I would like to press it.

The President.—The motion to adjourn is not debatable, and debate will not be allowed if the Delegate from the United States presses his motion.

Captain Shackford (United States).—Mr. President, I understood that this Resolution was to be read and that we would vote on it directly, and then I want to move to adjourn.

Mr. Hall (Great Britain).—Mr. President, could we not dispose of this one amendment? Of course I do not want to sit here if it does not suit the convenience of the other Delegates.

Captain Shackford (United States).—Mr. President, I simply want to say that I have other business to attend to besides this.

Mr. Goodrich (United States).—I desire to say that the Collocation Committee will meet at 5 o'clock.

The President.—The Resolution of the Delegate from France will now be read.
The Resolution is as follows:—

"*Resolved,*—That all amendments adopted by the Conference be placed in the Rules by the Collocation Committee, and a final Report furnished."

The President.—The Resolution will be again read so that it will be distinctly understood.
The Resolution is as follows:—

"*Resolved,*—That all amendments adopted by the Conference be placed in the Rules by the Collocation Committee, and a final Report furnished."

Dr. Sieveking (Germany).—Mr. President, would it not be advisable to vote upon this Resolution to-morrow? For this reason: in any case to prevent a misunderstanding as to the meaning of the Resolution which I take it is that the Report of the Collocation Committee is to be final in this sense, that no amendments are to be allowed, no amendments whatever, after the final Report and final wording of the Rules. That is a very great authority to give to the Collocation Committee. I do not know that all the members will agree to that, and I only desire to draw their attention to it. Perhaps they might do it, because the amendments are simple and only a matter of wording which is not very difficult, but I am sure, in order to prevent a misunderstanding, that it is my duty to draw the attention of the Conference to the fact that the meaning of this Resolution is that no amendment will be allowed after the Report of the Collocation Committee has been brought in.

Mr. Hall (Great Britain).—Mr. President, I take it that this is not the sole reason of this Resolution. I take it that these amendments have been moved and carried, and we have not left a single one of them for the Collocation Committee to deal with. As was pointed out by the learned Delegate from the United States, it was desirable that they should be carried here in such form as to be a part of the Rules. They will be put into the Rules by the Collocation Committee. I apprehend that it is not the intention that the Collocation Committee is to draw up a fresh Report, and then that is to be laid on the table, and then forty-eight hours are to be given, and then the final Report is to be discussed again. If that were so, may I ask when is the final reading to come? If a misprint is found in the general Report is that again to be sent to the Collocation Committee, and are they then to present their Report, and is there then to be forty-eight hours more elapse, and another discussion, and then another final Report? Really we must come to some conclusion. As my friend the gallant Delegate from France has pointed out, this is a third reading, and now all that remains to be done is simply clerk's work. I cannot help thinking that this is a very reasonable proposition, and if such work is to be done it is better that it should be done by the Committee. It is purely clerk's work.

Mr. Verney (Siam).—Mr. President, I understood by the word "final" that under no circumstances whatever should any word be altered in their Report which was going to be delivered. Perhaps I am wrong, but that is what I understand it to mean. I venture to suggest to this Conference that no such finality can be arrived at until the last amendment has been voted upon, and for this reason: an amendment which is proposed and adopted by the Conference may have some indirect effect upon what has gone before, and the Conference may find itself in the position of having passed an interim Report as a final Report,

Mr. Hall (Great Britain).—Mr. President, may I point out that this Resolution is dealing with all the amendments that are to be passed by the Conference on the third reading? It is only a proposition that when we have finished these amendments they shall be put into their proper place by the Collocation Committee. Some one will have to do it. The clerk will have to do it or the Secretary will have to do it, and this Resolution asks the Collocation Committee to do it, and they are willing to do it. They are only to carry into effect the decisions of the Conference and insert these amendments in the Rules in their proper places. As I say, that is purely clerk's work, and I cannot see why it should not be done.

Mr. Goodrich (United States).—Mr. President, I venture to suggest that if there should be any such glaring error or correction as has been suggested, it might be reconsidered, by unanimous consent, or this Resolution might be reconsidered.

Captain Richard (France).—Mr. President, I do not want the slightest doubt to exist regarding my intention when I proposed this Resolution. It was for the purpose of stopping further amendments. The discussion has been very long and sufficiently profound to permit us to look forward to winding up our labours.

Under those circumstances it will be necessary to have a final Report. The amendments which have been adopted will be inserted in the new Report, which will be a final one, and they will be inserted in such a manner as to express only what their authors intended they should express. We are here to pass judgment upon that point; we will still have the right, as we had in the Committees, to express our opinions in regard to the Report, and to cause our observations to be inserted at the end of the Report, if we deem it necessary. I do not think that this right can be denied us, and I therefore ask that the final Report be made.

Mr. Verney (Siam).—I have no objection whatever to that. It was with regard to the word "final" that I objected. Perhaps I misunderstood it.

Dr. Sieveking (Germany).—Mr. President, I certainly do not intend to oppose this proposition being a member of the Collocation Committee. It is a great compliment to the Collocation Committee to have this Resolution passed, and so there is no reason for me to oppose it. I only want to draw the attention of the members to the fact that they have placed this confidence in the Collocation Committee. If this proposal has been sufficiently discussed I think we can vote upon it at once.

The President.—Does the Delegate withdraw his proposition to postpone it?

Dr. Sieveking (Germany).—Mr. President, I do not make any proposition to postpone the vote.

Mr. Hall (Great Britain).—Mr. President, so far as I can see there is no one who proposes to postpone it. We shall meet at once in the Collocation Committee, if you authorize us to do it and deal with the work which has been done to-day, and put it into the Rules this evening.

The President.—The Secretary will read the Resolution.

The Resolution is as follows:—

"*Resolved,*—That all amendments adopted by the Conference be placed in the Rules by the Collocation Committee, and that such Report be final."

The President.—Does the Delegate from France accept that as his Resolution?

Captain Richard (France).—Yes, Sir.

The question was put to the Conference upon the adoption of the Resolution, and it was carried.

The Conference thereupon adjourned until Friday, December 20, 1889, at 11 o'clock A.M.

Washington, Friday, December 20, 1889, 11 *o'clock* A.M.

THE Conference was called to order at 11 o'clock A.M., Rear-Admiral Franklin in the Chair.

The President.—Amendment No. 26 is before the Conference. It will be read by the Secretary.

Amendment No. 26 is as follows:—

"Amendment to Collocation Report, proposed by Dr. Sieveking on behalf of the German Delegation, 14th December, 1889:

"In Article 18, strike out paragraph 2, and instead of the word 'It' at the beginning of paragraph 3, insert the words, 'This Article.'"

Captain Malmberg (Sweden).—Mr. President, it was said yesterday by the gallant Delegate from Germany that my objection to striking out paragraph 2 of Article 18, and especially the last three lines, was met by the first amendment in the fourth paragraph of the same Article; but I do not think so, because this sentence, and also the whole of paragraph 4, refers to steamers crossing, and not to steamers meeting, as does the second paragraph. Although the second paragraph is in part a reiteration of the first, it is, in my opinion, a good provision. I have, by long experience, gained a strong impression that the point of Article 2, as contained in the last three sentences, can never be too much impressed upon the minds of persons in charge of the steamers. I therefore wish that amendment No. 26 may not be accepted by the Conference.

The President.—The question is upon amendment No. 26. The Delegate from Germany being absent, the Chair hesitates to put the vote upon the amendment before he arrives. Does the other Delegate from Germany desire the vote to be put in the absence of Captain Mensing?

Dr. Sieveking (Germany).—Yes, Sir, if you please. I do not think it is necessary to postpone taking the vote.

The President.—The question is upon the amendment. The Secretary will please read the amendment before taking the vote.

235

Amendment No. 26 is as follows:—

"Amendment to Collocation Report, proposed by Dr. Sieveking on behalf of the German Delegation, 14th December, 1889:

"In Article 18, strike out paragraph 2, and instead of the word 'It' at the beginning of paragraph 3, insert the words, 'This Article.'"

The President.—Is the Conference ready for the question?
The question was put to the Conference upon the adoption of amendment No. 26, and it was lost.
The President.—Amendment No. 27 will now be read by the Secretary.
Amendment No. 27 is as follows:—

"Amendment to Collocation Report, proposed by Dr. Sieveking on behalf of the German Delegation, 14th December, 1889:

"In Article 21, instead of the words, 'and speed,' insert the words, 'and where one of two crossing vessels is to keep out of the way, the other shall keep her course and speed.'"

Dr. Sieveking (Germany).—Mr. President, this is an amendment which I would like to submit to the serious consideration of the Conference. The meaning of it, I think, is clear. The Rule as it stands, and as it has been passed by the Conference, says: "Where, by any of these Rules, one of two vessels is to keep out of the way, the other shall keep her course and speed." This Rule applies to overtaking vessels as well as to vessels crossing. There cannot be a doubt about that, because Article 24 says:—

"Notwithstanding anything contained in these Rules, every vessel overtaking any other shall keep out of the way of the overtaken vessel."

So an overtaking vessel comes under the Rule in Article 21, and an overtaken vessel shall keep her course and speed.

Our amendment is to have the Rule under Article 21 limited to crossing vessels; in other words, to take the overtaken vessel out of these Rules so far as to say that the overtaken vessel is to keep her course only, and not to keep her course and speed. When we discussed the principle of Article 21, I think the whole discussion turned, so far as I remember, upon the question of crossing vessels.

The reasons given for this Rule were taken upon the situation of crossing vessels, and no mention whatever has been made of an overtaken vessel. Because that has been the case, we have questioned whether it would be desirable to make the Rule apply to overtaken vessels as well as crossing vessels, and we now say it ought not to apply to them for the following reasons. The general principle given by common sense must be that the overtaking vessel ought to direct her movements or manœuvres so as to avoid the overtaken vessel. She is the faster vessel, and she looks ahead; and the overtaken vessel, merely taking the principle of common sense, ought not to be compelled in any way to manœuvre so as to assist the overtaking vessel to pass clear. That is the duty of the faster vessel. She ought not in any way to interfere with the intentions or with the movements of the vessel before her.

There are many cases imaginable where the duty of keeping her speed would be an injustice, in my opinion, to an overtaken vessel. I will mention two cases only. When an overtaken vessel is slackening or slowing in order to take a pilot, why should she in any way be prevented from doing so? It is the regular course of her voyage. She has arrived so far now as to be in a position to slow and take a pilot on board, and, if the Rule is applied as it stands now, she would first have to look out to see whether behind her there was an overtaking vessel, and, if so, she would not be allowed to slacken her speed. She would have to proceed until the overtaking vessel has passed clear by her. That is the plain consequence of this Rule as it stands, and everybody will say that is wrong. The overtaken vessel, of course, cannot in any way be prevented from slowing in order to take a pilot on board.

There is another case. Take two vessels proceeding up a river, one of which is following in the wake of the other. They are both subject to this Rule. The overtaken vessel arrives near the anchoring ground. She is about to drop her anchor, and slows, or even stops, to drop her anchor. But there is an overtaking vessel behind her, following her. She is not allowed to do so until the overtaking vessel has passed clear by her. Then there may be other vessels following, so the consequence of the Rule as it stands would be that she would have to wait until a happy opportunity occurs that no other vessel is behind her which is overtaking her. That is clearly quite contrary to common sense.

It might be said the present Rule must not be so applied as to lead to a consequence which is incompatible with common sense. But, then, I say it is better to frame the Law in a way which is compatible with common sense than to make a bad Law, and then leave it to the Judges to administer it in the best way they can. As we are legislators here in a certain sense, we ought to try to frame the Law, if we can, in such a way as to cover these cases. Now, what have we done in our amendment? If we take the overtaken vessels out of the rule of keeping their course and speed, let us see whether there are any consequences which might be of a serious nature, so as to make it inadvisable to adopt this amendment. The cases which I have mentioned would be covered. They would be guarded against.

Are there any consequences which would make it inadvisable to adopt the amendment? If we take the case where an overtaking vessel follows in the wake of the other vessel before her, I do not think there is any situation imaginable where it may be thought necessary to prescribe for the overtaken vessel that she shall keep her speed. "Keep her speed" means neither slacken nor increase her speed. To increase her speed would only lessen the danger of collision. No vessel slackens her speed unless there is a certain reason for it, as, for example, the reason which I have just mentioned of taking a pilot on board or dropping an anchor. In the open sea no vessel will slow or slacken her speed unless there are circumstances which compel her to do so. Then, again, the overtaking vessel, when she follows in the wake of the vessel before her, must put her helm over to one side or the other in order to pass, and when she puts her helm over I do not think there is any reason why her manœuvres should be influenced by the speed of the other vessel, because she has to pass on one side of the other vessel.

There is only one case imaginable, I think, where it might be doubtful, *primâ facie*, whether it would be advisable to make this rule of keeping her speed apply to an overtaken vessel, and that is the case where an overtaking vessel does not follow in the wake of the other vessel before her, but comes up at an angle and crosses the overtaken vessel, that is to say, within the dark arc as we have defined it. If she comes up at an angle to the course of the overtaken vessel there are two courses for her to follow. She may pass by the stern of the overtaken vessel or she may cross her bow. If she passes by the stern of the overtaken vessel, then she might say the overtaken vessel is not to be allowed to slacken her speed, because that shortens the distance. And if she intended to cross the bow, she might say the overtaken vessel is not to be allowed to increase her speed, because that lessens the distance.

In the first of these cases, where the overtaking vessel intends to pass by the stern of the overtaken vessel, I say what reason should there be, unless there is some particular reason given by circumstances—for example, the reason that the overtaken vessel has to take a pilot on board—for the overtaken vessel to slacken her speed. There is no reason for it whatever, and if there is any reason, then there must be a good reason, and the overtaking vessel ought to take into consideration that there might be some such reason, and therefore there is no reason why the overtaking vessel in such a case should claim this privilege, and impose this duty on the other vessel: that this other vessel is not to be allowed to slacken her speed; because you must consider that there may be instances which make it necessary for the other vessel to slacken her speed, and therefore she ought not to be so close to the other vessel that to slacken the speed of the overtaken vessel would have any effect upon the risk of collision.

Now take the other case, where the overtaking vessel intends to cross the bow of the overtaken vessel. That would, under any circumstances, be a very dangerous manœuvre, and I do not think that we ought to favour such a manœuvre. The Conference has already expressed its opinion clearly about it by establishing the general principle that a vessel is not to cross the bow of another vessel, and especially in the case of overtaking vessels. Certainly, an overtaking vessel ought not to be allowed to race, if I may be allowed to use this expression, with the vessel before her in such a way that she attempts to cross her bow, but she should, under all circumstances, pass under her stern.

Now, it may be said that there may be circumstances where she cannot do so. What circumstances? Another vessel is in the way. Then I say it is much more correct and according to justice to say—let the overtaking vessel wait until that danger of collision is past. Let her slow down and widen the distance until she can get clear of the other vessel or of the obstruction which is in the way, and pass under the stern of the vessel which is before her. I think that would not be demanding too much. I think the present Rule would impose on the overtaken vessel a duty which would not be in harmony with justice, and would give too great a facility to the overtaking vessel. Therefore, in my opinion, this case cannot be brought forward in order to oppose this amendment. The other cases, as I mentioned before, are very strong in favour of the amendment. Now, it might be said that, by the general rules of ordinary seamanship, the Court might arrive at a reasonable solution of the problem, and reach a decision in such cases which is in harmony with justice; still we thought it would be better to try and frame the Law in a good and sufficient way, and in a just way, rather than leave it to the ambiguities and doubts of Law Courts, and to the common sense of Judges, to construe the Law in a way which is, in some cases certainly, the very opposite of the wording of the Law as it stands.

Mr. Hall (Great Britain).—Mr. President, I regret that we are unable to accept the amendment which has been proposed by the learned Delegate of Germany, and I will state, as briefly as I possibly can, the reasons which have induced us to come to this determination. The learned Delegate has stated that this Rule is incompatible with common sense, and that it is desirable to steer clear of the ambiguity of the Law Courts. I will point out to the members of the Conference in a very few minutes that his amendment is open to the same ambiguity, and, if the original Rule is incompatible with common sense, so is his amendment. I will tell him why that is. But before I proceed to deal with his example of a vessel slowing to take a pilot on board and a vessel coming to anchor, I will call his attention to this fact. He has only cited exceptional cases. As to that, I will say, What is the use of the general Article, referring to special circumstances, unless it is to apply to such cases?

But before I come to these cases, may I point out, first of all, what the argument was in favour of this Rule, and why it was adopted? I venture to say that the strongest argument in favour of this Rule was the argument advanced by the Delegates from the United States—that there was a considerable difference of opinion, not only among sailors, but among lawyers and in the judicial decisions of the Maritime Powers, as to whether the words, "shall keep her course," mean "shall keep her course and speed," or not. That was the first point and the main point, I think, which was before us. It was argued thoroughly, and I confess that the illustrations I took principally were from the case of crossing vessels. It was argued that it was a good thing that a vessel should keep her speed. I also pointed out that I thought this was most important, having regard to the decisions in our Court, that the words "shall keep her course" did not mean "keep her speed." I also pointed out that we should put in these words so as to make it absolutely clear, not only to the sailors, but to the Courts, what was intended. I venture to say that that was the main reason which actuated the Conference in coming to this conclusion. I think the idea was this: to frame a general Rule that all vessels should keep their course and speed.

What would happen if you put in the words suggested by the learned Delegate from Germany?

You would emphasize it that a crossing vessel is to keep her course and speed, and the sailor would say, when he was on a crossing vessel: "I am bound to keep my speed at all hazards." I think you will find that the words in this amendment will emphasize it in such a way that a sailor may fairly say: "Crossing vessels are not merely to keep their course, but are to keep their speed, and therefore I am bound to keep my speed at all hazards." But, if we put it in a general Rule that they are to keep their course and speed, sailors, of course, will be influenced by the special circumstances of the case.

Now, what are the reasons given for confining this Rule to crossing vessels? There are only two which have been brought forward by the learned Delegate from Germany. There is a case of a vessel stopping for some purpose, like taking a pilot, and the second is a vessel going into a harbour. Now, it is said that this is a Rule which is incompatible with common sense. May I ask the attention of the learned Delegate from Germany on this point? If it is incompatible with common sense as it is applied now, why is it not incompatible with common sense as applied to crossing vessels, for a crossing vessel that is entitled to the right of way may want to stop and take a pilot on board. But, according to my friend's argument, he cannot stop, he is bound to go on and keep his course and speed. Now, a crossing vessel may be a holding-on vessel, and she may want to go into a harbour, or to drop her anchor, or to take a pilot, but, according to my learned friend's argument, she is not entitled to do so. She must keep on until the other vessel has gone by.

Now, I say, with great deference to the opinion of my learned friend, why does not exactly the same argument apply to crossing vessels as to an overtaken vessel, with regard to these two exceptional cases? If the Rule is to be construed hard and fast, and no attention is to be paid to the general Article for special circumstances, then I quite agree with him that a crossing vessel is bound to keep her speed. She is bound to go on until the other vessel gets out of the way, and she is not entitled to stop for a pilot nor to go into a harbour. But does any one believe for a moment that a rational seaman, if he wants to stop and take a pilot on board, will not take good care to notify the vessel behind him that he wants to stop and take up a pilot. Has any one any doubt that it would be gross negligence on the part of the overtaking vessel if she had such a bad look-out that she did not see that it was necessary for the vessel in front of her to slow or stop, in order to take a pilot on board? You may just as well say that the overtaking vessel would be justified in saying to the vessel in front: "You are obliged to keep your course, although you see you are running straight into a wreck. You are not allowed to alter your course."

Now, you cannot frame Rules to meet every possible circumstance. Let me take the ordinary case of an overtaking vessel, if there were no rule like this at all. There is no doubt that, *primâ facie*, when a vessel has got another vessel astern, she would be very much to blame if she suddenly stopped, Rule or no Rule. It, of course, does not want a Rule to tell us that. It is the ordinary common law. Take the case of a cabman driving up the street. Is he entitled to stop his cab suddenly when an omnibus is coming behind him? My learned friend shakes his head, but I venture to think that is a very good illustration. It is the common law of the land. A man is not entitled to block the way of any vehicle. A vessel under way must give some signal if she wants to stop, and every true seaman would do it. If so, I must confess I do not see why we should attempt to frame a special Rule to meet such circumstances. I have now dealt with the question of the pilot-vessel.

My learned friend says that a steamer is bound to go on if she is an overtaken vessel; she cannot stop for a pilot-boat; but I venture to say that the general Rule would apply there. Let me point this out. The only two illustrations which my learned friend has given to us are the cases of a pilot-vessel and of a vessel going into a harbour. And they are illustrations of themselves which would occur in such a place or in such a position that the other vessel would be near enough to watch and to see whether they were going to take up a pilot or whether they were going into a harbour. There is no possible suggestion that out in the open sea there is any difficulty with regard to this Rule. As I say, what we want is a general Rule. Sailors will understand, under this general Rule, that they are to keep their course and speed, and not merely their course. Whereas, if we insert these words proposed by the learned Delegate from Germany, you emphasize it, and you tell the holding-on crossing ships that they are to keep their course and speed, which would look as if it were a general order to them that, come what will, they are to keep their speed. That is, in my opinion, the result which would ensue from emphasizing the Rule in this way with regard to one particular vessel, instead of laying down a general Rule relating to all vessels which are to keep their course, and are also to keep their speed.

As I said before, I think one of the strongest arguments in favour of this Rule is to clear up the existing doubt which there is in the minds of many sailors and of many lawyers as to what the best meaning of the old Rule "keep your course," is. We have agreed that it is to "keep your course and speed," and, therefore, we have added the words "and speed." And I venture to think that, having come to that conclusion, and having been influenced greatly by that argument, we should be unwise if we were now to whittle the Rule down in such a way that every sailor would say, when he was on a crossing vessel, "I must keep my course and speed, come what will."

Mr. Goodrich (United States).—Mr. President, after the very careful and learned exposition of these two Delegates *pro* and *con* upon this subject it would be hardly necessary to add another word; but yet there is still a third point which had great influence in the passing of this amendment as originally proposed by the learned Delegate of Great Britain. That point was one which has had great weight with the Conference throughout all its deliberations upon this and cognate Rules, that the vessel which has the privilege, which has the right of way given to her by positive enactment, should advise her adversary exactly, as far as she may do, as to her position, intention, course, and speed. It is very easy if you meet a man in the street, if he positively and unhesitatingly and absolutely indicates his course, to avoid him, but if he hesitates and varies his course and turns to the left when he should turn to the right, then confusion exists. Now, what is the privilege given here not only to the overtaken vessel but to the privileged vessel as between crossing vessels? It is that, having that privilege, they shall not bother their adversary. Take a current like that of Hell Gate, especially before the obstructions were partially removed, and collisions occurred very frequently by reason of the uncertain course and speed of the vessel which was being overtaken. I know that in some cases it is very important that the overtaken vessel should keep her speed, and it is sometimes even more important than as between two crossing vessels. Let the overtaken vessel keep her course and speed, and her adversary or the following vessel can manoeuvre with safety.

The difficulty with this amendment of my learned friend the Delegate from Germany is that it limits the Rule. Why should the Rule be limited? There was no argument before us which showed the difference between the two cases, as suggested by the learned Delegate from Germany; and I am free to say that his very able expression of his views on this subject has not changed my opinion. Now, take the case, for instance, of a vessel wanting to stop. That may occur sometimes to an overtaken vessel which wants to stop. The law provides a signal for her. The twenty-ninth Rule says that she may give three signals indicating, "My engines are going full speed astern." The twenty-eighth Rule, as we have now adopted it, provides for special and extraordinary circumstances, which justify her in stopping and in altering her course either to starboard or to port. The overtaking vessel can easily see that alteration or the intention to take that course.

It seems to me further, Gentlemen of the Conference, that it is easier for the overtaking vessel to see the alteration, or proposed alteration, if you choose, in the course of the overtaken vessel than it is for the burdened vessel to see the intended alteration on the part of the crossing vessel, for this reason: the overtaking vessel has the overtaken vessel nearly, if not absolutely, ahead of her, and the slightest deviation of the overtaken vessel from her course is more instantly seen than is the case with the two crossing vessels, because the lines of the crossing vessels are not the same, or not parallel. These are circumstances which, it seems to me, render it advisable to leave this Rule in its broad character.

Let me go a little further, and make an additional suggestion to the one so ably pointed out by the Delegate from Great Britain in regard to the construction of this Rule by the Courts. It is undoubtedly true that the deliberations of this Conference and the contents of the Protocol are going o be regarded by the Admiralty Courts, flexible as they are, in the consideration of the Rules. I do not know what the learned Court in Germany will do, but I think I can say what the Court in the United States will do. That is my judgment absolutely and positively, from previous experience, as to what will be done by the Courts of Admiralty here. The Courts of Admiralty will refer to these Protocols for a judgment as to what the Conference meant by the Rules, and will see in the Protocols this state of things as to this Rule; first, the old Rule, second, the Rule as proposed by the Delegates of Great Britain and passed by the Conference, and, third, the amendment as suggested by the Delegate from Germany; and if it should pass, the fact that the Rule, as proposed by the Delegate from Great Britain, has been amended. Then comes the difficulty which was so clearly pointed out by the learned Delegate of Great Britain, that the action of the Rule and the force of the Rule are limited, and the duty is emphasized on the crossing vessel to keep her course and speed, and that duty is not put with equal force upon an overtaken vessel. These are difficulties which suggest themselves to my mind in regard to any change in the Rule, especially as it was so carefully considered in the previous deliberation of the Conference.

Dr. Sieveking (Germany).—Mr. President, allow me only a few remarks in reply. First, as to the remark of the learned Delegate from the United States as to the Protocol, and as to the interpretation of the Rules by the Protocol. Let us not attach too great importance to that. I am sure the Courts of Great Britain and the Judges would rule at once, when there is an ambiguity in the Rules, that the Protocols are not admissible evidence. The Courts of Germany, and I am also sure the Courts of the United States, would consider that the Rules derive their legal force not from what was meant by the Conference, but from what was meant by the legislative authority itself, that published the Rules and commanded its subjects to obey them. Can we expect that the legislative authorities of twenty-six countries here represented will not only read the Protocol, but carefully consider it, and will also be of the opinion that whatever is laid down in the Protocol as the meaning of the Conference is the true interpretation of the Rule?

I will now address a few remarks in reply to my learned friend the Delegate of Great Britain. He said it was the intention of their amendment to make clear what up to this time had been doubtful. He stated that the old Rule of keeping her course was considered to be doubtful and ambiguous as to whether it included course and speed or not. I do not think it ever was ambiguous. There are very clear decisions on this point that "course" does not include "speed" in England, because I take it——

Mr. Hall (Great Britain).—Mr. President, if the learned Delegate will pardon me, I will simply point out that I said there was a conflict of opinion between the Courts of Great Britain and the Courts of other Powers. We were told by the learned Delegate of the United States that it was held in a case in Pennsylvania that "keep her course" meant "keep her speed" also.

Dr. Sieveking (Germany).—Mr. President, of course there will always be some decision which will cast doubts upon that which is already well settled, but I think that the decisions of the Courts of Great Britain settle the question. There could not be any such mistake as this where the wording is clear. Now, it seems to me that the learned First Delegate from Great Britain has gotten a little afraid of his own Rule and the consequences of it, because he says we ought not to emphasize it as we would do if we accepted this amendment. Why not emphasize the Rule if the Rule is correct. Put it quite clear, and put it beyond all doubt. Do not leave any ambiguity with regard to it? But they say, it is better to leave the case a little in the dark. It is not so certain that we are right. There may be circumstances which would change our opinion. Do not emphasize it too much.

Now I should be very glad if the whole Rule had not been passed, but, as it has been, let us stand by it, and let us all say it is a just Rule, and it ought to be strictly adhered to, because I think the main principle of the Sailing Rules is that they ought to be clear to every sailor of the commonest understanding, and so that we could say: "These are the Rules you are to be guided by; you must adhere strictly to them." And I think the Rules must be framed so as to bear such an interpretation. It has been said against the amendment that crossing vessels may be quite in the same position as an overtaken vessel. If that were clear it would only imply that the Rule was bad for crossing vessels also. But I do not think that it is true, because there is a great difference between crossing vessels and overtaking vessels. The risk of collision between crossing vessels is determined in a very short time, and the risk of collisions between an overtaking vessel and an overtaken vessel may occupy a much longer time. That is quite clear, because the overtaking vessel wants a certain time, even if she is the faster vessel, to get clear of the overtaken vessel, and the risk of collision, according to the Rule which we have laid down, is only to be considered to be determined after the vessels are quite clear of one another.

I would not hesitate to say that crossing vessels ought to keep their speed even under the circumstance which I have mentioned when they intend to take a pilot on board. When these circumstances coincide with other circumstances, and at the same time there is risk of collision between the vessels, then they should not be allowed, by the Rule, to slacken. It is said here they are to be allowed to slow, but they must give a warning. But you see that has nothing to do with the amendment, and it is not an argument against the amendment, for this reason: if you say the overtaken vessel under such circumstances is allowed to depart from the Rule if she gives the warning, then you do not in the least alter the correctness of my statement that the Rule is not as good and just a Rule for all circumstances as it should be, and that is what we ought to try to make it. Then take the example of a man or of a carriage in the street, which has several times been referred to by the Delegate from Great Britain and the Delegate from the United States. Now I ask you to take the same example. You are out for a quiet walk in the street and you stop for some reason, whatever the reason may be. There is somebody coming behind you and he runs against your back. What would you say? Are you wrong, or is he wrong? I think the man is wrong that has run into your back, because we certainly must be allowed to stop for whatever reason we like when we are walking in the street. There may be many reasons for it; and has the man who walks on the street any right to ask for my reason? I do not think that he has; but he must walk in such a way as not to incommode any other man who is walking before him, even if this man wants to stop. That is only his legal right. Finally, it has been mentioned by the learned Delegate from the United States that this Rule has been introduced in order to give certainty, and in order to prevent the vessel which has got a privilege from manœuvring as she likes, and to prevent her from going from one side to the other. I need not say that these are cases which are entirely different. Changing her course falls under the old Rule, so that it is now only a question of changing her "speed." I must say that I do not think anything material has been brought against the amendment.

Mr. Verney (Siam).—Mr. President, may I make a few observations on this Rule? I think that if it is not passed, and it probably will not pass, and the learned Delegate from Germany and myself will be outvoted, there is one consolation we will have, and that is that there is a glorious ambiguity in this Rule as proposed which renders it entirely nugatory. The words, "keep her course," have long ago been decided to mean keep the course which a vessel is pursuing, exactly as if the other vessel were not in sight, and now she may also keep her speed as if the other vessel were not in sight. If she had intended to maintain the same course as when the risk of collision first began, then, no doubt, the learned Delegate from Great Britain would have so worded the Rule.

I cannot help thinking that there is lurking in the breast of the learned Delegate from Great Britain a consolation which he is going to offer hereafter. "Keep her course and speed" sounds extremely clear; but, in reality, I think it will be acknowledged by everybody who happens to read at the top of p. 415 in Marsden, that the words, "keep her course and speed," are extremely ambiguous under the decisions which are given to us in our English Law Courts. Therefore, I hope that if we are outvoted in this matter we shall have some consolation given us, and that not so much harm has been done as we anticipated. I venture to think that the old Rule is far the best, and that the old Rule, taken in connection with the old Article 23, meets every possible circumstance which it was necessary to meet. I have read over the Protocol very carefully, and have tried to follow with great care the arguments which have been delivered this morning. Of course, it is very bold for a man to get up and say so after this has been adopted by the Conference, but I venture to think that the old Rule is by far the best.

Mr. Hall (Great Britain).—Mr. President, perhaps I may follow the Delegate from Siam, in consequence of the startling statement which he has made with regard to the state of the English law. He says that we ought to read at the top of some page of a text-book upon the point, and that we would have been perfectly clear about it. But, Mr. President, there is no doubt whatever what the law is, and it is exactly contrary to what the Delegate from Siam has stated. If he will have the goodness to turn to the case of the "Beryl," he will see that the words, "keep her course," did not include "keep her speed," and that a vessel was held to blame for keeping her speed, although she justified it under that Rule. If he will look at the case of the "Beryl" he will find——

Mr. Verney (Siam).—I have read the whole of it.

Mr. Hall (Great Britain).—Mr. President, then I confess I am at a loss to understand how the learned counsel can say that the Rule as it stands is perfectly clear, that it means a vessel is to "keep her course and speed."

Mr. Verney (Siam).—Mr. President, I was not reading from a text-book at all. The text-book refers to the dictum of a learned Judge, which says that for a vessel to continue her course means that she is to continue the course she was pursuing, just as if the other vessel was not in sight. Now you insert the words "and speed," and you put them both together. How can it be argued the word "keep" does not mean the same thing when applied to "speed" as well as to "course"? If a vessel is to keep the same course as if the other vessel was not in sight, it is exactly the same thing, and she has to keep the same speed as if the other vessel was not in sight. The case of the "Beryl" has got

[93]

nothing to do with it. The case of the "Beryl" is an entirely different case, which I read through very carefully some weeks ago, and which I quoted from in connection with another matter. I venture to say that the Collocation Committee may do worse than to look into these words and see what they mean. I say once again that I believe the old Rule was much the best one, and that the old Rule, in connection with the old 23rd Rule, gave us all that we wanted. I have heard that said by sailors over and over again. I say that this wording is extremely unfortunate. It creates an ambiguity which did not exist before.

Mr. Hall (Great Britain).—Mr. President, I gave way to my learned friend the Delegate from Siam because he wished to correct me as to a statement of fact. He has now given us a second speech. I cannot sit here in silence and hear the Conference told that a point is perfectly clear, and it is impossible to conceive how anybody could argue that the word "course" does not include "speed." That point was decided in the case of the "Beryl," and the counsel who argued that the words, "keep her course," meant also "keep her speed," cited the case of the "Velocity." But the Courts distinctly decided that the words, "keep her course," did not include "keep her speed," and that, therefore, she was wrong in "keeping her speed." The "Beryl" was held to blame. I was counsel in the case myself. The "Beryl" was held to blame because she, being a crossing vessel, kept her speed as well as her course, because the master on board said he thought the Rule meant that he was to keep his course and speed. There is no doubt whatever of this fact.

Therefore, I cannot agree with the learned Delegate from Siam, who cannot conceive how it is possible to argue that the word "course" does not include "speed," because the Courts have decided the other way. I only rose because I thought it right that a statement as to what the English law was, which is made here, and to which I am unable to assent, should not be allowed to go uncontradicted; and I thought it my duty to point out that the Courts have decided an entirely different way. I have only one more remark to make. I want to quiet the apprehensions of my learned friend the Delegate from Germany. I can assure him that, so far as we are concerned, we are not in the condition which he has pictured. We may be in the dark, but we do not feel that we are in the dark at all about this. He assumed that we were a little bit afraid of this Rule, but I can assure him that we are not afraid of it at all. But we want it passed in its entirety, and not whittled away.

Mr. Goodrich (United States).—Mr. President, I think the illustration given by the learned Delegate from Germany in regard to a man stopping in the street is the best illustration of the necessity of applying this Rule to an overtaken vessel as well as to a crossing vessel. His question was what would be said by one of two men where one of them suddenly stopped in the street and another man ran into his back. My impression is that a very strong remark would follow from the man who ran into the other's back. He would say: "You fool! Why did you stop in a crowded fairway?" If that is true, the absolute necessity of applying this Rule as it is presented by the English Delegate to an overtaken vessel is pointed out by that little incident. Let me still insist upon the point which I made a few moments ago, because I deem it very important for many countries that this amendment shall not be passed, for I believe that the Courts of the United States will refer to the Protocol to ascertain the intention of the Conference in suggesting this Rule; although I know it is a little different from the ordinary discussions in legislative bodies upon a Statute, for the reason that the ultimate source of power upon these Rules is conferred by the Legislatures of the several Powers.

I have in my mind now a case upon which I base my assertion. When the Constitutions of the several States and of the United States were passed, there were Conventions in which the principles of the Constitutions were very carefully discussed. These discussions were embodied in Reports. These Reports are referred to to-day by the Courts in order to ascertain the intention of the framers of the Constitution under a particular sentence, or in a particular paragraph. The same Rule prevails with regard to the Code of the State of New York. The proceedings of the Legislature which passed that Code are continually referred to, and have for many years been referred to by the Courts to know what construction was put upon a particular sentence, and see what was intended by the Legislature which passed it; so that I do see a difficulty if any change is made here that the Courts will refer to the Protocol to understand what the Delegates meant, and what the Conference meant in making the change from the Rule they had already passed and change it into an entirely different one, limiting its force in one case, whereas it originally related to all cases of collision.

Admiral Kaznakoff (Russia).—Mr. President, we have had the pleasure of seeing our lawyers breaking their lances with one another, and it was a very agreeable sight. We thank them very much for the information they have given us; but what is the sailor thinking of? He is thinking how he will follow out that Rule. In my opinion it is better not to adopt this amendment; therefore I will vote against it.

Captain Mensing (Germany).—Mr. President, I am very glad indeed that the legal explanation which has been given us by the learned Delegates has been interrupted by the gallant Delegate from Russia. I believe that this question is an eminently practical one. I do not believe that in the decision of a Court composed of sailors there would be the slightest doubt as to the meaning of this Rule. With all due deference to the legal talent around here, and with the very great respect which I feel for what has been done by the Admiralty Courts of Great Britain, I do not know whether the meaning is not sometimes above the comprehension of ordinary mortals.

I remember a case that was brought up here, in which we were told that a ship which had to keep her course might in all other respects act exactly as she wished; that she might, even if by so doing she brought about a collision or was likely to do so, reverse, or stop, or do anything that she chose. We have been told that here. But I wish to be corrected if I am wrong when I say that no rational sailor would act as these learned lawyers have been instructing Courts to act with regard to this matter. I am not a lawyer, but I believe that this question will be correctly decided whenever the case comes up; and I am sure that if we knew that the distinguished First Delegate from England would have the case we would know how he would decide it. I wish that this point could be made clear to the sailors. We must remember that these men have got to go to sea, and that they have nothing to guide them but their common sense and these Rules. They have no time to discuss these things; they may not have time even to talk them over with their friends. Now, when they are out at sea they study these Regulations and these Rules, and they put such sense into them as they think is right. We have been told that the Rule should be taken in its broad sense. I should be very sorry if we were to adopt that. The sailor would say that he has asked us a clear question, and he wants to have a clear answer.

If I am not mistaken, I think the learned Delegate from the United States said that he thought it was a most dangerous thing for an overtaken ship to alter her speed. There is a conflict of opinion, as I take it, between the learned Delegate from the United States and the learned Delegate from Great Britain. One says, "Why, nobody thinks of putting this thing on an overtaken vessel." And the learned Delegate from the United States wants to keep this Rule as it stands now, because it seems to him that it is better that an overtaken vessel shall keep her speed. As my distinguished colleague has already pointed out, in crossing ships or in meeting ships the time when risk of collision occurs is short. The risk is passed, maybe, in two or three minutes. An overtaken ship takes a quarter of an hour. You will see that for a difference of speed of 4 miles it will take a quarter of an hour for the other ship to come up with her. These are practical points as I see them. As I say, I may have misunderstood the learned Delegate from the United States, but I certainly understood him to say that as the law stands now an overtaken ship must keep her course except under extraordinary circumstances. As a sailor I would say that I do not consider the stopping to take a pilot on board as an extraordinary circumstance, and I do not know whether old Article 23 could be taken into consideration in such a case.

Captain Malmberg (Sweden).—Mr. President, I have only a short remark to make about what has been said about an overtaken vessel. If you are in a fairway, and have ahead of you a steamer going at certain speed, the overtaking steamer can ascertain with certainty where she will be able to pass the overtaken steamer, but if the overtaken steamer suddenly slackens her speed, the overtaking steamer will thereby be led into great difficulty, if not into collision with the overtaken steamer. I hope, therefore, that this amendment will not be adopted by the Conference.

Mr. Flood (Norway).—Mr. President, may I, as a practical merchant sailor, say a few words on this subject? When the old Article 2 was altered, or rather when these words, "and speed," were added to the Rules, I had very great doubt whether they would work well. I may be excused for having those doubts, as I have manœuvred and navigated under the old Rule for over twenty years, and I have been nearly fifteen years an insurance agent, so I should be well versed in a good many cases; and yet I have never heard of anybody misconstruing the old Rule. But when the words, "and speed," were put into the Rule, I, of course, loyally bowed to it, and hoped that it would be a good addition to the Rules. But from what I have heard here to-day I am still more in doubt than I was at that time. I understood then and understand now that it was simply to be in circumstances where vessels were actually crossing each other; but as soon as I saw this amendment put forth by the German Delegate I thought it a very good thing to emphasize the fact that this "keeping her speed" only referred to crossing vessels. This has been so ably pointed out by the German Delegate that it will be unnecessary for me to further recommend this amendment.

I will only take the liberty to remind you of one fact more. When a vessel is overtaken by another, the crossing of these two ships will generally be less at a right angle, it will be in a slanting direction. The overtaking vessel will likely pass the other vessel to windward, and in doing so she will take away the wind from the overtaken ship's sails. First, she will take away the wind from her aftersails and she will bear off a little, and that will likely increase her speed if she is going by the wind. That is not so dangerous; but a few minutes afterwards the overtaking vessel will pass ahead and take away the wind from her foresails and the overtaken vessel will invariably fly up in the wind. This is a very difficult and dangerous position even in the open sea. I have repeatedly been under these circumstances. I think it, therefore, quite a necessary point to emphasize that this Rule must be applied when ships are crossing. I can for my part, from my personal experience, strongly recommend that this amendment be adopted by the Conference.

Mr. Goodrich (United States).—Mr. President, may I ask the gallant Delegate from Norway whether he believes the Courts would hold an overtaken vessel responsible for not keeping her speed when an overtaking vessel had taken away the wind from her and thus compelled her to slack up?

Mr. Hall (Great Britain).—Mr. President, I only want to point out this with regard to what has fallen from the gallant Delegate from Norway. He has reminded us to-day, as he has done on previous occasions, of his personal experience as having commanded sailing-vessels. But I am sure that I need not to remind him that a great many of the Delegates here have done the same thing. My gallant colleague here has commanded sailing-vessels, and the honourable Delegate who sits behind me has commanded merchant-vessels all his life, sailing-vessels as well as steamers: so that we have amongst us those who have also had great experience on board of sailing-vessels, and they differ from his views.

Captain Mensing (Germany).—Mr. President, I would be glad if the learned Delegate from the United States would answer my question. I would also like to refer to what Captain Malmberg has said. He has pointed out that this Rule here prescribes that a vessel should keep her speed. I have nothing to say against that, if that Rule should be made good. If it is the will of the Conference that the overtaken vessel shall keep her speed just as the crossing vessel, then let us say so. I only wish that this matter be made clear, and I hope that the able gentlemen of the law will so frame the Rule that it shall be clear, and that we shall know whether they really do believe that an overtaken vessel ought to keep her speed just as much as a crossing vessel.

Mr. Goodrich (United States).—Mr. President, may I ask the gallant Delegate from Germany what question he wants me to answer?

Captain Mensing (Germany).—Mr. President, whether in his opinion it is advisable for an overtaken vessel to keep her speed under all circumstances?

Mr. Goodrich (United States).—Mr. President, certainly not. But the 28th Rule, as we have adopted it, provides for that, especially when we have put in the words, "and collision," in addition to the Rule as it stood before. When my gallant friend the Delegate from Germany suggests that there was a difference of opinion between the Delegate from Great Britain and myself, I beg most respectfully to say to him that, with all the diligence of which I am capable, I have been endeavouring to find out what that difference is, and I fail to see any difference in his statement of the law and mine. If there should be any difference I bow with great deference to the large experience and learning of the First Delegate from Great Britain; but I do not see any difference of opinion. This may be what the Delegate refers to. I said in the discussion of this question at an earlier stage of the Conference that the Courts of Great Britain and one of the Courts of the United States were not in harmony upon this question. The learned Delegate from Great Britain referred to the case which I had in my mind a few moments ago. There is still another case where that question arises. The amendment suggested by the learned Delegate of Great Britain, and passed by this Conference, removes that lack of harmony. That lack of harmony being removed by the action which we have taken, do not let us throw the apple of discord into the arena again.

Mr. Flood (Norway).—Mr. President, the learned Delegate of the United States asked me awhile ago what I thought the Courts would do with the case which I mentioned where one vessel took the wind away from the other. At that time I did not think of the sailor's purgatory on earth, the Court, but when he mentions the Law Courts, I will say that I have heard so much swearing both ways that it is impossible to tell what to expect: I have had thirteen witnesses swearing one way and seven another, swearing right against each other in a collision case, and I have noticed that that has happened repeatedly. So I think the best way is to form our Rules so that we can avoid getting into the Courts. In regard to what the learned First Delegate of Great Britain has said, that there are a great many practical sailors present, I of course do not doubt that. I only wish that these practical sailors would speak for themselves and tell us their opinion. I should be very glad to be guided by their opinion.

Captain Sampson (United States).—Mr. President, I hope we can get a vote now.

The President.—Is the Conference ready for the question? The Secretary will please read the amendment.

Amendment No. 27 is as follows:—

"Amendment to Collocation Report proposed by Dr. Sieveking on behalf of the German Delegation, 14th December, 1889:

"In Article 21, instead of the words, 'and speed,' insert the words, 'and where one of two crossing vessels is to keep out of the way, the other shall keep her course and speed.'"

Dr. Sieveking (Germany).—Mr. President, I will call for the Yeas and Nays, if you please.

Mr. Flood (Norway).—Mr. President, before calling for the Yeas and Nays, may I be allowed to say that unfortunately my gallant colleague Captain Salvesen does not agree with me, so that Norway cannot vote on this matter?

The President.—The Yeas and Nays will be called. The Secretary will please call the roll.

The Yea and Nay vote is as follows:—

Austria-Hungary	... Nay.	Italy	...	... Nay.
Brazil	... Nay.	Japan	...	... Nay.
Belgium	... Nay.	Mexico	...	... Nay.
China	... Nay.	Norway	...	Did not vote.
Chile	... Nay.	Russia	...	... Nay.
Denmark	... Nay.	Spain	...	Did not vote.
France	... Nay.	Sweden	...	... Nay.
Germany	... Yea.	Siam	...	... Yea.
Great Britain	... Nay.	The Netherlands	...	... Nay.
Hawaii	... Nay.	United States	...	... Nay.

The President.—The vote stands 2 in the affirmative, and 16 in the negative, and two Powers did not vote. The amendment is lost.

Mr. Goodrich (United States).—Mr. President, before we come to the consideration of the next amendment I am going to ask the indulgence of the Conference to make one or two verbal alterations at the request of the Collocation Committee. We desire this in order that we may have our corrections of the Rules ready for the printer as quick as possible. On p. 4, Article 4, in the third line, the words, "in place of," are used, and in other parts of the Rules we have used the words, "in lieu of." That is a mere verbal correction. We are following out our principle of using the same words to express the same idea, and if we can have the unanimous consent of the Conference to make that amendment we shall be very much pleased. You will find a similar instance on p. 7, in subdivision 3, in the last line but one.

Mr. Flood (Norway).—Mr. President, may I propose "instead of" in place of "in lieu of."

Mr. Goodrich (United States).—Mr. President, perhaps some member of the Collocation Committee can tell me where these other words are.

The President.—The Delegate from Norway proposes "instead of" in place of "in lieu of."

Mr. Hall (Great Britain).—Mr. President, I think we adopted those words because the words, "in lieu of," are used in the old Rule, and we thought it better to adhere to the words used in the old Rule instead of putting in new words.

Mr. Goodrich (United States).—Mr. President, does the Delegate from Norway insist on this change?

Mr. Flood (Norway).—No, Sir; I do not.

Mr. Goodrich (United States).—Mr. President, then I ask unanimous consent to have the words, " in lieu of," instead of the words, " in place of," or, in other words, to substitute the word " lieu " for " place." Another suggestion which we have to make is on p. 6.

Captain Shackford (United States).—Mr. President, I would like to have these words, " in lieu of," changed to " instead of." I do not believe many sailors will know what the word " lieu " means.

Mr. Goodrich (United States).—You said a while ago that we must believe the sailors were men of common sense.

Captain Shackford (United States).—Mr. President, the sailor may be a man of common sense and yet not understand French.

Mr. Hall (Great Britain).—Mr. President, may I point out that these words have been in the Rules since 1863, and I do not know that there has ever been any doubt expressed as to what they mean.

Mr. Goodrich (United States).—Mr. President, may I call attention to the fact that on p. 6, in Article 7, we have made the amendment of yesterday as to small steam-boats, in subsection 2, making the present second paragraph, paragraph 3. Also in the amendment of yesterday proposed by the gallant Delegate of Italy, which will come in on p. 7, about vessels in the Mediterranean Sea. It reads: " In the Mediterranean Sea all vessels referred to in subsection (*b*) 2 may show the flare-up light instead of the pyrotechnic light." We want to change the words, " instead of," to " in lieu of," following up the suggestion which has just been made. The change follows from the assent of the Conference to the other change. On p. 8, Article 11, the Conference took out the words, " in a globular lantern of not less than 8 inches in diameter." It now reads, " a white light of such character." Unless an objection is made we will assume that it is the desire of the Conference that this change should be made. On p. 11——

Mr Hall (Great Britain).—Mr. President, before my learned friend goes on there is a word " Rules " and " Regulations " in Article 12 and in the note on p. 9. It should be " Rules " instead of " Regulations." We always use the word " Rules."

Mr. Goodrich (United States).—Mr. President, at the bottom of p. 9, in a note, the word " Regulations " should be " Rules." On p. 11, Article 23, the word " that " should be " which." Does the learned Delegate from Great Britain think we ought to speak of that amendment under Article 18 now, or after the discussion of the Committee on Collocation ?

Mr. Hall (Great Britain).—Mr. President, after the collocation discussion.

Mr. Goodrich (United States).—Mr. President, if the Conference will turn to p. 12, Article 26, they will find that it reads :—

" Sailing-vessels under way shall keep out of the way of sailing-vessels fishing with nets, lines, or trawls. In the daytime such mentioned vessels or boats, when under way, shall indicate their occupation by displaying a basket or other efficient signal where it can best be seen. But this Rule shall not give to any vessel or boat engaged in fishing the right of obstructing a fairway used by vessels other than fishing-vessels or boats."

We desire to transpose the paragraph commencing, " In the daytime," to Article 9, for the reason that such a course will put into Article 9 all of the Rules which refer to fishing-vessels. We should then read Article 26 as follows :—

" All vessels under way shall keep out of the way of sailing-vessels or boats fishing with nets, or lines, or trawls. But this Rule shall not give to any vessel or boat engaged in fishing the right of obstructing a fairway used by vessels other than fishing-vessels or boats."

In transposing this to Article 9 we have got to change the wording a little, so it will read as follows :—

" Sailing-vessels or boats fishing with nets, lines, or trawls, when under way, shall in daytime indicate their occupation to approaching vessels by displaying a basket or other efficient signal where it can best be seen."

The words, " to an approaching vessel," were put in simply for the reason that, in the Rule 26, the union of the two phrases indicates that the basket is only to be displayed when another vessel is approaching. If the Conference will consent to that proposition, the Collocation Committee will transpose that portion of the Rule to Article 9, and strike it out from Article 26.

Mr. Verbrugghe (Belgium).—Mr. President, may I thank the Chairman of the Committee on Collocation for having given effect to the suggestion which I had the honour to submit to him about this matter ?

The President.—If there should be no objections to these suggestions of the Chairman of the Collocation Committee, they will be accepted by the Conference. The Chair hears no objection, and they will be considered as accepted. The next amendment in order is amendment No. 28.

Admiral Viel (Chile).—Mr. President, I withdraw that amendment.

The President.—The Delegate from Chile desires to withdraw amendment No. 28. If there be no objection it will be withdrawn. The next amendment is No. 29, which the Secretary will please read.

Amendment No. 29 is as follows:—

"Amendment to Collocation Report, proposed by the Delegates for France:

"To eliminate Article 27 from the Regulations for preventing Collisions at Sea, and to add it to Appendix (B) of the Report as a Resolution recommended to the consideration of the Powers."

Captain Richard (France).—Mr. President, at a previous Session I explained to the Conference the technical reasons which led me to ask that Article 27, proposed by the British Delegates, should not be inserted into the Rules of the Road. I do not desire to renew this discussion, but I would ask the Conference to allow me to add a few additional reasons in regard to the disadvantages which would exist if this Article were left in the Rules of the Road. In proposing this I respectfully submit to the decision of the Committee, which disapproves of my proposition. I think that it would be well to submit this Article, before its adoption, to the consideration of our respective Governments, for the simple reason that it involves technical difficulties, the principal one of which, in my opinion, is that of delaying until the last moment the manœuvres which a war-vessel and a merchant-vessel should make to avoid a collision, which will take place when a merchant-vessel thinks it necessary to cross through a squadron which thinks that she is going to tack. The result of such manœuvres is that three-fourths of the time they necessarily lead to a collision.

From another standpoint I am afraid that, by adopting this Rule, this Conference will exceed its power, because it encroaches upon an international matter. It is impossible to give to war-vessels privileges of a similar nature unless all nations concur, because by so doing we go outside of the ordinary Rules, and we encroach upon international comity by granting to war-vessels a privilege which, when such vessels sail in squadrons, brings them under under international law. I know that war-vessels have already been given certain privileges, such as the right of search, and the right, when they are in a foreign port, to exercise police jurisdiction on board and to enjoy the sovereign rights of the State to which they belong. The right of way, as given by Article 27, seems to me of like character.

I believe that, with due regard to the decision of the Conference, we can (at least for the time being) eliminate this Article, which, in my mind, is a dangerous one, and ask that our Governments may pronounce their views in regard to the propriety of adopting it and introducing it into the Rules of the Road. Supposing one of our Governments should not adopt it, and all the others should agree to adopt it, then what would be the result? The Rules concerning lights on fishing-vessels (viz., Article 10) were not adopted at the same time with the other Rules, and the application of that Article did not enter into effect at the same time with the other Articles. Even now we are not entirely agreed in regard to the lights to be given to trawling-vessels, but this divergence of opinion upon the subject of lights for trawling-vessels is of but secondary importance, and the various Rules prescribed by different nations may be in operation at the same time without any serious difficulty; but can the same be said of Article 27? The nations which will not adopt it will allow their squadrons to be crossed by merchant-vessels of other nations, but they will claim the same favour for those of their nationality, and confusion will be increased. I therefore propose that the present Article 27 be stricken from the Rules of the Road, and placed in Appendix (B).

Mr. Hall (Great Britain).—Mr. President, as we had the honour of introducing this proposed Rule to the Conference, perhaps it is right that I should say a few words with regard to the position which we intend to take on this matter. We have considered very carefully the amendment of the gallant Delegate of France, and we think it desirable to support that amendment. We are of opinion that this is a most desirable Rule, but we recognize the fact that we ought not to introduce a Rule, and pass it, and stick to that Rule, against the wishes of the Powers represented in this Conference when it is on a perfectly new matter and a perfectly new principle. I think that we are entitled to hold to our opinion when it is a matter of an existing Rule or an improvement of an existing Rule; but we feel that we ought not to insist upon retaining this Rule merely because we have got a majority of the votes in favour of it, and endeavour to have it inserted in the Rules, however salutary we believe its effect may be. Therefore, we accede to the proposal of my gallant friend the Delegate of France to have it placed in Appendix (B), and we have firm hopes that the matter will be considered by the foreign Governments, and that they will come to our way of thinking when they have so considered it.

The President.—The question is upon the amendment of the Delegate of France.

The question was put to the Conference upon the adoption of amendment No. 29, and it was adopted.

Lieutenant Beaugency (Chile).—Mr. President, amendments Nos. 30 and 31, proposed by the Delegates for Chile, are about the squadron; and if the Conference intends to put that provision in Appendix (B), I wish that they may take this under consideration.

The President.—Does the Delegate withdraw his amendments?

Lieutenant Beaugency (Chile).—Yes, Sir.

The President.—Amendments Nos. 30 and 31 are withdrawn. The next amendment is amendment No. 32. The Secretary will please read it.

Amendment No. 32 is as follows:—

"Amendment to Collocation Report proposed by Captain Shackford (United States), 14th December, 1889:

"Article 29. Add following paragraph.

"'Whenever either the first two signals described are made by one of the vessels mentioned in this Article, the other must reply by sounding the same signal, in order that the vessel first signalling may know that the signal made has been heard and understood.'"

Captain Shackford (United States).—Mr. President, these signals under Article 27 having been made compulsory, it seems to me that it naturally follows that this amendment ought to pass. These signals are known as the American system, and have been in use in this country for about thirty years. The Law as it was originally passed, and as it continues now, reads in this way :—

"When steamers are approaching each other head and head, or nearly so, each shall pass to the right or port side of the other ; and the pilot of either steamer which may be first in determining to pursue this course thereupon shall give as a signal of his intention one short distinct blast on his steam-whistle, and the pilot of the other steamer shall answer promptly by a similar blast on his steam-whistle, and thereupon said steamers shall pass to the right or port side of each other."

This amendment is formally recommended by the Inspector-General of Steam-boats in this country, a man who has had a great many years' experience in these signals, and they are in universal use in this country in connection with the other signals. I do not think there is any doubt but that this amendment ought to pass now that we have made those signals compulsory.

Dr. Sieveking (Germany).—Mr. President, I think that we could not, under any circumstances, accept this amendment, and for this simple reason : endless confusion would ensue, and most disastrous confusion would be the consequence of adopting it. If one vessel communicates her intention by one short blast, it indicates that she is directing her course to starboard. The other vessel repeats the same signal by giving one short blast, and she would say, "I am directing my course to starboard." But now take the case of crossing vessels. One of the vessels is to keep her course, and is not allowed to deviate from her course unless under special circumstances. If she were to give this signal of one short blast, it would say, not, "I have heard what you have said," but it would say, "I am changing my course also." That, of course, could not be allowed. What has been said in support of this amendment refers only to vessels meeting end-on or nearly end-on. There, of course, it is quite right and quite acceptable, because vessels meeting end-on are "to put their helm so as to turn to starboard." You may make this even more complicated. Take the case where there are three or four vessels close to each other at the same time, and think what confusion would ensue if one vessel should give a short blast and the others should repeat it, each indicating by this blast that they are turning their helms to starboard. I think it is quite impossible for us to accept it.

Captain Shackford (United States).—Mr. President, I do not want to indulge in delightful personal reminiscences like the Delegate from Norway, but I should like to say that, after a good many years' experience with these whistles, and six years in the harbour of New York, I have never had any difficulty whatever with the confusion mentioned by the Delegate from Germany.

The President.—The question is upon the amendment of the Delegate from the United States. The Secretary will please read the amendment.

The amendment is as follows :—

"Amendment to Collocation Report proposed by Captain Shackford (United States), 14th December, 1889 :

"Article 29. Add following paragraph :

"'Whenever either of the first two signals described is made by one of the vessels mentioned in this Article, the other must reply by sounding the same signal, in order that the vessel first signalling may know that the signal made has been heard and understood.'"

The President.—Is the Conference ready for the question ?

The question was put to the Conference upon the adoption of the Amendment No. 32, and it was lost.

The President.—Amendment No. 33 is next in order.

Amendment No. 33 is as follows :—

"Amendment to Collocation Report proposed by Captain Sampson, 14th December, 1889 :

"Article 28. After 'of navigation,' in second line, omit the words, 'and collision.'"

Captain Sampson (United States).—Mr. President, after the discussion which took place yesterday morning upon the proposition of my colleague to insert the amendment suggested by the Delegate from Great Britain, I hesitate to defend the amendment which I have offered, because I have heard from the learned Delegate that these words, "and collision," are necessary in order to cover the case which they have in mind ; but to me it still appears that they are unnecessary in this Rule and misleading. The Rules which have heretofore been prescribed—the Steering and Sailing Rules—are intended to meet, and, as I believe, do meet, every possible case of vessels meeting. In whatever direction two vessels may be approaching each other, if the Steering and Sailing Rules which have been laid down are followed, no collision can result. But there are cases where these Rules cannot be applied, and this Article No. 28 is intended to cover those cases. There are two divisions of these cases. There are two sets of circumstances under which the Rules of the Road cannot be applied, and the first of these is when vessels are meeting and it becomes necessary for one of them to change her course to avoid a collision. But she is not required to do so if she thereby endangers herself, and the dangers which render the Rules inoperative are what are recognized as the dangers of navigation, that is, such dangers as are not provided for by the Steering and Sailing Rules, such dangers as shoals, rocks, wrecks, icebergs, or anything of that sort. If two or more vessels are meeting, and it becomes necessary for one of them, under the Rules, to change her course, and thus encounter such a danger, then the Rules are inoperative, and it becomes the duty of the vessel, which otherwise has the right of way, to manœuvre in order to avoid a collision.

The second set of circumstances under which these Steering and Sailing Rules do not apply are those which are originally set forth in amendment No. 1 of Great Britain, when two vessels find themselves close aboard of each other. As I said a few moments ago, if the Steering and Sailing Rules have been properly applied, two such vessels will not find themselves thus situated, but we can very readily understand that two vessels may meet in a fog, with the best intentions in the world, and they may misunderstand the direction of the sound of the fog-signals of each other, and suddenly find themselves close aboard of each other. Then the Rules for avoiding a collision become inoperative. They cannot be applied, and one or both of the vessels must manœuvre in order to avoid a collision.

These are the two sets of circumstances which it is intended to cover by this Rule, and I think that all other circumstances are covered by the Rules themselves. Therefore the provision that this Rule should apply when there is danger of collision, it seems to me, is quite wrong. If we read this Rule in another way it would be something like this: When two vessels are meeting with risk of collision, then our Rules shall not be operative. That is what it says. The Rules which have preceded this are made for the special purpose of avoiding collision. Therefore it seems to me that this Rule is intended to cover all cases except those which are covered by the Rules themselves.

Mr. Hall (Great Britain).—Mr. President, the gallant Delegate from the United States is quite correct in saying that this amendment was proposed in order to meet this want. I remind him of this: If he will look at the Protocol he will find that it was urged most strongly by two of his brother Delegates that it was very doubtful whether danger of collision was included in this Rule, and it was very doubtful whether a sailor was entitled to disobey the Rule in order to avoid a collision; that is to say, that the circumstances must be such, other than risk of collision, as, for instance, the risk of going ashore or of running into a wreck, &c. That was pointed out with great force by the learned First Delegate from the United States, and it was also pointed out by his colleague, the honourable Delegate who addressed us a short time ago; and it was suggested that it was very desirable that there should be no doubt on the subject. But the matter does not end there. As I pointed out before, a point arose in the discussion of a case in Great Britain, the case of the "Benares," in which the argument was raised, and the Court, although it did not deal with the point directly, gave an *obiter dictum*, which went so far as to suggest that risk of collision was included in this Rule. But it did not say distinctly that this Rule did include it. I think that the reason of their decision was that it did include it, but it did not say so in so many words.

I think it is most desirable that sailors should know that when there is risk of collision it may be necessary for them to act outside of the Rule. It is most desirable that the sailor should not be put into this position: Here are the Rules, I ought to obey them, and unless there is some special circumstance, other than risk of collision, such as a shore or a shoal, or something of that kind, I am going to obey these Rules, because I am not allowed to depart from them. The sailor might say: "You do not state here that special circumstances include collision, or that dangers of navigation include collision, and therefore I do not know whether I am to act under this Rule in order to avoid a collision or not."

But there is another and a much stronger reason. The Conference will remember that Great Britain proposed a Rule pointing out that when two vessels were so near to one another that it was necessary for both of them to act, both of them should act. We withdrew that, as I said before, very much in deference to the representation of our colleagues; but when we withdrew it we said that if we withdrew it we should ask to be allowed to put in the words, "and collision," in old Article No. 23, in order to point out most clearly to sailors that they are not entitled to insist upon a hard and fast rule, and say: "I am not bound to obey this Rule. The General Rules have not entitled me to do anything to prevent collision, because I am the holding-on vessel." That is the reason why we inserted these words in old Article 23. I then pointed out, I am afraid at very great length, the advisability of inserting these words, and the Conference came to the conclusion that they were desirable. I hope now that the Conference will not go back upon its decision and vote against the words, which were adopted for what I think were good and sufficient reasons.

The Conference here took a recess until 2 o'clock.

After Recess.

Captain Sampson (United States).—Mr. President, I have listened, as I always do, with great interest and respect to what has been said by the learned First Delegate from Great Britain. I think that we wish to accomplish precisely the same thing. It is only a question as to how it shall be done. I understand fully that the case which he has cited must be covered by this Rule. But it appears to me, still, that we are not accomplishing it in the right way. As I explained this morning—and, if I am allowed, I will repeat briefly what I said then upon this particular point—there are two distinct sets of circumstances which are provided for in this Rule. The Rule provides that in construing this Article due regard shall be had to the dangers of navigation; that is, when the dangers of navigation are such as to prevent the vessel whose duty it is to keep out of the way from manœuvring, then it becomes the duty of the holding-on vessel to assist her by manœuvring.

The second set of circumstances are those when, from any cause whatever, either from a fog or from neglect of the observance of the Rules, two vessels are found close aboard of each other, and it is impossible that, following the Rules, a collision could be prevented. Under these special circumstances the Rules are inoperative, and it becomes necessary that both of the vessels should manœuvre in order to avoid a collision. Now, it seems to me that that is clearly the case which is referred to in the last clause, which refers to special circumstances which may render departure from the above Rule necessary in order to avoid immediate danger. It will be noticed that immediate danger is collision, and nothing else. In the first clause the danger to be avoided is not collision, it is the danger of running ashore or running upon a wreck or upon a rock, and I think it would be a mistake to associate these two things as if they were the same. In the first part of the Rule a ship is allowed to disregard the Rules in order to prevent running ashore or to avoid a danger of navigation, and in the second part of the Rule, under special circumstances, which may produce the effect of bringing two ships close aboard of each other, they are then to disregard the Rules in order to avoid collision. This, as I said before, is the danger referred to in the second clause, and it refers to collisions, and nothing else. It seems to me that we would accomplish the object for which this Rule is made if we were to state the nature of the danger referred to in the second clause and substitute for the word "danger" the word "collision," leaving the Rule as it originally stood, and as it has been understood and read by sailors heretofore. The Rule would then read:—

"Due regard shall be had to the dangers of navigation and to any special circumstances which may render a departure from the above Rule necessary in order to avoid immediate collision."

Mr. Hall (Great Britain).—Mr. President, I said, in the course of the remarks which I made beforce recess, that this had been inserted to make the Rule perfectly clear, and I find that there was not only an opinion expressed by the learned Delegate from the United States that collision was not included, but I also find that it was pointed out by the gallant Delegate from the United States himself.

Captain Sampson (United States).—Yes, Sir; in the first clause, but not in the second.

Mr. Hall (Great Britain).—Mr. President, we have thought over this matter carefully in the Collocation Committee. I did originally put in the word "collision" at the end of the sentence, but it was pointed out by my learned friend the Delegate from Germany, and other members of the Committee, that it would be better to insert the word where it stands now than to insert it at the end. That was my original proposal, and I am very glad to find out that I am borne out in that by the gallant Delegate from the United States. But I am bound to say that my colleagues convinced me that it was better to put the words where they are now, and I gave way to their opinion. I would venture to say this: I think the discussion of yesterday makes it all the more necessary to put these words in. In the discussion of yesterday there were a good many expressions of opinion, showing that it was desirable for the sailors to have it clearly defined that collision was included within the meaning of this Rule, as well as outside danger.

Dr. Sieveking (Germany).—Mr. President, I do not think there is very much importance to be attached to this question. The words may be left as they are and they will not do any harm. I am rather inclined to state as my own opinion that it would be better to leave them out. The meaning of Article 23 is quite clear as it stands now, in the old Rule. The meaning is this: the law says to the sailors, "We give you certain Rules. We have given you these certain Rules, but of course there may arise circumstances where these Rules are not applicable, as unforeseen dangers of navigation or other circumstances, and in case of such circumstances you are to depart from the Rule. You must not stick to the Rule. Your principal object is always to avoid immediate danger, and of course that means to avoid immediate danger of collision." That is quite clear. If we say to avoid immediate danger of collision, it is superfluous.

The President.—Does the Delegate from the United States wish his amendment put to a vote just as it stands?

Captain Sampson (United States).—Yes, Sir.

The President.—The question is upon the amendment of the Delegate of the United States, amendment No. 33. Is the Conference ready for the question?

The question was put to the Conference upon the adoption of amendment No. 33.

The President.—The Yeas and Nays will be called upon this amendment.

Mr. Goodrich (United States).—Mr. President, in rising to explain my vote, I may say that my colleagues have instructed me to vote "Yea."

The Yea and Nay vote is as follows:—

Austria-Hungary ... ... Nay.	Italy ... ... Nay.
Brazil ... ... Yea.	Japan ... ... Nay.
Belgium ... ... Nay.	Mexico ... ... Nay.
China ... ... Nay.	Norway ... ... Nay.
Chile ... ... Yea.	Russia ... ... Yea.
Denmark ... ... Yea.	Spain ... ... Yea.
France ... ... Yea.	Sweden ... ... Nay.
Germany ... ... Yea.	Siam ... ... Yea.
Great Britain ... ... Nay.	The Netherlands ... ... Yea.
Hawaii ... ... Nay.	United States ... ... Yea.

The President.—Ten have voted in the affirmative, and 10 in the negative, so the amendment is not carried.

Mr. Goodrich (United States).—Mr. President, having finished the amendments in principle, I desire to call the attention of the Conference to one or two verbal corrections in the Report of the Collocation Committee resulting from corrections already made. On p. 5, in the last line of Article 4, the figures "32" should be "31," resulting from the striking out of Article 27, which makes also old Article 28 to be 27, old Article 29 to be 28, old Article 30 to be 29, old Article 31 to be 30, and old Article 32 to be Article 31. In Appendix (B), subdivision 5, the word "shall" in the first line must be "should," to make it correspond to all the other recommendatory Resolutions. If the Delegates will now turn to amendment No. 2, proposed by Dr. Sieveking, the principle of which was adopted by the Conference on day before yesterday, the Collocation Committee have formulated the following:—

"Side-lights should be so screened as to prevent the most convergent ray of the light from being seen across the bows more than half a point."

That is the formulating of the principle adopted by the Conference on the 18th December as Article 2. Referring to the amendment proposed by the Delegate of Norway with regard to the side-lights, the principle of the amendment having been adopted and ordered by the Conference to be put into the recommendation, the Collocation Committee have formulated the following: "The side-lights to be placed in steam-vessels not forward of the masthead-light." Old No. 8 of these Resolutions should be No. 10, No. 9 should be No. 11, and No. 10 No. 12. In consequence of the amendment of this morning, by which Article 27 was transferred from the Rules and Regulations of these recommendatory Resolutions, after the conversation with my colleagues, we shall follow the exact language of Article 27, with the exception of the word "should" for "shall," so as to make it read:—

"In clear weather, at sea, no vessel should attempt to cross the bows of the leaders of any squadron of three or more ships of war in regular formation nor unnecessarily to pass through the lines of such squadron."

Going back again to old Resolution No. 9, now Resolution No. 11, the Committee have inserted the words, "and bells," so that it now reads:—

"All steam-whistles, sirens, fog-horns, and bells should be thoroughly tested as to their efficiency."

The President.—If there be no objection to what has been suggested by the Delegate of the United States, these changes will be adopted.

Mr. Goodrich (United States).—Mr. President, I suppose now the Conference will proceed with the discussion of the amendments of the 1st class.

The President.—The next order of business before the Conference is amendment No. 1, Class 1. The Secretary will please read the amendment.

Amendment No. 1, Class 1, is as follows:—

"Amendment to Collocation Report proposed by Dr. Sieveking on behalf of the German Delegation, 14th December, 1889:

"In 'Preliminary,' instead of the words, 'and every steam-vessel which is under steam, whether under sail or not, is to be considered a vessel under steam,' insert the words, 'and every vessel under steam, whether under sail or not, is to be considered a steam-vessel.'"

Mr. Goodrich (United States).—Mr. President, I take the liberty of saying to the Conference that the Collocation Committee a little exceeded their duties in adding to the amendment, when printed, wherever they agreed to it, the printed words, "Agreed to in Collocation Committee." That was not designed to supersede the wishes or ideas of the Conference, but to expedite matters. May I suggest that, inasmuch as I supposed every member of the Conference has carefully considered these collocation amendments, that unless any Delegate desires to make some change in any amendment which has been agreed to by the Collocation Committee, that I may state these amendments as I have them on my draft Report, and if no one objects that we may assume them to be carried? I think we can run the most of them through in fifteen minutes.

The President.—If there be no objection on the part of the Conference, that course will be pursued.

Mr. Goodrich (United States).—Mr. President, in regard to this first amendment, the members of the Conference will perceive that it is only intended to make the Rules consonant with themselves and use the word "steam-vessel" in all the places where it refers to steam-vessel. The Collocation Committee have agreed to that. That would also amend Articles 18 and 19.

The President.—Should there be no objection it will be considered that the amendment is adopted. If any Delegate desires to object to the amendment he is at liberty to do so.

Mr. Hall (Great Britain).—Mr. President, will not the Chairman of the Committee now move to amend Articles 18 and 19, to insert the word "steam" before the word "vessel," and to leave out the words, "under steam"?

The President.—If the Conference does not object, those amendments will come in under the same principle as adopted in amendment No. 1. The Chair hears no objection, and the amendments are adopted. The next amendment in order is amendment No. 2. The Secretary will please read it.

The amendment is as follows:—

"Amendment to Collocation Report proposed by Dr. Sieveking on behalf of the German Delegation, 14th December, 1889:

"In Article 2 (*a*) insert after the words, 'on or in front of the foremast,' the words, 'or if a vessel without a foremast, then in the fore part of the vessel,' and after the words, 'not less than such breadth,' the words, 'so, however, that the light need not be carried at a greater height above the hull than 40 feet,' and strike out paragraph 2."

Mr. Goodrich (United States).—Mr. President, amendment No. 2 is designed to shorten the Article. Will the learned Delegate from Germany please explain the change in this principle?

Dr. Sieveking (Germany).—Mr. President, the amendment partially intends to shorten the verbiage of the Rule and partly to extend the principle, which is now confined to seagoing vessels without a foremast, to all vessels. Vessels without a foremast, according to Article 2 as it now stands, the breadth of which exceeds 40 feet, need not to carry the lights at a greater height than 40 feet. This certainly was not intended to be limited to vessels without a foremast; but the intention was that the light mentioned in Article 2 (*a*), in any case, by any vessel, need not be carried at a greater height than 40 feet. So this amendment only extends this principle, which has been adopted for vessels without a foremast, to all vessels.

The President.—If there be no objection, the amendment will be considered as adopted.

Mr. Goodrich (United States).—Mr. President, if there is no objection, I will read the Article as it would stand amended. Subdivision (*a*) reads :—

" On or in front of the foremast, or, if a vessel without a foremast, then in the fore part of the vessel, at a height above the hull of not less than 20 feet, and, if the breadth of the vessel exceeds 20 feet, then at a height above the hull not less than such breadth, so, however, that the light need not be carried at a greater height above the hull than 40 feet, a bright white light," &c.

Then strike out the next paragraph.

If there is no objection, I will call the attention of the Conference now to amendment No. 4, a little out of its order, for a reason which will appear.

The President.—Do you understand that this has been accepted?

Mr. Goodrich (United States).—Unless there is objection, yes, Sir.

The President.—If the Chair hears no objection, this amendment will be considered as accepted. The Chair hears none, therefore the amendment is considered as accepted. The Delegate from the United States desires now to have amendment No. 4 read.

Amendment No. 4 is as follows :—

" Amendment to Collocation Report proposed by Captain Shackford (United States), 14th December, 1889:

" Article 3:

" Second paragraph, second line : strike out 'guidance of its tow,' and insert, 'vessel being towed to steer by.' "

Mr. Goodrich (United States).—Mr. President, the Collocation Committee have assented to this because it seems to them to better express the meaning than the words adopted by the Committee. It should be stated that these are the words originally proposed by my colleague, Captain Shackford.

The President.—Should there be no objection on the part of the Conference, this amendment will be adopted. The Chair hears no objection, and the amendment is considered adopted. The Secretary will now please read amendment No. 3.

Amendment No 3 is as follows :—

" Amendment to Collocation Report proposed by Mr. Frederick W. Verney (Siam), 14th December, 1889:

" Article 3 to read as follows :

" ' A steam-vessel when towing another vessel shall, in addition to her side-lights, carry two bright white lights in a vertical line, one over the other, not less than 6 feet apart, the (upper—lower) one of which shall be carried at a height above the hull as directed by Article 2 (*a*). When towing more than one vessel, and when the length of the tow measuring from the stern of the towing vessel to the stern of the last vessel towed exceeds 600 feet, she shall carry an additional white light 6 feet above or below such lights, [but at a height of not less than 14 feet above the hull]. Each of these lights shall be of the same construction and character.

" Such steam-vessel may carry a small white light abaft the funnel or aftermast for the guidance of her tow, but such light shall not be visible forward of the beam."

Mr. Goodrich (United States).—Mr. President, the last clause of that amendment, I suppose, is obviated by amendment No. 4, which has been adopted; and I presume that the learned Delegate from Siam will withdraw that motion.

Mr. Verney (Siam).—Yes, Sir; certainly.

Mr. Goodrich (United States).—Mr. President, the other part of it the Collocation Committee do not assent to, after very careful consideration, because they do not see that the suggestions by the learned Delegate from Siam better the language adopted by the Conference, and it really embraces a new principle.

Mr. Verney (Siam).—Mr. President, I am very sorry to hear that statement, because I was entirely misled by the note which I see accompanies this amendment, " Agreed to in Collocation Committee."

Mr. Goodrich (United States).—Mr. President, the gentleman will see that it is placed in a different position. It, perhaps, might have been a little more specific, and is perhaps a printer's mistake. In the other amendment you will notice that the words, " Agreed to in Collocation Committee," are at the bottom of the page, because they embrace the whole Article ; but in this case it is attached to the last paragraph.

Mr. Verney (Siam).—Mr. President, I am very sorry. I need not say that I would be at a very considerable disadvantage to get up and argue in favour of this amendment when I was under the misapprehension that it had been agreed to in the Collocation Committee. I can only say that I do not wish to take up the time of the Conference, if the Conference is of the opinion that the other wording is better. It is a mere question of words. I ventured to entertain the opinion that this wording was the clearest, but if the other gentlemen do not think so I certainly do not intend to press this amendment on a mere question of verbiage. I do not for a moment mean to stand here in rivalry in a matter of that kind with others who are so much more able than myself to express themselves in English, and have a much greater command of the English language than I could possibly obtain. Therefore, I put myself entirely in the hands of the Conference.

Mr. Goodrich (United States).—Mr. President, do I understand the learned Delegate to withdraw the amendment?

Mr. Verney (Siam).—Mr. President, no, Sir ; I do not think I should do that. I should prefer to have a vote taken upon the subject.

[93]

Mr. Goodrich (United States).—Mr. President, I do not understand how the Delegate can put himself in the hands of the Collocation Committee and then ask to take a vote upon the amendment.

Mr. Verney (Siam).—Mr. President, I said that I would put myself in the hands of the Conference. I have taken a great deal of time in drawing and preparing this, and I should prefer to have a vote of the Conference upon it, and if it is decided against me I will not ask for the Yeas and Nays.

The President.—Is the Conference ready for the question upon amendment No. 3?

The question was put to the Conference upon the adoption of the first part of amendment No. 3, and the amendment was lost.

Mr. Verney (Siam).—Mr. President, perhaps I may save the time of the Conference if the same course is taken in Collocation Committee in regard to amendment No. 5, and I will withdraw it.

Mr. Goodrich (United States).—Mr. President, I want to say that the Collocation Committee have very carefully considered all the amendments of the learned Delegate from Siam, and have given them a great deal of attention, because he seems to have the happy faculty of using language, and one of them, at least, we shall ask the Conference to adopt, wherein we think he has very much improved upon the language of the Committee.

Mr. Verney (Siam).—Mr. President, I beg leave to withdraw the amendment.

The President.—The Delegate from Siam withdraws amendment No. 5. Amendment No. 6 will be read.

Amendment No. 6 is as follows:—

"Amendment to Collocation Report proposed by Dr. Sieveking on behalf of the German Delegation, 14th December, 1889:

"In Article 5, instead of the word 'light' in the last line, insert the word 'lights.'"

Mr. Goodrich (United States).—Mr. President, this is merely a verbal correction. It was a typographical error.

The President.—If there be no objection to amendment No. 6, it will be accepted. The Chair hears none, therefore the amendment will be considered accepted.

The next amendment in order will be No. 7. The Secretary will please read it.

Amendment No. 7 is as follows:—

"Amendment to Collocation Report proposed by the Delegates for Great Britain, 14th December, 1889:

"Article 5, last line, read 'lights' for 'light.'"

The President.—Amendment No. 7 will be accepted, unless the Chair hears objections. The Chair hears no objections, and therefore the amendment will be considered as accepted.

The next amendment is No. 8, which the Secretary will please read.

Amendment No. 8 is as follows:—

"Amendment to Collocation Report proposed by Mr. Verney (Siam), 14th December, 1899:

"Article 6. Instead of the words, 'and shall on the approach of or to other vessels,' insert the words, 'and they shall, on nearing, or being neared by, other vessels.'"

Mr. Goodrich (United States).—Mr. President, the Collocation Committee venture to suggest to the learned Delegate from Siam that to adopt that language will involve an alteration of five or six Rules. The Collocation Committee do not think that the words suggested by him make any difference in the Rules, and therefore we venture to hope that the learned Delegate will not press his amendment.

Mr. Verney (Siam).—Mr. President, I am quite aware that the words which I have suggested do not alter the meaning of the Rule in any way whatever, but I hoped that they would be able to accept them in the Collocation Committee. I wish to point out an objection to this amendment of my own, which the learned Delegate for the United States did not perhaps notice. That objection is this : we have now adopted in Article 8, the second paragraph, that "on the near approach of or to other vessels;" this Conference will see that that puts me in a difficulty, because it prevents me from using the phrase which I had originally intended. I think it is only fair to add that I have been trying to adapt my own phraseology to that which has been adopted by the Conference, and I confess that I am unable to invent words which would exactly embrace the meaning I desire. Still, I venture to say that the expression now used, "on the approach of or to," is not a very elegant one, and it is one which I, personally, regret to see adopted into the Rules. However, on the case as stated by the Delegate from the United States, I will withdraw my amendment, unless some one can help me in my difficulty.

The President.—Amendment No. 8 has been withdrawn. Amendment No. 9 is next in order. The Secretary will please read it.

Amendment No. 9 is as follows:—

"Amendment to Collocation Report proposed by the Delegates for the Netherlands, 14th December, 1889:

"Article 7. Strike out the words, 'and not fishing,' in the third line."

Mr. Goodrich (United States).—Mr. President, although the talismanic words, "Agreed to in Collocation Committee," are not on this amendment, yet the Collocation Committee last night, after very careful consideration, believe that this is a very proper amendment, and that it carries out the meaning of the Rule. Therefore to this amendment the Collocation Committee give their recommendation.

The President.—Is the Conference ready for the question upon this amendment?

The question was put to the Conference upon the adoption of amendment No. 9, and it was adopted.

The President.—The next amendment is No. 10. The Secretary will please read it.

Amendment No. 10 is as follows:—

"Amendment to Collocation Report proposed by Dr. Sieveking on behalf of the German Delegation, 14th December, 1889:

"In Article 7, 1 (*a*), instead of the word 'fitted,' insert 'fixed.'"

Mr. Goodrich (United States).—Mr. President, this is a mere verbal correction.

The President.—If there should be no objection, the amendment will be accepted. The Chair hears no objection, and the amendment is considered as accepted.

The next amendment is No. 11. The Secretary will please read it.

Amendment No. 11 is as follows:—

"Amendment to Collocation Report proposed by Admiral Bowden-Smith (Great Britain), 14th December, 1899:

"Article 7, subsection (*b*). Insert 'combined' before 'lantern,' in third line."

Mr. Goodrich (United States).—Mr. President, it is owing to the fact that the lantern described in the first two lines of that Article is to be described in the same way in all the Articles, and up to this time there has been no word given to it.

Mr. Hall (Great Britain).—Mr. President, that is the word which is used in our Navy Regulations. It is called a "combined" lantern.

The President.—As this has been agreed upon by the Collocation Committee, if there be no objection, it will be accepted. The Chair hears no objections, and the amendment will be considered as accepted. The next amendment is No. 12.

Mr. Verney (Siam).—Mr. President, I withdraw that amendment for the reasons I have before given.

The President.—The amendment No. 12 is withdrawn. The next amendment is No. 13. The Secretary will please read it.

Amendment No. 13 is as follows:—

"Amendment to Collocation Report proposed by Captain Norcross (United States), 14th December, 1889:

"Article 8. Second paragraph, strike out the words, 'show them temporarily,' and substitute, 'flash them at short intervals.'"

"In third paragraph, strike out 'shown temporarily,' and substitute, 'flashed at short intervals.'"

Mr. Hall (Great Britain).—Mr. President, that has been disposed of already.

The President.—This amendment having been disposed of, the next is amendment No. 14. The Secretary will please read it.

Amendment No. 14 is as follows:—

"Amendment to Collocation Report proposed by Dr. Sieveking on behalf of the German Delegation, 14th December, 1889:

"In Article 9 (*b*) 2, instead of the words, 'one of the pyrotechnic lights,' insert the word 'and.'"

Mr. Goodrich (United States).—Mr. President, and strike out the period after "second." It is simply a verbal correction.

The President.—If there be no objection, the amendment No. 14 will be accepted. The Chair hears no objection, and amendment No. 14 is accepted by the Conference.

The next amendment is No. 15.

Mr. Verney (Siam).—Mr. President, I withdraw that.

The President.—The amendment No. 15 is withdrawn. The next amendment is No. 16.

Dr. Sieveking (Germany).—Mr. President, Mr. Verbrugghe has been good enough to point out to me that this is a mistake, and I beg to withdraw it.

The President.—Amendment No. 16 is withdrawn by the Delegate of Germany. The next amendment is No. 17.

Dr. Sieveking (Germany).—Mr. President, amendment No. 17, after consideration with the Collocation Committee, I beg leave to withdraw, because it was pointed out yesterday that there might be a difference between a trawl and a drag-net.

The President.—Amendment No. 17 is withdrawn. Amendment No. 18 has been disposed of. Amendment No. 19 has been disposed of.

Mr. Goodrich (United States).—Mr. President, I should say, in regard to the acceptance of amendment No. 19 by the Collocation Committee, that they thought that no Government would adopt the signal and register and publish it in accordance with the provisions of Article 13, unless that Government was perfectly convinced that such signals did not cause confusion or mistake by reason of other signals adopted, either in this Code of Regulations or indeed a National Code.

The President.—If there are no objections, amendment No. 19 will be considered as accepted. The Chair hears none, and the amendment is considered as adopted by the Conference. The next amendment is No. 20. The Secretary will please read amendment No. 20.

Amendment No. 20 is as follows —

"Amendment to Collocation Report proposed by the Delegates for Great Britain, 14th December, 1889:

"Article 14. Strike out 'on or in front of the foremast,' and insert 'forward.'"

Mr. Goodrich (United States).—I do not know that I need explain that; the Delegates will see the object of it.

The President.—If there be no objection, amendment No. 20 will be adopted by the Conference. The Chair hears no objection, and it is considered as adopted. The next amendment is No. 21.

Amendment No. 21 is as follows:—

"Amendment to Collocation Report proposed by Dr. Sieveking on behalf of the German Delegation, 14th December, 1889:

"In Article 15 (*a*), instead of the words, 'under way,' insert the words, 'having way upon her,' and in Article 15 (*b*), instead of the words, 'not at anchor,' insert the words, 'under way.'"

Mr. Goodrich (United States).—Mr. President, will the learned Delegate from Germany explain that?

Dr. Sieveking (Germany).—Mr. President, the two cases which are stated in paragraphs (*a*) and (*b*) are not expressed correctly by the wording as we have it before our eyes. Paragraph (*a*) deals with a steam-vessel under way, and paragraph (*b*) deals with a vessel that has no way upon her, but is stopped. Now, a steam-vessel under way is not the same as a steam-vessel which has way upon her, because the general definition of under way is given in the beginning, where it is said that a vessel is under way when she is not at anchor or made fast to the shore or aground. But a vessel which is hove-to and which has no way upon her is under way, therefore, paragraph (*a*) must read in this way: "A steam-vessel having way upon her"—then she has to sound at intervals of not more than two minutes a prolonged blast; (*b*) must read: "A steam-vessel under way but stopped and having no way upon her shall sound at intervals," &c.

The President.—If there be no objection, this amendment will be considered as accepted by the Conference. The Chair hears no objection, and the amendment is considered as adopted. The next amendment will be No. 22. The Secretary will please read it.

Amendment No. 22 is as follows:—

"Amendment to Collocation Report proposed by the Delegates for Great Britain, 14th December, 1889:

"Article 15. Subsection (*c*):

"After the words, 'if a sailing-vessel,' add 'at intervals of not more than one minute.'

"Subsection (*g*):

"Substitute 'long' for 'prolonged.'"

Mr. Goodrich (United States).—Mr. President, the first amendment is to point the intervals of the blast of a sailing-vessel, limiting them to intervals of not more than a minute, as we do in another section, which the Conference will remember.

The President.—Should there be no objection to this amendment, it will be accepted by the Conference. The Chair hears none, therefore the amendment is accepted.

The next amendment in order is No. 23.

Mr. Carter (Hawaii).—Mr. President, I will withdraw that amendment.

The President.—The Delegate from Hawaii withdraws amendment No. 23. The next amendment is No. 24. The Secretary will please read it.

Mr. Verney (Siam).—Mr. President, I am very sorry indeed to ask the Conference to pause for a moment. They have been maintaining their course and speed with wonderful regularity for a little time past, but I must ask their kind attention while I say a few words upon this amendment. In the first place, I have to make a confession that this amendment as now proposed by me does not carry out the intention which I had when I put it on paper. As now proposed by me, on the paper before the members of the Conference, it would not meet my intention, and I venture to ask the Conference to allow me to alter the wording of the amendment, and to put other words, which are entirely germane to the subject, in place of the amendment I have presented. Therefore, if the Conference will allow me, I will hand up to the President a copy of the amendment, and I have had other copies made in order to save the Conference, as far as possible, the inconvenience of changing words on the printed amendment. I will hand the revised amendment round. It reads as follows:—

"The compass bearings of any vessel which appears to be approaching so as to involve risk of collision should, when circumstances permit, be carefully watched. If the bearing does not appreciably change, special caution is necessary."

Mr. Goodrich (United States).—Mr. President, may I rise to a question of order? With great respect to the learned Delegate of Siam, I doubt whether we can be called upon to consider a proposition of that kind without very careful examination. This is due to me. The Conference in the first place, and the Collocation Committee secondly, have given great attention to the language of this Rule, and have assented to one part of the proposition of the learned Delegate from Siam, namely, to the use of the word "circumstances" in place of "time," which, it seems to me, will meet all that he wants. I really suggest to him that it is of a little doubtful wisdom to consider a most important amendment hastily on a type-written paper which none of us has seen until this moment.

Mr. Hall (Great Britain).—Mr. President, may I also point out to the learned Delegate from Siam that these are not words chosen by the Conference, but they are words which have been adopted after consideration? I may say that we considered them several weeks before we proposed them to this Conference. We considered them most carefully in England before we came here, and are happy to know that they have received the consideration of very eminent people in this country. It is not as if we had proposed them in a hurry. Under these circumstances, I hope the learned Delegate from Siam will not think it necessary to press the new form of words upon us upon a matter which requires the very greatest care and attention in the words which are used.

Mr. Verney (Siam).—Mr. President, of course I know I am in the hands of the Conference, and if necessary I must argue my case on the words as originally chosen, although I should be extremely sorry to do so. These words are not by any means the best words which I can propose to the Conference, and I very much prefer the Conference to let me propose my second wording. I explained just now that the wording was adopted by me when I was not in a state to consider the subject as carefully as I have been since. I would not venture to occupy the time of this Conference for a single moment except upon a matter which I consider to be of considerable importance. If the Chair rules that I am out of order, I will take the original wording of the amendment and I will argue it if necessary upon those words.

The President.—What is the proposition of the Delegate from Siam?

Mr. Verney (Siam).—Mr. President, the proposition which I desire to make is to be permitted to argue my case upon the new amendment which I have proposed. But that I believe is opposed, and therefore I have not the power to do so.

The President.—By a three-fourths vote you could do so.

Mr. Verney (Siam).—Mr. President, I venture to make this proposition only because there is a strong reason for it in my own mind, although of course I may be overruled by the Conference.

Mr. Hall (Great Britain).—Mr. President, may I point out that if the learned Delegate from Siam wishes to argue that the present Rule is a bad one he certainly should have given notice of this principle in time? We are now merely dealing with questions of verbiage; if he can express what the Conference has adopted in better words, by all means let him do so; but if he intends to consider the question of whether this is a salutary Rule or not, it is open to objection, because we are now considering merely questions of verbiage, whether or not the words used in the Rule are the best words to be used.

Mr. Verney (Siam).—Mr. President, perhaps I may say that it was not my intention to argue merely a question of verbiage. I think it is a mistake that this amendment has been put into the place which it now occupies; but I had nothing whatever to do with that. The question is one of principle, and a very important principle. And I think it should have been inserted in the other class of amendments.

Mr. Hall (Great Britain).—Mr. President, then of course what should have been done is that the discussion of this should have been taken up while we were engaged in the discussion of the amendments upon principle.

Captain Shackford (United States).—Mr. President, I should like to say as a sailor that I hope the word "time" will be kept in there instead of the word "circumstances." It seems to me that circumstances will always permit it, to a careful officer, if he has the time. What does the word "circumstances" refer to? Does it refer to having his compass in its proper place, or what does it refer to? It really seems to me as if "time" was the word that should be kept there.

Mr. Goodrich (United States).—Mr. President, the idea of the Committee was that the word "circumstances" is more general in its character than the word "time," and embraces a good deal more. "Circumstances" relate to all the surrounding circumstances, the condition of the water, the proximity of other vessels, the distance between the vessels, the tide, and everything.

The President.—Does the Delegate of Siam wish a three-fourths vote taken upon the admission of his amendment?

Mr. Verney (Siam).—Mr. President, I have heard very strong opposition raised to that question, so that, perhaps, it is not worth while to have a vote taken upon it. I should be glad to be permitted to argue my case upon the words I have presented, but I warn the Conference that I shall argue it as a question of principle. I do not accept what has fallen from the learned Delegate from Great Britain, that it was necessary for me to get up and inform the Conference that it was not my intention to deal with this matter as a mere matter of verbiage, but as a matter of principle. I had nothing whatever to do with putting it in the place which it now occupies. My argument is this: that this is either a very important matter or it is not, that the compass bearing should be taken. There is no Rule passed by this Conference, and I do not know that there is a single Rule proposed to this Conference, where a mere permission has been given or a mere option left in a matter of vital importance. I have discussed this matter with several sailors, and they tell me that careful navigators do take the compass bearings, and that they ought to be taken. I have not heard a single dissenting word on that subject. If that is so, I will ask, why not put it in the Rules? A mere caution to sailors is an excellent thing in a nautical almanack, but it has no place, it seems to me, in the Rules for preventing Collisions at Sea.

Of course, it is very easy to say that this is a mere preliminary note, and that it does not form a part of the compulsory Rule. Well, Sir, what will it be when it comes into a Law Court? Our sailors will find out that it forms a very essential part of the Rule when it comes there. I venture to say that, if this note is put in, in every case of collision there will be the question raised, "Were the compass bearings taken, when were they taken, how often were they taken?" And woe betide the sailor who has not fulfilled what is intended to be his duty! As I read these Rules, this is not put in, as it should be, in the Rule itself, but it is introduced by a side wind into a preliminary note. I quite admit that is an objection to the word which I have ventured to put before the Conference. Now, in saying risk of collision should, when circumstances permit, be ascertained by watching the compass bearings of an approaching vessel, just consider what you impose upon a seaman. Then every vessel approaching another vessel, no matter how far off she is, has to be watched. That is an impossible burden to be put upon the sailors, and that is why I altered my wording. But the Conference will not allow me to argue upon my new wording. I see this objection, and would not be personally responsible for imposing such an obligation as that upon the commanding officer of a vessel, or upon any officer in charge. That is undoubtedly an objection to the amendment.

I feel very strongly that, by putting in this preliminary note, you are practically misleading—not, of course, intentionally, but practically misleading—a body of men who require to be told straight out exactly what you intend them to do. I have made that objection once before on another matter, and I will not repeat it. But I would remind this Conference that they are doing something more than putting in a preliminary note. They are adding a very vital and essential point, and putting it in in an indirect way, when I think it should be put in in a direct way. You are practically attempting here a definition of what constitutes risk of collision, and we are told by the most eminent and learned Judges that ever lived that that is impossible. Risk of collision, if this note is put into the Rule, is said to begin when the bearings are being taken of an approaching vessel. A master of a vessel takes the bearing of another vessel 5 miles off, and a second bearing 4½ miles off, and they do not appreciably change. But from that moment, according to this preliminary note, risk of collision commences, and the whole of the old Rules come into force. I venture to say that you introduce confusion which nobody can look forward to with pleasure who has to deal with these questions in Law Courts.

That, to my mind, is another serious objection to this preliminary note. I have tried to avoid that danger and that ambiguity in the revised wording which most of the members of this Conference have now in their hands. I regret very much that this amendment should have been considered as a mere matter of wording, and that it should have been put into the place which it now occupies. I cannot, of course, doubt that the vote will be given against me on this point. It appears that this matter has been discussed by the Collocation Committee, and has been carefully considered, and probably the vote will be given largely against me. I am very much obliged, however, to the Conference for their courtesy, and for hearing the opinions of one of their members.

Mr. Hall (Great Britain).—Mr. President, one part of the amendment of the Delegate from Siam is opposed, and the other part of the amendment of the honourable Delegate from Siam has been accepted by the Collocation Committee. Do I understand now that he wishes to have a vote taken on the wording of his amendment in the part which is objected to? The Delegate from Siam has proposed the words, "when circumstances permit," and we are all agreed to them, I think. There is no dispute about accepting those words, although, of course, the Delegate from the United States has pointed out that he prefers that the word "time" should remain.

Captain Shackford (United States).—Mr. President, I would only say that it all seems to me to come back to "time;" if you have time you will take the compass bearings. Every prudent watch officer, if he has the time, will take the bearings.

Mr. Hall (Great Britain).—Mr. President, then, of course, it might be that he would have time to take the bearings if he did nothing else; but he might be otherwise engaged for the moment. There might be sails in the way, or other difficulties. I can assure him that the word "circumstances" will include the word "time," so that we shall not be doing any harm by adopting these words, and I am in favour of adopting them.

Mr. Goodrich (United States).—Mr. President, I move an amendment to this amendment No. 24: that the words, "time permit," should be stricken out of the preliminary Article to Article 17, and that the words, "circumstances permit," should be inserted instead thereof.

The President.—That seems to be amending Article 17.

Mr. Goodrich (United States).—Mr. President, then I withdraw that motion, and ask you for a division on the question as to the use of the word "should."

Mr. Verney (Siam).—Mr. President, what the learned Delegate of Great Britain has said is true, and I have myself very strong objections to this wording; and, seeing them so strongly, I am not going to maintain it as a part of my amendment. I would like once more to state to the Conference that this amendment is not one which I would wish to hold myself responsible for, for the reason which I have already given. I do not in the least approve of it as it now stands, and I will withdraw it.

The President.—The amendment in which you insert the word "should" is withdrawn.

Mr. Goodrich (United States).—Mr. President, perhaps it would be best, inasmuch as the form of this amendment is changed, that it should be adopted upon the Protocol by a motion; and therefore I move that the portion of amendment No. 24 which is left after the withdrawal of the word "should" be adopted, so that the paragraph will read: "Risk of collision can, when circumstances permit."

The question was put upon the adoption of the amendment as above, and the amendment was adopted.

The President.—The next amendment is No. 25.

Mr. Goodrich (United States).—Mr. President, that has been adopted already by the assent of the Conference.

The President.—The Secretary will please read amendment No. 25.

Amendment No. 25 is as follows:—

"Amendment to Collocation Report, proposed by Dr. Sieveking on behalf of the German Delegation, 14th December, 1889:

"In Article 20, instead of the words, 'two vessels, one of which is a sailing-vessel and the other a steam-vessel,' insert the words, 'a steam-vessel and a sailing-vessel.'"

Mr. Goodrich (United States).—Mr. President, that is a mere clerical correction, to make the Article correspond with the other Articles where the same words are used to express the same idea as are now used in the present Article.

255

The President.—If there be no objection to the acceptance of this amendment, it will be accepted by the Conference. The Chair hears no objection, and the amendment is therefore accepted. Amendment No. 26 is next in order. The Secretary will please read it.

Amendment No. 26 is as follows:—

"Amendment to Collocation Report proposed by Dr. Sieveking on behalf of the German Delegation, 14th December, 1889:

"In Article 26, instead of the words, 'efficient signal,' insert the words, 'body of cylindrical shape.'"

Dr. Sieveking (Germany).—Mr. President, we have proposed this amendment thinking that it might be advisable to put in some more definite expression. But we have been informed by several of the Delegates that there may be objections raised to this proposal, and we do not consider it of sufficient importance to bring about a discussion, and therefore I beg to withdraw it.

The President.—Amendment No. 26 is withdrawn. The next amendment is No. 27. The Secretary will please read it.

Amendment No. 27 is as follows:—

"Amendment to Collocation Report presented by the Delegates for Great Britain, 14th December, 1889:
"Article 26. Omit word 'but' at commencement of last sentence."

Mr. Goodrich (United States).—Mr. President, that has already been disposed of by transposing the middle part of this Article to the Fishing Rules.

The President.—Amendment No. 27 having been disposed of, the next in order is amendment No. 28. The Secretary will please read it.

Amendment No. 28 is as follows:—

"Amendment to Collocation Report proposed by Mr. Frederick W. Verney (Siam), 14th December, 1889:
"Article 29. Instead of the words, 'in taking any course,' to 'or siren,' inclusive, insert the words: 'When vessels are in sight of one another, a steam-vessel under way, in taking any course authorized or required by these Regulations, shall indicate that course by the following signals on her whistle or siren.'"

Mr. Goodrich (United States).—Mr. President, the word "Regulations" in that sentence should be "Rules," to make it consonant with the other Articles. The Collocation Committee have had a good deal of discussion over the two signals, the one first adopted by the Conference and the one as proposed by the Delegate of Siam, and they finally came to the unanimous conclusion that the proposition contained in this amendment is, perhaps, a better phrase. And therefore we have, since this paper was printed, agreed to the adoption of this amendment, in place of the words in the Article previously adopted by the Conference.

The President.—The question is upon the adoption of amendment No. 28.

The question was put to the Conference for the adoption of amendment No. 28, and it was adopted.

The President.—The next amendment is No. 29. The Secretary will please read it.

Amendment No. 29 is as follows:—

"Amendment to Collocation Report proposed by Mr. Frederick W. Verney (Siam), 14th December, 1889:
"Insert Article 30 after Article 16."

Mr. Verney (Siam).—Mr. President, this is a genuine question of collocation. It was suggested to me by some of our gallant friends around the table that this was such an important Article that it was better, as a matter of collocation, to put this Article in the place which is here suggested, and I leave it to them, if they choose, to support this proposal.

Mr. Goodrich (United States).—Mr. President, will my friend let me suggest to him that if you bury this Article among the Rules——

Mr. Verney (Siam).—Mr. President, I want to disinter it.

Mr. Goodrich (United States).—Mr. President, in sound-signals for a fog you are not emphasizing it as you will if you close the whole argument by putting it at the end of the Rules, showing that this Rule holds, no matter what any one of the Rules or any half-dozen of the Rules have said.

Mr. Verney (Siam).—Mr. President, it is only a question between the learned Delegate from the United States and myself as to where the cemetery is to be. I think it is buried if it is put at the end end of the Rule, and he thinks it is buried if it is put in the middle of the Rule.

Mr. Goodrich (United States).—I do not know how it is as to the cemetery, but I am sure the symmetry of the Rules will be better if it is put in my way.

The question was put to the Conference upon the adoption of amendment No. 29, and it was lost.

The President.—Amendment No. 30 will be read.

Amendment No. 30 is as follows:—

"Amendment to Collocation Report proposed by Captain Norcross (United States), 14th December, 1889:
"Article 31. In third line strike out the words, 'harbour, river, or.'"

Captain Norcross (United States).—Mr. President, I withdraw that amendment.

The President.—Amendment No. 30 is withdrawn. Amendment No. 31 is next in order. The Secretary will please read it.

Amendment No. 31 is as follows:—

"Amendment to Collocation Report proposed by Captain Sampson, 14th December, 1889:
"Article 6. After 'at hand' in third line, insert the words, 'lighted and.'"

The President.—Does the Collocation Committee accept that amendment?

Mr. Goodrich (United States).—We do, Sir.

The President.—If there be no objection, the Collocation Committee having accepted this amendment, it will be accepted by the Conference. The Chair hears no objection; therefore the amendment will be accepted by the Conference. That ends the subject before the Conference.

Mr. Goodrich (United States).—Mr. President, I presume we shall all rejoice that the discussion on these Rules has now been finished, and I think the Chair had better announce its opinion as to whether the discussion upon these Rules is closed. Of course, it follows that if any such an overwhelming necessity arises that it would secure a three-quarters vote of this Conference to change these Rules, it could easily be secured if it were necessary. I make the motion that the Rules, as now severally adopted by the Conference, be adopted in whole.

The President.—I would suggest that you had better put in that the questions which have been considered in General Division I are now to be adopted.

Mr. Goodrich (United States).—Mr. President, I presume this also carries with it the recommendations in Appendix (B) of the Committee's Report; and to make it certain I suggest an amendment to my own motion by including in the motion the Resolutions contained in Appendix (B).

The President.—You had better word that very strictly and carefully.

Mr. Goodrich (United States).—Mr. President, I move to adopt the Report of the Collocation Committee as it has been amended by the Conference, and to adopt it as a whole.

The President.—It is moved to adopt the Report of the Collocation Committee, as it has been amended by the Conference, and to adopt it as a whole.

The question was put to the Conference upon the motion of the Delegate from the United States, and the motion was carried.

The President.—The Rules as adopted by the Collocation Committee, and as amended by the Conference, are now adopted by the Conference.

Mr. Goodrich (United States).—Mr. President, I presume that these Rules as now amended can be printed and presented to the Conference by Monday morning. There is no further business before us except, as I understand, the Report of the Committee on the later Divisions of the Programme, of which Captain Mensing is Chairman.

Dr. Sieveking (Germany).—Mr. President, I am sorry to say that Captain Mensing has been obliged to leave on account of his health, but I am able to say that he expects to have the work of the Committee finished so as to be able to lay the Report before the Conference on Monday week. That would be the 30th December. Then take forty-eight hours to consider the Report, and the result will be that the Conference would be in a position to consider the Report on the 31st December. Captain Mensing does not expect the discussion to be a very lengthy one. He does not think that it would extend over one day, so, perhaps, the whole Programme could be finished on the 2nd January.

Mr. Hall (Great Britain).—Mr. President, I am told by my gallant colleague, who is also a member of this Committee, and I understood from the gallant Captain the Delegate from Germany, that a part of the Report certainly will be ready in time for us to discuss it on Monday. There is only one matter left which the Committee has not yet finished their Report upon. There are various subjects before that Committee, and they can get a part of their Report printed in plenty of time for us to have it the required forty-eight hours and discuss it on Monday morning; that is, Monday week. That will enable us to finish up on New Year's Day; whereas, if we postpone it now, and do not meet until Thursday, some subject may come up which will prevent us from getting away at the end of that week, as I am certain a vast majority of us want to do.

What I venture to suggest is this: let us meet on Monday week and then consider such portions of the Report as are in print. So far as I can understand, certainly three-quarters of the Report will be in print and will have been on the table for forty-eight hours. I think it is very possible, from what I hear, that the remaining part of the Report of the Committee will be of such a character that it is possible we may not want forty-eight hours to consider it, but we can discuss it at once. At any rate, do not let us wait until Monday week and then come back and say we want forty-eight hours to read these papers. If the members want forty-eight hours, let them come back here on Saturday and read them, and have the papers ready to discuss on Monday week. I move that we meet here on Monday week to discuss this Report. Then I venture to think that we could get through with our work certainly by Tuesday night or Tuesday afternoon.

Admiral Nares (Great Britain).—Mr. President, may I say, as one of the members of this Committee, a few words upon this subject? The Delegates are aware how desultory our work has been. We have met for an hour or two, now and then. Now, practically, we shall be able to meet all day to-morrow and all day Monday, and, at least, we shall have two clear days. It is quite impossible even for the Chairman to foresee what we shall do in those two days. We will work reasonably hard, and we will hope to be able to get something ready for you and have it in print by Friday; then you will have forty-eight hours to finish before your Monday meeting. We have met so seldom, and at such irregular hours, that it is quite impossible to foresee how much work we can get through with; but, practically, you must leave it to us, and we will try to get something ready so that you will have it more than forty-eight hours—or at least forty-eight hours—before Monday week. I cannot promise to give you the whole of the Report; still, we will do what we can.

Mr. Goodrich (United States).—Then the desire of the gallant Admiral is to adjourn until Monday week?

Admiral Nares (Great Britain).—Mr. President, so far as the discussion goes, I am quite certain that we shall not have anything ready for discussion before Monday week. A part of the Report will be on the table Friday. How it will be gotten to the members so that they may have forty-eight hours to consider it, it is not for me to say.

Mr. Goodrich (United States).—Mr. President, I suppose the more practicable way is to adjourn until a week from Monday.

Admiral Nares (Great Britain).—Mr. President, with the understanding that if there is anything upon which we can report on Friday, it will be here on the table for the members to supply themselves.

Mr. Hall (Great Britain).—May I venture to suggest that, if the members will take the trouble, they can have the Report forwarded to them very promptly, if they wish to see it? If not, they can come back on Saturday or Sunday. I do not think that any member ought to say on Monday morning: "I have not read this Report, because I chose not to come back here until to-day, and therefore I am not ready to discuss it." Let us meet Monday and discuss this Report, when it has been on the table forty-eight hours.

Mr. Goodrich (United States).—Mr. President, the Secretary informs me that he will forward the Report to the members according to the addresses upon the address list, and that if any member desires to have it forwarded to some other place, he may give his address to the Secretary.

Admiral Nares (Great Britain).—Mr. President, of course I am not promising now to do something in the next two or three days. As I have said, our work has been going on in such a scattered way that we cannot say with perfect certainty that you shall have anything on Friday. I can only say that we will do the best we can.

Mr. Goodrich (United States).—Mr. President, I have omitted a very important matter. I have a Resolution here in regard to the duty of a vessel in a collision to stand by a vessel in distress. I am strenuous about that Resolution. I think it is a very important matter.

Mr. Hall (Great Britain).—Let us first finish discussing the question of adjournment. The motion is to adjourn until 11 o'clock A.M. on Monday week.

The President.—Is the Conference ready for the question?

The question was put to the Conference upon the motion to adjourn until 11 o'clock on a week from next Monday, and the motion was carried.

The President.—When the Conference adjourns it will stand adjourned until Monday week at 11 o'clock A.M. The Resolution presented by the Delegate from the United States will now be read by the Secretary.

[New section proposed by Mr. Goodrich (United States), November 26, 1889.]

"In every case of collision between two vessels it shall be the duty of the master or person in charge of each vessel, if and so far as he can do so without danger to his own vessel, crew, and passengers (if any), to stay by the other vessel until he has ascertained that she has no need of further assistance, and to render to the other vessel, her master, crew, and passengers (if any), such assistance as may be practicable and as may be necessary in order to save them from any danger caused by the collision; and also to give to the master or person in charge of the other vessel the name of his own vessel, and of her port of registry, or of the port or place to which she belongs, and also the names of the ports and places from which and to which she is bound. If he fails so to do, and no reasonable cause for such failure is shown, the collision shall, in the absence of proof to the c ( ) 11; to have been caused by his wrongful act, neglect, or default."

Mr. Goodrich (United States).—Mr. President, as I understand this provision, it is the law of England to-day, and has been since the 35th Victoria. This provision is taken bodily from that Act, because it seems to me to be a very beneficial provision, and to enforce the duty of common humanity. I have also understood that there is no objection to any part of this Resolution except the concluding paragraph—at least I have heard no opposition to any other part of it. I have not put into the present amendment any penalty that is prescribed by the Statute of 35th Victoria, which is a pecuniary penalty, and, if I mistake not, a misdemeanour which may be punishable by imprisonment. This is also the unwritten law of the Admiralty Courts to-day. Of course, I am speaking of the Courts of my own country. The Courts take cognizance of this duty in passing upon the merits of a collision at sea, and will often say that the running away of the vessel implies that she is at fault. The provision is also put into the Report of the Committee on Life-Saving Systems and Devices. I do not care about taking up the time of the Conference in discussing this. We all know what it means. I should like to have a vote upon it one way or the other. I am very much in favour of it in the interest of humanity, and if it is in the Rules the mariner will see it and obey it. If he has got to go to some other place to find it he will not necessarily do so.

Mr. Hall (Great Britain).—Mr. President, I need not say that I am in favour of this, because it is our law at present. But may I point out that I think the Delegate from the United States will get a unanimous vote if he does not press the last paragraph, viz.: "If he fails to do so, and no reasonable cause for such failure is shown, the collision shall, in the absence of proof to the contrary, he deemed to have been caused by his wrongful act, neglect, or default." If the last portion of it is opposed by any of the Powers, it is clear that it could not go into the Rules, because it interferes with their principle of law as well as of evidence. I venture to suggest to him much as I would like to see the proposition carried and inserted in the Rules, that he should not press it.

Dr. Sieveking (Germany).—Mr. President, the learned Delegate from the United States will perhaps allow me to suggest a very trifling amendment, and that is the insertion of the word "serious" before " danger."

Mr. Goodrich (United States).—Mr. President, I have no objection to that.

Dr. Sieveking (Germany).—Mr. President, the reasons are these: I do not think we ought to hasten too quickly over these Rules; and this is a law of great importance. We propose the insertion of the word "serious" because it is contained in the German law, which, apart from this word and apart from the last paragraph, is in the same wording as the English law. If we insert the word "serious" I do not think that we, in fact, alter the meaning of the English law, because every Judge would say that if there were a slight danger only it would not excuse a vessel leaving when there is danger of life or property being lost. I do not think that the real meaning of the law would be altered, but it would be if we omitted the word "serious," where it is in the German law. We have it provided for in the German law now, that a captain is not allowed to leave the other vessel in case of a collision unless there is *serious* danger to his own vessel; and if we alter that and say where there is danger to his own vessel, it would be quite clear that it is our intention to allow him to get away from the other vessel even if he should incur a slight danger only by standing by. He might always say that there was a slight danger, because every vessel which is on the sea is, in a certain degree, exposed to danger, and he might always have an excuse for saying that there was danger, not a serious danger, but some danger. That is not the meaning of the law, therefore I beg to suggest the insertion of this word "serious."

Mr. Goodrich (United States).—Mr. President, I can see no objection to the insertion of that word, and if it is desirable, I would suggest the amendment to the original proposition, by adding in the third line the word "serious" before the word "danger," and in the tenth line to strike out the word "or" and insert the word "and," that being a clerical mistake, and to strike out the last paragraph beginning "If he fails to do so."

The President.—The Secretary will please read the Resolution as amended.

The Resolution as amended is as follows:—

"In every case of collision between two vessels it shall be the duty of the master or person in charge of each vessel, if and so far as he can do so without serious danger to his own vessel, crew, and passengers (if any), to stay by the other vessel until he has ascertained that she has no need of further assistance, and to render to the other vessel, her master, crew, and passengers (if any), such assistance as may be practicable and as may be necessary in order to save them from any danger caused by the collision; and also to give to the master or person in charge of the other vessel the name of his own vessel, and of her port of registry, or of the port or place to which she belongs, and also the names of the ports and places from which and to which she is bound. If he fails so to do, and no reasonable cause for such failure is shown, the collision shall, in the absence of proof to the contrary, be deemed to have been caused by his wrongful act, neglect, or default."

Captain Richard (France).—Mr. President, I think that the Resolution as proposed, with a slight amendment introduced by the learned Dr. Sieveking, has already been voted upon by the Conference. I would like to know to what new use this Resolution is to be applied. I think that five or six days ago this Resolution as now proposed was voted upon, together with the Report of the Committee on Life-Saving Appliances, in which it is expressed. If I understand the honourable Mr. Goodrich's intention, he desires to introduce it into the Rules of the Road. I do not see what that proposition has in common with the Rules of the Road. What is required is a legislative sanction and the application of a penalty, the proper place for which is not in the Rules of the Road.

Mr. Goodrich (United States).—Mr. President, my own idea is that it should be put in as a new section to the Rules, and it would be section 32.

Captain Richard (France).—Mr. President, I do not see the advantage of placing this Resolution in the Rules of the Road, because you cannot give it any legal sanction. When a collision takes place, then, in order to punish the misdemeanour or the crime resulting therefrom, you will be obliged to bring the captain before the Court; but in some countries, including ours, this Rule is not a part of the law, and our Courts cannot reach a master in such a case, unless it be for culpable homicide; otherwise, if we cannot fasten this charge upon him, we are compelled to inflict a nominal fine for having failed to obey the Rules of the Road. In our country the infringement of the Rules of the Road is only considered by our Courts when damages are involved. Of course I do not mention the action of the Navy Department, which can always take away a certificate from a master as a measure of discipline. But so long as this Resolution has been adopted in our law, and simply forms part of a Decree, we cannot inflict a sufficient penalty. I would therefore ask that it be not introduced into the Rules of the Road. We must have an Article in our Code which will punish such an act, and I think that if we succeed in introducing such an Article into our Code, it will be far more effective than by simply inserting it in the Rules of the Road.

The President.—The question is upon the Resolution of the Delegate for the United States. Is the Conference ready for the question?

Captain Richard (France).—Mr. President, I propose that the Honourable Mr. Goodrich's proposition be inserted wherever it may be thought proper as a recommendation to our Governments, but that it shall not be inserted into the Rules of the Road, as for its proper observance a law should be made on the subject by each country interested in it.

Mr. Goodrich (United States).—Mr. President, unless it goes into the Rule it will be a *brutum fulmen*. If you put it in the Rule where the sailor can see it, he will obey the Rule, if it is where his attention is pointed to it, and where disobedience to it will cause him to suffer by way of damage. He would probably be pronounced against, *primâ facie*, if he did not obey this Rule.

Captain Richard (France).—Mr. President, I think our eminent and eloquent colleague is in error. It will be much easier to call a mariner's attention to the Article if it is made part of our laws. I am quite certain that an Article of a law is far superior, so far as enforcing the strict observance of a Rule, than anything that can be embodied in an official Circular or a Decree. For let it be understood that the Rules of the Road with us are only in the form of Decrees; you will then only have a positive safeguard in your law against the crime of inhumanity, which the proposition is aimed at.

Captain Salvesen (Norway).—Mr. President, I am quite of the same opinion as the gallant Delegate for France. In our country we have, as I said the other day, passed this Resolution as a law, and we have provided that if they fail to obey this they are to be tried by the common law, and can be punished by fine or imprisonment or hard labour; but the fact that it is a law does not prevent it from being printed, so that the sailor will have it in the same book where he has the Rules of the Road. I do not see any objection to the course proposed by the gallant Delegate from France.

Mr. Goodrich (United States).—Mr. President, I move that the principle of this Resolution be adopted, and that it be appended in the Resolutions already adopted by the Conference which are to be annexed to Appendix (B).

Captain Richard (France).—Mr. President, yes, I accept that proposition.

The question was put to the Conference upon adopting this Resolution and adding it to Appendix (B), and it was carried.

Mr. Goodrich (United States).—Mr. President, I would like to ask the attention of the Delegates of Great Britain. I presented a Resolution which instructed the Committee on Collocation of the Rules to prepare a general Report of the proceedings of the Conference. The Delegate from Great Britain suggested to me in private conversation that such a Report was unnecessary in his judgment, because the Protocol embraced a Report. I make this motion purely on behalf of the Secretary, and possibly because it seems to me that it would be well and that it would be wise to have something else than the Protocol to present to the different Powers. There is a Resolution already adopted by the Conference, as follows:—

"*Resolved,*—That such Rules and Regulations and amendments as this Conference shall finally approve shall be translated and published in the English, French, and Spanish languages."

It is possible that, inasmuch as all this work cannot be done in the recess between now and a week from Monday, that a proper Report could be drawn up, simply pointing to the Protocol, and so as to close the Protocol in good shape.

Mr. Hall (Great Britain).—Mr. President, may I point out this: that it is no part of our duty to make a Report of the proceedings of this Conference to any other Government but our own. I must positively decline to draw up a Report for any Government except our own. We are not sent here as Delegates for any other Government. We shall hand to our Government any such Report as we think necessary, but if I am to be asked to make a Report to any other Government, I must distinctly decline. It is no part of my duty, and I decline to do it. The Protocols will be handed by each Delegate to his Government. The United States' Delegates will, of course, make their Report to the United States' Government, and I most respectfully decline to make any Report to any Government but my own.

Dr. Sieveking (Germany).—Mr. President, I do not think that there is any form in which we, as a Conference, can enter into any direct communication with the different Governments. The Delegates can. They are appointed by the Government, and they are expected to give in their Reports to their respective Governments. But there is no connection between the Conference and the Government. What are the contents of the Report to be? Is it to be a letter addressed to the Governments signed by the President of the Conference? I do not think there would be any reason for such a correspondence. There has been no correspondence between the Governments and the Conference. They have never addressed us. Are we to address them? Then the question would arise: In what language are we to address them? I think it would be the better course to address them in twenty-six languages.

Mr. Goodrich (United States).—Mr. President, I do not suppose that the Report of the Collocation Committee of this Conference is a Report made by the Conference to the several Governments. It is a Report of the proceedings of the Conference which each Delegate takes to his own Government, and it strikes me that the learned Delegate from England might just as well say that he declined respectfully to hand the Protocol of the proceedings of this Conference to his Government as to say that he declined to make a Report to any other Government. I do not see the point of his remarks. It is true he does not make a Report to any other Government by making a Report to the Conference. It is a Report which will finish up the Protocol. Of course, I am free to say that this is the first International Conference which has been held, and I do not know that there is any precedent which could be cited as governing the course of the Conference, but all that I want is to round up the Protocol of the Conference in some apt way.

Mr. Hall (Great Britain).—Mr. President, may I point out that the course is universal in all Conferences. The Protocols are either taken, as they are here, in shorthand, and taken word for word—which, by the way, is a most exceptional course to pursue—or Minutes are drawn up by the Secretary, and these are signed by the members of the Conference. Where they are drawn up word for word, printer's errors and slight grammatical errors have to be corrected, and these Protocols form the record of the Conference. But I have never heard of any Conference in the world drawing up a final Report to anybody or from anybody. We have our Protocols, and we have our copy of the Reports of the Committees and the Resolutions which have been passed, and they all appear in the Protocols. We shall hand them to our respective Governments, and I take it for granted that the Delegates will draw up their Reports to their own Governments. That is quite enough for us to do, and I really must positively but respectfully decline to assist in drawing up a Report for any other purpose. I will report to my Government because I am sent here by my Government.

There is no Report required to wind up the proceedings of the Conference, as the learned Delegate from the United States suggests. I have no doubt the Secretary of the United States' Delegation will do exactly as we shall do. He will see to it that the Delegation reports the proceedings, and that, without any doubt, will be overlooked by the Delegation of the United States. They have their own Secretary, as we have our own Secretary, and each Delegation will draw up their own Reports and make them to their own Government. I do not wish to shirk work, but I must very respectfully state that it is not our duty, as Delegates, to report to anybody else but to our own Government.

Mr. Goodrich (United States).—Mr. President, I will withdraw the Resolution.

The President.—The Resolution is withdrawn. The Chair desires to call the attention of the Conference to one point. A Resolution was passed in the early days of the Conference, which the Secretary will read.

The Resolution is as follows:—

"*Resolved,*—That such Rules, Regulations, and amendments as this Conference shall finally approve shall be translated and published in the English, French, and Spanish languages."

The President.—This Resolution was passed at the suggestion of the Delegates speaking the Spanish language. The only way the Chair sees out of the difficulty is to have the Delegates who speak the Spanish language make out their own Report and let it be printed by the United States' Government.

Admiral Viel (Chile).—Mr. President, if you think there is nobody in the United States to translate into the Spanish language the action of the Conference——

The President.—The Chair did not say that. The Chair said that if the Delegation which speaks the Spanish language would make their own Report it could be presented to the State Department, and if they chose to publish it, upon the Resolution of the Conference, they could do so.

Commodore Monasterio (Mexico).—Mr. President, Admiral Viel has inquired whether the Collocation Committee would not make a translation of the Rules of the Road. As I was a member of that Committee, I was ready to undertake that work, but I did not think that that work would be approved, because it certainly could not be signed by the other members of the Committee, who were unfamiliar with Spanish, and therefore they could not take the responsibility.

Dr. Sieveking (Germany).—Mr. President, I think the best way out of this difficulty would be to cancel the Resolution which has been passed for these reasons: it is stated in this Resolution that the Rules and Regulations, as they have been passed by the Conference, are to be translated and published in three languages. I do not see what was the intent of publishing them. Where are they to be published, or in what paper, by whom, under what authority?—the authority of the Conference? I suppose that it was meant that it should be under the authority of the Conference. Then what would come of this is this: that we as a Conference have the duty of authorizing two translations, not only in the English text, but two other translations. I do not think the Conference would be a proper authority on that, because the greater part of us would not be able to master the Spanish language and the French language in such a way as to consider ourselves to be good judges or to be capable of making a good translation.

This is a question of very great importance, because if these texts are published in three languages under the authority of the Conference, one text would be, in point of law, on the same footing as the other, and if there was a difference, as might very easily occur, difficulties would arise and the Courts would be unable to say which is the proper text. Then the responsibility would rest on the Conference, which, I am sure, is not a proper body to bear this responsibility upon its shoulders. It would be a very difficult thing to make exact translations. I was very glad when the German language was not mentioned among those, as I very much prefer to have the translation made in Germany, and made by people who would bestow very much greater care upon it than this Conference could bestow. It is quite clear that the legislative authority of the Rules must rest upon each Government, and upon the legislative authority of each Government, and so let each Government publish the Rules in its own language, and care for the translation and publishing of them in its own language, and let the Delegates report to them from the Conference and attach to them the English text. Let the Delegates accompany it, if they choose, with the translation, or let them leave the translation to other persons. I do not think it is possible for the Conference to do it.

Señor Varella de Torres (Spain).—I quite agree with the learned Delegate from Germany in what he has just stated. Neither the Spanish Government nor the Delegates from Spain want to have the translation made here. For me it is enough to take the English text to my Government, and it is to the interest of the Government to have the translation made there.

Mr. Goodrich (United States). I move to reconsider this Resolution which has just been read. The Resolution is as follows:—

"*Resolved,*—That such Rules, Regulations, and amendments as this Conference shall finally approve shall be translated and published in the English, French, and Spanish languages."

The President.—Is the Conference ready for the question?

The question was put to the Conference upon the motion to reconsider the Resolution, and it was carried.

The President.—The question now is upon the Resolution.

Mr. Goodrich (United States).—I move to lay the Resolution on the table.

The President.—Is the Conference ready for the question?

The question was put to the Conference upon the motion to lay the Resolution on the table, and it was carried.

261

Mr. Goodrich (United States).—Mr. President, there was also a Resolution passed that the discussions and proceedings be conducted in English and French, and that the Protocol be printed in both languages. I move to reconsider that Resolution, the intention being to ask you to lay it on the table so far as the last part of the Resolution is concerned.

The President.—The question is upon the motion to reconsider the Resolution.

The question was put to the Conference upon the motion to reconsider the Resolution, and it was carried.

Mr. Goodrich (United States).—I now move to lay this Resolution on the table.

The President.—Is the Conference ready for the question?

The question was put to the Conference upon the motion to lay the Resolution on the table, and it was adopted.

The Conference thereupon adjourned until Monday, 30th December, at 11 A.M.

Washington, Monday, December 30, 1889, 11 o'clock A.M.

THE Conference was called to order at 11 o'clock A.M., Admiral Bowden-Smith, Delegate for Great Britain, in the Chair.

The Chairman.—Admiral Franklin has asked me to take the Chair for a short time, as he is engaged this morning at a funeral, and Captain Sampson is ill and unable to come. I have to announce to the Conference that Mavroyeni Bey, Delegate for Turkey, has appeared at the Conference this morning and taken his seat.

Captain Richard (France).—Mr. Chairman, I desire to ask a question, and thereafter to make a motion. That question is as follows: at our last session one of the Delegates from the United States made a proposition to annul a decision, which was passed on the 17th October at one of our first sessions, viz., not to print the Protocol in French and in English, but only in English. This Resolution was thereupon adopted by the Conference. I do not make a point in regard to this proposition being out of order, as it was made at the close of our labours. Neither will I ask why the Resolution of the 17th October had not, up to the end of the month of December, been carried out. I will ask for no explanation on that point. Besides, I voted with the other members of the Conference to suppress the French translation, because I have no confidence in such translation. But, on the other hand, a certain number of Delegates expressed themselves in French in this Conference. It is not my duty to speak in behalf of my colleagues, but it is only on my own behalf that I desire to ask this question. But the new state of affairs is such that I desire to know, and I think I am entitled to demand, if the remarks which I made before the Conference will be reproduced in French in the original text, which alone, so far as I am concerned, is entitled to credit, or whether there will be no other text than the English as it has already appeared in the Protocol. In the latter event, I am placed in a rather difficult position, which you will appreciate. I have only corrected the French text. So far as I am concerned, the French text is the only and original one, and I hope that the French text will appear side by side with the English. When I revised it, I had reason to suppose that the English translation would be of relatively little importance, and that the French text would have been put beside it for the purpose of corroborating the English text.

I now desire to ask the Chair whether it is the intention to reproduce my original language as uttered by me, or whether the Reports will only reproduce the English text of the translation which was made. This is the question which I desire to ask, and to which I should like to have an answer.

The Chairman.—In answer to the gallant Delegate from France, the Chair will state that he understands it is the intention to print them only in English. If anything further is desired the Chair would be glad to hear suggestions.

Captain Richard (France).—Mr. Chairman, if the original text is to be suppressed, and only the English to be printed, I desire to declare right here that I absolutely refuse to append my signature to the Protocol, there being no original text to clearly and distinctly corroborate the language which I used here. I will not accept the English text alone. Under those circumstances, the French text should have appeared together with the English in the Report of the proceedings. In other words, the speeches of the Delegates who spoke in French should have appeared in French in the same manner that those spoken in English were reported in English. Consequently, I make all reservations regarding my signature to the official Report.

Mr. Goodrich (United States).—Mr. Chairman, perhaps it will meet the views of the gallant Delegate from France if the proposition be limited to printing in French the remarks which have been made to the Conference in French.

Captain Richard (France).—Mr. Chairman, I have never claimed anything else. I simply ask that the speeches which I made before the Conference be printed in the original language in which I delivered them.

I should, moreover, say that it is not my intention to raise any difficulty here, and that in whatever manner satisfaction is given to me, I will be quite contented. Let the French text be placed opposite the English text; let it be inserted at the end; it makes little difference to me; all I ask is that it be inserted so that the English translation can be compared with the original text.

The Chairman.—The Chair understands that the gallant Delegate for France wishes what he has said before the Conference to be printed in French, and the Chair understands that it can be done, excepting what took place on the first two days of the Conference, and it will be done, excepting what took place during those first two days.

Mr. Goodrich (United States).—Mr. Chairman, I present the following Resolution, which will meet the views of the gallant Delegate from France.

Captain Richard (France).—Mr. Chairman, I do not think that any motion is necessary. I simply ask for an explanation, which should have been given at the outset. I do not see the necessity of any Resolution to that effect.

The Chairman.—The following Resolution will be read to the Conference, proposed by the Delegate for the United States.

The Resolution proposed by the Delegate from the United States is as follows:—

"*Resolved*,—That where remarks by members were addressed to the Conference in French, such remarks be printed in French."

The Chairman.—Is the Conference ready for a vote upon this Resolution?

The question was put to the Conference upon the Resolution proposed by the Delegate for the United States, and the Resolution was adopted.

Captain Richard (France).—Mr. Chairman, I now have a proposition to make. I desire to propose to the Conference "that a final Report be printed, establishing for each Division of the Programme, in the order of such Divisions, the Resolutions adopted by the Conference." No one in this assembly, I think, will contest the propriety of such a measure, which is the natural termination of our labours. If I am not mistaken, it would be in accordance with custom under like conditions. You know how our Resolutions have been scattered in a great number of Committee Reports and Protocols, and how convenient it would be to see at a glance all the Resolutions which have been adopted by the Conference. In addition to the usefulness of such a measure, I would attach a still higher importance to it. At our last session it was unexpectedly proposed to the Conference that a final Report be made. The Delegates from the Great Powers who sit on my right hand opposed this proposition. It is evident that we have to address a final Report only to our Government. To such Government alone must we render an account of our words, of our actions, and of our votes. And to it alone must we express our favourable and unfavourable criticisms in regard to the propriety and the value of the measures which have been voted upon and adopted by the Conference.

But, on the other hand, I am anxious that before breaking up, and at the moment that we are about to depart, that our attitude should not, outside of the pale of this Conference, give rise to unfair criticisms. I think that this Final Act should be drawn up to only include Resolutions already adopted which can give rise to no further discussions. As it will only include Resolutions which have been already adopted, and in regard to which there can be no further discussion, the work can be performed by the Secretary acting under the authority of the President.

By transmitting through the President a copy of this Report to the Government which he represents, the Conference will indicate that they consider their duties terminated, and that they desire to take leave of the Government which has received them, and of the country which has hospitably entertained them, with an expression of their high respect and deep gratitude.

Rear-Admiral Franklin, the President of the Conference, here took the Chair.

The President.—The Resolution submitted by the Delegate from France will be read.

Captain Richard (France).—Mr. President, I need hardly tell you that, although the Conference is impatient to set the time for its departure, this measure will not entail any delay in such departure, for this Report can be simply signed by the President and the Secretary, and our responsibility would be safely guarded by intrusting it to their care.

Mr. Hall (Great Britain).—Mr. President, I think the proposal from the gallant Delegate from France is one that ought to meet with our support, because it appears to me to be a very simple way of arriving at a proper conclusion. Of course the real evidence of our labours will be the Protocols, but they, I take it, would not be signed by the Delegates as a body, because I do not suppose that any one of us has had time or inclination to wade through the whole of these Protocols. We have corrected them so far as we are personally concerned, no doubt. What I understand to be the proposition of the gallant Delegate from France is that the Resolutions which have been carried by the Conference should be drawn up by the Secretary in their order, dealing with each of the Divisions numerically, and that such a digest, if I may so call it, when printed should be authorized by you as President. Of course, if that be done, and this digest be distributed by the United States to the Powers which have taken part in this Conference, it will be an authorized exposition of what has taken place in the Conference. I understand that this is the proposition of the gallant Delegate from France, and if I am correct in that supposition, I will give it my hearty support.

Mr. Goodrich (United States).—Mr. President, I may say that this is the proposal or the desire which I had in my mind when I presented a certain Resolution in regard to authorizing a similar thing to be done by the Collocation Committee; but I think the better course is the one suggested by the gallant Delegate from France, and the Resolution will have the assent of the Delegates for the United States.

The President.—The Secretary will please read the Resolution of the Delegate from France.

The Resolution is as follows:—

"Qu'un Acte Final soit imprimé, établissant pour chaque division du programme et dans l'ordre des divisions, les Résolutions votées par la Conférence.

"Cet Acte sera signé au nom de la Conférence par le Président et le Secrétaire."

Mr. Goodrich (United States).—Mr. President, I suppose it is not necessary to submit that to the Conference.

The President.—The Chair would suggest that it would be better to submit it to the Conference.

Captain Richard (France).—Mr. President, I do not see any reason for submitting this Report to the Conference. It will consist of Resolutions which have been voted upon, the text of which is absolutely settled, and which it is only necessary to put together. This work may be a long one for the

Secretary, but it is a labour which contains nothing new, and I do not see that the Conference can make any correction in it. I therefore think that any revision would be needless.

Mr. Hall (Great Britain).—Mr. President, I quite agree with what has fallen from the gallant Delegate from France. It is certainly not necessary for such a Report to be submitted to the Conference, and I apprehend that his object in asking you to be so good as to sign it and allow it to be issued is to prevent the necessity of having it submitted to the Conference. It would be absurd for us to wait here for the formal purpose of reading through a document compiled by the Secretary from the Protocols. I have no doubt that the work will be accurately done, and from the experience we have had in this Conference with the work of the Secretaries, we can make certain that it will be accurately done. Therefore I support the proposal that this document, when it be drawn up, as it will be drawn up by Mr. Cottman, when submitted to you shall be signed by you, and then it shall be distributed to the different Powers who have taken part in this Conference.

The President.—The Resolution of the Delegate from France is now before the Conference.

The question was put to the Conference upon the adoption of the Resolution of the Delegate from France, and was carried.

The President.—The next business in order will be the Report of Committee No. 3 upon General Division IX. The Secretary will please read the Report.

The Report of Committee No. 3 upon General Division IX is as follows:—

"*Report of the Committee upon General Divisions IX, X, XI, and XII of the Programme.*

"Sir, "*Washington, December* 28, 1889.

"In submitting their Report the Committee have thought it the most convenient plan to deal separately with each of the General Divisions which have been discussed and considered by them.

"GENERAL DIVISION IX.

"*Warnings of approaching Storms.*

"(*a.*) The transmission of warnings.
"(*b.*) The uniformity of signals employed.

"(*a.*) *The Transmission of Warnings.*—The Committee understand that the various Meteorological Offices in Europe are in frequent and intimate communication, and interchange telegraphic information for the purpose of weather forecasting on that side of the Atlantic Ocean; while the Meteorological Offices of the United States and the Dominion of Canada act in concert on the Western side; and also that a similar custom prevails in many Eastern countries.

"The preparation of weather forecasts and the transmission of warnings regarding expected storms must, by the very nature of the subject, be dealt with locally; and it is the opinion of the Committee very questionable whether any useful purpose would be gained by the adoption of uniformity of methods, except so far as the general progress of scientific knowledge indicates the direction of possible improvement; and this, it is hardly necessary to say, is more likely to be secured by work carried on independently rather than under any uniform system.

"(*b.*) *The Uniformity of Signals employed.*—Storm-warning signals were first introduced in the interests of the shipping or fishing-vessels lying at anchor in harbour or proposing to put to sea. Lately the same warning signals have been freely extended to coast stations, with a view to give information regarding the weather to passing vessels. Inasmuch as these may be local or foreign traders, the Committee are of opinion that such signals should, as far as possible, be in international agreement.

"The established signals originally in use in Europe are evidently founded on the seaman's knowledge of the 'law of storms,' and, while warning him of an approaching cyclone, indicate whether the northern or southern portion is expected to pass over the district. Experience proves that this was practically sufficient information for the masters of vessels in a neighbouring harbour, who would know whether the cyclone was approaching or had passed, but it is scarcely sufficient for coasting vessels, especially those proceeding on a course at right angles to the direction in which the cyclone is moving.

"In the opinion of the Committee it is therefore desirable that storm-signals displayed at coast stations should give to passing vessels some further information as to whether storms are approaching or have passed the station; and in reference to this, the Committee desire to call attention to the fact that this want has been supplied by the system now in use in the United States. The German system indicates four directions from which a storm is expected, and whether its probable course is to the right or the left. (See Appendix C.)

"In dealing with this matter the Committee have had the advantage of hearing the views of General A. W. Greely, the Chief Signal Officer, in charge of the United States' Weather Bureau, and he has summarized them in a Memorandum contained under cover of a letter dated the 23rd December, 1889, both of which are appended to this Report, and to which the Committee desire to draw special attention. (See Appendix A.)

"It will be seen that, in this Memorandum, General Greely has indicated the practical reasons for adopting, in lieu of cone-shaped signals, the use of coloured flags for notifying storm warnings on the coasts of the United States, which it is claimed can be seen (except in very calm weather) at a greater distance, and by means of which additional information can be given.

"The Committee consider that this subject is of such a technical nature that they are not prepared to express a decided opinion upon it. They recommend, however, the Conference to invite the various maritime countries to consider the best practical mode of signalling by day, whether by shapes,

[93]

coloured or black, by flags, or by the two combined, and by night, by means of lights, coloured or white, arranged to represent distinctive forms.

"Together with the Memorandum alluded to, General Greely inclosed a copy of 'General Order No. 29,' dated from the Signal Office, War Department, 11th November, 1889, from which a paragraph is quoted, and also a paper of diagrams showing the storm, cautionary, and wind-direction signals in use in the United States. These signals are reproduced in Appendix (B) to this Report.

"In recapitulation, the Committee recommend the Conference to invite the maritime countries interested to take into consideration the establishment of a uniform system of indicating storm warnings by day and by night, and that such a system should, as far as possible, include signals indicating whether the storm is approaching or has passed the station.

"Rear-Admiral S. R. Franklin, United States' Navy,
  "President, International Marine Conference, &c."

The President.—The Report of the Committee upon General Division IX is before the Conference.

Captain Mensing (Germany).—Mr. President, as Chairman of Committee No. 3, I would like to remark that in the Report of General Greely the list of storm-signal stations is not complete. You will find the list on pp. 9 and 10. Different changes have come into use since 1877, and the Committee have thought it worth while to have a list printed giving all the different storm-signals in use in the various countries at the present time. This list has been completed, but it was necessarily rather late because the information was received only during the last hours. It is ready to be printed, and if the Conference should think it of any value it can be printed and distributed to-morrow, and be attached to the Report. I would like to know the opinion of the Conference about it.

The President.—The Delegate from Germany suggests the printing of information received upon this subject at a late hour, and submits the question.

Mr. Goodrich (United States).—Mr. President, I should like to inquire of the gallant Delegate from Germany whether or not he himself considers it of sufficient value to be printed?

Captain Mensing (Germany).—Mr. President, I am quite sure about it, because there is not a single publication at the present moment which gives the actual list of storm-signals in use in the different countries. All of the lists which I have been able to look through and compare are incomplete. Some contain great errors and some small ones.

Mr. Hall (Great Britain).—Mr. President, I apprehend that we could perfectly well authorize the printing of the list and have it attached as an Appendix to the Report. I do not suppose that it would alter the Report at all.

Captain Mensing (Germany).—Mr. President, there will be no change in the Report at all. It is only for the information of the Governments, which, I believe, will be very glad to get such information.

The President.—The question is upon the motion of the Delegate from Germany to print the information relative to storm-signals.

The question was put to the Conference upon the motion of the Delegate from Germany, and the motion was carried.

The President.—The matter will be printed and appended to the Report of Committee No. 3 upon General Division IX. The Report of the Committee upon General Division IX is now before the Conference.

Mr. Goodrich (United States).—Mr. President, I move that the Report of the Committee upon the subject of General Division IX be adopted by the Conference.

The President.—It is moved that the Report of Committee No. 3 upon General Division IX be adopted by the Conference. Is the Conference ready for the question?

The question was put to the Conference upon the adoption of the Report upon General Division IX, and it was adopted.

The President.—The next order of business is the Report of Committee No. 3 upon General Division XII. The Secretary will please read the Report.

The Report of Committee No. 3 upon General Division XII is as follows:—

"GENERAL DIVISION XII.

"*A Uniform System of Buoys and Beacons.*

"(*a.*) Uniformity in colour of buoys.
"(*b.*) Uniformity in numbering of buoys.

"Owing to the absence of a uniformity in buoyage, mariners, up to very recent times, seldom attempted to navigate a district by means of the buoyage unless they were specially well acquainted with the local system. But now that a certain degree of uniformity on a fundamental basis prevails, mariners in general are more induced to navigate their vessel, trusting to it and the Chart of the district; it therefore becomes of greater importance that such uniformity should be extended as far as possible.

"Two principal characters are used for distinguishing buoys and beacons—colour and shape.

"The first object to be attained, from an international point of view, is uniformity. For that purpose colour is the best means, as applying to all systems of whatever kind, while the shape admits numerous exceptions. The colour is also applicable in all countries and with little expense, whereas the immediate adoption of shape would involve changes of several existing systems. Moreover, experience has proved that very many, if not the majority of channels, are now buoyed with sufficient distinctness without resorting to difference of form.

"For these reasons, and while the opinion prevails that at night and in thick weather difference in form is a better means of distinction than difference of colour, your Committee advise that uniformity in colour should be adopted as a general rule, and that the use of shape should remain optional.

"While, in the opinion of some members, the single colours of black and red are not so distinctive in contrast as a single colour used in connection with a parti-colour, experience gained in many buoyage districts, and particularly where used in conjunction with form, has proved that these dark colours are sufficiently distinctive for the safe navigation of districts where a more complicated system is not necessary. Single-coloured buoys are also more readily and cheaply repainted than parti-coloured buoys. We therefore recommend that the largely used red and black colours should be adopted generally for marking respectively the starboard and port sides of single channels.

"Many districts, however, require a more complicated system of buoyage to identify the several neighbouring channels one from the other, such as the entrances of rivers with numerous channels like the Thames, the outlying shoals off the coast of the North Sea, the numerous shoals separated from each other by complicated channels such as in the Baltic Sea, &c.

"In some of such districts a parti-coloured buoy is used, with much advantage, as a port-hand buoy. In a few—notably in England—a single black colour is used as a starboard-hand buoy. Inasmuch as a single black colour is in general use as a port-hand buoy in neighbouring districts visited by the same shipping, we suggest that the authorities of such countries should be invited to consider the great general advantages to shipping that would result from the adoption of uniformity in colour, by discontinuing this dangerous custom of using a black colour to denote a starboard-hand as well as a port-hand buoy.

"In some countries white is used as a distinctive colour, and with advantage when contrasted with a dark background. As this practice cannot lead vessels into danger, we hesitate to advise that it should be compulsorily interfered with.

"We are of opinion that where form is adopted, the two shapes, 'conical' and 'can,' are appropriate for marking the starboard and port sides of a channel, a spar-buoy taking the place of the can in certain cases.

"These forms are practically used in the United States, Germany, Canada, India, and Great Britain. But the various countries are not all in agreement as to which side of the channel is to be marked by a conical buoy, and which by a can or spar buoy.

"It follows that one or more of the countries would necessarily have to rearrange their system, but, if the work were done gradually, the Committee believe that this could be performed at a minimum of expense in no way comparable with the great advantage that would result to navigation.

"In connection with such a change of system we are informed that an extensive rearrangement in bouyage was recently carried out by Great Britain, the different shapes being changed from one side of the channels to the other side, the change being brought about without any casualty to navigation.

"As regards top-marks, we recommend that those countries whose buoyage is based on colour alone should, whenever top-marks are used to denote sides of a channel, use conical or can-shaped marks on the existing buoys or beacons.

"We are of opinion that the mode of distinguishing buoys from each other by names, numbers, or letters should be left to the decision of the various countries, but that all numbers and letters should be in consecutive order, commencing at the seaward end of the district.

"The Committee are of opinion that districts where the buoyage is so complicated as to have led the authorities to adopt a compass-system of marking, such as in the Baltic Sea, cannot, with a view to general uniformity, be coupled with the simpler systems found sufficient elsewhere; they therefore hesitate to recommend a fundamental change in such districts. But, after studying the 'Sailing Directions' and the publication of Mr. S. A. Philipsen, Copenhagen, on 'Beaconage and Buoyage of Different Nations,' which presents graphically the plans adopted by several nations, particularly those interested in the navigation of the Baltic Seas, the Committee find that the systems now in use, so far as colour and top-marks are concerned, are so similar that they recommend the Conference to suggest to the countries interested the desirability of the adoption of one uniform system, at least as regards colour.

"The Committee understand that the following are the colours and top-marks at present in use in the various districts using the compass-system to define the bearing of the mark or buoy from the danger it indicates:—

"Marks on the *north* side of a shoal:

| Norway, Sweden | Black. |
| Russsia, Finland, Denmark | White. |

"Marks on the *south* side of a shoal:

| Norway | White. |
| Sweden, Russia, Finland, Denmark | Red |

"Marks on the *east* side of a shoal:
- Norway ... Black.
- Sweden ... Black, with a white horizontal band.
- Russia ... Red, with white horizontal bands.
- Finland ... Half red and half white horizontal.
- Denmark ... Red.

"Marks on the *west* side of a shoal:
- Norway } White.
- Denmark }
- Russia ... White and black horizontal bands.
- Finland ... Half white and half red horizontal.
- Sweden ... Red.

"Marks on a *middle ground*, with fairway channels on either side:
- Norway ... Black and white horizontal bands.
- Finland } Red and white horizontal bands.
- Denmark }
- Russia ... Black.

"*Top-marks.*

"On buoys or marks on the *north* side of a shoal:
- Norway ... Brooms turned downwards.
- Russia ... Broom or brooms not systematically arranged.
- Finland ... A pole without a top-mark.
- Sweden ... A ball.

"On buoys or marks on the *south* side of a shoal:
- Russia }
- Finland } Broom turned upwards.
- Norway }
- Sweden }

"On buoys or marks on the *east* side of a shoal:
- Norway ... Broom turned downwards.
- Finland ... A pole without a top-mark.
- Sweden ... A ball.
- Russia ... Two brooms { upper one turned upwards. lower one turned downwards.

"On buoys or marks on the *west* side of a shoal:
- Norway ... Broom turned upwards.
- Sweden } Broom turned downwards.
- Finland }
- Russia ... Two brooms { upper one turned downwards. lower one turned upwards.

On marks on a *middle ground*, with fairway channels on either side:
- Norway } A ball.
- Russia }
- Finland ... A cross.

"Owing to the difficulty in choosing a fourth single colour—green being universally used to denote a wreck—it practically becomes necessary, in arranging for a general system, if four distinct modes of colouring are adopted to mark the four cardinal bearings of or from a shoal, to resort to one or more parti-colours to be used in conjunction with red, black, and white.

"On the principle of using four colours to mark the four sides of a shoal, the Committee put forward the following scheme, based on the least change that would be necessary in altering the present systems to a uniform plan; and they recommend the Conference to bring it to the notice of the countries interested, as an example, showing that uniformity is attainable if they will agree to consider the subject:

"All shoals, marked on the compass system, to be marked—

"On the *north* side by a single black or white colour.
   south side by red.
   east side by half red and half white combined.
   west side by half white and half black combined.

"On rocks in fairway, with channels on either hand, to be marked black or red, with horizontal bands.

"If such colours were adopted, then the following changes of colour would be necessary:

"The marks on the *north* side of a shoal would remain coloured black or white, as they now are in all countries using the compass system.

"The marks on the *south* side of a shoal would, in—

"Norway, have to be changed from white to red.

"The marks on the *east* side of a shoal would, in—

"Norway, have to be changed from black to half red and half white.

"Sweden, have to be changed from black and white to half red and half white.

"Denmark, have to be changed from red to half red and half white.

"The marks on the *west* side of a shoal would, in—

"Norway and Denmark, have to be changed from white to half white and half black.

"Sweden, have to be changed from red to half white and half black.

"Finland, have to be changed from white and red to half white and half black.

"The marks on a rock in *fairway*, with channel on either side, if a white horizontal band is generally adopted, would, in Russia, have to be changed from black to black or red with white horizontal bands, in agreement with other countries.

"The Committee advise the Conference to invite the various Powers interested to consider the following general principles, which they put forward as a basis on which to build up a uniform international bouyage system for districts other than those where the compass system is in use:—

"The term 'starboard hand' shall denote that side of a navigable channel which is on the right hand of the mariner entering from seaward; the term 'port hand' shall denote that side which is on the left hand under the same circumstances.

"*Colour.*—Buoys defining the starboard hand shall be painted a single red colour.

"Buoys defining the port hand shall be painted a single black colour or a parti-colour.

"Buoys defining middle grounds shall be painted with horizontal bands.

"*Form.*—Wherever form is used as a distinctive character—

"Buoys defining the starboard hand shall be conical, and those defining the port hand shall be can or spar.

"*Top-marks.*—Countries where form is not used as a distinctive character for buoys may adopt, as another distinctive feature for the buoys on either side of a channel, top-marks resembling a cone, to be used on the starboard side, or a cylinder on the port side of a channel.

"*Numbers and Letters.*—Numbers, letters, and names may be painted on the buoys, but they must never be so large as to interfere with their distinctive colouring.

"Wherever numbers and letters are used, they shall be in consecutive order, commencing from seaward.

"*Bouying and Marking of Wrecks.*—(*a.*) All buoys and the top sides of vessels used for the marking of wrecks shall be painted green, with a suitable white inscription.

"(*b.*) Where it is practicable, by day, one ball shall be exhibited on the side of the vessel nearest the wreck, and two placed vertically on the other side; three fixed white lights similarly arranged, but not the ordinary riding light, shall be shown from sunset to sunrise."

The President.—The Report is before the Conference for consideration.

Captain Norcross (United States).—Mr. President, before this Report is adopted, I would like to call attention to the third paragraph on the second page, which reads:—

"We are of opinion that, where form is adopted, the two shapes 'conical' and 'can' are appropriate for marking starboard and port sides of a channel, the spar buoy taking the place of the can in certain cases."

I would like to call attention to the fact that in many parts of the world can and conical buoys are entirely taken up in the winter time and replaced by spar buoys. I think this would be better if it should read in the last line: "the spar buoys taking their places in certain cases."

Captain Mensing (Germany).—Mr. President, the use of the spar buoy is different in different countries. In the United States they are only used in the winter time, but in other countries these spar buoys have been found, and are considered to be, one of the very best day marks that we can have, and on that account they have been adopted into the German system of buoyage on all the German coasts. It is different somewhat from the American spar buoy, in that the American spar buoy consists only of a wooden spar attached to the ground by some means. In Germany we only give them the general outline of a spar, and hence the name, but we make them of iron or steel, and give them sufficient height, so that they show above the water-line up to 9 metres, that is to say, 27 or 28 feet.

Now, this has been a most difficult subject. I do not believe that anybody who reads this Report can form really any conception of what a difficult task this has been for the Committee. The buoyage of the different countries represents an immense sum. I believe that the alterations which were introduced in Germany on the 1st of last year have cost them very near 3,000,000 marks, and the sums invested in this particular branch of service in other countries is even larger. It would have been very easy for the Committee to say, "There is no very pressing need, so we will let things be as they are; because in one country the system is based on colour, in another country form is put in the foreground, and in other countries different features are combined to make the system."

The Committee thought it would be better to try and find out whether it was not possible to come to some understanding, and to lay some foundation upon which to act in the future; and I will mention here (and I speak in the name of the Committee) that it is due to the gallant Admiral from Great Britain, Sir George Nares, that we have been able to come to some conclusion on this subject. He made propositions to us in this Committee, and the different systems were thoroughly discussed, and we came to the conclusion that we might try to have this one system adopted. You will see that colour is considered as being of the first importance. Now, for my personal opinion, I will say that I believe that form is better than colour, and that both combined are the best of all. But, at the outset, we found that there are different countries using the system based on colour, and that we could not change that system, because it is intimately connected with the system that is used on shoals to indicate the direction of a fairway through those most intricate channels to be found, for instance, on the French coast. That could not be given up, and so the question was, What can we do under the circumstances? Under the circumstances, we have placed colour first, because we found that we could all agree on that. But there had to be some changes made in order to bring uniformity in this direction.

The second question was, What could we do with regard to form? And if the honourable Delegate for the United States will be kind enough to read through the 7th paragraph on p. 5 he will find that it says there: "Wherever form is used as a distinctive character, buoys defining the starboard hand shall be conical, and those defining the port hand shall be can or spar." Now, if the United States do not see fit to introduce shape into their system, all that they have to do is to paint the buoys of the colours mentioned in the preceding paragraph. But, if they base their system, or if they declare that they base their system, on form and colour, then we thought that they should adopt either one of these forms. But, if they should base their system on form only, they could not use the spar buoy for sea-marking on the starboard hand. Now, as I said before, there has been considerable difficulty, and we found it to be quite out of the question that all countries should adopt this proposition; and therefore, in order to make it easier for these others to employ some other mark than the form of buoys, we have added the next paragraph, which speaks about top-marks, and there it says:—

"Countries where form is not used as a character for buoys may adopt as another distinctive feature for the buoys on either side of a channel top-marks resembling a cone, to be used on the starboard side, or a cylinder on the port side of a channel."

You see, all countries can introduce this, even if they do not want to introduce form. But, if they want to introduce a single feature for marking a channel, then everybody will be able in such cases to see whether the buoy is to be left on the starboard hand or the port hand by observing what the colour of the buoy is and what is the form of the top-mark used. After this explanation which I have given, I hope my gallant friend the Delegate from the United States will be satisfied.

Captain Norcross (United States).—Mr. President, I merely made that suggestion as a matter of convenience. I approve of the Report, and of everything contained in it. But I would call the attention of the gallant Delegate from Germany to the fact that I do not see how there could be any objection to allowing the spar buoys to take the place of the conical buoys when they are removed merely as a matter of convenience. This Report, as it now is, precludes the use of the spar buoy on the port hand.

Captain Mensing (Germany).—Mr. President, I apprehend there is really no difficulty in the way. The United States have simply to declare that they are entirely clear that they want to base their system on colour only, and then they may use their spar buoys on either side of the channel, and they may, as an additional safeguard, introduce top-marks, as mentioned here. But if they should declare that they would introduce form, then, of course, they must not place spar buoys upon both sides of the channel, in the winter time or any other time. I should like to assure my friend that in Germany we have, I suppose, just as thick ice as you have here, and we use our can buoys and our conical buoys and spar buoys all the winter through, by giving them proper anchors, and there has been found no difficulty whatever in keeping them in their positions.

Captain Malmberg (Sweden).—Mr. President, I only wish to state that I, as the Delegate for Sweden, do not find myself in a position to recommend to the consideration of the Swedish Government the adoption of the change of colour, as proposed in the Report of the Committee upon General Division XII. I merely desire to state this in order that it may appear upon the Protocol.

The President.—Has the Delegate from the United States any motion to make in connection with his remarks?

Captain Bisbee (China).—Mr. President, I think the objection of the Delegate from the United States can be gotten over in this way: that when buoys like conical and can buoys are replaced in the winter time by spar buoys, then the distinction of shape is not employed, and that of colour answers the purpose.

Captain Norcross (United States).—Mr. President, I will prepare an amendment.

The President.—The Delegate from the United States proposes to amend paragraph 3 on p. 2 of this Report in the last line. The Secretary will now read it.

The amendment is to have the last line read as follows: "the spar buoys taking their places in certain cases."

The President.—As this is an amendment, it must be printed and considered like any other amendment.

Admiral Nares (Great Britain).—Mr. President, may I say a few words? I think, perhaps, the honourable Delegate from the United States will not press this amendment. I should like to say a few words to calm his apprehensions. If he will read carefully the whole sentence he will find that we say "We are of the opinion that where form is adopted——" If form is adopted, what are the forms to be? You can only have two. If you end up the sentence by saying that then the spar buoy is to take the place of both these, the whole sentence must come out. Take the case of the Potomac. It is buoyed with spar buoys, red and black. The Potomac authorities, with only a single channel, do not want to adopt form, and there is no necessity for them to adopt form. What is the good of it to them? All that we recommend is that, if they do adopt form, then let us have two forms; and if the honourable Delegate from the United States can define any two better forms we will be ready to consider them. All that we say is that, whenever there are two forms, then we have given you what we think are the best forms. In the Potomac there is no reason at all to alter the spar buoys; they can still be red and black. After you get down the river, and you have two or three channels, I am not certain what the system is; but I believe that there you do have form, and you are very glad to adopt form, and then you come to the forms which we have given you.

Captain Norcross (United States).—Mr. President, I believe that what I have suggested does not alter the sense of that paragraph at all. I have no objection to form. We have already got spar buoys introduced into this paragraph. I merely want, as a matter of convenience, to have it read so that they can be used to take the place of conical or can buoys both, whenever these two are removed; and the wording of the Report as it stands now precludes the use of spar buoys when a conical buoy is removed. I cannot see why there should be any objection, because it really changes nothing. It merely provides that when the conical buoy is removed you can use your distinctive colours of red and black on the spar buoy.

Captain Mensing (Germany).—Mr. President, I would be glad if my honourable friend would explain to me how you could distinguish between them in the winter time if they had on both sides of the channel the same kind of buoy. I believe that he has skipped that question a little; but, if the system is introduced, of course it must hold in winter and summer, and under all circumstances as far as possible. I would ask my friend how he proposes to buoy a river in the winter time, so as to make both sides of the channel different in shape, if he uses but one kind of buoy.

Captain Norcross (United States).—By the difference of colour, simply. If the red colour will appear too much like the black, then use white on the other side. Why not permit the use of the spar buoys on both sides of the channel when it is impossible to keep any other buoys there?

The President.—Is the Conference ready for a vote upon this question at the present time?

Captain Mensing (Germany).—Mr. President, I would be glad if in this case the amendment should be printed and discussed here. It is out of order, and I believe it would be well to have it printed, and in that case everybody would come to a full understanding; and perhaps the Delegates from the United States will come to some understanding about the matter before the discussion is brought on.

Mr. Hall (Great Britain).—Mr. President, I think we ought to have no difficulty in taking the opinion of the Conference upon this point. We see what this Committee, which is a very strong Committee, have reported on this point. It has given us a very carefully prepared Report. I find on that Committee the name of a gallant Delegate from the United States, amongst others. Surely, I think, we can have no difficulty in coming to a conclusion upon this matter now. The proposal is a very simple one, but, as the gallant Delegate from Germany has pointed out, it will have a very disastrous result; and I cannot believe that with this Report before us we can have any doubt as to what view we ought to take with regard to it.

Mr. Carter (Hawaii).—Mr. President, may I point out that the amendment seems to be wholly irrelevant to the paragraph which it proposes to amend, for this speaks only of a matter of form, and the amendment suggests buoys of colour?

The President.—It is an amendment upon the same subject, and the Chair would consider it germane.

Captain Norcross (United States).—Mr. President, it is the usual practice in the winter time, when they are obliged to take in their buoys, to replace them by spar buoys; and I merely thought that, by leaving the words as they are now, that would be precluded.

Captain Mensing (Germany).—Mr. President, I agree to having the question taken on the subject now. I think it is not worth while to let it stand over.

The President.—Is the Conference ready for the question on the amendment of the Delegate from the United States? The amendment will be read.

The amendment of the Delegate from the United States is as follows:—

Page 2, last line of third paragraph to read as follows:

"The spar buoys taking their places in certain cases."

The question was put to the Conference upon the amendment of the Delegate from the United States, and the amendment was lost."

Captain Shackford (United States).—Mr. President, I would like to ask for information. In the fifth paragraph the Report says: "In connection with such a change of system we are informed that an extensive rearrangement in buoyage was recently carried out by Great Britain, the different shapes being changed from one side of the channel to the other side, the change being brought about without any casualty to navigation." I would like to ask if that means that the can-buoys were shifted to the starboard side of the channel?

Admiral Nares (Great Britain).—Mr. President, the adoption by Great Britain of the Resolution of 1882-83 of the Conference on Buoyage proposed first of all to bring the buoyage of Great Britain into one uniform system, with the hope that afterwards it would spread to a uniform system throughout the world. It was found out, when we examined it at that Conference, that ports within 20 or 30 miles of each other, navigated by the same ships, were practically buoyed on totally different principles. It gradually came around that shape was considered to be the best to introduce, and it was thought that perhaps in a few years afterward colour might be considered. Shape had only been used then in Ireland and to buoy the Mersey, and naturally the Committee proposing it took a selfish view, and proposed that these shapes should be introduced all over Great Britain.

When it came up in the Conference we looked a little further into the question, and found that most of the countries which had already adopted shape were buoyed on exactly the opposite principle, and the consequence was that the whole of the buoyage in Ireland and on the Mersey, and wherever else we had adopted shape, had to be changed again, and it was done without any casualty to navigation. But further than that, the colours which were chosen, which were the single colour for the starboard-hand buoy, and the parti-colour for the port-hand buoy, required a very great change in the different ports. It was a compromise, because we could not get Trinity House to establish the starboard red buoy and the port black buoy. So there was a compromise effected, and the single colour was adopted for the starboard side, and the parti-colour for the port side. Now, I think the time has come when Trinity House will be quite prepared to give up to a single colour on the port-hand buoy for the consideration of uniformity throughout the world. We shall have to give up all that.

However, I am now answering the gallant Delegate from the United States. A considerable change, both in colour and in form, has been carried out in Great Britain since 1883. They have taken three or four years about it, and by taking some length of time, notices to mariners have been published, and the mariners have been warned in time, and there has been no casualty in carrying out these changes.

If this is passed, the whole of the buoyage of the Thames will have to be altered, and the whole of the Irish buoyage will have to be altered. They happen to have the sides marked now with starboard and port buoys, and they will have to shift them from starboard to port and from port to starboard; and I have no doubt the changes can be carried out without any trouble.

Captain Shackford (United States).—Mr. President, do I understand the gallant Delegate from Great Britain to say that the buoys in the Mersey have been changed?

Admiral Nares (Great Britain).—Mr. President, I cannot answer right off, but whichever system the Mersey had in 1882, they have got a totally opposite system in 1889.

Captain Shackford (United States).—Mr. President, in 1882 the conical buoys were on the port side, and they will now be on the starboard side. Now, on p. 5 of the Report of the Committee there is a provision which, if carried out, means that the whole of the buoyage system of the United States will have to be shifted.

Captain Mensing (Germany).—Mr. President, so far as I know the system of the United States is based only on colour, and form has nothing to do with it. They need not introduce the form. If they consider their system the most perfect in the world, leave as it is, only do not say that it is based on form, because it is not.

Captain Shackford (United States).—Mr. President, the New York Bay system and the Delaware system are based on form, and the can buoys are on the starboard side and the conical buoys on the port side.

Captain Mensing (Germany).—Mr. President, I am perfectly willing to give the Delegate from the United States the information which has been laid before us, and I think he is very much mistaken. There is no such system of form used in the United States at the present day. It may be introduced in some parts of the waters, but it is not the system adopted for the whole United States, and it has not been pointed out to us by the gallant Delegate for the United States who took part in the deliberations of our Committee.

Captain Shackford (United States).—Mr. President, of course, I can only speak of the ports of the United States which I have been in. I have been in the Delaware and in New York Bay several hundred times, and I know that the channels there are distinguished by can buoys on the starboard and conical buoys on the port side. That is also the case in Charleston, Fernandina, Key West, and one or two other places.

Mr. Hall (Great Britain).—Mr. President, may I point out that in any arrangement such as this there must be give and take? When we are prepared to alter the whole of the buoyage to the entrance of the River Thames, and the whole of the buoyage of the coast of Ireland, I think we are undertaking to do just as much as the country which the gallant Delegate represents so well is asked to do. It is impossible for us to have a uniform system without many countries having to alter their systems of buoyage in some way or other, and the only way we can do it is by give and take. It is is perfectly true, as pointed out by the gallant Delegate from Germany, that it is possible that in some places there may be form used as a distinguishing mark in the United States; but we, as I say, shall have to make great alterations in our buoyage system if we adopt the whole of this Report, and the only way of reaching a satisfactory conclusion will be for the other Powers to do the same.

Admiral Nares (Great Britain).—Mr. President, I think the honourable Delegate for the United States is under a misapprehension. Wherever the United States have form for their buoyage, that form is for the starboard hand conical, and for the port hand can, and our Report is based practically on the principle of form as adopted in the United States. The principle of form, as adopted by the United States, so far as it was adopted, was the reason of our change in Great Britain in 1883, and if the honourable Delegate will study his charts he will find that I am correct.

Captain Shackford (United States).—Mr. President, I understand that a can buoy is a buoy with a flat top.

Admiral Nares (Great Britain).—Yes, Sir.

Captain Shackford (United States).—Mr. President, I think that if, when he goes out of the port of New York next week, the gallant Delegate from Great Britain will look at the buoys, he will find the conical buoy on the starboard hand and the flat-topped buoy on the port hand.

Admiral Nares (Great Britain).—Mr. President, may I say that we are talking about the same thing? We say that the starboard hand is the starboard hand when coming in from sea into port.

Captan Shackford (United States).—Mr. President, I understand that it means starboard hand when coming in from sea; but the can buoys in New York Bay are on the starboard hand coming in from sea and are flat-topped, and the buoys on the port hand are conical. The buoys on the starboard hand are certainly flat-topped buoys, unless they have been changed within the last two months.

Captain Mensing (Germany).—Mr. President, if this is the case, it would simply point to the fact that the system adopted in the chief port of the United States was in direct contradiction to the system which is published in the "Laws of Beacons, Buoys, and other Day Marks" in the Third Lighthouse District, which is a document published by the Government Printing Office, and which, I suppose, is an authoritative book. which the honourable Delegate from the United States, even with his great authority, will not be able to outweigh. Let me read to him what it says about shapes. It says: "In approaching a channel from seaward, red buoys with even numbers will be found on the starboard side of the channel, and they must be left on the starboard hand in passing in. On approaching the channel from seaward, black buoys with odd numbers will be found on the port side of the channel, and must be left on the port hand in passing in." I would like to call the attention of the honourable Delegate for the United States to the fact that the system of the United States is based on colour and not on shape also, and that shape is only an additional safeguard, which is spoken of in the next paragraph. "Different channels will be marked, as far as practicable, as follows: Principal channels by large nun buoys properly coloured and numbered, on the starboard side, and large can buoys on the port side; minor channels by small nun and can buoys and by spar buoys."

Now, suppose there are different channels; in one there may be only can buoys on either side; in the second channel there may be only conical buoys on either side, and in the third there may be only spar buoys on either side. If there is but one channel, then they are all to be "nun" buoys, which, I suppose, are the same as what we call "conical" buoys; and they are usually placed on the starboard side, and the can buoys on the port side. Now, that is a Regulation issued by the proper authorities; and I believe it to be the duty of the harbour authorities to conform with the Regulations laid down in this official book. We have not had anything else before us, and, as I have stated, the gallant Delegate for the United States, who has been a member of our Committee, has not thought it worth while to propose anything differing from this.

I should like to call attention to the fact that if our propositions are adopted, nothing in the system adopted by the United States would have to be changed with regard to single channels, because there we have already on the starboard hand, as it is declared here, the conical buoy, and on the port hand the can buoy. They would have to be painted in the regular way. There would have to be nothing changed except where there are several channels, and where there are buoys of the same kind used to indicate different sides of the channel.

Mr. Carter (Hawaii).—Mr. President, I move the adoption of the Report.

Lieutenant Beaugency (Chile).—Mr. President, before we take a vote upon that motion, will you allow me to call the attention of the Committee to paragraph (*a*) relating to buoying and marking of wrecks, where it says: "All buoys and top sides of vessels used for the marking of wrecks shall be painted green, with a suitable white inscription." I would suggest whether it would not be convenient to have in white numbers the number of cables a ship can anchor from this wreck with safety.

Captain Mensing (Germany).—Mr. President, I apprehend that there is no difficulty in doing this under the wording of the present section as it now stands. The white inscription, of course, must be chosen by the proper authorities in any way they see fit, and I believe that there would be some danger in making it compulsory, because, of course, if such a buoy should be anchored it would turn round, and sometimes the distance might be altered just by the swinging around with the tide; therefore I do not believe that it would be wise to make this provision compulsory. But it certainly is optional under the wording of the section as it now stands; and the form may be chosen by the proper authority.

The President.—Does the Delegate from Chile make any proposition?

Lieutenant Beaugency (Chile).—Not now, Sir; this explanation is sufficient.

The President.—It is moved that the Report of the Committee on General Division XII be adopted.

The question was put to the Conference upon the adoption of the Report of Committee No. 3 upon General Division XII, and the Report was adopted.

Mr. Goodrich (United States).—Mr. President, may I ask the gallant Delegate from Germany whether the remainder of his Report will be laid upon the table to-day?

Captain Mensing (Germany).—Mr. President, the Report has been finished by the Committee. It has been found that a list of the different Hydrographic Offices in the countries represented here might be given as a bit of information, and this list I have only finished so far as the material has been handed in before this morning. What came in yesterday is already in the hands of the Secretary or in the hands of the printer. The rest of the Reports are ready, and they will be handed to the members of the Conference before 5 o'clock this afternoon. The Committee have nothing to do with it any more. It is only the printers who require time. I do not see any reason why the Report should not be finished and ready for distribution this afternoon at 5 o'clock, although of course I am unable to give any definite promise.

Mr. Goodrich (United States).—Mr. President, I move that the remainder of the Report of Committee No. 3 be made the special order of business for to-morrow morning.

Captain Mensing (Germany).—Mr. President, I do not see any difficulty in going on with this Report. I think that we have taken a great deal of trouble in making it, and I believe there will be nothing in it which will give rise to any great number of alterations. I would like, however, to point out that there are quite a number of provisions contained in the Report which will have to be acted upon. I think there are about eighteen; and of course they may require the careful attention of some of the members. But at the same time I would like to remark that the Reports are a little more extensive than these two which have been before us. We have been unanimous in the adoption of the Report as it stands now, and I do not apprehend any difficulty in having it adopted by the Conference.

Mr. Goodrich (United States).—Mr. President, it seems to me that we might adopt this Rule, and thus commence the discussion of these two Reports to-morrow morning. We might then perhaps find it necessary or desirable to postpone a portion of the discussion until another day; but if the same unanimity prevails to-morrow with regard to the adoption of these other branches of the Report of Committee No. 3 as has prevailed to-day we shall have no difficulty with it; and, therefore, I see no objection to making this a special order for to-morrow morning.

The President.—The Delegate from the United States moves that the other two subjects contained in the Report of the Committee No. 3 be made a special order of business for to-morrow morning. Is the Conference ready for the question?

The question was put to the Conference upon the motion of the Delegate from the United States, and the motion was carried.

Mr. Goodrich (United States).—Mr. President, on behalf of the Collocation Committee I desire to state that a Report has been presented during the past week and laid on the table of the Delegates. The Collocation Committee have taken the liberty of making one or two manifestly verbal alterations, and I want to call the attention of the Conference to them that they may fully understand that in doing this we do it with your approval and permission.

In Article 4, subdivision (*b*), third line, the words, "in lieu of," are used instead of the words, "in place of." In the Report as laid before us it was "in place of." We have used here the same words as the Conference authorized in other portions of the Report, and we had it printed "in lieu of." Of course that is a mere verbal alteration. It was sanctioned in the first part of Article 4 by the Conference. On p. 9, Article 15, subdivision (*e*), the Conference have sanctioned the introduction of the words, " or if a sailing-vessel, at intervals of not more than one minute, two blasts with her fog-horn followed by ringing her bell." That necessitated a little change in the order of the sentences. If the Conference will turn to the previous Report of the Collocation Committee they will see how we have changed the order of the words. The old Article, commencing with the third line, reads as follows:—

"shall, at intervals of not more than two minutes, if a steam-vessel, sound two prolonged blasts on her whistle or siren, followed by ringing her bell, or if a sailing-vessel, at intervals of not more than one minute, two blasts on her fog-horn, followed by ringing her bell."

Apparently the word "sound" was governed by the words, "if a steam-vessel," and therefore the Committee changed the location of the several sentences, so that it reads in the new Report as follows:—

"shall sound, if a steam-vessel, at intervals of not more than two minutes, two prolonged blasts with her whistle or siren, followed by ringing her bell; or if a sailing-vessel, at intervals of not more than one minute, two blasts with her fog-horn, followed by ringing her bell."

It is a mere verbal correction, and the change is in the order of the sentences, but the meaning is in no sense changed.

In Appendix (B), paragraph 2, the word "ships" was used, and following the Rule adopted by the Conference the Committee have changed the word "ships" to "vessels." The word "greater," in the last line, has been substituted for the word "other," as it was in the original Appendix (B). Of course the other was nonsense, and this is good sense. In paragraph 5 the word "ships" has been changed to "vessels." Those are all mere verbal corrections, but the Collocation Committee want the approval of the Conference to those changes so that the Protocol may be regular.

The President.—If there be no objection, they will be considered as approved by the Conference. The Secretary will now read to the Conference a letter which has been received from the State Department.

The letter is as follows:—

"Sir,   "*Department of State, Washington, December* 27, 1889.

"I am instructed by the Secretary of State to inform you that the President will be pleased to receive the members of the International Marine Conference on the 1st proximo, at the Executive Mansion, at the hour of 11 A.M., and to request you to notify the members of the Conference of this arrangement.

"Attendance in uniform will be expected.

"It will not be necessary for you to send this notification to such members of the Marine Conference as are also members of the Diplomatic Corps, as they will attend at the same hour in their capacity as Representatives of foreign countries accredited to this Government.

"Please notify me of the receipt of this communication.

"I am, &c.
(Signed)   "WALKER BLAINE

"Lieutenant V. L. Cottman, United States' Navy,
    "Secretary of the International Marine Conference."

The President.—The Chair desires to know what action the Conference will take upon this letter, and as to whether the Conference would desire to go in a body from this point. The Chair would like to hear some expressions of opinion as to what will be the best course to pursue.

Mr. Hall (Great Britain).—Mr. President, I think we had better leave that to the individual opinion of the members of the Conference, as it is very possible a great number of us will not be here on the first of the new year. Of course, a great number of the Delegates would like the opportunity of showing their respect for the Head of the country, which is a mark of respect which, of course, would be followed by us all in whatever country we happened to be. But I do not think we can come to any resolution as to attending in a body, because it is so uncertain how many of us will be here

The President.—The Chair would suggest that there will be time enough to determine this matter to-morrow evening when we find out whether we have finished our business or not. Therefore, if there be no objection, the consideration of this subject will be deferred until after the proceedings of to-morrow.

Mr. Goodrich (United States).—Mr. President, the Collocation Committee assume that, inasmuch as the Conference have assented to the verbal changes which they have suggested, that there are no further amendments to be made to the Report of the Collocation Committee or to the Appendix (B) attached thereto. Therefore, I move that the final Report of the Collocation Committee be adopted.

Mr. Verney (Siam).—Mr. President, I am very sorry indeed to intervene on this occasion, and I do so under a very great sense of responsibility; but it is a responsibility which is not borne by myself alone, because some of the members of this Conference have been considering this Report, and while I desire to speak in terms of the utmost possible respect for the members of the Collocation Committee, I do not think I should be doing my duty if I should keep silent at this moment. I have read with very great care the Report of the Collocation Committee, and it would be extremely improper to say one single word which was wanting in respect to that Report and to the labours of that Committee; but at the same time there are ambiguities in this Report which might still be corrected with advantage; and I will ask the Conference to bear with me while I point out one or two of these cases.

This Report will go forth to the world, and will, of course, be criticized in many countries, and by experts in many parts of the world. I will ask the Conference to pause for one moment before they do that which is absolutely irrevocable, and listen to me while I put before them one or two things which have occurred to me whilst I have been reading through these Rules. I do not believe that any member of this Conference is aware of the fact that in Article 15 and the other Articles we have no less than five different kinds of blasts. I will refer to them Article by Article. We have blasts which are undefined in length in Article 9, subdivision (*g*), for fishing-vessels. In Article 15, subdivision (*c*), we have also blasts which are undefined in length for sailing-vessels; and even for steamers as well as sailing-vessels, under Article 15, subdivisions (*d*), (*f*), and (*i*), we have short blasts which are undefined in length. We have other blasts which are undefined in length, for instance, under Article 15, subdivision (*d*), there is a "long blast" for steamers not defined in length. We have, finally, "prolonged blasts," which are undefined in length, for sailing-vessels as well as steamers, under Article 15 (*a*), (*b*), and (*f*).

I will ask whether any member of this Conference is aware of the existence of this confusion, which cannot possibly be denied. We have had Reports placed before us by the highest authority, notably by Sir George Nares, in which he emphasizes the very great importance of having the blasts all of equal length and properly defined so that no mistake shall be made. I venture to think that if any one will take up the Committee's Report on Sound-Signals, and also read the eloquent and impressive speeches made by Sir George Nares and other great authorities, he will come to the same conclusion; and I think that this Conference does not wish to pass a whole series of blasts as now inserted in the Rules without a proper definition being applied to distinguish them. There are one or two small matters that could very easily be put right by the distinguished Collocation Committee, which has already done such valuable work for this Conference. There are one or two verbal alterations, as well as one or two alterations in principle, which would take them only a very short time to correct, and it would finish up and round off the work which has been done in such an admirable manner.

I will mention first, as a mere verbal alteration, of a very trivial kind, perhaps, a word which has evidently crept in by accident in one of these Articles, and that is the word "bright," which has been inserted in Article 9, subsection (*b*), paragraph 3. It is in the fifth line, the word "bright." I think that every member of the Conference will say that it ought to be stricken out. A "bright white light" means a bright light with a reflector behind it when used in these Rules elsewhere. Here it cannot mean this.

Mr. Goodrich (United States).—May I ask to what you are referring?

Mr. Verney (Siam).—Mr. President, I am referring to Article 9, subsection (*b*), paragraph 3, line 5. I have asked several members of this Conference whether I am wrong in thinking that the word "bright" is a mere accident; I believe it to be a mere accident. I stand ready for correction, of course, if I am wrong. There are other matters which are much more serious, and I find that member after member of this Conference is unwilling to accept some of the Rules as they now stand. I will mention one of these. In Article 7, paragraph 3, we have made it a necessity for every row-boat, however small, with only one single person rowing her, to carry a bi-coloured lantern. I am quite aware that some of these things have been discussed in this Conference; but before we separate I desire to enter my protest against that Rule as one which cannot and will not be obeyed; and I say, Sir, that it is of the greatest importance to this Conference not to separate without passing Rules which, within its own knowledge, ought to be and can be obeyed.

I shall possibly draw down upon me fire from both ends of the table. There is nothing so easy as to make sharp speeches against those who stand up alone; but I will appeal to my learned friends the Delegates to this Conference whether I have not got some truth on my side in proclaiming my belief that this is a Rule which will not be obeyed, and cannot be obeyed, as it is now passed. There are other matters in these Rules which I venture to allude to briefly before I sit down. There is, I think, an error in Article 7, paragraph (*b*). I think that Rule ought to read as follows:—

"Green and red side-lights constructed and fixed as prescribed in Article 2, (*b*) and (*c*), and of such a character as to be visible at a distance of at least 1 mile, or a combined lantern *constructed and fixed so as to show* a green light or a red light from right ahead to two points abaft the beam on their respective sides. Such lantern shall not be less than 3 feet below the white light."

If you do not put in the words, "constructed and fixed," the position of that lantern is not sufficiently definite. I will venture to ask the Collocation Committee to kindly take that into consideration.

This will then be put on the same level as every other Rule, and you will use the same language as you have used in the other Rules. I think that there can be no objection to that amendment.

There is one most important matter of principle which has slipped in against the intention of most, if not all, of the members of this Conference, and I will venture to refer to it. I do not believe that any member of this Conference really intends that a vessel which is 5 or 6 miles off from another should be possibly called a vessel which is in risk of collision with that other; and yet we have allowed a heading, or a preliminary note, which can mean nothing else than that a vessel 5 or 6 miles off may be called a vessel with which there is already risk of collision. I refer to the preliminary Article at the head of the Steering and Sailing Rules, and to call attention to the words, "if the bearings do not appreciably change, then risk of collision shall be deemed to exist." I venture to ask whether I am not right in my interpretation of that clause? Can there be any other interpretation put upon it than that if the bearing of another vessel is taken 5 or 6 miles away, and then a second one which does not appreciably vary from the first, from that moment risk of collision commences under these Rules? Is that the intention of this Conference? I am quite certain that it is not. I ask the members of this Conference to pardon me while I point out such matters as this, and ask them whether they really intend that these Rules shall go forth to the world with an interpretation of that kind stamped upon them?

Now, Sir, I do not wish to take up any of the time of this Conference more than seems absolutely necessary; but I will ask, on these accounts and for some other reasons which I would only be too glad to give the Collocation Committee, whether it would not be better once more to ask that Committee to take these Rules into their consideration, and to give them the few hours' work which is necessary in order that we may send them out to the world as the kind of Rules which we should be proud of, and which we shall recognize as being a start of a new era in maritime law for various countries. I am fully aware of the labour which the Collocation Committee has already bestowed upon these Rules, and I am deeply grateful, as we all are, for the labour which they have so freely given. Mr. President, I am very sorry indeed to have had to interrupt the proceedings of this Conference with these few remarks. They may meet with no support whatever from any gentleman around the table, and I have only made them under a sense of duty which, it seems to me, is imposed upon each member of this Conference, to speak out his own mind, whether his opinions are correct or incorrect.

Mr. Goodrich (United States).—Mr. President, I venture to ask the prolongation of this morning's session of the Conference for a few moments. I regret very much that the learned Delegate from Siam has thought it necessary to anticipate, somewhat plaintively, sharp speeches from any member of the Collocation Committee. There is no such intention, so far as I know, in the mind of any member of that Committee, and I am sure the whole course of this Conference renders such a reference as that entirely unjust and unfounded. The various subjects which the learned Delegate from Siam has presented to the Conference have all been carefully considered by the Collocation Committee, and if I had time or the courage at this late stage of the Conference to present the views of the Collocation Committee upon this subject to which the learned Delegate has referred, I think the Conference would be satisfied that all had received due attention. The Collocation Committee found certain Rules existing; they found certain principles added to the existing Rules by the Conference, and they found those principles elaborated by amendments; and after careful discussion they have formulated the Rules which they were instructed to ingraft into their Report. These Rules the Collocation Committee have followed.

The next question is: Have they made a mistake? That is, has the Conference itself and then the Collocation Committee made a mistake? I think not. The Conference has purposely left undetermined what blast was referred to in certain instances, notably the one referred to by the learned Delegate from Siam in Article 9, subdivision (*g*), on p. 7, where a fishing-vessel was directed to make a blast at intervals of not more than one minute. It was deemed wise to give no duration for that blast, because the Rule is given to mariners or fishermen who might be supposed not to be as conversant with the duration of blasts as are those who would be in command of larger vessels, and it was deemed wise not to make a hard and fast Rule which would bind them to a blast, the absolute duration of which should be fixed at a second, or a second and a-half, or two seconds. Wherever it was deemed wise to define a short blast, that duration was given.

In Article 28 there are three blasts, one short blast, two short blasts, and three short blasts. There it was deemed wise to fix the duration of the blast. Moreover, the whistle at such a time would be sounding, and the throat of the whistle would be clear. The whistle could be given instantly of a second's duration. But where, under the other Articles, a sudden blast is given when the throat of the whistle is not clear, it was deemed wise not to define the exact length of the duration of the blast. I do not see any trouble in these Rules, even if that principle is seen to have run into the minds of the Collocation Committee all through them.

The President.—The Chair desires to state that as this subject is likely to lead to discussion, the Conference might as well take a recess and return at 2 o'clock, unless the Conference desires to close this subject before recess.

Mr. Hall (Great Britain).—Mr. President, may I suggest that we might hear the rest of the remarks of the learned Delegate the Chairman of the Collocation Committee, because I think possibly he may satisfy us that it will not be necessary to reopen this discussion.

The President.—By general consent the Delegate will be permitted to proceed.

Mr. Goodrich (United States).—Mr. President, I do not deem it necessary to say anything further on the subject of these blasts. I may call attention to the other proposal of the Delegate from Siam with regard to the use of the word "bright" in Article 9, subsection (*b*), to which he referred. The use of that word is intentional, and has a specific object. The Article refers to small vessels. There is no provision anywhere in the Rule as to what the visibility of that light should be. Where the "white light" is referred to in other Articles, it is intended as a light which may be seen 2 miles, or in some instances a mile; but this is a small vessel which is carrying a light, and the word "bright" is really intended to point the attention of persons in charge of such vessels to the necessity of showing a white light; and it was deemed wise to add the word "bright," leaving it, of course, somewhat indefinite as to what light was intended, to point the attention of the mariner to the fact that he must show a bright white light. That was the object for putting the word "bright" into this Rule.

As to the criticism upon Article 7, subdivision 3, the Conference and the Committee have used the words, "combined lantern," because it describes the lantern which has been already referred to in the Rules, and it points attention to the lantern which is meant. When the learned Delegate from Siam says that this Rule will never be observed by fishermen——

Mr. Verney (Siam).—I did not say by fishermen only——

Mr. Goodrich (United States).—I think he is going a little beyond his knowledge. Whether it will be obeyed by fishermen or not is a matter which this Conference cannot determine, and is not within the province of this Conference to determine. It is for the Conference to say what lights boats shall carry, and if they fail to carry the lights and a collision ensues, the boat failing to carry them shall be held responsible. But that principle has been discussed by this Conference over and over again. It was discussed when the proposition was first made, and it was again discussed when the amendment was brought up, and again when the Report of the Collocation Committee was presented. It has been fully and carefully considered; but if the Conference see fit, by a three-fourths vote, to go back to that discussion, I am sure we shall be glad to stay here with you. But I really do not see any possibility of the Conference changing its opinion upon that point.

In regard to Article 7, paragraph 3, the point is made that it refers to all boats, to small rowing-boats, and that they shall exhibit a certain light. Well, that principle has been in the Rule since 1863, and I have only had, in my practice, one case where the Rule ever came under discussion, and that was a case where one of the Staten Island ferry-boats ran down a small boat, which was clearly held at fault for not having shown this light.

Admiral Bowden-Smith (Great Britain).—Mr. President, may I ask the learned Delegate for the United States where in the old Rules it occurs that row-boats are to show a red and green light, because I do not know of any such Rule?

Mr. Goodrich (United States).—I say a white light.

Admiral Bowden-Smith (Great Britain).—It is a red and green light which a row-boat has now to show.

Mr. Goodrich (United States).—Mr. President, this is a new principle as to the red and green lights. My last remarks were addressed to the subject of the white light to be carried by small boats, which is provided for in the old Rules of 1863.

Mr. Verney (Siam).—Mr. President, I foresee that my application is by no means a popular one, and I did not suppose it would be. I hope the Conference will pardon me if I said a single word which implied that every member of this Conference was not treated with absolute courtesy. If I said a word of that kind I wish to withdraw it, because it is not the fact. But I still must insist upon it that if the Collocation Committee had observed the rules which they laid down when they first started, we should not have had in all respects the Rules which we now have. I do strongly object to the use of that term "bright" in one sense in one Rule and in another sense in another Rule. The word "brilliant," or some other word, would do just as well, if they want to call attention to the kind of light or to the intensity of the light to be carried. The learned Delegate has not given any satisfactory reply with regard to paragraph (*b*) of Article 7. What I intended to say was that, as the Article now stands, it is not clear where the light there mentioned is to be carried.

That same remark applies to another Article, Article 11, the second paragraph. There the Rule has most carefully defined the height at which the forward of the two lights shall be put above the hull. You leave the second, or stern light, undefined. I think that is a serious omission in the Rule.

Mr. Goodrich (United States).—Mr. President, may I interrupt the learned Delegate from Siam to ask him what he considers the effect in Article 11 of the use of the words in the last line of the second paragraph: "another such light"?

Mr. Verney (Siam).—Mr. President, I consider that it refers to the first paragraph, that is to say, to a lantern so constructed as to show a clear, uniform, and unbroken light, visible all round the horizon at a distance of at least 1 mile. The lantern may be constructed so as to show a clear and uniform light. The construction may be perfect, but if it is not in the right place it will not show.

Mr. Goodrich (United States).—Then you would consider that it would be "another such light" if it were in the cabin?

Mr. Verney (Siam).—Certainly the lantern might be perfectly constructed, and unless the light was properly fixed it would not show. In every other case you have been providing for the lights to be fixed, as well as for their construction. These objections, as I said at the beginning, are merely objections which the Collocation Committee can take into their consideration, and which they could, in the course of a very few hours, make all right. I am not asking the Committee to remain in this country, or anywhere else, for an indefinite period of time. I do not want anything of that kind, but I want them to round off their work in a way which all of us know that they are abundantly capable of doing. I will not keep the Conference any longer at this time. I have deemed it to be my duty to say what I have said on this occasion, and if there is no support for it, I will not even bring a Resolution before the Conference, because it has always been my wish not to take up the time of the Conference for a single moment longer than is necessary for some practical purpose.

Mr. Goodrich (United States).—Mr. President, then I suggest that the order of business is the question upon the motion which I presented.

The President.—The question is upon the motion of the Delegate from the United States, that the final Report of the Collocation Committee be adopted.

The question was put to the Conference upon the motion of the Delegate from the United States, and the motion was carried.

Mr. Goodrich (United States).—Mr. President, I suppose we might now just as well adjourn until to-morrow morning.

Mr. Hall (Great Britain).—Mr. President, may I suggest that, perhaps, if an indication were made to the printers who are printing the Report for us that we are really now waiting for their Report, and have nothing else to do, they might possibly be able to expedite their work? I have no doubt that Mr. Cottman has used a great deal of influence already, and if that influence were backed up by an order from the President, I think, possibly, it might have due weight in that respect.

The President.—The Chair desires to state that the printer is in the hands of the Chairman of the Committee, and the Secretary has had nothing to do with the printing of their Report, therefore it rests with the Committee to have their work completed.

The Conference thereupon adjourned until Tuesday, 31st December, 1889, at 11 o'clock A.M.

Washington, Tuesday, December 31, 1889, 11 *o'clock,* A.M.

THE Conference was called to order at 11 o'clock A.M., with Rear-Admiral Franklin in the Chair.

The President.—The first business in order this morning is the consideration of the Report of Committee No. 3 on General Division X, which will be read by the Secretary.

The Report of Committee No. 3 on General Division X is as follows:—

" GENERAL DIVISION X.

" *Reporting, marking, and removing dangerous Wrecks or Obstructions to Navigation.*

" (*a.*) A uniform method of reporting and marking dangerous wrecks and derelicts.

" (*b.*) The division of the labour, cost, and responsibility among the several maritime nations, either by geographical apportionment or otherwise.

" Of the removal of dangerous derelicts;

" And of searching for doubtful dangers with a view of removing them from the Charts.

" The heading of this Division leaves it doubtful whether the Conference expect the Committee to consider measures dealing with dangerous wrecks and obstructions in territorial waters as well as on the high seas.

" The Committee are of opinion that it is not necessary or desirable to propose international action regarding territorial waters, except the marking of wrecks, which subject is treated under General Division XII.

" (*a.*) *A uniform Method of reporting and marking dangerous Wrecks and Derelicts.*

" Wherever the word 'wreck' is used in this Report it is meant to designate '*an abandoned vessel aground,*' and wherever the word '*derelict*' is used it is meant to designate '*a vessel afloat permanently abandoned.*'

" Wrecks are not always to be considered a source of danger to navigation. When lying outside of the fairways, as, for instance, on dangerous sands, or on coral reefs, they may even contribute to the safety of navigation by becoming conspicuous day marks; but when they are lying in a fairway, in water of not sufficient depth to allow vessels to pass without striking the hull or spars of the wreck, they become a serious danger to navigation.

" Derelicts are always a danger to navigation, as other vessels may run into them without any warning, particularly at night or during thick weather. Since the 1st January, 1889, five collisions with derelicts are known to have taken place in the North Atlantic Ocean alone, by one of which lives were imperilled. (See Appendix A, p. 16.)

" Undoubtedly the number of lives and the value of property lost through collision with derelicts at sea has been very considerable, and such losses might be greatly reduced if proper steps were taken to clear the seas of such dangers.

" Other dangerous obstructions (icebergs, newly-discovered shoals, reefs, &c.) would seem to be included under the heading of 'General Division X,' and although not alluded to in paragraph (*a*) should, in the opinion of the Committee, be discussed here, as they may constitute the most serious of all the dangers dealt with in this Division.

" *Reporting dangerous Wrecks and Derelicts.*

" The danger caused by wrecks and derelicts might be considerably lessened if their exact position were known to the mariner. For obvious reasons it is often most difficult to attain this end completely. Much, however, would be gained if as accurate a report as possible were secured and brought to the notice of mariners without loss of time.

" Regarding the manner in which such reports should be brought to the Central Office in charge of the distrubition of 'Notices to Mariners,' the Committee propose the following Resolutions:—

"1. That it is advisable to make it the duty of any of the officers or of the crew of a wreck o derelict to report, as soon as possible after landing, to the nearest harbour authority, if necessary through their Consul, as follows:

"(*a.*) Name of the vessel abandoned.
"(*b.*) Her distinguishing number.
"(*c.*) Name of her home port, port from which she sailed, and place of destination.
"(*d.*) General description of vessel and her rig.
"(*e.*) Place where abandoned (latitude and longitude as near as possible).
"(*f.*) Weather and current experienced before leaving the vessel, and, in case she was a derelict, the direction in which she would most likely drift.
"(*g.*) Whether or not it is intended to take any steps toward her recovery.

"2. That a similar Report should be made to the same authorities by the master of any vessel sighting a wreck or derelict, and a suitable entry made in the ship's log.

"3. Such Reports should be published in 'Notices to Mariners,' the daily press, and, if necessary, by giving telegraphic information to the ports which it most concerns."

Captain Mensing (Germany).—Mr. President, I beg leave to submit whether it would not be advisable to have every paragraph discussed as we go along, or every Division of the Report discussed in this way. For instance, there are several propositions made here, and perhaps it would help to clear up the matter if we go from one to the other. So I would like to propose that if there is any discussion of the propositions it should be disposed of now.

The President.—The Delegate from Germany suggests that any discussion on the propositions should be held as the Report is being read.

Captain Mensing (Germany).—Yes, Sir; from Division to Division.

The President.—Discussion will now be in order upon the two Divisions which have been read.

The Chair hears no suggestions. The Secretary will please read the next Division.

"*Reporting other Obstructions to Navigation, as Icebergs, newly-discovered Shoals, Reefs, &c.*

"Regarding the manner in which such Reports should be transmitted to the proper authorities, the Committee propose the following Resolution:—

"4. That it is advisable to make it the duty of every commander or master of a vessel to report the fact that an iceberg or dangerous field ice has been sighted, or a shoal, reef, or other obstruction has been discovered, to the harbour authorities or the Hydrographic Office of that country to which the port next reached belongs, giving a full description of the obstruction and all facts that may lead to the determination of its position; for instance, the time elapsed since the last reliable astronomical observation and the rate of the chronometer. If the obstruction be a shoal or reef, the depth of water actually obtained by sounding on it should be given. Also when land is in sight the position of any off-lying shoal or reef should be determined by compass bearings of fixed objects in view, the error of the compass being stated, with information as to how and when that error was observed. Angles should also be taken between such objects and a drawing of the coast, and the position of the observer be added.

"Regarding the reporting of ice met with in the vicinity of the Newfoundland Banks by signal from a vessel to other vessels, the Committee are aware that an 'Ice Code' has been published by a private individual, which, according to his own statement, is rather extensively used amongst steamers employed in the regular trade between the port of New York and the ports of Northern Europe.

"This Code seems to offer some advantages, but as there was no evidence before the Committee showing whether its use had been found to be beneficial or otherwise, they were unable to decide whether the introduction of this Code or a similar one could be recommended."

The President.—The subject of reporting other obstructions to navigation, as icebergs, newly-discovered shoals, reefs, &c., is now before the Conference for discussion. The Chair hears no proposition with reference to that section. The Secretary will please read the next Division.

The next Division of the Report is as follows:—

"*Marking Wrecks and Derelicts.*

"As it appears impracticable in most cases for the master and crew of a sunken vessel to mark the wreck in any effective manner, no such obligation should be imposed upon them; and it would also be a great burden, aside from the peril of the undertaking, to compel a passing vessel to mark a derelict. Neither does it seem feasible that any national Government should assume such a duty. But so far as possible means should be employed by which derelicts may be recognized at first sight, and with this end in view the Committee recommend the adoption of the following Resolution:—

"5. That whenever practicable it shall be the duty of the crew, before abandoning a vessel, (*a*) to hoist some distinctive signal, as 'B C F,' 'Abandoned by the crew,' or 'C R T G,' 'Derelict,' or a ball, shape, or other similar mark, where it can best be seen, and where it should not be mistaken for any other authorized signal; (*b*) to let go the sheets and halliards of such sails as are not furled."

The President.—The subject before the Conference for discussion now is "Marking wrecks and derelicts." The Chair hears no proposition with regard to it. The Secretary will please read the next Division.

The next Division of the Report is as follows:—

"Marking other Obstructions.

"At present it seems impracticable to mark shoals, reefs, &c., whether they be well known or only newly discovered, with the exception of those lying near the coasts of countries having a maritime commerce, and we consider it unnecessary to press for their being marked in other localities where they can be readily avoided by the exercise of ordinary skill and the usual precautions known to navigators. For this reason the Committee have no proposition to submit to the Conference beyond the introduction, so far as possible, of a uniform system of buoyage."

The President.—The subject before the Conference for discussion is "Marking other obstructions." The Chair hears no proposition with regard thereto. The Secretary will proceed to read the next Division of the Programme.

The next Division of the Programme is as follows:—

"(b.) *The Division of the Labour, Cost, and Responsibility among the several Maritime Nations, either by Geographical Apportionment or otherwise, of the removal of Dangerous Derelicts; and of searching for doubtful Dangers with a view of removing them from the Charts.*

"1. Derelicts, &c., on the High Seas.

"A geographical apportionment of the waters of the globe amongst the different maritime nations, in order to divide the labour and cost of removing wrecks and derelicts, or searching for doubtful dangers, cannot be recommended for adoption.

"In the open sea, with the exception of a part of the North Atlantic, derelicts and dangerous wrecks are exceedingly rare, and as these parts of the ocean are, comparatively speaking, not much frequented by vessels, the danger accruing from such obstructions is not one to warrant the expenditure of such sums of money as would be necessary to institute a regular service, sufficient to insure their removal from regions of such enormous extent. The news of having sighted a derelict is often a week or more old before it is received by the authorities; a rescuing steamer can often not be on the spot for another week; the position given is in many cases not accurate; and in most parts of the sea the drift of the derelict is exceedingly uncertain. It is, therefore, a most difficult task for a vessel sent out to search for a derelict to find it; and the expense incurred by such expeditions may often be out of all proportion to the small chance of finding and removing one.

"The geographical apportionment of the waters of the oceans might, besides this, easily lead to the supposition that the limits so defined would circumscribe, moreover, the sphere of political interest of the respective Governments."

The President.—The subject before the Conference for discussion is "Derelicts, &c., on the high seas." The Chair hears no proposition in regard to it. The Secretary will please read the next Division.

The next Division of the Report is as follows:—

"2. Derelicts in the North Atlantic.

"In the North Atlantic, particularly in that part of it bordering the North American coast westward of a line drawn from the Bermuda Islands to Cape Race, Newfoundland, derelicts are so frequently met with that they must be considered a serious danger to navigation.

"As in these waters the vessels whose safety is imperilled by their existence are exceedingly numerous, the number of persons on board of them very large, and the value of these ships and their cargoes very great, and as, moreover, the chances for locating derelicts and for determining the direction of their drift are particularly favourable, the Committee propose that the various Maritime Powers should come to some agreement respecting their removal.

"In case this proposition should be entertained, it is submitted that the respective Powers should also come to some understanding regarding the proprietary rights which may still exist, whether in the ship or in her cargo.

"Besides this, it seems desirable to point out that amongst other matters that will necessarily have to be considered it would be well to take steps to prevent the destruction of derelicts that might readily have been saved, and to make sure that in case destruction has been decided upon no evidence of crime should be destroyed also."

The President.—The subject before the Conference for discussion is "Derelicts in the North Atlantic." The Chair hears no proposition with reference thereto. The Secretary will please read the next Division.

The next Division of the Report is as follows:—

"3. Wrecks and Derelicts in Coast Waters.

"Regarding wrecks and derelicts in coast waters outside the territorial limits, the Committee submit that the duty of marking, and, if necessary, of removing wrecks, or such portions of them as obstruct navigation, has already been generally acknowledged by the Governments whom it concerns, and therefore no further propositions have to be made in this regard.

"It has, however, been brought to the notice of the Committee that Governments who by Treaty have acknowledged the exterritorality of subjects of other Powers and of their property are sometimes very much hampered by the consideration of private interests in their action regarding the removal of wrecks, even when the value of the wreck and cargo is very small, and there is scarcely a possibility that salvage operations can be successfully undertaken. The Committee are therefore of opinion that a Resolution should be adopted to the following effect: That in such cases the Consul or Consuls concerned shall not have the right of withholding his or their consent to the destruction of a wreck, or parts thereof, if it is shown that the wreck constitutes a danger to passing vessels, and if there is no apparent possibility that it will be removed within a reasonable time by the owners or by the Insurance Companies interested.

"As to derelicts in coast waters there seems to be little doubt but that private enterprise, in order to secure salvage, will prove sufficient to remove any of them. For this reason it would seem to be unnecessary that any proposition should be made which would interfere with the established custom.

"There was, in the opinion of the Committee, some doubt regarding the meaning of the word 'responsibility' used in this heading. They consider, however, that no Government would acknowledge any responsibility for the waters under discussion which had not been made the subject of some formal Agreement entered into after negotiations by the usual diplomatic methods."

The President.—The subject before the Conference is, "Wrecks and derelicts on coast waters," which is now open to discussion. The Chair will entertain any proposition upon this Division. The Chair hears no proposition. The Secretary will proceed to read the next Division.

The next Division of the Programme is as follows:—

"*4. Searching for doubtful Dangers with a view of removing them from the Chart.*

"The greater part of these dangers have been entered on the Charts from the report of single ships, and under the assumption that it is often better to do so rather than have the mariner entirely unwarned; though such Reports may have appeared from the very first of doubtful accuracy. In order to make sure that these dangers do not exist, it has been conclusively shown by experience that it is not sufficient to sail across the alleged position, but that it is necessary, at the same time, to take extensive soundings to prove beyond a doubt that nowhere in the vicinity of the alleged danger anything but deep water is found, and that it is therefore justifiable to remove the danger from the Chart. This has become the acknowledged custom of the different Hydrographic Offices.

"In order, therefore, to make such searches effectual, ships employed for this purpose should be fitted out with deep-sea sounding apparatus. Ordinary war-vessels are not usually supplied with such means, but only surveying vessels or vessels fitted out for scientific exploration. Such vessels will, as a matter of course, receive from their respective Governments instructions to search for dangers of this kind whenever they find them located in a position near which their special mission will take them. What is, however, most wanted at present are accurate surveys on coasts newly opened to trade and commercial enterprise in order to detect dangers whose existence is entirely unsuspected. The number of these that are yearly discovered (ninety last year), many by the expensive process of losing a ship on them, proves incontestably how imperfect the surveys of the world are.

"To divert ships engaged in such surveying work to scour the ocean in order to verify doubtful reports under international engagements would be to practically stop the production of improved surveys. Under these circumstances the Committee cannot recommend any action in the matter.

"If masters of vessels, when seeing indications of shallow water, would act in accordance with the Resolution we have placed before the Conference, on p. 3, instead of passing on their course without any examination, or even taking a cast of the lead, the number of these dangers reported as doubtful would be greatly lessened."

The President.—The subject before the Conference for discussion is "Searching for doubtful dangers with a view of removing them from the Chart." The Chair is ready to hear any suggestion or motion upon this subject. The Chair hears none. The Secretary will proceed to read the Resolutions regarding General Division X, submitted for the consideration of the Conference.

Captain Mensing (Germany).—Mr. President, these Resolutions are the same as have been given already in the text, and perhaps it will not be necessary to read them again.

The President.—Does the Delegate from Germany move that they be taken as a whole?

Captain Mensing (Germany).—Yes, Sir.

The President.—The Delegate from Germany moves that the Resolutions Nos. 1 to 7, inclusive, be taken as a whole for the consideration of the Conference.

"*Resolutions regarding General Division X, submitted for the consideration of the Conference.*

"1. That it is advisable to make it the duty of any of the officers or of the crew of a wreck or derelict to report, as soon as possible after landing, to the nearest harbour authority, if necessary through their Consul, as follows:—

"(*a.*) Name of the vessel abandoned.

"(*b.*) Her distinguishing number.

[93]

"(c.) Name of her home port, port from which she sailed, and place of destination.

"(d.) General description of vessel and her rig.

"(e.) Place where abandoned (latitude and longitude as near as possible).

"(f.) Weather and current experienced before leaving the vessel, and, in case she was a derelict, the direction in which she would most likely drift.

"(g.) Whether or not it is intended to take any steps towards her recovery.

"2. That a similar report should be made to the same authorities by the master of any vessel sighting a wreck or derelict, and a suitable entry made in the ship's log.

"3. That such reports should be published in 'Notices to Mariners,' the daily press, and, if necessary, by giving telegraphic information to the ports which it most concerns.

"4. That it is advisable to make it the duty of every commander or master of a vessel to report the fact that an iceberg or dangerous field ice has been sighted, or a shoal, reef, or other obstruction has been discovered, to the harbour authorities or the Hydrographic Office of that country to which the port next reached belongs, giving a full description of the obstruction, and all facts that may lead to the determination of its position; for instance, the time elapsed since the last reliable astronomical observation, and the rate of the chronometer. If the obstruction be a shoal or reef, the depth of water actually obtained by sounding on it should be given. Also when land is in sight the position of any off-lying shoal or reef should be determined by compass bearings of fixed objects in view; the error of the compas being stated, with information as to how and when that error was observed. Angles should also be taken between such objects, and a drawing of the coast and the position of the observer be added.

"5. That whenever practicable it shall be the duty of the crew, before abandoning a vessel, (a) to hoist some distinctive signal, as 'B C F,' 'Abandoned by the crew,' or 'C R T G,' 'Derelict,' or a ball, shape, or other similar mark, where it can best be seen, and where it should not be mistaken for any other authorized signal; (b) to let go the sheets and halliards of such sails as are not furled.

"6. That the different Maritime Powers interested in the navigation of that portion of the North Atlantic Ocean bordering the American coast and situated westward of a line drawn from the Bermuda Islands to Cape Race, Newfoundland, be invited to come to an agreement respecting the removal of derelicts in these waters under due official supervision.

"7. That in countries which, by Treaty, have acknowledged the exterritoriality of subjects of other Powers and their property, the Consul or Consuls concerned shall be instructed not to withhold his or their consent to the destruction of a wreck or parts thereof, if it is shown that the wreck constitutes a danger to passing vessels, and if there is no apparent possibility that it will be removed within a reasonable time by the owners or the Insurance Companies interested."

Mr. Carter (Hawaii).—Mr. President, I move the adoption of the Report and Resolutions.

The question was put to the Conference upon the motion of the Delegate from Hawaii, and it was carried.

The President.—The next order of business is the Report on General Division XI. The Secretary will please read it in Divisions.

The Report of Committee No. 3 on General Division XI is as follows:—

"GENERAL DIVISION XI.

"*Notice of Dangers to Navigation.*

"*Notice of Changes in Lights, Buoys, and other Day and Night Marks.*

"(a.) A uniform method of taking bearings, of designating them (whether true or magnetic), or of reporting them.

"(b.) A uniform method of reporting, indicating, and exchanging information by the several maritime nations—to include the form of 'Notices to Mariners.'

"(c.) A uniform method of distributing this information.

"All notices of changes in lights beacons, buoys, and other day and night marks require not only to be brought to the notice of the public of that country in whose waters these changes have taken place, but also to all other maritime nations, so that the authorities may be enabled to impart information for the benefit of their own seafaring population.

"This is usually done by publications to which the generic title of 'Notices to Mariners' has been applied. They are either issued whenever occasion demands it, or at regular intervals, with an extra edition when necessary.

"They may be further divided into (a) those published by the Department of Naval Affairs of the different countries, or, under its direction, by the Hydrographer; (b) those published by the authorities, central, provincial, colonial, or local, in charge of the lighthouses, beacons, and buoys.

"The publications mentioned under (a) are intended for the use of the mariner only, and the Committee do not consider it advisable to insist on any change regarding form or arrangement of 'Notices to Mariners.'

"What has been said regarding the publications mentioned under (a) is true as well regarding those mentioned under (b). These 'Notices to Mariners' are mainly intended for internal and local use in each country, and supply information not to mariners only, but to local officials, such as lighthouse keepers, inspectors of buoys, and others; and, considering that they are published for different objects, and to be used by men of very different classes and occupations, the Committee do not consider it feasible to insist upon uniformity in matters of detail."

The President.—The first Division of the Report is before the Conference for consideration. The Chair will hear any proposition with regard thereto. The Chair hears none. The Secretary will please read the next Division.

The next Division of the Report is as follows:—

"(a.) A uniform Method of taking Bearings, of designating them (whether True or Magnetic), and of reporting them.

"*Taking Bearings.*—In all countries, as far as we know, except Italy and Norway, the custom prevails that all bearings in 'Notices to Mariners,' and in 'Light Lists,' in order to locate a danger or to determine the limits of a light-sector, are given from seaward, that is, from the danger indicated towards the fixed objects by which its position is determined, or from the outer limit of visibility of a light towards the lighthouse.

"This mode of taking bearings has the advantage that it is in agreement with the mode in which they are used by the mariner, and the Committee recommend that the Resolution in this behalf appended to their Report be adopted by the Conference with a view to this custom being made universal.

"*Designating Bearings, whether True or Magnetic.*—The adoption of a uniform method of designating bearings, whether true or magnetic, offers the advantage that bearings given in the publications of any country can be transferred *verbatim* to similar publications issued in any other country without the necessity for any alteration or calculation. This is of importance in preparing publications the value of which depends in no small degree on the possibility of issuing them immediately after any changes have been made which require to be notified to mariners.

"All the evidence, however, which has been laid before your Committee tends unmistakably to the conclusion that it would be inexpedient for any country suddenly to adopt a new system of designating bearings in the place of one which has been sanctioned by the custom of many years and has become an essential part of the system of navigation generally adopted and taught in the nautical schools of the various countries.

"It has also to be borne in mind that such a change concerns not only experts and scientific men who can easily understand and adapt a new system to their requirements, but, in the vast majority of cases, it would affect seamen whose knowledge of matters regarding navigation is inseparably connected with the methods with which they have been familiar all their lives, and to whom any change of the kind indicated would be confusing and dangerous.

"For these reasons the Committee do not propose the adoption of a uniform method of designating bearings by giving them either true or magnetic.

"Uniformity might have been attained in another way, *i.e.*, by giving bearings both true and magnetic. It was shown, however, that the advantages of such a plan would be more than counterbalanced by a large increase in the bulk of the text, and by the possibility of errors amongst seafaring men unaccustomed to any but a single system, and who might mistake one set of bearings for another when read in a hurry.

"Having regard to these difficulties, the Committee do not propose to advise any action in this matter in the direction of uniformity beyond recommending that in all 'Notices to Mariners' and 'Light Lists' intended for exchange with other nations, whenever true or magnetic bearings are given, the variation shall be inserted.

"*Bearings to be given in Degrees or in Points and Fractions thereof.*—It seems that in the majority of maritime nations the custom prevails that all bearings are given in degrees. This has the advantage that if the variation, which is always expressed in degrees, has to be applied in order that the bearings be entered on a Chart, or when the variation has to be corrected for time elapsed since the date when it was determined, the result is more accurate than if the bearings were expressed in points.

"On the other hand, it has to be borne in mind that the 'Notices to Mariners' and 'Light Lists' which are most universally used retain the custom of giving bearings in points and fractions thereof.

"After a full discussion of this large and intricate question the Committee decided to adopt the following Resolution:—

"'That the bearings for cuts of different coloured sectors of lights, or of bearings of lights defining a narrow channel, should be expressed in degrees where practicable.'

"*Counting the Degrees.*—The custom adopted universally in geodesy is that of counting the degrees from the north to the right (or with the sun), beginning with 0° to 360°. In one country the steering compasses are also so marked, and directions with reference to the course of the vessel are so expressed. This method offers certain advantages, but it is contrary to the custom of the large majority of mariners, and on this account the Committee propose that the number of degrees used in designating bearings should be counted from north and south to east and west, beginning with 0° and ending with 90 degrees.

"North and south are universally designated by the letters N and S; but east is in some countries designated by the letter O, and west in others also by the same letter O. In order to make these designations uniform the Committee propose that all countries adopt, for use in the publications under consideration, the letter E to designate east, and the letter W to designate west, in uniformity with the Rules adopted already for publications of Meteorological Offices.

"*Designating Distances.*—The Committee advise that—

"Distances should be expressed in nautical miles and fractions thereof.

"The word 'cable' should mean the tenth part of a nautical mile."

The President.—The subject before the Conference for discussion is "A uniform method of taking bearings, of designating them (whether true or magnetic), and of reporting them." The Chair hears no proposition with reference thereto, and the Secretary will proceed with the next Division.

The next Division of the Report is as follows:—

"(*b.*) *A Uniform Method of reporting, indicating, and exchanging Information by the several Maritime Nations, to include the form of Notices to Mariners.*

"1. *Reporting Dangers to Navigation, Change of Lights, &c.*

"Reports of dangers discovered should be made as promptly and accurately as possible, and should be addressed to the proper authorities. This has been pointed out already in the Committee Report upon General Division X, p. 3.

"2. *Indicating Dangers, Changes of Lights, &c.*

"(*a.*) Several countries refer the longitude given in the publications under consideration to a prime meridian, whose difference from the meridians of Greenwich or Paris, on which most Charts in use by mariners are constructed, may be unknown to a sailor. In such a case, though he may have become acquainted with the fact of the discovery of a danger, the establishment of a lighthouse, &c. he may be unable to enter such information, with sufficient correctness, on his Chart.

"The Committee therefore propose that in all notices which refer to any other prime meridian but that of Greenwich and Paris, the difference in longitude between such meridians should be inserted.

"(*b.*) The visibility of a light is given in different ways. In some countries the number of miles given refer to the visibility of light in clear weather or in ordinary weather; in others, the visibility refers to a mean state of the atmosphere, *i.e.*, one which may be expected at that particular locality in fifty cases out of one hundred. The Committee had not sufficient evidence before them to decide as to the advantages of the two plans for general adoption; they, however, consider it desirable to bring the subject before the Conference in order that the attention of the different Maritime Powers should be called to it.

"(*c.*) In some 'Light Lists' the geographical range of light is given, *i.e.*, the distance resulting from the height of a light above high water, in connection with the curvature of the earth, together with or without the additional distance calculated for an observer supposed to be elevated above the sea at a certain height; in other 'Light Lists' the actual visibility of a light is given without any regard to the height of the light or the elevation of the observer; in some publications the lesser of the two distances is given, and in other cases both together.

"Each of these methods offers some advantage, and it seems inexpedient, at the present moment, to propose uniformity in this respect.

"It appears advisable, however, to adopt a standard height for the observer wherever the geographical range of a light is given in 'Light Lists' or in 'Notices.'

"The Committee therefore propose that the height of 5 metres be generally adopted in all countries where the metric system is in use, and that in other countries, where this is not the case, the height taken should be 15 feet of the measure of the country. This height seems to the Committee the best suited to the present requirements of navigation. The difference between these measures is of no practical importance.

"(*d.*) The lights of lighthouses are classified at present in 'Orders' according to the size of the lantern, or if dioptric, according to the diameter of the apparatus, though in this respect there exists considerable difference.

"Since the introduction of the electric light this classification has become inaccurate, and from a seaman's point of view misleading, for under its rules a third order electric light generally is much more powerful than a first order oil or gas light. Uniformity in this respect is desirable, and the Committee therefore propose that the several Maritime Powers interested should be requested to consider the question, in order to establish, if possible, a uniform classification of lights on the basis of the power of the light as seen by the mariner. At the same time it would be desirable to bring about a uniform classification as regards their character.

"3. *Exchanging Information by the several Maritime Nations.*

"It has become the custom for the Hydrographic Offices of the different maritime countries, with few exceptions, to ask for any information regarding their publications, 'Notices to Mariners,' 'Light Lists,' 'Charts,' 'Sailing Directions,' by direct application to the Hydrographic Offices of other countries, and to give such information in the same way.

"It is not easy to see how this information could be so speedily and conveniently given in any other way. But the Committee are not aware that this usage has ever been sanctioned by the proper authorities. They have on this account thought it well to call the attention of the Conference to this fact, and they submit that permission to exchange information regarding these publications direct, without the intervention of the Foreign Offices, should be granted to all central Hydrographic Offices in the home countries, as well as those in the provinces, Colonies, and dominions, and also to those central offices which administer lighthouses, beacons, and buoys of a country, and which publish such information. A list of the offices referred to in this paragraph which are known to the Committee will be found in Appendix (B).

"Some Maritime Powers are without any special Hydrographic Department. In such cases it would be well to designate some other office, for instance, that of Harbour-master of their principal ports, who could be addressed if occasion occurs.

"In some countries the 'Notices to Mariners' are published only in newspapers. It would be well if such notices were sent to the different Hydrographic Offices of the world.

"Contemplated changes in lights and buoys should be brought to public notice, if convenient, before the date on which such change is proposed to be made."

The President.—The subject before the Conference for discussion is "A uniform method of reporting, indicating, and exchanging information by the several maritime nations, to include the form of Notices to Mariners." The Chair is ready to hear any proposition with reference to this Division. The Chair hears none. The Secretary will please read the next Division of the Report.

Captain Mensing (Germany).—Mr. President, the list mentioned in this paragraph of the Hydrographic Offices in the different countries will be given in as soon as corrected. I may only say that, so far, we have received no answer from the Representatives of Nicaragua or Guatemala, but otherwise we have been able to complete the list of Hydrographic Offices in all countries. Up to this time we have not received a letter addressed to the Committee by the honourable Delegate from Venezuela. The list, when corrected, will be printed and added to this Report.

The President.—The Delegate from Germany then proposes to take no action except to append it to the Report?

Captain Mensing (Germany).—Mr. President, I only desire to mention it because the Report speaks of it as Appendix (B), and Appendix (B) has not yet been attached to the Report.

The President.—It will be appended to the Report, as requested. The Secretary will now read Division (c).

Division (c) is as follows:—

"(c.) *A uniform Method of distributing this Information.*

"The information contained in 'Notices to Mariners' is now brought to the knowledge of the seafaring population by sending copies of the same to the different shipping offices and Consulates, and to Captains of the navy, and to masters of the merchant fleet. The Committee have no evidence before them which points to the fact that the measures taken by each country do not fully satisfy the requirements of those interested."

The President.—The subject before the Conference for discussion is paragraph (c), under the heading, "A uniform method of distributing this information." The Chair hears no suggestions in regard thereto. Does the Delegate from Germany desire that a vote should be taken upon the Resolutions numbered 1 to 12, inclusive, as a whole?

Captain Mensing (Germany).—Mr. President, I think they are nearly the same as those contained in the text of the Report; but they are differently worded, and I think it would be advisable to have them read.

The President.—The Secretary will please read the Resolutions.

The Resolutions are as follows:—

"*Resolutions proposed to the Maritime Conference regarding General Division XI.*

"In recapitulation, the Committee recommend the Conference to invite the several maritime Powers to consider the following Resolutions with a view to establishing uniformity in the subjects treated in 'Notices to Mariners' and 'Light Lists':—

"1. That all bearings should be given from seaward.

"2. That the bearings of cuts of different coloured sectors of lights or bearings of lights defining a narrow channel should be expressed in degrees where practicable.

"3. That all bearings expressed in degrees should count from north and south, from 0° to 90°, towards east and west.

"4. That in designating bearings, the letter E shall designate east, and the letter W shall designate west.

"5. That whenever bearings are given, the variation of the compass at the place should be stated.

"6. That distances should be expressed in nautical miles and fractions thereof. The word 'cable' should mean the tenth part of a nautical mile.

"7. That whenever the longitude of a position is given, it should be stated which prime meridian is adopted, and if other than that of Greenwich or Paris, the difference of longitude should also be stated.

"8. That in defining the visibility of a light, it should be stated whether the distance is for 'clear' or 'mean' state of the weather.

"9. That where the geographical range of a light is given, it should be calculated as seen at high water from an observer 15 feet or 5 metres above the sea.

"10. That a uniform classification of lights based on luminous intensity and on the character as seen by the mariner should be adopted.

"11. That the central offices that issue 'Notices to Mariners' or 'Light Lists' should be permitted to correspond direct on such subjects.

"12. That from countries where 'Notices to Mariners' are published only in newspapers, copies of such papers should be sent to the various Hydrographic Offices."

Mr. Hall (Great Britain).—Mr. President, I rise to move the adoption of this Report, and in doing so I wish to take the opportunity of saying, on behalf of my colleagues and myself, how very much we are indebted to the gallant Delegate from Germany, the Chairman of this Committee, and the other members of the Committee, for the exceedingly able and interesting Report which they have given us. I think that no one can read this Report without seeing and feeling that it has necessarily been the result of very great labour indeed. The work which has been undertaken by the gallant Delegate and his colleagues is one from which many men would have recoiled; but for them it has been a labour of love, and the result, certainly, I am satisfied, will be of the greatest assistance to all the Maritime Powers of the world.

Captain Mensing (Germany).—Mr. President, on behalf of the members of the Committee and myself, I would like to state that we feel extremely grateful for the kind words which have been spoken by the distinguished First Delegate from Great Britain. As he has stated, we have given our best attention to the Report, and we hope that the work which is begun now, and which is but laying foundation-stones for the future, may be found to be of lasting benefit.

The President.—This last Report seems to conclude the labours of the Conference.

Captain Shackford (United States).—Mr. President, I would like to say a word about the statement I made yesterday about the buoyage of the harbour of New York. I made the statement that can buoys were on the starboard hand, going in from seaward. There seemed to be doubt in the minds of some of the members of the Committee on Buoys in regard to that. I have here the Sailing Directions for New York Bay and Harbour. The first channel mentioned here is Gedney's Channel. It says that there are several buoys passed, and then it says those to be left on the starboard hand are first-class can buoys painted red, and those to be left on the port hand are nun buoys painted black. Then it goes on to describe a number of different channels. I merely want to say that these are the Sailing Directions for New York Bay, and that the statement which I made yesterday was right.

Captain Mensing (Germany).—Mr. President, I would like to state that I never doubted that the statement made by the gallant Delegate of the United States was entirely right. What I meant to say was that in this case the buoyage was in contradiction to the official statement contained in the Report on Beacons, Buoys, and Stakes.

Mr. Hall (Great Britain).—Mr. President, now that the labours of the Conference are concluded, I would ask your permission to be allowed to move a Resolution, which, I can assure you, is not a mere matter of form. I wish to move a proposition which I am sure will be accepted without a single dissenting voice in this room, for it is a Resolution to tender a hearty and cordial vote of thanks to you, Mr. President, for your courteous, impartial, and able conduct in the Chair.

Now, Mr. President, I believe that there is not recorded in history any Conference at which so many Powers have attended, or at which they have been represented by so many Delegates, as that which has been under your direction for the space of nearly three months; and I am certain that in future years we shall all of us look back with pride and satisfaction to the fact that our proceedings have not been marred by a single unpleasant feeling, by a single angry thought or word. I wish to say on behalf of my immediate colleagues, the Delegates for Great Britain, that we have a very deep sense of the kindness and good feeling which we have received from all of our brother Delegates. We shall go away from here feeling that we have made many, many good friends, and with the firm belief and hope that we have not made a single enemy.

When I refer to the good feeling and harmony which have prevailed throughout, I desire to state that it is due not only to the Delegates themselves, but it is due in no little degree to the calm, judicial, and unbiassed manner in which you have conducted our proceedings, and it is with very great pleasure that I express our gratification and thanks to you for your conduct in the Chair. Mr. President, I would fain say more, but there are occasions when words will not come to the lips of the speaker, and I therefore content myself with moving that a cordial vote of thanks be tendered by the Conference to its President, Rear-Admiral Samuel R. Franklin, for his courteous, impartial, and able conduct in the Chair.

The President.—I thank you, Gentlemen, for the kind words which have just fallen from the learned First Delegate for Great Britain. Any language which I can command would inadequately express the feelings which I have upon this occasion. If I have administered the duties of my office to the satisfaction of the Delegates present, it is owing in a great measure to the kind courtesy which they have always displayed towards me, and to the courtesy which they have at all times extended to each other, even in the midst of the most heated debates. You have done your duty, Gentlemen, with great ability and with industry such as is rarely witnessed in a Conference of this kind. You have worked untiringly and unceasingly day and night. Now the results of your labours will come before the world, and I trust they will be found most satisfactory, as I hope and believe they will. In wishing you good-bye and a happy new year, I trust that you will find the Atlantic smooth for your passage across, and that you will be received at home by your Governments with the credit which you all so well deserve.

The motion of the Delegate from Great Britain tendering a vote of thanks to the President of the Conference was put to the Conference, after having been seconded by Admiral Kaznakoff (Russia), and unanimously adopted.

Dr. Sieveking (Germany).—Mr. President, I beg leave to propose a Resolution which I am sure will meet with the most cordial approval of all the members of the Conference. I beg to propose a vote of thanks to the Secretaries of the Conference, and to the officers detailed by the United States' Government to assist us. Their work, as we all know, has been a very extensive and important one. They have given us the whole of their time for nearly three months, since the very first day of their appointment to their duties, and the great number of Resolutions passed by the Conference, the many printed pages, and the many Committee Reports which have been laid before us, all testify to the fact that great zeal has been displayed by the Secretaries, and by the officers assisting them, in performing their most important duties.

I am sure that I am only expressing what is the general feeling of the Conference when I say that we never could have thought of arriving at the conclusion of our work in so satisfactory a manner and in so short a time without the valuable assistance they have rendered us. But I believe I would fail in fully expressing the feelings of the members of the Conference here present if I did not add that it is not only the zeal which they have bestowed upon the performance of their duty, but it is the very courteous manner in which they have met all the wishes of the Delegates, and they were very numerous and trespassed upon their time to a very great degree, which deserves to be gratefully acknowledged. The great courtesy, affability, and kindness in which they have met all our wishes, and the ability with which they have fulfilled them, certainly entitle them to the lasting gratitude of the Conference. I beg to propose that the thanks of the Conference be expressed to the Secretaries of the Conference and the officers detailed by the United States' Government for their services and the valuable assistance given by them to the work of the Conference.

Captain Richard (France).—Mr. President, I most heartily support the proposition which has been put before this Conference by the learned Dr. Sieveking. In so doing it is unnecessary for me to state the grounds which lead me to support it, and to repeat them. You are all familiar with them. It would evidently be difficult for me to say anything which the members of the Conference have not felt and thought for themselves. But among the Secretaries who have co-operated with us, there is a certain number of distinguished officers of the United States' Navy whose names have not appeared in any Reports of our sessions. I therefore ask that their names be set forth in Dr. Sieveking's Resolution as a testimonial of our gratitude both for the permanent and the temporary Secretaries who, either in the Conference or in the Committees, have assisted us with that courtesy and affability which Dr. Sieveking has so justly described.

I therefore ask that the names be mentioned of Lieutenant Cottman, Mr. Spring-Rice, Mr. Walter Blaess, Mr. Charles Ribière, Lieutenant Beatty, Lieutenant Bostick, Lieutenant Ridgely Hunt, Lieutenant Newton, and Ensign Howard.

If you are of the same opinion, of which I have no doubt you are, we will render to those gentlemen due justice, and the only testimony in our power of showing how we appreciate their enlightened and intelligent services.

If now, at the close of this year and on the eve of the morrow which will give light to a new one, I am allowed to express a wish, it is as follows: May they retain the same pleasant remembrances of us that we will retain of them.

The President.—If the Secretaries had a voice upon this floor I have no doubt they would suitably thank the Delegate from Germany and the Delegate from France for the kind words which they have spoken in their behalf. I therefore take occasion to thank the Conference for them for these kind words, and also to say that I have myself received a great deal of valuable assistance from them.

My first supposition was that the Conference would be adjourned *sine die*, but upon conversation with some of the Delegates I have had reason to change my mind. I will read a letter which I received from the Department of State this morning:—

"Sir, "*Department of State, Washington, December* 31, 1889.

"I have to acknowledge the receipt of your letter of the 31st instant, saying that the International Maritime Conference will probably conclude its labours on this date, and to state that you are hereby authorized to adjourn the Conference *sine die*, whenever in your judgment its labours are concluded.

"You will cause the Reports and conclusions of the Conference to be certified to this Department in the usual manner.

"In adjourning the Conference you may give suitable expression to the gratification of the Department at the harmony which has prevailed among the members thereof, and to the hope that the commercial world may be materially benefited by the results of its deliberations.

"I am, &c.,
"Signed   JAMES G. BLAINE.

"Rear-Admiral S. R. Franklin, United States' Navy, &c.,
    "International Maritime Conference."

I thought I could give no better expression to my views in regard to this matter than by reading this letter. There appears to be no further business before the Conference.

The Conference will now rise.

WITHDRAWN